119002

The Gospel
of John

The Gospel of John

Expository and Homiletical
Commentary

by
David Thomas

Two Volumes in One

KREGEL PUBLICATIONS
Grand Rapids, Mi. 49501

Gospel of John by David Thomas.
Copyright © 1980 by Kregel Publications
a division of Kregel, Inc. All rights reserved.

Library of Congress Cataloging in Publication Data

Thomas, David, 1813-1894.
  The Gospel of John.

  (Kregel limited edition library series)
  Reprint of the 1885 ed. published by R.D.
Dickinson, London under title: The Genius of the
Fourth Gospel.
  Includes index.
  1. Bible. N.T. John — Commentaries. 2. John,
Saint, apostle. I. Title.
BS2615.3.T43 1980   226'.5'07   79-15415
ISBN 0-8254-3809-8

Printed in the United States of America

Contents

vi / Contents

HOMILIES (Volume 2)   Page

ADDENDUM

INTRODUCTION TO GOSPEL OF JOHN

GERMS OF THOUGHT (Volume 1)

Contents / xi

THE AUTHOR'S CREED

AS EVOLVED FROM THE FOURTH GOSPEL

Faith

Not in Priesthoods, not on Creed,
  Is the Faith we need, O Lord!
These, more fragile than the reed,
  Can no rest for souls afford.
Human systems, what are they?
  Dreams of erring men at best;
Visions only of a day,
    Without substance, without rest.

Firmly fix it, Lord, on Thee,
  Strike its roots deep in Thy love;
Growing ever may it be,
  Like the Faith of those above.
Then, though earthly things depart,
  And the heavens pass away,
Strong in Thee shall rest the
    heart,
    Without fainting or decay.

Hope

Not on heaven, not on bliss,
  Should, O Lord, our hope be
    set;
Not on better worlds than this,
  Worlds that we might wish to
    get.
We would hope for goodness, Lord,
  Virtue mirrored out in Thee,
Beaming ever in Thy Word,
  Lighting up eternity.

Self-oblivious hope we need,
  Hope that springs from love to
    Thee,
Free from every sordid greed,
  From all selfish longings free.
Fix our hope on Thee, O Lord,
  On Thy likeness and Thy love,
This we know from Thy blest
    Word,
    Is the hope that reigns above.

Charity

Not on creatures high or low,
  Not on kindred e'en the best,
But on Thee, O Lord, we know,
  Should our chief affection rest.
Could our souls in love embrace,
  All the spirits dear to Thee,
Though they clasp'd all worlds in
    space,
    Empty, Lord, they still would
    be!

Oh, 'tis needful, it is right
  We should set our love on Thee;
Loving Thee with all our might,
  Makes the spirit strong and free.
This is love that fills the heart,
  Finds our powers full employ;
Breathes new life through every
    part,
    Floods the soul with heavenly
    joy.

Foreword

The pen of Dr. David Thomas was very highly regarded in the middle of the last century — and particularly by fellow preachers. His written works were unusual in two respects.

First (and most significantly) he concentrated entirely on producing homiletical commentaries rather than exegetical or philological ones.

In his comments he seldom asks, "What precisely does the original text say?" Dr. Thomas assumes that his readers are already well-furnished either with personal competence in the original languages, or with adequate aids and exegetical commentaries. Instead he asks, "What is the spiritual point and message of the passage? What does it say to me? What does the Holy Spirit intend to be preached from this portion of The Scriptures?"

Not surprisingly, therefore, this esteemed London pastor continued for more than thirty years to be editor of one of the best loved preachers' magazines of his day.

The second distinguishing feature of Dr. Thomas's works is the uncontrived, practical style for which he was so noted. It is a very humble, unaffected and even unmethodical style. So much so that it sometimes leads to these commentaries being sadly underestimated.

Too superficial a glance at this commentary of the *Gospel of John* might well result in the hasty impression that it is somewhat general and insubstantial. Nothing could be further from the truth — for no author concentrates more matter into such robust and practical explanations. Perhaps the best function this foreword can undertake is that of pointing to the very special value of almost any work by Dr. Thomas.

Fellow preachers and students of the ·Word — may I urge you to understand the style of the writer. You will find him in these pages, just as you would have found him in conversation in his book-lined study in London a century ago.

Let him unfold to you, in his inimitable style, the essential *purpose* of each passage. You will always be glad you listened, and even when you disagree you will find yourself strangely stimulated to think more deeply about the purpose of the passage.

If Dr. Thomas has recently preached the passage, you will find he is full of detail. If he has not, you will find him more analytical. He hardly ever quotes, but the more you listen to him the more you appreciate that he is steeped in the great tradition of Reformed commentators.

When you have drawn all possible assistance from exegetical discipline; and when your mind needs to be released from technicalities and to be helped to function as the mind of a pastor should, then you will value time with old Dr. Thomas. At such times you will realize just why he was such a favorite among the pastors of a hundred years ago.

SPURGEON'S METROPOLITAN TABERNACLE, LONDON   DR. PETER MASTERS

Preface

"THE GOSPEL OF JOHN IS BIBLE ENOUGH FOR ME." I am disposed to echo this, although, at the same time, far enough from thinking that it is the whole of the Bible.

Who was the author of this Gospel? Where, When, and Wherefore was it written? These questions, though rather speculative than *vital*, will be found discussed at the close of the Second Volume. No candid reader can peruse these volumes of mine, without finding that the LIFE recorded in this Gospel, the doctrines propounded, and the thoughts suggested, are sufficient in every way to meet the intellectual and spiritual exigencies of mankind. It has been said, that Christianity has no rudimental idea, either in religion or ethics, that is not found in connection with the teachings of Zoroaster, Buddha, Mahomet, Confucius, Seneca, Plato, and other ancient schools of spiritual thought. Were this granted, I unhesitatingly affirm that nowhere, throughout the whole domain of literature, ancient and modern, are those most vital and profound elements of truth, exhibited in forms so congruous with the reason, so fascinating to the heart, so commanding to the whole soul, as we have them in this Gospel of St. John. In this Logos they centre and radiate.

Some of the religious writers of the distant past emblematically represented this Gospel as the "*Eagle.*" So piercing is it in its vision, so broad in its sweep, so lofty in its flight, and withal so inspiring the sunny azure through which, with unrestricted freedom, it disports its pinions, that it may well be represented by the imperial bird.

Whilst I am increasingly convinced that the Four Gospels (notwithstanding certain discrepancies and apparent inaccuracies that may, peradventure, be found therein) contain the supreme Word of God, the "Word made Flesh," yet I think that, comparing them one with another, its phase in St. John is the most complete and spiritually educational. It suggests to me that the Christ exhibited in our Creeds, Churches, and Institutions, is as unlike the Christ of the Gospels, as the mechanical force of the manufacturing machine, throwing off commodities for trade, is unlike that vital energy in nature, that clothes the landscape with verdure, and fills the earth and the waters with countless tribes of life.

I am tempted to suppose that but few men of reflective minds, and honest purpose, will go through all I have written on this Book, and not conclude that John's Gospel is pre-eminently the field for preachers,—supplying themes not only of boundless variety, but of that soul-quickening, developing, and ennobling force, that can be found, not only nowhere else in the domain of general literature, but nowhere else in the book men call the Bible.

Christ is my Bible. And here, in the Gospel of John, I find Him in aspects that rouse my faculties and touch my heart, more intensely than when He appears to me elsewhere,—even in the Synoptic Gospels. Why preachers should be so untrue to their mission, and so indifferent to the paramount interests of humanity, as to preach their little creeds rather than this Christ, fills me often with amazement and with sore distress. Souls are everywhere crying out for the True "BREAD," and pulpits everywhere—with but few exceptions—are dealing out their little *theories* of this, the *Staff of soul-life.*

Some preachers (not a few, it has been said) habitually go to the Old Testament in quest of themes for pulpit discourse, and that because they find there so much of the sensational, always popular amongst the more sensuous and unthinking. I deplore this, not because I object to ministers selecting themes for lessons of usefulness anywhere,—from the history of nature or the history of man,—but because as a *habit*, it Judaises men's thoughts. Is conventional Christianity much better than Judaism? I trow not. Are not its prevalent ideas of priesthood more Aaronic than Christly, of kinghood, more Davidic than Divine?

By universal consent the Scriptures of the Jewish people have obtained an unwarranted power in Christendom; and by the concurrent judgment of ever-multiplying thinkers, that power must wane, as the Christ of the Gospels becomes more and more manifest to men.

Some years ago I published a Homiletic Commentary on the *First* Gospel, under the title of *The Genius of the Gospel*. That having run through numerous editions, is now out of print.* But it will in due course be re-published in this *Homilistic Library*. Should life be preserved, my articles on Mark and Luke will also appear in a short time. Thus my thinkings, such as they are, on the Four Gospels will be complete.

An Introduction, including a history of the Discussions relating to the Authenticity of this Gospel, Analysis of its Contents, etc., will be found at the close of the Second Volume; also a full *Index* of all the topics treated in this work.

October 1885.   **David Thomas**

*Reprinted 1980 as *Gospel of Matthew* by Kregel Publications, Grand Rapids, Michigan 49501. Other Thomas' titles are scheduled for reprinting.

Introduction

THE biography of true men is life-giving. The lives which great men—long since departed—lived on this earth, are amongst the most quickening and energizing forces of the age. Next in significance and usefulness to the life of Him Whose life " was the light of men," are the lives of the apostles; and of all the lives of the apostles that of John is not the least adapted to interest and bless posterity.

All that we have in Scripture concerning this " beloved disciple " we may gather up under three general heads.

I. The CIRCUMSTANCES OF HIS EARLY LIFE. As to his *birth-place*, it was probably in a small town upon the Lake of Gennesaret, called Bethsaida. The scenery in which he was brought up was picturesque and lovely, suited well to awaken the poetry of his nature, and make on his young heart impressions of the majesty of Him Who piled up the hills around, and poured forth the sea that rolled at his feet. As to his *family*, he was the son of Zebedee and Salome, and the brother of James. His parents were not poor. The fact that his father owned a ship and employed hired servants (Mark i. 20); that his mother was among those women who contributed towards the maintenance of Jesus (Matt. xxvii. 56); and that our Lord considered John to be in a position that would enable him to take care of His mother, lead us to the conclusion that if his family were not affluent they were in easy circumstances. His mother, if not his father, was godly. She attended our Lord in His circuit through Galilee, ministered to His bodily wants, followed Him to the Cross, and brought spices for His burial. No doubt such parents gave their son an education equal to their means. It is true that in Acts iv. 13 it is said that the council perceived of Peter and John " that they were unlearned . . men." This means, however, nothing more than that they had not been properly trained in schools of Talmudic theology. There are in this age narrow-minded men here in England, who consider some of our greatest scholars uneducated and unlearned because they have not been to Oxford or Cambridge.

The circumstances of his young life supplied most of the conditions of a noble character. He inherited, no doubt, a *good bodily organization*. His parents were not doomed to breathe the impure air of a pent up city. Their home was out in open nature; the fresh breezes of the hills and the sea breathed around their dwelling. Their habits were not those of self-indulgence and indolence which generate disease, nor on the other hand of hard brain work which tends to enervate the system. The work of the muscles and the limbs out upon the shore, the sea, and the field was their invigorating occupation. The child thus inheriting, what is almost essential to mental and moral greatness—a healthful frame—grew up amidst the same salutary and invigorating conditions. He breathed the same air, he sailed with his father in the skiff, and toiled with his father at the net. *His early impressions* from nature would be large and deep. Our greatness is determined by our ideas, and our ideas by our impressions. Small ideas can never make a great man, nor can great ideas grow out of small impressions. Large plants must have a deep soil. Hence some philosophers, not as I think without reason, maintain that, as a rule, a man must be brought up amidst grand scenery to have a grand soul. Be this as it may. To John's young eye nature towered in some of her most lovely and majestic aspects, and spoke, in the wail of trees, the howl of winds, and the roar of billows, strange and stirring poetry to his heart. His *religious* training, too, was undoubtedly favourable to future greatness. Whether his father was religious or not, it is clear that his mother was, notwithstanding the gust of ambition that once swept through her soul. Her services to Jesus, especially her following Him to the Cross, show that she was a woman of noble type, generous, loving, self-sacrificing, heroic. The mother, more than any other finite force, shapes the mind, moulds the character, and rules the destiny of the boy. Her sons are as clay in the plastic hands of her influence; John was trained religiously, and no doubt before he knew Jesus he had attended the ministry of the great forerunner. The fulminations of the Reformer would prepare his young heart for the serene and sanctifying ministry of Jesus of Nazareth. This is all that we know of his life prior to his connection with Christ. Notice—

II. The COURSE OF HIS CHRISTIAN LIFE. Here we have to mark him in several capacities.

(1.) As a *disciple.* He and his brother James were called by Jesus as they were mending their nets on board their little skiff. The call was *unexpected* but *effectual* (Matt. ix. 21, 22.) As a disciple he had to learn of Jesus. He was the most privileged of them all. He was not only one of the favoured three who witnessed the transfiguration, and had to watch in Gethsemane; but he was the only one who is said to have leaned on our Lord's bosom, he is called the "*beloved disciple.*" He had also the honour of taking charge of the Blessed Virgin.

(2.) As an *apostle.* He was called to this high office at the same time as the other eleven (Matt. x. 2—4). He was the youngest of the apostolic circle, the Benjamin of the twelve. His work was to preach and work miracles. Though we have but little recorded of what he did in this capacity, we may rest assured that he discharged his duties well.

(3.) As an *author.* If he wrote this wonderful gospel, he did it probably long after the destruction of Jerusalem, and after the decease of all the other apostles, about sixty years subsequent to the crucifixion of Christ. He wrote also the Epistles and the Apocalypse.

(4.) As a *bishop.* He had to superintend the Churches that had been planted in Asia Minor.

Such a life as his must have been most fruitful in stirring incidents, yet but few are recorded. It would seem from Gal. ii. 9 that he resided after the ascension of Christ in Jerusalem, where Paul finds him; there it is probable he remained until the death of our Lord's mother, which, according to Eusebius, took place A. D. 48. Some think that the great event which drew John at last from Jerusalem into Asia Minor was the death of the Apostle Paul (A. D. 65). Errors had grown up in the Church which Paul had planted, and they required the superintendence of such a bishop as John. It was during the period of his labours in Asia Minor that he was banished by one of the Roman Emperors to Patmos, in the Ægean Sea, where he wrote the Apocalypse. There on that lonely island, with the rugged aspects of nature before his eyes, and the saddening boom of the ocean in his ears, he received those revelations from Christ which are the wonder of all ages.

It is supposed that his exile to this desolate spot took place under Domitian (A. D. 96). He died at Ephesus, in the reign of Trajan, after he had reached a very great age; some say one hundred years, others one hundred and twenty. Notice—

III. THE CHARACTERISTICS OF HIS INNER LIFE. All seem to agree that John's mind had in it much of the woman's nature: retiring rather than demonstrative; receptive rather than originative; intuitive rather than logical; gentle and loving. One thing is certain, that love was the atmosphere of his soul after he became the disciple of Jesus Christ. The fact that his head rested on the Saviour's bosom, that Jesus is said to have loved him and committed His mother to his charge, shows that he was pre-eminently the *disciple of love*. Moreover, his writings are full of love. All his thoughts were generated in that region; every sentence he wrote was with a pen dipped in love. Tradition says that, when he had reached his extremest old age he became too feeble to walk to the meetings, and was carried to them by young men. He could no longer say much, but he constantly repeated the words, " Little children, love one another." When he was asked why he constantly repeated these words, his answer was, " Because this is the command of the Lord, and because enough is done if but this one thing is done."

Three remarks may be offered in relation to his Love.

First: His love was *capable of indignation*. We find his whole nature at one time in a flame of anger; he wished a Samaritan village to be burned up, because its inhabitants would not receive Jesus. There are passages also in his writings, especially in his epistles, which show that whilst he was a disciple of love he was a " son of thunder "—a Boanerges. He has been represented by many as a sentimental man, and has been painted as a youth of soft and effeminate features, but such was not John. There is a difference between an *angry man* and a man angry. An angry man is a man of malign, irritable temperament, whose whole nature is run to gall; but a *man angry* may be a man of the most loving nature. The Bible teaches us that there is an anger without sin. The anger of love is like fire from flint, it requires effort to bring it out, but as soon almost as it flashes it is extinct. In truth our capacity of loving is the measure of our capacity of indignation.

Genuine love has two sides, the lion as well as the lamb. The wrath most to be dreaded is the wrath of the lamb; it is oil in flames. The stronger a man's love the more you should dread his anger, for it has a depth, a virtue, a meaning, a divinity about it. Such anger is like the lightning, terrible, scathing and burning, because of the impurities of the universe. "Who is offended and I burn not?"

Secondly: His love was *divinely enlightening*. None of the apostles gave out loftier thoughts of God and Christ and immortality than John. His love bore him, as with the pinions of an eagle, into realms where he saw and heard things unknown to others. His writings are marvellous revelations of thought.

Three features distinguish his biography of Christ from those of the synoptists. It is *reflective, supplementary*, and *corrective*.

It is *reflective*. It does not merely record that in our Saviour's life which he saw and heard, but more, that about it which He thought and felt. He paints, as it were, the Christ as He appeared, not merely to his *outward eye*, but to his *inner soul*.

It is *supplementary*. He does not record all that the other evangelists wrote down; he omits much that they recorded, and gives more, in a form of stirring sublimity which escapes their notice, and perhaps transcends their conceptions. "Every man," says *Ebrard*, " may *see* the ineffable beauty of an alpine scene under the setting sun, but not every man can feel it, still less *paint* it. St. John had the nature of a living mirror which not merely received the full brightness of the Lord's glory, but could also reflect it."

His Gospel was also *corrective*. It was evidently written in order to put down the Gnostic, Labian and Judaic errors that had sprung up in the Churches. His epistles too are rich in the highest thoughts; they breathe the same spirit, throb with the same high thinking, wear the same literary features. His theology is not a thing of dry propositions, but of living realities. His loving heart saw God and he said, "God is light;" "God is love." A loving heart is the best interpreter of Divine truth; this he felt when he wrote, "He that loveth not, knoweth not God; for God is love."

"Love is blind," say some: this is a libel on this sublime affection. The more we love the more we see God—God and His universe then lie open to the loving heart. "O wonderful power of love," says *Novalis*, "organ of all spiritual knowledge, eye of the soul by which we gaze on God!"

Thirdly: His love was *sublimely heroic*. This may be inferred from the fact that he stood by the Cross when his Master was dying amidst the enraged fury of the mob. All the other disciples had fled, but John was there because he loved. He knew from experience what he said : " Perfect love casteth out fear." Love is courage; love is the essence of the truly heroic. There is a well-founded tradition concerning him which illustrates the invincible heroism of love. Clemens Alexandrinus, in his book, τίς ὁ σωζόμενος πλούσιος, narrates the following: " Listen to a story, or rather to a genuine tradition of the Apostle John, which has been faithfully treasured in memory. On his return from Patmos to Ephesus, he visited the neighbouring regions to ordain bishops and organize churches. While he was engaged in ex-horting and comforting the brethren in a city near Ephesus whose name is given by some, he noticed a handsome, spirited young man, toward whom he felt himself drawn so powerfully, that he turned to the bishop of the congregation, with the words, ' I commit him to you, who are witnesses of my heartfelt earnestness.' The bishop received the young man, promised to do all in his power, and John, at parting, repeated the same charge. The elder took the youth home, educated and watched over him, and finally baptized him. After he had given him this seal of the Lord, however, he abated in his solicitude and watchfulness. The young man, too early freed from restraint, fell into bad company. He was first led into lavish habits, and finally drawn on to rob travellers by night. Like a spirited steed that springs from the path, and rushes madly over a precipice, so did his vehement nature hurry him toward the abyss of destruction. He renounced all hope in the grace of God ; and as he considered himself involved in the same destiny with his com-panions, was ready to commit some startling crime. He associated them with himself, organized a band of robbers, put himself at their head, and surpassed them all in cruelty and violence. Some time after, John's duties again called him to that city. When he had attended to all the other matters, he said to the bishop : ' Well, bishop, restore the pledge which the Saviour and I entrusted to thee, in the presence of the congregation !' The bishop at first was alarmed, supposing that John was speaking of money, and charging him with embezzlement, But when John continued: ' I demand again that young man, and the soul of my brother,' the old man sighed heavily, and with tears replied : ' He is dead !' ' Dead !'

said the disciple of the Lord ; 'in what way did he die ?' 'He is dead to God,' responded the old man; 'he became godless, and finally a robber. He is no longer in the Church, but with his fellows holds the fastnesses of a mountain.' The Apostle, when he heard this, with a loud cry rent his clothing and smote his head, and exclaimed: 'To what a keeper have I committed my brother's soul!' He takes a horse and a guide and hastens to the spot where the band of robbers was to be found. He is seized by their outguard; he makes no attempt to escape, but cries out: 'I have come for this very purpose. Take me to your captain!' Their captain, completely armed, is waiting for them to bring him, but, recognizing John as he approached, flees, from a sense of shame. John nevertheless, forgetting his age, hastens after him with all speed, crying: 'Why, my child, do you flee from me—from me, your father, an unarmed old man? Have compassion on me, my child; do not be afraid. You yet have a hope of life. I will yet give account to Christ for you. If needs be, I will gladly die for you, as Christ died for us. I will lay down my life for you. Stop! Believe, Christ hath sent me.' Hearing these words, he first stands still and casts his eyes upon the ground. He next throws away his arms, and commences trembling and weeping bitterly. When the old man approaches, he clasps his knees, and with the most vehement agony pleads for forgiveness, baptizing himself anew as it were with his own tears: all this time, however, he conceals his right hand. But the Apostle pledging himself with an appeal to God for his truth, that he had obtained forgiveness from the Saviour for him, implores him even on his knees, and the hand he had held back he kisses as if it were cleansed again by his penitence. He finally led him back to the Church. Here he pleaded with him, earnestly strove with him in fasting, urged him with monitions until he was able to restore him to the Church—an example of sincere repentance and genuine regeneration."

This is true courage. Of the courageous man *Cowper* says :

> "He holds no parley with unmanly fears,
> Where duty bids he confidently steers,
> Faces a thousand dangers at her call,
> And, trusting in his God, surmounts them all."

Here is another anecdote concerning John narrated in Dr. Ellicott's "Commentary" which is too good to leave out. *Cassian* says : "The Blessed Evangelist was one day gently stroking a partridge, when a young man returning from hunting asked in astonishment how a man so illustrious could spend his time in such a manner? 'What have you got in your hand?' said the Apostle. 'A bow,' said the young man. 'Why is it not strung?' 'Because if I carried it strung always it would lose the elasticity which I shall want in it when I draw the arrow.' 'Do not be angry then, my young friend, if I sometimes in this way unstring my spirit, which may otherwise lose its spring and fail at the very moment when I shall need its power.'"

Homiletical Commentary on Gospel of John

John 1:1-18

CHRIST AND GOD

*(Preface to John's Gospel History.—*John i. 1—18.)

" In the beginning was the Word, and the Word was with God, and the Word
was God. The same was in the beginning with God."

EXEGETICAL REMARKS. — " Each
Evangelist," says *Godet,* " enters
upon his subject in the way which
corresponds best to the spirit of his
narrative. Matthew, whose purpose
is to demonstrate the right of Jesus
to the theocratic throne, begins with
His genealogy. Mark, who compiles
memorabilia, throws himself without
exordium *in mediam rem.* Luke,
who purposes to write a history properly so called, gives accounts to his
readers of his sources, aim, and method.
The prologue of John ought to be
equally in keeping with the general
viewpoint of his narrative. But to
determine this relation, requires the
profound study of that remarkable
piece which, more than any other
passage of our holy books, perhaps,
has exercised a decisive influence on
the conception of Christianity in the
Church down to our day." The
first eighteen verses of this chapter
constitute a prologue to the whole
work. The Logos of Plato and Philo
merely stood for a group of ideas.
But the Logos of John stands for the
real, the personal incarnate God Himself. "*In the beginning* (R. V. AT
FIRST) *was the Word.*" Christ is
spoken of as the Logos, the Word.
The Logos absolutely, as here, and the
Logos incarnate,—"made flesh," &c.
"*In the beginning.*" Of what? The
verbal revelation of God to man?
The appearance of the human race?
The origin of the universe? The context indicates the last. We are here
taken back into the immeasurable
abysses of time, or as Augustine has
it, "the topless mount of God."

HOMILETICS

The subject here is *Christ and God,* Christ as the Eternal
Revealer, Companion and *Self* of God. Notice—

I —THAT CHRIST IS THE ETERNAL REVEALER OF GOD

"*In the beginning was the Word,*"—the Logos. A word is the
revealer of the speaker. Christ here is called " THE WORD." God
has many words, many revealers. All the phenomena of nature,
all the operations of His power, all the dispensations of His government, are His words; His revealers. But Christ is *the Logos.* He

is not *a* word, but "THE WORD." As the Revealer, this Word is distinguished—

First: By its faithfulness. Christ is the *exact* Exponent of the Divine intellect and heart. There is not the slightest shade of discrepancy. He agrees with Eternal reality; thus He is called "*the* Truth," and "the faithful and true Witness." This Word is distinguished—

Secondly: By its fulness. Other words only speak partially of God. Some give intimations of His wisdom, some of His power, some of His goodness, &c. But Christ speaks out the *whole* God. "He is the express image of His Person." "So that he that hath seen Him hath seen the Father." The Word is distinguished—

Thirdly: By its forcefulness. Human words are sometimes powerful. They are not always air; they are sometimes a force. God's words in nature are *mighty*. The Psalmist speaks of the "voice of the Lord," as "breaking the cedars," "making Lebanon bound like a young unicorn," "dividing the flames," &c., &c. But Christ is a "*Word*," infinitely more powerful. As a "*Word*" He moves and sways the moral mind of the universe; and more, He calls dead souls to life. Christ is "the power of God:" He is then, the Eternal Logos.

We are here taught—

II —THAT CHRIST IS THE ETERNAL COMPANION OF GOD

"*And the Word was with God.*" The expression implies that He had a conscious existence distinct from the Absolute One. He was *with* Him.

First: Christ was with Him in the sense of agreement. God's volitions were His; God's thoughts His; God's aims His. There was a perfect concurrence.

Secondly: Christ was with Him in the sense of contact. Never out of His presence, living in His light, breathing His inspirations. He was in "the bosom of the Father." "I was by Him," says Wisdom, "as one brought up with Him," &c.

We are here taught—

III —THAT CHRIST IS THE ETERNAL SELF OF GOD

"*And the Word was God.*" This expression may, and no doubt does, mean a union with the Eternal so mysterious as to transcend all creature conception. Albeit there is a oneness which we can understand, and we can only speak of what we understand.

First: He was God in form. Deep, it would seem, in the constitution of the human soul, is the craving for some *form* of God. As He appears in the universe, He transcends the limits of human vision. Christ is the FORM He has assumed; the Form in which, in all probability, He appears to His intelligent universe as well as to man. He brings God within the sphere of human senses, sympathies, and conceptions.

Secondly: He was God in action. Through Him the Eternal volitions are carried out and realized. He is the Actualizer of God's Eternal ideas. "The Father worketh hitherto, and I work." "The Father hath life in Himself, and hath given the Son life in Himself, that all men might honour the Son even as they honour the Father." As identical as thought is with the mind of the thinker, and speech with the life of the speaker, so is Christ with God.

John 1:3

CHRIST AND THE CREATION

"All things were made by Him: and without Him was not anything made that was (R. V. HATH BEEN) made."

EXEGETICAL REMARKS.—The old Gnostic Christians held that the world was not created by the Great God, "but by Demiurgus, a spirit descending from the Æons, which were themselves derived from the Deity." John's statement stands in direct antagonism to this. He says, "*All things were made by Him*"—the Infinite Logos—"*all things.*" Some of the ancients said that part of the universe was made by a good, and part by an evil, principle. John's language stands opposed to this also. The work of creation is not a partnership work, it is the product of One Being. "*All things,*" organic and inorganic, animate and inanimate, material and spiritual, rational and irrational. "*And without Him was not anything made that was made.*" This covers all; whatever has been, whatever is, in the universe, sin excepted, He created. The universe had a *beginning;* it is not eternal, and it originated, not in *chance*, not in a *joint authorship*, but in the fiat of One Supreme Intelligence. Creation is ascribed to Christ in many other passages of Evangelic Writ: see Col. i. 16 ; Heb. i. 10, 12 ; Rev. iv. 11.

HOMILETICS

From this passage we infer—

I —THAT CHRIST IS OLDER THAN THE UNIVERSE

The worker must be older than his productions. How old then is the universe? Who shall go back enumerating ages until he reaches the initial hour of creation? If there be any truth in geology, this little globe was in existence before man appeared as its lordly inhabitant. But its Author is older than that; He was before all time, He was in "the bosom of the Father," in the solitudes of immensity alone—alone with the Infinite. "The Lord possessed me in the beginning of His way, before His works of old. I was set up from everlasting, from the beginning, or ever the earth was. When there were no depths, I was brought forth; when there were no fountains abounding with water," &c.

> The drops that swell the ocean,
> The sands that girt the shore,
> To measure His duration ;
> Their numbers have no power.

We infer from the words—

II —THAT CHRIST IS GREATER THAN THE UNIVERSE

As the architect is greater than his building, the author than his book, the artist than his productions, Christ is greater than the universe.

First: Greater in extent. How great is the universe in extent! Astronomers tell us that our solar system, as compared with the centres of systems that come within the view of their telescopes on a bright starry night, is as only one solitary leaf in a mighty forest. But what the strongest telescope discovers may be insignificant in proportion to that beyond the reach of vision. But Christ's being extends beyond the limits of the universe. The universe and all its parts are to Him as atoms in a boundless sea of sunbeams.

Secondly: Greater in force. What mighty forces there are in the universe, chemical, muscular, mental! But Christ's force is greater than all,—it is the breath and energy of all.

Thirdly: Greater in beauty. How lovely is the universe! Every part is crowded with beauty; it blooms in the plant, it sparkles in the mineral, the heavens and the earth are full of beauty. But all the beauty in the universe is but the effluence of His æsthetic nature, a touch of His pencil.

We infer from the words—

III —THAT CHRIST IS OWNER OF THE UNIVERSE

Production gives the highest right to possession! The produce of our energy we claim as our own, but what are our productions? Not creations, but combinations. The highest creature in the universe, possessing the largest amount of inventive genius and executive force, can only bring existing elements into new forms. Creatorship gives an absolute and indefeasible right to a production. Christ, therefore, *owns* the universe. "The sea is His, He made it, and His hands formed the dry land." On the same principle the universe is His, for He made it.

> "Praise ye the Lord.
> Praise ye the Lord from the heavens:
> Praise Him in the heights.
> Praise ye Him, all His angels:
> Praise ye Him, all His hosts.
> Praise ye Him, sun and moon:
> Praise Him, all ye stars of light.
> Praise Him. ye heaven of heavens,
> And ye waters that be above the heavens.
> Let them praise the name of the Lord:
> For He commanded, and they were created.
> He hath also established them for ever and ever:
> He hath made a decree which shall not pass."

John 1:4-8

CHRIST THE PRE-EMINENT AND ILLUMINATING LIFE

"In Him was life ; and the life was the light of men. And the light shineth in darkness, (R. V. THE DARKNESS) and the darkness comprehended (R. V. APPREHENDED) it not. There was (R. V. CAME) a man sent from God, whose name was John. The same came for a witness, to (R. V. THAT HE MIGHT) bear witness of the Light, that all men (R. V. OMIT) through him might believe. He was not that (R. V. THE) Light, but was sent to (R. V. CAME THAT HE MIGHT) bear witness of that (R. V. THE) Light."

EXEGETICAL REMARKS.— Ver. 4.— "*In Him was life.*" The word "*life*" occurs about sixty times in the productions of John's pen. "This expression," says *Godet*, " means that the world after having passed from nothingness to being by the power of the Word, continued to draw from Him the vivifying forces necessary for its preservation and progress. After having been the root of the tree, the Logos was also its sap." "*And the life was the light of men.*" "We are led from the relation of the Word to the universe, to His relation to mankind. That which to lower beings in the scale of creation was more or less fully life, as the nature of each was more or less receptive of its power, is to the being endowed with a moral nature, and made in the divine image, the satisfaction of every moral need." —*Watkin.*

Ver. 5.—"*And the light shineth in darkness, and the darkness comprehended it not.*" "This phrase," says *Westcott*, "is a startling paradox. The light does not banish the darkness : the darkness does not overpower the light. Light and darkness coexist in the world side by side."

Ver. 6.—"*There was a man sent from God, whose name was John.*" "The name is not uncommon, but it is striking that it is given here without the usual distinctive Baptist. The writer stood to him in the relation of disciple to teacher. To him he was *the* John. A greater teacher had not then appeared, but when He did appear, former teacher and disciple alike bear witness to Him."

Ver. 7.—"*The same came for a witness.*" "This idea of witness-bearing is one of the fundamental notions of our Gospel. It is inseparable from that of faith, and correlative with it."

Ver. 8.—"*He was not that Light.*" John was the mere reflector, simply a lamp.

HOMILETICS

From this passage we learn two things concerning Christ's Life—

I —HIS LIFE WAS PRE-EMINENT

"*In Him was life.*" The language seems emphatic. Is there not life in all living creatures ? Why, then, should the writer single out Christ and say, "*In* HIM *was life ?*" He means that in Christ was life in a pre-eminent sense.

First: "*In Him was life*" without beginning. Life in all existences had a commencement, but in Him it had no origin ; it was an eternal entity.

Secondly : "*In Him was life*" without dependence. Life in all other living things is conditional ; its support rests on things outside of itself. Not so with the life in Him ; it was before the universe. Were the universe to be no more, the life in Him would continue unabated in plenitude and power.

Thirdly: "*In Him was life*" without limitation. All created life has its limits; not so with His. His is without limit. (1.) As to kind. In His life were the germs and architype of all other life, material and spiritual. (2.) As to amount. All other life is circumscribed. In the highest creature it is scarcely more than a spark, but in Him it is an ocean of unfathomable depth and immeasurable breadth. (3.) As to communicativeness. His life was the great fontal Source of all life; He is the Fountain of all life—a Fountain ever outpouring, and eternally inexhaustible. (4.) As to duration. His life will never have a termination. "He is the same yesterday, to-day, and for ever."

II —HIS LIFE WAS ILLUMINATING.

"*And the life was the Light of men.*" Christ's life, whatever its variety and fulness, had in all a *moral character*, for He was a moral Being. It was under the control of moral principles, and directed for moral ends. Hence His *character* in the New Testament is called "*life.*" There are several things taught here concerning His life as *light*—

First: That this life was "*the Light of men.*" There are some lives that are not only like bodies opaque in themselves, but bodies incapable of reflecting light. Christ's life is the Fountain of moral light. It is to all intelligent beings in the universe what our sun is to our system. Two things are here suggested in relation to this "*Light of men.*" (1.) Man needed it. "*The light shineth in darkness.*" Humanity was in moral darkness: the darkness of depravity, guilt, and suffering. When Christ came into the world He came as a sun rising on man's dark heavens. The world never had such a Light before. Again, it is suggested—(2.) Man rejected it. "*The darkness comprehended it not*"—οὐ κατέλαβεν— did not take it in; apprehended it not. Man can shut out the material light of noontide from his house by darkening his windows, or even by closing his eyes, so men shut out this moral Light; close their eyes against it. Men were "sitting in darkness and the shadow of death;" while the Light was shining above and around they "*comprehended it not.*" It is here stated again—

Secondly: That this Light was heralded by the Baptist. "*There was a man sent by God, whose name was John. The same came for a witness, to bear witness of the Light, that all men through Him might believe.*" According to prophecy (Mal. iii. 1; Isa. xl. 3) John came as the forerunner of the Messiah; came as the morning star to announce the rising Sun. He pointed to the true Light. "Behold the Lamb of God!" It is here stated—

Thirdly: That this Light becomes available by faith. "*That all men through Him might believe.*" How is this Light to enter into the individual soul, scatter its clouds, and fill it with sunshine?

Unbelief closes the windows of the soul, and leaves all its apartments in moral gloom. He who would have this heavenly light
streaming into him must *believe*.

John 1:9

CHRIST THE LIGHT OF ALL THE LIVING

"That (R. V. THERE) was the true Light, (R. V. EVEN THE LIGHT) which lighteth
every man that cometh (R. V. COMING) into the world."

EXEGETICAL REMARKS. — "*True
Light.*" "The word for '*true*' is
remarkable, it means true as opposed
to spurious, not true as opposed to
lying. It is, in fact, the old English
'very,' *e. g.* 'very God of very *God.*'
All words about truth are very characteristic of John." "*Every man.*"
The light illumines each man singly,
not all collectively. God deals with
men separately as individuals, not in
masses. The verse, Hippolytus tells us,
was used by Basilides in defending
his doctrine.—*Plummer.*

HOMILETICS

The idea which these words give at the first glance is the true
idea. Certain Biblical critics, with judgment swayed by theological
predilections, have endeavoured to give them a meaning not manifest as they stand. I take them as being true to the original, true
to human history, and true to the general teachings of Divine
revelation.

The words contain two things—

I —THAT EVERY MAN COMES INTO THE WORLD WITH A LIGHT IN HIM

"The candle of the Lord" is in every human breast. It is very
dim in infancy; but there it is, ready to be fanned into a strong
flame by educational influences. It is very dark in heathenism;
but it glimmers there amidst the dense fogs of ignorance and
superstition. This Light may be said to reflect on three subjects.

First: On social obligation. There is in every human breast
a sense of right and wrong, a feeling that something is due. This
sense is often wrongly interpreted: but there it is—it burns on.
The wrong interpretation is but the coloured glass of ignorance
through which its beams are seen.

Secondly: On religious worship. The sentiment of a God is
universal; so much so, that man has been called a "Religious
Animal."

Thirdly: On future retribution. Man everywhere has an
instinctive reference to a life beyond this—a life of reward and
punishment. That all men have this Light altogether apart from

a written revelation is—(1.) Clear from *history*. Its rays are seen in the writings of Socrates, Seneca, and many other heathen authors; are seen in the Vedas of the Brahmins, and the sacred books of China and Japan; are seen even in the life of those most degraded of heathen tribes visited by Moffatt and Livingstone. (2.) Clear from the *Word of God*. "The invisible things of God from the creation of the world are clearly seen, being understood by the things that are made, *even* His eternal power and Godhead; so that they are without excuse: Because that when they knew God, they glorified Him not as God, neither were thankful; but became vain in their imaginations, and their foolish heart was darkened." "For when the Gentiles, which have not the law unto themselves: which show the word of the law written in their hearts, their conscience also bearing witness, and their thoughts the meanwhile accusing or else excusing one another; in the day when God shall judge the secret of men by Jesus Christ according to my Gospel." "It is absurd to deny the existence of this universal Light, this conscience, this moral monarch of the soul, because in some cases it burns so dimly, and under the glasses of ignorance and super-stition, throws a false hue on many of the great subjects of duty and destiny. The 'candle of the Lord' does not shine so clearly as it was wont; must it therefore be extinguished entirely? Is it not better to have its dimmest rays than to be in palpable and disconsolate darkness? It is but an old imperfect manuscript with some broken periods, some letters worn out; must they therefore, with an unmerciful indignation, rend it and tear it asunder? It is granted that the picture has lost its gloss and beauty, the oriency of its colours, the elegancy of its lineaments, the comeliness of its proportion; must it therefore be totally defaced? Must it be made one great blot?—and must the very frame of it be broken in pieces? Would you persuade the lutanist to cut all his strings asunder because they are out of tune?—and will you break the bow upon no other account but because it is unbended? Because men have not so much of reason as they should, will they therefore resolve to have none at all? Will you throw away your gold because it is mixed with dross? Thy very being, that is imperfect too; thy graces, they are imperfect, wilt thou refuse them also?" (See *Culverwell* on "The Light of Nature.") Observe—

II —THAT THE LIGHT IN EVERY MAN IS FROM CHRIST

"*That was the true Light, that lighteth every man.*" That what? The LOGOS—the Word, "which was in the beginning with God," which "was God," and which was "made flesh." He is the Light of humanity. This is what is here taught. Christ is not only the Light that shines in the Gospel, but the Light that shines in the human soul all the world over.

First: This fact exalts Christ to the position of a Creator of souls. This idea was in John's mind when he wrote these words, " Without Him was not anything made that was made." All souls come from the hand of Christ. He puts this inextinguishable light in them, and sends them into this dark world to have it so brightened by educational influences that it may shine a lustrous orb in its own sphere. The sentiments of causation, duty, religion, future retribution, which constitute the light of the soul, are from Christ. We bless Him for this " candle." It will never burn out; it will shine on when stars are extinguished. Christ is not merely the Light of Christendom, He is the Light of heathen lands.

Secondly: This fact reveals the responsibility of heathens. They are not left in utter darkness, Christ is amongst them. They have in them the elements of truth, and many of them without revelation attain to high spiritual intelligence ; may it not be that all who act up to the light they have are accepted of their Maker ? In expressing the hope that heathens will thus be saved, we are not making salvation independent of Christ, for He is the true Light of all. I rejoice to believe that the rays of Christ's mind and heart fall beyond the pale of Gospeldom.

Thirdly: This fact furnishes an argument for the congruity of Christianity with human nature. Both the natural light in human souls and the light in the Gospel come from the same Source—Christ. Though there are things in the Gospel which men could not have discovered by the light of nature, there is nothing that does not exquisitely harmonize with all their natural intuitions.

Fourthly: This fact supplies a motive to extend the light of the Gospel. Though Christ gave men this natural light, so deeply did He feel their need of a higher light, that He becomes flesh, and dies to give it. May the Light that " lighteth every man that cometh into the world " act with them as the strange star which the old Magi beheld rolling in the heavens—conduct them to the Incarnate God !

John 1:10-13

CHRIST AND MAN

" He was in the world, and the world was made by Him, and the world knew Him not. He came unto His own, and His own (R.V. THEY THAT WERE HIS OWN) received Him not. But as many as received Him, to them gave He power (R. V. THE RIGHT) to become the sons (R. V. CHILDREN) of God, even to them that believe on His name ; which were born, not of blood, nor of the will of the flesh, nor of the will of man, but of God."

EXEGETICAL REMARKS.—Ver. 10.— *was made by Him, and the world knew* " *He was in the world and the world* *Him not.*" " The language here is hardly less wonderful than the thought. Observe its compact simplicity and grand sonorousness—the *world* resounding in each successive member of the sentence—and the enigmatic form in which it is couched startling the reader, and setting his imagination a-working to solve the vast enigma of the world's Maker treading on and yet ignored by the world He made."—*Brown*.

Ver. 11.—"*He came unto His own.*" Who were they? The Jewish people, the descendants of Abraham. "*And His own received Him not.*" Their treatment of Him during His sojourn amongst them was to the last degree unjust, ungrateful, irreverent, and ruthlessly malignant.

Ver. 12.—"*But as many as received Him.*" But how few they were! They continued a "disobedient and gainsaying people." "*To them gave He power.*" Power of privilege and capability. "*To become the sons of God.*" They were aliens. Moral affiliation to God is the sublimest privilege, but this comes only through Christ.

Ver. 13.—"*Which were born, not of blood, nor of the will of the flesh, nor of the will of man, but of God.*" "The phrase appears to be parallel with as many as received. The act of reception coincided with the infusion of divine principle by which the later growth became possible."—*Westcott*.

HOMILETICS

These words give us *three* distinct classes of men in relation to Christ:—

I —THOSE WHO KNEW HIM NOT

This is stated as an extraordinary fact. Though "*in the world the world knew Him not.*" "*In the world:*"

First: In the operations of nature. Shining in its light, breathing in its life, and speaking in its voice.

Secondly: In the intuitions of souls. In the notions of causation, the sentiments of order, the propensities to worship, and the foreboding of conscience.

Thirdly: In the events of history. In the creations of literature, in the progress of science, in the growth of commerce, and in the advancing steps of civilization.

Fourthly: In the special revelations of heaven. Appearing as the Promised Seed to Adam, as the Shiloh to Jacob, as the Counsellor to Isaiah, and the Sun of Righteousness to Malachi, and yet "*the world knew Him not.*" This class comprehends Pagans. Another class of men here given are—

II —THOSE WHO KNEW HIM, BUT DID NOT RECEIVE HIM

"*His own received Him not.*" This class comprehends all who are mere hearers of the Gospel. To know Christ, and to reject Him, is to sin against—

First: The benevolent designs of God.

Secondly: The moral sentiments of our being. Such as justice, gratitude, and reverence. Sin against—

Thirdly: The higher interests of human nature.

The other class of men here given are—

III —THOSE WHO RECEIVED HIM, AND WERE DIVINELY AFFILIATED BY THE RECEPTION

" *To them gave He power to become the sons of God.*" He unites estranged humanity to God, by in-breathing His own filial disposition. A father may have twelve offspring, all young men, and yet there may be only six, or fewer, *sons.* Concerning those who have lost all filial affection for him, and who have grown hostile to him, he says, They are not my *sons,* they are lost to me; they are my enemies. These loving ones are my sons. *It is filial affection that makes the son.* All men are God's offspring, but the filial only are His sons. The end of Christ's mission was to inspire men with the *filial disposition,* and thus make them " *sons of God.*"

John 1:14

THE INCARNATE GOD

" And the Word was made (R. V. BECAME) flesh, and dwelt among us, (and we beheld His glory, the glory as of the only begotten of (R. V. FROM) the Father,) full of grace and truth."—i. 14.

EXEGETICAL REMARKS. — No less than thirteen introductory verses usher in this announcement of matchless interest to the universe and transcendent benefaction to humanity, announcing one of the grandest epochs. The *Logos* became man, veritable man, not as the ancient Docetae suppose, an apparent man, but a real man. Hence He displays all the features which characterize human nature. He slept, hungered, thirsted, wearied, grieved, &c. A great mystery this ! " Who can declare His generation !" " *Dwelt amongst us.*" Tabernacled with man. He had no settled residence, His stay on earth was transient. " *We beheld His glory.*" The mystic Shekinah radiated through the Temple. " *The glory as of the only begotten of the Father.*" " There is probably a special reference here to the Transfiguration. The glory is such as is the attribute of an only Son."—*Watkin.* " *Full of grace and truth.*" " Grace corresponds with the idea of the revelation of God as love, by Him Who is Life ; and truth with that of the revelation of God as light, by Him Who is Himself Light."—*Westcott.*

HOMILETICS

Here we have an account of the wonderful meeting of the human and the Divine in one Person—Christ. Two things are here taught concerning Christ as the *incarnate Deity—the God-Man—*

I —THE CHRIST OF GOD HAD A BEGINNING

" *The Word was made flesh.*" " *Flesh*" is used in very different senses in the Word of God. Sometimes it means all *animal nature,* —" The end of all flesh has come before Me." Sometimes *moral sensibility*—" I will take the heart of stone, and give a heart of flesh," &c. Sometimes *spiritual depravity*—" They that are in the flesh cannot please God," &c. Sometimes *human nature.* Thus—

"Thou hast given Him power over all flesh." The text means that the " Word," the Divinity, assumed human nature, body and soul. Human nature, however, not in its fallen state, with any taint of corruption in it; but human nature fresh and pure from the hand of God. "He was holy, harmless, undefiled, separate from sinners." Observe then—

First: Christ had human nature. He was not a mere apparition but a veritable Man. He had "flesh"—"He was made in all points like as we are; yet without sin."

Secondly: Christ was something more than human nature. He was a Man, but His humanity was only a constituent part of His personality. His humanity was no more Himself than the body is man.

Thirdly: Christ had the Divine and the human united in one personality. He was Divine, for the Word that became flesh, we are told, "*was God.*" But Divinity was no more Christ than the soul is man.

What then is Christ? He is the *union of man and Divinity in One Conscious Personality.* There was no actual Christ in the universe until the Incarnation, until the " *Word was made flesh.*" The term "*flesh*" is used rather than man, perhaps because it is impersonal. Christ took not some particular man or type of humanity, but human nature, and became One with the race, that all might have a share in Him. Observe—

II —THE CHRIST OF GOD LIVED AMONGST MEN

" *Dwelt amongst us.*" * εσκήνωσεν ἐν ἡμῖν. The word means tabernacled. He pitched His tent amongst men. Three things are here taught concerning this Christ-life among men—

First: This Christ-life was a manifestation of Divine glory to men. " *We beheld His glory.*" Jehovah of old revealed Himself to His people in the mystic radiance of the Shekinah, but now in the tabernacle or tent of Christ's humanity He reveals Himself to the human race. The glory of God was seen in His stately deportment, in His sublime doctrines, in His illustrious deeds, but especially was it seen in His transfiguration. "We were eye-witnesses of His majesty," says Peter (2 Peter i. 16, 17). The word seems to point to spectators in a theatre.

Secondly: This Christ-life was the only Divine production of the kind in the universe. " *The only begotten of the Father.*" This phrase is used by John in three other places, and by no other inspired writer. What does it mean? Some say—especially beloved. This is unsatisfactory. Others—eternal generation. This is confusion. The only intelligible idea we can attach to it is this: that God "*begot*" or effected the union between Himself and humanity, and that there is no other such union in the universe.

* See Germs of Thought, p. 22.

There is only *One* Christ throughout immensity. He is the "*only begotten of the Father.*" He stands in the creation as sublimely Unique—"*the only begotten.*"

Thirdly: This Christ-life abounded with grace and truth. "*Full of grace and truth.*" The word "*grace*" I take as standing for all that is genial, generous, and loving in temper: and the word "*truth*" as representing all that is substantial, real, and enduring in thought, habit, and life. The former is opposed to all that is cold, selfish, and malign; the latter to all that is hollow, fictitious, and ephemeral. They are two sides or sections of the same thing: and that thing moral goodness, the perfection of God, and the glory and happiness of His intelligent creation. Two remarks are suggested concerning this "*grace and truth.*"

First: They are deficient in man, and this is man's ruin.

(1.) Their deficiency is *unnatural.* Man's soul is formed for "*grace and truth.*" They are its native atmosphere, no other air will suit its life: its native orbit—in no other sphere will its faculties thrive and move harmoniously. Hence the soul in their absence declines in health—is pained with remorse, and groans under a terrible sense of emptiness.

(2.) Their deficiency is *universal.* This is too astoundingly evident to require argument or illustration. Selfishness and falsehood—their moral opposites—reign supreme in all unregenerate souls.

(3.) Their deficiency is *disastrous.* Their absence gives room for, and facilitates, the growth of every evil thought and passion. The soul in which "*grace and truth*" are not cultivated becomes like the sluggard's vineyard, overgrown with thorns and nettles and noxious weeds. It runs into a wilderness of evils. There is not a wrong institution, a corrupt system, a criminal act, that are not modifications of that selfishness and falsehood which pervade all the souls that are destitute of "*grace and truth.*"

Another remark suggested concerning "*grace and truth*" is—

Secondly: They are abundant in Christ, and this is man's hope. He is "*full of grace and truth.*" He overflows with those very blessings which fallen men most urgently require. There is an *empty* world: here is a *full* Christ. He has sufficient "*grace and truth*" in Him to fill up every graceless and untruthful soul.

(1.) He is full of "*grace.*" All that is generous, loving, compassionate, forgiving, fills Him to an overflow, and it streams from Him in every look, expression, and movement. (*a*) He is "*full of grace*" notwithstanding His immense *provocations.* Provocations soon exhaust all the kindness in our nature, or rather soon turn it to wrath. What provocations Christ received! Contemplate the treatment He met with from the men of His age!—yet after human enmity had done its worst, He sends offers of mercy to His murderers at Jerusalem. (*b*) He is "*full of grace*" notwithstanding

His immense *communications*. What millions has He enriched with His grace! Out of His fulness innumerable multitudes have received grace upon grace : yet the fountain in Him is unexhausted, and as full as ever.

(2.) He is "*full of truth.*" What is truth? Complete relative truth is *conformity of life to absolute reality*. Truth in *thought* is conformity to eternal *fact;* truth in *life* is conformity to eternal *law.* Christ was "*full*" of the "*truth.*" His thoughts about God and His universe : man, his constitution and condition, his duty and destiny, are in exact agreement with eternal reality. His life in every part was in exquisite harmony with absolute and eternal rectitude. He was the "TRUTH." He is the only perfect Teacher the world has ever had. "No man hath seen God at any time." Brothers, our duty and our interests agree, and are alike obvious. We need "*grace and truth*" to expel the demons of selfishness and falsehood, and there is only one Being in the universe that can supply our need, and that is Christ. He is "*full of grace and truth.*" "Lord, to whom shall we go?"

Germs of Thought
No. 1   John 1:14, Eph. 3:17

"And the Word was made flesh, and dwelt among us."
"That Christ may dwell in your hearts."

A DOUBLE INCARNATION

These two passages present to us two incarnations or Christ's two births—His birth into the world, and His birth into the human soul. Men think more of the former than of the latter— there is a period set apart in every year for its celebration. But the latter is equally momentous. The soul has its births. The rising into conscious existence of every latent sentiment is a birth. There was a time with us all when the *filial* sentiment had no conscious existence; it was not until we began to think that it was born. The connubial sentiment, as a vital power, is a new birth in the soul; so also is the parental; in childhood's heart this has no conscious life—it is a new birth. The highest birth of the soul is the birth into it of thoughts, sympathies, purposes, that are thoroughly Christlike—the birth of Christ.

Let us notice—

I —THE ANALOGY BETWEEN THESE TWO INCARNATIONS

First : Both result from Divine interposition. The child that was born in Bethlehem was begotten of the Spirit, so is His birth in the human soul. His advent to human hearts is in all cases the result of Divine power. "It pleased God," said the Apostle, "to reveal His Son in me."

Secondly: Both create great epochs. The birth of Christ in Bethlehem is the one period that tests the past and determines the future, the convergent and divergent point of all history. The B. C. meets in it; the A. D. starts from it. It is so with this advent in the soul; the greatest epoch in its history is in that event. All after-life takes its date, and derives its impulse from that.

Thirdly: Both awake antagonism. Christ's birth in Bethlehem roused the world to hostility. "Herod sought the life of the young Child." So long as He lived here the world was against Him; its enmity ultimately drove Him hence. It is so with His birth into the soul. It wakes up the antagonism of the depraved nature; old lusts, prejudices, habits, rose up against this young child, and would kill it in the cradle.

Fourthly: Both are manifestations of God. The Babe born in the manger was "God manifest in the flesh." The life of Christ on earth was "the brightness of His Father's glory." So with His birth into the soul. The nature is renewed after the Divine image. The man in whose heart Christ is, is the highest revelation of God on this earth.

Let us notice—

II —THE DISSIMILARITY BETWEEN THESE TWO INCARNATIONS

First: The one may become a curse to man, the other must be a blessing. Of all the afflicting and crushing memories that can fall on a lost soul, nothing is so terrible as the birth of Christ into the world. This fact aggravates the world's guilt, and augments the world's responsibility a thousand-fold. How many of the many millions in the lost provinces of God's universe may be ready to exclaim—"Would that the incarnation of Christ had never happened! Would that He had never visited the earth!" On the contrary, His advent to the soul is ever a blessing. It brings the spring and the sunshine of ever-advancing blessedness into it.

Secondly: The one occurred without man's choice, the other requires his seeking. Christ came into the world as the sun rises in the morning, as the seasons roll on—independent of all human choice. A few, it is true, expected Him; but their wishes and hopes had nothing to do with Him coming. He came. But in His advent to the soul He does not force His way into the heart; He waits to be invited. "Behold, I stand at the door and knock: if any man hear My voice, and open the door, I will come in to him, and will sup with him, and he with Me." "If a man love Me, he will keep My words: and My Father will love him, and We will come unto him, and will make our abode with him." You must open the door of your hearts, love Him, keep His commandments, and then He will "*dwell in you.*"

Brother, has this spiritual incarnation taken place in thy soul?

Is " Christ formed in thee ? " Is He in thee as " the hope of glory ? " Does " He dwell in thy heart by faith ? " This is the all momentous question. If this incarnation has taken place, thou hast a right to a happy Christmas, and a title to a happy destiny, and thou wilt have it. A true Church is an assembly of men in whom the " *Word has been made flesh* "—men who are the incarnation of Christ. Oh ! speed the hour when all the race shall be such incarnations !

John 1:15-17

CHRIST THE TRANSCENDENT ONE

" John bare (R. V. BEARETH) witness of Him, and cried, (R. V. CRIETH) saying, This was He of whom I spake, (R. V. SAID) He that cometh after me is preferred (R. V. BECOME) before me : for He was before me. And (R. V. FOR) of His fulness have (R. V. OMIT HAVE) all we received, and grace for grace. For the law was given by Moses, but grace and truth came by Jesus Christ."—i. 15—17.

EXEGETICAL REMARKS.—Ver. 15.— " *John bare witness of Him.*" This is John the Baptist, the son of Zacharias and Elizabeth, who was six years older than Jesus. " *This was He of whom I spake.*" " Twice on successive days had he heard these words from the lips of the Baptist ; three times within a few verses does he record them. They are amongst the words stamped on the hearts in the crises of life, and as fresh in the aged Apostle as they had been in the youthful inquirer. " *He that cometh after me, is preferred before me.*" " The precedence in dignity," says *Westcott*, "which Christ at once assumed when He was manifested, was due to His essential priority. He was in His essence (viii. 58) before John, and therefore at His revelation He took the place which corresponded with His nature."

Ver. 16.—" *And of His fulness have we all received.*" " The Evangelist had declared, in the 14th verse, that Jesus was full of grace and truth, and now he goes on to testify for himself and the disciples generally, that they had all received of His fulness of grace and truth." " *Grace for grace.*" Grace upon grace. " One and the same grace in its succession, in its constantly renewed impartation."—*Luthardt.* What a fulness of grace in Christ—a fountain copious, ever open, inexhaustible ! Take one drop from the ocean, and the mighty volume of waters is so much the less. But the mighty rivers of grace flowing from Christ leave the fountain in its inexhaustible abundance.

Ver. 17.—" *For the law was given by Moses, but grace and truth came by Jesus Christ.*" The " *law*" here stands in contrast to "*grace and truth ;*" the eternal law of right knows nothing of grace. Law concerns itself with duty ; grace with guilt and misery.

HOMILETICS

Here Christ appears as He has appeared before in this Gospel and will appear again—as He appears everywhere in the New Testament—the transcendent one.

The verses indicate—

I —THAT HE IS TRANSCENDENT IN GREATNESS

" *John bare witness of Him.*" This was his grand mission, as appears in the 7th verse. " *And cried,*" as the voice cried in the wilderness (Isa. xl. 3). He was earnest in his work as a witness, and what did he thus earnestly testify ? *"This was He of whom I spake, He that cometh after me is preferred before me: for He was before me."*

This last expression he repeats several times in this chapter. What does it mean ? Simply this,—*He that succeeds me in time transcends me in greatness.* Christ, though born after John, soon shows His superiority to John. John was a great man, he stands forth prominent and radiant. "Amongst those that are born of women," said Christ, "there is not a greater than John the Baptist." But great as he was, he will not bear comparison with Christ.

First: Christ is greater in person. John was a man, a good man, a man inspired by heaven; but still a man and nothing more. Christ united in His personality the human and Divine. "The "Word" so became "flesh," and the "flesh" so became "Word," that they constituted but one Personality.

Secondly: Christ is greater in character. John was a good man, though he shared, no doubt, to some extent, the imperfections common even to the best of men. But Christ was perfect. *Negatively* perfect. He never had sinned. "He was the holy, harmless, undefiled, separate from sinners." *Positively* perfect. "He fulfilled all righteousness." He was *"full* of grace and truth." *"Grace and truth"* came into John, they were imparted. They welled up in Christ as from their native fountain.

Thirdly: Christ is greater in position. John's office was that of forerunner. He had to go before the King in his march, level the hills, exalt the valleys, and announce the Royal approach. Christ was the illustrious King. John stood between his contemporaries and Christ, pointing them to Him. Christ stands between heaven and earth, and says,—"I am the Way, no man can come unto the Father but by ME." Well might John, therefore, say, *"He is preferred before me."*

The verses indicate—

II —THAT HE IS TRANSCENDENT IN BENEFICENCE

"And of His fulness have all we received, and grace for grace." Some read this, grace *instead* of grace. Others, grace *upon* grace. If the first is accepted, we have the idea of one grace taking the place of another, which is constantly occurring, in the experience of humanity. Take God's dealing—(1.) With the *world at large,* and we find one dispensation of grace taking the place of another. The Patriarchal taking the place of the Adamic, the Mosaic taking the place of the Patriarchal, the Gospel taking the place of the Mosaic; thus one dispensation of grace is taken away and another takes its place. Take—

(2.) The *personal experience* of the good, and the same change appears. God takes away temporal graces or gifts, and gives spiritual grace instead: He takes away secular property and physical health, and gives instead spiritual wealth, and moral life and vigour. And even spiritual graces He sometimes exchanges, according to the exigencies of His children. If the latter idea is accepted, viz.—grace *upon* grace, then we have the idea of abundance. Grace flowing in upon grace, like billow on billow in a rising tide, without intermission or end.

Indeed, whichever idea is accepted, three facts concerning Divine grace are suggested—

First: Constant succession. Grace following grace, without a break—following as drops in a river, as seasons follow seasons in the year; there is no pause, no break. *"Grace for grace"*—the river of grace is ever rolling on.

Secondly: Inexhaustible fulness. Paul speaks of the "unsearchable riches of Christ." His *"grace"* is an ocean that has no limits; as light is ever coming from the sun, grace ever flows from Him.

Thirdly: Relative adaptation. *"Grace for grace,"* according to the particular exigencies of mankind. One man requires a grace not so needful for another. Nay, the same man does not require the same grace at all times. What would serve him yesterday he may not need to-day; what he needs he shall have. "As thy day, so shall thy strength be."

Now the Evangelist says that of *"His fulness have all we received."* Who are the *"we"*? When he said this, the Gospel had been preached widely through the world. Churches had been planted in all the centres of civilization and influence. Paul had travelled from Jerusalem to Illyricum, and founded a Church even in the Imperial City. The converts to Christianity by this time constituted a multitude difficult to number. And the *"We"* includes them all. He speaks the experience of all the Christians then living, when he said, *"we have received."*

The verses indicate—

III —THAT HE IS TRANSCENDENT IN HISTORY

"For the law was given by Moses, but grace and truth came by Jesus Christ." This is given as a reason for the superabundant supply of grace. We are not to suppose either that there was no *"grace and truth"* in the communications of Moses, or that there was no *"law"* in the communications of Christ. This would not accord with fact. There was some portion of *"grace"* in the dispensation of Moses; there was some portion of *"law"* in the dispensation of Christ. The language must be taken in a comparative sense. The Evangelist points to the leading character-

istics of their dispensations. *Rigour and shadow* characterise the dispensation of Moses; *love and reality* that of Christ. Two remarks here may illustrate the passage—

First: The rigour and the shadows brought to the world by Moses were so important as to give him an elevated position in the world's history. Man wanted law, a code of enactments, positive rules for the regulation of his conduct. Man wanted, also, rites and ceremonies, symbols and shadows of the reality. What Moses taught in relation to religion was "a shadow of good things to come," and his law on the whole, says Paul, "worketh wrath" (Rom. iv. 15). Still the *severity* and the *shadow* of the things which Moses brought were so important as to give him a place in the world's history second to no other man's, however illustrious.

Secondly: The love and the reality brought to the world through Christ were so transcendently important as to give Him the highest position in the world's history. "*Grace and truth*," or love and reality, are the two grand essential elements for the spiritual culture and salvation of mankind. Grace for the heart, truth for the intellect. The one to quicken, inspire, develop, the other to direct, guide, and fashion. What have "*grace and truth*" done for humanity? All the real good that has ever appeared in the world, that is now, or ever will be, must be ascribed to the working of these two forces: and these "*came through Jesus Christ.*" He revealed them in His teaching, He incarnated them in His life, He glorified them in His death. What the sun is in the heavens, the name of Christ is in the world; not only infinitely more majestic than all the other objects, but the Source of all their radiance.

John 1:18

CHRIST'S RELATION TO THE GREAT FATHER

"No man hath seen God at any time ; the only begotten Son, which is in the bosom of the Father, He hath declared Him."—i. 18.

EXEGETICAL REMARKS.—"*No man hath seen God.*" "Not even Moses, or the greatest prophets. Intuitive glances of God all may have, perhaps all have occasionally, but a full sight of God none have but Christ. No man's views of God are to be taken as absolutely correct, but the views of Christ may be thus taken. '*The only begotten Son, which is in the bosom of the Father.*' The image is used of the closest and tenderest of human relationships. The '*bosom of the Father,*' like heaven, is a state, not a place."—*Westcott.*

HOMILETICS

These first eighteen introductory verses of this Gospel enshrine the sublimest views of the Son of God. The text is almost an epitome of the whole, and it leads us to look at *Christ in relation to the Infinite Father.*

I —HE IS THE NEAREST RELATION TO THE GREAT FATHER

" *He is the only begotten Son.*" This phrase occurs in three other places in John's writings (John i. 14; iii. 16 and 18; 1 John iv. 9). That the language implies an essential relation to the ABSOLUTE, perfectly unique, is obvious from two considerations—

First: The interpretation which the Jews attached to it. " Therefore the Jews sought the more to kill Him, because He not only had broken the Sabbath, but said also that God was His Father, making Himself equal with God."

Secondly: The most extraordinary manifestation of Divine love which the sacred writers saw in His mission. "He that spared not His own Son."

Several things connected with His history as recorded by the Evangelists show that He did sustain this essential and *unique* relation to the Great Father.

(1.) His *miraculous conception*. "The angel answered and said unto her, The Holy Ghost shall come upon thee, and the power of the Highest shall overshadow thee: therefore also that holy thing which shall be born of thee shall be called the Son of God."

(2.) *His entire history.* His whole life agrees with the wonderful account of His supernatural conception, and shows that He was the " *Son of God*" in a sense in which no other man was. His teaching everywhere assumes and asserts it. He speaks of Himself as the " bread " which came down from heaven, and declares over and over again His Oneness with the Father. His miracles attest it. He wrought works that no other man could ever perform. The phenomena, too, connected with His resurrection from the dead, and His ascension into heaven, all go to the same demonstration. The Great Father has many children. All souls human and angelic are His children, but this is His " *only begotten Son.*"

II —HE IS THE TENDEREST IN AFFECTION TO THE GREAT FATHER

" *He is in the bosom of the Father.*" He is not only the nearest in *essence*, but the nearest in affection with men, the " *only begotten Son* " may not have the closest relation with the father's heart. In many places Christ is represented as the most endeared object of the Divine affection—" *The Son of God.*" Speaking of the existence He had before all times and all worlds, He says, " I was daily His delight, rejoicing always before Him; " and of Him, the Great Father said in distant ages, " Behold My servant, whom I uphold; Mine elect in whom My soul delighteth." When Christ was inaugurated to His public ministry, a voice from the Father's heart was heard, " This is my beloved Son, in whom I am well pleased." Paul calls Christ God's " *dear* Son." From this we learn—

First: That God loves. He is not mere Infinite Intellectuality; He is Infinite Sensibility too. He has a heart. We learn from this—

Secondly: That Christ is the highest object of His love. What love is that? Who knows? It is not the love of pity, not the love of gratitude; it is the love of infinite complacency.

III —HE IS THE MOST ACCURATE IN THE KNOWLEDGE OF THE GREAT FATHER

"*No man hath seen God at any time.*" God is essentially invisible to creatures. "Who only hath immortality, dwelling in the light which no man can approach unto; whom no man hath seen, or can see: to Whom be honour and power everlasting." In Old Testament times we read of some personal manifestations of God that were seen, but not the absolute Deity. Christ alone hath "*seen God.*"

First: He alone is intellectually qualified to know God. Christ's intellect is vast enough to comprehend the Absolute Jehovah. The highest created spirit only knows God in *some* of His aspects. Christ knows Him in *all;* knows Him in His being.

Secondly: He alone is morally qualified to know God. He alone is sufficiently pure in heart, and the pure in heart only can see God. He alone is sufficiently powerful. Moses, Isaiah, John, could not stand a slight manifestation of God, much less could they stand the full vision. There is but one Being in the universe Who knows God thoroughly, and that is Christ.

IV —HE IS THE MOST COMPLETE IN THE REVELATION OF THE GREAT FATHER

"*He hath declared Him.*" "No man knoweth the Son but the Father, neither knoweth any man the Father save the Son, and he to whomsoever the Son will reveal Him." He is the "*Logos,*" the only word which can express the Divine heart. "He is the image of the invisible God, the express image of His Person." What is the revelation which Christ has given of the Father? It refers especially to two things—

First: To His Being. He is a Spirit, Almighty, All-wise, All-present, Invisible.

Secondly: To His relation. A Father, a governing, com-passionating, forgiving Father, feeling for humanity as the father of the prodigal felt for his lost son. If Christ is the complete revelation of God, observe—(1.) *That other revelations of God must be tested by His.* As neither Moses or any of the prophets saw Him as Christ saw Him, we must judge of their statements concerning Him by Christ's. We must interpret the Old Testament by the New, not the New by the Old. Observe—(2.) *That much that is prevalent in religious society must be repudiated as un-Christ-like.* Much in the opinions, in the spirit and institution of Churches are repugnant to the teaching of Christ. Observe—(3.) *That Christ must be held as the only Moral Master of souls*, He alone hath *" seen God,"* and can fully reveal Him. We must call no man master—no bishops, archbishops, or popes; no, not even Moses and the prophets. "One is your Master, even Christ."

John 1:19-34

JOHN THE BAPTIST AND THE JEWS

(The Testimony of John the Baptist to Jesus : John i. 19—34.)

"And this is the record of John,"

EXEGETICAL REMARKS.—Ver. 19.— *" And this is the record* (R. V. WITNESS) *of John, when the Jews sent priests and Levites."* Is this testimony addressed by John the Baptist to a Jewish deputation ? The *" Jews"* here may not mean the Jewish nation, but the Jewish rulers.

Ver. 20.—*"And he confessed, and denied not; but* (R. V. AND HE) *confessed, I am not the Christ."* Here he resisted what to ordinary men would have been a strong temptation. The people were ready to accept him as the Christ, and his acceptance would have given him enormous popularity and power.

Ver. 21. — *" And they asked him, What then? Art thou Elias?"* (R. V. ELIJAH). They had some expectation of the reappearance of Elijah, and would have been glad to welcome him. *"Art thou that* (R. V. THE) *prophet?"* The prophet referred to may be the one promised (Deut. xviii. 15). To these questions he gave a categorical no !

Ver. 22.—*"Then said they* (R. V. THEY SAID THEREFORE) *unto him, Who art thou? that we may give an answer to them that sent us. What sayest thou of thyself?"* As if they had said : "Thou art an extraordinary personage, and we are anxious to know who thou art ; we wish to carry back a definite report."

Ver. 23.—*"He said, I am the voice of one crying in the wilderness, Make straight the way of the Lord, as said the prophet Esaias,"* (R. V. ISAIAH THE PROPHET). I am the one that Isaiah describes (chapter xl. 3).

Ver. 24.—*"And they which were* (R. V. HAD BEEN) *sent of* (R. V. FROM) *the Pharisees."* "The statement," says *Watkin,* "is made to explain the question which follows, but it should be observed that in this Gospel, where the Sadducees are nowhere mentioned, the term Pharisees seems to be used almost in the sense of Sanhedrim."

Ver. 25.—*" And they asked him, and said unto him, Why baptizeth thou then, if thou be* (R. V. ART) *not that* (R. V. THE) *Christ, nor Elias,* (R. V. ELIJAH) *neither that prophet?"* Concluding from his replies to these questions, that he disclaimed any special connection with the Messiah's kingdom, they somewhat naturally demand his right to gather disciples by baptism.

Ver. 26. — *" John answered them, saying, I baptize with water : but there standeth One among you,* (R. V. IN THE MIDST OF YOU THERE STANDETH) *whom ye know not."* "The answer is in two parts, and suggestive rather than explicit. I baptize because the form of this baptism shows that, however striking outwardly, it does not belong to the work of Christ. My work is the work of a servant, and the work of a herald."—*Westcott.*

Ver. 27.—*" He it is, who coming* (R. V. EVEN HE THAT COMETH) *after me is preferred* (R. V. OMIT) *before me, whose shoe's latchet* (R. V. THE LATCHET OF WHOSE SHOES) *I am not worthy to unloose."* "The figure chosen," says *Luthardt,* "expresses the great difference between the two—I, with emphasis, in contrast with Him, am not worthy to do Him the least service."

Ver. 28.—*" These things were done in Bethabara* (R. V. BETHANY) *beyond*

Jordan, where John was baptizing." "This name (Judg. vii. 24) is a mere correction made as early as the end of the second century, for Bethany, which was probably an obscure village in Perea, and not to be confounded with the Bethany on the Mount of Olives. According to a possible derivation, Bethany may mean the house of the boat, as Bethabara the house of the passage, both equally marking the site of a ferry or ford across the Jordan.

HOMILETICS

In the interlocution between John the Baptist and the Jews two subjects worthy of note are suggested: *a proper question from society to a religious teacher,* and a *satisfactory answer from a religious teacher to society.*

I —A PROPER QUESTION FROM SOCIETY TO A RELIGIOUS TEACHER

Before we notice the question asked of John, a word must be said about the *questioners.* Who were they? They were, we are told, "*Priests and Levites from Jerusalem.*" These were the two classes of men who were generally employed in the Temple service, as we find in Joshua iii. 3. They came not of their own authority, but were, "*sent;*" they were delegated by a party of Jews from Jerusalem. At Jerusalem we know there were several religious parties, the chief of which were the Sadducees and Pharisees. These composed the two great powers in the Sanhedrim. Which of these parties sent these priests and Levites to John? The 24th verse tells us they "*were sent of the Pharisees.*" The Pharisees were rigorously exact in all ritualities. The Sadducees did not care much about such points. All ceremonialism was beneath the notice of their majestic intellects. Thousands upon thousands, it would seem, went out from Jerusalem, and the regions round about, and were baptized by John in the Jordan, and the Pharisees became ritualistically anxious on the subject, and consequently sent this deputation.

Now for their *question;* and this question may be divided into two parts; one part relating to John's *personal history,* and the other to his *religious authority.* The former begins with "*Who art thou?*" A very comprehensive question this; more comprehensive than they intended. "*Who?*" What is thy pedigree and pretentions, thy character and circumstances, thy principles and prerogatives? John having denied that he was the Christ, they continued to press the question. "*What then? Art thou Elias?*" —the man we expect to come down from heaven in person, to anoint the Messiah. Having denied that—for although he was an Elias (Mal. iii. 1), he was not *the* Elias they referred to, viz. Elijah, whose appearance they felt he resembled—they proceed. "*Art thou that prophet?*" means, "Art thou that prophet, like unto Moses, that we expect?" Having received a negative to this appeal, they continue still to press the question. "*Who art thou?*"

That we may give an answer to them that sent us. What sayest thou of thyself?" Such is the part of the question referring to John's *personal* history.

The other part of the question refers to John's *religious authority.* Having told them he was the mere "*Voice of one crying in the wilderness,*" and that he was not Christ, nor that prophet, they asked him for his authority in baptizing, "*Why baptizest thou then if thou be not that Christ, nor Elias?*" As if they had said, if thou art neither Christ, nor Elias, nor that prophet, what right hast thou to use this Jewish ceremony of baptism? Give us thine authority for presuming to officiate in the ritualistic department of Jewish worship.

Such was the question which Jewish society put to this new teacher that rose up in their country, a teacher who startled the nation by his eloquence, and commanded a vast popularity. Now, our position is, that this was a very *proper* question. We do not say that they put it in a proper spirit, or for proper reasons, but the question itself was undoubtedly right. Society should ever inquire well into the pretensions and doctrines of a public religious teacher. It should do so—

First: Because of the influence which religious teaching has upon the conduct and destiny of the community even in this life. Heretical religious principles are not only detrimental to the spiritual and future condition of humanity, but are immeasurably injurious to the temporal well-being of society. France, in all her revolutions, and in the last most of all, thunders out this truth. It behoves, therefore, those who are in authority, the guardians of public peace and order, to inquire into the character of the religious teaching to which the people is subjected. It should do so—

Secondly: Because the pernicious in doctrine should be suppressed, and the beneficent encouraged. It is said that every man has not only a right to form his own religious opinions, but to promote them; "that the prophet that hath even a dream should speak it," and that no government has a right by force to infringe on this liberty. Granting this, there is a *moral* power that is mightier than political force, which those in public can employ, aye, and which we think they are bound to employ;—the force of argument, the force of example, the force wielded by a pure literature, a sacred eloquence, a noble life. The time has come, we think, when English society should inquire a little concerning its religious teachers. In the name of Christianity, men are constantly rising up amongst us, with and without culture, hooting crudities and absurdities that insult the human understanding, misrepresent the genius of Christianity, blaspheme Infinite Love, prostrate the weak souls of our community to a miserable superstition, and drive the strong ones into indifferentism and infidelity.

In the interlocution here recorded between John and the Jews, we have suggested—

II—A SATISFACTORY ANSWER FROM A RELIGIOUS TEACHER TO SOCIETY

How did John stand this investigation? Did he treat it with a supercilious silence, or did he answer? If he answered, what kind of answer did he give? Here it is :—"*And this is the record of John, when the Jews sent the priests and Levites from Jerusalem to ask him, Who art thou?*" In John's answer, there are three things indicated which show him to be a true teacher, and which should characterize every teacher worthy of public attention :

First: Unquestionable sincerity. In answer to their interrogatory, he might have said: "I am Elias; or, I am that prophet like unto Moses. I am the Christ, the Messiah you expect." And saying this, in all probability they would have believed him. Anyhow, tens of thousands would have believed him; for he had moved the heart of the nation, and men were crowding about him from all parts. Had he been a false man, a charlatan, the temptation would have been irresistible. But without a moment's pause, in a most emphatic way, he disclaims all such pretensions. "*He confessed, and denied not ; but confessed, I am not the Christ.*" A Jewish idiom this, to express in the strongest possible way his negative answer. He "*confessed,*" he openly avowed it, he thundered it loudly from the banks of the Jordan in the ears of the multitude that crowded about him. Surely, here was a proof of his *sincerity.* He was an incorrupt soul. He could not swerve a hair's-breadth from the path of truth. Crowns and kingdoms were too poor to buy the conscience of a man like him. Sincerity is one of the most cardinal and essential qualifications for a religious teacher. The man who preaches what he does not believe, because it is popular, is often a grand preacher in the estimation of his shallow admirers, but a contemptible charlatan in the eyes of Him who is the Discerner of spirits. In John's answer there is indicated—

Secondly: Profound humility. "*He said, I am the voice of one crying in the wilderness.*" Here he speaks in manifest allusion to the passage (Isa. xl. 3), I am the mere voice of a herald in the Judean desert announcing some one to come. John does not say: —I am the truth; what I say is infallible; nor, I am the Word embodying the true thing. I am only a "*voice,*" a mere echo—nothing more. I don't originate what I say; it comes to me. I am its mere organ; I voice it, and that is all. "*I am the voice.*" This humility is another essential qualification for a religious teacher. No man is qualified to teach, who is not well-nigh overwhelmed with a sense of his own insufficiency. How many religious teachers there are who say, by their manner and mien: "I am the great linguist. I am the original thinker. I am the magnificent orator." Such are destitute of the spirit of a true preacher. " *I am the voice,*"—nothing more.

In John's answer there is indicated—

Thirdly: Supreme reverence for his Master. " *John answered them, saying, I baptize with water: but there standeth One among you, whom ye know not; He it is, Who coming after me is preferred before me, whose shoe's latchet I am not worthy to unloose.*" His reverence for Christ is here expressed in two ways. (1.) By intimating that his baptism was but a mere symbol of the baptism of Christ. " *I baptize with water: but there standeth One among you, whom ye know not;* HE *will baptize you with the Holy Ghost.*" As if he had said: All I do is simply to apply the *material* element to the bodies of men; but Christ, of Whom I am the mere herald—my Great Master, my All—He will apply the *spiritual* element of truth and righteousness to the soul. He will bring the very Spirit of God in contact with souls, in order to cleanse them. My ministry is material, symbolic, temporary. His is *spiritual, real, everlasting.* His reverence for Christ is here expressed (2.) By avowing his conscious inferiority to Christ. The people of the East wore only the sole of a shoe bound fast to the foot by strings passed over and round it. In tropic lands this was agreeable. It was the work of the humblest servant in the family to untie this thong. What John means to say is:— I am not worthy of doing even the meanest thing for Him. Christ to him was all, and in all. Thus it is with all true teachers. "God forbid," says Paul, "that I should glory, save in the cross of Jesus Christ, by whom the world is crucified unto me, and I unto the world."

CONCLUSION: Let society look well after its religious teachers, and see that they show that *sincerity* in their service, that *humility* of heart, that *reverence* for Christ, that came out in the answer of His illustrious Herald, on the banks of the Jordan, to the deputation of the Jewish Sanhedrim.

> " Would I describe a preacher such as Paul,
> Were he on earth, would hear, approve, and own,
> Paul should himself direct me. I would trace
> His master-strokes, and draw from his design :
> I would express him simple, grave, sincere :
> In doctrine uncorrupt, in language plain,
> And plain in manner : decent, solemn, chaste,
> And natural in gesture : much impress'd
> Himself, as conscious of his awful charge,
> And anxious mainly that the flock he feeds
> May feel it too : affectionate in look,
> And tender in address, as well becomes
> A messenger of grace to guilty men."—*Cowper.*

John 1:29-34

THE GLORIOUS WORK OF CHRIST AND THE SUPREME MISSION OF THE PREACHER

"The next day (R. V. ON THE MORROW) John seeth Jesus coming unto him, and saith, Behold the Lamb of God, which taketh away the sin of the world. This is He of whom I said, After me cometh a man which is preferred (R. V. BECOME) before me : for He was before me. And I knew Him not : but that He should be made manifest to Israel, therefore am I come (R. V. FOR THIS CAUSE CAME I) baptizing with water. And John bare record, (R. V. WITNESS) saying, I saw (R. V. HAVE BEHELD) the Spirit descending from heaven like a dove, (R. V. AS A DOVE OUT OF HEAVEN) and it abode upon Him. And I knew Him not : but He that sent me to baptize with water, the same (R. V. HE) said unto me, Upon whom (R. V. WHOMSOEVER) thou shalt see the Spirit descending, and remaining (R. V. ABIDING) on Him, the same is He which baptizeth with the Holy Ghost (R. V. SPIRIT). And I saw, and bare record (R. V. HAVE SEEN AND HAVE BORNE WITNESS) that this is the Son of God."

EXEGETICAL REMARKS. Ver. 29.— "*The next day.*" These words contain the testimony which John the Baptist addressed to his own disciples concerning Christ. It was delivered, we are told, "*the next day :*" that is, the day after the deputation from Jerusalem had visited him, detailed in the preceding verses, and which we have already noticed ; and it was, perhaps, immediately after the return of Christ from the wilderness, where He had been tempted by the devil. He appears now on the banks of the Jordan, after a terrible moral battle, in which He became the triumphant victor. "*Behold the Lamb of God.*" This is descriptive of the harmlessness and holiness of Jesus. Andrew calls Him the Messiah ; Philip the One predicted in the Old Testament ; Nathanael, the Son of God, the King of Israel ; John, here struck, it may be for the moment, as he saw Him in His calm, tender, yet stately aspect, speaks of Him as the "*Lamb.*"

Ver. 31.—"*And I knew Him not.*" The reference is to "whom ye know not" of ver. 26, and the assertion is not therefore inconsistent with the fact that John did know Him on His approach to Baptism.

Ver. 32.—"*I saw the Spirit descending from heaven like a dove, and it abode upon Him.*" "The Spirit comes down from heaven—that is, an influence passed from God to Jesus. It was not an influence starting from Jesus, not a mental excitement of Jesus, or the like, but an objective impartation of the Spirit of God to Jesus. The '*dove*' in the Scriptures is the figure of peaceable and pure simplicity. It serves to characterize the New Testament manner of the revelation of God in Jesus, perhaps in distinction from the fiery zeal of an Elijah."—*Luthardt.*

HOMILETICS

We shall regard these words as illustrating the *glorious work of Christ and the supreme mission of the preacher.*

I THE GLORIOUS WORK OF CHRIST

What is His work ? To appease Divine vengeance ? To give to the Eternal a certain kind and measure of suffering for a certain number of souls ? It is not said so here. It is to "*take away the sin of the world.*" Sin is in the world ; this is the dark fact in its history ; this is at once its curse and its ruin. Christ came "to put away sin"—as Paul has it: to put it away, not from a certain class or classes, not from particular sections, but from the WORLD. What does it mean? Not burying in oblivion the *fact* of sin—the dark fact will ever be memorable in the universe—but it means taking away its painful consciousness, its dominant power, its polluting influences, its damning issues.

First: This is the most difficult work. Senators, poets, sages, priests have tried a thousand times, and through a thousand ages, to put away sin; but they have failed—signally failed. Christ has commenced it, He is pursuing it, and He will do it.

Secondly: This is the most indispensable work. Sin is the fountain of all our intellectual, social, moral, political, and religious suffering. Until this fountain is dried up, the streams of misery will ever roll through the heart of the world. Sin must be taken away from our literature, our governments, our institutions, our hearts, before the world can be made happy. And this is Christ's work: for this He came into the world, suffered, died, rose, ascended into Heaven, and now manages the universe. Notice—

II THE SUPREME MISSION OF THE PREACHER

What is the great work of the preacher? Propounding theories, battling for theologies? No; but *pointing men to Christ*, as John did, saying, "*Behold the Lamb of God!*" There is no reason for supposing that John alludes here either to the Paschal lamb or to the lamb of daily sacrifices. His allusion, most probably, is to the 53rd chapter of Isaiah. The metaphor is descriptive, not necessarily of suffering or of sacrifices, but of spotless innocency and holy gentleness. John here directs his disciples to Christ—

First: As One Who was to deliver the world from sin. "*Behold the Lamb of God, which taketh away the sin of the world!*" Sin is a small word, but big with meaning. It always implies four things— (1.) The *existence* of law. (2.) The *means of knowing* law. (3.) The *capability of obeying* law. (4.) *Actual departure* from law. The preacher's work is to point men to Christ as the Sin-Deliverer. No one else can do it. "There is no other name given under heaven," &c.

Secondly: As One Who was greater than himself. "*After me cometh a Man which is preferred before me: for He was before me.*" This expression is the same as that in the 27th verse, and it means, as we have seen, the superiority of Christ. John means by it that He Who is after me in time is greater than me in the universe. Every true preacher should be deeply impressed with the transcendent superiority of Christ. How deeply did Paul feel this! "I am the least of all saints," &c.

Thirdly: As One Who was revealed to him by Heaven. "*And I knew Him not: but that He should be made manifest to Israel, therefore am I come baptizing with water. And John bare record, saying, I saw the Spirit descending from heaven like a dove, and it abode upon Him."* Christ was revealed to John by the Spirit, which descended from heaven like a dove. Up to that time, it would seem, he did not know Him. *"I knew Him not."* At the baptism He was revealed to him in all the beauty of His character and the grandeur of His mission. Unless God reveals Christ to us, we cannot preach Him. How can we make Him known to others unless we know Him ourselves? And God must impart this knowledge; "flesh and blood" cannot reveal Him to us.

Fourthly: As One Who was the true Baptizer of men. *"And I knew Him not: but He that sent me to baptize with water, the same said unto me, Upon whom thou shalt see the Spirit descending, and remaining on Him, the same is He which baptizeth with the Holy Ghost."* Deliverance from sin requires a baptism, a spiritual cleansing. This is the *real* baptism; other baptisms are but the shadows and symbols. This baptism is done by Christ, He *"baptizeth with the Holy Ghost."*

Fifthly: As One Who was the Son of God. *"And I saw, and bare record that this is the Son of God."* In the Synoptic Gospel Christ is termed the "well-beloved Son;" in St. Paul's writings He is called "God's own Son;" and in this Gospel He is called "the only begotten Son." It is a title expressive of His Divine essence, relationship, and dignity. Every true preacher must declare Christ to be superhuman and all-perfect. "I saw, and bare record that this is the Son of God." (See Liddon's "Bampton Lectures," page 246.)

CONCLUSION: Here, then, is our work as preachers: pointing men to Christ as the One Who is to deliver the world from sin, as the One infinitely greater than ourselves, as the One revealed to our souls by the Spirit of God, as the One Who is to dispense the true baptism to our souls, as the One Who is the Son of God.

John 1:35-51

CHRIST WINNING HIS FIRST TWO DISCIPLES

(Jesus gains Disciples.—JOHN i. 35—51.)

" Again the next day after (R. V. ON THE MORROW) John stood, (R. V. WAS STANDING) and two of his disciples ; and looking (R. V. HE LOOKED) upon Jesus as He walked, he (R. V. AND) saith, Behold the Lamb of God ! And the two disciples heard him speak, and they followed Jesus. Then (R. V. AND) Jesus turned, and saw (R. V. BEHELD) them following, and saith unto them, What seek ye ? They said unto Him : Rabbi, (which is to say, being interpreted, Master,) where dwellest (R. V. ABIDEST) Thou ? He saith unto them, Come and see (R. V. YE SHALL SEE). They came and saw where He dwelt, (R. V. ABODE) and abode with Him that day : for it was about the tenth hour. One of the two which heard John speak, and followed Him, was Andrew, Simon Peter's brother."

EXEGETICAL REMARKS.—Ver. 35.— *" Again the next day after John stood, and two of his disciples."* We need not suppose that these two were absent the previous day. Probably the words they heard the day before had so interested them that they came to see the Teacher Himself.

Ver. 36.—*" And looking upon Jesus as He walked, he saith, Behold the Lamb of God."* John, seeing Jesus walking, repeats the expression as in verse 29.

Ver. 37.—*" And the two disciples heard him speak, and they followed Jesus."* "Not as disciples leaving all as yet, but rather going after Him in the way of enquiry."

Ver. 38.—*" Then Jesus turned, and saw them following, and saith unto* them, *What seek ye?"* This the Great Teacher says to every man.

Ver. 39.—*" Come and see."* "The usual formula addressed by the Rabbi to his pupil, when he would invite his attention to some striking point or new doctrine." *" They came and saw where He dwelt."* "It may have been a house, a tent, or, as is often the case in Palestine, a cave."

Ver. 40.—*" One of the two was Andrew."* Andrew was a native of Bethsaida, and the brother of Simon Peter. The Evangelists give us a very small amount of information concerning him. He was present at the feeding of the five thousand : he with Philip introduced to Jesus certain Greeks who desired to see Him.

HOMILETICS

These words are memorable, inasmuch as they record the *first* men won as adherents by Him, Who came to "gather all men unto Himself." The untold millions of men who will complete the great Church at last began with these two whom Jesus now won to His doctrines, His enterprise, and Himself. Only the name of one is given, *" Andrew, Simon Peter's brother,"* whilst two disciples are referred to. Who was the other —the unnamed one ? Undoubtedly John—the tender, meditative, intuitional John, the "beloved disciple"—the author of this Gospel. He was too modest to mention his own name; he was one of those rare men who are too great to aspire after worldly fame. Genuinely great men seek goodness not greatness : their greatness is unknown to themselves, and by themselves undesired and unsought.

The text leads us to notice two things concerning them—

I —THEIR CONVERSION TO CHRIST

Here three things are worthy of note—

First: It was effected by their old master, John the Baptist. These two men were called John's disciples—*" The next day after John stood, and two of his disciples."* They had heard the terrible sermons of John, they had submitted to his baptism, but he now turns them to another Master, One *"whose shoe latchet,"* he told them, *"he was not worthy to unloose."* It is something uniquely grand, in this selfish world, to see a religious teacher turning his disciples to a Master of a higher type. Preachers of little souls are ever studiously anxious to keep their hearers entirely under their own influence, and when greater instructors appear in their circle, they rather warn their people against them, than direct them to their more enlightened ministry. Not so John the Baptist.

Secondly: It was effected by their old master through the proclamation of the grandest truth. That truth was this, "*Behold the Lamb of God, which taketh away the sin of the world!*" The meaning of this sublime expression we have already explained. The expression is tantamount to all that is contained in the cross, and the cross is the converting power. How did he pronounce these words, with what emphasis and tone! His eyes helped his voice to give effect to the proclamation, "*And looking upon Jesus as He walked, he saith, Behold the Lamb of God!*" The eye is a handmaid to oratory; its flash of feeling often feathers the arrow of a sentence, and bears it home to the heart of the hearer.

Thirdly: It was effected by the old master, after they had heard him without effect. "*And the next day after John stood, and two of his disciples.*" The "*day after,*"—the day referred to in the preceding paragraph, when John before directed his hearers to the "*Lamb of God.*" These disciples were undoubtedly present on that occasion; they heard his voice thundering out the same truth; but they were not then, it would seem, won to Christ. On the day before, there seems to have been a great multitude listening to John, but we have no account of any of the number accepting Christ; but now he speaks to *two* only, and the two were converted. "*And the two disciples heard him speak, and they followed Jesus.*" There are two lessons here for preachers—

(1.) Do not be discouraged. If you fail to convert sinners by one sermon, you may by the next. "Be instant in season," &c. (2.) Do not be influenced too much by the size of your congregation. John preached to multitudes on the previous day, apparently without effect. He preaches to two now, and the two "*followed Jesus.*"

The text leads us to notice—

II —THEIR FELLOWSHIP WITH CHRIST

First: Christ BEGAN the fellowship. "*Jesus turned and saw them following, and saith unto them, What seek ye?*" He knew they were seeking Him. He therefore means, What seek ye *with Me?*—not *whom* seek ye? By this question He touched their hearts. He showed that He knew they were seeking something. He gives them an opportunity to ask what they wanted. Christ always begins the fellowship with His disciples; He stimulates their inquiries.

Secondly: Christ ENCOURAGED the fellowship. He answers their question. "*They said unto Him, Rabbi, where dwellest Thou?*" Where art Thou staying? a question indicating a desire for a close fellowship,—and here is the answer: "*He saith unto them, Come and see."* He does not say here or yonder, but come with Me. Christ has nothing to conceal. He wishes the world to know all about Him, to follow all the windings of His life, and to peer into all the details of His history. *"Come and see."* This is, in truth, the voice of the whole Gospel to men. Do not judge from hearsay, search for yourselves.

Thirdly: Christ CONTINUED the fellowship. *"They came and saw where He dwelt, and abode with Him that day: for it was about the tenth hour."* The *"tenth hour,"* in the Jewish calculation, was about four o'clock in the afternoon. Ever memorable hour to them, that hour when they entered His lodging-place, and sat down to listen to His words; that was the beginning of a fellowship that has been going on until this day, and that may go on for millenniums, ever heightening, ever blest.

CONCLUSION: Behold the *"*day of small things;*"* despise it not. Here is the beginning of the Church; here is that seed that has already spread over many climes and many ages, and yielded unnumbered harvests. Here is the first drop of that fountain that has swollen into a majestic river.

John 1:41, 42

MAN'S WORK AND CHRIST'S WORK IN THE REFORMATION OF SOULS

" He first findeth his own brother Simon, and saith unto him, We have found the Messias, (R. V. MESSIAH) which is, being interpreted, the Christ. And he brought him to Jesus. And when Jesus beheld him, (R. V. JESUS LOOKED UPON HIM) He said, Thou art Simon the Son of Jona: (R. V. JOHN) thou shalt be called Cephas, which is by interpretation, A stone (R. V. PETER)."

EXEGETICAL REMARKS.—Ver. 41.— *" He first findeth his own brother Simon."* This means that the first thing Andrew did on the morning after visiting Christ at His dwelling, was to go in search of his brother. Beautifully natural this. The fraternal instinct. *" We have found the Messias."* What a sublime discovery to make to his brother! We have found Him—Him for whom the past ages have been looking, and by whom future ages will rise.

Ver. 42.—*" And he brought him to Jesus."* What better could he do for his brother than this? What better can any man do for another than this? *" And when Jesus beheld him, He said, Thou art Simon the Son of Jona."* "This is not necessarily a prophetic declaration by Divine knowledge. It rather means simply, This is your natural name. Some take the phrase interrogatively, 'Art thou?' ' *Thou shalt be called Cephas.*' Hereafter thou shalt win the name of Cephas. The Aramaic name is found in the New Testament, elsewhere, only in 1 Cor. i. 12 ; iii. 22 ; ix. 5 ; Gal. i. 18 ; ii. 9 ; xi. 14."—*Westcott.*

HOMILETICS

These words suggest two things—

I —MAN'S WORK IN THE CONVERSION OF SOULS

" He first findeth his own brother Simon, and saith unto him, We

have found the Messias, which is, being interpreted, the Christ. And he brought him to Jesus." "Brought him to Jesus;" this is man's part in the great work of converting souls. He has to bring men to Jesus—not to creeds, theologies, sects, churches, but to the Anointed of God. This work of Andrew was—

First: BENEFICENT. What a universe of good was involved in this simple act! (1.) What a service was rendered to Peter! His soul was translated into a new world. (2.) What a service to the disciples of Christ! The introduction into their society of a nature like his, warm, frank, generous, bold, thoroughly inspired with Christian sentiment, must have been a great gain to that little circle. (3.) What a service was rendered to the whole world! The Infinite alone can tell the good which Peter has accomplished. By his one sermon on the Day of Pentecost he converted three thousand souls. He became the disciple of Christ, and lovingly interested in all that pertained to the great kingdom of truth.

Peter preached the Gospel to the Gentiles. The Infinite alone can tell the amount of good which Peter has already accomplished in the universe. All this must be referred to the simple act of Andrew bringing him to Jesus. From one single human act may issue an influence for good that may go widening and deepening through the centuries. The highest service you can do on earth is to bring men to Jesus. The work of Andrew was—

Secondly: NATURAL. Andrew went to Peter, not as an *official*, but as a *man*, a brother. *"He first findeth his own brother Simon, and saith unto him, We have found the Messias."* All that is wanted to bring men to Christ is—(1.) *The common attributes of a man.* It does not require great genius, learning, or high culture, which distinguish only a few, but that which all men have—common sense. (2.) *Common love to Christ.* Andrew hastened to Simon with a heart touched and inspired with loving sympathies for Christ. What is wanted in this work is not the influence of man as a scholar, philosopher, priest, or bishop, but the influence of man as man. It is the *man*, not the *preacher*, who converts. When the man is lost in the preacher he has no power to win souls to Christ. In modern pulpits we want manhood redeemed from the fetters and grimaces of officialism. The work of Andrew was—

Thirdly: HONOURABLE. When Andrew went forth to Peter and persuaded him to come to Jesus, he did a work whose grandeur no seraph could transcend. To introduce a man to Christ is to introduce him to One Who in philosophy is infinitely greater than a Socrates, in wealth infinitely greater than a Crœsus, in royalty infinitely greater than a Cæsar. You bring him to One Who is the wisdom of God, One Who has "the unsearchable riches," One Who is "the Prince of the kings of the earth." The work of authors, sages, statesmen, warriors, is contemptible compared with the work of bringing men to Christ. The work of Andrew was—

Fourthly: EXEMPLARY. Andrew in bringing Peter to Christ is an example for universal imitation. (1.) *It is an example that all can imitate.* Though a glorious work, it is nevertheless so simple that it may be accomplished by a child. All that is wanted is a Christ-loving heart. (2.) *It is an example that all should imitate.* It is the duty of all Christians to bring men to Christ. It is not a work binding on any particular class, it is an obligation pressing on all. All relations—parents, children, brothers and sisters. All social grades, rich and poor. All intellectual types, the weak and the strong, the learned and the rude. The world is perishing with moral hunger. He is the BREAD OF LIFE. Our work is not to bring men to our little systems, sects, and churches, but to CHRIST. Unless we do this, services, however popular, are neither acceptable to Him nor of worth to human souls. Notice here—

II—CHRIST'S WORK IN THE CONVERSION OF SOULS

"*And he brought him to Jesus. And when Jesus beheld him, He said, Thou art Simon the son of Jona: thou shalt be called Cephas, which is by interpretation, A stone.*" All that we can do is to bring man to Christ: Christ must effect the great change. We can bring men to Christ, Christ brings men to themselves and to God. Christ did two things to Peter now in effecting the change—

First: Made him feel that he was personally known to Him. "*Thou art Simon, the son of Jona.*" Peter might have said, "How dost Thou know me? I have never met Thee before, and yet Thou knowest me." He felt, no doubt, that Christ had read him through and through, knew all within him and about him. Perhaps this is the first step in every conversion,—man is made to feel that God knows him. "God is in this place, and I knew it not."

Secondly: Gave him an ideal character to struggle, after. (1.) He was brought into contact with that type of character of which he was most *signally destitute*. (*a*) The type of character which Christ now held forth to Peter was Christian firmness. He said, "*Thou art Simon the son of Jona: thou shalt be called Cephas, which is by interpretation, A stone.*" "*A stone*" is the best emblem which the earth furnishes of firmness. Nothing more firm than granite rocks. What is Christian firmness? *Not obstinacy.* Obstinacy is such a pertinacious adherence to an opinion or a purpose as will yield neither to reason nor persuasion. Firmness is not *hardness.* It is foreign to the rough and harsh and insolent. It is allied to the deepest tenderness. He who set His face as "a flint" was tender. Christian firmness involves two things—enlightened convictions of Christian realities, and fixedness of affections upon the Christian's God. It is a rooting and grounding of the soul in truth and God. There is no *nobility* without firmness; whilst the obstinate man is despised, and the fickle man untrusted, the firm man commands reverence. Firmness is an essential element in all that is noble and heroic in character. There is no *usefulness* without firmness. The vacillating man is as "unstable as water," and cannot excel. Instability is failure in every department of life. The firm men do the work of the world. There is no *godliness* without firmness. Godliness begins in centering the soul upon the Supremely Good : " O God, my heart is fixed, I will sing and give praise." (*b*) *This firmness Peter sadly lacked.* Constitutionally Peter was a man of strong impulse and surging passion. He was therefore liable to vacillation and instability. This changefulness painfully shows itself even after his conversion. From impulse you may find him rushing to meet Christ, and endeavouring to walk on the sea, and from lack of faith about to sink into the whelming waters. No man confessed the Divinity of Christ with more explicitness and intensity than Peter, and yet after he denied Him thrice, and thrice with oaths. He was the first man to receive a Gentile into the Christian Church, and thus brave the opposition of the Jews; and yet, subsequently, we find him refusing to sit down at the Lord's table with converted Gentiles, and thus exposing himself to the righteous censures of St. Paul. Now, Christ in holding up to Peter at their first meeting firmness, held up that very phase of character which he most signally lacked. When Christ said, " *Thou shalt be called Cephas—a stone,*" his inmost soul must have responded, "I am not a stone ; rather than a rock, I am a reed shaken by the wind." When souls come to Christ He makes them feel their *missing* qualities of good, their lacking attributes of virtue. To the dishonest He holds forth righteousness; to the false, faithfulness; to the greedy, generosity; to the unclean, chastity ; to the sceptical, faith ; to the profane, reverence. Thus He touches the soul on its weak and vicious points. (2.) He is brought into contact with a type of character to *reach which is his destiny.* " *Thou shalt be called Cephas.*" Christian firmness was the idea now held forth to Peter's soul. It blazed as a Divine light before him. Ever afterwards we have no doubt he struggled earnestly to attain it. And the struggle involved a moral revolution within. In reading his history, his sermons, and his letters, we see his gradual progress towards this firmness, until in his martyrdom it reached its earthly consummation. On the day of Pentecost, how firm ! Standing a prisoner before the Sanhedrim, how firm ! How firm in his preaching to the Gentiles !—how firm in his first epistle ! We first meet with Peter uncertain as a shifting cloud, and as noisy as a tempest; we leave him as settled as a star, and as serene in soul as a summer's eve.

CONCLUSION.—First: Christ holds out to all His disciples an ideal. You have the ideal—(1.) In His teachings. (2.) In His example.

Secondly: This ideal is at variance with our natural dispositions. It was so now with Peter. In his case Christ held forth the morally firm to the fickle and the turbulent.

Thirdly: Though the ideal is at variance with our natural disposition, we must struggle after and reach it. What is our grand work in life? To realize those ideals of character that Jesus of Nazareth holds forth to our souls. Blessed be His name for those ideals, they are the lights of *the moral world*!

John 1:43-51

A GENUINE EVANGELIZER AND A GENUINE TRUTH-SEEKER

"The day following Jesus would (R. V. ON THE MORROW HE WAS MINDED TO) go forth into Galilee, and findeth Philip, and saith unto him, Follow Me. Now Philip was of (R. V. FROM) Bethsaida, the city of Andrew and Peter. Philip findeth Nathanael, and saith unto him, We have found Him, of whom Moses in the law, and the prophets, did write, Jesus of Nazareth, the son of Joseph. And Nathanael said unto him, Can there any (R. V. CAN ANY) good thing come out of Nazareth? Philip said unto him, Come and see. Jesus saw Nathanael coming to him, and saith of him, Behold an Israelite indeed, in whom is no guile! Nathanael saith unto him, Whence knowest thou me? Jesus answered and said unto him, Before that Philip called thee, when thou wast under the fig tree, I saw thee. Nathanael answered and saith unto him, Rabbi, Thou art the Son of God; Thou art the King of Israel. Jesus answered and said unto him, Because I said unto thee, I saw thee under (R. V. UNDERNEATH) the fig tree, believest thou? thou shalt see greater things than these. And he saith unto him, Verily, verily, I say unto you, Hereafter ye shall see heaven open, (R. V. THE HEAVEN OPENED) and the angels of God ascending and descending upon the Son of Man."

EXEGETICAL REMARKS.—Ver. 43.— "*The day following.*" This was the next day after Peter was called and designated, and the fourth day after what is recorded in the nineteenth verse. The scene of the events here recorded we are told was "*Bethsaida*," not the Bethsaida at the head of the Lake sometimes called Bethsaida-Julius, but the Bethsaida on the western side of the lake where Christ wrought many of His miracles, and which shared His denunciation with Capernaum on account of its unbelief.

"*Findeth Philip.*" Philip is referred to in three or four places in the New Testament. We find him present at the miracle of the loaves and fishes (John vi. 7). We find him appealed to by the Greeks, requesting an introduction to Jesus, and instead of going to Jesus, he goes to Andrew, to join him in the work (John xii. 22). We find him also present at the last supper (John xiv. 8).

Ver. 45.—"*Philip findeth Nathanael.*" We have but very little information concerning Nathanael. He is generally supposed to be the same as is sometimes called Bartholomew. The fact that in the first three gospels Philip and Bartholomew are commonly named together, and Nathanael is not mentioned, affords ground for the belief that the two names are the designation of the same person. We learn that he was a native of Galilee (John xxi. 2); that he was one of the twelve Apostles; that he was one to whom our Lord appeared at the Sea of Tiberias after His resurrection; and that he was also a witness of the Ascension, and returned with the other Apostles to Jerusalem.

Ver. 47.—"*Behold an Israelite, in whom is no guile.*" "The word of the Lord, addressed not directly to Nathanael, but to others on his approach. The reason why Nathanael is called a genuine Israelite is his freedom from falsehood. In the Jewish nature there was much guile."

Ver. 49.—"*When thou wast under the fig tree.*" "Jesus must have seen something in the spiritual posture of Nathanael under the fig tree which

marked the person of the Israelite without guile."—*Lange.*

Ver. 51.—"*Verily, verily.*" "We meet for the first time with the formula Amen, Amen, which is found twenty-five times in John, and nowhere else in the New Testament. Thence is derived the title of Jesus, the Amen."—*Godet.* "*Angels of God.*" "Angels are the instruments of Divine power in the domain of nature. This saying refers therefore to phenomena which, while passing the domain of nature, are due to a causality superior to the laws of nature."

HOMILETICS

Here we have—

I —A GENUINE EVANGELIZER

Philip represents this character. We find two things here connected with his history which are essential to every genuine Evangelizer.

First: He is called by Christ. "*Jesus would go forth into Galilee, and findeth Philip, and saith unto him, Follow Me.*" "*Follow Me;*" what words are these! (1.) Christ's masterhood is in them. They seemed to rise higher in authority than the words He had uttered just before—"*Come and see.*" Were He only a man this utterance would be the height of arrogance, but being Divine it is in beautiful accord with His character. "*Follow Me;*" I am your Teacher, your Chieftain, your Lord. (2.) God's law is in them. They are an epitome of the moral code of the universe; they contain the Decalogue and more. Christ is the Divine law of humanity, the law in human life, experience, and conduct. The whole duty of man is reduced to these two words, "*Follow Me.*" (3.) Converting force is in them. There went with these words an energy that not only arrested the attention but turned the whole nature of Philip to Christ. He began to follow Him at once, and continued doing so through his mortal life, and has not, I presume, paused in his Divine career through all the ages since. This is the first step a man must take to become a true Evangelizer.

Secondly: He calls men to Christ. "*Philip findeth Nathanael, and saith unto him, We have found Him of Whom Moses in the law, and the prophets, did write, Jesus of Nazareth, the son of Joseph.*" The same feeling that prompted Andrew to search out his brother Simon (ver. 41) prompted Philip now to find out Nathanael. He "*findeth Nathanael;*" this is his first Evangelic effort. No sooner does a man become a genuine follower of Christ than he feels at once an earnest solicitude to bring others to a knowledge of his blessed Master. Such is the influence which Christ's truth and love has upon the social affections of His disciples, that they feel at once the "necessity laid upon them" to preach the Gospel. Here then is the genuine Evangelizer. He is a man who first follows Christ, and then finds out others to join him in the moral march.

The other character which the narrative presents to us is:

II —A GENUINE TRUTH-SEEKER

Who is the truth-seeker? Nathanael. He puts the question to Philip, "*Can there any good thing come out of Nazareth?*" Observe three things in relation to him as a truth-seeker—

First, His efforts as a genuine truth-seeker.

(1.) He *hearkens to information* concerning the truth. "*Philip saith to him, we have found Him of whom Moses in the law,*" &c., and Nathanael listens. He listens attentively to the statement that One was found amongst them who was the substance of Him of whom Moses and the prophets did write. Christ is the Bible.

Philip in this language implies the opinion that Christ was the grand theme of the Old Testament writings. So, indeed, we are everywhere taught to regard Him. The ceremonies of the Mosaic system were shadows of which He was the substance. The predictions of the prophets were but sketches of a portrait of which He was the Original. Christ Himself taught this more than once, and especially to the disciples on the way to Emmaus after His resurrection; for in that conversation, "Beginning at Moses and all the prophets, He expounded unto them in all the Scriptures the things concerning Himself." Christ is the spiritual substance of the Bible. He that believes in Him believes in the Bible, though he may not be able to believe in all the statements contained in the Book. Nathanael hearkened to this wonderful intelligence concerning Christ.

(2.) He *renounces a prejudice* against the truth. "*And Nathanael said unto him, Can there any good thing come out of Nazareth?*" Bethlehem was the Messiah's predicted birthplace. Nazareth had no mention in the prophecies concerning Him, still Philip said Nazareth; and Nathanael felt that if He came from Nazareth He could not be the Messiah. "*Can there any good thing come out of Nazareth?*" The ill repute of Nazareth was proverbial. The prejudice that no good thing "*could come out of Nazareth*" started as the first opposition to the truth that Philip had propounded. This prejudice of Nathanael, like most prejudices, had but a poor foundation. It implies an exaggerated estimate of the power of social influence. It goes on the assumption that if the great bulk of a population is bad, no individual can be good.

But man, endowed as he is, with the power of independent thought and moral action, can break away from any social circle, take a path for himself, and make a character of his own. If he could not do so, he would not be responsible; and more, he has done so; and more still, he is morally bound to do so. Still, this prejudice was in Nathanael's way, and this prejudice he overcame.

(3.) He *prosecutes an inquiry* in search of truth. "*Philip saith unto him, Come and see. Jesus saw Nathanael,*" &c. Philip does not reason with him concerning the groundlessness of his prejudice, but merely invites him to "*Come and see*" for himself. Nathanael takes his advice, and goes with him. Jesus seeing him approaching goes forth to meet him, says of him, "*Behold an Israelite indeed.*" In pursuing his inquiry—(*a*) He is influenced by the words of Philip. "*Come and see.*" Such a common sense, straightforward, manly appeal as this he could not easily resist. (*b*) He is greeted by Christ. "*Behold an Israelite indeed.*" (*c*) He is struck by conviction. "*Whence knowest Thou me?*" He felt that his very heart had been read by Him Who had proclaimed him to be without "*guile*"—a sincere seeker for the truth.

Secondly: His success as a genuine truth-seeker. To his question, "*Whence knowest Thou me?*" Jesus replies, "*Before that Philip called thee, when thou wast under the fig tree, I saw thee.*" These words made him feel at once that he had found the Messiah. Nathanael had been under the fig tree, but did not suppose that any one saw him there. It was customary in those places at this period for students to meet their teachers in the morning and sit and study under the shade of the fig-tree. Nathanael had been there perhaps alone, studying the prophecies concerning the Messiah, and in a guileless spirit invoking Heaven for light. The declaration of Christ led him to exclaim at once, "*Rabbi, Thou art the Son of God; Thou art the King of Israel.*" Here is a full avowal of His Messiahship, and it shows that what he had been looking out for he now has. (*a*) A Divine Teacher. "*Rabbi, Son of God.*" (*b*) A Divine King. "*King of Israel.*"

Thirdly: His blessedness as a genuine truth-seeker. "*Jesus answered and said unto him, Because I said unto thee, I saw thee under the fig tree, believest thou? thou shalt see greater things than these. And He said unto Him, Verily, Verily, I say unto you, Hereafter ye shall see heaven open,*" &c. The language implies two things.

(1.) That *Nathanael now had seen great things.* What a revelation was made to his soul at this time! What a revelation of himself, and of the world, and of Christ! When a man first believes in Christ, great things rise on the horizon of his soul. All things appear in new lights; old things pass away.

(2.) That great as the things were that he now saw, *far greater things would be revealed to him in the future.* The key to this great saying is Jacob's vision (Gen. xxxiii. 12). Nathanael had called Christ the "*Son of God*," Christ calls Himself the "*Son of Man*." It is the first time He gives Himself this title, the title that He applies to Himself in almost all the subsequent parts of His history. "*The Son of Man*"—thoroughly human. Not the son of a Jew, or Gentile, or any particular tribe or race, but of *man*, the second Adam, the moral head of humanity. The promise is—(*a*) That he should see a new universe. "*Heaven open.*" (*b*) A new class of intelligence. "*The angels of God.*" (*c*) A new order of ministry. "*Ascending and descending*"—a ministry between heaven and earth. (*d*) A new centre of attraction. Angels ascend and descend on the "*Son of Man.*" What prospects are open to the *genuine* truth-seeker! The heavens of his soul will open wider, and grander visions will charm his existence.

John 2:1-11

THE GLORY OF CHRIST IN HIS FIRST MIRACLE
(*The marriage at Cana.*—JOHN ii. 1—11.)

"And the third day there was a marriage in Cana of Galilee; and the mother of Jesus was there: And both Jesus was called, (R. V. JESUS ALSO WAS BIDDEN) and His disciples, to the marriage. And when they wanted wine, (R. V. THE WINE FAILED) the mother of Jesus saith unto Him, They have no wine. Jesus saith unto her, Woman, what have I to do with thee? Mine hour is not yet come. His mother saith unto the servants, Whatsoever He saith unto you, do *it*. And (R. V. NOW) there were set there six waterpots of stone, after the manner of the purifying of the Jews, (R. V. AFTER THE JEWS' MANNER OF PURIFYING) containing two or three firkins apiece. Jesus saith unto them, Fill the waterpots with water. And they filled them up to the brim. And He saith unto them, Draw out now, and bear unto the governor (R. V. RULER) of the feast. And they bare *it*. When the ruler of the feast had tasted the water that was made (R. V. NOW BECOME) wine, and knew not whence it was : (but the servants which drew (R. V. HAD DRAWN) the water knew ;) the governor (R. V. RULER) of the feast called (R. V. CALLETH) the bridegroom, and saith unto him, Every man at the beginning doth set forth (R. V. SETTETH ON FIRST) good wine; and when men have well drunk (R. V. FREELY) then that which is worse: *but* thou hast kept the good wine until now. This beginning of miracles (R. V. HIS SIGNS) did Jesus in Cana of Galilee, and manifested forth (R. V. MANIFESTED) His glory ; and His disciples believed on Him."

EXEGETICAL REMARKS.—" Ver. 1.— "*The third day.*" From what? Undoubtedly from the incident recorded in the preceding verses. "*Cana of Galilee,*" not the Cana in Samaria. The place is now called Kana el-Jalib, a little town about eight or nine miles north-easterly of Nazareth. Nathanael was of this place. "*There was a marriage.*" There are several traditions as to the parties who were joined together at this time. Some suppose that St. John himself was the bridegroom—others, Simon the Canaanite—and others think that it was the marriage of Mary and Cleophas. The last is the opinion most probable, and most generally accepted. "*The mother of Jesus was there.*" Her husband Joseph does not seem to have been present. Probably he was dead, and she was a widow. Nothing has been heard of him for eighteen years, when he was in search of Jesus at the Temple.

Ver. 2.—"*Jesus was called, and His disciples.*" They were "*called,*" that is, invited. The twelfth verse gives us to understand that His "*brethren*" were also there. But it is not said that either they or His mother were "*called.*" Being relations, they seemed to have been there as a matter of course, and required no invitation. His disciples at this time were Peter and Andrew, James and John, Philip and Bartholomew, and they were all present.

Ver. 3.—"*And when they wanted wine, the mother of Jesus saith unto Him, They have no wine.*" Perhaps this marriage-feast continued longer than the usual time, or more guests attended than were first expected, or provided for. Such feasts as these lasted sometimes seven, or even fourteen days. "*They have no wine.*" Why did Mary go to Jesus with this statement? It is certain from her sublime song called the Magnificat, in Luke i. 46—56, as well as what she had often witnessed in the life of her Son, that she regarded Him as being endowed with Divine power. She might, therefore, have desired on such an interesting occasion to witness in her Son a striking manifestation of power.

Ver. 4.—"*Jesus saith unto her, Woman, what have I to do with thee? Mine hour is not yet come.*" "*Woman,*" this sounds to us like the language of disrespect or reproach; but on the lips of Christ it meant nothing of the kind. Citations from ancient authors show that this was a perfectly respectful address, though to us it sounds harsh. *Lange* expresses the thought thus:— "The Lord answered her, that is *my* concern, not thine, O woman; or, in other words, let *Me* alone, leave that to *Me;* thou'rt troubled, tender-hearted one."* "*Mine hour is not yet come.*" "Whatever our Lord intended by the fulness of these words, there was a present sense in which they were meant and received. My time for this public manifestation is fixed—is approaching; but it is *not yet come.*"

* See "Life of Christ," Lange, vol. ii. p. 202.

Christ seems to have had a programme —such a work for such an hour.

Ver. 5.—"*His mother saith unto the servants, Whatsoever He saith unto you, do it.*" His mother evidently understands His meaning, feels His authority, and bids the servants attend to His behests.

Ver. 6. "*And there were set there six waterpots of stone, after the manner of the purifying of the Jews, containing two or three firkins apiece.*" Why these six waterpots or urns were there is explained by the words "*purifying of the Jews.*" The Jews were accustomed to perform many ablutions, both of their persons and articles of furniture, both before and after meals. These earthenware urns were there for the purpose. The quantity of water in these vessels is supposed to have been about a hundred and twenty English gallons.

Ver. 7. "*Jesus saith unto them, Fill the waterpots with water. And they filled them up to the brim.*" Here could be no mistake. Water was not poured into empty or partially empty wine-casks that would give to it a wine flavour, but into common earthen wine-pots. All who were there, and John who records it himself being present, give the fact without any qualification.

Ver. 8.—"*And He saith unto them, Draw out now, and bear unto the governor of the feast. And they bare it.*" "*The governor.*" This term is used only in this chapter of the New Testament. It means the person (an honoured guest) who presided at the table. The tables had three sides, and the ruler of the feast sat or reclined at the head, opposite the open space. His was the honoured post. There was usually one on his right and one on his left. At the head the one leaning towards him on his right hand (as they all reclined on the left arm) was said to "bear on his bosom." (Ch. xiii. 23.) There were also three persons actually on each of the other two sides of the table.

Vers. 9, 10.—"*When the ruler of the feast had tasted the water that was made wine, and knew not whence it was: (but the servants which drew the water knew ;) the governor of the feast called the bridegroom, and saith unto him, Every man at the beginning doth set forth good wine; and when men have well drunk, then that which is worse : but thou hast kept the good wine until now.*" " It is clear from these words that the ruler of the feast did not know the miraculous origin of the wine, but he thought of its coming in the ordinary way from the grape. Notwithstanding this, he pronounced it better than the wine that they had previously taken, and was struck with the fact because it was contrary to general social usage. The general custom at feasts, he indicates, was to bring forth the best wine at first, when the keen tastes of the guests had not been deadened by an abundance, but here the best comes last. "This *wine* was not that fermented liquor which passes now under that name. All who know about the wines then used will understand rather the unfer-

mented juice of the grape. The present wines of Jerusalem and Lebanon, as we tasted them, were commonly boiled and sweet, without intoxicating qualities, such as we here get in liquors called wines. The boiling prevents the fermentation. Those were esteemed the best wines which were least strong. We may be sure that our Lord's wine would neither be *drugged*, nor *mixed* with deleterious ingredients, but *pure*. For *bread* He would give a *stone* as soon as for *wine* He would give poison." —JACOBUS.

Ver. 11. — " *This beginning of miracles did Jesus in Cana of Galilee, and manifested forth His glory; and His disciples believed on Him.*" There was no miracle before that. This miracle brought out the Divine glory of Christ. The sun of His Divinity which had been hidden by clouds now broke forth on the hearts of His disciples.

HOMILETICS

This first miracle is to be taken as an illustration of Christ's GLORY. Wherein does His " *glory* " appear in this extraordinary incident ? I think in the *sociality of His nature, the supernaturalness of His power*, and the *principle of His procedure*.

I.—IN THE SOCIALITY OF HIS NATURE

Christ was a full-orbed Man. He had not a particle of the misanthrope or ascetic in His nature. He was brimful of social love and sympathy. His social nature is here revealed—

First : In sanctioning a marriage by His presence. " Marriage," says Jeremy Taylor, " is the mother of the world." Without figure it is a dictate of nature, an ordination of God ; and coeval with the existence of the first human pair. Various sects have maintained the unlawfulness of marriage, from the Marcionites of old to the Shakers of modern times. Romanism even now denies its privileges to the sacerdotal class. There are thousands, too, in all ages who, having no theory as to the impropriety of marriage, are too lean natured to rejoice with those who enjoy matrimonial life. Christ, by attending a bridal feast, showed His interest in the relationship, and gave His sanction to it.

His social nature is here revealed—

Secondly : In promoting conviviality by His services. The beverage provision had run out, those entrusted with the responsibility of entertaining the guests had become anxious, and Christ interposes by a miracle, not only to meet the emergency, but to heighten the enjoyment. John the Baptist seemed to have been of an ascetic turn. He came "neither eating nor drinking," and some of John's disciples fell into the error of imagining that all the pleasures of life were to be eschewed, and that social festivities were wrong. They foolishly thought that the most effectual way to please God was to torment their bodies and destroy their natural inclinations. Such men have existed in all ages. The presence of Jesus at this feast was a protest against this absurdity and outrage. How the social nature of Christ shone on this occasion! How His sympathies and services heightened the festive hour! Christ was ever thus. He was no recluse. He mingled with men. He visited their houses, and He sat at their feasts. Had He not been thus social would He have been an example for us? Would He have had power to attract, comfort, or redeem?

In this miracle He "*manifested forth His glory*"—

II —IN THE SUPERNATURALNESS OF HIS POWER

Here He exhibits a power over nature in turning water into wine. The fact was so clear that no one doubted it, and the faith of the disciples was strengthened by it. Such power over the material world He often manifested afterwards. There is no way of explaining this result apart from His supernatural energy. When nature deviates from her wonted course, our intuitions and our reason force us to recognize a supernatural agency. Nature is a vast machine, and when its Maker arrests its progress or causes it to produce an unusual result, we call it a miracle. A result is not a miracle because of the greatness or amount of power involved in its production, for there is a larger amount of power *visible* in nature every day than in any of the miracles on record. There is infinitely more power seen, as St. Augustine intimates, in the wine that comes from the vine-trees every year through the vast and complicated workings of nature than in the converting this water into wine. The miraculousness consists in its being out of the ordinary course. Three things are noteworthy here in relation to Christ's miracle—

First: The ease with which it was performed. There is no excitement, no labour. It came as the result of a calm resolve.

Secondly: The timeliness of its occurrence. When Mary spoke to Him first, He said, "*My hour is not yet come ;*" an expression indicating that in His plan there was a special moment for such a work. Christ had a plan. He did not work by caprice or impulse. "The law—the programme—was written in His heart." Christ keeps the moral time of the universe. Every act of His rings out the hour of heaven's decrees.

Thirdly: The spirit of its accomplishment. Here is *independency*.

He did not, like Moses, Elias, and the apostles, look to another for power to achieve the work; the power was in Him. He did it Himself. Here is *unostentatiousness.* There is no demonstration, no aim at dramatic effect. Like God in nature, all sublimely quiet. In this miracle " *He manifested forth His glory* "—

III —IN THE PRINCIPLE OF HIS PROCEDURE

The narrative suggests two thoughts in relation to Christ's procedure with men—

First : He improves upon the best they have by nature. This family at Cana had water. Christ turned that water into wine. He gave it a new quality and a new flavour. This wine was *better* than water, inasmuch as one belonged to the mineral and the other to the vegetable domain. He turned the water of the human thoughts of the old prophets, historians, and apostles, into the wine of inspiration. Their thoughts were human ; but He gave them a new quality, a new aroma. So it is ever. What are the institutions of Churches, the writings of theologians, the thoughts of preachers ? They are mere water until He by His Spirit gives them a higher character. Christ always improves what we have by nature. There are natural virtues, but they are mere water until Christ touches them and changes them into spiritual wine.

Secondly : He improves upon the best that they have by attainment. The water which filled the urns was nature's gift, but the wine that they had drunk at the first part of the feast was that which they had obtained by their own ingenuity and work. And what does the " *governor of the feast* " say to that ? " *Thou hast kept the best wine of the feast until now.* " * The wine that Christ made was the *best* wine. It does not imply that their wine was bad, but it expressed the fact that His wine was better. In this the ruler of the feast, like Caiaphas afterwards, uttered an unconscious prophecy concerning Christ. This is the rule in Christ's kingdom of souls—a continuous progress from good to better, and from better to best. How different to worldly pleasures ! They pall upon the taste in the course of time. They get from bad to worse. For the Christian the better is always before him. Better, and better still, is always his motto, his destiny.

Conclusion : What think you of Christ, brother ? What a noble Man ! How grandly social ! What a Divine Man. Condescending to deviate from His ordinary procedure in order to gratify the wish and strengthen the faith of a few poor people by turning a little water into wine ! What a beneficent Worker ! Ever improving upon the best we have by nature, and making even the best things we have obtained by labour, better and better still !

* See Germs of Thought, p. 53.

Germs of Thought
No. 2   John 2:1-11

THE FIRST MIRACLE

" The third day there was a marriage. . ."   " This beginning of miracles did Jesus."

This first miracle suggests *four* lines of thought touching Christ's religion—

I —IT IS SOCIAL IN ITS GENIUS

All the *pre*-Christian religions, including the Jewish, were more or less ascetic. Most of the corrupt Christian religions also are. Christ, to show that His was sublimely social, *began* His miracles at a " *marriage feast*." Christianity is anti-ascetic. It is thoroughly human in its sympathies.

II —IT IS ORDERLY IN ITS PROGRESS

" *Mine hour is not yet come*." Christ does not move *arbitrarily* nor *capriciously*. He has a "time for everything," a plan of sequence. Why dost Thou not fulfil Thy prophecies? " *Mine hour is not yet come*." Why dost Thou not put all enemies under Thy feet? " *Mine hour is not yet come*," &c., &c.

III —IT IS HUMAN IN ITS INSTRUMENTALITY

" *Jesus saith unto them, Fill the water-pots with water*," &c. Christ does His work *for* man *by* man. " We have this treasure in earthen vessels," &c.

IV —IT IS IMPROVING IN ITS ENJOYMENTS

" *Thou hast kept the good wine until now*." The pleasures of the *world* decrease in their enjoyment as one passes on through years; but those of *personal Christliness* increase. It is from better to better. "The end is better than the beginning."

John 2:12, 13

THE SOCIALITY AND RELIGIOUSNESS OF CHRIST

" After this He went down to Capernaum, He, and His mother, and His brethren, and His disciples : and they continued there (R. V. THERE THEY ABODE) not many days. And the Jews' passover (R. V. THE PASSOVER OF THE JEWS) was at hand, and Jesus went up to Jerusalem."

EXEGETICAL REMARKS.—Ver. 12— " *After this*." That is, after the breaking-up of the marriage party of Cana in Galilee. " *He went down to Capernaum*." Capernaum was a city on the western shore of the Sea of Tiberias, and about ten hours' journey north of Cana. It was called His own city (Matt. ix. 1), because there He often resided ; some of His most wonderful works were wrought there ; also some of His grandest sermons were delivered there. (Mark ii. 1—28 ; John vi. 25 —70.) The neglect of its great privileges woke His most fearful denunciations, and brought on it a doom which has blotted almost every trace of it out of existence. " *He, and His mother*."

No mention is made of His father ; in all probability he had been "gathered to his fathers." "*And His brethren.*" Who were they ? Were they actual brethren, born of the same mother, or only near relatives, as cousins ? or were they, as some have supposed, sons of Joseph, His reputed father, by a previous marriage ? These are open questions, which the reader must decide for himself. "*And His disciples.*" Those whose names are mentioned in the previous chapter. "*And they continued there not many days.*" The time was short, because the feast of the Passover was just at hand.

Ver. 13.—"*And the Jews' passover*

was at hand." This was an institution ordained to commemorate the exemption, or passing over, of the families of the Israelites when the destroying angel smote the firstborn of Egypt ; also their departure from the land of bondage. It was one of the greatest religious festivals of the nation, and Jesus attended to this, as He did to all the others. With His attendance at this Passover His public ministry may properly be said to begin. "*Jesus went up to Jerusalem.*" It is said that He went *down* to Capernaum, but here He went "*up*" to Jerusalem. The description is true geographically and socially.

HOMILETICS

This fragment of Gospel history may be taken as illustrating the two sides of our Lord's life—the *social* and the *religious*. Notice—

I —HIS SOCIALITY

He goes down from Cana to Capernaum, which is a considerable distance, with his mother, brethren, and disciples, stays there a few days, and then returns, probably with them and others, up to Jerusalem (a greater distance still), in order to celebrate the Passover. Note here two things—

First : The great social advantages of Christ's friends. They are not only loving amongst themselves, as in this case, mother, brothers, and disciples, but they have Him with them. How delightful their journey must have been with "Him walking along in their midst ! " We should like to have had a record of their conversation. The remarks which probably He made on the beautiful scenery, on the significance of nature, on the character of the Infinite Father, on the object of His own mission, would surely so charm their spirits as to make them unconscious of distance and fatigue. All His disciples have this privilege ; He is with them always ; He not only talks to them by the way, but comes into them, and makes His abode with them. Note—

Secondly : The infinite condescension of Christ's love. What a sight ! God incarnate walking the dusty roads with men ! He seems to have gone to Capernaum on *their* account ; He could have wrought His miracles and propounded His doctrines at Cana of Galilee as well as at Capernaum, so far away. But probably these friends of His had business there. We know that Peter's home was there (Matt. viii. 14). He goes for their sake, not for His own. Anywhere would do for Him. We are made for society, but the best of our fellow-men fail to be companions that fully meet our social requirements, and justify our confidence. In Christ we have the society our social natures want; it is wise, immaculate, self-sacrificing, and almighty. Would that men would make Him their Friend, &c. Notice—

II —HIS RELIGIOUSNESS

He leaves Capernaum for Jerusalem in order to attend a great *religious* festival. He makes His way for the Temple : no doubt He meets with crowds who join Him on the way to the national festival, and reveals to them His spirit, doctrines, and glory. Religiousness lay at the root of Christ's spiritual life. It was deeper than His sociality—it inspired it, it ruled it. Men were near to Him, but the Father was infinitely nearer. He loved the former compassionately, because He loved the latter supremely. There is no true social love without religion : a man will never love his fellow-man as he ought until he love the Eternal with all his heart. Love for the Great Father is the only fire that can kindle in the soul true love for men. Genuine philanthropy is but one of the many branches of the majestic tree of piety which fills the glorious universe of the good. " He that saith he is in the light and hateth his brother is in darkness even until now." " If a man say I love God and hateth his brother, he is a liar."

CONCLUSION : Brother, wouldst thou have the *best* society, nay, the only society worth having ? Invite Christ into thy circle, make Him the centre and inspiration, and He will journey with thee on the rough road of life. Wouldst thou thyself be a good companion to others, a benediction to thy social sphere ? Let religiousness be thine imperial inspiration. Remember that He who gave a delightful inspiration to a *marriage* festivity at Cana, hastened His footsteps to a *religious* festivity at Jerusalem. Religion alone can make our society worth having. It hallows, beatifies, and immortalizes all human friendships.

John 2:13-17

THE IDEAL AND THE ACTUAL TEMPLE

(*At the Passover.*—JOHN ii. 13—17.)

" And the Jews' passover (R. V. PASSOVER OF THE JEWS) was at hand, and Jesus went up to Jerusalem, and found in the temple those that sold oxen and sheep and doves, and the changers of money sitting : and when He had made a scourge of small cords, He drove them (R. V. AND CAST) all out of the temple, and (R. V. BOTH) the sheep, and the oxen ; and poured out the changers' money, and overthrew the (R. V. THEIR) tables ; and said unto them that sold doves, (R. V. TO THEM THAT SOLD THE DOVES HE SAID,) Take these things hence ; make not My Father's house an house of merchandise. And His disciples remembered that it was written, The zeal of Thine house hath eaten (R. V. SHALL EAT) me up."

EXEGETICAL REMARKS.—Ver. 13.—
"And the Jews' passover was at hand, and Jesus went up to Jerusalem."
That is, went up from Capernaum. This seems to have been His first visit as a public teacher to the Holy City. *"And found in the temple those that sold oxen and sheep and doves."* "This was the most remarkable act of Jesus in Jerusalem at this time. By this act He entered upon His public ministry in the very centre of the Theocracy. He found in the temple, that is, in the precincts of the sanctuary, in the courts of the Gentiles, the dealers in oxen, sheep, and doves, as well as the money-changers sitting at their tables. These malpractices had gradually arisen from the wants, usages, and notions of the Jewish nation. Those persons who attended the festivals, or generally the Israelites who offered sacrifices, required animals for that purpose, and thus a cattle market was held. Besides that, according to Exodus xxx. 13, the Jews paid a temple tax, and in the temple coinage, a half shekel, according to the shekel of the sanctuary ; hence the money-changers were needed. Probably this temple market was originally in the neighbourhood of the outer court, and gradually brought within it."—*Lange.*

Ver. 15.—*"And when He had made a scourge of small cords, He drove them all out of the temple, and the sheep, and the oxen; and poured out the changers' money, and overthrew the tables."* His mode of procedure is remarkable. He makes a scourge of *"small cords."* This scourge He wields, not against men, but against the oxen and sheep, and against these animals naturally, not merely symbolically. It is a mark of His superiority that He drives the cattle out directly, as they had run of their own accord from the temple. In the same way He overturns the tables of the money-changers. He takes for granted that no tables ought to stand there.

Ver. 16.—*"And said unto them that sold doves, Take these things hence ; make not My Father's house an house of merchandise."* He does not deal in the same way with the doves. He commands them to be taken hence. Some see leniency here, and assign as the reason that the doves were sold for the poor. But the reason evidently was, that they were in cages, and to overturn them, as He had overturned the tables of the exchangers, would be to injure them, and they could not themselves break forth from their little prisons. Hence the command to their owners, *"Take these things hence."* *"My Father's house."* Thus He announces His Messiahship, by claiming a special relation to the Great God.

Ver. 17.—*"And His disciples remembered that it was written, The zeal of Thine house hath eaten me up."* The last clause is a quotation from Psalm lxix. When did the disciples remember this passage ? Now or after His resurrection ? At the latter period we think, when He Himself opened to them the Scriptures.

This cleansing of the temple is very similar to the purifying of the temple, as recorded by the other three evangelists. Was it the same event ? *Neander* and others suppose that it was so. But against that there are many strong objections.

HOMILETICS

As the event here recorded is so similar to that narrated (Matt. xxi. 1—16), upon which we have, in our "Genius of the Gospel" on Matthew (page 527), discoursed at length, our remarks now will be very brief. The subject of our discourse in the article referred to was the *Ideal and Actual temple*, under which heading we noticed "The Ideal temple, or the temple as it *should* be on earth ;" "The Actual temple, or the temple as *it is* on earth ;" and the "Cleansed temple, or the temple as it will one day *be realized* by Christ on earth."

We shall now look at the fact in three aspects—

I —AS THE REVELATION OF CHRIST'S GOD-HOOD

There is an air of Divinity about the whole of His procedure. Mark—

First: His boldness! What invincible courage it required for a poor Jewish peasant to enter the capital of His country, walk into the temple, the most sacred and majestic edifice in the whole city, around which the most tender and powerful associations of His contemporaries gathered, and strike a blow at once against the habits, the interests, and the prejudices of the people! Surely there is something superhuman in this indomitable daring. Mark—

Secondly: His power. The irrational creatures fled before Him, and the traders shrunk away at the moral majesty of His looks. The "*scourge of small cords*," says one, was taken up and formed into a species of whip rather as a symbol of His command than to be used either on man or beast. The mercenary barterers would have their consciences so stricken as to be overcome with fear. Was this clearing of the temple the achievement of a mere man in the aspect of a poor Hebrew peasant? Mark—

Thirdly: His authority. Observe His calmness. There is no perturbation, but the all-serenity of self-command. Observe His influence: The desecrators fled away abashed. Observe His words—words of command: "*Take these things hence.*" This is not the place for them. Remove them at once. Words, too, claiming especial relationship to the Infinite Father: "*Make not My Father's house a house of merchandise.*" Who does not see more than man in all this? Are not the beams of Divinity manifest in all?

Look at the fact—

II —AS AN EMBLEM OF CHRIST'S MISSION

This is an emblem of the work which He has to do. To cleanse religion of all that is mercenary and selfish. He is in His temple, and He does what Malachi had prophesied of Him—"He is as a refiner's fire, and as a fuller's soap; His fan is in His hand, and He is purging His floor." What He did now at Jerusalem is His great work in the world—clearing away all worldliness from the worship of God. Ecclesiastics have filled the modern Church with worldliness. Do not men bring traffic now into churches? If they drive not the actual cattle into the sanctuary, and set not up the tables of merchandise, do they not carry the schemes of the world in their brain, and the inspiration of the world in their heart! The great want of Christendom is a work by Christ similar to that which He now wrought in the temple at Jerusalem. We know that He is amongst us, and His object is to cleanse our temples; but as He works by moral means, the process seems depressingly slow.

Look at the fact—

III —AS AN EXAMPLE FOR CHRIST'S DISCIPLES

What Christ did we all should do—endeavour to drive worldliness from all the "*temples*" of men. The worldly spirit is antagonistic to the mind of God, and a curse to the human soul. This spirit must be exorcised. "He that loveth the world, the love of the Father is not in him." Let us drive out the world from the temple of our own natures. Let us do it as Christ now cleared the temple at Jerusalem—boldly, authoritatively, with all the might of our manhood, and with a burning "*zeal*" for the house of our Father.

> "Welcome, O welcome to our hearts, Lord ! here
> Thou hast a temple too, and full as dear
> As that in Zion, and as full of sin ;
> How long shall thieves and robbers dwell therein ?"

John 2:18-22

THE DEATH AND RESURRECTION OF CHRIST

"Then answered the Jews (R. V. THE JEWS THEREFORE ANSWERED) and said unto Him, What sign shewest Thou unto us, seeing that Thou doest these things ? Jesus answered and said unto them, Destroy this temple, and in three days I will raise it up. Then said the Jews, Forty and six years was this temple in building, and wilt Thou rear (R. V. RAISE) it up in three days ? But He spake of the temple of His body. When therefore He was risen (R. V. RAISED) from the dead, His disciples remembered that He had said this unto them ; (R. V. SPAKE THIS) and they believed the Scripture, and the word which Jesus had said."

EXEGETICAL REMARKS.—Ver. 18.— "*Then answered the Jews and said unto Him, What sign shewest Thou unto us, seeing that Thou doest these things?*" "This agrees with the demand which they afterwards made upon Him at the second cleansing. (See Matt. xxi.) They required to know by miracle His authority for such a proceeding, according to His claim in ver. 16, that the temple was His Father's house, and He of course the Son of God." (See my "Genius of the Gospel" on Matt. *in loco.*) What "*sign?*" Here is the unreasonableness of scepticism. Had these men not been visited with the most striking display of miraculous power in the clearing of the temple ? Yet these cavillers ask for more ; "captious men, they are like owls that hoot, and ask to see the sun at noon."

Ver. 19.—"*Jesus answered and said unto them, Destroy this temple, and in three days I will raise it up.*" "*This temple.*" What temple ? The Jewish temple at Jerusalem—that in which He had just performed the miracle of cleansing ? No ; the temple of His body. "*This temple.*" Some suppose that when he uttered these words He pointed to His body. His body was a "*temple,*" inasmuch as it was the dwelling-place and meeting-place of the great God. "*Destroy this temple.*" This must not be taken as a command to them to murder Him. The Holy One would not encourage such an enormity. It is, I think, hypothetical. If you "*destroy this temple,*" and you will do it, I will raise it again in three days. He means to say, I know you will destroy this body, and when you do it, in three days after "*I will raise*" *it up."* He repeats this (Matt. xii. 39): And this prophecy has been incontrovertibly fulfilled. In all history there is no fact better attested than the fact of Christ's Resurrection.

Ver. 20.—*"Then said the Jews, Forty and six years was this temple in building, and wilt Thou rear it up in three days?"* This temple restored and beautified, by Herod the Great, from the second temple of Zerubbabel, was begun in the eighteenth year of his reign, reckoning from the death of Antigonus. This would be sixteen years before the birth of Christ, or twenty years before our era. And counting thirty years after that, for our Lord's age at this time, we have forty-six years. As the temple was not yet finished, the meaning is that this structure had already been so many years in the course of building. When this saying was brought up against Him by the false witnesses

(Matt. xxvi. 61), their falsity consisted in putting a different sense to His words, and really altering them also, so as to make quite a different meaning. "I am able to destroy," &c., representing Him as an enemy to the temple; and some added that He "would raise another built without hands."

Ver. 22.—*"When therefore He was risen from the dead, His disciples remembered that He had said this unto them; and they believed the Scripture, and the word which Jesus had said."* The *"Scripture"* here refers to the Old Testament, the Law, the Prophets, and the Psalms. *"And they believed the Scripture, and the word which Jesus had said."* After what Christ had said to them (Matt. xix. 18; Luke xx. 32, 33), they saw that the Old Scriptures referred to the Resurrection of the Messiah, and they believed.

HOMILETICS

The words point to two of the greatest facts in the wonderful life of the world's Great Redeemer, namely, His *death* and *resurrection.* They are presented here in two aspects.

I —AS EVENTS PREDICTED

"Jesus answered and said unto them, Destroy this temple, and in three days I will raise it up." The words furnish four remarks in relation to their prediction.

First: They are given as an answer to scepticism. *"Then answered the Jews and said unto Him, What sign shewest Thou unto us, seeing that Thou doest these things?" "What sign?"* Had they not already received a *"sign"* sufficient to convince them of His Messiahship? Had He not driven from the temple not only the sheep and the oxen, but the mercenary men who trafficked within the Holy precincts? Could the poor and despised Nazarene of His own power have thus cleared the Temple as in a moment? What less than a flash of Divinity could have struck their consciences, and sent profane and sordid traders quailing from His presence? These events—namely, Christ's death and resurrection—are here and elsewhere given as the conclusive, ultimate, and crowning proof of His Messiahship. Another remark the words furnish in relation to the events predicted here, is—

Secondly: They are given in a metaphorical garb. *"Jesus answered and said unto them, Destroy this temple, and in three days*

I will raise it up." *" Destroy this temple"* is not, as we have seen, a command, but a prediction. It means you *will* destroy this temple. Christ's body was a *"temple"* in many respects. (1.) Divinity *specially built* it. The Temple of Jerusalem was built by God (1 Chron. xviii. 19). (2.) Divinity *dwelt in* it. In the Temple of Jerusalem the Shekinah, the symbol of the Divine Presence, majestically shone for ages. Christ's body was the shrine of the Eternal. In Him "dwelt all the fulness of the Godhead bodily." (3.) Divinity was *revealed through* it. The temple at Jerusalem was the scene of Divine manifestations, so was the temple of Christ's body. (4.) Divinity was *met* in it. The temple at Jerusalem was the place where men met with God, and communed with Him "from off the Mercy-seat." Another remark the words furnish in relation to their prediction, is—

Thirdly : They are given as suggestive of His Godhood. (1.) He here predicts the fact and authors of His own death. He means to say this temple will be destroyed, and you will do it. As if He had said, "I foresee My end : I know all about it. You are the men who will take away My life." This foresight certainly indicates super-humanity. (2.) He here predicts His own restoration. *" In three days I will raise it up."* Who amongst the untold millions of men who have lived and died have ever been able to raise themselves from the dead ? Christ here declares that He would, and history shows that He did so. Another remark the words furnish in relation to their prediction, is—

Fourthly : They are given but were misunderstood. *" Then said the Jews, Forty and six years was this temple in building, and wilt Thou rear it up in three days?   But He spake of the temple of His body."* They now, as ever, put a wrong construction on His words. They were too blinded by prejudice to perceive their spiritual import.

These two facts, therefore, in Christ's history, namely, His death and resurrection, were once mere predictions—events looming in the future, seen only by the eye of faith. But they are here presented also in a higher form, namely—

II —AS FACTS ACCOMPLISHED

"When therefore He was risen from the dead." He did rise. No fact in history is better attested than this. He realized His own predictions. The passage points to two good purposes which these important facts answered.

First : They threw light on the revelations of the past. *"His disciples remembered that He had said this unto them."* The facts of Christ's history light up all past Divine revelations. The old is to be understood by the new, not the new by the old. Christ's biography is at once the substance and interpretation of the Bible.

Secondly: They established confidence in the word of God. *"They believed the Scripture, and the word which Jesus had said."* (1.) In His word as contained in the Old Testament. Though they held the Old Testament as Divine before, they never saw its meaning so clearly as now in the light of these facts. (2.) In His word, as contained in the teaching of Christ. *"And the word which Jesus had said."*

Observe in conclusion—

First: That the genuine religion of humanity rests on FACTS. It does not rest on theories, speculations, or inferences, but on facts. It has, therefore, the same foundation as all true science.

Secondly: These facts refer specially to the history of ONE PERSONALITY. Christ's death and resurrection. These are the pillars. The latter, of course, involves the former.

Thirdly: These facts if accepted interpret PROPHECIES, AND ESTABLISH FAITH IN GOD. Experience solves enigmas. Christ's history throws light on the dark domain of ancient predictions.

John 2:23-25

CHRIST'S DISTRUST OF CERTAIN BELIEVERS AND HIS THOROUGH
KNOWLEDGE OF HUMAN NATURE

"Now when He was in Jerusalem at the Passover, in (R. V. DURING) the feast day, many believed in (R. V. ON) His name, when they saw the miracles (R. V. BEHOLDING HIS SIGNS) which He did. But Jesus did not commit (R. V. TRUST) Himself unto them, because (R. V. FOR THAT) He knew all men, And needed not that any should testify of (R. V. ONE SHOULD BEAR WITNESS CONCERNING) man: for He (R. V. HIMSELF) knew what was in man."

EXEGETICAL REMARKS.—Ver. 23.— *"Now when He was in Jerusalem at the Passover, in the feast day."* All religions seem to have their feasts. Amongst the Greeks and Romans these feasts were celebrated at the Olympian and other games. The Jews had three great feasts, the passover, the pentecost, and the feast of tabernacles. The first was held before the beginning of harvest. *"Many believed in His name, when they saw the miracles which He did."* "Miracles," whilst they philosophically cannot be considered a proof of the Divinity either of a messenger or message, were nevertheless designed and suited to promote faith : they arrested attention, roused the embruted soul of the thoughtless, and thrilled the witnessing multitudes with tokens of Divine power. What *"miracles"* they were we are not told, the other evangelists do not refer to them. We have only a fragment of Christ's voluminous biography. Probably His wondrous deeds animated them with such enthusiasm, that they were ready to proclaim Him king. They would feel that to fight on their way to Cæsar's throne, under the banner of a Man who could work such wonders, would be to fight without the possibility of defeat, and with the certainty of brilliant triumph.

Ver. 24.—*"But Jesus did not commit Himself unto them."* He read their motives and properly estimated the value of their enthusiasm. He knew the worth of the Hosannas of an empty crowd.

Ver. 25.—"*Because He knew all men, and needed not that any should testify of man: for He knew what was in man.*" Omniscience, attribute of the Absolute One, was His.

HOMILETICS

The verses contain two things:—*Christ's distrust of certain believers*, and *His thorough knowledge of human nature.*

I —CHRIST'S DISTRUST OF CERTAIN BELIEVERS

The thing to be well noted here is, that although men "*believed in His name,*" He,—"*Jesus did not commit Himself unto them.*" The sermons of some preachers abound with eulogies on "the believer," with enumerations of the trials of "the believer," the privileges of "the believer," the glory that awaits "the believer;"—the word has become a cant—its aroma is offensive. There is no virtue in a certain kind of believing, but often great sin.

First: The mere TRADITIONAL believer is distrusted by Christ. How much of the popular faith in Christianity is of this sort: people accept the dogmas that have been handed down to them from their ancestors, or presented to them by their religious teachers; and their faith implies no personal inquiry, and includes no spark of conviction. Such was the faith of the Jews in the days of Christ;—such is the faith of nominal Christians throughout Christendom. It is a base thing; it is the hotbed of bigotry and intolerance.

Secondly: The mere HISTORIC believer is distrusted by Christ. There are men who believe in the genuineness of Christ's biography (and we see not how any enlightened and faithful student of history could do otherwise), as they believe in Alexander, Augustus, or Napoleon. But their faith has no influence on their character—no more influence than faith in the existence of Julius Cæsar or of any other historic character. It has, therefore, no worth in it,—it is not to be trusted.

Thirdly: The mere DOCTRINAL believer is distrusted by Christ. Belief in what Christ has taught concerning God, man, and moral obligations, has no more virtue in it than belief in the principle of astronomy, or that of any other science. What is made obvious to man's intellect, man is bound to believe.

As it was eighteen hundred years ago, it is now: many who believe in His name Christ does not trust. He has no trust in the mere *traditional, historical,* or *doctrinal* believer. Is there a faith then that He can trust? Yes, it is this,—a loving, practical, and unbounded confidence in Him as the infallible Guide and the Divine Redeemer of the race. "When the Son of Man cometh, shall He find such faith on the earth?" He makes all virtue to depend upon believing *in Him;* not merely in what He has said or done, nor what people have said about Him, but *in Himself*. Notice here—

II —CHRIST'S THOROUGH KNOWLEDGE OF HUMAN NATURE

"*He knew all men, and needed not that any should testify of man: for He knew what was in man.*" The last clause may be read thus:—"For Himself He knew man." The magnificent edifice, amid whose halls, chambers, offices, corridors and courts we lose ourselves, is thoroughly understood by him who drew the plan: in the brain of the architect the whole existed in archetype before the foundation-stone was laid. The piece of intricate machinery, with its complication of wheels, springs, levers, convolutionary movements, fills us with perplexity: but the machinist who constructed it knows every part and pin. It is even so with MIND. The profoundest metaphysician understands it not, and hence the numerous and conflicting theories. But Christ the Architect knows it well. There are wonderful things *in* man, indefinite powers of action, innumerable germs of life, unsealed fountains of fathomless sympathies, unnumbered tribes of thought, and streams of emotion, both good and evil,—yet all are known to Christ.

From Christ's *thorough* knowledge of man, we may draw the following important truths—

First: That His sufferings and death must have been entirely voluntary. Christ's sufferings came not on Him by disease or accident as they come on us, but *by men,* and as He knew the inmost thoughts and purposes of all men, He certainly might have avoided them. His thorough knowledge of men demonstrates the voluntariness of His agonies and ignominious death. Another truth which we may draw from the fact is—

Secondly: That neither our obligations nor our trials will go beyond our capacities. As a just Sovereign, He proportions duty to power, and as a merciful Redeemer trials to strength. "He knoweth our frame." He knows both what we can *do* and what we can *endure.* Where capacity ends obligation ceases. Another truth which we draw from the fact is—

Thirdly: That a religion which is not of the heart is of no value in His sight. All formality and insincerity are not only worthless to His eye, but *abhorrent* to His heart. "He abhors the sacrifice where not the heart is found." Another truth which we draw from the fact is—

Fourthly: That His religious system must be in agreement with the spiritual nature and condition of man. He Who knows "*what is in man,*" and desires His system to spread, may be expected to fit it to man's nature and case. Christianity is fitted to the intellect, imagination, conscience, and heart of men, as well as to their circumstance as sinners. Another truth which we draw from the fact is—

Fifthly : That the transactions of the Judgment Day will proceed on a thorough knowledge of all the facts of man's history. Nothing will be done in doubt or darkness.

Sixthly : That the character of Christ is transcendently pure. "It would," says *Livermore*, "be an omission here not to take notice of the benevolent use to which Jesus ever applied His knowledge of mankind. While the brilliant poet, the ambitious writer, the artful statesman, and the unscrupulous money-maker, are so often guilty of employing their acquaintance with the human heart, to further their own sensual or selfish purposes, our Holy Master touched the secret springs of our nature only to bless and heal. He lighted the pure flame of love and truth on the altar of the soul, not the smouldering fires of lust and passion. He dealt as a brother with erring brethren, and never took advantage of their weakness or ignorance. God give us grace to imitate the magnanimous trait of our high Exemplar."

John 3:1-21

THE GOSPEL SCHOOL

(Our Lord's Discourse with Nicodemus.—JOHN iii. 1—21.)

"There (R. V. NOW THERE) was a man of the Pharisees, named Nicodemus, a ruler of the Jews : The same came to Jesus (R. V. UNTO HIM) by night, and said unto Him, Rabbi, we know that Thou art a Teacher come from God : for no man can do these miracles (R. V. SIGNS) that Thou doest, except God be with him," &c.

EXEGETICAL REMARKS.—"The connecting particle (δὲ), with which the original introduces this scene, should not have been omitted, as the Evangelist is now going to show, in continuation of his subject, that *all* the accessions to Christ during this, His first public visit to Jerusalem, were not like those of whom he had spoken at the close of the preceding chapter. It should have begun thus — 'But (or now), there was a man,' etc."— *Brown.*

Ver. 3.—"*Jesus answered and said unto him, Verily, verily, I say unto thee, Except a man be born again,* (R. V. ANEW) *he cannot see the kingdom of God.*" A reply this to the words of Nicodemus, singularly abrupt, emphatic, and startling. It struck a hard blow against the religion of the Pharisee. "*Verily, verily*"—an expression this found in none of the other Gospels. "*Born again.*" This phrase, as will be seen, was used to introduce Nicodemus to the true spiritual nature of Christ's kingdom, and by means of the terms and customs in use among the Jews, to open to him the higher sense. The Jews called those proselytes "new born" who were received by baptism in their Church—into the Messiah's kingdom, as they claimed their Church to be. But how infinitely below the true requirement was this ! The true regeneration lies not in any outward ordinance—in any boasted rite, as our Lord explains to this Jewish Rabbi. It is a new birth indeed. Christ means to say, You must begin a new life : it is not reformation but renovation you want ; not mending, but re-creating. "*The kingdom of God*" means the

Divine society, the grand confederation of holy souls. Man requires a new life before he can even *see* this kingdom ; the great spirit world is hid from the unregenerate.

Ver. 4. — *"Nicodemus saith unto Him, How can a man be born when he is old? can he enter the second time into his mother's womb, and be born?"* The figure of the new birth would have appeared clear enough to Nicodemus if Christ had referred to Gentile proselytes to the Jew's religion, for such proselytism was ever spoken of as a new birth ; but addressed to him as a Jew it was incomprehensible. It seemed to him as absurd as for a man to enter the second time into his mother's womb.

Ver. 5.—*"Jesus answered, Verily, verily, I say unto thee, Except a man be born of water and of the Spirit, he cannot enter into the kingdom of God."* "The next answer of Jesus has three noticeable features. (1.) The imperturbable confidence expressed in the repetition. (2.) The advance of the thought : the explanation of the birth from above as being born of water and Spirit. (3.) The entering into the kingdom of God instead of seeing it." —*Lange.* "*Water*" here does not mean baptism, it is used as a symbol of the means of moral cleansing, it is often so used.--Titus iii. 5 ; 1 Peter ii. 3 ; Ephesians v. 26 ; Heb. x. 22 ; John v. 6—8.

Ver. 6.—*"That which is born of the flesh is flesh; and that which is born of the Spirit is spirit."* "Like produces like. Man is naturally born into a life of the senses, in which the chief objects of pursuit and interest are visible and earthly. But he is spiritually born into a spiritual life, in which the leading aim and affections are of a spiritual and immortal nature : so that by the '*flesh*' is here meant what is corrupt and perishable, and by the '*Spirit*,' what is pure, divine, and everlasting. Some suppose an allusion to be made here to the Jewish boast of being by blood the descendants of Abraham."—*Livermore.*

Ver. 7.—"*Marvel not that I said unto thee, Ye must be born again.*"

(R. V. ANEW.) It would seem as if Christ saw astonishment on the brow of this Nicodemus, and He bids him not to *marvel*, and goes on to re-urge the necessity of the new birth.

Ver. 8.—"*The wind bloweth where it listeth, and thou hearest the sound* (R. V. VOICE) *thereof, but canst not tell* (R. V. KNOWEST NOT) *whence it cometh, and whither it goeth: so is every one that is born of the Spirit.*" "The laws which govern the wind have been partially discovered, but the risings, fallings, and change in different directions many times in the day of those gentle breezes here referred to will probably ever be a mystery to us ; so will be the operations of the new birth."—*Brown.* It has been suggested that a sudden blast might have blown at this moment, and given rise to this illustration.

Ver. 9.—"*Nicodemus answered and said unto Him, How can these things be?*" "From this moment," says *Stier,* "Nicodemus says nothing more, but has sunk into a disciple who has found his true Teacher."

Ver. 10.—"*Jesus answered and said unto him, Art thou a master* (R. V. THE TEACHER) *of Israel, and knowest* (R. V. UNDERSTANDEST) *not these things?*" The idea is that the high standing of Nicodemus as a master of Israel should prevent his amazement at these simple truths. He should have known that the spiritual change in the Jews was spoken of as a new birth.—Jeremiah xxxi. 31—33 ; Ezekiel xviii. 31 ; xxxvi. 26.

Ver. 11.—"*Verily, verily, I say unto thee, We speak that we do know, and testify* (R. V. BEAR WITNESS OF) *that we have seen ; and ye receive not our witness.*" Here we have the plural for the singular—"*we speak.*" Here is the personal certitude of Christ meeting the ignorance of Nicodemus. "*We*"—John and I, the Eternal Father and I. "*We know,*" we are conscious of what we affirm, "*we have seen.*"

Ver. 12.—"*If I have told you earthly things, and ye believe not, how shall ye believe, if I tell you of heavenly things?*" "In reference probably to the phrase being born again, which was in common use among the Jews, as signifying conversion from heathenism to their religion. Heavenly things, *i. e.* more advanced and spiritual views, as to the nature of the Messiah's kingdom, and the admission of the Gentiles to its privileges. You stumble in crossing the threshold of my religion, how then can you hope to penetrate its minor glories?"—*Livermore.*

Ver. 13.—"*And no man hath ascended up to heaven, but He that came down from heaven, even the Son of man which is in heaven.*" Local ascent and descent are not to be understood here. As a Divine Teacher Christ was in heaven as well as on earth. No mind but His Who came down from heaven. ever ascended up to heaven to bring down the heavenly truths.

Ver. 14.—"*And as Moses lifted up the serpent in the wilderness, even so must the Son of man be lifted up.*" Here He rises from the earthly thing, regeneration, to the heavenly thing, His own mediation. For the historic fact here used as a symbol, see Numbers xxi. 9.

Ver. 16.—"*For God so loved the world, that He gave His only begotten Son, that whosoever believeth in* (R. V. ON) *Him should not perish, but have everlasting* (R. V. ETERNAL) *life.*" No explanation can make these words clearer than they are: you cannot brighten the sun. "THE WORLD." Τὸν Κόσμον. This is to be taken in its widest sense. Here the Evangelist declares the love of God, the great originating cause of Christ's mission—"*everlasting life*"—the end of His mission. "The nature of the condemnation consists in rejecting the light and choosing darkness, not in being a Jew or a Gentile. This is the condemnation. Or it is itself a condemnation that light is come, &c. Profound disclosures of human nature are here made, which the experience of the whole world confirms. Men shrink from the light which exposes their moral deficiencies or deformities as the diseased eye from the shining of the sun. The images of light and darkness have been thought to be suggested by Nicodemus coming to Jesus by night."—*Livermore.*

HOMILETICS

This chapter may be regarded as exhibiting a good view of the *Gospel School.* It presents to us three things connected with this School: *a distinguished student, a glorious Master,* and *a characteristic theology.*

I —A DISTINGUISHED STUDENT

Notice—

First: His religious sect. He was a "*Pharisee.*" Of all religious sects that prevailed amongst the Jews, that of the Pharisees was the most proud, sanctimonious, exclusive and influential. John the Baptist had denounced them as a "Generation of Vipers," &c., Christ had warned His disciples against the leaven of their influence, and thundered at them many tremendous woes. They were the leading antagonists to the Son of God. To this sect Nicodemus belonged, as did Paul also. How interesting it is to see men breaking away from the shackles of old associations and the exclusiveness of a bigoted party. Notice—

Secondly: His civil position. He was "*a ruler of the Jews.*" He was one of the leading men of his age, a magnate in Jerusalem, a member of the Jewish Sanhedrim, the great council of the nation. A refreshing sight is this. A man, high in the society of his age and country, invested with civil authority, seeking knowledge at the hands of the reputed son of a carpenter. I see in this a picture of what ever ought to be, and what must be, ere the destiny of the race is complete. Ignorance in worldly power and splendour bowing before intelligence in lowliness and poverty. Nicodemus had come to feel that man could not live by bread alone, that he had deeper and more vital wants. Notice—

Thirdly : His moral timidity. "*The same came to Jesus by night.*" He came "*by night*" from fear of the Jews. He was a man that lacked at this stage of his history moral courage. Indeed, this seemed to be the great defect in his character. The question which he put in the council on one occasion (John vii. 13), "Doth our Lord judge any man ?" &c., indicates a sad lack of bravery. Why did he not protest in thunder instead of interrogating ? The secret way afterwards in which he came to Pilate to render respect to the crucified body of Christ, shows a craven heart. He loved truth, but he feared men. Still the love of truth was sufficiently strong in him to bring him to Christ in the night. This feature in his character cannot be admired, nor must it be imitated. We should like to have seen him go in open day before thousands of his countrymen to the poor Galilean in search of truth. Notice—

Fourthly : His respectful behaviour. "*He said unto Him, Rabbi.*" This title of respect is in some places rendered "Master." He recognized in Christ a moral Lord, and he approached Him with the utmost deference. Worldliness had not so closed his eyes as to prevent him seeing intellectual and moral greatness in the forms of poverty and meanness. As a rule wisdom has ever dwelt amongst the lowly and unpopular. Notice—

Fifthly : His evident sincerity. He acknowledges at once his conviction of the Divinity of Christ's mission. "*We know that Thou art a teacher come from God : for no man can do these miracles except God be with Him.*" He does not say that no man could perform miracles without God, but he says no man can do *such* miracles as Christ had wrought. His miracles were miracles of *mercy.* His miracles were the miracles of one Whose character was *perfect,* and Whose doctrines accorded with all that was morally intuitional in human souls.

Such is the distinguished student which we here find in this Gospel School. Here he sits at the feet of Christ. "Nicodemus," says Lange, "is better than his theology ; in theology he is the type of a rationalizing supernaturalism ; in character he is an inquiring child involved in the prejudices of old age."

We proceed now to notice—

II —THE TRANSCENDENT TEACHER

Christ, the great Founder of this Gospel School, was now present, and dealt directly with this distinguished inquirer. Concerning Him, we have to notice three things :

First : The spirit He exemplifies. (1.) Here is the spirit of *faithfulness.* In reply to the inquirer there is no circumlocution, no temporizing, no attempt to make truth palatable, but with the abruptness of a spirit fired with truth, He says, " *Verily, verily, I say unto you, Except a man be born again, he cannot see the kingdom of God.*" Words suited to shake his Pharisaism to its foundation. (2.) Here is the spirit of *earnestness.* The necessity of the change He repeats *thrice* in words of fire. (3.) Here is the spirit of *certitude.* " *We speak that we do know, and testify that we have seen.*" * Here is a consciousness of absolute knowledge. "What I say I know, not by the testimony of others, nor by the deduction of a fallible reason, but as a matter of direct vision from My Father." Christ said what He knew to be the truth : His doctrines were as real to Him as His own existence. Another thing indicative of his transcendent greatness is—

Secondly : The title He assumes. He calls Himself the Son of Man, and the only begotten Son of God. What does this mean ? † " *The Son of Man*"—not the Son of Jew, Greek, or Roman. The Son of Man—the ideal Man. The Son of God—the only begotten Son of God. A title this, whose meaning we can never penetrate : a relation whose import we can never fathom. Another thing indicative of His transcendent greatness is—

Thirdly : The wonderful mission He claims. He claims a mission from heaven. " *No man hath ascended up to heaven,*" ‡ &c. The meaning of this apparently paradoxical utterance is, that no man has got the truth by ascending to heaven : He only has got it who came down from heaven, and whose home is in heaven, even the Son of Man Himself. He claims a mission from God, to save the world. " *God so loved the world, that He gave His only begotten Son,*" &c. ‡

Such are briefly some of the indications we have here of the transcendent greatness of this Teacher sent from God, from whom Nicodemus was endeavouring to receive religious truth.

III —THE HEAVENLY THEOLOGY

What were the truths inculcated ? They comprehend the two great cardinals of His system, which theology designates *regeneration* and *reconciliation ;* in other words, a change in our moral character and in our moral relations—a subjective and an objective change. The former is developed in the first eleven verses,

---

* See our Notes on Chapter I. 18, also Germ on p. 71.
† See a full discourse at end of volume.　　　‡ See Germs, pp. 72, 73.

and the latter in the succeeding six. These doctrines are not only similar, but may be regarded as identical. In relation to the points of similarity, we notice three things. (1.) Both are indispensable. Without change of character there is no entering into the "*kingdom of God.*" Without change of relation, *i. e.* reconciliation to God by faith in Christ, there is no life. (2.) Both involve the Divine interposition; the one the agency of the Spirit, whose operations are as mysterious as the "*wind*"; the other the interposition of God's only Son. (3.) Both require faith in Christ, as the Messenger of God's love. This faith is essential both to regenerate and reconcile. But the two are so vitally connected that it is scarcely philosophical to regard them apart. Certainly Christ in this passage does not regard them as distinct, but treats them as one. The subjective change necessarily ensures the objective. Regeneration is reconciliation. The soul being made right in itself is right with God, and He regards it as such. The truths which Christ taught that night will perhaps come better out by disregarding the classifications and terminologies of theological systems. What then are the general truths which Christ taught Nicodemus?

First: That there is a necessity for a radical moral change in man's character. So thorough is the change that Christ represents it as a "new birth." The change is such a revolution in the governing disposition of the soul as involves a new life, experience, and history. Without it there is no entrance into the "*kingdom of God,*" the kingdom of spiritual truth, love, and blessedness. Christ intimates three things concerning this necessary change. (1.) It requires the agency of the Divine Spirit, which is *mysterious, sovereign,* and *mighty* in its operations. It must be accomplished by "*water and the Spirit,*" and that Spirit is as mysterious as the wind which "*bloweth where it listeth,*" &c. (2.) The non-understanding of it by believers in the Bible is a reprehensible matter. "*Art thou a master of Israel, and knowest not these things?*"* Thou professest to believe in the Old Scriptures, which are full of it, &c. (3.) The understanding of it is essential to the understanding of the higher aspects of Divine truth. "*If I have told you earthly things, and ye believe not,*" &c.* The earthly are those which come within the sphere of human consciousness; the heavenly, those which refer to the wonderful history of Christ, as the Messenger of God's love. Another truth here taught is—

Secondly: That the principle of eternal life involved in this change comes to men through the mission of Christ. The newborn life in the soul consists undoubtedly in supreme love to God. This love gives a new experience, a new history to man.

* See Germs, pp. 70, 71.

It is eternal life. It is everlasting blessedness in embryo. But it comes through Christ. (1.) Through looking at Him as the believing Jew looked upon the brazen serpent in the wilderness. "*As Moses lifted up*," &c.* (2.) Believing on Him as the Messenger of God's love. "*Whosoever believeth on Him*," &c. This "*eternal life*" then comes to the world through Christ. He who ascended to heaven, and came down from heaven, Whose home is heaven, He brought this eternal life to the world. This was the object of His mission. "As Thou hast given Me power over all flesh (mankind), that I should give to all flesh (mankind) that which Thou hast given Me—ETERNAL LIFE." Another truth taught here is—

Thirdly: That the mission of Christ to the world is to be ascribed to the infinite love of the Father. "*God so loved the world.*" Here is an immeasurable ocean, whose depths no intellect can fathom. "*So loved*," &c. Another truth taught here is—

Fourthly: That the world's treatment of this manifestation of infinite love determines its moral condition before God. "*He that believeth on Him is not condemned: but he that believeth not is condemned already*," &c.* "*This is the condemnation, that light is come into the world*," &c. We have only given here the bare outlines of the thoughts suggested by this passage. Every passage is a fertile text, and on many of them discourses appear below.

Germs of Thought
No. 3   John 3:9, 10

CULPABLE IGNORANCE

"Nicodemus answered and said unto Him, How can these things be? Jesus answered and said unto him, Art thou a master of Israel, and knowest not these things?"

The culpability of the ignorance of Nicodemus is seen by two facts.

I —HE HAD GREAT OPPORTUNITIES

He was brought up a Pharisee; he was trained in the Old Testament Scriptures; he ought to have known what spiritual renovation meant. The religious ignorance of some people is a misfortune; this man's ignorance was a crime.

II —HE MADE GREAT PRETENSIONS

He was a "*master of Israel.*" He professed to teach; he was, however, a mere letterist; he lived in the verbalities of truth, like many of the ecclesiastics of all ages. The language of Christ

* See Germs, pp. 72, 74.

savours of reproof. "*Art thou a master of Israel, and knowest not these things?*" Shame on thee to be ignorant of the spirit of that system in which thou hast been trained, in which thou hast assumed authority!

No. 4   John 3:11, 12

SPIRITUAL TRUTH

"Verily, verily, I say unto thee, We speak .that we do know, and testify that we have seen; and ye receive not our witness. If I have told you earthly things, and ye believe not, how shall ye believe, if I tell you of heavenly things?"

I —SPIRITUAL TRUTH HAS ITS ABSOLUTE TEACHER

"*We speak that we do know.*" As if Christ had said, Truth to Me is not a matter of speculation, theory, or reasoning, it is a matter of absolute certitude. We know it, and so "*we testify that we have seen.*" Physical truth has no absolute teacher. Spiritual truth has a teacher that speaks from holy consciousness.

II —SPIRITUAL TRUTH HAS ITS UNBELIEVERS

"*And ye receive not our witness.*" The Sanhedrim had not admitted the testimony of John nor the manifestations of Christ. Sad that men should accept the dogmas of the fallible and reject the doctrines of the infallible. But so it has been and so it is now.

III —SPIRITUAL TRUTH HAS ITS GRADATIONS

"*If I have told you earthly things,*" &c.; for "earthly" read "human," for "heavenly" read "Divine." What was the *earthly* or human thing referred to? *Regeneration.* This is a matter of human consciousness. All men must have known something of moral revolution. It is a human thing, a thing that comes within human reasoning, consciousness, experience. What was the *heavenly* or Divine thing referred to? Manifestly the *interposition of Christ.* His advent to the world was the effect and expression of God's infinite love. The facts which He states in the subsequent verses are all beyond human reasoning and consciousness, they are *Divine.*

IV —SPIRITUAL TRUTH HAS ITS LAWS OF STUDY

He who understands it must begin at the beginning. "*If I have told you earthly things, and ye believe not, how shall ye believe, if I tell you of heavenly things?*" Man must understand its human side before he can appreciate its Divine. In other words, he must know the nature and necessity of a radical moral change in him before he can appreciate the goodness, the wisdom, and the interposition of Christ.

No. 5   John 3:13

THE UNIQUE LIFE

"And no man hath ascended up to heaven, but He that came down from heaven, even the Son of man which is in heaven."

I —CHRIST CAME FROM HEAVEN TO EARTH

" *He that came down from heaven.*" He had a prior existence. He was "set up from everlasting." He was in the bosom of the Father. He came down. How infinite His condescension!

II —CHRIST WAS IN HEAVEN WHILE ON EARTH.

" *The Son of man which is in heaven.*" While He tabernacled on this earth He was still in heaven. His thoughts, sympathies, spirit were in heaven. He was in heaven, consciously in heaven, while He preached His sermons, wrought His miracles, offered His prayers, and endured His sufferings. Grand, sublimely grand was His life! Christ stands alone in the universe, there is no one like Him. *Every true teacher of the Gospel must be in heaven spiritually while he is on the earth.*

No. 6   John 3:14, 15

THE BRAZEN SERPENT AN EMBLEM OF HEAVEN'S ANTIDOTE FOR SIN

"And as Moses lifted up the serpent in the wilderness, even so must the Son of man be lifted up : that whosoever believeth in Him should not perish, but have eternal life."

From this passage we infer—

I —THAT THE ANTIDOTE PROVIDED IN THE GOSPEL IS FOR A LAMENTABLE EVIL

The affliction from which the Jews, bitten by the serpent, suffered resembled sin in three respects. It was *imparted*—it was *painful*—it was *mortal*. It was unlike sin in three respects. It was *material*, not spiritual—it was *a calamity*, not a crime—it was *transient*, not permanent.

II —THE ANTIDOTE PROVIDED IN THE GOSPEL ORIGINATED IN THE SOVEREIGNTY OF GOD

The brazen serpent did not originate with Moses, or any of the Jews, but with God; it is so with the Gospel. There are many points of difference in the antidote. (1.) The one was apparently arbitrary, the other was manifestly adapted. (2.) The one was insensible to the sufferer, the other was filled with sympathy. (3.) The one was local in its aspects, the other was world wide. (4.) The one was temporary in its efficacy, the other was abiding in its influence.

III —THE ANTIDOTE PROVIDED BY THE GOSPEL REQUIRES THE PERSONAL APPLICATION OF THE SUFFERERS

(1.) Personal application the most *simple*. The serpent required looking at—Christ believing in. (2.) Personal application the most *unmeritorious*. There is no merit in either looking or believing. (3.) Personal application the most *indispensable*. Those who did not look died; and those who do not believe are damned. (4.) Personal application is ever *efficacious*. Every Jew that looked was healed; every soul that believes is saved.

No. 7   John 3:16

LOVE

"For God so loved the world, that He gave His only begotten Son, that whosoever believeth in Him should not perish, but have everlasting life."

Here is *love :—*

I —IN ITS PRIMAL FOUNTAIN

Where does love originate? All streams from one fountain— God. God has a *heart*. He is not all sheer intellect. God's heart is benevolent, not unkind. Here is love:—

II —IN ITS HIGHEST FORM

Love for the good and the true is beautiful, but love for enemies!—This is amazingly grand! (1.) Here is love for guilty men:—Love for the corrupt, the criminal, the morally repulsive. (2.) Here is love for a world of guilty men:—Love for the world without any limitation. Here is love:—

III —IN ITS MIGHTIEST STRENGTH

Making the greatest conceivable sacrifice. "*He gave His only begotten Son.*" Who shall explain this? How omnipotent this love! Here is love:—

IV —IN ITS MORAL INFLUENCE

How is this love to influence men? To influence the guilty so as to absolve them, and the enemies so as to atone them, the lost so as to save them? Simply by *faith*. *The greatest love in the world can only move a moral being by faith.*

No. 8   John 3:17

FUNDAMENTAL FACTS OF EVANGELISM

"For God sent not His Son into the world to condemn the world; but that the world through Him might be saved."

Christianity is built on facts. These facts are connected with a person, and this person is the Son of God. There are three facts here:

I —THE FIRST FACT IS THIS, GOD SENT HIS SON INTO THE WORLD

This fact implies two things. (1.) That Christ is in some sense *separate* from the Father. There is a wonderful unity, but at the same time a distinction. (2.) Christ is in some sense *subordinate* of the Father. He is "*sent*" by the Father.

II —THE SECOND FACT IS THIS, THAT GOD SENT HIS SON INTO THE WORLD NOT TO CONDEMN IT

This is not what might have been expected. Two things might have led one antecedently to expect that if God had sent His Son into the world it would have been to damn it. (1.) The world's wickedness. (2.) The world's ill-treatment of previous messengers.

III —THE THIRD FACT IS THIS, THAT GOD SENT HIS SON INTO THE WORLD TO SAVE IT

What is salvation? It consists not in physical, intellectual, or local changes, but in the restoration in the soul of all that it has lost through sin;—lost freedom, lost harmony, lost love, lost happiness.

No. 9   John 3:18-20

CHRISTIANITY

"He that believeth on Him is not condemned : but he that believeth not is condemned already, because he hath not believed in the name of the only begotten Son of God. And this is the condemnation, that light is come into the world, and men loved darkness rather than light, because their deeds were evil. For every one that doeth evil hateth the light, neither cometh to the light, lest his deeds should be reproved."

These verses present Christianity to us in several aspects.

I —CHRISTIANITY AS THE GREATEST BLESSING

It is a "*light.*" Life is a great blessing. All feel this. "Skin for skin, all that a man hath," &c. But life without light, were it possible, would be worthless and intolerable. Moral light, light to see the eternal truths, the great God and the spiritual hierarchies, is infinitely more valuable than material light, which reveals but the shadows of the spiritual.

II —CHRISTIANITY AS THE GREATEST BLESSING ENTERING THE WORLD

"*Light is come into the world.*" This redemptive light was not always in the world. The world was once very dark. There were stars, or at least lunar rays, in heathen and Jewish times, but no true solar rays till Christ came, who is the "Light of the world,"— the "Sun of Righteousness."

III —CHRISTIANITY AS THE GREATEST BLESSING UNAPPRECIATED BY THE WORLD

" *Men loved darkness rather than light, because their deeds were evil.*" Corrupt men never did, and never will, appreciate the light of moral rectitude and holiness. It reveals their loathsomeness, and kindles within them the flames of remorse. As the foul birds of night, they hide themselves from its beams.

IV —CHRISTIANITY AS THE GREATEST BLESSING BECOMING A CURSE TO THE WORLD

" *This is the condemnation, that light is come into the world.*" Before the light came they were condemned and guilty, but now that the light is come, the guilt is augmented a thousandfold. " Woe unto thee, Chorazin !" The material sun becomes a curse to the burglar and the assassin when its bright beams lead to their discovery. Sinful men convert blessings into curses--this is what they are always doing. Christianity is a transcendent joy to the good. "But he that doeth truth cometh to the light, that his deeds may be made manifest, that they are wrought in God." Accept Christianity, brothers ! Reject it, and you act as madly as the drowning mariner who refuses to enter the life-boat which floats on the engulfing billows, touches his very hand, and comes within his reach.

John 3:22-36

A TWOFOLD MINISTRY. THE MINISTRY OF CHRIST, AND THE MINISTRY OF THE BAPTIST

(*Jesus remains in Judæa and baptizes. Further testimony of John the Baptist.* JOHN iii. 22—36.)

" After these things came Jesus and His disciples into the land of Judæa," &c.

EXEGETICAL REMARKS.—Ver. 22.— " *After these things came Jesus and His disciples into the land of Judæa; and there He tarried with them, and baptized.*" Who knows how many things were included in "*these things*"? We only know some ; such as the baptism of Christ by John (Matt. iii. 13—17 ; Mark i. 9—11 ; Luke iii. 21, 22) : His temptation of the devil in the wilderness (Matt. iv. 1—11 ; Mark i. 12, 13 ; Luke iv. 1—13) : His return into Galilee, and the call of Philip and Nathanael (John i. 43—50) : His first miracle at Cana (John ii. 1—11) : His presence at the first Passover, the cleansing of the Temple, and His discourse with Nicodemus at night (John iii. 1— 21). All these things are recorded, but how many in His fruitful life are unregistered ? " *Came Jesus and His disciples into the land of Judæa.*" He was in Judæa when He conversed with Nicodemus, but it was in the city— Jerusalem. It means here that He came into the territory of Judæa as distinguished from the metropolis. " *And there He tarried with them.*" It is supposed that He tarried in this Judæan district from the month of March till November or December, at least half a year. " *And baptized.*" He Himself we know baptized no one (see chap. iv. 2). He baptized, however, by His disciples. What a king's servants do is often spoken of as done by himself.

Ver. 23.—"*And John also was baptizing in Ænon near to Salim, because there was much water there: and they came, and were baptized.*" John, not the Apostle and the writer of this Gospel, but the Baptist. Although he had himself baptized Christ, and knew He had entered on His ministry, he continued his work in "*Ænon.*" This word signifies a fountain, "*because there was much water there.*" ὑδατα πολλὰ, "many waters." A place of many small streams. This circumstance proves nothing for or against immersion.

Ver. 24.—"*For John was not yet cast into prison.*" "From the first three evangelists one would naturally conclude that our Lord's ministry only began after the Baptist's imprisonment. But here, about six months probably after our Lord had entered on His public ministry, we find the Baptist still at his work. How much longer this continued cannot be determined with certainty, but probably not very long. This little verse is useful in harmonizing the Gospel and determining the probable duration of our Lord's ministry."—*Brown.*

Ver. 25.—"*Then there arose* (R. V. THERE AROSE THEREFORE) *a question* (R. V. QUESTIONING) *between some* (R. V. ON THE PART OF) *of John's disciples and the Jews about purifying.*" The different baptizing of John and our Lord so near together naturally led to a question concerning the two. John's disciples, it would seem, started the inquiry: they were perhaps jealous of the waning reputation of their master.

Ver. 26.—"*And they came unto John, and said unto him, Rabbi, He that was with thee beyond Jordan, to whom thou barest* (R. V. HAST BORNE) *witness, behold, the same baptizeth, and all men come to Him.*" "'*All men.*'∗ πάντες for οἱ πολλοί, very many. By an hyperbole usual in the language of those who speak under the influence of passion and prejudice."—*Bloomfield.* The spirit, perhaps, of their language

is: "He whom thou didst honour on the banks of the Jordan, when thou didst point men to Him as the true Messiah, is now requiting thy generosity by drawing away all thy followers; at this rate thou wilt soon have no disciples at all."—*Brown.* Perhaps they thought that as Jesus had sought baptism of John, He would become John's disciple, but instead of this He had arisen as a rival.

Ver. 27.—"*John answered and said, A man can receive nothing, except it be* (R. V. HAVE BEEN) *given him from heaven.*" "It is not from man, but from heaven, that the cleansing represented by baptism and gift of the Spirit must come. No one entrusted with a commission must exceed his commission."

Ver. 28.—"*Ye yourselves bear me witness, that I said, I am not the Christ, but that I am sent before Him.*" Perhaps John never plainly called Jesus Christ or the Messiah, but his language concerning Him always implied it.

Ver. 29.—"*He that hath the bride is the bridegroom: but the friend of the bridegroom, which standeth and heareth him, rejoiceth greatly because of the bridegroom's voice: this my joy therefore is fulfilled.*" "The subject is here illustrated by a similitude derived from common life (as in Matt. ix. 15; Mark ii. 19), in which the Baptist compares Christ to the bridegroom at a marriage feast, and himself to the παράνυμ φος or brideman, *i. e.* a friend who had been employed to negotiate the marriage, and had acted as his agent throughout the whole affair. The allusion at ἑστηκὼς χαίρει διὰ τὴν φωνὴν τοῦ νυμφίου is variously traced. But the words are, with most probability, supposed to allude to the ceremony of the formal interview, previous to marriage, of the betrothed pair, who were brought together by the bridemen into a private apartment, at the door of which they were themselves stationed, so as to be able to distinguish any elevation of voice on the part of the future bridegroom in addressing his intended bride, from which, and from the tone of it, they would easily infer his satisfaction at the choice made for him by them, and feel corresponding joy. The sense, then, may be thus expressed ; as at a marriage the bridegroom is the principal person, and his brideman willingly cedes to him the preference, and, rejoicing in his acceptance, is content to play an under part, so do I willingly sustain the part of an humble forerunner of Christ."

Ver. 30.—"*He must increase, but I must decrease.*" "*He increase,*" in labours, in authority, in disciples. "*Decrease :* ἐλαττοῦσθαι, be diminished. Noble freedom from envy. An admonition to His disciples."

Ver. 31.—"*He that cometh from above is above all: he that is of the earth is earthly*" (R. V. OF THE EARTH). "As the words in this last clause are precisely the same, they had better have been so rendered : ' He that is of the earth is of the earth ;' although the sense is correctly given by one translator, namely, that those sprung of the earth, even though Divinely commissioned, bear the stamp of earth in their very work ; but he 'that cometh from heaven is above all.' Here, then, is the reason why He must increase, while all human teachers must decrease. The Master cometh from above—descending from His proper element, the region of those heavenly things which He came to reveal ; and so, although mingling with men and things on the earth, He is not 'of the earth,' either in person or word. The servants, on the contrary, springing from earth, are of the earth, and their testimony, even though Divine in authority, partakes necessarily of their own earthiness. So strongly did the Baptist feel this contrast that the last clause just repeats the first. It is impossible for a sharper line of distinction to be drawn between Christ and all human teachers, even when Divinely commissioned and

speaking by the power of the Holy Ghost."—*Brown.*

Ver. 32.—"*And what he hath seen and heard, that he testifieth* (R. V. OF THAT HE BEARETH WITNESS) ; *and no man receiveth his testimony*" (R. V. WITNESS). *Bengel* says "that John so ardently desires Christ to have all, that, what the disciples call 'all men,' ver. 26, he calls mosa, 'no man.'"

Ver. 33.—"*He that hath received his testimony* (R. V. WITNESS) *hath set to his seal* (R. V. TO THIS) *that God is true.*" "A thing is sealed in common life for two objects : either to render it inaccessible and to place it under seal (Matt. xxvii. 66), or to confirm it. And thus there is in Scripture a double figurative and symbolical use of sealing. On the latter application of the seal, which alone can be regarded here, rest, *e. g.*, the following passages : John vi. 27 ; Rom. ix. 11 ; 1 Cor. ix. 2 ; 2 Cor. i. 22 ; Eph. i. 13 ; Rev. vii. 2."—*Hengstenberg.*

Ver. 34.—"*For He whom God hath sent speaketh the words of God : for God* (R. V. HE) *giveth not the Spirit by measure unto Him.*" Here is a sharp line drawn between Christ and all human inspired teachers. The inspiration of the one is limited, that of the other measureless.

Ver. 35.—"*The Father loveth the Son, and hath given all things into His hand.*" Here is the love of the Highest Being, for the highest object, conferring the highest gifts.

Ver. 36.—"*He that believeth on the Son hath everlasting life : and he that believeth* (R. V. OBEYETH) *not the Son shall not see life ; but the wrath of God abideth on him.*" These two clauses agree with our Lord's commission : "He that believeth shall be saved ; he that believeth not shall be damned." "*Wrath.*" God's wrath agrees with man's in nothing but repugnance to offensive objects.

HOMILETICS

The whole paragraph may be homiletically regarded as a representation both of the *ministry of Christ and that of John the Baptist,* and we have here their agreement and their dissimilarity.

I —THEIR AGREEMENT

First: Both were cleansing. Christ by His disciples "*baptized.*" John also "*was baptizing.*" * The application of water in both cases was but a symbol of *spiritual cleansing*. It represents two great cardinal truths: (1.) The moral uncleanness of men; and (2.) The necessity of the application of a cleansing element. Baptism was nothing but a symbolic act: an impressive way of striking home these moral truths to the souls of the masses.

Secondly: Both were Divine. John the Baptist was Divinely commissioned; and Christ in a higher sense was "*sent from God.*" "He came from above."

Thirdly: Both were ministering at the same time. While Christ's disciples were baptizing, John was also baptizing in Ænon near Salem; both were working near to each other at the same time. Their two ministries were like the sun and moon, which sometimes appear in the horizon at the same time, the moon sinking whilst the sun is rising. We have here—

II —THEIR DISSIMILARITY

John was inferior to Christ—

First: In office. (1.) He was "*not the Christ,*" * but the mere harbinger. A mere messenger preparing the way for the king. (2.) He was "*not the bridegroom,*" * but the mere friend; one to promote the union and to honour the marriage. Human souls were to be wedded not to John, but to Christ: betrothed to Him. It was John's work, as it is the work of all true ministers, to promote the wedding of souls to Christ. He was inferior to Christ—

Secondly: In influence. "*He must increase, but I must decrease.*" * As the star is lost when the sun rises, John's ministry was to be buried in the splendour of Christ's. He was inferior to Christ—

Thirdly: In origin. "*He that cometh,*" &c. John, like all men, was born of the flesh, and was nothing more than a man. Christ came from heaven. He pre-existed, He was above all in nature and in rank. John was inferior to Christ—

Fourthly: In truthfulness. "*What He hath seen and heard, that He testifieth. He that hath received his testimony hath set to his seal that God is true.*" He spoke *absolute* truth, truth so congruous with the reason, moral sense, and the conscious necessities of the soul, that it was felt at once to be true. The inward consciousness of the recipient would seal its truthfulness. John could not speak so. He was inferior to Christ—

Fifthly: In inspiration. "*For He whom God hath sent speaketh*

* See Germs, pp. 79, 81, 82.

the words of God: for God giveth not the Spirit by measure unto Him." There is no limit either to the amount of His inspiration or to His power of imparting it. John was inferior to Christ—

Sixthly: In relationship. *" The Father loveth the Son."* He is the Son of God. His relation to the Infinite is unique. We are all His offspring, but none His Son in the sense Christ was. John was inferior to Christ—

Seventhly: In authority. *" Hath given all things into His hand."* Christ is invested with universal dominion. John was inferior to Christ—

Eighthly: In character. *" He that believeth on the Son hath everlasting life: and he that believeth not the Son shall not see life; but the wrath of God abideth on him."* * *" The wrath of God !"* Who shall explain this? Who shall sound the abysses of its meaning? It is higher than heaven and deeper than hell. The language accords with other passages: see Psalms ii. 12; Rom i. 18; ii. 8, 9; 2 Thess. i. 8; Rev. vi. 15, &c., &c. His character is the *one great object* of soul-saving faith: John's character was not. Faith on Him determines the destiny of souls.

Germs of Thought
No. 10   John 3:22-24

SPIRITUAL CLEANSING

" After these things came Jesus and His disciples into the land of Judæa ; and there He tarried with them, and baptized. And John also was baptizing in Ænon near to Salim, because there was much water there : and they came, and were baptized. For John was not yet cast into prison."

These words present to us *spiritual cleansing* in two aspects :—

I —AS THE GREAT WANT OF MANKIND

Christ and John were now engaged in the work of *baptizing,* and that was only a symbol of the importance of spiritual cleansing. The "washing of regeneration" is the great need of men; the most comprehensive prayer a man can utter is, "Wash me thoroughly from mine iniquity, and cleanse me from my sin." Without this cleansing there is—

First: No spiritual vision. Moral defilement is such a dense atmosphere around the soul, that it shuts out the sunbeam, and obstructs all true spiritual vision. Without this cleansing there is—

Secondly : No spiritual health. Moral uncleanness is injurious to soul health. As sanatorial measures are necessary to physical health, the cleansing of the heart is necessary to the health of the soul. Without this cleansing there is—

* See Homily on these words at end of volume.

Thirdly : No holy fellowship. " Without holiness no man shall see the Lord." All unclean spirits are excluded from the kingdom of purity and bliss. Spiritual cleansing is presented here—

II — AS THE GRAND MISSION OF THE TRUE MINISTRY

Christ and John were now engaged in this work. What does this work require ?

First : The inculcation of spiritual truth. Men must believe at least two things : in the necessity of cleansing, and in the availableness of the cleansing element.

Secondly : The inculcation of these truths often requires the use of symbols. Christ and John now employed the symbol of *baptism*.

No. 11   John 3:25, 26

RELIGIOUS DISPUTES

"Then there arose a question between some of John's disciples and the Jews about purifying. And they came unto John, and said unto him, Rabbi; He that was with thee beyond Jordan, to whom thou barest witness, behold, the same baptizeth, and all men come to Him."

These words suggest four things concerning religious disputes :—

I — THEY ARE FREQUENTLY ABOUT MATTERS OF COMPARATIVELY TRIFLING MOMENT

It was now about purifying—mere ceremonial. The controversies in the Church have generally been of this order, about immersions and sprinklings, priestly costumes and attitudes, &c. How much controversy there has been on the question of dipping and sprinkling ! Another thing suggested concerning religious disputes is—

II — THEY ARE OFTEN INSTIGATED BY AN INFERIOR GRADE OF RELIGIONISTS

" *There arose a question between some of John's disciples and the Jews.*" Not between *Christ's* disciples. So it is ever, the lower the grade of intelligence and spiritual sympathy, the more ready generally for disputation. The highest order of saints in all ages have ever avoided controversy, and shunned sects. Another thing suggested concerning religious disputes is—

III — THEY ARE OFTEN TO BE TRACED TO SECTARIAN JEALOUSY

John's disciples were attached to their master, and were envious of what they considered to be a rivalry, the ministry of Christ. Another thing suggested concerning religious disputes is—

IV — THEY ARE OFTEN ASSOCIATED WITH EXAGGERATION

" *The same baptizeth, and all men come to Him.*" A very false statement. At this time Christ's followers were very few. The

curse of British Christianity is the existence of men in it who have
the spirit of John's disciples and the Jews.

No. 12   John 3:27, 28

TRUE MINISTERIAL SUCCESS

"John answered and said, A man can receive nothing, except it be given him
from heaven. Ye yourselves bear me witness, that I said, I am not the
Christ, but that I am sent before Him."

The words suggest two things concerning true ministerial
success :—

I —IT IS FROM GOD AND NOT FROM MAN

"*A man can receive nothing, except it be given him from heaven.*"
Men make sad mistakes about ministerial success, as John's
disciples did now. Crowds, excitement, noise, physical bustle,
these, to many, are regarded as the criteria of ministerial usefulness; but they are false, utterly false. Growth in spiritual
intelligence, in holy sympathy, in assimilation to God; there is no
usefulness apart from these, and these are ever from God, and not
from man. "A man can receive nothing" of these as a mere result
of his own labour. "Paul plants, Apollos waters, but God gives the
increase." Concerning true ministerial success—

II —IT SHOULD BE REJOICED IN, AND NOT ENVIED

This seems the noble spirit of John's words. The minister who
is really useful, whether he belong to "Our Church" or not, should
have our strongest sympathy and best wishes; we should rejoice
in his efforts, for he receives "*nothing, except it be given him from
heaven,*" and everything from heaven is a blessing to the race.

No. 13   John 3:29

CHRIST'S UNION TO THE RACE

"He that hath the bride is the bridegroom : but the friend of the bridegroom,
which standeth and heareth him, rejoiceth greatly because of the bridegroom's voice : this my joy therefore is fulfilled."—iii. 29.

Learn from this highly figurative language—

I —WHAT CHRIST'S RELATION TO ALL SOULS SHOULD BE

It is that of a "*bridegroom.*" A relation this implying three things.
First: Mutual affection.
Secondly: Agreement of sympathy.
Thirdly: Identity of interests. As husband and wife, all souls
and Christ should be one. Learn—

II —WHAT ALL MINISTERS' RELATION TO CHRIST SHOULD BE

"*Friend of the bridegroom.*" Their work should be to make such a representation of His unspeakable loveliness, supernal virtues, and matchless merits as to win for Him the love of all human souls.

No. 14   John 3:30

A SIGNIFICANT PREDICTION

"He must increase, but I must decrease."

Here is—

I —A PREDICTION THAT HAS BEEN FULFILLED

Christ has increased, and John has decreased. How? Not *personally*. Christ could never become greater in person, whilst the personality of John has perhaps been advancing in intelligence and moral nobility ever since. But *influentially*. John's influence has not waned, for he is more known and respected on this earth and in the universe now than he has ever been; but still his influence since he spoke these words, as compared with the influence of Christ, has been on the decrease. His influence, perhaps, then was greater than Christ's: the tide, however, has long since turned. His is a lake, Christ's an ocean. Here is—

II —A PREDICTION THAT WILL BE FULFILLED IN RELATION TO ALL HUMAN THINGS AND CHRIST

First: In relation to all religious systems. All the religious systems on this earth must decrease, while Christ's thoughts will grow and spread.

Secondly: In relation to all worldly principles. The maxims that ever have and still govern the world, must gradually give way to the glorious principles of Christ.

Thirdly: In relation to all human authorities. "The kingdoms of this world will become the kingdoms of our God and His Christ."

No. 15   John 3:35

THE HIGHEST LOVE

"The Father loveth the Son, and hath given all things into His hand."

Here is—

I —LOVE IN THE HIGHEST BEING

"*The Father loveth.*" The Infinite is not mere intellect, He has heart, and His heart is love. His love explains the *existence*, the *beauty*, and the *blessedness* of the universe. Here is—

II —LOVE SET ON THE HIGHEST OBJECT

"*The Son.*" Next to Himself the holiest and the greatest Being in the universe. It is the love of infinite complaisance and delight. Here is—

III —LOVE CONFERRING THE HIGHEST GOOD

" Hath given all things into His hand." " All things are delivered to Me of My Father." It means the whole administration of the Divine kingdom.

John 4:1-6

MAN'S HOSTILITY TO CHRIST

(John's imprisonment and Jesus' departure into Galilee.—MATT. iv. 12 ; MARK i. 14 ; vi. 17—20 ; LUKE iii. 19, 20 ; iv. 14 ; and JOHN iv. 1—3.)

" When therefore the Lord knew how the Pharisees had heard that Jesus made and baptized (R. V. WAS MAKING AND BAPTIZING) more disciples than John, (though Jesus Himself baptized not, but His disciples,) He left Judæa, and departed again into Galilee. And He must needs go (R. V. PASS) through Samaria. Then cometh He to a city of Samaria, which is called Sychar, near to the parcel of ground that Jacob gave to his son Joseph. Now Jacob's well was there. Jesus therefore, being wearied with His journey, sat thus on (R. V. BY) the well : and it was about the sixth hour."

EXEGETICAL REMARKS.—Ver. 1.— *" When therefore the Lord knew how the Pharisees had heard that Jesus made and baptized more disciples than John."* " The οὖν forms the connection with the preceding narrative, the central fact of which was, that Jesus had, during His stay in the land of Judæa, a greater following than John." —*Hengstenberg.*

Ver. 2.—*" Though Jesus Himself baptized not, but His disciples."* Baptism is of such inferior moment, that the Heavenly Teacher leaves it to His disciples. They baptize with water, He with the Holy Ghost.

Ver. 3.—*" He left Judæa, and departed again into Galilee."* The jealousy which He perceived rising in the Pharisees at His success, caused Him to withdraw from Judæa into Galilee. Matthew states (chap. iv. 12—17), that when our Lord heard that John the Baptist was imprisoned, He departed into Galilee. John's popularity was perhaps the great cause of his imprisonment, and as Christ's exceeded his, their indignation was waxing hot. He had been in Judæa from the time of His first Passover, about eight months : during those eight months we may rest assured He was most actively employed in carrying out His heavenly mission.

Ver. 4.—*" And He must needs go through Samaria."* " Needs" as a matter of convenience ; it was the shortest and most direct road. "Needs" as a matter of usefulness—there were souls in Samaria ripe for His influence.

Ver. 5.—*" Then cometh He to a city of Samaria, which is called Sychar."* " Sychar," or Shechem, was one of the most ancient cities of Canaan. The change to Sychar was made by the Jews to stigmatize the vices of the place, which were drunkenness, lying, and idolatry. Its more modern name is Neapolis. It was made the capital of the kingdom of Israel, in the reign of Jeroboam.

Shechem is associated with some of the most interesting events of patriarchal times. (Gen. xxxiii., xlix. ; Josh. xxiv. 1—32 ; Judges ix. 46—49, &c.) It belonged to Ephraim. At Shechem the tribes assembled to make Rehoboam king : and here, too, the tribes rebelled. Shechem was a city of refuge. It is situated between Mount Ebal on the north, and Gerizim on the south, about thirty-four miles from Jerusalem. The modern town, which has a population of about twelve thousand inhabitants, has many fine bazaars, and two long streets running parallel with the valley. The surrounding scenery is grand and imposing. Mahommed called it the Paradise of the Holy Land. *"Near to the parcel of ground that Jacob gave to his son Joseph."* From Gen. xxxiii. 18, we find that Jacob bought a field near Shechem ; and from Joshua xxiv. 32, we find that Joseph was buried in that very field, and it is said it became the inheritance of the children of Joseph.

Ver. 6.—*"Now Jacob's well was there."* The well in its present condition is nine feet in diameter, and one hundred and five deep ; when Maundrell visited it, it had fifteen feet of water. "It is a mile and a half from Nablous, the ancient Sychar, and was lately bought by Russia, for a site for a Greek Church."—*Van Doren.* *"Jesus therefore, being wearied with His journey, sat thus on the well : and it was about the sixth hour."* About twelve at noon. Some have said this is one of the most human of all the scenes in our Lord's history. Here He is a wearied traveller, seated on the old patriarchal stone under the scorching rays of noon.

HOMILETICS

We may regard this passage as illustrating *man's hostility to Christ.* Three facts are suggested.

I —MAN'S HOSTILITY TO CHRIST ESCAPES NOT HIS NOTICE

" When therefore the Lord knew how the Pharisees," &c. He *"knew"* the malign feelings that were beginning to burn in their hearts towards Him in consequence of His great spiritual influence. Perhaps they sought to conceal their rising indignation until they should organize it into a plan to effect His ruin; but His eye peered into their hearts, and He saw the rising wrath. *"The Lord knew."* How ? By *testimony?* It is probable that His disciples would tell Him what they had heard of the malign passions of the Pharisees in the prosecution of their mission. How ? By *His own observation ?* Did He learn it by the flash of the eye, the frown of the countenance, or the tone of the voice ? It is by testimony and observation that we learn the state of men's minds around us; but Christ knew the Pharisee mind in another and a higher way, viz. intuition. All souls are naked to His eye. He knows what is in men, "He understands their thoughts afar off." "He knew all men, and needed not that any should testify of man : for He knew what was in man." His thorough knowledge of souls is a truth which, like the pillar of old, has two sides, one terribly dark, the other cheeringly luminous. (1.) It is dark to the hypocrite. The hypocrite endeavouring to appear what he is not is labouring to do the impossible, and impiously insulting the Omniscience of Heaven. (2.) It is luminous to the genuine. The man of sincerity is sometimes misunderstood, and at other times misrepresented by his contemporaries, and often he finds it impossible to demonstrate to them the virtuous elements within him. His Master knows all, and credits him with all the goodness he has within him :

"Distance dissolves before His ray,
And darkness kindles into day."

Another fact suggested is—

II —MAN'S HOSTILITY TO CHRIST DEPRIVES HIM OF HIS PRESENCE

"*He left Judœa, and departed again into Galilee.*" He leaves them
not from *fear.* His courage was invincible; neither the rage of
earth and hell combined could strike terror into Him Whose breath
was the life of the universe. Not in *anger;* but rather in sadness
and compassion. He leaves them because their state of mind was
highly unfavourable to His spiritual influence. His mission was a
moral one. It was to be wrought out, not by force or coercion,
but by the spiritual influences of truth and love. They were at
present highly unsusceptible to such influences, and His ministry
amongst them would be a waste of labour. "*He left Judœa.*"
What a loss! A greater loss than if some terrible calamity had
stripped them of all their worldly possessions; yes, than if the sun
had left their heavens for ever. What service He could have
rendered, had He stayed and laboured amongst them, and had
their hearts been open to His influence! He could have given
them the "true liberty of the children of God," and honours and
joys as lasting as eternity.

Thus it will ever be; hostility to Christ will deprive men of His
blessed services. Those who continue to repel Him He will leave
sooner or later, He will turn from them for ever. Christ will not
continue long with His enemies. Kind Heaven forbid that He
should ever forsake us!

Another fact suggested is—

III —MAN'S HOSTILITY TO CHRIST DEPRIVES MAN OF HIS
MINISTRIES

"*Departed again into Galilee.*" Their opposition did not cool
the ardour of His zeal or weaken His determination to work out
His mission. He leaves them and turns to Samaria and to Galilee.
If they would not receive the blessings He offered, others might
and would. Though the sun sinks from our horizon, he breaks on
another hemisphere; and though Christ leaves Judæa, He ministers
elsewhere. The wickedness of Judæa brought the highest good
to Samaria and to Galilee. The worst of men, and the worst of
devils too, contrary to their spirit and determination, often do good
to others and to the universe at large. What service did Christ
render to Samaria? We shall find it as we proceed.

John 4:7-26

CHRIST AND THE WOMAN OF SAMARIA. THE TRUE WAY OF RECLAIMING THE MORALLY DEGRADED

(*Our Lord's discourse with the woman of Samaria. Many of the Samaritans believe on Him.*—JOHN iv. 4—42.)

"There cometh a woman of Samaria to draw water : Jesus saith unto her, Give Me to drink," &c.

EXEGETICAL REMARKS.—Ver. 7.— "*A woman of Samaria.*" This woman did not come from the city of Samaria, but from Sychar, an adjacent town. "*To draw water.*" In the East it was, and still is, customary for women to carry water. Christianity ameliorates the condition of women. "*Give Me to drink.*" It was high noon, the sun was pouring down his scorching beams, and the Holy One was thirsty. It is a remark of *Emerson*, in his Letters from the Egean, that "to him who has never panted beneath the burning sun of Asia, or trod its scorched and glowing soil, whose eye has never turned upon its cloudless skies, or shot wistfully along its parched and endless deserts, the frequent mention of water and its important uses in the Bible can come with but little weight ; and he alone who has toiled through the privations of India, or writhed beneath the withering sunbeams of the East, can enjoy in their full richness and luxury the sublime allusions of the Scriptures."

Ver. 8.—"*His disciples were gone away unto the city to buy meat*" (R. v. FOOD). This circumstance is mentioned probably to show how He came to ask water of her, a woman, as His disciples were not present. The city unto which the disciples were gone was Sychar, about half an hour's distance from the well.

Ver. 9.—"*Then saith the woman of Samaria unto Him, How is it that thou, being a Jew, askest drink of me, which am a woman of Samaria? for the Jews have no dealings with the Samaritans.*" A Jew was not accustomed to ask a favour of a Samaritan, neither would he eat or drink with one of that nation. The reason of this, probably, was that the Samaritans were not genuine

Israelites : they were a mixed race. (2 Kings xvii. 24—41.) Then, too, they rejected all the books of the Old Testament except the Pentateuch ; also they opposed the building of the Temple at Jerusalem. (Nehemiah ii. 19 ; v. 1—2 ; vi.) They built a rival temple, too, on Mount Gerizim. (Deut. xxvii. 12.) The enmity between these people is an illustration of a general principle, that the nearer religious parties approach each other in belief and worship the more bitter are their animosities.

Ver. 10.—"*Jesus answered and said unto her, If thou knewest the gift of God.*" Or better : "The favour of God in granting such an opportunity." "*Who it is that saith to thee, Give Me to drink.*" Herein He intimates that He was no common Jew, and that if she knew who He was she would feel the obligation to be on her side and not on His. "*Thou wouldest have asked of Him, and He would have given thee living water.*" That is, fresh running water. The Heavenly Teacher, with His wonted aptitude for drawing illustrations from objects around Him, here turns the conversation into a spiritual channel, and under the figure of living water reveals the spiritual blessings He came to communicate.

Ver. 11.—"*The woman saith unto Him, Sir, Thou hast nothing to draw with, and the well is deep.*" Travellers in the East are wont to carry bottles or buckets which, with cords, they let down into the well in order to get at the water they require. As yet she had not caught His spiritual meaning ; she was in the realm of earthly ideas, and thought only of material water, and the method of drawing it.

Ver. 12.—"*Art Thou greater than*

our father Jacob, which gave us the well, and drank thereof himself, and his children, and his cattle?" Samaritan and Jew were one in their respect for the memory of the illustrious patriarch. Who canst Thou be to talk of giving me living water? It would seem as if an impression by this time was coming over her that she was talking to no ordinary personage.

Ver. 13.—*"Jesus answered and said unto her, Whosoever* (R. V. EVERY ONE THAT) *drinketh of this water shall thirst again."* Our Lord proceeds to intensify the woman's inquisitiveness, and points to a sublimer element than lay down in the well. He does not say He is greater than Jacob, but suggests that He has better water to give than that which was in Jacob's well.

Ver. 14.—*" Whosoever drinketh of the water that I shall give him shall never thirst."* Here is water, a water that allays thirst for ever—*" shall never thirst;"* water that is in a man. Not, like the water in Jacob's well, outside of him, but water that springs in him, the water of everlasting life. Jesus opens in the soul a never-failing spring of improvement and happiness.

Ver. 15.—*" Sir, give me this water, that I thirst not, neither come hither* (R. V. ALL THE WAY) *to draw."* She has not yet extricated herself from earthly ideas, and risen to the meaning of Christ.

Ver. 16.—*"Jesus saith unto her, Go, call thy husband, and come hither."* This is His first step in granting her request—viz. an effort to convince her of her sin. He now strikes a deep chord in her nature, a chord that would ring out in her soul her past ungodly history.

Ver. 17.—*" The woman answered and said, I have no husband."* This was no new information to Christ; He knew it, He had read her heart: all the pages in the volume of her past life were open to Him.

Ver. 18.—*" Jesus said unto her, Thou hast well said* (R. V. SAIDST WELL), *I have no husband: for thou hast had five husbands; and he whom thou now hast is not thy husband: in that saidst*

thou (R. V. THIS HAST THOU SAID) *truly."* Christ recognizes that the five men with whom she had previously lived were, in a legal sense, her husbands, but the man with whom she was now living was in unlawful association with her.

Ver. 19.—*" The woman saith unto Him, Sir, I perceive that Thou art a prophet."* All trifling on her part was over; Christ had struck home to her conscience, and she saw in Him a prophet, a Divine Teacher.

Ver. 20.—*" Our fathers worshipped in this mountain; and ye say, that in Jerusalem is the place where men ought to worship."* Unwilling to dwell upon the sin with which her conscience now stung her, she turns to another subject, the question of worship. She broaches the great question which had been in dispute between the two nations for centuries. *" This mountain,"* that is, Gerizim.

Ver. 21.—*" Jesus saith unto her, Woman, believe me, the hour cometh, when ye shall neither in this mountain, nor yet at Jerusalem, worship the Father."* Here is an utterance of solemn earnestness. The worship of the Father was not to be circumscribed to any locality.

Ver. 22.—*" Ye worship ye* (R. V. THAT WHICH YE) *know not what."* That is, ye Samaritans. You are ignorant of true worship! You have only accepted a part of the Divine revelation—the Pentateuch, and you have rejected the further disclosures of God by the prophets. *" We know what we worship"* (R. V. WE WORSHIP THAT WHICH WE KNOW). Here He speaks of Himself as a Jew. *" For salvation is of* (R. V. FROM) *the Jews."* The Mosaic dispensation originated amongst the Jews, the prophets had spoken to the Jews, and the Messiah had risen from the Jews.

Ver. 23.—*" The hour cometh, and now is."* A new period in the history of worship has come, nay, it has dawned, and now is. Worship has no more to do with special places, persons, or periods. It is rather a spiritual state than a particular service, a life than a performance. *" In spirit.*" As distinguished from form. "*In truth.*" As distinguished from unreality. "*For the Father seeketh such to worship Him*" (R. V. FOR SUCH DOES THE FATHER SEEK TO BE HIS WORSHIPPERS). The Father is at once the Object and Claimant of worship.

Ver. 24.—"*God is a Spirit.*" Or rather, God is Spirit. The reference is not to His personality, but rather to His essence.

Ver. 25.—"*The woman saith unto Him, I know that Messias cometh.*" The Samaritans as well as the Jews looked for a coming deliverer — a Messiah. This woman participated in the general expectation. "*Which is called Christ.*" These are probably explanatory words thrown in by the Evangelist for the benefit of his readers. "*He will tell* (R. V. DECLARE UNTO) *us all things.*" She regarded the coming Messiah not as a political conqueror, but as a Divine Teacher who would "tell us all things." "All things" pertaining to the great question of worship.

Ver. 26.—"*Jesus saith unto her, I that speak unto thee am He.*" This is the first declaration that our Lord made of His Messiahship. It is remarkable that He should have first made this announcement to a woman, and to a Samaritan. But here in solitude, and alone, He could do it without the fear of any seditious movement.

HOMILETICS

Our subject is the *True way of reclaiming the morally degraded·* How to reach the masses so as to interest them in spiritual and eternal realities, is a question that presses on all earnest hearts, and agitates more or less most Christian Churches. Many methods are adopted, some unphilosophic, and some even immoral and degrading. The toiling millions of this country are confessedly outside of all churches, and for the most part out of sympathy with those things which are essential to spiritual culture and everlasting peace. Scheme after scheme is propounded in order to reach them, and bring these wandering sheep into the fold. Theatres are open for religious services, tales are introduced into religious journals in order to make (as is unwisely hoped) spiritual truth more palatable; ministers deliver secular lectures to the working classes, and exhaust their wit and their humour to make them interesting and attractive. In some cases, amongst the smaller brained and the more mawkish hearted of the religious world, efforts are adopted so ineffably silly as only to awaken the disgust of the more thoughtful of the working classes. Even the pulpit itself in some cases has been employed as the organ of miserable clap-trap, coarse humour, and silly jest. We may, perhaps, get at the true method by marking the way by which Christ reached this poor, degraded woman of Samaria.

I —HE APPROACHES HER ON THE BROAD GROUND OF HUMANITY

He did not speak to her as one of the lower classes, nor as a religious sceptic or schismatic, but He speaks to her simply as a *woman :* one inheriting human nature with all its wondrous relations, great possibilities, and deep spiritual needs. Mark here two things :

First: He asks a favour of her, and thus assures her that He does not despise her on the ground of her poverty. *"Jesus saith unto her, Give Me to drink."* It has been said that few things so touch the degraded and despised as asking a favour at their hands. The best way to interest a poor man is not by conferring on him a favour, but by asking him to bestow one. If a man in the most elevated station of life would touch my heart and win my sympathies, he would do it more effectually by condescending to ask me a service than in generously bestowing one. His gift to me would leave me feeling the distance still between us, but my gift to him, if he entered my humble cottage and sought it at my hands, would make me feel that he stood with me on the common level of our nature. You honour a man a great deal more by receiving his favours than in conferring upon him your own. You feel often humbled in the reception of a gift, but always exalted in the bestowment of one. Modern churches reverse this order, and degrade the poor by pressing on them their gifts.

Secondly: He asks a favour of her, though a Samaritan, and thus assures her He does not despise her on the ground of her sect. He had none of the narrow prejudices or sectarian feelings of the Jew who despised the Samaritan. The idea of her sect was lost in the grand idea of her humanity. Herein we should imitate Christ; we should not speak to men as *poor;* address them as the lower classes, and with gifts try to buy them over; nor speak to them as religious errorists, Catholics, Churchmen, or Dissenters, but deal with them as men; having nothing to do with their secular or religious distinctions. Another thing observable, and commanding our attention, in His method is—

II —HE ADDRESSED HER PERSONALLY WHEN SHE WAS ALONE

"His disciples were gone away unto the city to buy meat." * There is something sublimely affecting in the sight of the great Maker and Master of the race speaking to one lonely soul. Christ for some time holds a conversation with this woman, as if to Him she was a creature of transcendent importance. He sees Divinity, immortality, unbounded progress, and inexhaustible influence in one soul. In these modern times ministers seldom think it worth their while to preach to one. If when the church doors are opened for public worship there is only one lonely individual present, the service would most likely be adjourned. They can only catch inspiration in their ministry when they see a breathless crowd around them. Not so with the Great Master. The presence of a lone woman, and she a poor heretic, touched His great nature into earnestness. We lose the individual in the mass. He seems to have lost the mass in the individual. What we want now is this personal and

* See Germ, p. 91.

direct ministry. We have depended too much upon people congregating together in order to be spiritually influenced. The time has come when, if Christianity is to reach the masses, Christians must go to the individuals, meet them, if possible, alone, ply them with spiritual truths, and bring their own experiences in warm and conscious contact with theirs. Another thing observable, and demanding our attention, is—

III —HE PROPOUNDED TO HER SALVATION IN A WAY THAT MADE HER FEEL ITS NECESSITY

"*If thou knewest the gift of God*," &c., &c. He spoke to her *intelligibly;* He employed imagery—spoke of the well of living water. He did not talk to her in abstract language. He spoke to her *suggestively.* His words led her to ask, "*Whence then hast Thou that living water?*" He touched the spring of her intellect, and set her a thinking. He spoke to her *impressively*—"*Whosoever drinketh of the water*," &c., &c.* So impressed was she, that she exclaimed, "*Give me this water.*" Let us so speak to men—intelligently, suggestively, and impressively. Another thing observable, and demanding our attention, is—

IV —HE SO TOUCHED HER CONSCIENCE THAT SHE FELT THE DIVINITY OF HIS MISSION

"*Jesus saith unto her, Go, call thy husband*," &c., &c. This touched her conscience, called up the memory of her sins, and prepared her, by contrition, to receive the water of everlasting life. He did not condemn her; no word of denunciation escapes His lips. He holds the mirror of her depraved life before her, bids her to look, and thus compels her to condemn herself. "*I perceive that Thou art a prophet.*" Preach to men's experience, and they will perceive the Divinity of your mission. Another thing observable, and demanding our attention, is—

V —HE GAVE SUCH A REVELATION OF WORSHIP AND OF HIMSELF AS SILENCED HER CONTROVERSY

"*Our fathers worshipped*," &c., &c. She seemed full of the controversial spirit, but Christ puts an end to this—
First: By a revelation of true worship. He gives (1.) The true *Object* of worship. He is a "*Spirit*," and a "*Father.*" He gives (2.) The true *mode* of worship. "*In spirit and in truth.*" † He puts an end to this—
Secondly: By a revelation of His own Messiahship. "*I that speak unto thee am He.*" I am the Messias you are looking for. Thus He hushes all controversy, and the woman is reclaimed. Would that all Churches, and all Christians, would study this

* See Germ, p. 93.   † See article at end of volume.

method of morally reclaiming the vast masses lying outside all Christian influence.

Germs of Thought
No. 16   John 4:7

THE HUMANITY, FREEDOM, AND HUMILITY OF CHRIST

" Jesus saith unto her, Give Me to drink."

Observe here—

I —THE HUMANITY OF CHRIST

Wearied with His journey under the hot sun, He thirsted for water. He was a Man—the Son of man. " Made in all points like as we are, yet without sin." " The Word was made flesh." Observe—

II —THE FREEDOM OF CHRIST

Prejudice would have prevented any priest or Rabbi of His age and race from asking water of a woman. (1.) He appears free from the old prejudice against the *female sex*. He asks a favour of a woman. (2.) He appears free from the old prejudice of *nationality*. The Jew hated the Samaritan. (3.) He appears free from the old prejudice of *religion*. The worship of the Samaritan the old Jew loathed and deprecated. Observe—

III —THE HUMILITY OF CHRIST

He condescends to ask a favour of a poor, schismatic alien woman.

No. 17   John 4:8

THE DIVINITY OF SELF-HELP AND COMMERCE

" His disciples were gone away unto the city to buy meat."

We infer from these words—

I —THE DIVINITY OF SELF-HELP

Why had the disciples now to go under the broiling sun to Sychar to buy meat ? Could not their Master have supplied them by a miracle with all they required ? Truly so. But He never does for men what they can do for themselves. He helps them only by stimulating their own energies. This is the wisest method of helping men. (1.) The men who are thus helped are the most *effectively helped*. They work out their own faculties, and thereby get strength and independence. (2.) The men who are thus helped become the *best helpers of others*. They have risen themselves, and they know how to stimulate and direct others on the upward path.

II —THE DIVINITY OF COMMERCE

They went to "*buy*." Merchandise is a Divine ordinance, and a means of grace.

No. 18   John 4:9

SIMPLICITY SURPRISING

"How is it that Thou, being a Jew, askest drink of Me, which am a woman of Samaria ? "

No act could have been more *simple* than the request of a thirsty traveller for a little water to drink, and yet this simple act struck the woman with surprise. "*How is it that Thou, being a Jew ?*" What makes simplicity so surprising ?

I —ITS RARITY

The world is denaturalized by conventionalities. Christ here did what no other Jew would have done—allowed His nature to rise superior to the miserable prejudices of His race. He wanted water and He asks for it. How beautifully simple ! But the very simplicity startled this conventional woman. There has been, and still is, so much etiquette, ceremony, and masquerade amongst men, that when a real man appears, acts out his nature, and sets conventionalities at defiance, people are struck with surprise. How is it ?

II —ITS COURAGE

It requires great courage to go against the popular. There is nothing so beautiful as simple nature. No manners so graceful as those inspired by nature, no language so eloquent as that which expresses nature in her own tones. Sad for the world that simplicity should have the power to astonish men. Let us be simple.

No. 19   John 4:10

GOD'S SUBLIMEST GIFT

"He would have given thee living water."

Learn—

I —GOD'S SUBLIMEST GIFT

What is that ? Christ. (1.) Christ is *greater* to Him than the universe. By Him all things were created. (2.) Christ is *nearer* to Him than the universe. His only begotten Son. Learn—

II —MAN'S GREATEST NEED

What is that ? "*Living water*." What is the "*living water ?*" Moral goodness. This is like water in its origin and destiny, from ocean to ocean, from God to God in its flow and influence. Its flow is *natural* and *constant*, its influence *refreshing* and *beautifying*. Learn—

III —THE WORLD'S WORST IGNORANCE

"*If thou knewest the gift of God.*" (1.) No knowledge to man is so *necessary* as the knowledge of Christ. He may be saved without the knowledge of the sciences, but not without the knowledge of Christ. (2.) No knowledge is so *glorious* as the knowledge of Christ. It is to know the ROOT, the SOURCE, the SOUL of all things.

No. 20   John 4:14

THE CHRISTIANITY OF CHRIST

"But whosoever drinketh of the water that I shall give him shall never thirst ; but the water that I shall give him shall be in him a well of water springing up into everlasting life."

The biography of Christ is living and life-giving. At whatever point we touch Him in the sacred page we feel a quickening impulse; there is life in everything He does and says. That which to human eyes appears the merest incident, through His connection with it becomes a mighty epoch in history. The meeting with the woman of Samaria now at the well seemed the most fortuitous and simple affair; yet what results grew out of it, and still grow! It roused the Samaritan mind from the slumber of ages; it set hundreds at once to earnest thought. We are no judges as to the magnitude of events. A spark may burn a city ; a word may convulse an empire, and change the history of the world. The words of the text lead us to consider the religion of Christ in three aspects :—

I —AS AN INESTIMABLE BLESSING

It is here spoken of under the figure of "*water.*" Christ employed natural objects to represent spiritual realities. Thus by attaching Divine ideas to material things, the worth even of material nature is enhanced. The lily, the vine, the bird, the water, the stars, the sun, get a new value. He made them vehicles of those great thoughts with which He came to regenerate humanity. Here He speaks of His religion as *water*. And what so valuable as water ?

First : It is a life-giving power. We can scarcely wonder at old Thales referring all life to water. Wherever it is found, in the floating mists, the falling shower, the placid lake, the dancing brook, the rolling river, or the rushing cataract, it is fraught with a life-giving power. So is Christ's religion; it is life-giving. "The words that I speak unto you, they are spirit and life."

Secondly : It is a thirst-satisfying power. Physical thirst is of all animal sensations the most painful. The Oriental traveller on the burning sands has often told the tale of its scorching anguish. Material water alone can allay thirst. And the more *simple* its form the more effective. Man's soul is fired with a spiritual thirst, his one great burning desire is for happiness. Man has sought for the allayment of this thirst in wealth, fame, pleasure, literature; but all have proved in vain,—the passion burns on. The religion of Christ alone can satisfy this thirst; it has done so in millions of instances; it is doing so now, &c.

Thirdly: It is a nature cleansing power. Water is the great cleansing power of nature. Man's soul is polluted by sin; Christ's religion is the cleansing element. It is the fountain opened for the washing away of sin, &c.

The text leads us to look at Christ's religion—

II —AS A DIVINE COMMUNICATION

" *The water that I shall give him.*"

First: This godliness is imparted as the gift of Christ. He is the Giver of that system of truth that can alone produce it. In fact, He is not only the Author, but the very *substance* of the Bible. He, too, is the Giver of that Spirit, who so applies His Gospel to the heart as to make it a quickening power. It is then Christ's gift. In that great day of the feast, "Jesus stood and cried, saying, If any man thirst, let him come unto Me, and drink."

Secondly: It is imparted as the gift of Christ in connection with man's agency. " *But whosoever drinketh.*" Man must drink. The Oriental traveller will die of thirst though the crystal fountain bubble at his feet, unless he himself will drink. No one can drink for him; it is a personal act. The Gospel is the well, but men must drink of it before it can save them. The rock has been smitten in the wilderness, the refreshing streams wind along their path, and a thousand voices of mercy are heard issuing from its verdant banks: "Whosoever will, let him come and take of the water of life freely."

The text leads us to look at Christ's religion—

III —AS AN EVER-ACTING INNER LIFE

" *Shall be in him a well of water.*"

First: It is essentially active within. Godliness is an active principle. It is not like the sleeping lake or stagnant pool;— it is a well, a spring whose very essence is *activity*. Take away the activity of a spring and it ceases to be. The frosts of winter and the beams of summer will consume it. Godliness is activity.

Secondly: It is spontaneously active within. The spring is *free*. If you attempt to force the spring, you stir up impurities and destroy the clearness and the sweetness of the waters. You must not attempt to meddle with the free action of religion in the human soul. British legislation has done so ere now, and it has stirred up the worst passions of the soul and inflicted a serious injury on the cause of truth.

Thirdly: It is perpetually active within. "*Into everlasting life.*" It is a principle of endless evolutions. It originates a series of delightful operations that will multiply without end. It is a law of water that it will find its own level. The well is ever springing because of its connection with the great ocean. The highest mountains cannot prevent the water from rising to its level, and the springs from bubbling up. The godly soul will ever be happily active because of its connection with God, the great ocean of life.

All this is *within ;*—in you, and therefore independent of all outward circumstances. Whatever in the world leaves you,— friends, property, earthly joys,—this cannot be taken from you. You may leave the world, but you cannot leave this. You must lose your being ere you lose this. Death will tear down your earthly tabernacle; fires will devour these heavens and burn up this globe; but this will remain unhurt, amid the war of elements, the wreck of matter, and the crash of worlds. True happiness does not stream from without, but wells up within. Brother, trust not the *outward* to yield thee happiness. It cannot do so.

> "How oft the world's alluring smile
> Has tempted only to beguile!
> It promised health—in one short hour
> Perished the fair and tender flower:
> It promised riches—in a day
> They made them wings and flew away.
> It promised friends—all sought their own,
> And left my aching heart alone."—*Cunningham.*

John 4:27-34

A FOUR-FOLD THEME

"And upon this came His disciples, and marvelled that He talked (R. V. WAS SPEAKING) with the woman : yet no man said, What seekest Thou ? or, Why talkest Thou with her ? The (R. V. SO THE) woman then left her water-pot, and went her way (R. V. AWAY) into the city, and saith to the men, Come, see a man, which told me all things that ever I did : is not this (R. V. CAN THIS BE) the Christ ? Then they went out of the city, and came (R. V. WERE COMING) unto Him. In the mean while His disciples prayed Him, saying, Master (R. V. RABBI), eat. But He said unto them, I have meat to eat that ye know not of. Therefore said the disciples one to another, Hath any man brought Him ought to eat ? Jesus saith unto them, My meat is to do the will of Him that sent Me, and to finish (R. V. ACCOMPLISH) His work."

EXEGETICAL REMARKS.—Ver. 27.— "*And upon this came His disciples,* *and marvelled that He talked with the woman.*" The eighth verse informed us that they had been away to the city to buy meat, that is, the city of Sychar, about half an hour's distance from the well. The conversation with the woman had perhaps continued during the whole of their absence. We have only the record of a fragment of the conversation. Let us be thankful for what we have. The disciples, it would seem, found Him in conversation on their return, and they wondered. Why? Because it was not only contrary to the custom of the Orientals for men to talk to women in the street, but the Jews abstained from all intercourse with the Samaritans. The Rabbis despised the female sex as utterly without knowledge. In the Talmud it is said "no one salutes a woman," and again, "he who instructs his daughter in the law is like one who acts the fool." No wonder, then, the disciples marvelled when they saw Christ talking with the woman, or rather with a woman, for such is in the original. " *Yet no man said, What seekest Thou? or, Why talkest Thou with her?* " No one dared to put a question to Him on the subject; they were too reverential to pry into His procedure or plans.

Ver. 28.—" *The woman then left her water-pot, and went her way into the city.*" The thoughts Christ had breathed into her soon created a tide of emotions that buried for a time all thoughts of worldly things. She forgot her work, left her vessel at the fountain, and ran forth on a new mission.

Ver. 29.—" *Come, see a man, which told me all things that ever I did.*" She does not mean, of course, that He narrated to her every act of her life. No; strong emotions run into poetry. Christ had touched those central points in her history that brought up before her memory the leading chapters of her past life. " *Is not this the Christ?* " μήτι οὖτός ἐστιν ὁ Χριστός. "The grammatical form of this expression, which expects a *negative* answer, requires that it should be rendered : Is this—or rather—can this be the Christ? The woman put it thus, as if they

would naturally reply, Impossible! But beneath that modest way of putting it was the conviction, that if they would but come and judge for themselves, she would have no need to obtrude upon them any opinion of hers, which she well knew would be unworthy of attention. Thus by asking if this could possibly be the Christ, and so rather asking to be helped by them than pretending to be their teacher, she in reality drew their attention to the point in the least offensive and yet most effectual way." —*Brown.*

Ver. 30.—" *Then they went out of the city, and came unto Him.*" The conduct of the Jews had caused Christ to withdraw from Judæa, but here the Samaritans stream out from their city to meet Him.

Ver. 31.—" *In the mean while His disciples prayed Him, saying, Master, eat.*" Meanwhile, that is, during her absence, while she was away in the city telling out her new experience, the disciples urged Him to eat the food they had just brought with them from the city.

Ver. 32.—" *But He said unto them, I have meat to eat that ye know not of.*" The pronouns " *I*" and " *Ye* " are emphatically expressed to mark the contrast between His thoughts and theirs. They thought of the material bread, He of the spiritual.

Ver. 33.—" *Therefore said the disciples one to another, Hath any man brought Him ought to eat?*" They had not yet reached His meaning, they were thinking of the material food which they considered His exhausted physical nature required.

Ver. 34.—" *Jesus saith unto them, My meat is to do the will of Him that sent Me, and to finish His work.*" Here He explains. His whole living, His proper food and sustenance, His whole life and relish,—was to do His Father's will, as He had intimated already when a boy in the temple. It was then already more to Him than earthly parents or home.—Luke ii. 49.

HOMILETICS

In these verses there are four subjects worthy of note.

I —PREJUDICE CREATING WONDER

" *And upon this came His disciples, and marvelled that He talked with the woman.*" What was the cause of their marvelment? An old, foolish prejudice. The tradition that it was improper for a man to talk to a woman out of doors, and especially for a Jew to hold intercourse with a Samaritan, had been accepted by them without any inquiry. They had never examined the question for themselves, they had never reached the dogma as an intelligent conclusion. Hence the high and holy converse which their Divine Master held with this woman struck them with surprise, if not with confusion. They marvelled at Him, considered it perhaps beneath His dignity and inconsistent with His high pretensions. How often prejudice acts thus; how often it causes God's declarations and deeds to puzzle and astound! When we set up our own traditional notions as a standard by which to try the Eternal, His procedure will be always filling us with confusion. "Prejudice is a great obstruction to spiritual progress; it is like an undercurrent at sea, which, being stronger than the wind, resistlessly carries the vessel back; so that, instead of the mariner finding himself so many miles nearer home, he has really lost ground." So deep and strong is the under current of prejudice in some natures that the soul, in all her endeavours to advance, is baffled and confounded.

Another thing worthy of note here is—

II —REVERENCE LIMITING INQUIRY

" *Yet no man said, What seekest Thou? or, Why talkest Thou with her?*" Though they did not understand His conduct, they did not dare to question it. Though to them it seemed improper, they were so impressed with His superior character and judgment, that they refrained from inquiry. Genuine reverence will always limit inquiry; it will not allow the intellect to interrogate the Almighty, and to pry into the decrees of heaven. The intellect reposes on a well-grounded assurance of His unerring wisdom, inviolable rectitude, and unbounded love. Reverence implies some appreciation of the infinite disparity between the thoughts and ways of God and those of man, and therefore it becomes rather a humble listener than a busy critic.

Another thing worthy of note here is—

III —CHRISTIANITY WORKING IN LIFE

This is seen in the conduct of the woman. The conversation which Christ had with her broke the cerements of her soul, touched her into new life, set her on new trains of thought, and unsealed within her new fountains of emotion.

Mark how the new faith worked within her.

(1.) Emotionally. "*The woman then left her water-pot, and went her way into the city.*" All worldly concerns, for a time, seemed buried under the rising waves of newly-evoked sentiments and thoughts. The more Divine feeling we have within us, the less we care for worldly things.

(2.) Proselytingly. "*Went her way into the city, and saith to the men, Come, see a man,*" &c. A strong desire to bring others under the new influences which she now experienced grew up within her, and urged her forth as a messenger of mercy—a blessed missionary.

(3.) Religiously. She felt that He Who spoke to her was Divine. "*Come, see a man, which told me all things that ever I did : is not this the Christ ?*" She does not ask the question because she has any doubts, she knows that He is, for He has sounded the depths of her history. He had told her all things that ever she did.

(4.) Influentially. "*Then they went out of the city, and came unto Him.*" As she spoke to her townsmen and townswomen her words and looks were electric. Real earnestness wields a magic wand. A poor woman moving a city is indeed a grand sight.

Another thing worthy of note here is—

IV —MAN FEASTING ON THE INVISIBLE

"*I have meat to eat that ye know not of,*" &c. There are two facts which arrest our attention in reading this passage ; one is an ordinary *physical* fact in human nature, and the other is a rare *moral* fact in human nature.

The *common natural* fact is the influence of emotions on the physical appetite. It would seem that Christ had been for some time without food ; His disciples were anxious on this account, and "prayed Him, saying, Master, eat." His reply was, "*I have meat to eat that ye know not of.*" And afterwards He explains Himself and says, "*My meat is to do the will of Him that sent Me.*" His mind was obviously so thoroughly charged and engrossed with feelings of devout joy in relation to the will of God, and the progress of His truth in the world, that the natural craving for food was for the time not experienced. It is ever so. Such is the close connection between soul and body, that strong emotions, either of a painful or pleasurable character, will overcome for a time our animal appetites. I believe that physical disease and death, as well as physical health and life, are often in the emotions. In this incident, therefore, our Saviour showed that He was very Man, "made in all points like unto us, yet without sin."

The other fact which you have here is the *rare moral* fact in human nature. This is found in the cause of these powerful emotions. What fired and filled the heart of the holy Jesus with these all-absorbing affections? The consciousness of acting in harmony with the Divine will, the manifestation of a new life in the Samaritan mind, the indication which He saw in the multitude around Him of a rich and speedy harvest growing out of the principles which He had inculcated. Now this is a rare moral fact in human nature. It is common enough to see men's emotions overcoming for a time their physical appetites; but it is rare to see these emotions rising from such Divine considerations. The fires that kindle strong emotions in the world generally, are not spiritual and benevolent, but gross and selfish.

John 4:35-38

THE SPIRITUAL CULTURE OF THE WORLD

" Say not ye, There are yet four months, and then cometh harvest? behold, I say unto you, Lift up your eyes, and look on the fields ; for (R. V. THAT) they are white already to harvest. And he that reapeth receiveth wages, and gathereth fruit unto life eternal : that both he that soweth and he that reapeth may rejoice together. And (R. V. FOR) herein is that saying true, One soweth, and another reapeth. I sent you to reap that whereon ye bestowed (R. V. HAVE NOT, no labour : (R. V. LABOURED) other men (R. V. OTHERS HAVE) laboured, and ye are entered into their labours " (R. V. LABOUR).

EXEGETICAL REMARKS.—Ver. 35.— " *Say not ye, There are yet four months, and then cometh harvest?*" November, December, and January are the sowing seasons in Judæa, and from the seed-time to the harvest is generally about four months. "Four months to the harvest" was perhaps a proverbial expression amongst the Jews, hence our Lord rebuking says, "*Behold, I say unto you, Lift up your eyes, and look on the fields; for they are white already to harvest.*" As our Lord points them to the fields, it is highly probable that it was just seed-time ; and we are thus furnished with the date, to wit : that Jesus had remained in Judæa from April, when the Passover occurred, until November. "'I say' forms the antithesis to 'ye say'".—*Tholuck.* In the natural world we must wait four months—in the spiritual it is already the time of harvest. The fields were "already white." The spirit of religious inquiry was now at work in the Samaritan mind.

Ver. 36.—"*And he that reapeth re-*

ceiveth wages, and gathereth fruit unto life eternal.*" "Since the wages of the reaper are represented as given in this world, over against the gathering of fruit unto 'eternal life,' the primary idea is, the immediate spiritual blessings enjoyed by the harvesters—the communion of the converts themselves."—*Dr. Lange.* "*That both he that soweth and he that reapeth may rejoice together.*" The spiritual sower, as well as the spiritual reaper, shall have his reward. "*Together*"—at the same time, and in the same celestial scenes.

Ver. 37.—"*Herein is that saying true, One soweth, and another reapeth.*" Here Christ quotes another proverb. It seems that both the Greeks and the Hebrews had such a proverb. Christ now saw in the Samaritan mind its verification.

Ver. 38.—"*I sent you to reap,*" &c. Some expositors include in the sowers here not only the old prophets, but even the heathen philosophers who disseminated the seeds of truth. "*Other men laboured, and ye are entered into their labours."* He Himself is included in this "other men." The great teachers of past times had none of them laboured at such sacrifice and with such efficiency as He.

HOMILETICS

The subject of these verses is *The Spiritual Cultivation of Humanity*.

The words we have written on a former page may here be quoted as an introduction to this subject.

" There are two facts which arrest our attention in reading this passage ; one is an *ordinary physical fact in human nature, and the other is a rare moral fact in human nature.* The common natural fact is the influence of emotions on the physical appetite. It would seem that Christ had been for some time without food ; His disciples were anxious on this account, and 'prayed Him, saying, Master, eat.' His reply was, '*I have meat that ye know not of.*' And afterwards He explains Himself and says, 'My meat is to do the will of Him that sent Me.' His mind was obviously so thoroughly charged and engrossed with feelings of devout joy in relation to the will of God, and the progress of His truth in the world, that the natural craving for food was for the time not experienced. It is ever so. Such is the close connection between the soul and body, that strong emotions, either of a painful or pleasurable character, will overcome for a time our animal appetites. I believe that physical disease and death, as well as physical health and life, are often in the emotions. In this incident, therefore, our Saviour showed that He was very Man, 'made in all points like unto us, yet without sin.' The other fact which you have here is *the rare moral fact in human nature.* This is found in the cause of these powerful emotions. What fired and filled the heart of the holy Jesus with these all-absorbing affections? The consciousness of acting in harmony with the Divine will, the manifestation of a new life in the Samaritan mind, the indication which He saw in the multitude around Him of a rich and speedy harvest growing out of the principles which He had inculcated. With a heart bounding with inexpressible joy, He exclaims, 'Say not ye,' &c. As if He had said, 'I see the world's mind working up to higher thoughts, and worthier aims; I see how My Gospel takes hold upon the human mind : how it will win and conquer the world one day.' Now this is a rare moral fact in human nature. It is common enough to see men's emotions overcoming for a time their physical appetites ; but it is rare to see these emotions rising from such Divine considerations. The fires that kindle strong emotions in the world generally, are not spiritual and benevolent, but gross and selfish."

The subject to which I invite your attention is: The *spiritual culture of our race*. The Bible frequently represents the great work of spiritual renovation under the figure of husbandry. The simplicity of the process, so far as man's agency is concerned, and the dependency of all human effort upon the gracious agency of God for success; the capability of the soul to receive, quicken, and propagate Divine truth; and other circumstances, show the appropriateness of the figure. The text suggests four considerations in relation to this work—

I —THAT THE GREAT PURPOSE OF GOD WITH OUR WORLD IS ITS SPIRITUAL CULTURE

This is clear from the fact, that Christ was now absorbed in the work; and in the midst of it He says, "My meat is to do the will," &c. In chap vi. vers. 38—40, He states it more unequivocally still—" I came down from heaven, not to do Mine own will." There are two ways to ascertain the will or purpose of God concerning our world. By what He *does*, and by what He *says*. *The relation which He has established between the human mind and the outward universe shows it.* We come into this world with minds capable of receiving, and naturally craving for, those impressions of the Divine existence, attributes, and claims, which nature seems organized for the very purpose of imparting. Nature is a husbandman to the soul. It is fitted to mollify its soil, it has precious seeds to impart, it has the quickening sunbeam and the fertilizing shower at its command. Moreover, the history *of the providential economy under which we are placed indicates the same fact.* Providence deals as a husbandman with the soul. It ploughs and harrows, it uproots, plants, and waters. Still more, *The mission of Christ to the world and the representations of the Bible attest the fact.* He is the "SOWER" Whom the GREAT God has sent into the world. He is come to make the moral "wilderness bloom as Eden." The Bible speaks of the Jewish people as a "vineyard," the world as a "field," and the Church as "God's husbandry."

If we look to what He *says*, we shall find that His word through every part declares, without figure, that it is His will "that none should perish, but that all should come to repentance." And by the mouth of His holy prophets He has given us a view of the Paradisaic state of our world, when His purpose shall be fully realized. On every ground, then, we are bound to conclude that God wills the spiritual culture of our race:—that this is His grand purpose in relation to it. Yes, my brother, God's will concerning thine existence here is, not that thou shouldst become a great animal, a millionnaire, or even a sage, but a great, well-trained soul. If this be the Divine will, to obey God is to serve our race:—the cause of God is the cause of humanity.

II —THAT THE SERVANT OF GOD SHOULD EARNESTLY SEIZE EVERY OPPORTUNITY FOR ITS SPIRITUAL CULTURE

"Say not ye, There are yet four months, and then cometh harvest? behold, I say unto you, Lift up your eyes, and look on the fields; for they are white already to harvest." * The words imply two facts which illustrate the proposition, that it is our duty earnestly to seize every opportunity for promoting the cultivation of the race.

First: That moral seasons are not like material ones, independent of our agency. In Judæa, the husbandman was bound to wait for a fixed period—*"four months"*—before he could reap what he had sown. The natural seasons are independent of us. They will come whether we wish them or not. We cannot keep the winter back, we cannot retain the enchanting summer. Not so in the moral department. *"Say not ye,"* &c. Do not think or talk in the same way about *moral* seasons. You can change the temperature, you can bring on new seasons, in the moral world. You can turn the frigid winds of winter into the glowing gales of May; you can bring the moral sun to the meridian, and make it stand still to genialize the earth. "The good time coming," you may depend, will not come as the natural seasons come, independently of our efforts. We must roll the circling orbs of truth to hasten its cheerful dawn. We must create "our April day." The words imply—

Secondly: That the feeblest honest effort to improve the world will develop encouraging symptoms to persevere. The conversation which Christ now had with the woman seems to have stirred the heart of the city, and to have awakened a general spirit of inquiry. God alone knows the influence of true thoughts truly spoken; they increase the world's appetite and demand for the spiritual. The more you devoutly and honestly press Christianity upon the world, the more 'opening,' as the phrase is, the world will supply for it. In spirituals, the demand increases with the supply; the more you give, the keener the appetite, and the vaster the capacity. Hence from these two facts, it obviously appears to be our duty to seize every opportunity for promoting the moral cultivation of the world.

III —THAT A LONG SUCCESSION OF AGENTS ARE REQUIRED FOR ITS SPIRITUAL CULTURE

"One soweth, and another reapeth." "I have laid the foundation, and another buildeth thereon." "Paul plants, Apollos waters," &c. The great work is not accomplished at once. What one sows, another reaps. We enter into the labours of those who have gone before, and those who succeed will take up our humble endeavours and help to work them out:—and thus on and on, to the end.

* See Germ, p. 105.

Christ entered into the labours of the prophets. The disciples entered into His labours, &c. The proverb which Christ quotes embraces a universal principle in human history applicable to every department of conduct. *One generation sows what another reaps.* It applies to *sin.* "The fathers have eaten sour grapes," &c. It applies to *civilization.* Ingenious mechanicians, intrepid patriots, enterprising travellers, earnest philosophers, religious reformers, sowed seed in their day, whose rich fruits we are now reaping in the countless arts and privileges that bless our age. But it applies especially to religion. This principle is very suggestive.

First : It suggests the moral connection of the race. Not only does the physical existence of one generation spring from the loins of another, but the moral character of one grows out of the moral heart of the other. Man transmits his principles, as well as his nature. This age is reaping what previous ages have sown, and in its turn is sowing what all coming generations shall reap.

Secondly : It suggests the slow progress of moral principles in the world. Humanity requires ages to rise to the full appreciation of great truths. Principles which were considered as the dreams of brainless visionaries in one age, in the next a few will adopt as realities; but many ages must transpire before the majority will bow to them. Thus slowly does the work go on.

Thirdly : It suggests the humble part which the individual man plays in the history of the world. If we reap, it is not what we have sown. What we sow will not appear until we are dust, and time has blotted our name from the memory of the race. We pluck a few ripe ears from the great cornfield of life, drop a seed or two, and then pass away. Humility becometh us.

Fourthly : It suggests that results are not right rules of life. We see more of the effects of other men's labours than of our own. We cannot tell what will spring up in the world and grow from what we are doing now. We must leave consequences to the Eternal ;—with principles we have to do. What is right ? is our question ; and to follow it out will in the long run of ages be found essentially, exclusively, and for ever expedient. Let us in our short hour do the right thing, and speak the true thought.

> " The truth once uttered, and 'tis like
> A star new-born that drops into its place,
> And which once circling in its placid round,
> Not all the tumult of the earth can shake."

IV—THAT THERE IS A VITAL RELATIONSHIP BETWEEN ALL THE AGENTS THAT HAVE EVER BEEN ENGAGED IN THIS WORK OF SPIRITUAL CULTURE

" *He that reapeth receiveth wages, and gathereth fruit unto life eternal : that both he that soweth and he that reapeth may rejoice together.*"

First : They are all united in working out one common purpose. And this is the bond that unites all true workers; all follow out the same will, aim at the same object, and move by the same impulse.

Secondly : They are all united in participating in the same rewards. They shall all gather "*fruit unto life eternal.*" They shall all "*rejoice together.*" What is the common reward ? The expression "eternal life" includes all. It is eternal, well-being. "*Rejoice together ;*" eternal blessedness *together*. The true workers of every clime and age will meet. They will "*rejoice together.*" From east and west, from north and south, from every tribe, and every period, they shall meet and "*rejoice together.*" In that universal rejoicing there will be no under-rating of the service of the humblest, and the greatest will not glory in himself. Each will rejoice in another's labours rather than in his own, and all will ascribe their achievements to All-inspiring and Almighty love.

Brothers, let us feel that the master purpose of God with our world *is its moral cultivation.* For this the sun arises, the holy stars appear, the earth is kept in its circling path, all nature is sustained. For this Jesus appeared and wrought out His life of agony, the true men of every age and clime have toiled and prayed, and the Spirit of God is ever in earnest work. And further, let us blend our humble efforts with the mighty forces of God. The smallest effort is not lost. The coral insect that labours for an hour down in the depths of the ocean and dies, labours not in vain ; others appear, begin where it left off; and thus the work goes on until in the course of ages there rises above the vast solitary wilderness of dashing waves an island world, beautiful as Eden. Thus from the humblest labours of honest souls, there will one day rise from the deep, turbid, and turbulent sea of earth's depravity, a new world of moral beauty and blessedness.

> " 'Tis coming, coming up the steep of time,
> And this old world is growing brighter,
> We may not see its dawn sublime,
> Yet high hopes make the heart throb lighter.
> We may be sleeping in the ground
> When it awakes the world in wonder,
> But we have felt it gathering round,
> And heard its voice of living thunder.
>   'Tis coming, yes, 'tis coming ! "

Germs of Thought
No. 21   John 4:35

HARVEST

"Lift up your eyes, and look on the fields; for they are white already to harvest."

Harvest is a prolific subject for human thought; it is a many-sided theme, and from every side men may have most soul-quickening and soul-ennobling views. We shall look at it now as illustrating three great principles which are ever at work in the Divine Government. *The ripening, the compensatory, and the co-operative.*

I —THE RIPENING PRINCIPLE IN THE DIVINE GOVERNMENT

The fruits of the earth which have reached maturation were a few months ago in a most nascent state. From the time when the sower committed the seed to the earth up to the hour when the reaper thrust his sickle into the field of golden grain, there was a principle at work that never paused day nor night until culmination was reached. And this principle is not only at work in the vegetable kingdom, but in every other domain. It is at work in the *inorganic* realm. Astronomers tell us that our earth and the system to which it belongs are travelling to a crisis, approaching a ripened condition. It works in the *animal* realm. As the oak moves from century to century from the acorn to a point when its perfection is reached and decadence begins, all animal life passes from the embryo to an organization worn out with years. But it is in the *human* realm that we should ponder well its operations. Here it is seen—

First: In the body. From infancy to old age our bodies are ripening for the grave.

Secondly: In the character. The character of all men is ripening for a retribution, either of woe or bliss.

Thirdly: In institutions. Human institutions, whether good or bad, ripen and reach their culmination. They have their harvest. The tares are reaped and are cast into the fire of revolution. Thus, there is a ripening power at work. *Individuals* are ripening; the body for the grave, the soul for eternity. *Nations* are ripening; their end is approaching. The *world* is ripening; the harvest is the end of the world. The end of all things is at hand.

II —THE COMPENSATORY PRINCIPLE IN THE DIVINE GOVERNMENT

We see this principle rewarding the labourer according to the kind and the amount of his work.

First: According to the kind. What was sown has been reaped—not only the species, but the quality too. The field in harvest gives back to the agriculturist that which he gave it in spring. Nothing different in kind. This principle acts as rigorously in the *moral* sphere. "Whatsoever a man soweth, that shall he also reap. He that soweth to the flesh, of the flesh reaps corruption; he that soweth to the spirit, of the spirit reaps everlasting life." "Even as I have seen," says Eliphaz, "they that plough iniquity and sow wickedness, shall reap the same." The selfish, the sensual, the untrue, the profane, are sowing moral hemlock, and they shall reap the rankling poison.

Secondly: According to the amount. The sower who sows sparingly his seed, does not receive, other things being equal, back from nature the same as he who scattered with a more liberal hand. It is so in the *moral* department. He that soweth sparingly, reaps sparingly, &c. There are degrees in glory, and those degrees are regulated by the degrees of goodness. This retributive principle, gleaming in the harvest-field, shines everywhere through human life with more or less brightness. It is true it is dim here as compared with what it will be hereafter. Retributive justice, which is a mere star in our earthly sphere, will grow into a sun which shall flood with overwhelming brightness our eternity. "Be not deceived; God is not mocked; whatsoever a man soweth, that shall he also reap."

III —THE CO-OPERATIVE PRINCIPLE IN THE DIVINE GOVERNMENT.

In the harvest-field you have the result of a vast combination of agencies, animate and inanimate, human and Divine. The harvest demonstrates that man has been a *co-worker* with God. Had man not cultured the soil, and scattered the seeds, the golden crops would not have been here, and had not God given the sun, and dew, and shower, and genial temperature, man's industry and skill would have been vain. Indeed, even the agency of the agriculturists, though *free*, were Divine. God gave it, God sustained it, God directed it, so that to Him belongeth the praise. It is verily so in spiritual labour. "Paul planteth, Apollos watereth, but God giveth the increase."

John 4:39-42

THE WORLD'S REDEMPTIVE FAITH

"And many of the Samaritans of (R. V. FROM) that city believed on Him for the saying (R. V. WORD) of the woman, which (R. V. WHO) testified, He told me all (R. V. THINGS) that ever I did. So when the Samaritans were come unto Him, they besought Him that He would tarry (R. V. ABIDE) with them : and He abode there two days. And many more believed because of His own word ; and said unto the woman, Now we believe, not because of thy saying (R. V. SPEAKING) : for we have heard Him (R. V. FOR) ourselves, and know that this is indeed the Christ, (R. V. OMITS) the Saviour of the world."

EXEGETICAL REMARKS.—Ver. 39.—
"*Many of the Samaritans of that city.*"

This is a splendid commentary on the thirty-fifth verse, the fields are "white already to harvest." "*Believed on Him.*" Not merely as a good man, a great prophet, or a grand philosopher, but as the Messiah, the "Saviour of the world." "The Messiah," says *Hengstenberg*, "is represented as the Saviour of the world in that one of the few Messianic passages in the Pentateuch to which the Samaritans were restricted, Gen. xlix. 50. According to which the nations shall adhere to the Shiloh, the peaceful and peacebringer." "*For the saying of the woman, which testified, He told me all that ever I did.*" The brief record of the conversation of our Saviour with the woman at the well of Jacob does not contain all that He had spoken to her. In that conversation as recorded He told her of her domestic unchastities, but here she seems to have informed the Samaritans that He told her all things that ever she did. He spread out the moral of her whole life before her, so that she felt He was the Omniscient One. Because of her testimony concerning His thorough knowledge of her, the Samaritans believed.

Ver. 40.—"*So when the Samaritans were come unto Him.*" This woman had invited them in the twenty-ninth verse to come to Him, and now, according to her wish, they approach Him. They are brought face to face with that wonderful Person of whom she had been speaking. "*They besought Him that He would tarry with them: and He abode there two days.*" They pray, and He answers; they make a request, and He replies. He continued two days with them. We should like to have had a record of these two days' talking and working in the city of Samaria. How many disciples did He win during those two days? It is worthy of remark, that after His resurrection, whilst we only find a few who believed in Him in other places, that He appeared to five hundred brethren in Galilee (1 Cor. xv. 6). "The field was ripe unto harvest."

Vers. 41, 42.—"*And many more believed because of His own word; and said unto the woman, Now we believe, not because of thy saying: for we have heard Him ourselves.*" They had believed in Him to a certain degree because of the woman's word concerning Him, but now they arose to a higher faith; "*We have heard Him ourselves.*" "*And know that this is indeed the Christ, the Saviour of the world.*" "In the expression, ὁ σωτὴρ τοῦ κόσμου, 'the Saviour of the world' is signified, the universality of the Messiah's destination. That the people actually employed this expression cannot be maintained positively; nevertheless this very designation of a universal character was, on the ground of the Old Testament prophecies, acknowledged by every pious Israelite (Luke ii. 32)."—*Tholuck.*

HOMILETICS

The subject of these verses is *the world's redemptive faith.* The world has many faiths. Men are constitutionally credulous, and their curse is that they believe too much, rather than too little. Faith lies at the root of all human activities, institutions, pursuits; and the state of the whole world, socially, politically, and religiously, is according to its faith. All modifications in the outward life of the world must begin in an alteration of its faiths.

There is only one *redemptive* faith: faith to emancipate the soul from the bondage of prejudice, guilt, materialism, and moral depravity in all its forms, and that faith appears in these words.

Observe two things—

I —THE GRAND OBJECT OF THE WORLD'S REDEMPTIVE FAITH

That Object is Christ. Observe here three things concerning Him.

First: He thoroughly knows all pertaining to human life. "*He told me*," said the woman, "*all that ever I did.*" The conversation which the woman had with Him made her feel that He was thoroughly cognisant not only with all the items in her outward conduct, but with all the secret workings of her inner life. She felt that He had read her through and through, and her conclusion from the fact was that He was Divine, and the true Messiah. When she told the Samaritans His knowledge of her they seemed to believe at once in His Divinity. The object of the world's redemptive faith is One—a Person Who thoroughly understands it, knows all that it has ever done, knows its entire history from its roots, through all its ramifications.

Secondly: He is susceptible to human appeals. "*So when the Samaritans were come unto Him, they besought Him that He would tarry with them : and He abode there two days.*" He not only thoroughly knows the world, but He has a heart that inclines Him to yield to its appeals for help. The cry of Bartimeus arrested Him on His road; the entreaties of the travellers to Emmaus induced Him to turn in and tarry with them; and here the request of the Samaritans caused Him to abide with them two days.

Thirdly: He is the Restorer of mankind. "*This is Christ, the Saviour of the world.*" τοῦ κόσμου, the Saviour, not of the Jew only, but of the Gentile also; not of a class, but of all the races and sects that make up humanity.

Now this is the Object of the world's redemptive faith. It will never be saved by believing in Creeds, Churches, or Priesthoods; it must believe on *Him* Who knows it, feels for it, and came to save it. "He that believeth on Me shall be saved." Observe—

II —THE GRAND GROUNDS OF THE WORLD'S REDEMPTIVE FAITH

These grounds are here: one is testimony, and the other is consciousness; the one is a preliminary faith, the other is a perfect faith.

First: The *initiatory* faith. This faith is built on testimony. The Samaritans believed because "*of the saying of the woman.*" In their initial faith they accepted two things: (1.) Omniscience as a proof of Divinity. The saying of the woman was, "*He told me all that ever I did.*" She felt intuitively that He Who could tell out the whole history of human life was Divine. Who but God can read the heart? Every man feels that there is no one that can know him thoroughly but the God Who made him. You have only to convince me that such a being knows all about human life in order to establish my faith in His supernaturalness, nay, in His Divinity. They accepted (2.) The credibility of the woman's testimony. They believed what she said concerning Him was true. Why did they believe in her credibility? Because they could see that she believed. He who believes in a thing, and he only who believes in a Divine thing, has the power to inspire faith. This woman's faith was manifest in her movements, in her expressions, in the ring of her voice. She believed. The Word in her " became flesh," and was made manifest. Hence her influence. She seemed to have moved the city in a few hours. From what she said the Samaritans believed, came unto Him, and *" besought Him to tarry "* with them. Oh! the power of one earnest soul !

This initiatory faith was a faith in testimony, and here generally all faith in Christ begins : it is faith in the testimony of those who have seen and heard Him. A traditional faith is the faith of mere nominal Christians.

Secondly : The *consummating* faith. *" And many more believed because of His own word."* This faith was (1.) Intuitive. As soon as they saw and heard Christ for themselves, they felt at once that He was the Messiah. His truths agreed with their reason and their aspirations, and His character with their ideal. They required no argument; the Incarnate Word commended itself. This faith was (2.) Direct. *" We have heard Him ourselves."* We heard of Him through thee, thou woman of Samaria, and we intellectually accepted the fact that He is the Messiah; but now that *" we have heard Him ourselves"* we *know* He is. We know His voice; it chimes in with the Divine echoes of our nature. It is the voice we have been long craving to hear. This faith was (3.) Certain. *" And know that this is indeed the Christ."* We have no doubt about it. The man who has this faith, which springs from the felt congruity of Christ with the deepest things of his soul, is independent of all other evidences, and can stand firmly against all the hostile reasonings of infidelity. He says—All your logic is worthless; *" we know that this is indeed the Christ."*

CONCLUSION. Here, then, is the soul-redemptive faith,—faith in the all-knowing, all-loving Saviour of the world; faith grounded not merely on the testimony of others, but on the revelation of Himself to the human soul. This is the faith that is sadly lacking throughout Christendom. Traditional faith abounds, and it is often worse than useless. Oh, speed the day when God Who " commanded the light to shine out of darkness, shall shine into the heart of the world, giving it the light of the knowledge of the glory of God in the face of Jesus Christ ! "

John 4:43-45

MORAL USEFULNESS

(Jesus teaches publicly in Galilee.—MATT. iv. 17 ; MARK i. 14, 15 ; LUKE iv. 14, 15 ; JOHN iv. 43—45.)

" Now (R. V. AND) after two days He departed (R. V. WENT FORTH FROM) thence, and went into Galilee. For Jesus Himself testified, that a prophet hath no honour in his own country. Then (R. V. SO) when He was come into Galilee, the Galilæans received Him, having seen all the things that He did at (R. V. IN) Jerusalem at the feast : for they also went unto the feast."—

EXEGETICAL REMARKS.—The only difficult question in connection with this passage is this, What does the Heavenly Teacher here mean by "*country*"? (Πατριδι). There are several answers presented by different Biblical critiques to this question. (1.) "Galilee is to be taken in opposition to Nazareth. In this city, His own country, Jesus had no honour, but elsewhere in Galilee He was received as a prophet."—*Lightfoot, Krafft.* (2.) "Galilee is to be taken in opposition to Judæa. Judæa was His birthplace, and so His own country, and it was also the land of the prophets : but there He had found no reception, and had been compelled to discontinue His ministry. In Galilee, on the contrary, all were ready to honour Him."— *Ebrard, Norton.* (3.) "Galilee is His own country, where, according to the proverb, He would have had no honour, except He had first gone to Judæa and distinguished Himself there. It was His miracles and works abroad that gave Him fame and favour at home." —*Meyer, Alford.* We do not regard the subject of sufficient importance to canvass these conflicting views, or to advocate or propound a conclusion of our own.

HOMILETICS

The paragraph suggests to us certain practical thoughts concerning *man's moral usefulness in society.*

I —MAN MAY DO MUCH MORAL GOOD WITHIN A SHORT PERIOD

"*Now after two days He departed thence, and went into Galilee.*" Two days Jesus spent in Samaria, and what did He accomplish spiritually within that short period ? Many, we are told, "believed on Him for the saying of the woman," and "many *more* believed because of His own word." His words during that period broke the religious monotony of the Samaritans, set the minds of men to earnest and independent thinking. He won many at once to His cause, and He scattered those incorruptible seeds of truth which commenced germination at once, and which have yielded glorious harvests through all subsequent ages. The Infinite only can tell the amount of spiritual good that has resulted from Christ's ministry in Samaria during those "*two days.*" Every man may and *ought* to accomplish great spiritual good in "*two days,*"—not only by preaching to vast congregations and addressing multitudes through the Press, but even in a more private way—by indoctrinating the family with Christly sentiments, and distributing through the neighbourhood the "Bread of Life." We do not want a long life in order to be useful; in *"two days"* we may accomplish much. No man on the "great day" of trial will be able to plead the brevity of his mortal life as an excuse for not having been morally useful to his fellow-men. We may not have time enough to make fortunes, become scientific, or win fame, but we have time enough to be useful.

II —MAN'S EFFORTS TO DO GOOD ARE OFTEN OBSTRUCTED BY A STUPID PREJUDICE

" For Jesus Himself testified, that a prophet hath no honour in his own country." Christ here states a fact. Of course there are exceptions to it. Many men gain some kind of honour from their countrymen, but as a rule *prophets* do not. Home teachers are not so valued as the foreign. This is one of the great practical errors in all human society. There is no *good* reason for it. The doctrines of a teacher, whether true or false, salutary or pernicious, are independent of the country of the teacher. There are *bad* reasons for it. The prejudice springs from jealousy, envy, pride, and such vile passions.* Christ felt that this prejudice was against His usefulness, and prejudice in some form or other has been felt by every man endeavouring to do good to be one of his chief obstructions. Prejudices are fetters that enslave the intellect, clouds that obscure the vision, bolts that shut out the truth. Men in England are filled with prejudice concerning the elements of dignity, the means of happiness, the dogmas of theology, and the forms of worship.

III —MAN'S DESIRE FOR DOING GOOD SHOULD BE THE INSPIRATION OF HIS LIFE

Christ leaves Samaria, confronts a powerful prejudice, and enters Galilee—what for? In order to be useful. "He went about doing good." Spiritually to bless humanity was the one grand purpose of His sublime life. " I must work the works of Him that sent Me, for the night cometh, when no man can work." Such should be the grand aim of all men, and this for two reasons—

First: It is the *greatest* work. What work on earth is so Divinely grand as that of enlightening the human intellect, enfranchising the human will, purifying the fountains of the human heart, transforming the moral man into the image of God's own Son? All other occupations and enterprises are but puerilities compared with this.

Secondly: It is the *most recompensing* work. He that converteth a soul "covers a multitude of sins," wins the sympathies of immortal spirits, and secures the approbation of his own conscience and his God. The fruits of all other labours we leave behind at

---

*See remarks on this subject in *Gospel of Matthew*, p.320.

death, but from the field of spiritual usefulness we gather sheaves that will inspire us with ineffable delight when time shall be no more.

IV —MAN'S POWER TO DO GOOD INCREASES AS HIS PAST USEFULNESS GETS RECOGNIZED

" *The Galilæans received Him, having seen all the things He did at Jerusalem at the feast : for they also went unto the feast.*" Christ had done great things at Jerusalem, as we learn from chapter ii. 23. The Galilæans, to whom He now addressed Himself, had in the holy city witnessed the mighty wonders He had wrought, and now as He came amongst them they were prepared to receive Him, and they did receive Him. What they knew of Him disposed them to accept Him. We get power to do good amongst men as our past good works get recognized. Man's power of spiritual usefulness is cumulative; the more good he does the more his capacity for usefulness increases. There is no wearing out in the cause of spiritual usefulness. The more useful a man has been, the more useful he may yet be. His career is not like the growth of a tree, which, after its culmination, weakens and dies, but like that of the river, it becomes stronger and stronger as it proceeds to its destination.

> " Be useful where thou livest, that they may
> Both want and wish thy presence still.
> Kindness, good parts, great actions are the way
> To compass this.   Find out man's want and will,
> And meet them there.   All worldly joys go less
> To the one joy of doing kindnesses."—*George Herbert.*

John 4:46-54

THE HEALING OF THE NOBLEMAN'S SON

*(Jesus again in Galilee, heals the nobleman's son.—*JOHN iv. 46—54.)

" So Jesus came again into Cana of Galilee," &c

EXEGETICAL REMARKS.—Ver. 46.— " *So Jesus came* (R. V. HE CAME THEREFORE) *again into Cana of Galilee, where He made the water wine. And there was a certain nobleman, whose son was sick at Capernaum.*" This nobleman (βασιλικός) was probably connected with the royal household. Such as the centurion (Luke vii. 2) ; or Naaman. Josephus uses the term to distinguish the officers of the king from kings (as Herod), from those at Rome (Cæsar). He was probably a Jew.   " Some have taken this nobleman to be identical with the centurion of Capernaum " (Irenæus, Semler, Strauss, Baumgarten, Crusius). The office, the sick boy, the distant healing, are similar features. On the other side are these differences : (1.) The time : here, before the removal of Jesus to Capernaum ; there, long after it. (2.) The place of Christ at the time : here, Cana ; there, the vicinity of Capernaum. (3.) The characters: here, excited, weak, feebly believing ; there, calm, confident, strong of faith. Other differences by themselves considered, might be more easily wiped away. The υἱός here, the δοῦλος there (a distinction, however, which is not resolved by the common παῖς): here, the boy is a small boy, a child, ver. 49; there, a stout youth, there a Gentile; here, a miracle-believer, probably a Jew; yet these with the foregoing strengthen the difference. But the most decisive diversity is in the judgment of the Lord. The faith of the centurion He commends with admiration; the faith of the nobleman He must first subject to a trial." *—Lange.*

Ver. 47.—*" When he heard that Jesus was come out of Judæa into Galilee, he went unto Him, and besought Him that He would come down, and heal his son: for he was at the point of death."* From what Christ had done both at Jerusalem in cleansing the temple, and at Cana in turning water into wine, this nobleman had received such an impression of Christ's miraculous power as to have inspired the hope that He would restore his son that was dying.

Ver. 48.—*" Then said Jesus unto him, Except ye see signs and wonders."* These two words (σημεῖα καί) are significant: the former seems to express the *supernatural* character of an act, and the latter the demonstration which is promised of a Divine power. *" Ye will not* (R. V. IN NO WISE) *believe."* But he had believed to some extent. What but faith prompted him to come forth in quest of Christ? But his faith was very imperfect: it was only in embryo.

Ver. 49.—*" The nobleman saith unto Him, Sir, come down ere my child die."* The matter is serious; there is not an instant to lose. " While I am speaking my child is dying." But why *" come down?"* Will not thy faith enable thee to believe that the great Messiah can do His works without being on

the spot? This thou wilt believe, however, ere the work is done.

Ver. 50.—*" Jesus saith unto him, Go thy way; thy son liveth. And the man believed the word that Jesus had spoken* (R. V. SPAKE) *unto him, and he went his way."* " Both effects instantaneously followed; the man believed the word; and the cure, shooting quicker than lightning from Cana to Capernaum, was felt by the dying youth. In token of faith, the father takes his leave of Christ. In the circumstances this evidenced full faith."—*Dr. Brown.*

Ver. 51.—*" And as he was now going down, his servants met him, and told him, saying, Thy son liveth "* (R. V. SAYING THAT HIS SON LIVED). How this intelligence must have deepened his faith, as well as flooded his heart with parental delight!

Ver. 52.—*" Then* (R. V. SO HE) *enquired he of them the hour when he began to amend. And they said* (R. V. THEY SAID THEREFORE) *unto him, Yesterday at the seventh hour the fever left him."* The fact, though transporting to him as a parent, did not satisfy the new craving that his growing faith had gendered within him. He desires to seek out the cause.

Ver. 53.—*" So the father knew that it was at the same* (R. V. THAT) *hour, in the which Jesus said unto him, Thy son liveth: and himself believed, and his whole house."* Here is faith that has become so strong that it propagates itself through a whole family.

Ver. 54.—*" This is again the second miracle* (R V. SIGN) *that Jesus did, when He was* (R. V. HAVING) *come out of Judæa into Galilee."* Both were in connection with domestic life; the one was connected with a marriage, the other with a deathbed.

HOMILETICS

This narrative, though short, is full of interest and deep meaning; it throws up to our view several points of thought too important not to notice with some amount of attention. One point is this—

I —THAT THE HISTORY OF CHRIST OFTEN EXERTS A PRACTICAL INFLUENCE UPON MEN WHO ARE NOT AMONGST HIS GENUINE DISCIPLES

There were no doubt many genuine disciples in the neighbourhood in which this nobleman lived. In "Cana of Galilee," Christ in His first miracle had "manifested forth His power," and "many of His disciples believed on Him." But this disciple does not appear to have been amongst them. The faith that prompted him to go forth in search of Christ does not seem to have been recognized by the Messiah as of much worth. The man had undoubtedly heard so many floating stories in his neighbourhood concerning our Lord that he felt that peradventure He could and would help him in his domestic emergency. Up to this point he had no strong convictions against Him, or any vital sympathy with His spirit, His doctrines, or His aims. Certain facts about His life, which to him were more or less in shadow, alone influenced him up to the point of his leaving his home in quest of Christ. Christ's name had become a power in Galilee already. A noble name is evermore a wide, unconscious, and often unacknowledged social force for good. Christ's mere history has for eighteen centuries influenced millions of men whom charity cannot rank amongst His true disciples. His history to-day throughout Christendom affects the movements and external conduct of rulers, statesmen, authors, artists, and whole classes who have no living or practical sympathy whatever with Him or His cause. Another point that presents itself here is :—

II —THAT NO WORLDLY GREATNESS CAN SHIELD MEN FROM ANY OF THE COMMON CALAMITIES OF LIFE

Here is a nobleman *whose son is dying.* His son *"was at the point of death."* The young have ever been disposed to imagine that their parents must sicken and die before them,—that because they are young death is afar off. The cemeteries of the world prove that the vast majority of the human race die in childhood, and that but very few live to the age of fifty. The first grave dug on earth was not dug for a father, but a son. Aaron lost two in one stroke. David followed one after another of his children to the grave ; the patriarch of Uz was bereft of all his children in one short day. The agonies of the dying son were not the only sufferings in the mansion of that nobleman ; his own heart was breaking, and perhaps that of his wife and children as well. Such are ordinary trials, they are the common calamities of the race. Everywhere throughout the world you will find dying children and distressed parents. This man's wealth, position, influence, could not ward off such dire events. Death dares all opposition, and knows no adventitious distinctions, treats all alike, has an access as easy to the royal chamber as to a pauper's hut : " the rich man also died and was buried."

> " If hoarded gold possess'd the power
> To lengthen life's too fleeting hour,
> And purchase from the hand of Death
> A little span, a moment's breath,
> How I would love the precious ore !
> And every hour should swell my store ;
> That when Death came, with shadowy pinion,
> To waft me to his bleak dominion,
> I might by bribes my doom delay,
> And bid him call some distant day.
> But since not all earth's golden store
> Can buy for us one bright hour more,
> Why should we vainly mourn our fate,
> Or sigh at life's uncertain date ?
> Nor wealth nor grandeur can illume
> The silent midnight of the tomb."—*Thomas Moore.*

Another point that stands out in this narrative is—

III —THAT CHRIST'S TREATMENT OF MEN DIFFERS WIDELY FROM THAT OF AN IMPOSTOR

In a case of this kind how should we have expected an impostor to have acted ? Nay, how should we have expected even an ordinary religious teacher to have acted ?

First: We should have expected that He would have dealt somewhat obsequiously with this nobleman. To say nothing of an impostor, if a "*nobleman*" were to enter some of our chapels, how would the modern minister be likely to act towards him ? Would there be no fawning, no servile homage ? Alas ! there are popular preachers not unknown to us who follow the great as dogs their masters.

Secondly : We should have expected that He would have acceded at once to the request of this nobleman. Were a nobleman to ask a favour of some religious teachers which they could grant even with much inconvenience to themselves, they would render it at once with a proud exultation. Their vanity would be so much flattered that they would not only grant the boon in a moment, but emblazon the act as one of the most radiant incidents of their lives.

Thirdly : We should have expected that He would have looked for some compensation for any service that He might render to the nobleman. Few noblemen would feel that they would insult a religious teacher by rendering some tangible acknowledgment for services, and but few teachers would fail to look for such a manifestation. Naaman offered remuneration, nor were Elijah and Elisha above accepting acknowledgment for their services. But how stands the matter in relation to Christ as indicated in this incident? Did the humble Galilæan fall down before the nobleman when he appeared? Not He; but thundered in his ears a reproof, "*Except ye see signs and wonders, ye will not believe.*" Did He accede to his request at once? No; He seemed to repel him, and hence the nobleman became more importunate. "*Sir, come down ere my child die.*" Thus He acted too with Nicodemus, the Syri-Phœnicean mother, and others. He showed no servile anxiety to win adherents to His cause. Did He expect acknowledgment for His services? No. It is remarkable that not only do you not find in any part of the history of Christ a case where He asked for compensation for His numerous services, but what is more striking still, you will not find one who dared to insult Him by making such an offer. Strange that this nobleman, with the wonted generosity of the East, did not suggest remuneration; but he saw a moral majesty sitting upon the brow of that poor Galilæan that repelled the idea.

A little incident like this brings out to me Jesus of Nazareth in sublime contrast to all the religious teachers of the world ancient and modern, heathen and Christian. He stands above them, high as the ever-burning stars above the flickering gaslights of our streets.

Another point that stands out in this narrative is—

IV —THAT A GENUINE CONFIDENCE IN CHRIST HAS ITS PROGRESSIVE GROWTH

We find faith in this nobleman in three distinct stages—

First: In leaving his home to meet Christ. Unless he had possessed some amount of confidence in the capability of Christ to heal his son, would he have left his dying boy and gone out in search of Him? There was faith in germ.

Secondly: In leaving Christ to return to his home. "*Jesus saith unto him, Go thy way; thy son liveth. And the man believed the word that Jesus had spoken, and he went his way.*" Up to this time he had not believed that Christ could cure his son unless He went to the spot. Now he believed in that: "*Go thy way; thy son liveth.*" It is quite conceivable that on his way home he might have some misgivings, some doubt, as to whether the cure had taken place or not. Still he believed.

Thirdly: In influencing at once his household. On meeting the servants who told him that his son was living, and inquiring the hour when he began to mend, he found that the fever left the son the very hour at which Jesus spoke the words, "*Thy son liveth.*"

Here was another stage in his faith. Its roots must have struck deeply with this intelligence. So strong was his faith now, that he converted the whole household. Faith begets faith. In truth, a man must believe before he can make believers.

Thus genuine faith is progressive; it has the blade, the ear, and the full corn in the ear, and the full corn can multiply as in the case of the nobleman's family.

Another point that stands out in this narrative is—

V —THAT TRUE PRAYER CAN BRING TO THE SUPPLIANT
SUPERNATURAL RELIEF

Here is the prayer: "*He besought Him that He would come down and heal his son,*" and after an apparent rebuff it is repeated, "*Sir, come down ere my child die.*" Here is the relief: "*Thy son liveth,*" and the relief is obviously supernatural. Who could doubt this miracle? "It was performed at several miles distance, upon a person whom He had never seen, and where, therefore, there was no shadow of pretence for saying there was collusion or imposture. It satisfied the father of the child, who left him at the point of death. It satisfied those who remained at home and saw how instantaneously he recovered; and it ought to satisfy us, who live in this distant age and quarter of the world, that Christ by Divine power wrought this miracle, although we have not been witnesses to its effects."

Now prayer wrought this supernatural result. Indeed I scarcely know whether I should use the word supernatural, for as nature far transcends the reach of the greatest intelligence, and as there are confessedly elements at work both in the world of matter and the world of mind, which none of our philosophers can explain or even detect, it may turn out that what we call supernatural is only natural after all, and that Christ now sent relief to this young man through some regular law that has yet to be discovered. Modern scientists aver that the doctrine of answers to prayers is an absurdity only to be entertained by the ignorant and superstitious of mankind. They, from the lofty heights to which their scientific genius has lifted them, regard with supercilious compassion, if not with contempt, those who believe in the efficacy of prayer. Whilst upon me, as a believer in the power of prayer, they look down with scorn, I, in all sincerity, look up to them with reverence and thanks. The *true* Church of Christ, which can only live in the sun of intelligence, as well as the great world at large, owe them a deep and ever-increasing debt of gratitude. Their discoveries have thrown floods of light upon the pages of our Bible, and most of the arts that bless and adorn the civilized world must be traced to the results of their inquiries. Albeit, I fail to discover their scientific wisdom in their scoffings at prayer. Do they say that the "established order of nature" stands immovably against the doctrine of the efficacy of human supplication? Then I ask, how much of nature has come under the scrutiny of their own observation? Is it a yard as compared with an acre, or an acre as compared with a yard? I care not which, but ask, May it not be that just in the area, whether large or small, lying outside their personal observation, there may be natural phenomena not in harmony with their ideas of the established order of things?

Moreover, on the assumption that there is an intelligent First Cause pervading all space and permeating all existences, the force of all forces, the spring of all activities, is it not to the last degree absurd and presumptuous to deny the possibility of answers to prayers? And still yet, I inquire, is not the physical condition of mankind always more or less dependent upon the ideas that influence them? Are not human ideas the germs of all human institutions and the mainspring of all human activities? If so, you have only to operate on man's ideas in order to affect his physical condition. Is there anything, therefore, absurd in supposing that God, through prayer, can or does influence human ideas? But why reason on the subject, when the Bible, whose authority I hold Divine, abounds both with the assurance and examples of the fact that the "effectual fervent prayer of a righteous man availeth much"?

Where, it has been asked, is the necessity for prayer, since the great God is too loving to require persuasion, too intelligent to require information concerning our wants? Can prayer make the Infinitely Merciful more kind, the Omniscient more intelligent? "God," says a modern author, "undoubtedly knows all our wants; but that is not sufficient; we must know them ourselves, and feel our need of having them supplied, for the supply to be a real benefit to us." We all know that the value of a gift increases in the same ratio as the power of the recipient to appreciate it. Suppose a physician gave some medicine to two persons, one of whom felt himself dying, and who came entreating help; the other, although in exactly the same condition, was unconscious of it, and took the medicine merely to honour the doctor. The bodies of both may perhaps be equally influenced, but will their minds? The one will depart profoundly grateful, but the other self-complacent at his own supposed kindness of disposition.

> "There is an eye that never sleeps
> Beneath the wing of night;
> There is an ear that never shuts
> When smile the beams of light;
> There is an arm that never tires
> When human strength gives way;
> There is a love that never fails
> When earthly loves decay.
> That eye is fixed on seraphs' throng,
> That ear is filled with angels' song;
> That arm upholds the world on high;

> That love is throned beyond the sky.
> But there's a power which man can wield
> When mortal aid is vain,
> That eye, that arm, that love to reach,
> That listening ear to gain ;
> That power is prayer, that soars on high,
> And feeds on bliss beyond the sky."

Another point that stands out in this narrative is—

VI —THAT GREAT TEMPORAL CALAMITIES OFTEN LEAD TO THE HIGHEST SPIRITUAL GOOD

The temporal affliction of this nobleman brought himself and whole family to Christ. It was simply trial that impelled him in the first place to go to Christ. Probably, all healing resources at his command he had tried with his dying son, and they had failed, and now he was driven from the natural to the supernatural. Nature could do no more for him; his only hope was that the Miraculous Worker of Whom he had heard might come to his relief. Trials often act thus. For this purpose they are sent. When prosperous men are reduced to pauperism, and strong men to physical infirmity, and men accustomed to society to a state of absolute lonelihood, moral reflection is stimulated, spiritual inquiries are started, questions are asked about the spiritual and eternal. As the material vanishes from the man the spiritual becomes closer ; as the temporal recedes the eternal presses on. Men in all ages can say, "It is good for me that I was afflicted; before I was afflicted, I went astray." There is meaning in what an old Athenian is reported to have said : "I should have been lost if I had not been lost." Want drove the prodigal back to his father's house. Affliction brought Manasseh back to the God of Israel. Affliction deals with men as the parent eagle with her young when she takes them from her nest where they have been sheltered and indulged, and bears them off on her wings, into mid-heaven, and shakes them off into immensity, there to struggle for themselves.

When men are stripped of all physical good their spirits often begin to struggle on their way towards the Great Fountain of Life. Well does Sir Walter Scott say : " There are those to whom a sense of religion has come in storm and tempest, and there are those whom it has summoned amid scenes of revelry and idle vanity ; there are those who have heard its 'still small voice,' amid rural leisure and placid contentment. But perhaps the knowledge which cometh not to err is most frequently impressed upon the mind during seasons of affliction, and tears are the softening showers which cause the seed of heaven to spring and take root in the human heart."

John 5:1-9

THE POOL OF BETHESDA; OR, THE WORLD IN MINIATURE

(*The Pool of Bethesda, the Healing of the Impotent Man, and our Lord's Discourse.—v. 1—47.*)

"After this (R. V. THESE THINGS) there was a feast of the Jews; and Jesus went up to Jerusalem. Now there is at (R. V. IN) Jerusalem by the sheep market (R. V. GATE) a pool, which is called in the Hebrew tongue Bethesda, having five porches. In these lay a great multitude of impotent folk (R. V. THEM THAT WERE SICK), of blind, halt, withered, waiting (R. V. OMITS FROM THE WORD "WAITING" TO END OF VERSE FOUR) for the moving of the water. For an angel went down at a certain season into the pool, and troubled the water: whosoever then first after the troubling of the water stepped in was made whole of whatsoever disease he had. And a certain man was there, which had an (R. V. BEEN IN HIS) infirmity thirty and eight years. When Jesus saw him lie (R. V. LYING), and knew that he had been now a long time in that case, He saith unto him, Wilt (R. V. WOULDST) thou be made whole? The impotent (R. V. SICK) man answered Him, Sir, I have no man, when the water is troubled, to put me into the pool: but while I am coming, another steppeth down before me. Jesus saith unto him, Rise, take up thy bed, and walk. And immediately (R. V. STRAIGHTWAY) the man was made whole, and took up his bed, and walked: and on the same day was the Sabbath" (R. V. NOW IT WAS THE SABBATH ON THAT DAY).

EXEGETICAL REMARKS.—Ver. 1.— "*After this there was a feast of the Jews.*" Literally, "after these things," implying a succession of events. "Here closes," says *Lange*, "the first great ministry of Jesus in Galilee." The "*feast*" here is a subject on which expositors are not agreed. The probability, however, is that it was the Passover, the second of the four Passovers in our Lord's ministry. The point is of no practical moment. "*And Jesus went up to Jerusalem.*" He went up from Capernaum, where He called Matthew. (Mark ii. 13, 14.) Jerusalem occupied an elevated position, not only in a moral, but in a local sense; it was 200 feet above the sea on the boundaries of Judæa.

Ver. 2 —"*Now there is at Jerusalem by the sheep market a pool, which is called in the Hebrew tongue Bethesda, having five porches.*" As John wrote A.D. 96, he wrote after Jerusalem had been destroyed; still there stood the "*pool.*" This pool is generally regarded as that walled enclosure near St. Stephen's Gate, and is some 360 feet long, 130 feet broad, and 70 feet deep. It is called Bethesda, meaning a house of mercy. "*Five porches*"—

these, it would seem, were covered recesses around the pool for the shelter of the sick.

Ver. 3.—"*In these lay a great multitude of impotent folk, of blind, halt, withered.*" "*Impotent,*" the enfeebled and emaciated. "*Blind*"—blindness in the East is far more general than here. In Cairo it is said that one of every five is either blind or has diseased eyes. Some of the greatest men we have ever had have been blind—Homer, Ossian, Milton, the world's illustrious poets, were blind. John Metcalf, the great engineer, who lived in 1788, was blind. One of our greatest statesmen, Fawcett, was blind. "*Halt*"—the crippled and lame. "*Withered*"—paralyzed. "*Waiting for the moving of the water.*" Though this clause and the next verse are not found in the great majority of the ancient manuscripts, and are rejected by many modern critics, there is strong internal evidence in favour of its genuineness. It seems almost necessary to give meaning to the seventh verse. The statement of *Ebrard*, that much is gained by excluding the verse from the text, he does not satisfactorily sustain. (See "Gospel History," p. 294.)

Ver. 4.—" *For an angel went down.*" It is not said that an angel was seen doing this. There is nothing absurd in this. It is spirit that governs matter, and gives to matter its virtues.

Ver. 5.—" *And a certain man was there, which had an infirmity thirty and eight years.*" This fact is stated, probably, to show the extremity of the case, and to exhibit the power and mercy of Christ.

Ver. 6.—" *When Jesus saw him lie, and knew that he had been now a long time in that case, He saith unto him, Wilt thou be made whole?*" This man, perhaps, had never seen Christ before, and yet He knows all about him, and puts to him the question, " *Wilt thou be made whole?*"

Christ never acts contrary to the volition of men.

Ver. 7.—" *The impotent man answered Him, Sir, I have no man, when the water is troubled, to put me into the pool: but while I am coming, another steppeth down before me.*" He was utterly friendless as well as diseased and powerless, and those around him were all heartless and selfish. They cared not for him so long as they could push their way into the healing pool.

Ver. 8.—" *Jesus saith unto him, Rise, take up thy bed, and walk.*" He had no need to help him into the water, He could effect the cure by His mere volition, without any instrumentality whatever.

HOMILETICS

The remarkable incident here recorded may be legitimately and profitably used as an illustration of the *great world of mankind*. Indeed, in it you have the world in miniature. Looking at it in this light we observe—

I —THAT THE HUMAN WORLD IS GREATLY AFFLICTED

At this pool we have a great multitude of " *impotent folk*" lying, " *blind, halt, withered,*" &c. What was seen at Bethesda may be seen everywhere throughout the vast population of the earth. Men are everywhere in suffering—witness battle-fields, slavery, hospitals, prisons, &c. &c. Suffering is the background of the great picture of human life. The world's music is in the minor key. There is a wail in all its undertones; its history is tragic in the extreme. Two things should ever be remembered in relation to human suffering—

First: It is often the effect of sin. We say often, we could not say always. Human pains perhaps generally have their root in wrong. The connection between sin and suffering is a benevolent arrangement. To quench hell as long as sin reigns would be an injury to the creation.

Secondly: It is sometimes the means of holiness. It acts in some cases as the physician's curative cup and the Father's chastening rod.

Looking at the incident as a picture of mankind, we observe—

II —THAT THE HUMAN WORLD HAS ITS ALLEVIATING ELEMENTS

These suffering multitudes were at Bethesda—the house of mercy. Perhaps the waters in this pool had, like many waters, medicinal virtues, or perhaps healing power was given to them by the descending angel. In either case we have the fact in connection with alleviating elements. The world is indeed a Bethesda. Healing waters flow at the feet of every sufferer. What are they?

First: The medicinal properties of the earth. Science has discovered in the mineral, the vegetable, and animal kingdoms, elements to mitigate and remove for a time the diseases and pains of suffering men.

Secondly: The soothing influences of nature. There is much in the bright sky, the green fields, the wooded hills, the yellow shore, and the blue wave, the beauty of the garden, the grandeur of the forest, the music of the river, and the chorus of the groves, to allay the anguish of our suffering nature.

Thirdly: The ministry of social love. Corrupt as the world is, the fountain of its affections is not dried up, its healing streams circulate through all circles; kind words, loving looks, and tender hands of sympathy are alleviating forces ever at work.

Fourthly: The blessed Gospel of Christ. This, indeed, is the great panacea, this is the sovereign balm for every wound. Such are some of the alleviating elements of life, some of the healing waters that ripple at our feet.

Looking at it in this light, we observe—

III —THAT THE HUMAN WORLD IS PRE-EMINENTLY SELFISH

At the side of this pool there was one man who had had an infirmity for thirty-eight years, and amongst the crowd who seem to have gone there year after year he had found no one to help him: " *While I am coming, another steppeth down.*" One might have thought that if they were too selfish to help him before they were cured themselves, that on their return from the healing waters they would have done so. But no, each cared for himself. Sad picture this of the human world! Every man for himself! Selfishness is not only a regard for our own interest, but a disregard for the interest of others. Selfishness is *injustice*. He who is taken up entirely with himself keeps back powers which should be employed in the service of others. Selfishness is *impiety*. The selfish man makes self his god: he is at once the centre and circumference of his own activity. Selfishness is *misery*. All the fiendish passions which are the furies of hell spring from it.

Looking at it in this light, we observe—

IV —THAT THE HUMAN WORLD HAS A GLORIOUS DELIVERER

There was One Who appeared now amongst the sufferers, Who said to the impotent man, " *Arise, take up thy bed, and walk.*" Three remarks are suggested concerning this Deliverer—

First: He cures the greatest of all human sufferers. This

was a man afflicted for no less than thirty-eight years—a whole generation had come and gone during the period of his affliction. "Christ is able to save to the uttermost."

Secondly: He cures by virtue of His own word. *"Take up thy bed."* These omnific words carried with them the curative virtue. Without the intervention of any means the man became hale and strong at once. He took up the little pallet on which his suffering body had been wont to lay, and walked forth in manly vigour.

Thirdly: He cures in concurrence with the will of the patient. *"Wilt thou be made whole?"* Christ does not outrage our freedom. He asks us if we will be saved. He says to each, Wilt thou have thy guilt, thy ignorance, thy misery removed? If thou consentest, the work is done; if not, thou art left to suffer and to die.

Blessed be God, this glorious Deliverer is still in our suffering world. To each He says, *"Wilt thou be made whole?"*

John 5:10-13

RELIGIOUS BIGOTRY AND DIVINE PHILANTHROPY

"The Jews therefore (R. V. SO THE JEWS) said unto him that was cured, It is the Sabbath day: it is not lawful for thee to carry (R. V. TAKE UP) thy bed. He answered them, He that made me whole, the same said unto me, Take up thy bed, and walk. Then asked they him, What (R. V. WHO IS THE) man is that which said unto thee, Take up thy bed, and walk? And (R. V. BUT) he that was healed wist not Who it was: for Jesus had conveyed Himself away, a multitude being in that place."

EXEGETICAL REMARKS.—Ver. 10.— *"The Jews therefore said unto him that was cured, It is the Sabbath day: it is not lawful for thee to carry thy bed."* "In such cases the matter goes quickly through fanatics, informers, and subordinates to the chiefs. Here the hierarchical chiefs already seem to speak; according to Meyer and Tholuck, the Sanhedrists. Yet it is possible that the matter only gradually reached them. At first they attack only the man himself for his carrying, which was the most palpable."—*Lange.* *"Not lawful."* It was against the Jewish law to carry burdens on the Sabbath (Exod. xxxi. 13—17; Numbers xv. 32—36; Nehemiah xiii. 15 —19; Jeremiah xvii. 21).

Ver. 11.—*"He answered them, He that made me whole, the same said unto me, Take up thy bed, and walk."*

His answer implies that the Being Who had the power to heal him had the authority to command him. He felt that the Divinity that had cured him was superior to all ceremonial institutions.

Ver. 12.—*"Then asked they him, What man is that which said unto thee, Take up thy bed, and walk?"* *"What man?"* Who is the *man?"* The language seems to breathe a contemptuous spirit.

Ver. 13.—*"And he that was healed wist not Who it was: for Jesus had conveyed Himself away, a multitude being in that place."* Alford renders the last clause, "Jesus escaped his notice, a multitude being in the place." The idea is,—He slipped quietly out of the crowd that had gathered about Him.

HOMILETICS

In these verses we have a specimen of two things—*religious bigotry and Divine philanthropy.* We have here—

I RELIGIOUS BIGOTRY

This is illustrated in the conduct of these Jews in relation to this cured man. Religious bigotry is—

First: Always punctilious. It lives in words and rituals, it sacrifices the "spirit" to the "letter." It is very true that there was a law prohibiting the carrying of burdens on the Sabbath, but the spirit of the Sabbatic institution was that of universal benevolence. Christ taught that *true Sabbath-keeping was well-doing.** He who neglects a work of mercy on the Sabbath violates that holy day. The bigot is always quoting words, defending creeds, and observing rites. Religious bigotry is—

Secondly: Always heartless. Instead of rejoicing at seeing the poor man, who had been thirty-eight years a cripple, able to walk and to carry his pallet, they seemed to exult that they had caught a transgressor of their law. Bigotry eats up the humanity of men: nothing is more cruel. Not only has it tortured in all ages the best of men, but it transfixed the Son of Man Himself to a cross. "We have a law, and by our law He is to die." Religious bigotry is—

Thirdly: Always inquisitorial. *"What man is that which said unto thee, Take up thy bed, and walk?"* They did not ask, Who *healed* thee?—they had not sufficient humanity for that—but, Who bade thee take thy bed? We want to find the lawless profaner out in order to punish him according to our law. Bigotry always prys into the concerns of others; it built and sustained for ages the infernal Inquisition.

> "The bigot theologian—in minute
> Distinctions skilled, and doctrines unreduced
> To practice ; in debate how loud ! how long !
> How dexterous ! in Christian love how cold !
> His vain conceits were orthodox alone.
> The immutable and heavenly truth revealed
> By God, was nought to him : he had an art,
> A kind of hellish charm, that made the lips
> Of truth speak falsehood : to his liking turned
> The meaning of the text : made trifles seem
> The marrow of salvation : to a word,
> A name, a sect, that sounded in the ear
> And to the eye so many letters showed,
> But did no more—gave value infinite :
> Proved still his reasoning best, and his belief
> Though propped on fancies, wild as madmen's dreams
> Most rational, most scriptural, most sound :
> With mortal heresy denouncing all
> Who in his arguments could see no force."—*Robert Pollok.*

*See an article on this subject in my *Gospel of Matthew.*

We have here—

II —DIVINE PHILANTHROPY

Here in the work of Christ we have a glorious specimen of Divine philanthropy.

First: It is healing. It restored this "*impotent*" man, who had been lying at the pool of Bethesda for well-nigh forty years. Divine philanthropy does not expend itself in sighs of compassion and expressions of love: it works. It works amongst the suffering, and works with a power to restore the worst of cases. "Christ is able to save to the uttermost," &c.

Secondly: It is unrestricted. It is tied down by no letter or ceremony. All days and places are alike to it. Love is above all law; it is always lawful to do good. There is a thing called philanthropy on earth that is restricted by sects, bound by rules, and operates only through certain organizations: this is not the Divine thing. The Divine thing is as free as the air, and all-encompassing as the heavens.

Thirdly: It is commanding. "*He that made me whole, the same said unto me, Take up thy bed, and walk.*" The man obeyed, though he knew not Who it was that bade him. The love that restored him became a sovereign within him. No power has such a commanding influence over us as the power of love. This man knew as he walked forth on the Sabbath-day with his bed on his back that he set at defiance the prejudice of the people around him; yet love bound him to it and made him invincible. "The love of Christ constraineth us."

Fourthly: It is unpretending. "*Jesus had conveyed Himself away, a multitude being in that place.*" Crowds were about Him at this time. The knowledge of the fact would in all probability have evoked their hosannas. All this was distasteful to Christ, hence He glided away; so silently withdrew that the man lost sight of Him at once. Divine philanthropy courts not applause, and seeks no reward but in the good it does.

CONCLUSION. Such is Divine philanthropy, the "new commandment" Christ brought into the world. Would that it inspired all who call themselves by His name, and profess to do His work!

John 5:14, 15

ADVANTAGES OF ATTENDING THE TRUE CHURCH

"Afterward Jesus findeth him in the temple, and said unto him, Behold, thou art made whole: sin no more, lest a worse thing come unto (R. V. BEFALL) thee. The man departed (R. V. WENT AWAY), and told the Jews that it was Jesus, which had made him whole."

EXEGETICAL REMARKS.—Ver. 14.— "*Afterward.*" The term would indicate that it was at some period subsequent to the healing of the impotent man recorded in the preceding verses. "*Jesus findeth him in the temple.*" Perhaps the physical recovery he had experienced led him to religious reflection and worship. The temple must have been a strange place to him, for he had been a paralytic for thirty-eight long years: there would be a sublimity in his impressions and a freshness in his devotions. The temple was a fit place for the expression of a grateful heart. Hezekiah hastened to the temple to praise God for his recovery. Jesus resorted to the temple, and thus He sanctioned the ordinance of public worship. "*And said unto him, Behold, thou art made whole.*" Christ recognized him, knew that his cure was complete, and declares it for his encouragement and gratitude. "*Sin no more*"—language implying that his affliction was the fruit of some sin. Intemperance, impurity, inordinate passions, often afflict the body. "*Lest a worse thing come unto thee.*" Worse than thirty-eight years' suffering ! Thus a moral relapse is a terrible thing. However great our sufferings may be, there is something worse if we sin.

Ver. 15. "*The man departed, and told the Jews.*" The idea that some attach to this, that he went to the temple to betray his Benefactor as a Sabbath-breaker, is far too improbable to be entertained. His proclamation was dictated, no doubt, by a heart overflowing with gratitude. At the time he knew not the Author of his restoration. "*He that was healed wist not Who it was.*" But now he is made aware of it, and declares his Restorer. He told the Jews that it was Jesus, which had made him whole.

HOMILETICS

We take this incident to illustrate the *advantages of attending the true Church.* Whilst millions in this age neglect public worship altogether, those who attend to it are not sufficiently impressed with its obligation and advantages. Observe—

I —IN THE TEMPLE THIS MAN MET WITH HIS MERCIFUL DELIVERER

It was because he was in the temple Christ found him. Christ met His disciples in public worship. He has promised to do so. "Where two or three are gathered together in My name, there am I in the midst of them." "In all places where I record My name, I will come unto thee and bless thee." This old promise has received millions of realizations in every age, and is still being fulfilled in all the true Churches of Christendom every week.

> "He likes the tents of Jacob well,
> But still in Zion loves to dwell."

Now is it nothing to meet with the Great Deliverer; to meet with One Who can dispel all ignorance, correct all errors, chase away all sorrows, forgive all sins, overcome all enemies, and fill the soul with "joy unspeakable and full of glory" ?

II —IN THE TEMPLE THIS MAN RECEIVED DIVINE ADMONITIONS

Christ speaks to him and says, "*Sin no more, lest a worse thing come unto thee.*" What did he learn here ? (1.) That *sin was the cause of his affliction.* (2.) That he was *liable to fall into sin again.* (3.) That if *he fell into sin again, he would be worse off than ever.* These were solemn lessons—lessons of vital moment, lessons which every man needs to learn and ponder well. Such admonitions as these are addressed to congregations in every true Church. Who but God can tell the advantage of having those things proclaimed, enforced, and reiterated, Sunday after Sunday in England ?

III —IN THE TEMPLE THIS MAN LEARNT HIS OBLIGATION TO CHRIST

" *The man departed, and told the Jews that it was Jesus, which had made him whole.*" He did not know this until he went to the temple, and met with Christ. In the House of God men learn their obligations to Him Who loved them, and gave Himself for them.

> "Spirit ! whose life-sustaining presence fills
> An ocean, central depths by man untried.
> Thou for thy worshippers hast sanctified
> All place, all time ! The silence of the hills
> Breathes veneration ; founts and choral rills
> Of thee are murmuring : to its inmost glade
> The living forest with Thy whisper thrills,
> And there is holiness on every shade.
> Yet must the thoughtful soul of man invest
> With dearer consecration, those pure fanes,
> Which sever'd from all sounds of earth's unrest,
> Hear naught but suppliant or adoring strains,
> Rise heavenwards. Ne'er may rock or cave possess
> Their claim on human hearts, to solemn tendencies."
>
> *Mrs. Hemans.*

John 5:16, 17

CHRIST'S VINDICATION OF HIMSELF

"And therefore (R. V. FOR THIS CAUSE) did the Jews persecute Jesus, and sought to slay Him, (R. V. OMITS) because He had done (R. V. DID) these things on the Sabbath day. But Jesus answered them, My Father worketh hitherto (R. V. EVEN UNTIL NOW), and I work."

EXEGETICAL REMARKS.—Ver. 16.— "*And therefore did the Jews persecute Jesus.*" "For this cause the Jews persecuted Jesus." The expression is supposed to refer to a judicial arraignment. It would seem that there were minor Sanhedrims, exercising jurisdiction in Judæa, consisting sometimes of twenty, sometimes of seven, sometimes of three. Probably one of the smaller Sanhedrims were sitting in order to determine how best to put this Sabbath-breaker to death. "*And sought to slay Him.*" These words are struck out by the best critics, although they are retained in the

18th verse. "*Because He had done these things on the Sabbath day.*" "*What things?*" (1.) The healing of the invalid on the Sabbath. (2.) The commanding the healed man to carry his bed. It was directed in the law of Moses that a Sabbath-breaker should be put to death. (Exod. xxxi. 15 ; xxxv. 2.) But was a work of mercy on the Sabbath a violation of the fourth commandment ? Besides, He was Lord of the Sabbath.

Ver. 17.—"*But Jesus answered them, My Father worketh hitherto, and I work.*" "My Father worketh until now, and I work also." "A difficult answer," says *Lange*. "It undoubtedly asserts :—(1.) Christ's exaltation above the Sabbath law, like Mark ii. 28. (2.) The conformity of His work to the law of the Sabbath : in other words, His fulfilling of the Sabbath law—Matt. xii. 12. (3.) The relation of the working of God to His own working, as its pattern—ver. 20. (4.) His working out from God and with God, which makes their charge a charge against God Himself—ver. 19. The last idea has special emphasis."

HOMILETICS

Before studying the way in which the Great Son of God met this charge, it may be well for us to glance a moment at that *religious bigotry* which we just touched upon a few pages back. We have said that bigotry is heartless, punctilious, inquisitorial. It is further suggested by these words that it is *arrogant*. Here are a few ignorant men daring to sit in judgment upon One Who had manifested to their eyes the Divine attributes of mercy and power. Ignorance sitting in judgment upon wisdom, vice sitting in judgment upon virtue, human frailty upon superhuman power.

Christ met this charge by pleading the example of His Father : " *My Father worketh hitherto, and I work.*" Observe (1.) *God works*. He is essentially active, and His activity explains not only the existence but all the operations of the universe. God's works are *original, wise, mighty, boundlessly varied*, and *ever beneficent*. (2.) God works on *Sabbath days as well as on other days*. Were He to pause in His activity the heavenly orbs would stop in their courses, the air become stagnant, the ocean still, and all nature motionless as death itself. He never slumbers or sleeps. "He fainteth not, neither is weary." Christ's words imply two things in relation to God's *unremitting operation*.

I —THAT IT IS RIGHT

Christ pleads it as a justification for what He had just accomplished on the Sabbath. It is said that God "rested on the seventh day." But inactivity is not rest, non-working is not Sabbath-keeping. God works on the Sabbath, and therefore working on the Sabbath is right. The Infinite cannot do wrong. What He does is right because He does it ; there is no law of right outside of Himself. His actions are the expressions, the revelations, and the laws of absolute right. Well-doing is Sabbath-keeping. Another thing which is implied in Christ's words concerning God's *unremitting operation* is—

II —THAT IT IS EXEMPLARY

" *My Father worketh hitherto, and I work.*" What He does I am bound to do ; He is my Model. We are all commanded to be imitators of God, to be partakers of the Divine nature, to be "holy, even as He is holy." How can the finite imitate the Infinite ? Not in natural attributes, but in spirit and aim ; and though we cannot do what He does, we can have the spirit that inspires Him in all His procedure, viz. *love.* He is beneficent in all His operations, and so should we be. He pours tides of happiness on His universe on Sabbath-days as well as other days, and on that day our grand object should be to bless our fellow-men. Again, we repeat, *Sabbath-keeping is well-doing.*

John 5:18-31

CHRIST'S VINDICATION OF HIMSELF AGAINST THE CHARGE OF BLASPHEMY. (1.) THE NATURE OF HIS AUTHORITY

" Therefore the Jews sought the more to kill Him, because He not only had broken the Sabbath, but said also that God was His Father, making Himself equal with God," &c.

EXEGETICAL REMARKS.—Ver. 18.— " *Therefore* (R. V. FOR THIS CAUSE) *the Jews sought the more to kill Him, because He not only had broken* (R. V. BRAKE) *the Sabbath, but said also that God was His Father* (R. V. CALLED GOD HIS OWN FATHER), *making Himself equal with God."* πατέρα ἴδιον. It means that God was His own Father. The Jews considered that this claim meant His making Himself equal with God, and that therefore He was a blasphemer. Christ does not deny their interpretation, but proceeds to vindicate His claim to the high distinction. In this they discovered another reason for putting Him to death : for the law authorized the infliction of capital punishment not only for Sabbath-breaking, but for blasphemy as well.

Ver. 19.—" *Then answered Jesus and said unto them, Verily, verily, I say unto you, The Son can do nothing of Himself."* Christ here denies all action independent of His Father. He neither originates or pursues a course of conduct either in rivalry or apart from the Father. Their spirit and aim are identical. *" But what He seeth the Father do* (R. V. DOING): *for what things,"* &c. The meaning is, the Son doeth the same in the same way, or after the same fashion. Can there be a stronger assertion of His equality with the Father than this ? I see not how, after language of this kind, I can reject the Divinity of Christ, and not denounce His untruthfulness and pro-

fanity. If I hold His moral excellence I must hold His Divinity.

Ver. 20.—" *For the Father loveth the Son."* φιλεῖ is a word which denotes rather affection for the person than for the character. *" And sheweth Him all things that Himself doeth."* Love is ever communicative and confiding ; it has an instinct to reveal its deepest thoughts and aims to its object. *" And He will shew Him greater works than these."* "And greater works than these shall He shew Him."—*Alford.* What are the *" greater works"* ? Those undoubtedly referred to in the subsequent verses (21, 22) : those which *Stier* calls *" God's Regalia."*

Ver. 21.—" *For as the Father raiseth up the dead, and quickeneth them."* "One act in two stages, the resurrection of the body, and the restoration of life to it. This surely is the Father's absolute prerogative, if He have any." *" Even so the Son quickeneth whom He will."* "Not only doing the same Divine act, but doing it as the result of His own will, even as the Father does it. This statement is of immense importance in relation to the miracles of Christ, distinguishing them from similar miracles of prophets and apostles, who as human instruments were employed to perform supernatural actions, while Christ did all— as the Father's commissioned servant indeed, but—in the exercise of His own absolute right of action."—*Brown.*

Ver. 22.—" *For the Father judgeth*

no man (R. V. NEITHER DOTH THE
FATHER JUDGE ANY), *but hath committed* (R. V. GIVEN) *all judgment unto
the Son.*" Christ says here, Neither
doth the Father judge any man, but
hath committed all judgment, administration unto His Son.

Ver. 23.—"*That all men should* (R. V.
MAY) *honour the Son, even as they honour
the Father.*" "Theology of the Divine
administration. The Father manifests Himself in the acts of the Son,
because He manifests Himself in the
being of the Son. And the acts of the
Son unfold themselves in the total
works of salvation and judgment, to
the end that the Son may be honoured
and glorified as the Father, in order
that the Father may be glorified in
Him." "*He that honoureth not the
Son,*" &c. "Spoken most especially
against the Sanhedrists."—*Lange.*

Ver. 24.—"*Verily, verily, I say
unto you, He that heareth My word,
and believeth on Him that sent Me,
hath everlasting* (R. V. ETERNAL) *life,*"
&c. "*Verily, verily.*" St. Augustine
says these words were at that time an
oath. The idea of the verse is, that he
who accepts My doctrines, and trusts
Him Who sent Me, shall realize his
well-being for ever. "*And shall not
come into condemnation* (R. V. COMETH
NOT INTO JUDGMENT) ; *but is* (R. V.
HATH) *passed from* (R. V. OUT OF) *death
unto life.*" Faith in Him as the Messenger of the Almighty Father effects
this glorious transition.

Ver. 25.—"*Verily, verily, I say unto
you, The hour is coming* (R. V. COMETH),
*and now is, when the dead shall hear
the voice of the Son of God : and they
that hear shall live.*" The death here
evidently refers not to the corporeally
dead, as in the 29th verse, but to the
spiritually dead. For it is said, "*The
hour is coming, and now is.*" The soul-
quickening era of the Gospel has come
when all who will believe on Me, the
Son of God, "*shall live.*" "The present
manifestation of Christ's vivifying
power in the spiritual resurrection is
stated in contrast with the future
manifestation in the general resurrection. The hour was coming so far as
the Christian dispensation truly began
with the gift of Pentecost : but it was

already while Christ openly taught
among men."—*Westcott.*

Ver. 26.—"*For as the Father hath
life in Himself ; so hath He given* (R. V.
EVEN SO GAVE HE) *to the Son to have
life in Himself.*" What do these words
import but this—That the Eternal
Father, the Absolute Fountain of life,
has endowed Christ with a life with
which to quicken humanity ? "As
Thou hast given Him power, that He
may give eternal life to as many as
believe on Him." The "*logos*" is life.
He is *the* life, John xi. 25. The eternal
life, 1 John v. 20. The life which is
the essence of God. He is the Com-
municator of life, John i. 54.

Ver. 27.—"*And hath given Him*
(R. V. HE GAVE HIM) *authority to execute
judgment also, because He is the Son
of man.*" "This seems to confirm the
last remark that what Christ had probably in view was the indwelling of
the Son's essential life in humanity
as the great theatre and medium of
Divine display in both the great departments of His work—life-giving
and judgment. The appointment of
a judge in our own nature is one of
the most august and beautiful arrangements of Divine wisdom in redemption."—*Dr. Brown.*

Vers. 28, 29.—"*Marvel not at this :*"
—that is, at the appointment of the
Son as the great Judge of humanity—
"*for the hour is coming* (R. V. COMETH),
in the which all that are in the graves
(R. V. THE TOMBS) *shall hear His voice,
and shall come forth,*" &c. This points
to a period often referred to in the
sacred volume, Dan. xii. 2 ; John xi.
43, 44 ; 1 Cor. xv. 20—58 ; Rev. xxii.
15. We subjoin the following remarks
from Van Doren :—"The same person,
but not the identical body, will be
raised (*Locke*). Cannot literally be
the same body. (1.) Science shows
that in seven years the human body
has so totally changed that not one
atom remains : so that a man seventy
years of age has had ten bodies. (2.)
Shows that immediately after death
the various particles begin to liberate
themselves, and mix up as parts of
other bodies. (3.) In Oriental lands
the dead are burned, not buried, and
in process of combustion the greater

portions of the body pass off in gases, to mingle with other forms of existence. (4.) In the case of cannibals the parts of the body eaten assimilate with and become integral portions of other human bodies. St. Paul says, 'Thou sowest not that body that shall be.' What the Bible calls the resurrection body takes place at death (*Bush, Maurice*). In the buried body exists an indestructible germ (*Origen, Watts, Drew*). An immortal bone (*Ancient Jews and others*). A monad (*Leibnitz, Goethe*). In the spirit lies an ideal form of the body " (*Lange*).

Vers. 30, 31.—" *I can of Mine own*

self (R. V. MYSELF) *do nothing : as I hear, I judge : and My judgment is just* " (R. V. RIGHTEOUS), &c. " *I can of*—or :from (ἀφ)—*Mine own self do nothing* "—apart from, or in rivalry of, the Father, and in any separate interest of My own. " *As I hear, I judge : and My judgment is just,*" &c. " My judgments are all anticipated in the bosom of My Father, to which I have immediate access, and by Me they are only responded to and reflected. They cannot therefore err since I live for one end only, to carry into effect the will of Him that sent Me."—*Dr. Brown.*

HOMILETICS

The passage we have under consideration constitutes a part of our *Saviour's defence against the charge of blasphemy.* The whole defence has something like a logical arrangement. In the first part, extending over the whole of the verses before us, He states the *nature* of His authority; in the second part, running on to the end of the chapter, He points to the *proof* of His authority. Under the first head He claims five things : A special *unity* with the Father, the special *affection* of the Father, the special *revelations* of the Father, the special *prerogatives* of the Father, and special *devotion* to the Father.

Christ in this paragraph is vindicating Himself against the charge of blasphemy, and in His vindication He points both to the *nature* and *proof* of His authority. All the homiletical remarks that we have to make on the verses now before us may be treated under the general head of—

THE NATURE OF HIS AUTHORITY

And in connection with this subject He claims several things—

First : A special unity with the Father. " *Then answered Jesus and said unto them, Verily, verily, I say unto you, The Son can do nothing of Himself, but what He seeth the Father do.*" The solemn asseveration ἀμὴν ἀμὴν λέγω ὑμῖν occurs no less than three times in this very discourse, and must be regarded as expressing absolute certainty. The subject of the asseveration is unity with the Absolute Father, a unity which is something more than a unity of sympathy, will, action ; it is a unity of *being.* If the Son does nothing but what the Father does, nothing in the universe of matter or mind, and the Son does all that the Father does, since the activity of God is infinite, and since there cannot be two infinities, the natures must be one. Hence we find throughout the New Testament the same absolute attributes, the same governing and redeeming works ascribed alike to the Father and the Son. The charge of blasphemy which the Jews brought against Christ for claiming equality, He, instead of disclaiming, declares, with solemn emphasis. As Christ claims equality with God, if He is not God He is untruthful, dishonest, blasphemous, and must be discarded as the true moral leader of the race. I cannot reject the Divinity of His nature and hold the holiness of His character. He claims—

Secondly : The special affection of the Father. *" The Father loveth the Son."* Observe (1.) The Father loves. He is not a Being of cold intellectuality, He is a Being of infinite affection. Whilst He is wise in counsel, He is tender in love. The Creator of the universe is a loving Being, and His love is the fontal Source of all life and activities. "God is love." Whilst some scientists represent the Almighty as an infinite stoic, hard as iron, unbending as fate, and certain religionists as capricious and malevolent, the Gospel reveals Him as LOVE.

> "O love, the one Sun ! O love, the one Sea !
> What life has begun that breathes not in Thee ?
> Thy rays have no limit, Thy waves have no shore,
> Thou giv'st without measure to worlds evermore."

(2.) The chief object of the Father's love is the Son. His heart is centred on Him. *" This is My beloved Son, in Whom I am well pleased."* *" The Father loveth the Son."* But does He not love all ? Yea, but the Son especially. The Son is greater, better, nearer to Himself than all else in the universe. If the Infinite Father's heart is on the Son, let our hearts centre on the same Object, and then we in heart shall be one with the Great God. He claims—

Thirdly : Special revelations from the Father. *" He showeth Him all things that Himself doeth."* Communicativeness is the instinct of love. The deepest things of the heart we reveal to the chief object of our affection. The Infinite Father keeps no secret from Christ. (1.) All the great things that the Father has already done the Son knows. He has a complete insight into all the operations of the Infinite throughout immensity. Christ knows the universe thoroughly. Let us learn of Him. (2.) The greater things that the Father has yet to do, the Son will also know. *" Greater works than these."* "The works of the Lord are great, sought out of all them that have pleasure in them." What He has already done is great, incomprehensibly great, but what He has to do in the future is greater still. *" Greater works."* What the Eternal has done in the ages that are past may be only a faint indication of what He will do throughout the æons that are to dawn. Christ knows all. But perhaps the *" greater works"* mentioned here are the greater works in human history referred to in the following verses. And at these works men will *" marvel."* He claims—

Fourthly : Special prerogatives of the Father. Christ here seems to claim several prerogatives of the Father.

(1.) Power to awaken the dead according to His own will. "*As the Father raiseth up the dead, and quickeneth them; even so the Son quickeneth whom He will.*" Who but God can quicken life? An insect may destroy the majestic cedar of Lebanon, but God alone can restore the drooping flower.

This power Christ claims. The Son does the same as the Father—does it without restraint, control, or direction. "*Whom He will.*" Does it, "according to His own good pleasure." The worse death is the death of souls, and the most important work is the quickening of dead souls. This Christ does. And this is a Divine prerogative (Rom. iv. 17).

(2.) Authority to judge humanity and to receive its worship. "*The Father judgeth no man, but hath committed all judgment unto the Son: that all men should honour the Son, even as they honour the Father,*" &c. When it is denied that the Father judgeth men it is done in the same way in which, in verse 19, chap. vii. 17, it is denied that the Son can do anything of Himself—that is, in isolation from the Father. Christ is the Judge, Matt. xxv.; Acts xvii. 31. But whilst He has authority to judge the world, He has also authority to receive its worship. "*That all men should honour the Son, even as they honour the Father.*" Worship is here claimed by Christ. "Let all the angels of God worship Him." He is worshipped in heaven. "Blessing, and honour, and glory, and power," &c. "Every knee shall bow to Him of things in heaven and things on earth," &c. &c.

(3.) Capacity for redeeming humanity from condemnation and death. "*Verily, verily, I say unto you, He that heareth My word, and believeth on Him that sent Me, hath everlasting life, and shall not come into condemnation; but is passed from death unto life.*" Observe (*a*) That human souls are in a state of moral guiltiness and death. Their guilt is a matter of universal consciousness, and their death is proved by their insensibility to the beauty of holiness and the claims of God. (*b*) That Christ's word has the power to effect the restoration of human souls. "*He that heareth My word, and believeth on Him that sent Me,*" &c. And again, "The hour is coming, and now is, when the dead shall hear the voice of the Son of God, and they that hear shall live." Faith in Him is the soul-restoring power. All that the greatest of human or angelic teachers can do is to communicate information. Christ alone clears away guilt, and breathes new life—a life that is everlasting.

(4.) The possession of absolute life and judicial administration. "*As the Father hath life in Himself; so hath He given to the Son to have life in Himself; and hath given Him authority to execute judgment also, because He is the Son of man.*" Life in Himself, unoriginative, independent, eternal. "Who only hath immortality, dwelling in the light," &c. &c. Such life is the life of God, and

God only. Then judicial administration, too, is His: "*to execute judgment.*" * Not merely to judge, but to administer justice. Is not this a Divine prerogative? In His judicial capacity He will raise the dead and determine the destinies of mankind. "*Marvel not at this: for the hour is coming, in the which all that are in the graves shall hear His voice, and shall come forth.*" In verse 25 a spiritual resurrection was referred to.

There are at least three theories of the resurrection. One is the coming forth of the body, the very body that was committed to the grave. This idea is at once against science and against Scripture: the sameness between the buried and the resurrection body is not the sameness in particle and proportion, but the sameness in figure and function. Another idea is, the resurrection body is something that comes out of some indestructible "germ," or "bone," or "monad," which lay hid in the buried frame. And the other idea is that the resurrection body is the ideal form of the body which lies in the spirit, and goes out of it at death. Bush, Maurice, and others, regard the present body as the grave of the spirit, and that when the spirit departs in death it goes off to the spiritual world in a spiritual body. Without canvassing these theories, or pronouncing on their merits, the verse brings under notice four subjects: (*a*) The Resurrection *period.* "*The hour is coming.*" It is not something past: it awaits us. (*b*) The Resurrection *power.* "*His voice.*" This is the quickening force. (*c*) The Resurrection *subjects.* "*All that are in the graves.*" Not a class, not a generation, but "*all.*" (*d*) The Resurrection *issues.* "*They that have done good, unto the resurrection of life; and they that have done evil, unto the resurrection of damnation.*" Character, not creed, determines destiny. Well-doing—heaven: ill-doing—hell.

John 5:31-47

CHRIST'S VINDICATION OF HIMSELF AGAINST THE CHARGE OF BLASPHEMY. (2.) THE PROOF OF HIS AUTHORITY

"If I bear witness of Myself, My witness is not true. There is another that beareth witness of Me; and I know that the witness which He witnesseth of Me is true," &c.

EXEGETICAL REMARKS.—It must be kept in mind that Christ, from the 19th verse of this chapter, is vindicating Himself against the charge of blasphemy. His defence is logically arranged. It consists, first, of the *nature* of His authority, ver. 19—29; and, secondly, a statement of the *proof* of His authority. This statement extends from verse 30 to the end of the chapter, and this is the paragraph we have now to notice.

Ver. 32.—"*There* (R. V. IT) *is another that beareth witness of Me; and I know that the witness which He witnesseth of Me is true.*" Who is this? None other than the Father Himself, as appears in the sequel. He was well

* See Homily on these words at end of volume.

assured that the witness of His Father was true.

Ver. 33.—"*Ye sent* (R. V. HAVE SENT) *unto John, and he bare* (R. V. HE HATH BORNE) *witness unto the truth.*" In all probability Christ here refers to the deputation which the rulers sent to the Baptist, chap. iii. 26, and from whom they received a testimony concerning Christ.

Ver. 34.—"*But I receive not testimony from man*" (R. V. THE WITNESS WHICH I RECEIVE IS NOT FROM MAN). This does not mean that Christ rejected or undervalued the testimony of John, but that He did not need it, He was independent of it. "*But* (R. V. HOWBEIT) *these things I say, that ye might be saved.*" He referred to John's testimony, not for His own sake, but for theirs. They believed in John, and his testimony would tend to their salvation.

Ver. 35.—"*He was a burning and a shining light*" (R. V. THE LAMP THAT BURNETH AND SHINETH). "He was a lamp burning and shining. Christ is never called by the humble word here applied to John—a light-bearer, studiously used to distinguish him from his Master, but ever The Light (τὸφῶς) in the most absolute sense."—*Brown*. The Baptist was a lamp kindled by another antithetical to φως. "*And ye were willing for a season to rejoice in his light.*" There is a play of irony here referring to the hollow delight with which his testimony excited them.

Ver. 36.—"*But I have greater witness* (R. V. THE WITNESS THAT I HAVE IS GREATER) *than that of John: for the works which the Father hath given Me to finish,*" &c. He means the testimony of His miracles was the testimony of His Father Himself Who had sent Him.

Ver. 37.—"*And the Father Himself, which hath sent Me, hath borne witness of Me.*" Whether the reference is here to the testimony of His Father independent of His works or not, it is certain that Christ had a more direct testimony than that from the Father, as on the occasion of His baptism, when there came a voice from heaven, saying, "This is My beloved Son, in whom I am well

pleased." "*Ye have neither heard His voice at any time, nor seen His shape*" (R. V. FORM). So deaf are your spiritual ears, and so sealed your eyes, that you neither hear nor see the Eternal Father.

Ver. 38.—"*And ye have not His word abiding in you.*" "You lack permanent inward appreciation of His words," the true Messianic idea is not in you. "*For whom He hath sent, Him ye believe not.*" This is an effect and evidence of your not having the true idea within.

Vers. 39, 40.—"*Search the Scriptures* (R. V. YE SEARCH THE SCRIPTURES); *for in them ye think* (R. V. BECAUSE YE THINK THAT IN THEM) *ye have eternal life.*" You search the Scriptures expecting to find "*eternal life*" in them, that is in the mere letter of truth, but there is no life in the letter. "*They are they which testify* (R. V. BEAR WITNESS) *of Me. And ye will not come to Me, that ye might have life.*" Dr. Brown expresses the idea in the following words:— "With disregarding the Scriptures I charge you not: ye do indeed busy yourselves about them (He was addressing, it will be remembered, the rulers, ver. 16); rightly deeming them your charter of eternal life. But ye miss the great burden of them; of Me it is they testify: and yet to Me ye will not come for that eternal life which ye profess to find there, and of which they proclaim Me the ordained Dispenser."

Ver. 41.—"*I receive not honour* (R. V. GLORY) *from men.*" "Honour," that is, applause, glory. This was a fact. They did not honour Him, among other reasons because He had not that royal pomp and pageantry with which they associated their Messiah.

Ver. 42.—"*But I know you, that ye have not the love of God in you.*" He read their hearts, and discovered at once the cause of their spiritual blindness and depravity. They lacked love, love for God.

Ver. 43.—"*I am come in My Father's name, and ye receive Me not: if another shall come in his own name, him ye will receive.*" How strikingly has this been verified in the history of the Jews. "From the time of the true Christ to our time," says *Bengel*, "sixty-four false Christs have been reckoned, by whom the Jews have been deceived."

Ver. 44.—"*How can ye believe, which receive honour* (R. V. GLORY) *one of another, and seek not the honour that cometh from God only?*" (R. V. THE ONLY GOD YE SEEK NOT.) The idea is, So long as you set a high value upon the opinions of your fellow-men, you cannot honour Me with that virtuous honour that comes from God.

Ver. 45.—"*Do not think* (R. V. THINK NOT) *that I will accuse you to the Father: there is one that accuseth you, even Moses, in whom ye trust.*" "Referring, no doubt, to the accusations which they brought against Him, and the human trial which they put upon Him. Before the court He has assumed more and more the mien of a majestic judge. He has finally represented them as contradicting the testimony of God, as antichrists, pagans. They are disarmed by the authority and power of His words, and discharge Him. Now so far as He is concerned, He proposes to discharge them. He will not accuse them to the Father: but another, says He, will accuse you, even Moses, in whom ye hope. This is the last, the mightiest stroke. That very Moses on whom they set their hope will accuse them, and put their hope to shame. Not exactly the Holy Scriptures, but Moses himself, in his spirit as the representative of the legal basis of the Holy Scriptures. If they rightly searched the Scriptures they would find Christ, and only Christ, in the Old Testament, even in the books of Moses alone. But they find Moses in them, and only Moses, only law even in the prophets; and on this omnipresent Moses, whose all the Scriptures are in their view, that is on the legal element of the Holy Scriptures, they placed their self-righteous confidence."—*Lange*.

Ver. 46.—"*For had* (R. V. IF I) *ye believed Moses, ye would have believed Me: for he wrote of Me.*" If you believe Moses, you would believe Me. An important testimony, as *Alford* says, to the subject of the whole Pentateuch.

Ver. 47.—"*But if ye believe not his writings, how shall ye believe My words?*" "A remarkable contrast, not absolutely putting Old Testament Scripture below His own words, but pointing to the office of those venerable documents to prepare Christ's way to the necessity universally felt for documentary testimony in revealed religion, and perhaps, as *Stier* adds, to the relation which the comparative 'letter' of the Old Testament holds to the more flowing words of 'spirit and life' which characterize the New Testament."

HOMILETICS

The subject is, as we have stated, *Christ's vindication of Himself against the charge of blasphemy.* This subject extends from the 19th verse to the end of the chapter. In His vindication He makes a very full statement of His Divine authority. First: He discloses its *nature;* and Secondly: He states its *proofs.* Our attention has been occupied with the former in our preceding discourse on verses 19 to 29. We have now to consider the latter, viz.—

THE PROOFS OF HIS AUTHORITY

The proofs may be grouped under two general heads.

First: His absolute devotion to the Eternal Will. "*I can of Mine own self do nothing:*" *as I hear* —that is, as I hear the actual, the sentence of God—"*I judge, and My judgment is just.*" * I can do

* See Homily on these words at end of volume.

nothing; I feel Myself to be the mere organ of the Infinite Father. Love for Him is the inspiration of My being, His will is the absolute law that governs all My activities.

But how is this absolute consecration of Christ to the Divine Will, which He here asserts, an authentication of His Divine authority? Because such a life is the highest proof of the power and presence of Divinity. The diviner the life a man lives, the more manifest is God in his history.

Secondly: His authentication from the Eternal Himself. "*There is another that beareth witness of Me.*" Here the reference is undoubtedly to God the Father. He bore ample and mighty testimony to the Divine authority of Christ. And in these verses Christ refers to the means by which that testimony was expressed.

How? (1.) By John the Baptist. "*Ye sent unto John, and he bare witness unto the truth.*" Three things are here referred to concerning John. (*a*) His testimony. Where is that to be found? "John bare witness of Him, and cried, saying, This is He of whom I spake; He that cometh after me is preferred before me, for He was before me." "And this is the record of John when the Jews sent priests and Levites from Jerusalem to ask him, Who art thou? He it is Who, coming after me, is preferred before me, Whose shoe's latchet I am not worthy to unloose." "And John bare record, saying, I saw the Spirit descending from heaven like a dove, and it abode upon Him." (*b*) His influence. "*I receive not testimony from man: but these things I say, that ye might be saved.*" The idea is, I do not require the testimony of John or of any man, but I quote John because you believe in him. He has influence with you, and his testimony may induce you to believe in Me, in order that you may be saved. You must believe in My Divine authority to be saved. John has borne testimony to that. You believe in John, and therefore I point you to him as a witness. (*c*) His character. "*He was a burning and a shining light.*" He was a "*light*" that attracted to the Jordan all Judæa and the regions round about. He was a "*light*" that all regarded as Divine. "All hold John as a prophet." He was a "*light*" which even Herod the king reverenced. "He feared John, knowing that he was a just man and holy." He was a brilliant light, "for amongst those that are born of woman there has not appeared a greater than John the Baptist." Surely such a man's testimony was to be taken. Again, His Father authenticated His authority,—

(2.) By miracles. "*But I have greater witness than that of John: for the works which the Father hath given Me to finish, the same works that I do, bear witness of Me, that the Father hath sent Me.*" The miracles of Christ were confessedly great and numerous. "If all His mighty works had been written in a book," &c. &c. Three facts are to be noticed here. (*a*) That those miracles were wrought of God. They were Divine, not human productions. How can this be proved? 1. Man *instinctively* ascribes all miracles to God. Anything approaching the miraculous in nature, men everywhere—the savage and the civilized—involuntarily conclude to be products of Divine interposition. Though their logic would not perhaps take them to this point, their intuition always does. 2. Men must *logically* conclude that miracles of such a moral description, and wrought by such a high moral character as that of Jesus of Nazareth, are Divine. Had His miracles breathed malevolence, and tended to immorality and unhappiness, the logic of human nature would have denied their Divinity. Reason would have protested against the conclusions of instinct. But in the case of Jesus the moral character of the Miracle-worker was so sublimely pure and loving, and His mighty works so benign and virtuous, that you are bound to ascribe them to the primal Source of all power and goodness. Well might Christ say that "*the same works that I do, bear witness of Me, that the Father hath sent Me.*" Another fact to be noticed here is—(b) That the God, who wrought the miracles, they practically ignored. "*Ye have neither heard His voice nor seen His shape.*" These theoretic theists were practically atheists: they were without God in the world. The other fact to be noticed here is—(c) That they practically ignored this God because His word was not in their hearts. "*Ye have not His word abiding in you.*" If the word—the truth of God—had been in them as an all-animating power, they would have heard and seen God everywhere. If there is no God within, there is no God without. Men in whose hearts the Divine word is not, have no ears to hear the Infinite, though He speak in thunder, no eyes to see Him, though He fills up their horizon. Again His Father authenticated His authority—

(3) **By Scripture.** "*Search the Scriptures; for in them ye think ye have eternal life: and they are they which testify of Me.*"* The Scriptures did testify of Christ; Moses and the prophets were full of Him. These Jews did "*search the Scriptures,*" they made a habit, a conscience of this. "Ye search the Scriptures," says Christ. They searched the Scriptures, thinking that thereby they should have "*eternal life,*" but they had no life; they had not found Christ, Who is THE LIFE. Two things are suggested here. (a) There are men who search the Scriptures who never go to Christ. The Jews did so; and hundreds are to be found in this age who live in the study of the Scriptures, who have never gone to Christ. They find sometimes a theological Christ, or an ecclesiastical Christ, but not *the* Christ of God, the living, loving, personal Saviour of the world. Ye search the Scriptures "*and ye will not come to Me.*" The Scriptures, which are designed to bring men to Christ, often keep them away. (b) The reason men do not go to Christ is

* See Germ, p. 140.

because they are more in sympathy with the human than with the Divine. "*I know you, that ye have not the love of God in you.*" You have no sympathy with His character, His works and aims; on the contrary, your sympathies are all with the thoughts and doings of man. Worldly honours and worldly pleasures so occupy your minds that you cannot see the Divine. "*How can ye believe, which receive honour one of another, and seek not the honour that cometh from God only ?*" How solemnly true this is! Conventional ideas of honour and happiness blind the eyes of men to the honour and blessedness that come "*from God only.*" The world's heroes are evermore the incarnations of the world's thoughts, and those thoughts are, alas! far away from the immutable realities. He whose character and status are most in keeping with the popular sentiment will ever be the greatest magnate for the time. His Father authenticated His authority—

(4.) By Moses. "*Do not think that I will accuse you to the Father : there is one that accuseth you, even Moses, in whom ye trust,*" &c. (*a*) They professed the utmost confidence in Moses. Moses was their lawgiver, their prophet, their moral master; they said, We are Moses' disciples, and "we know that God spake unto Moses." (*b*) Moses testified to the Divine authority of Christ. "*Had ye believed Moses, ye would have believed Me, for he wrote of Me.*" He spoke of Me as the "seed of the woman," as the "Shiloh," as a "star out of Jacob," as a prophet that should be "raised from amongst His brethren." You believe in Moses, and Moses testified of Me. What then? If you reject Me : (1.) Moses himself will condemn you. "*Do not think that I will accuse you to the Father : there is one that accuseth you, even Moses.*" I need pronounce no judgment upon your conduct, I leave you with Moses. The man in whom you trust, he shall condemn you. (2.) My words will not be credited by you. "*If you believe not his writings, how shall ye believe My words ?*" After all your professions you believe not Moses, or else you would believe Me.

CONCLUSION. "This discourse of our Saviour presents some of the highest subjects for human thought, and some of the most impressive reasons why we, as well as the Jews, should believe in Him as the Messiah, the Son of God. The testimony of John the Baptist, the sublime miracles which Christ performed, the witness which God repeatedly gave Him, and the prophetic declarations of the Mosaic dispensation, still speak to us through the living page of the book of inspiration; and can any man innocently reject such various and overwhelming evidence ? Or, if any one is too hardened to be convinced by these arguments, though strong and conclusive, oh, let him not resist the pleadings of compassion and the merciful intercessions which broke forth from the quivering lips of the Divine Sufferer on the Cross. Let love persuade where reason cannot convince."

Germs of Thought
RUINOUS SEARCHING OF THE SCRIPTURES
No. 22   John 5:39, 40

"Search (R. V. YE SEARCH) the Scriptures ; for (R. V. BECAUSE) in them ye think ye have Eternal Life : and they (R. V. THESE) are they which testify (R. V. BEAR WITNESS) of Me.   And ye will not come to Me."

Christ, I take it, is not here commanding the Jews to "*Search the Scriptures*," but stating the fact that they did so.   The mood is to be taken as in the indicative, not in the imperative.   This is according to the Revised Version, which reads, "Ye search the Scriptures, because ye think that in them ye have eternal life, and these are they which bear witness of Me."

I—HERE ARE MEN SEARCHING FOR THE HIGHEST OBJECT

The object they were in quest of was "*eternal life*," which of course they considered to be something more than endless existence. Whatever it was, it was their *summum bonum*, their chief good. Christ's language implies that the good they sought would only be found in Him, and He was in the Scriptures : they testified or bore witness of Him.

II—HERE ARE MEN SEARCHING FOR THE HIGHEST OBJECT IN THE RIGHT PLACE

" *Ye search the Scriptures.*"   Observe—

(1.) *The highest search of man is for the chief good.*

(2.) The chief good is *only found in Christ.*

(3.) Christ is to be *found in the Scriptures.*   The Scriptures are not Christ, any more than the casket is the jewel, the field the pearl of great price, the palace the sovereign.   Where is Christ to be found ?   In the Gospel.

III—HERE ARE MEN SEARCHING FOR THE HIGHEST OBJECT IN THE RIGHT PLACE, AND UTTERLY FAILING

These men did not find Christ.   Instead of the Messiah, they found one whom they regarded as an impostor and a blasphemer, unfit to live.   Ah, me !   Thousands in every age "*search the Scriptures*," but they do not find the true Christ there.   They find their little creeds, their tawdry rites, and arguments to buttress their sects and their systems.   They do not find the living, loving, personal Son of God, the Saviour of the World.   Why is this ? Because their searching is—

(1.) *Technical, and not spiritual;*   (2.) *Speculative, and not practical;* (3.) *Desultory, and not persistent;*   (4.) *Perfunctory, and not earnest;* (5.) *Irreverent, and not devout.*   Men often find in the Bible what they do not seek,—they find a demon instead of a Christ, a curse instead of a blessing, damnation instead of salvation. The Scriptures have proved the ruin of thousands.

No. 23   John 5:40

THE SETTLED CONDITION OF A SINNER'S WELL-BEING

"Ye will not come to Me, that ye might have life."

Man's well-being here, and in various other places in the New Testament, is represented as "*life*." And what is the life? Supreme love to God. This man had at first; he lost it; and in its loss is spiritual death. The man who has this is truly alive, and he only. Observe two things in relation to it—

I — THE SETTLED CONDITION PROPOUNDED

How is it to be obtained? Only by coming to Christ. Christ alone can generate this supreme love to the Eternal Father in the human heart. He does it—

First: By furnishing the strongest demonstrations of *God's love to the sinner*.

Secondly: By furnishing the highest manifestation of *the lovableness of God's character*. They must come to Him; come to His teaching, as loyal pupils come to the teaching of their master; come to His life, as hero-worshippers come to the life of a great hero.

II — THE SETTLED CONDITION NEGLECTED

"*Ye will not come*." Why won't they come? Is it because the condition is too difficult? No; it is simple enough. They will go to their Shakspeare, their Cromwell, and their Luther. Are not Christ's thoughts more simple and more sublime than any of these? Is not His history more romantic and more heroic? Is it because they have discovered any other way to true well-being? No; no other way exists. All philosophy and experience show this. Why then?

First: They are too engrossed in other subjects.

Secondly: They are too prone to presume upon the advent of a better opportunity.

Thirdly: They are too much under the influence of the god of this world.

John 6:1-14

THE BENEFICENCE OF CHRIST

(*The twelve return. Jesus retires with them across the lake. Five thousand are fed.*—Matt. xiv. 13—21; Mark vi. 30—44; Luke ix. 10—17; John vi. 1—14.)

After these things Jesus went over the Sea of Galilee, which is the sea of Tiberias," &c.

EXEGETICAL REMARKS.—There are four independent accounts of this miracle. They beautifully agree in substance, though they differ in style, according to the peculiarities of each writer. Matthew shows that our Lord's retirement to the wilderness was immediately after the death of John the Baptist. Mark and Luke also speak of this. John adds the circumstance that the passover was at hand, which accounts for the great multitudes which were streaming to Jesus on their way to Jerusalem. For the other accounts see Matt. xiv. 13—21 ; Mark vi. 30—44 ; Luke ix. 10—17.

Ver. 1.—"*After these things.*" This does not mean, after the charge of blasphemy against Christ and His defence, as recorded in the preceding chapter ; but after the death of John the Baptist, &c., as recorded by Matthew. Upwards of a year had elapsed between this miracle and the things recorded in the preceding chapter. The third passover was at hand, and another year would bring the life of Jesus to a close. "*Jesus went over* (R. V. AWAY TO THE OTHER SIDE OF) *the sea of Galilee, which is the sea of Tiberias;*" called after the name of an ancient city on the west side. The present name is Tabarîyeh. It is so called by John for the benefit of those who are unacquainted with the geography of Palestine. Its shape is oval, thirteen miles long, and six broad. In the neighbourhood of the sea our Lord spent the greater portion of His public life. Nine cities stood on its shores, amongst which was Capernaum, "His own city." It was the most densely populated place in all Palestine.

Ver. 2.—"*And a great multitude followed Him, because they saw His miracles* (R. V. BEHELD THE SIGNS) *which He did on them that were diseased*" (R. V. SICK). The mere wonders in themselves would not necessarily attract many. Otherwise had they been malignant and destructive, they would have repelled ; but being beneficent they attracted, they drew men after Him.

Ver. 3.—"*And Jesus went up into a* (R. V. THE) *mountain, and there He sat with His disciples.*" The whole sea is skirted by a chain of hills on both sides, and the particular mountain cannot be ascertained. He ascended the mountain, probably to avoid the crowd and to enjoy the elevated delights of quiet and holy devotion.

Ver. 4.—"*And* (R. V. NOW) *the Passover, a* (R. V. THE) *feast of the Jews, was nigh*" (R. V. AT HAND). This is probably the third passover of our Lord's ministry. A great Jewish festival, causing at this time perhaps the gathering of the great multitudes. John alone states this.

Ver. 5.—"*When Jesus then lifted* (R. V. LIFTING) *up His eyes, and saw* (R. V. SEEING) *a great company come unto Him* (R. V. MULTITUDE COMETH UNTO HIM), *He saith unto Philip, Whence shall* (R. V. ARE WE TO) *we buy bread, that these may eat ?*" Being now in the region of Bethsaida Julius, of which Philip was a native, the question was naturally addressed to him concerning provisions for the famishing multitudes. "*Whence ?*" The object was to call attention to the great quantity that would be required. The question is put, not because He felt any difficulty, but because He sought to awaken their interest and their thoughts.

Ver. 6.—"*And this He said to prove him : for He Himself knew what He would do.*" By the question He wished to test and strengthen Philip's faith. "This gives us a glimpse into the educational method of the great Teacher." —*Watkin.*

Ver. 7.—"*Philip answered Him, Two hundred pennyworth of bread is not sufficient for them, that every one of them may take a little.*" The money here amounts to about £7 of our currency. This, it would seem, was all the money they had ; and he felt its utter insufficiency.

Vers. 8, 9.—"*One of His disciples, Andrew, Simon Peter's brother, saith unto Him, There is a lad here, which hath five barley loaves, and two small* (R. V. OMITS) *fishes: but what are they* (R. V. THESE) *among so many ?*" Andrew was one of the first of our Lord's disciples, but he seemed to have no more faith than Philip. Although both of them, in all probability, had seen Christ healing the nobleman's son (John iv. 46), giving the draught

of fishes (Luke v. 1), healing the
demoniac, the paralytic, and the leper
(Mark i. 21 ; Matt. viii. 2 ; Luke v.
19), restoring the man at Bethesda
pool (John v. 5), healing the withered
hand (Matt. xii. 9), and the centurion's
servant (Luke ii. 7), and raising the
widow's son at Nain (Luke vii. 11),
they did not seem to realize the fact
that He who put the question—their
Master—was fully able to meet the
difficulty.

Ver. 10.—"*And Jesus said, Make
the men* (R. V. PEOPLE) *sit down.*"
According to Mark and Luke, they
sat down in ranks or companies.
"*Now there was much grass in the
place.*" The ancient Hebrews were
in the habit of sitting on skins on the
ground to eat their food. These five
thousand sat down now on the fresh
grass that had sprung up through the
fertile rains of the season.

Ver. 11.—"*And Jesus took the
loaves; and when He had* (R. V. HAVING)
*given thanks, He distributed to the
disciples,* (R. V. OMITS) *and the disciples
to them that were set down.*" Bread
and fish in this miracle proved Him
Master both of earth and sea ; and
His giving thanks to His Father
pointed their minds to Him from
" Whom all blessings flow."

Ver. 12.—"*When they were filled,
He said unto His disciples, Gather up
the fragments* (R. V. BROKEN PIECES)
that remain, that nothing be lost."
"The Lord," says one, "is lavish of
His bounties, at the same time careful
of His gifts."

Ver. 13.—"*Therefore* (R. V. SO) *they
gathered them together, and filled twelve
baskets with the fragments of* (R. V.
BROKEN PIECES FROM) *the five barley
loaves, which remained over and above
unto them that had eaten.*" " In the
synoptic Gospels, the disciples gather
up the fragments of their own accord.
In this Gospel the order to do so
originated with Jesus. This was His
triumphant answer to the calculation
of Andrew and Philip."—*Godet.* Here
is a stupendous miracle, but such a one
as is going on in nature constantly.
A miracle not of creation, but of multiplication. Nature gives back to the
husbandman in harvest manifold more
than he committed to the earth in
spring.

Ver. 14.—"*Then those men, when
they had seen the miracle* (R. V. WHEN
THEREFORE THE PEOPLE SAW THE
SIGN) *that Jesus did, said, This is of
a truth that* (R. V. THE) *prophet that
should come* (R. V. THAT COMETH) *into
the world.*" John alone records this
effect of the miracle. It falls in with
his design, to show the Divinity of our
Lord. Here therefore he gives the
testimony of those who saw it wrought.
"*That prophet.*" The prophet like
unto Moses ; they meant undoubtedly
the Messiah. Is this narrative a
myth ? *Luthardt* says no. "The
idea of a myth is opposed by the fact
that this very event maintained its
position in the consciousness of the
early Christians as we perceive by
the four evangelical accounts."

HOMILETICS

As we have elsewhere * made remarks on this miracle as recorded
by Matthew, our observations now will be brief. We take the
miracle as suggesting certain remarks concerning the *Beneficence of
Christ.* Christ was not only benevolent, disposed to do good, but
beneficent, *always doing* good. "He went about doing good."

I —HIS BENEFICENCE IS A POWERFUL ELEMENT OF ATTRACTION
IN HIS CHARACTER

"*A great multitude followed Him, because they saw His miracles
which He did on them that were diseased.*" And then in the fifth
verse it is said, that "*He lifted up His eyes, and saw a great company.*"

*See *Gospel of Matthew,* p.337.

What attracted these multitudes? Not, as we have said, His wonders; for although wonders will ever arrest attention and excite curiosity, they will not attract unless they are beneficent. Had His miracles been works of wrath, devastation, death, and terror, they would have driven the multitudes in panic from His presence. The terrible wonders on the brow of Sinai did not tempt the millions at the base to climb to the summit; on the contrary, they were terrified exceedingly. It was the *beneficence* in Christ's miracles that drew after Him the multitudes. All His miracles were works of love. And this in His character is the great moral magnet that will one day draw all men unto Him. Beneficence always attracts. With what beauty and stirring force Job describes the influence of his own beneficence upon the men of his age amongst whom he lived. "The young men saw me, and hid themselves," etc. (Job xxix. 8—25). Ah! if what is called the Church of Christ on earth had, instead of indulging in acrimonious controversies cradling morbid and sanctimonious sentiments, and childishly attending to trumpery rites and ceremonies, exhibited Christly beneficence, how great the multitudes who would have followed after her! The captives would have looked to her for liberty, the poor for bread, the afflicted for healing, the naked for clothing, the oppressed for justice, and the sad everywhere for comfort and consolation. Why do not the multitudes follow the Church? Nay, why do they turn from her? This is a question that grows more pressing every day.

II —HIS BENEFICENCE WAS EVER INSPIRED BY THE TENDEREST COMPASSION

It is said in the other records of this miracle, that He "had compassion on the multitudes." This multitude was famishing for hunger. Though Christ crossed the sea in a vessel, they had to walk round on foot. It is probable they had journeyed all night, and when they reached Him on the other side they would be famishing for food. His compassion was moved as He beheld them. There are what are called beneficent acts that are done from *vanity*. The doers seek applause in their work. Such seek their gifts to be chronicled in records and trumpeted on platforms. Such acts are sometimes done from *avarice*. The doer seeks to win clients, patients, customers that will enrich his coffers, and administer to his greed. A large donation to a popular institution is one of the best commercial advertisements. And indeed such acts are not unfrequently stimulated by *superstition*. The doer seeks to win heaven and avoid hell by his benevolent deeds.

In sublime contrast to all this stands the beneficence of Christ. He was full of compassion—full, free, boundless compassion. Alas! how little of this compassion man has for man. In most cases man treats his brother with heartless indifference, and indeed in many cases with a ruthless and savage cruelty. There is a fact recorded of Napoleon which may be taken as typical of that cruel class of men that abound in all ages. Flushed with his victories, he sailed with a numerous fleet and army to the East. Everywhere the enemy fell before his triumphant troops. He came to Jaffa— the ancient Joppa—a town in Palestine. On the fourth of March, 1799, he assailed it: two days after, it was taken. Terrible was the carnage that took place. In the midst of the slaughter 4000 men took shelter in an old caravanserai, and called out from the windows that they would surrender on condition that their lives were spared. Napoleon's aides-de-camp agreed to this, and led them before their general. The ruthless demon in human form received them with a stern and relentless air. He decreed that all should die, and signed the fatal order, which was executed on March 10th. Four thousand men, firmly fettered, were marched to the sand-hills on the sea-coast, and mowed down by the musketry amid shrieks that rent the heavens. In vain they prayed for mercy: every man was put to death. The bones of the vast multitude lie there to this day; it is a field of blood—a sad scene of Christian atrocity from which the Arab turns away in horror and disgust. Alas! Christendom calls the Napoleons, the conquerors, great and glorious. Bishops make prayers for their success, and mock Heaven by thanks for their triumphs. How infinitely antagonistic to the spirit of Him Whom Christendom calls Lord and Master, Who when He " beheld the multitudes, had compassion on them, and fed them ! "

III — HIS BENEFICENCE TRANSCENDS BOTH THE FAITH AND NEEDS OF MEN

First : It transcends their *faith*. Philip said, "*Whence shall we buy bread ? "* and Andrew, another disciple, when he heard of the "*five barley loaves and fishes,*" said, "*What are they among so many?*"

Their faith went not beyond the means they had in actual possession. For the time they seem to have had no idea that Christ was equal to the occasion; when He said, "*Make the men sit down,*" perhaps they thought it was little less than mockery. How could starving men sit down and rest ?

Secondly : It transcends their *needs*. Jesus not only fed them, but after doing so, "*twelve basketfuls of fragments*" remained. Christ always gives more than is needed. In nature we have redundancy of light, and air, and water, and fruit, and beauty.

Nature that has fed the generations that are gone, has as much, if not more, for the generations yet to come. The fragments that remain are greater than the stock that has been used. " He is able to do exceeding abundantly above all that we ask or think," etc. His resources are exhaustless, His " riches unsearchable."

His blessings seem to increase by appropriation : the more they are used, the more they seem to multiply and grow; thus God's great universe becomes more affluent every day.

IV —HIS BENEFICENCE ALLOWS NO ENCOURAGEMENT TO WASTEFULNESS

" *Gather up the fragments that remain, that nothing may be lost.*" *
Use all, abuse nothing. In one sense nothing can be lost, not an atom of matter, not a thought of mind. Frugality is the duty of man both in his temporal and spiritual concerns.

V —HIS BENEFICENCE IS A CONVINCING TESTIMONY OF HIS MESSIAHSHIP

" *Then those men, when they had seen the miracle that Jesus did, said, This is of a truth that prophet that should come into the world.*" †
First: Mere miracles would not be a sufficient proof of His Divinity. Other beings besides God might perform that which man would regard as miraculous. Who can prove that no being but the Almighty could produce results that in the judgment of feeble man would be universally regarded as miraculous ? In truth, if the miracle was effected to enforce a doctrine repugnant to human reason and conscience, it would be spurned as undivine and devilish.

Secondly: Miracles that are beneficent are proofs of Divinity. These proofs were now felt by the people, and they said, " *This is of a truth that prophet.*" This was the evidence that Christ gave to the deputation that John sent to Him from prison. "Go and show John again those things which ye do hear and see : the blind receive their sight, and the lame walk, the lepers are cleansed, and the deaf hear, the dead are raised up, and the poor have the Gospel preached unto them."

Germs of Thought
No. 24   John 6:5-14

CHRIST FEEDING THE FIVE THOUSAND : HIS COMPASSION

"When Jesus then lifted up His eyes," &c.

This beautiful incident is fraught with glorious suggestions, and pulsates with the compassionate heart of Christ. Amongst the many subjects it illustrates, the chief is the benevolent interest of Christ in humanity. We learn—

I —THAT HIS COMPASSION EXTENDS TO MAN'S PHYSICAL WANTS

His love for souls, free, boundless, ever working, and ever-conquering, is the spirit of His glorious history; but here we learn that He is practically alive to the necessity of men's *bodies*. Here

---

* See Homily on these words at end of Volume.   † See Germ below.

was a great company that required food. His interest in man's physical wants is seen—

First : In the provision He has made for them in the constitution of nature. The world which He has made abounds with everything we want physically. His interest is seen—

Secondly : In the wonderful facts of His life. How He attended to their bodies while here! The interest Christ has shown in men's bodies is a *reproof* to the Church for neglecting the material exigencies of the population, and is an indication of what His disciples must do before they rightly manifest Him.

II —THAT HIS COMPASSION IS CONNECTED WITH AMPLE ABILITY TO SUPPLY

"*Five thousand*" were now fed. His ample power of supplying appears—

First : In the operation of ordinary laws. How abundant are the provisions of the earth! All come from Christ's liberal hand.

Secondly : In extraordinary incidents. Thus it appears not only in the case before us, but in innumerable instances besides.

III —THAT HIS COMPASSION IS EXERCISED IN CONNECTION WITH A DEVOUT SPIRIT

"*When He had given thanks*," &c. The lesson taught by this is, *that all temporal good comes from God.* This fact, practically realized, would sweeten for us the blessings of Providence, and give us an abiding impression of the presence and agency of God.

IV —THAT HIS COMPASSION IS EVER EXERCISED FOR MORAL ENDS.

"*Then those men when they had seen the miracles that Jesus did, said, This is of a truth*," &c. Christ blessed the bodies of men in order that He might bless their souls. So should we. He showed more favours than they could appreciate in order to prepare them to receive from His hands the higher blessing of eternal life.

John 6:15-21

MAN AND CHRIST

(*Jesus walks upon the water.*—MATT. xiv. 22—36 ; MARK vi. 45—54 ; JOHN vi. 15—21.)

"When Jesus therefore perceived that they would come and take Him by force, to make Him a king, He departed again into a mountain Himself alone," &c.

EXEGETICAL REMARKS.—Ver. 15.— " *When Jesus therefore perceived* (R. V. PERCEIVING) *that they would come and take Him by force, to make Him a king,* *He departed* (R. V. WITHDREW) *again into a mountain Himself alone.*" The facts recorded in these verses are also recorded with slight variation in Matt.

xiv. 22—36 ; Mark vi. 45—54.* The desire of the people to make Him a king was purely selfish and worldly. They wished it, not because of His pre-eminent intellectual and moral com-petency for ruling the nation righte-ously and usefully, but because of the material good which they expected from His reign. Jesus read their hearts, shrunk from their vulgar and gross ideas of power, and departed into a mountain alone. There, alone on the mountain, with His eye upon all the principles at work in society, He was infinitely more royal than all the Cæsars of the world. "Matthew and Mark add that He went to the moun-tain to pray. This juncture evidently coincides with the close of the 15th verse, and hence only a portion of the multitude, undoubtedly the more en-thusiastic, remained upon the spot." *Godet.*

Ver. 16.—" *And when even was now come* (R. V. EVENING CAME), *His dis-ciples went down unto the sea.*" Even-ing, with its deep shadows gathering on the little skiff, was not the most auspicious time to embark on the treacherous lake.

Ver. 17.—" *And entered into a ship* (R. V. BOAT), *and went over the sea toward* (R. V. WERE GOING OVER THE SEA UNTO) *Capernaum. And it was now dark, and Jesus was not come to them.*" In Matthew and Mark it is said that Jesus "constrained" His disciples to go into the ship, and to go before Him. So they went forth by His will, and they might have ex-pected a prosperous voyage. The ex-pression that it "*was now dark, and Jesus was not come to them,*" gives us to understand that they expected He would overtake them on the voyage, and join them on the way. Probably Christ promised He would do so, when He constrained them to depart; but night came on, and a storm was evi-dently brooding, but Christ had not come.

Ver. 18.—" *And the sea arose* (R. V. WAS RISING) *by reason of a great wind that blew.*" The lake, surrounded by hills and mountains, was always liable to sudden storms.

Ver. 19.—" *So when they had rowed about five and twenty or thirty fur-longs.*" Mark says, " And He saw them toiling (βασανιζομένους) in rowing ; for the wind was contrary unto them." " *Five and twenty or thirty furlongs.*" This is about four miles, according to our measurement; the vessel was therefore about half-way on its journey, and in the midst of the sea. " *They see* (R. V. BEHOLD) *Jesus walking on the sea, and drawing nigh unto the ship* (R. V. BOAT): *and they were afraid.*" Mark's account is more full than this. He says : " And about the fourth watch of the night He cometh unto them, walking upon the sea, and would have passed by them. But when they saw Him walking upon the sea, they supposed it had been a spirit (φάντασμα), and cried out: for they all saw Him, and were troubled."

Ver. 20.—" *But He saith unto them, It is I ; be not afraid.*" εἰμι, literally, "I am." *Who?* Whosoever you re-quire to help you. *What?* Whatso-ever you require to make you glorious, useful, and blessed here and yonder.

Ver. 21.—" *Then they willingly re-ceived* (R. V. THEY WERE WILLING THEREFORE TO RECEIVE) *Him into the ship* (R. V. BOAT): *and immediately* (R. V. STRAIGHTWAY) *the ship* (R. V. BOAT) *was at the land whither they went* " (R. V. WERE GOING). " *They re-ceived Him willingly.*" Literally, they were willing to receive Him into the ship, as they had not been at first, on account of their fear ; and imme-diately, by the calming of the sea, &c., through His providential favouring, the boat was at the land. Both Mat-thew and Mark proceed further with the history of this event.

HOMILETICS

Our subject is *Man and Christ.* Here we see man manifesting various states of mind in relation to Christ. Here we have—

*See *Gospel of Matthew,* p. 343. Kregel Publications, Grand Rapids, Mi. 1979

I —MEN VULGARLY ESTIMATING CHRIST

" *They would come and take Him by force, to make Him a king.*" They estimated Him according to their own views and feelings. Because they regarded worldly wealth as the highest position, worldly authority as the highest dignity, worldly pomp and pageantry as the highest glory, they thought that Christ would accept the office of a worldly monarch. Perhaps, as they approached Him with the offer of a worldly kingdom, they expected He would hail with enthusiasm the opportunity, and bound at once into regal splendour and power. But they were mistaken. " *He departed again into a mountain Himself alone.*" * His pure spirit recoiled from the grossness of the thought: hence He sends them away, and retires to the solitude and silence of the hills, to commune with the Infinite. The millions in all ages have always formed these worldly estimates of Christ. They are unable to form a correct idea of that kingdom which "consisteth not in meat and drink." but in "righteousness, and peace, and joy in the Holy Ghost"—a kingdom that "cometh not with observation;" a kingdom whose foundation is immutable rectitude ; which legislates for thoughts and moral motives ; whose authority is enforced, not by cannons, swords, or bayonets, but by love and truth. Oh, speed the day when men shall form a true estimate of Christ! Here we have—

II —MEN CONSCIOUSLY NEEDING CHRIST

" *It was now dark, and Jesus was not come to them. And the sea arose by reason of a great wind that blew.*" It was night—dark, bewildering, oppressive night ; and they, in a frail bark in the midst of the sea, were being beaten by the winds and dashed by the waves. Their perils were imminent and thickening. Who shall guide them safely to their destined haven ? They are painfully conscious of their own inability. Their strength is exhausted, and they are at their wits' end. They all feel that if Christ—He who had just fed five thousand with a few loaves and fishes—would come to them, He could rescue them, and He only. We may fancy how anxiously they looked out for Him. It is seldom so dark at sea but that you can see some distance. How they would strain their eyes, hoping for a glance at Him : how they would bend the ear, hoping to catch the echo of His voice ! The time hastens when every man will feel painfully conscious of his need of Christ. We are all on a treacherous sea. The night is coming on, and with the night, the storm.

> Be Thou my Guide on life's tempestuous sea,
> Be Thou my Guide ;

* See Germ, p. 151.

> The waves run high and all seems dark to me,
>   Be Thou my Guide.
> Take Thou the helm, and steer me safely o'er
> Life's surging sea to the celestial shore.

Here we have—

III —MEN IGNORANTLY DREADING CHRIST

"*They see Jesus walking on the sea, and drawing nigh unto the ship : and they were afraid.*" He needed no skiff to bear Him over the billows. "The Lord is mightier than the mighty waves of the sea." But why were they "*afraid*"? Matthew and Mark say they thought He was a spirit. Observe three things—

First: Man has a tendency to dread visitants from the spirit-world. Even Peter—bold Peter, who with his sword smote Malchus —trembles before an imaginary spirit. The vision of a supposed ghost never fails to strike terror into the heart of the spectator. Why should men be afraid of spirits? Are they not themselves spirits, and members of the great spiritual system? Is not their Father God Spirit? Why afraid? Consciousness of guilt: this is the philosophy of all the terror.

Secondly: This tendency to dread the supernatural is a great evil. It is the source of all superstition; and superstition has been, and still is, one of the greatest curses of the race. Superstitious fear is eternally opposed to all true spiritual knowledge, virtue, and progress.

Thirdly: Christ's mission is to eradicate from the human soul this dread of the supernatural. "*It is I; be not afraid.*" It is I; do not be afraid of anything in the universe, either spiritual or material, for I am absolute Master of all. Do not be afraid of God, for He has sent Me to demonstrate to you by My teaching, My life, and My death the unconquerableness and tenderness of His love to you. "*It is I; be not afraid*" of Me, for I am come, not to destroy, but to save. "*It is I; be not afraid.*" Thank God for this EGO EIMI!

Here we have—

IV —MEN CORDIALLY WELCOMING CHRIST

"*Then they willingly received Him into the ship.*" To receive Him was what they wished above all things. Because they had painfully felt their need of Him, they hailed Him with enthusiasm on board their little skiff. It is ever so. When once men have, by a deep conviction of their guilt, been overwhelmed by a sense of their moral danger, they will stretch out their arms widely to receive Him, crying, "Come, Lord Jesus; come quickly." It is when the soul feels itself sinking into the abysses of moral misery it will look to heaven, and say, "O Saviour, take the helm and pilot me." With Him on board they soon and safely reached port. "*Immediately,*" &c. &c. Brother, take Him on board thy bark, give Him the rudder, &c.

Germs of Thought
No. 25   John 6:15

CHRIST REJECTING POPULARITY, AND SEEKING SOLITUDE

"He departed again into a mountain Himself alone."

There are two things in the text concerning Christ remarkably significant.

I —HIS REJECTION OF POPULARITY

The popularity of Christ was now at its zenith. The feeding of the five thousand by the miracle He had just wrought, struck the populace for the hour with an enthusiastic admiration. "*They would take Him by force, to make Him a king.*" They would bear Him in their arms to Jerusalem, there to enthrone Him as the Monarch of their country. The world has nothing higher to give a man than a crown, and this the people of Judæa were anxious to confer on Jesus now. But how does He feel amidst all this thunder of popular Hosannas? Does He seize the offer made? No; He seems to recoil, with an ineffable disgust, both from their laudations and their proffered honours. Two things are suggested here—

First: The moral worthlessness of popularity. Christ peered into the souls of the multitude, and saw there nothing but worldly thoughts, corrupt feelings, and unvirtuous aims. "Jesus did not commit Himself unto them, because He knew all men, and needed not that any should testify of man : for He knew what was in man." All their notions of glory were grossly material. The ideas of spiritual sovereignty and spiritual honour which He inculcated had not touched their carnal souls. So long as the world is what it is, popularity is a worthless thing, a thing which only charlatans will pursue. Another thing suggested here is—

Secondly: The spiritual superiority of Christ. Whilst a few great men in every age may despise popularity, the millions prize it. Small men, both in Church and State, struggle after it as a prize, and worship it as a god. Why did Christ refuse the crown now offered to Him by enthusiastic admirers, and which His Almighty power would have enabled Him to wear with safety and splendour? Why? Because He was infinitely above such a worthless toy. Another thing in the text concerning Christ, remarkably significant, is—

II —HIS WITHDRAWMENT INTO SOLITUDE

" *He departed again into a mountain Himself alone.*" Christ often sought solitude. The stillness and secrecy of the hills at night would be thrice welcome to Him after the tumult of the day. In this Christ has left us an example, for we need solitude as well as society, to train our natures into Christ-like goodness.

First : Solitude is the best scene for self-communion.

Secondly : Solitude is the best scene for fellowship with the Eternal.

Thirdly : Solitude is the best scene for the formation of holy resolutions. "Enter into your closet, and shut your door, and the Father which seeth in secret will openly reward you." The soul resembles a tree in this, it requires the publicity of the open heavens, and the secrecy of the hidden depths, in order to grow to perfection. The spirit of the tree must go down into the dark quiet chambers of the earth to drink nourishment into its roots, and up into the lofty branches to be shone on by the sun, and tossed by the tempest.

John 6:22-27

MAN WRONGLY SEEKING CHRIST, AND CHRIST RIGHTLY DIRECTING MAN

(*Our Lord's discourse in the synagogue at Capernaum. Many disciples turn back. Peter's profession of faith.*—JOHN vi. 22—71 ; vii. 1.)

"The day following, when the people which stood," &c.

EXEGETICAL REMARKS.—Ver. 22.— "*The day following* (R. V. ON THE MORROW), *when the people* (R. V. MULTITUDE) *which stood on the other side of the sea saw that there was none other boat there, save that one whereinto His disciples were entered* (R. V. SAVE ONE, AND THAT JESUS ENTERED), *and that Jesus went not with His disciples into the boat, but that His disciples were gone* (R. V. WENT) *away alone.*" "The Evangelist here relates what the multitude had noticed as to the facts of Christ's departure—viz. that there was but one boat ; that this they saw go away without Christ : and hence, that as they found Him next day at Capernaum, He must have gone across in some unexplained manner. This statement is given to show how their observation of the facts correspond with the miracle."

Ver. 23.—" *Howbeit there came other boats from Tiberias nigh unto the place*

where they did eat (R. V. ATE THE) *bread, after that the Lord had given thanks.*" "These boats, perhaps, were driven by the contrary wind across the lake. Their coming probably explains the reference to the disciples in ver. 24. At first the multitude might have supposed that they had returned in one of them from some brief mission to the other side."—*Westcott.*

Ver. 24.—" *When the people therefore* (R. V. MULTITUDE) *saw that Jesus was not there, neither His disciples, they also took shipping* (R. V. GOT INTO THE BOATS), *and came to Capernaum, seeking for Jesus.*" These people had witnessed, we understand from the twenty-second verse, that Jesus did not go with His disciples into the boat, but that they went alone ; and they now felt anxious to find out the place where Jesus actually was. "*They also took shipping.*" It is not necessary to suppose that the whole five thousand *"took shipping;"* for although Josephus informs us there were about 230 vessels always crowding that sea, they would not have been sufficient to have conveyed such a vast multitude.

Ver. 25.—*" And when they had found Him on the other side of the sea, they said unto Him, Rabbi, when camest Thou hither?"* They were astonished at finding Him in that spot, and wondered how He could have gained the place, whether by land or water. They could not see how, unless He had travelled all night round the head of the lake alone, He could have reached Capernaum before they themselves arrived. They had no idea that He had walked on the waves of the sea, and hence they ask, *" When camest Thou hither?"* *" When?"* Here Thou art; but how couldst Thou reach this city so speedily?

Ver. 26.—*" Jesus answered them and said, Verily, verily, I say unto you, Ye seek Me, not because ye saw the miracles* (R. V. SIGNS), *but because ye did eat* (R. V. ATE) *of the loaves, and were filled."* He does not answer their question, He does not tell them how, in the might and majesty of the Godhead, He had trod the waters; nor does He even take notice of their question, but hits at once the miserable spirit that animated them—flippant, inquisitive, greedy.

Ver. 27.—*" Labour* (R. V. WORK) *not for the meat which perisheth, but for that* (R. V. THE) *meat which endureth* (R. V. ABIDETH) *unto everlasting* (R. V. ETERNAL) *life, which the Son of man shall give unto you: for Him hath God the Father* (R. V. THE FATHER, EVEN GOD, HATH) *sealed."* What meaneth the last clause? τοῦτον γὰρ ὁ πατὴρ ἐσφράγισεν ὁ θεός. *" Him hath the Father sealed."* *" Sealed."* Appointed, accredited as His Divine Messenger. He gave Him the stamp of Divinity, not merely by His sublime character and transcendent doctrines, but by His miracles and special declarations, as on the banks of the Jordan, on Tabor, and in the Temple. He is the authenticated Witness of the Father (Rev. i. 5).

HOMILETICS

These verses present to us two great subjects of vital and universal interest, viz. *Man wrongly seeking Christ, and Christ rightly directing man.*

I MAN WRONGLY SEEKING CHRIST

" When the people therefore saw that Jesus was not there, neither His disciples, they also took shipping, and came to Capernaum, seeking for Jesus." What was the spirit that animated these multitudes, that crossed the sea in quest of Christ? Was it a sincere love for His character, strong sympathy with His mission, or an earnest desire to understand the Divine Will concerning them? Not at all. The spirit that animated them seems to have been distinguished by two things—

First: *Curiosity.* His arrival at Capernaum so *speedily* after the miracle of the loaves and the fishes was a phenomenon that struck them with amazement, and roused their inquisitiveness. Men in all ages have been animated by this idle curiosity in their inquiries concerning Christ. The facts of His biography have appeared so wonderful to them, that they have been stimulated to investigation. Some have searched the facts in order to disprove them, and to show that they were mere myths and fables. Others, in order to explain away their supernaturalness, and to show that they can all be accounted for on the ordinary laws that govern the world. And others have prosecuted an inquiry into them in order to build up some ingenious theory. Now there is in man the instinct of inquisitiveness. This is what is called the philosophic spirit, and is the spring of all knowledge. It is intended by our Maker to lead us on in the attainment of truth, for ever on. But this instinct, like all other instincts of our nature, has been sadly perverted. In the case before us, it was inspired by unworthy motives, and it became mere idle curiosity. The spirit was distinguished by—

Secondly: *Greed.* "*And when they found Him on the other side of the sea, they said unto Him, Rabbi, when camest thou hither? Jesus answered them and said, Verily, verily, I say unto you, Ye seek Me, not because ye saw the miracles, but because ye did eat of the loaves, and were filled.*" They did not come to have further manifestations of His Divine nature and character, they did not come to Him for His sake, but for their own. By the miracle of the loaves and fishes they knew He could serve their material interests, and for this they sought Him. "*Loaves and fishes,*" these became their motives. Has not this selfish, this utilitarian principle animated thousands in every age in their searchings concerning Christ? Loaves and fishes make many Christian authors, preachers, bishops, and members of Churches. As Christianity grows in popularity, the temptation to follow it augments in force. It was never stronger than in England to-day.

II CHRIST RIGHTLY DIRECTING MEN

"*Labour not for the meat which perisheth, but for that meat which endureth unto everlasting life, which the Son of man shall give unto you: for Him hath God the Father sealed.*" The meaning of this is, work not supremely for mere material good. These words suggest three thoughts concerning spiritual sustentation—

First: That soul-food is provided for men. There is a "*meat which endureth unto everlasting life.*" What is this "*meat*"? Christ answers this question in the subsequent part of the chapter. He speaks of Himself as the "bread of life." "I am the bread of life." And again He says, "My flesh is meat indeed, My blood is drink indeed." What does this mean? The language, of course, is highly figurative; but the idea expressed is clear—namely, that there is something in Christ that we might take unto ourselves as the very nourishment of our souls. What is that something? *His moral spirit*, which is in truth His very life-blood;—the "blood shed for the remission of sins." What is that spirit? *Self-sacrificing love.* This was the very soul of His soul, and this is the spiritual food of humanity. We cannot live without it; for "he that hath not the spirit of Christ is none of His." Without it, Paul tells us, we are "nothing." It may be represented as food for two reasons—

(1.) *It satisfies the hunger of the soul.* As bread allays the gnawings of corporeal hunger, the moral spirit of Christ taken into us allays the spiritual, and nothing else can. This spirit is the water which quencheth the moral thirst. He who is filled with it has a blessed satisfaction.

(2.) *It invigorates the powers of the soul.* As bread strengthens the body, this spirit strengthens the soul. The man who is filled with the self-sacrificing love of Christ, is strong to suffer, strong to labour, strong in duty. He alone grows into the true hero.

Secondly: That soul-food requires the chief labour of man. "*Labour not for the bread that perisheth.*" This does not mean, of course, that we are to employ no effort to get our physical wants supplied; but that those efforts should not be so strenuous and persistent as those which are employed to get the higher good. Our chief labour should be for this—

(1.) *Because it is indispensable to our well-being.* Whatever else we have, if we have not this spirit in us, we have nothing that can make us fully and permanently happy.

(2.) *Because it can only be obtained by the most earnest efforts.* We can only get the spirit into us.—(1.) By meditation. Profound thinking upon the biography of Christ. (2.) By imitation. We must follow Him. (3.) By supplication. We must implore Him to fill us with the Spirit, that we may "become conformable to His death."

Thirdly: That soul-food is the gift of Christ. "*Which the Son of man shall give unto you: for Him hath God the Father sealed;*" that is, marked out and authenticated for the transcendent work of giving this food to hungry souls. Christ gives it—

(1.) *By His teaching.* Everywhere throughout His discourses does He inculcate the self-sacrificing love—the love which leads to the surrendering of everything, and of the taking up of the cross.

(2.) *By His spirit.* His spirit conveys it into the soul. Self-sacrificing love for God and man is indeed the gift of Christ. The world knew nothing of this spirit till He came and gave Himself a ransom for sinners. This spirit is in the highest sense the *moral* "flesh and blood of Christ." He poured forth this precious spirit upon the world to cleanse it from all sin. This spirit alone makes men truly happy and blest. "There never," says *Sir Walter Scott,* "did, and never will exist, anything permanently noble and excellent in a character which was a stranger to the exercise of resolute self-denial. Teach self-denial, and make its practice pleasurable, and you create for the world a destiny more sublime than ever issued from the brain of the wildest dreamer." *This is Christ's work.*

John 6:28, 29

EVANGELICAL FAITH

"Then said they (R. V. THEY SAID THEREFORE) unto Him, What shall (R. V. MUST) we do, that we might (R. V. MAY) work the works of God? Jesus answered and said unto them, This is the work of God, that ye believe on Him whom He hath sent."

EXEGETICAL REMARKS.—Ver. 28.— "*What shall we do?*" "The questioners appear to admit in word the necessity of the higher aim of work, and inquire as to the method of reaching it."— *Westcott.* As He had just exhorted them to concern themselves chiefly for another kind of food, they take Him up at His word, and ask what they are to do to comply with this that He proposes (the same word is used here as is rendered "labour" in ver. 27).

They seem to understand Him so far as to inquire what kind of work He exhorts them to do, and how they shall work such works of the law as God requires.

Ver. 29.—"*This is the work of God.*" He speaks not of works. They had thought of a round of legal works, which should be acceptable to God. There is but one work properly speaking, and this is no legal work.

HOMILETICS

We regard these words as illustrating a subject on which there is much talk, but little true intelligence, namely, *Evangelical faith.* The words present two facts explanatory of this subject.

I —EVANGELICAL FAITH IS FAITH IN THE PERSONAL CHRIST.

"*This is the work of God,*" said Christ in answer to the question of His hearers, "*that ye believe on Him whom He hath sent.*"

Evangelical faith is faith, not in *propositions,* whatever may be the amount of truth they embody, but faith in a *person,* and that person Christ Himself. This faith therefore stands in contradistinction to three things—

(1.) To faith in the *theology of any Church.* Millions in Christendom not only imagine, but propound the idea that evangelical faith consists in the acceptance of the articles of their Church. This is an error as pernicious as it is popular. This faith stands in contradistinction—

(2.) To faith in the *teaching of Christ Himself.* To believe in all the doctrines that Christ Himself propounded, is one thing; and to believe *in Him,* is another and very different thing. I may believe in the ethical teachings of Lord Bacon, and yet have no faith in him—in the scientific teaching of Stuart Mill, and yet have no faith in him—in the religious teaching of Calvin, and yet have no faith in him. In like manner, it is possible for me to accept the ethical and theological teaching of Christ, and yet have no faith in Him. This faith stands in contradistinction—

(3.) To faith in the *biography of Christ.* I may believe in all the facts of a man's life from his cradle to his grave, and yet have no faith in *him*. A man may accept the entire history of Christ as given in the Gospels, and yet have no trust in Him. Far enough am I from disparaging the importance of accepting as true the doctrines Christ propounded, or as real the facts of His history. Indeed, such acceptance I hold to be helpful if not indispensable to lead me up to a true faith in Him. Evangelical faith, then, I must maintain, is not faith in *propositions*, whether the propositions embody tenets of the most orthodox Church, or the teachings of Christ Himself, or even all the facts of His wonderful life. But it is faith in Him—

First: As the highest Embodiment of Divine excellence. We cannot set our entire faith on an imperfect being, still less on one of a corrupt character. To repose our utmost confidence in a being, we must not only be assured of his excellence, but that his excellence is absolutely complete—that he is all wise, all just, all loving, and all pure.

Secondly: As the faithful Revealer of the Great God. The Eternal has many revealers, but there is only One absolutely perfect. " No man hath seen God at any time : the Only Begotten of the Father, He hath declared Him." " He is the image of the invisible God, the express image of His person."

Thirdly: As the only Redeemer of mankind. Faith in Him means accepting Him as the only infallible Physician that can heal us of the malady of sin, the only Deliverer that can emancipate our spirits from the thraldom of depravity, the only sure Guide that can conduct us safely through the intricate, the shadowy, the perilous wilderness of life to a blessed immortality.

Such is the faith everywhere insisted upon by the teaching of Christ. " He that believeth in Me." This was His constant utterance. " In ME," not in what men say about Me, not merely in Mine—My teaching or My acts, but MYSELF. Such, and such only, He taught should be saved, should have life, should be useful.

II—FAITH IN THE PERSONAL CHRIST IS THE PARAMOUNT WORK OF MANKIND

" *This is the work of God.*" * Instead of faith standing opposed to work, it is *the* work of works. It is the spring and glory of all works. But, it is said, is not faith the " gift of God " ? Verily. But whilst God gives some things irrespective of our labour, such as existence, sun, air, water—other gifts, such as the crops of the husbandman, the daily bread of the labourer the mental attainments of the student, are only obtained in connection with human effort. So it is with this faith ; it requires work, and work of the hardest kind.

* See Homily on these words at end of the volume.

(1.) It is the work of *earnest investigation.* Before you can have faith in Christ, you must meet with Him; and you can only find Him out by resolute, honest, and persevering research. He is in the Bible; and the Scriptures must be searched. (2.) It is the work of *firmly holding.* When you find Him, you must hold Him fast. There are so many forces within and without, that turn you away from Him, that to hold on requires all the vigour of your soul. You must hold on as the drowning man holds on to the rope thrown out to his rescue. (3.) It is the work of *persistent following.* We must keep close to our Guide, or we shall be lost, follow our Commander, or we shall be slain in the battle. This is *the* work.

First: It is a work binding alike on all men. God legislates for our beliefs; and He demands that we should set our great faith on His Son. It is not a matter of indifference as to whether you shall believe on Him or not; it is a matter of urgent obligation. Non-believing on Him is the one great crime.

Secondly: It is a work performable alike by all men. It may be impossible for all men to believe on the same proposition—impossible for men to believe even in characters that are imperfect or corrupt. But all *can* believe in a character that embodies man's highest ideal of perfection.

Thirdly: It is a work indispensable alike to all men. This work is the great necessity of every man. It is indispensable to a man's own spiritual well-being. We are so constituted that nothing but faith can produce a reformation of the soul; no sacerdotal influences, no ritual observances, no mere legal efforts can do it. There must be faith. No faith in *propositions* can do it: there must be faith in a *Person,* and that Person must be none other than the Son of God. Hence the Apostles everywhere directed men to believe on Christ. "Believe on the Lord Jesus Christ, and thou shalt be saved." It is indispensable, also, in order to qualify a man to be spiritually useful to others. "He that believeth on *Me,*" saith Christ, "shall do the greater works." Why are ministers, why are Christians generally, so unsuccessful in their efforts to convert men? Simply because they either lack faith, or they set their faith on something short of Christ. Their faith is in obsolete dogmas, or hoary creeds, or their own little crotchets or superstitious dreams, and not in Christ as the living, loving, personal Son of God and Saviour of the world.

CONCLUSION. Here then is evangelical faith. It is faith in the Person of Christ, and this is the great work of mankind. Whilst I have no sympathy whatever with those morbid religionists the burden of whose addresses is "Only believe," I am profoundly convinced that the great want of the world is faith in Christ. Let us go for our faith, not to Churches, not to libraries, not to priesthoods, but to Judæa, and put ourselves in close and permanent contact with Him Who said, " All things are possible to him that believeth."

John 6:30-36

A TWOFOLD MANIFESTATION

" They said therefore unto Him, What sign shewest Thou then, that we may see, and believe Thee ? " &c.

EXEGETICAL REMARKS.—Ver. 30.— *" They said therefore unto Him, What sign shewest Thou then* (R. V. WHAT THEN DOEST THOU FOR A SIGN), *that we may see, and believe Thee ? What dost Thou work"* (R. V. WORKEST THOU) ? *" What dost Thou work ? "* Here they wished, as it were, to present again and give back to Christ the word *work*. We return it, and say, *" What dost Thou work ? "* " So rude and insolent is man ! The point would be far less fine if they had added the σύ, which is only carried on from what precedes. They have comprehended the greatness and difficulty of the demand which Christ makes upon them. In order to be able to require so much and to make upon us the demand to give up ourselves, Thou must do much greater works in proof of Thy authority than Thou hast yet done. Thou requirest infinitely more than Moses, and yet Moses did a much greater work. Thy feeding cannot compare with the miracle of the manna." — *Hengstenberg.* *" Thou,"* though not in the Greek, is emphatic. What dost *Thou* produce ?

Ver. 31.—*" Our fathers did eat* (R. V. ATE) *manna in the desert* (R. V. WILDERNESS) ; *as it is written, He gave them bread from* (R. V. OUT OF) *heaven to eat."* For accounts of this manna see Exodus xvi. ; Numbers xi. 7—9 ; Joshua v. 12. It continued for forty years, it had the taste of coriander-seed mixed with honey and olive oil : it fell on the dew, and was therefore preserved from the dust ; it fell daily, and became rancid if kept over the Sabbath; it amounted daily to about ninety-four thousand four hundred and sixty-six bushels, and that continued for forty years. They forgot that their fathers disbelieved Moses almost from the time

of their eating the manna, which descended miraculously, feeding two millions every day.

Ver. 32.—*" Then Jesus* (R. V. THERE-FORE) *said unto them, Verily, verily, I say unto you, Moses* (R. V. IT WAS NOT MOSES THAT) *gave you not that* (R. V. THE) *bread from* (R. V. OUT OF) *heaven ; but My Father giveth you the true bread from* (R. V. OUT OF) *heaven."* It was not Moses that gave you that bread ; he was the mere instrument, nor did it come from heaven. It came from the atmosphere, and then it was not the true bread, the bread that fed man as man.

Ver. 33.—*" For the bread of God is He* (R. V. THAT) *which cometh down from* (R. V. OUT OF) *heaven, and giveth life unto the world."* The *"bread of God,"* that is, the bread which God provides, is really of heavenly origin and quality, and it is He which cometh down from heaven. The manna which fell in the wilderness came from the clouds, the *" bread of God "* came from the spiritual heavens.

Ver. 34.—*" Then said* (R. V. THEY SAID THEREFORE) *they unto Him, Lord, evermore give us this bread."* " The similarity," says *Hengstenberg,* " of the answer of the Jews here to the answer of the Samaritan woman in John iv. 15, is explained by the fact, that it is the same Jesus who draws forth both the one and the other answer. On both occasions He had placed in prospect a glorious good—there a precious drink, here a precious food ; and not until He had called forth the expression of desire for it, did He explain the connection of this good with His own person."

Ver. 35.—*" And Jesus said unto them, I am the bread of life."* You ask for the bread of heaven, here it is,

I *am* that bread. " These words," said Luther, "should be written on the heart with golden letters." " *He that cometh to Me shall never* (R. V. NOT) *hunger; and he that believeth on Me shall never thirst.*" I satisfy for ever the deep craving of humanity.

Ver. 36.—*But I said unto you, That ye also have seen Me, and* (R. V. YET) *believe not.*" He means to say, You appropriate not the true bread because you believe not in Me. Although you see Me, you will not believe.

HOMILETICS

We have here a *twofold manifestation*—one of the *depravity of men*, and the other of the mercy of God.

I —A MANIFESTATION OF THE DEPRAVITY OF MEN.

The words which the Jews addressed on this occasion to Christ are a sad revelation of their moral wrongness. Mark—

First: Their *ingratitude*. *"What sign showest Thou?"* Why, only yesterday they had witnessed the miracle of the loaves and fishes, when five thousand people were fed, and basketfuls of fragments taken up unused. He had just, too, hushed the storm at sea, and walked upon the waves. All this, forsooth, they seem now to overlook and disregard. One might have thought that the wonders of mercy that they had already seen would not only have convinced them of His Messiahship, but overwhelmed them with gratitude and devotion. Ingratitude is one of the commonest and basest of vices.

> " Time hath a wallet at his back
> Wherein he puts alms for oblivion,
> A great sized mouther of ingratitudes ;
> Those scraps are good deeds past ; which are devoured
> As fast as they are made, forgot as soon as done."—*Shakspeare.*

Mark—

Secondly: Their *ignorance*. If they were in earnest for more miracles in order to believe, it showed their ignorance of what is necessary to produce faith. Mere miracles cannot insure faith. The history of the Israelites during their forty years' wanderings in the wilderness was a history of miracles, yet they believed not; their unbelief was their crime and their ruin. Furthermore the multiplication of miracles would destroy their effect. The power of miracles is in their rarity, not in their commonness. The men who are looking out—and they abound everywhere—for more evidence than they have, show, not only their ingratitude, but their ignorance as well. "If ye believe not Moses and the prophets, neither will ye believe though one rose from the dead." Mark—

Thirdly: Their *unspirituality*. "*Lord, evermore give us this bread.*" "They judged after the flesh," and concluded that the "*bread*" to which Christ had referred as the bread of God was mere material bread—bread to strengthen and satisfy their body.

They were too carnal to discover the truth which Christ propounded, namely, that He Himself was the true bread of the soul. Truly, "the carnal mind discerneth not the things of the Spirit, neither can he know them," for they are spiritually discerned. Alas that men, endowed with a spiritual nature, should be conscious only of corporeal wants, and crave only after material good !

Fourthly : Their *folly.* "*Evermore give us this bread.*" They desired to have this material food, irrespective of their efforts, given to them continually, as the manna in the wilderness, day by day. Their impression seems to have been, that to have the means of subsistence and satisfaction independent of labour was supremely desirable. Great folly this ! One of the greatest blessings of humanity is that Divine law which requires men to work for their livelihood. Labour is the condition of physical strength, intellectual development, and moral discipline.

Such are the bad moral attributes which the language of these Jews reveals; and such attributes, alas ! are as prevalent now. Ingratitude, ignorance, unspirituality, and folly mark the history of unrenewed men in all ages and lands.

We have here—

II —A MANIFESTATION OF THE MERCY OF GOD

First : *In the bestowment of a transcendent gift.* Observe (1.) The *necessity* of the gift. It is "*bread.*" The true bread from heaven. What material bread is to the body, Christ-spiritual bread is to the soul,—essential to its sustenance and satisfaction. It is a necessity of being. Men want bread, not theories of bread. Preachers throughout Christendom have been giving hungry souls theories (creeds) of Christ, and they are morally starving everywhere. The necessities of life are the invaluable things. (2.) The *nature* of the gift. What is the bread ? It is Christ Himself. "*I am the bread of life.*" Christ Himself is the food of souls. What a gift is this ! "God so loved the world, that He gave His only begotten Son." The universe is nothing in point of value to this. (3.) The *universality* of the gift. "*Giveth life unto the world.*" This bread is not provided for a class, but for the race : not for particular men, but for humanity. What a manifestation, then, of Divine mercy you have in this transcendent gift—a gift vital to the well-being of man. Nothing less than Christ Himself, and intended for the whole race.

This mercy appears—

Secondly : *In the simplicity of the condition on which the personal enjoyment of the gift depends.* That condition is represented here as coming to Christ, and as believing on Him. "*He that cometh to Me shall never hunger, and he that believeth on Me shall never thirst.*" Christ only becomes food for the human soul, appeasing its hunger, quenching its thirst, satisfying all its powers, so far as He is approached with unbounded confidence and love. And all may thus approach Him. It is no hard condition; nothing is more simple, in fact, than to trust the undoubtedly Trustworthy, and to love the undoubtedly Good. Men are made to believe, and made to love; and the more manifestly true and good a being is, the more easy the faith and the love.

CONCLUSION. O hungry and thirsty souls, come in love and faith to Christ, and you shall *never hunger, never thirst.* Believe me, there is nothing else on this round earth, nothing in the universe of God, that can support and satisfy your natures. "Where, but in the bosom of Christianity, has the heaven-born soul found its rest and peace, its cravings satisfied, its aspirations filled, and its highest heaven of hope realized? A bright cloud of witnesses respond, 'Nowhere but in Jesus Christ.'"

John 6:37-40

CHRIST IN RELATION TO THE ABSOLUTE WILL

"All that the Father giveth Me shall come to Me; and him that cometh to Me I will in no wise cast out," &c.

EXEGETICAL REMARKS.—Ver. 37.— "*All that* (R. V. THAT WHICH) *the Father giveth Me shall come to* (R. V. UNTO) *Me.*" The word "*all*" is in the neuter gender, and therefore does not necessarily include men. It may include power, dominion, success. Christ ascribes everything to His Father. He regarded the mediatorial power He received after His resurrection as from His Father. "All power is *given* unto Me." Even the political power that Pilate had to condemn Him to death, He ascribed to His Father. "Thou couldst have no power at all against Me except it were given thee from above." Indeed, Christ speaks of Judas as being given to Him. "Those that Thou gavest Me I have kept; but the son of perdition." We do not see Calvinian election here. "*Him that cometh to Me I will in no wise cast out.*" Here is the masculine gender. Whoever the man may be that comes to Christ, he will be received; on no account will he be rejected. A more faithful translation of the verse cannot perhaps be given than that of *Dean Alford:* "All which the Father giveth to Me

shall come to Me, and he that cometh to Me I will in no wise cast out."

Ver. 38.—"*For I came* (R. V. AM COME) *down from heaven, not to do Mine own will, but the will of Him that sent Me.*" Mark His origin. Heaven—where is that? Where the presence of the Eternal is especially manifest. Mark His mission: "*Not to do Mine own will, but the will of Him that sent Me.*"

Ver. 39.—"*And this is the Father's will which* (R. V. WILL OF HIM THAT) *hath sent Me, that of all which* (R. V. THAT WHICH) *He hath given Me I should lose nothing, but should raise it up again at the last day.*" Who can tell what the Father has given Christ? He has given Him the universe. Whatever He has given Him He will take care of,—answer for the whole at the "*last day.*" ἐσχάτῃ ἡμέρᾳ. Does Paul refer to this, when he says: "Then cometh the end when He shall have delivered up the kingdom to God, even the Father, when He shall have put down all rule and all authority and power." "*Raise it*"—not them —"*up again at the last day.*" On the last day there will be many resurrections besides the resurrection of men. The resurrections of buried truth, dead consciences, abused mercies, etc.

Ver. 40.—"*And* (R. V. FOR) *this is the will of Him that sent Me* (R. V. MY FATHER), *that every one which seeth* (R. V. BEHOLDETH) *the Son, and be-* lieveth on Him, may (R. V. SHOULD) *have everlasting* (R. V. ETERNAL) *life: and I will raise him up at the last day.*" Here is the condition of everlasting happiness. Seeing the Son, and believing on Him.

HOMILETICS

The subject of these words is, *Christ in relation to the absolute will.* The words teach, concerning the Father, the Great Head of the universe—(1.) He has a Will. He is not unintelligent force, blind and resistless; He is a free mind. He wills. (2). He has a Will in relation to humanity. He has not left men to chance or fate, but taken them into His purpose and plan. (3.) That Christ is the great Interpreter and Administrator of this Will. He came down from heaven to do it. Of all who ever trod this earth, He alone knows the whole will of the Father. He was in the bosom of the Father. He knows the inmost purpose of the Eternal fountain of life. The verses lead us to consider two things in relation to Christ and the Divine will.

I —CHRIST REVEALS HIMSELF TO MAN IN RELATION TO THE DIVINE WILL

The words teach,—

First: That He had a thorough knowledge of it. He speaks of it as a subject with which He was perfectly acquainted; He knew it in all its relations and bearings upon humanity through the ages.

Secondly: That He had unbounded confidence in it. "*All that the Father giveth Me, shall come to Me.*" * He knew that that will would never break down, but would be realized on every point. He knew that the Father intended Him to have power, and He would have it; success in His mission, and He would have it; genuine disciples, and He would have them; a spiritual kingdom, and He would have it.

Thirdly: He cordially acquiesced in it. "*Him that cometh to Me, I will in no wise cast out.*" It is His will that men should come to Me as their Teacher, Example, Redeemer, and I am willing to receive all. I will on no account "*cast*" any man away. I will not cast him away on account of the greatness of his age, or the number and enormity of his sins. When I come into possession of all that My Father wills Me to have, instead of using it to crush the sinner I will receive him, "*I will in no wise cast out.*"

Fourthly: He absolutely obeyed it. "*I came down from heaven, not to do Mine own will, but the will of Him that sent Me.*" † He was influenced by no personal consideration; He committed

* See Homily on these words at end of volume.　　† See Germ, p. 165.

Himself absolutely to the working out of the Divine will. His meat and His drink was to do the will of His Father.

II —CHRIST REVEALS TO THE WORLD THE DIVINE WILL IN RELATION TO HUMANITY

He taught that it was the will of God—

First: That they should be *everlastingly happy* through Him. " *This is the will of Him that sent Me, that every one which seeth the Son, and believeth on Him, may have everlasting life."* * Here is the true ground for belief in the immortality of the soul. Some men ground their faith in the immortality of the soul upon what they call its immateriality. But as no science can inform me what matter is : how can I predicate concerning immateriality ? Some ground their faith on the undeveloped powers of the soul at death. But do we not find everywhere, in the vegetable and animal kingdoms, millions of existences dying with undeveloped powers ? Some ground their faith on the instinctive longings of the human soul for a future state. But have not men on all hands instinctive longings here for things they can never have, and were never intended to have—such as long life, wealth, fame, dominion ? Some ground their faith on the idea that men have not justice done them here ; that the Divine government here makes no distinction between the righteous and the wicked. But does not the greatest sufferer feel in his conscience he has less punishment than he deserves ? I rest my faith in immortality on the revealed will of the Absolute One. All existences are either contingent or absolute, dependent or independent. There is but One Absolute Existence, and that is God ; and all others depend upon His " *will."* The only way in which I can ascertain the duration of any creature's existence, is to ascertain the Creator's will concerning him. If the Creator has willed that he shall go out of existence in a few years, or days, or hours ; then, however strong or robust in constitution, his being shall terminate for ever. But if He has willed that he shall continue for ever ; then, however fragile his constitution, he will run on through ages without end. Now, here I have the will of God on this question, stated by One who knew it thoroughly, and in language too unambiguous to misunderstand. " *This is the will of Him that sent Me, that every one which seeth the Son, and believeth on Him*, MAY HAVE EVERLASTING LIFE."

Secondly : That they should *recover everything that was lost* through Him. What do men lose here ? Their virtue, their freedom, their rights. Christ here says, that it is the will of His Father that He should " *raise it up at the last day,"* † whatever it be. They lose more. They leave the bodies through which they received their impressions and wrought out their character to

* See Germ, p. 165.   † *Ibid.* p. 166.

moulder in the dust. Christ says, in relation to every man who sees Him, that it is the will of His Father that He should "*raise him up at the last day.*" He will have a "restitution of all things."

Germs of Thought
No. 26   John 6:39

THE DIVINE WILL
"The Father's Will."

I —HERE IS AN EXPRESSED OBJECT OF THE DIVINE WILL

What is it?

That nothing of all that has been entrusted to Christ shall be lost. It is not His will that "one of the least of the little ones" shall perish. Destruction seems repugnant to the Divine mind. Matter seems indestructible; since the beginning of the world not an atom has been lost.

II —HERE IS A GLORIOUS DELEGATE OF THE DIVINE WILL

Who is He? Christ.

(1.) He is the Father's *Messenger*. (2.) He is the Father's *Steward*. "All which He hath given Me." Something has been entrusted to Him. What? "Power over all flesh" has been given to Him. Universal authority has been given to Him. "All power is given Me in heaven, and in earth." All who believe in Him as their Saviour are given Him. "All that Thou hast given Me I have kept." All truth has been given to Him. "I have given unto them the word which Thou gavest Me."

III —HERE IS AN ULTIMATE REALIZATION OF THE DIVINE WILL

Nothing that has been entrusted to Him shall be lost, but shall be raised up again at the last day. Christ will take care of everything that has been entrusted to Him, preserve all intact, and render up all at last to the great God. (1.) Not a soul entrusted to His care *will be lost.* (2.) Every soul entrusted to His care will be *exalted* in the last day. In this last day *God's* will concerning the redemption of the world will be fully realized.

No. 27   John 6:40

GOD'S UNALTERABLE DECREE IN RELATION TO MAN
" And this is the will of Him that sent Me, that every one which seeth the Son, and believeth on Him, may have everlasting life : and I will raise him up at the last day."

Much has been said and written about God's decrees. The dogmatism of narrow-minded theologians concerning them has made them something terrible to the common mind. But what are His decrees but the resolves of Infinite love ? The text leads us to make two remarks concerning them.

I —GOD DECREES THE WELL-BEING OF MANKIND

It is His "*will*" that we should have "*everlasting life.*" What does this mean ? Is it merely an existence without an end ? All, perhaps, will have that. But it means an *endless existence* in the *absence* of all *evil* and in *possession of all good*—physical, intellectual, social, religious.

II —GOD DECREES A SETTLED CONDITION FOR MAN'S WELL-BEING

The condition is *faith in Christ.* "*This is the will of Him that sent Me, that every one which seeth the Son, and believeth on Him,*" &c. In the days of His flesh thousands *saw* Him who did not believe on Him ; and now multitudes intellectually see Him who do not believe on Him. Faith in Him is God's condition. Faith in Him—

First : As the Divine Redeemer. One sent of God for the work of effecting the spiritual restoration of the world. Faith in Him—

Secondly : As the all-sufficient Redeemer ;—"One that is mighty to save." Faith in Him—

Thirdly : As the only Redeemer. "There is no other name given under heaven whereby ye may be saved." God's decree then is that man's well-being should be obtained through faith in Christ. God does not desire the misery of any man, but the happiness of all ; and as He has decreed that light shall come to the earth through the sun, He has decreed that true happiness shall come to humanity through faith in Christ.

No. 28   John 6:40

THE LAST DAY
"The last day."

There is the last day in everything in this life.

I —THERE IS THE "LAST DAY" IN BUSINESS

The last day comes to the tradesman in his shop, to the merchant on the Exchange, to the lawyer in his office, to the clerk at his desk, &c. &c.

II —THERE IS THE "LAST DAY" IN CHURCH

The last sermon heard, the last hymn sung, the last service attended, and the pew left for ever.

III —THERE IS THE "LAST DAY" IN LIFE

The whole of life dwindled down to one day in a certain year, month, week. The last refreshment taken, the last word spoken, the last breath drawn. The "*last day.*"

John 6:41-47

THE TENDENCY OF UNBELIEF

"The Jews then murmured at Him, because He said, I am the bread which came down from heaven," &c.

EXEGETICAL REMARKS.—Ver. 41.— *"The Jews then murmured at* (R. V. CONCERNING) *Him."* " A new section of the affair, occasioned by the Jews taking decisive offence at the preceding discourse. The οὖν is again very definitive. The verb γογγύζω, of itself, denotes neither, on the one hand, a whispering, nor, on the other, a grumbling or fault-finding ; but the murmuring is here the expression of fault-finding, and is made by the context ('among yourselves') and by the antagonism ('at Him') synonymous with it."—*Lange.* *" Because He said, I am the bread which came down from* (R. V. OUT OF) *heaven."* His claim here to have come down from heaven roused their rebellious spirits, His claim to be very God was insufferable to them.

Ver. 42.—*"And they said, Is not this Jesus, the son of Joseph, whose father and mother we know?"* *"Is not this Jesus,"*—who thus arrogates Divinity, represents Himself as coming down from heaven,—*"the son of Joseph,"* of Nazareth, a poor carpenter ? What does He mean ? *"How is it then that He saith, I came down from* (R. V. HOW DOTH HE NOW SAY I CAME DOWN OUT OF) *heaven ?"* His claim is false and impious.

Vers. 43, 44.—*"Jesus therefore answered and said unto them, Murmur not among yourselves. No man can come to Me, except the Father which hath sent Me draw him : and I will raise him up at* (R. V. IN) *the last day."* "Ἑλκύειν denotes all sorts of drawing, from violence to persuasion or invitation. But persons can be drawn only according to the laws of personal life. . . . Hence this is not to be taken in a high predestinarian sense." "The point of our Saviour's reply is, that all dispute about His person is fruitless, until the internal sense of want is experienced. In what this consists we are told in the forty-fifth and forty-sixth verses." *Luther :*—"You wish to subject Me to measure and square, and judge My word by your reason ; but I say to you, that is not the right way and path. You will not come to Him till the Father opens to you His great mercy, and Himself teaches you that from His Fatherly love He sent Christ into the world. [For] the drawing is not as a hangman draws a thief to the gallows, but it is a friendly alluring and drawing to Himself." *Tholuck :*—" Jesus therefore virtually says, Except the Divine works which the Father hath empowered Me to do, and the doctrines He has ordered Me to preach, induce men to believe in Me as a Teacher, commissioned by God to instruct them in heavenly truths, they cannot in any other way or by any other arguments do so."

Ver. 45.—*" It is written in the prophets, And they shall be all taught of God."* The particular reference is here to Isaiah liv. 13 ; but the sense of the statement runs through the prophets. (See Isaiah xi. ; Jeremiah xxxi. 33 ; Joel iii. 1.) It points to the gospel dispensation, when *"all"* are to be taught of God. *" Every man* (R. V. ONE) *therefore that hath heard* (R. V. OF THE FATHER), *and hath learned of the Father, cometh unto Me."* Here is a universal truth, every one that is in sympathy with the Father will come to the Son. All that pay attention to what the Father teaches, will not fail to be drawn with a loving interest to His Son. Like attracts like.

Ver. 46.—*" Not that any man hath seen the Father, save He which is of* (R. V. FROM) *God, He hath seen the Father."* Some suppose that Christ in this verse contrasts His seeing God with that of Moses ; others, that He means the inward manifestation of God supersedes the historical Christ ; others, that He indicates a difference in kind and degree of revelation ; others, that He indicates His transcendent nature in relation to the

Father. He only *"hath seen the Father."* Not Moses, not even the angels, have seen the Absolute Divinity.

Ver. 47.—*"Verily, verily, I say unto you."* A species of oath. *"Believeth on Me."* (R. V. OMITS ON ME.) The Divine redeeming Messenger from heaven. *"Hath everlasting* (R. V. ETERNAL) *life." "Hath"*—not shall have. Genuine faith in Christ puts man *now* and *here* in possession of everlasting goodness and blessedness.

HOMILETICS

In these verses there are several subjects which arrest attention and are worthy of serious meditation.

I —THE TENDENCY OF UNBELIEF

"The Jews then murmured at Him, because He said, I am the bread which came down from heaven. And they said, Is not this Jesus, the son of Joseph, whose father and mother we know? how is it then that He saith, I came down from heaven?"

"The Jews then murmured"—murmured in their own hearts, murmured to one another, and in all against Christ. Why did they murmur? Because of their reluctance to identify the Divine with the common. How could One whom they knew was from Nazareth be from heaven, One whose father and mother they knew as poor people be the Son of God? Had they not known the obscure scene of His nativity and the social lowliness of His parents, then,—had He performed such wonders as they witnessed, proclaimed such doctrines as they had heard,—they might have been disposed to have identified Him with the Divine. This feeling, which the Jews here displayed, is the tendency of unbelief, a tendency—

First: *Fearfully prevalent.* You may see it in the conduct of man in relation to the phenomena of *material nature.* Men may connect the idea of God with some majestic tree, but not with the daisy; with the lion, but not with the insect; with the thunderstorm, but not with the whispering zephyr. You may see it in the conduct of men in relation to their *contemporaries.* They are quick to catch what they consider glimpses of Divinity in the great of the land—in the high titled ecclesiastics, the bedizened nobles, the renowned orators and authors; but not a ray of the Divine can they see in humble life—in the devotion of parents, the innocent love of children, the streams of genuine sympathy that run through every sphere. Who does not recognize this tendency? Who does not feel it? It is a tendency—

Secondly: *Philosophically absurd.* Right reason assures us that Divinity, if anywhere, must be everywhere—as truly in the atom as in the globe, in the blade as in the forest, in the calm as in the tempest, in the fly as in the eagle; as truly with the poorest men as with the greatest, and that morally it flashes out in the life of the godly pauper more than in all the magnificent doings of mere worldly dignitaries. This tendency is—

Thirdly: *Morally reprehensible.* It is the duty of every man to see God everywhere, hear His voice in every sound, and behold His presence in every form, His energy in every motion. "Do not I fill heaven and earth? saith the Lord." "The earth is His temple." "God is a Spirit, and they that worship Him must worship Him in spirit and in truth." This tendency is—

Fourthly: *Spiritually pernicious.* It lessens our appreciation of nature, checks the growth of the sentiment in the heart of what is due to all men, shuts out God from the largest sphere of our activity, and reduces life to that of practical atheism. Let us seek to crush this tendency in our own hearts by a devout cultivation of the sense of God's universal presence.

Another subject which we find in these verses demanding our attention is—

II —THE DIVINITY OF CHRISTIANITY

" *Jesus therefore answered and said unto them, Murmur not among yourselves. No man can come to Me, except the Father which hath sent Me draw him: and I will raise him up at the last day.*" In these verses you have God doing two things—

First: Sending His Son to man. "*The Father which hath sent Me.*" Christ was "*sent,*" not by any secondary authorities. He came forth as a Messenger of the Eternal, came as the Result, the Revelation, and the Minister of God's free and boundless love to the world. He was sent, not contrary to His own will. He came as no reluctant Messenger. His heart was in full sympathy with that of the Eternal Father. His "delight was in the law of the Lord." His "meat and His drink" was to do the Divine will. He was "*sent,*" and He demonstrated the Divinity of His commission. "No man can do these miracles that Thou doest, except God be with Him," so said Nicodemus, and so says impartial and enlightened reason through all ages.

In these verses you have God doing another thing—

Secondly: Bringing man to His Son. "*No man can come to Me, except the Father which hath sent Me draw him.*" Man's well-being consists in being brought into a faithful, loving fellowship with Christ. Though Christ came, men stood aloof from Him. "He came to His own, and His own received Him not." Hence the Infinite Father draws men to Him. What meaneth this?

(1.) *Coercion* is not meant here. The great Creator treats all creatures according to the natures He has given them. He has endowed man with freedom, and He never has and never will infringe the principles of his liberty. He does not draw the soul

170 / Gospel of John

as the constable draws the prisoner into his cell, but as a loving mother draws her children to her arms.

(2.) *Partiality* is not meant here. It does not mean that He influences some to the exclusion of others. He shows no favouritism. All souls are His.

(3.) *Miracle* is not meant here. He draws souls by means and agencies in harmony with the laws of their nature, by the influences of events, material and spiritual, by the suggestions of thought, the workings of conscience, and the ministry of the gospel.

(4.) *Superfluity* is not meant here. This work is not unnecessary work. So destitute of sympathy with Christ is unregenerate humanity, and so potent and active are the influences of the flesh, the world, and the devil in drawing souls away from the Divine, that His drawing is indispensable. The human soul in this life is subject to two drawings—the one is *away from* Christ, the other is *to* Christ. The latter is Divine.

Another subject which we find in these verses demanding our attention is—

III THE PRE-EMINENCE OF JESUS

" *It is written in the prophets, And they shall be all taught of God. Every man therefore that hath heard, and hath learned of the Father, cometh unto Me. Not that any man hath seen the Father, save He which is of God, He hath seen the Father.*"

These verses teach two things illustrating the pre-eminence of Christ—

First : That all souls truly influenced by the Divine, will come to Him. "*Every man,*" etc. Christ gets the true men of every age, gets them as His disciples, His loyal servants, His devoted friends. Who are those that keep aloof from Him ? Not the best authors, statesmen, kings, citizens, fathers, mothers, husbands, wives, children, &c. No ; but the worst. The best come to Christ. And they will all come one day. "*It is written in the prophets, And they shall be all taught of God.*" "All men shall be drawn to Him, all nations shall call Him blessed."

Another thing taught in these verses concerning the pre-eminence of Christ is—

Secondly : That no one but Christ has any absolute knowledge of the Father. "*Not that any man hath seen the Father, save He which is of God, He hath seen the Father.*" God is the Mystery to all creatures, and will continue to be so for ever, after the study of millenniums. The most capacious intellect and the most diligent and successful student in the universe is ever ready to exclaim, "Who by searching can find out God ?"

> We cannot find Thee out, Lord,
> For infinite Thou art,

Thy wondrous works and word, Lord,
Reveal Thee but in part.
The drops that swell the ocean,
The sands that girt the shore,
To measure Thy duration
Their numbers have no power.
Thy nature is the mystery
In which all thoughts are lost,
Archangels wonder at Thee
Through heaven's unnumbered host ;
Unbounded is Thine essence,
All space is full of Thee,
And 'tis Thy Blessed presence
That suns immensity.

But Christ understands Him, and He alone. He was in the bosom of the Father. He knows Him, knows His nature, fathoms His thoughts, and comprehends His infinite purposes. He then is the Teacher of mankind, the Image of the Invisible God.

There is one more subject here demanding our attention, and that is—

IV. THE WELL-BEING OF HUMANITY

"*Verily, verily, I say unto you, He that believeth on Me hath everlasting life.*" Observe—

First : The nature of man's well-being. "*Everlasting life.*" Life is esteemed by all as the transcendent blessing. "All that a man hath will he give in exchange for his life." But this transcendent blessing may, and often does, become an intolerable curse; hence suicides. Aye, "*everlasting life,*"—taking life in the sense of existence, —may be an everlasting curse. But life here means happiness, well-being. It means everlasting well-being, living for ever in virtue, liberty, intelligence, dignity, progress.

Secondly : The condition of man's well-being. "*He that believeth on Me.*" *Me;* not what men say about *Me;* not My doctrines and history, but Myself.*

Conclusion. From this subject two things may be inferred—

First : That the true religion of man is essentially connected with the existence of Christ. There may be other intelligent creatures in the universe whose genuine religion has no connection with Jesus of Nazareth. In their case, it may be, that supreme sympathy with the Infinitely Good which was planted in their nature at first, has been nourished and developed under the influences of nature. This would have been the religion of man, had he not fallen; but now, all that is true in the religion of humanity has a vital relation to the character of Jesus Christ. He is its Example, Standard, and Inspiration.

Secondly : That the true religion of man is generated in the soul

* This subject has come under our attention in previous portions of this Gospel.

by the special agency of God. He sent Christ to man, and brings man to Christ for this purpose. The religion of unfallen intelligences requires no such special agency. In them it is but the development of their spiritual nature. Not so with man. By sin, he has quenched within him the true religion; and God's special effort is required to resuscitate, strengthen, and mature it. Hence in the Holy Scripture it is spoken of as a spiritual regeneration, resurrection, creation. He creates them "anew in Christ Jesus unto good works."

Thus, in fact, the true religion of man is the life of Christ in the soul, the life produced by the special agency of the Eternal Father. They are one with Christ,

> " And in their souls His image bear,
> Rejoicing in the likeness. As the sun
> Doth spread his radiance through the fields of air,
> And kindle in revolving stars his blaze,
> He pours upon their hearts the splendour of His rays."
>
> *Thomas C. Upham.*

John 6:48-58

CHRIST AS A DIVINE GIFT TO THE WORLD

" I am that bread of life. Your fathers did eat manna in the wilderness, and are dead," &c.

EXEGETICAL REMARKS.—Ver. 48.— " *I am that* (R. V. THE) *bread of life.*" This refers back to the previous announcement (ver. 35). "*That*" bread which came down from heaven, and which is necessary to the spiritual life of the world.

Vers. 49, 50.—" *Your fathers did eat manna in the wilderness, and are dead* (R. V. THEY DIED). *This is the bread which cometh down from* (R. V. OUT OF) *heaven, that a man may eat thereof, and not die.*" Here is a contrast between the life which the manna of Moses sustained and the spiritual life which is nourished by Christ, the living bread. All who ate the manna in the wilderness are dead centuries ago. None who partake of this true bread have or will ever die.

Ver. 51.—"*I am the living bread which came down from* (R. V. OUT OF) *heaven: if any man eat of this bread, he shall live for ever.*" Christ in this discourse repeats the same idea in different connections or phrases, in order to increase its force and intensify its emphasis. " *Living bread ;*" what

an expression ! Bread living ! Not only does it give life, but it is life. "*And* (R. V. YEA AND) *the bread that I will give is My flesh, which I will give for the life of the world.*" " The word '*flesh*' here must be taken as standing for Himself. It was often used in Scripture, sometimes without the word blood, to represent the whole man. What Christ means to say, therefore, is this,—'The bread that I give is Myself.' The flesh and blood of Christ are the historical Christ."— *Lange.*

Ver. 52.—" *The Jews therefore strove among themselves* (R. V. ONE WITH ANOTHER), *saying, How can this Man give us His flesh to eat ?*" The Jews were scandalized that a mere man should put forth such pretensions. " *How can this Man give us His flesh to eat ?*" The language to them seemed to be to the last degree absurd, and if it had a meaning, it meant blasphemy.

Ver. 53.—" *Then Jesus said* (R. V. THEREFORE) *unto them, Verily, verily, I say unto you, Except ye eat the flesh of the Son of man, and drink His blood,*

ye have no life· in you " (R. V. YOUR-
SELVES). " The Divine Teacher uses
these violent figures and bold para-
doxes powerfully to excite their attention, and to implant a seed of truth
which might afterwards germinate.
At present, He does not care to retain
among His disciples such mercenary
and earthly-minded followers. Hence,
instead of softening or explaining
expressions so offensive to their feelings and prejudices, He indulges in
others still more strange and paradoxical. He thus tested the faith of
His disciples, sifted His hearers, the
good from the bad, and inculcated
lessons of truth of inestimable value
to all ages."

Vers. 54, 55, 56.—" *Whoso* (R. V. HE
THAT) *eateth My flesh, and drinketh My
blood, hath eternal life; and I will raise
him up at the last day. For My flesh is
meat indeed, and My blood is drink
indeed. He that eateth My flesh, and
drinketh My blood, dwelleth* (R. V.
ABIDETH) *in Me, and I in him.*" Now,
the all-important question which one
has to determine here is, What does our
Saviour mean by "*flesh and blood?*"
He does not mean, of course, literally
the materials out of which His body
was built up, nor does He mean anything like what Papists hold, that the
bread and the wine employed at the
Lord's Supper become, after the invo-
cation of the priests, transmuted into
the flesh and blood of Christ. He
means, I imagine, simply this—Myself,
my life. "*Flesh and blood*" are employed in a large variety of passages
in the Bible to represent the life of
man. (See Psalm xiv. 4; lxv. 2;
Isaiah xl. 5, 6; Jeremiah xii. 12;
Luke iii. 6.) Again, we have such
expressions as these, "Flesh and blood
hath not revealed it" (Matt. xvi. 17);

"They twain shall be one flesh"
(Matt. xix. 5, 6)`; "No flesh shall glory"
(1 Cor. i. 29); "I conferred not with
flesh and blood" (Gal. i. 16); "The
children are partakers of flesh and
blood"(Heb. ii. 14) ; "Flesh and blood
cannot inherit the kingdom" (1 Cor.
xv. 50). In all these passages both the
words "*flesh and blood,*" sometimes
separately and sometimes together,
stand for human life. Hence, to ascertain the real meaning the words have
in His language, is to ascertain what
His life really was. What was the animating, ruling principle of His *being,*
that which marked Him off from all
other men, that in fact made Him Christ?
There is but one answer to this, namely,
Self-sacrificing love. The meaning
therefore I take to be this, that unless
you take into yourself *My life,*—My
self·sacrificing love,—you cannot live.

Ver. 57.—" *As the living Father hath
sent Me, and I live by* (R. V. BECAUSE OF)
*the Father : so he that eateth Me, even
he* (R. V. HE ALSO) *shall live by* (R. V.
BECAUSE OF) *Me.*" Christ here asserts,
not only that the living Father had
sent Him, but that the life of the
Father was in Him ; that is, the same
spiritual life—the life of disinterested
love that was in the Father—was in
Him, and that that life was the privilege of all who would participate of
His Spirit. The real life of a moral
intelligence is self-sacrificing love, that
life is the life of God, the life of
Christ, and, through Christ, is the life
of mankind.

Ver. 58.—" *This is that bread which
came down from* (R. V. OUT OF) *heaven :
not as your* (R. V. THE) *fathers did eat
manna, and are dead* (R. V. DID EAT
AND DIED) : *he that eateth of this bread
shall live for ever.*" A repetition, this,
· of former utterances.

HOMILETICS

These words present to us *Christ as a Divine gift to the world,*
and they lead us to look upon Christ in three aspects.

I —AS A SPECIAL GIFT FROM THE FATHER

Christ here speaks of Himself as "*the Living Bread which came
down from heaven,*" as sent by the living Father. He gives His

hearers to understand that He was the gift of God to the world, and this He taught elsewhere in various places and forms of expression. "God so loved the world, that He gave His only begotten Son." But are not all things the gifts of God—life, the universe, and every element that ministers to the well-being of sentient creatures? Yes; "every good and perfect gift cometh down from above." But Christ is a *special* Gift.

First: He is the greatest Personality in the universe. The whole material system is not to be compared in value to that of one intelligent, free, responsible, undying personality. The poorest child of man is greater than stars and systems. But some personalities are greater than others. An angel may be greater than a man. Christ is greater, infinitely greater than all. "He is the image of the invisible God, in Him dwells all the fulness of the Godhead bodily." The Father, in giving Him, gave a greater treasure than if He had given all He had beside.

Secondly: He is the dearest Personality to God in the universe. He is His "beloved Son in whom He is well pleased," the special object, channel, and minister of His love. What a gift is this! A gift the transcendent value of which no created intellect through eternal ages will ever be able fully to appreciate. Another aspect in which the passage leads us to look at Christ is—

II —AS A FREE GIFT OF SELF

Christ was not given as a slave, either without His will or against His will; but in the gift of the Father He gives Himself. "*The bread that I will give is My flesh, for the life of the world.*" Between the will of His father and Himself, there was a vital and inviolable harmony. The one gift is the free gift of both. "I lay down My life for the sheep, no man taketh it from Me" (John x. 15—18). "He gave Himself a Ransom for all" (1 Tim. ii. 6). "Who loved me, and gave Himself for me," says Paul. Christ is at once the *Gift*, and the *Giver* of the gift. This may transcend our reason, but it shocks it not. Children often willingly and lovingly give themselves to a work to which their parents devote them. The passage presents to us Christ in yet another aspect—

III —AS AN INDISPENSABLE GIFT FOR MEN

It is "*the Bread of life.*"

First: There is no spiritual life without it. "*Except ye eat the flesh of the Son of man, and drink His blood, ye have no life in you.*" *
The life of Christ, as we have seen, was that of free, disinterested, self-sacrificing love. Unless man takes this into him, he has no life. Love is the only true spiritual life. The loss of this is man's

* See Germ, p. 175.

damnation, its restoration is man's salvation. Christ came to restore it.

Secondly: This spiritual life is identical with that of God and Christ. "*He that eateth My flesh, and drinketh My blood,* dwelleth in Me, and I in him. As the living Father hath sent Me, and I live by the Father: so he that eateth Me, even he shall live by Me.*" In the moral universe there is but one true life, and that is the life of love. "He that dwelleth in love dwelleth in God, and God in him." The living Father is its perennial fountain. The Blessed Son incarnated it, and supplies it to all who are willing to receive it. *Love is the bread of life.*

Thirdly: This spiritual life includes man's well-being for ever. Mark the words: "*A man may eat thereof, and not die. If a man eat of this bread, he shall live for ever. He that eateth My flesh and drinketh My blood, shall live for ever, and I will raise him up for ever.*" Yes; in this our eternal well-being consists.

CONCLUSION. Oh, ye hungry, starving souls, "Wherefore do ye spend your money for that which is not bread, and your labour for that which satisfieth not? Hearken diligently unto Me, and eat ye that which is good, and let your soul delight itself in fatness." The bread of the soul, believe me, is not animal pleasure, not intellectual knowledge, not gold, not power, not fame. It is love —love as flowing from the heart of the Living Father, as embodied in the life and inculcated in the teaching of Jesus of Nazareth. He who lives in Christ, to use the language of another, stands at the focus of rejuvenation.

> "Why, man, pursue thy weary calling,
> And wring thy hard life from the sky,
> While happiness unseen is falling
> Down from God's bosom silently?"

Germs of Thought
No. 29   John 6:53

SPIRITUAL CANNIBALISM

"Except ye eat the flesh of the Son of man, and drink His blood, ye have no life in you."

Taking the expression flesh and blood as representing life, the subject here is participation in the life of Christ. Two remarks may give a meaning to this much misunderstood and misinterpreted expression.

I —THAT IT IS POSSIBLE FOR ONE MAN TO PARTICIPATE IN THE LIFE OF ANOTHER

What is the real life of a man? Not his corporeal organization,

* See Germ, p. 176.

but the *spirit* that animates and controls him—his *governing disposition.* Throughout all society men are spiritually living on one another. *Spiritual cannibalism* is universal. Every man is under the control of some disposition. It may be vanity, greed, ambition. Whatever it be, it is his life. On the productions of this life others feed and fatten. Notice—

II—THAT IT IS NECESSARY FOR EVERY MAN TO PARTICIPATE IN THE LIFE OF CHRIST

What was the life of Christ,—His governing disposition, that which marked Him off from all other men? *Self-sacrificing* love for mankind. This was in fact His flesh and blood—His very life. Had He not had this He would not have been Christ. Now this spirit, this life, is the food essential to human souls. *"Except ye eat the flesh."* It fulfils the twofold function of food.

First: It satisfies. Food allays the cravings of appetite, &c. No act that a man can perform can yield soul-satisfaction unless inspired by this self-sacrificing love. Conscience will not pronounce "well done" to any other, though it may awaken the hosannas of the crowd. If I want soul-satisfaction I must drink in the spirit, the self-sacrificing love of Christ.

Secondly: It strengthens. The other function of food is to strengthen. Food invigorates the frame, recuperates lost energy, and generates new force. It is only as a man gets within him this self-sacrificing love that he gets true moral force—force to endure magnanimously—and to battle invincibly. These thoughts show that there is no difficulty in reaching the practical meaning of these wonderful words. The words have no reference to the Lord's Supper or to any institution. Men of superstitious feeling and superficial thought, have in all ages expended many a valuable hour on discussions on transubstantiation, consubstantiation, and other miserable superstitions in connection with these words. But they have nothing to do with such fancies. The idea is, that unless a man takes into him the moral Spirit of Christ which is His life—His *"flesh and blood"*—he himself can neither grow or live.

No. 30   John 6:54

THE UNIQUENESS OF CHRIST'S BLOOD, OR HIS SACRIFICED LIFE

"Whoso drinketh My blood hath eternal life."

The expression *"Blood of Christ,"* is used by millions who have no accurate idea concerning its import. Blood is life; and the essential idea is *Christ's self-sacrificed life.* The expression is frequently used in the New Testament (see Col. i. 20; 1 John

i. 7 ; Rev. v. 9 ; vii. 14 ; xii. 11 ; Eph. ii. 13 ; Acts xx. 28). Two general remarks are suggested.

I —THAT IT IS SOMETHING SUBLIMELY UNIQUE IN ITS NATURE

Things are said of it here that could not possibly be said with propriety of the blood of any other man, in any age or time, who has sacrificed his life. Millions of men have been sacrificed, they have lost their life, but not in the way in which Christ was sacrificed. Some have been sacrificed by *assassination*, some by *war*, some by *capital punishment*, some by *accident ;* most against their will, although some voluntarily, either by suicide or superstitious fanaticism. But in the case of Christ's sacrificed life there was nothing like this. Two facts especially marked off His sacrificed life from that of any other sacrificed life.

First : It was in accordance with the eternal plan of God. He was the " Lamb slain from the foundation of the world." There was nothing accidental about it, nothing out of keeping with the eternal order of things.

Secondly : It was voluntary in the sense in which no other man's death was voluntary. Amongst the millions of men who have died *most freely*, not one has felt that he need not die at all if he choose, that he could continue here for ever. But this Christ felt. There was no law in heaven or earth to force Him to the fate. " I have power to lay down My life, and power to take it up again."

Thirdly : It was absolutely free from all imperfection. Not one of all the teeming myriads who have departed this life has been entirely free from sin. All have had on them, to a greater or lesser extent, the common stain. But Christ was immaculate. His greatest enemies could not convince Him of sin ; Pilate and all His judges could find no fault with Him. He was " holy, harmless, and separate from sinners." Another remark suggested concerning the Blood of Christ is—

II —THAT IT IS SOMETHING SUBLIMELY UNIQUE IN ITS EFFECTS

Results are ascribed to this blood which could not with any propriety, or the slightest approach to truth, be ascribed to the blood of any other man.

First : These effects are variously represented. His blood is sometimes represented as *reconciliation*. His sacrificed life was *the atonement*. It is represented as *purification*. " It cleanseth from all sin," and through it men are made white. " Unto Him that loved us, and washed us," &c. It is represented as an *essential element of soul-life*. *" Whoso drinketh My blood hath eternal life :"* something that has not only to be applied to the soul, but taken into it. It is represented as a *ransom*. " Redeemed us to God by His blood," "purchased by His blood." It is the power to deliver from the guilt and dominion of sin. It is represented as a *conquering force.* "Overcame by the blood of the Lamb." Of whose blood have these results ever been predicated or can ever be ?

Secondly : These effects are universal in their influence. His blood "cleanseth from all sin," it makes the great "multitudes that no man can number" "white." How extensive has been its beneficent influence on humanity already ! But its present area of influence, as compared with its future, is less than a little lake to the ocean.

Thirdly : These effects are eternal in their blessings. "*Whoso drinketh My blood hath eternal life.*"

> "Dear dying Lamb, Thy precious blood
> Shall never lose its power,
> Till all the ransomed Church of God
> Be saved, to sin no more."

CONCLUSION. The subject—

First : Serves to explain both the essence of the Gospel and the essence of personal holiness. Christ's sacrificed life *is the Gospel,* and hence the very effects that are ascribed to His blood are also ascribed to the Gospel, to the *truth* of the Gospel, to the *grace* of the Gospel, to the *word* of the Gospel : all these are said to cleanse, to redeem, to conquer, to make white, &c. Not only does it serve to explain the essence of the Gospel, but the essence of *personal holiness.* That principle of love which led Christ to sacrifice His life, must be appropriated by us as a vital ruling element if we would be holy. His sacrifice upon the cross will be worthless to us unless we sacrifice ourselves in love, hence we must become "conformable unto His death." The subject—

Secondly : Serves to correct the mischievous way in which the Blood of Christ is popularly represented. Men talk of Christ's Blood as if it was the crimson fluid that coursed through His veins that saves, washes, cleanses, &c., or at any rate that it was His blood which qualified Him to be a Saviour. It was not His Blood. The Blood was nothing, only as it expressed His self-sacrificing love. Supposing that the criminal law of Rome at the time in which Christ lived had required that capital offenders should be put to death by hanging or strangling, or suffocating, or by taking poison like Socrates. Had Christ been sacrificed in any of these ways, would the power of His self-sacrifice to save humanity be one whit the less ? Not so. It was His self-sacrificing love, not the form of His mortal agonies, that made Him the Saviour of the world.

John 6:59-65

GOSPEL REVELATION

"These things said He in the synagogue, as He taught in Capernaum," &c.

EXEGETICAL REMARKS.—Ver. 59.— " *These things said He in the synagogue, as He taught in Capernaum.*" The discourse recorded in the preceding verses was delivered in all probability on the Sabbath-day. The congregation was now broken or breaking up, and the incidents related in these last verses of the chapter occurred perhaps elsewhere and in private. The synagogue here perhaps was the building erected by the grateful centurion as an expression of his love for the Jewish nation.

Ver. 60.—" *Many therefore of His disciples, when they had heard this, said, This is an hard saying; who can hear it?*" The "*disciples*" here do not mean exclusively the twelve, but include those who generally attended His ministry in Capernaum. "*Hard saying.*" They regarded the words of our Saviour referring to the eating of His body and the drinking of His blood *literally*, and they could not understand them. "*Who can hear it?*" The thing is past comprehension.

Ver. 61.—" *When* (R. V. BUT) *Jesus knew* (R. V. KNOWING) *in Himself that His disciples murmured at it* (R. V. THIS), *He said unto them, Doth this offend you?*" (R. V. CAUSE YOU TO STUMBLE.) σκανδαλίζει, σκάνδαλον. "A snare laid for an enemy. In New Testament a stumbling-block, a scandal."—*Liddell and Scott.*

Ver. 62.—" *What and if ye shall see* (R. V. THEN IF YE SHOULD BEHOLD) *the Son of man ascend* (R. V. ASCENDING) *up where He was before?*" If ye are stumbled at what I have said, how will ye bear what I now say? Not that His ascension itself would stumble them more than His death; but that after recoiling from the mention of the one, they would not be in a state of mind to take in the other.

Ver. 63.—" *It is the spirit that quickeneth; the flesh profiteth nothing:*

the words that I speak (R. V. HAVE SPOKEN) *unto you, they are spirit, and they are life*" (R. V. ARE SPIRIT AND ARE LIFE). This verse is the key to unlock the meaning of the whole preceding discourse. He explains His seemingly violent expressions by telling them that they must understand Him figuratively, not literally; and that what was spiritual in His religion quickened men, and gave them life, not the literal flesh, which availed nothing to such an end. "*The words*"—"He proceeds to declare what He means by spirit and by life. It was His instructions, doctrines, truths, that would summon into action and progress man's spiritual life, and lead him onward to eternal blessedness."— *Livermore.*

Ver. 64.—" *But there are some of you that believe not. For Jesus knew from the beginning who they were that believed not, and who* (R. V. IT WAS THAT) *should betray Him.*" Jesus meant to say, It does not matter to some of you in what sense I speak, for ye will not believe Me. "*Jesus knew from the beginning.*" He read them through and through, His omniscience is elsewhere asserted (Rev. ii. 23; John ii. 24; Matt. ix. 4; xii. 25; Luke v. 22; vi. 8; ix. 47). He knew what Judas would do; his conduct did not take Him by surprise.

Ver. 65.—" *And He said, Therefore* (R. V. FOR THIS CAUSE HAVE I) *said I unto you, that no man can come unto Me, except it were given unto Him of My* (R. V. THE) *Father.*" "To be given of the Father," says *Whitby,* " is to be convinced by the miracles which God hath wrought by Him; to testify the truth of His mission, that He was the Messiah; and to be willing on these testimonies to own Him as such, laying aside all those unreasonable prejudices and carnal affections which obstructed their coming to Him."

HOMILETICS

The passage now under notice may be regarded as presenting to us *Gospel Revelation* in three aspects.

I —AS SENSUOUSLY INTERPRETED

These hearers of Christ gave a sensuous interpretation of His words concerning the eating of His flesh and the drinking of His blood. They considered that He meant a species of cannibalism. They did not penetrate into the spiritual meaning of the figure, and reach the grand principle of self-sacrificing love.

This sensuous interpretation—

First : Involved them in difficulty. *"This is a hard saying; who can hear it?"* As if they had said, It is beyond belief, it is an insult to our understanding. So in truth His language is, if literally interpreted. It is the sensuous or literal interpretation of Scripture that always makes it a *"hard saying"* to men. The literal interpretation of the metaphorical representations of God, as a Being *possessing human passions*, is a *"hard saying."* The literal interpretation of the metaphorical representations of the *millennium*, in which Christ is represented as coming in person to reign on the earth, and to accomplish by miracles what had not been done by moral ministries, is a *"hard saying."* The literal interpretation of the metaphorical *resurrection* of the race, in which every son of Adam is spoken of as coming forth from his grave in exactly the same body he had previous to his death, is also a *"hard saying."* The literal interpretation of the metaphorical representation of *hell*, in which the wicked are represented as burning in material flames for ever, is a *"hard saying."* In truth, no man who, like these hearers of Christ, gives a *literal* or sensuous interpretation of a book like the Bible, which is *pre-eminently metaphorical*, can fail to feel it a *"hard saying."*

This sensuous interpretation—

Secondly : Subjected them to unbelief. *"Who can hear it?"* Who can accept it, who can give it credence? Yes, who? To believe intelligently in the *literal* representations of the Bible is an utter impossibility. No class of men do more, perhaps, to promote infidelity amongst the people, than those writers and preachers who are proclaiming and urging sensuous interpretations of a highly figurative Book. I have sat in churches and chapels, and have heard such gross and material views of God, Christ, heaven, hell, set forth, as have led me to feel not only that they were a *"hard saying,"* I could not *"hear"* them, but that they were an outrage on reason, a calumny on the Book, and a libel on the Infinite.

This sensuous interpretation—

Thirdly : Was offensive to Christ. *"When Jesus knew in Himself that His disciples murmured at it, He said unto them, Doth this offend you? What and if ye shall see the Son of man ascend up where He was before?" "Doth this offend you?"* It need not; it only shows the carnality of your minds in putting a gross interpretation on My words. What makes it hard for you to understand, is the wrong in your own hearts, not the absurdity of My words. You are prejudiced, you are sensual, you "judge after the flesh," you do not understand Me although I am with you. How will you understand Me when I am gone? *"What and if ye shall see the Son of man ascend up?"* God deliver us from carnalizing the Holy Gospel! This has made Popery, this makes Ritualism, this fosters Infidelity. "The natural man receiveth not the things of the spirit of God, for they are foolishness unto him, neither can he know them, because they are spiritually discerned."

The passage now under notice may be regarded as presenting to us Gospel Revelation—

II —AS DIVINELY EXPLAINED

"It is the spirit that quickeneth; the flesh profiteth nothing: the words that I speak unto you, they are spirit, and they are life." The spiritual subject of My discourse is that which giveth life; the material form *"profiteth nothing."* The real subject of My discourse is spirit, not flesh or matter, true spiritual life, not carnal animal life. Paul expresses a similar idea when he says, "The letter killeth, but the spirit giveth life." What do "spirit" and "letter" mean here? Simply the word and the thought, the sentence and the sentiment. Christianity has letter and spirit. If it had no letter, it would be unrevealed to men, a thought shut up in the mind of God; and if it had mere letter and no spirit, it would be hollow sound, empty jargon. All essences, principles, spirits, are invisible to us; they are only revealed through letters or forms. The spirit of a nation expresses itself in its institutions; the spirit of the creation expresses itself in its phenomena; the spirit of Jesus in His wonderful biography. By letter, therefore, I understand the form of a thing in contradistinction to its essence; the word in contradistinction to its meaning; the institution in contradistinction to its genius. *"The flesh profiteth nothing,"* says Christ. By which He means to express the general idea that the mere forms and symbols of truth are worthless, if they fail to convey the ideas intended. But the *"spirit giveth life."* As the spirit of man vitalizes every part of his flesh during his life,—makes it warm, sensitive, and active,—so the spirit of truth and love and Christ quickens the human soul.

Christ's words *have spirit in them.* They are not mere facts and theories, but spirit itself. The words of some have nothing in them; of others, mere facts; of others, cold abstractions: not so with the words of Christ: they *are "spirit."* They throb with spirit. Christ's words are *quickening*. "It is the spirit that quickeneth." What quickening work in intellect, conscience, soul they have accomplished ere now! May we all so study the Holy Gospel that we may reach its "*spirit*," and feel its quickening energy!

The passage now under notice may be regarded as presenting to us Gospel Revelation—

III —AS PRACTICALLY DISBELIEVED

"*But there are some of you that believe not.*" Three remarks are suggested here.

First : Disbelievers are known to Christ from the commencement. "*For Jesus knew from the beginning who they were that believed not.*" Infidelity does not strike Him with surprise. No infidel, in any age or land, has ever appeared or will ever appear, whom He did not foreknow. His foreknowledge of their infidelity, however, interferes not with their freedom, influences not their character, and lessens not, in the slightest degree, their guilt. Infidels, Christ knows all about you!

Secondly : Disbelievers are capable of the most iniquitous con-duct. Christ not only knew who would not believe, but also who amongst the unbelievers "*should betray Him.*" One of the greatest crimes ever perpetrated on the earth was the betrayal of Christ, and that betrayal was the result of unbelief. No crime is too enormous for those to perpetrate who practically reject Christianity.

Thirdly : Disbelievers maintain a moral distance from Christ. "*And He said, Therefore said I unto you, that no man can come unto Me, except it were given unto him of My Father.*" Observe—(1.) That to believe in Christ's spiritual teaching, is to come to Him. The man who enters with all the love of his heart and the confidence of his being into the spiritual import of Christ's teaching, will feel himself brought into conscious contact with Him. He will "*come to Him.*" (2.) That the influence of the Father is necessary to enable him to believe. "*Except it were given unto him of My Father.*" Who but the Father can incline the depraved heart to look at the "truth as it is in Jesus," and to feel its quickening and saving power? This is the Father's work with all. By the influences of nature, by the events of Providence, by the discoveries of reason, by the workings of conscience, and by the ministry of truth, the great Father is ever working to bring His sons to Christ; and because His efforts are moral, they may be resisted.

> "We drive the furrow with the share of faith
> Through the waste fields of life, and our own hands
> Sow thick the seeds that spring to weeds or flowers.
> And never strong necessity nor fate
> Trammels the soul that firmly says, I will!
> Else are we playthings, and 'tis Satan's mock
> To preach to us repentance and belief."

John 6:66-71

THE TRANSCENDENT WORTH OF CHRISTIANITY

" From that time many of His disciples went back, and walked no more with Him," &c.

EXEGETICAL REMARKS.—Ver. 66.— *" From that time* (R. V. UPON THIS) *many of His disciples went back, and walked no more with Him." " Upon this"*—that is, on account of the discourse He had just delivered, which they by their carnal interpretations made absurd and abhorrent, they withdrew from His ministry.

Ver. 67.—*" Then said Jesus* (R. V. THEREFORE) *unto the twelve, Will* (R. V. WOULD) *ye also go away?"* How many of His hearers now went away, we are not told—perhaps hundreds ; and Christ, to test the twelve, turns to them and says, Do you also wish to go away ? Some see sadness in this question, and render the words, " Ye will not go away, will ye ? "

Ver. 68.—*" Then Simon Peter answered Him, Lord, to whom shall we go? Thou hast the words of eternal life."* Here is warm-hearted, impetuous Peter true to his nature again. " *Eternal life* " means eternal goodness, which is eternal blessedness.

Ver. 69.—*" And we believe* (R. V. HAVE BELIEVED) *and are sure* (R. V. KNOW) *that Thou art that Christ, the Son* (R. V. HOLY ONE) *of the living God."* Instead of the "*Son of the living God* " it should be, the Holy One of God, the One consecrated by and for the most Holy One.

Ver. 70.—*" Jesus answered them, Have not I chosen you twelve?"* (R. V. DID I NOT CHOOSE YOU THE TWELVE ?) A more definite exposition of the words of verse 67. " Not the language of reflection, but of sudden pain over the tragic result, in contrast with that joyful confession which Peter was convinced he could give in the name of all."—*Meyer.* " It probably refers, not to the tragic result, but to the moral alienation, the germ of apostasy, which from this time forth developed itself in Judas. The distribution of the

emphasis is very significant—' *I* ' is first, then '*You,*' then the ' *twelve.*' I, as the Holy One of God, have chosen you to the highest honours."—*Lange.* "*One of you is a devil.*" The words of *Dr. Farrar* on this subject deserve quotation. " The English version is unfortunate because it does not maintain the distinction between διάβολος, the word here used, and δαιμόνιον, which it usually renders ' devil,' *e. g.* in ' He has a devil.' Euthymius here explains ' devil ' by either ' servant of the devil ' or ' conspirator,' and the latter meaning seems very probable ; indeed, this very word ἐπίβουλος is used by the LXX to render the Hebrew Satan in 1 Kings v. 4; 1 Sam. xxix. 4. I have already noticed how much more lightly the Jews, and indeed all Orientals to this day, used the word Satan than we do ; this indeed may be almost called a *modus loquendi* among them ; and if Jesus spoke in Aramaic, and used the word שטנא, then the reproach is not one-tenth part so fearful as it sounds to us. Thus, the sons of Zeruiah are called a Satan to David (2 Sam. xix. 22), and Hadad is called a Satan to King Solomon (Kings xi. 23), where it is merely rendered 'adversary,' and in Matt. xvi. 23 the word is applied to Peter Himself. ' When the ungodly curseth Satan ' (*i. e.* an enemy), says the Son of Sirach (xxi. 27), ' he curseth his own soul.' All this is important in many ways. Further, we may observe that διάβολος occurs by no means frequently in the New Testament."

Ver. 71.—"*He* (R. V. NOW HE) *spake of Judas Iscariot the son of Simon.*" (R. V. ISCARIOT.) There was another Judas, the son of James ; but this was the son of Simon Iscariot. " *For he it was that should betray Him.*" About to betray Him. "*Being one of the twelve.*" In the three lists of the apostles it is added that he was the betrayer.

HOMILETICS

We may take these words as a whole to illustrate *the transcendent worth of Christianity*, and we remark—

I —THAT CHRISTIANITY PROVIDES FOR THE COMPLETE WELL-BEING OF HUMAN NATURE

" *Thou hast the words of eternal life.*" Life here does not mean mere existence; for existence itself may be a curse, and endless existence an eternal calamity. But it means, as we have said, eternal *goodness*, or holiness, which is happiness. It means an eternal existence, not only apart from all moral and natural evil, but in inseparable connection with all natural and moral good. It involves the totality of all that man requires to consummate his bliss. It is the true *summum bonum*. Now, Christianity has the " *words of eternal life.*" It has the means to *generate, sustain, develop,* and *perfect* in man this eternal goodness. Nothing else *can* do it. Science, literature, art, law, none nor all of those can effect it. Peter means to say, We want eternal life; and Thou hast it, and Thou alone. Yes, it is the want, the deep eternal want, of human nature. Now this Christianity provides for : it has " *the words of eternal life.*"

First : Its " *words* " revoke the sentence of self-condemnation to eternal death. The guilty conscience when awakened dooms man to a terrible future. Christ's words revoke in man this condemnation. "There is therefore now no condemnation," &c.

Secondly : Its " *words* " remove the moral disease which insures eternal death. The Bible teaches—(1.) That men are infected with the mortal malady. And (2.) That the Gospel removes it, and implants the seeds of eternal life.

Another fact here is—

II —THAT CHRISTIANITY RESPECTS THE FREEDOM OF HUMAN NATURE

" *Will ye also go away?* " Christ uses no coercion; He does not dragoon men into His service; He treats them according to their nature : men are made to act freely, and they never can act as men only as they are free. Hence Christ says, " *Will ye ?* "

First : Christ does not want our service. He can do without us. He could destroy the old creation, and create a new universe. Do not stay with Me from the idea that I want you.

Secondly : Christ will not accept forced service. (1.) Because there could be no moral virtue in such service. He requires us to serve Him because by doing so we become morally good. (2.) Because there could be no happiness in such service. He wishes our happiness. The gloomy looks and sepulchral tones of religious serfs are an abomination to Him. Be free then.

Another fact here is—

III —THAT CHRISTIANITY TAKES THE STRONGEST MORAL HOLD UPON HUMAN NATURE

"*To whom can we go?*" Though free, we are bound. What are its binding forces?

First: The gratitude it inspires. Gratitude ever binds to the benefactor.

Secondly: The love it enkindles. Love always binds the heart to its object, and the more excellences the object displays the stronger the tie becomes.

Thirdly: The hope it awakens. Hope binds the heart to the object promised. Christ makes wonderful promises.

Fourthly: The congeniality it produces. Christianity suits man in every respect—heart, conscience, intellect,—all. To whom, then, can the man "*go*" who has really secured Christianity? How can he extricate himself? To whom can you go? Will you go to Rationalism,—to Romanism,—to Paganism,—to Secularism? There is nowhere else you *càn* go to, if you would. Another fact here is—

IV —THAT CHRISTIANITY REJECTS NOT THE WORSE TYPES OF HUMAN NATURE

Christ had chosen Judas, who was a devil, and who betrayed Him. Christ gave Judas an opportunity of reaching "*eternal life.*" For three years He ministered to Judas. Judas heard His sermons, witnessed His miracles, sat at His feasts, and even had his feet washed by His hands. Observe—

First: The power of man to *misrepresent himself.* Judas for years appeared as a disciple, spoke as a disciple, prayed as a disciple; behaved in every way and appeared externally as a disciple, and yet the devil was in his heart. "*One of you is a devil.*" A bad man, like the devil, can transform himself into an angel of light. Observe—

Secondly: The power of man to *act against circumstances.* Circumstances more powerfully adapted to make a bad man good, you can scarcely imagine than those which acted upon Judas during the three past years. Notwithstanding this, he became a greater devil, became worse every day. No circumstances can make a man better or worse, irrespective of his own will.

"Our bodies," says Shakspeare, "are our gardens; to the which our wills are gardeners: so that if we will plant nettles, or sow lettuce; set hyssop, and weed up thyme; supply it with one gender of herbs, or distract it with many; either to have it sterile with idleness, or manured with industry; why, the power and corrigible authority of this lies in our wills."

John 7:1-10

INFIDELITY

(Jesus goes up to the Feast of Tabernacles—His final departure from Galilee—Incidents in Samaria.—LUKE ix. 51—56 ; JOHN vii. 2—10.)

" After these things Jesus walked in Galilee : for He would not walk in Jewry, because the Jews sought to kill Him," &c.

EXEGETICAL REMARKS.—Ver. 1.— *" After these things."* It will be observed from the harmony, that the year between the second and third passovers of our Lord is opened by John (chap. v.) and closed with this announcement ; so that John has only two chapters of his narrative falling within this second year of our Lord's ministry. The other evangelists have related the chief events of this year, embracing various important miracles. There are several parables, and also the sermon on the Mount, which are not given by John. *"Jesus walked in Galilee."* He continued to prosecute His labours in Galilee for a considerable time. " In this period of Galilean itineracy," says *Dr. Lange,* "fall the charges of heresy against Jesus in Galilee, and His contests with the hostile Pharisees there (Matt. xii.) ; most of His parables or sermons on the sea (Matt. xiii.) ; His interview with the deputation from Jerusalem, and the great gathering on the mountain which followed (Matt. xv.) ; the last contest with Pharisean power in Galilee ; the retirement of the Lord ; and His transfiguration (Matt. xvi. and xvii. 21)." *" He would not walk in Jewry* (R. V. JUDÆA), *because the Jews sought to kill Him."* The reason why He would not go into Jewry, or Judæa, is here stated, and also in chap. v. 18.

Ver. 2.—*" Now the Jews' feast of tabernacles* (R. V. THE FEAST OF THE JEWS, THE FEAST OF TABERNACLES) *was at hand."* The feast of tabernacles was the last of the three annual festivals, celebrated on the 15th of the 7th month, *i.e.* September. It was a celebration of the sojourn of Israel in the wilderness, when they dwelt in tents. It continued seven or eight days, and the last day became the great day of the feast.

Ver. 3.—*" His brethren therefore said unto Him, Depart hence, and go into Judæa, that Thy disciples also may see the* (R. V. BEHOLD THY) *works that* (R. V. WHICH) *Thou doest."* These brethren were undoubtedly the sons of Joseph and Mary, and their names were James, Joseph, Simon, and Judas. As Jesus was the eldest, the others must have been in fresh young manhood. The reason why His brethren requested Him to depart into Judæa and to do *"works"* there, was in all probability family vanity. They wished their Brother to avail Himself of a grand national occasion to impress their countrymen with His signal greatness. They became dissatisfied with His unostentatious life in Galilee.

Ver. 4.—*" For there is no man that doeth* (R. V. NO MAN DOETH) *any thing in secret, and he himself seeketh to be known openly. If Thou do* (R. V. DOEST) *these things, shew* (R. V. MANIFEST) *Thyself to the world."* Though they must be regarded as unbelievers, they seem to have had some kind of faith in His Messiahship, and they wished Him to be publicly recognized as such, by appearing at once on the open stage ; and they seemed to say, If Thou hast power of working miracles, do so on a large scale : let our nation recognize the fact.

Ver. 5.—*" For neither* (R. V. EVEN) *did* (R. V. DID NOT) *His brethren believe in* (R. V. ON) *Him."* Although afterwards they were numbered amongst His disciples (Acts i. 14), up to this point they had no true faith ; they were infidels so far as His Messiahship was concerned.

Ver. 6.—" *Then Jesus* (R. V. THERE-FORE) *said unto them, My time is not yet come.*" " *My time*"—there is no reason to believe that there is here any reference to His death. He had fixed upon a time when He should go to the feast, but it had not exactly arrived. The time He purposed challenging the nation and the metropolis with the fact of His Messiahship, His first public entrance into Jerusalem, was the entrance in the procession with palms. " *Your time is alway ready.*" Your time is your own, you have no plan in life, you acknowledge no Divinely-regulated law ; you can go where you please.

Ver. 7.—" *The world cannot hate you ; but Me it hateth, because I testify of it, that the* (R. V. ITS) *works thereof are evil.*" The world can have no reason to hate you. Not that they were particularly sinful, or complied wickedly with the practices and passions of the world ; but that they had done nothing to merit the resentment of the Jewish rulers, and call down the imprecations of the people. " *Because I testify of it.*" It was the freedom and honesty with which Jesus dealt with the bad, and probed their moral wounds, that awoke their fiery anger. His rebukes of the Scribes and Pharisees made them His unrelenting enemies till death. So always : "There is no surer way to involve one's self in the flames of persecution, than to reprove men for their sins, and advocate with unbending rectitude the great principles of the Christian code of morals and faith."—*Livermore.*

Ver. 8.—" *Go ye up unto this feast : I go not up yet unto this feast; for My time is not yet full come* " (R. V. FULFILLED). Some omit the word " *yet* " as it is not found in many of the ancient MSS. All that is meant is, I go not up at present to this feast, I am not ready.

Ver. 9.—" *When He had* (R. V. AND HAVING) *said these words* (R. V. THINGS) *unto them, He abode still in Galilee.*" This verse suggests that the conversation took place some days before the departure of His brothers for the feast.

Ver. 10.—" *But when His brethren were gone up, then went He also up unto the feast, not openly* (R. V. PUBLICLY), *but as it were in secret.*" He went, but He did not go with them, nor with the crowd in caravans, nor perhaps until nearly the close of the feast, which lasted seven days. He went up quietly and alone. "Some think to find a contradiction here, since, saying, 'I go not up to this feast,' He afterwards went." One solution makes Him to have had no intention at this time to go ; but afterwards He changed His mind and went. Another lays weight upon the use of the present tense, "I go not," which means, "I go not now, or yet ;" or, as given by *Alford,* "I am not at present going up." Another lays weight upon " this feast," which it is said He did not in fact attend except in its last days. Still another thus defines His words—"I go not up with you, or in public with the company of pilgrims," or "I go not up in such a way as you think or advise." The matter, to one who considers the scope of Christ's reply to His brethren, presents no real difficulty. They had said, "Go up to this feast, and manifest Thyself. Show Thyself to the world, and work Thy miracles in Judæa." He replied : "My time to manifest Myself is not yet come. I go not up to this feast with such intent. At some subsequent feast I shall manifest Myself." "As He had said, so He acted, going up to Jerusalem in a secret way, avoiding all publicity, nor arriving there till the feast was partially past. At the following passover He acted in substance as His brethren had advised, showing Himself to the world, and entering the holy city as a king, amid the shouts of the multitude."—*Andrews.*

HOMILETICS

These verses, thus explained, may be fairly taken to illustrate some phases of *infidelity.* It is said, that " *neither did His brethren believe in Him.*" They had no enlightened and genuine faith in His Divine Messiahship. The following remarks are suggested concerning infidelity—

I—THAT IT SELDOM LACKS EVIDENCE

These " *brethren* " must have had *ample* evidence to convince them of the Messiahship of Christ. As boys in their home at Nazareth, they must have seen every day a something that would sufficiently convince them that their Brother Jesus had elements of character transcending the human. Often, no doubt, had their mother and father pointed out to them extraordinary phases of His birth and His life ; and now, having come out into public life, they had been with Him in Galilee for a considerable period. In the first verse it is said, " *After these things Jesus walked in Galilee.*" He had travelled from the borders of Tyre and Sidon to the coasts of Decapolis, everywhere preaching sublime discourses and performing wondrous deeds. *Infidels* do not need evidence, they have plenty of it. Men who do not believe in God, do not lack evidence ; all nature is full of proof. Men who do not believe in the Divinity of Christianity do not need evidence. The congruity of Christ's biography with contemporaneous history, the congruity of His system with the conscience, reason, and deep-felt wants of humanity, and the immense and growing influence of His Gospel upon the sentiment, spirit, and character of mankind are certainly evidence enough. The cause of the infidelity is in the heart, rather than in the intellect, in all cases. Another remark here suggested concerning infidelity is—

II—THAT IT IS ALWAYS VAIN

These brethren of His, mainly from *vanity,* counsel Him to depart from Galilee, and go on a grand national occasion to Judæa, in order to make a display. " *Show Thyself to the world.*" Do not continue in such obscurity, do not be so unostentatious in Thy works, do something that will bring honour to Thee and to us. Let us be grand ! Infidelity is always vain ; the vainest speakers on platforms, the vainest authors in literature, the vainest members in society, are those who profess infidel opinions. They are vain of their imaginary intellectual independency, of their superior mental insight and grasp, of their superiority to current creeds. It must be so. The man who believes in nothing greater and sublimer than himself, will have both space and aliments in his mind in which his egotism can grow to the most offensive proportions. Faith in the infinitely great and good can alone burn out the native vanity of the corrupt heart. Infidelity is a negation. " Light empty minds," says *Leighton*, " are like bladders blown up with anything." Another remark suggested is—

III —THAT IT IS EVER IN AGREEMENT WITH THE WORLD

" *Then Jesus said unto them, My time is not yet come : but your time is alway ready.   The world cannot hate you ; but Me it hateth, because I testify of it, that the works thereof are evil.*" By the "*world*" is meant the prevailing ideas, spirit, and aims of corrupt humanity. And the mind of His brethren was in accord with this, but it was dead against Him. What is the spirit of the world ? (1.) Material-ism.—The body is everything. (2.) Practical atheism.—God is ignored. (3.) Regnant selfishness.—Self is supreme. Infidelity agrees with all this ; there is no moral discrepancy, no reason for mutual antipathies and battling. Another remark suggested is—

IV —THAT IT NEVER THWARTS THE DIVINE PURPOSE

" *But when His brethren were gone up, then went He also up unto the feast, not openly, but as it were in secret.*" Christ's plan was, not to go up to Jerusalem at the time they requested Him to go ; but He went up in His own time. Their counselling influenced Him not. He pursued His own course amidst their opinions and wishes, steady and majestic as the moon through opposing clouds. So it ever is. Infidelity can never modify, check, or retard the decrees of heaven. Infidels may in countless numbers combine together to arrest the progress of truth ; but He who sitteth in heaven and seeth the end from the beginning, hath said His " purposes shall stand," and He will " do all His pleasure."

CONCLUSION. Such is *infidelity* in some of its phases. It is a wretched thing. Enrich it with learning, energize it with the strongest logic, embellish it with the highest culture and genius, it is still a wretched thing. " I seem," says *Hume*, " affrighted and confounded with the solitude in which I am placed by my philosophy. When I look abroad on every side, I see dispute, contradiction, and distraction. When I turn my eye inward, I find nothing but doubt and ignorance. Where am I ? or what am I ? From what cause do I derive my existence ? To what condition shall I return ? I am confounded with questions, I begin to fancy myself in a very deplorable condition, surrounded with darkness on every side."

John 7:11-18

CHRIST'S FIRST TWO DISCOURSES AT THE FEAST OF TABERNACLES.
I. GREAT CONTRASTS

(Jesus at the Feast of Tabernacles.   His Public Teaching.—John vii. 11—53 ; viii. 1.)

"Then the Jews," &c.

EXEGETICAL REMARKS.—Ver. 11.— "*Then the Jews* (R. V. THEREFORE) *sought Him at the feast.*" By the "*Jews*" a heretic nation is meant, as headed by the rulers. "*Where is He?*" Where is that man? They had been waiting for Him at the feast in order to kill Him ; but He had not come. Crowds from all parts of the country had arrived ; but He was not to be seen. All looked out for Him.

Ver. 12.—"*And there was much murmuring among the people* (R. V. MULTITUDES) *concerning Him: for some said, He is a good man : others said, Nay;* (R. V. NOT SO) *but He deceiveth* (R. V. LEADETH) *the people.*" (R. V. MULTITUDE ASTRAY.) The people, including perhaps all classes, those who were friendly disposed and those who were hostile, all began to murmur or to whisper amongst themselves concerning Him. Some in an undertone daring to express their opinion that He was a "*good man,*" others declaring that "*He deceived the people.*"

Ver. 13.—"*Howbeit no man spake openly of Him for fear of the Jews.*" That is, none of His friends were bold enough to declare their faith in Him. All this time the mutterings and whisperings about Him go on, perhaps for three days after the feast had begun, then Christ appeared.

Ver. 14.—"*Now about* (R. V. BUT WHEN IT WAS NOW) *the midst of the feast Jesus went up into the temple, and taught.*" "*Midst of the feast,*" that is, at the close of the third, or beginning of the fourth day, probably the Sabbath. This would seem to have been His first public teaching at Jerusalem. Where in the temple did He take His stand? Probably in the great colonnade which surrounded the space before the courts, where the Sanhedrims had their chamber, and where there was a synagogue in which Rabbis discussed their points of doctrine and of duty.

Ver. 15.—"*And the Jews* (R. V. THE JEWS THEREFORE) *marvelled, saying, How knoweth this man letters, having never learned ?*" That is, having never learned in any Rabbinical school, like Paul under Gamaliel. Christ's discourse in the temple on this occasion is not given. No doubt it was, like that Sermon on the Mount, so original, so elevated, and so true to reason and consciousness, as to strike them with astonishment ; and captiously they inquire where He got His knowledge from, since He had not been technically trained.

Ver. 16.—"*Jesus answered them, and said, My doctrine* (R. V. TEACHING) *is not Mine, but His that sent Me.*" Our Lord takes up their challenge and indicates the vast difference between His "*doctrine*" and teaching and that of the Rabbis. He virtually says, I derive My "*doctrine*" from no human school, nor do I proclaim it on My own authority ; My Teacher is the Father. I teach under a Divine commission.

Ver 17.—"*If any man will* (R. V. WILLETH TO) *do His will, he shall know of the doctrine* (R. V. TEACHING), *whether it be of God, or whether I speak of* (R. V. FROM) *Myself.*" Alford renders the verse, "If any man be willing to do His will, he shall know concerning the teaching, whether it is of God, or whether I speak from Myself." The idea is, he who has the genuine desire to do the will of God, will have in him the test of the true "*doctrine.*"

Ver. 18.—"*He that speaketh of* (R. V. FROM) *himself seeketh his own glory : but He that seeketh His glory that sent Him, the same is true, and no unrighteousness is in Him.*" "*He that speaketh of himself,*" not concerning, but from himself—*ἀφ' ἑαυτοῦ.* Christ in this verse proposes another test of the truth of His claims, viz. : His freedom from the desire of self-aggrandisement, and His constant reference to the will of God in His ministry. The disinterestedness both of our Saviour and His Apostles in the promulgation of Christianity, furnishes an unanswerable proof of its Divine origin. "*No unrighteousness is in Him.*" Or no deceit is in Him. A contrast is drawn between the true prophet and a selfish impostor. "Some suppose Jesus to have met with an interruption between this and the following verse."

HOMILETICS

In these verses two striking *contrasts* are worthy of attention.

I —BASE COWARDICE AND SUBLIME COURAGE

Here is base cowardice ! "*The Jews*" (*i. e.* in all probability the leaders of the Sanhedrim, and not of the people) "*sought Him at the feast, and said, Where is He ? And there was much murmuring among the people concerning Him: for some said, He is a good man: others said, Nay ; but He deceiveth the people. Howbeit no man spake openly of Him for fear of the Jews.*" Here is cowardice. It was cowardice—(1.) For these chief men of the nation to be in cunning search for the life of one lonely man. "*Where is He ?*" We want Him. What for ? To listen to His doctrines ? honestly to test His merits ? to do honour to His person or His mission ? No ; but to kill Him. Here are a number of influential men banded together to crush one humble peasant ! How cowardly this ! It was cowardice—(2.) In the people meeting together in secrecy, and talking about Him. Why did they not speak their opinions openly, for or against ? They were afraid. Sin is always cowardly, virtue alone is courageous. Sin, it is true, puts on the form of courage. Its talk is swaggering, and its attitude often defiant ; but it is essentially craven-hearted. "Thou wear a lion's hide ! Doff it for shame, and hang a calf's-skin on those recreant limbs."—*Shakespeare.*

In contrast with this, we have the sublimest courage. "*Now about the midst of the feast Jesus went up into the temple, and taught.*" When the festival was at the height ; when its concourse had swollen to the greatest number ; when national enthusiasm for the old ceremonies and traditions blazed with the greatest intensity, this poor peasant Reformer appeared, stood up in their midst, and proclaimed doctrines that struck directly and mightily against the prejudices and spirit of the nation. He confronted public sentiment when its billows were thundering at high tide. Where in all history have you an example of courage comparable to this ? Truly "He set His face as a flint,"—He did not "fail, nor was He discouraged." The other contrast which we have in these verses is—

II — CONVENTIONAL SCHOLARSHIP AND GENUINE INTELLIGENCE.

First : Conventional scholarship. "*And the Jews marvelled, saying, How knoweth this man letters, having never learned ?*" The question breathes contempt. The idea is, He has never been to our seats of learning, never studied under our Rabbis, what can He know ? He is an uneducated man, and yet He forsooth presumes to teach. There has ever been much of this spirit amongst men. There are those who still hold the prejudice that a man cannot know much unless he has graduated at some University ; that he is unfit to teach unless he has sat at the feet of some Gamaliel. This is a great fallacy ; some of the most educated men the world has ever had, have never passed the college curriculum, and never won a university degree. This idea fills society with pedants, and often supplies our pulpits with men who have neither the kind of lore, faculty, or genius to preach the gospel of universal truth and love. In contrast with this we have—

Secondly : Genuine intelligence. "*Jesus answered them, and said, My doctrine is not Mine, but His that sent Me. If any man will do His will, he shall know of the doctrine, whether it be of God, or whether I speak of Myself.*" Three things are worthy of remark—(1.) God is the sole Teacher of the highest doctrine. "*My doctrine is not Mine, but His that sent Me.*" Although I have not studied under you, Rabbis, I have studied under the Infinite Father. I have got My knowledge directly from the Primal Source of all true intelligence. Yes ; God is the only True Teacher of Divine truth. Brother preacher, do not content yourself with sipping at the streams of conventional teaching, go to the fountain-head. (2.) Obedience is the qualification for obtaining the highest knowledge. "*If any man will do His will, he shall know of the doctrine.*" Philosophy and experience show the truth of this. "*Pars magna bonitatis est velle fieri bonum*" ("The essence of goodness consists in teaching to be good"), says *Seneca*. And well too has *Pascal* said, that "a man must know earthly things in order to love them, but that he must love heavenly things in order to know them." (3.) Entire devotion of self to the Divine is necessary in order to communicate the highest knowledge. "*He that speaketh of himself seeketh his own glory : but he that seeketh His glory that sent Him, the same is true, and no unrighteousness is in Him.*" It is only as a man becomes self-oblivious, and lost in the love and thoughts of God, that he can reflect the bright rays of Divine intelligence upon his fellowmen. We must allow ourselves to become mere channels through which the Divine will flow.*

* See a Homily on the True Theology, at the end of this volume.

John 7:19-30

CHRIST'S FIRST TWO DISCOURSES AT THE FEAST OF TABERNACLES (No. 2)—MURDER IN DESIRE

"Did not Moses give you the law?" &c.

EXEGETICAL REMARKS.—Ver. 19.— "*Did not Moses give you the law, and yet none of you keepeth* (R. V. DOETH) *the law? Why go ye about* (R. V. SEEK YE) *to kill Me?*" They profess to believe Moses. The law of Moses prohibited murder. "Thou shalt not kill" was one of its salient sovereign edicts, hence Christ's question, "*Why go ye about to kill Me?*" Where is your consistency?

Ver. 20.—"*The people* (R. V. MULTITUDE) *answered and said, Thou hast a devil: who goeth about* (R. V. SEEKETH) *to kill Thee?*" "*The people*," not the rulers, but the mixed multitude. These by implication deny any desire to kill Him, and charge Him with madness for supposing it. "*Thou hast a devil.*" Probably this was a proverbial expression, denoting gloominess, melancholy, brooding, suspiciousness. Perhaps they meant to say, "If Thou wert not mentally diseased, Thou wouldest not suppose that we intended to kill Thee." Mayhap these mixed multitudes had no intention to kill Him, and were ignorant of the malicious purpose of their rulers. As a rule it is not the people of the world that desire the slaughtering of men, but the rulers who have an interest in rapine and blood.

Ver. 21.—"*Jesus answered and said unto them, I have done* (R. V. DID) *one work, and ye all marvel.*" Christ disregards the interruption, and proceeds to show that there was no reason for them, as believers in Moses, to be indignant with Him for the miracle He wrought on the Sabbath day. The "*one work*" at which they did "*marvel*" was undoubtedly the miracle He performed on the Sabbath at Bethesda, as recorded in chap. v. vers. 1—9. Why should this "*one work*" offend them, for He had done many works? The reason was because it was wrought on the Sabbath day.

Vers. 22, 23.—"*Moses therefore* (R. V. FOR THIS CAUSE) *gave unto you circumcision; (not because* (R. V. THAT) *it is of Moses, but of the fathers;) and ye on the Sabbath day circumcise a man. If a man on the Sabbath day receive* (R. V. RECEIVETH) *circumcision, that the law of Moses should* (R. V. MAY) *not be broken; are ye angry at* (R. V. WROTH WITH) *Me, because I have made a man every whit whole on the Sabbath day?*" (R. V. OMITS DAY.) Every male child was circumcised on the eighth day after birth: and this eighth day would of course frequently fall on the Sabbath. Moses enjoined the circumcision, although the ordinance was of much higher antiquity, reaching back to the patriarchs. The argument of Jesus is this:—If it be right to perform such an external ceremony on the eighth day, as you are bound to admit it was; it certainly cannot be wrong to perform an act of benevolence upon a poor suffering man; nay, it is more justifiable, for the one is a work of mutilation, the other of restoration. The law of benevolence transcends ceremonialism and sets it at defiance. "*I have made a man every whit whole on the Sabbath day.*" Glorious work! the complete restoration of a man.

Ver. 24.—"*Judge not according to the appearance, but judge righteous judgment.*" Righteous judgment would justify the act; but righteous judgment cannot always be reached by appearances. A right judgment requires penetration into the moral meaning or spirit of the deed: and in this case, the spirit of the act being benevolence, was right in the Divinest sense.

Ver. 25.—"*Then said some* (R. V. SOME THEREFORE) *of them of Jerusalem, Is not this He, whom they seek to kill?*" The Jerusalemites seemed more favourably disposed towards Christ than the "people" mentioned in ver. 23. They seem to be mere onlookers, acquainted with the murderous designs of the rulers.

Ver. 26.—"*But* (R. V. AND), *lo, He speaketh boldly* (R. V. OPENLY), *and they say nothing unto Him. Do* (R. V. CAN IT BE THAT) *the rulers know indeed that this is the very* (R. V. OMITS VERY) *Christ?*" "They seem as an ultra party, to be solicitous even over the circumspection of the rulers, and to treat it with irony. They follow their ironical expression with their own judgment, which breathes the haughtiness of a hierarchical capital. As the Rabbis reproached the Lord with His lack of a regular education and graduation, these Jerusalemites cast up against Him His mean extraction."—*Lange.*

Ver. 27.—"*Howbeit we know this man whence He is: but when Christ* (R. V. THE CHRIST) *cometh, no man* (R. V. ONE) *knoweth whence He is.*" In the Old Testament there are passages such as Isaiah liii. 8 ; Micah v. 2, which convey the idea that the origin of the Messiah would be wrapped in mystery. Hence they mean to say that, inasmuch as they knew His origin, He could not be the true Messiah.

Ver. 28.—"*Then* (R. V. THEREFORE) *cried Jesus in the temple as He taught,* (R. V. TEACHING AND) *saying, Ye both know Me, and ye know whence I am:*

and I am not come of Myself, but He that sent Me is true, whom ye know not." Christ seems to have raised His voice above their disputatious din, and boldly avows His Divine mission. "*Ye both know Me, and ye know whence I am.*" Very likely you know My birthplace, My parentage, and earthly history ; but though you know My human side, you are ignorant of the Divine. "*I am not come of Myself, but He that sent Me is true, Whom ye know not.*" You know whence My human body came, but you know not whence I came. I came from God, and you know Him not.

Ver. 29.—"*But I know Him: for* (R. V. BECAUSE) *I am from Him, and He hath sent Me.*" His counsels, though unknown to you, are known to Me. "*I am from Him.*" My origin and commission are Divine.

Ver. 30.—"*Then they* (R. V. THEREFORE) *sought to take Him: but no man laid hands* (R. V. HIS HAND) *on Him, because His hour was not yet come.*" So exasperated were they at the bold avowal of His Divinity, that they sought to seize Him at once. Yet some mysterious force held them back. "*No man laid hands on Him, because His hour was not yet come.*" "*His hour,*" that is, the time of His death.

HOMILETICS

To gather all these verses together, in order to illustrate some one subject of thought, suited for public discourse, is a purpose which we feel to be important, albeit not a little difficult. The reigning passion of the various classes which Christ now addressed, and with which He in His remarks mainly contended, was a *desire to kill Him.* "*Why go ye about to kill Me?*" With this He starts His address ; and the Jerusalemites inquire, "*Is not this He whom they seek to kill?*" As if they had said, We know a mortal malignity towards some one reigns in the heart of our rulers ; is this the person ? The following remarks are suggested concerning the malignant passion that now reigned amongst the rulers of the Jews.

I —THIS DESIRE TO KILL HIM WAS INCONSISTENT WITH THEIR RELIGIOUS PROFESSION

They were all confessedly believers in Moses. His authority was supreme, his word was their law, he was their religious leader, their chief lawgiver, their illustrious prophet. But there was nothing in Moses that would sanction their malignant antagonism to Christ.

First : The *spirit* of their opposition was inconsistent with the moral law of Moses. *" Did not Moses give you the law, and yet none of you keepeth the law ? Why go ye about to kill Me ? "* You seek to kill Me, when the man whom you regard as your chief moral master has distinctly and in God's own name said, " Thou shalt not kill." None of you keepeth the law of Moses in this respect. Your malice towards Me is in direct opposition to the mandates of your acknowledged moral leader.

Secondly : The *proximate cause* of their opposition was inconsistent with the moral law of Moses. That which seemed to have exasperated them on this occasion was the healing of the impotent man at Bethesda, on the Sabbath day. This was the *" one work,"* the particular work of His numerous performances which now fired their indignation. He gave perfect restoration to a suffering man on the Sabbath day—*" made a man every whit whole,"* *—this was His offence. But what did Moses do ? Moses did what might have been considered something more objectionable than this. He circumcised children on the Sabbath-day, a work that inflicted a considerable amount of physical pain, and a great deal of manual labour. And not only did Moses do it, but your illustrious fathers, Abraham, Isaac, and Jacob, whose authority is of greater antiquity, did the same. Could it be right for Moses and your fathers to do all this work on the Sabbath day, the work of mere ceremony, and wrong for Me to do a work of mercy ? The crime and curse of religionists in all ages and lands have been, the exalting the ceremonial over the moral—the local, the temporary, and contingent above the universal, eternal, and absolute.

II —THIS DESIRE TO KILL HIM IMPLIED A GREAT ERROR OF JUDGMENT

" Judge not according to the appearance, but judge righteous judgment." † Judging from appearance, they concluded :

First : That a mere ordinary peasant had no Divine mission. Some of them, perhaps most of them, knew His humble birth-place and parentage, and concluded from His lowly appearance that He was a poor man, and nothing more. They were too blinded to discover beneath such apparently abject forms, a Divine spirit, character, and mission. It has ever been so. Men who judge from appearances have always failed to discern anything great or Divine in those who occupy the humbler walks of life. And thus the men of highest genius, the greatest intellect, Divinest inspirations and aims, have been counted by their contemporaries as

* See Germ, p. 198. † See Homily on these words at end of volume.

the "offscouring of all things." Judging from appearance, they concluded—

Secondly : That a ritualistic religion was a religion of righteousness. Had there been in connection with the ceremonies of the Temple the healing of the sick on the Sabbath day, they would have esteemed the work as highly sacred. None of the ceremonies of their ritualistic religion could they regard as of doubtful or even secondary importance. But the religion of ritualism is not always the religion of righteousness ; but otherwise it is sometimes the religion of immorality. When men attend even to the divinest ceremonies of religion, merely as a matter of custom or form, they degrade their own spiritual natures, and insult Omniscience. "God is a Spirit, and they that worship Him, must worship Him in spirit and in truth." The religion of righteousness is the religion of love, not of law. Judging from appearance, they concluded—

Thirdly : That by killing a teacher, they would kill his influence. Why did the Jews and the rulers seek to kill Christ ? Because of the doctrines He proclaimed—doctrines which not only clashed with their prejudices, but struck against their greed, popularity, and influence. They knew that if His doctrines spread, their authority would crumble, and from the elevated seat of Moses, they would pass into scenes of social degradation. Hence they thought that by killing Him they would kill His doctrines. Men who have judged from appearance have ever thought so, hence they have martyred unpopular teachers. But facts, as well as philosophy, show that such judgment is not a "*righteous judgment.*" The blood of the martyrs has always been the "seed of the Church." The doctrines of a true teacher get fire, force, and sweep by inflicting on him a martyr's death. Christ's death was as a grain of corn that fell into the earth, there grew, spread, multiplied a thousandfold, and will multiply for ever. Do not judge by appearances. "Things are not what they seem."

III —THIS DESIRE TO KILL HIM INVOLVED THEM IN PERPLEXITY

"*Then said some of them of Jerusalem, Is not this He, whom they seek to kill ? But, lo, He speaketh boldly, and they say nothing unto Him. Do the rulers know indeed that this is the very Christ ? Howbeit we know this Man whence He is : but when Christ cometh, no man knoweth whence He is.*" There seems much confusion and bewilderment here. They thought they knew Him, yet they felt they did not know Him. They wondered, too, how a Man whom their rulers desired to kill should speak so boldly, without being arrested at once by them. Minds under a wrong-leading passion are sure to get into confusion. A corrupt passion spreads a deep haze over the whole region of intellect, and makes its path intricate and perplexing. No moral spirit can have its intellectual region clear and bright, and its path straight and sunny, that is not under the control of benevolent dispositions. All the conflicting theories of the world concerning God, spirit, and morals, have their origin in a wrong state of heart. The intellectual confusion of hell grows out of malevolence. What they could not understand, Christ explains. *"Then cried Jesus in the temple as He taught, saying, Ye both know Me, and ye know whence I am: and I am not come of Myself, but He that sent Me is true, whom ye know not."* As they had no love in them, they could not see God; and as they could not see God, they could not understand Him who came from God, and was sent by Him. Observe what Christ asserts—

First: That He knows the Absolute. He is the only Being in the universe that knows Him.

Secondly: That He was a Messenger from the Absolute. *"He that sent Me."* This is the great spiritual Ministry of the world. What are Popes, Cardinals, Archbishops, to Him? "This is My beloved Son, hear ye Him." Whoever else you disregard, "hear ye Him."

IV —THIS DESIRE TO KILL HIM WAS DIVINELY RESTRAINED

"Then they sought to take Him: but no man laid hands on Him, because His hour was not yet come." Why did not their malignant desire work itself out at once? It was wide and strong enough; it glowed in all the breasts of the rulers of the nation, and perhaps in not a few of the men of Jerusalem, and the general population of the country. Why did they not at once seize Him and strike the fatal blow? The answer is, *"because His hour was not yet come."* There was an unseen hand that held them back. He who holds the "wind in His fist," and the waters "in the hollow of His hand," turns the hearts of men as the rivers of water. With God for everything there is a season. Man may wish to hurry events and to go before the appointed time, but there is a power that holds him back until the hour strikes. The power that governs every wavelet in the ocean, controls every passing passion of mankind. "There is a power unseen that rules the illimitable world."

Conclusion. Learn—

First: That being hated by society is not always a proof of hateworthiness. Here is One, "Who did no sin, neither was guile found in His mouth, holy, harmless, undefiled," hated with a mortal hatred. To be hated by a corrupt society is to have the highest testimony to your moral purity and goodness. The world loves its own, and hates all moral aliens. It worships the Herods as gods, and stones the Stephens as wretches unfit to live. "Marvel not if the world hate you; it hated Me before it hated you." Learn—

Secondly: That being hated by society is no reason for neglecting our mission. Though Christ knew that in the leading men of Jerusalem there flamed the fiercest fires of indignation towards Him, yet to Jerusalem He goes, enters the Temple on a great public occasion, and fearlessly delivers His Divine message. That love for truth, God, and humanity, which inspired and ruled the heart of Christ, raised Him above the fear of men, made Him intrepid and invincible in the prosecution of His mission.

Germs of Thought
No. 31   John 7:23

EVERY WHIT WHOLE

"I have made a man every whit whole."

We detach these words and take them to illustrate two subjects—

I —THE GREAT WANT OF MAN

What is his great want? To be made "*whole.*" Man is unsound in every part.

First: He is corporeally unsound. Some men's physical organizations are healthier and haler than others, but even the strongest are unsound. The seeds of disease and death are in all. There is a canker-worm gnawing at the vitals of the most robust. The strongest man is, as compared to the weakest, like an oak to a fragile reed; but ever at the roots of the oak there is a rotting disease that is working its way up.

Secondly: He is intellectually unsound. The man who has the strongest mind is the subject of some mental infirmity. He lacks elasticity, freedom, clearness of vision, courage, and independency. He cannot see things completely, or hold them with a manly grasp. The stronger intellects are the most conscious of their unsoundness.

Thirdly: He is socially unsound. Socially, men were made to love their fellow-men, and to be loved by them, and thus be harmoniously united in reciprocal affection and services of mutual goodwill and usefulness. But it is not so. Socially, man is unsound in every point. The social heart is diseased with greed, envy, jealousy, ambition, and malice. So that the social world is rife with discords, contentions, and wars.

Fourthly: He is morally unsound. Morally, man has lost at once the true idea of right, and the true sympathy with right. His conscience is dim, infirm, torpid, buried in the flesh, "carnally sold under sin." Thus man in every part is unsound. He is lost, not in the sense of being *missed*, for God knows where he is; nor in the sense of being *extinct*, for he lives a certain kind of life; nor in the sense of being *inactive*, for he is in constant labour; but in the sense of *incapacity* to *fulfil the grand object of his being.* He is lost, in the sense that the gallant ship is lost, when no longer sea-worthy; that the grand organ is lost, that has no longer the power to pour out music. We take these words to illustrate—

II.—THE GRAND WORK OF CHRIST

What is it? It is to make "*man every whit whole.*" He makes man—

First: Corporeally whole. It is true that He allows the human body to go down to dust, but the essential personality He will re-animate. "It is sown in corruption, it is raised in incorruption," &c. He makes man—

Secondly: Intellectually whole. Here He begins the healing of the intellect. He clears away from it the moral atmosphere of depravity, and opens its eyes so that it may see things as they are. Christ is working here to give man a sound intellect. In the future world it will be "*every whit whole,*" free from prejudice, from errors, and from all the fogs of depravity. He makes man—

Thirdly: Socially whole. He restores men to social soundness by filling them with that spirit of true philanthropy which prompts them not to seek their own things, but the things of each other, and to labour for the common good of men as men, irrespective of creeds, countries, races or religions. This He is doing now, this He will continue to do on this earth, until men shall love each other as brethren, and nations beat their "swords into ploughshares," "their spears into pruning-hooks," and hear of war no more. He will make the world, even here, "*every whit whole,*" socially, and in the Heavenly Jerusalem above the social soundness and order will be perfect. He makes man—

Fourthly: Morally whole. He will make man sound morally by bringing him under the control of SUPREME LOVE FOR THE SUPREMELY GOOD. Thus: He will take away the heart of "stone," and give it a heart of "flesh." At last He will cause all men to stand before Him without "spot or wrinkle, or any such thing."

CONCLUSION. What a Physician is Christ! He cures all manners of diseases. No malady can baffle His skill. The world has never wanted men who have tried to make people sound. It has its *corporeal* doctors, *intellectual* doctors, *social* doctors, *moral* doctors; but those who succeed most in their respective departments only prove by their miserable failures that they are miserable empirics. Here is a Physician that makes a "*man every whit whole.*"

John 7:31-36

CHRIST'S FIRST TWO DISCOURSES AT THE FEAST OF TABERNACLES
(No. 3)—THE FAVOURABLY DISPOSED AND THE MALIGNANTLY
OPPOSED TO CHRIST

" And many of the people believed," &c.

EXEGETICAL REMARKS.—Ver. 31.—
'*And many of the people* (R. V. BUT
OF THE MULTITUDE MANY) *believed.*"
Their belief means perhaps nothing
more than a passing impression that
He was the Messiah, and does not
include that faith in Him which secures
everlasting life. "*When Christ cometh*
(R. V. THE CHRIST SHALL COME), *will He
do more miracles* (R. V. SIGNS) *than
these* (R. V. THOSE) *which this Man hath
done?*" This implies that there was
—(1.) A general belief that the true
Messiah would work miracles. The
Old Testament gave them to understand this (Isa. xxxv. 5, 6). (2.) A
general acknowledgment that Christ's
miracles had already been great.

Ver. 32.—"*The Pharisees heard that
the people murmured* (R. V. THE MULTI-
TUDE MURMURING) *such* (R. V. THESE)
*things concerning Him ; and the Phari-
sees and the Chief Priests sent officers to
take Him.*" Here the actuating motive
of the persecutors of Jesus is revealed.
They feel a species of rivalry against
Him ; they fear the loss of their popularity and authority, and never can
pardon Him for gaining the affections,
and even, in some measure, the belief
of His countrymen. Death—the death
on the cross—alone can make reparation.

Ver. 33.—"*Then said Jesus* (R. V.
JESUS THEREFORE SAID) *unto them.*"
To whom? To the officers, or to the
Pharisees who gave information, or to
the whole assembly? Probably to the
whole, with the chief priests especially
in view : "*Yet a little while am I with
you, and then I go unto Him that sent
Me.*" Probably He meant by this language to intimate to His enemies that
they need not be in a hurry to seize
Him, as His departure by death was
just at hand. But although they would
lose Him from their midst, He would
not be in the grave, but with His
Father.

Ver. 34.—"*Ye shall seek Me, and
shall not find Me : and where I am,*
thither (R. V. OMITS THITHER) *ye cannot
come.*" You will one day search earnestly for Me, but I shall not be found.
When the judgment of Heaven falls
on your nation (Matt. xxiv. 23) you
will be anxious to find Me, as your
Deliverer. "*Thither ye cannot come.*"
I shall be beyond the reach of your
malicious and murderous designs, in a
state for which you possess no congeniality, and into which you cannot enter.

Ver. 35.—"*Then said the Jews* (R. V.
THE JEWS THEREFORE SAID) *among
themselves, Whither will He* (R. V. THIS
MAN) *go, that we shall not find Him?
will He go unto the dispersed* (R. V.
DISPERSION) *among the Gentiles* (R. V.
GREEKS), *and teach the Gentiles?*" (R. V.
GREEKS.) "The mocking malice of their
reply (in vain questioned by Meyer)
rises into a climax of three clauses : (1.)
Whither will He go, that we might
not follow Him? (Into Paradise?) (2.)
Whither will He seek His fortune?
Among the Jewish dispersion?—among
the Gentiles?—with the less orthodox,
less respectable and intelligent Jews?
(3.) Or will He even teach the Greeks,
to whom indeed, judging from His conduct towards the law, and His liberal
utterance, He seems rather to belong
than to us? But what they say in
mockery must fulfil itself in truth.
They prophesy like Caiaphas (chap.
xi. 50, 51), and Pilate (xix. 19) : 'Unto
the dispersed among the Greeks.' The
διασπόραν (dispersion, *abstract, pro
concret*) Τῶν Ἑλλήνων (genitive of re-
moter relation), not the dispersed Gentiles (*Chrysostom*), or Hellenists, or Jews
(*Scaliger*) ; but according to Greek specific usage (Jas. i. 1 ; 1 Pet. i. 1), the
Jews dispersed in the Gentile world."

Ver. 36.—"*What manner of saying
is this* (R. V. IS THIS WORD) *that He
said, Ye shall seek Me, and shall not*

find Me: and where I am, thither (R. V. OMITS THITHER) *ye cannot come?"* Literally, What is this saying that He said? They felt the dark mystery of the words, and wished, probably, to regard them as nonsense.

HOMILETICS

We have in these verses two classes of men in relation to Christ: those *who were favourably disposed,* and those who were *malignantly opposed to Him.*

I THOSE WHO WERE FAVOURABLY DISPOSED

"*And many of the people believed on Him, and said, When Christ cometh, will He do more miracles than these which this Man hath done?*" These people were the commonalty, as we should say; the lower classes, who were more or less unsophisticated and free from religious prejudices and vested interests in existing institutions. Elsewhere it is said, these common "people heard Christ gladly." These people's faith in Him did not in all probability go farther than to dispose them favourably towards His teaching. It did not prompt them to commit themselves entirely to Him, to follow Him through evil as well as "good report." They were sufficiently instructed in religion to know that the Messiah would be a Miracle Worker, and they had witnessed so many of the miracles of Christ that they were disposed to regard Him as the promised One, the Anointed of God. They did not say, He is indeed the Christ;—but, "*Is not this He?*"

First: Their favourable disposition towards Him was grounded upon facts. There does not seem to be any question even amongst His malignant opponents as to the reality of His miracles. None seemed to deny them, or even to question them.

Secondly: Their favourable disposition toward Him intensified the opposition of His enemies. "*The Pharisees heard that the people murmured such things concerning Him; and the Pharisees and the Chief Priests sent officers to take Him.*" They felt that if the people believed in Him, their influence would wane, their authority depart, and all the honours and amenities connected with their elevated position would vanish. Hence the good opinions expressed now by the people fell as oil on the flames of their malignity.

Now, through all Christendom there has always been a large class of people favourably disposed towards Christ; and their good opinions are based upon undeniable facts concerning Him. This class, even as in the days of Christ, intensify the opposition of enemies. When the atheist, the scientific infidel, the worldling, and the profligate, mark the favourable disposition of the people towards Christ, they, like these Pharisees and Chief Priests, only become the more anxious to banish Him from the world. Were it not for the favourably-disposed people, Christianity would soon be extinguished. Popular sentiment is our bulwark against infidelity. The other class here are—

II —THOSE WHO WERE MALIGNANTLY OPPOSED

These were the "*Pharisees*" and the "*Chief Priests.*" Three remarks are suggested concerning them.

First : They were to be deprived of the fellowship of Christ. "*Then said Jesus unto them, Yet a little while am I with you,*" &c. But six months after this, Christ was crucified, and afterwards ascended to heaven, and returned to the bosom of His Father. It was only a "*little while*" that He was in their midst; it would have been well for them if they had availed themselves of that "*little while.*" The period of redemptive mercy with all men is but a "*little while.*" When He departed they lost Him for ever. Their sympathies and characters excluded them from all future fellowship with Him.

Secondly : They would vainly seek the help of Christ. "*Ye shall seek Me, and shall not find Me.*" The hour is approaching when the Roman legions would invade their country, destroy Jerusalem, and overwhelm their land with such desolation as had never been before, and perhaps will never be again. Then they would look out for Divine deliverance, but none would come. "*Ye shall seek Me, and shall not find Me.*" There is a time to " seek the Lord," a time when He may be found ; and there is a time when He will be sought, and will not be found. " Many shall say to Me at that day, Lord, Lord ! " &c.

Thirdly : They misunderstood the meaning of Christ. "*Then said the Jews among themselves, Whither will He go, that we shall not find Him? will He go unto the dispersed among the Gentiles, and teach the Gentiles? What manner of saying is this that He said, Ye shall seek Me, and shall not find Me : and where I am, thither ye cannot come?*" Observe—

(1.) They started from His words an ungenerous conjecture. "*Will He go unto the dispersed among the Gentiles, and teach the Gentiles?*" That is, " Will He go amongst the Jews who are scattered amongst the Gentiles, or the Gentiles dispersed over all the world? In either case He will go to a contemptible class of men—men to be treated with disdain. If He leaves our glorious country, where else can He go but amongst such despicable people?" (2.) They failed to attach to His words the true idea. "*What manner of saying is this?*" They had not reached the idea of His Divine mission and destiny; they were carnal, and judged after the flesh.

Thus it ever is with this class, the malignant opponents of Christ; they are deprived of His fellowship. Their worldly, corrupt natures exclude them from all intercourse with Him. Where He is, they cannot come. He is in the sublime region of purity, righteousness, and benevolence : they are down in the depths of depravity. They must all seek the help of Christ one day, when it will be too late. On the last great day they shall agonize to enter in at the "strait gate" of His kingdom, and shall not be able, for the Master will have risen up and shut the door. They all misunderstood His meaning. They have "eyes but see not, ears but hear not." They judge after the flesh, they live in the "letter."

CONCLUSION. To which of these classes dost thou belong, my reader ? Most probably the former. Albeit to be merely favourably disposed to Christ is not enough ; there must be decision, consecration, vital affinity. Shouldst thou, peradventure, belong to the latter, ponder thy condition ere it be too late. "*Yet a little while,*" and the day of grace will be over ; then thou wilt seek Him, but wilt "*not find Him.*"

John 7:37-39

CHRIST'S FIRST TWO DISCOURSES AT THE FEAST OF TABERNACLES.

(NO. 4)—THE TRANSCENDENT PHILANTHROPIST

" In the last day, that great day of the feast, Jesus stood and cried, saying, If any man thirst, let him come unto Me, and drink," &c.

EXEGETICAL REMARKS.—Ver. 37.— "*In* (R. V. NOW ON) *the last day, that* (R. V. THE) *great day of the feast.*" The last day of the feast of tabernacles was the closing feast day of the year (Lev. xxiii. 39). It was distinguished and sanctified by very remarkable ceremonies. "The generally joyous character of this feast," says *Olshausen,* " broke out on this day into loud jubilation, particularly at the solemn moment when the priest, as was done on every day of this festival, brought forth, in golden vessels, water from the stream of Siloam, which flowed under the temple-mountain, and solemnly poured it on the altar. Then the words of Isaiah xii. 3 were sung : 'With joy shall we draw water out of the well of salvation,' and thus the symbolical *reference* of this act, intimated in ver. 39, was expressed." "So ecstatic," says *Lightfoot,* "was the joy with which this ceremony was performed, accompanied with sounds of trumpets, that it used to be said, whoever had not witnessed it had never seen rejoicing at all." "*Jesus stood and*

cried, saying." On this grand occasion He probably stood on some eminence, so that all could see Him, and hear Him utter the sublime words,—"*If any man thirst, let him come unto Me, and drink.*" "*If any man,*" Jew or Gentile, "*thirst,*" craving for a higher life, "*let him come unto Me, and drink.*"

Ver. 38.—"*He that believeth on Me.*" Not on what men say *about* Me ; not merely on the facts of My history ; not on the doctrines of My teaching ; but on *Me*—the living, loving, personal Son of God. "*As the Scripture hath said, out of His belly shall flow rivers of living water.*" The words, "*as the Scripture hath said,*" point perhaps to no particular passage, but to the general strain of Scripture in relation to Himself. (See Isa. lviii. 11 ; Joel iii. 18 ; Zech. xiv. 8 ; Ezek. xlvii. 1— 11.) Most of these Scriptures refer to waters issuing from beneath the Temple. The aim is, to apply the typical waters to their now-present Antitype, proclaiming that the hour of their grand fulfilment has come. "*Out of His belly,*" 'Εκ τῆς κοιλίας αὐτοῦ. Out of His body, or inner self; that is, out of His inner nature, shall flow the quickening influences of God.

Ver. 39.—"(*But this spake He of the Spirit, which they that believe on Him should* (R. V. BELIEVED ON HIM WERE TO) *receive: for the Holy Ghost* (R. V. THE SPIRIT) *was not yet given; because that Jesus was not yet glorified.*)" "*For the Holy Ghost was not yet given.*" Beyond all doubt the word "*given,*" or some similar word, is the right supplement here, if we are to insert any supplement at all. In chap. xvi. 7, the Holy Ghost is represented, not only as the gift of Christ, but as a Gift the communication of which was dependent upon His own departure to the Father. Now, as Christ was not yet gone, so the Holy Ghost was not yet given. "*Because that Jesus was not yet glorified.*" This is one of those explanatory remarks of our Evangelist himself, which constitute a marked feature of this fourth Gospel. "The word '*glorified*' is here used advisedly, to teach the reader, not only that the departure of Christ to the Father was indispensable to the giving of the Spirit, but that this illustrious Gift, direct from the hands of the ascended Saviour, was God's intimation to the world, that He whom it had cast out, crucified, and slain, was His Elect in whom His soul delighted; and it was through the smiting of that Rock, that the waters of the Spirit, for which the Church was waiting, and with pomp at the feast of tabernacles proclaiming its expectation, has gushed forth upon a thirsty world."—*Dr. Brown.*

HOMILETICS

In these words, Christ appears as a *Transcendent Philanthropist.* "*In the last day of the feast,*" amidst assembled thousands, Jesus appears and offers with earnestness, and on the easiest conditions, the one great blessing which humanity requires, to make it holy, great, and happy, viz. the spiritually quickening influences of God.

I —HE OFFERS THEM THE HIGHEST BLESSING

What is it? Water. "*If any man thirst, let him come unto Me and drink.*" Water is the most precious element in nature: a life-giving, thirst-satisfying, nature-cleansing, and supporting element. What is the water Christ here offers?

First: It was a Divinely refreshing influence. "*This spake He of the Spirit,*" *i. e.* the Spirit of God, that "quickeneth all things:" the spirit of love, and truth, and peace, and righteousness. This is that which alone can satisfy the burning thirst of human souls. A soul without this spirit is like an Oriental traveller on the burning sands with no water.

Secondly: It was a Divinely refreshing influence that would roll through the centre of human nature. "*Out of his belly*"—out of himself—"*shall flow rivers of living water.*" The spiritual influences which Christ gives will not only allay the thirst, but stream forth in all directions to refresh and quicken the spirits of others. A good man is a fountain of life.

Thirdly: It was a Divinely refreshing influence that only came in its plenitude after the ascension of Christ. "*The Holy Ghost was not yet given, because that Jesus was not yet glorified.*" The

Holy Spirit was not yet given in all its power and fulness ; it came not until the day of Pentecost, when the influence came down like showers upon the new-mown grass.

Behold this Philanthropist ! How He transcends all the most illustrious benefactors of the race ! Who ever bestowed such benedictions as He ? He brings the refreshing influences of God into the human soul, and thus blesses it in order to make it a fountain of blessing to others. He fills the human with the Divine.

II —HE OFFERS THEM THE HIGHEST BLESSING WITH INTENSE EARNESTNESS

" *Jesus stood and cried.*" A term used to denote a proclamation with peculiar boldness and emphasis. Christ's invitation was the opposite to all that is cold and formal. His own soul—which was on fire—went out with the cry. Would that we had heard His voice : how loud, how tuneful, how thrilling ! Loud as thunder, sweet as music, piercing as agony. Christ was no half-hearted philanthropist. He did not form a scheme to help the world, and work at it methodically, or with spasmodic earnestness. From beginning to end He was earnest : " I must work the works of Him that sent Me, while it is day : the night cometh, when no man can work." He travailed in soul to regenerate the world. Does incessant labour prove earnestness ? Does enormous sacrifice prove earnestness ? Does grappling with the fiercest foes prove earnestness ? Does soul-absorbing, self-sacrificing, unremitting struggle prove earnestness ? Then Christ was an earnest Philanthropist : " He poured out His very soul unto death." " *Jesus stood and cried.*" And He stands now before humanity, and cries through nature, through providence, through reason, through conscience, and through the blessed Gospel, and says to all : " *If any man thirst, let him come unto Me, and drink.*" To Me, not to the caterers for public amusements, not to priests, philosophers, or poets, but to *Me*.

III —HE OFFERS THEM THE HIGHEST BLESSING ON THE EASIEST CONDITION

" *He that believeth on Me.*" He does not require great struggling, great labour, great sacrifice, as the condition of its bestowment, but simple faith in Him. Observe—

First : Faith in a proposition that is obviously true is one of the easiest acts of the mind. It is as easy for me to believe an evident truth as it is to open my eyes and behold the light. In addition to this, we have all a natural craving to believe. Man is a credulous creature, so much so that his crime and curse is, that he believes too much rather than too little.

Secondly: Faith in a person that is obviously good, is easier still. Faith in men is a universal instinct. We are made to trust in each other. We do so through all the stages of life, from the dawn of childhood to the night of age. True, as our experience advances, our faith in some men is severely tried and often shipwrecked; but to others we hold on until the last gasp. Now did ever a Being appear in history so easy to confide in as Christ—a Being so obviously perfect in love, truthfulness, tenderness, wisdom? All that is wanted, then, is to "*believe*" on Him, in order to get this highest good: this quickening, refreshing, satisfying influence of God. "*He that believeth on Me.*" Who cannot believe on Him? None but those who do not study Him as He appears on the pages of His biographers.

CONCLUSION. Blessed be heaven for such a Philanthropist as this! Why need the world be unhappy? Why need men be damned, either here or yonder, with such a Philanthropist?

John 7:40-53

CHRIST'S FIRST TWO DISCOURSES AT THE FEAST OF TABERNACLES

(No. 5)—DIFFERENT IMPRESSIONS PRODUCED BY CHRIST'S TEACHING

"Many of the people therefore, when they heard this saying, said, Of a truth this is the Prophet," &c.

EXEGETICAL REMARKS.—Ver. 40.— "*Many of the people* (R. V. SOME OF THE MULTITUDE) *therefore, when they heard this saying* (R. V. THESE WORDS), *said, Of a truth this is* (R. V. THIS IS OF A TRUTH) *the Prophet.*" There was an expectation amongst some of the Jews that one of the old prophets would appear and precede the Messiah. Many of them thought that Jesus was one. They felt certain of this.

Ver. 41.—"*Others said, This is the Christ.*" Some of the Jews held that the prophet who was to come was different from the Messiah, and was to herald His coming. Others held that He was the same with Christ. Here they seemed to be distinguished. Some took Jesus for the prophet, and others for the Christ Himself. "*But some said.*" "These objectors were always ready, ever stifling by the Scripture itself the yearnings of faith. A true sample this of the world's wisdom in things spiritual. Knowing so much, and yet knowing so little— ready enough to bring forward diffi- culties and pick flaws, but not at all ready with the proper explanations, even when they are plain to a child." —*Jacobus.* "*Shall Christ* (R. V. WHAT DOTH THE CHRIST) *come out of Galilee?*" Those who put this question insinuated falsehood or a desire to pervert facts. Christ did not come "*out of Galilee*" in the sense of being born there. He was born in Bethlehem. He was brought up, it is true, in Nazareth in Galilee, but not born there.

Ver. 42.—"*Hath not the Scripture said, That* (R. V. THE CHRIST) *Christ cometh of the seed of David, and out of the town of* (R. V. FROM) *Bethlehem, where* (R. V. THE VILLAGE WHERE) *David was?*" (Isaiah xi. 1; Jer. xxiii. 5; Micah v. 2.) "*Where David was*" (1 Sam. xvi.).

Ver. 43.—"*So there was* (R. V. AROSE) *a division among the people* (R. V. IN THE MULTITUDE) *because of Him.*" "This division, or violent split, among those who accorded recognition to the Lord in different degrees, must be distinguished from the division between all those who are friendly to Him and the enemies of whom (ver. 44) John goes on at once to speak, or the analogous divisions in ch. ix. 6 and x. 18. There were at first but a few among the people who made common cause with the hostile Pharisees." —*Lange.*

Ver. 44.—"*And some of them would have taken Him.*" "*Some.*" Who? Not any of the two preceding classes; but the people who heard His words and were exasperated. "*No man laid hands on Him.*" Why not? What held them back? Conscience, and the restraining force of justice.

Ver. 45.—"*Then came the officers* (R. V. THE OFFICERS THEREFORE CAME) *to the Chief Priests and Pharisees.*" These "*officers*" are the same in all probability as those spoken of in verse 32, who were sent by the Sanhedrim to take Him. They had been on the watch for some hours during this public excitement. Why did they pause so long? This is the question the Chief Priests and Pharisees asked them. "*Why have ye not brought* (R. V. DID YE NOT BRING) *Him?*" Why? They could not, for the causes that prevented some of the people from taking Him.

Ver. 46.—"*The officers answered, Never man spake like this Man*" (R. V. NEVER MAN SO SPAKE). This was their answer, and explains the reason why they had not brought Him, viz. the impression they had received of His transcendent excellence as a Teacher. There was a grandeur, an independency, a purity, a power, and a catholicity in His words that impressed them with the surpassing greatness of the Teacher.

Ver. 47.—"*Then answered them the Pharisees* (R. V. THE PHARISEES THEREFORE ANSWERED THEM), *Are ye also deceived?*" (R. V. LED ASTRAY.) Is it possible that you, our servants, our officers, are cheated by this Impostor?

Ver. 48.—"*Have* (R. V. HATH) *any of the rulers or of the Pharisees believed on Him?*" This means, Since none

of the rulers or the Pharisees believed on Him, how monstrous it is that such men as you, ignorant hirelings, should yield in any way to His claims.

Ver. 49.—"*But this people*" (R. V. MULTITUDE). The language is contemptuous, this ignorant rabble. "*Who* (R. V. WHICH) *knoweth not the law are cursed.*" They are utterly ignorant of all law, are "*cursed,*" that is, We, who are the religious lawgivers, have cursed them.

Ver. 50.—"*Nicodemus saith unto them.*" He was a member of the Sanhedrim. "(*He that came to Jesus by night* (R. V. HE THAT CAME TO HIM BEFORE), *being one of them.*)" We have an account of his appearing to Christ in the third chapter. This timid and cowardly disciple, instead of thundering condemnation in their ears, puts a question.

Ver. 51.—"*Doth our law judge any* (R. V. A) *man, before it* (R. V. EXCEPT IT FIRST) *hear him* (R. V. FROM HIMSELF), *and know what he doeth?*" As if he had said, You talk about law, but where is the law in your conduct? Law requires an honest trial, before ever a criminal is condemned (Exod. xxiii. 1; Deut. i. 16, 17; xix. 15).

Ver. 52.—"*They answered and said unto him, Art thou also of Galilee?*" This fierce rejoinder of the Pharisees strikingly and solemnly contrasts with the very feeble defence which Nicodemus had put forth. It expresses utter scorn for the man who in any way sympathized with Jesus. "*Search, and look: for* (R. V. SEE THAT) *out of Galilee ariseth no prophet.*" Here they showed their ignorance; for was not Jonah a prophet, and Elijah a prophet, and came they not out of Galilee? Besides, Christ did not come out of Galilee in the sense of being born there, He came out of Bethlehem.

Ver. 53.—"*And every man went unto his own house.*" (R. V. OMITS THIS VERSE HERE AND INSERTS IT AT COMMENCEMENT OF CHAP. VIII.) Finding their malignant attempts so far unsuccessful, the members of the Sanhedrim went to their own houses.

HOMILETICS

The incidents recorded in the verses before us present certain facts connected with Christ's discourses at the feast of tabernacles additional to those which have already been noticed. These facts indeed are generally developed through the *teaching of Christ* in every age and land. And in relation to His Teaching it appears—

I —THAT IT PRODUCED A VAST VARIETY OF OPINIONS CONCERNING HIM

"*Many of the people*," &c. Some of His hearers on this occasion said He was a "*prophet;*" some, that He was the "*Christ;*" whilst many denied that He was either, and were ready to wreak vengeance on Him as an impostor. So there was a "*division*," a schism amongst them. Diversity of opinion amongst the hearers of Christ is shown on another occasion. "Jesus said, Whom do men say that I the Son of Man am? And they said, Some say that Thou art John the Baptist: some, Elias; and others, Jeremias, or one of the prophets" (Matt. xvi. 13, 14). The variety of speculative opinion which Christ's teaching has always produced reveals—

First: The great diversity in the minds of men. No two minds are exactly alike in the kind or measure of faculty and tendency. Nor have any two minds passed through exactly the same educational process. Hence it is almost impossible for any two minds to form exactly the same opinions concerning any person or proposition. This variety gives a freshness to the great field of human thought, and it should teach man to treat the conclusions of his brother with respect, however much they may differ from his own. It should also warn those ecclesiastics and rulers who presume to govern the opinions of men, of their folly and their wickedness.

> Let those who sit in priestly state
> As lordlings over mind,
> And by the notions they dictate
> The thoughts of men would bind,
> Remember well that on this earth
> It must be ever heard,
> The Lord hath yet more light and truth
> To break forth from His Word.—"*Biblical Liturgy.*"

This reveals—

Secondly: The moral perversity in the souls of men. Wrong opinions in all cases on moral subjects indicate a perversion of judgment. The broad eternal principles of moral virtue are so self-obvious and radiant, that wrong conclusions concerning them are inexcusable in the case of all to whom they are presented. Christ's life was at once the incarnation and brightest revelation of those principles; and hence diversity of opinion in relation to His character implies perversity of heart. Were all men, whatever their diversity of mind, to give to Him a proper study, they would say, "Master, we know that Thou art true." This reveals—

Thirdly: The intellectual freedom which Christ allows men. Mighty as He is in power, far-reaching as His influence is in the depths of the human soul, and potent as are His truths, He does not coerce thought, does not compel men to believe, He leaves them free. "Will ye also go away?"

In relation to His teaching it appears—

II —THAT IT PRODUCED A PROFOUND IMPRESSION AS TO HIS TRANSCENDENT WORTH

"*Never man spake like this Man.*" This was the utterance of the rough Roman officers who were sent forth by their masters to seize Him; and it is the language that impartial minds in all times and lands must adopt; there never was such a Teacher. "*Never man spake like this Man.*" * So original, so independent, so suggestive, so natural, so tender, so faithful, so devout, so soul-commanding. As a Teacher, in all these respects He throws the greatest sages of antiquity in the shade, and makes modern scientists dwindle into insignificance.

"*Never man spake like this Man.*" Such is the opinion of the greatest men—legislators philosophers, and poets—of the world. He stands alone. The thoughts of the greatest thinkers of all times are, as compared to His, only as the frail productions of human art compared to the magnificent organizations of living nature. "The whole world," says a modern author, "has confirmed this sentence. Believers have felt its truth, as they have imbibed the instructions of their heavenly Master; and infidels have not been able to suppress their admiration at the Sermon on the Mount, the Golden Rule, the Parables of the Good Samaritan, the Prodigal Son, and the prayer of Jesus with His disciples before His death. May it not be found at last that He lifted up in vain His voice of sweet persuasion and awful warning, to plead with our negligent and hardened hearts, and to win us to God and heaven; but, hearing, may we understand; and understanding, feel; and feeling, practise the precepts of life and immortality."

In relation to His teaching, it appears—

III —THAT IT PRODUCED A DEADLY HOSTILITY TOWARDS HIM

"*Some of them would have taken Him,*" &c. In the hostility which the teaching of Christ roused in the minds of these Chief Priests and Pharisees we discover several evils.

First: Intolerance. Exasperated by the doctrines He proclaimed and the influence He was exerting upon the people, they wickedly resolved to crush Him. "*Some of them would have taken Him.*"

*See *Gospel of Matthew* on these words.

Deep and strong was the desire they had to arrest His progress, cripple His energies, and even destroy His very existence. Antagonism to Christianity is ever associated with intolerance; it denounces argument and betakes itself to violence. Another evil we discover is—

Secondly: Superciliousness. "*Have any of the rulers or of the Pharisees believed on Him?*" The spirit of this language is: What is the worth of your opinions compared with ours—the "*rulers*" of the people? They are beneath contempt. With what haughtiness the enemies of Christianity have always treated its disciples! They have branded them as fools and fanatics; they deem themselves the wise, forsooth! Another evil we discover is—

Thirdly: Insolence. "*But this people who knoweth not the law are cursed.*" "*This people!*" Meaning this rabble, this ignorant mob. The enemies of Christianity have always treated its adherents as the "offscouring of all things." Another evil we discover is—

Fourthly: Ridicule. "*Art thou also of Galilee? Search, and look: for out of Galilee ariseth no prophet.*" These words were addressed to Nicodemus, whose mean spirit their hostility had stirred up to a little courage, sufficient to say in their presence, "*Doth our law judge any man, before it hear him, and knoweth what he doeth?*" But little respect have I for such discipleship as that of Nicodemus. He was too mean-spirited and craven. "*Doth our law judge any man, before it hear him?*" Why ask such a question? O Nicodemus, why didst thou not say, "Our law condemns your conduct? You are perpetrating the greatest moral enormity in treating with heartless indignity the Holy Son of God! Woe to you!" So far as he was concerned, their reply served him right. "*Art thou also of Galilee?*" Art thou one of the despicable Galileans? Ridicule has often been one of the ready instruments of the opponents of Christianity. Another evil we discover is—

Fifthly: Humiliation. "*Every man went unto his own house.*" So far the malignant plans of the Chief Priests and Pharisees were baffled, and they retired home no doubt with spirits chagrined and humbled. Such will be the condition of all the opponents to Christianity sooner or later.

Such are some of the evils connected with the hostility which the teaching of Christ awakened in the minds of those old bigoted leaders of the Jewish people.

CONCLUSION. How stand we in relation to Christ? Are our minds merely taken up with speculative opinions concerning Him; or are our hearts centred in Him by a living faith? True faith is something independent of what are called "the evidences." It comes by a soul recognition of Christ in the glory of His person, and the adaptation of His teaching to the intellect, conscience, and deep-felt needs of the heart.

> " A man of subtle reasoning asked
> A peasant if he knew
> Where lies the internal evidence
> That proved his Bible true.
> The terms of disputative art
> Had never reached his ear ;
> He laid his hand upon his heart,
> And only answered ' Here ! ' "

John 8:1, 2

CHRIST AS A RELIGIOUS TEACHER

" Jesus went unto the mount of Olives. And early in the morning He came again into the temple, and all the people came unto Him ; and He sat down, and taught them."—viii. 1, 2.

EXEGETICAL REMARKS.—Concerning the genuineness of these and the following ten verses of this chapter, which is questioned by some and denied by others, we shall offer remarks in our next section. Meanwhile we shall confine our attention to these two verses.

Ver. 1.—*"Jesus went unto the Mount of Olives."* Some say that this ought to have been at the conclusion of the preceding chapter, following the words, " every man went unto his own house." Whilst the people had perhaps all their own houses to go to, and to them they retired, Jesus had no home, but withdrew to the *" Mount of Olives."* " This spot is a high hill rising quite abruptly from the valley of Jehoshaphat, and overlooking Jerusalem on the east side. At its foot between the city and the hill, is the brook Kedron ; and on its slope, just across the brook, is the garden of Gethsemane. A winding footpath leads over the hill to Bethany on the other side. Our Lord seems to have passed the night on the Mount, perhaps at Bethany, where He was wont to resort, away from the bustle and the turmoil of the crowded city, and from the malice of His enemies." From Luke xxii. 37 we learn that He was in the habit of spending the night on the Mount of Olives during His last residence at Jerusalem.

Ver. 2.—*" And early in the morning."* Ὄρθρον. " John writes elsewhere, πρωΐα (xviii. 28) ; πρωΐ (xx. 1) ; Luke, on the contrary, ὄρθρου. It is to be observed here, however, that the term ὄρθρου denotes more precisely the dawn of morning, and that it is intended to denote just this time."—*Lange.* *" He came again into the temple, and all the people came unto Him ; and He sat down, and taught them."* Though He had been persecuted in the temple, as we find in the twenty-fifth verse of the preceding chapter, with undaunted courage He resorts thither again in order to teach the people.

HOMILETICS

The two verses suggest to us a few thoughts concerning *Christ as a Religious Teacher.*

I —HE WAS AS A TEACHER DEVOUTLY STUDIOUS

It was from the solitudes of the Mount of Olives, where He had spent the previous night, that He went to the temple to preach. Christ often had recourse to the lonelihood of the hills for holy meditation and communion with the Eternal. There, in those profound silences where alone the voices of truth are heard, He poured out His thoughts upon the loftiest themes, and opened His heart to the influences of His great Father's loving mind.   Devout solitude is the scene where preparation for public speaking can be best attained.   Without this, Theological Halls and Elocutionary Schools are worse than useless.   It is only in solitude that a man can break the shells and reach the germs of the higher truths of life and destiny.   There only, by bathing them in the living current of devotion, can he make them so real to himself as to make them realities to others.   There are three things that seem essential in order properly to preach the Gospel, and these can come only by seasons of *devout solitude*.

First : Self-formed conviction of Gospel truth.   Gospel truth is our great instrument of social usefulness; that without which nothing else will be of any service.   It is the "power of God unto salvation."   But how is this to be wielded ?   By circulating copies of the Scripture, or by a mere recitation of their contents, or by repeating what other people have said and written concerning those truths ?   All these may be and are useful in their way.   But there is one thing indispensable, even to do these things effectively, and that is, *self-formed convictions*.   Heaven has so far honoured our nature, that the Gospel, in order to obtain its grand victories, must pass as living beliefs through the soul of him that employs it.   If we would effectually use the Gospel to help society, we must see, taste, and handle it with our own souls. The men who speak the Gospel without such convictions,—and there are thousands of such amongst conventional preachers,—can never enrich the world.   They are echoes of old voices; what they say was in the world before they came into it.   They are but mere channels through which old dogmas flow.   But he who speaks what he believes, and because he believes, speaks in some sense a new thing to the race.   The doctrine comes from him instinct and warm with life.   His individuality is impressed upon it.   The world never had it in that exact form before, and never would have had it so had he not believed and spoken.   Now, devout solitude is necessary to turn the Gospel into this power of living conviction; you can never get it elsewhere.   Alone with God, you can search the Gospel to its foundation, and feel the congruity of its doctrines with your reason, its claims with your conscience, its provisions with your wants.

Secondly : Unconquerable love for Gospel truth.   There is an immense practical opposition to Gospel truth in society.   Men's pride, prejudice, pleasures, pursuits, and temporal interests are now, as ever, against it.   It follows, therefore, that those who think more of the favour and applause of society than of the claims of truth, will not deal with it honestly, earnestly, and therefore successfully.   The man only who loves truth more than popularity, fortune, or even life, can so use it as really and everlastingly to benefit mankind. In devout solitude you can cultivate this invincible attachment to truth, and you may be made to feel with Paul, who said—" I count all things but loss for the excellency of the knowledge of Christ."

Thirdly: A living expression of Gospel truth. We must be "living epistles." Our conduct must confirm and illumine the doctrines which our lips declare. Gospel sermons which are the expressions of life, are life-giving. Gospel truth must be embodied; the "Word must become flesh;" it must be drawn out in living characters in all the phases of our every-day existence; its spirit must be our inspiration, if we would make it instrumental for good. Now, for the production of such sermons, I am convinced there must be seasons of devout solitude; hours when, under the silent sunbeams of eternity, ideas run into emotions, circulate as a vital current through every vein of the soul, and form the very stamina of our being. It is said of Moses, "that the skin of his face shone while he talked with God." But in seasons of devout solitude our whole nature may grow luminous, and every phase of our character coruscate with the deep things of the Spirit. John the Baptist gained his invincible energy in the lonely wilderness; Paul prepared to be an apostle in the quiet of Arabia; and it was in the awful midnight solitude of Gethsemane that an angel from heaven came to strengthen Jesus for His work. It is beneath the earth's green mantle, in secret and silence amongst the roots, that the trees of the forest turn the elements of nature to their own advantage. And it is down in the quiet depths of spiritual realities, alone with God, that the soul only can turn this world to its true use. The verses suggest that—

II —HE WAS AS A TEACHER SUBLIMELY COURAGEOUS

"*He came again into the temple.*" In that temple during the previous days, His life had been threatened. It is said that " they sought to take Him " (chap. vii. 30); that is, to kill Him. Officers had been despatched on the previous day from the Sanhedrim in order to seize Him. Yet, notwithstanding this malignant determination to destroy Him, with a noble daring He goes "*early in the morning*" of the next day "*into the temple.*" You must distinguish this spirit of fearless daring from that which the world calls courage.

First: Brute courage is dead to the sacredness of life. The great bulk of the armies of Europe is formed of men who have gone into the profession (as it is called) without any deep conviction as to the sacredness of human life. They are men, for the most part, who hold life cheaply. Their courage is an animal and a mercenary thing. Soldiers are not spiritual men, but sanguinary bipeds who have sold themselves to carnage. This was not the courage that Christ possessed and displayed. Deeply did He feel, and frequently did He teach, the sanctity of life. He came, not to *destroy* men's lives, but to *save* them. "What," said He, "shall it profit a man, if he shall gain the whole world, and lose his own soul? Or what shall a man give in exchange for his soul?"

Secondly: Brute courage is indifferent to the grand mission of life. The man of brute valour is not penetrated, still less inspired, with the question, What is the grand object of my life? Wherefore was I sent into the world? Am I here to work out the great designs of my Maker, and to rise into angelhood, or to be a mere fighting machine? On the contrary, Christ's regard for the grand mission of His life made Him courageous. He held the will of His Father as a dearer thing to Him than His mortal existence. He came to "bear witness to the truth;" and to fulfil this work He dared the fury of His enemies, and willingly risked His own mortal life.

Thirdly: Brute courage is always inspired by mere animal passion. It is when the blood is up the man is daring. And the blood, what is it? The mere blood of the enraged tiger or the infuriated lion. When the blood cools down, the man's courage, such as it is, collapses. Not so with the valour of Christ. His courage was that of deep conviction of duty. His excitement was not animal, but spiritual—not malign or ambitious, but reverent and benign. "As Luther," *Dr. D'Aubigné* informs us, "drew near the door which was about to admit him into the presence of his judges (the Diet of Worms), he met a valiant knight, the celebrated George of Fruendsberg, who, four years later, at the head of his German lansquenets, bent the knee with his soldiers on the field of Pavia, and then, charging to the left of the French army, drove it into the Ticino, and in a great measure decided the captivity of the King of France. The old General, seeing Luther pass, tapped him on the shoulder, and shaking his head, blanched in many battles, said kindly, 'Poor monk, poor monk! thou art now going to make a nobler stand than I or any other captain have ever made in the bloodiest of our battles. But if thy cause is just, and thou art sure of it, go forward in God's name, and fear nothing. God will not forsake thee.' A noble tribute of respect paid by the courage of the sword to the courage of the mind."

Nothing is more necessary for a religious teacher than courage, for his mission is to strike hard against the prejudices, the self-interests, the dishonesties, the cherished passions and sinful pursuits of the masses. No man without an invincible valour of soul can do the work of a religious teacher in this age. The popular preacher must, more or less, be cowardly and conciliatory. The less force of conviction a preacher has, the more he is fitted for popularity.

Dead fish flow with the stream ; it requires living ones with much inner force to cut up against the current. The verses suggest that—

III —HE WAS AS A TEACHER EARNESTLY DILIGENT

"*Early in the morning.*" Elsewhere we are informed that He rose up "a great while before day." He did not indulge Himself in sleep. When sleep, which generally does its refreshing work in a few hours, had left Him, and the sun struck his rays upon the horizon, He was up at His great work. "I must work the works of Him that sent Me, while it is day : the night cometh, when no man can work." * Two things should make a teacher earnestly diligent—

First : The transcendent importance of his mission. What has he to do ? To enlighten and regenerate imperishable spirits that are in a morally ruinous condition. What is involved in the loss of one soul ?

Secondly : The brevity of his life. How short the time, even in the longest lived men, for the prosecution of this the greatest of all human undertakings ! Oh that all preachers of the Holy Word were inspired with something of the earnestness of Christ's spirit ! Then indeed they would be earnest in season and out of season, &c. No time would be wasted in sleep, in self-indulgence, or even in occupations that had not a salutary bearing on the great mission.

> "Oh ! let all the soul within you
> For the truth's sake go abroad.
> Strike ! let every nerve and sinew
> Tell on ages—tell for God."

The verses suggest that—

IV —HE WAS AS A TEACHER BEAUTIFULLY NATURAL

"*He sat down, and taught them.*" There was nothing stiff or official in Christ's manner of teaching. All was free, fresh, and elastic as nature.

First : He was natural in attitude. Modern rhetoric has rules to guide a public speaker as to his posture, how he should move his hand, point his finger, and roll his eyes. All such miserable directions are not only to the utmost degree unlike Christ, but degrading to the moral nature of the speaker, and detrimental to his oratoric influence. Let a man be charged with great thoughts, and those thoughts will throw his frame into the most beseeming attitudes.

Secondly : He was natural in expression. He attended to no classic rule of composition ; the words and similes He employed were such as His thoughts ran into at first, and such as His hearers could well understand. To many modern preachers composition is

* See a reading on early rising, "The Practical Philosopher." Published by R. Dickinson.

everything. Words the most select and ornate, sentences the most polished, and periods the most rounded, paragraphs the most finished and brilliant, they scrupulously regard. How unlike Christ ! and what solemn trifling with Gospel truth !

Thirdly : He was natural in tones. The tones of His voice, we may rest assured, rose and fell according to the thoughts that occupied His soul. The voice of the modern teacher is often hideously artificial. Just so far as a speaker goes away from his nature, either in language, attitude, or tone, he loses self-respect, inward vigour, and social force.

John 8:3-11

THE WOMAN TAKEN IN ADULTERY

*(Jesus in Jerusalem.—Account of the woman taken in adultery.—*JOHN viii. 3—11.)

" And the Scribes and Pharisees brought unto Him a woman taken in adultery ; and when they had set her in the midst, they say unto Him, Master, this woman was taken in adultery, in the very act," &c.

EXEGETICAL REMARKS.—On the question of the genuineness of this paragraph we cannot do better than by presenting our readers with a summary of the arguments as given by Dr. Farrar: " I. ARGUMENTS AGAINST ITS GENUINENESS.—(1.) It is not found in some of the best and oldest MSS. ; (2.) nor in most of the Fathers (*e.g.* Origen, Cyril, Chrysostom, Theophylact, Tertullian, Cyprian) ; (3.) nor in many ancient versions (*e.g.* Sahidic, Coptic, and Gothic) ; (4.) in other MSS. it is marked with *obeli* and asterisks, or a space is left for it, or it is inserted elsewhere ; (5.) it contains an extraordinary number of various readings ('variant singula fere verba in codicibus plerisque.'—*Tischendorf*) ; (6.) it contains several expressions not elsewhere found in St. John ; and (7.) it differs widely in some respects—particularly in the constant use of the connecting δὲ—from the style of St. John throughout the rest of the Gospel. Several of these arguments are weakened, (i.) by the fact that the diversities of readings may be reduced to three main recensions ; (ii.) that the rejection of the passage may have been due to a false dogmatical bias ; (iii.) that the silence of some of the Fathers may be accidental, and of others prudential. II. ARGUMENTS IN FAVOUR OF ITS

GENUINENESS.—(1.) It is found in some old and important uncials, and in more than 300 cursive MSS., in some of the Itala, and in the Vulgate ; (2.) The tendencies which led to its deliberate rejection would have rendered all but impossible its invention or interpolation ; (3.) It is quoted by Augustine, Ambrose, and Jerome, and treated as genuine in the Apostolic Constitutions. St. Jerome's testimony is particularly important, because he says that in his time it was found 'in multis et Græcis et Latinis codicibus,' and it must be remembered that nearly all of these must have been considerably older than any which we now possess. The main facts to be observed are, that though the dogmatic bias against the passage might be sufficient to account for its rejection, it gives us no help in explaining its want of resemblance to the style of St. John. A very simple hypothesis will account for all difficulties. If we suppose that the story of the woman accused before our Lord of many sins,—to which Eusebius alludes as existing in the Gospel of the Hebrews,—is identical with this, we may suppose without any improbability, either (i.) that St. John (as Alford hesitatingly suggests) may here have adopted a portion of current synoptic tradition, or (ii.) that the story may have been derived originally from Papias, the pupil of St. John, and having found its way into the Gospel of the Hebrews, may have been adopted gradually into some MSS. of St. John's Gospel. Many recent writers adopt the suggestion of Holtzmann, that it belongs to the ' Ur-marcus,' or ground doctrine of the Synoptists. Whoever embodied into the Gospels this traditionally remembered story deserved well of the world." *

Ver. 3.—"*And the Scribes and Pharisees brought unto Him* (R. V. BRING A WOMAN) *a woman taken in adultery; and when they had* (R. V. HAVING) *set her in the midst.*" These Scribes and Pharisees had tried to entrap Him before, but were foiled. A death penalty was involved in the act here charged against the woman. We may therefore suppose that the Sanhedrim moved now in the matter.

Ver. 4.—"*They say unto Him, Master, this woman was* (R. V. HATH BEEN) *taken in adultery, in the very act.*" Alford's reading of this verse is as follows : "The priests say unto Him, tempting Him that they might have to accuse Him, Master, this woman hath been taken in adultery, in the very act."

Ver. 5.—"*Now Moses in the law commanded us, that such should be stoned* (R. V. TO STONE SUCH): *but what sayest Thou ?*" (R. V. WHAT THEN SAYEST THOU OF HER ?) σὺ οὖν τί λέγεις, "What now sayest Thou ?"

Ver. 6.—"*This they said, tempting Him, that they might have* (R. V. WHEREOF) *to accuse Him.*" That is, putting Him to a test in order to have ground for accusation against Him. They thought that their question was such that, whatever answer He gave, He would involve Himself in guilt. If He said, "Stone her," they would charge Him with assuming a political authority that did not belong to Him. If He said, "Let her alone, do nothing with her," they would charge Him with encouraging immorality and abrogating their law. "*But Jesus stooped down,*"—He was in a sitting posture

before,—"*and with His finger wrote on the ground.*" This gesture was familiar to antiquity as a representation of deep thinking, languor, or absence of mind (see the representation in Lücke, page 269). Perhaps by the act Christ meant to express disregard of their question. "*As though He heard them not*" (R. V. OMITS). This clause is not in the original, it is supplied by our translators. It should be struck out, as it conveys the idea that Christ meant to deceive.

Ver. 7.—"*So* (R. V. BUT) *when they continued asking Him, He lifted up Himself, and said unto them, He that is without sin among you, let him first cast a stone at her.*" "*Without sin.*" Without this sin, in spirit if not in act ; and whose conscience acquits him of any such sin, "*let him first cast a stone.*" Thus He turns the tables upon them. Under the law (Deut. xvii. 7) the stone in such a case was to be hurled by the witnesses of the guilt ; and this in order that they might feel the responsibility of giving evidence.

Ver. 8.—"*And again He stooped down, and* (R. V. WITH HIS FINGER) *wrote on the ground.*" What wrote He ? No one knows. Did He stoop and write merely to give the accusers of this woman an opportunity to slink away unobserved ? Probably so. Anyhow they availed themselves of the occasion.

Ver. 9.—"*And they which* (R. V. WHEN THEY) *heard it, being convicted by their own conscience,* (R. V. OMITS THIS) *went out one by one.*" It is historically stated that at this time many prominent Rabbis were living in adultery, hence the words of Christ caused them to be convicted by their own conscience. "*Beginning at* (R. V. FROM) *the eldest,*" or rather at the elders in the official sense, and not the seniors in age. "*Even unto the last.*" One by one they slunk away. They did not dare to wait until Christ rose from His bent attitude and looked lightning and spoke thunder to them. "*And Jesus was left alone, and the woman standing* (R. V. WHERE SHE WAS) *in the midst.*" Only the band of accusers ran away, the disciples and the people probably

* See "Life of Christ," by Dr. Farrar, vol. ii. p. 62.

remained and were looking on. Why did not the accused run away ? Christ had His grasp upon her conscience ; she felt chained to His judgment-seat.

Vers. 10, 11.—" *When Jesus had* (R. V. AND JESUS LIFTED) *lifted up Himself, and saw none but the woman,* (R. V. OMITS THIS) *He said unto her, Woman, where are those thine accusers?* (R. V. WHERE ARE THEY ?) *hath no man condemned thee?* (R. V. DID NO MAN CONDEMN THEE?) *She said, No man, Lord. And Jesus said unto her, Neither do I condemn thee: go, and sin no more* " (R. V. GO THY WAY ; FROM HENCEFORTH SIN NO MORE). " What inimitable tenderness and grace ! Conscious of her own guilt, and till now in the hands of men who had talked of stoning her, wondering at the *skill* with which her accusers had been dispersed, and the *grace* of the few words addressed to herself, she would be dis-

posed to listen, with a reverence and teachableness before unknown, to our Lord's admonition. Jesus pronounces no pardon upon the woman, like, ' Thy sins be forgiven thee,' ' Go in peace,' much less does He say that she had done nothing condemnable. He simply leaves the matter where it was. He meddles not with the magistrate's office, nor acts the judge in any sense. But in saying ' *Go, and sin no more,*' which had been before said to one who undoubtedly believed (chap. v. 14), more is probably implied than expressed. If brought suddenly to conviction of sin, to admiration of her Deliverer, and to a willingness to be admonished and guided by Him, this call to begin a new life may have carried with it what would ensure and naturally bring about a permanent change."—*Dr. Brown.*

HOMILETICS

Amongst the thoughts which this wonderful narrative suggests, there are three worthy of notice, which are true whether the narrative is genuine or not.

I —THAT THE VILEST SINNERS ARE OFTEN THE GREATEST ACCUSERS

Who were the accusers of this adulteress ? The Scribes and Pharisees ; and according to Christ's judgment, and according to the judgment of all who would look at actions through His system of morality, they were, of all sinners, the greatest. It is true that on this occasion their accusation of the woman was inspired by their dislike to Christ, rather than a dislike to her or a hatred of her crime. " *They say unto Him, Master, this woman was taken in adultery, in the very act. Now Moses in the law commanded us, that such should be stoned : but what sayest Thou ? This they said, tempting Him, that they might have to accuse Him.*" They sought by this to entrap Him, to get Him to do or say something in the matter on which they could found a charge that would lead to His ruin. If He acquitted her, they would accuse Him of violating the law of Moses ; and if He condemned her, they would accuse Him of political usurpation—for the power to condemn to death was invested entirely in Roman authority. But whether their conduct in this instance was prompted by a dislike to Christ, or a dislike to the woman, it suggests and illustrates the truth, that the greatest sinners are generally the greatest accusers. The more base and corrupt a man is, the more ready he is to charge crimes on others, and the more severe he is in his censures on the conduct of his fellow-men. The more unchaste, untruthful, dishonest a man is, the more ready is he to suspect the chastity, truthfulness, and probity of others. Take care of social accusers—the demon of the old Scribes and Pharisees is in them! Were there worse men in Judæa or on the round earth than these Scribes and Pharisees, and members of the Sanhedrim, who now accused this woman? It is ever so: the more base and corrupt a man is, the more ready to charge crimes on others, and the more severe in his censures.

II —THAT THE SEVEREST JUDGE OF SINNERS IS THEIR OWN CONSCIENCE

" *They which heard it, being convicted by their own conscience, went out one by one.*"

See how Jesus touched the consciences of these sinners! He " *stooped down, and with His finger wrote on the ground, as though He heard them not. So when they continued asking Him, He lifted up Himself, and said unto them, He that is without sin among you, let him first cast a stone at her. And again He stooped down, and wrote on the ground. And they which heard it, being convicted by their own conscience, went out one by one, beginning at the eldest, even unto the last: and Jesus was left alone, and the woman standing in the midst.*" Observe two things—

First: Christ's method of awakening their conscience. (1.) He expresses by a symbolic act His superiority over their malignant purposes. They were full of unholy excitement. Evil was in them now a passion, and they were impatient for Him to commit Himself, but He is sublimely calm. He stoops down as if He were utterly indifferent to their miserable aims. They must have felt this. There is often a power in holy silence which no words, however eloquent, can carry. (2.) He puts the question of the woman's punishment upon their *own* consciences. " *He that is without sin,*" &c.

As if He had said: "I do not defend her conduct; stone her if you like. But let her be stoned by those who are free from sin, for it is monstrous for one sinner to stone another. Are you without sin? Then stone her. If not, take care." This touched them. Observe—

Secondly: The force of their awakened consciences. They were convicted, and " went out one by one." Conscience-smitten, they went out from the presence of Christ as if scared by His majestic purity. This conscience for a time confounded their purposes, and abashed them with their own wickedness. " *One by one,*" they skulked away. Ah! there is no judge so severe and crushing in his sentence as that of a guilty conscience.

III —THAT THE GREATEST FRIEND OF SINNERS IS JESUS CHRIST

The accusers are gone, but the accused remains with Jesus alone. Observe—

First: He declines pronouncing a judicial condemnation upon her. *"Neither do I condemn thee."* He does not mean that He did not disapprove of her conduct and condemn her *morally,* but judicially. He declines to pronounce judgment. He neither possessed nor claimed any jurisdiction in civil or criminal affairs. He left the work of the magistrate for the magistrate to do. He did not come to stone bodies to death, but to save souls to life.

Secondly: He discharges her with a merciful admonition. *"Go, and sin no more."* An expression, this, implying (1.) That she had sinned. Adultery is confessedly a crime. (2.) That He forgave her. *"Go."* I absolve thee. (3.) That her future should be free from sin. *"Sin no more."* Let bygones be bygones; let oblivion cover thy past; let virtue crown thy future. Thus Jesus deals with sinners. Desolate, branded, forsaken of all, He alone will stand by thee. He recriminates no penitent.

John 8:12

THE LIGHT OF THE WORLD
*(Further public teaching of Our Lord.—*JOHN viii. 12—59.)

"Then spake Jesus again unto them, saying, I am the light of the world: he that followeth Me shall not walk in darkness, but shall have the light of life."

EXEGETICAL REMARKS.—Ver. 12.— *"Then spake* (R. V. AGAIN THEREFORE JESUS SPAKE) *Jesus again unto them, saying, I am the light of the world: he that followeth Me shall not walk in* (R. V. THE) *darkness, but shall have the light of life."* This verse should perhaps chronologically follow ver. 52 of the preceding chapter, for it is a continuation of that discourse. Some suppose that Christ here, speaking of Himself as the "Light," alludes to the large golden chandeliers in the court of the women of the temple, the light of which illuminated the whole city.

"He was," says *Dr. Farrar,* "seated at that moment in the Treasury, either some special building so called, or that part of the court of the women which contained the thirteen chests with trumpet-shaped openings called *shopherôth,* into which the people, and especially the Pharisees, used to cast their gifts. In this court therefore close beside Him were two gigantic candelabra, fifty cubits high and sumptuously gilded, on the summit of which nightly during the Feast of Tabernacles lamps were lit which shed their soft light over all the city. Round these lamps the people, in their joyful enthusiasm, and even the stateliest priests and Pharisees, joined in festal dances; while, to the sound of flutes and other music, the Levites, drawn up in array on the fifteen steps which led up to the court, chanted the beautiful psalms which early received the title of 'Songs of Degrees.' In allusion to these great lamps, on which some circumstance of the moment may have concentrated the attention of the hearers, Christ exclaimed to them, '*I am the Light of the world.*' It was His constant plan to shape the illustrations of His discourses by those external incidents which would rouse the deepest attention and fix the words most indelibly on the memories of his hearers." Stier, however, thinks that the allusion is not to the light of the chandelier, but to that of the great sun itself. It might be so, for in the second verse of the chapter we are told that it was "early in the morning" that Christ came to the temple. The festal lights of the temple were probably extinguished, and the glorious sun was ascending the horizon and throwing his radiance upon the marble temple, and He might have meant, What that sun which is now breaking upon us is to the earth, that, and more than that, am I to the whole sinful world.

"The glorious morn from height to height
Shoots the keen arrows of the light;
And glorious in their central shower,
Palace of holiness and power,
The temple on Moriah's brow
Looks a new-risen sun below."

Elsewhere this same Evangelist calls Him the true "Light." The Logos is the true light. "All," to use the language of another, "that has really enlarged the state of intellectual truth or of moral goodness among men, all that has ever lighted any soul of man, has radiated from Him. He proclaims Himself to be the '*Light of the world,*' and the Truth ; and His apostle, speaking of the illumination shed by Him upon the Church, reminds Christians that the darkness is passing, and the true Light now shineth."

HOMILETICS

Observe, that Christ is *The Light for the World,* that is, the Light for humanity. Κόσμος stretches over all time, as over all space. The lights of the candelabra only irradiated the temple, or at most part of the city ; however effulgent, they left the surrounding regions in darkness. But Christ as the "*Light*" is not confined to a district, but radiates a globe ; not for a tribe, but for the race ; not for a time, but for all times the *Light of the World.* His doctrines are fitted for universal reason, His precepts for universal conscience, His provisions for universal needs. Christ is no more the property of any particular community or tribe than the natural sun is ; He belongs to the race.

I —CHRIST AS A "LIGHT" IS WONDROUSLY REVEALING

Light is a revealing element. When the sun goes down and darkness reigns, the whole of the beautiful world is concealed, all on ocean and on land are hidden with a veil which no eye can pierce. The sun arises, and all stands forth distinctly to view. What does Christ reveal? God, a spiritual universe, a moral government, a future state of retribution, a remedial system by which fallen humanity can be restored to the knowledge, the image, the friendship, and the enjoyment of the eternal Father. Men have appeared here in different ages and regions who have been called lights. Prophets were lights ; John the Baptist was called a light ; the apostles were lights ; some of the heathen sages were lights ; and many of the modern philosophers and scientists may be called lights. But Christ is *the* Light. Other lights are borrowed; He is the original Fountain. Other lights only reveal dimly a few things in some narrow space; He reveals all things fully through all regions of moral being. Other lights shone a little, and, like meteors, went out; He burns on for ever—the " *Light of the world.*"

II—CHRIST AS A "LIGHT" IS HUMANITY-GUIDING

" *He that followeth Me shall not walk in darkness.*" The sun may shine in its noontide radiance, and yet men may walk in darkness; they may shut their eyes or keep in cells or caverns. It is so with Christ. Though He is the moral Sun of the world, the millions " *walk in darkness.*" Christ is to be followed (1) *doctrinally,* (2) *ethically,* (3) *spiritually.* Men who follow Him thus will always be in the " *light.*"

III—CHRIST AS A "LIGHT" IS SPIRITUALLY QUICKENING

The natural sun is the fountain of life to the world; his beams quicken all. Christ is the Life of the world. " In Him was life." He quickens the *intellect,* the *conscience,* the *soul.* There is no spiritual life apart from Him.

CONCLUSION. How great the obligation of the world to Christ! What would this earth be without the sun? Its condition would be wretched beyond conception; and yet it would be better off than humanity without Christ. Were all that Christ has been to humanity, and still is, to be withdrawn, into what a Stygian condition it would sink. " Thanks be unto God for His unspeakable gift!"

John 8:13-19

CHRIST'S SUPERHUMAN CLAIM

" The Pharisees therefore said unto Him, Thou bearest record of Thyself; Thy record is not true," &c.

EXEGETICAL REMARKS.—Ver. 13.— " *The Pharisees therefore said unto Him, Thou bearest record* (R. V. WITNESS) *of Thyself; Thy record* (R. V. WITNESS) *is not true.*" In Deut. xvii. 6 we have this Jewish law. " At the mouth of two witnesses, or three witnesses, shall he that is worthy of death be put to death; but at the mouth of one witness he shall not be put to death." This law did not mean that what one man said was necessarily untrue because not confirmed by other men, for truth is independent of witnesses. Nor does it mean that a statement is necessarily true because a number of men will affirm it; for in corrupt society it is not difficult to get almost any number of men, on certain conditions, to swear to a falsehood. This has been done over and over again in human history, and is being done the world over this very day. The intention of this law seemed to be to guard human life from the stroke of a hasty vengeance. The Pharisees, however, seem to refer to this law as a reason for rejecting what Christ had asserted concerning Himself being the " Light of the world." They do not say that His evidence is insufficient because it is unsupported by a second party, but that it is not true.

Ver. 14.—" *Jesus answered and said*

unto them, Though (R. V. EVEN IF) *I bear record* (R. V. WITNESS) *of Myself, yet My record* (R. V. WITNESS) *is true."* This seems to contradict what our Saviour said in chapter v. 31—" If I bear witness of Myself, My witness is not true." He does not mean there, not true in itself; but, not true in your judgment, according to your law. Here He asserts broadly, that though He had no witness, yet His *" record was true."* What He said was true, though the world itself denied it. He knew it to be true. *" I know whence I came, and whither I go; but ye cannot tell* (R. V. KNOW NOT) *whence I come, and whither I go."* "Light," says *Augustine,* " both shows itself and other things. Light affords witness to itself. It opens sound eyes and is its own evidence." Then also, only he who knows can witness, and Jesus alone knew this. He, as it were, said, I know perfectly My origin, My mission, and My plans, and no human evidence could be free from any possibility of error, or have such absolute certainty as Mine. *" But ye cannot tell."* His origin in God and His return to God were Divine actions which surpassed all human knowledge, and could not be reached except through Divine revelation, which they would not receive.

Ver. 15.—*"Ye judge after the flesh."* They judged from appearances; a most deceptive rule of judgment this, for things are not what they seem. All their notions of worth, happiness, honour, success, were carnal. *" I judge no man,"* i. e. I judge no man as you judge man. He came, " not to condemn the world," but that the world through Him might be saved. He had not even condemned the adulteress to death, but preached to her repentance, forgiveness, salvation.

Ver. 16.—*" And yet* (R. V. YEA AND)

if I judge, My judgment is true." *"Yet if I judge,"* καὶ ἐὰν κρίνω δὲ ᾽Εγὼ. The *" I "* is emphatic. *" For I am not alone, but I and the Father that sent Me."* He felt Himself so personally associated, so essentially One with His Father, that His acts as well as His testimonies had the highest confirmation.

Ver. 17.—*" It is also written in your law"* (R. V. YEA AND IN YOUR LAW IT IS WRITTEN). He now puts the case home to them on their own principles, that the law requires a double witness. Deut. xvii. 6; xix. 15. The emphasis is upon *" your "*—the law which they had made so completely their own, and in which they boasted. *" That the testimony* (R. V. WITNESS) *of two men is true."* It was in the mouth of two or three witnesses that every word should be established. This allowed of two as enough. He claims that He has two.

Ver. 18.—*" I am One* (R. V. HE) *that bear* (R. V. BEARETH) *witness of Myself, and the Father that sent Me beareth witness of Me."* As if He had said, According to your law, which requires a second witness, you should believe Me, for My Father is My witness.

Ver. 19.—*" Then said they* (R. V. THEY SAID THEREFORE) *unto Him, Where is Thy Father?"* This question was evidently put in derision, spoken in the same spirit as Pilate exclaimed, "What is truth?" You have no Father but an earthly one like ourselves; if so, where is He? *" Jesus answered, Ye neither know Me, nor My Father: if ye had known* (R. V. KNEW) *Me, ye should have known* (R. V. WOULD KNOW) *My Father also."* The same spiritual light and darkness would suffice to reveal to the mind or to hide from it at once the Father and the Son, the Sender and the Sent.

HOMILETICS

The subject of these words is *Christ's superhuman claim.* That claim is stated in the preceding verse which we have already discussed, it is the claim of being the *" Light of the world."* Here we have this claim—

I —DENIED BY THE PHARISEES

" *The Pharisees therefore said unto Him, Thou bearest record of Thyself; Thy record is not true.*" We make two remarks upon their denial—

First: It was, from their view of Him, somewhat *natural.* Though it must be admitted that they had plenty of evidence to convince them that He was anyhow superhuman, they regarded Him only as a man, and therefore such words as, " *I am the Light of the world,*" falling from the lips of a mere man, would strike them as an arrogant and impious falsehood. Imagine the wisest and the best man that ever lived coming to you and uttering such words, how would you feel, and what would you say? Would you not be likely to regard him either as a brainless fanatic or as an impious impostor? You would repudiate his utterance and recoil from his presence. These Pharisees, therefore, regarding Him as they did, as a mere man, we wonder not at their statement, " *Thy record is not true.*" Another remark we make concerning their denial is—

Secondly: The reason for it was somewhat *absurd.* What was the reason? It lacked the corroboration of another witness. " *Thou bearest record of Thyself.*" We cannot accept this mere self-assertion: Thy single testimony on such a subject as this we cannot accept. We do not suppose for a moment that if all the disciples and a thousand more had stood by Christ and asserted the truth of His utterance, they would have accepted it. No number of men can make a truth more true, or turn a falsehood into truth; and hence their reason is absurd. The fact was, that their unbelief in Christ was a thing of the heart, and they were ready to formulate some reason to justify its existence. So it has ever been, and so it is now. The reasons men assign for their infidelity are not the cause of their unbelief; the cause is deeper down in their nature, down in the region of prejudices, pre-possessions, likings and dislikings. Here we have this claim—

II —VINDICATED BY CHRIST

In His vindication, He states four things—

First: That His assertion was true, independent of any witness. " *Jesus answered and said unto them, Though I bear record of Myself, yet My record is true: for I know whence I came, and whither I go; but ye cannot tell whence I come, and whither I go.*" That He was the " *Light of the world* " was not with Him an ambitious dream, or an idea that had come to Him from the testimony of others; it was with Him an absolute fact of *personal consciousness.* " *For I know whence I came.*" As men know that they have minds because they think, feel, and resolve, Christ knew that He was the " *Light of the world.*" It was true independent of all testimony for or against. He was conscious of it. "*Though I bear record of Myself, yet My record is true.*" In His vindication He states—

Secondly: That their judgment on the question was carnal, His was true. "*Ye judge after the flesh ; I judge no man. And yet if I judge. My judgment is true.*" The judging of the Pharisees was without significance or weight, for it was by appearances; and appearances are ever deceptive. They judged Christ by His mere bodily aspect and mien, a poor, wan, dejected man; and therefore His declaration that He was the "*Light of the world*" would appear incredible to the last degree. He that judgeth by appearances, in a world like this, will generally judge wrongly. Thus Christ judged not. His eyes penetrated through all appearances and phenomena, clearly discerned and estimated those everlasting principles that inspire the heart of the Absolute One, and that move and manage the universe. In His vindication He states—

Thirdly: That whilst His assertion was true, independent of a witness, it was nevertheless backed by the testimony of the Eternal Father. "*It is also written in your law, that the testimony of two men is true. I am One that bear witness of Myself, and the Father that sent Me beareth witness of Me.*" Jesus had up to this point vindicated the validity of His own testimony. Here He asserts that His testimony was affirmed by the Highest Being —the Father. In His words here we have a conclusion *a minori ad majus ;* "If, according to your law, the testimony of two men who may be deceived is sufficient, how much more the testimony of two witnesses who are highly exalted above all suspicion of error or deception." God's testimony in favour of Christ's teaching goes on through the ages, comes out in nature, in science, in human history and consciousness. In His vindication He states—

Fourthly: That they were in utter ignorance both of His Father and Himself. "Their question seemed to indicate that His Father was something Utopian, that His conceit of being God's Son was an idle fantasy, without any reality. Christ intimates to them that they, by the wicked position which they assumed towards Him, closed against themselves the way to the knowledge of His Father. Whosoever places himself in opposition to Christ can never know the Christian and only true God, the Father of Jesus Christ; for Christ is the bridge to that God Whom not to know is to be without life and without salvation. In reference to the manner of the Jews' coming. Quesnel remarks, 'All may desire and seek the knowledge of God and His mysteries in humble and sincere prayer, or with a mind full of evil design and unbelief, as we see here, and among the learned of this world.'"—*Hengstenberg.*

John 8:20

DIVINE PROVIDENCE

"These words spake Jesus (R. V. HE) in the treasury, as He taught in the temple : and no man laid hands on (R. V. TOOK) Him ; for (R. V. BECAUSE) His hour was not yet come."

EXEGETICAL REMARKS. — "*These words spake Jesus* (R. V. HE) *in the treasury, as He taught in the temple.*" Jesus is still in the temple, and continuing His discourse, notwithstanding repeated interruptions. Indeed the interruptions and interrogations, captious as most of them were, seem to stimulate utterances of truth which otherwise, perhaps, the world would never have heard. He was in that part of the temple called the "*treasury.*" This was the court of the women, in which there were thirteen chests into which the worshippers cast their offerings. In this court there were the great chandeliers which had been lighted at the feast, and from which Jesus had just drawn an illustration of Himself as the "Light of the world." What courage Christ had, to stand in the most public place on the most public occasion, in order to utter truths that struck at once against the secular interests and religious prejudices of the people !

HOMILETICS

The words present to us the subject of *Divine Providence,* and suggest two thoughts concerning it.

I —THAT IT EXERTS A RESTRAINING POWER ON WICKED MEN

"*No man laid hands on Him.*" Why ? Jewish rage was almost at its height. The Sanhedrim and many of the people were thirsting for His blood, the thirst was becoming intense. Why did they not lay hands upon Him now ? They neither lacked the disposition, the muscular power, nor the public co-operation. Why ? "*His hour was not yet come.*" There was a subtle mysterious power on their spirits, holding them back ; there was an invisible hand restraining them. In relation to this restraining power in God's moral government of the world, three remarks may be offerep.

First : It is not always a matter of consciousness. Sometimes, it may be, men feel that they are reined in, that there is a curb on them, some mysterious power preventing them from doing what they most fervently desire. History presents us with monsters that have felt themselves like caged lions. But as a rule the restraining force is so subtle, so delicate, that men are unconscious of it.

Secondly : It interferes not with human freedom. A man is not free from the guilt of a wrong act because he has not the power or the opportunity to embody it. The guilt is in the desire, the volition. "As a man thinketh in his heart, so is he." At first sight it seems morally absurd that God should restrain a man from committing a crime, and yet hold him guilty for it. The solution is here : *The crime is in the wish.*

Thirdly : It is an incalculable advantage to the race. What was in the Alexanders, the Caligulas, the Napoleons, the Lauds, and the Bonners, is for the most part in every unregenerate soul. Were there no restraining hand upon depraved hearts, all social decency, order, peace, and enjoyment would be at an end. The world would be a Pandemonium. We rejoice that He Who reins in the ocean and keeps it within bounds, holds in the passions and impulses of the depraved soul. " The king's heart is in the hand of the Lord, as the rivers of water : He turneth it whithersoever He will." Another thought concerning Divine Providence suggested is—

II —THAT IT HAS SETTLED PERIODS FOR THE DEVELOPMENT OF EVENTS

" *For His hour was not yet come.*" Christ seemed practically to recognize the fact that there was a particular hour or crisis for everything He had to do. There was an hour for the commencement of His miracles, an hour for His baptism, an hour for His death. His death was the hour of hours. " Father, the hour is come." God has appointed scenes in space, and ordained seasons in duration for all things that occur in His vast dominion. Nothing He allows to be done in one scene that is intended to occur in another ; nothing in one season that is fixed for another. There is a season for everything. " To every thing there is a season, and a time to every purpose under the heaven." Every orb that rolls through immensity has a point it is bound to reach, and a certain fixed period and " *hour*" ; it is never behind its time. So it is, not only in the epochs and eras of human history, but in all the events of individual life. ' Man's decrees and purposes," says a modern author, " often fail from the fickleness of his own mind, from his want of foresight, and from his want of power. When the period contemplated for carrying them into effect arrives, he has already, perhaps, laid them altogether aside ; or, if they are still entertained, he finds, it may be, the circumstances unfavourable to the carrying out of his design. It is altogether otherwise with the designs of the Almighty. When His set time for working comes, not all the power in the universe can stay His hand. When we first look abroad, indeed, upon the busy field of human affairs, and observe the numerous actors upon the scene, all moving energetically to and fro, planning, arranging, adjusting the course of things, we may be tempted for the moment to imagine that destiny itself is in their hands. But when we have looked a little longer, and have seen all their schemes deranged, and all their contrivances thwarted, and all their devices turned to foolishness, and a result emerging the very opposite, it may be, of what they had been labouring to produce, we begin to discover that there is a power out of sight mightier than all—One Whose purposes are "from everlasting to everlasting," Whose "counsel shall stand, and Who will do all His pleasure."

John 8:21

CHRIST AND MEN

"Then said Jesus again (R. V. HE SAID THEREFORE) unto them, I go My way (R. V. AWAY), and ye shall seek Me, and shall die in your sins (R. V. SIN): whither I go, ye cannot come."

EXEGETICAL REMARKS.—Ver. 21.— "*And ye shall die in your sins*" (R. V. IN YOUR SIN). It does not mean, you shall die *for* your sins, but in your sins, in your moral guiltiness. "If they persisted in their unbelief and rejection of Him, they could have no salvation, they must die in their sin, because they rejected the one Saviour from the power and curse of sin."

HOMILETICS

The subject of this verse is *Christ and Men;* and there are three things here worthy of attention.

I —THE WITHDRAWMENT OF CHRIST FROM MEN

First: Christ had a "*way.*" "*I go My way.*" By His "*way*" He undoubtedly means His way through the Cross up to His Father's presence and His native heavens. As if He had said, I have a "*way*" clearly defined, though rugged and distressing in some parts. In that "*way*" I go, in it I shall not pause, and from it I shall not swerve. What a "*way*" was His! It will be the study of eternity.

Secondly: Christ pursued His "*way*" voluntarily. "*I go.*" You cannot force Me. I am not the victim of coercion, I am free. (1.) The voluntariness of Christ's death is no extenuation of the guilt of His murderers. "The Son of man indeed goeth, as it is written of Him, but woe to that man by whom He is betrayed!" (2.) The voluntariness of Christ's death is the glory of His history. Why has Christ's death the power, not only to save humanity, but to thrill and charm the universe? Because it was *free.* "I have power to lay down My life, and power to take it up again."

A more terrible calamity cannot happen to men, than the withdrawment of Christ from their midst. A greater calamity far than if the sun were to withdraw from the heavens, and leave them in sackcloth. There is a sense in which Christ withdraws from impenitent men now. Another thing here worthy of attention is—

II —THE FRUITLESS SEEKING OF CHRIST BY MEN

"*Ye shall seek Me, and shall die in your sins.*" This is a repetition of what Jesus had before said in the previous chapter. "Ye shall seek Me, but shall not find Me." When I am gone, and the judgments of heaven will descend on your country, you will be seeking Me, but you will not find Me; you will have filled up the measure of your iniquity, "the things that belong to your peace will be hid from your eyes."

First: This fruitless seeking is possible. There is a *fruitless* seeking for Christ. The day of grace closes with some men even while they are in the world. In the judgment He will be earnestly sought, but will not be found. "Many shall say unto Me on that day," &c. &c.

Secondly: This fruitless seeking is lamentable. " *Ye shall die in your sins.*" Sin is like quicksand, the man who walks on it must ultimately sink and be lost. "It sometimes happens on the coast of Britain or Scotland that a person walking on the sand will suddenly find a difficulty in walking. The shore is like pitch, to which the soles of his feet cling. The coast appears perfectly dry, but the footprints that he leaves are immediately filled with water. Nothing distinguishes the sand which is solid from that which is not. He passes on, unaware of his danger. Suddenly he sinks. He looks at his feet: the sand covers them. He wishes to turn back, but with every effort sinks more deeply. With indescribable terror he finds he is involved in a quicksand. He throws down his burden; but it is already too late. The slow burial of hours continues; the sand reaches to his waist, to his chest, to his neck; now only his face is visible. He cries; the sand fills his mouth, and all is silent." What a striking emblem of the danger of sin! Another thing worthy of attention here is—

III —THE ETERNAL SEPARATION OF CHRIST FROM MEN

" *Whither I go, ye cannot come.*" The separation will be complete and irreversible. " *Ye cannot come.*" Christ had said this before (vii. 34), and He refers to it again (xiii. 33). So that to Him the words had a terrible meaning. More terrible words than these could not be sounded in human ears, " *Ye cannot come.*" It means incorrigible depravity, hopeless misery. Separation from Christ is hell. The commission of every sin contributes to the construction of the impassable gulf.

John 8:22-24

ASPECTS OF UNBELIEF

"Then said the Jews (R. V. THE JEWS THEREFORE SAID), Will He kill Himself? because (R. V. THAT) He saith, Whither I go, ye cannot come. And He said unto them, Ye are from beneath; I am from above: ye are of this world; I am not of this world. I said therefore unto you, that ye shall die in your sins: for if ye believe not (R. V. EXCEPT YE BELIEVE) that I am He, ye shall die in your sins."

EXEGETICAL REMARKS.—Ver. 22.— " *Will He kill Himself?*" "They evidently," says *Dr. Brown*, "saw more in His words than when He spake thus before (vii. 34), for their question now is more malignant and scornful." They malignantly hint that He was going to commit what they considered one of the greatest crimes, viz. suicide, a crime which, though the Greeks and Romans thought little of, was regarded by the Jews with supreme horror.

Ver. 23.—"*And He said unto them, Ye are from beneath; I am from above: ye are of this world; I am not of this world.*" By these words He seemed to imply that they could not go, as He had said, to Him because they belonged to different worlds. They were "*from beneath.*" Not perhaps in a physical and local sense, but in a *moral* sense. Their spirits were down in the infernal regions of guilt, prejudice, and profanity. On the other hand, He was from above, up in the realms of Divine purity and love. Because of this, He said, "*Whither I go, ye cannot come.*" We have nothing morally in common.

Ver. 24.—"*I said therefore unto you, that ye shall die in your sins: for if ye believe not that I am He.*" "*He*" is not in the original. ὅτι ἐγώ εἰμι, I am.

HOMILETICS

In these words we have *Aspects of unbelief.* Here is,—

I —THE PERVERSITY OF UNBELIEF

"*Then said the Jews, Will He kill Himself?*" They were either sincere or insincere in this interrogative: in either case the perverseness of their hearts is manifest. If they saw the meaning of Christ, they were perverse in giving it this turn; if they did not, they were perverse in being so dull of comprehension, for His words were plain enough. It is evermore the characteristic of unbelief, that it perverts truth. "If any man will do His will he shall know of the doctrine whether it be of God." We have here—

II —THE DEGRADATION OF UNBELIEF

"*He said unto them, Ye are from beneath; I am from above,*" &c.* As if He had said, You will not understand Me, and cannot come to Me; because you live in a different moral region. Observe—

First: The world in which a man lives is his character. The habitual thoughts, paramount desires, leading purposes of the soul, is the world of the soul. Thus, every soul builds up its own world. It creates for itself either a Gehenna or an Eden.

Secondly: The character of one man may be so different to another as to constitute different worlds. As soon may the earth enter into the orbit of Mars or Jupiter, and live and flourish there, as a bad character enter into the orbit and live in the presence of a character that is Christly and pure. These characters have different centres, different orbits, the one *cannot* come into the other. This is what Christ seems to mean, and this is a profound truth. We have here—

* See Germ, p. 231.

III — THE DISASTROUSNESS OF UNBELIEF

"I said therefore unto you, that ye shall die in your sins." *
Mark—(1.) The *inevitable.* Every man must die : this is assumed.
"It is appointed for all men once to die." What is it to die ? Ah,
what ? (2.) The *optional.* The option is this : whether you should
"die in your sins" or not. To die in sin is very terrible. To die
in confusion, anguish, self-crimination, black despair. But, thank
God ! you need not *"die in your sins."* *Believe !*

Germs of Thought
No. 32 John 8:23

CHRIST'S MORAL ELEVATION

"Ye are from beneath ; I am from above."

This expression is susceptible of two interpretations : the one,
physical or local ; the other, ethical or spiritual. Does Christ
mean *"from above"* in a *local* sense ? Does He mean that He
came from the heavenly world, and that they—the Jews—had
their origin on the earth ? It is true that Christ had a pre-
existence ; but it is not true that men had no heavenly origin, that
they grew out of the earth. This is modern materialism. All
human souls—we take it—as truly come from God as Christ came
from the bosom of the Father to this earth. In a *moral* sense we
must take the words. The language applies to *character :* its
elevation and degradation. His moral character was from above ;
it was lofty, Divine : the character that makes heaven, and is Godlike. On the other hand, their character was *"beneath."* It was
mean, selfish, low as hell. The word *"above"* is frequently used in
a moral sense. Paul says, " Seek those things that are above,"—
that is, not things that are socially or locally above, but that are
spiritually elevated. Truth, love, &c.—these are the elevated things
in God's universe. Indeed, the next clause sustains this view :
"Ye are of this world ; I am not of this world." In moral character
Christ was as *distant* from His age, the Jews, and all unregenerate
mankind as heaven from hell. Paul says He was " separate from
sinners." Concerning this distance we make three remarks—

I — IT WAS MANIFESTED IN HIS EARTHLY LIFE

First : It was seen in the conduct of the Jews in relation to Him.
The evangelical record abounds with many striking incidents
illustrative of the felt disparity between Christ's character and
the character of the people with whom He lived. He enters a
synagogue at Nazareth, His native place. All there knew His
humble pedigree, and regarded Him as one of their peasant townsmen ; but there was such a moral originality of goodness about

* See Germ, p. 234.

Him, that, after He had closed the book He read from, "the eyes of all them that were in the synagogue were fastened on Him" (Luke iv. 14—27). A Roman centurion—"a man under authority" —felt the same awe in the presence of Jesus; felt that between him and the Peasant there was a distance that made him humble; and he said, "Lord, I am not worthy that Thou shouldest come under my roof!" (Matt. viii. 5—13.) Those who sold and bought in the temple felt this, and struck with terror, they hurried off (Matt. xxi. 12). The Scribes and Pharisees who accused the woman taken in adultery, could not stand before the unearthly purity of Christ's character, and they went out one by one (John viii. 1—11). The Roman ruffians who came into the garden of Gethsemane to take Him by force, felt it; and they fell as dead men before Him. Pilate felt it, struggled against it, but it overwhelmed him at last. The spectators of the Crucifixion felt it. Luke tells us that "all the people that came together to that sight, beholding the things which were done, smote their breasts and returned." Even Peter, after he had partially assimilated to Him, declares it: "Depart from me; for I am a sinful man, O Lord." Whence arose this felt distance? It cannot be accounted for—(1.) On the ground of *miraculous manifestation;* His miracles were attractive. Nor (2.) On the ground of social *superiority:* He was known as a humble peasant. Nor (3.) On the ground of His *non-sociality.* He mingled with the people. It was simply distance of character. His incorruptible truthfulness, His immaculate purity, His calm reverence, His warm and overflowing benevolence, struck them with awe.

Secondly: It was seen in the conduct of Christ in relation to the people. He felt, He manifested, a moral loneliness. In the crowd He felt solitary. "Of the people there was none with Him." They had nothing in common with Him morally. What they honoured, He despised; what they loved, He hated; what they pursued, His whole nature recoiled from. All their idols were to Him abomination. Hence, He only felt akin to those who had to some extent kindred sympathy. "My mother and brethren are these which hear the Word of God and do it." Hence, too, His frequent withdrawal from the people to pour out in lonely solitude His sorrows to the everlasting Father. And in His lonely hours He bewails the moral character of His age: "O righteous Father, the world hath not known Thee." He was morally above them. They were mere flickering lamps, dim and sooty; He rolled as a bright star above them. Concerning Christ's distance from sinners, notice—

II—IT WAS DEMONSTRATIVE OF HIS REAL DIVINITY

Whence came such a character as this? *Intellectually* it has been proved over and over again, that there was nothing, either in the Jewish or Gentile mind, to give rise to such a doctrinal system as that propounded by Jesus of Nazareth. His revelation of God's love transcended all human conception. "Eye hath not seen; ear hath not heard." And, *morally,* it is equally evident there was nothing in His age to produce such a character. How could immaculate purity come out of an age of corruption—incorruptible truth come out of a world of falsehood—self-sacrificing love out of a world of selfishness? Men's characters are formed on the principle of imitation; but Christ's character could not be thus formed. He had no perfect form to imitate. Even the best of the patriarchs and the holiest of the prophets were imperfect. How can you account for the existence of such a character as His? Tell me not that it came of the earth. Do grapes grow on thorns? Did the flaming pillar in the wilderness grow out of the sand? His perfect moral excellence was universally felt, not because there was no effort employed to discover imperfections in Him. The keen eye of His age was always on the watch, in order, if possible, to descry some moral defect. And Pilate, who had every facility for knowing Him, and every motive for condemning Him, said, "I find no fault in Him." And this moral excellence, too, was retained to the last, not because He was not assailed by temptation. Never came the great tempter to any man in a more powerful form than he came to Christ in the wilderness. How then is it possible to account for such a character as this? Only on the principle that He was indeed the "Son of God." Concerning Christ's distance from sinners, notice—

III —IT WAS ESSENTIAL TO HIS REDEEMERSHIP

Had He not been thus morally "*above*" His age and above mankind, He had lacked the qualification to redeem souls. Holiness has the power to convict, to renovate, to sanctify, and to save. A man who is one with sinners, morally standing on the same platform, can never save them. Christ has regenerated millions, and will regenerate millions more, because of the *holiness* of His character. Because He is "*above*" them, He rolls His moral thunders down to alarm the careless; pours His sunbeams to quicken the dead; rains His fertilizing showers to make moral deserts blossom as the rose. As the well-being of the earth depends upon the heavens, so the spiritual progress of humanity depends upon that Character that is stretched over us like the sunny skies.

CONCLUSION. The subject—

First: Predicates the way to true elevation. Men are endowed with aspirations; they have an instinct for progress, an inborn desire to rise. But what altitudes should they scale to reach true dignity? Commerce, literature, scholarship, war? No; from all these heights man must fall—fall like Lucifer, the son of the morning. The altitude of imitating Christ is that which conducts to glory. Seek the things "*above.*" Press on to assimilation to that Character that is above you. It will always be above you, and so far it meets the unbounded moral aspirations of your heart. "Be ye holy, even as God is holy." Christ's character is everlastingly saying to you, "Come up hither." The subject—

Secondly: Reveals the only way by which we can regenerate the world. Keep at a moral distance from mankind. Let the people amongst whom we live, feel that we are morally above them. In this age, what is called the Church is morally so identified with the spirit that moves the world, that it is on the same moral plane as the market, and the theatre. The subject—

Thirdly: Presents motives for the highest gratitude. The grandest fact in the history of our planet is, that a perfect moral character has been here, wearing our nature. Though His physical personality is gone, His character is here still, and ever will be.

No. 33   John 8:24

THE GREATEST CALAMITY

"Die in your sins."

These words imply—

I —THAT TO DIE IN ONE'S SINS IS THE GREATEST OF CALAMITIES

To *die* is a terribly solemn thing. Solemn, for it involves the separation from the home, the business, the acquaintance, the world, and the very body itself;—solemn, for it involves an introduction into a mysterious, untried, spiritual state of retribution. But "*to die in sins,*" this adds immeasurably to its solemnity. Sin is the *sting* of death. To die in one's sins, what does it mean?

First: It means to die having *misused this life with all its blessings.* The grand purpose of life is the cultivation of a holy character; for this physical blessings are given—health, time, the influences of nature. All *social* pleasures, and all happy interchanges of thought, feeling, and soul; all *mental* blessings also—literature, science, poetry, schools, &c. All *redemptive* blessings, moreover—the Gospel, with its soul-saving appliances. He who dies in "*his sins*" has *abused* all.

Secondly: It means to die *with all the conditions of misery.* Conflicting passions, a tormenting conscience, a dreaded God, foreboding anguish. If this is not hell, what is it? *To "die in sins"* —why, better a thousand times to die in a pauper's hovel, or in a martyr's tortures, than to die in sin. The words imply—

II —THAT UNBELIEF IN CHRIST RENDERS THIS GREATEST OF CALAMITIES INEVITABLE

" *If you believe not that I am He,*" &c. It is easy to show, on philosophical grounds, that belief in Christ, as the Revealer of God, is essential to the deliverance of man from the guilt, the power, and the consequence of his sins. Three facts may be sufficient to indicate this.

First: Deliverance from sins requires the awaking in the soul of a *supreme* affection for God. Love to God is the only expulsive power. This only can destroy the "old man," &c.

Secondly: A supreme affection for God requires a certain *revelation* of Him. In what aspects must the Eternal appear to man before this love can be awakened within him? I answer, He must appear *personally, forgivingly,* and *sublimely perfect.*

Thirdly: This certain revelation of God, which is essential to love, is *nowhere* but in Jesus Christ. He alone reveals God in aspects to awaken this love. He brings close to the eye of the heart a *personal, forgiving, perfect* God. Belief in Him, therefore, is essential to a deliverance of the soul from sin. "Believe in the Lord Jesus Christ, and thou shalt be saved."

John 8:25-27

CHRIST'S TEACHING

"Then said they (R. V. THEY SAID THEREFORE) unto Him, Who art Thou? And Jesus saith unto them, Even the same that I said (R. V. THAT WHICH I HAVE ALSO SPOKEN) unto you from the beginning. I have many things to say (R. V. SPEAK) and to judge of (R. V. CONCERNING) you : but (R. V. HOWBEIT) He that sent Me is true ; and I speak to the world those things which I have heard of Him (R. V. AND THE THINGS WHICH I HEARD FROM HIM THESE SPEAK I UNTO THE WORLD). They understood (R. V. PERCEIVED) not that He spake to them of the Father."

EXEGETICAL REMARKS.—Ver. 25.— "*Then said they unto Him, Who art Thou?*" A fair and very important question this, as it stands—a question for the race. But what was the spirit that inspired it in this case? Was it an earnest desire to ascertain the truth, as it was in Paul's case when he put the question, "Lord, who art Thou?" No. Jesus had told them oftentimes who He was. It is rather in the spirit of derision that the question is here put. "*And Jesus saith unto them, Even the same that I said unto you from the beginning.*" Τὴν ἀρχὴν ὅ τι καὶ λαλῶ ὑμῖν. "This clause is in the original somewhat obscure, and has been variously rendered and much discussed. But the sense given in our version seems the true one, and has on the whole the best support." *Dr. Davidson* renders the clause, "Altogether such as I am telling you." The idea is, undoubtedly, "that which I have told you all along from the commencement I am." "Jesus does not wish to make the reply, 'I am the Messiah,' because they adhered so strongly to a dead positive idea ; and as they would not find this verified in Him, they would only have been the more hardened against Him. He refers them therefore to His discourses. First of all in these discourses was He to be recognized."—*De Wette.*

Ver. 26.—"*I have many things to say and to judge of you: but He that sent Me is true; and I speak to the world those things which I have heard of Him.*" "The sense is somewhat obscure, but is perhaps best conveyed in the paraphrase of *Bloomfield,* 'I could say much more in reference to you and your unbelief, but I shall content Myself with declaring that, as I am sent from the great Father of truth, so what I publicly aver is from Him and therefore must be true.'"

HOMILETICS

These words suggest a few thoughts concerning *Christ's Teaching.* Notice—

I —IT IS CONSISTENT

"*The same as I said unto you from the beginning.*" Probably His interrogators desired that He should make a proclamation concerning Himself inconsistent with His former utterances: if so, they were disappointed. All that Christ said concerning Himself is beautifully consistent. There is no real discrepancy, not a shadow of contradiction; it is a beautiful whole. All His utterances concerning Himself meet in Him as the rays meet in the sun. This consistency is very remarkable when we consider two things.

First: The various and often trying circumstances under which He spoke. His utterances often came forth under intense suffering and great provocation, and often in answers to men who did their utmost to make Him contradict Himself.

Secondly: The diversity in the minds and circumstances of those who reported His utterances. How different in faculties, taste, culture, habits, circumstances, and angles of observation were His four biographers; and yet their reports agree. These words suggest another thought concerning *Christ's Teaching*—

II —IT IS PROGRESSIVE

"*I have many things to say and to judge of you.*" Christ suited His teaching to the capacities and characters of His hearers. In His mind there was an Infinite treasury of truth. But His administration of it was *gradual.* Indeed, no finite intelligence could take in all that was in the mind of Christ: it would take eternity to unfold all His wonderful thoughts. Christ has been teaching John for millenniums, but He has "*many things to say*" to him yet.

First: The progressiveness of His teaching supplies a motive to stimulate human inquiry. Christ will teach you according to your capacity. The more you learn of Him the more He will teach you.

Secondly: The progressiveness of His teaching shows His suitability as a Teacher for mankind. Men have naturally a craving for knowledge; and the more they know the more intense the craving becomes. They therefore want a teacher of unbounded resources. Another thought suggested concerning *Christ's Teaching* is—

III —IT IS DIVINE

" *He that sent Me is true ; and I speak to the world those things which I have heard of Him.*" He taught, not human things, but the things of God—absolute realities. "No man hath seen God at any time, the only begotten of the Father, He hath declared Him." The things He taught were things concerning God, things relating to the Divine government, character, claims. The last thought suggested concerning *Christ's Teaching* is—

IV —IT IS NOT ALWAYS UNDERSTOOD

" *They understood not that He spake to them of the Father.*" In this they represent an enormous class of men in every age, who understand not Christ, who misrepresent, misinterpret Him.

CONCLUSION. Have we put to Christ in earnest the question, " *Who art Thou ?*" and have we received in docility, faith, and love back into our own hearts an answer from Him ? Do we know Him, "Whom to know is life eternal ?" Do we know Him Whom flesh and blood cannot reveal to us ?

John 8:28, 29

CHRIST FORECASTING HIS DEATH AND DESTINY

"Then said Jesus (R. V. JESUS THEREFORE SAID) unto them, When ye have lifted up the Son of man, then shall ye know that I am He, and that I do nothing of Myself ; but as My (R. V. THE) Father hath taught Me, I speak these things. And He that sent Me is with Me : the Father (R. V. FOR HE) hath not left Me alone ; for I do always those (R. V. THE) things that please (R. V. ARE PLEASING TO) Him."

EXEGETICAL REMARKS.—Vers. 28, 29.—" *Then said Jesus unto them, When ye have lifted up the Son of man.*" This is the plainest intimation He had yet given in *public* of the *manner* and the *authors* of His death. "*Then shall ye know that I am He, and that I do nothing of Myself; but as My Father hath taught Me, I speak these things.*" That is, they should find out, or have sufficient evidence, how true was all He said, though they would be far from owning it. "*And He that sent Me is with Me: the ·Father hath not left Me alone ; for I do always those things that please Him.*" "To you who gnash upon Me with your teeth, and frown down all open appearance for Me, I seem to stand uncountenanced and alone ; but I have a sympathy and support transcending all human applause ; I came hither to do My Father's will, and in the doing of it have not ceased to please Him ; therefore is He ever by Me with His approving smile, His cheering words, His supporting arm."—*D. Brown, D.D.*

HOMILETICS

In these verses we have *Christ forecasting His death and destiny ;* and in relation to the language which He here employs we offer four remarks.

I —HIS LANGUAGE REVEALS HIS SUBLIME HEROISM IN THE PROSPECT OF A TERRIBLE DEATH

" *When ye have lifted up the Son of man.*" He refers undoubtedly to His elevation on the cross, where He was to be nailed as a malefactor between two thieves. On another occasion He speaks of His crucifixion in a similar way, " The lifted up," &c. His death by crucifixion was—

First : The culmination of human wickedness. Human wickedness could not reach a higher point than the putting to death of the Son of God. It was—

Secondly : The culmination of human suffering. The crucifixion involved ignominy, insult, cruelty, torture. Yet how calmly Christ speaks of this terrible death ! " He endured the cross, despising the shame." With what elevated calmness and ineffable composure of soul He speaks of the terrible event which awaited Him ! There was no faltering note, no syllable of complaint, no ripple of perturbation. He faced the cross with all its horrors, and felt no dismay.

II —HIS LANGUAGE EXPRESSES HIS UNSHAKEN FAITH IN THE TRIUMPH OF HIS CAUSE

" *Then shall ye know that I am He.*"

First : He was not discouraged by apparent failure. To the world, His life, ending in crucifixion, would appear a stupendous failure. To Him, however, it was a success. His death was a seed falling into the earth.

Secondly : He did not despair of man's improvability. He believed that there would come a reaction in men's minds concerning Him. When He was gone, they would begin to think, recognize, and give Him credit for excellency, which they did not when He was among them.

Thirdly : He was not doubtful of ultimate success. He saw the day of Pentecost ; saw the results of apostolic labours ; witnessed the triumph of His truth through all subsequent ages ; at last, saw His character moulding the race to His own ideal. Christ is certain of success.

III —HIS LANGUAGE IMPLIES A PRINCIPLE OF CONDUCT COMMON IN ALL HISTORY

The principle is this, that good men, undervalued in life, are appreciated when gone. We see this principle in the *family*. Members of a family may live together for years ; and through the infirmity of tempers, the clashing of tastes, and the collision of opinion, excellences may be entirely overlooked. One dies,—the father, mother, brother, sister,—and then attributes of goodness come up to the memory of the survivors that never appeared before. We see it in the *State*. Public men, devoted to the common good, and loyal to conscience, so clash with popular opinions and prejudices, that they are regarded with odium, and denounced with bitterness—they die, and their virtues emerge, and fill the social atmosphere with fragrance—Burke, Hume, Cobden, are amongst the illustrations and examples of this. We see it in the *Church*. A minister labours for years amongst a people. He may be too thoughtful to be appreciated by the thoughtless, too honest to bow to current prejudices ; so that, during his life, his labours pass unacknowledged and unrequited. He dies. His memoir is written ; his discourses are printed; he has a moral epiphany. It was so with Arnold of Rugby and Robertson of Brighton.

IV —HIS LANGUAGE INDICATES A CONSCIOUSNESS OF HIS PECULIAR RELATION TO THE ETERNAL FATHER

" *As My Father hath taught Me, I speak these thiⁱgs. And He that sent Me is with Me : the Father hath not left Me alone ; for I do always those things that please Him.*"

First : He was the *Pupil* of the Father. " *As My Father hath taught Me, I speak these things.*" The ideas, principles, purposes, that I have, I have derived from the Infinite Father. This you will know when I am gone. You will learn after My crucifixion that My teaching is Divine.

Secondly : He was the *Companion* of the Father. " *He that hath sent Me is with Me.*" Though He has sent Me, I am not distant from Him, He is with Me. He has not left Me alone. He is with Me, not only in sympathy and aim, but in loving, close, personal intercourse. " I and My Father are one."

Thirdly : He was the *Servant* of the Father. " *I do always those things that please Him.*" I am His " beloved Son, in Whom He is well pleased." Whatever I do meets with His approval. He delights in My services for humanity. Though I displease you, I do " *always those things that please Him.*"

CONCLUSION.

First : This subject reveals the sublime uniqueness of Christ. Who, amongst all the millions of men that have appeared on the earth, could use such language as this ? Who could forecast such a terrible future with such perfect accuracy and sublime calmness of soul ? Who could claim such a relationship to the Infinite Father as He proclaims for Himself ? Christ stands alone, sublimely alone in the history of humanity. As our solar system has but one sun, our universe has but one Christ.

Secondly : This subject suggests the Christ-verifying force of human history. What Christ here predicts, history has established.

Through His crucifixion ever-increasing multitudes of men have been convinced that He is the true Messiah, the Messenger, the Revealer, the Companion of the everlasting Father.

In connection with what is said here and elsewhere about Christ, the remarks of Stuart Mill, who was considered by some to be an infidel, will prove interesting.

" About the life and sayings of Jesus there is a stamp of personal originality, combined with profundity of insight, which, if we abandon the idle expectation of finding scientific precision where something very different was aimed at, must place the Prophet of Nazareth, even in the estimation of those who have no belief in His inspiration, in the very first rank of the men of sublime genius of whom our species can boast. When His pre-eminent genius is combined with the qualities of probably the greatest moral reformer and martyr to that mission who ever existed upon earth, religion cannot be said to have made a bad choice in pitching upon this man as the ideal representative and guide of humanity ; nor even now would it be easy even for an unbeliever to find a better translation of the rule of virtue from the abstract into the concrete than the endeavour so to live that Christ would approve our life. When to this we add that to the conception of the rational sceptic it remains a possibility that Christ was actually what He supposed Himself to be,—not God, for He never made the smallest pretension to that character, and would probably have thought such a pretension as blasphemous as it seemed to the men who condemned Him,—but a man charged with a special, express, and unique commission from God, to lead man to virtue and truth, we may well conclude that the influences of religion on the character, which will remain after rational criticism has done its utmost against the evidences of religion, are well worth preserving, and that what we lack in direct strength as compared with those of a firmer belief is more than compensated by the greater truth and rectitude of the morality they sanction."

John 8:30-32

GENUINE CHRISTIAN DISCIPLESHIP

"As He spake these words (R. V. THINGS), many believed on Him. Then said Jesus (R. V. JESUS THEREFORE SAID) to those Jews which believed on (R. V. HAD BELIEVED) Him, If ye continue (R. V. ABIDE) in My word, then are ye (R. V. TRULY) My disciples indeed (R. V. OMITS) ; and ye shall know the truth, and the truth shall make you free."

EXEGETICAL REMARKS.—Ver. 30.— *"As He spake these words, many believed on Him."* "This is not to be wondered at. The wonder is, that such unearthly language, spoken with such calm majesty, did not strike conviction into the hearts of all."

Ver. 31.—*"Then said Jesus to those Jews which believed on Him, If ye continue in My word, then are ye My disciples indeed."* "Continue," that is, not merely "continue to believe," as *Lange* has it, but according to the spirit of the Word, and in obedience with the word which He spoke. A mere hearing of the Word, or a deep passing interest in the Word, or an intellectual belief in the Word, or an occasional devotion to the Word, will not constitute genuine discipleship, but a practical continuance in its spirit and aim.

Ver. 32.—*"And ye shall know the truth, and the truth shall make you free."* "He that doeth the will of God shall know of the doctrine." "If they proved steadfast in their discipleship, they would attain to new and exalted views of truth, which would emancipate them from their present errors and sins. For it is eminently the property of truth, to make men free in all respects—physic- ally, socially, civilly, and spiritually. The reference here, however, is undoubtedly to the freedom which the Gospel imparts from the bondage of sin."

HOMILETICS

The subject of these words is *Genuine Christian Discipleship.* Three remarks are suggested concerning it.

I —IT GROWS OUT OF A PRACTICAL CONTINUANCE IN CHRIST'S WORD

" *If ye continue in My Word, then are ye My disciples indeed.*" " *My* WORD." What is that? It is no small thing. Its dimensions are infinite; it embraces all that is true in the words of prophets and apostles. It has in it a philosophy that comprehends all that is true in all the philosophies of the world,—a morality that embraces all that is just and righteous in all the laws and ethics of humanity. This " *Word* " is large enough to supply thought, inspiration, and direction for the loftiest of created geniuses. It takes God Himself into it. Now, to be a genuine disciple, you must " *abide in this Word;* " it must be the home, the dwelling-place of your soul.

(1.) There are some who regard themselves as disciples, who never enter it. They live in its *letter*, they never penetrate its spirit, itself. The letter of this " *Word* " is the mere rough materials of which the buildings are composed, not the spacious, elegant, and costly furnished rooms.

(2.) There are some who enter it, only as passing visitors. Like travellers in an hotel, they only enter one apartment, and tarry only as brief sojourners. They do not dwell in this house of the Lord. They do not visit its unnumbered apartments, and inspect its countless treasures. Neither of these classes are genuine disciples. The genuine disciple is he who continues in Christ's Word —continues just as the devoted merchant continues in the commercial spirit, as the devoted artist continues in the spirit of his art. To abide in Christ's Word, is to abide in Him: and if any man abide in Christ he is a "new creature." "Old things are passed away; behold all things are become new."

Another remark concerning genuine Christian discipleship is—

II —IT QUALIFIES FOR A RIGHT APPRECIATION OF DIVINE TRUTH

" *Ye shall know the truth.*" The man who continues in Christ's Word gets the faculty for discerning and appreciating *truth* in the world of falsehoods, *reality* in the world of shams. Truth is reality, and reality is covered by a thick veil in the whole world of unregenerate men. Men walk in a vain show, they live in fiction. Ever since the Fall, the father of lies rules the world. Lies are its imperial laws. Men's ideas of religion, happiness, power, are all fictitious, and not in accord with eternal realities. Now, the man who *continues* in Christ's "*Word*," acquires the faculty of taking off the mask from things and seeing them as they are. He accepts what Christ taught—that happiness consists not in what man *has*, but what he *is;* that greatness is in not commanding, but serving; that worship is not an occasional service, but the living spirit. Now, to be in conscious contact and loving sympathy with reality, is essential to our well-being. All falsehoods, social, political, religious, intellectual, are as fleeting as the visions of the night, as shifting as the clouds. Souls want realities—want substances to embrace, rocks to stand upon, eternal principles of truth, beauty, and goodness as their living elements. They can only live, grow, and flourish behind the shifting scenes of phenomena, upon those immutable principles that lie at the root of all things.

Another remark concerning genuine Christian discipleship is—

III —IT ENSURES THE ENJOYMENT OF PERFECT LIBERTY

"*Ye shall know the truth, and the truth shall make you free.*" "*Make you free.*" (1.) Free from the bondage of *fashions.* The millions are the mere serfs of fashion; fashion is their iron master. But the man who knows *reality*, sets fashion at defiance. (2.) Free from the bondage of *false opinions.* Prejudices built on falsehoods are amongst the greatest despots of the soul. The man who knows reality hurls them from their throne and breaks out into intellectual liberty. (3.) Free from the bondage of *animal propensities.* The flesh rules the millions who have no convictions of morality; "they are carnally sold unto sin." The man who *knows the truth* treads down his lusts and enthrones his conscience. (4.) Free from mere *forms and ceremonies.* Forms and ceremonies in social life, as well as religion, hold thoughtless millions in subjection. But a man who knows the truth becomes independent of all appearances.

CONCLUSION. Who would not be a genuine disciple of Christ? A sublimer character know I not than this. No one sustains a position so truly honourable and blessed as this. What a contrast between conventional Christianity and genuine Christian discipleship! The one is a huge falsehood, the other a sublime reality: the one subjects the soul to a miserable slavery, the other lifts it into the "glorious liberty of the sons of God."

> "He is the freeman whom the truth makes free,
> And all are slaves besides."

John 8:33-36

MORAL BONDAGE

" They answered (R. V. UNTO) Him, We be Abraham's seed, and were never (R. V. HAVE NEVER YET BEEN) in bondage to any man : how sayest Thou, Ye shall be made free ? Jesus answered them, Verily, verily, I say unto you, Whosoever (R. V. EVERY ONE THAT) committeth sin is the servant (R. V. BONDSERVANT) of sin. And the servant (R. V. BONDSERVANT) abideth not in the house for ever : but the Son abideth (R. V. FOR) ever. If the Son therefore shall make you free, ye shall be free indeed."

EXEGETICAL REMARKS.—Ver. 33.— " *They answered Him, We be Abraham's seed, and were never in bondage to any man.*" Here the hostile part of His audience interrupts Him in the kind and instructive words which He addresses to those who have believed. " *We be Abraham's seed.*" This was the darling idea of the Jews. Ever did they boast of their descent from the great Father of the Faithful. " *We were never in bondage to any man.*" An utterance, this, revealing their characteristic pride and falsehood too. "*Never in bondage to any man !*" Were they not slaves in Egypt, captives in Babylon ? and were not the Romans now their masters ?

Ver. 34.—" *Jesus answered them, Verily, verily, I say unto you, Whosoever committeth sin is the servant of sin.*" " *Whosoever*" ($\pi\tilde{a}\varsigma$ *ό*), every one that does sin. Sin is not here to be taken as a simple act, but as a habit, a course of life. He conveys to them the idea that He did not mean political servitude, but moral ; assures them that sin is the real tyrant of man.

Ver. 35.—" *And the servant abideth not in the house for ever : but the Son abideth ever.*" " The Saviour here alludes to a common occurrence in life, by which he illustrates this moral truth of the slavery of the wrong-doer. A slave has no permanent residence in a family, but is liable at any time to be sold or sent away ; whereas a son is the heir, and therefore remains stationary. Only those, therefore, that are God's genuine children can inherit His promised blessings." *Dr. Brown's* remark on this verse is good. " A very glorious statement, the sense of which may be thus expressed : ' And if your connection with the family of God be that of BONDSERVANTS, ye have no *natural* tie to the house ; your tie is essentially *uncertain* and *precarious*. But the Son's relationship to the Father is a *natural and essential* one ; it is an indefeasible tie ; his abode in it is *perpetual* and of *right.*' That is my relationship, my tie. If then ye would have your connection with God's family made *real, rightful, permanent,* ye must by the Son be *manumitted,* and *adopted* as sons and daughters of the Lord Almighty." In this sublime statement there is no doubt a subordinate allusion to Gen. xxi. 10, " Cast out this bondwoman and her son : for the son of this bondwoman shall not be heir with my son, even with Isaac." Compare Gal. iv. 2—30.

Ver. 36.—" *If the Son therefore shall make you free, ye shall be free indeed.*" There is a supposed allusion here to an ancient custom by which a son had the power to liberate the slave in the household. " *Ye shall be free indeed*" (*οἰκία*) ; clearly the house or household of God. " If your character, your relationship to the master of the house, be that of slaves, there is no indissoluble bond connecting you with him, and therefore your abode in his house is precarious. The condition of a son is widely different ; his relationship to the master is indefeasible, his abode in the house perpetual and of right. If, then, the Son, the Heir, sets you free, and that by adoption, so that you become the recognized children of the family, you become free indeed, partakers even of His character and privileges (Gen. xlv. 1). The allusions to the manumission of slaves and adoption of strangers into families, practised among the Romans, need no explanation."—*Webster and Wilkinson.*

HOMILETICS

The great subject of these words is *Moral bondage;* and they suggest three facts concerning it—

I —THAT THE SUBJECTS OF MORAL BONDAGE ARE UNCONSCIOUS OF IT

In the midst of Christ's address on freedom, the hostile Jews broke in and exclaimed, "*We be Abraham's seed, and were never in bondage to any man;*" as if they had said, "Why talk of freedom to us? we are free men." But, in truth, they were slaves; and to the eye of Christ they were in the most miserable captivity.

It is common here in England to hear men boast of *religious liberty,* who have no religion. Some of the most strenuous professional advocates of religious liberty are manifestly destitute of that spirit of reverence for the Infinite and charity to all men, which constitutes the very essence of true Christliness. These men will say that they have never been "*in bondage to any man,*" when in truth they are "*in bondage*" to their own prejudices, exclusiveness, love of fame or gain. Nor is it uncommon to hear men boasting of *civil freedom,* who are moral slaves. Men who are under the absolute tyranny of their own lusts and greed, who are even governed, as Carlyle says, "by a pot of heavy wet" and a clay pipe, peel out in thunderous chorus,—"Britons never shall be slaves." In truth, the worst part of this moral bondage is, that men are *unconscious* of their thraldom. Hence they are mere creatures of circumstances. Like rotten logs of wood on the river, they are being borne down to the great oceanic future. Hence their inner man, their moral *ego,* is "carnally sold unto sin." This unconsciousness is the more sad because it precludes any aspiration or effort for self-manumission; and it is only self-effort that can liberate. Other men may deliver the prisoner from his dungeon, or the domestic slave from his tyrant, or the political serf from his despot; but no one can deliver him from bondage but himself—

"He who would be free, himself must strike the blow."

Another fact suggested by the text in relation to moral bondage is—

II —THAT THE SUBJECTS OF MORAL BONDAGE ARE THE AUTHORS OF IT

"*Whosoever committeth sin is a servant of sin.*" "*Whosoever,*"— each one. It is not the sin of another man that makes me a slave, it is my own. Solomon says, "that his own iniquities shall take the wicked himself, and he shall be holden with the cords of his sins." And Paul says, "Know ye not, that to whom ye yield yourselves to obey, his servants ye are to whom ye obey, whether of sin unto death, or of obedience unto righteousness." "Vice is imprisonment," says *Shakspeare.* This is verily so : "Can the Ethiopian change his skin, or the leopard his spots ? Then may ye also do good that are accustomed to do evil." Every sin a man commits, forges a new link in the chain to manacle his soul, creates a new despot, for he strengthens the reins of the despot within him. The longer a man pursues a certain course of conduct, whether it be good or bad, the more wedded he becomes to it, and the less power he has of abandoning it. Every time an action is repeated, a new web has been woven binding us to it. Habit is a cord ; it is strengthened with every action. At first it is as fine as silk, and can be broken with but little effort. As it proceeds it becomes a cable, strong enough to hold a man-of-war steady amidst boisterous billows and furious winds. Habit is a momentum ; it increases with motion. At first a child's hand can obstruct the progress. As the motion increases it gets a power difficult for an army of giants to overcome. Habit is a river. At its head spring you can arrest its progress with ease, and turn it in any direction you please ; but as it approaches the ocean it defies opposition, and rolls with a thunderous majesty into the sea.

Another fact suggested by the passage in relation to moral bondage is—

III —THAT THE SUBJECTS OF MORAL BONDAGE CAN BE DELIVERED FROM IT

" *If the Son therefore shall make you free, ye shall be free indeed."* How does Christ make the soul "*free ?* " This question may be answered in many ways, and in many ways it is answered. Some answers are wise, and some are foolish. The answer most satisfactory to my intellect is this : *By generating in the human heart supreme love to the Supremely Good.* It is a law of mind, to have some permanent object of affection ; and that object, whatever it is, limits the field of its operation. The man who loves money most, will have all his faculties confined to that region ; or fame most, the same ; or pleasure most, the same. In whatever the heart centres its affections, to that it binds the intellect, the imagination, the sympathies, the whole soul. It will not, it cannot, go beyond that object. But all these objects are limited. Hence the soul is hemmed in as in a cage. In order to have freedom, the heart should be centred upon an infinite object, and this Christ does. He generates in the human soul supreme love for God ; and with God as the Centre of the heart all the faculties and the powers have unbounded scope for their operation. Christ is the only One that can do this, and He does it effectively. "*Ye shall be free indeed."*

CONCLUSION. Ponder well the fact, that all souls which are not made free by Christ are in slavery. Even the heathen considered the virtues essential to true freedom. *Cicero* said, "The wise man alone is free." *Plato* represents the lusts as the hardest tyrants. *Seneca* speaks of the passions as the worst thraldom, *Epictetus* said, "Liberty is the name of virtue." And this virtue is obtained only through Christ. *"If the Son therefore shall make you free, ye shall be free indeed."*

John 8:37-44

THE PRIMAL PARENTS OF MORAL CHARACTER

"I know that ye are Abraham's seed ; but (R. V. YET) ye seek to kill Me, because My word hath no (R. V. NOT FREE COURSE) place in you," &c.

EXEGETICAL REMARKS.—Ver. 39.— *"They answered and said unto Him, Abraham is our father"* (R. V. OUR FATHER IS ABRAHAM). This was their darling thought. As a people, they prided themselves on being descendants of Abraham. On account of this, they considered themselves the special favourites of Heaven. *"Jesus saith unto them, If ye were Abraham's children, ye would do the works of Abraham."* Though they were the descendants of Abraham, our Saviour reminds them they were not his children. A father may have many offspring, but only a few children. They only are children who have the true spirit of children. All men are God's offspring ; but only those who have the true filial spirit are His sons. *Physical* lineage is one thing, *ethical* lineage is another, and very different.

Ver. 40.— *"But now ye seek to kill Me, a man that hath told you the truth, which I have heard of* (R. V. FROM) *God : this did not Abraham."* Abraham was generous and loving, you are malignant and cruel ; and although physically you are his descendants, morally you are not his children.

Ver. 41.— *"Ye do the deeds* (R. V. WORKS) *of your father."* Who this father is appears in the sequel. You have a parentage different to that of Abraham. *"Then said they to Him, We be* (R. V. WERE NOT) *not born of fornication."* What they mean is, We are not bastards—who were excluded from the congregation (Deut. xxx. 22)—but we are the genuine offspring of Abraham. *"We have*

one *Father, even God."* Being the true descendants of Abraham, we have one God, as he had,—the same God. The one paternity ensures the other.

Ver. 42.— *"Jesus said unto them, If God were your Father, ye would love Me."* All true children of God will love His Son, not seek to murder Him as you do. *"For I proceeded* (R. V. CAME) *forth and came* (R. V. AM COME) *from God ; neither came I of Myself, but He sent Me.* "For from God I proceeded, and am come." He was conscious of being sent by God, both ontologically and ethically.

Ver. 43.— *"Why do ye not understand My speech?"* "Λαλιά, in distinction from λόγος, the personal language, the mode of speech, the familiar tone and sound of the words, in distinction from their meaning. From its original idea of talk, babble, λαλιά here preserves the element of vividness, warmth, familiarity. It is the φωνή, the tone of spirituality, and tone of love in the shepherd voice of Christ. They are so far from recognizing this loving tone, that they are incapable of even listening to the substance of His words with a pure, undistracted, spiritual ear. Fanaticism is characterized by false hearing, and words primarily by false hearing."— *Lange.* *"Even because ye cannot hear My word."* λόγος means His doctrine, His word concerning spiritual things.

Ver. 44.— *"Ye are of your father the devil."* Alford remarks, that this is one of the most decisive testimonies to the objective personality of the devil. By "father," Christ means, not the fatherhood of being, but the fatherhood of character. "*And the lusts of your father ye will* (R. V. IT IS YOUR WILL TO) *do.*" Ye *desire* to do. The impure, malignant, untruthful propensities of your father ye are disposed to do. "*He was a murderer from the beginning.*" From the beginning of what ? Not of his existence ; if so, the Infinite Creator is the author of sin. But from the beginning of human history. His spirit is malignant, he is the inspirer of all murderers. "*And abode* (R. V. STOOD) *not in the truth.*" "And stands not in the truth."—*Dr. Davidson.* The expression does not mean that he was once in the truth, and fell from it— this is a great Biblical fact ; but that he does not now stand in the truth. He is out of the truth, out of sympathy with eternal realities. "*Because there is no truth in him.*" He is utterly untrustworthy, filled with falsehoods. "*When he speaketh a lie, he speaketh of his own.*" Some render it, "he speaks of his own nature ;" and others, "of his own resources, or treasures." "*For he is a liar, and the father of it*" (R. V. THEREOF). Who is the father of lies ? not the Creator of the universe,—He is the truth ; but the devil, and all the lies in this world are from him.

HOMILETICS

The grand subject which we shall use these words to illustrate, is *Moral Ancestry ;* and three facts are suggested concerning it.

I —THAT THE ANCESTRY OF A MAN'S CHARACTER, IS FOR MANY REASONS MORE IMPORTANT TO HIM THAN THAT OF HIS CORPOREAL EXISTENCE

When the Jews here referred to Abraham, their physical ancestor, in a spirit of proud exultation, Christ brought forward their moral ancestry as something far more worthy of their consideration. As if He said, What does it matter from whose loins you came ? The great question is, From whose *spirit* did you derive your character ? The father of a man's corporeal existence is not always the father of his character. These men came from Abraham corporeally, but they had not the faith, the nobleness, the moral generosity of their ancestor. It is often so. Holy fathers have sometimes children corrupt in character, and the reverse.

(1.) It is natural that children should have the moral character of their parents. The moral susceptibility of a child's nature, its filial instinct to love and imitate its parent, and the special opportunities which the parent has to instil his principles and breathe his spirit into the young heart, might naturally lead one to expect, that the moral character of the child would be but a reproduction of that of the parent. (2.) When it is so, it is either a blessing or a curse. If the child inherits the character of a truly Christly parent, the advantage is inexpressibly great, and the reverse. (3.) In either case, where the moral character of the child is not that of the parent, it proves the natural freedom of the human soul. What more powerfully demonstrates the natural liberty of the human soul, and its consequent responsibility, than the power of a child to form a character essentially different to that of the parent ? If any being in the universe could make a moral character for us, that being would be our natural parent; but he has no absolute power in this work. Hence every soul is free, and amenable to moral government. But our point is, that the ancestry of *character*, is for many reasons more important to man than that of his corporeal existence. The following reasons may be suggested—

First: That a man is responsible for his moral parentage, and not for his corporeal. We had no choice whatever in our earthly ancestry, whether we should descend from the loins of princes or paupers, scoundrels or saints. The man who boasts of his physical ancestry is simply a fool. As a native of this island, what merit or demerit belongs to me, whether I descended from the hungry vagrants that William the Assassin brought to these shores, or from the grand old Druids, the Celtic aborigines of the island? But it does matter to me where my *character* has come from; for this I am responsible. I am responsible for my convictions, the moral spirit, tenour, and habits of my life. My moral father has been to me, more or less, a matter of choice.

Another reason may be suggested—

Secondly: That corporeal existence will prove an intolerable curse if the character is bad. "It had been good for that man if he had not been born," says Christ. It would be a thousand times better that a man had never come into existence, if during his probationary period he constructs a character opposed to the will of God. Better never to have been, than to have been wicked. Existence apart from virtue must become an intolerable curse.

Another reason is—

Thirdly: That character survives corporeal existence. All that we derived from our earthly parents we give back to the earth, we leave in the dust; but our character we carry with us wherever we go. And as our character, so will be our position in the universe, and our relation to the Infinite for ever.

Another fact suggested by the passage is—

II —THAT IN THE ANCESTRY OF CHARACTER THERE ARE TWO PRIMAL PROGENITORS

Christ speaks of these under the titles "*devil*" and "*God.*"

First: He speaks of both as personal existences. He speaks of the *devil* as a personality. "*Ye are of your father the devil,*" &c. In these modern times there are men professing faith in Christianity who deny the personality of the great *evil one;* they reason his tremendous agency down into principles, abstractions of the brain. I accept the authority of Christ on this question. He knew the devil, He was at his creation. He speaks of God as a Person. "*If God were your Father.*" Again, "*which I have heard of God.*" Ontologically, the relation of these great personalities in the universe is that of the Creator to the creature; ethically, that of holiness to wickedness.

Secondly: He speaks of both as morally antagonistic. (1.) The devil is malignant. A "*murderer.*" Malevolence is his inspiration; he is a "roaring lion, going about seeking whom he may devour." God is good; He is love; love is the spring of all His activities. (2.) The devil is untruthful. He "*abode not in the truth.*" There is no truth in him. Once he was in the truth.

> "High in the midst of all the throng,
> Satan, a tall archangel, sat."

He "kept not his first estate." He renounced moral facts for fictions. He is not only false in himself, but the promoter of falsehood. "*When he speaketh a lie, he speaketh of his own.*" On the other hand, God is truth. He is the absolute Reality. (3.) The devil is Christ-hating. Jesus said unto them, "*If God were your Father, ye would love Me.*" You hate Me, and thus prove your moral descent from the devil, who hates Me. The devil hates Christ. On the other hand, God loves Christ. "This is My beloved Son, in Whom I am well pleased."

Now, these two personal existences are the primal progenitors of all moral character in this world. Morally, every man is either the child of the devil or the child of God. Every man can say morally, either, "Our Father, Who art in *heaven*," or, "Our Father, who art in *hell.*"

The other fact suggested by the passage is—

III — THAT EVERY MAN'S PRIMAL MORAL ANCESTOR IS DEMONSTRATED BY HIS LIFE

"*If ye were Abraham's children, ye would do the works of Abraham.*" From Christ's language we may infer—

First: That the man of falsehood is a child of the devil; the man of truth is the child of God. Alas, the overwhelming majority of mankind are at once the subjects, the agents, the advocates of lies. Their whole life is a lie, out of harmony with eternal fact; they walk in a vain show, they are the children of the devil. On the other hand, the man of truth is the child of God. Truth to him is everything; he will sacrifice everything to it, even life itself. He is the child of God. Like Paul, he says: "I count not my life dear unto me."

Secondly: That the man of malice is a child of the devil; the man of love is the child of God. "*Ye seek to kill Me.*" "*The devil was a murderer from the beginning.*" What malice there is in the world—political, commercial, religious! The millions have ever been ready to "*kill*" men for entertaining and propagating religious convictions opposed to their own prejudices. There are many ways of killing. Parents kill their children, husbands their wives, masters their servants, &c. &c., by an intolerant persecuting spirit in daily life. These are the children of the devil. All the loving and the tender are of God.

Thirdly: That the man hating Christ is a child of the devil; the man loving Christ is the child of God. "*If God were your Father, ye would love Me.*" The unregenerate millions hate Christ; and although few demonstrate their hatred in their talk or writing, yet in their spirit and life they manifest their enmity. What though a man declare his friendship for me, if he habitually pursues a course of conduct hostile to my wishes, views, interests, reputation; is he not my foe? All haters of Christ are the children of the devil. On the other hand, those who love Christ in sincerity and truth are the children of God.

CONCLUSION. What an unveiling of the moral universe is here! In Christ's view of life, all men are either the children of the devil or the children of God. All other distinctions, social, intellectual, religious, are lost in this distinction. On this little planet there are two great moral families, those of the devil, and those of God. Man, thou canst change thy moral father.

John 8:45-48

THE RATIONALE OF UNBELIEF

"And because I tell you (R. V. SAY) the truth, ye believe Me not. Which of you convinceth (R. V. CONVICTETH) Me of sin? And if I say the truth (R. V. IF I SAY TRUTH), why do ye not believe Me? He that is of God heareth God's words (R. V. THE WORDS OF GOD): ye therefore (R. V. FOR THIS CAUSE YE) hear them not, because ye are not of God. Then answered the Jews, and said unto Him, Say we not well that Thou art a Samaritan, and hast a devil?"

EXEGETICAL REMARKS.—Ver. 45.—"*And because I tell you the truth, ye believe Me not.*" Here Christ tells the Jews that, like their diabolic father, they were out of sympathy with truth, and would not believe Him who spoke the truth.

Ver. 46.—"*Which of you convinceth Me of sin?*" What does He mean by sin (ἀμαρτίας) here—mere intellectual error, or moral falsehood and wrong? He means, I presume, sin in its widest sense—all that is untrue in thought, improper in feeling, wrong in life. "Which of you convinceth Me of any sin," either of judgment, feeling, speech, or act? Perhaps Christ means here to say, I am free from any moral wrongness, and therefore could not

be untruthful. "*And if I say the truth, why do ye not believe Me?*" Since you cannot find anything morally wrong in Me, it is clear that I only speak the truth; and if I do, why do ye not believe Me?

Ver. 47.—"*He that is of God heareth God's words.*" "A syllogism; but not with this conclusion: I now speak God's words (*De Wette*); but you are not of God. That Jesus speaks the word of God is presupposed in the foregoing. An attentive hearing and reception of the word of God is meant. This is conditioned by being from God, by moral relationship with God; for only kindred can know kindred. The being of God has been more particularly characterized as a being drawn by God (chap. vi. 44), being taught by Him (ver. 45), as showing itself by doing truth in God (chap. iii. 21)."—*Lange.* " *Ye therefore hear them not, because ye are not of God.*" It is because you have no moral affinity with God, no sympathy with Him, that you hear Him not.

Ver. 48.—" *Then answered the Jews, and said unto Him, Say we not well that Thou art a Samaritan, and hast*

a devil?" "What intense and virulent scorn! The '*Say we not well*' is a reference to their former charge, Thou hast a devil (chap. vii. 20). '*Samaritan*,' here, means more than no Israelite at all. It means one who pretended but had no manner of claim to connection with Abraham, retorting perhaps to His denial of their true descent from the father of the faithful." —*Dr. Brown.*

HOMILETICS

These words help to give us an insight into the *Rationale of unbelief.* There are five things discoverable in these words, which go a great way toward the generating and sustaining of unbelief in the Gospel.

I —REPUGNANCE TO THE TRUTH

"*Because I tell you the truth, ye believe Me not.*" If He had given them popular dogmas or speculative disquisitions, they might have believed in Him; but He gave them truth—REALITY. And the truth He gave them was not intellectual and speculative, but moral and regulative—truth that addressed itself with an imperial force to the central nerves of their being. They were living in falsehood, appearances, and shams, far away from the awful region of spiritual realities. This truth came in direct collision with their associations, their prepossessions, their pride, their interests, their habits; it was therefore repugnant to them, and they would not have it.

First: Man's repugnance to truth reveals his abnormal condition. His soul is as truly organized for truth as the eyes are organized for light. Truth is its natural atmosphere, natural scenery, natural beverage, natural food.

Secondly: Man's repugnance to truth suggests his awful future. The soul and truth will not always be kept apart. The time must come, in the case of every man, when the intervening fiction and falsehoods shall melt away as clouds, when the interspacing gulfs shall be bridged over, and when the soul shall feel itself in vivid, conscious, eternal contact with moral realities. Another thing discoverable in this passage is—

II —THE PURITY OF CHRIST

" *Which of you convinceth Me of sin ?* " * Christ is the Substance of the Truth, the Truth itself; and His invincible intolerance to all sin, and His refulgent purity, repel the depraved heart. " Men love darkness rather than light, because their deeds are evil." The first beams of morning are not half so uninviting and repulsive

* See Ullman, on the " Sinlessness of Jesus," published in 1863.

to the midnight burglar, as the moral rays of Christ's truth are to a corrupt heart. Moral purity makes the hell of depravity. Its effulgent beams, as they fall directly on the elements of moral corruption in the soul, kindle the unquenchable flames of gehenna. We discover in this passage—

III —ESTRANGEMENT FROM GOD

" *He that is of God, heareth God's words.*" " *Of God* " in a moral sense, born of God, having the true filial sympathies warm and regnant. Such sympathies are essential to true faith. The more love a child has in him, the more credulous he is in relation to the utterances of his parent. Men in their unregenerate state have not this sympathy. Hence their unbelief. They do not like to "retain God in all their thoughts." Love is the foundation of all true faith. I only believe in a man in proportion to the strength of my love for him; and I can only trust God as I love Him. "He that loveth not, knoweth not God, for God is love." Another thing discoverable in this passage is—

IV —PRIDE OF INTELLECT

" *Then answered the Jews, and said unto Him, Say we not well that Thou art a Samaritan, and hast a devil ?* " They had said this before (viii. 20), and here they pride themselves on their sagacity. " *Say we not well ?* " Are we not clever ? Can we not discern spirits ? What insight we have into character ! How we can peer into the springs of action ! We cannot be deceived. Is not this ever the spirit of unbelief ? Infidels have ever been too scientific to believe in miracles, too philosophic to require a special revelation, too independent to require even the invaluable aid of Christ, too moral to need any inward reformation. " *Say we not well ?* " This is their spirit. It comes out in their books, in their lectures, in their converse with their fellow-men, and in their daily life. "We are the wise men, and wisdom will die with us." This pride is essentially inimical to true faith. "Whosoever shall not receive the kingdom of God as a little child, he shall not enter therein." Another thing discoverable in the passage is—

V —UNCHARITABLENESS OF DISPOSITION

" *Thou art a Samaritan, and hast a devil.*" Suppose He was a Samaritan : are not Samaritans men, and have they not a claim to human sympathy ? Are all Samaritans bad, and are there none good amongst the thousands ? All Samaritans have devils. Thou art a Samaritan, therefore Thou " *hast a devil.*" This was their uncharitable reasoning, and it has ever characterized infidelity. All Christians are hypocrites, all preachers are crafty mercenaries, all Churches are nurseries of superstition, all ecclesiastics are cunning worldlings, robing themselves in sanctity and fattening on the toils of the millions : hence we will have nothing to do with this Christianity. Far enough are we from wishing men to believe in the corrupt, the crafty, and the vile. True charity is often rigorous in its criticism, and inexorable in its denunciations of wrong. True charity is never blind; it is all eye. Uncharitableness is evermore a barrier to faith, for it is always suspicious, and loses the power of trusting. "Infidelity," says *Robert Hall*, "is the joint offspring of an irreligious temper and unholy speculation, employed, not in examining the evidences of Christianity, but in detecting the vices and imperfections of professing Christians."

CONCLUSION. Such are some of the causes of unbelief; and perhaps those causes were never more rampant in any age or land than now and here. Years ago, Sharon Turner, a high-class thinker, and distinguished author, summed up infidelity in the following words : "It is the champion of matter against mind—of body against spirit—of the senses against the reason—of passions against duty—of self-interest against self·government—of dissatis-faction against content—of the present against the future—of the little that is known against all that is unknown—of our limited experience against boundless possibility."

John 8:48-51

THE ANTI-DIABOLISM OF CHRIST

"Then answered the Jews, and said unto Him, Say we not well that thou art a Samaritan, and hast a devil? Jesus answered, I have not a devil; but I honour My Father, and ye do dishonour (R. V. YE DISHONOUR) Me. And (R. V. BUT) I seek not Mine own glory : there is one that seeketh and judgeth. Verily, verily, I say unto you, If a man keep My saying (R. V. WORD), he shall never see death."

EXEGETICAL REMARKS.—Ver. 48.— "*Then answered the Jews, and said unto Him, Say we not well that Thou art a Samaritan, and hast a devil?*" "The Samaritans are here regarded as unsound in faith, or heretics. And the heresy of Jesus they found in the fact that He, although a man, made Himself God (ch. x. 33). '*Thou hast a devil,*' or evil spirit (comp. ch. vii. 20), refers to the enthusiastic manner in which He proclaimed His delusion. Similar charges had been alleged by the ungodly against the prophets of the Old Testament. In 2 Kings ix. 11, the servants of his lord said to Jehu, when a prophet had been with him, 'Wherefore came this mad fellow

to thee?' 'Every man that is mad and maketh himself a prophet,' is the style in which a false prophet writes concerning the true."—*Hengstenberg*. Why did they call Him a Samaritan? They knew He was not a Samaritan, for they had reproached Him before as being a Galilean and a Nazarene. The reason was this : their vocabulary of abuse furnished no stronger epithet. To be a Samaritan, to them, was to be a demon, one inspired with a diabolic spirit.

Ver. 49.—"*Jesus answered, I have not a devil*" [δαιμόνιον, "demon"]. "What calm dignity is here! Verily, 'when reviled, He reviled not again' (1 Pet. ii. 23). Compare Paul before

Festus: 'I am not mad, most noble Festus' (Acts xxvi. 25). Our Lord adds not, 'Nor am I a Samaritan,' that He might not even seem to partake of their contempt for a race that had already welcomed Him as their Christ, and begun to be blessed by Him."—*Dr. Brown.* "*But I honour My Father, and ye do dishonour Me.*" Christ honours His Father by ascribing His distinguished excellences to the Divine within Him. But they dishonoured Him—Christ—by attributing all that was peculiar in Him to a diabolic source.

Ver. 50.—"*And I seek not Mine own glory: there is one that seeketh and judgeth.*" He seems to intimate that He leaves His δόξα, "glory," in the hands of the Father.

Ver. 51.—"*Verily, verily, I say unto you, If a man keep My saying, he shall never see death.*" This he had expressed many times before, not however in such a bold and naked form.

HOMILETICS

The subject that the words suggest, is *The Anti-diabolism of Christ.* Notice —

I —CHRIST HONOURS THE FATHER; THE DEVIL DOES NOT

"*I honour My Father, and ye do dishonour Me.*" How does Christ honour the Father?

First: By a faithful representation of the Father's character. He was "the faithful and true Witness:" the highest Revelation of God in the universe. The revelation of the Infinite which the material creation gives, is very dim and limited, compared with that revelation given by Jesus Christ. He was the "brightness of His Father's glory, the express image of His person." "In Him dwelt all the fulness of the Godhead bodily." He honoured Him—

Secondly: By supreme devotion to the Father's will. He came to this world in order to work out the Divine will in relation to humanity, to substitute in all human hearts truth for error, purity for pollution, benevolence for selfishness, spirituality for materialism, God for the devil. He came, in one word, "to put away sin by the sacrifice of Himself," to sweep moral evil clean out of the earth.

Now this is just what the devil does not do. On the contrary, the devil seeks to dishonour God by misrepresenting Him, dealing out calumnies into every ear that will listen to them; by opposing with might and main the Divine will. He dares Omnipotence "to arms." "He is a liar, and the father of it." The words suggest—

II —CHRIST SEEKS NOT HIS OWN GLORY; THE DEVIL DOES

"*I seek not My own glory.*" Personal ambition and self-seeking had no place in the heart of Christ. "He made Himself of no reputation, but took on Him the form of a servant, and became obedient unto death, even the death of the cross," &c. Love to the Infinite Father seemed to swallow up His *ego*-ism. He was self-oblivious. Often does He say, "I seek not My own will." Had He sought His own earthly glory, He would have been the triumphant Leader of all armies, the absolute Emperor of all nations, instead of which, He was born in a stable, lived without a home, and died upon a cross.

All this is anti-diabolic. Ambition is the inspiration of Satan. His motto is, "Better reign in hell than serve in heaven." He cares for no one else, and would kindle hells for a thousand generations in order to maintain his own dominion and gratify his own ambition. Just so far as a man loses his own *ego*-ism in love for the Infinite, he is Christ-like. Just so far as he is self-conscious and aiming at his own personal ends, he is devil-like. The words suggest—

III —CHRIST DELIVERS FROM DEATH ; THE DEVIL CANNOT

"*If a man keep My saying, he shall never see death.*" What does He mean by death here ?

First : Does He mean the dissolution of soul and body ? Not so ; for all the millions that "*kept His saying*" have gone down to the grave.

Secondly : Does He mean extinction of existence ? If He does, it is in all probability true. It is morally certain, to say the least, that all genuine disciples of Christ will inherit perpetual existence. This He Himself has taught. "This is the will of Him that sent Me, that every one that seeketh the Son, and believeth on Him, may have everlasting life."

Thirdly : Does He mean the destruction of that which makes death repugnant to man's nature ? If so, the dying experience of millions demonstrates its truth. "The sting of death is sin." Take sin away, and the event of the dissolution of soul and body becomes one of the brightest prospects in the pilgrimage of souls. It is a mere step over a beautiful river from a wilderness into a Canaan ; it is the mere opening of the door from a cell into palatial apartments. Now, does the devil deliver from death ? No, he cannot. He *cannot* raise a dead insect to life, nor make a fading flower re-bloom ; and if he could, he would not. The work of destruction is the gratification of his malignant nature. He goes about " seeking whom he may devour."

CONCLUSION. How essentially antagonistic are the inspirations of good and evil : the kingdom of the devil, and the kingdom of Christ ! The one is God-honouring, the other God-dishonouring ; the one self-abnegating piety, the other blasphemous ambition ; the one death extinction, the other death production. Kind Heaven ! inspire the world with the spirit of anti-diabolism, the spirit of Christ.

John 8:52-59

CHRIST GREATER AND OLDER THAN ABRAHAM

"Then said the Jews unto Him, Now we know that Thou hast a devil. Abraham is dead, and the prophets ; and Thou sayest, If a man keep My saying (R. V. WORD), he shall never taste of death," &c.

EXEGETICAL REMARKS.—Ver. 52.— "*Then said the Jews unto Him, Now we know that Thou hast a devil.*" ἐγνώκαμεν. We are sure, have found out. δαιμόν ἔχ. "His implied claim to a dignity greater than that of Abraham and the prophets, and His assertion of supernatural virtue in His words were, as they affected to believe, a proof that He was a raving fanatic, possessed with an evil spirit that prompted Him to such extravagances." —*Webster and Wilkinson.* "*Now we know.*" As if they had said, We stated this just now, and we were almost frightened by our rashness, but now we are certain that "*Thou hast a devil.*"

Ver. 53.—"*Art thou greater than our father Abraham, which is dead ?*" &c. The Jews understood Him to mean merely bodily death. Their meaning seems to be: Thou sayest that if a man keep Thy words he shall never die. Abraham kept *God's* words, and yet he died. So did the prophets ; they kept God's words, but died. Yet Thou sayest, those that keep Thy sayings shall never die ; who then art Thou ? What arrogance, what blasphemy !

Ver. 54.—"*Jesus answered, If I honour* (R. V. GLORIFY) *Myself, My honour* (R. V. GLORY) *is nothing: it is My Father that honoureth* (R. V. GLORIFIETH) *Me ; of whom ye say, that He is your God.*" "These words seem to be uttered in order to prepare the way for the more startling declaration which follows in verse 56. 'Honour Myself.' If My honour is, as you say, self-fabricated. '*Is nothing.*' It is the nothing you pronounce it. '*Your God.*' The Source of My true dignity is the God of Abraham, of the prophets, of Israel, and, as ye claim, of yourselves. Your quarrel is therefore with them and Him."—*Whedon.*

Ver. 55.—"*Yet* (R. V. AND) *ye have not known Him; but I know Him: and if I should say, I know Him not, I shall be a liar like unto you: but I know Him, and keep His saying*" (R. V. WORD). "He implies that He cannot so speak of God as to disguise the fact of His intimate knowledge of Him, without speaking untruly, and imitating them, who spoke of God as their God and Father, whereas they knew him not. ὅμοιος ὑμῶν. The ordinary construction is with the dative ; but the genitive is used by classical authors : it makes the idea of comparison more prominent. τὸν λ. α τηρῶ. If we take these words in connection with verse 51, He implies by them that He also lived by keeping His Father's word, as men should live by keeping His. Comp. vi. 57 ; xv. 10."

Ver. 56.—"*Your father Abraham rejoiced to see My day.*" Exulted or exceedingly rejoiced that he should see : that is, exulted to see it by anticipation. "*And he saw it, and was glad.*" Does this mean that he saw it in prophetic vision, or that he saw it in his disembodied spirit from the sphere of celestial blessedness ? Or that he saw it in the familiar intercourse which he had with the "angel of the Lord" when he appeared to him in his tent at Mamre ? It scarcely matters. However, I incline to the last opinion. In either case, he saw it.

Ver. 57.—"*Then said the Jews* (R. V. THE JEWS THEREFORE SAID) *unto Him, Thou art not yet fifty years old, and hast thou seen Abraham ?*" Alford remarks that our Lord's age at this time cannot be inferred from this statement. Fifty years was with the Jews the term of ripe manhood ; it was the age when the Levite ceased to officiate. All that is meant here is, You are not yet past middle life, not even on the verge of old age, and how canst Thou say that Thou hast seen Abraham ?

Ver. 58.—"*Jesus said unto them, Verily, verily, I say unto you, Before Abraham was, I am.*" *Dr. Brown's* remarks on this verse seem a faithful explanation. "*Before Abraham was,* πρὶν 'Αβραὰμ γενέσθαι. Before Abraham came into existence, *I am.* ἐγώ εἰμι. The difference between the two verbs applied to Abraham and Himself in this great saying is to be carefully observed. Before Abraham was brought into being, I exist. The statement, therefore, is not that Christ came into existence before Abraham did, as Arians affirm is the meaning : it is, that He never came into being at all, but existed before Abraham had a being ; which of course was as much as to say that He existed before all creation, or from eternity, as in ch. i. 1. In that sense, beyond all doubt, the Jews understood Him, as will appear from what follows."

Ver. 59.—" *Then took they up stones* (R. V. THEY TOOK UP STONES THERE-FORE) *to cast at Him: but Jesus hid Himself, and went out of the temple, going through the midst of them, and so passed by*" (R. V. OMITS THIS CLAUSE). The last clause of this verse is considered by the best critics to be spurious. It is clear from the fact that the Jews took stones to cast at Him, that they considered the expression "*Before Abraham was, I am*" as expressive of His eternity, and His claim therefore to Godhead. This they regarded as blasphemy, and for the sin of blasphemy they felt justified in stoning Him. While the Jews were in the act of selecting the stones, it would seem that Jesus moved away by a route which interposed projecting objects between them and Him, and so He escaped from the temple.

HOMILETICS

These words present to us the fact that *Christ is both greater and older than Abraham.* The passage shows—

I —THAT CHRIST IS GREATER THAN ABRAHAM

" *Then said the Jews unto Him, Now we know that Thou hast a devil. Abraham is dead, and the prophets ; and Thou sayest, If a man keep My saying, he shall never taste of death. Art Thou greater than our father Abraham, which is dead ?* "

Three things are to be noticed here—

First : The implied denial of the Jews that Christ was greater than Abraham. In their implied denial we see—(1.) A sensuous interpretation. "*Abraham is dead.*" They took death in its mere *material* sense, the death of the body; they had no profounder idea of death than the dissolution of mind from matter. The dissolution of mind from truth, virtue, happiness, God—*which is of all deaths the worst,* which is of truth death—had not entered their carnal souls. The dissolution of soul from body—or corporeal death—is but the *palpable type* and the probable result of the separation of the human soul from the life of holiness and God. This is death—the death to which Christ referred; and this the carnal Jews misunderstood. Christ asserts that the man who practically obeyed Him would not taste of this death, nor will he, nor can he. "This is life eternal, to know Thee." In the implied denial we see—(2.) Their ancestral pride. " *Art Thou greater than*

our father Abraham, which is dead?   And the prophets are dead."
Their pride of ancestry led them to believe that Abraham was the
greatest man in the universe.   We are the greatest people in the
world, for we descended from the loins of the greatest man, and
that was Abraham.   Ah me! these two things—sensuous interpretation and ancestral pride, have been in all ages, and still are,
amongst the greatest obstructions to the spread of truth.   Notice—
Secondly : The reply of Christ to this implied denial.   In His
reply three things are noteworthy.   (1.) He asserts that He honoured the Father, they did not.   *"If I honour Myself, My honour is
nothing."*   (2.) He knew the Father, they did not.   *" Yet ye have
not known Him ; but I know Him : and if I should say, I know
Him not, I shall be a liar."*   He knew the Father.   He was the
only Being who knew Him.   "No man hath seen God at any
time," &c.   (3.) He served the Father, they did not.   *"I know
Him, and keep His saying."*   His "meat and drink was to do the
will of His Father."   Notice—
Thirdly : The declaration of His superiority to Abraham.   *" Your
father Abraham rejoiced to see My day: and he saw it, and was
glad."* *   However he saw it, He means it was a wonderful sight to
him ; Christ's day was a period that rejoiced him.
The passage shows—

II —THAT CHRIST IS OLDER THAN ABRAHAM

" Before Abraham was, I am."   This declaration struck them—
First : As absurd.   *" Thou art not yet fifty years old, and hast
Thou seen Abraham ?"*   Abraham lived thousands of years ago,
how could he see Thy day ? or how couldst Thou see Abraham ?
How absurd, for a man who had not reached middle life, to give
Himself a patriarchal age !   This declaration struck them—
Secondly : As blasphemous.   *" Then took they up stones to cast at
Him."*   They evidently understood Him to mean that He existed
before Abraham, and therefore put Himself on an equality with
God.

CONCLUSION.   How sublimely unique is Christ in the history
of the human race !   *Greater* than Abraham.   Abraham was great,
one of the most illustrious of the human family, the " friend
of God," the ancestor of a wonderful race of men.   Christ is
older than Abraham.   Abraham lived upwards of thirty centuries
before ; but Christ lived before Abraham.   *" Before Abraham was,
I am."*   "In the beginning was the Word," &c. &c.

* See Germ, p. 259.

Germs of Thought
No. 34   John 8:56

CHRISTIAN PIETY IN RELATION TO THE FUTURE

"Your father Abraham rejoiced to see My day : and he saw it, and was glad."

The text leads us to consider the aspect of Christian piety in relation to the future, and we infer—

I THAT CHRISTIAN PIETY TURNS THE SOUL TOWARDS THE FUTURE

"Your father Abraham rejoiced to see My day." Piety seems to have turned Abraham's mind to the "*day*" of Christ. This refers undoubtedly to Christ's Incarnation, personal ministry, and spiritual reign. Nineteen long centuries rolled between Abraham and the period of Christ's Incarnation. Still he saw it. Christian piety does two things in the mind in relation to the future.

First : It gives an interesting revelation of the future. Science, poetry, literature, shed no light upon the on-coming periods of our being; but the Bible does. It opens up the future history of the race to us.

Secondly : It gives a felt interest in the blessedness of the future. It gave Abraham a felt interest in the "*day*" of Christ. It gives the good a felt interest in the glories that are coming. And what glorious things are on their march ! We infer—

II —THAT CHRISTIAN PIETY FASTENS THE SOUL UPON CHRIST IN THE FUTURE

"*My day.*" To the godly, Christ is everything in the future. "The glory of their brightest days, and comfort of their nights." Do the rivers point to the sea ? Does the needle point to the pole ? Do the plants point to the sun ? Does hunger cry for food ? Does life pant for air ? Even so does the heart of Christly piety point to Christ in the future. Christ has a "*day*" in the future, His universal day on earth, the day of His glorious revelation at the judgment. We infer—

III —THAT CHRISTIAN PIETY BRINGS JOY TO THE SOUL FROM THE FUTURE

"*Your father Abraham rejoiced.*" It made Abraham "*glad.*" He was glad with a *benevolent* gladness; he knew the world would be blessed by Christ's advent. He was glad with a *religious* gladness; he knew that God would be glorified by His advent. Several reasons might make us glad when we think of the coming day of Christ. (1.) In His day there will be a solution of all difficulties; everything will be explained. (2.) In His day there will be the termination of all imperfections, physical, mental, spiritual. (3.) In His day there will be the consummation of unending blessedness. "They shall hunger no more." Learn from this subject—

First: The congruity of Christianity with the prospective tendency of the soul. The soul is everlastingly pointing to the future. Christianity meets this tendency, ministers to it, satisfies it. Learn—

Secondly: The antidote of Christianity to the forebodings of the soul. Some souls are constantly boding evil, and well all ungodly souls may. Christianity lights up the future. We learn—

Thirdly: The fitness of Christianity to the aspirations of the soul. Wonderful is the good after which some souls are aspiring in the future. The present and the material have lost for them their attractions. They have done with them, they have thrown them away, as boys who have sucked the orange throw away the peel. Christianity meets these loftiest aspirations. Man cannot aspire after anything higher than that which Christianity supplies: "Eye hath not seen, ear hath not heard," &c.

John 9:1-7

THE MAN BORN BLIND

TYPES OF CHARACTER IN RELATION TO CHRIST'S WORK

(NO. 1)—THOSE WHO CONSCIOUSLY NEED CHRIST'S WORK

(*The blind man healed on the Sabbath. Subsequent discourses at Jerusalem.* JOHN ix. 1—41; x. 1—21.)

"And as Jesus passed by, He saw a man which was blind from his birth," &c.

EXEGETICAL REMARKS.—Ver. 1.— "*And as Jesus* (R. V. HE) *passed by.*" Either on His way from the temple after the attempted assault, or, as some think, on the next Sabbath. "*He saw a man.*" This man probably sat where beggars were accustomed to resort, in the neighbourhood of the Temple. "*Which was blind from his birth.*" It would seem a notorious fact that he was born blind.

Ver. 2.—"*And His disciples asked Him, saying, Master* (R. V. RABBI), *who did sin, this man, or his parents, that he was* (R. V. SHOULD BE) *born blind?*" "As the doctrine of the pre-existence of souls and that of the metempsychosis—the transmission of the soul of one person into the body of another—though held by certain of the more philosophical Jews, was never a current belief of the people,

we are not to understand the disciples here to refer to sin committed in a former state of existence; and probably it is but a loose way of concluding that sin somewhere has surely been the cause of this calamity."—*Brown.*

Ver. 3.—"*Jesus answered, Neither hath* (R. V. DID) *this man sinned* (R. V. SIN), *nor his parents: but that the works of God should be made manifest in him.*" "But that," ἀλλ' ἵνα, namely, to this end, was he born blind. The ultimate object of evil, as of things in general, is the glorification of God. Christ does not say that neither the blind man nor his parents had sinned, but that special sin was not to be charged on either in consequence of his blindness.

Ver. 4.—"*I* (R. V. WE) *must work the works of Him that sent Me, while it is day: the night cometh, when no man can work."* These words imply that Christ regarded Himself as having a special Divine work to do on earth, and to that work He must consecrate Himself with persevering diligence.

Ver. 5.—*"As long as* (R. V. WHEN) *I am in the world, I am the light of the world."* "He evidently knew that the spiritual effect of His coming into the world would be typified by the act He was about to perform. The connection between these words and the preceding may be thus expressed : When My death removes me, so that I shall no longer perform My Father's work among you, then will that light be removed which at present creates for you a spiritual day ; and so in xi. 9, 10. ὅταν . . . ὦ. The expression denotes indefinite frequency, and must therefore be understood, in a general sense, applicable to present circumstances. Let Me be at any time in the world, I am at such time the light. It is not meant that in consequence of His special mission He was at that particular time the light of the world ; but that, being in the world, He was, in consequence of His nature and origin, the light of the world. φῶς εἰμι, 'My character is light.' "

Ver. 6.—*" When He had thus spoken, He spat on the ground, and made clay of the spittle, and He anointed the eyes of the blind man* (R. V. HIS EYES) *with the clay."* What is the object of such actions as these ? Why did He, Who could by a word open the eyes of the blind, here spit on the ground, make clay, and anoint the man's eyes with clay, and send him to wash in the pool of Siloam ? Probably to deepen the

impression of the miracle. For this reason, probably, Moses used the rod to get water from Horeb, and the tree to sweeten the waters of Marah. For this reason, too, probably Elijah used his mantle to divide the waters (2 Kings ii. 8). All this exertion, too, on our Saviour's part would strike against the superstitious sentiments which the Pharisees had in relation to the Sabbath.

Ver. 7.—*"And said unto him, Go, wash in the pool of Siloam."* This is a pool or a small pond in an oblong form, at the lower end of the Valley of Jehoshaphat, overlooked by the wall of Mount Zion. Its sides are built up with stones, and a column stands in the middle, indicating that a chapel was once built over it. It is in length 54 feet by 18 in breadth. It is fed probably by water from the temple mount. "(*Which is by interpretation, Sent.*)" It can hardly be doubted but that the Evangelist was guided by some sense of the appropriateness of the name of the pool to the occasion. Either the character of Jesus as the Sent of God, or the character to be assumed by the blind man in order to obtain his cure, the sent by Jesus, would seem to be intimated. Reference to the similar cure and the whole case of Naaman renders the latter the more probable. It should be observed, that in Isaiah viii. 6 this pool is spoken of emblematically. "The waters of Shiloah that go softly." *"He went his way* (R. V. AWAY) *therefore, and washed, and came seeing."* It does not appear that he came to Jesus, nor did he see Jesus at all until his expulsion from the synagogue (ver. 35).

HOMILETICS

As this chapter is the history of one event, opening and closing (unlike most other chapters) with reference to the same object, viz. that of a man *"born blind,"* homiletically it may be divided into several sections ; each section may be used to represent certain classes of men in relation to Christ. These sections may be designated those who *consciously need* the work of Christ ; those who are *speculatively interested* in the work of Christ ; those who are *malignantly prejudiced* against the work of Christ ; those who are *heartily interested* in the work of Christ; and those who are *experimentally restored* by the work of Christ.

These seven verses we take to represent *those who consciously need the work of Christ.* Looking at the poor blind man before us, as representing the consciously needy class, two things are noteworthy—

I —THE WRETCHEDNESS OF THEIR CONDITION

First : This man was afflicted with blindness. "*A man blind from his birth.*" He had never enjoyed the blessings of vision. Those windows through which the human soul looks out upon the universe had, in his case, never been opened. Those doors through which the soul lets in the beauty of God's creation had been barred from his birth. Unknown to him was the glory of the heavens, the majesty of the mountains, the sublimity of the sea, the beauty of the emerald meadows, the waving forest, the floral vales. The world to him was a great, black, monotonous cave. To him never came—

> " Day, or the sweet approach of even or morn,
> Or sight of vernal bloom, or summer rose."

Secondly : This man was afflicted with beggary. Day by day, perhaps from his earliest childhood, he sat near the temple in darkness, begging for the mere necessaries of life. He lived on the cold, precarious charity of those who visited the temple. There, pinched with hunger, shivering in the cold, and scorched in the strong rays of the Eastern sun, he sat in the unbroken night of blindness, seeking relief of the passers-by. How great the affliction of this man ! The world abounds with subjects of affliction to a greater or less extent. The blind, the deaf, the destitute, the diseased, we meet in all the walks of daily life. The question has often been asked, Why, under the government of God, should such cases as the one in the text occur ? Why should the Great One send men into the world sometimes without the use of their limbs—cripples ; sometimes without the use of their ears—deaf ; sometimes without the use of their eyes — blind ; sometimes without the use of their reason—idiots ? These questions I have endeavoured to answer elsewhere.*

Thirdly : This man was afflicted with social heartlessness. The question of the disciples, " *Who did sin, this man or his parents ?* " indicated a heartless disregard to his wretched condition. If the question fell on his ear, as in all probability it did, it must have struck pain into his heart. Their question involved a great error, viz. that present sufferings are the results and measures of individual sins. That suffering always implies sin, is peradventure an unquestionable fact ; and that the sin of parents often entails sufferings on their

---

*See *Acts of the Apostles*, p. 46. Kregel Publications, Grand Rapids, Mi. 1980

children, is too patent to admit of disputation. But that individual suffering is always the result of individual sin, is an egregious and pernicious error. It was indeed a common notion amongst the Jews. The whole book of Job seems to have been written in order to correct it. Christ Himself exposed the error (Luke xiii. 1—4). The sufferings of individuals are no just criteria of moral character. Their question involved a positive absurdity. Part of this question was very absurd. How could the blindness of a man *"born blind"* be the result of his sin ? How could he sin before he was born ? Did they believe in the Pythagorean doctrine of metempsychosis, or the transmigration of souls from one body to another, that they spoke of a man sinning before he was born ? If so, their question was consistent with their faith ; but it is not likely that the poor fishermen of Galilee held such a philosophical dogma.

This man, then, consciously required the help that Christ alone could render ; he was blind, indigent, despised. Spiritually, all men in their unregenerate state are in as urgent a need of the aid of Christ as this man. Alas ! but few realize their necessity. Another thing presented here is—

II —THE NATURE OF THEIR DELIVERANCE

We learn—

First : That the deliverance is the pre-determined work of God. *" Jesus answered, Neither hath this man sinned, nor his parents : but that the works of God should be made manifest in him."* Christ does not mean that either this man or his parents were free from sin, but that their sin was not the cause of the man's blindness. His blindness was a Divine result for a Divine purpose ; it was to afford scope for His remedial agency. God's restorative agency reveals Him often in more striking aspects than even His creating and preserving. God should be studied as a *Restorer.* We learn—

Secondly : That the deliverance was effected by Jesus Christ. *" I must work the works of Him that sent Me."* * Those works were redemptive works. His work was to finish transgression and to make an end of sin ; to heal all the diseases of mankind ; to wipe away all tears from all faces.

(1.) This work He did *systematically.* He did not proceed in a capricious and desultory manner. He worked by a Divine programme. He did the right work in the right place, on the right person, at the right time. (2.) This work He did *diligently.* " *While it is day.*" He knew His work was great, and the period Divinely allotted for its accomplishment limited. These works of Christ suggest three truths of importance. (*a.*) There is a Divine *purpose* in every man's life. (*b.*) There is a Divine *work* for every man's life. (*c.*) There is a Divine *limit* to every man's life. (3.) This

* See Germ, p. 264.

work He did *appropriately*. "*As long as I am in the world, I am the Light of the world*." He assumes a character corresponding with the exigencies of the sufferer. To the thirsty woman at Jacob's well, He was the "*living* water;" to the mourning sisters at the grave of Lazarus, He was "the *resurrection* and the life;" to this poor blind man, He was the "*Light of the world*." He is the central Light in all the spheres of being. The material heavens borrow their brightness from Him. The beams of reason are but the radiation of His intelligence; the rays of moral goodness are but emanations from Him, the "Sun of Righteousness." (4.) This work He did *unasked*. It does not appear that the blind man besought His interposition. "*As Jesus passed by, He saw a man which was blind*." He looked, perhaps, stedfastly at him as he sat there in destitution and darkness, as He looked at the poor widow of Nain following her only son to the grave, as He looked at the fainting multitudes whom He fed by a miracle. Though the Jews had just taken up stones to cast at Him as He was leaving the temple, yet as He "*passed by*," He tenderly observed the poor blind sufferer. The violence that raged around Him did not disturb the calm flow of His compassion for sufferers. Ill-treatment from our fellow-mortals tends to make us miserable and misanthropic. Not so with Him. The fountain of His love was so infinite, that it admitted of no diminution. In this man's case He was "found of one who inquired not after Him." (5.) This work He did *instrumentally*. "*When He had thus spoken, He spat on the ground, and made clay of the spittle, and He anointed the eyes of the blind man with the clay, and said unto him, Go, wash in the pool of Siloam*." These means were very simple. No chemical compounds were applied, no surgical operations were performed. Clay! Why such means were employed, who can tell? All we know is, that the healing virtue was not in the means, but in Himself. It is the prerogative of Christ to produce grand results by feeble instrumentalities. The man went, after the application of the clay to his eyes, to Siloam, as directed. "*He went his way therefore, and washed, and came seeing*." A new world opened round the man, and new and strange emotions came rushing into his soul. All this may be regarded as symbolic.

Germs of Thought
No. 35   John 9:4

MORAL SIGNIFICANCE OF LIFE

"I must work the works of Him that sent Me, while it is day: the night
cometh, when no man can work."

These are the words of Christ, and they suggest truths of importance to us all.

I —THERE IS A DIVINE PURPOSE IN EVERY MAN'S LIFE.

Christ said that God had sent Him into the world, and so He has sent every man that exists. We come into this world, not by accident, not by necessity, nor by our own choice. Every man is " *sent* " here.

First : Then he has a right to be here. Who has a right to send him hence ? Every man is sent here.

Secondly : Then he has some distinct mission. What is it ? The words suggest—

II —THERE IS A DIVINE WORK FOR EVERY MAN'S LIFE

" *The works of Him that sent Me.*" What are the works which God requires us to do ? Not works of any particular class, intellectual or manual, mercantile or mechanical : all these works may either be the devil's work or God's, according to the *spirit* in which they are performed. The works of God are works prompted and controlled by *supreme love* to Himself and regard for the good of His universe. " Whatsoever we do in word or deed, we should do all to the glory of God." The words suggest—

III —THERE IS A DIVINE LIMIT TO EVERY MAN'S LIFE

" *While it is day : the night cometh, when no man can work.*" There is an appointed time for man upon earth.

First : It is very short. It is a mere " *day.*" How brief is life !

Secondly : Its business is very urgent. In this day how much must be done, if it is ever done. There is business to be done in the day of our mortal life which cannot be done afterwards.

John 9:8-13

THE MAN BORN BLIND

TYPES OF CHARACTER IN RELATION TO CHRIST'S WORK

(No. 2)—THOSE WHO ARE ONLY SPECULATIVELY INTERESTED IN THE WORK

" The neighbours therefore, and they which before had seen him that he was blind, said, Is not this he that sat and begged ? " &c.

EXEGETICAL REMARKS.—Ver. 8.— " *The neighbours therefore, and they which before had seen him* (R. V. SAW HIM AFORETIME) *that he was blind* " (R. V. A BEGGAR). Here follows an account of what befell this blind man. The account is so minute, distinct, lifelike, that one must conclude that the biographer had it from the very lips of the blind man himself. " *Is not this he that sat and begged ?* " It would seem that they had been in the habit of seeing him as a blind man and begging.

Ver. 9.—" *Some* (R. V. OTHERS) *said, This* (R. V. IT) *is he : others said, He is* (R. V. NO, BUT HE IS) *like him : but he said, I am he.*" The diversity of opinions is readily accounted for by the great difference in his appearance which would be made by the removal of the most deforming of blemishes, and the bestowal of the most distinguishing of features. The very difficulty which they had in believing that he was the blind beggar proves the perfection of the cure.

Ver. 10.—" *Therefore said they*

(R. V. THEY SAID THEREFORE) *unto him, How were* (R. V. HOW THEN WERE) *thine eyes opened?"* A very natural question.

Ver. 11.—*"He answered and said, A* (R. V. THE) *man that is called Jesus,"* &c. "He is therefore not acquainted with the Messianic character of Jesus. He however emphasizes the name of Jesus. He has immediately noticed the significant name, which was not the case with the impotent man of Bethesda (chap. v.). The form of his already budding faith in the prophetic dignity and Divine mission of Jesus, declares itself in verses 17 and 33; he as yet does not know Him as the Messiah (ver. 35). '*I received sight.*' Ἀναβλέπειν means to look up, to see again. Meyer maintains against Lucke's explanation, 'I looked up' (Mark xvi. 4), the '*I received sight again.*' For this there is no ground in verses 15 and 18, although the explanation of Grotius, '*Nec male recipere quis dicitur, quod communiter tributum humanæ naturæ ipsi abfuit,*' is ingenious."—*Lange.*

Ver. 12.—*"Then said they* (R. V. AND THEY SAID) *unto him, Where is He?"* From this it would appear that Jesus, after the attempt to stone Him, had retired from the Temple, and still kept Himself from the public eye. The motive for asking the question was not hostility, but a natural interest, to see and to know the author of such a work. "*He said* (R. V. SAITH), *I know not.*" The man had heard the voice, but had never seen the person of his Benefactor, until revealed in verse 37.

Ver. 13.—*"They brought* (R. V. BRING) *to the Pharisees him that aforetime was blind"* (πρὸς τοὺς Φαρισαίους). Probably to the Sanhedrim, which sat daily, and the principal members of which were the leading Pharisees.

HOMILETICS

The healing of this poor blind man was a very influential fact. As a stone cast into a lake throws the whole mass of water into agitation, producing circle after circle to its utmost bounds, this fact stirred into excitement the whole social sphere in which it occurred. It broke the monotony of ordinary life, it touched the springs of many minds, and filled the neighbourhood with strange thoughts and feelings. This is a striking illustration of the fact that no man "liveth to himself." What affects one, will affect many. Society is a chain, of which every man is a link; the motion of one link may vibrate through the whole chain. Society is a body, every man is a member; the pulsation of one heart will throb through every limb. There were circumstances connected with this man's healing, that tended to heighten its exciting power. He was well known. For many years, probably, he sat near that old temple; he had been seen by thousands who periodically visited that sacred spot, and had been the subject of remark by many a passer-by; he was a kind of institution, one of the well-settled and most notable objects in that great thoroughfare. The removing of his blindness was miraculous. Such an event had never been known before. Cases of blind men whose sight had been restored might have occurred ere then, within the knowledge of some; but this was not restoration, for he had never seen, never had a vision. It was a kind of creation; it was altogether wonderful; it stood out as one of the most marvellous things that had ever happened.

Hence the greatness of the interest awakened. The feelings produced, however, were very various.

The representative class which we have in these verses are those who are only *speculatively interested in Christ's work.* Notice three things concerning this class—

I —THE LACK OF EARNESTNESS IN THEIR INQUIRIES

Their inquiries were confined to three subjects.

First : To the identity of the restored man. " *Is not this he that sat and begged ?* " The question seems to be asked in the mere spirit of curiosity. "*Some said, This is he : others said, He is like him.*" Their difficulty in deciding his identity would arise partly perhaps from the change that the opened eye would make in his countenance, for the eye gives a character to the face, it kindles in every feature a new glory. The human eye in the face is as the moon in the night firmament, changing the whole aspect of things. And partly, and probably mainly, from the unaccountableness of the result. Though they might have felt that in nearly every respect he was like him, yet they could not believe because of the marvellousness of the change. Their inquiries were confined—

Secondly : To the method of his restoration. " *How were thine eyes opened ?* " In this question there is no ring of earnestness; it seems dictated by nothing but an ordinary curiosity. Their inquiries were confined—

Thirdly : To the whereabouts of the Restorer. " *Where is He ?* " Not, What is He ? All they meant was, We should like to see this Man, who has wrought such a wonderful cure. Those who have a *mere* speculative interest in Christianity are constantly asking such questions as these. Is it so and so ? How did it occur ? Where is the cause ? And all this with no deep genuine thirst for truth. Notice—

II —THE LACK OF GENEROSITY IN THEIR INQUIRIES

They utter no congratulatory word to the restored man. There was no gush, as one might have expected, of sympathy and gratitude for the merciful deliverance. Had they been true men, the event would have thrilled them with emotions that would have touched them into the enthusiasm of social affection. But there is not one spark of it. Their intellect seems to move in ice. So it is ever with those who are merely speculatively interested in Christianity. There is no exultation of heart on account of the millions it has blessed. It is mere cold inquiry about details. Notice—

III —THE LACK OF INDEPENDENCY IN THEIR INQUIRIES

" *They brought to the Pharisees him that aforetime was blind.*" They brought him to the judicial court, to try the question of his identity. They were not earnest enough in the matter to reach a conclusion that would satisfy themselves as to his identity. In that court to which they took him there would not be much difficulty in proving that the man was not himself, but some one else. Hostile judges can prove to a servile and ignorant jury that the man who says "*I am he*," is not himself but some one else. This has been done, I think, in England only within the last few years.

CONCLUSION. Truly lamentable it is, that there are men to be found who are *only* speculatively interested in the wonderful works of Christ. What these men saw and heard should have led them to a hearty acceptance of Jesus as the true Messiah, and their consecration to Him as their Lord and Master.

John 9:14-18

THE MAN BORN BLIND

TYPES OF CHARACTER IN RELATION TO CHRIST'S WORK

(NO. 3)—THOSE WHO ARE BITTERLY PREJUDICED AGAINST CHRIST'S WORK

"And it was the Sabbath day when Jesus made the clay, and opened his eyes," &c.

EXEGETICAL REMARKS.—Ver. 14.— "*And* (R. V. NOW) *it was the Sabbath day* (R. V. ON THE DAY) *when Jesus made the clay, and opened his eyes.*" This fact, that the miracle was done on the Sabbath, is here noted in connection with the tribunal; and the making of the clay is probably mentioned as a species of labour, which their law pronounced illegal. "Jesus had certainly of set purpose chosen the Sabbath for His work of healing. He designed to give matter of offence to the Pharisees, who, by their exaggerated severity in the external rites of the Sabbath festival, sought to compensate for their lacking spiritual service. (Augustine: *Sabbatum carnaliter observabant spiritualiter sistebat.*) And He would teach the people how the Sabbath was really to be used. His polemic in act was not directed against Moses, but against the caricature into which Pharisaism had turned the Mosaic Sabbath. The Sabbath was a rest from evil, as also from servile works, which centre in ourselves. But it was not to be a day of rest when the honour of God and the furtherance of our neighbour's good were concerned."—*Hengstenberg*.

Ver. 15.—"*Then again* (R. V. AGAIN THEREFORE) *the Pharisees also asked him how he had received his sight.*" This question had been propounded by the "neighbours" in verse 10. And it is again repeated by the Pharisees. "*He said unto them, He put clay upon mine eyes, and I washed, and do see.*" The answer which the man gives is according to the fact as recorded in verses 6, 7.

Ver. 16.—"*Therefore said some of the Pharisees* (R. V. SOME THEREFORE OF THE PHARISEES SAID), *This Man is not of* (R. V. FROM) *God, because He keepeth not the Sabbath day* (R. V. OMITS DAY). *Others said, How can a man that is a sinner do such miracles?*" (R. V. SIGNS.) "*Therefore.*" "That is, in consequence of the man's unflinching statement. They had hoped that he would invalidate the miracle by his testimony; but failing of this, they proceed to invalidate it against testimony by reasonings of their own. '*Others said.*' One party said, He is a sinner; and this cannot be a miracle. The other party said, This is a miracle; so He cannot be a sinner. Had the deed truly been a sin, the reasoning of the first party would have been correct.

The premise of the second party proved, not only that Jesus was no sinner, but that He was a messenger of God."

Ver. 17.—" *They say* (R. V. THERE-FORE) *unto the blind man again, What sayest thou of Him, that* (R. V. IN THAT) *He hath opened thine eyes?* " Stress is to be laid on the word "*thou.*" " *What sayest thou?* " The reply of the others was contradictory, and therefore did not satisfy inquiry. What sayest *thou?* No doubt, in appealing thus directly to him, they expected he would say something un-favourable to Christ. But they were disappointed. " *He said, He is a prophet.*" Without any circumlocution, he declared Him to be a "*prophet.*"

Ver. 18.—" *But the Jews* (R. V. THE JEWS THEREFORE) *did not believe con-cerning him, that he had been blind, and* (R. V. HAD) *received his sight, until they called the parents of him that had received his sight.*" Thus discon-certed, failing to obtain any informa-tion that went to condemn Christ, they adopt the pretext of appealing to his parents, hoping no doubt that they could extract from them the confession that he was not "*born blind.*" They "*did not believe until they called the parents;*" not as if they would have then believed. "The meaning is, that unbelief led them to this procedure."—*Hengsten-berg.*

HOMILETICS

The types of character in relation to Christ's work which are represented in these verses, are *Those who are bitterly prejudiced against His work.* Such were the Pharisees. They were determined if possible to deny the fact that the man's eyes were opened; and if they failed in this, to prove that Christ was exposed to punish-ment because He broke the Sabbath. Four facts marked the conduct of these men.

I —THEY WERE TECHNICAL RATHER THAN MORAL, IN THEIR STANDARD OF JUDGMENT

" *Therefore said some of the Pharisees, This man is not of God, because He keepeth not the Sabbath day.*" Christ had performed the miracle on the Sabbath. In this He struck a blow at the pre-judices of those hypocrites, and declared, " The Sabbath was made for man, and not man for the Sabbath." These Pharisees, instead of thanking God that their poor brother before them had his eyes opened, and expressing a solicitude to get a knowledge of Him Who had accomplished such a wonderful work, endeavour to make the whole thing a ceremonial crime. They had a greater respect for ceremonies than for souls. The Pharisees exalted the " letter " above the spirit, the ritual above the moral. Their sympathies were more with dead ceremonies than with living men.

Another fact which marked the conduct of these men was—

II —THEY WERE BIASSED RATHER THAN CANDID, IN THEIR EXAMINATION OF EVIDENCE

They made up their minds not to believe the fact; and all their examination, their questionings and cross-questionings, were in-tended to throw discredit upon it. They did not want evidence.

If evidence came up, they would endeavour to suppress or misinterpret it. The uncandid spirit breathes through the whole of their conduct. This endeavour to reject the truth which clashes with prejudices is, alas! too common in every age. The conduct of the Pharisees on this occasion shows the blindness of prejudiced minds and the heartlessness of technical religion.

Another fact which marked the conduct of these men was—

III —THEY WERE DIVIDED, RATHER THAN UNITED, IN THEIR CONCLUSIONS

"*There was a division among them.*" There were some, perhaps Joseph of Arimathea and Nicodemus, touched a little with the sentiment of justice and candour, who could not but see something of the Divinity of the act. Infidels ridicule Christians for their divisions, whilst they themselves are never agreed. Error is necessarily schismatic; evil has no power to unite: it is as changeable as the chameleon. Examine the theories of infidelity. The other fact which marked the conduct of these men was—

IV —THEY WERE MALIGNANT, RATHER THAN GENEROUS, IN THEIR AIMS

If their purpose had been generous they would have been disposed to believe in the mission of a Divine Restorer. Instead of which, they are determined to repudiate the fact. Their heartless treatment of the young man in brow-beating him, the readiness and delight with which they seized the conclusion that Christ was a sinner, and the violence with which they cast out of the synagogue those who believed on Him, all show that the malign, and not the benign, was their inspiration.

CONCLUSION. This class of men is not extinct. There are those who are bitterly prejudiced against Christianity in every region of Christendom. The most patent facts they dispute and deny. They are proof against all argument. Prejudice turns a man into a kind of behemoth whose heart is as "firm as stone," as hard as a piece of molten millstone. All our "sling stones" of argument are turned "with him into stubble." He "laugheth at the shaking of your dialectic spear."

John 9:19-23

THE MAN BORN BLIND
TYPES OF CHARACTER IN RELATION TO CHRIST'S WORK
(NO. 4)—THOSE WHO PRACTICALLY IGNORE CHRIST'S WORK

" And they asked them, saying, Is this your son, who ye say was born blind?" &c.

EXEGETICAL REMARKS.—Ver. 19.— "*And they asked them, saying, Is this* *your son?*" The parents are now brought forward in this ecclesiastical court. They are compelled to give evidence on the question before the Sanhedrim. What the court wanted the parents to depose was, that it was a great mistake to suppose that he was born blind, that he was only a little dim, and that having washed in Siloam he had been cured. *" Is this your son, who ye say was born blind ?"* This is the first question they put. This they could not deny. The fact was too patent, they had already admitted it. They had a strong temptation to deny it.

Ver. 20.—*" His parents answered them and said, We know that this is our son, and that he was born blind."* Here they declare the two facts that he was their son, and that he was born blind. "Thus," says *Chrysostom*, "the truth becomes strengthened by the very snares which are laid against it. A lie is its own antagonist, and by its attempts to injure the truth sets it off to greater advantage. So was it here. For the point which might have been urged, viz. that the neighbours knew nothing for certain, but spake from a mere resemblance, is cut off by the introduction of the parents, who could of course testify of their own son."

Ver. 21.—*" But by what means* (R. V. HOW) *he now seeth, we know not."* This is their reply to the third question, viz. "How then doth he now see ?" *" Or who hath opened his eyes, we know not."* Here is an evasion. "Yet they hint that they have heard of one who has opened his eyes." *" He is of age; ask him: he shall speak for himself."* "The son must speak for himself. The whole reply is characteristic of parents who are honest and sensible, but at the same time timidly and selfishly cautious. Something of their son's intellectual humour is perceptible in their answer, which, however, especially testifies to their pride that their son has wit enough to give them correct information with regard to the last question. The thrice-repeated αὐτὸς (αὐτοῦ ἡμεῖς, αὐτὸν, αὐτὸς) is in the highest degree significant. On the one hand it tells of their confidence in their son, but on the other hand, also of their fear. That they hereby jeopardize him or leave him in the lurch, is truly a selfish trait. They lack strength to prove their gratitude for the healing of their son by uniting their testimony to his, although they clearly indicate by the tartness and touchiness of their reply, but they are thoroughly observant of the bad intentions of the inquisitors." —*Lange.*

Ver. 22.—*" These words spake* (R. V. SAID) *his parents, because they feared the Jews."* Standing before such an august tribunal, brow-beaten, and knowing the consequences of their avowal, they had not the courage to declare the fact. *" For the Jews had agreed already, that if any man did* (R. V. SHOULD) *confess that He was* (R. V. HIM TO BE) *Christ, he should be put out of the synagogue."* "There were two or three kinds or degrees of excommunication among the Jews. The lighter species consisted of a kind of suspension from some of the privileges of worship and social intercourse, while the heavier was an utter and final exclusion, attended with terrible curses and maledictions that were pronounced in the fearful words, Anathema Maranatha (1 Cor. xvi. 22)."

Ver. 23.—*" Therefore said his parents, He is of age; ask him."* At the age of thirteen, among the Jews, a person was qualified to give evidence on disputed points. In this way the parents exposed their son to the danger from which they shrank.

HOMILETICS

The previous paragraphs of this chapter we employed to illustrate three classes of men in relation to the work of Christ; viz. those who consciously need His work, those who are speculatively interested in His work, and those who are malignantly prejudiced against His work.

These words we shall use to illustrate another class; viz. *Those who practically ignore His work.* This class is represented by the parents, who were called into court, and who, instead of avowing that Christ had given eyesight to their son, evaded the question for fear of the Jews. That they felt some interest in Christ can scarcely be doubted. He Who had conferred such a benefit on their son could scarcely fail to attract their special attention, and to have made on them some special impression. But their interest in Him was not strong enough to make them courageous for the truth. They practically ignored Him. The great majority of men in England, aye, in Christendom, belong to this class. They have no strong prejudice against Christ, still less are they malignant opponents; but they lack that vital interest in Him necessary to induce them to avow Him. We offer three remarks in relation to this class, as suggested by the conduct of these parents.

I —THEY IGNORED CHRIST'S WORK, ALTHOUGH THEY HAD EVERY OPPORTUNITY OF KNOWING IT

It cannot be doubted for a moment that these parents had the means of knowing Christ. He was no stranger in the neighbourhood. Often, in all probability, they had seen Him, heard Him speak, and witnessed some of His beneficent works. They were present, too, without doubt, when He wrought the miracle on their son; and from the lips of their son, we may infer from the sequel, they had heard, with the emphasis of gratitude and delight, the marvel which Jesus of Nazareth had wrought. This is the case with the millions that belong to this class; they practically ignore Him, not because they lack opportunities of knowing the mighty works He has achieved and is still achieving. Wherever they look, they can discover monuments of His beneficent operations. In every social circle which they enter, they can scarcely fail to find some faithful disciple who will proclaim and extol His name. Another remark in relation to this class, as suggested by these parents, is—

II —THEY IGNORED CHRIST'S WORK, WHEN GRATITUDE SHOULD HAVE URGED THEM TO ACKNOWLEDGE IT

Under what an obligation had He placed these parents, in conferring on their son the inestimable privilege of vision! By this He had not only given their child a new world of enjoyment, but had given him a capacity to contribute to their comfort and interests in such a way as he never could have done in a state of blindness. One might have thought that common gratitude would have impelled them, not only to acknowledge Him, but to glory in His name. Have not all the members of this class in Christendom, and especially in England, the strongest reasons for cherishing gratitude to Christ ? All that is salutary and righteous in their government, all that is pure and ennobling in their literature, all that is fair and honest in their commerce, all that is true and loving in their friendships, all that is progressive in their intelligence, morality, and happiness, must be ascribed to Him. Take from England to-day all that she owes to Christ, and you will leave her in all the ignorance, the confusion, horrors, and cruelties of the heathen districts of the world. What base ingratitude, then, to ignore Christ ! Another remark in relation to this class as suggested by these parents, is—

III —THEY IGNORED CHRIST'S WORK, FROM A COWARDLY MEANNESS OF SOUL

" *They feared the Jews.*" They were afraid of the Sanhedrim ; they were afraid to be truthful, honest, and hence their reply, " *He is of age ; ask him.*" They were willing for their son to bear alone all the danger that the avowal of the truth would entail.

Why do members of this class now ignore Christ ? Does not selfish fear lie at the root of their baseness—fear of losing property, sacrificing friendships, and injuring their position and their influence ? Fear, that prompted Peter to deny Christ, inspires the multitudes to ignore Him. Strange to say, thousands who have the courage to confront an army, are too cowardly to avow Christ. " He that is ashamed of Me and of My cause," &c.

"The cure of the blind man," says *Sears,* "and the incidents and conversations which followed thereupon, are transactions as full of nature as they can hold. Here was a miracle right under the eye of the Sanhedrim, and in the Temple court, and the people have seen it. It will not do to arrest and execute this man, unless the fact can be accounted for or explained away. They appeal to the parents, hoping the parents will deny that there was any blindness in the case. They evade most ingeniously, and are non-committal. All we know about it is, that he was born blind, and that he now sees. Who opened his eyes ? ' *He is of age ; ask him.*' Then follow the cross-examination of the young man himself, and his excommunication, and the rebuke of Jesus to the Pharisees for their own incurable blindness, ascending as usual from natural things to spiritual. The miracle is only the nucleus of a whole texture of natural events, and the discoursings which proceed from them, which are indissolubly bound together with the plainest marks of historic certainty, and the most subtle shadings of human character."

John 9:24-38

THE MAN BORN BLIND

TYPES OF CHARACTER IN RELATION TO CHRIST'S WORK

(No. 5)—THOSE WHO ARE CONSCIOUSLY RESTORED BY THE WORK

" Then again called they the man that was blind, and said unto him, Give God the praise," &c.

EXEGETICAL REMARKS.—Ver. 24.— " *Then again called they* (R. V. SO THEY CALLED A SECOND TIME) *the man that was blind.*" Calling him the second time indicates that he had been excluded from the court during the examination of his parents. They were rigorous in their judicial procedure. " *And said unto him, Give God the praise*" (R. V. GLORY TO GOD). This is not to be taken, we presume, as a devout exhortation, calling upon him to thank Jehovah and to give no attention to the impostor who he thought had cured him, but it is the language of adjuration, obliging him, on a solemn oath, to tell the truth. They wished to overawe him, so that he might declare what they desired, which was, that " *this Man is a sinner.*"

Ver. 25.—" *He answered* (R. V. THEREFORE ANSWERED) *and said, Whether He be a sinner or no, I know not.*" He is not to be shaken from the truth. Without taking upon himself to discuss with the judges as to whether the " Man" was a sinner or not, he declares his experience : " *One thing I know, that, whereas I was blind, now I see.*" They could not dissuade him from a fact of which he was conscious.

Ver. 26.—" *Then said they to him again* (R. V. THEY SAID THEREFORE UNTO HIM), *What did He to thee? how opened He thine eyes?*" They seemed to despair of making him deny the miracle, and now they question him as to how the work was done. And this, no doubt, to bring out the charge again, that He was a Sabbath-breaker.

Ver. 27.—" *He answered them, I have told you already* (R. V. I TOLD YOU EVEN NOW), *and ye did not hear: wherefore would ye hear it again? will* (R. V. WOULD) *ye also be* (R. V. BECOME) *His disciples?*" The man perseveres in maintaining his ground, unterrified by the dangers hanging over his head, until at last, provoked by their repeated and wearisome interrogation, he loses his patience, and puts the ironical and irritating question, whether they wish to be "this Man's followers."

Vers. 28, 29.—" *Then* (R. V. AND) *they reviled him, and said, Thou art His disciple; but we are Moses' disciples* (R. V. DISCIPLES OF MOSES). *We know that God spake* (R. V. HATH SPOKEN) *unto Moses: as for This Fellow* (R. V. MAN), *we know not from whence He is.*" His manliness heightens their indignation, and they break out in taunts and censures against him, and declare their adhesion to Moses. Dost thou ask us to become His disciples—the disciples of an impostor ? We are the disciples of Moses. We know that Moses was sent by God, and that his doctrines are true and Divine. " *As for This Fellow, we know not from whence He is.*"

Ver. 30.—" *The man answered and said unto them, Why herein is a marvellous thing* (R. V. THE MARVEL), *that ye know not from whence He is, and yet He hath opened mine eyes.*" " Why herein," for herein, is a "marvellous thing." As if he had said, You believe that whoever performs a miracle must be sent from God. My cure is confessedly a miracle, and yet you say you know not " *from whence He is.*"

Ver. 31.—" *Now we know that God heareth not sinners,*" &c. A miracle not only proves that He is Divine, but that He is pure from sin, for God does not hear sinners, and no one can perform a miracle but by the power of God.

Vers. 32, 33.—" *Since the world began was it not* (R. V. IT WAS NEVER) *heard that any man* (R. V. ONE) *opened the eyes of one* (R. V. A MAN) *that was born blind. If this Man were not of* (R. V. FROM) *God, He could do nothing.*" What he means is, Here is a great miracle, such a thing as had never occurred before ; and the doer of the miracle must be from God.

Ver. 34.—" *They answered and said unto him, Thou wast altogether born in sins, and dost thou teach us?*" All along, these Pharisees had assumed that this man's blindness was a punishment for his sin : they go beyond this now, and declare he was "*born in sins,*" that he was thoroughly depraved in body and soul. "*And dost thou,*" thus so constitutionally vile, "*teach us?*" "*And they cast him out.*" This was according to their threat (ver. 22). They excommunicated him, thrust him, not only from the court-room, but from the synagogue, the temple, and from all worship.

Ver. 35.—"*Jesus heard that they had cast him out.*" Christ heard of his expulsion, and hastened in search of him. "*And when He had found him* (R. V. FINDING HIM), *He said unto him, Dost thou believe on the Son of God?*"

Davidson translates, " Son of man." That is, the Messiah. This voice the blind man had heard before in the words, "Go, wash in the pool of Siloam." No doubt he at once recognized its tones.

Ver. 36.—"*He answered and said, Who* (R. V. AND WHO) *is He, Lord, that I might* (R. V. MAY) *believe on Him?*" As if he had said, I am ready to believe on Him if I knew Him ; but I must know who He is.

Vers. 37, 38.—"*And Jesus said unto him, Thou hast both seen Him, and it is He that talketh* (R. V. HE IT IS THAT SPEAKETH) *with thee. And he said, Lord, I believe. And he worshipped Him.*" It is remarkable that Jesus declared Himself as the Messiah to the woman of Samaria, to His disciples, and now to this man, while He made no such explicit announcement to the Jews at large. The reason, no doubt, was, that He would not subject Himself to the tumult incident upon making such a profession to the mass of the people. "*Worshipped Him.*" Paid Him obeisance, probably by prostrating himself on the ground according to the Eastern manner.

HOMILETICS

We have already noticed four classes of persons in relation to the work of Christ as suggested by this chapter—those who consciously need His work, those who are speculatively interested in His work, those who are malignantly prejudiced against His work, and those who practically ignore His work.

The verses now before us suggest another class, viz. *those who are consciously restored by the work of Christ.* The young man himself is the type of that class. He was blind, and now he saw. Not only was there in his case the restoration of physical vision, but of spiritual. He met Christ, "*And he said, Lord, I believe. And he worshipped Him.*" We find this man doing two things which characterize all who are spiritually restored by Christ.

I MAINTAINING TRUTH IN THE FACE OF FIERCE OPPOSITION

Nothing could exceed the determination of these rulers to reject the fact that this blind beggar was restored by Christ. After having had him before them once, and questioned and cross-questioned him, in order to destroy the credibility of the fact, and having summoned to their presence afterwards his parents with the same attempts, and again been thwarted, they recall the young man, and try in every way to get rid of Jesus Christ as the Restorer. But see how he holds his own.

First: He maintained the truth in a noble spirit. His conduct stands in sublime contrast to that of his parents and others concerning this matter.

Mark his *candour*. Hearing men disputing about the miracle, some saying he was like the blind man, and others that he was the blind man, without mincing or hesitation, he exclaims, "*I am he.*" Outspokenness is the ring of a great nature. Mark his *courage*. In defiance of the prejudices and the wishes of the Sanhedrim, he declares repeatedly that Jesus, Whom they hated, wrought the cure. The genuine alone are brave: honest souls dread a lie more than the frowns of a thousand despots. Mark his *consistency*. In spite of all the questions, cross-questions, and brow-beating he never varies in his statements. He never flinches from his first assertion. He is consistent throughout. His honest soul, though put through hottest furnaces, will come out nothing but metal. Truth is that subtle element which alone gives unity to all the varied parts of a man's life. Error makes man contradict himself, makes his utterances and deeds jostle against each other like logs of wood on the dashing wave. Verily the spirit which this young man manifested throughout is noble, and shows that the most abject poverty, aggravated by blindness, does not necessarily unman the soul. There may be grandeur of soul where there is social obscurity and physical infirmity.

Secondly: He maintained the truth by sound argument. (1.) His argument was built upon consciousness. "*He answered and said, Whether he be a sinner or no, I know not: one thing I know, that, whereas I was blind, now I see.*" No one could convince him to the contrary. All the new sensations that the light of heaven had poured into him rose in rebellion against any doubt on the subject. The logic of a college of Aristotles could not disturb his conviction. It is so with the true Christian: he *feels* the change, and no argument can touch it. (2.) His argument was formulated by common sense. His judges pressing him again with the question, "*What did He to thee? how opened He thine eyes?*" he reproves them for repeating the questions which he had already answered; and with withering irony says, "*Will ye also be His disciples?*" He states his argument thus:—that his cure, of which he was conscious, was a miracle. "*Herein is a marvellous thing, that ye know not from whence He is, and yet He hath opened mine eyes.*" Here is a miracle of which I am conscious, which you cannot deny, and you ask whence He is that wrought it? Is it not a doctrine with you, that no one who has not Divine authority can perform miracles? Why ask such questions? He goes on to state that not only had the Author of the miracle Divine authority, but also a *holy* character. "*Now we know that God heareth not sinners.*"

Such is the spirit of the argument with which this man maintained the truth in the face of fierce opposition; and all men who are consciously renewed will in some such way defend the truth. They will exemplify a noble spirit, and will employ arguments drawn from their own experience—arguments which to themselves no logic can refute.

Another thing which we find this man doing, which characterizes all who are spiritually restored by Christ, is—

II —FOLLOWING CHRIST WHEN CAST OUT FROM MEN

Noble as was his spirit, and strong as were his arguments, instead of convincing his judges, he only irritated them, and intensified their opposition. "*They answered and said unto him, Thou wast altogether born in sins: and dost thou teach us? And they cast him out.*" The best men in every age are always "*cast out*" by the ungodly. But, when cast out, what became of him?

First: Christ sought him. "*Jesus heard that they had cast him out; and when He had found him.*" Christ found him out. Sometimes men seem to have found Christ out by their own searching; such was the case with Zaccheus and blind Bartimeus. But here Christ finds the man out, as He found out the woman of Samaria, irrespective of his search.

Secondly: Christ revealed Himself to him. "*He,*" that is Jesus, "*said unto him, Dost thou believe on the Son of God? He answered and said, Who is He, Lord, that I might believe on Him? And Jesus said unto him, Thou hast both seen Him, and it is He that talketh with thee.*" Christ must show Himself, to be known.

Thirdly: Christ was followed by him. "*And he said, Lord, I believe. And he worshipped Him.*" Out with the world, and in with Christ. *Calvin* says: "We have known the same thing in our own time; for when *Dr. Martin Luther,* and others of the same class, were beginning to reprove the grosser abuses of the Pope, they scarcely had the slightest relish for pure Christianity. But after the Pope had cast them out of the Roman synagogue by terrific Bulls, Christ stretched forth His hand and made Himself fully known to them."

John 9:39-41

CHRIST'S MISSION TO THE WORLD

"And Jesus said, For judgment I am come into this world, that they which see not might see; and that they which see might be made blind," &c.—

EXEGETICAL REMARKS.—Ver. 39.— "*And Jesus said, For judgment I am* come (R. V. CAME I) *into this world, that they which see not might* (R. V.

MAY) *see.*" Rising to that sight of which the natural vision communicated to the youth was but the symbol. "*And that they which see might be made* (R. V. MAY BECOME) *blind.*" "Judicially incapable of apprehending and receiving the truth to which they have wilfully shut their eyes."—*Brown.*

Ver. 40.—"*And some* (R. V. THOSE) *of the Pharisees which were with Him heard these words* (R. V. THINGS), *and said unto Him, Are we blind also?*" "We, the authorized guides of the country in spiritual things, '*are we blind?*'" "Jesus was here, as usual in His visits, surrounded by an immense multitude. (Comp. ch. x. 19—21.) Among these were found a number of Pharisees who were wont to follow the Lord as spies, and watch all His steps and movements (Luke xi. 54; xiv. 1). These well understood that the declaration of Jesus bore the character of a challenge, and was meant for them. They also rightly discerned that, if they were to become blind through Christ's manifestation, it must follow that they had been before, although in a certain sense seeing, yet in another and more im-

portant sense blind; just as in Matt. xv. 14 they were exhibited as blind leaders of the blind, apart from their relation to Christ, through which they only became more blind. For nothing but such a previously existing blindness could, as being misunderstood and denied, bring down upon them the judgment of blindness. And it was this charge on the part of Christ that excited the pride of the Pharisees to the extreme of rebellion. But this moral perturbation was itself a proof how well grounded was the reproach. 'It was a manifest sign of their blindness,' says *Quesnel,* 'that they knew not that they were blind.'"—*Hengstenberg.*

Ver. 41.—"*Jesus said unto them, If ye were blind, ye should* (R. V. WOULD) *have no sin: but now ye say, We see; therefore your sin remaineth.*" This seems to mean, If you were spiritually blind for want of capacity, or means to obtain sight, ye would have no sin; as in chap. xv. 22. "*No sin;*" that is, none of the guilt of shutting out the light. But inasmuch as you say that you do see, that you claim vision, and at the same time you are rejecting Me, you seal your guilt of unbelief.

HOMILETICS

These verses present to us *Christ's Mission.* Christ Himself tells us why He came into the world; and it is certainly well to have an explanation of the reason of His advent from His own lips. In relation to His advent, as here stated, two remarks are suggested.

I —THAT HIS MISSION TO THE WORLD HAS TWO APPARENTLY OPPOSITE RESULTS

It was to give sight, and to make blind. "*That they which see not might see; and that they which see might be made blind.*"

First: The one result is the greatest *blessing;* the other, the greatest *curse.* "*That they which see not might see.*" All men in an unregenerate state are spiritually blind: God and the great spiritual universe are as much concealed from them as the ten thousand objects and beauties of this mundane scene are from those who from their birth have been physically blind. They walk in darkness, and have no light. They grope their way through this life and stumble on into the great future. A greater blessing is not conceivable than the opening of the spiritual eye. It involves the translation of the soul into the real Paradise of being. This

Christ came to do, this was His purpose. The other result is a great curse. " *That they which see might be made blind.*" Which means this:—that those who are unconscious of their blindness, and conceitedly fancy they see, are still stone-blind, and would be incalculably injured. By rejecting the remedial agency of Christ, they would augment their guilt and intensify their moral gloom. These two results of Christ's mission are taking place every day. The Gospel must prove either the "savour of life unto life," or of " death unto death."

Secondly: The one result is *intentional,* the other *incidental.* The grand purpose of Christ was, to give spiritual illumination. He came to preach "the recovery of sight to the blind." But the other result is *incidental,* and directly opposed to His supreme aim. It comes because Christ does not coerce men, does not interfere with their liberty, treats them as free agents, and also because of the perversity of the unregenerate heart. Spiritual illumination takes place *by* His will, spiritual blindness *against* His will. In both cases the human will is free. As men may get food out of the earth or poison, fire out of the sun that shall burn them to ashes, or a genial light that shall cheer and invigorate them, so men might get salvation or damnation out of Christ's mission. It is suggested—

II —THAT HIS MISSION TO THE WORLD IS MISINTERPRETED
AND ABUSED

First: Misinterpreted. " *And some of the Pharisees which were with Him heard these words, and said unto Him, Are we blind also?* " Dost Thou mean to say that *we*—educated men trained in the laws and religion of our forefathers and devoted to the work of teaching the nation—are *blind?* They did not seem to understand that our Saviour meant by spiritual blindness, blindness of heart. So it has ever been. Men misinterpret the grand purpose of Christ's mission. Some treat the Gospel as if its grand object is to give a speculative creed, an ecclesiastical polity, a civil government, or a social order and refinement, while they practically ignore the fact that its *grand* object is to open the spiritual eyes of men, so that they may see, not the mere forms and phenomena of being, but the spiritual realities that underlie all existing substances. His mission to the world is—

Secondly: Abused. " *Jesus said unto them, If ye were blind, ye should have no sin: but now ye say, We see; therefore your sin remaineth.*" Notwithstanding My mission, " *ye say, We see.*" With Me you have the opportunity of being spiritually illuminated; if you had not such an opportunity, your blindness would be a tremendous calamity, but now it is a crime. " *Therefore your sin remaineth.*" If, like the man whose physical eyes I have just opened, you were without the power of seeing, and had not the opportunity of being cured, you would have no sin; for no man is required to use a power he does not possess. Your spiritual blindness is a crime. What should we think of a man living in the midst of beautiful scenery, with the light of heaven streaming on him every day, and possessing eyes healthy and powerful enough to descry all the beauties, but refusing day after day for years to open those eyes? We should say he was either mad or under the influence of some strange enchantment. But the case of men who are spiritually blind, with the faculties of reason and conscience and the sun of the Gospel streaming on them, is worse than this. " Men love darkness rather than light because their deeds are evil."

John 10:1-16

THE GOOD SHEPHERD

"Verily, verily, I say unto you, He that entereth not by the door into the sheepfold, but climbeth up some other way, the same is a thief and a robber," &c.

EXEGETICAL REMARKS.—Ver. 1.— " *Verily, verily, I say unto you, He that entereth not by the door into the sheepfold* (R. V. FOLD OF THE SHEEP), *but climbeth up some other way, the same is a thief and a robber.*" This discourse on the Good Shepherd seems a continuation of the closing verses of the preceding chapter. The figure of a shepherd and sheep was familiar to the Jewish ear (see Jer. xxiii. ; Ezek. xxxiv. ; Zech. xi. &c.). " 'This simple creature, the sheep,' says *Luther*, as quoted by Stier, 'has this special note among all animals, that it quickly hears the voice of the shepherd, follows no one else, depends entirely on him, and seeks help from him alone, cannot help itself, but is shut up to another's aid.' "—*Dr. Brown.* Christ here exposes the hypocrisy of the religious teachers of the Jews, by stating what He as a true Teacher was. " *The shepherd that entereth not by the door into the sheepfold, the same is a thief and a robber.*" He means to say that there were such shepherds, He was not. In all ages there have been those who have intruded themselves into the Church of God as pastors. Ver. 2.—" *But he that entereth in*

by the door is the shepherd of the sheep." "There is a right and legitimate way into this high office, and he who enters through that way is the true shepherd."

Ver. 3.—" *To him the porter openeth.*" To him the man authorized to guard the entrance gives a free and ready access. " *And the sheep hear his voice.*" In the East the shepherd and his flock are so identified that they easily detect his voice from all other human voices. " *He calleth his own sheep by name, and leadeth them out.*" As we give names to some of our cattle, so the Eastern shepherd gives names to each of his flock ; he calleth them by name and they follow him.

Ver. 4.—" *And when he putteth forth his own sheep* (R. V. WHEN HE HATH PUT FORTH ALL HIS OWN), *he goeth before them, and the sheep follow him: for they know his voice.*" In this country, and in Greece, the shepherds drive the sheep before them. But not so in the East. There is a closer affinity between them, and the sheep follow him.

Ver. 5.—" *And a stranger will they not follow, but will flee from him: for they know not the voice of strangers.*" Strangers will frighten them away.

" What is said in these three verses, though admitting of important *application* to every faithful shepherd of God's flock, is in its direct and highest sense true only of the 'Great Shepherd of the sheep,' who in the first five verses seems plainly; under the simple character of a true shepherd, to be drawing His own portrait."— *Brown.*

Ver. 6.—" *This parable spake Jesus unto them : but they understood not what things they were which He spake unto them.*" What Christ said was totally incomprehensible to the Pharisees because of the idea which they entertained of their office.

Ver. 7.—" *Then said Jesus* (R. V. JESUS SAID THEREFORE) *unto them again, Verily, verily, I say unto you, I am the door of the sheep.*" Here is the explanation, which He introduces in a solemn way. " *Verily, verily.*" " Christ is both the Door and the Shepherd and everything ; no one else can suffice."—*Bengel.*

Ver. 8.—" *All that ever came* (R. V. ALL THAT CAME) *before Me are thieves and robbers: but the sheep did not hear them.*" Does He mean by this, that all religious teachers that preceded Him—the patriarchs, Moses, and the prophets—were unauthorized teachers? Such was the interpretation of the ancient Gnostics, a professedly Christian sect. Dr. Davidson's translation, " All that ever came are thieves and robbers ; but the sheep did not hear them," does not meet the difficulty. But Dr. Lange's, " All that ever came instead of Me (ἦλθον πρὸ ἐμοῦ) are thieves and robbers," does. All who profess to take Christ's place, to fulfil His mission, are thieves and robbers. The words, I think, must be taken as they stand. There is no authority for any alteration.

Ver. 9.—" *I am the door : by Me if any man enter in, he shall be saved, and shall go in and out* (R. V. GO OUT), *and find* (R. V. SHALL FIND) *pasture.*" Shall go in and out into all the duties and privileges of life freely, and find safety and nourishment in all.

Ver. 10.—" *The thief cometh not, but for to* (R. V. THAT HE MAY) *steal, and to kill, and to destroy.*" False teachers are dishonest and destructive to the Church of God. " *I am come* (R. V. CAME) *that they might* (R. V. MAY) *have life, and that they might* (R. V. MAY) *have it more* (R. V. OMITS MORE) *abundantly,*" or in more abundance. The true Shepherd comes, not only to give them true life, but true life in abundance.

Ver. 11.—" *I am the good Shepherd : the good Shepherd giveth* (R. V. LAYETH DOWN) *his life for the sheep.*" I, Ἐγώ emphatically repeated, am the ideal Shepherd (Ps. xxiii. ; Isa. xl. 11 ; Ezek. xxxiv. 11).

Vers. 12, 13.—" *But he that is an hireling, and not the* (R. V. A) *shepherd, whose own the sheep are not, seeth* (R. V. BEHOLDETH) *the wolf coming, and leaveth the sheep, and fleeth : and the wolf catcheth* (R. V. SNATCHETH) *them, and scattereth the sheep*" (R. V. THEM). The hireling, the man who does his work for filthy lucre, is no true shepherd. He does not care for the flock, but for the fleece. Hence, when the wolf or any threatening destroyer appears, scattering the sheep, the hireling, instead of risking his life, fleeth.

Ver. 14.—" *I am the good Shepherd, and know My sheep* (R. V. I KNOW MINE OWN), *and am known of Mine*" (R. V. MINE OWN KNOW ME). " The proof of this character : *I know them that are Mine;* and the fact of the indissoluble connection with the flock, with true believers, whom the Father has given Him, here expressed by the relation of *mutual acquaintance.* True, this knowing does not mean *loving;* but it is still an emphatic expression, by which a loving knowledge is implied. It is the expression of the personal, Divine cognition of kindred personalities. The grace of Christ is such a cognition of His own on His part. Faith, on the other hand, is a corresponding cognition of Christ on their part."—*Lange.*

Ver. 15.—" *As the Father* (R.V. EVEN AS THE FATHER) *knoweth Me, even so know I* (R. V. AND I KNOW) *the Father.*" This verse is connected with the former, and the idea seems to be, that there is some similitude between the mutual love subsisting between Him and His Father. " *I lay down My life for the sheep.*" So far from being an hireling, He is self-sacrificing to the highest degree.

Ver. 16.—"*And other sheep I have, which are not of this fold : them also I must bring, and they shall hear My voice; and there shall be one fold* (R. v. SHALL BECOME ONE FLOCK), *and one Shepherd.*" "*Other sheep !*" Who are they ? Undoubtedly the Gentiles, the heathen. Christ has an invisible Church even in heathendom. All good men will one day meet and form one fold, and have one Shepherd.

HOMILETICS

Let us gather up all the wonderful things that are said here by this Good Shepherd Himself concerning His flock. At the outset, we have here to remark on the amazing *self-assertion* of Christ. "*I am the good Shepherd,*" He says, and more,—He proclaims all that ever came before Him as "*thieves and robbers.*" Nor is this self-assertion here singular in Christ's utterances. Elsewhere He says, "I am the Light of the world ; " I am the "Bread of Life." Again, "I am the Resurrection," &c. &c. Were any mere man to speak of himself in this way, we should denounce him as an inflated egotist. And yet His title, "Son of God," the wonders He performed, His resurrection from the dead, &c., all seem to justify such utterances from Him. They chime in with His whole biography. But what does He say Himself about the "*Good Shepherd*"?

I —THAT THE "GOOD SHEPHERD" APPROACHES HIS FLOCK IN AN HONEST WAY

He does not, like "*the thief*" and the robber, scale the fences, but He "*entereth in through the door.*" Christ comes to men *honestly.* He declares who He is, and every part of His life furnishes the credentials. There is not the slightest shadow of the cunning, the dissimulating, the sophistic, which characterize all impostors. His statements are unmistakable, His character transparent, His whole life as open as the day. He stands before humanity and challenges their most rigorous scrutiny. To all He says, "Which of you convinceth Me of sin ? " No religious teacher so interpretable in His utterances, so frank in His life, as Jesus of Nazareth. He "*entereth in through the door ;*" He deals with men honestly. He teaches—

II —THAT THE "GOOD SHEPHERD" AND HIS FLOCK MUTUALLY RECOGNIZE EACH OTHER

"*The porter openeth ; and the sheep hear his voice : and he calleth his own sheep by name, and leadeth them out. And when he putteth forth his own sheep, he goeth before them, and the sheep follow him : for they know his voice.*" "In this northern England," says *Robertson,* " it is hard to get the living associations of the East, or the relation between the shepherd and the sheep. The pastoral life and duty in the East is very unlike that of the shepherds on our bleak hillsides and downs. Here the connection between the shepherd and the sheep is simply one of pecuniary interest. Ask an English shepherd about his flock, he can tell you the numbers and their value; he knows the market in which each was purchased, and the remunerating price at which it can be disposed of. They are before him so much stock, convertible into so much money. Beneath the burning skies and the clear starry nights of Palestine, there grows up between the shepherd and his flock an union of attachment and tenderness. It is the country where at any moment sheep are liable to be swept away by some mountain torrent, or carried off by hill-robbers, or torn by wolves. At any moment their protector may have to save them by personal hazard. The shepherd-king tells us how, in defence of his father's flock, he slew a lion and a bear; and Jacob reminds Laban how, when he watched Laban's sheep in the day, the drought continued. Every hour of the shepherd's life is risk. Sometimes for the sake of an armful of grass, in the parched summer days, he must climb precipices almost perpendicular, and stand on a narrow ledge of rocks, where the wild goat will scarcely venture. Pitiless showers, driving snows, long hours of thirst; all this he must endure, if the flock is to be kept at all. And then there grows up between the man and the dumb creatures he protects a kind of friendship. For this is, after all, the true school in which love is taught—dangers mutually shared, and hardships borne together; these are the things which make generous friendship—risk cheerfully encountered for another's sake. You love those for whom you risk, and they love you; therefore it is that, not as here, where the flock is driven, the shepherd goes before, and the sheep follow him. They follow him in perfect trust, even though he should be leading them away from green pasture, by a rocky road, to another pasture which they cannot yet see. He knows them all, their separate histories, their ailments, their characters."

"*He leadeth them out.*" He does not drive them. He always goes before His disciples. He is always in advance. They follow Him; there is a moral magnetism; they know His voice. "*They know his voice, and a stranger will they not follow.*" As the loving child knows the tones of a mother's voice, the genuine disciple recognizes the voice of Christ. They cannot be deceived. There is a spiritual instinct that is an infallible guide—the instinct of love, the instinct of intense mutual sympathy. He teaches—

III —THAT THE "GOOD SHEPHERD" IS TO HIS FLOCK THE
MEDIUM OF ALL GOOD

"*I am the door.*" "*Then said Jesus unto them again, . . . I am the door of the sheep.** *All that ever came before Me are thieves*
* See Germ, p. 285.

and robbers: but the sheep did not hear them. I am the Door: by Me if any man enter in, he shall be saved, and shall go in and out, and find pasture. The thief cometh not, but for to steal, and to kill, and to destroy." This could be explained philosophically.

First: Without supreme sympathy with God, no man can find real liberty, safety, and nourishment in anything. A man whose heart is dominated by love to the mighty Maker of the universe, can *"go in and out"* everywhere, into business and out of business, into church and out of church, into literature and out of literature, into recreation and out of recreation, and not only feel *free*, but be *safe* and *nourished*. But no man without this love can do it. He will feel more or less fettered in everything, in peril everywhere, and lacking the true food of his being.

Secondly: Without Christ, no man can get this supreme sympathy with God. He alone can generate it. This He has done in millions of instances, this He is doing now, hence He is the *" door."* He is the door into the enjoyment of nature, life, and God. *"I am the door: no man cometh unto the Father but by Me."* He teaches—

IV —THAT THE " GOOD SHEPHERD " HAS SELF-SACRIFICING LOVE FOR HIS FLOCK

" The thief cometh not, but for to steal, and to kill, and to destroy : I am come that they might have life, and that they might have it more abundantly.* I am the Good Shepherd : the Good Shepherd giveth his life for the sheep." The Church in all ages has had pastors that have acted the *" thief."* They have been religious impostors and crafty priests. It has had those, too, who have acted the *hireling*, doing their work merely for filthy lucre, mercenary ministers.

"The hungry sheep look up and are not fed."

It has had those, also, that have acted the wolf. Like Laud and Bonner, they have been bloody persecutors, devouring the flock. In sublime contrast with this, Jesus says, *" I am come that ye might have life, and that ye might have it more abundantly."* He came, not only to give them life and happiness, but abundance or fulness of an endless felicity. He teaches—

V —THAT THE " GOOD SHEPHERD " HAS AN INTERPRETING SYMPATHY WITH HIS FLOCK

Love laone can interpret love. "If any man love God, the same is known of Him" (1 Cor. viii. 3). *"I am the Good Shepherd, and know My sheep, and am known of Mine. As the Father knoweth Me, even so know I the Father: and I lay down My life for the sheep."* This means, We know each other as the Father and I know each other, by a deep mysterious sympathy. Elevating and consolatory

* See Germ, p. 288.

is the fact that Christ not only knows His disciples—knows all about each, all the actualities and possibilities of their being—but He reads their hearts—knows their inner selves. "*He calleth His own sheep by name.*" As God gave names to all the hosts of heaven and knows all about them, so Christ has given names to His disciples. He knows not only who they are and where they are, but *what* they are, and what they will be through all the ages of the future.

> "As the good shepherd leads his sheep
> Through paths secure,
> And, while a-fold by night they sleep,
> Doth keep them sure ;
> So the true Shepherd, Christ, our souls doth guide,
> Safe in His eye, protected by His side."

He teaches—

VI—THAT THE "GOOD SHEPHERD" GATHERS HIS SHEEP, WHEREVER THEY ARE, INTO THE COMMON FOLD

"*And other sheep I have, which are not of this fold : them also I must bring, and they shall hear My voice ; and there shall be one fold, and one shepherd.*" "*Other sheep I have.*" Where are they ? Where are they not ? Is there a tribe or a race under heaven where they are not found ? "They shall come from the east, and from the west, and from the north, and from the south, and shall sit down" with Abraham, Isaac, and Jacob in the kingdom of heaven.

"I beheld, and lo, a great multitude, which no man could number, of all nations, and kindreds, and people, and tongues, stood before the throne, and before the Lamb, clothed with white robes, and palms in their hands " (Rev. vii. 9).

Germs of Thought
No. 36   John 10:9

CHRIST THE DOOR
"I am the door."

Wonderful is the condescension as well as the wisdom of Christ in representing Himself to man under a vast variety of imagery. He not only selects some of the grandest objects in nature, the loftiest offices in social life, and the greatest things in human art, to set forth some aspects of His transcendent character, but also some of the most insignificant objects are chosen to emblemize Himself. Here, for example, He speaks of Himself as the "*door.*" Using the figure we observe—

I—HE IS THE "DOOR" INTO THE FULL ENJOYMENT OF NATURE

We lay it down as a fact that admits of no rational debate, that supreme sympathy with the Creator is an essential qualification for a full enjoyment of nature. The impression which a beautiful painting makes upon us is wondrously heightened by a love for the artist : our admiration for a noble poem is strongly intensified by a love for the author. Productions looked upon through a love for the author have attributes of power and fascination of which otherwise they are entirely destitute. Men of poetic sensibility may be charmed with certain features and phases of nature ; men of science may admire the exquisite wisdom displayed in infinite variety in all its arrangements; but it is only the man whose soul is filled with a supreme love for his Maker that can enter fully into its enjoyments. Nature to him is the production and the photogram of the chief object of his love, the garden in which his spirit walks in the cool of the day, and feels all to be vocal with the loving sentiments of his Father. Now who can generate this supreme sympathy in the human heart towards its Maker but Christ ? This He does—(1.) By the most powerful demonstration of Divine love : and (2.) By the most commanding manifestation of Divine excellence.

II —HE IS THE " DOOR " INTO AN UNDERSTANDING OF PROVIDENTIAL DISPENSATIONS

Heaven's system of dealing with man in this world is a long series of insoluble inquiries viewed apart from Christ. There is no way of reconciling its ever-transpiring events either with our innate sense of justice, *à priori* conclusions of reason, or with our deductions of expediency as drawn from the experience of mankind. Now Christ teaches two things concerning Providence which gives a grand consistency to the whole system.

First: He teaches that it is *mediatory*. He gives us to understand through the whole of His Gospel that men are not dealt with here now on the ground of their own character, but on the ground of merciful *mediation*.

Secondly : He teaches that it is *disciplinary*. His Gospel gives us the idea that human life here is a school for the ignorant, a hospital for the diseased, &c. Hence the mingling of so much of the painful with the agreeable. " Our light affliction, which is but for a moment," &c.

III —HE IS THE " DOOR " INTO A TRUE MEMBERSHIP WITH THE CHURCH

Some would represent the *Church* as the door of Christ. This is a great mistake. By the Church of course I do not mean a mere ecclesiastical institution, whether Papal, Episcopal, Presbyterian, Independent, or Wesleyan. Into such, men may and do enter, by subscription to certain dogmas and submission to certain rites. But by the Church I mean the great community of regenerated spirits who are represented as the friends of Christ, the children of God.

Members of this *community* are limited to no particular ecclesiastical system; they are in heaven as well as on earth. They are the saved ones; they are the flock of which Christ is the Shepherd, the kingdom of which Christ is the King. This is the Church, and none other. Now it is obvious that into this Church none can enter but through Christ. He is "*the door*": through Him and Him only men are regenerated in spirit, adopted into the family of heaven, and saved from all that imperils the interest and the happiness of their souls. The Church is not the "*door*" to Christ, nor is any priesthood the "*door*" to the Church. Christ is "*the door*." We do not ask what conventional Church you have entered, for all are more or less defective; but we ask, Have you entered the Church of which you are a member through this "*Door*"? If so, well.

IV —HE IS THE "DOOR" INTO THE UNIVERSAL PARADISE OF GOD

Through Christ man comes into the possession of "all things." "All things are yours," said the apostle. The Christian man has a priceless property, and a vital interest in all things—all things in this world, and in the world to come also. The kingdom of universal goodness is prepared for him; he enters even into the "joy of his Lord," and sits down upon the throne with Him. He has access direct to that fruit of the tree of life, which is at once the ornament and sustenance of the spiritual universe. He has access to that river which rolls from beneath the throne of God. This is heaven, and Christ is the "Way"—the only Way thereto. Not one of all the millions of sainted spirits above has entered the celestial world but through Christ.

Brother: Christ is in truth the "*Door*" to all enjoyment. Nothing is of any real or permanent service to thee but as thou approachest it through Christ; and whatever thou reachest through Him, however apparently insignificant and worthless, will contribute to thy highest weal. Entering thus through Him, thou art safe and free, and hast pasture everywhere. "By Me if any man enter in"—into business, recreation, science, literature, or religion—"he shall be saved, and shall go in and out"—move freely through the universe—"and shall find pasture"—shall get good out of everything. Enter whatever thou dost enter—business, religion, or recreation —through Christ, and thou shalt be free, safe, and fed in everything.

> "Is He a door?—I'll enter in,
> Behold the pasture, large and green:
> A paradise divinely fair,
> None but the sheep have freedom there."—*Watts.*

No. 37   John 10:10

THE PHILANTHROPY OF CHRIST'S MISSION

"I am come that they might have life."

These words suggest at the outset three ideas about Christ—

First: That He existed before His appearance in our world. *"I am come."* Whence? *Plato* entertained the idea that all souls had an existence anterior to their connection with the body. This may be true or false. But Christ's pre-existence is distinctly taught—(John i. 10; iii. 13; xvii. 5; Eph. iii. 3; Phil. ii. 5—6; Col. i. 14—17).

Secondly: That His existence in our world is the result of His own voluntary determination. *"I am come."* Not one of our race can be said to have *"come"* into the world. We have been sent. We had no voice or power in the question as to whether we should be, or not be, or as to whether we should be here or elsewhere—this or that. But Christ had this power.

Thirdly: That His determination to come into our world was swayed by love for man. *"I am come that they might have life."* The subject which we shall now give attention is—the *Philanthropy of Christ's mission;* and in illustrating this we make three observations—

I —THAT THE OBJECT OF HIS MISSION IS CONTRARY TO WHAT MIGHT HAVE BEEN EXPECTED

Let us suppose that we are told, for the first time, two things. (1.) That there is in God's universe a province of moral beings who had renounced their allegiance to their Maker, and who for forty centuries had rebelled against His authority, spurned the overtures of His mercy, and persecuted the messengers of His love. (2.) That He resolves upon visiting that province in a special and extraordinary way—going down in person to it. Having been informed of these two things, suppose the question were propounded to us: What will be the object of His mission? We think that the answer would be prompt and decisive. We should say *punishment:* He would descend robed in terror with the sword of justice. Two things would urge us to the conclusion:—(*a.*) That justice must some day show herself in connection with sin. She will not sleep for ever. (*b.*) That mercy had been exercised sufficiently long towards that province. Four thousand years is a long period for mercy. All this applies exactly to our world; and yet Christ comes *"that we might have life."*

II —THAT THE OBJECT OF HIS MISSION WAS THE BESTOWMENT OF THE HIGHEST BLESSING ON HUMANITY

"That they might have life."

First: He gives corporeal life. Corporeal death comes by sin. I will grant three facts, and yet hold this Biblical doctrine intelligently and tenaciously. (1.) That death was in the world before sin. (2.) That the human body, like all material organizations, tends to decomposition. (3.) That this globe is not adequate to the sustentation of a perpetual multiplication of the race. Albeit on one indisputable fact I base my faith : that the continuation of a creature's existence, for a day, a millennium, or for ever, depends entirely upon the purpose of the Creator. And His purpose is that we "*might have life.*" And this includes *corporeal* life. It is true that you do not see the accomplishment of this purpose yet. The graveyard is as still and quiet as ever. But the purpose of the faithful and Almighty mind is formed and virtually done. "One day with Him is as a thousand years." Christ has the key of every grave at His girdle. The trumpet will one day sound, and the graves will be opened; "the hour cometh, and now is, when all that are in their graves," &c. By resurrection is not necessarily meant the resurrection of the relics of the buried body.

Secondly : He gives spiritual life. Men are represented as spiritually dead. The valley of "dry bones" is not an inappropriate representation of the state of souls. Why is the depraved spirit represented as dead ? Another question will answer this : What are the ideas you generally attach to death ? (1.) Perhaps you say the extinction of some *principle.* You look at the corpse, and you feel that the mysterious something which coursed through those veins, moved those limbs, beamed through those glazed eyes, is gone out. It is so with the soul. Love to God, the principle of spiritual life, which once inspired and worked those faculties is gone out. (2.) Perhaps you say *separation.* [You look at the corpse, and you feel the soul is gone from it,—the agent has left the instrument, and the instrument is therefore silent and motionless. The branch is cut from the root, and is withered; the star is turned from its centre, and is in darkness. So with the soul separated from God. (3.) Or perhaps you say *subjection.* You look at the corpse, and you see that which, when life was in it, subordinated the outward elements to its own health and vigour, now the sport of all. The sunbeam that cheered it, the air that heaved its lungs with life, all the gases that contributed to its energy, now contribute to its utter corruption. So it is with the soul. The outward circumstances in which it is placed, which were intended to brace and strengthen it, subordinate it to their capricious forces, and work out its ruin. (4.) Or perhaps you say *loathsomeness.* That dead body which a few days ago was so beautiful, is now offensive. Love itself says, "Give me ground to bury my dead out of my sight." So it is with the depraved soul. Its falsehood, vanity, selfishness, and carnality render it loathsome to all living souls. "Do not I hate them, O God, that hate Thee ? " When you say, therefore, that the soul is dead, it is no figure.

Corporeal death is in truth but a faint symbol and figure of this. Now Christ is come, that we might have spiritual life. He is come to resuscitate the extinct principle, to unite it to its true Source of life—God; to invest it with a power to subordinate all outward circumstances to its use; and to adorn it with the beauties of holiness.

Let us look for a moment at this blessing, in order to value the gift of Christ.

(*a*) Life is the divinest thing. Wherever there is life, there is God in an especial sense. No one can give life but Him. Art has reached wonderful perfection; it can mimic life in the marble and on the canvas. The picture of Cowper's mother seems to have been a very perfect one: on the reception of it the filial poet exclaimed—

"Those lips are thine; thine own sweet smile I see."

But as he looked at it in all the hue and form and expression of life, with her sweet eye fastening as it were upon her son, he felt that it was only a picture. No warm blood coursed through those veins, there was no motion in those limbs, no vision in those eyes; and with sadness he exclaims again—

"O that those lips had language!"

Life is the emanation of God—no creature can give it. Life is the Divinest thing on this earth. Spiritual life is Divine.

(*b*) Life is the dearest thing. Every living creature struggles to preserve it. Sometimes I fancy that even the grass beneath my tread shrinks at the injury I inflict. It is so with spiritual life; where it is there is a constant struggle to preserve it.

(*c*) Life is the mightiest thing. The storm is mighty; but life is mightier: the trees of the forest get strength from its fury. Gravitation is mighty; but life is mightier. The power that chains the ocean to its bed, and binds planets to their centre, is conquered by the little lark that pours down her music from the clouds. Take her life from her, and gravitation will bring her down.

Because life is thus the Divinest, the dearest, and the mightiest thing in the world, the great blessing which Christ imparts is called Life. Notice—

III —THAT THE OBJECT OF HIS MISSION IS TO BESTOW THE HIGHEST BLESSING ON HUMANITY IN AN ABUNDANT DEGREE

"*That they might have it more abundantly.*" The idea I take to be this, that Christ will not only restore lost life to man, but restore it in a greatly advanced measure—that He will give back to man more than sin took away. "Where sin abounded, grace will much more abound."

Let us, to illustrate this, draw a comparison between spiritual life in its original form in Adam, and spiritual life in its Christian form in the restored.

First: It is more abundant in the guarantees of its continuance in the Christian form. In Eden what a feeble thing it was—what a slight circumstance destroyed it! We, if Christians, resist temptations every day, a thousand times as strong as those which Adam yielded to. Take Adam and Paul. A little prohibited fruit is presented to Adam,—he yields. The greatest persecutions, obloquy, insults and perils, are presented to Paul to turn him away; and he says, "None of these things move me," &c. "I give unto My sheep," says Christ, "eternal life: neither shall any pluck them out of My hands."

Secondly: It is more abundant in the amount of benevolent inspiration in the Christian form. The circumstance that Adam, to excuse his own guilty act, referred the blame to the partner of his life, shows that his soul could never have been the seat of very broad generous sympathies. It is contrary to the laws of mind to suppose that the soul passes at a bound from broad benevolent sympathies to the meanest selfishness. Compare with this the benevolent sympathies which Christianity gives. On one occasion Peter came to Christ (Matt. xviii. 21) and said, "Lord, how oft shall my brother sin against me, and I forgive him? till seven times." The Apostle, no doubt, thought this marvellously generous, but Christ said, "Seventy times seven," *i. e.* there is to be no limit. Take Stephen when dying, &c.

Thirdly: It is more abundant in the honours it secures in the Christian form. I know not what honours man might have inherited if he had retained his innocence; no doubt he would have moved on for ever in a progressive course of dignity and blessedness; but he never would, I think, have seen his own nature in personal connection with God. This we see. Who is in the midst of the throne now?—*A Man.* Who will judge the world at last?— *A Man.*

Fourthly: It is more abundant in the influence which it exerts in the Christian form. Spirit life in Adam would not have been powerful enough to convert sinners. It had neither the argument nor the impulse; but in Christianity it has. "It casts down every imagination; every thing that exalts itself."

Brothers, under what obligation are we to Christ! He is our Life! What a test you have by which to determine whether the object of His mission has been realized in your case! Have you this Life? How clearly does it point out what should be the grand aim of our existence! It is to give Life.

John 10:17, 18

THE TRANSCENDENT ELEMENT IN MORAL CHARACTER

"Therefore doth My Father love Me, because I lay down My life, that I might take it again. No man taketh it from Me, but I lay it down of Myself. I have power to lay it down, and I have power to take it again. This commandment have I received of My Father."

EXEGETICAL REMARKS.—Ver. 17.— *"Therefore doth My* (R. V. THE) *Father love Me, because I lay down My life, that I might* (R. V. MAY) *take it again."* What cause? Christ's self-sacrificing love for His sheep. *"I lay down My life"*—devote it to the good of mankind. In order that I might take it again. This has been suggested to mean—"This evidence will there be of My Father's love to Me, that, having laid down My life, I shall receive it again."

Ver. 18.—*"No man* (R. V. ONE) *taketh it from* (R. V. AWAY FROM) *Me,*

but I lay it down of Myself. I have power to lay it down, and I have power to take it again." Here He announces absolute power over His own existence, and His voluntary sacrifice of that existence. He did not die by necessity. He died because He willed it ; He rose because He willed it. *"This commandment have I received* (R. V. RECEIVED I) *of My Father."* His self-sacrifice and His resurrection from the dead were by the will of His Father. "Him, being delivered by the determinate counsel and foreknowledge of God," &c.

HOMILETICS

Our subject is *the transcendent element in moral character.*

In these words we find Christ declaring four of the most significant and important facts that can possibly engage our attention.

I —THAT HE HAD AN ABSOLUTE POWER OVER HIS OWN EXISTENCE

"I have power to lay it down, and I have power to take it again." Of all the millions of men that ever appeared on this earth, Jesus of Nazareth was the only Man that could justly claim His own existence. He was His *own Proprietor.* All other men are bound to say, We "are not our own." Not a particle of the body, not a faculty of the mind can we claim as our own : all belongs to another ; all souls are His. But whilst men are the mere trustees of their existence, Christ was the Owner of His. Being thus His own, He had a right to do with Himself whatever accorded with His desires. He could lay down this possession and take it up whenever, however, and wherever He pleased. Wonderful property ! Life ! a far greater thing than to own a world.

He declares—

II —THAT THE LAYING DOWN OF HIS OWN EXISTENCE WAS ENTIRELY HIS OWN VOLUNTARY ACT

"No man taketh it from Me." His whole biography shows, and the mighty miracles that He performed, that no human power could take His life from Him if He had willed otherwise. He did not die because of disease or age or human violence, but because He

willed to die. Indeed, in laying down His life, there was something more than *willingness* on His part. We have read of good men—aye, we have known them—who have been willing to die. They have said with Paul, "I desire to depart." But all these men knew right well that death in their case was *unavoidable,* that they could not live here for ever. All that their willingness meant, therefore, was, that they would as soon die then and there, as somewhere else and at some other time. It was not so with Christ. There was no necessity for His dying. He might have lived here or anywhere else for ever. He died simply because He willed it; He willed His life away. "Father, into Thy hands I commit My spirit." It is this voluntariness that gives infinite moral might and merit to His. death. It invests His cross with a force sublimely unique and ever growing—a force that has already wrought mighty revolutions in the world, and that will one day work out the spiritual reformation of humanity.

He declares—

III —THAT ON ACCOUNT OF THIS VOLUNTARY SELF-SACRIFICE HIS FATHER LOVED HIM

"*Therefore doth My Father love Me,*" &c. The relation of the Father to the Son is an impenetrable mystery. We can only think of them as distinct from each other, and one holding a position in some way subordinate to the other. The Father *loves.* He is not sheer intellect or heartless force, but has *sensibility,* and His sensibility is instinct with love. He *is* love. He loves His Son. His great heart seems to centre in Him. Why does He love Him? Because there is something morally lovable in Him. What is that? Here we are told what that is—*His self-sacrificing spirit.* This spirit is the very essence of all virtue, and the fountain of all goodness and beneficence. It is the very inspiration of God Himself, as is demonstrated in the works of nature. No moral intelligence in the universe who has it not can be by Him loved with esteem. Christ had it in an immeasurable degree. Hence His unbounded love for Him. "*Therefore doth My Father love Me, because I lay down My life, that I might take it again.*" Would we secure the love of the Infinite? Let us free ourselves from all selfishness, and come under the dominion of that "charity which seeketh not her own."

He declares—

IV —THAT HIS SELF-SACRIFICING SPIRIT WAS ACCORDING TO THE WILL OF THE ETERNAL

"*This commandment have I received of My Father.*" It was God's will that Christ should be so actuated by this spirit as to give His life for the moral redemption of mankind. And the "*commandment*" that Christ received of the Father is binding on every living man. Conscience and the Bible tell us this. Every man should be "conformed to His death," should have that same spirit that led Him to the cross. Unless we have in us His self-sacrificing spirit, His sacrifice on the cross will be no service to us. "Bear each other's burdens, and so fulfil the law of Christ." "If any man have not the spirit of Christ, he is none of His." "He died for all, that they which live should not henceforth live unto themselves, but Him which died for them, and rose again." "Hereby perceive we the love of God, because He laid down His life for us: and we ought to lay down our lives for the brethren." Such passages as these assure us that "*this commandment*" we too have received of the Father, and should act in all things with self-sacrificing love.

CONCLUSION. Where are the Churches, where are the ministers, who are ruled by "*this commandment*"? When this "*commandment*" governs the Churches, the world will be converted—not before.

John 10:19-21

A BAD SPIRIT AND A SOUND ARGUMENT

"There was a division therefore again among the Jews for these sayings. And many of them said, He hath a devil, and is mad; why hear ye Him? Others said, These are not the words of Him that hath a devil. Can a devil open the eyes of the blind?"

EXEGETICAL REMARKS.—Ver. 19.—"*There was* (R. V. AROSE) *a division therefore again among the Jews.*" Christ having finished the discourse in which He was interrupted by the Pharisees (in chap. ix. ver. 40), that discourse including reproofs, monitions, and sublime truths in relation to His death, the crowd seemed to continue about Him all the while, and often interrupted Him, as in chap. ix. 17—43. Their opinions concerning Himself and what He said were by no means in accord. And here at the close there is a division—literally, a *schism*.

Ver. 20.—"*And many of them said, He hath a devil, and is mad; why hear ye Him?*" He hath a devil, a demon. This they seem to have said, not to Him, but about Him behind His back; and they resolved to treat Him henceforth as a madman: treat His utterances as beneath their notice.

Ver. 24.—"*Others said, These are not the words* (R. V. SAYINGS) *of Him that hath* (R. V. ONE POSSESSED WITH) *a devil. Can a devil open the eyes of the blind?*" These belonged to the party who regarded Him as possessed with an evil spirit, a madman, and they adduced an argument, and the argument was sound until a demon opened the eyes of the blind.

HOMILETICS

In these verses we have two things worth note—*a bad spirit and a sound argument.*

I —A BAD SPIRIT

First: Here is a schismatic spirit. "*There was a division.*" Sad, that Christ and His doctrines should divide men into sects.

One might have thought that, as His life was so manifestly, so pre-eminently pure, loving, and morally commanding, and His doctrine so congruous with human reason and conscious spiritual wants, that all men would have centred in Him. Schism amongst men in relation to Christ is bad. The sects are a calumny on the Gospel, and a curse to the race.

Secondly : Here is a blasphemous spirit. "*And many of them said, He hath a devil, and is mad.*" Here is the old accusation, "He casteth out devils by Beelzebub." There are, to use the language we have elsewhere employed, two great evils which men commit on the question of moral causation—

(1.) *Some ascribe bad deeds to God.* The warrior who has rifled cities and slain his thousands, appears after his bloody achievements at the altar, to return thanks to that God Who has commanded us not to *kill*, and declared that all wars arise from "*the lusts*" of the wicked heart. The priest who presumes to stand between God and the people, by his sacerdotal services professing to propitiate Almighty Justice, ascribes his crafty deeds to God. The Islam and the Mormonite leaders, who impose upon the credulity of the ignorant, profess to have derived their authority and doctrines from Heaven. How much kingly despotism, military slaughter, priestly craft, religious imposture, and international plunder and oppression are enacted in the sacred name of God !
(2.) *Some ascribe good deeds to Satan.* These cavilling and malicious men did so. Irritated with jealousy at the impression which Christ's miracles made upon the people, so favourable to His own growing popularity, they said, with contemptuous indignation, "This fellow doth not cast out devils, but by Beelzebub, the prince of the devils." They could not deny the miracle, it was too patent to all ; the only plan they had, therefore, to resist its influence amongst the people, was to ascribe it to Satanic agency. This they did. They traced a good act to a bad cause, a Divine act to the arch foe of God. This was heinous sin. Yet the principle of this has been too common in every age. What is the conduct of those who assign all the good effects which Christianity has produced upon the world, the moral miracles it has achieved amongst the various tribes and nations of the earth, to the ingenuity and craft of impostors, and who designate the Bible a " cunningly devised fable ? " What, too, is the conduct of those who, alas ! abound in all times and lands, who are ever disposed to ascribe good acts to bad motives, and brand as hypocrites the most holy and useful men ? Why, such conduct is exactly the same in principle as that which these blaspheming scribes and Pharisees now committed.

Thirdly : Here is an intolerant spirit. "*Why hear ye Him ?*" The spirit which has characterized bigots and bloody persecutors through all Church history breathes in these words, and this spirit

296 / Gospel of John

is, alas! not extinct. *"Why hear ye Him?"* So one sect now says, in relation to a preacher of another sect.

In these verses we have,—

II —A SOUND ARGUMENT

"Others said, These are not the words of Him that hath a devil. Can a devil open the eyes of the blind?" There is no reason to believe that the devil could give eyes to the blind; and if he could, there is every reason to believe that he would not. The principle on which these men reasoned, was that which Christ Himself enunciated, "Ye shall know them by their fruits." This is an infallible test. As in the material so in the moral, men reap what they sow. Every tree beareth its own kind; a corrupt heart will have a corrupt life. The argument of these men may be thrown into a syllogistic form. An essentially malevolent being does not perform genuinely merciful deeds; the desire is essentially malevolent, and therefore this merciful deed, namely, the giving eyes to a blind man, cannot be his act. Evil deeds come from evil beings. Christianity will bear this test. Judge Christianity by its works. This is the test with which Christ sought to overcome the rising scepticism of John the Baptist. Christ says, "Go your way, and tell John what things ye have seen and heard; how that the blind," &c. &c.

John 10:22-30

RELIGIOUS SCEPTICISM

(Jesus in Jerusalem at the Feast of Dedication. He retires beyond Jordan.)
JOHN x. 22—42.
"And it was at Jerusalem the feast of the dedication, and it was winter," &c.

EXEGETICAL REMARKS.—Ver. 22.— *"And it was at Jerusalem the feast of the dedication, and it was winter."* The feast of dedication succeeded the feast of tabernacles after an interval of two months. It was established under Judas Maccabæus, after it had been desecrated by Antiochus Epiphanes, about 167 years before Christ. That monarch had trampled upon the Jewish religion, burned the books of law, established idolatry in the holy place, and offered swine's flesh upon the great altar. Judas, the triumphant hero of the Jews, having conquered him in battle, re-dedicated the temple at a period answering to our 15th of December. Hence *"it was winter."*

Ver. 23.—*"And Jesus walked* (R. V.

WAS WALKING) *in the temple in Solomon's porch."* A porch, this, outside of the temple proper, where persons could walk without exposure, and where they could be sheltered both from storms and scorching sunbeams. Here Jesus was now walking alone, not only to be sheltered from wintry blasts or showers, but no doubt to indulge in calm and devout meditation. Some of the pagan temples of Greece had porticoes for the convenience of those who attended them. Here, independent of the weather, they could stand or walk, indulge in lonely reverie, or engage in social converse. "It is curious to remark," says a modern expositor, "that from two of the words used in this verse, περιεπάτει and στοά, two philosophical sects were named respectively Peripatetics and Stoics."

Ver. 24.—" *Then came the Jews* " (R. V. THE JEWS THEREFORE) (that is, we presume, the rulers of the Jews, chap. i. 19) " *round about Him, and said unto Him, How long dost Thou make us to doubt?* " (R. V. HOLD US IN SUSPENSE.) I cannot agree with *Lange* in regarding these Jews as sincere now in their inquiry. They did not seek for truth, but they sought to entrap Him. Their religious malice thirsted for some utterance from Him that contained blasphemy, and would consequently justify them according to their law in stoning Him to death. " *If Thou be* (R. V. ART) *the Christ, tell us plainly.* " How often had He told them plainly?

Ver. 25.—" *Jesus answered them, I told you* " (in substance He had so told them, chap. vii. 37, 38 ; viii. 35, 36—58), " *and ye believed* (R. V. BELIEVE) *not : the works that I do in My Father s name, they* (R. V. THESE) *bear witness of Me.* " My works are the credentials of My Messiahship.

Ver. 26.—" *But ye believe not, because ye are not of My sheep, as I said unto you.* " (R. V. OMITS THE LAST CLAUSE.) The " *ye* " is emphatic, and stands in contrast to the sheep.

Ver. 27.—" *My sheep hear My voice, and I know them, and they follow Me.* " The meaning of this expression has been explained in the sketch on verses 1—16.

Ver. 28.—" *And I give unto them eternal life.* " I give, not I *will* give, but I impart the blessing to them now. The word " *life* " here must be taken in an ethical rather than a physical sense. Eternal existence is no blessing in itself, it may be a curse. Moral goodness is life, and moral goodness is eternal. " The soul's endless being," says *Dr. Young*, " is in intelligence, rectitude, purity, love, and all goodness." * " *They shall never perish, neither shall any man pluck* (R. V. NO ONE SHALL SNATCH) *them out of My hand.* " The soul with eternal goodness in it can " *never perish,* " nor can it ever be taken out of the " *hand* " of Christ. It is possible for Him and His Father to give it up, and then it would " *perish ;* " but will They ? Never. It is the Divine Will, and that Will is immutable and omnipotent, that not one of the " least " of His little ones shall perish.

Ver. 29.—" *My Father, which gave* (R. V. HATH GIVEN) *them Me, is greater than all ; and no man is able to pluck* (R. V. NO ONE IS ABLE TO SNATCH) *them out of My* (R. V. THE) *Father's hand.* " My Father, Who has given them to Me. If He has given them—(1.) He is their absolute Proprietor. This is undeniable ; all souls are His. If He has given them,—(2.) It must be in harmony with their own free consent. Souls cannot be given away as material objects can. They are essentially free, and the great Father would not outrage the nature of His offspring. If He has given them—(3.) It is not in such a way as to involve the renunciation of His claim upon them. When we give a thing away, we cease to have any right to it. God will never relinquish His claim to the existence, love, reverence, and service of souls. Indeed, Christ in this very passage, after speaking of them as being given to Him, says they are in His Father's hand.

Ver. 30.—" *I and My* (R. V. THE) *Father are one.* " One in moral consciousness, one in spirit, one in will. In the original it seems to mean, not one person, but one thing. The expression is analogous to that in 1 Cor. iii. 8, " He that planteth and he that watereth are one." That is, oneness of design and purpose. *Calvin* says concerning this passage : " That the ancients wrested it to prove that Christ was the same in Being with the Father ; but Christ is not discussing concerning His unity of substance, but His unity of will with the Father, to wit, that whatever was done by Him would be confirmed with power by the Father." Though other passages, I think, abundantly prove that Christ is God, this does not.

* See " The Christ of History," by Dr. Young, p. 109.

HOMILETICS

The conduct of the Jews, as recorded in these verses, suggests a few general truths in relation to *religious scepticism*.

I.—IT DOES NOT LACK EVIDENCE

"*And it was at Jerusalem the feast of the dedication, and it was winter.* And Jesus walked in the temple in Solomon's porch. Then came the Jews round about Him, and said unto Him, How long dost Thou make us to doubt? If Thou be the Christ, tell us plainly? Jesus answered them, I told you, and ye believed not: the works that I do in My Father's name, they bear witness of Me.*" Christ appeals to His works in proof of His Divine authority and oneness with the Father. His works were such as no mere man had ever performed or could ever accomplish. They were not only the productions of Divine power, but expressions of Divine benevolence. "What," to use the language of another, "is the extent of the evidence arising out of Christ's works? The circle of Christ's power over nature seems a free circle. Was the eye blind? He opened it. The ear deaf? He unstopped it. The tongue bound? He loosed it. The brain lunatic? He regulated it. Food scarce? He multiplied it. Wine wanting? At His touch the water blushed into it. The storm up? He laid it. Kindred dead? He raised them. Mortals suffering the ills 'flesh is heir to'? Among the sick hosts on hosts that crowded His steps, probably every variety of disease fled from His healing hand. And in the parting of body and soul on His cross, as its miraculous might went out of the world, it rent it and veiled its light. What was wanting to describe this power as it were round the whole sphere of nature, but that the very hands and lips that had held it, after death's damp had passed through them, should break through bars of rocks to do and speak again in the world of their benediction? When throughout the power of the world yields to a mightier power, the thin crust is broken that parts us from the Infinite and Eternal. We know God's presence; we see the vision of the wheels Ezekiel saw, which had a living spirit in them moving them every way. We judge that God moves what at every point He stops—that He is in the tempest He makes sink at His Son's bidding—that He lights up the luminary He darkens before His Son's cross."

If the works that Christ had accomplished in His day were sufficient evidence, how much more the *moral* works which He has accomplished since in Christendom? For eighteen centuries those works have been multiplying. To sceptics who say, How long are we to be held in doubt? we answer, If you are sincere in your inquiries, you need not be held in suspense a day longer.

It is suggested in relation to religious scepticism that—

* See Germ, p. 300.

II — IT LACKS SYMPATHY WITH TRUTH

" *Ye believe not, because ye are not of My sheep, as I said unto you. My sheep hear My voice, and I know them, and they follow Me.*" * This lack of sympathy with truth—and not the lack of evidence— is the cause of scepticism. The sympathy of these Jews was with the formulæ and conventionalities of religion, and not with truth itself. The wish is "evermore the father of the thought." The facts that are uncongenial to the temper of the heart, the intellect is always disposed to question and deny. Men are sceptics because they have not sympathy with the truth. Why are men atheists? Because they do not "like to retain" God in all their thoughts. Why are men anti-Christians? Because they do not like Christ: He is too pure, too honest. "Ye will not come unto Me, that ye might have life." Are men responsible for this lack of sympathy with Christ? As well ask, Are men responsible for not being truthful, just, and virtuous? Their own consciences are bound to answer in the affirmative.

It is suggested in relation to religious scepticism that—

III — IT EXPOSES TO ENORMOUS LOSS

" *I give unto them eternal life; and they shall never perish, neither shall any man pluck them out of My hand.*" This implies—

First: That they, the sceptics, would *not* have eternal *life*. That they would not have everlasting goodness, freedom, perfection, and joy. That they would not have that, the absence of which meant to "*perish*." It is implied—

Secondly: That they, the sceptics, would *not* have eternal *security*. His sheep, the true genuine believers, would be safe in the hands of Christ and His Father. Safe from ruin and misery. But those who were not His sheep would be insecure and in a perilous condition.

CONCLUSION. See here—(1.) How *hypocritical* is scepticism! These Jews professed to be in search of truth, when, in fact, they were only in quest of some pretext upon which they could destroy truth. They wanted to entrap Christ. Observe—(2.) How *irrational* is scepticism! It refuses to accept the most overwhelming evidence in favour of truth: the mighty and ever-multiplying works of Christ. Observe—(3.) How *immoral* is scepticism! It springs from the state of the heart, destitution of sympathy with Christ. Observe—(4.) How *egregiously foolish* is scepticism! It risks eternal life and eternal security.

* See Germ, p. 300.

Germs of Thought
No. 38   John 10:22

WINTER AS AN EMBLEM OF DEATH

" And it was winter."

Winter is an emblem of death.   Observe—

I —WINTER IS DREARY OF ASPECT

So is death.   The leaden cloud, the ungenial air, the leafless branches, the shivering creatures of earth and air, invest winter with a sombre and saddening aspect.   How dreary is death!   The body—once rosy, warm, agile, sensitive in feeling, eyes beaming with intelligence, nerves quivering with emotion—pallid, cold, rigid, motionless, insensible as marble.   Nothing on this earth so dreary as a human body stretched out in its coffin, and prepared for the grave.

II —WINTER IS DEVELOPMENT OF LIFE

So is death.   Winter is not death; it is only nature stripping itself of its old costume to prepare another.   It is life going to rest for a short space, in order to spring into new vigour and beauty.   There is no extinction.   So is it with death.   It is but a pause in life's march, a halt on the road to eternity, a sleep; or rather, it is a birth into a new world.   It is—

> " A moulding
> Of forms, and a wondrous birth,
> And a growing and fair unfolding
> Of life from life, and life from death.
> For death, a mother benign,
> Transformeth, but destroyeth not,
> And the new thing fair of the old is wrought."

III —WINTER IS A LAW OF NECESSITY

So is death.   Without winter there would be no spring, and no summer, and no golden autumn.   Winter is a necessity of nature. Death is necessary.   From death the higher life comes.   It is so *mentally.*   How much in a man's mind must die—conceit, prejudice, etc.—before it can advance!   It is so *morally.*   There must be a crucifixion of passions and lusts before there can be a resurrection.   It is so with the body: " Flesh and blood cannot inherit the kingdom of God."

No. 39   John 10:27

MORAL IMITATION

" Follow Me."

The following remarks will show the importance of following Christ :—

I —THAT MAN'S MORAL CHARACTER DETERMINES HIS DESTINY

"As a man thinketh in his heart, so is he." So is he in his *experience*, whether happy or miserable; in his *prospects*, whether terrific or inviting; in his *influence*, whether useful or pernicious; in his *relation to God*, whether approved or condemned; to the *world*, whether a blessing or a curse. Out of character springs destiny; blooms the Paradise, or flames the Gehenna. It must be ever so. As is the moral state of the soul, so is God, and the universe to it.

II —THAT MAN'S MORAL CHARACTER IS FORMED ON THE PRINCIPLE OF IMITATION

So strong is the imitative instinct in children that they draw, as it were, the ruling spirit of those around them into themselves, and it shows itself in their tones, their prattle, and their gait. The seed of a child's action is not in the principles his parents inculcate, but in the acts he performs. "An example," says *Walpole*, "is like the press; the thing done is the thought printed : it may be repeated, it cannot be recalled. It has gone forth with a self-propagating power, and may run to the end of the earth, and descend from 'generation to generation.' The ancient Romans recognized this force of the principle of imitation in their youth, and hence placed in the vestibules of their houses the busts of their great men, that the young men might be reminded of their noble deeds and illustrious virtues. Parents mould the character of their children, and hence families have a likeness that is moral as well as physical."

III —THAT THE FORMATION OF A GOOD CHARACTER REQUIRES A PERFECT MODEL

It is said that Sir Joshua Reynolds found, after years of studying his art, that he had been imitating, not Titian, whom he had desired to make his model, but the productions of one who had forged his style. On this he resolved to make nature his model, and thus he became himself a great master of the art. Man morally must have a model, and according to his model so will he be. One reason, perhaps the chief, why the moral character of men the world over, has been and still is, so depraved and undivine, is because the world for four thousand years never had a perfect model, and that now the only perfect model is but little known and less appreciated.

IV —THAT THE ONLY PERFECT MODEL IS JESUS CHRIST

Some have said that He is too sublime a character, too "separate from sinners" to be imitated by man. But this is a mistake : no character is so imitable as the character of Jesus of Nazareth. Who is the most imitable character ? I answer—

First : He who has the strongest power to command my admiration. We always imitate men in proportion to our admiration for them.

Secondly : He who is the most transparent in character. We can never become thoroughly like one whose character is shadowy and vague, whose leading principles and aims are not salient.

Thirdly : He who is most unchangeable in the spirit that animates him. We can never become thoroughly like a man who is constantly changing, for if we resemble him to-day we shall be unlike him to-morrow.

I maintain that we cannot completely become like any one in character, who has not the power of commanding our highest admiration, who is not transparent in spirit, and unchangeable in purpose. Christ *alone* is all this. Hence He is infinitely the most imitable Model.

CONCLUSION. *"Follow Me."* This is an epitome of all the moral laws of God concerning men. Herein, too, is man's life and perfection. Imitate Him, not by trying to do what He did, or talk as He talked, but by inbreathing that moral spirit of His which has given Him a "name above every name."

John 10:31-38

RELIGIOUS INTOLERANCE

"Then the Jews took up stones again to stone Him. Jesus answered them, Many good works have I showed you from My Father ; for which of those works do ye stone Me ?" &c.

EXEGETICAL REMARKS.—Ver. 31.— *"Then the Jews took up stones again to stone Him."* They had sought to destroy Him before (v. 18 ; viii. 59).

Ver. 32.—*"Jesus answered them, Many good works have I showed you from My* (R. V. THE) *Father ; for which of those works do ye stone Me ?"* or, as some render it, "are ye stoning Me ?" They had, in all probability, brought stones with them for the purpose ; and although, perhaps, they had not actually cast the stones at Him, they were about doing so.

Ver. 33.—*" The Jews answered Him, saying, For a good work we stone Thee not ; but for blasphemy ; and because that Thou, being a man, makest Thyself God."* It is evident from this that they understood Christ to represent Himself as God. *" Thou, being a man, makest Thyself God."* "The Jews," says an ancient writer, "understood

Him better than the Arians." *" But for blasphemy."* Stoning was the legal punishment for this crime (Lev. xxiv. 16). To represent Thyself as God is blasphemy : this Thou hast done, and for this we are about to stone Thee.

Ver. 34.—*" Jesus answered them, Is it not written in your law, I said, Ye are gods?"* Christ here quotes Psalm lxxxii. 6. The Jews included the Psalms in what they termed their law. Christ passes no opinion for or against their law, but He quotes the passage because it was with them an authority.

Vers. 35, 36.—*" If he called them gods, unto whom the word of God came, and the scripture cannot be broken ; say ye of Him, whom the Father hath sanctified, and sent into the world, Thou blasphemest ; because I said, I am the Son of God?"* You cannot deny your own Scriptures ; you are bound to recognize them. The quotation from Psalms reads as follows : " I have said, Ye are gods ; and all of you are children of the Most High. But ye shall die like men." The words were addressed to the judicial magistrate. "Christ here," says a modern expositor, " draws the irresistible conclusion, that if the rulers of Israel were called gods, because they were the commissioned heralds of the word of God, then how much more properly was He, Whom the Father had specially sanctified, and set apart, and sent into the world as the Founder of a new religion, to be called the Son of God ? " The argument seems to be this : If your law —that which you hold in authority— call those gods who are prophets, or magistrates, or both, do I blaspheme in representing Myself as being one with the Father, Who has consecrated Me to the office of Prophet, and authorized Me to assume this character ?

Vers. 37, 38.—" *If I do not the works of My Father, believe Me not. But if I do* (R. V. THEM), *though ye believe not Me, believe the works: that ye may know, and believe* (R. V. UNDERSTAND), *that the Father is in Me, and I in Him* " (R. V. THE FATHER). There was in Christ's works, independently of any miracles, a self-evidencing truth, majesty, and grace, which those who had any spiritual susceptibility were unable to resist (chap. vii. 46 ; viii. 30). But for those who wanted this, the " *works* " were a mighty help. When these failed, the case was desperate indeed. " *That ye may know and believe, that the Father is in Me, and I in Him.*" " He is reiterating His claim to essential oneness with the Father, which He had only seemed to soften down that He might calm their rage and get their ear again for a moment."—*Dr. Brown.*

HOMILETICS

The subject presented in these verses is *Religious Intolerance;* and three remarks are suggested concerning it.

I —IT PERSECUTES A MAN SIMPLY ON ACCOUNT OF HIS RELIGIOUS OPINIONS

" *Then the Jews took up stones again to stone Him.*" Why did they do this ? Merely because He had proclaimed a doctrine concerning Himself which agreed not with their opinions ; nay, which was repugnant to their prejudices, interests, and pride. He said He was the " *Son of God.*" They would not believe this, and called it " *blasphemy.*" In every age of the world this religious intolerance has been rampant ; and although it has not at its command the instrumentality with which to inflict suffering, as it once had, its spirit is as rife now as ever, and it employs means more impalpable and subtle, but not the less powerful, to wound the supposed heretic.

To persecute a man on account of his opinions is—

First : Most absurd. Such are the constitutional differences between minds in the kind and measure of their capacity, and such is the difference in the educational process through which all minds pass, that it is absolutely impossible for any two minds to have exactly the same view of the same subject. There must be, therefore, a diversity of opinion. This diversity is interesting and useful, it stimulates discussion and promotes thought. Were all to think alike, how monotonous would be the social life of the universe !

To persecute a man on account of his opinions is—

Secondly : Most arrogant. Greater audacity know I not than that which is displayed in the man, or the Church, who attempts to bring all men's opinions to his own theological standard. Who was Calvin ? who was Luther ? who was John Knox ? who was Wesley ? that men should be bound to accept their opinions? " Jesus I know, and Paul I know, but who are ye ? " Let every man be " fully persuaded in his own mind."

Another remark suggested here concerning religious intolerance is—

II —IT PERSECUTES A MAN ON ACCOUNT OF HIS OPINIONS, HOWEVER EXCELLENT HIS LIFE MAY BE

" *Jesus answered them, Many good works have I showed you from My Father ; for which of those works do ye stone Me ?* " Numerous were the works that Christ had wrought amongst them. So numerous, that the Evangelist says, that "if they had been written in a book, the world itself would not contain the books." All these works were *good* works—works to bless men, both in body and in soul. " He went about doing good." These persecutors did not deny this; nay, they tacitly admitted it. In truth, deny it they could not, for His " *good works* " were patent to all. And yet, though they knew He was the greatest Benefactor amongst them, and His character was one of exemplary excellence, simply because His doctrine clashed with their opinions, they stoned Him. Good men here in England are stoned now on account of their opinions— stoned, not with flint or granite, but with the tongue of slander and subtle social influences that damage reputation and depreciate influence. Bigots in all sects throw their stones at men, not because they are not good, but because they are not Baptists, not Independents, not Wesleyans, or not Episcopalians. " *For a good work we stone Thee not,*"—we stone Thee because Thou art not one of us. Read the so-called religious journals, and you will find that this *stoning* is rampant even here in England, and now.

The other remark suggested concerning religious intolerance is—

III —IT PERSECUTES A MAN ON ACCOUNT OF HIS OPINIONS, HOWEVER STRONG THE ARGUMENTS IN THEIR FAVOUR

Christ reasons with these bigots. " *Jesus answered them, Is it not written in your law, I said, Ye are gods? If He called them gods, unto whom the Word of God came, and the Scripture cannot be broken ; say ye of Him, whom the Father hath sanctified, and sent into the world, Thou blasphemest ; because I said, I am the Son of God ?* " Christ seems to say, that even on the assumption that He was nothing more than a man, there was no " *blasphemy* " in His calling

Himself a *"god,"* according to their own authority. Their law called men who were magistrates, *"gods."* And if they allowed that, what *blasphemy* was there in Him, Who was *"sanctified by the Father," "one with the Father,"* and Who, as they were bound to acknowledge, performed works which those whom their law called *"gods"* never had accomplished, and never could ? If your Scriptures call men gods, *"unto whom the word of the Lord came,"* surely there can be no blasphemy in Me representing Myself as God, Who am the Word of God itself—the *Logos. Lange* thus states the argument: *"A minori ad majus.* In what respect ? (1.) From those blameworthy judges and their lofty title to Christ; (2.) From those who derived their dignity from the Mosaic institution, to Him Whom God hath sanctified; (3.) From those to whom the λόγος τοῦ Θεοῦ did but come, to Him Whom God sanctified and sent into the world, *i. e.* Whom he has actually made His λόγος to the world ; the Logos-nature of Christ is here implied, though not expressed. This last we hold to be the only correct conception, the only one satisfactory to the Old Testament Christology." But His argument went for nothing although it was very clear and very conclusive, quite sufficient to show that He was no blasphemer.

CONCLUSION. What an accursed thing this religious intolerance is ! Absurd, arrogant, cruel, regardless of moral excellence, dead to argument, alive only to what it deems heresy.

John 10:39-42

MORAL INCORRIGIBILITY AND POSTHUMOUS USEFULNESS

"Therefore they sought again to take Him : but He escaped out of their hand," &c.

EXEGETICAL REMARKS.—Ver. 39.— *" Therefore they sought again to take Him : but He escaped* (R. V. AND HE WENT FORTH) *out of their hand."* He did not retract His statement, or seek to conciliate them. He stood His ground. And as He saw they were determined to lay violent hands upon Him, He escaped (ἐξῆλθεν), "went or passed away out of their grasp, just when they thought themselves sure of having Him."

Ver. 40.—*"And went* (R. V. HE WENT) *away again beyond Jordan into the place where John at first baptized* (R. V. WAS AT THE FIRST BAPTIZING) ; *and there He abode."* "The place is Bethabara. *'First'* was to distinguish it from the second place of

baptism, in chap. iii. 23. Why Jesus went away from Jerusalem is plainly enough intimated in what precedes. He must die in Jerusalem, and not elsewhere ; but not before the passover. As "His hour was not yet come," He retired for a season from the now mad rage of His enemies. But why did He go to Bethabara in particular ? What follows gives the reason. John had there uttered his first testimony concerning Jesus. The circumstance of our Lord's going there must have brought the fact visibly to the people's remembrance."—*Hengstenberg.*

Ver. 41.—*"And many resorted* (R. V. CAME) *unto Him, and said, John did no miracle* (R. V. INDEED DID NO SIGN): *but all things that* (R. V. WHATSOEVER)

John spake of this Man were true." Many resorted unto Him. "Bengel : *Fructus posthumus officii Johannis.* But we must not overlook the fact that Christ had before sojourned in Peræa and worked there. John did no miracle; nevertheless he is attested by Christ Himself in what he said of Him. And thus his testimony to Christ lives again and continues working to the furtherance of faith."— Lange.

Ver. 42.—"*And many believed on Him there.*" He found in that region an audience made susceptible by the teaching and influence of John the Baptist.

HOMILETICS

Two subjects of thought are here presented to us—*moral incorrigibility* and *posthumous usefulness.*

I —MORAL INCORRIGIBILITY

What was the result of the appeal of Christ to the good works He had performed amongst them, and His appeal to their "*Law*"? What was the effect of His noble life and strong logic? Were their prejudices broken down? was their opposition overcome? No; here it is: "*Therefore they sought again to take Him : but He escaped out of their hand.*" Their opposition was rather intensified, and their determination to stone Him to death grew stronger. The mightiest ministry of the Son of God was lost upon these men. There are undoubtedly men on this earth who have reached the stage of moral incorrigibility. Their opinions are fossilized, their habits are confirmed, their characters are stereotyped. Did not Christ teach this when He said, "Give not that which is holy unto the dogs, neither cast ye your pearls before swine, lest they trample them under their feet, and turn again and rend you?" And again, when weeping over Jerusalem, He spoke of the "things that belonged to peace" as hid from the eyes of the doomed city. Indeed, examples of such characters lie thickly around us all. There are men so canine in temper, so swinish in materialism, that to argue with them on spiritual subjects would be waste labour, and expose to insult and persecution. With these characters the day of grace is over, retribution has already got them in its iron grasp. Two evils befell these men now to which all such characters are liable—

First: Disappointment. "*They sought again to take Him : but He escaped out of their hand.*" They made all arrangements to stone Him; and when their plans were complete, they looked for Him; but He was not, He had gone. The incorrigible sinner is irrevocably doomed to disappointment. Sooner or later he will discover that all his calculations are false. He will have all his plans thwarted, his purposes broken, and his hopes blasted. Another evil which befell these men was—

Secondly: The loss of Christ. Christ had withdrawn from their midst. He was not afraid of them, but His time had not yet come. When the hour struck He would voluntarily again fall into their hands. Meanwhile they lost Him. The greatest calamity that can happen to a man or a community is the withdrawal of Christ; and this must happen sooner or later to the incorrigible. "My spirit shall not always strive with man." When He withdraws from the human soul, it is as if the sun withdrew from its orbit, and all the planets rush into black, fathomless, thunderous chaos.

The other subject of thought here is—

II—POSTHUMOUS USEFULNESS

"*Jesus went away again beyond Jordan into the place where John at first baptized; and there He abode. And many resorted unto Him, and said, John did no miracle: but all things that John spake of this Man were true. And many believed on Him there.*" This Bethabara was a town on the east bank of Jordan, where there was a ford across the river, whence the name—house-of-passage, or ferry-house. It was thirty miles north-east of Jerusalem. Here the Israelites crossed the Jordan, and here John baptized and fulfilled his mission.

Now the ministry of a man who had been perhaps some time in his grave had prepared the population of this neighbourhood to receive Christ.

First: The ministry of this dead man was *remembered.* The appearance of Christ in their midst and His deeds and doctrines brought John the Baptist and his ministry up to the memory of these people. He was alive again amongst them. His extraordinary *personnel* became vivid to their imaginations, and his rousing voice re-echoed its thunders in their hearts. The ministry of faithful ministers will never be forgotten by their hearers. Preachers must live in the memory of their hearers.

Secondly: The ministry of this dead man was *useful.* (1.) It served to set off to the minds of the people the superiority of Christ's ministry. "*John did no miracle.*" His ministry was purely moral. The effects he produced were directly on mind, and by the tremendous force of his oratory. But Christ, it would seem, performed miracles among them, as well as preached doctrines, and they were struck with His superiority. John was great, they felt, but Christ was greater. When John and Christ appeared in their presence, a few months before, John would strike them as the greater, for before their eyes John baptized Him in that Jordan. But now He was the greater. (2.) It served to confirm the Messiahship of Christ. "*All things that John spake of this Man were true.*" They remembered what John had said concerning His supernal character and mission; and now they felt that John's words were realized. The consequence was, that "*many believed* on *Him there."* And *"there He abode."* How long, we are not told. How delightful must have been the intercourse which His genuine disciples had with Him there ! "They were choice Sabbatic hours, where no police-officers watched them in the crowd. There, across the desert, some thirty miles from Jerusalem, they were free and secure.

CONCLUSION. Faithful ministers may take courage from the fact that, as in the case of John the Baptist, their ministry will be operating for good when they are in their graves. John was dead and buried; but his ministry was working in Bethabara, and working so as to prepare men to receive Christ and to believe on Him.

John 11:1-6

THE FAMILY AT BETHANY —(NO. 1.)

(The raising of Lazarus at Bethany.—JOHN xi. 1—46.)

" Now a certain man was sick, named Lazarus, of Bethany, the town of Mary and her sister Martha," &c.

EXEGETICAL REMARKS.—In the last verses of the preceding chapter we find that, in order to elude the malignant purposes of the Pharisees in Jerusalem, Christ went away beyond Jordan, where John had baptized, a distance of between twenty-five and thirty miles from the city. Here He seems to have continued for some time ; in fact, to have continued until a message reached Him of the sickness of His friend Lazarus. "The narrative of the raising of Lazarus," says *Westcott,* "is unique in its completeness. The essential circumstances of the fact in regard to persons, manners, results, are given with perfect distinctness. The history is more complete than in chapter nine, because the persons stand in closer connection with the Lord than the blind man ; and the event itself had in many ways a ruling influence on the end of His ministry."

Ver. 1.—" *Now a certain man was sick, named Lazarus, of Bethany, the town* (R. V. THE VILLAGE) *of Mary and her sister Martha."* Bethany was a small village lying at the foot of Mount Olivet, and a road leads from it into the metropolis, crossing the brook Kedron by a rustic bridge, winding up amidst a host of vineyards. From the fact that it is called the "*town of Mary and her sister Martha,"* it has been inferred by some that not only their parents were dead, but that they were people of property, and that they were well-known in the neighbourhood. The probability that this is the case, that Mary, at a feast held in honour of Jesus, poured on the feet of Jesus a box of ointment valued by Judas at 300 pence—a sum amounting in our money to about £50—is of itself sufficient to show that they were at any rate in easy, if not affluent, circumstances ; and the fact that a large number of Jews came to comfort the sisters after the death of their brother Lazarus, suggests that they had considerable social influence.

Ver. 2.—" *(It* (R. V. AND IT) *was that Mary which anointed the Lord with ointment, and wiped His feet with her hair, whose brother Lazarus was sick.)* " This fact, which is given elsewhere (Matt. xxvi. 7 ; Mark xiv. 3 ; chap. xii. 3), seems to have become so notorious, that John mentions it here in passing as a well-known incident. Why the Synoptists make no mention of the resurrection of Lazarus, has been variously accounted for. It has been suggested that as they lived when the event occurred, the record of it might have involved Lazarus in persecution :

whereas John did not write for a considerable time afterwards. The attempts that have been made to identify Lazarus with any other person mentioned in the New Testament and to identify Mary with Mary Magdalene are questioned.

Ver. 3.—" *Therefore his sisters* (R. V. THE SISTERS THEREFORE) *sent unto Him, saying, Lord, behold, he whom Thou lovest is sick.*" Nothing is said of the messenger who carried the information ; and the message bears no request. The sisters seem to have had such faith in the love of Christ for their brother, that all that was necessary was to intimate to Him that Lazarus was ill, in order to draw Him at once from Bethabara to Bethany.

Ver. 4.—" *When Jesus heard that* (R. V. BUT WHEN JESUS HEARD IT), *He said, This sickness is not unto death, but for the glory of God, that the Son of God might* (R. V. MAY) *be glorified thereby.*" "Remarkable language this," says *Dr. Brown*, " which from creature lips would have been intolerable. It means that the glory of God manifested in the resurrection of the dead Lazarus would be shown to be the glory, personally and immediately, of the Son."

Ver. 5. —" *Now Jesus loved Martha, and her sister, and Lazarus.*" Jesus loved all men. The love here is special ; it is the love of private friendship. This statement gives the lie to the charge that Christ's ethical teaching excludes the virtue of private friendship.

Ver. 6.—" *When He had heard* (R. V. THEREFORE HE HEARD) *therefore that he was sick, He abode two days still* (R. V. AT THAT TIME) *in the same place where He was.*" Beyond all doubt, this was just to let things come to their worst, in order to display His glory." It is weak of Strauss to suggest the moral impropriety of Christ in allowing Lazarus to die, in order to raise him. How immoral, then, must the Infinite One be, to allow whole generations to die without any immediate resurrection ! " *Abode two days.*" "There appears," says a modern expositor, "something quite felicitous in the identification by Wieseler of these two days with the to-day and to-morrow of Luke xiii. 32. And then the passage, Luke xiii. 22, will be identified with this present journey to Bethany. And the profoundly interesting details of Luke xiii. 22 ; xvii. 10, are a narrative of Jesus' teaching after the reception of this message from the sisters of Bethany. And we see why in the parable Lazarus is the name chosen (Luke xvi. 20) for one desired to be raised from the dead. While the man He loved is dying, Jesus is performing His living mission preparatory to His own death and resurrection."

HOMILETICS

These words direct us to the *Family at Bethany.* The verses bring under our attention four things.
Notice—

I —THE PRIVATE FRIENDSHIP OF CHRIST

" *Now a certain man was sick, named Lazarus, of Bethany, the town of Mary and her sister Martha.*" From this verse, as well as from the other verses in this chapter, it will appear that Christ was on the most friendly terms with this family at Bethany. It is not unlikely that He was on terms of friendship with other such families, although there is reference to no such fact. We have only fragments of His wonderful biography. It has been said, as an objection to Christ, that He never inculcated the duty of friendship. Here He gives a fine example of it. Endowed as He was with all the instincts and capacities of our common nature, He yearned for friendship. He sought its encouragements and inspirations. As a rule, the greatest natures are always the most social, and crave most for friendly sympathy and intercourse; and in proportion to their labours the more they yearn for the opportunity of retiring into the circle of social love, where they can throw off all professional formality and stiffness, and unbend their faculties in the freedom of love and confidence. Two things in relation to this friendly social circle are worthy of note.

First: None of its members seem to have been amongst His professed disciples. We do not read of them following Him about, nor were they at the last supper. There are many good people who are not formal professors of religion, who notwithstanding are worthy of our confidence and friendship.

Secondly: All of its members were different from each other. They were different in *sex*. Indeed, there could scarcely be a social circle without the two, the woman and the man. Apart from fleshhood, there is a love of sex. The true woman in nature has those spiritual attributes of sensibility, delicacy, affection, intuition, which must ever awaken in a true man, who is endowed with spiritual attributes of another sort,—such as energy, resolution, boldness—special sympathy and regard. The one, in fact, supplements the deficiency of the other; and hence the *real marriage is that of souls*. Any other idea of marriage is degrading and brutish. Hence it is said here, Christ "*loved Martha and Mary*." The greatest and the purest men, it has been said, have always had the most pleasure in that female society where the ideal of true womanhood is realized. There is no home without a woman. There is a difference, not only in the sex, but in the *attributes* of the members of this circle. Lazarus seemed to have been a reticent man. He does not talk. He represented, perhaps, *thought*. Mary seems to have been of a pensive turn. Her nature was full of quiet affection. Martha, on the other hand, was energetic. She went forth to meet Christ, she served at table, &c. In these three, it has been said, we have represented *thought, feeling,* and *action*. Such were the members of Christ's friendly circle. Into this circle, no doubt, He frequently retired, after the toils and insults of the day, to interblend His thoughts and sympathies with loving hearts.

Notice—

II —THE CHIEF HONOUR OF LIFE

"(*It was that Mary which anointed the Lord with ointment, and wiped His feet with her hair, whose brother Lazarus was sick.*)" Whatever were the respective excellences of Lazarus and Martha, Mary here stands out in honourable distinction. The narrative of the anointing is given in Mark, as well as in the next chapter of this Gospel. Here it is referred to as something well known, a fact that had become notorious, and therefore had realized the words of our Lord, Who said, "Wheresoever this Gospel shall be preached throughout the whole world, this also that she hath done shall be spoken of for a memorial of her." That act of Mary not only gave a distinction to the other two, shed a glory on them, but made her name fragrant for ever in the Universal Church. The distinction of goodness is the true distinction, is the only praise-worthy and lasting distinction. She obtained immortal honour because she was good ; she was good because she loved Christ. The distinctions of wealth, birth, titles, or even of intellect, genius, learning, what are they before the distinction of moral goodness ? Little flickering rushlights that must go out, compared to the imperishable star that burns on through the ages. It will be found at last that many of the titled Right Honourables of the earth are Right Abominables in the universe. The only heroes in the great spiritual empire are those who are distinguished by moral goodness. For example, the countless thousands of the men whom Frederick the Great brought into his Seven Years' War included most of the monarchs and nobles and magnates of Europe. But what were they morally ? Greedy, grovelling swine, wallowing in the filthiest mud of depravity. And what are they to-day, looked at through history ? Caged brutes with which we play and laugh as they grin and snarl at us. Contemptible creatures truly ! (See " Frederick the Great," by Carlyle.)

Notice—

III —THE APPARENT INCONSISTENCY OF LOVE

" *Therefore his sisters sent unto Him, saying, Lord, behold, he whom Thou lovest is sick.** When He had heard therefore that he was sick, He abode two days still in the same place where He was.*" Two things seem to be inconsistent with His friendship—

First : His permission of the sufferings and death of the brother. It is obvious that they regarded Him as having power sufficient to have kept off pain and mortality from their dwelling. " *If Thou hadst been here, my brother had not died,*" said Martha. As if she had said, "Thy power could have prevented such a heart-breaking catastrophe befalling us : oh, why didst Thou not come ? " We can scarcely avoid the impression, that during the four days of their anguish, their confidence in His love would be greatly shaken.

Secondly : The tardiness with which He came to their relief after their message to Him. " *Lord, behold, he whom Thou lovest is sick.*" It is true that the message did not contain an ex-plicit request to Him to visit them—so strong, perhaps, was their confidence in His love of their brother and themselves, that they

* See Germ, p. 312.

deemed such a request unnecessary : the mere intimation that he
was sick, they thought, would have been enough. In giving the
message to the bearer, perhaps they said, " Only say he is sick :
that is enough : He will be here : such love as He has for us
requires no entreaties." But He came not. The sickness goes on ;
Lazarus dies, and is buried ; and well-nigh four long days are gone,
and Christ does not appear. And then, when He comes into their
village He does not repair at once to their house of mourning,
but stops at some other place.

The inconsistency, however, is only apparent. In this case, the
permission of the death, and the tardy way in which relief came,
which seemed to be inconsistent with love, turned out to be a great
blessing. So it has ever been. " Our light afflictions, which are
but for a moment," &c. " Whom the Lord loveth, He chasteneth."

Notice—

IV —THE ULTIMATE PURPOSE OF PROVIDENCE

" *This sickness is not unto death, but for the glory of God, that the
Son of God might be glorified thereby.*" It would seem from this
that Christ knew all about the sickness of Lazarus before the
sisters had sent unto Him. " *Not unto death.*" But he did die,
and perhaps was dead at the time. What does He mean ? Is it not
this, the end of his sickness is not death—but the " *glory of God ?*"
Death is the most impressive event in human history. But it is
a mere incident ; not the end. It is an occurrence passing on to
something grander and more sublime—the " *glory of God.*" So with
all the events of life. What is the " *glory of God ?* " What but the
happiness of His loyal subjects ? And all things tend to this. " All
things work together for good to them that love God."

Germs of Thought
No. 40   John 11:3

THE SICKNESS OF LAZARUS

" Therefore his sisters sent unto Him, saying, Lord, behold, he whom Thou
lovest is sick."

The words before us present—

I —A PRIVILEGE OF INCOMPARABLE VALUE

What is that ? To be loved by Christ. " *He whom Thou lovest.*"
To be loved by some beings is of no advantage : their love is carnal,
selfish, fickle. But what is Christ's love ?

First : It is *tender.* So tender that in all the afflictions of its
objects He is afflicted. They are as dear to Him as Himself.
" Inasmuch as ye have done it unto one of the least of these My
brethren, ye have done it unto Me."

Secondly : It is *constant*. His love is not founded upon any mistakes as to our characters : as to what we have been, what we are, or what we shall be; He knows all about us. Men sometimes withdraw their love because they discover in us imperfections which they never anticipated.

Thirdly : It is *all-sufficient*. It has at its command ample resources to supply all our wants; ample power to sustain, guard, and bless us through all the future of our being. "He is able to do exceeding abundantly," &c. To be loved by Christ ! The words before us present—

II —A TRIAL STRIKINGLY SUGGESTIVE

Why did He permit Lazarus, His loved friend, to be sick ?

First : Not because it was agreeable to His heart. The sufferings of those we love are always painful to our heart. Is it not so with Him ? "He doth not afflict willingly, nor grieve the children of men."

Secondly : Not because He could not have prevented it. He Who hushed the storm and raised the dead had power to keep off disease from this loved one. Why then ? It was for some useful end. "Whom the Lord loveth, He chasteneth." The affliction of Lazarus was a blessing both to himself and his sisters. It strengthened their faith and intensified their joy. The words present to us—

III —A FAITH OF REMARKABLE POWER

"*His sisters*" uttered the words of the text, and they did so, what for ? To induce Him to visit the afflicted one. They used no argument, they urged no entreaty, they employed no persuasion. So strong was their faith in His love that they only said, "*he whom Thou lovest is sick.*" So assured were they of the genuineness and strength of His love, that they felt that the mere statement of the illness was enough ; that persuasion was unnecessary, and would be, perhaps, an offence to His heart. True love requires no persuasion : only state the fact. Where there is true philanthropy no persuasion is necessary to relieve distress. The appeals to benevolence that stream hourly from the press, and that are sounded almost every Sunday from pulpits, imply a sad lack of faith in their authors in the philanthropy of the land. Such appeals are an insult to genuine love.

John 11:7-16

THE FAMILY AT BETHANY   (No. 2.)

"Then after that saith He to His disciples, Let us go into Judæa again," &c.—

EXEGETICAL REMARKS.—Ver. 7.— "*Then after that* (R. V. THIS) *saith He* to His (R. V. THE) *disciples, Let us go into Judæa again.*" There was an

eternal chronometer that seemed to
guide the movements of Christ; hence,
in one place in this Gospel He says,
"Mine hour is not yet come;" and
again, "My time is not yet fully come."
He had an hour for everything, and
the hour for His going back to Judæa
had now struck.

Ver. 8.—"*His* (R. V. THE) *disciples
say unto Him, Master* (R. V. RABBI), *the
Jews of late sought* (R. V. WERE BUT
NOW SEEKING) *to stone Thee; and goest
Thou thither again?*" At each of the
last two visits to Jerusalem, viz. when
He attended the Feast of Tabernacles,
and when He attended the Feast of
Dedication (chap. viii. 59; x. 31), the
Jews had sought to stone Him. His
disciples intimate that He ought not
to venture any more.

Vers. 9, 10.—"*Jesus answered, Are
there not twelve hours in the day? If
any* (R. V. A) *man walk in the day, he
stumbleth not, because he seeth the light
of this world. But if a man walk in
the night, he stumbleth, because there
is no light* (R. V. THE LIGHT IS NOT)
in him." "As precisely as the sun
measures off the twelve hours, so does
God mark out for man his exact time
and mission. In that mission he is
Divinely safe; for death itself, being
in the mission, would be true safety.
A man is 'immortal until his work is
done.' Opposed to this *day* of mission and duty there is a night side of
darkness and wandering. It is the
hemisphere outside man's true life.
'*No light in him.*' A man's divinely-
assigned path is a divinely-illuminated
path. The light is a blended light,
combining rays of reason, conscience,
Scripture, Providence, and the blessed
spirits. And it is not only a light
around a man, but a light *in* him.
The dark wanderer with no light in
him, stumbleth."—*Whedon.*

Ver. 11.—"*These things said* (R. V.
SPAKE) *He: and after that* (R. V. THIS)
*He saith unto them, Our friend Lazarus
sleepeth* (R. V. IS FALLEN ASLEEP); *but
I go, that I may awake him out of
sleep.*" "Sleepeth," κεκοίμηται. Men of
all times and countries have been

struck with the resemblance between
sleep and death. In Christ's mind,
the death of Lazarus was a sleep, inasmuch as it waited an awakening. How
did Christ learn now that Lazarus
was dead? In the same way that He
knew all things.

Ver. 12.—"*Then* (R. V. THE DIS-
CIPLES THEREFORE) *said His disciples*
(R. V. UNTO HIM), *Lord, if he sleep* (R.
V. IS FALLEN ASLEEP), *he shall do well*"
(R. V. HE WILL RECOVER). There is
no reason to risk Thy life by going
up again to Jerusalem.

Vers. 13, 14.—"*Howbeit Jesus spake*
(R. V. NOW JESUS HAD SPOKEN) *of his
death: but they thought that He had
spoken* (R. V. SPAKE) *of taking of rest
in sleep. Then said Jesus* (R. V. THEN
JESUS THEREFORE SAID) *unto them
plainly, Lazarus is dead.*" "εἰρήκει,
was speaking. περὶ τῆς κοιμήσεως τοῦ
ὕπνον, the rest of sleep. The beauty
of the narrative is impaired in English
by the want of a word corresponding
to κεκοίμηται in verse 11. Is at rest,
does not convey an idea closely enough
associated with sleep; but it would
be better than sleepeth, for the sake
of the explanatory remark that follows
in this verse. So awaken, on the other
hand, or raise from sleep, Wicl., Rh.,
would better express ἐξυπνίσω than
awake him out of sleep, which makes
the idea of sleep too prominent by its
repetition."—*Webster and Wilkinson.*

Ver. 15.—"*And I am glad for your
sakes that I was not there, to the intent
ye may believe; nevertheless let us go
unto him.*" Christ here expresses His
gladness at an opportunity of performing a miracle that would be of
service to their faith.

Ver. 16.—"*Then said Thomas,
which* (R. V. THOMAS THEREFORE WHO)
is called Didymus (R. V. SAID), *unto
his fellowdisciples, Let us also go, that
we may die with Him.*" The language
implies that the return of his Master
to Jerusalem rendered His death inevitable; and that his love for Him
was stronger than death, and that life
was nothing without Him.

HOMILETICS

In this portion of the account of the *Family at Bethany* we have three subjects for reflection—the walk of duty, the character of death, and the self-sacrifice of love.

Notice—

I —THE WALK OF DUTY

"*Are there not twelve hours in the day? If any man walk in the day, he stumbleth not, because he seeth the light of this world. But if a man walk in the night, he stumbleth, because there is no light in him.*" In Palestine, each day throughout the year was divided into twelve hours. Perhaps the first hour of the day was just breaking when these words were uttered. It may be that the allusion of our Lord is, to the day of human life, or the day of duty. Does He mean,—I have a work to do within a certain period, and to that work I must devote myself without any loss of time? Three remarks are suggested concerning the walk of duty.

First: It is a walk of light. "*Walk in the day.*" The man who, from proper motives and with a single eye, pursues his mission in life, moves in open day. No dark cloud shadows his path, no thick haze hangs over him, he knows what he is about. His race-course lies clearly before him, and he sees the goal.

Secondly: It is a walk of safety. "*If any man walk in the day, he stumbleth not.*" "He," says *Luthardt,* "who moves within the bounds of duty, does not stumble, makes no false steps; for the light of the world—that is, the will of God—enlightens him. But he who walks outside of the limits of his vocation will err in what he does, since, not the will of God, but his own pleasure, is his guide."

Thirdly: It is a walk that must be pursued. Though the disciples warned Him of what was likely to occur on His return to Jerusalem, instead of being deterred, Christ says, "*Are there not twelve hours in the day?*" I have got time to do the work that is given Me to perform, and pursuing that work I am safe; for it is the work of day, and I shall not stumble. The path of duty is the path of safety. I shall pursue that path whatever be the result. My duty is to go to Bethany, and I am not afraid of what will happen to Me at Jerusalem.

We have all our "*twelve hours;*" and if in those "*twelve hours*" we pursue the path of duty, we shall move in daylight; we shall not "*stumble.*" Ah me! what stumbling there is amongst the millions in these twelve short hours! The moment a man steps aside from the true path, he is in "*darkness,*" and he stumbles.

Notice—

II —THE CHARACTER OF DEATH

Two things are suggested here concerning death.

First: It is not necessarily terrible. "*Our friend Lazarus*" *sleepeth; but I go, that I may awake him out of sleep. Then said His disciples, Lord, if he sleep, he shall do well. Howbeit Jesus spake of his death: but they thought that He had spoken of taking of rest in sleep. Then said Jesus unto them plainly, Lazarus is dead."* That event, which comes to most men grim and ghastly, robed with terrible associations, is, in the view of Christ, only a "*sleep*," the herald of a coming morning and of renovated activity. There is nothing *alarming* about sleep; nay, the wearied worker hails it. There is nothing *injurious* about sleep; nay, it refreshes and re-invigorates. There is nothing *final* about sleep; nay, it is a step to renewed inspiration and labour. "*Our friend Lazarus sleepeth.*"

Another thing suggested here concerning death is—

Secondly: It is ever expedient. "*I am glad for your sakes that I was not there, to the intent ye may believe; nevertheless let us go unto him.*" That death is an event not only expedient in this world, but even necessary, will scarcely be doubted. In a sinful world like this, were there no death, human existence would soon become intolerable, and earth a pandemonium.

But we have to do with the death of Lazarus, concerning which Christ said He was "*glad;*" and glad, because of the high moral end which He knew it would answer. "*I am glad for your sakes that I was not there.*" Incidentally we may remark, that it would seem from this, that if Christ had been there Lazarus would not have died, as if death could not take place in His presence. It has been remarked, that the process of death is prolonged by the clinging sympathy of friends, that the strong love of attendant friends will retain the spirit in the clay. If so, how much more powerful is the presence and sympathy of Christ to detain the spirit to its dissolving tenement! But the point here is, that the death of Lazarus was expedient for moral ends, "*to the intent that ye may believe.*" The greatest moral need of humanity, is faith in Christ; and whatever promotes that end is a transcendent blessing. The resurrection of Lazarus tended to that. It would deepen and strengthen the faith-roots, not only of Lazarus, his sisters, and the disciples, but of men in succeeding times. I cannot here forbear quoting a paragraph from a discourse on this passage by one of my dear old ministerial friends, who some twenty years ago was one of the ablest ministers in London.* "Herein is a picture of Providence. God does these things many times with men. There was transformation here of evil into good. And this is the light which Jesus and His word throw on evil. It is not evil only, or for ever. There is a soul of good in things evil. He may tarry at a distance, but it is only to get nearer soon—nearer to the heart than if He had gone at once. He may answer not a word, as in

---

* Rev. Alfred Morris, of Holloway. For the discourse from which the extract is taken, see "The Open Secret," published by Miall & Co., p. 96.

the case of the Syro-phœnician woman, but it is only that He may have to say, 'O woman, great is thy faith!' These are the sayings of the Word of life, 'tribulation worketh patience, and patience experience, and experience hope.' He chastens us for our profit, that we might be partakers of His holiness; the 'light affliction which is but for a moment, worketh out a far more exceeding and eternal weight of glory.' There was elevation here. The material made instrument of the spiritual. The body and the grave were made sacramental by the power of Christ. And thus, as in the world of matter, we get transparent glass from hard flints, and nearly all the properties of gold and platinum, the most precious metals, in a metal (aluminium) obtained from common clay; and the brightest lights reside in lumps of coal and blocks of wood; and the diamond is only charcoal—so in the world of mind and morals, purest lustre and richest worth are, by the faith which worketh by love, extracted from things which in their natural state are both offensive and pernicious. There was *fellowship* here. One sickening and dying for the health, and joy, and higher life of many. 'For us they suffer, and for us they die.'"

Notice—

III —THE SELF-SACRIFICE OF LOVE

" *Then said Thomas, which is called Didymus, unto his fellow-disciples, Let us also go, that we may die with Him.*" Thomas assumes that Christ's death was inevitable; that no sooner would He reach Jerusalem—and He would be there now in a few hours —than He would meet with a violent death from the hand of His enemies; and with that heroism of soul which can spring only from love, he exclaims, Let us follow Him unto the scene of danger, confront His enemies, and die with Him.

Many years ago I remember reading a very remarkable sermon on this text in the works of the celebrated *John Howe.* I regret to find I have not the book by me, or would indicate the plan, which I then deemed one of distinguished excellence.

This expression of Thomas may be looked upon in two aspects.

First: That love for Christ can overcome the fear of death. Thomas loved Christ, and that love buried all selfish feeling, all dread of death. The love of goodness should always be in man stronger than the love of life. When it is so,—and not otherwise, —man grows into the heroism of true sainthood.

Secondly: That the test of genuine discipleship is readiness to follow Christ into the greatest dangers. Let no man conclude that he is a genuine disciple of Christ, who shrinks from any amount of trial and danger to which the following of Him exposes.

CONCLUSION. How are we morally walking in these "*twelve hours*" of our life? Is it in the straight path of duty? If so, the daylight will be on us, and our steps will be secure. Do we regard death as an end, or as a means to a moral end, as Christ regarded the death of Lazarus? Are we prepared, like Thomas, to go with Christ even unto death?

John 11:17-27

THE FAMILY AT BETHANY (No. 3.)

"Then when Jesus came, He found that he had lain in the grave four days already," &c.

EXEGETICAL REMARKS.—Ver. 17.— " *Then* (R. V. SO) *when Jesus came, He found that he had lain* (R. V. BEEN) *in the grave* (R. V. TOMB) *four days already.*" It was customary for the Jews to bury the corpse soon after death, because decomposition proceeds rapidly in warm climates.

Ver. 18.—" *Now Bethany was nigh unto Jerusalem, about fifteen furlongs off.*" About two miles of our distance.

Ver. 19.—" *And many of the Jews came* (R. V. HAD COME) *to Martha and Mary, to comfort* (R. V. CONSOLE) *them concerning their brother.*" The family being so much respected, and their home so near to Jerusalem, no doubt a goodly number of mourners came. Seven days were allotted in Palestine to lamentations after the death of a friend.

Ver. 20.—" *Then Martha* (R. V. MARTHA THEREFORE), *as soon as* (R. V. WHEN) *she heard that Jesus was coming, went and met Him : but Mary sat still* (R. V. STILL SAT) *in the house.*" This verse indicates the characteristic difference between the two sisters, the one energetic and practical, the other meditative and devout. How Martha came to know that Christ was in the neighbourhood we are not told. Perhaps a secret message was brought her, and she hurried forth at once.

Vers. 21, 22.—" *Then said Martha* (R. V. MARTHA THEREFORE SAID) *unto Jesus, Lord, if Thou hadst been here, my brother had not died. But* (R. V. AND EVEN NOW) *I know, that even now, whatsoever Thou wilt* (R. V. SHALT) *ask of God, God will give it Thee*" (R. V. GIVE THEE). Wonderful is the faith in Christ which Martha here indicates. She meant to say, that death could not have occurred in the presence of Christ; and that at His presence death even would be overcome.

Ver. 23.—" *Jesus saith unto her, Thy brother shall rise again.*" Here is a promise transcending her hope, as appears from the next verse, although she had intimated that He could, through invoking the Eternal, do something for their relief in so great a sorrow.

Ver. 24.—" *Martha saith unto Him, I know that he shall rise again in the resurrection at the last day.*" She understood His words to refer to the resurrection of the body, and expresses her belief in the general resurrection at the last day.

Vers. 25, 26.—" *Jesus said unto her, I am the resurrection, and the life : he that believeth in* (R. V. ON) *Me, though he were dead* (R. V. HE DIE), *yet shall he live : and whosoever liveth and believeth in* (R. V. ON) *Me shall never die. Believest thou this ?*" 'Εγώ εἰμι, &c., &c. "It is clear that He is first speaking of natural life and death, then of spiritual. ἡ ζωή, therefore, is not to be understood merely of renewed life. It expresses what is afterwards implied in ὁ ζῶν as well as in ζήσεται. His power to convey or restore life is not limited to times and seasons. Resurrection from death, as well as original life, depends entirely upon Him. He, and not a succession of physical causes and effects, produced all life at the beginning; and He, and no operation of material forces or natural laws, will re-animate the dead at the resurrection. He therefore, at His pleasure, can give or restore life at any time. In Him, independently of time, is the whole truth and reality and power of the resurrection. ὁ πιστεύων. In the words '*live*' and '*die*,' as understood of natural life and death, there is here an obvious and intentional paradox : 'The believer in Me, if you suppose him to die, shall live; while the living believer, ὁ ζῶν καὶ πιστεύων, shall never die;' or, 'Belief in Me shall ensure life after death, and ensure life against death.' ζῶν καὶ is introduced to give effect to the apparent paradox, by marking the supposed contrast of the two cases. The solution is, that in reality there is no such thing as death to the believer in Christ. And this fact is stated in two forms : first, that the believer, though he die in the body, yet for all that he shall live; secondly, that the life of the believer is continuous and eternal, not subject to anything that can be rightly called death. The former statement is meant to meet the case of the departed, as dead in the body. The latter, to meet our own case, as living both in the body and the spirit. The life spoken of in the words ζωή and ζήσεται, is not to be confounded with the resurrection of the body, much less to be limited to it. The life is more and higher than the resurrection, involving it, however, as part of its manifestation.

It is to be observed that our Lord first spoke of the present and temporary resurrection of Lazarus (ver. 23). Martha then spoke of the future and general resurrection (ver. 25). Then He rises beyond this to the source and cause of spiritual and eternal life, quits the specific idea of resurrection, and concentrates His and our attention upon that of life in Him which the living and the departed believers equally enjoy. κἂν ἀποθάνῃ, 'though he die,' ζήσεται, 'shall live again,' as in Matt. ix. 18, εἰς τὸν αἰῶνα, rendered in the Collect of the Burial Service, 'Shall not die eternally.' And doubtless this is the true meaning of the promise here given. We must interpret the phrase, however, as signifying simply never, as in the parallel passage, chap. viii. 51, 52."—*Webster and Wilkinson.*

Ver. 27.—"*She saith unto Him, Yea, Lord : I believe* (R. V. I HAVE BELIEVED) *that Thou art the Christ, the Son of God, which should come* (R. V. EVEN HE THAT COMETH) *into the world.*" "*I believe*," literally, I have believed. This was her settled faith. Augustine, paraphrasing this, says, "When I believed that Thou wert the Son of God, I believed also that Thou wert the resurrection and the life, with all the corresponding benefits to us."

HOMILETICS

In this portion of the account of the *Family at Bethany* we shall consider the social sadness of death, the extraordinary claim of Christ, and the noble confession of faith.

I —THE SOCIAL SADNESS OF DEATH

The death of Lazarus had made many sad, spread a dark shadow over the hearts of not a few. Whilst Martha's grief took the form of restless excitement, Mary's held her at home in silent solitude. The neighbours too were affected with the saddening touch of sorrow : "*Many of the Jews came to Martha and Mary, to comfort them concerning their brother.*" The God of love has implanted in human hearts such a mighty and mystic tie of sympathy, that a painful event personal to one will touch many into grief; the groan of one will vibrate on the heart-chords of many. The noble mother of a large family writhes in agony on her death-bed. By her pure life and beneficent ministries she has won the love of all around her; her neighbours "called her blessed." Who is the sufferer? Not merely the dying mother, but all who loved her suffer. The mental anguish of her dear children and attached husband is in some respects far deeper and intenser than the physical pains of the dying one. There is an enormous amount of vicarious suffering in the human family. The bodily sufferings of one become the mental anguish of many. In all the lanes, alleys, and streets of social life there are those moving about who are bearing in their hearts the miseries of others. The more love a man has in him, the larger the amount of vicarious suffering that he will endure in a world of trial and sorrow. Hence, He Who had more love in Him than all the race besides—Who was love itself, Divine, incarnate, unbounded love—became while here a "Man of sorrows and acquainted with grief." "Surely He hath borne our griefs, and carried our sorrows." To suffer for others by sympathy is not only natural, but Christly. We are commanded to "bear each other's burdens, and so fulfil the law of Christ."

The words lead us to consider—

II —THE EXTRAORDINARY CLAIM OF CHRIST

"*I am the Resurrection and the Life.*" What words are these? Such words never sounded on this earth before. No man before ever gave utterance to such language. Had any other but Christ pronounced them, they would have sounded as astounding arrogance and blasphemy the most revolting. But from Him they seemed to flow naturally; they chime in, not only with His professions, but with His antecedent life of superhuman excellence. What can they mean? Interpreters disagree. Who shall penetrate into their import? Who shall sound their abyss? It is clear, I think, from the circumstances under which Christ uttered these words, as well as from the interpretation of them by Martha, that Christ did not mean *moral* death, but *physical*—the death of the body. But if this be the case, how can it be explained that he that believeth on Him shall never physically die; or, that if he had physically died, he should live again? We suggest three facts which seem to be implied in the expression—

First: That death, whatever it is, is a great evil. What is death in the Bible sense? It is not the mere dissolution of the body, the return of the organized dust back to its primitive elements. This dissolution seems to be a natural event—as natural as birth and growth. It is, for many reasons, highly probable that, had man never sinned, this dissolution would have taken place. Like all organized bodies, man's body would have gone back to dust. The death, I take it, threatened as the consequence of his sin, is something over and above this, something that gave it a moral significance and a terror which it otherwise would not have possessed. "In the day thou eatest thereof, thou shalt surely die," which means literally, *dying thou shalt die.* The language implies the idea of *intensity* rather than of certainty. It seems to me to mean this: Thy death, man, in case thou sinnest, shall indeed be death —shall be a far more terrible thing than the death of those creatures that thou seest expiring around thee. It is sin that invests this event with its terrible significance. Sin is its "sting," that which gives it virus and agony to the man. Sin clothes this event with many terrible attributes, such as—(1.) *Physical sufferings.* Had there been no sin, the body might have returned to dust without any pain. (2.) *Grievous disappointments.* Had man not sinned, he would have returned to the dust without any broken purposes. (3.) *Social disruptions.* Had man not sinned, he would have returned to dust without the rupturing of any tender ties; he would have passed away in the full hope of meeting the survivors soon again. (4.) *Moral forebodings.* Two things make death especially terrible to us—the fear lest it should be the end of our being, and the fear lest it should be the end of our happiness.

Take away all these elements from physical dissolution—take away from it its physical suffering, mental disappointments, social disruptions, and its moral forebodings, and what is it? A simple natural event, that might be hailed as a blessing. These things make death *death;* and this, I think, is what is meant by death everywhere in the New Testament. It is not the event; it is the *curse,* the misery, the wretchedness connected with it. Perhaps the word *death* might in the Scriptures be rendered *curse.* "In the day thou eatest thereof thou shalt surely *be cursed.*" "By one man sin entered into the world, and *the curse* by sin." This view of death will throw light on many ambiguous passages, such, for instance, as "the wages of sin is death." If death there meant only physical dissolution, the wages are both inadequately and generally very tardily paid. Again: "To be carnally minded is death." All ungodly men are "carnally minded"; and there is no physical death in that state of mind. Again, we read that "Christ hath abolished death," &c. Now, if death in these cases means physical dissolution, there is scarcely truth in it; for that goes on. Men die as regularly since His advent, eighteen centuries ago, as they did before. Death is as great a conqueror as ever. But if it means curse, or misery, then it is true that Christ hath destroyed and abolished all that in the experience of His disciples. The fear is removed; the sting is gone. Another fact suggested is—

Secondly: That from this evil Christ is the great Deliverer. "*I am the Resurrection and the Life.*" Christ is life,—the original, fontal, absolute life. "I am He that liveth," &c. He is the resuscitating life too—the *Resurrection,* Not only does He create new life, but He resuscitates the old. Now, understanding death in the sense indicated, viz. as the curse of sin, we know that Christ is the "*Resurrection*" in this respect: He delivers men from sin. "Forasmuch, then, as the children are partakers of flesh and blood, He also Himself likewise took part of the same; that through death He might destroy him that had the power of death, that is, the devil; and deliver them who through fear of death were all their lifetime subject to bondage." Again: "He hath abolished death." In the experience of all those in all ages who have trusted in Him, He has been the "*Resurrection and the Life.*" He has taken away the sting of death, turned the forbidding monster into an attractive friend, so that they have desired to depart, &c. The other fact suggested is—

Thirdly: That from this evil He delivers on the condition of trust in Him. "*He that believeth in Me, though he were dead yet shall he live: and whosoever liveth and believeth in Me shall never die.*" *
He that trusteth in Him,—not in what men say about Him, not merely in the facts of His life, or the doctrines of His teaching, but *in Him*, as the living, loving Son of God, the Saviour of the world —shall never die; that is, shall never know the curse of death, that which makes death terrible. St. Paul, as well as hundreds more, have experienced this. He said, "O death, where is thy sting? O grave, where is thy victory? The sting of death is sin: but thanks be unto God, which giveth us the victory through our Lord Jesus Christ." The words lead us to consider—

III —THE NOBLE CONFESSION OF FAITH

"*Believest thou this? She said unto Him, Yea, Lord, I believe that Thou art the Christ, the Son of God, which should come into the world.*" The preceding verses show that before this Martha had a certain amount of faith. She believed that Christ had the power to *prevent death*.

"*If Thou hadst been here, my brother had not died.*" Whether she had as yet risen to the true conception of His Messiahship or not, she evidently regarded Him as endowed with supernatural power. Of what man that she had ever known had she entertained the idea that he could prevent death? She had, like all, seen death going on around her: men dying in her village, dying in the neighbouring city of Jerusalem; and she had witnessed efforts of skill and loving attention to prevent death. But no one had appeared who could do it. But here, in Christ, she knew there was One Who could have done it. Moreover, she believed in the possibility of Christ securing the interposition of God on her behalf. "*But I know that even now, whatsoever Thou wilt ask of God, God will give it Thee.*" She knew that all life was in the hands of God, and believed that Christ had the power to secure His interposition.

* See Germ, p. 323.

She had acknowledged her faith in a *general resurrection of the dead.* A belief in a general resurrection was prevalent among the Pharisees. But now her faith struck a deeper root and pulsated with a new vitality. "*I believe that Thou art the Christ, the Son of God.*" This is the true confession of faith,—faith in Christ.

Germs of Thought
No. 41   John 11:26

DEATH AVOIDED

"Whosoever liveth and believeth in Me shall never die."—xi. 26.

What does this mean ? Does it mean—(1.) Freedom from *corporeal death ?* Nothing does the world dread so much as death, and nothing would it hail with greater exultation than a deliverance from it. Albeit so long as men continue sinful, a deliverance from corporeal mortality would be an evil rather than a good. Death seems to arrest the course of sin, and to prevent the world from becoming a Pandemonium. Does it mean—(2.) Freedom from *annihilation ?* We are in no danger of this, and this in itself is no boon : non-existence is better than a miserable existence. What then does it mean ? Generally it means this : that nothing that gives value to life, nothing that makes life worth having shall ever die, if we truly believe in Christ.

I —THE HEALTHY ACTION OF OUR SPIRITUAL POWERS WILL NEVER CEASE

What is life without activity ? Worthless. And what is activity unless it be healthful ? Misery. Faith in Christ secures the healthy action of all our spiritual faculties ; the *perceptive, reflective, imaginative, recollective, anticipative,* will work harmoniously for ever.

II —NOTHING VALUABLE IN OUR SPIRITUAL ACQUISITIONS WILL EVER BE LOST

What is life without ideas, emotions, memories, habits ? A blank. And what is it with those if they are not of a truly virtuous character ? Despicable and wretched. But when these acquisitions are holy, life is blessed. Faith in Christ secures the permanency and perfection of all true ideas, affections, principles, habits, &c. "Our works do follow us." We cannot labour in vain in the Lord.

III —ALL THE SOURCES OF TRUE PLEASURE WILL CONTINUE FOR EVER

What are the sources of true enjoyment ? *Intellectual*—study, &c. *Social*—friendship, usefulness, &c. *Religious*—communion with God, worship. Faith in Christ then :—in *Him,* not in propositions concerning Him ; not in what theologians say about Him ; but in *Him* as the living, loving, personal Son of God and Saviour of mankind, is the condition of a happy immortality.

John 11:28-32

THE FAMILY AT BETHANY (No. 4.)

" And when she had so said, she went her way, and called Mary her sister secretly, saying, The Master is come, and calleth for thee," &c.—xi. 28—32.

EXEGETICAL REMARKS.—Ver. 28.— " *And when she had so said, she went her way* (R. V. AWAY), *and called Mary her sister secretly, saying.*" "*Secretly*" implies, perhaps, a mere whisper. Probably Mary had retired to some secluded chamber of the house, as far as possible away from the presence of the Jews who had come to mourn. " *The Master.*" Some render it, "the Teacher," or " our Teacher." This family regarded Christ, not merely as their Friend, but as their moral Master, Teacher. " *Is come, and calleth for thee.*" It would seem as if Christ required Mary to go forth to Him as unobserved as possible, in order to awaken no public excitement.

Ver. 29.—" *As soon as* (R. V. AND SHE WHEN) *she heard that, she arose quickly, and came* (R. V. WENT) *unto Him.*" With all the promptitude of affection, she hastened to obey the voice of love.

Vers. 30.—" *Now Jesus was not yet come into the town* (R. V. VILLAGE), *but was in that* (R. V. STILL IN THE) *place where Martha met Him.*" Bengel remarks, that Jesus did everything with a suitable delay. His tarrying outside the village, somewhere near the burial-ground, which was always outside the town, brought the whole company of Mary's comforters to Him. As they followed her toward the grave, they found themselves in the presence of the Master, and were thus brought into a situation to behold the wondrous miracle.

Ver. 31.—" *The Jews then which were with her in the house, and comforted* (R. V. WERE COMFORTING) *her,* *when they saw Mary, that she rose up hastily* (R. V. QUICKLY) *and went out, followed her, saying, She goeth* (R. V. SUPPOSING THAT SHE WAS GOING) *unto the grave* (R. V. TOMB) *to weep there.*" It is customary in the East for survivors to resort for several days to the tombs of their friends, there to pour out their grief at their graves. Nothing was more natural, therefore, for the mourners, when they saw Mary withdraw, than to conclude that she was gone to the grave to weep, and to follow her thither.

Ver. 32.—" *Then when Mary was come* (R. V. MARY THEREFORE WHEN SHE CAME) *where Jesus was, and saw Him, she fell down at His feet, saying unto Him, Lord, if Thou hadst been here, my brother had not died.*" " The first stroke of character which distinguishes Mary from Martha is seen in the expression, she '*fell down at His feet.*' The second is, that she says nothing further than, ' Lord, if Thou hadst been here, my brother had not died.' While Martha added to these words, 'and even now I know,' &c. (ver. 22). Mary bursts into tears. Martha may at first strike us as the one who possesses the greater joy in believing; but Mary is the more human and warm in her feelings, and there is more of devotion in the expression of her faith. Her kneeling posture and her tears are more eloquent than the words of Martha. The saying that both utter constitutes a precious trait from life. They made this remark to each other over and over again at the deathbed of Lazarus: ' If He were here !'"—*Lange.*

HOMILETICS

In this portion of the narrative concerning *The Family at Bethany*, we have what may be justly considered *the Gospel message to every man;* and we have it here clearly stated, properly delivered, and rightly received. We have it—

I—CLEARLY STATED

"*The Master is come, and calleth for thee.*" *   What Martha said to Mary may be regarded as a glorious truth addressed to all men. First: "*The Master is come.*" Come from heaven, come to this earth, come for every man. "This is a faithful saying, and worthy of all acceptation, that Christ Jesus came into the world to save sinners." Of all the facts in the history of the world, none is better attested, more important, or more glorious than this.

Secondly : The Master *invites individuals.* "*And calleth for thee.*" It is as true that Christ invites individual men to Him now as that through Martha He invited Mary to Him. He "*calleth for thee*" in the operations of nature, in the events of history, in the workings of conscience, in the ministry of His servants. He "*calleth for thee,*" to heal thy diseases, to break thy chains, to enlighten thy judgment, to cleanse thy conscience, to purify thy heart, and to save thy soul. "Come unto Me, all ye that labour, and are heavy laden," &c. We have this Gospel message—

II—RIGHTLY DELIVERED

The way in which Martha delivered the message to her sister is worthy of the imitation of every Gospel minister.

First: She did it *undoubtingly.* She had just seen the Master; she had confessed her faith in Him. "*I believe that Thou art the Christ, the Son of God;*" and she proceeds direct from His presence, filled with the spirit of her mission, to Mary. "*When she had so said*"—that is, when she had made the confession—"*she went her way, and called, Mary.*" He who delivers the message without being assured of its truth, is no genuine preacher ; that Christ has come and calls for men, must be amongst the most settled convictions in his mind. Any doubting on this subject is a disqualification for the work.

Secondly : She did it *judiciously.* She "*called Mary her sister secretly.*" Why she did it "*secretly*" does not appear. We may be sure it was not from fear on her part; for love is heroic. Probably an interview with Him, before the crowd gathered to witness the grand transaction, was needful to establish her faith, and calm her spirit. There is a prudence necessary in delivering the Gospel message, a prudence which has regard to *times, circumstances,* and *moods of mind.* We have here this Gospel message—

III—PROPERLY RECEIVED

How did Mary receive this message ? Just as every hearer of the Gospel should.

First: Promptly. "*As soon as she heard that, she arose quickly, and came unto Him.*" She did not wait to consult her companions

* See Germ, p. 327.

who were with her in the house: without the pause of a moment, she crossed the threshold of her house and hastened forth to Christ. The Gospel call demands instant attention. "Immediately I conferred not with flesh and blood." The delay of a moment after the call has come, is at once wrong and perilous. "To-day, if ye will hear His voice."

Secondly: Resolutely. "*Now Jesus was not yet come into the town, but was in that place where Martha met Him.*" On an occasion so full of excitement, it required no little nerve for Mary to leave her home, pass beyond the boundaries of her village to the spot where Jesus stood in sublime solitude. It requires that the Gospel call should be attended to with a determination of soul. There are so many opposing forces, so many unfavourable considerations, that nothing less than invincibility of purpose is required. "I will follow Thee whithersoever Thou goest."

Thirdly: Fearlessly. "*The Jews then which were with her in the house, and comforted her, when they saw Mary, that she rose up hastily and went out, followed her, saying, She goeth unto the grave to weep there.*" Well she knew that her going forth to meet Jesus would be contrary to the wish of the Jews in her house, if they knew it. Indeed, when she broke away from them, they did not seem to have the slightest suspicion that she was going to Jesus; they concluded that she was going to weep at the grave of her brother. Defiant of their prejudices and wishes, she obeys the command. Thus it must be with those who would comply with the invitations of the Gospel; they must be fearless of all opposition; they must dare persecution, if need be.

Fourthly: Devoutly. "*Then when Mary was come where Jesus was, and saw Him, she fell down at His feet.*" At His feet she broke into tears, not mere tears of grief for her brother, but rather, perhaps, of ecstasy and delight at seeing once more Him Who was more to her than brother, or sister, or the world—the Christ, the Son of God. "*Lord, if Thou hadst been here, my brother had not died.*" Thou art mightier than death. My brother had been living, hadst Thou been here.

CONCLUSION. Here is—(1.) A fact in which humanity should rejoice. "*The Master is come, and calleth for thee.*" Thank God for the advent of this Heavenly Teacher, man's Moral Master, Guide, and Saviour. What fools are those—alas! how numerous—who accept not His invitation, and hasten not to His presence! Here is—(2.) An example which preachers should imitate. Like Martha, they should proclaim the advent and sound the invitation, and do so undoubtingly, fired with the spirit of the message, yet with godly judiciousness. Here is—(3.) Conduct which Gospel hearers should follow. Like Mary, they should go promptly, resolutely, fearlessly, and devoutly, to meet the Heavenly Teacher.

Germs of Thought
No. 42   John 11:28

THE LATEST ARRIVAL *

"The Master is come, and calleth for thee."—xi. 28

I shall draw my illustrations from the facts narrated in this chapter, as I proceed to ask and answer the following questions :—

I —WHO HAS COME ?

" *The Master* "—One who rules, governs, directs, or has supreme authority.   How appropriate the title !   He is Master of man and all his surroundings; Master of the mighty forces of nature and the laws by which they are governed; Master of this mighty planetary system and all the stellar universe; Master of all animate and inanimate existences, " whether they be thrones, dominions, principalities, or powers ; for all things were created by Him and for Him."

II —HOW DID HE COME ?

In our perfect humanity—able to sympathize with us in our sorrows as a Man, and as God to take them away—able to enjoy the innocent festivities of a marriage feast, and to stand weeping with sisters beside their brother's grave ; His heart in each case beating in unison with the company.   He came along the dreary road of poverty, persecution, and pain, while every step brought Him nearer to a death of the most awful and ignominious character. This was necessary, that He "might be a merciful and faithful High Priest in things pertaining to God, to make reconciliation for the sins of the people."

III —WHEN DID HE COME ?

Not until human sympathy and skill had done their best, and utterly failed.   Lazarus is dead.   Those loving sisters left nothing undone, kind friends did what they could, and the physician's skill was taxed to the uttermost, but all in vain, for Lazarus grew worse and worse ; soon was still in death.   So *spiritually*.   With all the tonics and stimulants of natural religion, the genial aid of poetry, the bracing power of science, philosophy, and varied culture, man continued to grow worse and worse ; so that when the Master came, He found the nations "dead in trespasses and sins," and beyond the power of human recovery.

IV —WHAT DOES HE SAY ?

He comes to inquire after the cause of our trouble : " *Where have ye laid him ?* "   He wants to get face to face with the cause of all

* In revising this germ the author has some doubts as to whether it is really his, although there are some expressions that are undoubtedly his own.

our trouble and sorrow, that He may take it away. My brother, "*the Master is come,*" and is inquiring after that evil heart of yours which has caused you so much sorrow. God help you to bring Him right up to it, and say, "Blessed Master, here it is—foul and polluted ; but if Thou wilt, Thou canst make me clean, and here I give Thee unrestricted sway." Do this, and you will feel the pulsations of an imparted life which will lift you out of your spiritual sepulchre, and enable you to throw off your carnal grave-clothes, with a new song in your mouth, even praises to our God.

V —FOR WHOM DOES HE CALL ?

"*For thee.*" Learn from this, religion is a *personal* thing. "The Master is come, and calleth for *thee.*" Take a note of this,—*for thee.* My brother, unless you heed the call of this blessed Master, and come personally in contact with Him, and bring Him face to face with your polluted guilty spirit, His arrival will but deepen your condemnation and make darker your doom. "*The Master is come.*" His stay may not be long, but He "*calleth for thee.*"

> "He now stands knocking at the door
> Of every sinner's heart."

John 11:33-38

THE FAMILY AT BETHANY (No. 5.)

" When Jesus therefore saw her weeping, and the Jews also weeping which came with her, He groaned in the spirit, and was troubled, and said," &c.—xi. 33—38.

EXEGETICAL REMARKS.—Ver. 33.— "*When Jesus therefore saw her weeping, and the Jews also weeping which came with her, He groaned in the spirit, and was troubled.*" ἐνεβριμήσατο τῷ πνεύματι, καὶ ἐτάραξεν ἑαυτόν. Some regard the verse as expressing indignation, some grief ; *Alford* regards it "to be moved with indignation." Dr. Samuel Davidson translates it, "greatly moved in spirit." But who can analyze the emotions of a Mind which so infinitely transcends our minds, both intellectually and morally ?

Ver. 34.—"*And said, Where have ye laid him ?*" A question asked, not, of course, for the sake of information ; but in order to awaken interest, according to His custom.

Ver. 35.—"*Jesus wept.*" One of the shortest of sentences, but fraught with an unfathomable meaning.

Ver. 36.—"*Then said the Jews* (R. V. THE JEWS THEREFORE SAID), *Behold how He loved him !*" These bystanding Jews interpreted the flowing tears of Jesus as a demonstration of His love for Lazarus ; but had those tears no reference to the ravages of sin, the unbelief and the moral corruption to be seen in the men around Him ?

Ver. 37.—"*And* (R. V. BUT) *some of them said, Could not this Man, which opened the eyes of the* (R. V. HIM THAT WAS) *blind, have caused that even this man* (R. V. THIS MAN ALSO) *should not have died ?*" (R. V. DIE.) Some interpreters regard this speech as having malice in it, and as intended to express the idea that Christ either lacked the disposition or the power to prevent death. Perhaps they wished to insinuate that His inability to raise Lazarus, proved by His tears, was sufficient to show that He never opened the eyes of the blind, as reported, and that therefore He was an impostor. Others, however, give another interpretation, and regard the expression as indicating no malicious disposition, no doubt of His past miracles, but simply wonder that this miraculously endowed Being should allow a friend to die.

Ver. 38.—"*Jesus therefore again groaning in Himself cometh to the grave* (R. V. TOMB). *It* (R. V. NOW IT) *was a cave, and a stone lay upon* (R. V. AGAINST) *it.*" In some ancient nations cremation was practised, and the burnt ashes of the dead were deposited in urns. This, however, was not the custom of the Jews ; they buried in the earth. Survivors closed the eyes, washed the body, perfumed it, swathed

it in numerous folds of linen with spices enclosed. Burial-places were always without the cities, but within easy reach ; they were caves, either natural or hewn. In some of these caves several persons could stand upright. In such a cave the body of Lazarus was placed, and its mouth was closed with a massive stone fitted to the aperture. The tomb that is now pointed out to travellers as the tomb of Lazarus, is a chamber in a rock underground, entered by twenty-six irregular, rough, winding steps cut out in the rock. But there are serious doubts as to whether this be the real spot.

HOMILETICS

In this portion of the narrative concerning the *Family at Bethany,* we are led to consider three subjects.

I —DEATH'S INFLUENCE UPON HUMAN HEARTS

"*When Jesus therefore saw her weeping, and the Jews also weeping which came with her, He groaned in the spirit, and was troubled.*" The death of Lazarus was an event that touched the hearts of the sisters, of the Jews, and of Jesus, and made them *all* weep. Here is a community of feeling and of tears. How many wept now ! One weeper will make others who are present weep, even though they neither know nor feel the cause of distress. It has been said, that what will have but little influence on a few persons will often thrill an assembly of thousands. "There is a kind of sympathetic electricity in a crowd, by means of which the small agitations are united, so that, like a wave, they strike each soul with a force equal to the sum of all their forces." The weepers here did not weep for the same reasons. The reason of Mary's tears was not felt by the unbelieving Jews ; and the reason of our Saviour's tears was different to that, not only of the Jews, but of the sisters also. All tears are not of the same character ; there are tears of reality, which are the automatic and involuntary expressions of the heart, and tears of falsehood, feigned and hypocritical and therefore voluntary. There are the tears of joy as well as sorrow, tears of disappointment and tears of hope, tears of love and tears of anger, tears of grief and tears of rapture, tears of weakness and tears of power. Tears show the mysterious connection between the soul and the body. One solitary thought springing up involuntarily in the mind, can open at once the lachrymose fountains and make showers run down the face.

But the one great event that affected all the hearts here, was death. And this event has lost none of its power; it strikes sadness into all souls. Hardened as humanity is, there are, I trow, but few in any age whose hearts death has not smitten. Who amongst the giddiest has ever laughed in the presence of a corpse? Who amongst the most callous has not had convulsive throbs as he felt the cold touch of death? Why should death thus produce this distress in men? Other creatures seem to look on it with calmness. They will tread on the dead bodies of their young with indifference. Is it because death is repugnant to our nature? or because of the ideas we associate with it? Perhaps both. The words lead us to consider—

II —MAN'S MISINTERPRETATION OF DIVINE PHILANTHROPY

"*Jesus wept. Then said the Jews, Behold how He loved him! And some of them said, Could not this Man, which opened the eyes of the blind, have caused that even this man should not have died?*"

"*Jesus wept.*" This short sentence is a sun in a spark, a universe in an atom. The word is not the same as when He wept over Jerusalem; there it means He wept aloud, here He wept silently. He wept in sympathy with the other weepers. Oh those tears of His! they were drops from the boundless ocean of His love! The Jews regarded the tears as an expression of His love for Lazarus. "*Behold how He loved him!*" And His love was to them a wonder. "*And some of them said, Could not this Man, which opened the eyes of the blind, have caused that even this man should not have died?*"

First: The difficulty which they now felt has always been prevalent. It was this: Why—seeing that Jesus so loved Lazarus—did He allow him to die? It could not be from the lack of power, for He had wrought other miracles, such as opening the eyes of the blind. Where is Christ's consistency in loving a man, and yet allowing him to suffer and to die? Now this has always been a difficulty with men. Men are always asking why, if Christ loves us, does He allow us to be afflicted with diseases, distressed by disappointments, crushed by poverty, heart-broken by bereavements? Is the suffering which is everywhere prevalent amongst His disciples, consistent with His love?

Secondly: This prevalent difficulty is capable of solution. Why? Not because suffering in any form can be pleasing to His benevolent nature; not because He could not prevent it; but because His disciples need it. "No suffering for the present is joyous, but grievous; nevertheless it worketh out the peaceable fruits of righteousness to them that are exercised thereby." Pain is a beneficent minister. Pain whips the dormant intellect into action; indeed, all our sciences owe their existence to pain. Pain rouses us to action against evils that would prove our ruin. Pain detaches our sympathies from the material and the evanescent, and turns them to the spiritual and the eternal. Pain is often the curative element in the cup of life. What could the world of corrupt humanity do without pain ? Hence its existence is love : "Whom the Lord loveth, He chasteneth." You may say to Christ, " *He whom Thou lovest* " is heart-broken with disappointment, is writhing with agony, is overwhelmed with sorrow, is famishing with hunger. Very well, the loved one needs it, and love does it.

The words lead us to consider—

III —CHRIST'S LAMENTATION OVER HUMAN UNBELIEF

" *Jesus therefore again groaning in Himself cometh to the grave.*" Why did He groan ? Not because Lazarus was dead, for that event He could have prevented. Not because Lazarus was in his grave, for He was conscious of the power to raise him, and He was now about to exercise it. Was it because of the ravages of sin which He saw everywhere around Him—saw in the ages past and the world over ? No doubt this would deeply affect Him. Indeed He seemed always affected when He came into conscious contact with this, even in its smallest aspects. Thus, for example, we read in Mark vii. 34, when a man deaf and dumb was brought to Him, that He " *sighs.*" Looking over Jerusalem, He seemed to break into a wild agony of grief; and down in Gethsemane He falls prostrate under the sense of the enormity of the ravages of sin, and exclaims : "My soul is exceeding sorrowful." But perhaps that which was the immediate cause of His present sorrow, was the unbelief of the people around Him. This unbelief even the sisters had exhibited, when they said, "Lord, if Thou hadst been here, my brother had not died." As if they had said, Thou mightest have prevented his death, but Thou canst do nothing now, for Thou canst not restore him. And again they showed it when they exclaimed, "Lord, by this time he stinketh : for he hath been dead four days." The expression of the Jews : "Could not this Man, which opened the eyes of the blind, have caused that even this man should not have died ? " is full of unbelief. Why is the unbelief of men so distressing to the heart of Christ ? Why does it make Him groan and shudder ?

First : Because, unless they believe in Him, He cannot save them. Faith in Him, we are assured, both by philosophy, history, consciousness, and the Bible, is essential to lift the human soul into sympathy and fellowship with the Eternal Fountain of purity and blessedness.

Secondly : Because, unless they believe in Him, His beneficent mission into the world is frustrated. He could not do "many mighty works " in one place "because of their unbelief." In all departments of action men's unbelief prevents God helping them.

Would the agriculturist have God to perform mighty works on his fields, covering them in autumn with abundant crops, then he must have faith in the laws of nature and the capacity of the soil. Would the poor man have God to perform mighty works for him, raise him from penury and obscurity to wealth and influence, he must have faith in the principle that the "hand of the diligent maketh rich." Would the statesman have God to perform mighty works for his country, he must in all the measures that he proposes and the laws he enacts, have faith in the truth that " righteousness exalteth a nation." It is so in everything. Read Hebrews xi.

John 11:39, 40

THE FAMILY AT BETHANY (No. 6.)

" Jesus said, Take ye away the stone. Martha, the sister of him that was dead, saith unto Him, Lord, by this time he stinketh : for he hath been dead four days. Jesus saith unto her, Said I not unto thee, that, if thou wouldest believe, thou shouldest see the glory of God ?"—xi. 39, 40.

EXEGETICAL REMARKS.—Ver. 39.— " *Jesus said, Take ye away the stone. Martha, the sister of him that was dead, saith unto Him, Lord, by this time he stinketh : for he hath been dead four days.*" "The fearful reality of the grave in which her brother has lain four days disturbs the practical woman, and shakes her faith. She thinks a scandal may result from the bursting forth of the odour of corruption, especially in the presence of so many people from Jerusalem. True, it follows from the reason she assigns for her remark, that she does not already perceive this odour. For he hath been dead four days. It is a proverb in the Talmud and the Targum, that corruption sets in the third day after death. As the sister of the dead man, she shudders at the thought of seeing her brother in a putrefying state, of witnessing the exposure of that countenance upon which corruption has already set its seal."— *Lange.*

Ver. 40.—" *Jesus saith unto her, Said I not unto thee, that, if thou wouldest believe* (R. V. THAT IF THOU BELIEVEDST), *thou shouldest see the glory of God !*" God's glory is the manifestation of Himself ; and this manifestation to the individual soul depends upon faith. We need not understand that the miracle depended on her faith ; but her perception of the glory of God depended on her faith.

HOMILETICS

There are two subjects of thought in this portion of the narrative concerning the *Family at Bethany.*
Here we have—

I —CHRIST'S CONDESCENSION IN EMPLOYING MAN IN CARRYING OUT HIS PURPOSES

" *Take ye away the stone.*" Could not Christ do this Himself? Yes; not only by the touch of His hand, but by the volition of His mind. Does He need help in performing a miracle? The idea is absurd. He did it, not for His sake, but for theirs. In doing it they would not help Him, but help themselves. No principle is more clearly revealed throughout all sentient existences than this, that God does not do for a creature that which He has given the creature power to do for itself. He carries food to the plants because they cannot go in search of it; but all to whom He has given the power of locomotion must go in search of their food or die. This principle is manifestly true in relation to man. He requires man to work out the powers with which He has endowed him. In this ordinance man is both honoured and helped.

First : Christ could *feed* us without our labour. He Who fed by miracle multitudes on the height of Capernaum of old, could feed all human beings on the face of the earth without any labour or effort of their own. He could bring the necessary daily meal into every homestead. But He does not do so, and this is well for man. The mental devisings and the physical toilings necessary under the present system to get food are scarcely less essential, not only to man's strength but to man's subsistence, than food itself. To the lazy farmer, whose grounds are a wilderness, God says, " *Take ye away the stone.*" You do your work, and I will do Mine.

Secondly : Christ could *enlighten* us without our labour. As He has given to every insect a sufficient instinctive light to secure its well-being, He might have given us a sufficient knowledge on all the questions necessary to our interests. He might have planted in our mental heavens the stars of all true science, physical, intellectual, and moral. But He has not done so. This also is well. The intellectual and moral effort, the study and the perseverance required to master even the simplest of the sciences, are better for us than the possession of all knowledge. The ideas we get for ourselves are infinitely more valuable to us than those that are imparted to us; convictions self-produced are a thousand times more valuable than all the creeds of Christendom. Hence, to the ignorant men, whose mental domain is, like the vineyard of the sluggard, in ruins, God says, " *Take ye away the stone,*" go and work.

Thirdly : Christ could have given us the means of *spiritual improvement* without our labour. He could have caused Bibles and the best books to come down like the manna of old and surround our dwellings. He could have planted churches and chapels, schools and libraries, in every mountain, in every corner of every street in every town. But He has not done so ; this also is well. We must buy our Bibles, procure our books, establish our libraries, build our churches and our schools : and all this is priceless discipline. To a man destitute of the means of spiritual improvement, God says, " *Take ye away the stone,*" and set to work. The process is better than the result. In the deed there is the blessedness.

The verses suggest—

II —HUMAN UNBELIEF IN SUGGESTING DIFFICULTIES AS TO THE FULFILMENT OF HIS PURPOSES

" *By this time he stinketh.*" How can it be done ? Not only are the senses dulled, the blood frozen, the limbs sealed, but decomposition has taken place, the disintegration of the particles is proceeding. No doubt Martha felt the difficulties were insuperable, and that there was no hope.

Now there is a tendency everywhere in men to suggest difficulties in relation to the fulfilment of Christ's purposes. Christ has proposed to work out the moral reformation of mankind, to " put away sin " from all institutions, books, trades, professions, tribes, nations, and individuals on the face of the earth. This, and nothing else, is His purpose. But what difficulties are suggested on all hands ! We are pointed to the obstructions, and told that they are insurmountable. We are pointed to their *number*, errors, habits, lusts, prejudices, institutions, domestic, political, social, and religious— add them together, and how great the sum ! We are pointed to their *strength*, fixed as firmly as the granite mountains, more deeply and firmly rooted than the oaks of the forest. We are pointed *to the little progress His purpose is making.* It is said that after the lapse of nearly nineteen centuries the obstructions are as numerous and as firm as ever ; and that notwithstanding the progress of intelligence and civilization the cause of real moral reformation has made but little advance. Well, moral humanity is in the grave, its sepulchre is deep, and massive is the stone which covers it up ; and, like Martha, we may say it " *stinketh.*" And truly its disgusting odour loads the atmosphere. Still, be not faithless, but believing. Christ is approaching the tomb. "The hour cometh, and now is, when all that are in their graves shall hear His voice."

John 11:41-44

THE FAMILY AT BETHANY (No. 7.)

"Then they took away the stone from the place where the dead was laid," &c.

EXEGETICAL REMARKS.—Vers. 41, 42.—" *Then* (R. V. SO) *they took away the stone from the place where the dead was laid.* (R. V. OMITS THIS CLAUSE.) *And Jesus lifted up His eyes, and said, Father, I thank Thee that Thou hast heard* (R. V. HEARDEST) *Me. And I knew that Thou hearest Me always : but because of the people* (R. V. MULTITUDE) *which stand by* (R. V. STANDETH AROUND) *I said it, that they may believe that Thou hast sent* (R. V. DIDST SEND) *Me.*" " This is the only instance in which our Lord uttered a prayer before performing a miracle. Nothing can be more dignified than His communion with His Father in these words, which are such as no other person could have employed. He thanks Him for the result before it was obtained ; and by implying that there was no necessity for formal prayer on His own account, He further implies His perfect union in the Spirit with the Father. *διὰ τὸν ὄχλον.* The people were to be taught now, by a great example, a phenomenon, the meaning of such assertions as those, v. 19—21, 36, 37 ; viii. 16."—*Webster.*

Ver. 43. —"*And when He thus had* (R. V. HAD THUS) *spoken, He cried with a loud voice.*" It does not seem to have been His custom to speak loudly : " He did not cause His voice to be heard in the street," &c. He did so now, not because He would move the dead by it more than by a silent volition, but in order to call the attention of the multitude to the stupendous miracle He was about to perform. "*Lazarus, come forth.*" How must this voice have affected the multitude, thrilling all hearts !

Ver. 44.—"*And he that was dead came forth, bound hand and foot with graveclothes.*" He came forth entangled in the graveclothes from which, it seems, he could not disengage himself. "*Jesus saith unto them, Loose him, and let him go.*" "It is the remark of *Ferness,* that at first view there seems to be here a descent in the narrative to a trifling particular ; but when it is considered into what consternation the bystanders must have been thrown at the sight of the dead man coming to life, rendering them, by the palsy of fear, incapable for the moment of assisting Lazarus in his vain struggles to free himself from the folds in which he was wrapped hand and foot, the sublime self-possession of Jesus appears in the important command by which He quietly bade them loose the graveclothes and set the newly risen man at liberty. *Priestly* observes, that there was a natural gradation in the three miracles by which Jesus raised persons to life. The first was a person just dead, the second was one who was carried out to be buried, and the third had been dead and buried four days." —*Livermore.* It was an early legend of the Church, that Lazarus was now thirty years of age, and lived after his resurrection another thirty years.

HOMILETICS

In this portion of the narrative of the *Family at Bethany,* we have the *Remarkable words of Christ at the grave of Lazarus.* Notice—

I —THE WORDS WHICH HE ADDRESSED TO HEAVEN

"*Jesus lifted up His eyes, and said, Father, I thank Thee that Thou hast heard Me. And I knew that Thou hearest Me always.*"

In this solemn and sublime appeal to Heaven we have—

First : His recognition of God as His Father. He was the Son of God in a higher sense than any other moral creature ever has been, or perhaps ever will be—a relationship of mutual resemblance and love. (1.) A higher mutual *resemblance.* He was "the express image of His person." (2.) A higher mutual *love.* The Father loved Him in a sense higher than that in which He loved any other human being. "This is My beloved Son, in whom I am well pleased." And He loved the Father supremely. The Father's will was the absolute law of His life.

Secondly : His consciousness of His Father's regard for Him. "*I thank Thee that Thou hast heard Me. And I knew that Thou hearest Me always."* Ever in close communion with His Father. And to every aspiration of His He felt His Father's response. *"Always"*—no exception, not a word of true prayer is ever lost.

Thirdly: His consideration for men in giving utterance to His devotions. *"But because of the people which stand by I said it."* Audible words, though not *essential* to worship, and having no influence on the Infinite Father, still are often useful to our fellow-men. *"Because of the people which stand by I said it."* *Clarke* supposes that the audible prayer here to God was intended to show that the miracle was not by Satanic power, but truly Divine. Words in prayer are accidents, not essential. Prayer is a spirit, a spirit of dependence on God, ever abiding, ever inspiring and controlling. It uses words, not to inform or influence the Infinite, but to stimulate devotion in self and others. The prayer of Christ on this occasion is not recorded; probably it had no words. His words of thanksgiving, which were for the good of the bystanders, are recorded. We have here—

II —THE WORDS WHICH HE ADDRESSED TO THE DEAD

"And when He had thus spoken, He cried with a loud voice, Lazarus, come forth." Observe—

First: His words to the dead were personal. *"Lazarus."* He calls him by name. When He called back to life the daughter of Jairus, He did not pronounce her name, but said, "Maid." When He spoke life to the widow's son, He made no mention of his name, but said, "Young man." But here the name is mentioned. Why? "He calls him by name, lest He should bring up all the dead," says *Augustine*. What a silly remark for a man of acknowledged genius to make! Observe—

Secondly: His words to the dead were earnest. *"Cried with a loud voice."* He could have done it with a whisper, nay, with a silent volition; but He raised His voice, probably to the highest note. And how high was that? Probably His voice had a force and a fulness that would reverberate among the hills and be heard afar. He spoke thus undoubtedly for the sake of the bystanders, to startle them into solemn thought. Observe—

Thirdly: His words to the dead were mighty. They struck life into Lazarus, made the still heart beat again, and the frozen blood glow and bound through the veins. *"He that was dead came forth, bound hand and foot with graveclothes."*

It is trifling to say, as some do, that Lazarus was only apparently dead; or with *Strauss*, that this is a myth. Lazarus was literally dead. Poetry has thus described the scene:—

> " And instantly, bound hand and foot,
> And borne by unseen angels from the cave,
> He that was dead stood with them. At the word

Of Jesus the fear-stricken Jews unloosed
The bands from off the folding of his shroud :
And Mary, with her dark veil thrown aside,
Ran to him swiftly, and cries, *Lazarus !*
My brother Lazarus ! And tore away
The napkin she had bound about his head,
And touched the warm lips with her fearful hand,
And on his neck fell weeping. And while all
Lay on their faces prostrate, Lazarus
Took Mary by the hand, and they knelt down
And worshipped Him Who loved them."—*Willis.*

Here we have—

III —THE WORDS WHICH HE ADDRESSED TO LIVING MEN

"*Jesus said unto them, Loose him, and let him go.*" Here again,
as in the command, "Take ye away the stone," we have the principle of man co-operating with the Divine. Men could not raise
Lazarus from the grave, hence Christ did it; but they could
unloose the bands with which his limbs were bound, and this for
their own sake He required them to do. "Christ had great
respect for human agency, and employed it when He could. Men
must cast in the net, though the draught of fishes is miraculous;
men must carry the baskets, though the bread is Divinely provided; men must fill the water-pots with water, though Jesus
turns it into wine ; and men must open the grave and unbind the
body, though He only ' quickeneth Whom He will.' And it is so
still, and in all things. The use of man's agency is an ordinance
of God. It is not that God needs it, for God provides it: it is
that men need it, and therefore, as a merciful appointment, in
every department of life, we have to do what our hand findeth to
do, the thing to which it is fitted, and for which it is competent;
and in connection with that we may expect His rich and varied
blessing."—*A. J. Morris.*

Were the resurrection of Lazarus to be looked at as an illustration of the moral resurrection of a dead soul, then three facts
might be noted.

First : That the resurrection of a dead soul is effected by Christ.

Secondly : That a dead soul, when raised, may still be entangled.
Just as the body of Lazarus, after he had left the grave, was bound
in graveclothes, so old prejudices, associations, habits, often en-
tangle a risen soul.

Thirdly : That the disentangling of a risen soul requires the aid
of the living. "*Loose him, and let him go.*" The work of the
living Church and a living ministry is to loose encumbered souls.
"*Loose him, and let him go.*"

John 11:45, 46

DIFFERENT EFFECTS OF THE SAME REVELATION UPON DIFFERENT MEN

" Then many of the Jews which came to Mary, and had seen the things which Jesus did, believed on Him. But some of them went their ways to the Pharisees, and told them what things Jesus had done."—xi. 45, 46.

EXEGETICAL REMARKS.—Ver. 45.— " *Then many* (R. V. MANY THEREFORE) *of the Jews which came to Mary, and had seen the things which Jesus* (R. V. BEHELD THAT WHICH HE) *did, believed on Him.*" In the case of many of the Jews the grand moral end of the miracle was answered, it produced faith—faith in Christ as the true Messiah, and with this faith a new and glorious life in the souls of the believers. As Lazarus was raised from the material grave, they were raised from the grave of prejudice, worldliness, and unbelief. In their case it was true as Christ had said : " This sickness is not unto death, but for the glory of God."

Ver. 46.—" *But some of them went their ways* (R. V. AWAY) *to the Pharisees, and told them what* (R. V. THE) *things* (R. V. WHICH) *Jesus had done.*" Whilst many were convinced, there were those who remained in unbelief. Thus is illustrated the passage that those who would not believe Moses and the prophets would not believe " though one rose from the dead." The statement here is an incidental argument in favour of the honesty of the evangelical historian. A partisan would have concealed the fact that such a mighty miracle did not convince all, but left some hardened and hostile.

HOMILETICS

We have here *Different effects of the same revelation upon different men.*

First : Many believed. "*Many of the Jews which came to Mary, and had seen the things which Jesus did, believed on Him.*" They were convinced that He was the true Messiah, the Son of God, and became His disciples. (1.) In their case the moral end of the miracle was answered. They saw the " glory of God." (2.) In their case the end of Christ's mission was answered. He became their Saviour. " He that believeth on Me hath everlasting life."

Secondly : Some did not believe. "*But some of them went their ways to the Pharisees, and told them what things Jesus had done.*" Here is an illustration of the words, " If they hear not Moses and the prophets, neither will they be persuaded though one arose from the dead." The Pharisees had interests and predilections opposed to Christ. They knew that His prosperity would be their ruin.

Now the different effect of the same revelation upon different minds is—

I —A COMMON OCCURRENCE

Concerning those who heard Paul's sermon at Athens, it is said : " Some mocked : and others said, We will hear thee again of this matter. So Paul departed from among them. Howbeit certain men clave unto him, and believed " (Acts xvii. 32—34).

It has ever been so, and is so now. The Gospel is to some the

" savour of life unto life," to others the " savour of death unto death." In every congregation there are believers and unbelievers, those who receive and those who reject. The results of the Gospel are nowhere uniform. It is in this respect like the sunbeam; while it wakes the vital germ in the grain of corn, and calls into being a beautiful and manifold life, it draws poisonous vapours out of bogs and morasses; it brings life out of some objects on which it falls, and death into others. This is—

II —A SIGNIFICANT OCCURRENCE

It indicates several things—

First : Diversity in men's minds. If all men were alike, the same cause acting upon them would produce the same results. But they are not alike.

They are not alike *naturally*. No two have the same kind and measure of faculty. They are not alike *morally*. No two have exactly the same quality and force of disposition. They are not alike *educationally*. No two have passed through exactly the same process of education. Hence it is that no two minds can see the same things in exactly the same aspect, or feel the same things with exactly the same force. St. Paul, in giving an account of his conversion on his way to Damascus, says : " They that were with me saw the light and were afraid, but they heard not the voice of Him that spoke to me." Here is an extraordinary circumstance which is common in life. Everywhere there are men hearing the same voice, but receiving different impressions; seeing the same lights, but observing different objects. A voice fraught with deep meaning to some, is mere empty sound to others ; a light revealing the grandest realities to some, discloses nothing to others. There is everywhere through human society diverse subjectivity, where there is identical externalism. It indicates—

Secondly : The moral force of depravity. Men, through prejudices, sinful habits, and carnal tendencies, become strong enough to resist the mightiest evidence and appeals. " Ye do always resist the Spirit of God." It indicates—

Thirdly : The uncoerciveness of the Gospel. The Gospel is the power of God ; but it is not a *resistless* force. It does not outrage the natural freedon of the human soul. It reasons and persuades, but does not compel or coerce. " Will ye also go away ? " &c. It indicates—

Fourthly : The need of perseverance in the preacher of the Gospel. Do not be discouraged because *some* do not believe : *others* will. " Sow your seed beside all waters, for ye know not which shall prosper, this or that."

John 11:47-52

CAIAPHAS; OR, A GLANCE AT GOVERNMENT, HUMAN AND DIVINE

(*The Council of Caiaphas against Jesus.   He retires from Jerusalem.*

"Then gathered the Chief Priests and the Pharisees a council, and said, What do we? for this man doeth many miracles," &c.—xi. 47—52.

EXEGETICAL REMARKS.—Ver. 47.— "*Then gathered the Chief Priests and the Pharisees* (R. V. THE CHIEF PRIESTS THEREFORE AND THE PHARISEES GATHERED) *a council.*" "*Council.*" This means the court of the Sanhedrim, the chief judicatory of the nation. This court was accustomed to assemble in a hall of the temple; the full number was seventy-one, but twenty-three could transact business. "*What do we?*" What are we to do? Something must be done; things are coming to a crisis. "*For this man.*" Probably contemptuously expressed. "*Doeth many miracles*" (R. V. SIGNS). A most important concession, coming from His bitterest enemies. His miracles were undeniable facts.

Ver. 48.—"*If we let Him thus alone, all men will believe on Him.*" Here again is an admission that His miracles had a commanding power,—power to command their faith. "*And the Romans shall* (R. V. WILL) *come and take away both our place and nation.*" "*Place*" may refer to the temple, their pride and their glory. They feared that Jesus would involve them in fatal hostilities with Rome.

Ver. 49.—"*And* (R. V. BUT A CERTAIN) *one of them, named Caiaphas* (R. V. OMITS "NAMED"), *being the High Priest that same year.*" That office was an annual one; persons considered suitable were chosen every year to fill the post. "*Ye know nothing at all.*" What haughty insolence! It means this, What do you know of political expediency? I am the authority.

Ver. 50.—"*Nor consider* (R. V. DO YE TAKE ACCOUNT) *that it is expedient for us* (R. V. YOU), *that one man should die for the people.*" "As much as to say, The source of all our trouble lies in this One Person. If He were put out of the way, the nation would be safe. What doubt, then, can there be that it is best for us to put Him to death, in order to save the people? As there was no alternative in his mind, he counsels the death of Christ on this plea." "*That the whole nation perish not.*" His plan was, to sacrifice Christ for the good of the nation.

Vers. 51, 52.—"*And this spake he* (R. V. NOW THIS HE SAID) *not of himself: but being High Priest that year, he prophesied that Jesus should die for that* (R. V. THE) *nation,*" &c. "*Not of himself,*" &c., but by impulse from a higher power. "St. John clearly implies that the prophetic impulse was connected with the pontifical office. Whether this was a popular notion or not, is not, as some assume, the question. It is John's idea of the fact. It was the High Priest who anciently drew responses from the Urim and the Thummim. Both Josephus and Philo are quoted by Alford as sustaining the belief that the priesthood was occasionally prophetic. The momentary gift belonged not to the impious man, but to the office. Nor did he even know the supernatural import of his own expression. The devil instigated his thoughts, but God overruled his words. 'As Pilate (*Stier* in substance says), the representative of the secular power, testified by the superscription to Jesus as King; so Caiaphas, the head of the ecclesiastical system, symbolized Jesus as the true priest and sacrifice.'

"But is it necessary to regard the utterance as Divine? Does it mean anything more than the foresight of an able man in office? As a public man, he saw that the death of Jesus would not only tend to save the nation, but to collect the scattered Jews together, here called the 'children of God.'"

HOMILETICS

Our subject is *Caiaphas; or a glance at government, human and Divine.* In these words we see—

I —AN INIQUITOUS POLICY IN THE GOVERNMENT OF MAN

Christ had now obtained such a command over the mind of His country as to strike alarm into the hearts of the members of the Sanhedrim. Hence they met to deliberate as to what they should do. At this meeting two things were admitted—

First: The fact of His mighty deeds. " *This man doeth many miracles.*" Secondly: The fact of His power over the people. " *If we let Him thus alone, all men will believe on Him.*" These admissions by enemies are very important as evidence, and significant as lessons. At this meeting, Caiaphas, being the High Priest that year, submitted the proposition that it was " *expedient* " that Christ should die. Now, in relation to this policy, we offer three observations—

First: That it was apparently adapted to the end. Christ was alienating the people from the institutions of the country, and shaking their faith in its authorities; and the most effective plan for terminating the mischief *seemed* to be to put Him to death. This would appear to strike the evil at the root. When this was done, public excitement would soon subside, and the feeling of the people soon flow back to its old level, and roll on monotonously in the old channel, as heretofore. It was, anyhow, plausible. Observe concerning their policy—

Secondly: That though seemingly adapted to the end, it was radically wrong in principle. What right had Caiaphas to propose the death of any man, however criminal that man may be ? And even assuming his right, as a governor, to put *a criminal* to death— a prerogative, however, which we deny to all but God—certainly there was no *show* of right in proposing the death of One Who, like Christ, had never violated any law; Who had wronged no one, but blessed all. The *apparent* fitness of a measure to an end does not make it right. The only standard of right is the Will of God. Concerning their policy observe—

Thirdly: That being radically wrong, it was ultimately ruinous. Did the putting of Christ to death avert the dreaded calamity ? Did it secure Judæa from the invasion of the Romans ? Did it serve in any way even the temporal interests of the country ? No, no; it hastened the flight of the Roman eagle; it brought on them judgments which speedily broke up their commonwealth, and beneath which the Jewish people have been groaning to this hour. Ah ! what seems " *expedient* " to-day may prove in the future to have been most disastrous. Eternal principle is the only pillar to guide short-sighted creatures in their endless path. Let governments study the policy of Caiaphas! Here is—

II — A STUPENDOUS FACT IN THE GOVERNMENT OF GOD

"*It is expedient for us that one man should die for the people.*" The very words in which Caiaphas propounds his own sinful policy, unconsciously predict a great fact in God's administration—namely, that the death of Christ was necessary to the salvation of others. Wicked men often express great truths; and truth is not the less important because uttered by the lips of folly and crime. We need not cite passages in proof of the fact here predicted—namely, that the death of Christ is essential to the salvation of others. The Bible is full of it. It is the central truth of the Bible. What does the death of Christ do towards man's salvation?

First : It does not change the mind of God in relation to man. It is sometimes represented as appeasing the anger and awakening the compassion of God. This is a fearful blasphemy. The death of Christ is not only the effect of God's love, but the expression, proof, and medium.

Secondly : It does not relax the claims of law. There are some who represent the death of Christ as freeing man from the claims of law. This is absurd. Nothing can remove a moral being from the claims of law but annihilation.

Thirdly : It does not mitigate the enormity of sin. In truth it increases the enormity of sin in the experience of a Christian.

Fourthly : It does not change the necessary conditions of spiritual improvement. It does not make men good and great in any miraculous or mystical way. The necessary conditions of spiritual improvement for all intelligences, are the intellectual study of Divine truth, the heart application of Divine truth, and the devotional practice of Divine truth. Angels advance in this way. The death of Christ does not alter these conditions. What, then, does the death of Christ do towards our salvation? (1.) It gives a new revelation of God. What is the new revelation? His love for SINNERS. This idea you can read nowhere else. (2.) It gives new motives to obedience. "Ye are not your own : ye are bought with a price," &c. (3.) It supplies new helps to spiritual culture. (a) It gives the highest ideal of excellence. The character of Christ reaches higher than the highest created conceptions of goodness. (β) It gives the highest incentives to excellence—gratitude, esteem, benevolence. (γ) It gives the highest minister to excellence—God's Spirit.

John 11:53-57

THE CROWNING CRIME OF HUMANITY, AND THE MANIFOLD
ASPECTS OF WICKEDNESS.

(*Jesus arrives at Bethany six days before the Passover.*—JOHN xi. 55—57 ;
xii. 1, 9—11.)

" Then from that day forth they took counsel together for to put Him to
death," &c.

EXEGETICAL REMARKS.—Ver. 53.—
" *Then* (R. V. SO) *from that day forth
they took counsel together for to* (R. V.
THAT THEY MIGHT) *put Him to
death.*" " *Then,*" οὖν, after the speech
of Caiaphas, which they regarded as
decisive, and heartily approved. It
was no longer a matter of discussion
as to whether Christ should be put to
death or not, that was decided. The
question now was ways and means.

Ver. 54.—" *Jesus therefore walked
no more openly among the Jews ; but
went* (R. V. DEPARTED) *thence unto a*
(R. V. INTO THE) *country near to the
wilderness, into a city called Ephraim,
and there continued* (R. V. TARRIED)
with His (R. V. THE) *disciples.*"
" Ephraim is sometimes spoken of in
conjunction with Bethel (2 Chron.
xiii. 19 ; Joseph. *Bell. Jud.* iv. 99). It
lay some distance north of Jerusalem
—eight miles according to Eusebius ;
twenty to the north-east according to
Jerome. The place was, on account
of its retired situation and its proximity
to the desert, favourable to the design
of our Lord. He might there prepare
His disciples in solitude for His approaching end, and, if pursued, retire
to the desert. This desert is, as Lange
remarks, the northern extremity of
that barren strip by which the table-
land of Judah and Benjamin is separated in its whole length from the
valley of the Jordan and the Dead
Sea. From this locality Jesus might,
at the time of the Passover, either join
the pilgrims from Galilee who were
going to Jerusalem by the direct route
through Samaria, or go down to
Jericho, in the plain of the Jordan,
and put Himself in front of the caravan
from Perea. We know from the
Synoptists that He took the latter
step. μετά (ver. 54) is not synonymous with σύν ; the meaning is : He
there confined Himself to the society
of His disciples ; and not merely He
was there with them."—*Godet.*

Ver. 55.—" *And the Jews' Passover
was nigh at hand* (R. V. NOW THE PASS-
OVER OF THE JEWS WAS AT HAND):
*and many went out of the country up
to Jerusalem before the Passover, to
purify themselves.*" " *The Jews' Passover* (compare ii. 13 ; vi. 4) led many
ἐκ τῆς χώρας (' out of the country ')—
that is, again, the open country, in
contrast with the capital (Lücke, De
Wette, Meyer, Godet), and especially
the neighbourhood in which Jews had
dwelt (Bengel, Olshausen) ; for it is
a resumption of χώρα (ver. 54), even
before the feast, to Jerusalem, in order
to subject themselves to Levitical
purifications on behalf of the passover
(compare Exod. xix. 10 ; Num. ix.
10 ; 2 Chron. xxx. 17)."—*Luthardt.*

Ver. 56.—" *Then sought they* (R. V.
THEY SOUGHT THEREFORE) *for Jesus,
and spake among themselves* (R. V. ONE
WITH ANOTHER), *as they stood in the
temple, What think ye, that He will
not come to the feast ?* " " (ἐζήτουν)
' were seeking and saying.' Many
from the country, having heard of the
great miracle lately wrought near
Jerusalem, would expect to find Jesus
there or in the neighbourhood (xii.
18). Hence, perhaps, their expression
of disappointment and doubt, though
the time of the feast had not arrived.
(Τί δοκεῖ ὑμῖν, ὅτι, &c.) ' What think
ye ? (do ye think) that ?' &c."—
Webster.

Ver. 57.—" *Now both the Chief
Priests and the Pharisees had given a
commandment, that, if any man knew
where He were* (R. V. WAS), *he should
show it, that they might take Him.*"
The " *Chief Priests*" were the authorities from whom the command officially
emanated ; the evangelist adds " *the
Pharisees,*" because they were its
actual authors.

HOMILETICS

Our subject here is—*The crowning crime of humanity, and the manifold aspects of wickedness.*

I —THE CROWNING CRIME OF HUMANITY

" *Then from that day forth they took counsel together for to put Him to death.*" The murder of Christ stands unmatched in the world's black catalogue of human enormities. It was the culmination of human wickedness. Three remarks are here suggested concerning it—

First: It was sanctioned by religion. Caiaphas had just pronounced in favour of it. It was a religious act. A thing is not good because it is called religious. A religious institution is often the corruptest institution; a religious man the worst. The greatest crimes ever perpetrated have been in the name and by the agency of religion. Christliness is the only true religion.

Secondly: It was pursued with deliberation. " *They took counsel together.*" When murder is perpetrated by the impulse of passion, it is an awful crime; when by cold deliberation, it is worse; when by the deliberation of one man, it is terribly hideous; but when by the deliberation of an assembly, its enormity is enhanced. "*They took counsel.*" Took counsel as to the best way of murdering the most pure, the most benevolent, the most noble Being that ever trod the earth.

Thirdly: It was delayed by Christ. "*Jesus, therefore, walked no more openly among the Jews.*" Christ knew their murderous design, and knew also that its execution was inevitable; but by withdrawing He delayed it for a few days. He withdrew, not from cowardice, not with the hope of escaping it, but to spend a few quiet hours with His disciples and His Father. Notice—

II —THE MANIFOLD ASPECTS OF WICKEDNESS

" *The Jews' Passover was at hand.*" This shows that John was writing for Gentiles rather than Jews. The approaching festival was one at which Jesus was to be crucified. In the wickedness of the people now concerned in seeking Christ's death we discover—

First: Wretched superstition. The object of this ritual was to prepare for the Passover. They could not partake of it if they were defiled. But here are men with murder in their hearts careful to attend to mere ceremony. With superstitious earnestness they hastened to observe a ritual, whilst their souls thirsted for the blood of innocence. Wickedness often runs into superstition. We discover—

Secondly: Profane curiosity. " *What think ye, that He will not come to the feast?*"* The people began to speculate as to the pro-

* See Germ, p. 345.

bability of His coming to the feast. Some of them thought that He would come perhaps, and some that He would not appear. "It is like a sort of betting," says *Lange*, "whether He would come or not." These people seem to have no reverent thoughts on the subject; no genuine desire to see Christ. They were mere speculators. Wickedness often takes the form of speculation. We discover here—

Thirdly: Organized malice. "*Now both the Chief Priests and the Pharisees had given a commandment, that, if any man knew where He were, he should show it, that they might take Him.*" A resolution had been passed by the Council, authorizing any man that should meet with Christ to take Him. They evidently expected that He would at this time be at or about the temple. It was in accordance with this order of the Sanhedrim that Christ was at length delivered up. "Judas, which betrayed Him, knew the place," &c.

Germs of Thought
No. 43   John 11:56

FESTIVITIES

"What think ye, that He will not come to the feast?"

The feast referred to here was the feast of the Jewish Passover, one of the great religious festivals of the Hebrew people. Crowds from all parts of Judæa assembled in Jerusalem on this occasion. Christ had retired into solitude, and His enemies knew not where He was. Preparations were being made for the feast, which was to take place in six days' time, and at which Christ's enemies determined to put Him to death. Hence the question, "*What think ye, that He will not come to the feast?*" They knew not where He was. They were anxious He should be present on that occasion, that they might effect their fiendish purpose. His presence at that feast was a matter of anxious speculation with them. "*What think ye?*"

We have our festivals; and the question which these Jews asked each other, it may be well for us to ask, though in a different spirit and for a different purpose. Will Christ be at our feasts? "*What think ye?*" In answer to this question I may observe—

I—HE WILL CERTAINLY BE AT OUR FEASTS AS A JUDICIAL SPECTATOR

As God, He is everywhere. "He looketh to the ends of the earth, and seeth under the whole heaven. Neither is there any creature that is not manifest in His sight: but all things are naked and open unto the eyes of Him with Whom we have to do." The Apostle John saw Him. "His eyes were as a flame of fire." He has been present at every festive scene ever held by man, and will be present at all our feasts. He will witness the gluttonies that degrade, and the inebrieties that paralyze the reason. The irreverent joke, the profane oath, the filthy song, and all the noisy revelries of unholy lusts will fall on His ear.

He will know the whole, see it through and through, thoroughly understand the moral character and bearing of every feast. He will "bring every work into judgment, and every secret thing, whether it be good, or whether it be evil." He will "bring all the hidden things of darkness to light." "We must all appear before the judgment seat of Christ," &c. We need not speculate as to whether He will be at our feasts or not; we need not say to each other, "*What think ye?*" He will come; He must come. No granite walls, no doors or bolts of iron can keep Him out. He will be there. He has flaming eyes peering through all the avenues of the heart.

II—IT IS POSSIBLE FOR HIM TO BE AT OUR FEASTS AS A LOVING FRIEND

There is nothing on His part to prevent it. (1.) He is pre-eminently *social* in His nature. There is nothing of the insulating spirit of the recluse in Him. "The Son of man came eating and drinking." His social feelings were deep and strong. (2.) He *personally attended* feasts while on earth. He joined a bridal party at Cana of Galilee; He was present at a great feast in Levi's house; He supped with the family at Bethany; and after His resurrection He had a parting meal with His disciples on the open shores of Galilee. (3.) He has *promised to be present* in the social gatherings of His people through all future times. "If a man love Me, he will keep My word; and My Father will love him; and We will come unto him, and make our abode with him." "Wheresoever two or three are gathered together in My name, there will I be to bless them." If He does not come to your feasts it is *your* fault: it is because you do not wish Him. Your idea of a feast does not agree with His. and you wish your idea to be carried out. You are afraid that His presence will have too sobering and chastening an influence upon the party. You wish the utmost license in the frolic of the hour. Do you ask, "*Will He come to our feast?*" I ask, "Have you *invited* Him?" All the other guests are invited, but is He? He waits for the invitation only. "Behold, I stand at the door and knock."

III—IF HE DOES NOT COME AS A LOVING FRIEND, WE HAD BETTER NOT HAVE THE FEASTS AT ALL

(1.) If He is absent it would be an affair unworthy of our natures. Eating and drinking, talking nonsense and scandal, discoursing upon the paltry questions of time, and tickling each others risibilities, are unworthy the dignity of human nature. (2.) If He is absent, it will be an affair pernicious to us. The devil is sure to be there as the presiding genius; he will supply the excitations to weaken and degrade our higher nature, and to strengthen the lower. The Christless feast is a miserable affair when it is over, in its effects upon character, and in its hideous aspects in the reminiscences of conscience. Infinitely better a "feast of herbs" with Christ, than the banquet of kings without Him.

Friends, invite Christ to your festivities; His presence will chasten and hallow the scene, unseal the deepest fountains of your social nature, and bring the souls of your guests together in the closest relations, and sanctify and immortalize the friendships of the joyous hour.

John 12:1-11

THE TRUE CHURCH

(*The Rulers conspire. The Supper at Bethany. Treachery of Judas.*—MATT. xxvi. 1—16 ; MARK xiv. 1—11 ; LUKE xxii. 1—6 ; JOHN xii. 2—8.)

"Then Jesus six days before the Passover came to Bethany, where Lazarus was which had been dead, whom He raised from the dead," &c.

EXEGETICAL REMARKS.—Ver. 1.— " *Then Jesus* (R. V. JESUS THEREFORE) *six days before the Passover came to Bethany, where Lazarus was which had been dead, whom He raised from the dead* " (R. V. WHOM JESUS RAISED FROM THE DEAD). " *Then,*" after leaving Ephraim. (See xi. 54.) He went from Ephraim, on the borderland between Samaria and Galilee, to join the caravans going down by the Jordan, through Jericho, to the Passover at Jerusalem. " *Six days before the Passover.*" A short period of time, but embracing wonderful events, discourses, and deeds. It was the Passion Week. All the events recorded from this chapter on to the 19th, occurred during the six days preceding our Lord's death.

Ver. 2.—" *There* (R. V. SO) *they made Him a supper* (R. V. THERE) ; *and Martha served : but Lazarus was one of them that sat at the table* (R. V. MEAT) *with Him.*" We are not told who made the supper. This supper at Bethany was, according to the best computation, on the first day of the week. The crucifixion occurred on the following Friday.

Ver. 3.—" *Then took Mary* (R. V.

MARY THEREFORE TOOK) *a pound of ointment of spikenard, very costly* (R. V. PRECIOUS), *and anointed the feet of Jesus, and wiped His feet with her hair : and the house was filled with the odour of the ointment.*" " Matthew and Mark tell us that, being in Bethany, in the house of Simon the leper, as He sat at meat, He was anointed by a woman, not mentioning her name. John, however, tells us it was Mary. Lazarus sits as the guest, Martha serves at table, Mary performs the ceremony, and glorifies the feast by the anointing. After the anointing, Matthew says, an 'alabaster box of very precious ointment,' and Mark gives the same account. That this is not the same anointing as recorded by Luke (vii. 38), is generally agreed, as that was in a different place, probably Capernaum ; and the whole record is different, the occasion and purpose of the anointing being different. The woman in that case also is represented as a notable 'sinner,' and 'a woman of the city.' It was such a transaction as could easily have occurred more than once." " *The feet.*" Matthew says she poured it on His head, so also Mark. John records the additional fact that she anointed His feet, because it was the greatest proof of love and reverence.

Ver. 4.—"*Then saith one of His disciples, Judas Iscariot, Simon's son, which should betray Him*" (R. V. BUT JUDAS ISCARIOT, ONE OF HIS DISCIPLES, WHICH SHOULD BETRAY HIM, SAITH). John is the only one of the evangelists who names Judas as the objector. "*Which should betray Him.*" This is mentioned here because the feeling that he displayed was worthy of the traitor.

Ver. 5.—"*Why was not this ointment sold for three hundred pence, and given to the poor?*" About eight pounds of our money.

Ver. 6.—"*This* (R. V. NOW THIS) *he said, not that* (R. V. BECAUSE) *he cared for the poor; but because he was a thief, and had* (R. V. HAVING) *the bag, and bare* (R. V. TOOK AWAY) *what was put therein.*" "The same love of money which disposed Judas to be the treasurer of the little fraternity, led him, by its unchecked indulgence, to petty frauds in his office, and finally to the awful step of selling his Master for a paltry sum of silver."—*Livermore.*

Ver. 7.—"*Then said Jesus, Let her alone* (R. V. JESUS THEREFORE SAID, SUFFER HER TO KEEP IT): *against the day of My burying hath she kept this.*" Christ defends the pious act.

He knew her spirit, and appreciated it. He would not suffer a spontaneous act of generosity and reverence to be blamed.

Ver. 8.—"*For the poor always ye have* (R. V. YE HAVE ALWAYS) *with you; but Me ye have not always.*" He would not have the poor unremembered; but opportunities for serving them were always at hand, while the opportunity for honouring Him was departing. He was impressed with a view of His impending doom.

Ver. 9.—"*Much people* (R. V. THE COMMON PEOPLE THEREFORE) *of the Jews therefore knew* (R. V. LEARNED) *that He was there: and they came not for Jesus' sake only, but that they might see Lazarus also, whom He had raised from the dead.*" No wonder people crowded to that spot. At that feast there was not only a man who had been in his grave, but the Mighty Man Who had raised him from the tomb.

Vers. 10, 11.—"*But the Chief Priests consulted* (R. V. TOOK COUNSEL) *that they might put Lazarus also to death; because that by reason of him many of the Jews went away, and believed on Jesus.*" The hostility of these priests knew no bounds. They sought to destroy not only the Agent, but the subject of the miracle, and this, no doubt, to blot both from the memory of the living.

HOMILETICS

Here is a wonderful social scene, which we shall employ to illustrate *The true Church.* Viewing it in this light, two things are notable—its internal aspect and its external influence.

I —ITS INTERNAL ASPECT

Looking into this feast in the house at Bethany, we observe—

First: Christ as the central figure. "*They made Him a supper.*" Whilst Lazarus would of course attract considerable notice, Christ was the Object on Whom all eyes were specially fixed, and in Whom all special interest centred. In the *true* Church, Christ is the central figure: in all things He has the "pre-eminence." He is in the "*midst.*" Again, we observe—

Secondly: A variety of guests. Lazarus was there, who had undergone a wonderful experience. Naturally he seems to have been a reticent man. It is wonderful that no word of his is recorded, especially on such an occasion. Martha is there, busy in waiting, and perhaps anxious to serve as ever. Mary is there, thoughtful, tender, overflowing with devotional sentiment. Judas is there, covering his avaricious heart with the mantle of philanthropy. Simon the leper is there. It was in his house, Matthew informs us, that the feast was held. Probably Christ had healed him of his disease, and he was bounding with gratitude. No doubt others were there whose names are not recorded. The true Church embraces all *varieties* of character, the male and the female, the intellectual and the emotional. "There is neither Jew nor Greek, neither bond nor free, neither male nor female, for ye are all one in Christ Jesus." We observe—

Thirdly : The presence of an incongruous character. Judas is there. He sits at the banquet, he participates in the viands ; perhaps he joins in the festive talk. But he is utterly destitute of any sympathy with the genius of the scene. He soon reveals his utter incongruity of spirit ; for when Mary, in the affluence of her love, broke the precious box of ointment, and "*anointed the feet of Jesus*," he exclaimed with a greedy snarl, "*Why was not this ointment sold for three hundred pence, and given to the poor ?*" Not that he cared for the poor ; the Evangelist says, "*he was a thief, and had the bag.*" This man shows three base things. (1.) A false estimate of property. Why was this waste ? Worldly men will of course agree with the idea of Judas, that money laid out in the cherishing of mere devotional feeling is waste. But what is wasted money ? The money that is laid out in magnificent houses, gorgeous apparel, and sumptuous fare, or that which is laid out in the cultivation and development of all the *moral sentiments* of the soul ? Assuming that man is an accountable and undying spirit, the waste is in the former case. He shows—(2.) A hypocritical philanthropy. Did Judas care for the poor ? Not he ; so the Evangelist states, so his history shows. (3.) A heartless intrusion. What right had he to make the remark, to interfere with the outflowing of this woman's love ? Hence Christ says, "*Let her alone.*" Why trouble ye her ? No man has a right to trouble another on account of his religious services. In the *true* Church on earth such an incongruous character is not, alas ! uncommon. Indeed, his characteristic selfishness under the garb of benevolence, and his selling truth and principle for money, are too prevalent in every Christian assembly. I fear there is no power either in Church or State more prevalent than this Iscariotism. We observe—

Fourthly : The display of genuine devotion. This we discover in Mary, in her anointing of Christ and wiping His feet with her hair. Her devotion was (1.) *Generous.* The ointment was costly. (2.) *Spontaneous.* It was unsought. (3.) *Open.* It was done in the presence of all the guests. (4.) *Right.* It comes out in the narrative as sweetly natural. This woman was doing the right thing. It was right in *principle.* She wrought a good work. It was right in *extent.* She did what she could. It was right in *reason.* "*Against the day of My burying.*" * So far, then, this social scene represents the true Church. Regarding it as a portrait of the true Church, another thing noticeable is—

II —ITS EXTERNAL INFLUENCE

This banquet at Bethany acted powerfully upon the classes outside. Its influence could not be confined to the limits of the banquet house. It broke forth, touched and roused into excitement populations around.

First: Some were attracted by curiosity. "*Much people of the Jews therefore knew that He was there: and they came not for Jesus' sake only, but that they might see Lazarus also, whom He had raised from the dead.*" They had undoubtedly a strong desire to see the man who was raised from the dead; as well, no doubt, as to see Him Who had wrought the miracle, Whose name perhaps was on the tongue of all, and Whose wondrous life they probably regarded as drawing rapidly to a close. The true Church has never failed to excite the curiosity of those outside of it. The wonderful facts on which its theology is founded, as well as the moral revolutions which it is constantly effecting, have a natural tendency to rouse the inquisitiveness of outsiders. Hence the questions that are started, the criticisms that are instituted, and the discussions that constantly occur in social circles, in public halls, and in the current literature of the day.

Secondly: Some were attracted by malice. "*But the Chief Priests consulted that they might put Lazarus also to death; because that by reason of him many of the Jews went away, and believed on Jesus.*" As the popularity of Christ advanced, the spirit of religious intolerance and animosity gained power. It had become so irrepressible that it resolved not merely to murder Christ, but to murder Lazarus as well. We can understand why they hated Christ and determined to put Him out of existence; but why should they hate Lazarus? There was no proof that Lazarus had ever come into collision with them, had ever struck against their prejudices, or denounced their spirit. He seems to have been always a reticent, inoffensive man. They hated him because of his connection with Christ. He was now a mighty, living witness of Christ's power and Divinity, and attracted general notice. Their determination—(1.) Was very *wicked.* Whilst Christ had never done them an injury, but had proved Himself the Great Friend of their race, Lazarus had in no way injured them. How daring the

*See *Gospel of Matthew,* in loco.

impiety, not only to strike a blow at the Great Miracle-Worker Who had proved Himself Divine, but upon one who had been in the grave, and who, if struck down, might rise again. Their determination—(2.) Was *foolish*. Why did they determine to destroy these two? In order to prevent the spread of Christ's doctrines and spirit. But how absurd! Truth cannot be struck down by physical force. Might cannot manacle thought. As soon employ argument to arrest the progress of the incoming tide as to employ mere force to check the march of truth. The true Church has always attracted men by malice as well as curiosity. Multitudes have pursued it with a malignant spirit. Never perhaps were its enemies more numerous, more determined, and more crafty than now.

CONCLUSION. Are we in the true Church? If so, are we true men in the true Church? or, like Judas, false?

John 12:12-19

THREE CLASSES IN RELATION TO CHRIST

(Our Lord's public entry into Jerusalem.—MATT. xxi. 1—11, 14—17; MARK xi. 1—11; LUKE xix. 29—44; JOHN xii. 12—19.)

"On the next day much people that were come to the feast, when they heard that Jesus was coming to Jerusalem," &c.

EXEGETICAL REMARKS.—Ver. 12.— " *On the next day much people* (R. V. ON THE MORROW A GREAT MULTITUDE) *that were* (R. V. HAD) *come to the feast, when they heard that Jesus was coming to Jerusalem.*" The festal party broken up, the banquet over, the next day Jesus proceeds to enter Jerusalem for the last time. The Synoptic Gospels give a fuller account of this wonderful event. The "*next day*" means the "first day" in the week, the day we call Sunday. There is a little diversity in the accounts given by the Synoptists and that given by John. "John mentions that part of the palm-procession which issues from Jerusalem, while the Synoptists give prominence to the portion accompanying Jesus, *i. e.* the Galilæan. Since the same story is here told us by the Synoptists and by John, it becomes very evident that it was John's intention to supplement their accounts. However, the Synoptists themselves distinguish between a part of the procession that preceded Jesus, and a part

that followed Him. By the former attendants, those seem to be meant who set out from Jerusalem, intending to bring Jesus into the city. John, on the other hand, likewise discriminates between two divisions (vers. 17 and 18)—citizens of Jerusalem and festal pilgrims who are already at Jerusalem."—*Dr. Lange.* "*Much people that were come to the feast,*"—great multitudes; the Feast of the Passover was one of the grand national festivals.

Ver. 13.—"*Took branches of palm trees, and went forth to meet Him.*" "The meaning of palm-branches we learn from Lev. xxiii. 40. There the children of Israel were commanded, in the Feast of the Tabernacles, to take green branches of *palms* and the boughs of thick trees; and they were to rejoice before the Lord seven days. The present festal rite was therefore an expression of joy, the object of which was the coming of the so long expected King."—*Hengstenberg.* As this entrance to Jerusalem occurred about the first day in the week before the Passover, the Sunday before Easter is termed in the ecclesiastical register Palm Sunday. The scattering of branches of palm and of other trees was not unusual in triumphant processions. Such tokens of honour were shown to Eastern kings. When Mordecai went forth from the gate of the king, we are told, the streets were covered with myrtle, and the porches with purple. They sang a jubilant passage from Psalm cxviii., which was chanted at the Feast of the Tabernacles. Indeed, at the Feast of Tabernacles we are informed (Lev. xxiii. 40) the Jews were " commanded to take palm branches, and rejoice before the Lord their God." " *Hosanna: Blessed is the King of Israel that cometh in the name of the Lord* " (R. V. HE THAT COMETH IN THE NAME OF THE LORD, EVEN THE KING OF ISRAEL). " *Hosanna.*" Matthew says, " Hosanna to the Son of David ;" Mark, " Hosanna ;" Luke, " Hosanna in the highest."

Vers. 14, 15.—" *And Jesus, when He* (R. V. HAVING FOUND) *had found a young ass, sat thereon,*" &c. The particulars are given by the other Evangelists, and John seems to suppose that his readers were familiar with the other accounts.

Ver. 16.—" *These things understood not His disciples at the first: but when Jesus was glorified, then remembered they that these things were written of Him, and that they had done these things unto Him.*" As it is written :

But when Jesus was glorified, *i. e.* after His resurrection and ascension. All was done at the time spontaneously, without reference to the fulfilment of any prophecy ; but after the descent of the Holy Spirit, which was sent to " teach them all things, and to bring all things to their remembrance," they thought they saw the agreement of these events with their Scriptures.

Ver 17.—" *The people* (R. V. MULTITUDE) *therefore that was with Him when He called Lazarus out of his grave* (R. V. THE TOMB), *and raised him from the dead, bare record* " (R. V. WITNESS). Here John states a fact which the Synoptists had altogether omitted. Indeed, they give us no account at all of the resurrection of Lazarus ; but John does give a very detailed statement.

Ver. 18.—" *For this cause the people also* (R. V. ALSO THE MULTITUDE WENT AND) *met Him, for that they heard that He had done this miracle* " (R. V. SIGN). John here states the fact that that wonderful miracle attracted the crowds.

Ver. 19.—" *The Pharisees therefore said among themselves, Perceive ye how* (R. V. BEHOLD HOW) *ye prevail nothing? behold* (R. V. LO), *the world is gone after Him.*" The popular enthusiasm displayed on this occasion struck the intolerant leaders of the people with dismay. " *The world is gone after Him*"—have become His followers. The language seems to be almost the language of vexation and alarm.

HOMILETICS

Two things strike us at the outset in connection with this wonderful scene.

First : The highest majesty under the garb of meanness. Christ, as a *mere* Man, was great. But how does this great Being, " Prince of the powers of the earth," enter Jerusalem ? In a triumphal chariot ? On a stately, prancing steed, accompanied by a magnificent cavalcade ? No ! On " *an ass.*" The more truly kingly a man is, the less he cares for conventional pageantry. Your great men have never cared for jewellery. The more ornaments are coveted and dress is studied, the more mean and impoverished the soul. Heart of oak requires neither veneer nor varnish. *A great age has never been an age of millinery and gold rings.* The kingly soul does not care for the robe or the crown. To me it argues terribly ill in this age, that England's Prime Minister should have such low ideas of the true dignity of men as to offer high-sounding titles to them, and that there should be found in a realm calling itself Christian, bipeds destitute of sufficient manhood to resist with scorn the offer of such tawdry distinctions. Human butchers, brewers, technical lawyers, millionnaires, and such, are entitled Sirs, and Lords, Honourables, &c. Bah !

> "Howe'er it be, it seems to me,
> 'Tis only noble to be good,
> Kind hearts are more than coronets,
> And simple faith than noble blood."

Secondly : An eternal idea developed in an apparently incidental appearance. It seemed perfectly casual that Christ should have required a creature to ride upon, and that there should be such a creature at hand ; but all this, some have said, was but the carrying out of what seemed a very old idea ; an eternal plan that an old writer indicated some six hundred years before. "Rejoice greatly, O daughter of Zion ! " Caprice and impulse had no part in the control of Christ's life. The life of virtue is never that of impulse or accident, it is always the unfoldment of an eternal idea.* We have here *Three classes in relation to Christ*—the *populace*, the *disciples*, the *Pharisees*.

I —THE POPULACE

"*On the next day much people that were come to the feast, when they heard that Jesus was coming to Jerusalem*," &c. Who these people were, we are not told. Some, no doubt, who had heard Christ preach in some parts of the country. All had heard of Him. Amongst all there had arisen a strong desire to see Him on this occasion. Many perhaps were of those who asked the question a day or two before, " What think ye, that He will not come to the feast." (chap. xi. 56) ? Having heard that Christ was coming to the feast, they hurried out with rapturous hearts to meet Him. These may be regarded as a type of the unsophisticated masses of mankind. Those who are unbiassed by religious prejudices both doctrinal and ecclesiastic. These men—

First : Saw Divine royalty under the garb of secular meanness. In the poor Man pursuing His journey on an "*ass*," they descried a moral majesty before which their spirits bowed. Men in our age and land are so blinded by worldly pride and religious prejudice, that they can discover no moral greatness under the tattered garb of poverty. But an unsophisticated soul can with the eye of conscience peer through all forms into the realm of moral realities. These men—

*See *Gospel of Matthew.* p.401.

Secondly : Became enraptured with the morally great for its own sake. "*Took branches of palm trees.*" Conscience, which is in truth the core of human nature, the inner man, is bound by the law of its constitution to exult in the morally right and the morally great. "I delight in the law of God after the inner man." Conscience feels bound to admire and adore the right, and to shout "*Hosanna!*" whenever it appears. These men—

Thirdly : Felt the reality of Christ's miracle. "*For this cause the people also met Him, for that they heard that He had done this miracle.*" The sophisticated and prejudiced tried to argue the miracle away, and refused to believe it. But the fact to these people was clear. They were "with Him when He called Lazarus out of his grave." They had no interest to serve in denying it.

Thus the "*people*" went with Christ, and followed and honoured Him when He appeared. And this, methinks, the people will always do, if Christ is presented to them as He really is, not as metamorphosed by Churches and creeds, but as He appears in the pages of His inspired biographers.

Another class which we have in relation to Christ is—

II —THE DISCIPLES

"*These things understood not His disciples at the first : but when Jesus was glorified, then remembered they that these things were written of Him, and that they had done these things unto Him.*" Two things are suggested concerning these disciples—

First : They were partially informed. They were at this time utterly ignorant of what Zechariah (ix. 9) is supposed to have uttered in relation to Christ. Though they had been with Christ for nearly three years and heard Him expound their Scriptures, they were yet very ignorant. Even His disciples, the most enlightened of them, were greatly in the dark, and knew but little of their Sacred Books. "The Lord hath yet more light and truth to break forth from His word."

Secondly : They were enlightened by history. "*When Jesus was glorified, then remembered they that these things were written of Him.*" After He had ascended to Heaven and the Spirit came down, a new light dawned on them. The facts of His life were brought up vividly to their minds, and these facts they compared with their old Scriptures, and they saw in them, as they thought, the fulfilment of ancient predictions. History—not Churches, not even Biblical critics—is the best interpreter of prophecy. Let us study prophecy and the old Hebrew Scriptures in the light of Christ's biography, not His life in their hazy atmosphere.

Another class which we have in relation to Christ is—

III —THE PHARISEES

" *The Pharisees therefore said among themselves, Perceive ye how ye prevail nothing? behold, the world is gone after Him.*" These men were the most powerful of the nation, and from the first they set their hearts against Christ, and had lately planned His destruction. His growing popularity heightened their indignation and increased their alarm. They now met in council, and the pressing burden of their business is the advancing influence of Christ. " *They said among themselves, Perceive ye how ye prevail nothing?* " The language is peevish and fretful in the extreme. It would seem as if one was criminating the other. " *Ye prevail nothing.*" Your efforts have been planned, bold, and determined, but to no avail. " *Behold, the world is gone after Him.*" Here is a testimony to the tremendous power which Christ had obtained during His three years' ministry. These men were—

(1.) Bound to acknowledge the failure of all their efforts. " *Ye prevail nothing.*" All the antagonists of Christianity will have to acknowledge this sooner or later. (2.) Bound to acknowledge a most disagreeable fact. " *The world is gone after Him.*"

CONCLUSION. The subject suggests—
First: The moral obstruction to the spread of Gospel truth. What is that? The religious sophistication of the masses of the people. Religious hierarchies and sects have made them the victims of religious conventionalities. All these things are to be swept away from their horizon before they will see the moral glory of Christ. The subject suggests—
Secondly: The work of the true preacher. Present Christ to men as He appears in the Gospel. Do not dress Him up in your tawdry robes of ritualism or rhetoric. He is mighty in His humility, majestic in His worldly degradation. The subject suggests—
Thirdly: The folly of the truth opposer. " *Ye prevail nothing.*" Every blow put forth to crush the truth will not only rebound upon the head of its author, but give a new impetus to quicken its speed.

John 12:20-23

THE MORAL CRAVING, THE GRANDEST WORK, AND THE SUBLIMEST TYPE OF HUMANITY

(Certain Greeks desire to see Jesus.

"And there were certain Greeks among them that came up to worship at the feast," &c.

EXEGETICAL REMARKS.—Ver. 20.— " *And* (R. V. NOW) *there were certain Greeks among them* (R. V. THOSE) *that came* (R. V. WENT) *up to worship at the* feast.*" "Among all the facts which took place between the solemn entry and the Thursday evening before our Lord's death, St. John has preserved but one, omitted by the Synoptists—viz. the attempt of certain Greek proselytes to approach Him, and the discourse in which He expressed the feelings to which this unexpected circumstance gave rise."—*Dr. Godet.* "*Certain Greeks.*" Were these Jews dwelling in foreign parts, or Gentiles who were proselytes to Judaism, or Gentile idolaters? No one can determine with certainty. *Milman* regards the term as comprehending all who were not of Jewish descent. Perhaps they were Gentile converts, technically called "proselytes at the gate."

Ver. 21.—"*The same came therefore* (R. V. THESE THEREFORE CAME) *to Philip, which was of Bethsaida of Galilee, and desired* (R. V. ASKED) *him, saying, Sir, we would see Jesus.*" "If they were from Galilee, which was partly inhabited by Gentiles, we might imagine them to have been previously acquainted with Philip; yet (Grecianized) Syrians inhabited the country from Lebanon to Lake Tiberias (Josephus, *De Bello Jud.* iii. 4, 5); Peræa had Greek cities (Joseph., *Antiq.* xvi. 11. 4). Philip's consultation with Andrew must be attributed to the unusualness of seeing the Master hold intercourse with Gentiles (Matt. x. 5); for the uncircumcised proselytes of the gate were still so considered (Acts. x.)."—*Tholuck.* It is worthy of note that the two disciples now appealed to by

these Greeks are the two disciples alone whose names are of Greek origin.

Ver. 22.—"*Philip cometh and telleth Andrew: and again Andrew and Philip* (R. V. ANDREW COMETH AND PHILIP, AND THEY) *tell Jesus.*" Here we see the cautious character of Philip, who would not take on himself the responsibility of acceding to the request without consulting his brother Andrew. We find these two disciples together on other occasions, chap. i. and iv.

Ver. 23.—"*And Jesus answered* (R. V. ANSWERETH) *them, saying, The hour is come, that the Son of man should be glorified.*" "It is not said whether the Greeks were admitted to converse with Jesus; but it seems probable that these words were spoken to Philip and Andrew in reply, and in the hearing of the strangers and of the disciples. It may have been, indeed, after receiving Greeks and conversing with them, that this discourse was delivered. His answer was suggested by the appearing of these Gentiles. He is led to look upon these heathen hungering after salvation, as the first-fruits of that abundant harvest which His death would produce."—*Tholuck.* "*The hour is come*"—the eternally predestined period. Heaven has a set time for all things. "*The Son of man should be glorified.*" Chap. xvii. 5 is a commentary on these words.

HOMILETICS

There are three things here worthy of our notice, in relation to *Humanity.* Here is—

I—THE MORAL CRAVING OF HUMANITY

"*And there were certain Greeks among them that came up to worship at the feast: the same came therefore to Philip, which was of Bethsaida of Galilee, and desired him, saying, Sir, we would see Jesus.*" These Greeks were not Jews speaking Greek, but Gentiles and Greeks by race. Whatever their station in life or philosophic opinions, they seemed to be amongst those free men in religion who are ready to render homage to the institutions of the place. They were at Jerusalem, and desired to fall in with the religion of Jerusalem. They "*came up to worship at the feast.*" It is manifest that they felt a deep religious want, a restless craving of nature. They wanted something more than their philosophies could supply, more even than Jewish ritualism could supply ; for after the feast they came to Philip and said, " *We would see Jesus.*" They wanted— (1.) Some one who could *solve their moral problems.* (2.) Some one on whom to *centre their supreme love.* (3.) Some one to *correct the moral evils of which they were conscious.* (4.) Some one to *guide them rightly on the way of life.* In all hearts, the world over, there is a craving for such an one, and such an One is Jesus, and He only. He is man's true Christ.

We have here—

II —THE GRANDEST WORK OF HUMANITY

In that work we see Philip and Andrew engaged. " *Philip cometh and telleth Andrew, and again Andrew and Philip tell Jesus.*" To bring men to *Christ* is something more than to bring them to science and art. Though this ministry we disparage not, we highly prize it. Something more than bringing them to a Church or a sect. Numbers are actually engaged in this work; their inspiration is sectarianism, and their efforts are often immoral and pernicious. To bring men to Christ is to bring them—(1.) *To the Only infallible Physician.* (2.) *To the Only efficient Educator.* (3.) *To the Only qualified Redeemer.* No work on this earth is so important, so beneficent, so sublime as this. But to bring to Christ, you must be *Christlike.* You may bring crowds to your Church by clap-trap. You can only bring them to Christ by a life of Christly stateliness, inspiration, and influence.

We have here—

III —THE SUBLIMEST TYPE OF HUMANITY

" *And Jesus answered them, saying, The hour is come, that the Son of man should be glorified.*" " *The Son of man,*" not the mere son of a Jew or Gentile, not the son of a nation, a Church, or a sect; but the " *Son of man,*"—sustaining the same relations to all, having the same love for all—*the Model Man.*

First : He speaks with magnanimity, in prospect of His death. Gethsemane and Calvary were before Him. And yet with what sublime composure He fronts them !

Secondly : He speaks with triumph in prospect of His glory. " *The Son of man should be glorified* "—glorified in His resurrection from the dead, His exaltation to heaven, His moral victories over all the errors, the curses, and miseries of the world.

John 12:24-26

THE GRAIN OF WHEAT —CHRISTLINESS

" Verily, verily, I say unto you, Except a corn of wheat fall into the ground and die, it abideth alone,"

EXEGETICAL REMARKS.—Ver. 24.— *" Verily, verily, I say unto you, Except a corn* (R. V. GRAIN) *of wheat fall into the ground* (R. V. EARTH) *and die, it abideth* (R. V. BY ITSELF) *alone: but if it die, it bringeth forth* (R. V. BEARETH) *much fruit."* As it is necessary that a seed should be buried in the bosom of the earth, and to all human appearance die, in order that it may become a fruitful plant, and multiply itself a hundred-fold, so was it essential that Jesus should die, that His religion might triumph, and its saving influences be disseminated far and wide to bless mankind, that—

" Millions of souls might feel its power,
And bear it down to millions more."

" It abideth alone." It remaineth a single grain, without increase.

Ver. 25.—*" He that loveth his life shall lose* (R. V. LOSETH) *it; and he that hateth his life in this world shall keep it unto life eternal."* "The egotism that clings to the outward life of appearance, and lives for that, loses its true life, which is conditional on surrender to God; the spirit of sacrifice, which does not cleave to its life of self, nay, which hates it in its old form in this old world—*i. e.* joyfully sacrifices it, the sooner the better, and even hates it, if it be about to become a hindrance—regains it unto a higher, eternal life."—*Lange.*

Ver. 26.—*" If any man serve Me, let him follow Me; and where I am, there shall also My servant be: if any man serve Me, him will My* (R. V. THE) *Father honour."* The way to serve Christ, is to follow Him; and following Him will secure His eternal fellowship and the honour of His Father. " If we suffer with Him we shall reign with Him."

HOMILETICS

These verses may be fairly regarded as representing what genuine religion really is. It is not a theory, however Scriptural; not a ritual, however beautiful; not a passing sentiment, however powerful and devout; not an outward service, however consistent with prescriptive law, but *Christliness.* The most un-Christly things in literature, institutions, and men I know, are those labelled Christian. Christliness stands in these days in startling contrast to the Christian. But what is *Christliness?* The words suggest three things concerning it—it is the death of selfishness—the following of Christ—the guarantee of blessedness.

I —IT IS THE DEATH OF SELFISHNESS

His self-sacrifice is here represented in a symbol and in a statement.

First : In a symbol. *" A corn of wheat."* The fact in nature to which Christ refers is patent to all, and practically recognized in all labours of the agriculturist. It is this—*that the grain, in order to multiply itself, must go down into the earth, and its wrappage or husk die.* This fact might be taken as a symbol of several things.

1. As a symbol of the history of Jesus Christ. For His doctrines to obtain wide, regal influence over the minds of men, His death seemed necessary; that event struck home in thunder His truths to the understanding and conscience. Christ means to say, that His death was as necessary to the extension of His truths in the world, as the death of the seed to the multiplication of its kind; and it was verily so. "Ought not Christ to have suffered?" The fact may be taken—

2. As a symbol of the history of moral truth. A great truth, to grow and multiply, must go deep into the soil of the soul, and there its logical *husks* and *wrappages* must die and rot; and then by quiet reflection it shall germinate and grow.

3. As a symbol of the history of a true soul. The fact admirably illustrates this. (1.) It is simple in its appearance. How plain and unattractive is the grain of corn! How unostentatious is a true soul! it makes itself of "no reputation." (2.) It is unbounded in possibilities. What possibilities does a single grain possess! Harvests slumber in one seed; forests repose in one shell! What wondrous potentialities lie within the human soul! (3.) It is developed by self-abnegation. Unless the soul dies to self, loses all its egotism, becomes self-oblivious, it will never rise into freedom, power, and perfection.

But it is as the symbol of the first, namely, Christ's self-sacrifice, it is here employed. It was not necessary that He should merely die in order that His beneficent influence might spread, and His disciples multiply through the earth, but that He should die the death of *self*-sacrifice. If He had died by accident, or disease, or force, its moral influence would be worthless. He gave Himself, He laid down His life. His self-sacrifice is here represented—

Secondly: In a statement. "*He that loveth his life shall lose it.*" A strong way, this, of saying, he that loveth his own interests as the primary end of life will be ruined, whereas he that hateth—that is, in a comparative sense—his mere personal interests, will secure his everlasting well-being. "The term," says *Dr. Godet*, "μισεῖν, *to hate*, here includes the idea of a generous contempt, and well characterizes the noble ambition which aims higher than this world." The self-seeking spirit is moral ruin, the self-sacrificing spirit is moral salvation. The reigning spirit of Christ was that of self-sacrificing love. "If any man hath not the spirit of Christ, he is none of His."

The words suggest concerning Christliness that—

II —IT IS THE FOLLOWING OF CHRIST

"*If any man serve Me, let him follow Me*," or, as some render it, "If any one minister to Me, let him follow Me;" that is, let him become self-sacrificing as I am; let him die to all selfish and personal considerations as I have. You cannot follow Christ in the vastness of His intelligence, in the might of His arm, in the force and extent of His authority ; but you can in His master aims and motives. His aim is the universal reign of holiness, the happiness of humanity, the good of the universe, and the glory of the Father. All should aim at this, and all should work for this, animated by disinterested affection. Without this love, this charity, we are "nothing." (See 1 Cor. xiii.)

The words suggest concerning Christliness that—

III —IT IS THE GUARANTEE OF BLESSEDNESS

" *Where I am, there shall also My servant be. If any man serve Me, let him follow Me,*" &c. What does it involve ?

First : Fellowship with Christ. " *Where I am.*" To be with Christ is heaven. What will it be to dwell with Christ for ever ? It involves—

Secondly : The highest dignity. " *Him will My Father honour.*" What is it to be honoured by the Infinite Father ? Eternity alone can reveal.

CONCLUSION.—Here then is genuine religion. It is Christliness, nothing else. We must die to live, as a grain of wheat—die to self and to all worldly ambitions, and live the life that Christ lived, that of supreme love to God and self-sacrificing love for man.

John 12:27-31

A TWO-FOLD CRISIS

" Now is My soul troubled ; and what shall I say ? Father, save Me from this hour," &c.

EXEGETICAL REMARKS.—Ver. 27.— " *Now is My soul troubled ; and what shall I say?*" To whom does He speak ? *Himself.* It is profound self-consultation. " *Father, save me from this hour.*" " He seemed to have had," says Meyer, " a momentary abhorrence of the pains of death, induced by weakness." He seemed to have had the same feeling as in Gethsemane, when He exclaimed, "Father, if possible, let this cup pass from Me." " *But for this cause came I unto this hour.*" His sensitive nature cried for exemption, but His higher spirit realized the greatness and necessity of His mission. "The soul, ψυχὴ, is the seat of the natural, as *spirit*, the πνεῦμα, is that of the religious emotions. Jesus here used the first of these terms, because

it was the prospect of His personal sorrows which at this moment moved Him. The perfect, τετάρακται, *is troubled,* indicated the condition into which the Lord found Himself plunged. This inward trouble revealed itself to Him especially by the unusual hesitation which He experienced when about to pour out His feelings in prayer."—Godet.

Ver. 28.—" *Father, glorify Thy Name.*" He rises now as a conqueror of His temporary weakness. He loses all the horrors of His death in His lofty aspirations for His Father's glory. " *Then came there* (R. V. THEREFORE) *a voice from heaven, saying, I have both glorified it, and will glorify it again.*" Each time that the Son performed a great act of personal consecration, the

Father answered by a sensible mani-festation of approval. Thus, at the baptism and the transfiguration. What was the voice? It was Divine. It came from heaven. It communicated glorious encouragement; "I am glori-fied, and will glorify again." It is not only audible, but loud.

Ver. 29.—" *The people* (R. V. MULTI-TUDE) *therefore, that stood by, and heard it, said that it thundered* (R. V. HAD THUNDERED): *others said, An angel spake* (R. V. HATH SPOKEN) *to Him.*" It was not mere sound, though it was articulate thunder. Voices from heaven are frequently noticed in the Bible (1 Kings xix. 11, 12 ; Dan. iv. 31 ; Matt. iii. 17 ; xvii. 5 ; Acts ix. 7 ; x. 13 ; Rev. i. 10 ; iv. 5). The hearers formed different conceptions of the voice ; some regarded it as mere thunder, others as the utterance of an angel.

Ver. 30.—" *Jesus answered and said,* *This voice came not* (R. V. HATH NOT COME) *because of Me* (R. V. FOR MY SAKE), *but for your sakes.*" Christ did not require the thundering sound in order to assure Him of the answer. He had it in His own soul. But those about Him required that He should come in thunder.

Ver. 31.—" *Now is the judgment of this world : now shall the prince of this world be cast out.*" " As to the world, this hour was one of deepest revolution. It was the signal, first, of its judgment (ver. 31) ; then of the expulsion of its ancient master (ver. 31) ; and lastly, of the accession of its new Sovereign (ver. 32). The word *νῦν, now,* at the beginning of the first two propositions, expressly brings out the decisive nature of the present moment with respect to the human race." Satan's empire over the world is shattered with the death and resurrection of Jesus.

HOMILETICS

All things have their crises, some periods which determine a new course in their history. *Inanimate nature* has its crises. It has periods when it seems to oscillate between opposite points. There are times when the subterranean fires seem to hesitate as to whether they shall burst into fury, cleave the mountains, or decline—times when the storms of heaven reach a point, and they either rise to greater fury or die away. The various strata of the earth indicate the critical periods to which material nature has ever been exposed. All *life* has its crises. Every living creature has its critical periods. Indeed our life is but a perpetual oscilla-tion between health and sickness, life and death. *Human history* has its crises. In the life of the individual man they are found. " There is a tide in the affairs of men." There are moral moods on which the destiny of some depend. In the investigations of science, in the progress of empires, and in the march of commerce, critical times are manifest. This passage leads us to consider *a twofold crisis*—a crisis in the history of the Son of God and a crisis in the history of our fallen world.

I —A CRISIS IN THE HISTORY OF THE SON OF GOD

" *Now is My soul troubled,*" &c. Our Lord seemed to hesitate now as to whether He should advance or recede. Four facts are here suggested in relation to this crisis.

First : This crisis was caused by mental suffering. As yet there were no wounds inflicted in His body, the hand of violence had not touched His physical frame. Bodily sufferings are not to be compared to mental. Whatever Christ's mental sufferings were, they had not in them the elements of remorse, malignity, or despair. His sufferings were—(1.) Those of a holy and exquisitely susceptible nature in the presence of a world of sin. In proportion to the purity of a mind will be the poignancy of the pain which the view of sin inflicts. Paul's soul was "stirred" within him, &c. (2.) Those of an exquisitely tender and benevolent nature in view of misery. This Christ manifested when He wept over Jerusalem. Christ saw the world as no other Being ever saw it. (3.) Those of a merciful Saviour endured on behalf of humanity. Suppose the whole history of *one* sin made known to a holy soul—its rise, progress, and bearings upon the universe, as well as upon the individual—the tremendous woes and miseries it would produce—what agony it would strike into that heart! But Christ saw the agonies which would spring from *every* sin of *every* man. These sufferings brought Christ's soul to a crisis—and what a crisis!

Another fact suggested is—

Secondly: This crisis proved the strength of His love for humanity. It is only for a moment that His love for the race seemed to give way. "*What shall I say?*" How long did He hesitate? With the very next pulsation of the heart He said, "*Father, glorify Thy Name.*" Not, Father, deliver Me from this woe, take away My sufferings; but, "Thy will be done."

Thirdly: This crisis displayed the efficacy of prayer. It was by prayer He came off victorious. Oh, how He prayed! (Luke xxii.)

Fourthly: This crisis explains His history. "*But for your sakes.*" He endured His sufferings, not for His own sake, but for the sake of man.

Here is—

II —A CRISIS IN THE HISTORY OF OUR FALLEN WORLD

"*Now is the judgment of this world: now shall the prince of this world be cast out.*" Christ knew the power of the devil to be that of a prince. To Him he appeared a being of tremendous power. Before his fall he was great. He was created pure, for benevolence never created an unholy thing. In heaven he commenced his career. He learnt his lessons in the smiles of infinite love and light.

> "High in the midst of all the throng
> Satan a tall archangel sat."

But his fall does not seem to have deprived him of his natural power. The loss of his innocence left him a mental Hercules in the universe, a gigantic prince. But how does the death of Christ cast him out?

First: It gives a new force to Redemptive Truth. Satan rules by error. Error in relation to religion, error in relation to happiness, error in relation to glory. Remove these errors, and you break his power. His empire is founded on falsehood. Error cannot stand before truth. Christ embodied truth in a holy life and a noble death.

Secondly: It gives a wider theatre to Redemptive Truth. Moral truth, under the Law, was limited in its range. Christ universalized it, sent it through the world. Moral truth, under the Law, was only as a dim lamp hung up in the heavens of the Israelitish people. In the Gospel it broke forth as a sun in the heavens of humanity.

Thirdly: It gives a mightier advocacy of Redemptive Truth. Every genuine believer in Christ becomes a propagandist.

CONCLUSION.—Brothers, ponder this crisis. Whereunto shall I liken Christ's position? I think of the *Physician*, when the disease of his patient has reached a crisis, and when he feels that his next prescription will determine the fate of one who is the father of a large family, or the ruler of a great people. I think of the *Pilot* who, under the starless vault of heaven, and amid the fury of the hurricane, with the foaming billows dashing against his vessel, feels, that on his next direction the fate of all on board depends. I think of the *General* who, after many encounters with his foe, is determined to make another and a last; who feels, that on the calculations of that hour the fate of armies and the existence of empires are suspended. But such crises are but as faint shadows to this! "*What shall I say?*" It would seem as if there were an inclination to retreat; but if He had retreated? His pledges would have been broken, all the hopes of the world would have gone out.

John 12:32-37

THE CRUCIFIXION OF CHRIST

" And I, if I be lifted up from the earth, will draw all men unto Me. This He said, signifying what death He should die," &c.

EXEGETICAL REMARKS.—Ver. 32.— " *And I, if I be lifted up from the earth.*" Κἀγώ, "*and I.*" The *I* is emphatic, and stands in contrast with the ejected prince, referred to in the preceding verse. The lifting up does not point, as some suppose, to His ascension to Heaven, but to His crucifixion upon the cross. " As Moses lifted up the serpent in the wilderness." The "*if*" (ἐὰν ὑψ.), the conditional particle, does not indicate the doubtfulness of the event expressed by ὑψωθῶ, but the certainty of the event represented as contingent upon it. " *Draw all men unto Me* " (R. V. MYSELF). " We suppose," says *Lange*, " this to be indicative of the totality of the nations, in antithesis to the firstlings of the Greeks who have here inquired after Him."

Ver. 33.—" *This* (R. V. BUT THIS) He said, signifying what death He should die* " (R. V. BY WHAT MANNER

OF DEATH HE SHOULD DIE). (See chap. xviii. 32.)

Ver. 34.—*"The people* (R. V. MULTITUDE THEREFORE) *answered Him, We have heard out of the law that Christ* (R. V. THE CHRIST) *abideth for ever: and how sayest Thou, The Son of man must be lifted up? Who is this Son of man?"* "The people—the multitude (ὄχλος)—answered Him, 'We have heard out of the law,—meaning the Scriptures of the Old Testament; referring, no doubt, to such places as Psalms lxxxix. 28, 29; cx. 4; Dan. ii. 44; vii. 13, 14, '*that Christ abideth for ever: and how sayest Thou, The Son of man must be lifted up? Who is this Son of man?'* How can that consist with this 'uplifting?' They saw very well both that He was holding Himself up *as the Christ*, and a Christ to die a violent death; and as that ran counter to all their ideas of the Messianic prophecies, they were glad to get this seeming advantage to justify their unyielding attitude." Perhaps the allusion is especially to Daniel, who describes Him as coming in the "clouds of heaven with great glory." And they meant, How can this be the Son of man who is going to die the death of crucifixion?

Ver. 35.—*"Then Jesus* (R. V. JESUS THEREFORE) *said unto them, Yet a little while is the light with* (R. V. AMONG) *you. Walk while ye have the light, lest* (R. V. THAT) *darkness come upon you"* (R. V. OVERTAKE YOU NOT). Christ, ignoring their quibblings, exhorts them to a proper use of their opportunity. He was the *Light*, and He was with them now. He would soon leave them, and this was their opportunity. *"He that walketh in darkness knoweth not whither he goeth."* This implies, that whoever avails himself not of the "*Light*" which Christ reflects, walks in darkness; and whoever walks in darkness walks in peril.

Ver. 36.—*"While ye have* (R. V. THE) *light, believe in* (R. V. ON) *the light."* Which means, "While ye have Me, believe in Me; you will not have Me long." *"That ye may be the children* (R. V. SONS) *of light."* The recipients and the reflectors of the true light. *"These things spake Jesus, and departed, and did hide* (R. V. HE DEPARTED AND HID) *Himself from them."* Why did He hide Himself? To talk more with them would be waste of time and energy. Whither did He go to hide Himself? Probably He retired to Bethany. (See Matt. xxi. 17; Luke xxi. 7.)

HOMILETICS

The subject of these verses is *the Crucifixion of Christ*. The most extraordinarily suggestive and morally powerful fact in the history of mankind—a fact that may be viewed *historically*, *theologically*, and *ethically*—a fact to which all the past seemed to point, and from which all that is beneficent in the future seems to start. There are many ways of looking at this fact. The passage before us seems to present it to us in three aspects—

I —AS AN INSTRUMENT TO ATTRACT ALL

"*Draw all men.*" Though in the original "men" are not mentioned, men are meant, for "all" is in the masculine gender. Observe—

First: The Cross is to draw "*all men.*" It does not say, all the *elect*, nor all the *Jews*, nor all of this *nation*, or of this *Church*, or this *tribe*, but "*all men*" of every land and time. The Cross is for *humanity*. Observe—

Secondly: The Cross is to draw "*all men*" to Christ. "*Unto Me.*"

Not merely to My system of doctrine, purpose, or government, but to *Me*, the living, loving Son of God, the Saviour of the world. As gravitation draws all rivulets to the sea, the Cross is to draw all men to Christ. (1.) The Cross has the power to draw the *intellect* of all men to Him. As the most stupendous phenomenon in history, it challenges the investigation of all. (2.) The Cross has the power to attract the *hearts* of all. As the centre of infinite interest, it is potent enough to awaken the profoundest sympathies of all. All! Does this furnish a hope for the moral restitution of all human souls? Would it were so. Another aspect in which the passage presents the Crucifixion is—

II — AS AN EVENT MISUNDERSTOOD BY SOME

" *The people answered Him, We have heard out of the law that Christ abideth for ever: and how sayest Thou, The Son of man must be lifted up? Who is this Son of man?* " " *Out of the law,*" that is, by the reading as well as by the explanation of their Scripture. They considered perhaps that Psalm cx. 4; Isaiah ix. 7; Daniel vii. 13, referred to Christ. In such passages the person is spoken of as the " Ancient of days; " as " One that is to continue for ever; " One " whose kingdom is to have no end." Their question would be therefore, " If Thou art to die, how canst Thou be the Messiah? " " *Who is this Son of man?* " We know who the Son of man in the Old Testament is; but who is *this* Son of man? Men have always misunderstood the Cross. It is "foolishness to the Greek, and a stumblingblock to the Jew." (1.) Some now speak of the Cross as a transaction that will appease the wrath of the Almighty; (2.) Some, as a transaction that will purchase human souls; (3.) Some, as the procuring cause of God's love for the world. Whereas the Cross is the *effect*, the *demonstration*, and the *channel* of God's love for man. Another aspect in which the passage presents the Cross is—

III — AS A FACT EXPLAINED BY CHRIST

How does He explain their difficulties? Not by descending into logical disquisition. But by exhorting them to practise holiness. " *Walk in the light.*" * It is the pure heart, not the logical understanding, that solves the great problems of Christianity. " He that doeth the will of God shall know of the doctrine." " The carnal mind discerneth not the things of the Spirit, neither can he know them, for they are spiritually discerned." He seems to urge the spirit of holiness on three considerations—

First: Their possession of a special advantage. They had the " *light* " with them. From His presence, words, deeds, and spirit, holiness beamed brightly on them. They were moving in the rays of the highest moral excellence.

* See Germ, p. 366.

Secondly : Their special advantage was only temporary. "*Yet a little while.*" He would not be with them long. A few days more, and He would be gone ; the moral Sun would set. Men's opportunities for spiritual improvements are very temporary. Their light soon grows dim.

Thirdly : The departure of their special advantage would expose them to danger. "*He that walketh in darkness knoweth not whither he goeth.*" To walk on in moral darkness to the great eternity, how dismal and how dangerous !

Fourthly : The right use of their advantage would fill them with light. "*Believe in the light, that ye may become the children of light,*" or sons of light. Trusting in Christ, the true light will fill the soul with Divine illumination. "The entrance of Thy Word giveth light !" Sons of light ! All luminous.

CONCLUSION. Thank God for the Cross. Hold up the Cross to draw the world to Christ. Solve men's difficulties concerning the Cross, not by argumentation, but by the strongest exhortation— the life of practical holiness. "It is an endless work," says *Mr. Robertson* of Brighton, "to be uprooting weeds. Plant the ground with wholesome vegetation, and then the juices which would have otherwise fed rankness will form themselves into a more vigorous growth : the dwindled weeds will be easily raked out then. It is an endless task the refuting error. Plant truth, and then the error will pine away."

Germs of Thought
No. 44   John 12:36

SONS OF LIGHT

" While ye have light, believe in the light, that ye may be the children of light."

Notice three things here—

I —THE GREATEST PRIVILEGE OF HUMANITY

" *While ye have the light.*" That is, the light of Christ's character. His character includes of course all He taught, did, and suffered. The whole forms the moral light of humanity. All the light of philosophy is dimness to this. It is not only luminous to the intellect, but light to the conscience and heart.

II —THE GREATEST WORK OF HUMANITY

" *Believe in the light.*" Faith in Christ does not mean mere intellectual credence. There is neither effort or virtue in this ; but a practical trust in Him : not what men say about Him in old creeds and theologies, but in Him.

III —THE GREATEST HONOUR OF HUMANITY
" *That ye may be the children of light*," or sons of the light. Light
in the Scripture is the emblem of intelligence, purity, joyousness,
usefulness.

John 12:37-46

A GUILTY UNBELIEF, A COWARDLY FAITH, AND A REDEMPTIVE
TRUSTFULNESS

(*The unbelief of the Jews.*—JOHN xii. 37—50.)

"But though He had done so many miracles before them, yet they believed
not on Him," &c.

EXEGETICAL REMARKS.—It is the
manner of our Evangelist alone, as has
been frequently remarked, to record
his own reflections on the scenes he
describes. But here having arrived
at what was virtually the close of
Our Lord's public ministry, he casts
an affecting glance over the fruitfulness of His whole ministry on the
bulk of the now doomed people.

Ver. 37.—"*But though He had done
so many miracles* (R. V. SIGNS) *before
them, yet they believed not on Him.*"
Christ had done great signs amongst
them. These signs were intended
and adapted to settle their faith on
Him, but had failed to do so.

Ver. 38.—"*That the saying of Esaias*
(R. V. WORD OF ISAIAH) *the prophet
might be fulfilled, which he spake, Lord,
who hath believed our report? and to
whom hath the arm of the Lord been
revealed?*" The passage referred to
may be found in Isaiah vi. 10. St.
Chrysostom truly says, it is not
because " Esaias said so they did not
believe, but because they would not
believe Esaias said this." Because it
was thus predicted, the Evangelist
speaks as if they so acted in order
to make the prediction true.

Vers. 39, 40.—"*Therefore* (R. V. FOR
THIS CAUSE) *they could not believe,
because* (R. V. FOR) *that Esaias* (R. V.
ISAIAH) *said again, He hath blinded
their eyes, and hardened* (R. V. HE
HARDENED) *their heart; that they should
not* (R. V. LEST THEY SHOULD) *see with
their eyes, nor understand* (R. V. AND
PERCEIVE) *with their heart, and be converted* (R. V. SHOULD TURN), *and I should
heal them.*" They could not believe, not
because of what Esaias had said, nor

because there was a Divine purpose that
they should not, but because of the state
of their hearts. Their inability to believe was moral, not physical—a crime,
not a misfortune. It grew out of the
self-contracted blindness of mind referred to in the verses. The quotation
here, it should be observed, does not
follow exactly either the Hebrew or
the Greek of the passage in Isaiah.

Ver. 41.—"*These things said Esaias*
(R. V. ISAIAH), *when*(R. V. BECAUSE) *he
saw His glory, and spake* (R. V. HE
SPAKE) *of Him.*" (See Isaiah vi. 1.)
It was the Messianic glory that Esaias
saw filling the temple.

Ver. 42.—"*Nevertheless among* (R. V.
EVEN OF) *the chief* (R. V. OMITS CHIEF)
*rulers also many believed on Him;
but because of the Pharisees they did
not confess Him* (R. V. IT), *lest they
should be put out of the synagogue.*"
"The chief rulers (καὶ ἐκ τῶν ἀρχόντων)
rather, even of the rulers, such as
Nicodemus and Joseph, many believed
on Him; but because of the Pharisees,
that is, the leaders of this sect, for
they were of it themselves, they did
not confess Him—or confess it (οὐχ
ὡμολόγουν)—did not make an open confession of their faith in Jesus, lest they
should be put out of the synagogue."

Ver. 43.—"*For they loved the praise*
(R. V. GLORY) *of men more than the
praise* (R. V. GLORY) *of God.*" "A
severe remark, considering that several
at least of these persons afterwards
boldly confessed Christ. It indicates
the displeasure with which God regarded their conduct at this time,
and with which He continues to
regard similar conduct." — *Webster
and Wilkinson.* Some read, they

loved the glory that is of men more than the glory that is of God.

The following remarks of *Godet* on vers. 37, 38 are pertinent and philosophical : " As to the relation of Jewish unbelief to the Divine prevision (vers. 37 and 38), St. John does not point out the metaphysical theory by means of which he was able to reconcile God's foreknowledge and man's responsibility, but simply accepts these two data—the one of the religious sentiment, the other of the moral consciousness. But if we reflect that God is above time—that, properly speaking, He does not *foresee* a fact which, so far as we are concerned, is still future, but *sees* it absolutely, as we contemplate one present—that, consequently, when He announces it at any moment, as well before as after its accomplishment, He does not *predict*, but describes it as a spectator and witness—the apparent contradiction of the two *apparently* contradictory elements vanishes. Undoubtedly the fact, once predicted, cannot fail to happen, since the sight of God cannot show Him as *being* that which will not be. But the fact does not take place because God saw it ; but, on the contrary, God said it because in His eyes it *is*. Hence the true cause of that Jewish unbelief which God announced was not His foreseeing it. This cause in its ultimate analysis was the moral state of the people themselves. It was that state which, when it had once become permanent, necessarily involved the final unbelief of Israel, as being on the one hand its deserved punishment, and on the other the condition of the salvation of the Gentiles."

Ver. 44.—"*Jesus* (R. V. AND JESUS) *cried and said.*" If possible with greater earnestness, solemnity, and in a louder tone, Christ now speaks. What is here recorded to the end of the chapter He has uttered before more than once. "*He that believeth on Me, believeth not on Me, but on Him that sent Me.*" "A perfect antithesis," says *Lange*, "to the honour-seeking party of the Jews which was the cause of their unbelief, is here presented to us in the testimony of Jesus concerning Himself." The faith He required in Him, was faith in the living God.

Ver. 45.—"*And he that seeth* (R. V. BEHOLDETH) *Me, seeth* (R. V. BEHOLDETH) *Him that sent Me.*" I am the incarnation, the image of God ; God is to be seen in Me—"I and My Father are one."

Ver. 46.—"*I am come a light into the world, that whosoever believeth on Me should* (R. V. MAY) *not abide in darkness.*" This He had often said before. Faith in Him is the moral light of men.

HOMILETICS

These verses bring under our attention three subjects for thought —*a guilty unbelief, a cowardly faith, and a redemptive trustfulness.* Here we have—

I —A GUILTY UNBELIEF

" *But though He had done so many miracles before them, yet they believed not on Him.*" Why did they not believe ?

First : Not for the want of evidence. For "*many miracles*" and signs had been wrought amongst them. I grant that a miracle itself cannot prove the Divinity either of the person or doctrine of the worker, unless it could be proved, as it cannot, that—(1.) No being but God can perform what we call miracles, and—(2.) If no one but He could do so, that He would never except to establish the true. Who can prove this ? Suppose a being whose character was repugnant to our ideas of virtue, and whose doctrines were repugnant to our ideas of truth, were to perform what we consider a miracle, his miracle could not by any possibility prove to us that he was a Divine messenger. A miracle only becomes a proof as the character of the miracle-worker accords with our idea of Divine power and excellence. Whilst He did works, therefore, which no other man could do, He lived a life of sublime excellence which no other man ever lived. His miracles were therefore evidences, powerful evidences. These evidences they had in abundance—"*many miracles.*" "If they should be written every one, I suppose that even the world itself could not contain the books that should be written." Why did they not believe?

Secondly: Not for the want of warning. Their Scriptures abounded with examples of the evils of unbelief. Esaias preached; and so unbelieving were his hearers that he exclaimed, "*Lord, who hath believed our report? and to whom hath the arm of the Lord been revealed?*" * What judgments the unbelief of the hearers of the old prophet brought upon themselves! They must have known this, and should have taken the warning. The preaching of Esaias, instead of enlightening them, blinded their eyes; instead of filling them with contrition, "*blinded their eyes and hardened their heart, that they should not see with their eyes, nor understand with their heart.*"† The ministry, then, that was intended by God, and fitted by Him, to bring them to spiritual knowledge and repentance, they by their depravity turned to opposite results. Here then was warning enough for them. Hence the guiltiness of their *unbelief.* When a man has not three things—*evidence*, the *capacity* for examining evidence, and the *opportunity* for doing so—his unblief is not guilty unbelief. This is not the unbelief in England to-day; it is not innocent, but criminal.

Another subject here presented is—

II—A COWARDLY FAITH

"*Nevertheless among the chief rulers also many believed on Him; but because of the Pharisees they did not confess Him, lest they should be put out of the synagogue,*" &c. These men had not the courage to utter their convictions. Two things made them cowardly.

First: Fear of men. "*Because of the Pharisees.*" The Pharisees were the leaders of the sect—men of great influence in the State, and of intolerant spirits. These rulers, such as Nicodemus and Joseph, had not the courage to say to the face of these men, We believe in Christ. Alas! how many in every age, and how many now, are found whose faith in Christ is too cowardly for confession. They are afraid of their contemporaries, their associates. Verily, this is a poor kind of faith. I question whether it has any virtue in it. The other thing that made them cowardly was—

*See *Gospel of Matthew.* † See Germ, p. 370.

Secondly : Love of popularity. "*For they loved the praise of men more than the praise of God.*" Perhaps the word "glory" would be better than the word "*praise*" in both instances. Observe—(1.) It is implied, between the glory of men and the glory of God there is an essential difference. What is glory in the estimation of men ? Wealth, fame, titles, pageantries, &c. &c. In the eye of God, these are worthless rubbish. What is the glory of God ? Moral holiness. When Moses asked Jehovah of old to show him His glory, His answer was, "I will cause all My goodness to pass before thee." Observe—(2.) It is implied that a higher appreciation of the glory of men than the glory of God is inimical to a courageous faith. Hence these rulers had no heroism in their convictions. The faith of Peter when he stood before the Sanhedrim and exclaimed, "We cannot but speak the things which we have heard," is faith of the true type. Another subject here is—

III —A REDEMPTIVE TRUSTFULNESS

Two remarks are suggested concerning this kind of faith.

First : It is faith in His identity with the Father. "*He that believeth on Me, believeth not on Me, but on Him that sent Me.*" Christ claimed no position independent of the Father. "*And he that seeth Me, seeth Him that sent Me,*" which means, in Me the Eternal is to be seen. "He that hath seen Me hath seen the Father." Between the spirit, purpose, and character of Christ and that of the Father there was a perfect oneness : "I and My Father are One." A redemptive trustfulness therefore must have faith in Christ, not only as the Divinely sent, but as the Divinely-imaged and Divinely-natured. Another remark is that—

Secondly : It is faith, the absence of which tends to a terrible doom. "*Shall not abide in darkness.*" What is it to abide in darkness ?—in the darkness of ignorance, remorse, and despair ! Ah, what ?

Germs of Thought
No. 45   John 12:38-41

THE GOSPEL REPORT

"That the saying of Esaias the prophet might be fulfilled, which he spake, Lord, who hath believed our report ? and to whom hath the arm of the Lord been revealed ? Therefore they could not believe, because that Esaias said again, He hath blinded their eyes, and hardened their heart ; that they should not see with their eyes, nor understand with their heart, and be converted, and I should heal them. These things said Esaias, when he saw His glory, and spake of Him."—xii. 38—41.

In connection with what I have written on this passage, the following general remarks may tend to clear up difficulties and enforce solemn truths. The word *"report"* here I take to mean Redemptive Truth, or the *Gospel,* and on it offer the following remarks.

I —THAT THE GOSPEL REPORT IS TRUE AND DIVINELY MIGHTY

First : It is true because it is implied that it ought to be *"believed."* What is genuinely believable must be true.

Secondly : It is Divinely *"mighty,"* for it is called the *"arm of the Lord."* There is Divine power in Redemptive Truth. It is "the power of God unto salvation."

II —THOUGH TRUE, ITS TRUTH IS OFTEN UNBELIEVED AND UNFELT

It was so in the days of the prophets, the days of Christ, the days of the apostles, and through all subsequent times. *" Therefore they could not believe."* Why ? Not because of Esaias' prediction, not because of any Divine decree, but because of the state of their minds. They had *" blinded their eyes, and hardened their heart,"* &c. So long as men are in the depths of moral corruption they can neither see nor feel Divine things. A malignant nature cannot see love, and a mercenary, avaricious nature cannot feel and see the generous and disinterested.

III —THESE MORAL STATES OF MIND INIMICAL TO FAITH ARE OFTEN INTENSIFIED BY LISTENING TO THE REPORT

" He hath blinded their eyes, and hardened their heart." These words are quoted several times in the New Testament. Christ quotes them in Matt. xiii. 14, and Paul quotes them in Acts xxviii. 26. It is a fact proved by the nature of things, and patent to the observation and consciousness of all, that the hearer of the Gospel that believes not; is made more blind and hard by listening. Men, as free agents, have the power of counteracting the moral tendency of things, turning blessings into curses, and curses into blessings. The unbelieving man is ever doing the former, and the man of genuine faith the latter.

IV —THE AWFUL RESULTS OF THE GOSPEL UPON MEN POSSESSING THESE STATES OF MIND ARE ALL FOREKNOWN OF GOD

The prophet was told what would be the fate of his *" report."* God knew that men would be morally injured by the report He commanded the prophet to deliver. He foresees all, the good and the bad. But His foreknowledge did not render the result *necessary,* interfered not with their freedom of action, nor lessened in the least the amount of their guilt.

V —ALTHOUGH GOD FOREKNOWS THE TERRIBLE CONSEQUENCES
OF THE GOSPEL UPON THE UNBELIEVING HEARER, HE STILL
COMMANDS IT TO BE PREACHED

In the prophecy here quoted we have these remarkable words,
" Go and tell this people, Hear ye indeed, but understand not ;
and see ye indeed, but perceive not. Make the heart of this people
fat, and make their ears heavy," &c. Christ Himself said (John ix.
39), " I am come into this world, that they which see not might
see ; and that they which see might be made blind." The proclaiming of Gospel truth is a good in itself, and a good to the
universe, though it may enhance the guilt and misery of millions.
Though He knows that storms will spread fearful devastation over
sea and land, yet He sends forth storms. Man is not the only
creature in the universe to be served, nor yet the chief creature,
although in our egotism we fancy him the being for whom the
world was made. Men once thought that this earth was the centre
of the system to which it belongs, that all the heavenly bodies
moved around it, and were attendant on it. That geocentric theory
has vanished as a dream. It will be so one day with that egotistic
theory that man is the moral centre of Divine Providence, that all
things are made to serve him.

John 12:47-50

ASPECTS OF CHRIST'S WORDS

" And if any man hear My words, and believe not, I judge him not," &c.—

EXEGETICAL REMARKS.—Ver. 47.—
" *If any man hear My words* (R. V.
SAYINGS), *and believe not* (R. V. KEEP
THEM NOT), *I judge him not : for I
came not to judge the world, but to save
the world."* God sent not His Son to
condemn the world. (See chap. iii. 17.)
Ver. 48.—" *He that rejecteth Me,
and receiveth not My words* (R. V. SAY-
INGS), *hath one that judgeth him : the
word that I have spoken* (R. V. SPAKE),
*the same shall judge him in the last
day."* Because Christ, in His Person,
life, and teaching, is the perfect manifestation of God's mind, His teaching
will be the grand and only criterion in
the day of judgment. Christ Himself
is now, and ever will be the standard
of judgment by which our character
will be tried.
Ver. 49.—" *For I have not spoken*
(R. V. SPAKE NOT) *of* (R. V. FROM) *My-*

*self; but the Father which sent Me, He
gave* (R. V. HATH GIVEN) *Me a commandment, what I should say, and
what I should speak."* Here is assigned
the reason why His word shall be the
rule in the last judgment.
Ver. 50.—" *And I know that His
commandment is life everlasting* (R. V.
ETERNAL): *whatsoever I speak* (R. V.
THE THINGS THEREFORE WHICH I
SPEAK) *therefore, even as the Father
said* (R. V. HATH SAID) *unto Me, so I
speak."* Our Lord here in closing His
public discourses sets this solemn seal
to His message : His commandment
is " *life everlasting."*
Through the remainder of this entire Gospel, including chapters xiii.—
xxi., nearly the half of the whole, we
have only the *private* ministry of
Christ. His public ministry is now
closed. Hence on He addresses Him-

self to those who have been called His apostles and colleagues ; and then He was tried, condemned, crucified, buried, rises from His grave, says a few more wonderful words to His disciples, and the curtain falls. He is in heaven.

HOMILETICS

This passage leads us to look at the *Words of Christ* in several aspects—

I —AS LAWS TO BE OBEYED

" *If any man hear My words, and believe not.*" * The words of Christ are not like poetry for entertainment, or abstract science for speculative thought; they are laws to be *kept ;* not so much a *creed* as *a code.* They come with Divine authority, they demand obedience. It is only as His words are translated into actions and embodied in actual life, that their mission is answered, that they are of any real and lasting service to man. Look at the words—

II —AS A MEANS OF SALVATION

" *For I came not to judge the world, but to save the world.*" Had He come to "*judge the world*" His words would not have been what they are now, they would have breathed the indignation of insulted justice. But He came to save, and hence His words are full of all that can restore man to holiness and to God. ·The salvation which Christ speaks of is not the miserable thing that it is represented from popular pulpits—a salvation from eternal fire to some local paradise—but a restoration from *spiritual ignorance to intelligence,* from *selfishness to benevolence,* from *bondage to freedom,* from *inward conflict to inner harmony,* from *social perniciousness to social utility.* This is the salvation which Christ came to effect, and for which His signs and words are adapted. " *Save the world* " —not a class. Look at the words—

III —AS CRITERIA OF JUDGMENT

" *He that rejecteth Me, and receiveth not My words, hath one that judgeth him : the word that I have spoken, the same shall judge him in the last day.*" † The man to whom Christ has spoken, and who *rejects,* or nullifies His word, needs no other judge than His words. These words will judge him—judge him in his own conscience ; they will condemn him for his *ingratitude, folly, rebellion.* Look at the words—

IV —AS EXPRESSIONS OF THE FATHER

" *For I have not spoken of Myself :* ‡ *but the Father which sent Me, He gave Me a commandment.*" Christ's thoughts He does not ascribe to the fertility of His own intellect, but traces to the Infinite Source of all truth and intelligence. Whatever other

* See Germ, p. 374.   † See Germ, p. 375.   ‡ See Germ, p. 375.

teacher ever said this? And are not His ideas such as to justify Him in ascribing them to God, so congruous, when rightly interpreted, with *à priori* reasonings, moral intuitions, conscience, and the deep-felt exigencies of the human soul? They are as true to the soul as the sun is to the eye, as the vital air is to the heaving lungs. Look at the words—

V —AS DEPOSITORIES OF LIFE

"*And I know that His commandment is life everlasting.*" Or, eternal life; which is better. Christ's words are spirit and life; they are the "incorruptible seed which liveth and abideth for ever;" they have in them the germs of a blessed immortality.

CONCLUSION. "See that ye refuse not Him that speaketh." Ponder Christ's words; do not let the interpretations of a sectarian theology take you away from their deep moral significance. Let His words enter you, dwell in you, and reign within you, for they are "*life everlasting.*"

Germs of Thought
No. 46   John 12:47

A GREAT PRIVILEGE, AND A TERRIBLE POSSIBILITY

"And if any man hear My words, and believe not, I judge him not."—xii. 47. Observe here three momentous subjects.

I —THE GREATEST SPIRITUAL PRIVILEGE THAT A MAN CAN HAVE ON THIS EARTH

To "*hear the words*" of Christ. It is a priceless privilege to hear the words of any great sage, poet, moralist. But what are the best human words compared with the words of Christ? They are "Spirit" and "Life," more pure than crystal, more refreshing than the morning breeze, more quickening than the sunbeam, they are re-creative forces. What have they accomplished ere now? Observe here—

II —THE GREATEST CRIMINAL NEGLECT OF WHICH A MAN CAN BE GUILTY

"*If any man hear My words, and believe not,*" or keep them not. The man who hears Christ's words and keeps them not is guilty of —(1.) The most *egregious folly*. (2.) The most *heinous ingratitude*. (3.) The most *hardened impiety*. Observe here—

III —THE MOST TERRIBLE DOOM THAT A MAN CAN APPREHEND

"*I judge him not.*" The meaning of this is—I as a Saviour have nothing more to do with him; I leave him to the retributive treatment of My Father. Mercy leaves him, and justice apprehends him.

No. 47   John 12:48

THE REDEMPTIVE BECOMING RETRIBUTIVE

"He that rejecteth Me, and receiveth not My words, hath one that judgeth him : the word that I have spoken, the same shall judge him in the last day."—xii. 48.

Observe—

I —CHRISTIANITY MAY BE REJECTED NOW

"*He that rejecteth Me.*" There are millions still rejecting Christ. They do not accept Him as the only spiritual Redeemer and supreme moral Commander. Christendom to a great extent accepts Him in creed, and rejects Him in conduct.

II —THOSE WHO REJECT CHRISTIANITY NOW, MUST BOW TO ITS JUDICIAL FORCE HEREAFTER

"*The word that I have spoken, the same shall judge him in the last day.*" "*The last day*" is the *retributive period that awaits us all.* In that period the "*word*" that has been trodden under foot rises from the dust and takes the throne. (1.) *There is nothing arbitrary in the decision or the procedure of the last judgment.* The glorious words of mercy which are rejected will spring from their graves, and conscience will invest them with the authority of an inexorable judge. (2.) *Man should be profoundly cautious as to how to treat the words of Christ now.* His words are not sounds, but things— terrible things; not vocables, but vitalities. They must live for ever in every soul into which they have fallen. Old sermons will be preached again by memory many ages on. Old preachers will reappear. "How shall we escape, if we neglect so great salvation ?"

No. 48   John 12:49

CHRIST AS A TEACHER

"For I have not spoken of Myself ; but the Father which sent Me, He gave Me a commandment, what I should say, and what I should speak."—xii. 49.

Here we have Christ as a Teacher—and notice—

I —HIS PROFOUND HUMILITY

"*For I have not spoken of Myself.*" As if He had said, I take no credit for the thoughts that I have addressed to men : they are not the flashes of My own genius or the conclusions of My own reason. I am not their fountain, but their channel. A teacher is *great and Divine just in proportion to his humility.* Alas! the vanity of preachers has become proverbial. Notice—

II —HIS CONSCIOUS DIVINITY

"*But the Father which sent Me, He gave Me a commandment.*" He felt that what He said was not His own. It did not spring up within Him, but came to Him as from a Divine messenger. It is a general truth, that no man is a true spiritual teacher who is not conscious that the thoughts he utters are not his own, but God's. As he loses his egotism in preaching, he alone rises to an efficient ministry. "When I am weak, then am I strong."

John 13:1

SOME OF THE WONDERS OF CHRIST'S DEATH

(*Jesus washes the feet of His disciples. Jerusalem.*—JOHN xiii. 1—20.)

"Now before the feast of the Passover, when Jesus knew that His hour was come that He should depart out of this world unto the Father, having loved His own which were in the world, He loved them unto the end." —xiii. 1.

Here begins the *second division* of John's gospel. In the first division Christ is revealed in His works, discourses, and conflicts with the Jews. In all these He appears in superhuman glory. In this second division He appears in a more private capacity. Communion with His disciples, interceding with the Everlasting Father, betrayed, tried, condemned, crucified, rising from the dead, reappearing to His disciples, and continuing with them for forty days.

EXEGETICAL REMARKS.—Ver. 1.— "*Now before the feast of the Passover.*" "It was past three o'clock, the commencement of the (Matthew, Mark, Luke) first (Matthew, Mark) day of unleavened bread (Matthew, Mark, Luke),—at a later period of which, as the Law enjoined (Luke), men were in the habit of killing the Paschal lamb (Mark), when the disciples joined Him (Matthew). Where, asked they (Matthew, Mark),—or Peter and John, in response to His command to go and get ready the Passover for Himself and His disciples (Luke),—were preparations to be made ? He bade (Matthew, Mark, Luke) them (Matthew), or two of them (Mark),—these the two just mentioned (Luke),—go into the city (Matthew, Mark, Luke), to such an one (Matthew), whom they would discover by following a man who met them carrying a pitcher of water (Mark, Luke), and tell him that the Master's time was at hand, that at his house was He keeping the Passover with His disciples (Matthew); inquiring in His name for the guestchamber in which to hold the feast. They would be shown a large upper room, furnished (Mark, Luke) and prepared after the custom of that season (Mark). There they were to make ready. They went, and found as their Master had indicated (Mark, Luke). They did as He commanded (Matthew), and made ready the Passover (Matthew, Mark, Luke), though a full day before the regular time for the feast (John). At the commencement of the second evening (Matthew, Mark), at the appointed hour of six o'clock (Luke), Jesus came along with the twelve and sat down (Matthew, Mark, Luke)." (See "Historical Sketch of the Life of our Lord," by W. Ireland Gordon, M.A., B.D.) "*When Jesus knew* (R. V. KNOWING) *that His hour was come*"; or, according to Lange and Godet, Jesus knowing that His hour was coming. "Jesus knowing that." "These words show the prevailing thought of our Lord's mind during these highest manifestations of His love. He knew that the hour of His return to the Father and His separation from His disciples was at hand."—*Dr. Godet.*

Jesus had withdrawn Himself; but now, as the great public religious feast was at hand—the Passover,—He was drawn forth by the consciousness that *"His hour was come."* It is the fourth Passover, and it is the last that He will ever attend. The festival began on the fifteenth of the month, and lasted seven days. *"Depart out of this world unto the Father."* What a blessed change! leaving a scene of moral pollution, enmity, and tumult, and entering into the presence of Infinite purity, love, and peace. *"Having loved His own which were in the world, He loved them unto the end."* This expression does not mean, "as He had loved them, He continued to do so;" but, "if He had loved them before, it was now that it was fully seen how much He loved them." "The expression *His own*, expresses the value His heart attached to these beings given Him by the Father,

whom He was about to leave in so critical a position. Εἰς τέλος does not seem to have in Greek the meaning *unto the end*. At least Passow does not give this meaning, nor does the N.T. seem to furnish an example of it. In the two passages, Luke xviii. 5, and 1 Thess. ii. 16, we must translate *at last*, or *to finish*, a sense which this phrase has also in classical Greek (Passow), but which is inappropriate here. The usual meaning of εἰς τέλος in good Greek is, *to an extreme, to the greatest degree;* and this is also the most suitable in this verse. At these last moments, the manifestations of His affection attained a degree of intensity which they had not hitherto reached; they went so far as to completely pour forth this feeling, and, in some sort, to exhaust it. This is the sense which we have endeavoured to give in our translation."—*Dr. Godet.*

HOMILETICS

This verse suggests three wonderful facts in relation to *Christ's death.*

I—HE HAD A DIVINE PRESENTIMENT OF THE EXACT TIME OF HIS DEATH

" When Jesus knew that His hour was come," or knowing that His hour was come. All men have the sentiment that they must die sooner or later. This, like a law, is written in them. It throws a shadow along the path of life, from the beginning to its close. It mingles with all our earnest thinkings, it colours our ideas, it often chills the heart, and sends a quiver through every nerve. But we have not the presentiment as to the exact *time* of our dissolution. This in mercy is hidden from us. If we had it, we should be rendered utterly unfit to enjoy the blessings or to discharge the duties of life. But Christ had this presentiment. He knew the *"hour."* It stood before His mind with all its attendant horrors. Now, it is worthy of remark, that with this presentiment, instead of shrinking from death or endeavouring to avoid it, He comes forth to meet it. In the preceding chapter (verse 36) we are informed that He had gone into concealment. But now, at the great religious festival of the nation, He leaves His solitude and comes forth to meet His destiny. This argues at any rate His superhumanity. What mere man would have done this—done it with such heroic calmness?

II —HE HAD A GLORIOUS VIEW OF THE NATURE OF HIS DEATH

He did not think of His death with a particle of horror, but as a grand moral mission. It was going from the world to the Father, " *that He should depart out of this world unto the Father.*" To Him—

First : It was a departure from this world. With the exception of the ten thousand beauties and countless blessings of the earth, and the splendour of the heavens that encircle it, there was everything in the world that must have been in the highest degree repugnant to His moral tastes and aims. It is a world of rebels against the government of His Father, a world of enemies to Himself, and to all that is pure and good. To Him it must have been more uncongenial than the cell to the prisoner, the foul lazaretto to the man of health. To leave such a scene as this could not have been a matter of regret; it was rather a matter of earnest desire and strong expectation. May not every good man look upon death in this aspect ? What is there in the *human* world to interest him ? To Him—

Secondly : It was going to His Father. The language seems to imply that one who lives in a corrupt world, however pure he may be, is to some extent separate from the Father. The senses and our corrupt character seem to some degree to shut out the spiritually pure and beautiful. The Father is everywhere, but is only seen by those who can extricate themselves from the materialistic and immoral. (1.) In going to the Father, He would get the highest approbation of His work. He had come into the world to do the " will of His Father," and that will He had wrought out to the death. Here He heard no approving voice save that of His own conscience. Now He is to have the "Well done, good and faithful servant," of His Father. (2.) In going to the Father, He would enjoy the sublimest fellowship. We are told that " In His presence is fulness of joy," and " At His right hand there are pleasures for evermore." May not every good man take this view of death ? passing out of the world to the Father ? Why, then, mourn the death of the good ? They have not gone out of existence, but rather passed from a corrupt scene of existence into a pure and blessed one.

III —HE HAD A SUBLIME MOTIVE FOR MEETING WITH HIS DEATH

What was that ? Love for humanity. " *Having loved His own which were in the world, He loved them unto the end.*" Who were " *His own?* " Some say, His few disciples then existing. Some say, the elect. Others say, the whole human world. One thing is certain, that " *His own* " are those in every land and age who consecrate themselves to the will, the service, and glory of that God whose we are. They are "*His own.*" Love for such,—and all men are *potentially* such,—was His motive. He loved the world and gave Himself for it. "He tasted death for every man." This was the sublime motive, and this sublime motive carried Him on to the end of His mission. "*Loved them unto the end*" (extremely), or, according to *Godet,* "*He perfectly manifested His love to them.*" He went on to the full demonstration of it on the cross. His love bore Him on, until, on the cross, He exclaimed, "It is finished." What love was this! Unmerited, compassionate, unbounded, unconquerable love! "*Unto the end.*" It continues—(1.) To the end of every man's existence; (2.) To the end of the mediatorial system. Nay, will it ever have an end? Never in *essence,* but in *achievement.*

John 13:2-7

CHRIST WASHING HIS DISCIPLES' FEET (No. 1.)

"And supper being ended, the devil having now put into the heart of Judas Iscariot, Simon's son, to betray Him," &c.—xiii. 2—7.

EXEGETICAL REMARKS.—Ver. 2.— "*And supper being ended*" (R. V. DURING SUPPER). It is clear from verses 25 —28 of this chapter that supper was not "*ended*" at this point; and it is necessary therefore to ask whether the Original does not admit of a better translation. It does so, as some of the best scholars aver. Godet, for example, translates thus: "And supper having taken place." Ellicott: "And it now becoming supper-time." The idea perhaps is, supper having arrived or being in process. "*The devil having now* (R. V. ALREADY) *put into the heart of Judas Iscariot, Simon's son, to betray Him.*" Some read as if the "*heart*" here meant the heart of the devil: the devil having now decided in his heart. But this meaning cannot be justified either on philological or theological grounds. Our version, however, gives the true sense as well as the true translation. The devil having now put into the heart of Judas Iscariot, Simon's son, that he should betray Him. "*Judas Iscariot, Simon's son.*" "The name is given here in the sad fulness of this mournful record. The fact is recorded here to explain the references to Judas which follow in our Lord's words (verses 10, 18, 21, 26, 27, 30)."—*H. Watkins, M.A.*

Ver. 3.—"*Jesus knowing that the Father had given all things into His hands, and that He was come* (R. V. CAME FORTH) *from God, and went to* (R. V. AND GOETH UNTO) *God.*" "This '*knowing*' corresponds with that of verse 1; and here, even more frequently than in the latter passage, commentators are wont to paraphrase it as 'though knowing.' But this is in our opinion a still graver misconception of the Evangelist's meaning, as well as that of Jesus Himself, than at verse 1. It was not, notwithstanding His Divine greatness, but because of that greatness, that Jesus humbled Himself in the manner about to be related. Feeling Himself the greatest, He also felt that it was for Him to give the example of true greatness by humbling Himself to fulfil the office of the lowest: for greatness in the Messianic kingdom as He had come to establish it would consist in voluntary abasement. This was a kind of greatness hitherto unknown in the world, and which His own were now to behold in Him, that His Church might never acknowledge any other. It was therefore, *inasmuch as* He was Lord, and not *though* He was Lord, that He was about to fulfil the office of a slave."—*Godet.*

Ver. 4.—"*He riseth from supper,*

and laid (R. V. LAYETH) *aside His garments; and took a towel, and girded Himself.*" In Luke xxii. there is the record of a strife among the disciples as to whom among them should be accounted the greatest; and now Christ, by an acted parable, shows them that greatness is in service. Here He Himself not only serves, but puts on the garb of a servant. He strips Himself of His outward garments and girds Himself with a towel. *Tholuck* understands "that our Lord had already reclined at the table, and that, as they had no servants, the feet-washing would naturally have been done by one of the disciples. The things necessary for it were at hand. As the disciples are debating who shall undertake it, Jesus no longer remains in His reclining posture, but rises Himself to perform this duty of a servant, to show His condescending love in this closing transaction."

Ver. 5.—"*After that* (R. V. THEN) *He poureth water into a* (R. V. THE) *bason, and began to wash the disciples' feet, and to wipe them with the towel wherewith He was girded.*" Such a vessel would of course be at hand, as it was the custom at feasts to wash the feet of guests (1 Sam. xxv.). The reason of this custom is obvious: travelling in a hot country with sandals, exposed the feet to dust. "Did not the feet-washing at other times precede the supper? We remark, in reply, that the fact that

they had already gone to the table by no means implies necessarily that this washing did not precede their eating: it was customary to wash the outstretched feet as the guests lay upon the cushions, as in Luke vii. 38."— *Tholuck.*

Ver. 6.—"*Then cometh He* (R. V. SO HE COMETH) *to Simon Peter: and Peter* (R. V. HE) *said unto Him, Lord, dost Thou wash my feet?*" The sense of Christ's moral superiority which came out in an exclamation of Peter's on a former occasion (Luke v. 8), "Depart from me, for I am a sinful man, O Lord," he now felt perhaps when Christ approached him in order to wash his feet. "*Lord, dost Thou wash my feet?*" Is it possible that Thou art so condescending as this? *Thou* is to be strongly emphasized.

Ver. 7.—"*Jesus answered and said unto him, What I do thou knowest not now.*" Here both the pronouns are emphatic, and convey a rebuke to Peter. His words had almost implied that the Lord's act was wholly out of place, as of one who knew not what he was doing. The opposite was really the case. "*But thou shalt know* (R. V. UNDERSTAND) *hereafter,*" *i. e.* in the teaching which is to follow (vers. 13—17). The word rendered "*hereafter*" is different from that rendered "*afterwards*" in verse 36. The precise meaning is, "after these things." The sense is then, "What I do thou knowest not now; but thou shalt come to know presently."

HOMILETICS

Our subject is *Christ washing His disciples' feet*. In this paragraph we have three subjects of great interest and importance, a great crime suggestively stated, a great character infinitely condescending, and a great truth symbolically expressed.

I —A GREAT CRIME SUGGESTIVELY STATED

"*And supper being ended, the devil having now put into the heart of Judas Iscariot, Simon's son, to betray Him.*" An account of this criminal transaction we have more fully given in the Synoptists (Matt. xxvi. 14—16; Mark xiv. 10, 11; Luke xxii. 3—6). It had taken place some hours before the supper. The traitor had struck the bargain with the chief priests in the temple, and pledged himself to the guilty act for thirty shekels of the sanctuary, the mere price of a slave. We have here the *genesis* of this crime: there are *two factors*, the devil and Judas. A pretty full description is given of Judas. He was Judas Iscariot, and Simon's son. Thus he is marked off from every other man of his name. This man, like many sons, by his infamous conduct brought disgrace upon his father's name. As to the devil—the other factor —much is said in Scripture about him. This being, who in Greek is Diabolos, is in Hebrew Satan. The Bible assumes that he is not a principle, but a personality, and he is represented as an accuser, a murderer, a liar, the arch-enemy of God and man. Now the expression here, that "*the devil put into the heart of Judas,*" shows three things.

First: The accessibility of this infernal spirit to the human soul. He has ways of entering it, he knows its avenues, and avails himself of them. Through the bodily senses and the inner propensities, he can touch the springs of human activity, inject thoughts that will fire the passions and turn the will. His "fiery darts" are numerous, and from his bow they go forth, silent as the night, rapid as the sunbeam. Let us beware of his "devices." The expression shows—

Secondly: The tendency of the human soul to be influenced by Satanic impressions. In spiritual natures that retain their pristine innocence, and all those who advance without any swerving in the paths of holiness, there is no tendency to yield to evil impressions. Of course the susceptibility of feeling them is there, otherwise they would not be responsible; but the tendency of yielding to them is not there, this has come through the Fall. When the evil spirit assailed Christ, Christ's nature felt his demon touch, but He resisted it. "The prince of this world cometh, and hath nothing in Me." On innocence the "fiery darts" of the devil fall as on water, and are quenched; on depravity they fall as on tinder, and become a blaze. The expression shows—

Thirdly: The possibility of the two uniting in a common crime. Both now acted jointly in the betrayal of Christ. The suggestion perhaps came from the one, the execution from the other. Two remarks may be offered on this subject—(1.) The unity of action *might not have sprung from exactly the same motives.* It does not appear that Judas had any positive hatred towards Christ; on the whole, perhaps, he was interested in Him, and his sympathies were on His side. Not so with Satan: this evil spirit seems to have had a burning dislike to Christ, hence we hear him exclaim at one time, "I know Thee who Thou art: art Thou come to torment me before the time?" The two are constitutional antagonists, in nature, in sympathy, and in purpose. (2.) The unity of action *did not lessen the responsibility of either.* Though Judas was instigated by Satan, yet Judas was *free:* of his freedom in the action he was conscious. Hence, after the crime, how deep and intense was his remorse! "Then Judas, which had betrayed Him, when he saw that He was condemned, repented himself, and brought again the thirty pieces of silver to the chief priests and elders, saying, I have betrayed the innocent blood. And they said, What is that to us? see thou to that. And he cast down the pieces of silver in the temple, and departed, and went and hanged himself." In this paragraph we have—

II—A GREAT CHARACTER INFINITELY CONDESCENDING

Look here at two things—

First: See what this great character really was. He was One into Whose hands "*the Father had given all things*," Who had "*come from God, and went to God*." He was Divine in His authority, which was universal, and Divine in His mission and destiny. "*Come from God, and went to God*." Of this He was profoundly conscious. "*Jesus knowing*."

Secondly: See what He was actually doing. "*He riseth from supper, and laid aside His garments; and took a towel, and girded Himself. After that He poureth water into a bason, and began to wash the disciples' feet, and to wipe them with the towel wherewith He was girded*." He does the work of a slave with the towel of a slave. Here is an illustration of that wonderful passage in the writings of the Apostle Paul (Phil. ii. 6—8): "Who, being in the form of God; did not think equality with God a thing to be grasped at; but emptied Himself by taking upon Him the form of a servant, being made in the likeness of men: and being found in fashion as a man, humbled Himself, having become obedient even unto death, and that the death of the cross" (*Dr. Samuel Davidson*). In this paragraph we have—

III—A GREAT TRUTH SYMBOLICALLY EXPRESSED

What is the truth expressed by this washing of the disciples' feet? It is this, that *in the spiritual kingdom of Christ, to be truly humble is to be truly great.* That in His kingdom the lowest kind of service, if properly rendered, is sublimely dignified. The disciples had just been striving amongst themselves as to who should be the greatest. In answer to this, Christ had said, "The kings of the Gentiles exercise lordship over them: and they that exercise authority upon them are called benefactors. But ye shall not be so. But he that is greatest among you, let him be as the younger: and he that is chief as he that doth serve. For whether is greater, he that sitteth at meat, or he that serveth? Is not he that sitteth at meat? but I am among you as he that serveth." And here by a symbolic action He further illustrates the statement. True humility is true greatness, and the lowest services properly rendered are Divinely dignified. Observe two things—

First : Christ's idea of greatness condemns the general conduct of mankind. In the kingdoms of the world, men are considered great in proportion to their wealth and their influence. Hence, to break down the individual independency of men and reduce them to mere instruments to be wielded at pleasure, has ever been the aim and effort of the ambitious and the proud. The antithesis of this is true greatness. Its measure is not determined by the numbers that servilely attend on us, but rather by the numbers that we benevolently attend upon. Its mission is to minister, not to master : to give, not to govern. Its sceptre is love, not force, its throne is in the heart and its empire over souls. Observe—

Secondly : Christ's idea of greatness agrees with the moral reason of our nature. The greatness of Christ—Who "made Himself of no reputation," Who gave Himself to save the world—and the greatness of Paul, is the greatness which commends itself to the unsophisticated reason of the world. He that "humbleth himself" to do good is "exalted" in the estimation of universal conscience. Disinterestedness is the soul of greatness. Observe—

Thirdly : Christ's idea of greatness was startling even to His disciple. *"Peter saith unto Him, Lord, dost Thou wash my feet ?"* Peter could not suppose for a moment, that He Whom he regarded as Master and Lord—that He Whom he expected would restore Jerusalem and build up a kingdom that should make the Jews everywhere a free and triumphant people—would condescend to do the work of a slave and to wash the feet of His guests. He could not see greatness in that. Hence, startled, he exclaims, *" Dost Thou wash my feet ?"* To this our Saviour replies, *" What I do thou knowest not now ; but thou shalt know hereafter."* * As if He had said, Wait a little, and thou shalt know the doctrine of true greatness.

Germs of Thought
No. 49   John 13:7

EXISTING IGNORANCE AND APPROACHING KNOWLEDGE

" What I do thou knowest not now ; but thou shalt know hereafter."—xiii. 7.

The special reference here is to Peter ; and the promise of future knowledge was fulfilled in his own experience. Let us look at the words in a wider application.

I —THEY INDICATE THE EXISTING IGNORANCE OF THE GOOD

There is much that the best man knows not now.

First : There is much in nature he knows not now. How little does the most scientific man know of the substances, lives, laws, operations, extent of the universe ! How deeply did Sir Isaac Newton feel his ignorance !

* See Germ, below.

Secondly : There is much in moral government he knows not now. The reason for the introduction of sin, the suffering of innocence, the prosperity of the wicked, the afflictions of the good, the tardy march of Christianity, is wrapped in utmost obscurity.

Thirdly : There is much in Divine revelation he knows not now. What Peter said of Paul's writings, we feel to be true of the whole Book. There are " many things hard to be understood." There are discrepancies that we cannot remove, there are doctrines that transcend our intelligence, towering high above our reason as the heavens above the earth.

Fourthly : There is much in his own experience he knows not now. Why should he be dealt with as he is ? Why such alternations of sorrow and joy, friendship and bereavement, health and sickness ? Why such conflicting elements in his nature ? Thus a thick cloud of darkness covers man's intellectual heavens, narrows his horizon, and renders the things most near at hand almost too obscure even for a superficial recognition.

II —THEY INDICATE THE APPROACHING KNOWLEDGE OF THE GOOD

" *Thou shalt know hereafter.*" This implies that there is a "*here-after*" for man, and that that hereafter will be a sphere of knowledge. "*Thou shalt know hereafter.*" There will be—(1.) Sufficient *time* for knowing. (2.) Sufficient *facilities* for knowing.—All existing obstructions will be removed, and the immeasurable field of truth wide open under a never-clouded and a never-setting sun.

John 13:8-11

CHRIST WASHING HIS DISCIPLES' FEET (No. 2).

" Peter saith unto Him, Thou shalt never wash my feet," &c.

EXEGETICAL REMARKS.—Ver. 8.— "*Peter saith unto Him, Thou shalt never wash my feet.*" Again the self-will of the apostle developes into contradiction and disobedience, as on the occasion when Jesus announced that He was about to tread the path of suffering (Matt. xvi. 22). The connection between the two passages is discoverable, on the one hand, in the great attachment and reverence which Peter entertained for the Lord ; but on the other hand also in his cleaving to the external glory and sovereignty of Christ, and in coveting a share thereof for himself. Christ now began practically with His self-humiliation to turn Peter's moral view of the world "upside down." " Peter, meanwhile, instead of divining the blessing of the Cross enfolded in this act, struggled with anxious forebodings against its pricks Christ's washing of the disciples' feet was an affair utterly repugnant to his soul. Never : properly to eternity, with the œon, *εἰς τὸν αἰῶνα.*"—*Lange.* The emphasis here is not to be on the "*Thou*" or the "*my*," but on the "*never.*" " The incidental touches of character, where individual apostles are named in this gospel, are in striking agreement with the more fully-drawn character of the other evangelists ; and the value of their evidence for the authorship cannot be over-estimated. They are perfectly artless, but are beyond the most consummate art. He feels that it is the loving, impulsive, but self-confident Peter of the earlier gospels who is speaking here. He does not wait for that after-knowledge which our Lord promises him. He sees no ground on which our Lord's act can possibly be one which he can permit." "*Jesus answered him, If I wash thee not, thou hast no part with Me.*" That Christ meant His act to be symbolic of the spirit of self-sacrifice and humility, in opposition to the spirit of self-seeking and pride, is here manifest. What He means is, If I do not impart to thee this spirit of self-sacrifice and humility, thou "*hast no part with Me.*" Christ's spirit of self-sacrifice is the soul-cleansing element, the washing of regeneration.

Ver. 9.—"*Simon Peter saith unto Him, Lord, not my feet only, but also my hands and my head.*" Peter has not yet penetrated the meaning of that symbolic act, nor rightly interpreted the words that had just been spoken to him. He does not understand what this washing means; but inasmuch as Christ has said that, unless he submits to it, He will cease to have any further connection with him, his loving and impulsive nature prompts him to yield whatever Christ commands. "*Not my feet only, but also my hands and my head;*" as if he had said, I will submit to anything Thou commandest, rather than forfeit my connection with Thee.

Ver. 10.—"*Jesus saith to him, He that is washed* (R. V. BATHED) *needeth not save to wash his feet, but is clean every whit: and ye are clean, but not all.*" "This answer," says Godet, "has naturally a double meaning. As in His conversation with the Samaritan woman, He passed with a rapid transition from the material to the spiritual. Just as one who, having bathed in the morning, considers himself clean, and does not repeat this total ablution at meal-time, but is contented with washing his feet on entering, to remove such accidental defilement as he may have contracted by the way; so he who, by sincerely attaching himself to Christ, has found pardon for his sins, needs nothing else than a daily and continual purification from the moral defilement of which he becomes conscious during the course of his life. Peter was clean, because he sincerely believed in Christ. The purpose, then, of what Jesus was now doing for him was, not to reconcile him to God, but to remove from him, by such an example of humility, that particular defilement, the desire for earthly power and greatness, which Jesus at that very moment observed in His own. With this evil tendency Peter could not labour in the work of God, nor even sit down one day at the table of Christ." "*He that is washed*"—better, he that has been bathed. "λοῦσθαι, in contradistinction from νίπτεσθα, signifies, not washing, but bathing, and refers therefore to the purification of the entire body, and not of a portion merely." A man whose whole body has been bathed in water is clean all over, "*every whit,*" and need not have any particular part cleansed. Peter need not, therefore, have requested his feet, hands, and head washed, if he had been thoroughly bathed. If the whole has been done, every part has been done; if the soul is saturated with self-sacrificing love, every part of the soul is so cleansed.

Vers. 10, 11.—"*And ye are clean, but not all. For He knew who* (R. V. HIM THAT) *should betray Him; therefore said He, Ye are not all clean.*" This is the first reference to the betrayal during the feast (Matt. xxi. 18).

HOMILETICS

The subject of these words is *Christ washing His disciples' feet,* and the verses suggest to us five topics worthy of meditation—

I —THE MIXTURE OF EVIL IN THE EXPERIENCE OF THE GOOD

Peter, on the whole, was a good man; and his language, "*Thou shalt never wash my feet,*" expresses something that was really good.

The feeling that came out on another occasion, "Depart from me : for I am a sinful man, O Lord" (Luke v. 8), implying the sense of Christ's greatness and his own unworthiness, is expressed here. Just before, as Christ approached him, he exclaims, "Lord, dost Thou wash my feet ?" Every word is emphatic. *Thou,* Son of the living God ! *My* feet. I, a poor, worthless man ! *"Thou shalt never wash my feet."* I cannot allow it. Thy condescension overwhelms me. This is good. But associated with this there is some amount of evil. There is the want of reflection. His characteristic impulsiveness shows itself. There is the want of ready acquiescence. He ought to have felt such unbounded confidence in Christ as to submit to His wish without any reluctance. Thus, see how evil mixes with the best things within us. The subject suggests—

II —THE NECESSITY OF SPIRITUAL CLEANSING

When Peter, from a mistaken humility, refused to have his feet washed, Christ says, *" If I wash thee not, thou hast no part with Me."* Spiritual cleansing is the great want of man. This will appear from two facts. (1.) Divine fellowship is essential to happiness. The true happiness of all spiritual intelligences consists in a loving fellowship with their great Father. (2.) Spiritual purity is essential to Divine fellowship. "The pure in heart alone shall see the Lord." "Without holiness no man shall see the Lord." Spiritual cleansing, then, is the great want of the world. Hence the command of God is, "Wash you, make you clean," &c. The prayer of good men is, " Purge me with hyssop, and I shall be clean." The words show two things concerning this spiritual cleansing, so essential to the race.

First : It is pre-eminently the work of Christ. The application of water to the disciples' feet now, symbolizes the fact that it was His great work to cleanse men of their sins. *" If I wash thee not."* I must wash thee : this is My work. This is Christ's work. His blood—His self-sacrificing love—alone "cleanseth from all sin." He receives the praises of eternity for this cleansing work of His. " Unto Him that loved us, and washed us."

Secondly : It extends to the whole life of man. *" Simon Peter saith unto Him, Lord, not my feet only, but also my hands and my head. Jesus saith to him, He that is washed needeth not save to wash his feet, but is clean every whit : and ye are clean, but not all."* Literally, the words mean, Your hands and your head, Peter, have been already washed in the bath (it was customary to take a bath before supper), you only need now to have the dust that has since gathered on your feet taken off. Spiritually, it means, Those who have been truly regenerated, as you have, still need the cleansing of some part of their life : the cleansing of the feet from defilements in the walk of common life. Though a man is regenerated, he is not perfect : every day brings its defilements, and every day requires its purifications. At that table on this occasion there were (*a*) The *perfectly* clean. This was Christ. (*β*) The *partially* clean. These were the disciples: the vital parts of their natures had been cleansed, but the extremities, their feet, still required washing. (*γ*) The entirely *unclean*. This was Judas. The subject suggests—

III —THE POSSIBILITY OF A RIGHT FEELING LEADING TO EVIL

The humility of Peter on this occasion was right, but through his want of reflection it led him to oppose Christ. A sense of our own unworthiness, and of God's greatness, right in itself, may, and often does, lead to wrong results.

First : Some reject the doctrine of *Christ's mediation* from this feeling. So deeply do they profess to feel the worthlessness of human nature, and the greatness of God, that they refuse to believe that the Maker of the great universe sent His Son into this little planet to die for a world of rebellious worms.

Secondly : Some reject the doctrine of *God's personal providence* from this feeling. There are some who say that God is too great, man too little, to render it credible that He should superintend the affairs of individual men. The great God has only to do with the great.

Thirdly : Some reject *Christian consolation* from this feeling. Many devout souls in suffering refuse to apply to their own use the promises of God from a sense of their own unworthiness. Thus a right feeling for the lack of intelligent reflection may lead to evil results. The subject suggests—

IV —THE RAPIDITY WITH WHICH THE SOUL CAN PASS INTO OPPOSITE SPIRITUAL MOODS

At one moment we hear Peter exclaim, " *Thou shalt never wash my feet,*" and the next, " *Lord, not my feet only, but also my hands and my head.*" What a bound ! We are all conscious of this power of rapid change—some temperaments more than others, still all have it.

First : This power indicates the greatness of human nature. We know of no other creature on earth that can pass through such changes. All irrational creatures move in a rut from which they cannot go. Man has a power to defy time and space, to live in the future, and to revel in the distant. " I knew a man in Christ fourteen years ago, whether in the body or out of the body I cannot tell, God knoweth."

Secondly : This power shows the necessity for human reflection. If men reflect not, they will be ever at the mercy of external influences. Thoughtless men of impulse are like feathers on the wind ; they are the sport of circumstances. The subject suggests—

V—THE NECESSITY OF AN INCREASE OF DIVINE KNOWLEDGE FOR PERFECTION IN CHARACTER

What brought Peter from the wrong to the right mood of soul? New light. After Christ had said, "*If I wash thee not, thou hast no part with Me,*" he exclaimed, "*Lord, not my feet only, but also my hands and my head.*" Just before, Jesus had said to him, "What I do thou knowest not now; but thou shalt know hereafter." He was in the dark when he said, "*Thou shalt never wash my feet.*" A new light had dawned on him when he said, "*Lord, not my feet only, but also my hands and my head.*" More light from heaven. More light: this is what we want: let us "follow on to know the Lord." Knowledge.

John 13:12-17

WHAT CHRIST REQUIRES OF HIS DISCIPLES

"So after He had washed their feet, and had taken His garments, and was set down again, He said unto them, Know ye what I have done to you?" &c.

EXEGETICAL REMARKS.—Ver. 12.— "*So after* (R. V. WHEN) *He had washed their feet, and had taken His garments, and was set* (R. V. SAT) *down again.*" That is, when He placed Himself in the reclining position which was customary among the Jews at meals (Luke xi. 37; xxii. 14; John vi. 10; xxi. 20). "*He said unto them, Know ye what I have done to you?*" That is, Do you understand the spiritual meaning of My conduct in washing your feet?

Ver. 13.—"*Ye call Me Master and Lord: and ye say well; for so I am.*" Here begins the explanation. The word "*Master*" refers to His position as their Teacher: the word "*Lord,*" to the reverence which they paid Him. You profess to recognize Me as your Teacher and Lord, and so I am. I claim to be that.

Ver. 14.—"*If I then, your* (R. V. THE) *Lord and* (R. V. THE) *Master, have washed your feet; ye also ought to wash one another's feet.*" The argument is *à fortiori*. If I have humbled Myself to do the work of a servant

for you, how much more ought you to humble yourselves to serve one another!

Ver. 15.—"*For I have given you an example, that ye* (R. V. ALSO) *should do as I have done to you.*" This does not mean that they were to copy His action, but to inbreathe His spirit. The example is in the inner principle, not in the overt act.

Ver. 16.—"*Verily, verily, I say unto you, The* (R. V. A) *servant is not greater than his lord; neither he* (R. V. ONE) *that is sent greater than he that sent him.*" (See Matt. x. 24; Luke vi. 40; John xv. 20.)

Ver. 17.—"*If ye know these things, happy* (R. V. BLESSED) *are ye if ye do them.*" What things? The things He had taught them in verses 13 to 16. The greatness of humility, the duty of rendering loving service to the poorest, and the obligation to imitate Christ, are the "*things.*" These things may be known and not be performed; but in the practical development of them is true happiness alone found.

HOMILETICS

These verses serve to illustrate what *the conduct of Christ's disciples should be;* and they teach us four things in relation to it.

I —IT SHOULD BE INTELLIGENT

" *So after He had washed their feet, and had taken His garments, and was set down again, He said unto them, Know ye what I have done to you?* " Virtually the question is, Do you know the meaning and intent of this act of Mine? He does not propound the question in order to get from them an answer at once, but to draw their attention to it, and to impress them with the fact that it had a meaning, and that meaning they should understand. Sometimes the actions of men have *no* meaning; they are impulsive and purposeless. Sometimes they have a *bad* meaning; they have selfish and sensual aims. Sometimes they have a *good* meaning; they are benevolent and pure in their motives. Christ's actions *always had a meaning.* There was nothing purposeless in what He did; and His acts had always a good meaning, holy and beneficent. The duty of His disciples is, to *find out* their *meaning,* and therefore, as Christians, always to act intelligently. There are two classes of professed Christians who act wrongly in this respect.

First: Those who attach *no* meaning to Christ's works. When they are brought under their notice, they may receive an impression of their outward form and the circumstances connected with them; but as to the eternal idea that underlies them and beats through them all, this they never reach, and seldom attempt to reach. Another class is—

Secondly: Those who attach a *wrong* meaning to Christ's works. What absurd, and in some cases blasphemous, ideas are current in Christendom concerning many of the works which Christ wrought when on this earth! Now, in opposition to this, it is the duty of every man who names the name of Christ to endeavour to penetrate the meaning of His deeds, and to act accordingly. Christians should be intelligent in their conduct, should " prove all things," and hold fast that which is true; be always prepared to give a reason for the " hope that is in them." To act from blind impulse, from superstitious passions, from old customs and prejudices, is to act unchristianly. Another thing in relation to this conduct which is taught here is—

II —IT SHOULD BE CONSISTENT

" *Ye call Me Master and Lord: and ye say well; for so I am. If I then, your Lord and Master, have washed your feet; ye also ought to wash one another's feet.*" The idea is this, If I, Who, according to your own profession—and your profession in this case is true—am so superior to you as to be your " *Master and Lord,*" condescend to wash your feet, is it not reasonable and right in you to engage in such lowly work? If I, Who am the Lord of all, am not degraded by it, can you esteem it unworthy of your humble position ? The general principle suggested is, that *Christ's disciples should act consistently with their professions.* There should be a perfect harmony between what they profess to be and what they are. Let creed and conduct be agreed; " live as becometh the Gospel of Christ." The discrepancy between the creed and the conduct of Christendom is at once amongst its greatest crimes and curses. Look into our own country as an example, and what do we see ? The millions by profession calling Christ Master and Lord, and yet in daily life denying His doctrines and disobeying His will. He denounces war, they practise it ; He denounces worldliness, they practise it ; He denounces selfishness, they practise it ; He denounces subjection to the flesh, they practise it. Thus—

> With lip they call Him Master,
>   In life oppose His word ;
> They every day deny Him,
>   And yet they call Him Lord.
>
> No more is their religion
>   Like His, in soul or deed,
> Than painted grain on canvas
>   Is like the living seed.

We extol the Reformation from Popery to Protestantism, but that Reformation is not half so important nor half so necessary, as the reformation from Protestantism to the *true* Gospel, from conventional Christianity to the Christliness of Christ. Another thing in relation to this conduct which is taught here is—

III —IT SHOULD BE CHRISTLY

" *For I have given you an example, that ye should do as I have done to you.*" *Do* what ? Not the exact special bodily work I have now done in washing your feet, but do what is practised in the spirit and embodied in the act, the spirit of disinterested self-abnegating humility. Some fools have thought, and still think, that they obey this precept of Christ by washing the feet of one another. In the Popish Church it is made a sacrament, and the Pope washes the feet of twelve beggars every year ; and even in the Moravian fraternity such a ceremony seems to have been practised. What Claudius has said of ceremonies that are empty, may be said of this, " They are the little flags which reach forth over the water, and mark where a ship with her rich lading has sunk." To do in spirit as Christ did, is to follow His example. It may be possible for a man to speak all the words that another has ever uttered, to perform all the actions that another has ever performed, and yet to be essentially different. Were we to do all that Christ ever did, we may still be out of harmony—aye, and in antagonism—with His spirit. The only way to imitate His example, is to imbibe His spirit; for if "any man hath not the spirit of Christ, he is none of His." The way for a student artist to become like a great painter, is not to copy most accurately all the strokes and shadings of his model, but to catch the genius that inspired the master. With that genius—though he produced no painting exactly like his ideal—he may produce others of equal, if not superior, excellence. Christ's spirit is the genius of all works of moral beauty and excellence; and if we catch that, we shall be "fruitful unto all good works." Another thing in relation to this conduct which is taught here is—

IV —IT SHOULD BE HAPPY

" *Verily, verily, I say unto you, The servant is not greater than his lord; neither he that is sent greater than he that sent him. If ye know these things, happy are ye if ye do them.*" The first clause is a self-evident proverb, it is the last that deserves remark— "*happy are ye if ye do them.*" What things? Things that grow out of the spirit embodied in this conduct of Mine. It is implied here that you may know them, and yet not do them. And it is stated, if you know them and do them you will be happy. Observe—

First : That Christ desires the happiness of His disciples. " *These words have I spoken unto you, that your joy may be full.*" " He came that we might have life [or happiness], and that we might have it more abundantly." Those who profess His name and are gloomy, discontented, murmuring, are an offence to Him, a misrepresentation of Him—are not His. To them He says, " I know you not." His religion is designed and fitted to inspire the highest joy—"Joy unspeakable and full of glory." Observe—

Secondly : That the doing in love the things of His loving heart ensures true happiness. " *Happy are ye if ye do them.*" The labour of love is the music of life. Yes; whatever the labour may be—whether it be the washing of disciples' feet, penetrating the foul dungeons of prisoners, or visiting the hospitals of the sick and the dying—happiness is the outcome of all. Love is happiness.

John 13:18-20

A FOURFOLD THEME

" I speak not of you all : I know whom I have chosen," &c.

EXEGETICAL REMARKS.—Ver. 18.— "*I speak not of you all : I know whom I have chosen.*" The pronoun *I* is emphatic : I, for My part, know whom I have chosen. The chosen included Judas as well as the rest, for in chap: vi. 70 we have these words, " Have not I chosen you twelve, and one of you is a devil ?" " *That the Scripture may be fulfilled.*" " Wonder not that one has been introduced into your number who is none of Mine. It is by no accident ; there is no mistake ; it is just that He might fulfil His predicted destiny." "*He that eateth* (R. V. MY) *bread with Me*"—"that did eat of My bread" (Ps. xli. 9), as one of My family ; admitted to the nearest familiarity of discipleship and of social life. "*Hath lifted up his heel against Me*"—turned upon Me, adding insult to injury. (Comp. Heb. x. 29.) In the Psalm the immediate reference is perhaps to Ahithophel's treachery against David (2 Sam. xvii.). "The eating bread," says *Stier* (with whom, as with others who hold that Judas partook of the Lord's Supper, we agree), "derives a fearful meaning from the participation in the Sacramental Supper, a meaning which must be applied for ever to all unworthy communicants, as well as to all betrayers of Christ who eat the bread of His Church" (*Dr. Brown*).

Ver. 19.—"*Now* (R. V. FROM HENCEFORTH) *I tell you before it come* (R. V. TO PASS), *that, when it is come to pass, ye may believe that I am He*." Christ knew that when one of their number—one whom He had chosen —should prove treacherous and betray Him, their own faith might be shaken in Him as the Messiah, and that He would be crushed under the traitorous act of a pretended friend. Hence He forewarns them, and fortifies them against the coming shock.

Ver. 20.—"*Verily, verily, I say unto you, He that receiveth whomsoever I send receiveth Me; and he that receiveth Me receiveth Him that sent Me*." "The connection here seems to be, that, despite the dishonour done to Him by Judas, and similar treatment awaiting themselves, they were to be cheered by the assurance that their office, even as His own, was Divine." The words spoken when they were called to be apostles—though one of their number would fall—would still hold true. Their honour and encouragement as apostles are in the fact that they are apostles from Him as He is an Apostle from the Father.

HOMILETICS

We have here a *fourfold theme* for thought—a solemn truth, a lamentable fact, a beneficent warning, and a glorious assurance. Here is—

I—A SOLEMN TRUTH

"*I know whom I have chosen*." Christ knows His disciples, knows both the true and the false. He not only knows their works, but knows their hearts. We are told that He "knew what was in man ; " and that He knew from the beginning who they were who believed not, and who would betray Him. In the Apocalypse He says, "I am He that searcheth the reins and hearts." And to the seven Churches He says, "I know thy works." He knows all that we have been, all that we are, and what we shall be through all the centuries of our future. The fact that Christ knows His disciples may lead us to infer—

First : That He does not require from us what will out-measure our faculties. He loves us too much; nay, He is too just in Himself to do this. He only demands what is equal to our powers. He is not a "hard Master, reaping where He has not sown." We infer—

Secondly : That the services that are not rendered to Him from the heart are of no worth in His sight. Formality and insincerity are worse than worthless; they are sinful, and expose to His righteous indignation. We infer—

Thirdly : That every one that names His name should depart from evil. Let us strip ourselves of all hypocrisies and pretensions, knowing that all things are "naked and open to the eyes of Him with Whom we have to do." In human service inner motives go for little. The employer does not concern himself with the spirit of his *employées*, but with their labours, whether they are profitable or not. He will pay the man who is successful in the work which he has set him to do, though he may know that the man in his heart cares nothing for him. On the other hand, he will discharge from his service the man whose work is of no value to him, even although he knows that he loves him. In sublime contrast to this, is Christ's estimate of labour in His service. It is not the amount of outward work done, but the amount of inward love felt. "Many will say to Me in that day, Lord, have we not prophesied in Thy name, and in Thy name done many wonderful works ? And I shall say, Depart from Me, I never knew you"— never approved of your works.

> "The painted hypocrites are known
> Through the disguise they wear ;
> Nothing but truth before His throne
> In honour can appear."

Mark, Christ is here said to have chosen the twelve, including Judas. Good reasons could be assigned (which we have elsewhere noticed) for His choosing Judas as a member of His circle. There are men who build their assurance of heaven at last upon persuading themselves that they are amongst the chosen ; but Judas was "*chosen*" and was damned. Here is—

II —A LAMENTABLE FACT

"*That the Scripture may be fulfilled, He that eateth bread with Me hath lifted up his heel against Me.*" Whatever may be the meaning of the expression, "*that the Scripture may be fulfilled,*" it cannot be entertained for a moment, that Judas betrayed Him in order to fulfil the Scripture. In the first place, there is no proof that the Scripture quoted was a prophecy at all ; in the second place it is not quoted accurately ; and in the third place the writer states a fact in his own history of some one whom he had served—a professed friend who had proved false and traitorous. That Judas should have acted thus, is, we say, a lamentable fact, lamentable because it involves—(1.) *The basest ingratitude.* How kind Christ had been to him in taking him into His circle ! It involves—(2.) *The guiltiest avarice.* The lowest greed was the inspiration of his act. "What will ye give me ?" It involves—(3.) *The most daring impiety.* Well he must have known that Christ was more than a man. His Divinity was manifest in His mien, His spirit, His work. Notwithstanding this, Judas betrays Him. Such a fact as this—

First: Shows a possibility that should lead us all to the most rigorous heart scrutiny. Here we see that a man may be in close contact with Christ, live in intimate association with Him for three long years, be impressed by His wonderful words and superhuman bearing, and yet have no vital spiritual connection with Him. Well may we all ask, "Lord, is it I?" Such a fact—

Secondly: Shows that Christ coerces no man into His service. He leaves each of His disciples to act for himself. "Will ye also go away?" Here is—

III —A BENEFICENT WARNING

"*Now I tell you before it come, that, when it is come to pass, ye may believe that I am He.*"

First: The warning here was against a probable danger to the other disciples. Had the conduct of Judas broken suddenly on them, the probability is, they would have received a moral shock that would go far to shake their faith. When they saw Him betrayed into the hands of the Roman ruffians by one of their own number, would it not be natural for them to conclude that their Master was overwhelmed and crushed, and that all their hopes of His being a triumphant Messiah were at an end? But this warning would prepare them for it.

Secondly: The warning here would make the very betrayal the means of fortifying their faith in the Messiah. Feeling that the betrayal was only the fulfilment of His word, they would feel that His very forecast was an additional proof of His Messiahship. The warning was therefore beneficent; to be forewarned is to be forearmed. All Christ's warnings were of this character. Here is—

IV —A GLORIOUS ASSURANCE

"*Verily, verily, I say unto you, He that receiveth whomsoever I send receiveth Me; and he that receiveth Me receiveth Him that sent Me.*" He assures them that,—

First: His faithful disciples were identified with Him. "*He that receiveth whomsoever I send receiveth Me.*" The treatment they receive, whether considerate, generous, or otherwise, I take as being rendered to Me. "Inasmuch as ye have done it unto one of the least of these My brethren, ye have done it unto *Me.*" "Why persecutest thou *Me?*"

Secondly: His faithful disciples were identified with Him as He was identified with His Father. (1.) By official work. Ambassadors. As He represented the Father, they were to represent Him. (2.) By a vital sympathy. They are to be one with Him—one in feeling, spirit, purpose, work.

John 13:21-30

CHRIST IN SADNESS, THE DISCIPLES IN ANXIETY, AND THE TRAITOR UNMASKED

(*Jesus points out the traitor—Judas withdraws—Jerusalem.*—MATT. xxvi. 21—25 ; MARK xiv. 18—21 ; LUKE xxii. 21—23 ; JOHN xiii. 21—35.)

" When Jesus had thus said, He was troubled in spirit," &c.

EXEGETICAL REMARKS.—" In this paragraph we have the detection and dismissal of Judas. We have another work performed by Jesus from love to His disciples. So long as Judas was present, His feelings were under restraint, and He could not give free course to the Divine treasures with which His mind was filled. Ver. 31 vividly expresses the feeling of relief which He experienced at seeing the traitor depart ; and it was then that those full effusions of His inmost heart contained in chaps. xiv.—xvii. took place. These last moments of friendly intercourse were necessary to our Lord's work. In the circle of the twelve, Judas had been the representative of that spirit of carnality which was directly opposed to that which Jesus had just sanctioned by washing the disciples' feet. If he would not humble himself and renounce this spirit, he must depart ; and it was the spirit of the false, of the Jewish Messiah, of Antichrist, which departed with him."—*Godet.*

Ver. 21.—"*When Jesus had thus said, He was troubled in* (R. V. THE) *spirit, and testified.*" " His higher nature became agitated with a mysterious sorrow, agitated as the troubled sea. The inmost life of His human spirit was invaded by horror at the unprecedented fact of His approaching and imminent betrayal. The sight of the crafty one, and of his connection with the circle of disciples, most of whom were without suspicion of his guilt, and had trusted implicitly to his fidelity, tempted Him to despise the whole race of mankind, and tended to produce in Him an exasperation of spirit which He must summon all His energies to resist."—*Lange.* " *Verily, verily, I say unto you, that one of you shall betray Me.*" Who shall tell the

agony of spirit in the discovery and the disclosure of this fact ? The awful secret is out now. Perhaps His frame was convulsed, His lips quivered, and His eyes wept tears as He proclaimed this terrible fact.

Ver. 22.—" *Then the disciples looked one on another, doubting of whom He spake.*" In Matthew it is said that they were exceedingly sorrowful at this dreadful moment (xxvi. 22). Luke says they began to inquire among themselves which of them it was that should do this dreadful thing (xxii. 23). And Mark says they began to say unto Him, one by one, " Is it I ? " (xiv. 19.) But whilst all the others asked the question, each perhaps in his turn, was Judas silent ? Could he brave singularity ? No. Judas last of all answered and said, " Lord, is it I ? " To this Christ responded, " Thou hast said " (Matt. xxvi. 24, 25). Heart-searching, awful hour this !

Ver. 23.—" *Now there was leaning on* (R. V. THERE WAS AT THE TABLE RECLINING IN) *Jesus' bosom one of His disciples, whom Jesus loved.*" As Jesus certainly loved all the eleven, this must mean a peculiarly, dear love which Jesus had for John (comp. chap. xi. 3, 4, of Lazarus). " Once and again does our Evangelist thus denote himself. Doubtless it was on account of this love that Jesus placed him next to Himself in His own '*bosom*' at the table. But it is alluded to here to explain the facility which he had from his position of asking his Lord quietly what He meant."—*Brown.* " This is the moment," says *Rev. W. Watkins,* " which has been caught in Leonardo da Vinci's famous masterpiece in the refectory of the Dominican Fathers at Milan. The painting itself has almost passed away, but, perhaps, no work of art is so widely known,

The three apostles mentioned in the text are all on the right of our Lord. John is nearest to Him, and leaning towards Peter, who stretches behind Judas to speak to 'the disciple whom Jesus loved.' Judas, clutching the bag and upsetting the salt, declaring in every feature of that wondrous face—which cost Da Vinci a whole year's study in the lowest quarter of the city—that he is the traitor, is on the right hand of John, and between him and Peter. This verse can have no better comment than a study of this great picture, accompanied by the chapter in Lanzi's 'Storia Pittorica,' or Mrs. Jameson's ' Sacred and Legendary Art,' would provide ; and Englishmen have a noble copy of it in their own National Gallery. But Leonardo's picture is in one respect misleading, and, like most paintings of the Lord's Supper, has not represented the method in which the guests reclined rather than sat at table. Each leaned on his left arm, leaving the right arm free. The feet were stretched out behind the guest on his right hand, and the back of his head reached near to the bosom of the guest on his left. The Jews followed this Persian method of reclining on couches at meals from the time of the Captivity ; and this method of eating the Passover had the special significance and security and possession of the Promised Land, as opposed to the attitude of one undertaking a journey, which was part of the original institution (Exod. xii. 11)."

Ver. 24.—" *Simon Peter therefore beckoned* (R. V. BECKONETH) *to him, that he should ask who it should be of whom He spake* " (R. V. SAITH UNTO HIM, TELL US WHOM IT IS OF WHOM HE SPEAKETH). The words are in the present tense in the original, and should therefore be translated, "Simon Peter beckons," that is, makes a sign. John and Peter were old friends. They had been disciples together of John the Baptist, and among the first who gave in their adherence to Christ, and we therefore may suppose their intercourse was pretty free. Peter makes a sign to him.

Ver. 25.—" *He then lying* (R. V.

LEANING BACK AS HE WAS) *on Jesus' breast saith unto Him, Lord, who is it ?* " Let us know who is the man amongst us that is to betray Thee.

Ver. 26.—" *Jesus answered* (R. V. THEREFORE ANSWERETH), *He it is, to* (R. V. FOR) *whom I shall give a sop, when I have dipped it* (R. V. I SHALL DIP THE SOP AND GIVE IT HIM). *And* (R. V. SO) *when He had dipped the sop, He gave* (R. V. TAKETH AND GIVETH) *it to Judas Iscariot, the son of Simon* " (R. V. ISCARIOT). The sop was a piece of bread soaked in the wine ; and the giving now of the sop to Judas answered John's question, and told him that Judas Iscariot, Simon's son, was the betrayer.

Ver. 27.—" *And after the sop* (R. V. THEN) *Satan entered into him.*" In a preceding verse we were told that the devil had already put it into his heart to betray his Lord ; but now the Evil Spirit advances farther, enters into him, and takes possession of him, and gives full effect to his diabolic purpose. The hypocrite now stands exposed and self-committed. " *Then said Jesus* (R. V. JESUS THEREFORE SAITH) *unto him, That thou doest, do quickly.*" This may mean, " Away, *i. e.* begone, here thou art out of thy sphere ;" or it may also mean, " I dare thee to do thy worst ; do it quickly."

Vers. 28, 29.—" *Now no man at the table knew for what intent He spake this unto him. For some of them thought* (R. V. SOME THOUGHT), *because Judas had the bag, that Jesus had said unto him, Buy those* (R. V. WHAT) *things that we have need of against* (R. V. FOR) *the feast ; or, that he should give something to the poor.*" This is the biographer's comment as he remembered the solemn scene and the impressions of that night.

Ver. 30.—" *He then having received the sop went immediately out* (R. V. OUT STRAIGHTWAY) : *and it was night.*" " The words doubtless state the physical fact that at the time when Judas left the room the darkness of night had already come on. He went out, and went out into the darkness of night. We cannot say that the writer meant them to express more than this; and yet we feel that there is in them a fulness of meaning that cannot have been unintentional. It was night, and he stepped forth from light into darkness, from the presence and guidance of the Light of the World, to be possessed by and guided by the Prince of Darkness. It was night, and John could hardly have written these words without remembering those he had written but a short time before, 'If a man walk in the night, he stumbleth, because there is no light in him.' "—*Ellicott's Commentary.*

HOMILETICS

In these verses we have three things worthy of notice—*Christ in sadness, the disciples in anxiety, and the traitor unmasked.*

I —CHRIST IN SADNESS

" *When Jesus had thus said, He was troubled in spirit, and testified, and said, Verily, verily, I say unto you, that one of you shall betray Me.*" What was the spirit-trouble of Christ on this occasion? Though an answer to this question may be impossible, an attempt to realize it in some measure may not be unjustifiable or unuseful. We can safely predicate two things concerning it.

First: It was the distress of intense holiness in the presence of foul depravity. Holiness makes the soul intensely sensitive; and the more holy a man is, the more deeply grieved and pained is he at the discovery of the false and the vile. With the body, sometimes the optic nerve becomes so sensitive that the touch of the sunbeam will produce the greatest pain; and the auricular nerve so tender that the softest sound yields agony. And in some diseases the whole nervous system becomes so exquisitely tender that even a breath of air will throw the whole writhing frame into anguish. The whole moral being of Christ was rendered so exquisitely sensitive by His holiness, that every sin grieved Him to the heart. Now, with Judas under His eye, perhaps a shock of horror sent a quiver through all the nerves of His pure soul.

Secondly: It was the distress of the highest benevolence in the presence of a lost soul. The more love a being has in him, the more, by the law of sympathy, he feels and bears the sufferings of others. Christ's love was deep, tender, and immeasurable; and it brought on His great heart the woes of the world. He knew what a lost soul meant, He comprehended all the evils and miseries involved therein; and a lost soul stood before Him. We wonder not that He was "*troubled in spirit.*" In these verses we have—

II —THE DISCIPLES IN ANXIETY

When Christ said, "*One of you shall betray Me,*" all seemed startled into the deepest solicitude. "*Then the disciples looked one on another, doubting of whom He spake. Now there was leaning on Jesus' bosom one of His disciples, whom Jesus loved.** *Simon Peter therefore beckoned to him, that he should ask who it should be of whom He*

* See Germ. p. 399.

spake. He then lying on Jesus' breast saith unto Him, Lord, who is it?" Matthew and Mark add to our information concerning the anxiety of the disciples, they were "exceeding sorrowful;" and they tell us, too, that every one of them put the question, "Is it I?" The question implies two things.

First : Self-suspicion. Had they been certain of their incapability to perpetrate such an enormity, they would not have made such an appeal. None of them had an undoubted confidence in his impeccability. This self-suspicion is well founded in all souls this side of the grave, and it is a help to our spiritual progress and safety. "Let him that thinketh he standeth, take heed lest he fall." The question implies,

Secondly : A desire to know the worst. Cowardly natures close their eyes on the worst, and delude themselves with the idea that all is right. It is to the spiritual interest of every man to know the worst concerning himself here and now, for here and now the worst can be rectified. "Search me, O God, and know my heart : try me, and know my thoughts; and see if there be any wicked way in me, and lead me in the way everlasting." In these verses we have—

III —THE TRAITOR UNMASKED

Observe here four things—

First : The means of his detection. "*Jesus answered, He it is, to whom I shall give a sop, when I have dipped it. And when He had dipped the sop, He gave it to Judas Iscariot, the son of Simon.*" There is no reason for supposing that these words were spoken in an undertone to the beloved disciple who was leaning on Jesus' breast. The "*sop*" was a morsel of food dipped in the water in which the bitter herbs had been boiled, and always used at the Passover supper, and now on the table for use. Is it implied that Christ did not hand the sop round to others, or that after His words Judas was the first person to whom He gave the sop? Anyhow, the sop was given to Judas, and with that act the traitor stood unmasked. Observe—

Secondly : His domination by Satan. "*And after the sop Satan entered into him.*" Before this we read that Satan had put the wicked deed into his heart; now it would seem as if the infernal spirit entered and took possession of his soul. We are told that this evil spirit filled Ananias and Sapphira to lie, and he now filled Judas to betray Jesus. Observe—

Thirdly : His defiance by Christ. "*That thou doest, do quickly.*" As if Christ had said, "I dismiss thee forthwith, and I defy thee to do thy worst. There is no time to lose; quickly bring the infernal drama to a close, and let the curtain fall." It appears from the two following verses that none of the other disciples understood what Christ meant by these words. " *Now no man at the table knew for what intent He spake this unto him,*" &c. (vers. 28, 29). They thought—as some provisions were still required to be made for the festival, and as Judas had the money, and the Sabbath was at hand, when there could be no merchandise—that Christ meant to say to Judas, " Go quickly, and procure the necessary supplies." Observe—

Fourthly: His lamentable doom. " *He then having received the sop went immediately out: and it was night.*" He obeyed the request of Christ, " *and went immediately out* "—out before the Lord's Supper, which took place after the Paschal meal. " *And it was night.*" The night immediately preceding that day of the Crucifixion, when the Son of God suffered on the cross. It was the night in which, in the garden, he executed his diabolical purpose; it was the night of all the nights on earth, the darkest in his soul. Remorse swept all brightness from his sky, and mantled his being in the sackcloth of despair.

Germs of Thought
No. 50   John 13:25

FAMILIARITY WITH CHRIST

" He then lying on Jesus' breast saith unto Him, Lord, who is it ? "—xiii. 25.

This remarkable incident reveals great *familiarity* with Christ— John leans on the Saviour's bosom. Personal Christianity is an *intimate* connection with Christ. To be a true Christian is to be more familiar with Christ than with fathers, mothers, brothers, sisters.

I —THIS FAMILIARITY INVOLVES THE MOST AMAZING CONDESCENSION

Little magnates of earth deem it a great condescension to allow the humble and lowly to speak to them even at a distance. But here is the AUTHOR and PROPRIETOR of the universe, the Infinitely Holy as well as transcendently Great, permitting poor frail sinful man to lean on His bosom. " Though He is high, yet hath He respect unto the lowly." The humblest soul is dear to Him.

First: Let this condescension *inspire us with adoring gratitude.*

Secondly: Let this condescension consume *that pride which prompts man to keep the poor at a distance.*

II —THIS FAMILIARITY INVOLVES THE SUBLIMEST PRIVILEGE

To be so closely allied to Christ as this, is to be in the safest and most honourable position. What honour to recline on the bosom of the " King of kings, and Lord of lords!" Paul said, " To be with Christ is far better." Yes; to be with Christ is to be secure, joyous, and dignified.

III —THIS FAMILIARITY INVOLVES THE PROFOUNDEST REVERENCE

John addresses Christ as Lord. *"Lord, who is it?"* Familiarity with men, the proverb says, breeds contempt. We know it often breeds discontent. So imperfect are the best of men, that, as a rule, the more we know of them the less reverence we have. Not so familiarity with Christ; the more we know of Him, the profounder our reverence. *"Lord, who is it?"*

John 13:31-33

THREE IMPORTANT FACTS IN RELATION TO CHRIST

"Therefore, when he was gone out, Jesus said, Now is the Son of man glorified, and God is glorified in Him," &c.—xiii. 31—33.

EXEGETICAL REMARKS.—Vers. 31, 32.—"*Therefore, when* (R. V. WHEN THEREFORE) *he was gone out, Jesus said* (R. V. SAITH), *Now is the Son of man glorified, and God is glorified in Him*" (R. V. SHALL GLORIFY HIM), &c. The traitor is gone; all breathe more freely; even Christ Himself feels a restraint removed: and He speaks with greater freedom and flow. Now from His lips there roll, clear as crystal, those rich streams of living and quickening truths which continue to flow during the whole of the supper, until He enters the last stage of His great work, the scene in the garden. Now that the betrayer is gone, and the little circle is united in truth and love, about what does Jesus speak? Does He make any reflections on the conduct of the traitor? No. Does He deplore the awful agonies that were about to break on Him and crush Him into the grave? No. His words are those of triumph. Five times in two sentences does He use the word "*glorify.*" "The Son of man glorified," &c. His soul goes on to His triumph over the grave, His ascension to

heaven, His mediatorial reign, and all the ever-brightening glories of an interminable future.

Ver. 33.—"*Little children, yet a little while I am with you. Ye shall seek Me: and as I said unto the Jews, Whither I go, ye cannot come; so now I say to* (R. V. UNTO) *you.*" Amidst thoughts of His own glory He does not forget the condition of His disciples, their state of orphanage and exposure to persecution when He shall have departed. Hence with exquisite tenderness He addresses them with the endearing title, "*little children.*" These words, which John well remembered as coming from the lips of His Master, he frequently uses in his epistles (See 1 John ii. 1, 12, 28; iii. 7, 18; iv. 4; v. 21). Probably what Christ means here is, My bodily presence is about leaving you; very soon you will not see Me as you now see Me. I shall go to the Father, and shall be far beyond the reach of your senses. Though you seek for a view of Me then, you will not find Me; where I am—upon the throne of the universe—ye cannot come.

HOMILETICS

There are in these verses *Three facts which we discover in relation to Christ.*

I — A PAINFUL OPPRESSION REMOVED FROM HIS HEART

" *Therefore, when he was gone out, Jesus said.*" With the departure of Judas, Jesus seems to have felt a relief.

First: An object of moral offence had been removed from His vision. In human experience it is never felt to be a pleasant thing to have in your social circle a corrupt man, still less one whom you know to have plotted against you. The exit of such a man is felt to be a relief. Christ must have felt somewhat thus now when Judas had departed. His presence had oppressed and pained Him.

Secondly: An obstruction to the free utterance of His love had been removed from amongst his hearers. Parents have often things to say to their children which they will not utter when a stranger is amongst them, still less when the stranger is an enemy. It is even so with Christian pastors, they have often something to say to their loving people, which the presence amongst them of a known enemy would restrain. All this Christ seems to have felt. The presence of Judas had oppressed His heart, and checked the free flow of His loving utterances to His disciples. The traitor has departed, His spirit is relieved and His tongue free. Another fact in relation to Christ which we discover in these verses is—

II — A GLORIOUS CONSUMMATION OF THE GREAT PURPOSE OF HIS LIFE

" *Now is the Son of man glorified, and God is glorified in Him.*" " *The Son of man.*" This expresssion occurs no less than sixty-six times in the Gospel histories. " *Son of man*"—not the Son of a *tribe,* otherwise He would have tribal idiosyncrasies; not the Son of a *nation,* otherwise He would have national peculiarities; not the Son of a *sect,* or He would have sectarian predilections and marks; but the "SON OF MAN." He is a Man, realizing the Divine ideal of what a man is and what a man ought to be. Now this Son of man felt that the grand object of His mission here was so near realization that He exults in it as a consummation. " *Now is the Son of man glorified.*" Two remarks are here suggested—

First: *That the true glory of a man is the realization of the Divine purpose of his life.* Whatever existence realizes the Divine purpose, is thereby glorified. The bright heavens, the lovely landscapes, and mighty oceans, are glorious and glorified because they realize the Divine purpose. Thus "the heavens declare His glory." The Gospel is glorified when it realizes its grand purpose with men by transforming them into the image of God. Thus the Apostle speaks of its having "free course and being glorified." Man can only glorify God as he realizes in his life the Divine purpose concerning his creation.

Secondly : That the man who realizes the Divine purpose in his life, not only glorifies himself, *but glorifies God also*. The real glory of man and of God are identical. What really glorifies man, glorifies God. Where do we see most of the glory of God ? In the life of that man who works out the Divine will and developes the Divine purpose. Well then would it be for us all to remember, that we glorify God, not by endeavours to prove His existence, or illustrate His attributes, or vindicate the justness of His procedure to man, or by panegyrizing His name by singing psalms and offering prayers, but by living a *godlike life*—a life in which the grand purpose of God toward us is wrought out in living characters. This is what Christ felt now. His mission to the universe was about being realized, and He triumphantly exclaims, "*Now is the Son of man glorified.*" Another fact in relation to Christ which we discover in these verses is—

III —A TENDER CONSIDERATION FOR THE COMING TRIAL OF HIS DISCIPLES

"*Little children, yet a little while I am with you. Ye shall seek Me: and as I said unto the Jews, Whither I go ye cannot come; so now I say to you.*" The great trial awaiting them was His departure from their midst. They had been with Him for three years. He had won their hearts, changed the whole current of their thoughts and sympathies; they had resigned their worldly avocations, renounced their old fellowships, and excited the flaming ire of their rulers and their countrymen on His account. So long as He was with them they were amply supplied and well guarded. But now He was about to leave them, and they would be left as sheep without a shepherd to the ravenous wolves of a ceremonious and an intolerant religion. Two days more, and Christ would be in His grave; and about seven weeks afterwards He would be away in the holy heavens beyond their ken. With tender consideration He here prepares them for this trial.

First : By informing them of it. "*Yet a little while I am with you.*" A trial that would crush us if it came suddenly and unexpectedly, may fall lightly if we have known of its approach, and realize it to some extent before it comes. Christ knew this, and thus He foretells them of His exit. He here prepares them for the trial—

Secondly : By informing them of it in language of endearment. "*Little children.*" You are My children; I speak to you with the tenderness of a Father; you are My little children, dear to Me as infants to their mother. How tender is Christ ! He "carries the lambs in His arms, and gently leads those that are with young."

John 13:34, 35

THE NEW COMMANDMENT, OR GENUINE ALTRUISM

"A new commandment I give unto you, That ye love one another," &c.—
xiii. 34, 35.

EXEGETICAL REMARKS.—Ver. 34.—
"*A new commandment I give unto you, That ye love one another; as I have loved you.*" "This commandment is called new, not so much in relation to the Old Testament, as to the teaching of Christ, and to the new standard it sets up, viz. that love should go so far as even to make one lay down life for those one loves, or ought to love. (Compare 1 John iii. 16.) Thus the newness consists in adding, '*as I have loved you.*' Hitherto to follow Jesus, step by step, had been the disciples' rule of conduct, and

this implied love ; but now they could follow Him no longer, since He was leaving them ; and therefore He lays before them a summary of duty. Compare, as to praying, chap. xvi. 24 ; as to calling them friends, chap. xv. 15 ; as to the hatred of the world, chap. xvi. 4. Hence the law of love is called the law of Christ, Gal. vi. 2."

Ver. 35.—"*By this shall all men know that ye are My disciples, if ye have love one to another.*" Christly love is the mark, the only infallible mark, of genuine discipleship.

HOMILETICS

The subject here is *The New Commandment,* or *Genuine Altruism.* Christ is the world's Monarch, the Prince of all the kings of the earth. All Christendom professes to regard Him as such. " Ye call Me Master and Lord : and ye say well ; for so I am." Now, what is the great law of this King of kings, the cardinal law, the law that should fashion all other laws, and that all are bound to obey ? It is the law of *brotherly love,—altruism.* In relation to this law the words suggest three things.

I —IT IS A NEW THING TO THE WORLD

" *A new commandment I give unto you, That ye love one another ; as I have loved you.*" * It is not new in its *essence* or objects ; for the old law required that we should love our neighbour as ourselves. Its newness is in its rule or model, "*As I have loved you.*" What was the character of Christ's love towards men ? It was—

First : Absolutely disinterested. The love which man shows to man has in it generally, if not always, some amount of selfishness. There is in it the hope of some advantage. Not so with the love which Christ had for man. He had no personal interest to serve. Men could confer no benefit on Him ; nor could their wrath, though it raged with the fury and force of hell, injure Him. His love towards men was—

Secondly : Unexcited by merit. The love of man for man has generally in it the recognition of some merit. Man is loved on account of some real or imaginary excellence, such as amiability, uprightness, intelligence, or trustfulness. But in man Christ saw nothing to merit His love. To His eye all men were corrupt,

* See Germ, p. 405.

hell-deserving, and enemies to Himself. He loved His enemies. His love towards man was—

Thirdly : Self-sacrificing in power. Man's love for man developes itself, for the most part, in warm conversation, in free inter-visitations, and in kindly offices, sometimes involving some amount of self-sacrifice. But Christ's love was a practical force, a force that urged on to the sacrifice of Himself. "He loved us, and gave Himself for us." "Scarcely for a righteous man will one die," &c. His love towards man was—

Fourthly : Essentially forgiving. His love was a forgiving love, for He loved His enemies. Even on the Cross He prayed for His murderers, "Father, forgive them, they know not what they do." Man's love for man has seldom in it the forgiving power to any great extent. One or two offences will destroy it and replace it by revenge. When Peter asked the question of our Lord, "How often shall my brother sin against me, and I forgive him, till seven times ? " he thought that to forgive a man seven times was a wonderful display of love—a display that Christ would commend. But what was the reply ? "I say not unto thee, until seven times : but until seventy times seven."

Here then is the "*new commandment.*" Men are bound by the law of Christ to love their brethren with a love absolutely dis-interested, entirely unmerited, practically self-sacrificing, and essentially forgiving. This kind of love is the great cardinal supreme law under which humanity is placed by Christ. In relation to this law the words suggest—

II —IT IS A CRITERION OF DISCIPLESHIP

"*By this shall all men know that ye are My disciples.*"

First : This is a simple test. Had the test been the adoption of a certain set of beliefs, or conformity to certain rites, it would have been too complicated to be of easy application or of practical use ; but here how simple ! The question is not, Do you believe in this or that ? Do you belong to this sect or that ? Do you attend to this rite or that ? but, Do you love your brother man as Christ loved him ? "He that loveth not his brother whom he hath seen, how can he love God whom he hath not seen ? "

Secondly : This is an infallible test. Other tests, even the best, are of doubtful accuracy ; their application may lead to wrong conclusions. But this is infallible. "Bear ye one another's burdens, and so *fulfil* the law of Christ." It is the test which will determine the destiny of all men on the last day. Whether men on that day will rise to heavenly happiness or descend to hellish sadness, will be determined by their practical conduct towards their fellows while on this earth—whether they clothed the naked, visited the prisoner, &c. (Matt. xxv.).

Thirdly : This is a solemn test. If we apply it to the Christians of this age and country, where men hate each other, cheat each other, fight each other, how few will be proved to be genuine disciples! Could all men stand this test, the human world would be a Paradise. In relation to this law the words suggest—

III —IT IS THE PATH TO HEAVEN

These words were uttered immediately after our Saviour had said, "Whither I go, ye cannot come; so now I say to you. *A new commandment,*" &c. The implication seems to be, if you obey this "*new commandment*" we shall meet again; you will reach the scenes whither I am going. True; the path of Christly love is the only path to heaven.

CONCLUSION.—Read, in connection with this subject, Paul's chapter on charity, or love. That chapter is not only a glorious illustration, but a cogent enforcement of this law of love.

Germs of Thought
No. 51   John 13:34

TRUE SOCIAL LOVE

" A new commandment I give unto you, That ye love one another ; as I have loved you, that ye also love one another."—xiii. 34.

These words lead us to consider *true social love,* the love that men ought to have for their fellow-creatures.

I —ITS MODEL

How should man love his brother ? Here is the answer—"*As I have loved you.*"

First: Initially. Christ loved man before man loved Him. "Herein is love ; not that we loved Him, but that He loved us." Because others do not love us, it is no excuse for not loving them.

Secondly : Practically. His love did not evaporate in sentiment, did not exhaust itself in speech. (1.) His love expressed itself in His works. In His life "He went about doing good." (2.) His love expressed itself in His death. "Greater love hath no man than this, that a man lay down his life for his friends." "Scarcely for a righteous man will one die."

Thirdly : Constantly. His love is an everlasting love. "The mountains shall depart, and the hills be removed," &c. Thus we are to love each other. This is the model. We are not to hate men ; we may hate their characters, but not their being. We are not to love them with a passing feeling, but with a practical affection.

These words lead us to consider—

II —ITS OBLIGATION

"*A new commandment I give unto you.*" It is a "*commandment,*" not a suggestion, not an advice. And it is a "*new commandment.*" How is it new ?

First: It is new to the world's idea. *Plato,* in his "Republic," asked the question, If when a poor man is ill, whether it is our duty to help him? and the answer is *no,* because he is not worth the trouble. And *Celsus,* the famous antagonist to Christianity, declared that "it must be nothing short of madness to believe that Greeks, and barbarians, Europe, Asia, and Libya, can ever be united in the bond of a common religion." To *" love one another"* is a new idea. It had no residence in the brain of men of past times.

Secondly: It is new to the world's feeling. To love men as Christ loved them, was an affection which but very few of even the best of men of ancient times ever experienced.

Thirdly: It is new to the world's practice. Point me to any age preceding the Christian, where love built schools to educate the ignorant, infirmaries for the diseased, asylums for the poor, refuges for the destitute; or point me, even in modern times, to any part of heathendom where such institutions exist.

John 13:36-38

PETER'S INQUIRY AND IMPULSE, AND CHRIST'S RESPONSE AND CORRECTION

(*Jesus foretells the fall of Peter and the Dispersion of the Twelve. Jerusalem.—* MATT. xxvi. 31—35 ; MARK xiv. 27—31 ; LUKE xxii. 31—38 ; John xiii. 36—38.)

"Simon Peter said unto Him, Lord, whither goest Thou?" &c.

EXEGETICAL REMARKS.—Ver. 36.— *"Simon Peter said* (R. V. SAITH) *unto Him."* Peter speaks here ; Thomas, Philip and Judas in chap. xiv. 5, 8— 22 ; and all the disciples in chap xvi. 29. The very conversations mentioned in chap. xiv. seem to indicate that Peter and John had not returned from making ready the Passover. Yet John seems to have had no more difficulty in describing them than Luke had in relating the particulars contained in the first chapter of his gospel. Who could undertake an exact setting forth of these colloquies, even had he heard or read them a hundred times? This power then was Divinely conferred on the sacred writers. But, supposing the conversation mentioned in chap. xiv. to have taken place *before* Peter and John went into the city, the remaining narrative remains undisturbed ; but, in this case, the rest of the discourse must be separated from the short clause, *" Lord, whither goest Thou?"* Peter asked in the hope that he might follow. Peter's heart

clave to Jesus (chap. vi. 68 ; xxi. 7). *"Jesus answered him."* Jesus answers the questions at intervals (chap. xiv. 2, 28 ; xvi. 5). *"Whither I go, thou canst not follow Me now."* Neither the state of the case nor the weakness of Peter permitted him ; but it was the latter objection only to which the words referred. Peter did follow Jesus (chap. xviii. 15), but at a distance, and not unscathed (Matt. xvi. 58). *"But thou shalt follow Me afterwards."* (R. V. OMITS THE LAST 'ME.') (Chap. xxi. 19—22.)

Ver. 37.—*"Peter said* (R. V. SAITH) *unto Him, Lord, why cannot I follow Thee* (R. V. EVEN) *now? I will lay down my life for Thy sake"* (R. V. THEE). Here is Peter, impulsive Peter, true to his nature, warm, emotional, unguarded. I have no doubt that he was sincere in this avowal.

Ver. 38.—*"Jesus answered him* (R. V. ANSWERETH), *Wilt thou lay down thy life for My sake?"* (R. V. ME.) Some have seen irony in these words of Christ. I know thee better; thou art deceiving thyself. "*Verily, verily, I say unto thee, The cock shall not crow, till thou hast denied me thrice.*" Lay down thy life for Me! Thou wilt not so much as confess Me; but before the cock crows on the approaching day thou shalt deny Me thrice.

HOMILETICS

These verses bring under our notice, *Peter's inquiry and Christ's response, Peter's impulse and Christ's correction.*

I.—PETER'S INQUIRY AND CHRIST'S RESPONSE

Two remarks here—

First: The inquiry was natural. "*Simon Peter said unto Him, Lord, whither goest Thou?*" Christ had just said to His disciples, in Peter's presence, "Whither I go, ye cannot come," and previously he had heard Him refer to His departure from the world. Peter evidently did not exactly understand what the departure meant, and he inquires, "*Whither goest Thou?*" Thou sayest Thou art going to leave us; the idea of Thy departure distresses me; tell me whither Thou art going. Evidently he had no clear conception of what the departure of Christ really meant. He ought to have known. Frequently had he heard his Master say that He was going to leave them and return unto His Father. But his Jewish prejudices had blinded his mind on the subject.

Secondly: The response was significant. It indicated—(1.) Christ's voluntariness. "*Whither I go;*" not "Whither I am *driven.*" To preach Christ as a *Victim*, is not to preach the Gospel; it is to misrepresent, to blaspheme Him. He was the sublimest moral Hero. Not a poor *Victim*, but a Mighty *Victor*. Goethe has said somewhere, that evangelical preachers *trade* in those physical sufferings of Christ from which the Sun veiled itself. He came into the world of His own independent choice; He walked it with a free step; and He left it of His own accord, and in His own way. "I have power to lay down My life, and I have power to take it again." The response indicates—(2.) Christ's wisdom. "*Whither I go, thou canst not follow Me now; but thou shalt follow Me afterwards.*" Christ does not answer Peter's question, does not tell him distinctly where He is going to, does not satisfy his curiosity, but rather checks his impetuosity, and says, "*Thou canst not follow Me now.*" Peter's faith and hope are appealed to here. (1.) His faith. "*Thou canst not follow Me now.*" I do not tell thee why; but trust Me. There were reasons, no doubt, why Peter could not. (*a*) He was not fully prepared to go into the other world with Christ. There was considerable discipline of soul required in him yet. (β) He had much to do in the world before he could leave it. He had to bear witness to Christ, not only to the Jews, but also to the Gentiles. He had to preach at Jerusalem, and at Antioch, &c. There is a good reason for keeping good men in the world. "I pray not Thou shouldest take them out of the world," &c. Christ appeals to—(2.) His hope. "*Thou shalt follow Me afterwards.*" A few years afterwards Peter did follow his Master, followed Him probably in the very mode of his death, followed Him into one of the mansions or abodes which Christ prepared for His people in the heavenly world. Do not be discouraged, "*thou shalt follow Me.*" "Where I am, thou shalt be also." If we are genuine disciples, though we cannot enter heaven now, we shall. Let us take hope. Notice—

II —PETER'S IMPULSE AND CHRIST'S CORRECTION

First: Peter's impulse. "*Peter said unto Him, Lord, why cannot I follow Thee now? I will lay down my life for Thy sake.*" As if he had said, "I walked with Thee upon the waters, I ascended with Thee the Mount of Transfiguration, why cannot I follow Thee now? Why? Is there danger? I will brave it. Is there death? I will face it." No doubt his love was genuine as well as strong.

Secondly: Christ's correction. "*Jesus answered him, Wilt thou lay down thy life for My sake? Verily, verily, I say unto thee, The cock shall not crow, till thou hast denied Me thrice.*" Observe here—(1.) Peter's self-ignorance. Instead of doing this, thou wilt not even acknowledge Me. How ignorant are we of our own hearts! "Is thy servant a dog?" &c. Lay down thy life for Me, indeed! In two or three hours hence, in the break of morning, before the cock has crowed, announcing the first beam of day, thou wilt have "*denied Me thrice.*" (2.) Christ's foreknowledge. What Christ now foresaw actually occurred. (See Matt. xxvi. 69—75; Mark xiv. 66—72; Luke xvii. 55—62; John xviii. 16—18, 25—27.) This warning seems to have hushed Peter into silence, for he does not seem to have spoken once during the whole of the long subsequent discourse.

CONCLUSION. Let us not speculate about the Divine procedure, but rather trust in the Divine character, and hope in the Divine promise. Let us be cautious of our best impulses, and trust not even to our own hearts, but practically live the prayer, "Create in us clean hearts, O God, and renew a right spirit within us."

Homiletical Commentary on Gospel of John

John 14:1-3

HEAVEN

(Jesus comforts His disciples. The Holy Spirit promised.—JOHN xiv. 1—31.)

"Let not your heart be troubled : ye believe in God, believe also in Me," &c.

EXEGETICAL REMARKS.—" We now come," says *Olshausen*, "to that portion of the Evangelistic history which we may with propriety call its 'Holy of holies.' Our Evangelist, like a consecrated priest, alone opens to us the view into this sanctuary. It is the record of the last moments spent by the Lord in the midst of His disciples before His last passion, when words of heavenly thought flowed from His sacred lips. All that His heart, glowing with love, had still to say to His friends was compressed into this short season. At first the intercourse took the form of conversation. Sitting at the table they talked familiarly together. But when the repast was finished, the language of Christ assumed a loftier strain ; the disciples assembled around their Master, listened to the words of life, and seldom spoke a word. At length, in the Redeemer's sublime intercessory prayer, His full soul was poured forth in express petitions to His heavenly Father, on behalf of those who were His own. It is a peculiarity of these last chapters that they treat most exclusively of the most profound relations—as that of the Son to the Father, and both to the Spirit; that of

Christ to the Church ; of the Church to the world, and so forth. Moreover, a considerable portion of these sublime communications surpassed the points of view to which the disciples had at that time attained: hence the Redeemer frequently repeats the same sentiments in order to impress them more deeply upon their minds, and because of what they still did not understand, points them to the Holy Ghost, who would remind them of all His sayings, and lead them into all truth."

Ver. 1.—"*Let not your heart be troubled.*" No doubt the little company were at this moment greatly troubled. Christ had told them He was going to depart,—that would trouble them. Judas—one of their number—had been convicted as a traitor and had left ; that would trouble them. Peter had been told that in the early morning, before cock crow, he would deny Christ thrice ; this would trouble them. Christ propounds an antidote for their trouble, viz. trust in His Father and Himself. "*Ye believe in God, believe also in Me.*" Whether these words should be taken in the indicative or the imperative is a question not easily settled, and scarcely worth discussion. The meaning is, trust in God the Father and the Son, and this will support you under all your trouble. Trust in Him as the absolute Truth. Trust in Me as the image and Revealer of that Truth.

Ver. 2.—"*In My Father's house.*" The Greek word used for house here is slightly different from that used for the material temple on earth, in chap. ii. 16. The exact meaning will be at once seen from a comparison of 2 Cor. xv. 1, the only other passage in the New Testament where it is used metaphorically. The Jews were accustomed to the thought of heaven as the habitation of God, and the disciples had been taught to pray, "Our Father, which art in heaven." (Comp. Ps. xxiii. 13, 14 ; Isa. lxiii. 15 ; Matt. vi. 9 ; Acts vii. 49, and especially Heb. ix.) "*Many mansions.*" Abodes or dwellings. The word does not refer to diversity of abodes, but to number. The idea is amplitude, room enough for all. "*If it were not so, I would have told you.*" Otherwise I would have told you.—*Davidson.* "*I* (R. V. FOR I) *go to prepare a place for you.*" "It is not enough that the Father's house is spacious, access to it must be open to them, and an abode there assured them. For this purpose Jesus will precede them. (Comp. Heb. vi. 20, Christ as the Forerunner.) It is under this image that He teaches them to regard His death, first as that which will open to them by its atoning efficacy an entrance into heaven, and then as His elevation to that Divine condition in which He will make them sharers by the gift of Pentecost."—*Godet.*

Ver. 3.—"*And if I go and prepare a place for you, I* (R. V. COME AGAIN) *will come again and receive you unto Myself.*" This means, when I shall have gone to prepare a place for you, I will come again.

HOMILETICS

Things were now converging to a crisis in the life of Christ and in the spiritual history of humanity. The "hour was come," the hour to which all past economies pointed, and the hour from which all future improvements in human history would derive their impulse and take their date. It is the last meeting of Christ with those few poor men whom He at first called into His confidence and made His disciples. He had taken them away from their avocations, social friendships, and secular duties, and wrought such a thorough change in their spiritual sympathies and aspirations, that those things that once pleased them had lost their fascination and their charm. By joining Him they raised their country and their age in fierce opposition against them. And, now He was about leaving them. Jesus knew their feelings, observed every billow of anguish that surged through their hearts, and He mercifully condescended to minister the necessary relief. "*Let not your heart be troubled.*" The subject of these verses is *Heaven.*

They lead us to consider—

I —THE COMMON HEAVEN FOR ALL THE GOOD

Christ calls this His "*Father's house.*" The old temple was called His house, the true Church is called His house. He dwells in His people. But here the reference is to some magnificent district in His great universe. Heaven is a *place* as well as a state. In truth, we cannot conceive of existence apart from space. This place is sometimes represented in the Bible as a *garden,* implying that it is the choicest spot in the creation; as *a city*, implying that it is a scene of glorious social existence; sometimes as a *palace*, where the Infinite is on the throne, and holy intelligences are in loyal attendance; and sometimes as *an inheritance.* Three thoughts are here suggested concerning it.

First: It is a scene of family life. It is the *"Father's house."* Wherever that region is, all within its precincts are members of *one* family. Christ is the Head :—of "Whom the whole family in Heaven and earth is named." A family is something more than a *Society.* A society may be based on some common interests, and held by some compact; but a family is based on *natural affinities.* Souls are linked together by a vital tie; all hearts centre in one head. It is a *large* family. The Bible teaches that there are celestial intelligences of countless number and vast variety—"an innumerable company of angels," "thrones, principalities," &c. It is a *holy* family. All are pure, free from selfishness, from error and sin. It is a *harmonious* family. Though mixed and of vast gradations, they are all united in thought, sympathy, and aim. A family society is not like political, ecclesiastical, commercial, literary societies. These are organized by rules and laws, but this is united by vital affinities. It is an *undying* family. Death never enters that circle. It is an *ever increasing* family. Who can tell how many worlds of intelligent beings are created every day, and how many *are added to this family?* Another thought suggested is—

Secondly: It is a scene of great amplitude. *"Many mansions,"* or dwelling-places, these are the abodes in God's great *"house."* Every orb that rolls throughout immensity, from the smallest to the largest, may be one of these *"mansions."* Astronomy shows that the multitude of those orbs baffle all arithmetical calculations. Where is heaven? Wherever God is, and holy beings are. Hell in the universe is only as one miserable hut in an immeasurable city of palaces, one withered leaf in the boundless forest. Heaven is a large place. It is, moreover, suggested here—

Thirdly: It is a scene of undoubted reality. *"If it were not so, I would have told you."* It is no poet's dream, no fictitious realm. The word of Christ attests its existence, what other proof is needed?

(1.) He is too intelligent to be mistaken. He knows every part of the universe. He existed before the creation. He knew it in archetype. "I was set up from everlasting," &c. (2.) He is too truthful to misrepresent. In Him there is no motive to deceive. *He* is truth, unerring and unerrable truth. (3.) He is too kind to delude. *"I would have told you."* Two things should be remembered. (*a*) His knowledge. I speak from knowledge; I know every part of the universe. "I was set up from everlasting," &c. (*b*) His sincerity. He had no disposition to deceive. *"Were it not so, I would have told you."*

Such is the universal heaven of the good—a scene of family life, of vast amplitude and undoubted reality. The text leads us to consider—

II.—THE SPECIAL HEAVEN FOR CHRIST'S DISCIPLES

" *I go to prepare a place for you.*" * Amid the "*many mansions*," I will "*prepare a place for you.*" Learn—

First: Man's heaven is a scene which Christ prepares. Christ, in a way which I cannot explain, prepared a "*place*" in God's great universe especially for His disciples. " When Thou didst overcome the sharpness of death, Thou didst open the kingdom of heaven to all believers." It is not necessary to suppose they live alone, shut off from communion with other intelligences. Whilst they have a particular apartment, they are still in the same vast house or palace, and may be permitted to pay visits to all, and receive visits from all that dwell in other apartments of the Great " *House of the Father.*"

Secondly : Man's heaven is a scene into which Christ introduces him. " *I will come again, and receive you unto Myself.*" What is the death of a true disciple ? The advent of Christ. He comes to take His children home from school. He comes to you in the school of affliction, and says, Come away with Me, my young brother, to our " *Father's house*"—your education is finished ; you are qualified to take office in the eternal kingdom ; the days of your minority are over ; come away to your inheritance. Here the soul is imprisoned in the body. He comes and opens the prison-doors and lets the prisoner free.

Thirdly : Man's heaven is a scene in which Christ's fellowship is enjoyed. " *Where I am, there ye may be also.*" The heaven of man is to be where Christ is.

CONCLUSION. What consolation we have for troubled souls in these verses ! Christ says in effect to all such,—Trust in My Father and in Me for the present, and look for perfection in the future. Faith and hope will soothe and sustain you. How many sorrowing souls have these words comforted ! Sir Walter Scott just before his death desired to be drawn into his library, and placed by the window that he might look down upon the Tweed. To his son-in-law he expressed a wish that he should read to him. " From what book shall I read ? " said he. " Can you ask ? " Scott replied. " There is but one." " I chose," says his biographer, " the fourteenth chapter of John. He listened with mild devotion, and said when I had done : 'Well, this is a great comfort. I have followed you distinctly, and I feel as if I was to be myself again.'"

* See Germ, p. 5.

Germs of Thought
No. 52   John 14:2, 3

CHRIST IN RELATION TO HEAVEN

" In My Father's house are many mansions," &c.

We present another plan of treatment of these verses, and use them to illustrate *Christ in relation to heaven.* From the text we infer—

I —CHRIST REVEALS MAN'S HEAVEN

He reveals it here—(1.) As a scene of family life. " *My Father's house.*" (2.) As a scene of great amplitude. " *Many mansions.*" (3.) As a scene of undoubted reality—" *If it were not so, I would have told you.*" Christ knows the universe too well to be deceived, and He is too incorruptibly honest to deceive. " *I would have told you.*" He reveals man's heaven; He draws the veil, and gives a glimpse of it.

II —CHRIST PREPARES MAN'S HEAVEN

" *I go to prepare a place for you.*" (1.) All places in the universe would not suit us *physically.* There are worlds unsuited to our organization. (2.) All places would not suit us *intellectually.* They would not present the class of truths we crave for, or in the forms we need. (3.) All places would not suit us *emotionally.* They would not suit our sentiments of admiration, love, and worship. Christ prepares a place for us, suited for us in every respect. The mother of a large family has just received a letter from a loved son who has been for years in a distant land, informing her he will be home on a certain day. What preparation forthwith she sets about! She thinks of his tastes, his wants, what will please him, what will supply his needs, and yield him joy. Father and brothers and sisters join her in the work. One says he likes music, and a piece of music is studied wherewith to charm him; another remembers that he loves flowers, and splendid bouquets are collected; another recollects he is fond of some outdoor sport; another thinks of drawings and paintings; another of poetry; and so on the preparations are made. Love makes preparations for the known tastes of the loved one. Thus our *Great Brother* in the other world prepares a place exactly suited for us after death.

III —CHRIST INTRODUCES INTO MAN'S HEAVEN

" *I will come again, and receive you unto Myself.*" What is the death of the good man? The advent of Christ. Christ comes and opens the material door which encloses our spirits, and conducts us to the world He has prepared. He takes us (1) *Gently,* (2) *Securely,* (3) *Triumphantly.* What matters the distance, what matters the labyrinthian path, if He is with us as our Convoy?

IV.—CHRIST CONSTITUTES MAN'S HEAVEN

"*That where I am, there ye may be also.*" This is His desire.
"Father, I would that they may be with Me where I am." And
this is their desire. They feel to be with Christ is "far better."

> "Let me be with Thee where Thou art,
>   My Saviour, my eternal Rest,
> Then only will this longing heart
>   Be fully and for ever blest.

> "Let me be with Thee where Thou art,
>   Where none can die, whence none remove,
> There death nor sin my soul shall part,
>   From Thy blessed presence and Thy love."

John 14:4-7

THE WELL-BEING OF HUMANITY

"And whither I go ye know, and the way ye know," &c.

EXEGETICAL REMARKS.—Ver. 4.—
"*And whither I go ye know* (R. V. THE
WAY), *and the way ye know.*" Jesus
seems to say that now He had answered
their question in chap. xiii. 2—36,
both as to whither He was going, and
the way for their going thither. He
had plainly stated it in the foregoing
words. He was going to His Father's
house. There was room there for
them all. He was going with the
express object of arranging everything
for their arrival. And He assured
them of His coming again to take
them to Himself, that they might be
there also. If they were not utterly
blinded, they must see what He had
made so plain.

Ver. 5.—"*Thomas saith unto Him,
Lord, we know not whither Thou goest;
and how can we know* (R. V. KNOW WE)
the way?" "Our Lord's words had laid
stress upon the '*way.*' Thomas lays
stress upon the '*whither.*' His mind
seeks for measured certainty. In all
that he has heard of the Father's house
of 'many mansions,' of being with
the Lord, there is much that he cannot
understand. The Messiah, he thought,
was to reign upon earth. There was
this vast royal home, with dwelling-
places for all, to which Christ was
going first, and to which they were to
follow. They know not whither, and
without that knowledge they cannot
even think of the way."—*Watkins.*

Ver. 6.—"*Jesus saith unto him, I*
am the Way, (R. V. AND) *the Truth,
and the Life.*" "*I,*" emphatic. *Lange*
regards "truth and life" here as ex-
plicative, and as meaning the truth as
well as the life of this way. Christ
is the *Truth* of this way: its clear
manifestation, its life, and its animating power. "*No man* (R. V. ONE)
cometh unto the Father, but by Me."
Thomas thought of the "*Way*" to the
"mansions" of which Christ had
spoken; Christ here virtually says
the way to the Father, to *His* presence
and friendship, is the way to the mansions. To be with the Father is to be
at home. This is the grand end, the
chief good, and to this end Christ
leads the way.

Ver. 7.—"*If ye had known Me, ye
should* (R. V. WOULD) *have known My
Father also.*" "The thought here is
made quite plain by what has preceded;
but the form in which it is expressed
demands attention. The emphasis of
the first part of the sentence is not
upon '*Me,*' as is generally supposed,
but upon '*known.*' In the second part
the emphatic words are '*MY FATHER.*'
The English word 'known' represents
two Greek words in the latter text,
which are not identical in meaning.
The former means, to know by observation; the latter to know by reflection. It is the difference between
connaître and *savoir;* between *kennen*
(ken, *know*) and *wissen* (wit, wisdom).
We may express the meaning more

exactly thus, 'If ye had *recognized* Me, ye would have known *My Father* also.' If ye had recognized who I really am, ye would have known that I and My Father are one." "*And from henceforth ye know Him, and have seen Him.*" "See 1 Cor. xiii. 31, where the glorifying of the Son of man is regarded, as in the future which is immediately present. He can, therefore, say that from this time onwards, after the full declaration of Himself in verses 6 and 9 *et seq.*, they know and have seen the Father."

HOMILETICS

The subject of these words is *The Well-being of humanity.*— Notice—

I —THE END ESSENTIAL TO MAN'S WELL-BEING

What is that? Fellowship with the Father. It is not merely being conveyed into one of the " many mansions," for if we are not with the Father even there, we shall be desolate and miserable. "*Cometh unto the Father.*" What does this mean? Not that the Father is distant from us. He is "not far from every one of us." He is *locally* near. We are in constant contact with Him. He is *relationally* near. Nearer to us than any other relation. He is our Proprietor; aye, our very life. He is *sympathetically* near. No one feels such a deep interest in us as He does. But it means that we are morally estranged from Him. We are without God. "He is not in all our thoughts." Coming to Him means cherishing a supreme sympathy with Him, assimilation to His character—a growing consciousness of His presence, His love and fellowship. To be with the Father is to be in light, freedom, and perfect blessedness. To be away from Him is to be in darkness, thraldom, and misery. "In Thy presence is fulness of joy : at Thy right hand there are pleasures for evermore!" Another thought suggested is—

II —THE MEANS ESSENTIAL TO MAN'S WELL-BEING

By what means are we to come to the Father? Here is the answer. "*I am the Way, the Truth, and the Life : no man cometh unto the Father, but by Me.*"

First : Christ is the " *Way*" to the Father. "*I am the Way, the Truth, and the Life.*" The "*Way*"*—to a supreme sympathy with God, to an experimental knowledge, to a loving sympathy and perfect friendliness with Him. He is the " *Way*"—(1.) Because He is the " *Truth.*" † No unrealities can conduct us to the Father. He is the " *Way*"—(2.) Because He is the " *Life.*" ‡ No inanimate force can lead us to Him. It requires the most animated, the most inspiring life. Christ is that Life. Without a way there is no progress, without truth there is no certainty, without life there is no motion.

Secondly : Christ is the only " *Way*" to the Father. "*No man cometh unto the Father, but by Me.*" § These words coming from the

---

* See Germ, p. 8.   † See Germ, p. 9.
‡ See Germ, p. 9.   § See Germ, p. 10.

lips of any mere man, however exalted in intelligence and character, would fall on our ears as the utterance of blasphemous presumption; but from the lips of One Who displayed the attributes, Who lived the life, Who wrought the works that Christ did, they come with exquisite naturalness and simplicity. "*No man.*" (1.) The nature of the case shows this. Where else can you find that Divine force of character, that sublime energy of thought and passion, that mighty moral influence suited to win souls back to the Father, but in Christ? "*No man.*" (2.) The history of the race shows this. Have any of the millions of the race been brought back to the Father, but through Christ? If so, who?

CONCLUSION. How profoundly thankful should we be for this passage! It teaches us what no other system has ever taught mankind—*Man's chief good, and the true way of attaining it.* His chief good is friendship with the ever loving Father, and the true way is practical faith in the Lord Jesus Christ.

Germs of Thought
No. 53   John 14:6

CHRIST THE WAY TO THE FATHER

"I am the Way."

Christ is man's "*Way*" from spiritual ignorance to knowledge, spiritual bondage to liberty, spiritual degradation to dignity, spiritual misery to blessedness. But here He speaks of Himself as the "*Way*" to man's spiritual fellowship with the Father, and this involves all the rest. That He is the "*Way*" to the Father, will be seen if we consider, what keeps men away from the Father.

I —INDIFFERENTISM

The great bulk of mankind are utterly indifferent concerning God; they are without God. "God is not in all their thoughts." Who can remove this indifferentism? No one but Christ. He comes to the soul, and gives such a revelation of the Father, as stirs its sympathies and excites its interest.

II —DREAD

Men are afraid of God. "I heard Thy voice in the garden, and was afraid." The soul flees from the object it dreads. Who but Christ can remove this dread? He comes and reveals God not as a heartless tyrant or a vindictive judge, but as a Father full of tenderness and love. He comes to the soul in the name of God and says—"It is I, be not afraid."

III —ENMITY

The object you dread you are sure ultimately to hate. By a law of mind, you invest him with the most hideous attributes—

attributes which you loathe and curse. Thus men hate God : "the carnal mind is at enmity with God." So long as they hate God they will keep away from Him, they will shun Him. Who can destroy this enmity? Christ. He comes and assures them that the Object they hate loves them, and always has done.

CONCLUSION. Inasmuch as *Indifferentism, Dread,* and *Enmity,* keep the soul away from God, and Christ alone can destroy these, He is, with emphasis, the " *Way* " to a loving fellowship with the Father.

No. 54   John 14:6

CHRIST THE TRUTH
"I am . . . the Truth."

The human world abounds with *unrealities :* " Every man walketh in a vain show." Christ is the great Reality in the human world —*the Truth.*

I —HE IS THE TRUTH IN ITS MOST IMPORTANT FORM

There is truth in relation to nature, and its passing phenomena, but Christ is Truth in relation to the grandest realities of being.

First : He is " *Truth* " in relation to *God.* He gives a *true* idea of God ; no one else has ever done so, or ever can. " No man hath seen God at any time." You see what God is by looking at Him. Hence he that has seen Him has seen God.

Secondly : He is " *Truth* " in relation to *man.* There are a thousand theories concerning Man, but Christ is the Truth. Truth concerning—(1.) His origin ; (2.) His wonderful nature ; (3.) His solemn obligations ; (4.) His moral condition. He is the " *Truth* " in all these points. " He came to bear witness to the truth."

II —HE IS THE TRUTH IN ITS MIGHTIEST FORM

Truth in every form is powerful. Truth in propositions is powerful ; truth in example is more powerful. Truth in the example of a child is powerful ; truth in the example of a great man is more powerful ; truth in the example of the great God is *moral omnipotence.* Here is Eternal Truth embodied in a Divine life.

No. 55   John 14:6

CHRIST THE LIFE
"I am . . . the Life."

There are untold millions of lives, lives of every species, and of every degree of importance in the universe—plant life, brute life, mind life. But there is *One* life above all others in the world of mind. " *The Life.*"

I —HE IS THE ONLY QUICKENING LIFE

Human souls in a spiritual sense are dead ; dead in relation to the higher—(1.) Claims; (2.) Enjoyments; (3.) Engagements, and (4.) End of being. Christ is the only Quickener of such souls. His words, "they are spirit and life." His life is life-giving.

II —HE IS THE ONLY MODEL LIFE

No other life ever appeared on earth that has realized the perfect ideal of manhood. There have been men good in some respects, but bad in others. Such were even the best of the patriarchs, the prophets, even the apostles. But Christ was good in *all*, the only perfect Example. Perfect assimilation to Him is at once our grand obligation and our perfect blessedness. "Follow Me," &c.

III —HE IS THE ONLY SUSTAINER OF LIFE

"I am the Bread of life." His ideas, and spirit, and character are as essential to the life of the soul, as bread is to the life of the body. *His life is the Grand Necessity.* It is only as we drink in His soul-inspiring thoughts that we can live : apart from Him we die.

No. 56   John 14:6

MEDIATORIAL RELIGION, THE RELIGION OF MAN

"No man cometh unto the Father, but by Me."

We shall endeavour to develop the meaning of this remarkable expression by the statement of three facts :

I —THAT A SPIRITUAL CONNECTION WITH THE ABSOLUTE FATHER, IS THE SUPREME INTEREST OF ALL MORAL INTELLIGENCES

The language implies, that to come to the Father is the highest destiny of souls. But what is meant by coming to the Father ? (1.) It does not mean coming to His *being*, for He is ever *with* all, and *in* all. (2.) It does not mean coming to His *influence*, for "His constant visitation preserveth our spirits." *It means an approximation—*

First : To His moral attributes. An assimilation to His character ; becoming partakers of His nature. It means an approximation—

Secondly : To a deeper consciousness of His love. It means an approximation—

Thirdly : To an entire identification with His will. Having our wills lost in His, He becoming the "*all in all*" of our thoughts, emotions, and activities.

Three things show that this approximation is the *supreme* interest of moral intelligence. (1.) Instinct. The profoundest desire of the soul is for a God. "Show us the Father" is the deepest cry of humanity. (2.) Reason. This approximation is *right*. We are the offspring of God, and *ought* we not thus to come to Him ? It is *necessary* as well as right. From the constitution of our nature we cannot be happy without. (3.) The Bible. "In Thy presence is fulness of joy."

II — THAT SUCH A CONNECTION BETWEEN THE ABSOLUTE FATHER AND MAN DOES NOT GENERALLY EXIST

This is implied. Man is not with the Father, otherwise there would be no meaning in the language. Do not observation and experience show that he is not with "*the Father?*" (1.) Does his character agree with the moral attributes of God? (2.) Has he a consciousness of God's love? Is his *guilty conscience* not rather alarmed with a sense of His displeasure? (3.) Is his will identified with the will of God? Is he not a rebel? Is not the language of his heart, "Who is the Lord, that I should obey Him?" Alas! man is not in spiritual connection with the absolute Father. This is his crime and ruin.

III — THAT THIS SPIRITUAL CONNECTION BETWEEN THE ABSOLUTE FATHER AND MAN IS OBTAINED THROUGH CHRIST

"*No man cometh unto the Father, but by Me.*" There are four classes of men who seek to come to the Father.

First: Those who seek to come *without* any Mediator. Deists are of this class.

Secondly: Those who seek to come through a *wrong* Mediator. Pagans, Catholics, Jews. These have their priests and sacrifices.

Thirdly: Those who seek to come through a *right Mediator in a wrong way.*

Fourthly: Those who seek to come through a right Mediator *in a right way.* What a position does Christ assume! He stands between the everlasting Father and humanity, and says, "*No man cometh unto the Father, but by Me.*" *No* man, be he sage or sovereign.

John 14:8-11

MAN'S CRY AND CHRIST'S RESPONSE

"Philip saith unto Him, Lord, shew us the Father, and it sufficeth us," &c.

EXEGETICAL REMARKS. — Ver. 8. "*Philip saith unto Him.*" There is not much recorded of this Philip in the Holy Word. There are a few little incidents which throw some light upon his character, and give us the impression that he was a doubting, irresolute, diffident man. He was of the city of Andrew and Peter, and was at first a disciple of John the Baptist, and heard the testimony which John had given concerning the Messiah. He was called to follow Christ the day after the call of An-drew and Peter, and was the fourth who attached himself to Jesus as His disciple, and left all and followed Him. The first act recorded of him is one of interest and instruction. He brought Nathanael, who is supposed to have become an apostle under the name of Bartholomew, to Jesus. In Nathanael's case he had a prejudice to contend with which he overcame in an exemplary manner. "Philip findeth Nathanael, and saith unto him, We have found Him, of Whom Moses in the law, and the prophets, did write,

Jesus of Nazareth, the Son of Joseph" (chap. i. 44—47). The next incident which we find recorded of Philip is in connection with the miraculous feeding of the five thousand (chap. vi. 1—7). We find that Christ on that occasion singled Philip out from the rest and put this question to him, "Whence shall we buy bread, that these may eat?" This question, we are told, Christ put to prove him, to try his faith. There were five thousand men assembled on the mountain, weary, and wanting food. The question of our Lord was a perplexing one. Philip's answer was, "Two hundred pennyworth of bread is not sufficient for them, that every one of them may take a little." His answer indicated that he entertained no idea that Christ's miraculous agency would meet the case. The next account we have of him is in chap. xii. 22, 23. Certain Greeks came to him, wishing to be introduced to Christ, saying, "Sir, we would see Jesus." Philip does not take the responsibility of the introduction, but gets Andrew to assist him. The only other mention of him is in this verse, and the question he here puts to Christ, and the answer given, constitute one of the most precious sections in the revelation of mercy. "*Lord, shew us the Father, and it sufficeth us.*" Two of the disciples had already interrupted Christ at the supper on this His last evening, Peter and Thomas, and now Philip. Such interruptions undoubtedly show how much they felt at ease in the presence of their loving Master. Philip was evidently materialistic in his idea of God. He wanted a *visible* manifestation of Him, and thought that such a manifestation would be all-satisfying.

Ver. 9.—"*Jesus saith unto him, Have I been so long time with you,* and yet hast thou not known (R. V. DOST THOU NOT KNOW) Me, Philip? he that hath seen Me hath seen the Father; and how sayest thou then, Shew us the Father?*" Philip had been upwards of three years with Him. Their intercourse was free and frequent, and yet Philip failed to see the Father in Him. There seems to be a wail of love in this utterance of Christ, as if He had said, Alas, after My three years' manifestation of the Father in Me, thou art ignorant of Him, and this on My last night.

Ver. 10.—"*Believest thou not that I am in the Father, and the Father in Me? the words that I speak* (R. V. SAY) *unto you I speak not of* (R. V. FROM) *Myself: but the Father that dwelleth* (R. V. ABIDING) *in Me, He doeth the* (R. V. HIS) *works.*" Whatever these words mean, they cannot mean personal oneness. *Hooker* says, the "Son is in the Father, as light in that light out of which it floweth without separation; the Father is in the Son as the light in the light which it causeth and leaveth not." We can understand something of one soul dwelling in another, each making the other the paramount object of its love, the dominant subject of its thought, the primary mover of its actions.

Ver. 11.—"*Believe Me that I am in the Father.*" In affection, thought, purpose. "*And the Father in Me.*" As His image and organ. "*Or else believe Me for the very works' sake.*" "The meaning of our Lord's reply," says *Godet*, "is that the true Theophany has long been before your eyes in My character, teaching, and works." "Observe," says *Dr. Brown*, "how this expression of the Mutual In-being of the Father and the Son, passes almost insensibly from the words He said to the works He did."

HOMILETICS

The passage may be looked upon as containing the *Spiritual cry of man, and the glorious response of Christ.*

I —THE SPIRITUAL CRY OF MANKIND

"*Shew us the Father.*" We may take Philip here as representing all men in their deepest spiritual experiences. For what in truth is the cry of the world, but the cry of spiritual orphans after a lost Father ? This is the spring and spirit of all its cries, the wail of the world's heart. It goes forth from different lands and in different languages, but the meaning is the same. The soul has lost its great Father, deeply feels its loss, and cries after Him. " O that I knew where I might find Him ! " The cry implies an underlying belief—

First : In the existence of a Great Father. " *Shew us the Father.*" There is no *atheism* in the human heart. *Atheism* is a phantom of the brain, not an instinct of the soul. The idea of God is at the root of all ideas ; it is the axle on which the wheels of reason turn. Nor is'there any *pantheism* in the human heart. A father is a personality. The heart holds its faith in a father as distinct from the universe as the author from his works. It shows, further, that there is no *Molochism* in the human heart. There are theologies that represent God as cruel and malignant, burning with anger, that can only be appeased by torture and anguish, the Draco of the universe. Some of the popular theologies of Christendom thus misrepresent and blaspheme the Infinite Father. Deep in the heart of man is the belief that the God of the universe is the Father of the soul. You cannot reason this instinctive belief away ; it is the deepest hope of the sinner on his deathbed, of the criminal on the gallows. The heart turns to it as the flower to the sun. This cry implies an underlying belief—

Secondly : In the sufficiency of the Father's manifestation. " *It sufficeth us.*" Until the Father comes the soul will have a gnawing hunger and an aching void. (1.) It will satisfy the *intellect.* It will solve the problems our reason seeks to solve in vain, and whose crushing weight philosophy but augments. (2.) It will satisfy the *affections.* It will unfold, purify, harmonize, and centralize all the affections of our moral nature. The repentant prodigal was flooded with joy in the warm caresses of his father's love. As the genial sun of May sets the choristers of the grove into music, the presence of the Father will not only hush all the cries of the child, but fill the heart with filial rapture. The passage contains—

II —THE SATISFACTORY RESPONSE OF CHRIST

" *He that hath seen Me hath seen the Father.*" " He was God manifest in the flesh and the brightness of His glory." In Christ the Father of man appears to man in man's nature.

First : This was now amply attested. " *The words that I speak unto you I speak not of Myself : but the Father that dwelleth in Me, He doeth the works.*" " *Believest thou not that I am in the Father ?* " *
Who but the Father could have wrought those works which He accomplished ? Who but the Father could have inspired those

* See Germs, p. 14, 15.

sublime doctrines which He proclaimed? Who but the Father could have produced such a character as He manifested?

Secondly: This was now practically ignored. *"Have I been so long time with you, and yet hast thou not known Me, Philip?"* Two things are to be observed here. (1.) A criminal neglect of means. *"Have I"*—the medium of His power, the organ of His love, the Revealer of His thoughts, and the Image of His character—*"been so long time with you, and yet hast thou not known Me?"* (2.) The finality of revelation. *"How sayest thou then, shew us the Father?"* There is no other revelation of the Father to come, "No man hath seen God at any time: the only begotten Son, He hath declared Him." If you cannot find the Father in Me you will never find Him. You will not find Him abroad in the universe, nor in the speculations of philosophy.

CONCLUSION. The great want of our nature is fellowship with the Father. Without this, whatever else thou hast, thy destitution is terrible. No amount of worldly wealth, no measure of social influence, no degree of intellectual culture, will be of any real or lasting service to thee without this. Unless thou art brought back to the home, the bosom, the embrace of thy Father, thou wilt be of all orphans the most wretched for ever and ever. Brethren, our work is, as far as we can, to show men the Father. The unsophisticated millions yearn for a Father, and neither in church or chapel do they often find Him, and they retire and avoid such scenes altogether. One preacher will present a *Partial Deity* instead of a Father, and tell men that the Supreme One chooses the few and damns the many. Another preacher will present an *Infinite Merchant* as the Father, and represent Him as having disposed of a certain number of human souls on stipulated conditions to Christ, that they only will be saved, and the others damned. Another preacher presents Him as an *Avenging God*, burning with such wrath towards the sinner as can only be quenched by the blood of His innocent Son. The unsophisticated men when they come, hear such representations, recoil with revulsion and horror from such a God, and still cry out—*"Shew us the Father."* We need a Father.

Germs of Thought
No. 57   John 14:10

CHRIST IN THE FATHER

"Believest Thou not that I am in the Father?"

Christ is—

I —IN THE FATHER'S AFFECTIONS

He loves Christ more than He loves the universe. "This is My beloved Son." As a loving child lives in the affection of his parent, so Christ in an infinitely higher degree lives in the heart of God. Christ is—

II —IN THE FATHER'S THOUGHTS

What an intelligent being loves most he will think most about. (1.) He is the Logos, the Revealer of the Divine thought. As the word is in the mind before it is sounded, Christ is in God. (2.) He is the Executor of the Divine thought. By Him His creative and redemptive thoughts, His governing, and His retributionary thoughts, are carried out,—"*I am in the Father.*"

No. 58   John 14:10

THE FATHER IN CHRIST
"I am in the Father, and the Father in Me."

Christ probably means to say, "*The Father in Me,*" as—

I —HIS SPECIAL TEMPLE

He Whom the "Heaven of Heavens cannot contain" has a special dwelling in Me. In Me, He manifests Himself in a fulness and glory in which He is seen nowhere else. He is in Me as—

II —HIS SPECIAL ORGAN

As the soul dwells in the body He dwells in Me, and works by Me. He is in Me as—

III —HIS SPECIAL REVEALER

"I am the brightness of His glory, the express image of His person." I reveal His power, His wisdom, His moral character, which is all pure, just, tender, and compassionate. He is in Me as—

IV —HIS SPECIAL DEVOTEE

He is the Object of My supreme love. I subordinate all My thoughts, and powers, and aims, to Him. I am devoted to His will. He is "My all in all."

No. 59   John 14:11

GOD IN CHRIST
"The Father in Me."

The Father, is He not in all? In every tree, stream, and star? Verily, He is in all. There is no life in which He is not. But Christ says, He is in Me. And this in a higher sense than He is in any other existence. He is in nature as the animating principle. He is in holy souls as an inspiring influence. But He is in Christ as a Divine Personality. In Him He is "God manifest in the flesh."

I.—THE FATHER IS IN HIM AS AN APPRECIABLE PERSONALITY

It is difficult, if not impossible, to realize the Divine personality in nature. He seems so vast and so boundless. But in Christ He comes within the range of our (1) *senses*, (2) *sympathies*, and (3) *experiences*. He has " bowed the heavens," and come down in our midst.

II —THE FATHER IS IN HIM AS AN ATTRACTIVE PERSONALITY

Does *Wonder* attract ? He is " the Wonderful." Does *Love* attract ? He is the tenderest, the strongest, the most self-sacrificing and unconquerable love. Does *Beauty* attract ? He is the " altogether lovely." In Christ there is the power to draw all men to Him.

III —THE FATHER IS IN HIM AS AN IMITABLE PERSONALITY

Our obligation and our well-being require us to become like God, partakers of the Divine nature, " holy even as He is holy." In Christ He appears pre-eminently imitable. (1) His love wins our hearts, (2) His principles command our consciences, (3) His moral glories inspire our admiration. Thus we can imitate Him.

John 14:12-14

THE SPIRITUAL REFORMATION OF HUMANITY

" Verily, verily, I say unto you, He that believeth on Me, the works that I do shall he do also," &c.

EXEGETICAL REMARKS.—Ver. 12.— *"Verily, verily, I say unto you, He that believeth on Me, the works that I do shall he do also."* It must be remembered that Christ was consoling His disciples in prospect of His departure. It was His final meeting with them before His death. Deeply, no doubt, did they feel how much they would lose, when a Friend, Who had wrought amongst them such mighty works, would withdraw. Virtually He says to them, "Let not your hearts be troubled about this matter, because when I am gone," *"the works that I do shall he do."* You shall perform miracles if you believe on Me. This promise was fulfilled. *"And greater works."* The word *"works"* here should be omitted, although it is implied. What were the greater works ? Not greater miracles, for their history shows that the miracles they wrought after His departure were not so great in their nature or number as His. The works, undoubtedly, refer to those connected with the *Spiritual Regeneration* of the world : in other words, the conversion of mankind. Witness, for example, the moral wonders of the day of Pentecost. *" Because I go*

unto My (R. V. THE) *Father."* This refers to His re-entrance into the heavenly world.

Vers. 13, 14.—*"And whatsoever ye shall ask in My name, that will I do,"* &c. "This prayer is thought of as addressed to the Father, but the answer here, and still more emphatically in the following verse, is thought of as coming from the Son, Who is one with the Father. The width and limitation of the promise are both to be noted. It is, *'whatsoever ye shall ask;'* and it is ask *'in My name.'* This means as My representatives on earth, as doing My work, living in My Spirit, seeking, as I have sought to do, the will of My Father. It follows from this that personal petitions are not contemplated here, except as far as they are for the glory of God ; and that petitions asked in ignorance may be most truly answered when they are not granted."—*Watkins.* The essence of these verses may be given as follows, I think : WHATSOEVER IN CONNECTION WITH THIS GREAT WORK YOU HEARTILY DESIRE FOR MY SAKE, I WILL DO, AND THUS GLORIFY THE FATHER.

HOMILETICS

The great subject of these words is *the Spiritual Reformation of Humanity,* and they suggest three facts in relation to this great work.

I —THAT IT IS A "GREATER WORK" THAN THE PERFORMANCE OF A MIRACLE

"*Greater works than these shall he do.*"
Another fact suggested concerning this "*greater work*" is—

II —THAT FAITH IN CHRIST WILL QUALIFY ANY MAN TO ACHIEVE THIS "GREATER WORK"

"*He that believeth on Me, the works that I do shall he do also.*"
The other fact suggested concerning this "*greater work*" is—

III —THAT THE ASCENSION OF CHRIST TO HEAVEN IS THE GUARANTEE FOR ACCOMPLISHMENT OF THIS "GREATER WORK"

"*Because I go unto My Father. And whatsoever ye shall ask in My name, that will I do.*" *

John 14:15-27

THE DIVINITY OF A CHRIST-LOVING SOUL

"If ye love Me, keep My commandments," &c.

EXEGETICAL REMARKS.—Ver. 15.— "*If ye love Me.*" "Me" is emphatic. "*Keep* (R. V. YE WILL KEEP) *My commandments.*" Probably He especially refers to the precepts He was addressing to them in this discourse.

Ver. 16.—"*And I will pray the Father.*" I will ask the Father. The words imply nearness and familiarity. "*And He shall give you another Comforter.*" Paracleton. This word means "advocate," and it is used here (and in verse 26, also chapters xv. 26 ; xvi. 7) for the Divine Spirit, Who is here spoken of as a person. John in his epistle (1 chap. ii. 1) applies the word to Christ Himself. The word "*another*" points to an advocate or "*Comforter*" in some sense distinct from Himself. He had been a "*Comforter*" or Advocate to them up to this point, but now He was about leaving them and departing to His Father, and He would send them some other person, or, as some suppose, He would in some

other way come and comfort them. *Help* would perhaps be the best word. "*That He may abide* (R. V. BE) *with you for ever.*" He, their "Comforter," in the person of a Man, was now leaving them, but He would come again in the person of the Paraclete, and in this spiritual way He would remain with them (Matt. xxviii. 20).

Ver. 17.—"*Even the Spirit of truth.*" "Compare chaps. xv. 26 ; and xvi. 13 ; 1 John v. 6. He is called the '*Spirit of Truth,*' because part of His special office is to bring truth home to the hearts of men, to carry it from the material to the moral sphere, to make it something more than a collection of signs seen or heard, a living power in living men."—*Watkins.* "*Whom the world cannot receive, because it seeth* (R. V. BEHOLDETH) *Him not, neither knoweth Him.*" "It was by no arbitrary act that the Spirit came down upon one hundred and twenty only, on the day of Pentecost, and not on

---

* A fuller development of these thoughts will be found in Homily at end of volume.

all the inhabitants of Jerusalem, the former having alone undergone the indispensable preparation. Jesus explains wherein this preparation, which the world is without, consists ; before receiving they must have seen and known the Spirit. The Spirit identifies Himself too closely with our individual life to be merely a bestowed gift ; if He is to dwell in us He must be desired and summoned by us."— *Godet.* "*But ye know Him ; for He dwelleth* (R. V. ABIDETH) *with you, and shall be in you.*" The words imply that they already had some knowledge and experience of this Paraclete or Helper. So they had of Christ.

Ver. 18.—"*I will not leave you comfortless*" (R. V. DESOLATE). *Orphanous,* —orphans. "*I will come to you*" (R. V. I COME UNTO YOU). I will return to you. Here, undoubtedly, it is implied that He Himself is the Paraclete, Who will in spirit return and administer to His disciples. "The Holy Spirit," says *Tholuck,* "is only the Person of Jesus spiritualised."

Ver. 19.—"*Yet a little while, and the world seeth* (R. V. BEHOLDETH) *Me no more ; but ye see* (R. V. BEHOLD) *Me.*" Though I shall be beyond your physical vision you shall see Me in the spiritual presence of the Paraclete. "*Because I live, ye shall live also.*" For I live, and ye shall live. His life is the Source of all spiritual life in His disciples.

Ver. 20.—"*At* (R. V. IN) *that day ye shall know that I am in My Father, and ye in Me, and I in you.*" "*That day*" indicates a definite period, particularly the day of Pentecost. That was the day of Christ's spiritual advent to the world, the most important of all His advents. His advent in the flesh was only for a short period, and confined Him to certain limits ; but His advent in the Spirit, or in the Paraclete, is for indefinite ages, and for the wide and ever-growing world of humanity. In this period His disciples will know the vital identification of Christ with the Father, and they with Him.

Ver. 21.—"*He that hath My commandments, and keepeth them, he it is*

that loveth Me : and he that loveth Me shall be loved of My Father, and I will love him, and will manifest Myself to* (R. V. UNTO) *him.*" The meaning is that obedience to Him will demonstrate their love for Him, and their love to Him will ensure both the love and the manifestation of the Father.

Ver. 22.—"*Judas* (R. V. NOT ISCARIOT) *saith unto Him, not Iscariot.*" That he was not Iscariot is mentioned to distinguish him beyond all possibility of confusion, from him who had gone out into the darkness, and was no longer one of their number (chap. xiii. 30). He is commonly identified with Lebbæus, whose surname was Thaddæus, and was a brother or son of James (Luke vi. 15). "*Lord, how is it* (R. V. WHAT IS COME TO PASS) *that Thou wilt manifest Thyself unto us, and not unto the world ?*" The word "*manifest*" started to the mind of Judas, as the word "See" to the mind of Philip, thoughts of a material manifestation of God ; such as Moses desired. But the manifestation which Christ meant was a spiritual one—the manifestation of the moral reign of God in the soul. Christ's words seem to have taken Judas by surprise : he says virtually, "What has happened that Thou wilt manifest Thyself to us ?"

Ver. 23.—"*Jesus answered and said unto him, If a man love Me, he will keep My words* (R. V. WORD) : *and My Father will love him.*" Here the condition necessary to a consciousness of the Divine Presence and Power is once more repeated,—it is love and obedience. "*We will come unto him, and make our abode with him.*" This language is perhaps an allusion to God as dwelling in symbol, in the sanctuary of old among His people.

Ver. 24.—"*He that loveth Me not keepeth not My sayings*" (R. V. WORDS), &c. No man that does not love Christ will obey Him, and no man that does not obey Him can enjoy this intimate connection with Himself and the Father.

Ver. 25.—"*These things have I spoken unto you, being yet present with you.*" (R. V. WHILE YET ABIDING WITH YOU.)

I tell you these things while I am in the flesh.

Ver. 26.—"*But the Comforter, which is* (R. V. EVEN) *the Holy Ghost* (R. V. SPIRIT), *whom the Father will send in My name, He shall teach you all things, and bring* (R. V. TO YOUR REMEMBRANCE) *all things to your remembrance, whatsoever I have* (R. V. ALL THAT I SAID) *said unto you.*" This Paraclete was to be sent to them by the Father; sent by the Father in the name of Christ; sent in the name of Christ in order to reproduce in their memory and consciousness all things Christ had said.

Ver. 27.—"*Peace I leave with you, My peace I give unto you,*" &c. "The immediate context speaks of His departure from them (vers. 25 and 28), and it is natural therefore to understand these words as suggested by the Common Oriental formulas of leave-taking. Men said to each other, when they met and parted, Shalom! Shalom! (Peace, Peace) just as they say the Salaam! Salaam! in our own day (1 Sam. i. 17 ; Luke vii. 50 ; Acts xvi. 36 ; Eph. vi. 23 ; James ii. 16 ; 1 Peter v. 14 ; 3 John i. 15)."—*Watkins.* Peace is His legacy. A peace unlike that of the world.

HOMILETICS

These verses may be looked upon as unfolding the *Divinity of a Christ-loving soul.* Here such a soul is represented as living a Divine life, possessing a Divine Helper, enjoying Divine companionship, and participating in Divine peace.

I —AS LIVING A DIVINE LIFE

The life is that of practising Divine commandments. "*If ye love Me, keep My commandments.*" It is taught in this paragraph that this obedience is at once the effect and evidence of love to Christ.

First : It is the effect. "*If ye love Me, keep My commandments.*" Here is a law of mind. He who really loves another is naturally desirous of acting in accord with the wishes and the will of the object loved. Without such a desire there is no true love. It may be mere sentiment, passing emotion, but infinitely remote from love of the right stamp. The child that really loves its parent wishes to act out the will of its parent, and thus at once gratify and prove its affection. Love is always hungering for an opportunity to reveal itself to its object in some practical way. And this is its happiness. Obedience to Christ's commandments, if not the effect of love is not obedience at all.

Secondly : It is the evidence. "*He that hath My commandments, and keepeth them, he it is that loveth Me.*" He, and no one else. There may be the most glowing songs of praise, the sublimest language of adoration, and the most vigorous observance of the mere letter of His law, but all this would not necessarily prove the existence of *love.* Love is only proved by practical obedience. Hence, then, the Christ-loving soul is ever living a Divine life, carrying out in all the plans and pursuits of daily existence the laws of the Divine. He is, in a sense, the Divine "word made flesh," the will of God embodied and wrought out. How unlike the life of mere worldly men. They embody and work out only

the current ideas and notions of their age. " I will run the way of
Thy commandments when Thou shalt enlarge my heart." Here
the Christ-loving soul is represented—

II — AS POSSESSING A DIVINE HELPER

" *And I will pray the Father, and He shall give you another
Comforter, that He may abide with you for ever ; even the Spirit of
truth.*" This is promised to the Christ-loving soul and to no other.
Four things are taught in the passage concerning this " *Comforter,*"
Advocate, or Helper.

First : He is the Gift of the Father. " *I will pray the Father,
and He shall give you another Comforter.*" The " *Father,*" Who " so
loved the world as to give His only begotten Son," so loves those
who love His Son, as to send this spiritual Helper. It is a gift, a
free, sovereign, priceless gift. Another thing taught concerning
the " *Comforter* " is—

Secondly : He is the Messenger of reality. " *Even the Spirit of
Truth.*" The human world is under the dominion of falsehoods
and shams ; error rules it. " Every man walketh in a vain show."
False ideas of life, and duty, and God, and happiness, and greatness
everywhere prevail. This is its guilt and its ruin. This Paraclete
comes as the messenger of reality, comes to scatter delusions, and
to bring souls into contact with the morally real. Christ's Kingdom
is the kingdom of truth. " I came to bear witness of the truth."
Another thing taught here concerning the " *Comforter* " is—

Thirdly : He is exclusively for the Christ-loving. " *Whom the world
cannot receive, because it seeth Him not, neither knoweth Him : but ye
know Him ; for He dwelleth with you, and shall be in you.*"* This
love is at once the receptive and the recognizing faculty : without
it He can never be received or seen. Love opens the eyes of the soul
to see, and the doors of the heart to welcome. " The natural man
receiveth not the things of the Spirit of God : for they are foolishness unto him : neither can he know them, because they are
spiritually discerned " (1 Cor. ii. 14). As soon may a man who has
not attained the faculty of reading, see in " Paradise Lost " the genius
of Milton that breathes in it all, as the man who has not the love
of Christ see and receive the Spirit of God, the glorious Paraclete.
Another thing taught here concerning the " *Comforter* " is—

Fourthly : He is the spiritual presence of Christ. " *I will not
leave you comfortless : I will come to you.*"† Though My body will
depart from you, and pass beyond the reach of your senses, " *I will
come to you* " in Spirit. " Lo, I am with you alway, even unto the
end." Christ is as truly here with His genuine disciples now as
He was when He tabernacled among them in the flesh. The
other thing taught here concerning the " *Comforter* " is—

* See Germ, p. 22.   † See Germ, p. 22.

Fifthly: He instructs in the things of Christ. "*He shall teach you all things, and bring all things to your remembrance, whatsoever I have said unto you.*" In another place Christ said, "He will guide you into all the truth." The things that Christ has said He would bring to "*remembrance*," re-produce with new vitality and vigour, and into the regions of undiscovered truths He will lead them as their Guide. Here the Christ-loving soul is represented—

III —AS ENJOYING DIVINE COMPANIONSHIP

"*At that day ye shall know that I am in My Father, and ye in Me, and I in you.*" "*My Father will love him, and we will come unto him, and make our abode with him.*" Love to Christ makes the soul the residence of God. Such a soul He enters not as a passing visitor, but as a permanent guest. "Know ye not that ye are the temple of God, and that the Spirit of God dwelleth in you?" (1 Cor. iii. 16.) And here He says, "*We will come unto him,*" the Father and the Son. "If any man hear My voice, and open the door, I will come in to him, and will sup with him." What a companionship is this!

> "In secret silence of the mind,
> My Heaven and there my God I find."

Truly "our fellowship is indeed with the Father and with His Son Jesus Christ." Here the Christ-loving soul is represented—

IV —AS PARTICIPATING IN DIVINE PEACE

"*Peace I· leave with you, My peace I give unto you: not as the world giveth, give I unto you.*" "*Peace,*"—what a blessing! Peace with our own conscience, peace with society, peace with God. "*Not as the world giveth, give I unto you.*" (1.) Not as to *quality*. The world gives *inferior* gifts. Christ gives the highest. The world gives *non-essential* gifts. Men can do without the best things that the world can give; they cannot do without Christ's gifts. (2.) Not as to *manner*. (*a*) The world gives *selfishly*. It looks for something in return. Christ gives from infinite disinterestedness. (β) The world gives *limitedly*. It cannot give much; it has neither the heart nor the capacity. Christ gives unlimitedly. He openeth His liberal hand. (γ) The world gives *occasionally*. It is only now and then by moods. Christ gives constantly. (δ) The world gives to its *friends*. It loves its own. Christ gives to His enemies.

Germs of Thought
No. 60   John 14:17

THE SPIRIT WITH YOU AND IN YOU

" He dwelleth with you, and shall be in you."

Three remarks are suggested.   It is implied—

I —THAT A MAN MAY HAVE THE DIVINE SPIRIT WITH HIM, BUT NOT IN HIM

The Divine Spirit was now with the disciples in the Person of Christ. He was the temple of the Godhead. Every man on the earth has the Divine Spirit *with* him. With him—(1.) In the operations of nature. With him—(2.) In the revelations of the Bible. With him—(3.) In the events of history. With him—(4.) In the biography of all good men.   It is implied—

II —THAT IT IS A GREAT PRIVILEGE FOR A MAN TO HAVE THE SPIRIT OF GOD WITH HIM

What a privilege it was for the disciples to have the Spirit of God with them in the person of Christ ! When the Spirit of God is with us, we have one at our side Who is ever ready to Guide us, Protect us, Strengthen us, and Perfect us.   It is implied—

III —THAT IT IS A GREATER PRIVILEGE FOR A MAN TO HAVE THE SPIRIT OF GOD IN HIM

Christ had unfolded to His disciples an infinite system of truth ; but His doctrines lay cold and dead in their memories. He deposited precious seed in the soil ; but the soil lacked that warmth and sunshine that the Spirit of God alone could give. When the Spirit of God is in you, you have spiritual *Life, Satisfaction, Power*. Compare the difference between the apostles when Christ was *with* them before His death, and when He came *into* them at the Pentecost.

No. 61   John 14:18

SOUL ORPHANHOOD

" I will not leave you comfortless : I will come to you."—xiv. 18.

Ορφάνους is the original word here, and it is a pity that the translators should have rendered it "*comfortless.*" The text leads us to offer some remarks on soul orphanhood.

I —SOUL ORPHANHOOD CONSISTS IN MORAL SEPARATION FROM GOD

This seems to be implied. We say *moral* separation, not *local*, for God is everywhere, and no spirit can flee from His presence. Not *physical ;* for as an existent it has its life and force in God.

But *morally* it may be distant from Him, and in the case of the unregenerate is ever distant from Him. It is alienated from Him in sympathy, purpose, and pursuit. It is without God. "God is not in all its thoughts." The ungodly world is a world of orphans. They are without a father's fellowship and guidance.

II —SOUL ORPHANHOOD IS AN EVIL OF STUPENDOUS MAGNITUDE

The language of Christ implies, that His disciples would feel this orphanism to be the greatest of evils; and a terrible evil in truth it is.

First : Orphanism, so far as human parents are concerned, is a *calamity; but this is a crime.* A child bereft of its parents, left alone, disconsolate, and desolate in this cold world, is truly an object of commiseration, but not of blame. The Great Disposer of life deprived him of his earthly guardians. But in the orphanage of soul there is guilt. The soul has broken away from its Father: the Father has not gone from it.

Secondly : Orphanism, so far as human parents is concerned, may *have its loss supplied by others, but this cannot be supplied.* Society in many cases supplies the poor orphan with friends, and does more for his happiness than his parents could. Thank God, society in this age has loving hearts, and wholesome food, and comfortable clothing, and good homes for orphans. But nothing on earth can relieve *soul orphanhood:* nothing in the universe; —nothing can take the place of God in relation to the soul. Oh! there is no evil comparable to it. The starving child at night in a wilderness, teeming with beasts of prey, crying for food, protection, and guidance, is not in a condition half so terrible as an orphan soul—a soul without God : such a soul is benighted, perishing, lost.

III —SOUL ORPHANHOOD IS REMOVED BY THE PRESENCE OF CHRIST

"I will not leave you comfortless: I will come to you." Here Christ speaks of Himself not merely as the Substitute of the Father, but as the Father Himself; as if He had said, "My coming to you will be as the coming of the Father to you, for I and My Father are one." "Show us the Father, and it sufficeth," said Philip. Christ answered, "Have I been so long time with you, and yet hast thou not known Me, Philip? He that hath seen Me hath seen the Father also." Christ brings the soul into a loving, joyous, blessed fellowship with God. The deep cry of humanity is the cry of the orphan for the Father. The response to that cry is the advent of Christ.

John 14:28-31

CHRIST'S EXIT FROM THE WORLD

"Ye have heard how I said unto you, I go away," &c.

EXEGETICAL REMARKS.—Ver. 28.— "*Ye have* (R. V. YE HEARD) *heard how I said unto* (R. V. TO YOU) *you, I go away, and come again* (R. V. I COME) *unto you.*" Christ had in verse 12 said, "I go unto My Father." In fact, He had stated it more than once, with more or less distinctness (see also ver. 19, 20). "*If ye loved Me, ye would rejoice* " (R. V. HAVE REJOICED). "The words," says *Godet,* " '*If ye loved Me,*' are exquisitely tender. The Saviour uses them to make their joy the duty of affection ; He calls their attention to His approaching exaltation (compare xiii. 3, 31, 32). What friend would not rejoice to see his friend raised to a position truly worthy of him ? And if they rightly understood the extent of this change in their Master's situation, they would at the same time rejoice for themselves. It implied that His departure would, in some way, be to His advantage, therefore, though His separation from them might be painful to them to some extent, inasmuch as they loved Him, they should rejoice. It is the eternal law of true love to rejoice in the good of its object. '*My* (R. V. THE) *Father is greater than I.*' This is an expression which is much controverted. It is difficult for those who hold the tenet that the Son is the very God of the substance of the Father, begotten before all worlds, to accept the idea of His inferiority here expressed. Distinctness of personality from the Father, and subordination to Him, is here declared. At the same time, His transcendent greatness is undoubtedly implied. What should we think of the greatest men that ever lived, Paul, Plato, Socrates, &c., thus comparing themselves with the Infinite One, and saying, He is greater, &c. ? Calvin supposes that the inferiority here implied is not in His *personality,* but in His *condition.* His words are, 'Christ does not here compare the Godhead of His Father with His own, nor His

human nature with the Divine essence of the Father, but His present condition with that heavenly glory into which He was soon to be received.' " The Father's condition in the universe is infinitely glorious and blessed. But Christ's condition when on earth was one of humiliation. He appeared without any form of comeliness, "a Man of sorrows, and acquainted with grief."

Ver. 29.—"*And now I have told you before it come to pass, that, when it is come to pass, ye might* (R. V. MAY) *believe.*" Here again, He tells them the event before the accomplishment, that it may serve to strengthen their faith. "Two interpretations of this verse are possible. (1.) That He told them of the coming of the Advocate to teach all truth, and bring all things to their remembrance, in order that in the fulfilment of this they might, with increase of faith, believe in Him. (2.) That He told them of His going to the Father in order that when the hour of departure came they might believe that He had gone to the Father. Upon the whole, and especially considering the close parallel with chap. xiii. 29, the first seems the more probable meaning."

Ver. 30.—"*Hereafter I will not talk* (R. V. I WILL NO MORE SPEAK) *much with you.*" I will say but little more to you. My words are coming to a close. My teaching is approaching its end. My voice you will soon hear no more. "*For the prince of this* (R. V. THE) *world cometh, and* (R. V. HE HATH) *hath nothing in Me.*" Here the existence, the personality, and world-wide authority of the evil spirit is unmistakably taught by the Infallible Teacher. Elsewhere he is called "the Prince of the power of darkness, that worketh in the children of disobedience." The "*Prince of this world cometh,*" cometh with hostile intent, cometh for a last grand attack. Foiled in his first deadly assault he had "departed," but for a season only. (See Luke iv. 13.) That season is now all but come, and his whole energies are to be once more put forth —with what effect the next words sublimely express. "*And hath nothing in Me.*" Nothing of his own in Me, nothing of sin on which to fasten as a righteous cause of condemnation. As the prince of this world he wields his sceptre over willing subjects, but in Me he shall find no sympathy with his objects, no acknowledgment of his sovereignty, no subjection to his demands.

Ver. 31.—"*But that the world may know that I love the Father; and as the Father gave Me commandment—even so I do.*" The most probable arrangement of this verse is to omit the period after "*So I do,*" and to consider all down to this point as governed by "*that.*" We shall read them thus,— "*But that the world may know that I love the Father; and that as the Father gave Me commandment, so I do, arise, let us go hence.*" He has asserted, in the previous verse, the sinlessness which makes His act wholly self-determined. He now expresses the subordination of His own to the Father's will. The words seem to point back to the "prince of the world" who has just been mentioned. The prince cometh, but it is to a defeat, and the very world over which he has ruled will see in the self-sacrifice of Jesus the love of the Father. That love will reclaim them from the bondage of the oppressor, and restore them to the freedom of children.

HOMILETICS

The following remarks are here suggested concerning *Christ's Exit from the World:*—

I—HIS DEPARTURE WAS OF HIS OWN FREE CHOICE

"*Ye have heard how I said unto you, I go away.*" "*I go.*" I am not driven or forced from the earth, but I go out of it unforced and free. Thus indeed He came into the world at first. "I am come that ye might have life." All other men were *sent* into the world. They had no choice. But He came of His own free will, came at His own time, into the sphere and condition in which He appeared. During His sojourn on this earth He moved freely, went hither and thither according to His own good pleasure, and now He departs from it with a free step. "*I go away.*" This fact exposes the moral impropriety, nay, the blasphemy of representing Him as the *victim* of forces over which He had no control, an object to be compassionated, to be wept over with the tears of pity. Christ even upon the Cross should be preached, not as *a Helpless Victim,* but as a victorious Hero fighting the moral battles of humanity. How often did He assure His hearers of this during His public ministry! "No man taketh My life from Me. I have power to lay it down, and take it up again. For this purpose I came into the world, to bear witness of the truth." To pity Him even in His greatest agonies is impiety. To adore Him as the Commander of the people, and the "Captain of human salvation," is that state of mind which He deserves, demands, and alone approves.

Observe here—

II —HIS DEPARTURE WAS ONLY FOR A BRIEF PERIOD

"*I go away, and come again unto you.*" Christ comes to His disciples in two ways—

First: By His Spirit. "I will not leave you comfortless: I will come to you." Thus He comes into their souls in all Righteous admirations, all Holy aspirations, all True consolations, and all Purifying and Uplifting influences. He comes in to the spirit of His disciples with the advent of every truth.

Secondly: By their dissolution. "I will come," He says, "and take you unto Myself." "In such an hour as ye think not the Son of man cometh." Yes, He comes at death, dis-imprisons the spirit from its mortal cell, leads it through the "valley of the shadow of death." His departure therefore was very temporary. He withdrew His body from their senses, only that His Spirit might enter their souls. Indeed it is ever true that the withdrawal of the bodily forms of our friends by death serves to bring them not only near to our hearts, but into the very chamber of our spirits. When a godly friend dies he virtually says, "*I will come again unto you,*" and verily he does come and dwell as a Permanent Resident in our memories.

III —HIS DEPARTURE WAS A RETURN TO HIS FATHER

"*If ye loved Me, ye would rejoice,* because I said, I go unto the Father: for My Father is greater than I.*" What does He mean by going to the Father? Was not the Father always with Him? Yes. But there were certain obstructions to the closest fellowship and the fullest enjoyment: obstructions which death alone could remove. What were they?

(1.) *There was the body with its infirmities.* His body was, as it were, a material veil which lay between Him and the Infinite Father. His hungerings, thirstings, fatigues, tended no doubt to interrupt the fellowship. (2.) *There was the sinful condition of the world in which He lived.* The evils of falsehoods, dishonesties, impieties, blasphemies, which crowded the moral atmosphere of the age in which He lived, tended, no doubt, to interfere with His fellowship with the Father. (3.) *There was the influence of the principalities and powers of darkness.* Satan, "the prince of the power of the air," never perhaps deserted Him, assailing Him at every point of His soul. Though he could not tempt Him, yet he teased Him. No doubt, therefore, His fellowship with God here was interrupted. Now all these things interrupt the fellowship of the good man with God here. Every good man has—
(*a.*) The body with its thick veil intervening. (*b.*) A sinful world whose exhalations darken his moral sky. (*c.*) Satanic influence

* See Germ, p. 28.

pressing him away from the Father. But in connection with all this, the godly man has something more. He has what Christ had not,— *Worldly cares, Inward depravity, Corrupt habits.* At death, however, these things are removed, the soul passes away from the material and corrupt into the immediate presence of its God. We should not sorrow for the departed good. Indeed, if we love them, we ought to rejoice because they have gone to the Father. They are with their Father. Away from clouds and storms and enemies, they are "for ever with the Lord."

IV —HIS DEPARTURE WAS MERCIFULLY FORETOLD

"*And now I have told you before it come to pass, that, when it is come to pass, ye might believe.*" To be forewarned is to be fore-armed. Suppose all the horrors connected with Christ in the garden of Gethsemane, and before His judges, and in His dying agonies on the cross, had come upon His disciples unawares, could their faith have stood the revelation? Would they not have been tempted to feel that He Whom they had been following as the Messiah was but a feeble man, therefore a gross impostor? Christ knew the danger, and here forewarns them; tells them that He knew all that was before Him; that nothing would come upon Him as a surprise; that with all His coming agonies He was perfectly acquainted; and into the roaring fiery tempest He entered freely. This foretelling of the whole prepared them so, that when the storm came, instead of shaking their faith it deepened and strengthened it.

V --HIS DEPARTURE WAS AN ENCOUNTERING OF SATAN

"*Hereafter I will not talk much with you: for the prince of this world cometh, and hath nothing in Me. But that the world may know that I love the Father. . . Arise, let us go hence.*"* He had before grappled with Satan in the wilderness when He was an hungered forty days and forty nights, but now He was to encounter him in more terrible forms. He was to meet this gigantic fiend, who works in the children of disobedience, in the treachery of Judas, in the violence of the Roman ruffians in the garden of Gethsemane, in the slanders and insolence of His judges, Caiaphas, Herod, Pilate, in the mockeries and insults of the maddened rabble that surrounded His Cross. Truly on His way out of the world to the Father He had a terrible battle with this fiend. Yet He conquered, He spoiled their principalities and powers, and "made a show of them; openly triumphing over them in His cross."

CONCLUSION. The departure of truly good men from the world is in some respects like the departure of Christ. It is more or

* See Germ, p. 30.

less voluntary. "I am ready to be offered, and the time of My departure is at hand." It is a going to the Father, in "Whose presence there is fulness of joy; at Whose right hand there are pleasures for evermore." It is an encountering of Satan in his bitterest opposition, knowing that it is final; knowing that if they leave this world uncrushed by him they pass beyond his reach for ever.

Germs of Thought
No. 62   John 14:28

THE DEATH OF THE GOOD A REASON FOR JOY
"If ye loved Me, ye would rejoice, because I said, I go unto the Father."

There are three things connected with this verse which strike us at the outset.

First: The view which Christ had of His death. "I go away." *"I go unto the Father."* *Whence* does He go? From this world, where He had been so wickedly treated, &c. *Whither* does He go? To *"the Father,"* not to *destruction,* not to eternal solitude, not to fellowship with minor souls. But to *"the Father."* *How* does He go? He is not *driven*—He is not forced against His will. *"I go."* Other men are sent to the grave. Christ went—freely went.

Secondly: The sadness of His disciples at the prospect of His death. The eleven were with Him now on the eve of His crucifixion, and sorrow filled their hearts—the sorrow of sympathy, the sorrow of fear. They were troubled; and no wonder.

Thirdly: The consolatory thought which He here addresses to them. That was, that He was going to His Father, going into the happiest conceivable state, into conscious fellowship with Infinite Love. The text contains three general truths.

I —THAT GENUINE LOVE REJOICES IN THE HAPPINESS OF ITS OBJECT

"If ye loved Me, ye would rejoice." The love that is more ready to weep with those that weep, than rejoice with those that rejoice, is not of the genuine type. It is of the essence of tried love to yearn after, to struggle for, and to rejoice in, the happiness of its object. To make happy is the supreme wish of love. This fact is so true to our consciousness that it requires no proof. Its illustrations are manifold. It finds its illustrations—

First: In the creation. Whence sprung the universe? From love. Love created in order to diffuse happiness. Love rejoices in the happiness of the creation.

Secondly: In Christ's mission. Christ came into the world to make happy the objects of Infinite Love. He was love's Messenger to banish the sufferings of humanity, and to fill the world with heavenly joy.

Thirdly: In Christian labour. The strongest wish of all Christian souls, the great end of all Christians, is to make people happy. Happiness is the grand end of all true Church work. Another general truth contained in this passage is—

II —THAT THE HAPPINESS OF MEN DEPENDS UPON FELLOWSHIP WITH THE FATHER

"*I go unto the Father.*" "In Thy presence is fulness of joy; at Thy right hand are pleasures for evermore." It is as impossible for the human soul, constituted as it is, to be happy without God, as it is for the stream to flow on cut off from the fountain, the tree to grow uprooted from the soil, the star to shine severed from its great centre orb. The Infinite Father is the Fountain of all true joy.

First: Happiness is in love. Where there is no love there can be no happiness.

Secondly: The love to produce happiness must be directed to the Father. His perfection delights it; His goodness reciprocates it.

Thirdly: Love for the Father yearns for fellowship with Him. Love always craves for the presence of its object. The happiness of the soul is to be with the Father. The great end of Christ's mediation was that "the Lord God might dwell amongst men." Another general truth contained in this passage is—

III —THAT DEATH INTRODUCES THE GOOD INTO A SPECIALLY CLOSE FELLOWSHIP WITH THE FATHER

"*I go unto the Father.*" But had He not always been with the Father? Yes; but there had been obstructions to the closest fellowship. What were they? As we have already said—

First: There was the body with its infirmities. His body was, as it were, a material veil which lay between Him and the Infinite Father. His hungerings, thirstings, fatigues, tended no doubt to interrupt the fellowship.

Secondly: There was the sinful condition of the world in which He lived. The evils of falsehoods, dishonesties, impieties, blasphemies, which crowded the moral atmosphere of the age in which He lived, tended no doubt to interfere with His fellowship with the Father.

Thirdly: There was the influence of the "principalities and powers of darkness." Satan, the prince of the power of the air, never perhaps deserted Him, assailing Him at every point of His soul. Though He could not tempt Him, yet he assailed Him. No doubt, therefore, His fellowship with God here was interrupted. Now, all these things interrupt the fellowship of the good man with God here. (1.) He has the body with its thick veil intervening. (2.) He has a sinful world whose exhalations darken his moral sky. (3.) He has Satanic influences pressing him away from the Father. But in connection with all this, the godly man has something more. He has what Christ had not. (1.) Worldly cares. (2.) Inward depravity. (3.) Corrupt habits. At death, however, these things are removed ; the soul passes away from the material and corrupt into the immediate presence of its God.

CONCLUSION. We need not sorrow for the departed good. Indeed, if we love them, we ought to rejoice because they have gone to their Father. They are with their Father. Away from clouds and storms and enemies, they are " for ever with the Lord."

No. 63 John 14:31

THE CALMNESS OF CHRIST

" Arise, let us go hence."

" *Go hence.*" Whither ? To the horrors of Gethsemane, to the tortures of hostile tribunals, to the insults of infuriated mobs, to the agonies of the Cross. Considering His *whither*, what a spirit of sublime calmness breathes in these words ! The moral calmness of Christ appears everywhere in His history ; it breathes in His answers to insulting and malignant men, in His sublime silence before His hostile judges, in His unperturbed bearing amidst infuriated mobs. It is indeed the story of His life. His calmness suggests—

I —HIS CONSCIOUSNESS OF THE RECTITUDE OF HIS CHARACTER AND PROCEDURE

Had He been guilty of any moral impropriety, of any wrong against God or man, conscience would have disturbed Him, for remorse creates inner storms. Or, had He had any misgiving as to the rectitude of His procedure in endeavouring to work out the moral restoration of mankind, He might have been disturbed. His calmness, inasmuch as it was not stoicism, or indifference, or the lack of sensibility or passion—for Christ was exquisitely sensitive and emotional—shows that He had a profound sense of the rectitude of His procedure. His calmness suggests—

II —A SETTLED SENSE OF HIS SUBLIME SUPERIORITY

Well He knew the ignorance and depravity, the feebleness and wretchedness of those who were dealing out to Him their scoffings and insults on every hand, and He rose above all; He felt His superiority. Their stormy insults awoke no ripple upon the deep translucent lake of His great nature. His calmness suggests—

III —AN INWARD ASSURANCE OF HIS ULTIMATE SUCCESS

He had an end to accomplish, and had laid His plans by which to reach it. All the opposition which He met with had entered into His calculations before He commenced this sublime enterprise. "He set His face as a flint, and would not fail or be discouraged." He knew that He would "see of the travail of His soul, and be satisfied." He set at defiance all opposition. Though "the heathen raged, and the people imagined a vain thing," He laughed them to scorn. His calmness suggests—

IV —THE HARMONY OF ALL HIS IMPULSES AND POWERS

Because in our depraved natures there are two elements warring against one another—the law of the flesh and the law of the spirit— we are constantly being disturbed, right wars against policy, conscience against impulse, and we are subject to constant tempests, and we get like the troubled sea. Not so with Him. All the elements of His soul moved as serenely and harmoniously as move the planets. He was at One with Himself as well as with His God and the universe. His calmness suggests—

V —HIS COMMANDING CLAIM TO OUR IMITATION

Had He been subject to disturbances of passion, had He been irritated with the conduct of His contemporaries, had He been thrown into a tumult of indignation by the conduct of His enemies, or of fear at the prospect of His awful sufferings and death, He would have failed as an example to us, for we feel that moral calmness is what we all want. God enable us to imitate Christ in this calmness! To be calm amidst the surges of human passion, calm in the prospect of death, what a blessing! A lady once asked Mr. Wesley, "Supposing that you knew that you were to die at twelve o'clock to-morrow night, how would you spend the intervening time?" "How, Madam?" replied he, "why, just as I intend to spend it now. I should preach this evening at Gloucester: and again, at five o'clock to-morrow morning. After that I should ride to Tewkesbury, preach in the afternoon, and meet the societies in the evening. I should then repair to friend Martin's house, who expects to entertain me: converse and pray with the family as usual, retire to my room at ten o'clock, commend myself to my Heavenly Father, lie down to rest, and wake up in glory." "*Arise, let us go hence.*"

John 15:1-8

THE TRUE SPIRITUAL LIFE IN MAN

*(Christ the true Vine, &c.—Jerusalem.—*JOHN xv. 1—27.)

"I am the true Vine, and My Father is the Husbandman," &c.

EXEGETICAL REMARKS.—After the words, "Let us depart hence," it is likely that Jesus and the disciples withdrew from the upper chamber and directed their steps to Jerusalem, at the declivity which descended into the valley of Kedron, near to Gethsemane. Vines abound in this neighbourhood, and it may be that Jesus stopped at one loaded with branches, saw in it an emblem of the vital connection between Him and His genuine disciples.

Ver. 1.—" *I am the true Vine, and My Father is the Husbandman.*" "The point of comparison between Christ and the vine is that organic union by which the life of the trunk becomes that of the branches. As the sap in the branches is that which they draw from the vine, so will the life in the disciples be the life they will derive from Jesus glorified. This comparison might undoubtedly have been borrowed from any other plant. But the vine has a special dignity, resulting from the nobleness of its sap and the excellence of its fruit."—*Godet.* "*The true Vine.*" The word here translated "*true,*" rather means original than genuine. Elsewhere Christ calls Himself the "True Bread," the "True Light," here the true (or original) "*Vine.*" Other men, "from whose thoughts and spirit people may derive some kind of spiritual life," are mere copies, imitations. He is the grand original. Or perhaps, He means this natural vine before Me, is but a shadowy symbol of Myself as a Source of all true spiritual life. "*My Father is the Husbandman.*" Eternal Father, at once the Proprietor and Cultivator of the vine.

Ver. 2.—" *Every branch in Me that beareth not fruit He taketh* (R. V. IT) *away: and every branch that beareth fruit, He purgeth* (R.V. CLEANSETH) *it, that it may bring forth* (R.V. BEAR) *more fruit.*" "Two classes of Christians are here set *forth*—both of them *in Christ*—as truly as the branch is in 'the vine ; but while the one class bears fruit, the other bears none. The natural husbandry will sufficiently explain the cause of this difference. A graft may be *mechanically attached* to a fruit-tree, and yet take no vital hold of it, and have no *vital connection* with it. In that case, receiving none of the juices of the tree —no vegetable sap from the stem—it can bear no fruit. Such merely mechanical attachment of the True Vine is that of all who believe in the truths of Christianity, and are in visible membership with the Church of Christ, but having no living faith in Jesus nor desire for His salvation, open not their souls to the spiritual life of which He is the Source, take no vital hold of Him, and have no living union to Him."—*Brown.*

Ver. 3.—" *Now* (R. V. ALREADY) *ye are clean through* (R. V. BECAUSE OF) *the word which I have spoken unto you.*" " *Ye,*"—My disciples, in contradistinction to others. The vine-dresser has two things to do—cut off the rotten and the redundant branches, and trim the others of all excrescences that may hinder growth. These disciples had been thus pruned or cleansed.

Ver. 4.—" *Abide in Me, and I in you.* As the branch cannot bear fruit of itself, except it abide in the vine ; no more* (R. V. SO NEITHER) *can ye, except ye abide in Me.*" If I withdraw from you, you would die ; if you withdraw from Me, you would wither and rot. We must remain in vital connection.

Ver. 5.—" *I am the Vine, ye are the branches : He that abideth in Me, and I in him, the same bringeth forth* (R. V. BEARETH) *much fruit.*" Here is a repetition of what He had said before, and perhaps it is repeated in answer to some question which His previous remarks had started. " *For without* (R. V. APART FROM) *Me ye can do nothing.*" What can the branch produce cut off from the trunk ?

Ver. 6.—" *If a man abide not in Me, he is cast forth as a branch, and is withered.*" When a branch is cut from the trunk, of what service is it but to be burnt ? And when a soul is detached from Christ it is utterly worthless.

Ver. 7.—" *If ye abide in Me, and My words abide in you, ye shall ask what ye will, and* (R. V. ASK WHATSO-EVER YE WILL) *it shall be done unto you.*" Here is a large promise—a promise to have whatever we ask for, if we remain in vital connection with Christ.

Ver. 8.—" *Herein is My Father glorified, that ye bear much fruit ; so shall ye be My disciples."* Fruitfulness, in spiritual virtues and usefulness, is the grand end to be secured by this connection with Christ. This fruitfulness honours the Father.

HOMILETICS

This beautiful passage suggests the following remarks in relation to *The True Spiritual Life in Man* :—

I —THAT MAN'S SPIRITUAL LIFE IS DERIVED FROM CHRIST

Religion is not a mere creed or form ;—it is a life, and the life is a *"branch"* of Christ's life. It grows out of Him. The vital sap—the spirit—comes from Christ as the Root, and runs through every branch, leaf, and fibre. There is no true spiritual life where Christ's Spirit is not the inspiration. "Without Me," &c. It teaches—

II —THAT MAN'S SPIRITUAL LIFE IS DEVELOPED IN FRUITFULNESS

" Every branch in Me that beareth not fruit He taketh away." The production of fruit is what is required ; it is not to pass off in foliage and blossom—it is to yield fruit. Unless we yield fruit we are worthless, and doomed to destruction. What is the fruit ? " Love, joy, peace, long-suffering, gentleness, goodness, faith, meekness, temperance." It teaches—

III —THAT THIS FRUITFULNESS IS PRODUCED BY THE JOINT AGENCY OF GOD AND MAN

First : Man must seek an abiding connection with Christ in order to produce it. *" The branch cannot bear fruit of itself, except it abide in the vine."* Cut the branch from the tree, it will wither and rot. Abide in Me.

Secondly : God must act the part of the great Husbandman in order to produce it. The mere abiding in Christ will not do of itself. *" Every branch in Me that beareth not fruit He taketh away : and every branch that beareth fruit, He purgeth it, that it may bring forth more fruit."* He prunes : " Unto him that hath shall be given."

John 15:9-11

CHRIST'S LOVE FOR HIS DISCIPLES

" As the Father hath loved Me," &c.

EXEGETICAL REMARKS.—Ver. 9.— *" As* (R. V. EVEN AS) *the Father hath loved Me, so have I* (R. V. I ALSO HAVE) *loved you."* (See chap. xvii. 26.) " As the Father loved Me, I also loved you : abide in My love."—DAVIDSON. *"Con-tinue* (R. V. ABIDE) *ye in My love."*

That is, continue to love Me : abide in the possession, the enjoyment of it.

Ver. 10.—*" If ye keep My com-mandments, ye shall abide in My love ; even as I have kept My Father's com-mandments, and abide in His love."* Here is a law. The way not only to retain but strengthen the love that we have for another is to practise, as far as we can, his wishes and his will. Disobedience is the death of love.

Ver. 11.—"*These things have I spoken unto you, that My joy might remain* (R. V. MAY BE) *in you.*" The joy that He had in loving and obey-ing His Father He would have them to possess and enjoy. "*That your joy might* (R. V. MAY) *be full*" (R. V. FULFILLED). The highest joy of an intelligent being is in loving and being loved—loving the best Being, and being loved by Him.

HOMILETICS

The subject of these words is, *Christ's Love for His disciples;* and there are three remarks suggested concerning it.

I —THAT IT IS LIKE THE LOVE THE FATHER HAS FOR HIM

"*As the Father hath loved Me, so have I loved you.*"

"This is My beloved Son, in Whom I am well pleased." No being in the universe is so dear to the Infinite heart as Christ. Does Christ mean by this—

First: That as *Really* as the Father loves Me, I love you? The reality of the Father's love for Him was a grand reality attested by His own consciousness. He could not doubt it. It was proved to Him in a thousand ways, in every faculty and fact of His life. But not less really did He love His disciples. His love for them was a mighty, ever-operating force within Him. Or does He mean—

Secondly: That as *Disinterestedly* as the Father loves Me, I love you? The Father's love for Christ was absolutely and spontaneously unselfish, so was Christ's love for His disciples. There was nothing in them to merit His affection, nothing in them to render Him more glorious or more happy. Another remark suggested concerning Christ's love for His disciples is—

II —THAT IT IS PERPETUATED BY OBEDIENCE TO HIS COMMANDS

"*If ye keep My commandments, ye shall abide in My love; even as I have kept My Father's commandments, and abide in His love.*" How does Christ retain the love of His Father? By working out His will. It would seem as if the Father's love, great though it be, would wane and die if the Son ceased to obey. So with Christ's love towards His disciples. Its continuance depends upon a practical fulfilment of His will. It seems almost a law of mind that love must work to live. If it remain in the mind merely as a sentiment or emotion, it would perish. The mother's love is kept alive by working for her children. When the work ceases the maternal affection wanes. If we would keep the love of Christ strong in the heart we must keep His commandments. No emotion of the soul will strike root, live and grow, only as it is translated into acts. Love only lives in deeds. Still more, another remark suggested concerning Christ's love for His disciples is—

III — THAT IT YEARNS TO MAKE ITS OBJECTS HAPPY

" *These things have I spoken unto you, that My joy might remain in you, and that your joy might be full.*" It is the essence of love to glow with desires for the happiness of its object. See this in the unwearied services of parents; see it also in the countless efforts of genuine philanthropy. In Christ's love for man this desire is unquenchable and ever-operating. To make men happy was the grand object of His advent to earth. He was not so much the Teacher of the intellect, as the Inspirer of the heart. He poured ideas into the understanding in order that they might kindle love in the soul. He knew and He taught that men could only be happy as they loved, as He loved, disinterestedly, continuously, practically. No truth is more profoundly philosophic, than that human happiness is in love. No truth is more clear in the Scripture than this, that Christ came to fill the human heart with Divine love. "I am come that ye might have life." "He came to heal the broken-hearted, preach deliverance to the captives, recovery of the sight to the blind, to set at liberty them that are bruised, and to preach the acceptable year of the Lord." Christ wishes His disciples not only to be happy, but to be full of happiness. " *That your joy might be full.*" All saddening emotions are foreign to Christliness. Christliness is sunshine, music, rapture.

John 15:12-16

BROTHERLY LOVE

"This is My commandment, That ye love one another," &c.—xv. 12—16.

EXEGETICAL REMARKS.—Ver. 13.— "*Greater love hath no man than this, that a man lay down his life for his friends.*" There is a greater love than this; the love which Christ had, for He laid down His life for His enemies. But no mere man has a greater love than that which sacrifices life for friends. "Scarcely for a righteous man would one die; yet peradventure, for a good man, some would even dare to die." Love shows its strength in sacrifice. Never does it appear so strong as when it sacrifices life.

Ver. 14.—"*Ye are My friends, if ye do whatsoever*(R. V. THE THINGS WHICH) *I command you.*" The accent is not on the condition, "*if ye do,*" but upon the statement, "*Ye are My friends,*" as though Jesus meant to say, "It was not without a reason that I just now

said *for his friends* (ver. 13), for this is really the relation I have borne to you." And what is there more touching in domestic life, than a master who, finding a servant really faithful, raises him to the rights and title of a friend?

Ver. 15.—"*Henceforth I call you not* (R. V. NO LONGER DO I CALL YOU) *servants; for the servant knoweth not what his lord doeth: but I have called you friends; for all things that I have heard of* (R. V. I HEARD FROM) *My Father I have made known unto you.*" This proves the reality of the statement. He had bestowed upon them an unbounded confidence, by communicating to them all that the Father had revealed to Him regarding the great work for which He sent Him.

"Undoubtedly there were still many

things of which they were not yet informed (xiv. 12). But it was not from want of confidence and love that He had not revealed these also, but to spare them in their state of weakness, and because another alone could fulfil this task. The title, "*My friends*," used in Luke xii. 4, long before the present moment has been adduced in objection to this 'ou'kéti' (I *no more call you*) ; as though the tendency to make them His friends had not existed from the very first, and could have failed to manifest itself from time to time ! It has also been objected that the apostles continued to call themselves *servants of Jesus Christ*, as though when the master chooses to make his servant a friend, the latter is not at all the more bound to remind himself and others of his real condition."—*Godet*.

Ver. 16.—"*Ye have not chosen* (R. V. DID NOT CHOOSE) *Me, but I have chosen* (R. V. CHOSE) *you*." "*Chosen*," here, does not point to eternal predestination, but to the fact that He selected these disciples of His from their various worldly avocations, such as fishermen, tax-gatherers, &c. "*And ordained* (R. V. APPOINTED) *you*." Appointed you for what ? To be fruitful : "*That you should go and bring forth* (R. V. BEAR) *fruit*." To be permanently fruitful. "*Your fruit should remain*" (R. V. ABIDE). And be successful in prayer : "*That whatsoever ye shall ask of the Father in My name, He will* (R. V. MAY) *give it you*." "*In My name*." This may mean in My character, in My spirit. It is certain that the man who prays to the everlasting Father in the true spirit of Christ, will have what he requires, for he will ask for the right *thing* in the right *spirit*, and for the right *reason*.

HOMILETICS

The subject of these words is *Brotherly Love*. "*This is My commandment, That ye love one another*." This is repeated in verse 17 also. "I command you, that ye love one another." The following remarks are suggested concerning the love that Christ's disciples should have for one another :—

I —THAT IT HAS THE HIGHEST MODEL

"*As I have loved you*." How did Christ love ?

First : Disinterestedly. There was not a taint of selfishness in His love. He looked for no compensation, no advantage.

Secondly : Earnestly. It was an all-pervading, all-commanding passion. It was a zeal consuming Him.

Thirdly : Practically. It was a love that slept not as an emotion in the heart ; not a love that expended itself in words and professions ; it was a love that worked all the faculties to the utmost ; a love that led Him to the sacrifice of Himself. This is the kind of love we should have one toward another. This is the brotherly love that unites Christ's disciples together, honours Him and blesses the world with the most beneficent influences. Concerning this love it is suggested—

II —THAT IT FORMS THE HIGHEST FRIENDSHIP

"*Greater love hath no man than this, that a man lay down his life for his friends.** *Ye are My friends, if ye do whatsoever I command*

* See Germ, p. 37.

you. Henceforth I call you not servants." * It not only establishes a friendship between themselves, but a friendship between them and Christ. *"I call you not servants, but I have called you friends."*

First: A true friendship between man and man is the greatest blessing on earth.

Secondly: A friendship between man and Christ is the consummation of man's well-being. If Christ is my Friend what want I more? Concerning this love it is suggested —

III —THAT IT HAS THE HIGHEST SOURCE

" Ye have not chosen Me, but I have chosen you." We did not chose to love Christ first, but He chose to love us. His love to us generates our love to Him. *" We love Him because He first loved us."* He chose His first disciples from their worldly avocations and called them into His circle; this inspired them with His love. Men will never love one another properly until Christ sheds abroad His love in their hearts. He is to all His disciples what the sun is to the planets; around Him they revolve, and from Him derive their life and unity. They are united one to another by the bonds that unite them to Christ. Concerning this love it is suggested—

IV —THAT IT REALIZES THE HIGHEST GOOD

First: Spiritual fruitfulness. *" Ordained you, that you should go and bring forth fruit."* The fruit involves two things—(1.) The highest excellence of character. (2.) The highest usefulness of life. Rendering others the highest service.

Secondly: Successful prayer. *" Whatsoever ye shall ask of the Father in My name, He may give it you."* There is no true prayer that is not offered in the name and spirit of Christ, the spirit of reverence, humility, earnestness, submission to the Divine will. And no such prayer is offered in vain. The Father gives whatever you ask.

Germs of Thought
No. 64   John 15:13, 14

DEMONSTRATION OF FRIENDSHIP DIVINE AND HUMAN

" Greater love hath no man than this, that a man lay down his life for his friends. Ye are My friends, if ye do whatsoever I command you."—xv. 13, 14.

In the text Christ indicates the strength of His friendship for His disciples. There is a real friendship between Christ and His people. There is between them (1.) a mutual love, (2.) a concurrence of sympathy, (3.) a unity of aims. The words lead us to make two remarks—

I —CHRIST DEMONSTRATES HIS LOVE TO MAN BY DYING

" Greater love hath no man than this, that a man lay down his life for his friends." Here He states—

* See Germ, p. 39.

(1.) The utmost limit of human love. Nothing is felt by man to be more precious than his life. Everything he has will he sacrifice for this. A love that will lead to the sacrifice of this is a love in its highest human measure. History has very few examples of it. Indeed there is only one instance known to me in the whole history of eighteen centuries, and even that may be fabulous. I refer to Damon and Pythias, two bold Pythagoreans of Syracuse. It is said that Pythias being condemned to death by Dionysius, the tyrant of Syracuse, begged to be allowed to go home for the purpose of arranging his affairs. Damon pledged his own life for the re-appearance of his friend. Dionysius accepted the pledge, and Pythias returned just in time to save Damon from death. This noble example of friendship so struck the ruthless tyrant that he not only pardoned Pythias, but desired to be admitted into their friendship. According to Christ, Damon in this instance showed the highest degree of human love. Perhaps had occasion required it, the friendship existing between David and Jonathan would have risen to the same degree.

(2.) Christ's love transcended the limits of human love. He laid down His life for *enemies*. "God commendeth His love to us, in that while we were yet sinners, Christ died for us." There is nothing in human history approaching this. "Scarcely for a righteous man would one die, yet peradventure for a good man some would even dare to die." The sublimest imagination cannot conceive of a higher love than this: "Heaven is love." This transcendent love is—

First: The love of *compassion*. There could be neither gratitude nor esteem in it, for the subjects are all enemies, and hideous in wickedness. This transcendent love is—

Secondly: The love of *disinterestedness*. He had nothing to gain by it. His glory and happiness were infinite, and admitted of no enhancement. "Ye know the grace of our Lord Jesus Christ," etc.

II —MAN DEMONSTRATES HIS LOVE TO CHRIST BY OBEYING

" *Ye are My friends, if ye do whatsoever I command you.*" Surely all men ought to love Christ. The demonstration of His transcendent love is not only designed to destroy all indifference towards Him, but to generate in every heart the highest measure of love to Him. Where this love exists, and it should exist everywhere, it demonstrates itself in *obedience*. The obedience will always be marked by three things—

First: By *heartiness*. Obedience will be nothing more than the expression of love. It will be a thing not of "letter," but of spirit. Not so much a thing of outward act as an inspiration of soul. "Love is the fulfilling of the law." Where love is, there will be obedience to Christ, though the tongue be sealed, and the hand be paralysed. The obedience should be marked—

Secondly: By *cheerfulness*. Where this love is, obedience to Christ is the highest *gratification* of the soul. The first question love asks is, What shall I do to please the object? "Lord, what wilt Thou have me to do?" When the heart is "enlarged" with love, man runs in the way of Christ's commandments. Obedience to Christ is the "meat" and "drink," the bread and wine, of a loving soul. Practical Christianity is happiness. The obedience should be marked—

Thirdly: By *entireness*. "*Whatsoever I command you.*" Love does not sort duties, does not weigh and measure them, does not say, "I will do so much, and no more." It bounds into the "*whatsoever.*" Whatsoever the object wishes, even unto death, it shall be done. Hence Christian martyrdom.

CONCLUSION. This subject—

First: Supplies the test of Christian piety. Christian piety is not a ritualism, however becoming; not a theology, however Scriptural; it is a *love* to Christ that shows itself in a hearty, cheerful, universal obedience. This subject—

Secondly: Indicates the true method of preaching. What is the true work of the Gospel minister? So to exhibit Christ's love to human souls as to awaken in them love to Him. Love is the central doctrine of Christianity: love is the renovating power of souls; love is the soul of all excellence and the fountain of all joy.

> "Love is God's seal upon the universe,
> The hand and sign of His omnipotence;
> And hearts enshrining love the most on earth,
> Find here the most of heaven."—*Swain.*

No. 65 John 15:15

MAN'S RELATION OF SERVITUDE AND FRIENDSHIP TO CHRIST COMPARED

"Henceforth I call you not servants, ... but I have called you friends."—

The whole human race may be divided into two classes, and these are represented by the two words in the text, "*Servants*" and "*Friends.*" All human beings have to do with Christ, and their service must be either that of slaves or of friends. Our Lord here intimates the superiority of the one relationship to the other. This superiority will be obvious by comparing the relationships together.

I—THE ONE IS LEGAL, THE OTHER IS LOVING

The master treats his slave, and the slave treats him, according to legal contract. The servant works by rule, and the master treats him accordingly; the slave lives and works in the letter of the contract, he goes not a step beyond it. But the service of the *friend* is irrespective of all prescriptive rules, of all legal arrangements. He does not feel himself to be under the law at all, and although he does more real hard work in the service of his friend than that of the slave in the employ of his master, he does it neither by enactment or law; love is his inspiration, and love is his law.

II —THE ONE IS WATCHED, THE OTHER IS TRUSTED

The master keeps his eye upon the slave; he knows that he is not the character to be trusted, he is a mere eye-servant. If the contracted work is to be done he is to be kept up to it by force. Not so with the friend; he is trusted, he is thrown upon his love, upon his honour, his sense of gratitude and justice. Thus Christ treats His disciples; He does not tell them how much to do, or how to do it. He trusts to their love, knowing that if they love Him they will keep His commandments. This is the true way to treat men—trust them. Thus Dr. Arnold treated his boys at Rugby, and thus all whom Providence has put in authority over men should treat their subordinates, in order to get from them the highest service they can render.

III —THE ONE IS DISTANT, THE OTHER IS NEAR

The master keeps his servant at a distance, he stands on his authority, gives out his orders, and insists on their discharge. They live not only in different apartments, but in different mental worlds. Not so with the friend—the friend is near to the heart. An old philosopher defined friendship as the existence of two souls in one body. Thus near are Christ's disciples to Him. "The servant," He says, "knoweth not what his Lord doeth, . . but all things that I do I have made known unto you." How close and vital the connection! "Shall I hide from Abraham that thing which I do?" said God.

IV —THE ONE IS USED, THE OTHER USES

The master uses his slave, uses him as he does a piece of machinery; he has no tender interest in him. All he cares for is what benefits he can extract from his service; the slave is used— used as a beast of burden. But the friend is *using*. All his services, as a true friend, answer his own purpose, conduce to his own happiness of soul. He acts from love, and love, like the philosopher's stone, turns the commonest things into moral gold, to enrich his own heart. Thus it is with Christ's disciples: all their efforts to serve Him serve themselves. "All things are yours," life, death, &c. Everything turns to the real use of those who are the friends of Christ.

V —THE ONE IS COERCED, THE OTHER IS FREE

The slave is not free in his work; he would not serve his master if he could help it. He is placed under considerations that force him to do his work. But the service of the friend is free, he would not but do what he does, and his desires to render service transcend his abilities. Thus it is with Christ's disciples. "He that is joined to the Lord is one spirit." The love of Christ constrains them; they welcome the slightest intimation of duty from their Lord.

CONCLUSION. What is our relationship to Christ—that of servitude or friendship? All must serve Him, either *against* their will, or *by* their will. The former is the condition of devils, the latter that of holy Saints and blessed Angels.

John 15:17-25

KOSMOS: UNREGENERATED HUMANITY

"These things I command you, that ye love one another," &c.—xv. 17—25.

EXEGETICAL REMARKS.—Ver. 17.— "*These things I command you, that ye love* (R. V. MAY LOVE) *one another.*" This is a repetition of the twelfth verse. The duty of brotherly love is here re-stated, probably with a view to the persecutions which Christ proceeds to foretell. The meaning may be, Love one another, for the world hates you.

Vers. 18, 19.—"*If the world hate* (R. V. HATETH) *you, ye know that it hated* (R. V. HATH HATED) *Me before it hated you. If ye were of the world, the world would love his* (R. V. ITS) *own: but because ye are not of the world, but I have chosen* (R. V. CHOSE) *you out of the world, therefore the world hateth you.*" "The '*if*' suggests no doubt of the fact, but prepares them for the terrible reality, and furnishes them the antidote." The word "*world*"— *Kosmos*—here does not mean the physical frame of the world, the globe, nor the human race which it is frequently employed to represent, but the corruptive portion of the race —unregenerate humanity. It is used five times in this nineteenth verse. It is that vast section of humanity of which Satan is the prince; it is the kingdom of evil.

Ver. 20.—"*Remember the word that I said unto you, The* (R. V. A) *servant is not greater than his Lord. If they have persecuted Me, they will also persecute you; if they have kept My saying* (R. V. KEPT MY WORD), *they will keep yours also.*" Elsewhere it is said, "If they have called the master of the house Beelzebub, how much more shall they call them of his household." (Matt. x. 25.)

Ver. 21.—"*But all these things will they do unto you for My name's sake, because they know not Him that sent Me.*" The Christians in the opening of the second century were put to death for professing to be Christians, and because they would not renounce the name. Pliny wrote to Trajan, that this was his practice in Bithynia. Athenagoras pleaded before the heathen magistrates that the Christians should not be punished for bearing the name when in other respects they were blameless. Tertullian says in the second century, even the name was hated in men perfectly innocent. The disciples were called Christians, and Peter says, "If any man suffer as a Christian, let him not be ashamed." (1 Peter iv. 16.) James asks, "Do they not blaspheme that worthy name by which ye are called?" (James ii. 7.)

Ver. 22.—"*If I had not come and*

spoken unto them, they had not had sin: but now they have no cloke (R. V. EXCUSE) *for their sin.*" Our Lord here declares that their sinfulness was wonderfully augmented in consequence of His appearing amongst them. Had He not come they would have been amongst the ordinary class of sinners, which God of old overlooked in the times of ignorance. (Acts xv. 31.)

Ver. 23.—"*He that hateth Me hateth My Father also.*" Hatred against the disciples is hatred against their Master, and hatred against Him is hatred against God the Father.

Ver. 24.—"*If I had not done among them the works which none other man* (R. V. OMITS MAN) *did, they had not had sin: but now have they both seen and* hated both Me and My Father." What wonderful works He did ! (See chaps. v. 36 ; ix. 3, 4 ; x. 21—37 ; xiv. 10.) His great works were great proofs of His superhuman power, and mission.

Ver. 25.—"*But this cometh to pass, that the word might* (R. V. MAY) *be fulfilled that is written in their law, They hated me without a cause.*" The word "may" is better than might: and the words, *this cometh to pass*, which are italicised should be omitted. The sense is, not that their hatred came to pass in order to fulfil an old Scripture, but it so turned out that an old Scripture was illustrated by it. The passage referred to is found in Psalms lxix. 4 ; and xxxv. 19. There was no just reason for their hatred of Him.

HOMILETICS

These verses present this *Kosmos* or *Unregenerate Humanity* in two striking aspects, as glowing with hate and as loaded with responsibility.

I —AS GLOWING WITH HATE

"*The world hateth you.*"

The words suggest the following remarks concerning this hatred.

First: It was a hatred of goodness. To hate the mean, the selfish, the false, the dishonest, and morally dishonourable would be right. But evil was not the object of their hatred. (1.) It was good as embodied in the life of Christ. "*It hated Me before it hated you.*" How deep, burning, persistent, and cruelly operative was the enmity which unregenerate men exhibited towards Christ, from His birth in Bethlehem to His Cross on Calvary ! (2.) It was good as reflected in His disciples. Just so far as they imbibed, and reflected, the spirit of Christ were they hated. "*All these things will they do unto you for My name's sake.*" Because of what they see of Me in you. The words suggest—

Secondly: It was a hatred developed in persecution. It was not a hatred that slumbered in a passion or that went off even in abusive language ; it prompted the infliction of the greatest cruelties. The history of true Christians in all ages has been a history of persecution. The words suggest—

Thirdly : It was a hatred without a just reason. "*They hated Me without a cause.*" Of course they had "*cause.*" The doctrines of goodness clashed with their deep-rooted prejudices, the policy of goodness with their daily procedure ; the eternal principles of goodness flashed on their consciences and exposed their wickedness. But their "*cause*" was the very reason why they ought to have loved

Christ. Christ knew and stated the cause of the hatred. "*If ye were of the world, the world would love his own: but because ye are not of the world, but I have chosen you out of the world, therefore the world hateth you.*"* The words suggest—

Fourthly : It was a hatred forming a strong reason for brotherly love amongst the disciples. Christ begins His forewarning them of it by urging them to love one another. "*These things I command you, that ye love one another.*" As your enemies outside of you are strong in their passionate hostility towards you, be you compactly welded together in mutual love. Unity is strength.

The verses present Unregenerate Humanity,—

II —AS LOADED WITH RESPONSIBILITY

"*If I had not come and spoken unto them, they had not had sin.*" These words must of course be taken in their comparative sense. Before He came amongst them the guilt of their nation had been augmenting for centuries, and they had been filling up the measure of their iniquities. But great as was their sin before He came, it was trifling compared to it now since His advent amongst them.

First : Had He not come, they would not have known the sin of hating Him. Hatred towards the best of beings, the incarnation of goodness, is sin in its most malignant form ; it was the culmination of human depravity. But had they not known Him they could not have hated Him ; the heart is dead to all objects outside the region of knowledge.

Secondly : Had He not come, they would not have rejected Him. "He came to His own, and His own received Him not." The rejection of Him involved the most Wicked Folly, the most Heartless Ingratitude, the most Daring Impiety. "If they which despised Moses' law died without mercy under two witnesses, of how much sorer punishment suppose ye shall he be thought worthy that hath trodden under foot the Son of God, and done despite unto the Holy Ghost ? "

Thirdly : Had He not come, they would not have crucified Him. What crime on the long black catalogue of human wickedness is to be compared to this ?

CONCLUSION. (1.) Good men, accept the moral hostility of the unregenerate world. Your great Master taught you to accept it. It is in truth a test of your character, and an evidence of your Christliness. "Woe unto you when all men speak well of you." (2.) Nominal Christians, read your doom ! Christ has come to you, and you have hated Him ; you have rejected Him ; you have crucified Him "afresh," and your responsibility is tremendous. "Woe unto thee, Chorazin ! woe unto thee, Bethsaida ! for if the mighty works which were done in you had been done in Tyre and Sidon, they would have repented long ago."

* See Germ, p. 44.

Germs of Thought
No. 66   John 15:19

THE PEDIGREE AND POSITION OF TRUE MEN

"If ye were of the world, the world would love his own : but because ye are not of the world, but I have chosen you out of the world, therefore the world hateth you."—xv. 19.

The text leads us to make two remarks concerning the *Pedigree* and *Position* of true men.

I —THE PEDIGREE OF TRUE MEN

They have been brought out of the world by Christ. "*I have chosen you out of the world.*"

First: They were once in the world. They were members of that vast assemblage of human beings who are in the "gall of bitterness, and in the bond of iniquity." That world is characterized by three things—(1.) Practical atheism. They who make up this world are practically without God. Though some of them may not be avowed atheists, they live without Him, and form their plans and work them out as if He existed not. "God is not in all their thoughts." They go "into this city and that, and buy and sell, and get gain," and never take Him into their counsels or calculations. It is characterized by—(2.) An imperial materialism. They have no practical recognition of a spiritual universe, spiritual relationship, and spiritual obligation. They are canopied by matter. They "walk after the flesh;" they live to the flesh. They seek their happiness, their wealth, their dignity, in earthly things. They endeavour to get the bread of their being, the supreme good, out of stones. It is characterized by—(3.) A dominant selfishness. Each one is governed by selfish interests. Self-interest is the goal towards which each directs his steps; self is the idol at whose shrine each renders his devotions.

Secondly : They have been brought out of the world by Christ. Out of this world, from this vast body of human beings, whose lives are all characterized by practical atheism, imperial materialism, and dominant selfishness, Christ brought His disciples, and brings all true men now. No one but Christ can bring men out of such a state. Philosophy, civilization, natural religion—all these are powerless. Christ alone has proved equal to the task. He penetrates men with the idea of the true God. He draws the curtain of materialism, and reveals the spiritual world. He destroys the selfishness, and constrains men with His own love. This work of Christ is represented by an Emancipation, a Resurrection, a Regeneration, a Creation—and none of these appellatives are too strong.

The words lead us to notice—

II —THE POSITION OF TRUE MEN

They are rendered repugnant to the world by Christ. "*Because ye are not of the world, but I have chosen you out of the world, therefore the world hateth you.*" The words imply—

First : That the hatred of the world to true men is of the same *kind* as that which Christ experienced. Towards Christ it showed itself in slander, ridicule, misrepresentation, insults, and cruelties. Its genius is persecution. The forms of persecution change, but the spirit remains. If it is prevented from mangling the body, it will mangle the reputation. Venom rankles on from age to age, in the serpent's seed against that of the woman. The words imply—

Secondly : That the hatred of the world to true men is for the same *reason* as that which Christ experienced. Why did the world hate Christ ? Because (1.) His purity condemned their depravity, (2.) His benevolence their selfishness, (3.) His humility their pride, (4.) His truth their prejudices, and (5.) His spirituality their carnal pleasures. For these reasons, now, the world hates true men. "Cain was of that wicked one, and slew his brother." And wherefore slew he him ? Because his own works were evil, and his brother's righteous. This is the philosophy.

John 15:26, 27

THE GREAT WORLD-RESTORING SPIRIT

"But when the Comforter is come, whom I will send unto you," &c.— xv. 26, 27.

EXEGETICAL REMARKS.—Ver. 26.— "*But when the Comforter is come.*" Read Advocate instead of Comforter. "*Whom I will send unto you from the Father.*" What childish and withal presumptuous speculations have technical theologians indulged in, in what is called the *procession* of the Holy Ghost ! For example, the Greek Church held the dogma that the Spirit proceeded from the Father only through the Son : while the Latin Church insisted that He proceeded from the Father and the Son : and the one short word *Filioque*, which the latter would exclude and the former insert in the Creed, was the cause of the great schism between the Eastern and the Western Churches. "*Even the Spirit of truth, which proceedeth from the Father.*" Truth is a small word, but it is an infinite thing ; it is the underlying, unchangeable

reality in the great universe of thought. In character this Spirit is eternal reality in the universe of shadows, semblances, and phenomena. "*He shall testify* (R. V. BEAR WITNESS) *of Me.*" Dr. *Browne* says :—"This refers to that glorious Pentecostal attestation of the Messiahship of the Lord Jesus which in a few days gave birth to a flourishing Christian Church in the murderous capital itself, and the speedy diffusion of it far and wide."

Ver. 27.—"*And ye also shall bear* (R. V. ALSO BEAR) *witness, because ye have been with Me from the beginning.*" "The apostles should bear witness by their inspired records of Christ's life, which we have in the Gospel narratives. This they should do, not independently of the Spirit, but under His prompting, and yet individually, giving each his own testimony."

HOMILETICS

Here we have presented to us *The Great World-Restoring Spirit*, the Spirit that was striving with men in the antediluvian age, and with men in every subsequent age, and that came with new arguments and power after our Saviour's ascension to heaven. Here we have—

I —HIS ADVENT FORETOLD

" *When the Comforter is come, whom I will send unto you.*"

First: The prediction here given was to comfort them in the prospect of the persecution to which He had just directed their attention. They are given to understand that however great their approaching trials may be, and though He Himself was about departing from them, One would soon come to them from His Father, Who would be *all sufficient* for their help.

Secondly: The prediction here given was strikingly fulfilled on the day of Pentecost, in connection with the preaching of Peter. " And when the day of Pentecost was fully come, they were all with one accord in one place. And suddenly there came a sound from heaven as of a rushing mighty wind, and it filled all the house where they were sitting. And there appeared unto them cloven tongues as of fire, and it sat upon each of them. And they were all filled with the Holy Ghost, and began to speak with other tongues, as the Spirit gave them utterance." Here we have—

II —HIS CHARACTER PORTRAYED

" *The Spirit of Truth.*" There is a spirit of *lying* abroad in the world, sowing the seeds of error in human souls, and cultivating them into briars and thorns, into poisonous weeds, and Upas trees. But here is the Spirit of Truth, who is also abroad and at work.

First: He is *infallible* truth. Truth without any admixture of error or impurity. His ideas and His affections, so to say, are in perfect accord with eternal fact.

Secondly: He is *redemptive* truth. His truth is to open the eyes of ignorance, to break the chains of bondage, to cleanse the heart from impurities, to deliver the conscience from guilt! In one word, to restore the soul to the Knowledge, the Image, the Friendship, and the Enjoyment of the great God. Here we have—

III —HIS WORK INDICATED

First: His work is that of an *Advocate*. He goes into the Court of human conscience, and there He pleads for spirituality, benevolence, righteousness, God, against worldliness, selfishness, wrong, the devil. Sometimes He pleads in whispers, sometimes in thunder. Always is He earnest and persevering. He inspires

His ministers to say, "We beseech you in Christ's stead, be ye reconciled unto God."

Secondly : His work is that of a *Witness.* A witness for Christ, for the perfection of His character, the purity of His doctrines, and the beneficence of His influence. He does this through the teaching, the miraculous works, the moral triumphs, and the noble lives of those whom He inspired as the Apostles of Christ.

CONCLUSION. Let the assurance that this Restoring Spirit is in the world encourage us in our efforts to spread truth, and in our trials to be magnanimous and patient.

John 16:1-6

CHRIST'S METHOD OF PREPARING HIS DISCIPLES FOR HIS DEPARTURE

(*Persecution foretold further promise of the Holy Spirit.—Jerusalem.—*JOHN xvi. 1—33.)

"These things have I spoken unto you, that ye should not be offended," &c.

EXEGETICAL REMARKS.—Ver. 1.— "*These things have I spoken unto you, that ye should not be offended*". (R. V. MADE TO STUMBLE). "'*These things.*' The reference appears to be not to the whole revelation of the vital union of the believer with Christ."—*Westcott.* "We find here expressed the ultimate aim of all that has been said from chap. xv. 18 onwards, and the point of view is here shown under which all must be viewed. The design was, namely, to obviate the offence which the hatred of the Jews could not fail to occasion, especially as authority and scientific knowledge were on their side. '*These things*' do not refer merely to the fore-announcement of their hatred; it includes also everything that had been said to place their hatred in the true light, as well as the help which had been promised in the sending of the Paraclete."—*Hengstenberg.* Ver. 2.—"*They shall put you out of the synagogues: yea, the time* (R. V. HOUR) *cometh, that whosoever killeth you will* (R. V. SHALL) *think that he doeth God service*" (R. V. OFFERETH SERVICE UNTO GOD). He will think that he is offering a religious service unto God, as Saul of Tarsus did (Acts xxvi. 9, 10 ; Gal. i. 9, 10 ; Phil. iii. 6).

Ver. 3.—"*And these things will they do unto you, because they have not known the Father, nor Me.*" The persecution will result from ignorance. This is nearly a verbal repetition of chap. xv. 21. Ver. 4.—"*But these things have I told* (R. V. SPOKEN UNTO) *you, that when the time* (R. V. THEIR HOUR) *shall* (R. V. IS) *come, ye may remember that I told you of them* (R. V. HOW THAT I TOLD YOU). *And these things I said not unto you at* (R. V. FROM) *the beginning, because I was with you.*" "You will be confirmed in your faith, and strengthened in courage. He had said it pretty clearly (Luke vi. 22), but not so nakedly as in ver. 2." —*Brown.* Ver. 5.—"*But now I go My way to* (R. V. I GO UNTO) *Him that sent Me ; and none of you asketh Me, Whither goest Thou ?* " As I gave you to understand in chap. xiv., and none of you asketh Me where I go. They were inquisitive while they thought only of His going to some city to be crowned King, or otherwise ; but now that He had opened to them the plan for departure, that He was going to the Father, they are mute on the subject; and are overcome with sorrow on their own account, when they ought to be glad."

Ver. 6.—" *Because* (R. V. BUT BE-CAUSE) *I have said* (R. V. SPOKEN) *these things unto you, sorrow hath filled your heart.*" The sorrow was reason-able, but the word *filled* implies that it was excessive and reprovable. But He goes on to express with a stronger emphasis the consolation He had already proffered, namely, the coming of the Comforter.

HOMILETICS

These verses furnish us with a specimen of *Christ's Method of dealing with His disciples.* Observe—

I —CHRIST FORETELLS HIS DISCIPLES OF APPROACHING EVILS, NOT TO TERRIFY THEM, BUT TO STRENGTHEN THEM

The evils which He here foretells as approaching were indeed tremendous. Tremendous—

First: On account of the injuries they would sustain. Here is —(1.) Banishment from the synagogue. " *They shall put you out of the synagogues.*" Their most sacred associations were connected with the synagogues, and to be shut out of them would imply degradation and loss. (2.) Destruction of their life. " *Whosoever killeth you.*" "Skin for skin, yea, all that a man hath will he give for his life." Martyrdom is the culmination of all physical suffer-ings. Not only were the evils tremendous on account of the injuries they would sustain, but—

Secondly: On account of the spirit which inspired the men who inflicted them. " *Whosoever killeth you will think he doeth God service.*" No passion in the human breast is so strong when excited, so savage and so cruel, as religious fanaticism. Take Saul of Tarsus as an example. It maddened him; it gave him an intense thirst for blood; he breathed out slaughter, and thought he was doing " *God service.*" But these tremendous sufferings are here foretold, not in order to alarm or distress them, but in order to encourage and strengthen them. " *These things have I spoken unto you, that ye should not be offended.*" They were foretold in order—

(1.) To prepare them so that they should not be surprised, and at their wits' end. To be forewarned is to be forearmed.

(2.) To establish their confidence in Christ when they came. When they came, instead of having their faith shaken in their Master, it would be deepened and strengthened with the assurance that He was Divine, because cognizant of the future.

II —CHRIST REPROVES THE DEFECTS OF HIS DISCIPLES NOT WITH ANGER, BUT WITH TENDERNESS

These defects seem to have been twofold.

First: An apparent indifference to His departure. " *None of you asketh Me, Whither goest Thou ?*" His departure to Him was a sublimely solemn event, both in His history, and in the history of the race, and yet they did not seem to have any deep concern in it.

Secondly: A sadness on account of His approaching absence. They seemed to be sorry on their own account that He was going to leave them. He had been with them for three years, and so long as He was with them they knew they would be well protected. But now when He left them what would become of them? "*Sorrow hath filled your heart.*" In this reproof there seems not only the utter absence of all anger, but a spirit of deep and touching tenderness. It is as if He had said, Why don't you ask Me concerning the scenes into which I am going? If you did I would tell you and give you all information. Don't be so sad, there is no just cause for it. My departure will turn out to your advantage.

III—CHRIST DEPRIVES HIS DISCIPLES OF SOME BLESSINGS NOT FOR THEIR INJURY, BUT FOR THEIR BENEFIT

Of what was He going to deprive His disciples now? Of nothing less than His own personal presence. To them this would seem, undoubtedly, an unspeakable loss. But why did He do it? Not to injure them, but to bless them by preparing them for the Divine Spirit, which would always be with them, teaching, comforting, and strengthening them.

John 16:7

THE GREATEST TRIALS LEADING TO THE GREATEST BLESSINGS

"Nevertheless I tell you the truth," &c.

Exegetical Remarks.—Ver. 7.—"*Nevertheless I tell you the truth.*" In the preceding verse Christ says to His disciples, "Sorrow hath filled your heart." They were indeed in trouble, in deep, sad distress on account of His apprehended departure from thence, and here He means to say: "It must be so; I tell you the truth; I who know all your badness, and all your needs, and all that is best for you; I tell you the truth." "*It is expedient for you that I go away.*" My departure need not distress you; it is in truth necessary for you, "*it is expedient.*" "*For if I go not away, the Comforter will not come unto you; but if I depart* (R. V. GO), *I will send Him unto you.*" "We may not indeed," says an able modern author, "fathom the deep counsels of God in which the reason of these words is to be found; but the order fixed in these counsels was that the Son of man should complete His work on earth, and offer the sacrifice of Himself for sin, and rise from the dead, and ascend to the Father's throne, before the Advocate should come. The Son of man was to be glorified before the Spirit was to be given. Humanity was to ascend to heaven before the Spirit could be sent to humanity on earth. The revelation of saving truth was to be completed before inspiration was to breathe as the breath of life into man's soul. The conviction of sin, righteousness, and judgment could only follow the finished work of Christ."

HOMILETICS

The subject of these remarkable words is *The Greatest Trials leading to the Greatest Blessings*, and the following general truths are suggested :—

I —THAT THE GREATEST TRIAL MAY PROVE THE GREATEST BLESSING

First : The departure of Christ from His disciples was felt by them to be a most grievous trial. "Sorrow," He said, "hath filled your heart." He had been with them for three years, won their affections, changed their whole history, both their inner experience and their outward circumstances. And now He was leaving them. What a bereavement ! The Sun of their souls sinking beneath the horizon, and their world left in darkness and desolation.

Secondly : The advent of His Spirit to His disciples would be the greatest blessing. He was the "*Comforter,*" the Spirit of Truth. He would enter the inner temple of their nature and reproduce all the impressions that Christ had made, bring all things to their remembrance, and abide with them for ever. His advent more than compensated for the departure of Christ. Thus it ever is, ever has, and ever will be, with great trials to the good. So it was with Abraham, Daniel, Paul, &c. "Our light afflictions." Another truth suggested is—

II —THAT THE GREATEST TRIAL MIGHT BE NECESSARY TO THE GREATEST BLESSING

"*It is expedient for you that I go away.*" * The departure of the One was necessary to the advent of the Other. To attempt assigning the reasons in the Eternal Mind for this would be manifestly presumptuous. Albeit, we can discover certain things which seem to render it necessary. What rendered it expedient ?

First : It seemed "*expedient*" in order to give a more vivid meaning to the life of Christ. Never does the life of a loved friend come with such meaning and might into the heart as when death has removed him from the sphere of our observation. Death which takes our friend from our outward eye, enshrines him in the soul, and there he assumes lovelier forms, and yields a more potent influence. It was so with Christ. When He ceased to be seen without, He became formed within them, the "*Hope of Glory.*"

Secondly : It seemed "*expedient*" in order to dissipate all their material and local conceptions of Him. So long as He was with them corporeally, and judged after the flesh, their religion was sensuous. The impressions of His form, voice, and touch formed the greater part of their religious experience. Even Mary, after

* See Homily at end of Volume.

His resurrection, wanted to *touch* Him, embrace Him only after the flesh. His kingdom was to them *local*, confined to Judæa, Jerusalem its seat. Spiritual virtue, the cause of truth, and the well-being of their souls, required all these sensuous and local conceptions to be swept away from their minds. His departure tended at once to spiritualize and universalize their conceptions.

Thirdly: It seemed *"expedient"* in order to stimulate them to study the eternal principles of duty. So long as our teacher is with us in person, we are contented to have our duty pointed out to us from day to day. Like children we shall be controlled by verbal rules and voices from without. But when he is gone there is a sphere and a stimulus for the use of our faculties. We must study for ourselves, enquire in the great temple of truth all the days of our life. How inferior is the mind moving by prescriptive rules to one that is ruled by universal principles!

Fourthly: It seemed *"expedient"* in order to throw the soul upon the help of its own faculties. Man only really grows and advances as he works his own faculties, and becomes self-reliant. Up to a certain period parental watching and superintendence are indispensable to the well-being of a child; but if it is extended beyond the proper age it becomes an evil. The law of nature is evidently that the parent, after a certain time, should withdraw, not his *affections*, but his exclusively supporting agency, so that the child may be brought to realize the importance of self-reliance. It is a wise law, yes, a *kind* law, though painful at times, which requires one child after another to withdraw from the parental roof where everything has been supplied, and seek out whatever is needed for himself. It was so in relation to the disciples. I do not think that they would have made much advancement if they had continued to depend upon the personal direction of the Lord, and not upon great principles. Look at them on the Galilean lake in the storm. Where did they rest? Not upon principles, but upon a Person. Look at Peter whilst Jesus was yet on earth. When in the stillness of the night the Roman band approached Gethsemane, when his Master was bathed in tears and blood, he "forsook Him and fled;" and that very same night, with the spirit of a coward, he in the court exclaimed before Caiaphas, "I know not the Man." A few weeks rolls away. Jesus has left the world; He has been crucified; He has been buried; He has risen from the dead; He has ascended to Heaven; He appears no more in their midst; they see not His form, they hear not His words;—He is gone; the clouds have received Him up out of their sight. The disciples now begin to examine for themselves: they *meet*, and *read*, and *think*, and *pray*, and thus grow in strength. The day of Pentecost dawns—men from all parts of the world are gathered together to celebrate that ancient festival. And now look at Peter; look at the man who, but a few weeks before, trembled at the question of a servant-maid, standing up with an indomitable heroism before that mass of anti-Christian men, and charging upon them the guilt of Christ's crucifixion (Acts ii. 22, 23). A few days pass on, and he is brought a prisoner before the very men who crucified his Lord, into the very hall where he too *denied* Him. But how different his spirit! (Acts v. 28—31.)

The principle that the greatest trials may be *necessary* to the greatest blessings, illustrated in the departure of Christ and the Advent of the Spirit, is capable of a very wide and general application to human history. It is often necessary for a man to lose his *friends, property, health,* and even *liberty* to prepare him for the great blessings of eternal life. The words suggest—

III —THAT THE GREATEST TRIALS AND THE GREATEST BLESSINGS ARE ALIKE UNDER THE DIRECTION OF CHRIST

First: The greatest trial is under His direction. *"I go away."* There is no compulsion, no driving ; *"I go away."* Christ was free in His death. "I have power to lay down My life," &c. Sublime power this! *"I go"*—through Gethsemane, over Calvary, down into the grave, up through the clouds, on to the central throne of the universe. *"I go."* All power is in His hand.

Secondly: The greatest blessing is under His direction. He sends the Spirit. *"I will send Him unto you."* *Him ;* not *it.* A *person,* not an *influence.* He " hath received gifts for men." Our destiny is in the hands of God in Christ. Let us trust in Him. The whole of our life is made up of loss and gain ; but if we are His, He takes away one good thing in order to give us a better. Trust Him, my brother !

> " Trust Him in days of sorrow,
>   And meekly tread the thorny way ;
> It may be thou wilt see to-morrow,
>   The love that chastens thee to-day."—*Maurice.*

John 16:8-15

THE DIVINE SPIRIT IN RELATION TO THE REDEMPTIVE DISPENSATION

"And when He is come, He will reprove the world of sin," &c.

EXEGETICAL REMARKS.—Ver. 8.— "*And when* (R. V. AND HE WHEN) *He is come, He will reprove* (R. V. CONVICT) *the world* (R. V. IN RESPECT OF) *of sin, and of righteousness, and of judgment.*" Convict the human world, the unregenerated race, mankind. "This conviction of the world is by witness concerning Christ (chap. xv. 26). It is the revelation to the hearts of men of the character and work of Christ, and therefore a refutation of the evil in their hearts. The result of this conviction is twofold, according as men embrace it, accept its chastening discipline, and are saved by it : or reject it, and in the rejection harden their hearts, and are thus condemned by it (comp. 2 Cor. ii. 15, 16). The effect of St. Peter's sermon on the day of Pentecost is the first great historical comment on this verse, but the comment is continued in the whole history of the Church's work. The last part of the verse enumerates the three steps in this conviction, which are more fully defined in the three following verses." "*Righteousness.*" Ideal righteousness, righteousness as embodied and exemplified in the character of Christ. Righteousness the antithesis of sin. "*Of judgment.*" Retribution. Convince them that both from sin and righteousness retributive results will spring.

Ver. 9.—"*Of sin, because they believe not on Me.*" Unbelief in Christ is in itself a sin, and is the prolific source of sin.

Ver. 10.—"*Of righteousness, because I go to My* (R. V. THE) *Father, and ye see* (R. V. BEHOLD) *Me no more.*" When I am gone to My Father the Spirit will convince you of My righteousness. "The special reason of the conviction of righteousness is the resurrection and ascension of our Lord. Man called Him a sinner (chap. ix. 24), and His crucifixion was the world's assertion that He was a malefactor (chap. xviii. 30), and even when He was hanging upon the cross, there came to the centurion's mind the conviction, 'Truly, this Man was innocent,' and His return to the Father was heaven's witness to His righteousness. For the way in which this conviction was brought home to the hearts of the apostles, and through them to the hearts of mankind, comp. especially Acts ii. 27, 31, 36. Also Acts iii. 14 ; vii. 52 ; 1 Peter iii. 18 ; 1 John ii. 1—29 ; iii. 7."

Ver. 11.—"*Of judgment, because the prince of this world is* (R. V. HATH BEEN) *judged.*" "*The prince of this world,*" the old serpent, the devil, the "prince of the power of the air." The completion of Christ's work on the earth, His triumph over death, His ascension to heaven, effected a terrible retribution on Satan, and this retribution proves a retribution upon all his

adherents. The sin of the world, the rectitude of Christ, the judgment or retribution following the wrong, are the great subjects with which the Divine Spirit was to carry profound conviction into the souls of men.

Ver. 12.—"*I have yet many things to say unto you, but ye cannot bear them now.*" Christ reveals to men just so much as they have the capacity for receiving, and no more. Let the capacity expand, and more light will come.

Ver. 13.—"*Howbeit when He, the Spirit of truth, is come, He will* (R. V. SHALL) *guide you into all* (R. V. THE) *truth : for He shall not speak of* (R. V. FROM) *Himself ; but whatsoever* (R. V. THINGS SOEVER) *He shall hear, that* (R. V. THESE) *shall He speak : and He will shew* (R. V. SHALL DECLARE UNTO) *you things* (R. V. THE THINGS THAT ARE) *to come.*" This means probably the truth. All the truth, essential to the spiritual restoration of mankind. "*For He shall not speak of* (R. V. FROM) *Himself.*" The meaning is not He shall not speak concerning Himself, but He shall not speak *from* Himself, in the sense immediately to be added.

Ver. 14.—"*He shall glorify Me.*" "The pronoun is here full of emphasis. The thought is that the future guidance of the Spirit promised in verse 13 will be the revelation of the many things of Christ Himself which they cannot hear now" (verse 12). "*For He shall receive* (R. V. TAKE) *of Mine, and shall shew* (R. V. DECLARE) *it unto you.*" Better as in ver. 13, announce it unto you. This is the test of the Spirit, "Every spirit that confesseth that Jesus Christ is come in the flesh is of God, and every spirit that confesseth not Jesus is not of God." The revelation of Christ is not an imperfect revelation which the Holy Spirit is to supplement. It is a free revelation imperfectly received, and His office is to illuminate the heart and bring home to it the things of Christ."

Ver. 15.—"*All things that* (R. V. WHATSOEVER) *the Father hath are Mine : therefore said I, that He shall take* (R. V. TAKETH) *of Mine, and shew* (R. V. DECLARE) *it unto you.*" These words I think do not express the relation of the Son to the Father, but the amazing plenitudes of truth which the Father had communicated to Him. "*All things*" refers, I am disposed to think, to the things connected with Christ's mission, character, purposes, and deeds, His whole his-tory, and this the Spirit was to present to the world when He was gone. Reproduce not merely the revelations that He had made to them, but unfold revelations that He had yet to make. (See *Watkins, Lange, Godet, Stier, and Westcott*, &c.)

HOMILETICS

These verses bring under our notice the *Divine Spirit in relation to the Redemptive Age*. Observe—

I —HIS ADVENT INTO THE WORLD IN CONNECTION WITH THIS AGE

This Divine agent here called "*Comforter*" or Advocate, the "*Spirit of truth*," had always been in the world. He had been working in its *material* department. He evolved this bright and lovely world out of chaos. He spread out the heavens, poured out the oceans, and piled up the hills. He had been working in its *mental* department, teaching men how to build houses, cultivate lands, and establish order, live holy and noble lives.* He strove with the antediluvians, He worked in bad men, in Balaam, Cyrus, Saul, &c., stimulated them to good actions. He inspired patriarchs and prophets to noble deeds and sublime utterances. But *now* in con-nection with this redemptive dispensation, He comes because Christ had finished His work, left the earth, and ascended to heaven. He came to work upon humanity through the biography of Christ, to press that biography in all its sublimest significance and quickening forces on the souls of men. The Gospel was a new organ through which this Divine agent was to work in the world. He came on the day of Pentecost through this Gospel and worked wonders, and has been working in the world ever since : so that the Gospel comes to the world now not in word only but with "much assurance," and with "the power of the Holy Ghost." Observe—

II —HIS MINISTRY IN THE WORLD IN CONNECTION WITH THIS AGE

First : His ministry is that of moral conviction. "*Reprove the world of sin*." Though the world is well acquainted with sin, for its hideous form and terrible results are everywhere, it has no deep conviction of it, and a conviction of its terrible enormity is the first step to its abandonment, the first impetus to an effective struggle for the true, the beautiful, and the good. "*Of righteousness*." Christ's righteousness. The righteousness which rung in His every

* See a service entitled the "Holy Spirit," p. 150, in "Biblical Liturgy," published by Higham.

word, shone in His every look, beamed and bounded in every act of His life, was the righteousness of which the world required the deepest and strongest conviction. It required this in order to see the ghastly heinousness of sin, and the grand ideal which it should endeavour with intense earnestness and perseverance to attain. "*Of judgment*"—retribution. The world required a conviction of this, that men have not done with deeds as they perform them, but that those deeds by an eternal law bring after them momentous consequences. "Whatsoever a man soweth that shall he also reap." Such are the convictions which the Divine Spirit through the Gospel has to burn into the souls of living men.

Secondly: His ministry is that of spiritual guidance. "*He will guide you into all truth.*" The world lives in the realm of shadows, dreams, fictions, unrealities, it walks in a "vain show." The work of the Spirit is to take it into the universe of eternal realities, and especially to bring out those vital truths which Christ had to communicate, but which His disciples at present were incapable of receiving. "*I have yet many things to say unto you, but ye cannot bear them now.*" An expression this which indicates—(1.) That Christ's disciples are not ignorant for lack of knowledge in their Teacher. "*I have yet many things to say.*" Ah, how many! A universe to communicate. (2.) That Christ's disciples are ignorant because of their incapacity to receive. "*Ye cannot bear them now.*" A man's capacity to receive knowledge depends upon his attainments, the lower those the less capable; the higher, the more. Hence the duty to study. The deeper the cavity in the earth the more water the clouds can pour into it.

Thirdly: His ministry is that of Christ—glorifying. "*He shall glorify Me.*" How will He glorify Christ? Here is the answer. "*He shall receive of Mine, and shall shew it unto you.*" To reveal Christ is to glorify Him. To take of the things of an inglorious and a degraded being would be to bring him into contempt. But to take of the things of a Being Who is Himself glorious, and reveal them is to glorify Him. The Sun is glorified by the rays that it pours out on the rolling orbs that reflect its brightness, and Christ is glorified by having Himself revealed.

CONCLUSION.—Such, then, is the advent and mission of this Divine agent. Has this Divine agent come to us through the Gospel, producing convictions, guiding into all the truth, and glorifying Christ, revealing Him to our inmost souls? Has He given permanent impressions of Christ's glory to us? We are told that the inventor of photography found at first a great difficulty in fixing his sun pictures. The solar beams came and gave the image, but when the tablet was drawn from the camera the image had vanished. What he wanted was, that which has since been obtained—a fixing solution to arrest and retain the fugitive impressions. This is what we want with the impressions that Divine truth makes upon the soul, and this is the work of the Spirit. He forms Christ in the heart, the Hope of Glory.

> Flow down, Thou stream of Life Divine,
>   Thy quick'ning truths deliver,
> Oh, flow within this soul of mine
>   For ever and for ever.
>
> Flow down, and cause this heart to glow
>   With love to God the Giver ;
> That love in which all graces grow,
>   For ever and for ever.
>
> Flow down, as flows the ray and rain,
>   In vital work together,—
> Refreshing roots and quickening grain,
>   For ever and for ever.
>
> Flow down, as flows the living sun
>   Upon the sparkling river,
> Whose crystal wavelets chiming run,
>   For ever and for ever.
>
> Flow down, revive this famished soul,
>   And bear away all error,
> That I may praise Thee, God of all,
>   For ever and for ever.

John 16:16-24

THE RELATION OF CHRIST TO THE INTELLECTUAL PERPLEXITIES OF HIS DISCIPLES

" A little while, and ye shall not see Me," &c.

EXEGETICAL REMARKS.—Ver. 16.— *" A little while, and ye shall not see Me* (R. V. BEHOLD ME NO MORE) : *and again, a little while, and ye shall see Me."*— The two expressions *" see Me"* here are from two different Greek words,' the former from a word signifying seeing either by the bodily or mental eye, the latter signifying mere bodily sight. He here points either to His departure from them by death and His return forty days after His resurrection, or to His departure from them at His ascension, and His return to them at the Pentecost, at their death, or at the final judgment. Probably the reference is to the Pentecost and His appearing in the Paraclete, for it is of this advent the whole context speaks. The expression *" little while"* does not settle which, but, " one day

with Him is as a thousand years," &c. *" Because I go to the Father."* (R. v. OMITS THIS CLAUSE.) "The majority of the better MSS. omit these words at this place. They have probably been inserted here from the end of next verse."

Ver. 17.—*" Then said some of His disciples among themselves* (R. V. SOME OF HIS DISCIPLES THEREFORE SAID ONE TO ANOTHER), *What is this that He saith unto us?"* &c. They did not understand Him, they were perplexed.

Ver. 19.—*" Now Jesus knew* (R. V. PERCEIVED) *that they were desirous to ask Him, and said unto them, Do ye enquire among yourselves of* (R. V. CONCERNING THIS) *that I said?"* &c. " Jesus here gives them a last proof of His superior knowledge, not only by showing them that He was conscious of the questions which were engrossing their thoughts, but also by solving in this last conversation all the enigmas by which they were tortured."—*Godet.*

Ver. 20.—"*Verily, verily, I say unto you, That ye shall weep and lament.*" These last two words represent the intense grief of the Apostles between His crucifixion and resurrection. "*But the world shall rejoice.*" While they were weeping the Jewish world was rejoicing. When they saw Him fastened in the grave, they thought He was finally crushed, and their triumph was complete. "*And ye shall be sorrowful, but your sorrow shall be turned into joy.*" Not only shall your sorrow be followed by joy, but it shall itself be transformed into joy.

Ver. 21.—"*A woman when she is in travail hath sorrow, because her hour is come.*" "The Greek is more exactly, 'the woman hath pangs'—that is, the woman in the well-known illustration. This figure was of frequent use in the prophets. (Comp. Isa. xxi. 3 ; xxvi. 17, 18, and especially lxvi. 7, 8 ; Jer. iv. 31 ; xxii. 23 ; xxx. 6 ; Hos. xiii. 13, 14 ; Mic. iv. 9, 10.) '*That a man is born into the world.*' The word is the wider word for human being. The thought is of the joy of maternity swallowing up the pangs of childbirth. These cease to exist, but that continues ; she forgets the one in the fulness of the other."—*Ellicott's Commentary.*

Ver. 22.—"*And ye now therefore have sorrow: but I will see you again, and your heart shall rejoice, and your joy no man* (R. V. ONE) *taketh* (R. V. AWAY) *from you.*" Elsewhere we are told that at His appearing to them after His resurrection the "disciples were glad when they saw the Lord." How joyous, too, were they after His Pentecostal appearance in the Paraclete. "And they continuing daily with one accord in the temple, and breaking bread from house to house, did eat their meat with gladness and singleness of heart, praising God, and having favour with all the people. And the Lord added to the Church daily, such as should be saved " (Acts ii. 46, 47).

Ver. 23.—"*And in that day ye shall ask Me nothing.*" This seems in all probability to refer to the whole period of the Spirit's dispensation, commencing with the Pentecost. "*Verily, verily, I say unto you, Whatsoever ye shall ask* (R. V. IF YE SHALL ASK ANYTHING OF) *the Father in My name, He will give it you* " (R. V. HE WILL GIVE IT YOU IN MY NAME). "*Whatsoever*" must, of course, have its limitations. Nothing, of course, that would involve an alteration in the established laws of nature or the purpose of God will be given. "*In My name.*" In My spirit and purpose.

Ver. 24.—"*Hitherto have ye asked nothing in My name : ask, and ye shall receive, that your joy may be full*" (R. V. FULFILLED). "They had not up to this time received the Holy Spirit. When He came He was as the presence of Christ dwelling in them. Under His influence their will became the will of Christ, and their thoughts the thoughts of Christ, and their prayers the prayers of Christ."

HOMILETICS

The passage leads us to consider the *Relation of Christ to the Intellectual Perplexities of His disciples.* They did not understand what He meant by the reference to His departure and return, "*in a little while.*" The passage suggests three remarks—

I —CHRIST FREQUENTLY OCCASIONS THE PERPLEXITY OF HIS DISCIPLES

He did so now, "*What is this that He saith ?*" "Seven times does the phrase '*a little while*' occur in these chapters, and at this point their query is specially fixed upon that clause, but not that clause only. They take His last expressions by piecemeal, and toss them from one to another. They would be glad to know, but dare not interrogate the Lord."

Christ often, by His symbolical and enigmatical language, threw His hearers into intellectual perplexity. Thus, when He speaks of soul redemption as a new birth, Nicodemus says, "How can these things be?" Thus, when He speaks of His death and resurrection as the destruction and rebuilding of the temple, His hearers considered He meant literally the destruction and re-building of the temple at Jerusalem in three days. When He speaks of His absolute necessity for human souls, in the figure of eating His flesh, and drinking His blood, His hearers said, "This is a hard saying, who can hear it?" But the examples are too numerous to quote. Constantly did our Saviour throw His hearers and His disciples into intellectual perplexity. He puzzled them. This must have been intentional. We can see good reasons for this.

First: It would serve to impress them with their ignorance. It is scarcely conceivable that any could have heard Him without being impressed with the greatness of His intellect and the affluence of His knowledge. The hearing, therefore, of utterances from Him that baffled their understanding could scarcely fail to impress them with their ignorance. The first step to knowledge is a consciousness of ignorance.

Secondly: It would serve to stimulate their thoughts. It would break the monotony of their minds, set them thinking, urge them to inquiry. The great object of His teaching was to educate His hearers. Difficulties are essential to educational work. The schoolbook that is mastered by the pupil ceases to be educational, and becomes obsolete. There never lived a Teacher so potent in stirring the mental faculties into vigorous action as Jesus of Nazareth. He broke the monotony of mind and set the wheels of thought agoing. Almost every word of His roused inquiries, and His answers to the inquiries constituted a very large portion of His public ministry. The passage suggests—

II —CHRIST IS ALWAYS ACQUAINTED WITH THE INTELLECTUAL PERPLEXITIES OF HIS DISCIPLES

"*Now Jesus knew that they were desirous to ask Him, and said unto them, Do ye enquire among yourselves of that I said?*" Christ "knew what was in man." Before they spoke He knew their doubts and difficulties. And more, we are told that He knew from the beginning who they were that should betray Him. No other Teacher ever showed, or ever had, such a thorough acquaintance, with the unspoken thoughts that coursed through the mind of His hearers. Indeed, so frequently are they ignorant that they often infer that where there is scepticism, there is faith; where there, is impiety, there is religion. Not so with Christ: no hearer ever deceived Him, for all souls are more open to Him than the tropical seas are to the beams of the sun. This fact should have two effects upon us.

First: It should encourage us to search the Scriptures. The difficulties we have in endeavouring to understand the writings of the great authors of antiquity, are not known to them, when we ponder perplexed over their utterances, nor have they the power to help us in our difficulties. Not so with Christ. He not only knows our difficulties in studying His Word, but is ready if we ask Him, to yield a satisfactory solution.

Secondly: It should urge us to cultivate sincerity in our thoughts. For us to profess to know things of which we are ignorant, to believe in things of which we are sceptical, is to insult His Omniscience. Our prayer should be, "Teach me, O God, and know my heart; try me, and know my thoughts, and see if there be any wicked way in me, and lead me in the way everlasting." The passage suggests—

III —CHRIST WILL FURNISH A SATISFACTORY SOLUTION OF THE INTELLECTUAL PERPLEXITIES OF HIS DISCIPLES IF DESIRED

"*Now Jesus knew that they were desirous to ask Him.*" And because they were "*desirous,*" He here gives a full explanation. In His explanation concerning His departure and return, He states three things—

First: That His departure would involve them in great sorrow, whilst the world would be rejoicing. "*Verily, verily, I say unto you, That ye shall weep and lament, but the world shall rejoice.*" Who can tell what poignant agony they endured when they saw Him on the Cross, and heard His expiring groans, and beheld Him conveyed to the grave? On His way to the Cross we are told, "there followed Him, a great company of people, and of women who also bewailed and lamented Him." Do you want to know— as if Christ had said—what I mean by the "*little while, and ye shall not see Me?*" I will tell you in order to prepare you, that that period will be a time of sore distress for you, "*ye shall weep and lament.*" You will soon know all about it, from bitter experience. The event is just at hand. Yes; you will indeed "*lament,*" even while the world is rejoicing. My enemies will revel in unholy delight when they know that death has done its work on Me. He states—

Secondly: That His return will change their sorrow into high rejoicing. He indicates here two or three things concerning their joy at His return. (1.) It will be intensified by their previous distress. "*A woman when she is in travail hath sorrow, because her hour is come: but as soon as she is delivered of the child, she remembereth no more the anguish, for joy that a man is born into the world.*" The anguish of the mother is lost in the rapture she feels, when she presses to her bosom the new-born babe. So it will be with all the sorrows and trials of the good man on earth. They will be lost and forgotten in the celestial felicities of the future. (2.) It will be beyond the power of man to take away. "*Your joy no man taketh from you.*" It will be in them as "a well of water, springing up into everlasting life." A man may take away your property, your health, your life, but your joy never. "God shall wipe away all tears from their eyes, and there shall be no more death, neither sorrow, nor crying, neither shall there be any more pain; for the former things are passed away." (3.) It will be associated with the power of obtaining all spiritual blessings from the Father. "*In that day ye shall ask Me nothing. Verily, verily, I say unto you, Whatsoever ye shall ask the Father in My name, He will give it you.*" "*That day,*" that long day beginning with the Pentecost, running on through all the ages of redeemed spirits. With the Spirit working in you, you shall obtain from the great Father, the primal Source of all goodness, whatever you shall require.

Thus Christ, without going minutely into particulars concerning His departure and return, states facts abundantly sufficient to set their souls at rest.

CONCLUSION. If we are genuine disciples of the Holy Christ we shall have a full and satisfactory solution of all our perplexities and difficulties one day. What we know not now, "we shall know hereafter." Wait a little.

John 16:25-28

THE DAY OF THE SPIRIT

"These things have I spoken unto you in proverbs," &c.

EXEGETICAL REMARKS.—Ver. 25.— "*These things have I spoken unto you.*" Perhaps the things He had just spoken, beginning at ver. 16. "*In proverbs,*" or as in margin "parables." "There is a sense," says an able modern expositor, "in which it is necessarily true of all Christ's teachings and indeed of all teaching in words. They are but parables, until the truth which they contain has been thought out by the man who hears them. To the disciples much of Christ's teaching remained in a parabolic form until the Spirit came, and uncovered their meaning." "*But the time* (R. V. HOUR) *cometh, when I shall no more speak unto you in proverbs, but I shall shew* (R. V. TELL) *you plainly of the Father.*" The time referred to is the time of the Spirit, the Paraclete, who should carry the naked truth there amidst souls.

Ver. 26.—"*At* (R. V. IN) *that day ye shall ask in My name: and I say not unto you, that I will pray the Father for you.*" These words have often been taken to mean, "that I will pray the Father for you is a matter of course which I need not tell you;" but this sense is excluded by the following verse. The thought is rather, "I do not speak of praying for you, because in the presence of the Advocate you will yourselves be able to pray in My name to the Father." "His prayer is thought of as not necessary for them, and yet the form of the words implies that He will pray for them, if it should be needed. While their hearts are the temples of the Holy Ghost, and they maintain communion with the Father, they will need no other advocate, but 'If any man sin, we have an Advocate with the Father, Jesus Christ the righteous' (1 John ii. 1). Compare chapters xiv. 16 and xvii. 9, which refer to the time which precedes the gift of the Holy Ghost."—*Ellicott's Commentary.*

Ver. 27.—"*The Father Himself loveth you, because ye have loved Me,*

and have believed that I came out from God" (R. V. FORTH FROM THE FATHER). The love here of the Father must be something more than that general philanthropy that embraces the whole human race, for it refers to individual men, and these men are those who loved Christ, and believing, regard Him as coming forth from the Father. The language seems to teach that God has a special love for all those who love His Son, and bless His messenger.

Ver. 28.—"*I came forth* (R. V. OUT) *from the Father, and am come into the world: again, I leave the world, and go to* (R. V. UNTO) *the Father.*" He came from the Father to this earth, and He returns to the Father. He came and He goes, for the spiritual restoration of mankind.

HOMILETICS

The passage suggests a few thoughts concerning *The " Day " of the Spirit.* The day is here referred to in the expression, "*at that day.*" This is a long day; it began on the Pentecost, and runs on through the ages until the "restitution of all things." It is the best day that has dawned on humanity since the fall; better than the day when God "spake unto the fathers through the prophets," running on for forty centuries; better than the day of Christ's personal ministry on the earth. It is a day that will grow brighter and brighter until it floods all souls with the sunshine of infinite love. The prophets call it the "notable day of the Lord," the "great day of the Lord," and sometimes the last day; it is a day in which moral wonders multiply every hour. There is no day after this, it runs into the endless ages of retribution. Two thoughts are here suggested concerning this day of the Spirit—

I —IT IS A "DAY" IN WHICH CHRISTLY TEACHING BECOMES MORE AND MORE INDEPENDENT OF WORDS

" *The time cometh, when I shall no more speak unto you in proverbs, but I shall shew you plainly of the Father.*" Proverbs, words, language, are not truth; at best they are the mere vehicles. They are no more truth than the water-pipes are water; the pipes may be broken into atoms, but the waters continue as free and as boundless as ever, and will work their way through other channels. They continue to flow in rivers, bound in oceans, sail in clouds. The Bible itself, even its most inspired utterances, is not *truth*— it is the mere shell, symbol, channel. Christ used words in order to convey truth to His disciples. Sometimes His words did convey truths to their spirits, and sometimes they did not. When He says, therefore, "*I will no more speak unto you in proverbs,*" He points to a more direct, more thorough, and more effective way of conveying His truth to human souls, the way in which the Paraclete would do it—bring all things that He had said to their remembrance, make His very "*proverbs*" blaze in their consciousness. He would take the sense out of the sound, the spirit out of the letter, of even inspired language, and convey them into the inmost depths of their spiritual nature. The men who are most under the influence of this Paraclete are seldom able to trace their most sacred impressions, most devout aspirations, most godly resolves, most elevated experiences to any words, even the words of Christ Himself. "*The Comforter, which is the Holy Ghost, Whom the Father will send in My name, He shall teach you all things.*" "The anointing which ye have received of Him abideth in you, and ye need not that any man teach you." "Ye have an unction from the Holy One, and ye know all things." Christ says here, "*I shall shew you plainly of the Father.*" To see the Father is to see all truth, and to see that is the supreme necessity of human nature. But how can the Father be plainly shown? Not in words, for no words can reveal the Father. The Father can only be seen with the heart; a loving, pure heart. "Blessed are the pure in heart, for they shall see God." Another thought suggested is—

II —IT IS A "DAY" WHEN FELLOWSHIP WITH THE FATHER BECOMES MORE AND MORE INDEPENDENT OF MEDIATION

Christ seems to say in illustration of this—

First: That His disciples in this day will pray in His name, and therefore will not require Him to pray for them. "*At that day ye shall ask in My name.*" He had just before said, "Hitherto have ye asked nothing in My name." Why? They had not at that time received the Paraclete. But when He came it was stated that they would pray in His name, which means, I presume, that the Spirit would so inspire them with the sentiments and purposes of Christ that they would always pray in the spirit of Christ, and therefore their prayer would be real and effective. Because of this He says, "*I say not unto you that I will pray the Father for you.*" It is not necessary; you will have My spirit in you, and will pray as I should pray. Christ had prayed for them, and was just about interceding for them again, but after this it is implied that His prayers would be unnecessary. The coming of the Paraclete was, in fact, the *second advent of Himself.* Thus He represents it, " I will not leave you comfortless, but will come unto you." It is His coming, not as at the first, into their sensuous region, but into their spiritual natures, into their souls.

Hence His intercession is intercession in their souls, and intercession with them on behalf of the claims of God. "The Spirit maketh intercession for us with groanings which cannot be uttered." Popular theology represents Christ as engaged in one constant earnest prayer to His Father on behalf of the world, as if His Father's malignity was so deep and strong, that it required long ages of Christ's earnest intercession in order to melt His heart into mercy.

> "Lift up your eyes to the heavenly seats
> Where your Redeemer stays;
> Kind Intercessor there He sits,
> And loves, and pleads, and prays."

Such sentiments as these are still sung in some so-called churches. Is this a Divine fact or a godless fiction? Undoubtedly the latter. Christ seems to say—

Secondly: That His disciples in this day will have such a sense of the Father's love that they will not feel the need of the intercession of others on their behalf. *"For the Father Himself loveth you, because ye have loved Me, and have believed that I came out from God."*

Observe, incidentally—(1.) That God loves men individually. *"The Father Himself loveth you."* He loves all, but He does not overlook the individual in the millions. His love embraces each, as if the each were the whole. (2.) That God loves the individuals especially who love His Son. *"Because ye have loved Me."* He loves all, whether they love Christ or not, but it would seem from this He has a *special* love for those who love His Son. In truth no man can love the Father who does not love the Son, who is His Revealer and Image. And no man who does not love the Father can be conscious of the Father's love for him; and if he is conscious of the Father's love, why should he require an intercessor with God to entreat Him to bestow that of which he is in conscious possession? Under the ministry of the Paraclete all Christ's disciples will have the blessed and ever-deepening consciousness that the great Father loves them, and with this consciousness there will be *direct* communion between the Father and His children. Another thought suggested is—

III —IT IS A "DAY" IN WHICH CHRIST CAME FROM THE FATHER AND WILL RETURN TO HIM AGAIN

"I came forth from the Father, and am come into the world: again, I leave the world, and go to the Father." * He came from the Father as the expression, evidence, and channel of the Father's love for the world; came to reveal the regenerating thoughts, the quickening sympathies, the glorious purposes of that love to estranged humanity, in order to win it back to filial loyalty and

* See Germ, p. 64.

unbounded trust. When He had done His work on earth He left a history which constitutes the gospel of the world. He returns to the Father in order that the Paraclete—Himself—may come in Spirit to apply effectively that history to the men of all coming times.

CONCLUSION. Such is the Day of the Spirit. How are we using this day? It is the day of grace, the day of salvation.

> O Spirit, descend
>   As the beams of the morn,
> In the brightness of God
>   Our natures adorn.
> Come down as Thou didst
>   On chaos of old,
> Bring forth those creations
>   Thy prophets foretold.
>
> O Spirit, descend
>   As the rain and the dew,
> That the beauties of Eden
>   May spring up anew.
> Come down as the wind
>   On the dry bones of old,
> Breathe life into souls
>   That are withered and cold.
>
> O Spirit, descend
>   As on Pentecost hour,
> When thousands that met
>   Were changed by Thy power.
> Come down as a fire
>   From Thine altar above,
> Re-kindle within us
>   The flames of Thy love.—*"Biblical Liturgy."*

Germs of Thought
No. 67   John 16:28

FROM THE FATHER TO THE FATHER

"I came forth from the Father, and am come into the world : again, I leave the world, and go to the Father."

These are remarkable words in a remarkable address, delivered on a remarkable occasion. They reveal a history sublimely unique and infinitely profound. Of all the millions of men that have appeared on this earth, none but Jesus Christ could say, "*I came forth from the Father, and am come into the world : again, I leave the world, and go to the Father.*"

The text contains three facts—

I —CHRIST HAS BEEN HERE ON THIS EARTH AND GONE

"*I came.*" . . . . "*I leave.*"

First: This is one of the best attested facts in the world's history.

It is attested by collateral history, by numerous truthful and contemporaneous witnesses, and by the mighty and accumulating moral and social influences of eighteen centuries. That Christ has been here and gone is better proved than that Socrates, Aristotle, Cæsar, Alexander, Napoleon have ever lived and wrought on this earth. Christ has been here. The fact is engraven in imperishable characters all round the beaming brow of growing Christendom.

Secondly: This is the most glorious fact in the world's history. No fact has so blest the world. It was the creation of a Sun in man's moral heavens, the opening of a Fountain in man's moral desert. What has it done? All that is wholesome in the governments, pure in the morals, benevolent in the institutions, holy in the spirit and manners of the world, owes its existence to this fact. Insignificant as this Planet is, as compared with other orbs in the fields of immensity, the fact that Christ has trod its soil, and breathed its air, has given it a moral lustre that pales the brightness of them all. Notice—

II —CHRIST HAS BEEN HERE ON THIS EARTH, AND GONE BY HIS OWN CHOICE

"*I came. . . . I leave.*" What man amongst the millions that have appeared could say this? All have been *sent* here, irrespective of their choice or effort, and all in the same way have been despatched to other scenes. But Christ *came*. He fixed His own *time*, His own *birthplace*, His own *country*, His own *parentage*, His own *circumstances*. He might have come or not come, might have come as an angel or as a man, as a prince or as a pauper. All rested with Him—" Lo, I *come*." In the same way He departed —"*I leave*." I leave *when* I please, now or in the distant future. "*I leave*" *how* I please. By a natural death, or by the hands of violence. " I have power to lay down My life, and power to take it up again." What man could ever say this? We are sent away; often by means most revolting, and at a time most dreaded. "No man hath power over his spirit," &c. We are in the hands of another absolutely, as " clay in the hands of the potter." Observe—

III —CHRIST, IN VISITING THIS EARTH AND DEPARTING FROM IT, WAS THE CONSCIOUS MESSENGER OF THE FATHER

"*I came forth from the Father. . . . . I leave the world, and go to the Father.*" What does this mean? It does not mean that while on this earth He was *absent* from the Father. The Father was always with Him. " I am not alone, for the Father is with Me." The language suggests two things—

First: The life of true souls. "*I came forth from the Father and go to the Father.*" Coming from the Father with our motives, inspirations, and directions for His service, and returning with the results of our labours. As rivers have their existence by rolling from the ocean to ocean, so the true life of souls is in consciously moving *from* the Father *to* the Father : the Cause and End of all activities. The language suggests—

Secondly : The interference of the world with this life. Christ speaks as if, when in the world, He was away from the Father. There were circumstances in His history which seem to eclipse His Father's face ; hence, on the cross He exclaims, " Why hast Thou forsaken Me ? " There is much in the experience of every holy man, connected with his life here, which obscures Divine presence, and interferes with Divine communion :—the power of the senses, physical sufferings, secular engagements, and social trials. The Father does not always seem to be with us whilst on this earth ; but when we leave this world we go to Him. We shall no longer see " through a glass darkly ; we shall see Him face to face."

CONCLUSION. With what holy gratitude should we celebrate the advent of Christ to this earth! He is the great redeeming Man Who came here from the Great Father, and returned to Him again, having accomplished His mission. We rejoice that He is with the Father ; and all who serve the Father as He served Him return also into His beatific presence. Alas ! how many who come into this world return not to the Father, but to the devil.

John 16:29-33

NOTEWORTHY ASPECTS OF CHRIST AND HIS DISCIPLES

"His disciples said," &c.

EXEGETICAL REMARKS.—Ver. 29.— "*His disciples said unto Him* (R. V. HIS DISCIPLES SAY), *Lo, now speakest Thou plainly, and speakest no proverb.*" "They are heartily rejoiced at their own understanding ; they congratulate themselves that they can gladden their Master by the declaration that they can understand Him. They recognize in their understanding a foretaste of the fulfilment of the promise given in ver. 25 to which they verbally refer. Now they breathe freely, and inhale the fresh air."— *Hengstenberg.*

Ver. 30.—"*Now.*" This is emphatic. "*Are we sure* (R. V. KNOW WE) *that Thou knowest all things, and needest not that any man should ask Thee: by this we believe that Thou camest forth from God.*" They recognized in their acquaintance with His

thoughts, and in the new light which He brings them, the Divinity of His mission. They seemed to feel as if the day had already dawned when they need ask for nothing, for He knows all things, and would communicate to them all necessary truths.

Ver. 31.—"*Jesus answered them, Do ye now believe?*" The question does not mean that He doubted their avowal, for He knew the state of their hearts. He knew, however, that the hour of their full illumination had not yet dawned. "Their present light," to use the language of another, "was as the flash of a meteor, brilliant but passing away." He knew that clouds were still gathering round them, and a storm that must break over their heads.

Ver. 32.—"*Behold, the hour cometh, yea, is now come, that ye shall be scat-*

tered, *every man to his own, and shall leave Me alone."* He refers to the hour of His crucifixion, when they were all so overwhelmed with terror that they forsook Him and fled, and He was left alone. *"And yet I am not alone, because the Father is with Me."* In a sense He was away from them. Such a soul as His must have felt isolation in the midst of crowds.

Ver. 33.—*"These things I have spoken unto you, that in Me ye might* (R. V. MAY) *have peace."* Freedom from all anxieties and apprehensions, and a settled faith in the immutable and all-loving Father. *"In the world*

ye shall have (R. V. YE HAVE) *tribulation."* Afflictions, and sorrows, and persecutions are always the lot of true disciples. *"But be of good cheer; I have overcome the world."* "The last and crowning act of His victory, indeed, was yet to come. But it was all but come, and the result was as certain as if it had been already over — the consciousness of which, no doubt, was the chief source of that wonderful calm with which He went through the whole of this solemn scene in the upper room." — *Dr. Brown.*

HOMILETICS

In these verses we have certain *Noteworthy aspects both of Christ's disciples and of Himself.* Here we have—

I —CHRIST'S DISCIPLES IN NOTEWORTHY ASPECTS

They appear here—

First : As professing satisfaction with the explanations of their Master. *"His disciples said unto Him, Lo, now speakest Thou plainly, and speakest no proverb. Now are we sure that Thou knowest all things, and needest not that any man should ask Thee : by this we believe that Thou camest forth from God."* Some say that the language of the disciples here is not that of sincerity; that they did not really appreciate the meaning of Christ, as their subsequent history shows; that they only professed to do so. If they were really assured in their own minds that Christ knew *"all things,"* and did really believe that He came *"forth from God,"* all the better for them ; but if their avowal was a mere pretension, most daring was their impiety. At the same time, alas, in this they would only be types of the teeming millions in every age, whose religion is but that of empty profession. How many to-day in England profess to understand the teaching of Christ, who are utterly ignorant of His spiritual meaning ! They appear here—

Secondly : As unconsciously nearing a terrible crisis. *"Jesus answered them, Do ye now believe ?"* Are you really sincere ? Then I tell you, *"Behold, the hour cometh, yea, is now come, that ye shall be scattered, every man to his own, and shall leave Me alone."* The truth of your confession will soon be tested ; you are soon to pass through a terrible trial. The reference here is of course to the crucifixion, which was just at hand. How did they stand the test ? We are told elsewhere (Matt. xxvi. 56) that "all the disciples forsook Him and fled." Panic-struck, they hurried *"every man to his own"* home, and left their Master *"alone."*

A time comes in the experience of every professor of religion to test the falsehood or reality of his religion, in great afflictions and dying hours. Here we have,

II—CHRIST HIMSELF IN NOTEWORTHY ASPECTS

First : Forsaken by all. *"Shall leave Me alone."* Alone, when just as a Man, His human heart would yearn for the presence of His friends. Perhaps the words of an Old Testament writer will express His experience in this dark hour. "I looked for some to take pity, and there was none, and for comforters, but I found none." There is a sense in which the highest natures must always feel themselves *alone*, unapproached by inferior souls. Of Christ this was true in a pre-eminent degree. No one could enter into His thoughts and feelings. Here He is represented as—

Secondly : In communion with His Father. *"Yet I am not alone, because the Father is with Me."* *"With Me"* in all My deepest experiences. Philosophy shows that if there be a God He is with all men : leaves none alone. Conscious guilt shows that God is present as a righteous and inexorable Judge, but piety evermore recognizes His presence as a Father. *"The Father is with Me,"* said Christ. If the Father is with us we have all we need. Here we see Him as—

Thirdly : Giving encouragement to His disciples. He does this in three ways, by—(1.) Warning them of the tribulations they would meet with. *"In the world ye shall have tribulation : but be of good cheer."* *"In the world,"* that is, in their *outward* life. Great and overwhelming were the trials into which the disciples were about to plunge, and the history of the true Church in all ages has been a history of tribulation. Christ here prepares them for it by forewarning them, and to be "forewarned is to be forearmed." Trials rushing upon them suddenly and unexpectedly would crush them ; but here they are led to expect tribulation, and this was an element of encouragement. He encourages them by—(2.) Promising them peace in Him. *"That in Me ye might have peace."* Peace for the *intellect :* no sceptical distracting thoughts need trouble you. Peace for the *heart :* all your affections harmonized and centred in Me. Peace for the *conscience :* no more remorseful reminiscences and forebodings. This peace is to be found in Christ, *"in Me"*—not in Churches, not in priesthoods, not in creeds, but *"in Me."* How peaceful are the planets whose Sun is their centre ! The mightiest hurricanes of the earth cannot touch them, nor can the most terrible earthquakes shake them in their peaceful orbits. Emblem this of the peace of that man even under the greatest trials of earth whose soul is centred on Christ. He encourages them by—(3.) Assuring them of His mastery over the world. *"I have overcome the world."* Christ often speaks of what is to come as if it had already transpired, so certain was He of the future. The world for a few hours longer would be in fierce antagonism with Him, insulting Him, wounding Him, and murdering Him ; but, sure of the result, He says, *" I have overcome the world."*

John 17:1-3

SUPREME THINGS IN MAN'S SPIRITUAL HISTORY

(Christ's Last Prayer with His disciples.—JOHN xvii. 1—26.)

"These words spake Jesus," &c.

EXEGETICAL REMARKS.—Ver. 1.— *" These words* (R. V. THINGS) *spake Jesus."* Of all the grand and touching passages that make up this, the grandest of all books, the Bible, this chapter stands pre-eminent, so simple in language, that a child can interpret it ; so sublime in ideas and sympathies as to surpass the grasp of an angel's intellect. It reveals the heart of Christ as it points up to the Infinite Father, and looks down through all the scenes and ages of the race. It is a prayer for Himself, the Apostles, and for the universal Church. *"And lifted* (R. V. LIFTING) *up His eyes to heaven."* " The words ought not to be taken to imply that He looked up to the sky, and must therefore have been in the open air. The upward look is naturally expressive of feeling, and irrespective of place." It would seem that the preceding words of Christ were spoken on the way from Jerusalem to Gethsemane ; and now, as He was about crossing the Brook of Kedron, He lifts His eyes to heaven, and pours out His great soul in prayer. *"And* (R. V. HE) *said, Father, the hour is come."* The hour which He had often referred to, the hour of His crucifixion. This hour was one of the greatest epochs in the history of our world ; to it all past events pointed, and from it all future history would take its date and derive its influence. *" Glorify Thy Son."* " What is meant by glorifying the Son is further explained in ver. 5. But this implies the dark path of death, which has to be trodden before that glory will be attained." *" Thy Son,"* in a unique sense, in a sense that transcends all human conception. *" That Thy* (R. V. THE) *Son also may glorify Thee."* The prayer is absolutely disinterested. What He invokes is something that would enable Him to glorify the Infinite Father. " The glorifying of the Father by the Son is the manifestation of God's glory in the completion of the Messianic glory by the mission of the Advocate, and the future victories of the Church." (See *Luthardt.*)

Ver. 2.—*"As Thou hast given Him power* (R. V. EVEN AS THOU GAVEST HIM AUTHORITY) *over all flesh."* What is the idea here ? Is it that power over all mankind in order that He may bestow upon some—viz. the elect—*"Eternal life?"* This is the current idea in what is called orthodox theology. But the words do not convey this idea. The translation of Dr. Samuel Davidson is : " That Thy Son may glorify Thee, even as Thou gavest Him authority over all flesh, that whatsoever Thou hast given Him, He should give to them life everlasting." The following criticism explains this : " ' All flesh ' represents a Greek translation of a Hebrew phrase. It occurs again in Matt. xxv. 22 ; Mark xiii. 20 ; Luke iii. 6 ; Acts ii. 17 ; Rom. iii. 20 ; 1 Cor. i. 29 ; and xv. 39 ; Gal. ii. 16 ; 1 Pet. i. 24. St. John uses it in this place only. Its special signification is humanity as such, considered in its weakness and imperfection." *" That He should give eternal life to as many as Thou hast given Him"* (R. V. THAT WHATSOEVER THOU HAST GIVEN HIM, TO THEM HE SHOULD GIVE ETERNAL LIFE). "Literally, 'That all whom Thou gavest Him, He may give to them eternal life'

70 / Gospel of John

(comp. ver. 6). The word '*all*' is in the Greek a neuter singular, and signifies collectively the whole body of humanity given to Christ. The word for '*to them*' is masculine and plural, and signifies the individual reception on the part of those to whom eternal life is given." (See "Commentary for English Readers," by Bishop Ellicott.) Dean Alford's version is: "According as Thou hast given Him power over all flesh, that whatsoever Thou hast given Him, to them He should give eternal life." To me the idea seems to be this: INASMUCH AS THOU HAST GIVEN HIM AUTHORITY OVER ALL MANKIND, THAT HE SHOULD GIVE TO ALL MANKIND WHAT THOU HAST GIVEN TO HIM,—ETERNAL LIFE.

Ver. 3.—"*And this is life eternal, that they might* (R. V. SHOULD) *know Thee the only true God, and Jesus Christ, whom Thou hast sent*" (R. V. HIM WHOM THOU DIDST SEND, EVEN JESUS CHRIST). From what Christ here says of eternal life, it would seem it is not a physical but a moral quality; is not an endless state of being, but an endless moral mood of soul, consisting in a true knowledge of the great God and His blessed Son. Moral goodness is eternal life, and moral goodness consists in the highest spiritual intelligence. "Eternal life consists in the knowledge of the Father as the only Being answering to the ideal thought of God." — (See Ellicott's "Commentary.")

HOMILETICS

These wonderful words may be taken as setting before us some of the *Supreme things in Man's Spiritual History*. We have here suggested—

I —THE SUPREME PURPOSE OF EXISTENCE

What is that? To glorify the Father. For this Christ prays, "*Glorify Thy Son, that Thy Son also may glorify Thee.*" What is it to glorify God? It is not laudation, however enthusiastic and continuous. Because vain men are pleased with panegyrics and eulogiums, they foolishly imagine they will be acceptable to the Almighty, hence they compose laudatory hymns, set them to music, and call their productions "Services of Song." It is not contributing in any way to the blessedness of His nature, or the grandeur of His being. This cannot be done! To *glorify* Him is to reveal Him in our character and life. Whatever creature works out the nature which God has given him in harmony with His will, glorifies Him. Thus the "heavens declare His glory." The soul that lives as God intended it to live manifests His glory. Thus we are commanded to glorify God in our body and our spirits, which are His. It is here indicated that we can only glorify God as He glorifies us. "*Glorify Thy Son, that Thy Son also may glorify Thee.*" As if He had said, I cannot glorify Thee, unless Thou wilt glorify Me. This is true of men; unless God will glorify us by enabling us to live according to His will, we cannot glorify Him. Were it possible for the orbs of heaven to reverse their course and rush into chaos, they would not show forth His glory; it is only as His creatures move in harmony with His eternal law that they radiate His glorious character. "Whatsoever ye do in word or deed, do all to the glory of God." There is more of God seen in a

Divinely inspired and righteously regulated soul, than is seen in all the splendour of the heavens, the grandeur of the ocean, or the beauties of the earth. We have here suggested—

II —THE SUPREME MISSION OF CHRIST

What is the grand object of this mission? To give to all men that which the Father gave Him—"*eternal life*," that is, eternal goodness. "*As Thou hast given Him power over all flesh, that He should give eternal life to as many as Thou hast given Him.*" In this verse there seem wrapt up several glorious truths.

(1.) That Christ is the Master of the human race. "*Power over all flesh.*" "All power is given to Him in heaven and on earth." His authority is absolute and independent, yet never interfering with the freedom of any of His subjects, and ever more estimating their services, not by their amount, but by their motive.

(2.) That Christ is the Master of the human race by Divine appointment. "*Thou hast given Him power.*" "The Father loveth the Son, and hath given all things into His hands." The Divine right of human kings is an *impious fiction*, but Christ reigns by Divine right, and therefore we should obey Him, and rejoice in His government.

(3.) That Christ is the Divinely-appointed Master of the human race in order to make us happy. "*That He should give eternal life.*" "*Eternal life*"—or goodness, is the supreme necessity of human nature. Moral goodness is essentially eternal, because God is eternal. Goodness is the incorruptible seed, the perennial river of life, the unfading crown. Sin is death, goodness is life, and goodness is everlasting. So long as God continues it will endure.* We have here suggested—

III —THE SUPREME SCIENCE OF MAN

What is that? "*And this is life eternal, that they might know Thee the only true God, and Jesus Christ, whom Thou hast sent.*" Science abounds, the science of the organic and the inorganic, the science of matter and the science of mind; and these sciences are promoted and extolled amongst us. But unless a man knows the true God and His Christ—not with a mere speculative knowledge, but with a spiritual, sympathetic, and practical knowledge—all other knowledges are but meteors that flash across the heavens of mind, and leave the darkness more profound. I only really know the man with whose character I have an intense sympathy, and without this sympathy I know not God; and if I have this sympathy I have moral goodness, and this is "*eternal life.*" The man who has this supreme science has "*eternal life.*" Has it— not the means to it—but itself; has it, not will have it—it is his; he has it already in possession.

* See Homily at end of the volume.

John 17:4, 5, 22

TRUE SOUL GLORY

" I have glorified Thee on the earth : I have finished the work which Thou
gavest Me to do," &c.

EXEGETICAL REMARKS.—Ver. 4.—
" *I have glorified* (R. V. I GLORIFIED)
Thee on the earth : I have finished
(R. V. HAVING ACCOMPLISHED) *the
work which Thou gavest* (R. V. HAST
GIVEN) *Me to do.*" Observe—(1.)
Christ came into the world to accomplish a certain Divine work. This
is true of every man ; every man
has a Divine mission. (2.) This
Divine work He had now finished.
He had fulfilled His Divine mission ;
this is what every man ought to do.
(3.) Having finished the work, He
glorified God, and ceased His earthly
life. God is glorified in the execution
of His will, and when that is done, so
far as that will relates to earth, our
connection with earth terminates. It
was so now with Christ. Though
He had not at this time left the
earth, and would not for upwards of
forty days, yet He speaks of Himself
as having actually departed. His
work on the earth had *finished*, and
He regarded His connection with the
earth as over. If a man could do all
that God intended him to do on the
earth, however long he continued on
the earth after, the earth would
become heaven to him.

Ver. 5.—"*And now, O Father,*
glorify Thou Me with Thine own self."
As I have finished My work on earth,
and thus glorified Thee, I ask Thee,
O Father, to glorify Me. " *With the
glory which I had with Thee before the
world was.*" We are far enough from
saying that Christ had not an eternal
existence, but the words do not convey that idea. They only convey the
idea of a pre-existence. He might
have existed before all time, before
the creation, and yet not from eternity.
(See chap. i. 18 ; Phil. ii. 4, 9.) One
expositor says : " That there can be no
explanation of verses 1 to 5 of this
chapter, which denies that Christ
claims for Himself that He was Divine
and co-eternal with the Father."
Though we disclaim Unitarian views
on this point, honesty compels us to
say that there can be such an explanation. The words do not necessarily
convey the idea of co-eternity with
the Father.

Ver. 22.—"*And the glory which
Thou gavest* (R. V. HAST GIVEN) *Me I
have given* (R. V. UNTO) *them ; that they
may be one, even as We are one.*" Here,
again, the future is regarded by Christ
as present. What is the glory ? Ideal
goodness, moral excellence, that which
is as we shall see, the glory of God.

HOMILETICS

We have brought verse twenty-two in connection with the
fourth and fifth verses, because it has to do with the same grand
subject, viz. the glory of God, or *True Soul Glory*.

Glory implies the manifestation of something that is adorable.
There are manifestations of the adorable where the adorable does
not exist. Worldly pomp, glitter, and pageantry, the thoughtless
render homage to these manifestations, as if there was something
really intrinsically adorable behind them. Whereas, if the thing
behind the vanity, the selfishness, the superstition, and the ignorance were truly seen, men would recoil from the manifestation
with disgust. Now, what is the really adorable thing, the thing
which, if manifested, would excite honour and reverence and
praise ? It is MORAL EXCELLENCE. This is the glory of God.

When Moses besought God to show him His glory, what was the reply? Was it, " I will show thee the Almightiness of My power, the infinity of My wisdom, the immensity of My dominion, the boundlessness of My wealth?" No. Men cannot from their souls *adore* these things. But He said: " I will cause all My *goodness* to pass before thee." *God's glory is His goodness,* His infinite moral perfection. Hence the passage suggests two things in relation to true glory—

I —IT IS THE SAME IN ALL MORAL BEINGS, WHEREVER IT EXISTS

We are taught here that—

First : In *God* it is the manifestation of moral excellence. "*I have glorified Thee on the earth.*" Take from the Infinite His disinterested love, His absolute purity, His inflexible rectitude, and though you leave Him in possession of His Omnipotence, His Omniscience, and His Almightiness, you have stripped Him of all that moral souls can really adore. We are taught here that—

Secondly : In *Christ* it is the manifestation of moral excellence. "*And now, O Father, glorify Thou Me with Thine own self with the glory which I had with Thee before the world was.*" (1.) Christ had it as the *eternal* Logos. He was the Word, the Logos that was with God "in the beginning." He was, so to say, the organ, through which the absolute and unknowable One revealed Himself in the creation of worlds. "By Him were all things made that were made." This was the glory He had with the Father in the beginning, the glory of creating innumerable worlds, and systems, and myriads of existences to manifest Him who "dwelleth in the light which no man can approach unto, Whom no man hath seen, nor can see." (2.) Christ seeks it now as the *incarnate* Logos. "*And now, O Father, glorify Thou Me with Thine own self with the glory which I had with Thee before the world was.*" He would now ascend to the same power and influence that He had before. He "humbled Himself, and became obedient unto death." He would have His nature now raised into the full effulgence of eternal excellence. That glory had been, to a great extent, under a cloud during the days of His flesh ; the cloud was about breaking, and He yearned for the original refulgence. We are taught here that—

Thirdly : In *man* it is the manifestation of moral excellence. "*And the glory which Thou gavest Me, I have given them.*" Man is glorious only as he realizes, embodies, and manifests the eternal *ideal of excellence.* True glory, then, wherever it exists, is the same—the *same* in *God,* the *same* in *Christ,* the *same* in *Humanity ;* there is no other glory worth the name. To be glorious is to be good, and to be good is to be like God. The passage suggests in relation to true glory that—

II —WHEREVER IT EXISTS ON EARTH, IT COMES THROUGH CHRIST FROM GOD

"*And the glory which Thou gavest Me, I have given them;* * *that they may be one, even as We are one.*" How does it come through Him?

First: He reveals it to men. "We beheld His glory, the glory as of the only begotten of the Father, full of grace and truth." He revealed the moral perfections of the Eternal, not only in His teaching, but in the whole of His life. He was not only the incarnate *Logos—reason,* but the *eternal life—*goodness. In Him was "life, and the life was the light of men." He was the "express image" of the invisible God. All the elements of spiritual excellence were in Him livingly, harmoniously, and constantly. Never did spiritual excellence appear before men in such a radiant and regnant manner. Sages had reasoned about it, poets had sung about it, but it was all in haze and weakness.

Secondly: He inspires it in men. He implants its germ in the human soul, or, rather, He kindles its flame. "God, Who commanded the light to shine out of darkness, hath shined in our hearts, to give the light of the knowledge of the glory of God in the face of Jesus Christ."

Germs of Thought
No. 68   John 17:22

TRUE GLORY

"And the glory which Thou gavest Me I have given them."

This chapter is the sublimest prayer that ever ascended from this earth to heaven—the prayer of Christ. It reveals at once—(1.) The purpose of God; (2.) The heart of Christ; and (3.) The wants of humanity. Every sentence is a text, and the sentence we have selected is not the least significant. It leads us to make three remarks concerning true glory.

I —TRUE GLORY IS THE SAME IN ALL MORAL INTELLIGENCES

"*The glory which Thou gavest Me.*" The prayer in the chapter refers to several grand *Unities.* It speaks of *one life.* The life of God, and Christ is here spoken of as *One.* It speaks of *one truth* —"Thy truth." Truth has many sides, but it is one essential whole. What are called truths, are but phases of the one truth, of which God is the centre and circumference, the root and the branch. It speaks of *one Church*—"that they all may be one." There is but one Church. The Christly in all sects, countries, worlds, are but members of one grand spiritual whole: one family, of which Christ is the Head.

* See Germ, below.

> " The Church on earth and all the dead
> But one communion make."

It speaks of *one love.* That "the love wherewith Thou hast loved Me may be in them, and I in them." Benevolence has many modifications—justice, mercy, forbearance. But in essence it is the same in all minds. *Love* is one, as God is one. In the text it speaks of *one* glory. " *The glory which Thou gavest Me.*" The glory which Christ had was the glory of God, and this glory He imparts to mankind. What is true *glory?* It is the glory of *moral goodness.* In the eye of conscience, in the light of the Bible, and in the estimate of the great God and His holy universe, the good only are glorious.

II —TRUE GLORY IS COMMUNICABLE FROM ONE BEING TO ANOTHER

The glory which Christ had came from God, and was now being imparted to His disciples. Three things are necessary to its communication.

First : The manifestation of it. Were the Eternal to conceal His glory, no creature intelligence could participate in its rays. Goodness, to be communicated, must be revealed. A good being, to make others good, must show his own goodness.

Secondly : The contemplation of it. What boots it, if glory is manifested, if no eye observes it, no mind contemplates it ? The man who in noontide splendour shuts his eyes, is as truly in darkness, as he who gropes his way in the depths of midnight.

Thirdly : The imitation of it. There must be an effort on the part of the observer to imbibe, cherish, and develop the Divine spirit of goodness and of glory. Thus true glory is communicated. It comes not to us irrespective of our choice and effort. It requires attention, study, practice.

III —TRUE GLORY COMES TO MAN THROUGH JESUS CHRIST

" *I have given them.*" Christ was the *only perfect Revealer* of true glory. "We beheld His glory, the glory as of the only begotten of the Father, full of grace and truth." "He was the brightness of His Father's glory." No other being revealed God to man as Christ did. "No man hath seen God at any time : the only begotten Son, He hath revealed Him." It is by studying Him, and imitating Him, that men become glorious. "For we all with open face beholding, as in a glass, the glory of the Lord." There is no true glory for man dissociated from Christ.

IV —TRUE GLORY IS CONSISTENT WITH CIRCUMSTANTIAL SUFFERING

The disciples had received their glory from Christ, yet what were their *circumstances* in the world ? They were poor, tried, persecuted, regarded as the "offscouring of all things." Ultimately, most of them left the world through the agonies of martyrdoms. Yet, in all their struggles and toils, in all their afflictions and dangers, in all the obloquies they received, in all the tortures they met with from enemies, they *were glorious*. In affluence of heavenly thought, in force of holy will, in peace and energy of conscience, in purity and disinterestedness of love, in an unconquerable power of endurance, in an invincible heroism, in free fellowship with God, in high hopes of immortality, in a fame that corruscates and in an influence that widens and deepens through the ages, they were glorious. Glorious, too, were they in their achievements. "Through faith they subdued kingdoms, wrought righteousness, obtained promises, stopped the mouths of lions, quenched the violence of fire, and escaped the edge of the sword, out of weakness were made strong, waxed valiant in fight, turned to flight the armies of the aliens." To their bloodless victories we owe our liberty, our Bible, our schools, our asylums, our Christendom.

John 17:6-8

THE APOSTOLIC COMMUNITY

"I have manifested Thy name unto the men which Thou gavest Me," &c.—

EXEGETICAL REMARKS.—Ver. 6.— "*I have manifested* (R. V. I MANIFESTED) *Thy name.*" Thy holy character. "*Unto the men which* (R. V. WHOM) *Thou gavest Me out of the world.*" Christ here regards His Apostles as a body separated from the world, and entrusted to His spiritual care. "*Thine they were, and Thou gavest them* (R. V. TO) *Me; and they have kept Thy word.*" "The meaning of these words is that they were morally prepared by the earlier manifestation of God for the fuller manifestation in Christ. They were God's in more than name, and therefore when Christ was revealed to them, they recognized Him of whom Moses and the prophets did speak (compare chap. i. 37)."—"New Testament Commentary," by Bishop Ellicott.

Ver. 7.—"*Now they have known* (R. V. KNOW) *that all things whatsoever Thou hast given Me are of* (R. V. FROM) *Thee.*" Christ here asserts what they had just before attested. "Now we are sure (know we) that Thou knowest

all things, and needest not that any man should ask Thee" (chap. xvi. 30). He acknowledges their faith, feeble as it was.

Ver. 8.—"*For I have given unto them the words which Thou gavest Me* (R. V. THE WORDS WHICH THOU GAVEST ME I HAVE GIVEN UNTO THEM); *and they have received them, and have known surely* (R. V. KNEW OF A TRUTH) *that I came out* (R. V. FORTH) *from Thee, and they have believed* (R. V. THEY BELIEVED) *that Thou didst send Me.*" "From their perception of the absolutely Divine character of His word, they had risen to that of the Divine origin of His person and of His mission. These sayings also breathe that sentiment of inward joy and lively gratitude which Jesus had but a few moments since experienced ; for it was but quite recently that the glorious result for which He gave thanks to His Father had been obtained (xvi. 29—31). The harvest seemed undoubtedly scanty : eleven Galilean peasants after three years' labour !

But it is enough for Jesus, for in these eleven He beholds the pledge of the continuance of God's work upon earth. '*They have received,*' upon the author- ity of My testimony ; '*they have known,*' by their own moral discernment ; '*they have believed,*' by the surrender of their whole being."—*Godet.*

HOMILETICS

Christ here states two great facts in relation to the *Apostolic Community,* the college or training school which He had established for the diffusion of His doctrines and Spirit. A school infinitely superior to the schools established by Epicurus or Zeno, or by any other philosopher of ancient or modern times. He states certain facts concerning these men—

I —THAT THEY ARE GIVEN TO HIM BY THE FATHER

"*I have manifested Thy name unto the men whom Thou gavest Me out of the world : Thine they were, and Thou gavest them Me.*" What is the meaning of these words ? The answer by a certain, and, alas ! a popular school of theology, is—that far back in the "counsels of eternity" (as the phrase is) the Absolute One gave over to Christ a certain number of human souls to be saved, on the condition that He would become their Substitute, and endure all the penalties attached to the laws which they had broken. This is called the "covenant of redemption." I confess that such a covenant I have been unable to discover in any part of the Sacred writings, and it seems to me derogatory to the Infinite Father of souls, who Himself is Love. It is a mere theological fiction, a fiction, I fear, that has wrought immeasurable spiritual mischief. Whatever is meant by God giving men to Christ, it cannot mean the three following things :

First : It cannot mean that men are so given to Christ as to interfere in any measure with their perfect freedom as responsible beings. To give a man is to give a being whose very essence is freedom. Take away his liberty of action, and you take away his humanity ; and at best he is a mere animated machine, he is not a man.

Secondly : It cannot mean that men are so given to Christ as to lessen to the smallest extent God's claim upon them. When we, in good faith, bestow any object unconditionally on another, we sink our claim to it ; the thing given is no longer ours, it is the property of the recipient. God's claim to the supreme love and service of all moral intelligences can neither be abrogated or lessened.

Thirdly : It cannot mean that men are given to Christ in such a way as to render their salvation absolutely certain. The expression—"All that the Father giveth Me shall come to Me," has been so interpreted as to favour this blasphemy. If the Father has given them to Christ they shall come to Him, it matters not where they live, when they live, or how they live ; they shall "*come.*"

But the very language of Christ in the context shows that such an idea as this is inadmissible to the last degree. If their salvation is certain, why does Christ here pray for them? Why does He say, "Holy Father, keep through Thine own name those whom Thou hast given Me?" Moreover, why does He say that Judas, who had been given Him, was lost, and had become the "son of perdition?"

Denying all these ideas, I can attach a sublimely impressive meaning to these words; *Christ, as the Model of piety, ascribes everything He has to His Father.* It is the instinct of piety to trace all things up to the primal Source—God. Indeed, even sufferings He regarded as the gift of God. The political power of Pilate to condemn Him He regarded as the gift of God. "Thou couldest have no power to condemn Me, except My Father gave it." The cup of suffering He drank in the garden of Gethsemane He traced up to His Father as His gift. "The cup which My Father has given Me, shall I not drink?" Christ traced everything, but sin, up to the Father. He says, "*All things are given unto Me.*" "All power is given unto Me." Piety always does this. A congregation has been deprived of its minister; another has come to occupy his place whom they consider pre-eminently suitable. The piety of the Church says, God has given us another pastor. A godly man is in great distress; a man visits him in his sufferings who heartily sympathizes with him, alleviates his anguish, and removes his burden, and he says, God has given me a friend. The words of Christ must, therefore, be taken not as the language of a spurious theology, but as the natural expression of the highest piety. "God is All and in All." Christ states the fact—

II —THAT THEY ARE BELIEVERS IN THE FATHER THROUGH HIM

" *They have believed that Thou didst send Me* "

First: They believed in the Father so as to obey His will. "*And they have kept Thy word.*" "Though it is still necessary that they should be sifted, they have stood the main test, and have not suffered themselves to be entangled in the apostasy of Judas. To Christ's eyes they do already issue victorious out of temptation."— *Lange.*

Secondly: They believed in the Father so as to accept Christ as His Messenger. "*For I have given unto them the words which Thou gavest Me; and they have received them, and have known surely that I came out from Thee, and they have believed that Thou didst send Me.*" They were led to regard Christ as the Administrator of the Father's blessings, and the Revealer of the Father's character. Through Christ they heard the Father, they saw the Father. "*Have known surely that I came out from Thee.*" They were thoroughly convinced of this fact.

CONCLUSION. Profoundly interesting are those facts connected with the members of that Training School which Christ established —a school which teaches the sublimest doctrines which can engage the thoughts of men, and the most elevated ethics, congruous at once with reason and with conscience ; ethics embodied in a spotless life. Oh! that all men were disciples in this school! "There is but one apostolic Christianity, and none besides; whoso will not have that has none. That unity of the Father and Son is, therefore, not simply a type, but a true and effective *cause* of the oneness of Christianity. If the Church of Christ stood forth as a harmonious community of brethren, where nought but order and love ruled, it would be so unique a phenomenon that every one would be forced to acknowledge that here was Divine work. All doubts as to, and accusations against, Christianity must perforce hold their peace."—*Heubner.*

John 17:9-19

THE DIVINE SUPPLIANT

"I pray for them : I pray not for the world," &c.

EXEGETICAL REMARKS.—Ver. 9.— *"I pray for them: I pray not for the world, but for them which* (R. V. THOSE WHOM) *Thou hast given Me; for they are Thine."* Christ did pray for others. In this chapter He says, "Neither pray I for these alone, but for them also which shall believe on Me through their word." And on the cross He prayed for His enemies. "Father, forgive them, for they know not what they do." But here He intimates that His prayer is confined entirely to the apostles.

Ver. 10.—*"And all* (R. V. THINGS THAT ARE) *Mine are Thine, and Thine are Mine."* "Any man," says a modern expositor, "may say, What is mine is thine, but only the Son can say, What is Thine is Mine." This is not quite correct, for there is a sense, and a very profound sense, in which every godly man may truthfully say to the Father, What is mine is Thine. Of this more hereafter. *"And I am glorified in them."* "This expression has been variously understood. There is no reason for departing from the constant meaning of the term to be glorified. Notwithstanding His form of a servant, Jesus had appeared to their hearts in all His beauty as the

Son of God ; even before having been restored to His glory, He had regained it in them by the fact that they had recognized Him for what He truly was."—*Godet.*

Ver. 11.—*"And now I am no more in the world, but* (R. V. AND) *these are in the world, and I come to Thee."* "The immediate future is still regarded as present. The words have a special reference to the interval between His death and the Day of Pentecost, which would be for the disciples a time of darkness and danger, when they would have special need of the Father's care. '*Holy Father.*' (Comp. verses 1, 24, 25.) There is a special fitness in the word '*holy*' here, as in opposition to the world. The disciples were left in the world, but they were not of the world. These were spiritually God's children separated from the world, and He commits them to the Holy Father that He may keep them from the evil of the world. '*Holy Father, keep through* (R. V. THEM IN) *Thine own name* (R. V. THY NAME) *those whom* (R. V. WHICH) *Thou hast given Me.*' The reading is slightly doubtful, but if we take what would certainly seem to be the true text, the rendering should be, 'Keep them in Thy name which Thou hast given Me.' (Comp. verse 12.) The Authorized Version renders the same words by '*through Thy name*' in this verse, and by '*in Thy name*' in verse 12. The thought appears to be that the revelation of the nature of God by Christ to the world (verse 6), was that which He Himself received from the Father. 'I have not spoken of Myself, but the Father which sent Me gave Me a commandment, what I should say and what I should speak.' '*That they may be one as* (R. V. EVEN AS) *We are.*' This clause depends upon the words, '*Keep them in Thy name.*' They had so far realized the revelation of God that they had known Christ's whole life to be the utterance of God to their spirits. He prays that they may be kept in this knowledge in order that they may so know the Father through Him, as to become themselves one with the Father." (See *Watkins, Olshausen, Stier*, &c.)

Ver. 12.—"*While I was with them in the world* (R. V. OMITS IN THE WORLD), *I kept them in Thy name.*" I have now done with the world, My mission is finished, and I am no more in the world, but these are in the world. "*Those that Thou gavest* (R. V. WHICH THOU HAST GIVEN) *Me I have kept* (R. V. AND I GUARDED THEM), *and none* (R. V. NOT ONE) *of them is lost* (R. V. PERISHED), *but the son of perdition.*" *Webster* and *Wilkinson* observe on this expression, that "it is not implied that Judas was one of those whom the Father had given to the Son;" but I think if language means anything it is implied. "*That the Scripture might be fulfilled.*" What Scripture? It is not given. I know of no inspired prediction pointing to this event. It is probable therefore that the Heavenly Teacher had some infallible prediction before His mind with which we are utterly unacquainted.

Ver. 13.—"*And now come I* (R. V. BUT NOW I COME) *to Thee; and these things I speak in the world, that they might* (R. V. MAY) *have My joy fulfilled in themselves.*" "The world is far behind, the agony is past, He stands

upon the Mount of God, approaching His Father's smiling face. But all this is upon a conceptual standpoint, for He immediately adds, '*these things I speak in the world.*' Why speak them in the world? The words immediately following explain, that His apostles might hear, that one apostle might record, so that their joy, and the joy of the future Church, whom they represent, may be fulfilled."

Ver. 14.—"*I have given them Thy word; and the world hath hated them, because they are not of the world, even as I am not of the world.*" (See on chap. xv. 18—21.)

Ver. 15.—"*I pray not that Thou shouldest take them out of* (R. V. FROM) *the world.*" Though their departure would be a gain to them, it would be a loss to the world. "*But that Thou shouldest keep them from the evil*" (R. V. EVIL ONE). That is, from all moral evil.

Ver. 16.—"*They are not of the world, even as I am not of the world.*" (See on verses 6—9, and chap. xv. 13.)

Ver. 17.—"*Sanctify them through Thy* (R. V. IN THE) *truth: Thy word is truth.*" Not only keep and guard them, but sanctify them. Make them holy. Truth here means God's truth as revealed in Christ.

Ver. 18.—"*As Thou hast sent* (R. V. DIDST SEND) *Me into the world, even so have I also sent* (R. V. SENT I) *them into the world.*" "As their mission was designed for no other end than to carry into effect the purpose of His own mission in the world, so He speaks of the authority by which He was sending them into the world, as but an extension of the same authority by which Himself was sent of the Father. As He was the Father's Ambassador and Agent, so they were to be His. Nay, He represents them as already sent, just as He represents His own personal work on earth as already at an end: and what His soul is now filled with and looking forward to is the coming fruit of that work, the travail of His soul, and His satisfaction therein."—*Dr. Brown.*

Ver. 19.—"*And for their sakes I sanctify Myself; that they* (R. V. THEM-

SELVES) *also might* (R. V. MAY) *be sanctified through the* (R. V. IN) *truth."* Christ consecrates Himself to the service of His disciples, and consecrates Himself in order that they may be consecrated.

HOMILETICS

Our subject is *The Divine Suppliant.* There are certain truths implied in this part of Christ's prayer that cannot be too prominently or powerfully set forth. What are they?

I —THAT THE SUPREME GOOD OF MAN IS SPIRITUAL, AND NOT TEMPORAL

The blessing that Christ here seeks for the disciples is entirely spiritual. It is that they may be "*kept from the evil,"*—that they may be thoroughly "*sanctified,"*—that is, made holy; that they may be all spiritually united, "*all may be one,"*—made one with themselves, with Him, and with their Father. He does not pray that they may be healthy in body, prosperous in circumstances, or enjoy a long life in this world. He does not undervalue these things, but temporal prosperity to Him was of very insignificant importance, compared with spiritual. There are good reasons for this.

First: Temporal prosperity is utterly insufficient to satisfy the cravings of the human soul. "A man's life (happiness) consisteth not in the abundance of things which he possesseth." "What shall it profit a man?" &c.

Secondly: Temporal prosperity often leads to spiritual adversity and ruin. How often it happens that the higher a man rises in worldly things, the lower he sinks in moral destitution and degradation. Hence He does not pray for this temporal prosperity, nor does He anywhere encourage it. On the contrary, His command is, "Seek ye first the kingdom of heaven and His righteousness." Another truth implied here is—

II —THAT THERE IS A COMPLETE UNITY OF INTEREST, BETWEEN CHRIST AND HIS FATHER

"*And all Mine are Thine, and Thine are Mine; and I am glorified in them."* The first part of the verse is—

First: True, absolutely. God is the universal Proprietor. All spiritual existences, even the highest, are bound to say with Christ, "*All Mine are Thine."* We have nothing that we can call our own. We are trustees, not owners. The second part of the verse is—

Secondly: True, subjectively. "*And Thine are Mine."* Genuine goodness in all good creatures has both an instinct and capacity to appropriate not only all things that belong to God, but God Himself. What an old Hebrew writer said, all genuine saints can say. "The Lord is my portion, oh, my soul." Though in a worldly sense they may be indigent, in a spiritual sense they "inherit the earth," they "possess all things." "All things are yours; whether

Paul, or Apollos, or Cephas, or the world, or life, or death, or things present, or things to come; all are yours; and ye are Christ's; and Christ is God's." The language of deep love to its object is, "*all that is Mine is Thine.*" "His are the mountains, and the valleys His," &c. I rejoice in Thy possessions, more, I claim them as my own. This appropriation of God in His universe is the glory of man. "*I am glorified in them.*" Another truth implied here is—

III —THAT SINCE THE DEPARTURE OF CHRIST FROM THIS EARTH, THE PRESERVATION OF A GOOD MAN IN HIS GOODNESS, DEPENDS UPON THE AGENCY OF THE GREAT FATHER

"*And now I am no more in the world, but these are in the world, and I come to Thee. Holy Father, keep through Thine own name those whom Thou hast given Me, that they may be one, as We are.*" The meaning is, "I have taken care of them until now. Now I am leaving them, and commend them to Thee." Two things are here indicated—

First: The way of keeping them. "*Through Thine own name.*" That is, His moral character, which is His name. His moral excellence is at once the power to convert them to goodness, and to "*keep*" them in goodness. Would that preachers would practically recognize this, and preach like Paul at Athens. "Him declare I unto you," not their little dogmas and speculations.

Secondly: The reason for keeping them. "*That they may be one, as We are.*" We are "*one*" in a supreme purpose, inspiring spirit, and moral character. Let them be kept that they may be "*one*" with us. Real unity of soul consists of oneness of aim, spirit, and character. What attraction is in the material world, binding all things together, the vast and the minute, the proximate and the remote, disinterested love is in the moral system. Another truth implied here is—

IV —THAT AMONGST THOSE WHO ARE GIVEN BY GOD TO THE SCHOOL OF CHRIST, THERE ARE BAD MEN AS WELL AS GOOD

"*While I was with them in the world, I kept them in Thy name: those that Thou gavest Me I have kept, and none of them is lost, but the son of perdition; that the Scripture might be fulfilled.*" Judas was with the disciples, and perhaps there has ever been a Judas in all the communities of Christian discipleship. In the gospel field there are tares as well as wheat; in the fold goats as well as sheep; in the net the unclean as well as the clean. All are God's gifts. Bad men as well as good are the *property* of God; He can give them. Bad men as well as good are under the *direction* of God. Judas did not go into the school of Christ by accident, but "*that the Scripture might be fulfilled.*" Bad men as well as good are *employed* in the *service* of God. Judas did a useful work. Bad men in the school of Christ *must meet with a terrible end.* Judas was lost; the *"son of perdition"* went to his own place. It is better for a man to fall from the level sands than from a lofty cliff; it is better for a soul to fall into ruin from the corrupt world, than from the height of Christian privilege and profession. Another truth implied here is—

V —THAT THE GRAND DESIRE OF CHRIST IS, THAT ALL HIS DISCIPLES SHOULD PARTICIPATE IN HIS JOY

"And now come I to Thee; and these things I speak in the world, that they might have My joy fulfilled in themselves." Christ had joy. Though in one sense He was a "Man of sorrows and acquainted with grief," no man ever walked this earth who had so much joy as He had. The joy of an innocent conscience, of an approving God, of a disinterested love, of close and unbroken fellowship with the Everlasting Father. He had "meat to eat" of which other men knew nothing. Now His desire is that all His disciples should participate in this joy, and at last all His faithful ones will "enter into the joy of the Lord." As there is but one glory in all moral beings—the glory of moral excellence, there is but one joy, "the joy of the Lord." Another truth implied here is—

VI —THAT THE FAITHFUL CARRYING OUT OF CHRIST'S DESIRE, WILL EXCITE THE WORLD'S HATRED

"I have given them Thy word; and the world hath hated them, because they are not of the world, even as I am not of the world." (See my remarks on chap. xv. 8.) The *"world"* here of course does not mean the physical world, but the unregenerate race of mankind, and this world is a world of practical atheism, practical selfishness. It is in direct antagonism to the ethical teaching and the ideal life of Christ. The man therefore who will act out the teaching of Christ will ever come in direct antagonism with all the passions and prejudices of the world. "If the world hate you," says Christ, "ye know that it hated Me before it hated you." Yes; it did hate Him with a malignant and mortal hatred. The conduct of a truly godly man acts upon the sensibilities of the corrupt as the noontide sun on diseased eyes, as strains of music on diseased auricular nerves.

Another thing implied is—

VII —THAT IT IS POSSIBLE SO TO LIVE IN THE WORLD, AS NOT TO BELONG TO IT

"They are not of the world, even as I am not of the world." * In the current language of life there is a difference between a man of

* See Germ, p. 88.

the world and a worldly man. By a man of the world is generally meant not a man of sordid avarice, but of certain habitudes of life —a man who has made use of the world to enrich his experience, deepen his insight of life, polish his manners. He stands opposed to the clown, the pedant, the recluse, the sectary. He is supposed to be a man free from crotchets, angularities, a man of breed, soul, and genial humour. By the worldly man, on the other hand, is meant one who lives *for* the world, and *to* the world, and in the selfish spirit of the world. The wealth he covets, the honours he aspires to, the pleasures he seeks, the society he cultivates, are all worldly. He is of the world; he loves it. Christ did not belong to the world in either of these senses, neither do His disciples. The world in which a man really lives is the realm of his *governing purpose*. Whatever is a man's chief aim, that is his life. To it all his sympathies tend, in it all his activities operate, to it he renders all his circumstances subservient. Now the main purpose of Christ and His disciples is to "do the will of their Father" in heaven. But the purpose in which worldly men live is their own self-gratification. Hence it is that though the disciples of Christ are in the world, they are not of the world. The world is *practically atheistic;* it has no God. Christ and His disciples are *intensely theistic*. The world is practically *materialistic,* it judges after the flesh, it "walketh after the flesh." Christ and His disciples are *intensely spiritual*. Another truth implied here is—

VIII —THAT FOR A GOOD MAN TO BE KEPT IN THE WORLD, IS NOT SO DESIRABLE, AS THAT HE SHOULD BE KEPT FROM ITS EVIL

"*I pray not that Thou shouldest take them out of the world, but that Thou shouldest keep them from the evil.*" Observe—

First : That it is not always desirable for a good man to leave the world.

(1.) It is not always desirable on *his own account*. Until good men reach maturity of character they require this world. This world is furnished with all the appliances for spiritual training. Serious evils have, we conceive, arisen from what has long been, and still is, a popular notion in the Christian world, namely, that there is a necessary opposition in this world to true religion. The existence of monasteries is based upon this absurd opinion : and the current excuses which even the majority of Christian men urge for their not being more spiritual and devoted, are grounded upon the same foolish and miserable notion. Indeed, from the pulpit this dogma is frequently proclaimed. The truth is, the necessary claims of business, and the avocations of this life, instead of being opposed to spiritual culture, are amongst the most important means of grace and facilities for spiritual training. The man, for example, who has to work hard on the soil, and by the sweat of his brow obtain the means of subsistence for himself and family, is called by that very labour to put into exercise those principles of self-dependence, perseverance, and endurance, which are essential elements in the Christian character. So he who has to take his stand in the market and engage in the barter of business, has a noble opportunity for rousing his energies, testing his honesty, sharpening his powers, and, through the conduct of buyer and seller, attaining a practical knowledge at once of the nature and character of man. All experience shows that the necessary labour in these departments of operation is highly conducive to spiritual training. The men who say business is against religion, are men who are not acting on the true principles of business. The man who works in the field, the shop, or the senate-house, on the principle of godly honesty, must by the effort grow in vigour of character.

The notion we are combating is derogatory to the Divine character. Were the necessary duties of this life absolutely opposed to our spiritual interests, where would be the wisdom, goodness, and justice of God in sending us into such a state, and at the same time demanding from us the cultivation of a character opposed by all the circumstances of our being? Nor is the notion more derogatory to the Divine character than it is injurious in its bearings upon man. Men are everywhere making excuses for their religious indifference upon the supposed opposition which the world offers to it. Christians, you need the world in order to perfect you. You need its trials to humble you; you need its storms to purify the atmosphere of your heart; you need its difficulties to challenge your powers to action; you need its changes to remind you that this is not your home; you need its labour to invigorate your brain, on whose healthful action both your intellectual power and moral character depend. Do not, as too many do, indulge in morbid sentiments of dissatisfaction with the world; you cannot dispense with it. Use it, therefore, as the farmer uses the field, to produce fruit, that shall abound in after-life; as the pupil the school, to attain a knowledge that shall fit him for high offices in time to come. Use it as the mariner the winds and waves, to bear him on to the desired haven.

(2.) It is not always desirable on account of *others*. The truly good are social benefactors. For them to "remain in the flesh is needful." They are the correctors of the evil, and the conservators of the good. They are the lights of the world. They break through the clouds of the world's errors, sensuality and vice, and bring to bear on it the radiance of eternal truth. They are the "salt of the earth." They penetrate with their influence the mass, and prevent it from sinking into entire corruption. When good men leave the world, the world loses their prayers, sympathies, and personal presence. The death of a good man is the quenching of a light in our sky, the drying-up of a fountain on our earth. Observe—

Secondly: That it is always desirable for a good man to be kept "*from the evil.*"

(1.) Evil is in the world. Its introduction is a mystery, but its fact is patent to all. The history of the world is little less than a history of evil. It is a serpent enfolding all things in its deadly coil; it is a dark, cold mist hanging over every scene, intercepting the rays of the sun, and checking the growth of nature; it is a miasma impregnating the atmosphere, and causing disease and death in every breath.

(2.) Into this evil good men are liable to fall. This is clearly implied in the prayer. Evil here is the ascendant principle. It is everywhere. It presses all into its service—the loftiest genius and the greatest talent. It adorns itself in all the attractions that art can furnish. It speaks in the strains of music. It appears in all the fascinating forms of beauty. It promises sensual gratification, social power, and secular affluence. The prizes of the world are in its hand. In addition to this there is in the bosoms of even the best of men a susceptibility of being influenced by it. There are combustible elements which the fires of evil can kindle; latent germs slumbering within which outward evil can quicken into life and power. "The law in the members" is a lever in the human system always within its reach.

Add yet to this fact, *that there are infernal agents of evil*—agents whose numbers are overwhelming, whose skill and powers are immense, and whose efforts are incessant—availing themselves of every opportunity to contaminate and seduce. All these considerations are quite sufficient to show that good men while here are in danger of falling into evil. Meek-souled Moses was overcome by a gust of passion and carnal impulse. Peter, brave and bold, crouched into fear, and passed from cowardice to falsehood, ingratitude, and blasphemy. Indeed, the history of humanity only furnishes us with the example of ONE Who passed through the world uninfluenced by its evil. "The prince of the world cometh, and findeth nothing in Me." Temptation fell on His nature as dewdrops on Etna's fires; as sparks on ocean waves.

(3.) The falling of a good man into evil is immensely injurious. To yield to one temptation, to swerve from one principle, to give up one element of truth, is a most serious thing. It is to break down the moral fences of the soul, and lay it open to every enemy. One sin may destroy peace of mind, self-respect, and send us mourning all our days. It injures our power of usefulness. One sin greatly incapacitates for good. It weakens the arm, takes emphasis from the voice, and influence from the life. And, in addition to all this, it unfits for Heaven. "Without holiness no man can see the Lord." "And there shall in no wise enter in any thing that defileth, neither whatsoever worketh abomination, or maketh a lie: but they which are written in the Lamb's book of life" (Rev. xxi. 27).

(4.) The power of God is necessary to prevent this falling into evil. Christ invokes the Almighty to keep them from it. Who else can? What arm but His can hold us above the surging waves? What wisdom but His can guide us safely through? "Now unto Him that is able to keep you from falling, and to present you faultless before the presence of His glory with exceeding joy, to the Only Wise God our Saviour, be glory and majesty, dominion and power, both now and ever." Another truth implied here is—

IX —THAT BETWEEN THE COMMISSION OF CHRIST AND THAT OF GENUINE EVANGELIC MINISTERS, THERE IS A CORRESPONDENCE

"*As Thou hast sent Me into the world, even so have I also sent them into the world.*"

First: They correspond in their authority. Both are of Divine authority. God sent Christ into the world, and Christ sends the Church. Christians have a *right* to go into every part of the world, to unfurl their banner on every shore, and fight the battles of the Lord. We want no licence from bishops or potentates to authorize us to preach the gospel.

Secondly: They correspond in their principle. What induced Christ to come into the world, and inspired Him in working out His mission? *Love:* all-embracing, disinterested, unconquerable love. The same feeling must influence the Church, and no other feeling.

Thirdly: They correspond in their object. Why did He come? "To seek and to save the lost." This is our work. We have to save from ignorance, sin, the devil.

Fourthly: They correspond in their mode. (1.) Both are spontaneous. (2.) Both are self-denying. (3.) Both are persevering. (4.) Both are diligent. (5.) Both are devout.

Fifthly: They correspond in their *encouragements.* (*a.*) Christ had the Divine presence, so has the Church. (*b.*) Christ had the highest sympathy, so has the Church. (*c.*) Christ had the assurance of success, so has the Church. Another truth implied here is—

X —THAT THE HOLINESS OF MAN INVOLVES THE AGENCY OF DIVINE TRUTH, AND THE CONSECRATION OF CHRIST

"*Sanctify them through Thy truth: Thy word is truth. And for their sakes I sanctify Myself, that they also might be sanctified through the truth.*" The word "*sanctify*" means to render holy, and to render holy by an inward consecration to God, and this consecration is effected—

First: By *God's truth.* "*Thy truth.*" What truth? All truth is God's. All truth in physical and mental science is God's truth. But the truth here must be regarded as the "truth as it was in Jesus," as it appears in the incarnate *Logos,* His redemptive truth —the Gospel. The Gospel is the truth, its doctrines are in accord with the eternal realities; its morality in accord with the immutable principles of rectitude; its provisions in accord with the spiritual exigencies of fallen human nature. The consecration is effected—

Secondly : By God's truth in connection with the consecration of Christ. "*For their sakes I sanctify Myself,*" &c. The consecration of His entire life to the spiritual interests of humanity is the soul and essence of redeeming truth. Here, then, is the power to make men holy, to put men in possession of that moral excellence which is the glory of God, the glory of Christ, and the glory of all moral beings.

Germs of Thought
No. 69   John 17:16

THE UNWORLDLINESS OF CHRIST
" I am not of the world."

What does this mean ?

It does not mean—

First : That He cared nothing for mankind. There are men so utterly selfish, so utterly absorbed with their own personal concerns, that in a sense they may be said to be "*not of the world.*" The great human world about them they care nothing for. Christ was not unworldly in this sense. He was intensely interested in the condition of all the men about Him. " He went about doing good." He healed all manner of diseases; He wept over Jerusalem. It does not mean—

Secondly : That He did not appreciate the natural blessings of the world. There are austere and ascetic souls who are "*not of the world*" in this sense : its innocent amusements they regard with a pietistic horror; they have a superstitious fear of eating and drinking lest they should give their body an advantage over their soul. The spirit of Christ was foreign to this. He came eating and drinking, and hence He was called a Samaritan, a glutton, a winebibber by the ascetic men of His time. What is the world ? The human world is—

I —PRACTICALLY ATHEISTIC

It is "without God." Not *theoretically,* for the laws of the human mind render atheism as a conviction, an impossibility. But *practically* men are now "without God," and have been since the Fall. His presence is not practically recognized. His authority is not practically acknowledged. His will is not practically consulted. So thoroughly atheistic is the world in its everyday life that were it to be assured to-day that no God existed, its life would remain unaltered. Christ was not of the world in this sense. He was *intensely theistic.* The Father ever filled His whole horizon. His presence was the sun through which He saw everything. "I am not alone," He says; "the Father is with Me." The Father was never out of His mind : His communings were with Him, His works were by Him, His sermons were about Him, His inspiration was from Him. The moment the soul feels God to be in the world, the world assumes a new from. "Surely God is in this place," &c., says Jacob. The human world is—

II —PRACTICALLY MATERIALISTIC

Men ever since the Fall "judge after the flesh," "walk after the flesh," "live after the flesh." Christ was *intensely spiritual.* Men are "carnally minded."

First : Their pleasures are material. "What shall we eat?—what shall we drink ?" Christ's pleasures were spiritual. "I have meat to eat that ye know not of."

Secondly : Their honours are material. The highest honour is an earthly crown ; the highest victories are those of the sword. Christ's kingdom was "not of this world." He did not war after the flesh. He was a King, but His empire was Spirit. He was a Conqueror, but His weapons were truth, and His soldiers legions of angels. The material world to Christ was but the symbol and scene of spiritual existences and operations. He lived whilst here not so much amongst the things " seen and temporal," as amongst the things "unseen and eternal." The human world is—

III —PRACTICALLY SELFISH

Every man seeks his own. There are as many interests in the world as there are men; hence the collisions, domestic, social, ecclesiastic, national. Selfishness, which is the fountain of all crime, is the law of every man's life. Christ was "*not of the world*" in this sense. He was Love, tender, disinterested, compassionate, unconquerable love. He "pleased not Himself."

Thus Christ was "*not of the world.*" Though corporeally in it, He was spiritually out of it. He was at an infinite distance from its ruling spirit, its moral heart. The subject furnishes—

First : A test of genuine Christianity. He only is a *true Christian* who, like Christ, is "*not of the world.*" "Be not conformed," &c.

Secondly : A guide as to man's grand interest. What is it ? To get out of the moral spirit of this world, which is the Babylon of the soul. "Arise ye, and depart," &c.

John 17:20-24

CHRIST IN RELATION TO HIS DISCIPLES IN ALL FUTURE TIMES

" Neither pray I for these alone," &c.

EXEGETICAL REMARKS.—Ver. 20.— " *Neither pray I for these alone* (R. V. FOR THESE ONLY DO I PRAY), *but for them also which shall believe* (R. V. THAT BELIEVE) *on Me*." "The true reading here is one we should not have expected, 'for them which believe on Me,' πιστευόντων, not πιστευσόντων. But the evidence in its favour is decisive, while the received reading has but feeble support. Of course the sense is the same ; but this reading exhibits the whole company of believers as already before the eye of Jesus in that character—a present multitude already brought in, and filling His mighty soul with a Redeemer's satisfaction. How striking is it, that while all future time is here viewed as present, the present is viewed as past and gone."—*Dr. Brown.* " *Through their word.*" Their testimony concerning Him. He had manifested the character of God, and they had believed, and now His disciples must through all times bear witness to the same ideal.

Vers. 21.—"*That they all may* (R. V. MAY ALL) *be one; as Thou* (R. V. EVEN AS THOU), *Father, art in Me, and I in Thee, that they also may be one in us*" (R. V. MAY BE IN US). Not theologically or ecclesiastically one, but morally one : one in master-purpose and supreme desire. " The design," says *Lange*, " is triply intensified : (1.) All one ; (2.) One as We ; (3.) One in Us." Here is the unity of the Father and the Son. " *As Thou, Father, art in Me, and I in Thee.*" The union of all disciples into that unity, " *that they also may be one in Us,*" and the union of the disciples amongst themselves, " *that they may be one.*" " *That the world may believe that Thou hast* (R. V. DIDST) *sent* (R. V. SEND) *Me.*" Such a unity would carry the conviction to the outlying world of the Divinity of Christ's mission.

Ver. 22.—" *And the glory which*

Thou gavest (R. V. HAST GIVEN) *Me I have given them ; that they may be one, even as We are one.*" (For remarks on this verse see article on *True Soul Glory*, page 72.)

Ver. 23.—" *I in them, and Thou in Me, that they may be made perfect in* (R. V. MAY BE PERFECTED INTO) *one; and that the world may know that Thou hast* (R. V. DIDST) *sent* (R. V. SEND) *Me, and hast loved* (R. V. LOVEDST) *them, as* (R. V. EVEN AS) *Thou hast loved* (R. V. LOVEDST) *Me.*" All but the last clause of this verse is a repetition of preceding utterances. This cannot mean that exactly the same affection as the Eternal had for the Son He had for the disciples. But rather that as truly as He loves His Son, so does He love His disciples.

Ver. 24.—"*Father, I will.*" θέλω. This does not seem to be so much the language of determination as purpose. " *That they also, whom Thou hast given Me, be with Me where I am*" (R. V. THAT WHICH THOU HAST GIVEN ME, I WILL THAT WHERE I AM THEY ALSO MAY BE WITH ME). In chapter xiv. 3, He had assured His disciples that they should be with Him. He said, " I will come again, and receive you unto Myself ; that where I am, there ye may be also." " *Where I am.*" I shall be somewhere, I shall not cease to be, and I will that they shall be with Me. " *That they may behold My glory, which Thou hast given Me : for Thou lovedst Me before the foundation of the world.*" The glory, δόξα, of a moral being, as we have said, is excellence or goodness. It is in God as its Source, in Christ as its Medium, in His disciples as its recipients and reflectors. To desire men to behold this glory, has nothing of vanity in it ; it is a pious desire that all men should adore God, the Eternal Source. A man whose only glory, such as it is, is in some material, social, or mental distinction, is often inspired by vanity to request men to come and behold his glory. But where there is true glory no such a desire could exist ; the *ego* is lost in the infinitude of goodness.

HOMILETICS

The words lead us to look at *Christ in relation to His Disciples in all Future Times.* Observe—

I —HIS REALIZATION OF THEIR ACTUAL EXISTENCE

The only disciples living were the eleven, but He prays for them which shall hereafter " *believe* " on Him " *through their word.*" How many have believed " *through their word* " during the last 1800 years, and how many more will believe before humanity shall cease on earth ! It will verily be " a great multitude which no man can number." And yet all these seem *present* to Christ at this moment; they come within the range of His far-reaching vision; His great soul realized each in his distinctive personality, and for them He prays. To a soul in vital fellowship with God, and inspired with the spirit of Omniscience, *time and space* are of little account. The old Hebrew seers threw their glance far away into the distant centuries, and had a glimpse of generations and kingdoms yet to come. But none of them saw the future so clearly and realistically as did the Son of God, the incarnate *Logos.* A Being Who thus knows the future can never be disappointed ; He will have all His purposes realized, and He is now " sitting down in the heavens expecting His enemies to be made His footstool." In relation to His disciples in all future times, observe—

II —HIS METHOD OF CALLING THEM INTO HIS SCHOOL

" *Believe on Me through their word.*"

First : They must " *believe* " on Him. Not on what men say about Him, not on priesthoods, but on Him, the living, loving Son of God, and the Redeemer of the world. This is the way of becoming a disciple, there is no other way ; it has ever been so, it is so now, and will continue to be till the end. " He is the Way, the Truth, and the Life."

Secondly : They must " *believe* " on Him " *through their word.*" That is, their testimony of Him. By their " *word,*" which is the word of inspired truth, He will be made known to men. It is a witnessing word. How can they believe on Him of Whom they have not heard, and how can they hear without a preacher, and how can they preach unless they be sent ? This is the method. Do not expect any other. Observe, in relation to His disciples of the future—

III —HIS SUPREME DESIRE THAT THEY SHOULD BE UNITED ON EARTH, AND DWELL WITH HIM IN HEAVEN

First : That they should be united on earth. " *That they may be one, as Thou, Father, art in Me.*"

Observe—(1.) The *nature* of this unity. (*a.*) It is a unity that is very vital. One living in another. "*I in them, and Thou in Me, that they also may be one in Us.*" There is nothing mysterious or uncommon in the idea of one soul living in another. The object we love most, without figure, lives in us, not as a mere form, but as a living force. Friend lives in friend; the parent lives in the loving child. Love brings the distant object near, bears it over oceans, and often from the other world, and enshrines it in the heart. Thus, those who love Christ have Christ in them, and those whom Christ loves are in Him; and as Christ and His disciples both love the Infinite Father, He is in them, and He loves them that are in Him. (*β.*) It is a unity of the Infinite with the finite, of the Creator and the creature. As attraction links the smallest atom to the highest orb of immensity, love links the humblest disciples to the great heart of the Infinite, and He to them. Observe—(2.) A *reason* for this unity. "*That the world may believe that Thou hast sent Me.*" No argument could be formulated by all the logicians in the universe to convince the world of the Divinity of our Saviour's mission, so mighty as a thorough union of soul in all the professed disciples of Christ. Unphilosophic religionists have endeavoured to create a doctrinal unity. This is impossible. But could it be done, it would be highly mischievous to souls. They have sought, too, and to some extent succeeded, in creating ecclesiastical unity, which is a huge imposture, and a terrible bane. Hence various denominations and churches, and sects universal, that put professed disciples in antagonism one with another, and thus create a universal scepticism. The union wanted, and the only real union that can exist, is a *moral* union—a union in purpose, sympathy, and inspiration. This is the union to convert the world. Christ's supreme desire is—

Secondly: That they should dwell with Him in heaven. "*Father, I will that they also, whom Thou hast given Me, be with Me where I am; that they may behold My glory which Thou hast given Me: for Thou lovedst Me before the foundation of the world.*" (1.) With Me in *person* as well as in *sympathy.* With Me as disciples, as friends, as brethren. (2.) With Me, to "*behold My glory.*" That they may see Me as I am. My glory is the glory that "*Thou hast given Me;*" it is a gift and a reflection of Thyself. Thou hast given it Me, "*for Thou lovedst Me before the foundation of the world.*" The world had a "*foundation.*" Christ was before all worlds, and before all worlds the Father loved Him. "He was in the beginning with God," the "first-born of every creature."

John 17:25, 26

THE "AMEN" TO THE SUBLIMEST OF ALL PRAYERS

"O righteous Father, the world hath not known Thee," &c.

EXEGETICAL REMARKS.—Ver. 25.— "*O righteous Father.*" The "*O*" should be omitted, say some. "*The world hath not known Thee* (R. V. KNEW THEE NOT) : *but I have known Thee* (R. V. I KNEW THEE), *and these have known* (R. V. THESE KNEW) *that Thou hast sent* (R. V. DIDST SEND) *Me.*" All this being regarded as past. I knew Thee, these disciples knew Thee, but the world knew Thee not.

Ver. 26.—"*And I have declared* (R. V. MADE KNOWN) *unto them Thy name, and will declare it* (R. V. WILL MAKE IT KNOWN) : *that the love where-with Thou hast loved* (R. V. LOVEDST) *Me may be in them, and I in them.*" "The last word of the Lord's prayer corresponds with the last word of His discourses (xvi. 33). He is Himself the Source of victory and life."— *Westcott.*

HOMILETICS

Sincere prayer reveals the heart of man ; inspired prayer reveals the heart of God as well. In this, the sublimest prayer ever breathed from this planet, we have a reflection of all that is glorious in the human heart, and all that is loving and tender in the heart of God. These verses give us the *Amen to the Sublimest of all Prayers.* The following subjects are here suggested to our reflection : God and the world, Christ and His school, the preacher and his mission.

I —GOD AND THE WORLD

First : Here is *God. "O righteous Father."* Here is a subject for thought ; this is infinitely the grandest, the most invigorating and ennobling subject that can be brought within the range of creature intellect. Notice—

(1.) His relationship. "*Father.*" No relationship more intelligible, attractive, morally assimilating than this. It means *causation, affection, resemblance.* Christ never represents God as an inexorable Judge, a mighty Monarch governing the universe by rigorous laws, but as a Father full of the tenderest concern for the well-being of His children. His God was not a cold King upon the throne, but a loving Father Whose heart yearns for the return of His prodigal children. Ah me ! How theologians have calumniated this God ! Notice—

(2.) His character. "*O righteous Father.*" There is such a thing as rectitude in the universe ; the sentiment of right is co-extensive with the moral creation. What is right ? Not something in-dependent of God, some principle outside of Him. The idea is pre-posterous and pernicious. (*a*) His existence is the Foundation of all right, (*β*) His will the Standard of all right, (*γ*) His works and word the Revelation of all right. Our Father not only never has done wrong, but never can do wrong. All consciences in the universe, however fallen and miserable, are bound to admit that "just and right is

He." Let us trust our Father, He will never wrong us. His righteousness is not opposed to love ; nay, it is love itself. Justice is love sternly resisting all that will injure the moral universe ; aye, and sometimes overwhelming in ruin the resisting forces. It is love uprooting the weeds out of the paradise of virtue. Love often binding corrupt spheres of intelligences in the iron band of frost, in order that the spring may be more free from the pestiferous, and more abundant with the beautiful and the good.

Secondly : Here is *the world.* " *The world hath not known Thee.*" That is, unregenerate humanity. What ignorance is this—the worst of all ignorances !

This ignorance is—(1.) *Most universal.* The *barbarian* world " *hath not known Thee,*" did not know Thee, and does not know Thee. It is sunk in idolatry, superstition, and gross sensuality. The *civilized* world " *hath not known Thee,*" nor does now. When this confession was made, Egypt, Greece, and Rome had worked their intellects, made discoveries, and advanced considerably in civilization. They had their philosophies, their religions, and their arts, but even in Athens, the eye of Greece, God was the " unknown." The *conventionally Christian* world " *hath not known Thee.*" Its science often denies Thee ; its literature, commerce, and politics ignore Thee ; its creeds and its Churches malrepresent Thee.

This ignorance is—(2.) *Most inexcusable.* Men may have just excuses for not being scholars, historians, scientists, but they have no excuse for not knowing God. Nature is made to reveal God, and it does so everywhere, in every form that strikes the eye, or sound that falls on the ear. The soul is made to know Him, its eyes and ears and touch are given for this purpose. He is ever with us, and we in Him. The blindness of the man who shuts his eyes to the sun is not more inexcusable than the ignorance of the man who knows not God.

This ignorance is—(3.) *Most ruinous.* The man who is ignorant of God is in moral midnight. The distinguishing germs and faculties of his soul are as dead as the buried seed on which the quickening sun of heaven never falls. Ignorance of God is the " blackness of darkness." Another subject here is—

II —CHRIST AND HIS SCHOOL

First : Christ. " *I have known Thee.*" From any lips but those of Jesus how presumptuous would these words sound ! Through the teeming millions of the race, including the greatest scholars, geniuses, sages of all ages, who could say this to his Maker ?

(1.) No one had the *opportunity* of knowing God that Christ had. He was in the " bosom of the Father." He knew the motive that prompted the creative act, and the plan on which the whole was organized. (2.) No one had the *capacity* of knowing God that Christ had. Looking at Him merely as a Man, and judging of Him by His sublime utterances, what an intellect He had!—how keen and how far-reaching its vision, how immeasurable its sweep, how firm its grasp, how amazing its fertility! What is the greatest human intellect to His? What is a blade of grass to the majestic cedar, a bee to the imperial eagle, a rush light to the noontide sun? (3.) No one had the *heart* for knowing God that Christ had. No person can really know another unless he has heart sympathy with him. To know all the facts of a man's history is not to know the man. You must be one with a man in soul in order to understand him. Christ was one with God in a transcendent sense. "*I and My Father are One*"—one in heart, spirit, and purpose. Notice—

Secondly: Christ's school. "*These have known that Thou hast sent Me.*" All His genuine disciples know this. Without this knowledge, indeed, they could not enter His school. How did they know it?

(1.) By the mighty works which He wrought. "We know that Thou art a Teacher come from God, for no man can do these miracles that Thou doest." (2.) By the sublime doctrines He propounded. His ideas about God, the universe, duty, destiny, were not only sublimely original, but so accordant with the reason, conscience, the moral intuitions, and the deep felt wants of humanity, that people were constrained to ask the question, "Whence had this Man this wisdom?" (3.) By the manner of His teaching. "Never man spake like this Man." There was something so natural, so unconventional, so spontaneous, so rational, and devout in His manner, that all His hearers felt He was not like the Scribes and Pharisees; they had never heard such a Teacher before. They felt He was the Master of their souls. (4.) By the matchless purity of His character. There was a moral halo about Him which all felt detached Him from them. Though He mingled with them, sat with them, feasted with them, they all felt that morally He was not "of them," that He was made higher than they. Even Peter said, "Depart from me, for I am a sinful man." The ruffians in the garden fell prostrate before the majesty of purity that sat upon His brow.

Notice—

III —THE PREACHER AND HIS MISSION

What Christ did is the genuine work of every true preacher. What was the work?

First: A persistent declaration of the Divine character. "*I have declared unto them Thy name, and will declare it.*"* To declare self, theories, or speculations, about God is what Churches do, but to

---

* See Germ, p. 93.

declare His "*name*," His moral character, the *essence* of which is love, is what Christ did and does. All His moral perfections, all His true glory are rooted in love.

Secondly: A persistent declaration of the Divine character, in order to transfuse Divine love into human souls. "*That the love wherewith Thou hast loved Me may be in them.*" Alas! how many there are who so preach God as to transfuse into the minds of their hearers terror, abhorrence, loathing, atheism. He only is the true preacher, who so presents God to his hearers as to transfuse into them God's love.

CONCLUSION. I have thus gone through this wonderful Prayer —a prayer which reveals at once the heart of man and the heart of God. We see in it all that is glorious in renewed human nature, and all that is loving and tender in the heart of the Infinite.

I have assumed that the prayer here is a genuine record of the devout utterances of Jesus. Men have asked, How could they have been recorded? There is no proof that the apostle had a pencil in hand to note down the sublime words as they fell from those sacred lips. Be it so. Was not John present, and the other ten disciples? Would they not all be profoundly interested in Him, and in all they heard Him say? Would not every tone be marked, every sigh noticed? Does not memory always seize and hold most tenaciously everything in which the heart is most deeply interested? Since most of us know men who can repeat whole sermons from memory, is it not likely that every listener to this prayer would retain it? And then when they met together—which probably they would—immediately at its close, would not each one repeat to the other what he heard, and thus, in comparing their recollections, would it be possible for a single word to be lost?

Profoundly conscious am I of my lack of qualifications, both intellectual and moral, to do anything like justice to such a transcendent composition as this. Yet I have not dogmatized. I have endeavoured to free myself from all theological predilections in looking through the words. In consulting the expositions of others, both ancient and modern, I have been saddened at discovering the prejudicial theological influence under which most expositors have laboured. They have spoken of the "counsels of eternity," and the contract between God and His Son before the "foundation of the world" was laid, or the wheels of time commenced their revolutions. They have penetrated the Divine essence, and laboured to expound the mysterious connection between Christ and the Father. All this I regard as impiously presumptuous, and fruitful only in the pernicious.

It would be well for all theologians to take to heart the words of *Thomas Carlyle :—*

"Is this what thou namest 'Mechanism of the Heavens' and 'System of the World;' this, wherein Sirius and the Pleiades, and all Herschel's Fifteen-thousand Suns, per minute, being left out, some paltry handful of Moons and inert Balls had been looked at, nicknamed, and marked in the Zodiacal Way-bill; so that we can now prate of their Whereabout; their How, their Why, their What, being hid from us, as in the signless Inane? Systems of Nature! To the wisest man, wide as is his vision, Nature remains of quite *infinite* depth, of quite infinite expansion; and all Experience thereof limits itself to some few computed centuries and square-miles. The course of Nature's phases, on this our little fraction of a Planet, is partially known to us, but who knows what deeper courses these depend on; what infinitely larger Cycle (of causes) our little Epicycle revolves on? To the Minnow every cranny and pebble, and quality and accident, of its little native Creek may have become familiar; but does the Minnow understand the Ocean Tides and periodic Currents, the Trade-winds, and Monsoons, and Moon's Eclipses; by all which the condition of its little Creek is regulated, and may, from time to time (*un*-miraculously enough), be quite overset and reversed? Such a Minnow is Man, his Creek this Planet Earth; his Ocean the immeasurable All; his Monsoons and periodic Currents the mysterious Course of Providence through Æons of Æons. Metaphysical Speculation, as it begins in No or Nothingness, so it must end in Nothingness; circulates and must circulate in endless vortices, creating, swallowing—itself! Which of your Philosophical Systems is other than a dream-theorem; a net quotient, confidently given out, where divisors and dividend are both unknown? What are your Axioms, and Categories, and Systems, and Aphorisms? Words, words. High Air-Castles are cunningly built of Words, the Words well bedded also in good Logic-mortar; wherein, however, no knowledge will come to lodge. Like a God-created, fire-breathing Spirit-host, we emerge from the Inane, haste stormfully across the astonished Earth, then plunge again into the Inane. But whence? O Heaven, whither? Sense knows not; Faith knows not, only that it is through Mystery to Mystery, from God and to God."

Germs of Thought
No. 70   John 17:25

THE DIVINE CHARACTER
"I have declared unto them Thy name."

The *"name"* of God is His moral *character*. His character is the stability and glory of the universe. These words present it—

I —AS THE HIGHEST OBJECT FOR REVELATION

" *I have declared,*" &c.

Paul said at Athens, "Him declare I unto you." Not only is it the highest function of the material and angelic universe to manifest God, but also of *Christ the greatest Being.* These words present the Divine character—

II —AS THE GRAND ORGAN OF REFORMATION

Why is it manifested? " That the love wherewith Thou hast loved me," &c. God's character is the reformative force. Observe—
(1.) Moral reformation consists in the transfusion of Divine love into souls. (2.) This transfusion of love can only be accomplished through a manifestation of the Divine character. God's character alone generates love.

John 18:1-10

A MOST REMARKABLE MEETING

(*Departure to Gethsemane—Betrayal and Imprisonment—Mount of Olives.—*
MATT. xxvi. 30—36, 47—56 ; MARK xiv. 26, 42—52 ; LUKE xxii. 39—53 ; JOHN xviii. 1—12.)

" When Jesus had spoken these words, He went forth," &c.

EXEGETICAL REMARKS.—It does not seem that John intended to give a complete narrative of our Lord's Passion. In all probability he was perfectly acquainted with the details as given by the Synoptists. It might be that through the whole of his narrative he had in view the accounts of his predecessors.

Ver. 1.—" *When Jesus had spoken these words, He went forth with His disciples over the brook Cedron* (R. V. KIDRON), *where was a garden, into the which He entered, and* (R. V. HIMSELF AND) *His disciples.*" " Kedron, a deep dark ravine to the north-east of Jerusalem, through which flows the small storm-brook, or winter torrent, and which in summer is dried up." Though John here refers to the garden, he does not give all particulars of the sufferings of the Lord there as did the Synoptists.

Ver. 2.—" *And* (R. V. NOW) *Judas also, which betrayed Him, knew the place : for Jesus ofttimes resorted*

thither with His disciples." " John alone states the fact that Judas was familiar with the place, as he had often accompanied our Lord in His retirement there. Often had Jesus sought this retreat from the bustle and persecution of the city. The wretch who could plot to betray our Lord, could take a guilty advantage of such sacred privacy."—*Jacobus.*

Ver. 3.—" *Judas then, having received a* (R. V. THE) *band of men* (R. V. SOLDIERS) *and officers from the Chief Priests and Pharisees, cometh thither with lanterns and torches and weapons.*" " The other gospels tell us of a great multitude. John uses the technical word for the Roman cohort. It was the garrison band from Fort Antonia at the north-east corner of the temple. This well-known band is mentioned again in the New Testament. The torches and lamps were part of the regular military equipment for night service. Dionysius describes soldiers rushing out of their tents with torches and lamps in the same words which are used here."—*Ellicott's Commentary.*

Ver. 4.—"*Jesus therefore, knowing all things* (R. V. THE THINGS) *that should come* (R. V. WERE COMING) *upon Him, went forth, and said* (R. V. SAITH) *unto them, Whom seek ye?*" "Not that Jesus did not know whom they sought. Not that their leaders did not know Him by the traitor's kiss. He speaks to make them confess their object, and then to show that they can attain it only by His active permission."

Ver. 5.—"*They answered Him, Jesus of Nazareth. Jesus saith unto them, I am He. And Judas also, which betrayed Him, stood* (R. V. WAS STANDING) *with them.*" "The band of disciples was stationed within the garden in two divisions like a watch. The three intimates of Jesus were in the background, the eight others near the entrance. From the standpoint of these latter, to whom Matthew belonged, the most striking occurrence was the pressing of the troop with Judas at their head into the garden; from the standpoint of the three Jesus hastens to meet the throng."—*Lange.*

Ver. 6.—"*As soon then as* (R. V. WHEN THEREFORE) *He had said* (R. V. HE SAID) *unto them, I am He, they went backward, and fell to the ground.*" "The whole action," says *Westcott,* "represents the effects of fear, awe, veneration, self-humiliation, not of external force; the exaggeration which describes the men as 'falling backwards' is utterly alien from the solemn majesty of the scene."

Ver. 7.—"*Then* (R. V. AGAIN THERE-FORE) *asked He them again, Whom seek ye? And they said, Jesus of Nazareth.*" "By a Divine authority He pushes their impotence with these same questions."

Ver. 8.—"*Jesus answered, I have told* (R. V. I TOLD) *you that I am He: if therefore ye seek Me, let these go their way.*" "This is an intimation to the armed crowd what playthings they might be in His hand. He then points to the disciples, sacrificing Himself, but saving others."—*Whedon.*

Ver. 9.—"*That the saying* (R. V. WORD) *might be fulfilled, which He spake, Of them which* (R. V. THOSE WHOM) *Thou gavest* (R. V. HAST GIVEN) *Me have I lost none*" (R. V. I LOST NOT ONE). What was the word to be fulfilled? It is to be found in chapter xvii. 4, 12.

Ver. 10.—"*Then Simon Peter* (R. V. THEREFORE) *having a sword drew it, and smote* (R. V. STRUCK) *the High Priest's servant, and cut off his right ear. The* (R. V. NOW THE) *servant's name was Malchus.*" "The Jews," says *Westcott,* "among the company seem to have been foremost in the arrest. The incident is described by all the Evangelists, but John alone mentions the names of Peter and Malchus. It is easy to see why these were not likely to be particularized in the original oral gospel while both were alive and at Jerusalem. It was not lawful to carry weapons on a feast day." Who was *Malchus?* No one knows. What particular office did he hold? No one can tell. He was struck by Peter no doubt on account of his prominent position amongst the rabble.

HOMILETICS

It will be seen John records some most suggestive circumstances in Christ's biography that are not recorded by the Synoptists. It is true he omits other circumstances connected with the Memorable Night which the other biographers distinctly record. I cannot see how this difference in the narrations can, in any just way, be regarded as invalidating the testimony of either. It seems to me to give an air of naturalness and reality to the statements of all. Fabricators of a history would never have acted thus: they would have been studious in their endeavours to make their respective testimonies agree—not only in their essence, but also in their accidents. Indeed, had there been this uniformity, there would have been reason for suspecting their veracity. Many, if not most of the events of Christ's life, occurred in connection with turbulent multitudes and immense excitement. Under such circumstances it would have been almost impossible for the observers to detail them in the same order. From the nature of the case, each would have a stand-point peculiar to himself, would be struck with a circumstance which the other would not have an opportunity of observing, and be in a position to receive a deeper impression from some incident which the other, perhaps, would scarcely deem worthy of note. Hence this *formal* diversity would almost necessarily take place in the honest statements of independent and trustworthy witnesses. The fact is, the narrative of each of our Lord's biographers naturally differs by greater or less fulness, as each regarded the events from his own point of view. Our remarks will be confined entirely to John's utterance, as elsewhere we have referred to the statements of other Evangelists on the narrative.*

We have, therefore, before us an account of a *Most Remarkable Gathering*, and in connection with the gathering three things are noteworthy—

I —THE SCENE OF THE GATHERING

"*He went forth with His disciples over the brook Cedron, where was a garden, into the which He entered with His disciples.*" "As it is in the reflective Gospel only that the circumstance of His crossing the brook Kedron is mentioned, we can hardly doubt that to the Evangelist's own mind there was present the somewhat analogous crossing of the same dark streamlet by another sufferer (2 Sam. xv. 23); possibly, also, certain other historical associations (see 2 Kings xxiii. 12)." "Thus surrounded," says *Stier*, "by such memorials and typical allusions, the Lord descends into the dust of humiliation and anguish." To this garden, Jesus, it is said, went forth with His disciples. (1.) *Whence?* In John xiv. 31 we have these words, "Arise, let us go hence." Go hence. From this room where I have been speaking to you, praying for you, feasting with you. From this city—Jerusalem—away from the haunts of men. (2.) *Whither?* Into the solemn grandeur and deep hush of nature. To this garden we are here told He "*ofttimes resorted with His disciples.*" Some have supposed that this spot belonged to a friend, and that it was a favourite resort of Christ and His disciples. Thither Jesus had retired. There overshadowed by the silent hills, amidst the deep hush of midnight, with the pale rays of the full moon falling on His brow, He passes

*See *Gospel of Matthew*, in loco.

into a mysterious agony of soul, and pours out His heart in prayer. "*Jesus ofttimes resorted thither with His disciples.*" Great souls often sigh for solitude, and all souls morally require it. (3.) *Wherefore?* He went there to commune with His Father, to realize His awful mission, and to confront His doom. His going forth with His disciples to this scene, and for this purpose, reveals two elements in His nature—

First: His sublime courage. Terrible are the scenes before Him, yet with a fearless step He goes forth to meet them. Conscious virtue is always fearless. His going forth reveals—

Secondly: His social sympathy. He goes forth with His disciples. He takes Peter, James, and John with Him that they may be near Him in His agonies. As a Man He yearned for and valued the presence of sympathetic friends in His great trials. Another noteworthy thing here is—

II —THE PERSONS IN THE GATHERING

In imagination enter this secluded spot. Though night, it was not dark, the moon was at its full, throwing its silvery rays upon the scene. The group is not large, but wondrously diverse; diverse in Character, Passion, Purpose.

First: Christ and His disciples are there. He is the central figure, poor and sad in aspect, but Divinely grand. On Him all eyes are fixed, to Him all thoughts are directed. Peter, James, and John are there. On them, in all probability, there rests a heart-sinking impression that something awful, they scarcely know what, is about taking place, that something terrible is to happen to the One they love best of all.

Secondly: Judas is there. He, "having received the sop," at the table, we are told, "went immediately out: and it was night." He went out for the purpose of meeting Christ in this garden, His usual resort, there to betray Him to His enemies. In him we see here a threefold development of *greed*, for it was greed that prompted him to this infernal step. "What will ye give me?" this was his reigning impulse.

In his case we find greed running—(1.) Into *base ingratitude.* What favours Christ had conferred upon this man! But the passion of greed buried them all in oblivion. Gratitude and greed cannot co-exist. Here we find greed running—(2.) Into *heartless cruelty.* Judas handed his Benefactor over to ruthless ruffians, and intolerant bigots, to be crucified. Greed is ever cruel, it tramples on the rights and lives of men in quest of its object. Here we find greed running—(3.) Into *atrocious treachery.* In Matthew xxvi. 49 we are informed that Judas came to Jesus and said, "Hail, Master, and kissed Him." His greed overcame all sense of truth and honour, and even moral decency. Greed is always treacherous, always false; it fills the markets and senates of the world with lies and deceptions.

Thirdly: Unprincipled hirelings are there. "*A band of men and officers from the Chief Priests and Pharisees cometh thither.*" The word "*men*" is superfluous, and not in the original. Two bodies are here mentioned, meaning the detachment of the Roman cohort on duty at the festival, for the purpose of maintaining order, and the officials of the ecclesiastical authorities, the captain of the temple, and armed Levites. These men, perhaps, had no personal impressions concerning Christ, no hostile feeling towards Him, but they were there to do their *duty*, meaning by duty, the orders of their masters. In the sacred name of Duty what crimes have been enacted under these heavens! Soldiers rifle innocent homes, burn villages and cities, shed oceans of human blood, create millions of widows and orphans, in the name of Duty,—meaning by duty the commands of men lost to the claims of humanity, the sense of moral right, and of responsibility to their Maker. Such were the men now in the garden, venal hirelings. Notice—

III —THE TRANSACTIONS AT THE GATHERING

Four classes of deeds were here enacted.

First: Those *against* a conviction of duty. What Judas did in conducting the band into the garden, and there betraying Jesus with a kiss, must have been against his convictions of right: well he knew he was perpetrating an atrocious crime. Hear his own confession: "When he saw that He was condemned, he repented himself, and brought again the thirty pieces of silver to the Chief Priests and elders, saying, I have sinned in that I have betrayed the innocent blood" (Matt. xxvii. 3, 4). To sin against conscience is to sin with the most aggravated heinousness. Another class of deeds here enacted were—

Secondly: Those *without* any conviction of duty. These were the deeds of the "*band and the officers of the Chief Priests,*" who came with their "*lanterns and torches and weapons*" to seize Christ and to drag Him to the tribunal. These men were like "dumb, driven cattle," they were mere tools. Such men are ready for anything at the bidding of their masters; they have no will of their own; no convictions concerning the right and wrong of actions. Alas, how numerous are such men in every age! Wretched serfs, on them despots build their thrones. The other class of deeds here enacted were—

Thirdly: Those by a *right* conviction of duty. Such were the deeds of Christ. (1.) Mark His intrepidity. "*Jesus, therefore, knowing all things that should come upon Him, went forth, and said unto them, Whom seek ye?*" He does not wait for their approach. After Judas had given the treacherous kiss, he retreats perhaps among the band who followed him, who stand in hesitation. With calm and sublime heroism Jesus steps forward and confronts them with the question, " *Whom seek ye ?* " He does not propound this question for His own information, for He knew their purpose well, but in order that they may confess their object, and to impress them with the fact that they could only attain their object by His voluntary permission. (2.) Mark His dauntless confession. " *They answered, Jesus of Nazareth. Jesus saith unto them, I am He.*" Here I am. Here by My own power and choice ; here not as a Victim, but as a Victor. I am prepared to meet you : fulfil your mission, do your worst, My time has come. " No hostile hand can antedate My doom." (3.) Mark the moral force of His expression. " *As soon as He had said unto them, I am He, they went backward, and fell to the ground.*" What struck them down ? Not physical force, not miraculous agency, it was the flash of His pure soul upon their guilty consciences. They came with deadly "weapons" to seize His body ; He by the moral majesty of His looks seized their souls, and they fell as Saul fell on his way to Damascus ; fell like the sentinels at the tomb before the angels' withering glance (Matt. xxviii. 4). (4.) Mark His tender consideration. " *Then asked He them again, Whom seek ye ?** *And they said, Jesus of Nazareth. Jesus answered, I have told you that I am He : if, therefore, ye seek Me, let these go their way.*" They seem to have recovered from the shock, and are on their feet again. And again to impress them with the terrible wickedness and impiety of their mission, He repeats the question, " *Whom seek ye ?* " They reply, " *Jesus of Nazareth.*" If you want Jesus of Nazareth, " *I have told you I am He.*" Seize Me, but let My disciples escape. Perhaps some of the Roman cohort, not knowing Jesus personally, were about to lay hold on His disciples, and Jesus thus shields them. Thus the "Shepherd seeth the wolf coming, and fleeth not, because he careth for the sheep." In all this our Lord acted *by the conviction of right,* by the conviction that He was doing the will of His Father in heaven, which was the grand object of His mission to earth. The other class of deeds here enacted were—

Fourthly : Those by a *wrong* conviction of duty. " *Then Simon Peter having a sword drew it, and smote the High Priest's servant, and cut off his right ear. The servant's name was Malchus.*" No doubt Peter did this under the impression that he was doing the right. A conviction of duty probably gave force to the impulse to strike in defence of his Master. But the deed was wrong.

To which of these classes do our actions belong ? Are we acting *against* the sense of right, or *without* the sense of right, or by a *right* sense of right, or by a *wrong* sense of right ? Crucial question this !

* See Germ, p. 104.

Germs of Thought
No. 71   John 18:4-8

THE MAJESTY AND FORCE OF RIGHT

"Jesus therefore, knowing all things that should come upon Him," &c.

This incident serves to illustrate two things—

I—THE MORAL MAJESTY OF RIGHT

This is seen in two particulars—

First: In the heroic manner in which Christ, single-handedly, met His enemies. Jesus, instead of fleeing from their presence, or manifesting the slightest perturbation, goes forth magnanimously to meet them; and looking them, perhaps, directly in the face, says, "*Whom seek ye?*" What great offender are you in search of, at this late hour of the night? "*Jesus of Nazareth,*" said they; a name of reproach. As if they had said, 'We are in search of that infamous carpenter's Son from Nazareth; the Blasphemer, Who is representing Himself as the Son of God and the true Messiah. We want "*Jesus of Nazareth.*"' What was the reply? Did Christ in any way attempt to evade them? No! "*I am He.*" I shrink not from that name, though clothed with obloquy, though the object of imprecation with priests and populace. I am neither ashamed of My abused name, nor of Nazareth, My humble home. "*I am He.*" I shun not My past history; I am ready to have it scrutinized in open day. I, Jesus of Nazareth, have been in poverty, but never in disgrace; despised, but never depraved; assailed by the tempter, but never incited to sin.

Moral majesty is seen here—

Secondly: In the tender consideration which Christ displayed for His friends under the most trying circumstances. "*If ye seek Me, let these go their way.*" As if He had said, "Whatever injury you are going to inflict on Me, save them, though they have neglected Me, and "could not watch with Me one hour." I would not have them injured; and though I should like them to be with Me in this hour of My trial, to sustain Me with their presence and their sympathy, yet for the sake of their safety I forego the gratification; "*let these go their way.*" "Touch not Mine anointed, and do My prophets no harm."' He forgets Himself in His disciples. Is there not moral sublimity here? Who that has a soul within him, does not see the highest moral majesty, in Christ thus heroically meeting, single-handedly, His enemies, and seeking the safety of His unfaithful followers, at the moment when His own life was in most imminent peril?

The question which here comes up, and is worthy of a moment's thought, is, What was it that made Jesus so calm and powerful in this terrible hour? What is the philosophy of this majestic bearing? (1.) It was not *ignorance* of His perilous position. Men are sometimes calm in the midst of dangers, because they are unconscious of their situation. But it was not so with Christ; for we are told that He "*knew all things that should come upon Him.*" All the horrible events which were now to crowd into a few short hours of His life passed distinctly under His vision. The Hall of Caiaphas, the baseness of Annas and of Pilate, the maddened fury of the populace, the agonies of the Cross; He knew all these things, and knew that they were all coming upon Him at once— and yet He was calm. (2.) It was not *stoical insensibility* to His perilous position. The composure of some in trying circumstances is nothing but a stolid obduracy of heart. But it was not so with Christ. He was sensitiveness itself; His soul was all nerve. What then is the cause? It is the consciousness of rectitude. He knew that He was right with Himself, with the universe, and God. And with this consciousness of rectitude, there can never be any moral forebodings or apprehensions as to the future. With this, the future is evermore bright and attractive. With this consciousness of rectitude, moreover, there is always an assurance of God's presence and favour. Hence Christ might exultantly exclaim, "I have set the Lord always before Me; because He is at My right hand, I shall not be moved." This incident illustrates—

II—THE MORAL FORCE OF RIGHT

"*As soon then as He had said unto them, I am He, they went backward, and fell to the ground.*" What was it that now struck them down? What was the force that laid prostrate these strong men? Was it Miraculous Power? I think not, for the following reasons—

First: Because this supposition does not agree with the general use of Christ's miraculous agency. All the miracles of Christ were characterized by Mercy. The destruction of the barren fig-tree was the only exception. He did not employ His energy to injure, but to bless.

Secondly: Because this supposition is opposed to that general spirit of non-resistance, which He constantly exemplified and inculcated. We never find Him putting forth His hand to resist. He practised the principle He enforced, of returning good for evil.

Thirdly: Because this supposition is not necessary to account for the phenomenon. We think that the Divine and glorious bearing of Christ, when He approached them with His mighty words and piercing looks, was quite suffiecint to excite such a rush of violent emotion in their guilty spirits, as would produce the effect here stated. In support of this view, think of three things—

(1.) That violent and sudden emotions always tend to check the current of life. It is a physiological fact, that both sudden and extreme joy and terror, have often paralyzed the physical organs, and produced death. There are instances of culprits who, on receiving tidings of pardon under the gallows, have fallen dead in a moment, as if struck with a thunderbolt. Sudden and extreme terror produces the same effect. Notice—

(2.) The probable state of the minds of these men, when they entered the garden. They must have known and felt that they were doing wrong. Men when they are engaged in wrong work are always timid—always disposed to be alarmed;—"a guilty conscience makes cowards of us all." The nocturnal burglar moves to the door, you may be sure, with a tremulous step and a timid soul. The faintest sound has often broken the purpose of the midnight robber, and paralyzed the arm of the assassin. These men, perhaps, like all cowards, talked very bravely as they wended their way through the streets of Jerusalem, and crossed the brook of Cedron; but we may be certain there was a moral nervousness within.

(3.) The unexpected and morally dignified way in which Christ met them. They expected *resistance*—and then they would have put forth some resolute effort. But, instead of this, when He walked calmly up to them, and spoke in kind and dignified tones, they were taken aback. They felt that there was Divinity in His transcendent bearing, and this roused their guilty souls. Shame, remorse, terror, foreboding, rushed up from the depths of their moral heart like a tempest, before which they fell. It was the Force of Right that struck them down. This subject teaches—

First : The *supreme importance* of being Right. There is nothing of such moment to man as rectitude. This gives value to everything else. Apart from this—wealth, social influence, knowledge, and even life itself, are worthless. Our great want is a "right spirit within us." Nothing will enable us to meet the future but this. There is a Gethsemane before us all; the last night of our existence will come; and foes will approach us then more formidable than those which now surround us. Would we in that solemn moment be calm and firm? Then must we be made right.

Secondly : The *Divine method* of promoting Right. How are men to be made to feel its power? Not by force and violence, but by a calm display of itself.

Thirdly : The *ultimate triumph* of Right. The falling of these men before the moral majesty of Christ seems to prefigure what must one day be the case everywhere. The Right must conquer. The *Right is might,*—Divine might. Almightiness is with the right thought, act, and life. The wrong cannot stand before it : it must fall, as the colossal image in Nebuchadnezzar's dream fell at the touch of the little stone. The wrong in science, literature, government, institutions, religion, must fall before the Right.

Fourthly: The *folly of opposing* the Right. Priests and princes may rise up against it. Intrigue and violence, armies and navies, may be employed to put it down; but fruitless will prove all their efforts. The Triumphal Car of Right must roll over the dust of the Herods, Caiaphases, Julians, Neroes, Alexanders, and Napoleons of the world.

John 18:10, 11

PETER'S SWORD

"Then Simon Peter having a sword, drew it," &c.

EXEGETICAL REMARKS.—Ver. 11.— *"Then said Jesus* (R. V. JESUS THERE- FORE SAID) *unto Peter, Put up thy sword into the sheath: the cup which My* (R. V. THE) *Father hath given Me, shall I not drink it?"* "The image of the cup used to designate a lot to be submitted to, recalls the similar expression in the prayer in Gethsemane."—*Godet.*

HOMILETICS

We have three things here worthy of notice—

I —AN IMPULSE MANIFESTLY GENEROUS, WRONGLY DIRECTED

"*Then Simon Peter having a sword drew it, and smote the High Priest's servant.*" This fact is recorded by all the evangelists. John alone records that it was done by Peter, and the name of the servant of the High Priest—Malchus. The motive that prompted Peter to this act was not greed, ambition, or personal vengeance, it was that of sympathy for his Master; a generous desire to protect Him. But this impulse, *good* in itself, was *improperly* directed: directed to bloodshed and murder. How much good feeling is wrongly directed in this world!

First: There is *parental affection.* How generally is this employed to the advancement of a child's temporal good, rather than to his spiritual; to pamper his appetites rather than to discipline his heart; to make him independent of labour, rather than to train him to habits of honest industry; to make him a great figure in the world, rather than a good man in the universe; to enrich him with the wealth of the world, rather than with the wealth of a Christly character, which is the heaven of the soul!

Secondly: There is *religious sympathy.* Religious sympathy is one of the most glorious attributes of humanity. But how often is it directed, not to the making of our own characters so great and Christlike as to be witnesses or God wherever we go, but to formulate and promote theological dogmas, and establish and nourish little sects!

Thirdly: There is *philanthropic sentiment.* A love for humanity is an instinct as universal as the race. But this instinct, instead of being directed in endeavours, first to improve the moral heart of humanity, and then working from the heart to the whole outward life, and from the individual to the race, is directed to the creation and support of costly machinery for lopping off branches from the Upas, applying salves to the ulcers, and whitening the sepulchres of depravity. No man can be improved, only by first improving his heart; the fountain must be cleansed before the streams can be pure. We have here—

II —A VIOLENCE ENTIRELY DEFENSIVE, DIVINELY CONDEMNED

"*Then said Jesus unto Peter, Put up thy sword into the sheath.*" Did Peter expect his Master to say, "Well done, Peter, I value thy generous effort on My behalf?" If so, he was disappointed: strong words of disapproval came instead. "*Put up thy sword.*" In Matt. xxvi. 52, we have an addition to this: "All they that take the sword, shall perish by the sword." The words from Matthew may be taken in one of two senses, either as a *prediction* or as a *law* of humanity. If taken in the former sense, almost every chapter in the history of the world supplies abundant fulfilment. The nations of the earth that have practised war, have ultimately been ruined by wars. If in the latter sense, we find instincts in the human soul which lead to the result. Anger begets anger, love begets love, and "with what measure we mete, it is meted again." But clearly the words imply on Christ's part disapproval of Peter's deed. How could He approve of such an act? It was contrary to the old law, "Thou shalt not kill," and contrary to the law He introduced, to return "good for evil." We have here—

III —A RESIGNATION ABSOLUTELY FREE, SUBLIMELY DISPLAYED

"*The cup which My Father hath given Me, shall I not drink it?*" Christ was in His present condition not by necessity, but as a matter of free choice. He had "power to lay down His life, and power to take it up again." Matthew reports Him as saying on this occasion—"Thinkest thou not that I could pray to My Father, and He would send Me twelve legions of angels?" &c. Notwithstanding this, He submits with filial loyalty to overwhelming sufferings. "*The cup which My Father hath given Me, shall I not drink it?*" * Observe—

First: The sufferings of the good are a "*cup*," not an ocean. Happiness is an immeasurable sea, misery is only a "*cup*" in the universe: an exhaustible and exhausting quantity. Observe—

Secondly: The sufferings of the good are a gift from the Father. They are not a curse from the devil. It is an instinct of genuine piety to trace up all evil as well as good to the Father. "What

* See Germ, p. 109.

son is he whom the Father chasteneth not?" All hells are benevolent institutions. Observe—

Thirdly: The sufferings of the good are to be accepted with filial resignation. "*Shall I not drink it?*"

Germs of Thought
No. 72   John 18:11

THE RIGHT WAY TO VIEW AND ACCEPT SUFFERING

"The cup which My Father hath given Me, shall I not drink it?"

Christ was an Example to us in Suffering, The significant and somewhat tragic exclamation of the text shows how He viewed and accepted affliction.

I.—TAKING HIM AS OUR EXAMPLE, WE SHOULD REGARD SUFFER-INGS, EVEN WHEN INFLICTED BY WICKED MEN, AS COMING FROM GOD

A band of officers from the Chief Priests, led on by a treacherous disciple, had come down from the garden to arrest Him; and of this assault He speaks as the "*cup*" which His Father gave Him. As no suffering can come upon us without the Divine Knowledge and Permission, it is reasonable and right to recognize God's hand in it. In persecutions, trials, aye in martyrdom itself, we should recognize a "*cup*" in the hand of God.

II.—TAKING HIM AS OUR EXAMPLE, WE SHOULD ACCEPT SUFFERINGS, HOWEVER INEXPRESSIBLY DISTRESSING, AS COMING FROM GOD AS A FATHER

"*My Father hath given Me.*" It is not held out to Me by the hand of an Iron Necessity, or of an Indignant Judge, but by the hand of a Father. "*Shall I not drink it?*" (1.) Shall I not drink it without *reluctance?* Take it freely and in filial confidence. (2.) Shall I not drink it *thankfully?* I know it is for My good. The bitterest cup has curative elements.

John 18:12-14

PHASES OF A CORRUPT GOVERNMENT

(*Jesus before Caiaphas—Peter's Denial—Jerusalem.*—MATT. xxvi. 56, 57, 69—75; MARK xiv. 53, 54, 66—72; LUKE xxii. 54—62; JOHN xviii. 13—18, 25—27.)

"Then the band and the captain and officers," &c.

EXEGETICAL REMARKS.—Ver. 12.— "*Then* (R. V. SO) *the band and the captain* (R. V. CHIEF CAPTAIN) *and officers of the Jews took* (R. V. SEIZED) *Jesus, and bound Him.*" The record of the examination before Annas is peculiar to John. He no doubt was present; the enumeration of the band, the captain and the officers, show that, however different they were in many respects, they were one in their antagonism to Christ. The band was in all probability a cohort.

Ver. 13.—" *And led Him away* (R. V. LED HIM TO) *to Annas first ; for he was father in law to Caiaphas, which was the High Priest that same year*" (R. V. THAT YEAR). " The former relations which Annas had sustained to the high priesthood, both in himself and in his family, would make him an honorary officer still. He had been high priest eleven years, five of his sons had succeeded him in the office which was now held

by his son-in-law, and he himself was probably a vice high priest : besides, this was so special a case, it seems fit that he should be consulted."—*Jacobus.*

Ver. 14.—" *Now Caiaphas was he, which gave counsel to the Jews, that it was expedient that one man should die for the people.*" " John here doubtless refers to the counsel of Caiaphas, to show that he was fully prepared to carry out whatever orders Annas might give for the destruction of Christ."—*Whedon.* (See our notes on xi. 50.)

HOMILETICS

In these words we have several *Phases of a Corrupt Government in its Endeavours to Crush the Right.* " *Then the band and the captain and the officers of the Jews took Jesus, and bound Him.*" Why did the government of Judæa desire so earnestly, and labour so indefatigably, for the destruction of Christ ? Was there anything in His *genealogy* to account for it ? No. He was One of their own race—a Jew, Who by birth came down from the most illustrious of their ancestors. The blood of Abraham quivered in His veins. Was there anything in His *appearance ?* Was He hideous in form or countenance, somewhat monstrous or repulsive in presence ? Not so, I trow. In bodily presence I imagine Him to have been beauty idealized, " altogether lovely." Why then ? He was the Embodiment and fervid and fearless Advocate of RIGHT—right between man and man, and man and God. The Government was wrong—wrong to its very core—and it could not bear the right. The Right flashed on its corrupt heart, as sunbeams on diseased eyes. Hence they were determined to put an end to it, to kill it, to bury it, and to seal it down so that it should rise no more. Corrupt governments are always against the Right, hence the persecutions and the martyrdoms. A corrupt government appears here *endeavouring to crush the Right*—

I—BY THE EMPLOYMENT OF HIRELINGS

Who are now employed ? " *The band and the captain*" were the Roman cohort, and the " *officers*" were the apparitors. There are in all countries and under all governments, multitudes of men so utterly dead to the sense of justice, and the higher instincts of manhood and independency, that they are ready at any hour to sell themselves for pay, to services the most dishonourable and unrighteous. These have ever been, and still are, the ready tools of despots.

From these come, for the most part, the soldiers who, at the command of the authorities for the time being, will engage in the most iniquitous crimes, with malignant enthusiasm and ruthless cruelty. Alas, that creatures, formed in the image of God, endowed with grand possibilities, commissioned by heaven for services of justice and beneficence, should be thus so embruted and fallen! As we look upon them trooping forth, at the bidding of their masters, bearing with them the implements of cruelty and death, we are urged to cry out with the prophet, "Can these dry bones live?" Can these Thoughtless Bipeds, who sell themselves to the work of plunder and murder for thirteen pence a day, ever become *men*, alive with the sense of manly independence, and personal responsibility? A corrupt government appears here *endeavouring to crush the Right—*

II — IN THE NAME OF LAW

"*And led Him away to Annas first, for he was father in law to Caiaphas, which was the High Priest that same year.*" This Annas is pronounced by Josephus to have been the most fortunate man of his times. He had occupied the post of high priest for not less than fourteen years, and four of his sons had also filled that eminent office, and now his son-in-law Caiaphas occupied the distinction. His venerable age, and his ancient title to the priesthood, invested him with great legal authority. Because the enemies of Christ wanted their diabolical conduct and intentions towards Him to be sanctioned by law, they now commanded their hirelings to take Him to Annas and Caiaphas. They gained their purpose, and went forth to enact the infernal tragedy of Calvary under the authority of Law.

The greatest crimes ever perpetrated under these heavens have been perpetrated under the sanction of law. "We have a law, and by our law He ought to die." Despots say that the Law must be respected and sustained, or as their cant is, "law and order." But no; if your law and order are built on moral falsehood and wrong, tread them in the dust. The progress of the world requires this. The heroes of imperishable renown have given themselves to this work. What is wrong in morals, can never be right in any Government. A corrupt government appears here *endeavouring to crush the Right—*

III — UNDER THE PRETEXT OF A MISERABLE EXPEDIENCY

"*Now Caiaphas was he which gave counsel to the Jews, that it was expedient that one man should die for the people.*" In relation to this "*counsel*" three remarks may be offered.

First: That it was *apparently adapted* to the end. Christ was alienating the people from the institutions of the country, and shaking their faith in its authorities. The most effective plan for terminating the mischief *seemed* to be to put Him to death.

This would appear to strike the evil at the root. When this was done public excitement would soon subside, and the feeling of the people speedily flow back to its old level, and roll on monotonously in its old channel as heretofore. It was anyhow plausible.

Secondly : Though seemingly adapted to the end, it was *radically wrong in principle.* What right had Caiaphas to propose the death of any man, however criminal that man might be ? And even assuming his right as a governor, to put a criminal to death— a prerogative, however, which we deny to all but God,—certainly there was no show of right in proposing the death of One Who, like Christ, had never violated any law, Who had wronged no one, but blessed all. *The apparent fitness of a measure to an end does not make it right.* The only Standard of Right is the will of God.

Thirdly : Their policy being radically wrong, was *ultimately ruinous.* Did the putting of Christ to death avert the dreaded calamity ? Did it secure Judæa from the invasion of the Romans ? Did it serve in any way even the *temporal* interest of the country ? No, no ; it hastened the flight of the Roman eagle ; it brought upon them judgments which speedily broke up their commonwealth, and beneath which the Jewish people have been groaning to this hour. Ah ! what seems *"expedient"* to-day may prove in the future to have been most disastrous. Eternal principle is the only pillar to guide shortsighted creatures in their endless path. Let Governments be warned by the policy of Caiaphas.

John 18:15-18

A TEMPORARY FAILING OF TRUE COURAGE
"And Simon Peter followed Jesus, and so did another disciple," &c.

EXEGETICAL REMARKS.—Ver. 15.— *"And Simon Peter followed Jesus, and so did another disciple: that* (R. V. NOW THAT) *disciple was known unto the High Priest, and went in* (R. V. ENTERED) *with Jesus into the palace* (R. V. COURT) *of the High Priest."* It is generally supposed that by the *"other disciple,"* John is speaking of himself. Peter and John are often found in special connection with each other ; they now followed Jesus. How John was *"known to the High Priest"* is not stated, although in Acts iv. 6 his name appears amongst the kindred of the High Priest.

Ver. 16.—*"But Peter stood* (R. V. WAS STANDING) *at the door without."* He remained outside with the crowd. Jesus, as a Prisoner, and the other dis-

ciple as a friend of the High Priest, went into the court. *"Then went out that other disciple* (R. V. SO THE OTHER DISCIPLE), *which was known unto the High Priest, and spake unto her that kept the door, and brought in Peter."* It is customary even at the present day, in the East, for the doors of the wealthy to be superintended by a portress, who receives a fee for her services from the visitors.

Ver. 17.—*"Then saith the damsel* (R. V. THE MAID THEREFORE) *that kept the door unto* (R. V. SAITH UNTO) *Peter, Art not thou also* (R. V. ART THOU ALSO) *one of this man's disciples? He saith, I am not."* There is no charge brought against him ; it is simply an inquiry.

Ver. 18.—*"And* (R. V. NOW) *the*

servants and officers stood (R. V. WERE
STANDING) there, who had made (R. V.
HAVING MADE) a fire of coals; for it
was cold: and they warmed (R. V. WERE
WARMING) themselves: and Peter stood
(R.V. ALSO WAS) with them (R. V. STAND-
ING), and warmed (R. V. WARMING)

himself." Probably the "other disciple"
had gone forth and followed Christ
up, and entered the house. But fear
compelled Peter to mix with the
officers and servants, desiring that he
should be regarded as one of them.

HOMILETICS

Our subject is *The Temporary Failing of True Courage.* Observe here—

I —HERE IS TRUE COURAGE NOBLY DISPLAYED

"*And Simon Peter followed Jesus, and so did another disciple, into the palace of the High Priest,*" or the court. Here is heroism. To follow One Who was cursed by the nation, and was being dragged in bonds by Roman ruffians to undergo a mock trial, and Who in a few hours would, amid the fury of a maddened multitude, undergo the agonies of a terrible crucifixion, revealed a bravery of heart of no mean character. They stood firm and faithful to Him in "Whom they believed," although they knew that the spirit of their age and the rulers of their country were against Him.

II —HERE IS TRUE COURAGE TEMPORARILY FAILING

"*But Peter stood at the door without. Then went out that other disciple, which was known unto the High Priest, and spake unto her that kept the door, and brought in Peter.*" It would seem that at this stage Peter's courage began to fail, for he halted at the door, so that John had to go and take him in. As he entered he was recognized by the portress, who said to him, "*Art not thou also one of this man's disciples? He saith, I am not.*" Here is fear seeking to protect itself by falsehood. "*And the servants and officers stood there, who had made a fire of coals; for it was cold: and they warmed themselves: and Peter stood with them, and warmed himself.*" Fear had taken possession of Peter, and to protect himself, he halted by the fire, and mingled with the servants and officers who stood there, desiring, it may be, that he should be regarded as one of them.

Now here is a failure of courage which led to a terrible false-hood thrice repeated, even with curses. *Fear,* perhaps, is one of the most *prolific parents* of lies. *Greed* is a parent of lies; it fills the market with fallacies. *Vanity* is a parent of lies; it fills all social circles with misrepresentations. *Malice* is a parent of lies; it hatches the slanders that destroy reputations and often break hearts. But perhaps *fear* is the most fruitful source of lies, though these lies, in my judgment, are not the most venal. They are not aggressive, but defensive. Still they cannot be justified, although some good men have sought to justify them. Their influence is pernicious. The influence of Peter's falsehood upon John, his fellow-disciple, must have been most distressing, and the influence upon himself was to injure his self-respect, and to sting him with remorse.

But this fear was only *temporary*, his failing courage was soon restored. The look of Christ rallied the drooping forces of his moral manhood, and ever afterwards he appears as a hero amongst heroes in the cause of his Master. Witness his conduct before the Sanhedrim when he said to his accusers, " Whether it be right in the sight of God to hearken unto man rather than unto God, judge ye." Witness his sermon on the day of Pentecost, &c.

CONCLUSION. Learn—

First : The liability of a good man to moral reactions. Here is Peter, who was almost constitutionally bold and courageous—so that He Who knew what " was in man " called him a " rock "—struck with cowardice and trembling before the breath of a silly maid. So it often happens, men of great faith have sceptical moods, men of great hope desponding seasons, men of generous natures have misanthropic feelings. Learn—

Secondly : Whatever the moral reactions, the good element will ultimately prevail. The cowardice of Peter was only a passing mood. Courage lay at the root of his nature, and this courage came out in his after life in many a form sublimely inspiring. In his martyrdom, too, as given by tradition, the heroism of his soul shone in splendour.

John 18:19-23

A CONVENTIONAL JUDGE, AN INSOLENT SYCOPHANT, AND AN UNIQUE PRISONER

(Jesus before Caiaphas—He declares Himself to be the Christ—Jerusalem.—MATT. xxvi. 59—68 ; MARK xiv. 55—65 ; LUKE xxii. 63—71 ; JOHN xviii. 19—24.) " The High Priest then asked Jesus of His disciples, and of His doctrine," &c.

EXEGETICAL REMARKS.—Ver. 19.— " *The High Priest then asked Jesus of His disciples, and of His doctrine* " (R. V. TEACHING). Luke calls both Annas and Caiaphas high priests in Acts iv. 6. " It is easy to imagine," says *Westcott,* " that arrangements had been made for a private examination in the chamber of Annas, at which Caiaphas was himself present, and in which he took part. At the close of the unofficial proceeding, Annas sent Jesus to Caiaphas for a formal trial. The preliminary examination was directed to the obtaining of materials for the formal accusation which was to follow."

Ver. 20.—" *Jesus answered him, I spake* (R. V. HAVE SPOKEN) *openly to the world; I ever taught in the synagogue* (R. V. IN SYNAGOGUES), *and in the temple, whither* (R. V. WHERE ALL) *the Jews always resort* (R. V. COME TOGETHER) ; *and in secret have I said* (R. V. SPAKE I) *nothing.*" His preaching had been in the regular public places, the synagogue and the temple. He had no conspiracy, no secret society.

Ver. 21.—" *Why askest thou Me ? ask them which* (R. V. THAT HAVE) *heard Me, what I have said* (R. V. WHAT I SPAKE) *unto them : behold, they know what I said"* (R. V. THESE KNOW THE THINGS WHICH I SAID). "Jesus claims that the examination should proceed in due order by the calling of witnesses."

Ver. 22.—" *And when He had thus spoken* (R. V. SAID THIS), *one of the officers which stood by* (R. V. STANDING BY) *struck Jesus with the palm of his hand* (R. V. WITH HIS HAND), *saying, Answerest Thou the High Priest so?"*

It was not one of the servants, but one of the High Priest's attendants, or possibly one of the band who had brought Him thither.

Ver. 23.—" *Jesus answered him, If I have spoken evil, bear witness of the evil: but if well, why smitest thou Me?"* "If I have said anything improper, stand forth as a witness against Me ; but if not, why employ brute force towards Me?"

HOMILETICS

These verses present to us three subjects of thought, *A Conventional Judge, An Insolent Sycophant,* and *An Unique Prisoner.* Here we see—

I —A CONVENTIONAL JUDGE

Whether Annas had any right to exercise judicial authority at this time, or assumed it because he had long exercised it, and was of great experience and extensive influence, he now assumes that authority, and subjects Christ to interrogations. I discover three very censurable elements in the conduct of this conventional judge on this occasion. Here is—

First : Officiousness. If he had been in possession of judicial authority at this time, he had no right whatever to ask the prisoner concerning *"His disciples, and of His doctrine."* His business was with His personal conduct. Was He personally guilty of any sin against ecclesiastic or civic laws, or not ? But, inasmuch as in all probability he was not in possession of any judicial authority, his officiousness was *indecent* and *offensive.* Another element discoverable in this conventional judge is—

Secondly : Craftiness. The question was evidently designed to entrap Christ into some statements that might be used against Him at His trial; some statements that might involve Christ in something like a self-crimination. Craftiness is one of the most despicable attributes of character, and scarcely anywhere is it so prominent and prevalent as in Courts of Law, and on the Judicial Bench. In sooth it is regarded too much as a qualification for judicial work. Another censurable element discoverable in this conventional judge is—

Thirdly : Heartlessness. It might have been supposed that an old man, who had been brought up from childhood in the religion of the patriarchs, and who, long before Christ was born, occupied the highest position, in order to vindicate its rights and extend its influence, would have been touched into the tenderest compassion at seeing a young Man Whose countenance had no trace of vice, but radiated with virtue, bound in chains, and awaiting a terrible doom. But no, his old heart is callous. The atmosphere of the high office which he had sustained for many a long year had frozen within him all the fountains of humanity. In a Conventional Judge, sad to say, there is nothing very rare in this. How often do we find an old man on the bench, who seems to gloat over every new contribution of evidence that goes to convict the prisoner, and with the black cap on his head, will pronounce sentence of death with heart unthrilled, and a voice unquivering. It is said that justice is cold. This is a libel on the celestial attribute. Justice is a ray of love, it is indeed a modification of love, it is rooted in love, and cannot live without the root. Quench love in the soul, and what is called justice becomes statutory rigorousness.

> "The calm Divinity of justice sits
> And pities while she punishes mankind."

The words present to us—

II —AN INSOLENT SYCOPHANT

" *One of the officers which stood by, struck Jesus with the palm of his hand, saying, Answerest Thou the High Priest so ?* "

First : Here is an act of Sycophancy. This man was one of those mean craven souls, who are ever ready to flatter superiors. He wished Annas to think, that he saw in the reply of Christ the want of that respect which such a high dignitary should always have ; and the miserable lacquey considered that he would be pleased by a prompt recognition and avengement of the same. No doubt this was the spirit that actuated this man. A more despicable and pernicious character than this, know I not : *despicable* because it implies the lack of all manly independence ; *pernicious*, for it degrades the possessor, deceives others, and impedes the progress of individuals and communities. But whilst it is despicable and pernicious, it is, alas, prevalent not only in courts, but in all circles society through. Parasites abound, the Calibans count their millions.

> "Deceitful, smiling, fawning flatterers,
> Like rats oft bite the holy cords in twain,
> Too intricate to unloose : soothe every passion
> That in the nature of their lords rebels :
> Revenge, affirm, and turn their halcyon beaks
> With every gale and vary of their masters."

Secondly : Here is an act of Insolence. He " *struck Jesus with the palm of his hand.*" Mark the heartless insolence of this creature : he struck an innocent Man Who stood before him bound as a prisoner ; more than that, he struck incarnate Divinity. The lowest-natured persons are always the most insolent. Men who are the most ready to flatter those above them, are ever most disposed to treat with the greatest rudeness those of a humbler grade. The reason is obvious, the sycophant can have no true respect for himself, for being an abject toady he finds nothing in himself to respect, and much with which to feel self-disgust. He who respects not himself has neither the desire, nor the qualification to respect others. At the bidding of those in power, the servile multitudes will deal out insults, not only to every passer-by, but even to those in the higher ranks of intelligence and morality.

The words present to us—

III—AN UNIQUE PRISONER

First : Mark His Reply to the Conventional Judge. *" Jesus answered him, I spake openly to the world ; I ever taught in the synagogue, and in the temple, whither the Jews always resort ; and in secret have I said nothing. Why askest thou Me ? ask them which heard Me, what I have said unto them : behold, they know what I said."* In this Reply three things are observable.

(1.) *Manly Independency.* There is no bowing down before this venerable official, nothing crouching or craven. He speaks to him as man to man. It is noteworthy that Christ pays no respect to mere Office. In these last days, men have come to think that an elevated office of itself has a just claim to respect and honour. A huge fallacy this. Legislative, administrative, regal offices, what are they worth if not occupied by morally worthy men ? Nothing ; they are simply contemptible. The more elevated the office is, the more dishonourable the man who occupies it, if not intellectually and morally qualified. Ignorance and depravity are bad everywhere ; bad in the poor and the obscure, but a thousand times more abhorrent in the legislator, the judge, and the king. Mere office is an abstraction ; it is the man who makes the office worthy or unworthy. Christ had no respect for this man as a man, and therefore no respect for him as a judge. In this Reply we see—

(2.) *Conscious Honesty.* Christ's referring the question to His disciples indicates that He had nothing to fear. *" Why askest thou Me ? ask them which heard Me, what I have said."* I am no conspirator : what I have said and done has been in the face of all the world, in the synagogues of the Jew and in the temple at Jerusalem, in the face of open day have I said what I had to say. Does not this indicate conscious honesty ? It was this that made Him fearless and invincible. In this Reply we see—

(3.) *Faith in Humanity.* No one had such an overwhelming and painful sense of the moral depravity of the men of His age as Christ had, yet He was prepared to trust to their verdict. He seemed to feel that it would be impossible for them, if they had any remnant of conscience left, to accuse Him of anything underhanded or conspiratory. Confidence in human nature is the effect and evidence of conscious honesty. Treat every man as a rogue until you find him honest, is the maxim of the world. Christ acted on the converse, He treated every man as honest until He found him otherwise. The greatest rogues are ever the most suspicious.

Secondly : Mark His Reply to the Insolent Sycophant. *"Jesus answered him, If I have spoken evil, bear witness of the evil: but if well, why smitest thou Me ?"* Though a miserable retainer, the base minion of bloated authority, albeit Christ treats him as a man, and says virtually, " If I have said anything improper, stand forth as a witness against Me, but if not, why employ brute force towards Me ?" If this man had a soul, this rebuke must have shaken its every fibre. An Unique Prisoner this ! In truth, He was only a Prisoner in form and aspect. The conventional judge and his insolent sycophant, they were, in reality, the prisoners ; their little souls were manacled by chains stronger than adamant. He was the true Judge, the Sublime Judge of all Mankind.

John 18:24-27

THE TWO DENIALS OF PETER

" Now Annas had sent Him bound unto Caiaphas the High Priest," &c.

EXEGETICAL REMARKS.—On the termination of Christ's pre-examination by Annas, he sent Him bound in chains into the hall of Caiaphas, which was contiguous, and probably under the same roof. " Our evangelist, it would seem, had nothing to add to the ample details of the trial and condemnation of the Lord Jesus, and the indignities with which He was thereafter treated. And next to nothing on the sad fall of Peter in the midst of these transactions. With all this he holds his readers already familiar through the records of the three preceding evangelists."

Ver. 24.—*"Annas sent Him bound unto Caiaphas the High Priest."* The private interrogation at which Caiaphas had assisted, led to no decisive result. Annas therefore sends Him on to the High Priest officially.

Vers. 25, 26, 27.—*"And* (R. V. NOW) *Simon Peter stood* (R. V. WAS STANDING) *and warmed* (R. V. WARMING) *himself. They said therefore unto him, Art not thou also* (R. V. ART THOU ALSO) *one of His disciples? He denied it, and said, I am not. One of the servants of the High Priest, being his kinsman whose ear* (R. V. OF HIM WHOSE EAR) *Peter cut off, saith, Did not I see thee in the garden with Him? Peter then* (R. V. THEREFORE) *denied again: and immediately* (R. V. STRAIGHTWAY) *the cock crew."* " Although John relates in the briefest terms two of Peter's denials, and the crowing of the cock, this is merely to supply one small but striking particular, which had not been noticed in the preceding gospels : how one of those who charged Peter with being a disciple of Jesus was able to identify him, by his own relationship to the man whose ear Peter had cut off in the garden, and who saw him do it." — *Dr. Brown.* The fact that the other Synoptists record the three denials of Peter at the house of Caiaphas, and John, only two here can be explained by the fact that Annas and Caiaphas in all probability occupied the same sacerdotal palace, and that the passage from the presence of the one into that of the other would occupy scarcely any time, and the three denials therefore would be regarded as successive.

HOMILETICS

There are four things here in connection with *Peter's Denial,* on which we may profitably fasten our attention.

I —HE HAD STEPPED AT THE OUTSET INTO A TEMPTING SOCIETY

First : In that Hall he would meet with a rank of men *Superior to his own grade.* No doubt there were present some of the magnates of Jerusalem, some perhaps even members of the Sanhedrim, and others their acquaintances and friends. Peter was a poor fisherman ; his pedigree was obscure, and his circumstances were impoverished. One poor man in the presence of magnates could scarcely fail to feel that influence ; would, whilst listening to their words and marking their stately manners, involuntarily cower in their presence. The poor are ever disposed servilely to honour and imitate the rich.

Secondly : The rank of men that Peter would meet in that Hall were all *Hostile to Christ.* He would hear not only their disparaging remarks concerning Him, but their language of ridicule, scorn, and contempt. Arguments, too, conducted perhaps with logical power, would fall on his ears, to show from the Old Testament Scriptures that Christ was a blasphemous impostor. In such a social atmosphere as this, his confidence in Christ would be shaken ; grow cold and weak. Sad for thee, Peter, that thou shouldst enter such a circle ! " Evil companionships corrupt good manners." " One rotten apple," says *Feltham,* " will infect the store ; the putrid grape corrupts the whole sound cluster. If I have found any good companions I will cherish them as the choicest of men, or as angels which are sent as guardians to me. If I have any bad ones, I will study to lose them, lest by keeping them I lose myself in the end." Another circumstance here worth noticing is—

II —HIS PERILS INCREASED THE LONGER HE CONTINUED

Peter might well have concluded that if his Master were to be actually crucified, his own ruin would be terrific and inevitable. The devotees of the universally hated One would be hated ; of the murdered One would be destroyed. And all this because very likely every hour the clouds were becoming more and more widespread and black, all the stars of hope had set, the sky was black —blackening into midnight. How could he continue in his devotion to Him in such a tremendous hour ? Fear impelled him to deny, and deny he did. Fear emasculates a man, strikes down his courage, takes the heart out of him ; it makes the most open nature often quiver in every fibre.

"I feel my sinews slackened with the fright,
And a cold sweat trills down o'er all my limbs,
As if I were dissolving into water."—*Dryden.*

Another circumstance here deserving remark is—

III —HE WAS RECOGNIZED BY THE BROTHER OF HIS ENEMY

"*One of the servants of the High Priest, being his kinsman whose ear Peter cut off, saith, Did not I see thee in the garden with Him?*" It was bad enough for him to have been recognized by the portress as Christ's disciple, bad enough that those who stood by while he was warming himself should ask, "*Art thou not one of His disciples?*" but far more distressing was it to be recognized by an official, the ear of whose kinsman his sword had cut off. "*Did not I see thee in the garden with Him?*" This was scarcely a question of curiosity, scarcely a question put for the sake of information : it breathes vengeance. It means perhaps this, Dost thou mean to say that I, whose brother thou hast injured, did not see thee in the garden with Him? Did I not stand by thee, and glare at thee with indignation when thou didst assault my brother? Terrible stroke this for Peter! Perhaps when he entered this Hall he congratulated himself upon his good fortune ; it was warm in the cold night, and he stood side by side with great men. "Thou art more fortunate," says *Gossner,* "in having a friend who preventeth thee from going in to men of the world, than in possessing one who procureth thee access to them, and introduceth thee into their dwellings." The other circumstance that is noteworthy here is—

IV —HE WAS UNEXPECTEDLY ROUSED TO THE SENSE OF HIS SIN

"*Peter then denied again : and immediately the cock crew.*" The cock crew in the very climax of his infidelity. Twice before the shriek of this bird had filled his ear, now it fell like a thunder-clap on his conscience. God can give the most innocent object in nature an arrow to pierce the soul, the most feeble voice a power that shall rouse the sleeping conscience into fury. Elsewhere it is said, "Peter remembered the words of Jesus," and when he thought thereon "he wept." And, again, it is said he "went out and wept bitterly." He went out from the companionship of ruffians, and the scene of bigotry and injustice—he went out from the circle where he had been tempted to a course of wickedness, whose memory now struck him with horror and alarm—he went out into the solitudes of nature, under the quiet vault of night, to weep his tears at the foot of justice, and to breathe his sighs into the ear of mercy. He went out to unburden himself of that load of guilt which he had contracted, and to consecrate his being once more to the will of his Maker. He wept bitterly, and his tears were

> " Like blessed showers
> Which leave the skies they come from
> Bright and holy."

John 18:28

SPURIOUS SANCTITY

(The Sanhedrim lead Jesus away to Pilate—Jerusalem.—MATT. xxvii. 1, 2 ; MARK xv. 1—5 ; LUKE xxiii. 1—5 ; JOHN xviii. 28—38.)*

" Then led they Jesus from Caiaphas unto the hall," &c.

EXEGETICAL REMARKS.—Ver. 28.— "*Then led* (R. V. THEY LED THERE-FORE) *they Jesus from Caiaphas.*" It is noteworthy that John does not record Christ's trial before Caiaphas ; the Synoptists do. " *Unto* (R. V. INTO) *the hall of judgment* " (R. V. PALACE). This was the official residence of the Roman governor. His private home was at Cæsarea, but during the Passover season there was an influx of strangers and consequent general excitement, so that he felt it his duty to be present in the city, that peace and order might be preserved. The *cere-mony* referred to here is the Pass-over. "*That they might* (R. V. BUT MIGHT) *eat the Passover.*" Because all the other Evangelists assured us that Jesus had eaten the paschal lamb the night before, viz. on the Thursday evening ; John's statement here that it was eaten on the present day, viz. on the Friday, is difficult to be un-derstood. Sceptics have discovered a damaging contradiction. Various theories have been propounded by Biblical critics for solving the diffi-culty. I agree with a modern ex-positor, who says that "the simplest and most satisfactory solution is found in the different meanings of the word ' *Passover.*' It no doubt often did signify simply the paschal lamb. But it also had a more extensive mean-ing, so as to include the entire festival of the Passover week." Such is the obvious meaning in John ii. 13—23 ; vi. 4 ; xi. 55 ; xii. 1 ; xiii. 1. So also in 2 Chron. xxx. 22. " They did eat throughout the feast seven days, offer-ing peace offerings." Now during the Passover week, there was to be on each day a burnt offering : two young bul-locks, one ram, and seven lambs ; also a meat offering, and one goat for a sin offering. Unleavened bread was to be eaten through the week. There was also the *chigagah,* which was a festive thank offering made by private individuals and families. To partake of these during any day of the festival was to keep or eat the Passover. That John did not disagree with the other Evangelists in holding the supper on the night of Christ's betrayal to be the *Passover* we have good historical proof. For his disciple Polycarp, in a discussion of the question occurring in his day, expressly declared that " John himself celebrated the Easter supper on the fourteenth of Nixan, the time of the Jewish Passover." (On the whole subject read Excursus F., in Bishop Ellicott's " Commentary for English Readers," vol i. p. 559.) The *sentiment* is vastly more import-ant than either the scene or the ceremony. "*And they themselves went not into the judgment hall* (R. V. PALACE), *lest they should be* (R. V. THAT THEY MIGHT NOT) *defiled.*" They sent Christ in the custody of Roman officers ; these remained outside, " *lest they should be defiled.*"

HOMILETICS

These wretches who were thirsting for the blood of Him Who was " harmless," " holy," undefiled, " separate from sinners," Who was the Son of God Himself, were afraid of being ceremonially " *defiled* " if they entered the apartments of a heathen majesty.

Here is a *Spurious Sanctity.* In relation to this wretched state of mind, I predicate the following facts—

I —IT IS COMMON

How many religionists there are in Christendom, of almost every creed and sect, who are afraid to enter certain places, lest their holy souls should receive a taint! Papists stand aloof from all Protestant scenes of worship; and Protestants from a similar sentiment avoid all churches of the Catholic order. Nor are the numbers few amongst the adherents of the Episcopal Church of England, who would not enter the churches of Nonconformist communions, "*lest they should be defiled.*" As if, forsooth, those who every Sunday proclaim themselves in the great congregation to be "*miserable sinners,*" felt themselves at the same time so pure as to dread defilement in entering Churches, where such men as John Foster, Robert Hall, John Howe, Caleb Morris and Dr. Chalmers preached; where Milton sang, and Cromwell knelt! Nor are Nonconformists free from this miserable sentiment. There are thousands of narrow souls in the region of Dissent, who avoid Episcopal Churches lest they should receive a taint. The men, of this Spurious Sanctity, Who are they? Are they lawyers, who never take advantage of their clients; merchants who never practise dishonesty on their customers; doctors who never impose on their patients; servants who never cheat their masters; mistresses who never deal unkindly and unjustly with their servants; aristocrats who are never haughty, overbearing, and licentious? I trow not. The chances are, the high probability is, that the men of spurious sanctity belong to these classes. For no order of men had the Divinest of all Teachers and the Noblest of all Characters a profounder contempt. "Woe unto you," &c. To His all pure and piercing eye they were "whited sepulchres." Verily, the most soul-polluted men and women I know are those of this class. I could not trust them. All healthy moral virtues have quitted their natures, and their graces are all shams. I predicate another fact in relation to this Spurious Sanctity, and that is—

II —IT IS IRRATIONAL

First: It is founded on an absurd idea of *localities.* It presupposes that some places are in themselves more holy than others. Is St. Peter's in Rome more holy than St. Paul's in London? Or is St. Paul's in London more holy than the Methodist Chapel in the City Road, or any other place, shop, or sanctuary? Nay, all places are alike: every spot on which we tread is "holy ground," for the Holy God made it, and is present with it every minute. True, the purpose for which a certain place has been consecrated, or set apart, may be good or bad, but the place is the same whether it be for a Cathedral or a Market. The notion that one place on this round earth is more holy than another, is an offence to reason, an insult to common sense.

Secondly: It is founded on an absurd idea of *human obligation*. It supposes that a man is bound to be more holy in one place, or in one period, than in another; more holy in the church than in the shop; more holy on the Sunday than on the other six days of the week. This notion, which is terribly prevalent, is a superstitious phantom, a preposterous fiction. Man, though of complex elements and faculties, is but *one* being, and *moral* in all and evermore. Even all his physical voluntary actions have a moral quality, and so have all his volitions, whether referring to the movements of bodily organs or of mental faculties. "Whatsoever he does in word or deed," whether in business or in worship, he is bound to do all to the "glory of God."

Thirdly: It is founded on an absurd idea of *mind*. It supposes that the human mind is some passive substance that can be defiled by some outward element or agent, irrespective of its own choice and effort—a kind of fabric, a piece of ware or stone that you can daub or wash. But it is not so. Nothing outward can affect the mind irrespective of itself, no force can soil or cleanse it independent of its own efforts. It can make itself filthy in scenes and services supposed to be the most holy; it can wash itself from its pollution in scenes considered the most corrupt and vile. There is a power in the body, when in a healthy state, to appropriate whatever goes into it from external nature that is wholesome and necessary, and to expel that which is noxious and superfluous. The soul has a power analogous to this—a power to appropriate the wholesome and to expel the injurious. This power we call the *transformative*. Let us use it rightly—use it as Noah used it, who, amidst the blasphemy and ridicule of a corrupt generation, "walked with God," and fulfilled a noble destiny; as Paul used it at sceptical Athens, and dissolute Corinth, and in Pagan Rome, who from experience left the world this testimony: "All things work together for good to them that love God." Another fact I predicate in relation to this *Spurious Sanctity* is—

III—IT IS PERNICIOUS

First: This spurious sanctity is a positive injury to its subject. The religionist who moves about the world with the dread of having his soul "*defiled*" by outward things, is like a man who enters a sick room, afraid of inbreathing the disease of the sufferer; he is nervous, and feels oppressed by the atmosphere, his buoyancy and brightness for the nonce have quitted him. The spurious saint lacks naturalness, buoyancy, and elasticity of soul. There is no joyous humour in the eye, no manly ring in the voice; there is the pietistic face, the whining voice, and the moody eye. He is afraid of being "*defiled*," and he shuns the scenes of innocent recreation, he trembles all over in the presence of heretics and schismatics. Poor creatures, quit the world and retire to the scenes of monks or nuns !

Secondly : This spurious sanctity is a calumny on true religion. The religion of Christ is happiness. "These things have I spoken unto you that your joy may be full." He came to bring the soul out into perfect freedom, and to pour into it "joy unspeakable and full of glory." I am disposed to believe that the teeming thousands of sanctimonious men and women, that crowd churches and chapels, talking in sepulchral tones and pulling long faces, are far greater obstructions to the progress of Christianity, than all the sceptics of the day, for they *misrepresent* the Son of God.

CONCLUSION. Among the many practical lessons that may be drawn from this subject, there is one applicable especially to *Parents*. It is always a deeply anxious period in the history of a pious parent, when the time comes to send his children out in the wide world, to engage in such pursuits as may be the most conducive to their advancement and usefulness in life. This profession is thought of and given up, because of the temptations with which it is associated. That business, though lucrative, is renounced because of the fallacious and dishonest principles on which it is conducted, and the depraved circle with which it stands connected. There is not a single department of secular life, that can be thought of as suitable for the child, that is not beset with perils to his innocence and virtue. And when, after much anxious thought and prayer, the parent decides on that which is least objectionable, on moral grounds, still he is anxious. Which is the way to meet this parental difficulty ? Teach the child that his Maker has endowed him with powers of mind and thought, that will enable him to stand against all outward temptation; that if he is true to the spiritual nature which Kind Heaven has given him, he can pass through the most fiery assaults of the devil unscathed, move through the most polluted scenes without a moral taint. Teach him, that his safety is in reliance upon the right use of his own faculties and in the blessing of his God. Teach him, that it is not the unchaste conversation, the filthy song, the profane expression that may go into his ear, that will *defile* him; but the *use* he makes of these. Teach him, that he has a power to turn wickedness to his own spiritual advantage, that he may

> "Gather honey from the weed,
> And make a moral of the devil himself."

John 18:29-32

THE TWOFOLD APPEAL OF PILATE TO THE ENEMIES OF CHRIST, AND THEIR RESPONSE

"Pilate then went out unto them," &c.

EXEGETICAL REMARKS.—Ver. 29.— "*Pilate then* (R. V. THEREFORE) *went out unto them, and said, What accusation bring ye against this man?*" Though Pilate might have a general knowledge of the accusation, it was their place formally to present it. "Bound to respect the Jewish customs, the Procurator steps forth to them."—*Tholuck.*

Ver. 30.—"*They answered and said unto him, If He were not a malefactor* (R. V. IF THIS MAN WERE NOT AN EVIL DOER), *we would* (R. V. SHOULD) *not have delivered Him up unto thee.*" They are getting impatient, and will not wait for a formal process, and are quite unprepared for the governor's hesitation.

Ver. 31.—"*Then said Pilate unto them* (R. V. PILATE THEREFORE SAID UNTO THEM), *Take ye Him* (R. V. TAKE HIM YOURSELVES), *and judge Him according to your law. The Jews therefore said unto him, It is not lawful for us to put any man to death.*" Pilate means to say, "If He is to pass for a criminal simply in accordance with your sentence, then execute Him also according to your law." "This reply of Pilate compelled on their part the humiliating confession that the nation since the subjection to Roman power had been deprived of judicial authority over life and death."

Ver. 32.—"*That the saying* (R. V. WORD) *of Jesus might be fulfilled, which He spake, signifying what* (R. V. BY WHAT MANNER OF) *death He should die.*" See chap. xii. 32; comp. Matt. xx. 19.

HOMILETICS

As the Spurious Sanctity of these Scribes and Pharisees who thirsted for the blood of Christ, would not permit them to enter the Prætorium, or the "hall of judgment," into which they had forced Christ to appear before Pilate as a Prisoner, Pilate comes forth to them and asks, "*What accusation bring ye against this Man?*" In this position outside of the Prætorium we have *Two Distinct Appeals which Pilate makes to the Enemies of Christ, and their Response.* Let us notice—

I —PILATE'S FIRST APPEAL TO THE ENEMIES OF CHRIST, AND THEIR RESPONSE

"*What accusation bring ye against this Man?*" It is probable that Pilate had a general knowledge of the charge which they had to bring; but now, as he has to enter on the business of a judge, he would require something more specific. As the Roman procurator, he demands to know the specific crime Christ had committed against the Roman law.

What response did these intolerant bigots make to the appeal? Here it is. It is very characteristic and very significant. "*They answered and said unto him, If He were not a malefactor, we would not have delivered Him up unto thee.*" Look with an analytic eye into this utterance, and we shall detect three elements of moral depravity—

First : Baseless Calumny. *" If He were not a malefactor,"* an evil-doer. Meaning that He was an evil-doer was a well-attested fact. As if they had said, that He is a great criminal is patent and notorious. But what evil had He done ? what crime had He perpetrated ? None whatever. Here, then, is a vile calumny implied rather than expressed. Thus slander generally works. It unblushingly assumes wrong in the character it traduces, and expresses it, not in intelligible language, but in oblique innuendo, a nod of the head, a shrug of the shoulder, and an expression of the countenance. Here is—

Secondly : Arrogated Superiority. *"If He were not a malefactor, we would not have delivered Him up unto thee."* *" We"* could not have done such a thing. As if they had said, 'So vital is our sympathy with rectitude, that we should have recoiled with abhorrence from charging crime on an innocent man.' *" We would not have delivered Him up."* *" We,"* oh no, not for the world !

There is a great social influence in arrogated superiority, whether intellectual or moral. Let a man assume before his fellows that he is a great thinker, a great scholar, and the thought-less circles in which he lives will accept him as such, and ring out his transcendent merits. Let a man assume to be pre-eminently holy, and in the especial confidence of heaven, and he shall be accepted as a saint of the first rank, and the chief of all the prophets. The credulous fools in the sphere in which he moves, whether large or small, will regard his prayers as having the power to reverse the laws of the universe, and his dogmas as having an efficacy to rescue souls from damnation. As a rule, alas, our contemporaries take us, not for what we *are*, but for what we *assume* to be. Here is—

Thirdly : Crouching Sycophancy. *" We would not have delivered Him up unto thee "*—thee, the great judge. "Their demand," says *Lange,* "was intended to convey the right of a greater inde-pendence. If we come before thy tribunal that is an honour for thee, in return for which thou canst surely do us the honour to recognize our sentence without further ceremony." Corrupt men always work out their base designs by a crawling servility to men in power. The devil himself is the prince of sneaks and sycophants. Let us notice—

II —PILATE'S SECOND APPEAL TO THE ENEMIES OF CHRIST, AND THEIR RESPONSE

" Then said Pilate unto them, Take ye Him, and judge Him according to your law. The Jews therefore said unto him, It is not lawful for us to put any man to death." Pilate's words here seem

to be an ironical reply to their assumption. They assume that the very fact of their bringing Jesus before him, was in itself a proof of His criminality. Pilate virtually says, "Very well, then, this being so, dispose of Him if you dare, do not trouble me." What was their reply? *"It is not lawful for us to put any man to death: that the saying of Jesus might be fulfilled, which He spake, signifying what death He should die."* Two remarks here concerning these enemies of Christ.

First: They were animated by a mortal malice. Their hatred to Christ had become so hot and rampant, that nothing short of His death would satisfy them. *"It is not lawful for us to put any man to death,"* and His death we want. For this we come to thee. Nothing but His death will satisfy us. To what a height had the tide of their depravity risen!

Secondly: Their mortal malice was restrained by Providence. Two things seem to have restrained them: (1.) Public law. They would have inflicted on Him capital punishment themselves, but the Romans had taken away that power. *"It is not lawful for us to put any man to death."* They were restrained by (2) A Divine decree. *"That the saying of Jesus might be fulfilled, which He spake, signifying what death He should die."* Christ had frequently predicted that He should die the death of crucifixion. But crucifixion was the Roman mode of inflicting capital punishment. Had it been left to the Jews to put Him to death, it would have been by stoning (Lev. xxiv. 16; 2 Kings vi. 17; Acts i. 16). There was, therefore, a Divine purpose as well as a Roman law, that *restrained* them from putting to death the Son of God.

Sinners live under a grand system of restraints. They are held back from fully gratifying their passions or realizing their aims. It is well that it is so, otherwise the world would soon become a Pandemonium. Even the devil himself, like some fiery steed, is reined in with bit and bridle.

John 18:33-35

CHRIST'S REPLY TO PILATE'S ADDRESS, AND PILATE'S REMARK ON CHRIST'S REPLY

"Then Pilate entered into the judgment hall," &c.

EXEGETICAL REMARKS.—Ver. 33.— *"Then Pilate* (R. V. PILATE THEREFORE) *entered into the judgment hall* (R. V. PALACE) *again, and called Jesus, and said unto Him, Art Thou the King of the Jews?"* "Pilate," says *Hengstenberg*, "had set the alternative before the Jews, either to bring a formal accusation against Jesus, or to judge Him according to their own law. They declined the latter, and we may suppose they adopted the former." Pilate, therefore, entered again into the Prætorium or palace, and summoned Jesus before him. No honest investigation could he carry on amidst the intolerant religionists and roaring rabble, hence he repairs into the palace where the Jews could not enter, for a private examination. Pilate puts the question directly, "*Art Thou the King of the Jews?*" As if he said, this is the charge against you. Luke tells us, "They began to accuse Him, saying, We found this fellow perverting the nation, and forbidding to give tribute to Cæsar, saying that He Himself is Christ a King." Pilate's question therefore means, Is this the case?

Ver. 34.—"*Jesus answered him, Sayest thou this thing* (R. V. THIS OF) *of thyself, or did others tell it thee of* (R. V. CONCERNING) *Me?*" "The most probable interpretation of the question is," says a modern expositor, "that which regards it as establishing a distinction between the title '*king of the Jews*' as spoken by Pilate, and the same title as spoken by Jesus. In the political sense in which Pilate would use it, and in this sense only, the claim would be brought against Him in Roman law, He was not King of the Jews. In the theocratic sense in which a Jew would use that title He was King of the Jews." *Grotius* seems to hit the meaning of our Lord's words

here. "Thou hast been so long a ruler, and so careful a defender of the Roman majesty, and hast thou ever heard anything that would impeach Me of a design to usurp authority against Rome? If thou hast never known anything of thyself, but others have suggested it, beware lest thou be deceived by an ambiguous word."

Ver. 35.—"*Pilate answered, Am I a Jew? Thine own nation and the Chief Priests have delivered Thee unto me: what hast Thou done?*" Pilate seems here to speak in a tone of a little irritation, at the very suspicion that he paid any attention to the distinctions in a Jewish quarrel: as if he had said, "Do you suppose I am a Jew?" "He gets out of patience," says *Godet*. "What have I to do with all your Jewish subtilties?" There is a supreme contempt in the antithesis, ἐγώ ... Ἰουδαῖος (I . . . a Jew!) Then dismissing the Jewish jargon, which he had allowed the accusers to impose on him for a moment, he examines as an open straightforward Roman. "Come to business. What crime hast Thou committed?"

HOMILETICS

Here we have *Pilate's Address, and Christ's Reply.* Notice—

I—CHRIST'S REPLY TO PILATE'S ADDRESS

To Pilate's question, "*Art Thou the King of the Jews?*" Christ says, "*Sayest thou this thing of thyself, or did others tell it thee of Me?*" This is not said in the spirit of insolence or disrespect, for that would be foreign to His holy nature. But said, no doubt, as a warning to Pilate, not to be prejudiced against Him on account of the reckless charges of the intolerant Jews. "*Sayest thou this thing of thyself?*" Knowest thou anything thyself concerning My history, to make you suppose that I presume to call myself a King in a political sense? We may legitimately use the words as suggesting an appeal to two classes of men in relation to Christianity.

First: To the *Infidel.* To the infidel we may say when he urges his objections to Christianity, "*Sayest thou this thing of thyself, or did others tell it thee?*"

(1.) When he objects to the Divinity of the Bible. When he talks of its difficulties and discrepancies, states how he thinks the manuscripts were produced, and how they were compiled, all in order to show that the book cannot be Divine, we say to him,

"*Sayest thou this thing of thyself, or did others tell it thee?*" Art thou stating all these things on hearsay, or hast thou thoroughly and honestly investigated the question for thyself? If thou hast not done this, be silent, it is a *personal* question. The men from whom thou hast heard thy objections, perhaps, never examined them for themselves, but received them from others, and they also from others, and so on. Hush! *think for thyself.*

(2.) When he objects to the doctrines of the Bible. When you hear him dilate on the absurdity of the Incarnation, the Atonement, the Resurrection, ask him, "*Sayest thou this thing of thyself?*" Hast thou examined these doctrines so as to get an independent judgment? If not, hold thy tongue. In these questions every man should be "fully persuaded in his own mind." We know of no better way to deal with modern infidels than this; silence them in their babblement by saying, "*Sayest thou this thing of thyself, or did others tell it thee?*" As for us, "we speak that we do know, and testify what we have seen." The words suggest an appeal to be made—

Secondly: To preachers. When you hear men talk nonsense, even blasphemy, in the pulpit in the name of the Bible; when you hear them advocate sacramentalism, reprobation, Divine wrath to be quenched only by the blood of the innocent, the literal purchase of a certain number of souls to salvation, by the mysterious agonies of the Son of God, and all such blasphemous absurdities as these, say to them, "*Sayest thou this thing of thyself?*" Hast thou found out these things from the Word of God by thine own devout, honest, independent, inductive study, or have others told thee? Hast thou not got all these horrid dogmas, that misrepresent Christianity, outrage the intellect, and shock the moral reason of mankind, from "*others,*" from old theologies, hoary creeds, and floating traditions? No man is a True Preacher who does not utter the things which he has "seen and felt and handled for himself." Half the pulpits in England would be shut if the people asked the preacher, "*Sayest thou this thing of thyself, or did others tell it thee?*" We have here—

II —PILATE'S TREATMENT OF CHRIST'S REPLY

There are two things here worthy of notice—

First: A haughty scorn that is always contemptible. "*Pilate answered, Am I a Jew?*" Who does not see his curled lip and hear his arrogant tone in this? "Do you suppose that *I* belong to that despised and conquered race? No, I am of Roman birth, and represent Cæsar, not only the master of this petty province, but the master of the race." This is very contemptible. There is a scorn that is right and noble, a scorn for all that is mean, and base, and false. But to scorn birth is to the last degree despicable.

Albeit it is *common*. Those who are born in what are called the higher social circles, look with disdain upon the grades below, though from the grades below they all sprung, and by them they are all supported. Albeit amongst them there are often those who, like Garfield, have a moral splendour before which all the brilliancy in castles and courts grows dim. Oh, Pilate, with all thy disdain for the men of Israel, there were greater ones among them than were ever found in Rome—Moses, Solomon, Daniel, Paul! Can you find their match in those grandees who at any time trod the streets of the imperial city? Another thing noteworthy in Pilate's treatment of Christ's reply is—

Secondly : A judicial procedure that is commendable. "*Thine own nation and the chief priests have delivered Thee unto me: what hast Thou done?*" With their miserable prejudices, and conventional distinctions, I do not concern myself. Tell me from Thy own lips, "*What hast Thou done?*" Let me hear the truth from Thee, tell out all.

Now this procedure in a Judge is most commendable. Common sense and common justice tell us that in all cases the prisoner ought to be thus treated. But, to the disgrace of our Courts of Judicature, the mouth of the accused is closed. Charges are brought against him in the court; these are urged with legal skill and oratory; but he is not called into the private presence of his judge at the outset, and asked, "*What hast thou done?*" Tell me the whole truth about thyself, especially in relation to the charge brought against thee.

John 18:36, 37

THE MORAL EMPIRE OF CHRIST

"Jesus answered," &c.

EXEGETICAL REMARKS.—Ver. 36.— "*Jesus answered.*"—These words are the reply of Jesus to the question of Pilate, "What hast Thou done?"— "*My kingdom is not of this world.*" Ἡ βασιλεία ἡ ἐμή. The "*My*" here is emphatic. This kingdom of Mine. He does not say it is not in or over, but, it is not of this world, ἐκ τοῦ κόσμου, τούτου, that is, in its origin and nature, and so is no such kingdom as need give thee or thy master the least alarm. "*If My kingdom were of this world, then would My servants fight, that I should not be delivered to the Jews.*" Were it an organism like the Roman Empire or other political governments, military force would be employed. The political kingdoms of

men are established, sustained, and defended by force. Probably He here makes an allusion to the scene of His arrest in the garden which had just occurred, when He bade Peter, who was in the act of employing force for His defence, to put up the sword. "*But now is My kingdom not from hence.*" As if He had said, The fact is, it has neither its origin nor its support from the world. It has been remarked that the word "*My*" here is emphatic, and occurs no less than four times in this one verse, thrice of His kingdom, and once of Himself. "MY *kingdom*," "MY *servants*," &c. It is in contradistinction to all worldly empires and ministries.

Ver. 37.—"*Pilate therefore said*

unto Him, Art Thou a king then?"
I see no reason to believe that there
is any sarcasm or contempt in this
interrogatory ; it is rather the expression of surprise and inquiry.
"*Jesus answered, Thou sayest that I
am a King.*" Or, "Thou sayest it
because I am a King." "*To this end
was I* (R. V. HAVE I BEEN) *born, and
for this cause* (R. V. TO THIS END) *came*

*I into the world, that I should bear
witness unto the truth.*" "To be a king
have I been born, and to be a king
came I into the world, in order that I
may bear witness unto the truth."
"*Every one that is of the truth heareth
My voice.*" All, in all times and lands,
of a truthful loving spirit, that shall
hear My voice, will recognize it as
the response to all earnest inquiries.

HOMILETICS

These words bring under our attention the *Moral Empire of
Christ*, and there are three facts suggested concerning it—

I —IT IS SPIRITUAL IN ITS NATURE AND MINISTRIES

First : It is "*not of this world.*" This does not mean—

(1.) That *His empire should exert no influence on "this world."*
This would be contrary to Christ's *teaching*, for He taught that
His principles were the "leaven," the "salt," the "light" of the
world. This is contrary also to *fact*, for His system has modified
the political institutions of the world. His ideas will continue
to work upon the heart of humanity, until the "kingdoms of this
world shall become the kingdoms of our God," &c. Nor does it
mean—

(2.) That *His subjects have nothing to do with the political duties
of the world.* He does not interdict His disciples from the office of
magistrate, statesman, king. On the contrary, His teaching binds
them to avail themselves of all positions favourable to the diffusion
of their heavenly principles. Nor does it mean—

(3.) That *He Himself has no control over the kingdoms of the
world.* "He is exalted far above all principalities and powers," &c.
But it means that His kingdom is not *like* Worldly kingdoms,
built on compromise and force, and sustained in the same way.
His empire is an empire over minds and hearts, over thoughts,
and feelings, and volitions.

Secondly : It does not employ violence. "*If My kingdom were
of this world, then would My servants fight.*" Christ's language
merely states the well-known *fact* of national wars, He does not
sanction them. Christ's empire is not only foreign, but hostile,
to all violence. He condemns the sword to the scabbard ; His
weapons are not carnal. He does not sanction, but merely
describes the conduct of human governments. He does not say,
as war advocates would have Him say, that it is right for
governments to employ violence ; He only expresses their general
conduct. All history shows that human thrones have been reared
and supported by force. Their foundations are down in the blood

and sacrificed rights of millions conquered by the sword. His weapons are the weapons of truth and virtue, which work as silently and as mightily as the noiseless dew and the genial ray. His battles are fought, not against the lives and rights of men, but against their crimes and curses, against falsehood and oppression. Another fact concerning this Moral Empire of Christ is—

II —IT IS WON BY THE TRUTH, OF WHICH CHRIST WAS A WITNESS

" *To this end was I born, . . . that I should bear witness unto the truth.*" What do we mean by " *truth ?* " Truth may be regarded in two aspects—as an *absolute reality*, and as a *relative experience*. As an *absolute reality*, its seat is in God Himself; it underlies the universe, it is the soul and substance of all. It is independent of all minds, yet that for which all minds naturally hunger and thirst. "Where shall wisdom be found ?" &c. As a *Relative Experience, it is conformity in thought and speech and life to the absolute truth.* The man who thus conforms to the great reality is " *of the truth* " a True man. There is truth of *sentiment*, conformity of thought to the reality; there is truth of *speech*, conformity of language to the inner sentiment; there is truth of *life*, conformity of the man's character in all his thoughts, utterances, and actions, to the eternal reality. In this form truth appeared in Christ : hence He is called " *the Truth*." Two thoughts here are worth note, and are suggested—

First : That the world is under the *rule of falsehood*. Men live in fictions, fallacies fill the atmosphere, the " father of lies" rules the world. Men live in a wilderness of phantoms. Lies have become the laws of human activity. Man's ideas of religion, pleasure, dignity, power—the world over—have no agreement with the eternal realities. This explains its social babblings, its ecclesiastical controversies, its national convulsions. Its crime and curse are that it rolls in an orbit of fiction. Observe—

Secondly : That the grand object of Christ's mission was to bring man under the *reign of reality*. " *To this* END *was I born.*" Christ says His mission is to " *bear witness to the truth,*" to shatter shams, to make men real. He was the " *Truth,*" eternal Truth, incarnate, breathing, living, acting, before men. Truth is the mirror of God. The teachings and the lives of the truest men, are but broken pieces of that mirror reflecting only a fraction of the Eternal, and that fraction in a distorted form. Christ's life was the complete mirror. In Him, "as in a glass, we behold the glory of the Lord." How directly was His teaching against the popular ideas and feelings of mankind concerning Greatness, Happiness, Worship ! He taught that happiness is not in what a man *has*, but what he *is*. He taught that greatness is not in *commanding*, but in *serving ;* that worship is not an occasional *service*, but a *living spirit*. Thus

He bore *"witness to the truth."* Thus He builds up His empire and explodes the reign of fiction. The other fact concerning this Moral Empire of Christ is—

III —IT HAS AMONGST ITS NUMBERS ONLY THE CHILDREN OF THE TRUTH

"Every one that is of the truth heareth My voice."

First: There are men *"of the truth."* In a world of fiction there are men—few, it is true, in number—who are of the truth, to whom truth is everything; men over whom forms, dogmas, sect-peculiarities, logical definitions, have no dominion, to whom truth is everything; men who are prepared to make any sacrifice on its behalf, and who will listen to its voice from whatever quarter it may come. Their moral intuitions are not so clouded by reason, interest, or prejudice, as to prevent them recognizing Truth, whether it comes garbed in plebeian rags or royal costume. These men are the "salt of the earth."

Secondly: These men *"of the truth"* recognize Christ's voice. He speaks to their common sense, their deep spiritual wants, and they respond to His call. Hence it was not from the conventional religionists and theologues that Christ won His disciples; it was from the unsophisticated people: the "common people heard Him gladly."

CONCLUSION. Mark that none are subjects of this glorious and ever-growing empire of Christ but *true men*. It does not embrace charlatans, hypocrites, men of pretence or sham, but only the men who are practically loyal to the Real. You are not to estimate their number by those enrolled in Church books, but by those who follow Truth to whatever Calvaries it may conduct. Truth has no sectarian limits or geographic boundaries; it is not the property of sects, or classes. The man who has it feels it to be Divine, and that he is a citizen of her holy empire, and bound to promote her sway.

> "How sure it is,
> That if we say a true word, instantly
> We feel 'tis God's, not ours, and pass it on
> As bread at Sacrament : we taste and pass,
> Nor handle for a moment, as indeed
> We dared to set up any claim to such."—*E. B. Browning.*

John 18:38-40

A THREEFOLD SUBJECT FOR SOLEMN REFLECTION

(*Pilate seeks to release Jesus. The Jews demand Barabbas. Jerusalem.*—MATT. xxvii. 15—26 ; MARK xx. 6—15 ; LUKE xxiii. 13—25 ; JOHN xviii. 39, 40.)

"Pilate saith unto Him, What is truth ?" &c.

EXEGETICAL REMARKS.—Ver. 38.— *"Pilate saith unto Him, What is truth?"* Lord Bacon and others see a jesting spirit in these words. "What is truth? says jesting Pilate, and would not stay for an answer." Others see an earnest inquiry in these words. In his experience as a Roman, and especially in his position as a judge, he had heard so many conflicting theories, that he was unsettled and anxious concerning truth : and he asks, What is it? As if he had said, I shall be glad to know it. "*And when he had said this, he went out.*" He does not seem to have waited for an answer to his question ; a fact which gives plausibility to Lord Bacon's interpretation. "*He went out again unto the Jews, and saith unto them, I find in Him no fault at all.*" (R. V. NO CRIME IN HIM.) What is meant is, I find no ground for the criminal charge of which you accuse Him.

Vers. 39, 40.—"*But ye have a custom, that I should release unto you one at the Passover: will ye therefore that I release unto you the King of the Jews?*" "These words are immediately connected by John with those of verse 38, because the sending to Herod was preceded as well as followed (Luke xxiii. 4, 14) by a declaration of the innocence of Jesus. These two declarations might be blended in one. The very abridged account which John gives of the episode of Barabbas serves as a link of connection between his narrative and that of the Synoptics. The origin of the custom referred to in Pilate's offer is unknown. It is probable, since the custom was connected with the feast of the Passover, that it contained an allusion to the deliverance of the Jews from their Egyptian captivity. The words ἐν τῷ πάσχα, at the Passover, by no means contain the proof, as *Lange, Hengstenberg,* &c. allege, that the Passover feast was by this time celebrated. The 14th Nisan already formed part of the feast. It is even more probable that the deliverance of the prisoner took place on the 14th than on the 15th, that he might be able to take part in the Paschal feast with all the people. In making this offer to the Jews, Pilate counted on the popular sympathy for Jesus, which had appeared so remarkably on Palm-day. For it was to the entire people that the favour was granted,

and Pilate knew perfectly well that it was from envy that the rulers wished the death of Jesus (Matt. xxvii. 18), and that the feeling of part of the people was against them. In the designation, "*King of the Jews,*" irony prevails, as in verse 14. Only the sarcasm is not addressed to Jesus, for whom Pilate from the beginning feels a growing interest and respect, but to the Jews. Their King? What! This, then, is the only rival whom this people with their national pretentions have to set up against Cæsar? But it is said in Mark xv. 11, "The chief priests moved the people that he should rather release unto them." The friends of Jesus remained mute, or their weak voices were drowned in those of the rulers and their creatures. Some resolute agitators imposed their will on the multitude. This is explained in John's πάντες, all, which corresponds to Luke's παμπληθεί. The πάλιν, *again*, the authenticity of which is established by the principal documents of both families, is remarkable. Thus far, in John's account, the Jews have uttered no exclamation. It was otherwise in the Synoptics (Comp. Mark xv. 8, ἀναβοήσας ὁ ὄχλος, and Luke xxiii. 5, 10). "They were the more fierce, saying . . . they vehemently accused Him." Here again John's narrative expressly assumes that of his predecessors—Λῃστής does not always signify robber, but a violent man in general. According to Mark and Luke, Barabbas had taken part in an insurrection in which a murder had been committed. The gravity of the choice made by the people is indicated by one of those short propositions whereby John describes a crisis of peculiar solemnity (Comp. xi. 35 ; xiii. 30). The name of the man who was set up along with Jesus, for the choice of the people, admits of two etymologies. Barabbah, son of the father (either God or any Rabbi), or *Bar-rabban*, son of the Rabbin. In the first case we must double the *b*, in the second the *r*. The MSS. and Talmudic orthography favour the first etymology. The name is not infrequent in the Talmud. According to Mark's narrative, there occurred at this point something like a rush of people demanding spontaneously the application of the custom, whereby a prisoner was released unto them ; and Pilate sought to turn this incident to his purpose—the liberation of Jesus. In any case, whether this incident was suggested or simply turned to account by Pilate, thus to deliver Jesus was to commit a denial of justice. For He should have been released as innocent. This first weakness was soon followed by a graver."—*Godet.*

HOMILETICS

These verses present to us *A Threefold Subject for Solemn Reflection.* Here is—

I —A POWERFUL VINDICATION OF CHRIST

Pilate leaves the court in which he had earnestly and carefully examined Christ, stands before the assembled multitude, and says, " *I find in Him no fault at all.*" What stronger testimony could be given to the blameless character of Christ than this ? For—

First : He had ample means of knowing all about Christ. Pilate was the Roman governor of Judea, the representative of Cæsar. His position would enable him, and his duty would require him, to make himself acquainted with all the facts concerning a notorious rebel. There was no man who for the last two or three years had roused the popular mind more than Jesus. His name had been on the lips of all : all charges against Him would undoubtedly be brought under the notice of the Procurator. This being so, his testimony was founded on intelligence.

Secondly : He had every inducement to discover His faults if He had any. He was a lover of popularity, and all the influential men over whom he ruled, as well as millions of the commonalty, desired to convict Christ of crime, in order that He might be put to death. If Pilate, therefore, declares His faultlessness, His non-criminality, who can justly allege any charge against Him ? Another subject for thought which these verses present to us is :—

II —A REPREHENSIBLE TREATMENT OF CONSCIENCE

Personally convinced as he was of Christ's innocence of the charge, what ought Pilate to have done ? To have come out as a man before His accusers, denounced their wicked conduct and delivered Him. But what did he do ? He tried to compromise the matter, and proposed to release Jesus, not on the ground of right, but on the ground of an old Roman custom. " *But ye have a custom that I should release unto you one at the Passover : will ye therefore that I release unto you the King of the Jews ?* " Oh, Pilate ! where is thy courage ? where thy manhood ? Instead of a man thou art a servile minion, controlled by outward circumstances, rather than by inward convictions. When men treat conscience thus—(1.) They *contract guilt.* (2.) They *lose self-respect.* (3.) They *endanger their souls.* The other subject for thought which these verses present to us is—

III —A SCANDALOUS POPULAR ELECTION

" *Then cried they all again, saying, Not this man, but Barabbas. Now Barabbas was a robber.*" Who was this Barabbas? A notorious brigand, who was at this time in prison on account of sedition and murder. Now the question that Pilate submitted to the choice of the people was, which of the two should he release, set at freedom, to mingle amongst them? Hear their decision, their vote, "*Not this man, but Barabbas.*" * Not the just, the pure, the tender, and the merciful, but the outrageously dishonest, the disgustingly foul, the morally malignant. Such was their choice, and such, alas, has been too often, and still is, the choice of the people. They prefer the blustering brigands to men of modesty and truth, brute force to moral power. "Who are the chosen of our race," says *Dr. Archer Butler*, "that poetry crowns with its halo of glory, and every young imagination bows to worship? Who but the laurelled Barabbases of history, the chartered robbers and homicides that stain its pages with blood, and that after 1800 years of Christian discipline the world has not yet risen to discountenancing? Remove the conventional discredit that attaches to the weaker thief, exalt him to the majesty of the military despot, and how many would vote for Barabbas, how many linger with the lowly Jesus?"

So long as the people are morally uneducated, and destitute of practical sympathy with the Right, so long, *vox populi vox diaboli*, will continue to be true. Heaven deliver any country from the suffrage of a democracy, unconverted and unenlightened !

John 19:1-16

A THREEFOLD TYPE OF SINNERS

(*Pilate delivers up Jesus to death. He is scourged and mocked. Pilate again tries to release Him. Jerusalem.*—MATT. xxvii. 26—30 ; MARK xv. 15—19 ; JOHN xix. 1—16.)

"Then Pilate therefore took Jesus, and scourged Him," &c.

EXEGETICAL REMARKS.—Ver. 1.— "*Then Pilate therefore took Jesus, and scourged Him.*" In order to conciliate the intolerant and bloodthirsty bigots, Pilate had before proposed chastising Christ. "I will therefore chastise Him and release Him" (Luke xxiii. 10). The chastisement here referred to was in all probability the scourging which he now inflicted. "The scourging," says *Philo Judaes*, "was that inflicted on the worst criminals." Monuments show that this scourging was a custom in ancient Egypt. Moses legalized the custom, but limited it to forty lashes. "Scourging," says a modern expositor, "as practised among the Romans, was so cruel a punishment that the prisoner very often succumbed to it. The scourge was formed of switches or thongs, armed at the extremity with pieces of bone or lead. The prisoner received the strokes while fastened to a small post, so as to have his back bent, and the skin on the stretch. The back became quick flesh, and the blood spurted out with the first strokes." Pilate now inflicted this chastisement, not as a punish-

---

* See Homily on *Pilate and the Crucifixion* at end of volume.

ment—for as yet Christ had not been pronounced a criminal—but in order to conciliate the persecutors, and thus, if possible, to avoid that which he felt in his own conscience would be a crime, viz. pronouncing on Him the sentence of death.

Vers. 2, 3.—*"And the soldiers platted a crown of thorns, and put it on His head, and they put on Him a* (R. V. ARRAYED HIM IN) *purple robe* (R. V. GARMENT), *and said* (R. V. AND THEY CAME UNTO HIM AND SAID), *Hail, King of the Jews! and they smote* (R. V. STRUCK) *Him with their hands."* The crown of thorns and the purple robe, and the reed, which Matthew tells us they put in His right hand, are the expressions of their malignant mockery and derision. It is not said that Pilate commended or even sanctioned them in this, but it was no doubt done under his eyes.

Vers. 4, 5.—*"Pilate therefore went forth again* (R. V. AND PILATE WENT OUT), *and saith unto them, Behold, I bring Him forth to you, that ye may know that I find no fault* (R. V. CRIME) *in Him. Then came Jesus forth* (R. V. JESUS THEREFORE CAME OUT), *wearing the crown of thorns, and the purple robe* (R. V. GARMENT). *And Pilate saith unto them, Behold the Man!"* The object which Pilate had in thus bringing Jesus forth, all bleeding from the scourging, wearing in mockery the insignia of royalty, was no doubt so to assuage their wrath, and evoke their pity, that they might willingly let Him go. He bids them look upon Him in His wretched condition and be satisfied. Ecce Homo! "The solemn presentation of Jesus before the world preceding His final delivery to death, has produced a most powerful impression upon the minds of the Church of all Christian ages. The pencils of the great masters of Christian art have selected it as a choice subject. Pre-eminently He stands forth, the Man, the Representative of the race, the memento of our sins, the exhibition of our misery."

Ver. 6.—*"When the* (R. V. WHEN THEREFORE) *Chief Priests therefore and officers saw Him, they cried out, saying, Crucify Him, crucify Him. Pilate saith*

unto them, Take ye Him (R. V. TAKE HIM YOURSELVES), *and crucify Him: for I find no fault* (R. V. CRIME) *in Him."* "The spectacle of the agonized Prisoner failed to touch their savage natures; like Shylock, they must have their 'pound of flesh.' In bringing Christ forth and calling their attention to Him, Pilate seems to say, 'Here, here is your Man! Look at Him bleeding from the scourge and mocked by the fictitious emblems of a royal crown and royal robe. Surely that is enough. Let Him creep away to His delusions in peace.' But when this unjust judge perceives that the sop he would throw to Cerberus only makes them more furious, he drops all remaining care for their Victim, throws off the case entirely from his jurisdiction, and cries with mingled vexation and scorn, 'Well, then, take the Man yourselves, I wash my hands of Him, though I tell you again, I find no fault in Him.'"—*Prebendary Griffiths, A.M.*

Ver. 7.—*"The Jews answered him, We have a law, and by our* (R. V. THAT) *law He ought to die, because He made Himself the Son of God."* It was a custom of the Romans to enjoy their own laws and institutions. The Jews here take their stand on this ground, and appeal to an article in their code (Lev. xxiv. 15), an article which condemns blasphemers to death. *"He made Himself the Son of God."* Therefore He is a blasphemer, and now we demand that as thou wilt not condemn Him as the King of the Jews on political grounds, thou wilt condemn Him on the ground of our law as a blasphemer.

Vers. 8, 9.—*"When Pilate therefore heard that* (R. V. THIS) *saying, he was the more afraid; and went again* (R. V. HE ENTERED) *into the judgment hall* (R. V. PALACE), *and saith unto Jesus, Whence art Thou?"* The *"Son of God"* had a meaning to Pilate that struck him with terror. Once more he returns to the judgment hall—the Prætorium, and addresses to Christ a question referring to His personal origin, *"Whence art Thou?"* He seemed to feel that He had some supernatural origin, for he knew well concerning His natural origin, viz.

that He was a Galilean. "*But Jesus gave him no answer.*" Christ had virtually answered the question over and over again ; further words would be useless. There is a moral majesty in His silence.

Ver. 10.—"*Then saith Pilate* (R. V. PILATE THEREFORE SAITH) *unto Him, Speakest thou not unto me? knowest Thou not that I have power to crucify* (R. V. RELEASE) *Thee, and have power to release* (R. V. CRUCIFY) *Thee?*" Pilate seems to have felt the silence of Christ, felt it as a reproach, felt it to the quick, and perhaps with indignant haughtiness asserts his power. Thy destiny is in my hands.

Ver. 11.—"*Jesus answered, Thou couldest* (R. V. WOULDEST) *have no power at all against Me, except it were given thee from above.*" "Thou thinkest too much of thy power, Pilate. Against Me that power is none, save what is meted out to thee by special Divine appointment for special ends." "*From above*"—not from the Roman Emperor, but from heaven. "*Therefore he that delivered Me unto thee hath the greater* (R. V. HATH GREATER) *sin.*" He, that is Caiaphas, the High Priest, including also all who were acting with him. The whole Sanhedrim is included in this "*he.*"

Ver. 12.—"*And from thenceforth* (R. V. UPON THIS) *Pilate sought to release Him.*" He had sought to release Him before, he could have released Him by his own powers, but he wanted to do it in a way that would insure their consent. The more he saw of Jesus the more he was impressed with the fact of His innocence, and with His supernatural bearing. "*But the Jews cried out, saying, If thou* (R. V. EVERY ONE THAT) *let this man go* (R. V. RELEASE THIS MAN), *thou art not Cæsar's friend: whosoever maketh himself a king speaketh against Cæsar.*" Here they struck the blow that would bend the soul of Pilate to their purpose. "They have noted his pliability, they work upon it now by arousing his fears. What! snatch out of our hands a wretch, whom we as friends to Cæsar have publicly denounced before the representative of Cæsar, for conspiring against Cæsar ? Remember

if you let such a man escape, you are not one of Cæsar's friends. And this was enough."—*Prebendary Griffiths.*

Ver. 13.—"*When Pilate therefore heard that saying* (R. V. THESE WORDS), *he brought Jesus forth* (R. V. OUT), *and sat down in the judgment seat in* (R. V. AT) *a place that is called the Pavement, but in the Hebrew, Gabbatha.*" His mind was now brought to their purpose, and he brings Jesus forth, takes the judgment seat and pronounces the sentence against the prisoner. "*The Pavement*" was a hall laid with mosaics or tessellated, on which the throne stood. "*Gabbatha*" signifies an elevation.

Ver. 14.—"*And* (R. V. NOW) *it was the preparation of the Passover, and* (R. V. IT WAS) *about the sixth hour.*" "The day before the Jewish (Saturday) Sabbath ; that is Friday, the day of crucifixion. As the Jewish Sabbath commenced on the evening of the preceding Friday, so the latter part of Friday was originally devoted to a preparation for the Sabbath. But gradually the line of preparation was extended, and finally the whole day became the preparation. It was the Sabbath preparation in the Passover week." The "*sixth hour*" means towards noon. "*He saith unto the Jews, Behold your King!*" Here Pilate rebounds from compassion and respect, and flies back to contempt and mockery, and with bitter irony exclaims, "*Behold your King!*" There He is.

Ver. 15.—"*But they* (R. V. THEY THEREFORE) *cried out, Away with Him, away with Him, crucify Him.*" King or not, man or not, they will crucify Him. Nothing else will satisfy them. "*Pilate saith unto them, Shall I crucify your king?*" He thus avenges himself for the act of baseness and vengeance to which they had forced him. "*The Chief Priests answered, We have no king but Cæsar.*" Alford remarks that those who thus cried died miserably in rebellion against Cæsar forty years after.

Ver. 16.—"*Then* (R. V. THEREFORE) *delivered he Him therefore unto them to be crucified. And they took Jesus, and led Him away."* "Against all justice, against his own conscience, against his solemnly and repeatedly pronounced judicial decision, that He was innocent, Whom he now gave up.

And so amid the conflict of human passions and the advancing tide of crime, the Scripture was fulfilled which said, 'He is led as a lamb to the slaughter.'"—*Dr. Brown.*

HOMILETICS

Here we have *a Threefold Type of Sinners.* Perhaps all sinners of all ages may be brought into a threefold class or group: those who sin *Against* conviction, those who sin *From* conviction, and those who sin *Without* conviction.

I —THOSE WHO SIN AGAINST CONVICTION

To this class Pilate belonged. How often does he here and in the preceding chapter publicly declare to the Jews that he could *"find no fault"* in Christ! And how manifest, from his various attempts to deliver Christ, was his deep conviction of His innocence. Notwithstanding this he ultimately condemns Him, and thus perpetrates an act in direct antagonism to his profound convictions.

First: To sin against convictions is very *hard* work. How difficult did Pilate find it!—how his better nature struggled against the popular cry that was urging him on to the terrible deed! How many attempts he made to avoid its perpetration, but at last his love of popularity and his dread of Cæsar overbore his conscience, and urged him to that from which his moral nature recoiled. Perhaps the greatest difficulty he encountered was the conduct of Christ in his last interview with Him. The *silence* of Christ to his question, *"Whence art Thou?"* must have shaken him to the centre of his soul. *"Jesus gave Him no answer."* How terribly eloquent that silence! There is a silence which is often more eloquent than speech. It means more than any words, and speaks ten times more powerfully to the heart. Such, for example, is the silence when the heart is too full for utterance, and the organs of speech are choked by the whelming tide of emotion. The sight of a great man so shaken and quivering with feeling, that the tongue can give no voice to what the heart feels, is of all human rhetoric the most potent. Such also is the silence of a wise man, challenged to speak by those whom he feels unworthy of his words. The man who stands and listens to the language of stolid ignorance, venomous bigotry, and personal insult, addressed to him in an offensive spirit, and offers no reply, exerts a far greater power upon the minds of his assailants, than he could by words, however powerful. His silence reflects a moral majesty, before which the hearts of his assailants will scarcely fail to cower. Such was the silence which Christ now maintained in the Hall. He knew the utter futility of their charges, He understood their malignant spirit,

He knew the truth they wanted not, and that to reason with men of their animus would only be to "cast pearls before swine." Sublime magnanimity I see in this silence of Jesus. In His bright consciousness of truth, all their false allegations against Him melted away as the mists from the mountains in the summer sun. His Divine soul looked calmly down upon the dark and wretched spirits in that hall, as the queen of the night looks peacefully upon our earth, amid the rolling clouds and the howling winds of nature in a passing storm. And then His speech. "*Thou couldest have no power at all against Me, except it were given thee from above.*" Thus pointing his guilty Judge to the God Who is over all.

Secondly: To sin against conviction is a very *fiendish* work. Satan and his legions pursue their course of wickedness in opposition to their moral convictions. Truly this is the worst class of sinners. "He that knoweth his master's will and doeth it not, shall be beaten with many stripes." What millions here in England are sinning *against* their convictions! Another class of sinners are—

II —THOSE WHO SIN FROM CONVICTION

Such were the Chief Priests and officers, and members of the Sanhedrim. "*When the Chief Priests therefore and officers saw Him, they cried out, saying, Crucify Him, crucify Him. . . . We have a law, and by our law He ought to die, because He made Himself the Son of God.*" These men seem to have had a conviction that Christ was a religious impostor, and that according to their law they were bound to put Him to death (Deut. xviii. 20). Thus Saul of Tarsus said when he was persecuting the Church he thought he "ought to do many things contrary to the name of Jesus." Whilst there is no true religion without sincerity, there is often sincerity where there is no religion. It is not enough for a man to believe he is doing right, he must have sufficient evidence that he is right.

Innumerable heathens, heretics, persecutors, sin from conviction. They believe they are doing right, whilst they are perpetrating the greatest enormities on which the sun has ever shone. On the world's long black roll of crime there are no crimes greater than those enacted from religious convictions. Another class of sinners are—

III —THOSE WHO SIN WITHOUT CONVICTION

Such were the soldiers who "*platted a crown of thorns, and put it on His head, and put on Him a purple robe, and said, Hail, King of the Jews, and they smote Him with their hands.*" Such also the thoughtless rabble who led Him to the brow of Calvary and nailed Him to the cross. In these men conscience was dormant; they had no moral convictions; they were the miserable hirelings of Pilate and the Chief Priests. From sordid considerations they sold themselves to the infernal enterprise. They wove a crown of piercing thorns, and placed it on the tender brow of Jesus, and put on Him a purple robe, and said, " *Hail, King of the Jews! and they smote Him with their hands,*" &c. Besides the *injustice* and *cruelty* of all this, there are two elements of character which the conduct of these soldiers develops, always the most contemptible and ever too prevalent—*ridicule* and *obsequiousness.* Foolish and wicked men! they trifled with the sublimest reality in the universe in order to *please their masters.* These two elements are often conjoined ; ridicule is frequently the handmaid of servility. The men who deal most in banter, burlesque, lampoon and satire, have generally masters whom they are seeking to please. They lack manly independence. These soldiers seem to have had no conviction ; they did what their superiors told them, and what they knew would please. This class of sinners is very numerous ; it comprehends all thoughtless assistants in commerce, who cheat the customer in order to please their Employer ; all political officers who perpetrate moral wrong to serve their Sovereign ; all soldiers who sell their conscience to their General. The millions in almost every age are like "dumb, driven cattle," mere instruments of their masters ; they will work in the most immoral trades, in the most diabolical professions, in the most infernal enterprises in order to please their masters, and to get gain.

CONCLUSION.—Here, then, we have a picture of the wicked world. Here are the three great classes of sinners, to one of which every sinner belongs.

John 19:16-18

THE MORALLY WRONG EVER INEXPEDIENT

*(Jesus is led away to be crucified—Jerusalem.—*MATT. xxvii. 31—34 ; MARK xv. 20—23 ; LUKE xxiii. 26, 33 ; JOHN xix. 16, 17.)

" Then delivered he Him therefore unto them to be crucified," &c.

EXEGETICAL REMARKS.—Ver. 16.— " *Then delivered he* (R. V. THEREFORE HE DELIVERED) *Him therefore unto them to be crucified. And they took Jesus, and led Him away* " (R. V. OMITS THIS CLAUSE). It was not John's intention to give all the details of Christ's crucifixion. He only states those circumstances which the other three biographers have omitted, and thus fills up the narrative. Pilate, in now delivering up Christ, had ridded himself for a time of a difficulty that had been pressing heavily on his heart for many anxious hours. But in doing this, what a crime he committed, and what immeasurable issues came therefrom ! The Jews now had what in their intolerant malignity they had been hungering for, for many a long month, and what they had clamoured for with a vehemency of soul. They led Him as a "lamb to the slaughter." He seems to have made no resistance whatever.

Ver. 17.—" *And He bearing His cross* (R. V. WENT OUT BEARING THE CROSS FOR HIMSELF) *went forth into*

(R. V. UNTO THAT) *a place called the place of a skull, which is called in the Hebrew Golgotha.*" It was called the place of a skull, not because of the executions which took place there, but because of the rounded form and bare aspect of the hill. John does not say anything here of that which the other evangelists inform us, that a great crowd of women followed, and the tears of compassion which they wept at the tragic scene, nor does he say anything about Simon of Cyrene, in Lybia, who was compelled to bear the cross part of the way. "The cross had the form of a T. It was of no great height. The condemned man was raised to the desired elevation by means of cords (*in crucem tollere*), the hands were nailed to the transverse pieces of wood, either before or after he was raised. *Keim* quotes the following words from a Latin author: '*Patibulo suffixus in crucem crudeliter erigitur,*' which show that the hands were usually nailed *before* its erection to the top of the cross. That they might not be torn by the weight of the body, the latter rested on a block of wood, fastened to the shaft of the cross, and on which the prisoner sat as on horseback. There has been great discussion in modern times as to whether the feet were also nailed. The passages of the ancients quoted by Meyer (see in Matt. xxvii. 35) and Keim are decisive ; they prove that, as a rule, the feet were nailed. Luke xxiv. 39 leads to the conclusion that it was so with Jesus. Sufferers lived usually on the cross for twelve hours, sometimes till the third day."—*Godet.*

Ver. 18.—"*Where they crucified Him, and two other with Him, on either side one, and Jesus in the midst.*" Why was this? Did the Jews demand that He should die in the midst of two malefactors, in order to enhance the ignominy, or did Pilate do it in order to humiliate them? Who knows?

HOMILETICS

Our subject is *The Morally Wrong ever Inexpedient*. Here we have—

I —A DIFFICULTY REMOVED, DESTINED TO APPEAR IN MORE TERRIBLE FORMS

"*Then delivered he Him therefore unto them to be crucified.*" In this, Pilate, I have no doubt, felt that he had got rid of a difficulty, that had weighed heavily upon him ever since Christ was brought under his notice. How to meet the claims of his Imperial Master, maintain his popularity with the Jewish people, and at the same time satisfy his own conscience, constituted a difficulty that had distracted him beyond measure. Now, handing Him over to the Jews, he would probably feel somewhat relieved, breathe freer, and have nothing more to do with this Jesus of Nazareth. Alas! Pilate, the difficulty is only temporarily shifted, and pushed for a moment out of sight, but not removed, or even lessened in bulk or hideousness, but otherwise becoming more huge and revolting. It only passed out of the region of immediate actuality, into the awful realm of moral memory, where it will appear and reappear in aspects of ever-increasing horror as ages roll on. Thus it is ever, no difficulty can be removed by outraging, or even ignoring the immutable principles of rectitude. Most men have certain difficulties pressing upon them. A desire to remove them is natural, but every effort will prove fruitless, unless accordant with that everlasting law of Right, which binds the universe together, and on which the throne of the Almighty is settled.

One man has a *financial* difficulty; accumulated debts weigh him down, he knows not how to deliver himself from his embarrassments. He makes himself bankrupt, or forges a bill, and foolishly fancies that he has ridded himself of his difficulty. Not so. Another man has a *social* difficulty. By amorous impulses and reckless vows, he has committed himself to some one whom he comes to loathe as an intolerable infliction. In an evil moment, he does, what is being done almost every day,—uses the razor,. or administers the poison, foolishly supposing that the difficulty is got rid of. But the old tormentor, though buried under the earth, is alive in memory to haunt him for ever. Another man has a *moral* difficulty; he is oppressed with the sense of his guilt, his conscience is a torment, he seeks to remove this difficulty by resorting to the inebriating cup, and revelling in scenes of gaiety and debauch. His moral nature gets benumbed, remorseful sensations are gone. But is his difficulty removed? No. That sleeping conscience shall break in thunder, and flash in flame. Believe me, there is no getting rid of any difficulty, by any effort, however skilful and earnest, in deviating one iota from the right. No means in such cases can sanctify the end, but frustrate the end and overwhelm with confusion the doer. Pilate, He Whom thou hast delivered up to the Jews must come back to thee! Here we have—

II —A CONQUEST ACHIEVED WHICH MUST OVERWHELM THE VICTORS IN ULTIMATE RUIN

"*And they took Jesus, and led Him away.*" The Jews were now triumphant, they had gained what they had been seeking for many months. How earnestly they had wrought to "get a case against Him!" With lynx eyes they had watched Him, they had employed spies and suborned witnesses. At last they had gained the day. He was in their ruthless hands, and law was on their side. The cross on which He was to be executed was on His shoulders, and Golgotha was in sight. With what fiendish exultation they wended their steps onward to the scene of torture and death. But of what worth to them was this conquest? How transient their exultations! Their very conquest would rebound on their own heads and overwhelm them with ruin.

Even in this life they felt the *temporal* rebound. A very few years on, not more than forty, and the Roman battalions led on by Titus and Vespasian would ravage their country, flood their city with human blood, set their temple in flames, break up their commonwealth, and scatter their survivors as vagrants over the face of the earth. Truly the "triumphing of the wicked is short." History abounds with instances of conquests reversed, and conquerors conquered. "He that taketh the sword shall perish by the sword." In modern times the anti-slavery reformer in South America is a remarkable illustration. The slaveholders martyred that noble man, John Brown, thereby foolishly imagining that they had dealt an effective blow against all slave-liberating forces in the United States. But in the course of one brief year or two, that hellish deed rebounded on their own heads. The whole slave-holding system was shivered to atoms, and every bondman was made free. The principle is this, that whatever is wrongfully achieved must lead to ruin. A man struggles for a fortune, he achieves it, but how? Struggles for senatorial, or perhaps regal power. He gains it, but how? The *how* is the question. All the produce of human labour, however valuable and magnificent, if unrighteously obtained, the justice of the universe turns into stone that will grind the possessors into powder. Here we have—

III —AGONIES ENDURED, TENDING TO IMMEASURABLE GOOD

"*And He bearing His cross went forth into a place called the place of a skull, which is called in the Hebrew Golgotha, where they crucified Him.*" Who shall depict the agonies of the crucifixion! All nature seemed to groan in sympathy with the mysterious Sufferer. The heavens darkened at high noon, the solid rocks rent asunder, the buried dead started to life. But the good issuing from all this anguish will brighten the universe with joy, and fill the ages with rapture. "Worthy the Lamb that was slain."

All the streams of happiness that flow through human souls, quickening them into life, and clothing them with beauty, issue from the deep, dark fountain of the Redeemer's anguish. "These are they that have come out of great tribulation, but have had their robes washed," &c. &c.

In truth, no man can really be happy without enduring personal sufferings of some kind or other. But they must be endured in the spirit of the Cross. Trials tune our hearts to music, tribulation fits us for the skies. "Our light afflictions which are but for a moment," &c.

> "Oh, let me suffer, till I know
> The good that cometh from the pain,
> Like seeds beneath the wintry snow,
> That wave in flowers and golden grain.
> Oh, let me suffer, till I find
> What plants of sorrow can impart,
> Some gift, some triumph of the mind,
> Some flower, some fruitage of the heart.
> The hour of anguish passes by ;
> But, in the spirit there remains
> The outgrowth of its agony,
> The compensation of its pains.

> In meekness, which suspects no wrong,
> In patience, which endures control,
> In faith, which makes the spirit strong,
> In peace and purity of soul."—*Thomas C. Upham.*

Here we have—

IV —A SIMILARITY OF CIRCUMSTANCES, BUT CHARACTERS UNSPEAKABLY DIVERSE

" *They crucified Him, and two other with Him, on either side one, and Jesus in the midst.*" Here are three men condemned as criminals by their country, side by side, each nailed to a cross and enduring, apparently, the same kind of physical torture. They are enduring the most inglorious and excruciating death that the most malignant spirits could devise; their whole weight is suspended by rugged iron driven through the most exquisitely tender nerves of the system. There above the heads of a fiendly maddened crowd they hang in agony to die. There is a great *outward* similarity; they all appear to be dying the same kind of death. But how *different* are they in their *souls!* Each mind has a world of its own. He, Who is in the midst, in being and character, stands at an infinite distance from the other two. He is the God-Man. Invisible worlds pause and wonder at His sufferings, the material universe vibrates with His groans. Of those on His side, one of them is a stricken penitent, struggling his way up to a virtuous and a happy life in the future, and will soon be in the Paradise of the blest; the other is a hardened wretch, ripe for destruction, and will soon fall into the nethermost hell. Characters so diverse, where circumstances are so alike, should—(1.) Guard us from the error of making external circumstances the test by which to determine our spiritual position. And—(2.) Show us the native power of each soul over the external circumstances in which it is placed.

John 19:19-22

THE SUPERSCRIPTION ON THE CROSS

(*The Crucifixion.*—*Jerusalem.*—MATT. xxvii. 35—38 ; MARK xv. 24—28 ; LUKE xxiii. 33, 34 ; JOHN xix. 18—24.)

" And Pilate wrote a title, and put it on the cross," &c.

EXEGETICAL REMARKS.—Ver. 19.— " *And Pilate wrote a title, and put it on the cross. And the writing was* (R. V. THERE WAS WRITTEN), *Jesus of Nazareth the King of the Jews.*" The " *title*" which John here tells us was placed over the Cross of Christ, was an inscription to give information of the crime for which the malefactor was sentenced. Matthew calls it the " accusation ;" Mark and Luke the

"superscription ;" but the word "*title*" or τίτλος was the customary term. Some suppose that the "*title*" which Pilate wrote was borne on the person of Christ on His way to execution, and then, when He was suspended, was fastened on the Cross.

Ver. 20.—"*This title then* (R. V. THEREFORE) *read many of the Jews: for the place where Jesus was crucified was nigh to the city: and it was written in Hebrew,"*—that is, Syro-Chaldaic, the language of the country ; *" and Greek,"*—the current language ; *" and Latin,"*—the official language. "These were, then, the chief languages of the earth, and this secured that all spectators should be able to read it." —*Dr. Brown.*

Ver. 21.—*" Then said the Chief Priests of the Jews* (R. V. THEREFORE SAID) *to Pilate, Write not, The King of the Jews; but that He said, I am King of the Jews."* This request of the Chief Priests shows that the superscription was odious to the Jews ; they could not endure that the men of Jerusalem and Judæa should be informed, as they looked upon the Sufferer on the Cross, that He was their King ; and they virtually say to Pilate, do not let the people be informed that He was King, but that He merely pretended to be a King.

Ver. 22.—*" Pilate answered, What I have written I have written."* He had yielded already too much to them. By their importunity he had acted contrary to his conscience in pronouncing the sentence of death ; but no longer would he be pliable, but inexorable, and with all the haughtiness of an imperious Roman he says, *" What I have written I have written."* Thus he wreaks on them his revenge.

HOMILETICS

Our subject is *The Superscription on the Cross.* The incident under our notice presents several objects which deserve most thoughtful attention. Here is—

I —A GLORIOUS FACT UNCONSCIOUSLY PUBLISHED TO THE WORLD

The royalty of Christ is here proclaimed. He is a *" King; "* the *" King of the Jews."* This poor dying Man on the Cross, this Jesus of Nazareth, is a Royal Personage. This is one of the most glorious truths in the Bible of God ; He is " King of kings, and Lord of lords." All worlds, systems, beings, and forces, are under His almighty sway. Pilate did not *mean* this, did not believe that there was even any political royalty about Christ. On the contrary, he writes,—*" King of the Jews "* in sarcasm and scorn, to wound the pride of the Jewish people, especially the ecclesiastics. How often men, even worthless men, unconsciously utter the highest truths ! Some event strikes on the soul and brings out truths, as steel brings fire from the stricken flint. An old writer says, " The venerable eulogy and epitaph set upon our Saviour's Cross, proclaimed Him King of all religion, having reference to the Hebrews ; of all wisdom to the Greeks ; of all power to the Latins."

The universal spirit of Truth flows through all moral beings, and hence the utterances even of ungodly men may repay attention, inasmuch as in them some hidden truth may be discovered. What a wonderful subject for study is the human soul !

In this incident there is another fact that deserves attention, viz. :—

II —A REVENGEFUL PASSION GRATIFYING ITSELF BY FRAUD

The Jews, as the preceding verses show, had by their importunity urged Pilate to pronounce sentence of death upon One, Whom in his conscience he regarded as innocent and just. This must have stung him with many a remorseful thought and ghastly foreboding. Now that it was over, revenge on his tempters breaks into passion. How does he gratify it? By writing such a falsehood that would strike torment into the instigators of his crime. He called Him "*King of the Jews.*" He did not believe He was "*King of the Jews,*" or King of any class, but he knew this would insult and degrade the Jews. Thus he sought revenge by fraud, and fraud, perhaps, is more frequently the instrument of revenge than violence.

No passion in the human breast is more malignant than revenge, more ravenous for satisfaction. Fraud, in the form of slander, chicanery, and poisonous innuendo, is, in these days, more the weapon of revenge than the pistol or the poignard. The revengeful man, though he does not carry with him the stiletto as in days gone by, and in other lands, carries with him the lying tongue and the libellous lip.

Another fact in this incident that deserves attention is—

III — A WICKED TRANSACTION BRINGING ITS OWN PUNISHMENT

These Chief Priests, who sought an alteration in the superscription, were guilty of the greatest wickedness in causing the death of the Son of God. They crucified the Prince of Life, and no sooner was the act accomplished than punishment, to some extent, overtakes them. What a poignant sense of humiliation these proud ecclesiastics must have experienced, when they saw written over the cross of a malefactor, exposed in the most public position, for men of every language to read, that this was the "*King of the Jews!*" "We, the descendants of the illustrious patriarchs, over whose sires the greatest monarchs of the world swayed their sceptres, to be represented as having been ruled by a malefactor!" How intolerable the insult! How bitterly, too, would they feel the haughty reply of Pilate to their request, "*What I have written I have written.*" As if he had said, "I have been pliable towards you in working out your malignant designs, but now I am inexorable. Say no more to me, I scorn you." Thus a small instalment of their retribution came at once.

Evermore sin brings with it its own punishment. "Be sure your sin will find you out." The other fact in this incident that deserves attention is—

IV — A MORAL OBLIQUITY WHICH ESTIMATES WHAT IS TRULY GLORIOUS A DISGRACE

These Chief Priests felt themselves disgraced and degraded by this superscription, but had they seen things in a right light they would have gloried in it. That Malefactor was "the glory of His people Israel." As a Sage, a Saint, a Hero, a King, there never had been in all Israel, and never would be again, any approaching Him. Instead of feeling themselves humiliated, they should have felt exalted. Depraved men are, alas, ever acting thus ; ever estimating the most glorious realities as worthless and contemptible ; and the reverse. Sinners see degradation where there is nobility, shame where there is glory, worthlessness where there is value ; and the reverse. If men saw things as they are, they would often see pauperism in mansions, affluence in huts, ignominy on thrones, and royalty in the beggar's cot.

John 19:23, 24

ONE EVENT WITH MANY REVELATIONS

"Then the soldiers, when they had crucified Jesus, took His garments," &c.

EXEGETICAL REMARKS.—Ver. 23.— *" Then the soldiers* (R. V. THE SOLDIERS THEREFORE), *when they had crucified Jesus."* Chronologically this passage ought to have succeeded verse 30, inasmuch as the account of His crucifixion follows. *" The soldiers."* These were the executioners of Pilate's sentence, who acted no doubt under the command of the Centurion. Mere hirelings, they were to perpetrate crimes which their masters had planned. *" Took His garments, and made four parts, to every soldier a part."* John was an eye-witness of the scene, and no doubt describes it with literal accuracy. It would seem that by the Roman law the *" garments"* of the executed malefactor were allowed as perquisites to the executioner. The term *" garments"* describes the outer loose garment or cloak worn in the East. "It is a long piece of cloth thrown round his shoulders, sometimes fastened at the neck, and used also as a covering for the night. Here it is spoken of in the plural as we speak of one's *robes* for robe."* It has been remarked that " between this full statement of John and the briefer one of Mark, there is variation but no contradic-

* *Holy Coat of Trèves.*—This relic is alleged to have been the seamless coat of our Saviour, and to have been discovered in the fourth century by the Empress Helena (mother of Constantine the Great), and by her deposited at Trèves, at that time the capital of Belgic Gaul, and residence of later Roman Emperors. Concealed in a crypt, from the Normans, in the 9th century, it was re-discovered in 1196, and then exhibited ; not exhibited again till 1512, when Leo X. appointed it to be exhibited once in every seven years. The Reformation and wars prevented the observance for some time, but the celebration was attended in 1810 by a concourse of 227,000 persons, and by a large number in 1844, when Archbishop Arnoldi announced a centenary jubilee. Not only were miraculous cures asserted to have been wrought by this relic, but this celebration is otherwise memorable for the reaction which it produced, leading to the secession of Johann Rouge, and the German Catholics from the Church of Rome. The dimensions given on an engraving published at Trèves, in 1844, are, from the extremity of each sleeve, 5 feet 5 inches ; length, from collar to lowermost edge, 5 feet 2 inches. In parts it is tender or threadbare ; and some stains upon it are reputed to be those of the Redeemer's blood. It is a loose garment, with wide sleeves, very simple in form, of coarse material, dark brown in colour, probably the result of age, and entirely without seam or decoration.

tion." Mark says, "They parted His garments, casting lots upon them what every man should take." Here the garments are viewed in a mass as being "*parted*," and as "*casting lots*" upon them. Whether the "*cast lots*" affected the whole, or only a part, is not said. Still less is there a contradiction of Matthew, who says they "parted His garments, casting lots." This only affirms that there was a casting lots, more or less in the process of division. These two statements are indefinite, but John's precise. "*Also His* (R. V. THE) *coat: now the coat was without seam, woven from the top throughout.*" This was the under-garment or vest, called the tunic. It was generally woven of linen or wool, like Aaron's vest, as described by Josephus. It was made of two pieces, a front and a back, with two sides open, fastened with clasps or laced with cords. *Webster* and *Wilkinson* regard it as a garment denoting considerable skill and labour, and fabricated by one or more of those women who ministered such things to Him (Luke viii. 3).

Ver. 24.—"*They said therefore among themselves* (R. V. ONE TO ANOTHER), *Let us not rend it, but*

cast lots for it, whose it shall be." Perhaps each man's name, token, or lot, was placed in some receiver, such as an urn, or a helmet, and the receiver was either to shake out the lot, or the lot was fortuitously drawn. "*That the Scripture might be fulfilled, which saith, They parted My raiment* (R. V. GARMENT) *among them, and for* (R. V. UPON) *My vesture they did* (R. V. DID THEY) *cast lots.*" "*Fulfilled*" here must mean one of two things ; either that the passage quoted in the Psalms was an inspired prediction of this very event, or that it was a suggestion to the soldiers as to how they should divide the garments. There are many difficulties in the way of entertaining the former idea. (1.) There is no certain proof of any reference whatever to the history of Jesus of Nazareth, and (2.) Those Roman ruffians who seem to have uttered these words were not likely either to know or respect the Divine application. The probability is that the words had somehow got into the minds of these men, and that the dread transaction in which they were now engaged brought them up fresh to the memory.

HOMILETICS

We have entitled our subject *One Event with Many Revelations*. This event reveals—

I —THE SPOLIATION OF DEATH

Christ is crucified. Death has completed its work. There was nothing more for it to do in His case. What had it done ?

(1.) It had *not destroyed His existence*. He had gone in the full personality and plenitude of His powers to His God and our God. (2.) It had *not destroyed His character*. Christ, during His stay on earth, like all men, had formed a moral character—a character, however, unlike that of ordinary men—Divinely perfect in all its elements and proportions. Death cannot rob us of our character. This indeed is the only property we have. We have formed it ourselves. It is our own production, and we have an absolute right over it. Death cannot deprive us of it. It is the only property we can carry with us out of this world, over the river, and into the Æons before us. What then does death take from us ?

First : Our material *frames*. Here was Christ's body torn from

Him, the body through which He looked out at the universe, through which He received His sensations, and by which He delivered His sublime doctrines, and wrought His marvellous deeds. A precious thing to every man is this body, and yet death takes it from every man. However much we appreciate it, we must lose it. It must go back to the dust from which it came, and take its part in the sublime chemistry of nature. It takes from us—

Secondly : Our material *property*. The garments of Christ were His only *earthly* property, but of them He was stripped. No doubt He valued them, not merely on account of their utility, but on account of those hands of love and tenderness that had woven and presented them.

Such is the *spoliation of death*. "We brought nothing into this world, and it is certain we can carry nothing out." "Naked came we into the world, and naked must we return." All of the earth which men struggle for and gain, they must lose. This event reveals—

II —THE DESECRATIONS OF AVARICE

What avarice is displayed in the gambling of these Roman soldiers over the garments of the Son of God! If aught of this earth were sacred, the garments worn by the Son of God were; yet avarice seizes them, gambles over them, and turns them to its own sordid ends. Avarice has ever traded in the *sacred*, and does so now more than ever. It not only trades in coal, corn, metals, and manufactures, but in philanthropic and religious institutions. Preaching has become a trade; temples, houses of merchandise; charitable societies, organs of worldly greed. Avarice, perhaps, makes more money by trading in the Gospel, by preaching, printing, publishing, building, and by authorship, than any other commodity, &c. A thing this to be wept over by all thoughtful souls !

> "Canst thou tell what is insatiable ?
> The greedy eye of avarice !
> Were all the universe a loaded table,
> It never, never could fill this ! "

This event reveals—

III —THE CULMINATION OF WICKEDNESS

Here, in this scene, you see human wickedness ripened, crowned, and achieving all it could. Beyond this point it could not go.

Where can you see baser *ingratitude* than in putting to death One Who "went about doing good?" More outrageous *injustice* than in putting to death One "Who did no sin, neither was guile found in His mouth?" More appalling *impiety* than in striking down God's own Son, the Prince of Life? More savage *malignity* than in torturing One Who was exquisite in tenderness and over-flowing with mercy for all? Truly the Crucifixion of Christ is sin's culmination. Wickedness could not go beyond it. In it, its tree is fully and completely developed, it is full of the poisonous fruits of retribution. And yet it is marvellous that the most consummate production of human wickedness should be made, by God, the instrument by which to banish it from the world. By the Cross of Christ the world is to be converted. Thus sin frustrates its own purpose and destroys its own existence. This event reveals—

IV —THE REPETITIONS OF HISTORY

"*That the Scripture might be fulfilled.*" It might be inferred from this, that concerning the conduct over the "*garments*" of Christ there had been similar transactions aforetime. History, it has been said, repeats itself; so it has ever done, so it does. The reasons are obvious—

First: That all men, of all climes and lands, are, in the main, actuated by the same class of motives. Another reason is—

Secondly: That similar circumstances will cause these motives to take similar forms. Hence no wonder that we run in circles, and "that which hath been is now," and what is now will be again until the old class of motives becomes extinct. When the world's corrupt motives are consumed by the fire of Gospel Truth, then a new system of things will appear, "a new heaven, and a new earth, wherein dwelleth righteousness."

John 19:25-27

A MANIFOLD REVELATION OF LOVE

(*The Jews mock at Jesus on the Cross.—He commends His mother to John.—* MATT. xxvii. 39—44; MARK xv. 29—32; LUKE xxiii. 35—37; 39—43; JOHN xix. 25—27.)

"Now there stood by the cross of Jesus His mother, and His mother's sister, Mary the wife of Cleophas," &c.—xix. 25—27.

EXEGETICAL REMARKS.—Ver. 25.— *Now there stood* (R. V. BUT THERE WAS STANDING) *by the cross of Jesus His mother, and His mother's sister.*" This tenderly touching and sug-gestively significant incident in the biography of Christ is recorded only by John, the other evangelists take no note of it. The reason of this, perhaps, is that John alone was present on the occasion. "*Mary the wife of Cleophas* (R. V. CLOPAS), *and Mary Magdalene.*" "This Clopas is usually identified with Alpheus (comp. Matt. x. 3; xxvii. 56). The question arises, Are there three or four women men-tioned? *i. e.* is '*Mary the wife of Clopas*' sister of Mary the mother of our Lord? or does St. John mean by '*His mother's sister,*' an unnamed woman who may not improbably be his own mother, Salome, whom he nowhere mentions? The question cannot be answered with certainty, but, upon the whole, the balance of evidence inclines to the view that we have four persons here mentioned in two pairs,—"His mother and His mother's sister; Mary the wife of Clopas, and Mary Magdalene. As early as the second century the Peshito-Syriac version adopted this view and inserted 'and' after the word sister."—*Dr. Ellicott's Commentary.*

Ver. 26.—"*When Jesus therefore saw His mother, and the disciple standing by, whom He loved.*" It is clear from chapter xiii. 23 that the disciple here referred to was John himself. "Now there was leaning on Jesus' bosom one of the disciples whom Jesus loved." "*He saith unto His mother, Woman, behold thy son!*" This "*woman*" was Mary, His mother; she was now standing by His Cross. Already her husband had departed,

and she was a widow, and now her Son was leaving the world. With tender compassion He directs her to John, who henceforth would care for her as a son.

Ver 27.—"*Then saith He to the disciple, Behold thy mother!*" This is addressed to John. He commends the dearest object of His heart, His mother, to that disciple whom He loved best of all. "*And from that hour that* (R. V. THE) *disciple took her unto his own home.*" Though he seems, from verse thirty-five, to have been at the Cross after the soldier had "pierced His side," John probably took Mary away at once from the scene of agony, and left her somewhere near, in order that he might return to see the end of the tragedy.

HOMILETICS

In these verses we have a *Manifold Revelation of Love.* We have here a revelation of Moral Heroism in love, Parental Distress in love, and Christian Obedience in love. Here we have—

I —A REVELATION OF MORAL HEROISM IN LOVE

The presence of the mother of Jesus, and the other women, together with John, now at the Cross, strikingly reveals the Heroism of Love. Scarcely could they have placed themselves in a more perilous position. To stand by One Whom the nation abhorred, and against Whom it was launching its fiercest thunders of indignation, displayed a grand invincibility of soul. *Love is the soul of courage.* On this earth there is no power for magnanimous endurance and fearless achievements, equal to calm, tender, womanly affection. Such love you can trust. The thing that is called love, which comes out in florid utterances, in spasmodic effort you cannot trust; it is all sound and show. It is the quiet love like that of contemplative John and of these unassuming women you can trust. Such love clings to its object as the ivy to the old castle; holds on to it midst the scorchings of summer and the blastings of winter; survives even the ruin of its object, and spreads a beauty over its grave. It is said that a woman has more nerve than a man; it is love that steels her nerves and makes her heroic in trial. The man with a giant frame, if he have not love in him, will be a moral coward. Love is the root of true heroism. Here we have—

II —A REVELATION OF PARENTAL DISTRESS IN LOVE

What must have been the feelings of Mary as she now witnessed the agonies of her wonderful Son! Now in her experience was fulfilled the prophecy of old Simeon, who, when he took her child in his arms, said,—"This child is set for the rising of Israel; yea, and a sword shall pierce thine own heart." There are few, if any, trials in life more poignant than the sufferings of an affectionate mother in the death-throes of her child. Rachels, the world over, weep for their children and refuse to be comforted.

But there are circumstances which sometimes mitigate the distress. Should, for instance, the child die in unconscious innocency, or should he be one of a large number of children, or should he gradually die in maturity amongst his friends, the distress would not approach in intensity the circumstances connected with Christ's death. Mary's Son was now in the prime of life; He was dying a violent death amongst malignant foes and by their hands. It is said of Socrates that he spent his last hours amongst his friends, and that even his executioner was touched with sympathy when he gave the fatal cup of hemlock into his hand. But Christ died amongst His enemies, and by their hand. Then, too, perhaps He was Mary's only Son; no one could take His place. Besides all this, her husband Joseph was sleeping in his grave. Truly here is parental distress in love. Love has its agonies. Here we have—

III—A REVELATION OF FILIAL COMPASSION IN LOVE

"Woman, behold thy Son!" As if Jesus had said, I am leaving the world, but John My beloved disciple will supply My place, he will be a son to thee. These words must have been as a gleam of unearthly sunshine to Mary, calming the fury of the tempest. From them we may infer four things—

First: That no sufferings, however great, can quench love. The sufferings of Christ at that moment in intensity and aggravation surpass all conception. Every nerve of His frame in torture, a mysterious load of sorrow on His heart, yet all this did not drown the memory of His Mother. Her uplifted, tearful, loving face met His eye and pierced His heart. He seemed to forget His sufferings in the tears of His mother. Children, learn a lesson from this! Plead no personal inconvenience as a reason for neglecting your parents. We infer from the words—

Secondly: That no engagements, however vast, can justify the neglect of domestic duties. How vast were Christ's engagements now! He was fighting the moral battles of the universe. Earth, heaven, and hell were interested in His position. It was *"the hour."* A crisis in the history of moral creation. Notwithstanding this, He was alive to His domestic duties. He attended to the needs of His aged mother. Let none plead—statesmen, ministers, or reformers—the vastness of their engagements as a justification for neglecting home duties. We infer from the words—

Thirdly: That no legacy, however precious, is equal to the

Legacy of Love. Christ could have made His mother the mistress of an empire; but He bequeathed to her what was better—Love; the affection of a noble and a loving soul. What is equal to this? Give me cities, empires, continents: what are they compared to the friendship of one loving soul? We infer from the words—

Fourthly: That no argument, however plausible, can justify us in regarding Mary as an object of worship. The mothers of Paul and Luther, or of any great men, I hold in high veneration. Albeit, ought I to regard this poor destitute, desolate woman whom Jesus commended to the care of John as the Queen of Heaven? Here we have—

IV.—A REVELATION OF CHRISTIAN OBEDIENCE IN LOVE

" *From that hour that disciple took her to his own home.*" Tradition says that John never forsook the dear trust which his dying Saviour had bequeathed to him, and that he never went beyond the borders of Palestine until the mother of his dying Lord had breathed her last. His obedience was prompt and full. "*From that hour.*" He felt the sanctity of the dying request.

There are only three admissible reasons supposable for not attending at once and fully to Christ's commands, as John did now. (1.) If the command is found to be inconsistent with the eternal principles of right. Or (2.) If there are such difficulties in the way of obedience which procrastination is certain to remove. Or (3.) If there is good ground to expect an amount of help in the future which is not obtainable now. Such reasons, though admissible, do not exist, and therefore, like John, we should at once commence obedience.

John 19:28-30

THE MODEL DEATH

(*Darkness prevails.—Jesus expires on the Cross.—Jerusalem.*—MATT. xxvii. 45—50 ; MARK xv. 33—37; LUKE xxiii. 44—46 ; JOHN xix. 28—30.)

" After this, Jesus knowing that all things were now accomplished," &c.

EXEGETICAL REMARKS.—Ver. 28.— " *After this, Jesus knowing that all things were now accomplished* (R. V. FINISHED), *that the Scripture might be fulfilled*" (R. V. ACCOMPLISHED). It would seem that Christ had a programme of His life ; understood it well ; knew the last item ; and now He was conscious that He had fully realized it. There is a Divine programme for every life, but Christ, of all the men that ever lived, knew of that programme, and none but He

have ever filled it up—fully "*accomplished*" it. "*I thirst.*" He had refused the usual stupefying draught at Crucifixion (Matt. xxvii. 34—38). Now that all is finished He seeks relief for His thirst.

Ver. 29.—"*Now there was set* (R. V. THERE WAS SET THERE) *a vessel full of vinegar.*" "This vessel of the ordinary sour wine drunk by the Roman soldiers was placed near, in order to be given to those who were crucified. Thirst was always an accompaniment of death by crucifixion, and that the vessel of wine was prepared for this purpose, is made probable by the mention of the sponge and hyssop." "*They filled a spunge with vinegar, and put it* (R. V. SO THEY PUT A SPUNGE FULL OF THE VINEGAR) *upon hyssop, and put* (R. V. BROUGHT) *it to his mouth.*" "This detail is peculiar to St John. *Bochant* thinks that the plant was marjoram, or some plant like it, and he is borne out by ancient tradition. The stalks, from a foot to a foot and a half high, would be sufficient to reach to the Cross. The plant is named in another passage of the New Testament (Heb. ix. 29), and is frequent in the Greek of the Old Testament. The Hebrew word is *ezau*, and the identification must always be uncertain, because we cannot know whether the Greek translation is based upon an identification of the plant, or upon a similarity in the sound of the names."—*Bishop Ellicott's Commentary.*

Ver. 30.—"*When Jesus therefore had received the vinegar, He said, It is finished : and He bowed His head, and gave up the ghost*" (R. V. HIS SPIRIT). "The order of the seven words of the cross will be—(1.) 'Father, forgive them, for they know not what they do.' (Luke xxiii. 34.) (2.) 'Verily I say unto thee, this day shalt thou be with Me in paradise.' (Luke xxiii. 43.) (3.) 'Woman, behold thy Son.' (John xix. 26.) (4.) 'Eli, Eli, Lama Sabachthani ?' (Matt. xxvii. 46 ; Mark xv. 34.) (5.) 'I thirst.' (Ver. 28.) (6.) 'It is finished.' (Ver. 29.) (7.) 'Into Thy hands I commend My spirit.' (Luke xxiii. 46.)"—(*Ibid.*) "It is remarkable," says *Dr. Brown*, "that while we have this glorious saying only in the fourth Gospel, we have the manner in which it is uttered in the first three and not in the fourth."

HOMILETICS

Though all men must die, all do not die in the same way. Over the *fact* of death man has no control, die he must ; but over the *mode* of dying he has power. Man's life shapes his death. Hence he may die virtuously or wickedly, nobly or ignobly, happily or miserably.

In these verses we have the *Model Death*. Four things are to be noticed in this, the end of our Saviour's life—

I —LIFE ENDING WITH A CONSCIOUSNESS OF HAVING REALIZED ITS MISSION

"*After this, Jesus knowing that all things were now accomplished, ... said, It is finished.*"

(1.) All life has a mission. The most insignificant ephemera is not made in vain, but has some part to play in the great drama of being. To every man that appears on the stage of life there is a Divinely allotted work, something that he has himself to accomplish. (2.) The form in which the mission is wrought out differs with different men. (*a.*) No two men have exactly the same class of *faculties.* Some are distinguished by the imaginative, some by the metaphysical, and some by the logical faculty, &c. They cannot do the same kind of work, or in the same manner. (*b.*) No two men are under exactly the same class of *circumstances.* Hence the needs, motives, and opportunities of work will be necessarily varied to some extent. (3.) The accomplishment of the mission is not in the kind or amount of work done, but in the *spirit* which inspires and guides it. Hence two men may perform a work, identical in *appearance* but different in *essence*,—essentially distinct. In the one case the life of the man shall be accomplished, "*finished;*" in the other it will be a miserable failure. All depends on the spirit.

Now Christ's work was *peculiar* to Himself; His faculties were peculiar to Himself. The conditions under which He had worked those faculties were peculiar, consequently His mission in form varied from that of any other man. What was the work given Him to do? Who knows all? None but Himself. We shall only mention two things which we can anyhow partially comprehend.

First: He had to work out a *moral character* which imperatively demands the *imitation* of mankind. Man's destiny depends upon his character; out of it blooms his Paradise or flames his hell. Moral character is evermore formed on the principle of imitation. But mankind never had a character worthy of *complete* imitation, and therefore demanding it, until Christ gave it. Every man now looking at the character which Christ wrought out, is bound to feel that in it his highest ideal is realized, and that in conformity to it, his highest happiness is secured. When He said, "*It is finished,*" He had rounded, completed, and burnished a moral character, that must command the admiration of ages, and by which all men's destinies must ultimately be determined.

Secondly: He had to demonstrate a *Divine love* that would bring the *heart* of mankind into sympathy with God. Men, the world over, are morally estranged from their Maker; this estrangement is at once their sin and their ruin. How is this estrangement to be overcome? Only in *one* way, and that is by convincing men that the God Whom they hate, loves them with a deep, tender, incomparable love. This Christ *demonstrated* on the Cross, and belief in this is that which will "draw all men unto Him;" hence "God is in Christ, reconciling the world unto Himself."

This is the work, then, that Christ accomplished which we can understand. When we are told by theology that His work was to appease the wrath of God, to render it possible for the Almighty to pardon, and that He suffered as a Legal Substitute for the sins of men, we can only say we cannot understand this, and what we cannot understand we had better not talk about. Notice here—

II —LIFE ENDING CALMLY IN THE MIDST OF PHYSICAL TORTURES

"*I thirst.*" This is the cry of anguish, poignant, deep, inexplicable. "Thirst is a deeper suffering than hunger. After the bloody sweat of Gethsemane, the sleepless night of His trial, the scourgings, the loss of blood, and the unknown mental agonies, the fluids of His system became exhausted." But notwithstanding this how sublimely calm He is in soul! "*He bowed His head, and gave up the ghost."* That such a life should end in such suffering is—

First : A distracting perplexity. Antecedently one might have thought that in proportion to the perfect excellence of character, and usefulness of life, would be the painlessness and calmness of the end; that every signally good man would be, if not translated like Enoch, freed from all the pains attendant on dissolution. But here we find the best Man that ever lived, dying in the midst of physical sufferings. That such a life should end in such suffering is—

Secondly : A Christian encouragement. Who has not had friends and dear relatives whose dying agonies have racked the heart ? But inasmuch as Christ endured the same, they are no indications of moral delinquencies. Nor when our end comes, if it be given to us to endure great suffering, let us conclude that we are not approved of Heaven. "What son is he whom the father chasteneth not ?" But in the midst of all may we be blest with that calmness of soul, that repose in God, which our Great Example now manifested when *"He bowed His head, and gave up the ghost !"* Notice here—

III — LIFE ENDING IN A SURRENDERING OF THE SPIRIT TO THE FATHER

"He bowed His head, and gave up the ghost,"—Spirit. This utterance throws light on three things.

First : On the nature of His existence. *"He gave up the ghost."* The language indicates that—(1.) He had a Spirit independent of His body. In this respect He resembled all men. (2.) His Spirit would survive the body. The body was all but extinct, the last spark was all but gone out, but He felt that His Spirit would live. (3.) His Spirit was destined for the Eternal. The body "must return to dust, but the soul to God Who gave it." "Into Thy hands I commit My spirit." The words throw light—

Secondly : On the voluntariness of His death. *"He gave up."* The spirit was not wrested from Him, it was not snatched away by force, He *gave* it up. He had "power to lay down" His life and power to "take it up." The words throw light—

Thirdly : On His confidence in God. What unbounded confidence do these words express ! (1.) Confidence in His *Presence.* He feels that God is near Him, in immediate contact with Him—so close that He could put His Spirit at once into His hands. (2.) Confidence in His *Power.* He feels that He has that Almighty capacity necessary to guide, to guard, and bless His immortal spirit through all the future of its wondrous history. (3.) Confidence in His *Love.* His trust in His Fatherly affection is as strong as His trust in Almighty power. Hence He yields Himself into His hands. In His death He makes the Eternal the Trustee of that which is

of infinitely more value than worlds and systems—Himself. Such
confidence as this in God is the characteristic of the highest piety,
and the philosophy of an easy death. Piety is this self-dedication
to God, not in death only, but in life as well; and when this is
done in life, there will be a calm and triumphant death.

John 19:31-37

A FRAGMENT OF A WONDERFUL HISTORY

(*The taking down from the Cross.—The Burial.—Jerusalem.*—MATT. xxvii. 57
—61 ; MARK xv. 42—47 ; LUKE xxiii. 50—56 ; JOHN xix. 31—42.)
" The Jews therefore, because it was the preparation, that the bodies should not
remain upon the cross on the Sabbath day," &c.

EXEGETICAL REMARKS.—Ver. 31.
—" *The Jews therefore, because it was
the preparation, that the bodies should
not remain upon the cross on the Sabbath day*" (R. V. SABBATH). The day
of the crucifixion is described by all
four evangelists as "*the preparation,*"
—that is, as we imagine, the preparation for the passover. In John xix.
14, it is so represented. By the Jews
here, we are to understand the rulers
of the Jews. The passover was on the
Saturday, which was the Sabbath of
the Jews, and Christ was crucified on
the Friday. "*For that* (R. V. FOR
THE DAY OF THAT) *Sabbath day was
a high day.*" The Sabbath was now
dawning, and it was a "*high day.*"
It was the first Sabbath of the feast
of the unleavened bread, the most
sacred season in the whole of the
Jewish year. The Mosaic law required
that the body of one hanging on a
tree, for any sin worthy of death,
should not remain all night on the
tree, but should be buried that night,
"for he that is hanging shall be
moved, that thy land be not defiled "
(Deut. xxxi. 21—23). These hypocrites
who, in crucifying Christ, perpetrated
the greatest crime on which the sun
ever shone, were afraid of ceremonial
defilement. "*Besought* (R. V. ASKED
OF) *Pilate that their legs might be
broken, and that they might be taken
away.*" "The breaking of the legs
by means of clubs was a Roman
punishment, known by the name of
crucifragium, which sometimes accompanied crucifixion, and appears
also to have been used as a separate

punishment. It is not otherwise clear
that its purpose was, or that its effect
would be, to cause death, but this is
the impression we derive from the
present context " (verse 33).

Ver. 32.—" *Then came the soldiers*
(R. V. THE SOLDIERS THEREFORE), *and
brake the legs of the first, and of the
other which was crucified with Him.*"
This act of barbaric atrocity was
usually done with clubs or iron
mallets. Crucifixion was a very
lingering death, and this act was
employed to hasten it.

Ver. 33.—" *But when they came to
Jesus, and saw that He was dead
already, they brake not His legs.*" He
seems to have died sooner than the
rest. "There were," says *Dr. Brown,*
" in His case elements of suffering
unknown to the malefactors, which
would naturally hasten His death,
not to speak of His exhaustion from
previous care and suffering, all the
more telling on the frame now from
its having been endured in silence.
' *They brake not His legs.*' This is a
fact of vast importance, as showing
that the reality of His death was
visible to those whose business it was
to see to it."

Ver. 34.—" *But* (R. V. HOWBEIT)
*one of the soldiers with a spear pierced
His side.*" It does not appear that
they pierced the sides of either of the
other two malefactors. In Christ's
case, probably, they did it to make
sure of His death. Medical science
has attested that He could not have
lived after this piercing. "*And
forthwith* (R. V. STRAIGHTWAY) *came*

thereout blood and water." There does not seem to be anything miraculous in this, for physiology teaches that this was the lymph of the pericardium, or the watery blood of the pleura which follows a mortal wound. " The infliction of this death-wound," says a modern expositor, "was an important point of evidence for all time as to Christ's death and resurrection. There were those in this apostle's time who held that Jesus was only an apparition, and had not a real body. This testimony may have been intended also for them."

Ver. 35.—" *And he that saw* (R. V. HATH SEEN) *it bare record* (R. V. HATH BORNE WITNESS), *and his record* (R. V. WITNESS) *is true: and he knoweth that he saith true, that ye might* (R. V. YE ALSO MAY) *believe.*" "This solemn way," says *Alford*, "of referring to his own testimony in this matter was at least intended to call attention both to the fulfilment of Scripture in these particulars and to the undeniable evidence he was thus furnishing of the reality of Christ's death, and consequently of His resurrection; perhaps also to meet the growing tendency in the Asiatic Churches to deny the reality of our Lord's body, or that 'Jesus Christ is come in the flesh.'" (1 John iv. 1—3.)

Vers. 36, 37.—" *For these things were done* (R. V. CAME TO PASS), *that the Scripture should be fulfilled, A bone of Him shall not be broken.*" "The Israelites ate the paschal lamb in haste as if on a journey, and, therefore, broke not its bones. The evangelist quotes the Scripture as illustrative of the fact that the bones of Jesus were not broken. (Ex. xii. 46; Num. ix. 12.)" "*And again another Scripture saith, They shall look on Him whom they pierced.*" "Another quotation after the same method of accommodation. (Zech. xii. 10.)"—*Livermore.*

HOMILETICS

There are three subjects suggested by this startling *Fragment of a Wonderful History.*

I —THE IMMORALITY OF TECHNICAL SAINTHOOD

The Jews here, the members of the Sanhedrim, were, in a conventional and ceremonial sense, very great saints: such they esteemed themselves and felt themselves to be. They were strict in all religious observances, and in their charitable distributions,—they gave alms to the poor, &c. Referring to the mere *letter* of duty they could say with the young lawyer who sought Christ, "All these things have I kept from my youth up." Verily, great Saints were these men! They lived in their doctrines and their ritualities. Albeit they were utterly destitute of genuine morality; they would lie and cheat, rifle their fellow-men of their rights, devour widows' houses, and, in heart, utterly disregard every precept of the moral decalogue.

It has ever been so. There is a close connection between a mere technical sainthood and an immoral life, hence inquisitions and persecutions. Even Calvin could murder Servetus. There is a pietism that eats out the heart of humanity, and turns men into bigots and persecutors. Show me the man who regards himself as a saint above the rest, and you will show me a man whose morality I could not trust. "Many will say to Me on that

day, have we not prophesied in Thy name, and done many
wonderful works?" &c. Another subject here presented is—

II —THE SERVILITY OF STATE HIRELINGS

Those soldiers who nailed the Son of God to the cross, and now
plunged the spear into His side, had sold themselves to the State.
Like all soldiers they had sold their whole individuality, and given
up their will and independency to their employers. They had no
higher idea of duty than to obey their masters. The spirit of true
manhood was extinct within them; they became machines, nothing
more,—machines to plunder and to kill. Alas! how are we fallen!
"The crown is fallen from our head," &c. The spirit of servility
is the disgrace of humanity and the curse of nations. In proportion
to the servile spirit of a people is the strength of tyranny amongst
them, and their utter inability to break their fetters and become
free. Fawning sycophancy paralyses true patriotism. Ah me!
how rampant is this even in our England! It steams everywhere
and fills our social atmosphere with an aroma abhorrent to all
honest souls. Another subject presented is—

III —THE CERTITUDE OF THE GREATEST FACT

"*And he that saw it bare record, and his record is true: and he
knoweth that he saith true, that ye might believe.*" Observe—
First: The greatest fact in history is the death of Christ. To
it all past events pointed, and from it all future take their rise and
have their date. It is the supreme epoch in the world's history.
It has created moral influences in the world, whose rivers multiply,
widen, and deepen every day. It will become "a sea of glory, and
spread from pole to pole." Observe—
Secondly: The most competent witness of that fact was John.
"*His record is true.*" No one amongst men was—(1.) More
intellectually competent. No one was so much with Christ, no one
was so intimately acquainted with Him. No one was—(2.) More
morally competent. He was incorruptibly honest and incontrovertibly disinterested. Another subject presented is—

IV —THE PHILOSOPHY OF EVANGELICAL PENITENCE

"*And again another Scripture saith, They shall look on Him
Whom they pierced.*" There is here a reference to a passage in
Zechariah xii. 10, which reads thus: "They shall look upon Him
whom they have pierced, and they shall mourn for Him." If
John had finished the quotation, the idea of penitence would
have been the point of his reference. He who looks with the
eye of faith on Christ upon the Cross, as the demonstration of
human wickedness, and the mighty expression of God's compassion
for sinners, is in a way to have his heart broken with contrition
on account of his sins.

Professor Plumtre's Explanatory Notes on
THE CRUCIFIXION OF OUR LORD
As given by Rev. F. Watkin, M.A.

(1.) The narratives of the First Three Gospels, and that of the Fourth agree in the statement that on the night that immediately preceded the betrayal or the Crucifixion of our Lord, He and His disciples met together at a supper. As to what that supper was, they seem at first to differ. The first Three agree in speaking of it as the first day (Matthew and Mark), or *the* day (Luke) of the feast, known as that of unleavened bread, the day when "the Passover must be slain" (Mark, Luke). The disciples ask where they are to prepare the Passover. They are sent to the owner of the upper room, where they are met with the message that their Lord purposes to eat the Passover there. When they arrived they "made ready the Passover" (Matthew, Mark, Luke). As they begin, He tells them that He has eagerly desired to eat that Passover with them before He suffered (Luke xxii. 15). At a certain stage of the meal, which corresponded with the later ritual of the Paschal Supper, He commands them to see in the bread and the cup which He then blessed, the memorial feast of the New Covenant. The impression, *primâ facie*, left by all the Three, is that our Lord and His disciples partook, at the usual time, of the Paschal Supper. In St. John, on the other hand, there is no record of the institution of this memorial feast. The supper is introduced as "before the feast of the Passover" (John xiii. 1). When Judas leaves the room the other disciples think that he is sent to buy what is needed for the feast (John xii. 29). When the priests are before Pilate they shrink from entering into the Prætorium, lest they should be defiled, and so be unable to eat the Passover (John xviii. 28). The impression, *primâ facie*, left by St. John's Gospel is, that our Lord's death coincided with the sacrifice of the Paschal lamb; that left by the Three is that the Paschal lamb had been sacrificed the previous evening.

(2.) The difference has been regarded by many critics as altogether irreconcilable, and conclusions have been drawn from it unfavourable to the authority of one or both the narratives. Those who look on the Gospel of St. John as the work of a writer of the second century, see in this discrepancy a desire to give a sanction to the local usage of the Church of Ephesus, or to force upon his readers, as in his relation of "a bone of Him shall not be broken" (John xix. 36), the correspondence between the Passover and the death of Christ. Those who accept the Gospel as St. John's, wholly or in part, see in his narrative a correction, designed or undesigned, of the narrative of the Three, and look on that narrative accordingly as more or less untrustworthy. Some even of those who shrink from these conclusions have been content to rest in the conviction that we have no adequate *data* for the solution of the problem. Some minor difficulties gather round the main question. It was not likely, it has been urged, that on the very night of the Passover the high priests should have taken the counsel and the action that led to the capture in Gethsemane; nor that on the day that followed, "a day of holy convocation" (Ex. xii. 16), they should have sat in judgment and appeared as accusers before Pilate and Herod; nor that Simon of Cyrene should have come from the country (Mark xv. 21); nor that Judas should be supposed to have been sent, if it were the Paschal Supper, to make purchases of any kind—as if the shops in Jerusalem would on such a night be open (John xiii. 29).

The day of the crucifixion is described by all four Evangelists, as "the preparation," which, it is assumed, must mean "the preparation for the Passover." In St. John (xix. 14) it is definitely spoken of as "the preparation of the Passover."

(3.) Some solutions of the problem, which rest on insufficient evidence, may be briefly noticed and dismissed. (*a.*) It has been supposed that our Lord purposely anticipated the legal Paschal Supper, and that the words, "With desire I have desired to eat this Passover with you before I suffer" (Luke xxii. 15), were an intimation of that purpose. Against this, however, there is the fact that the disciples, who could have no such anticipatory purpose, ask the question where they are to prepare, and then actually prepare the Passover as a thing of course, and that the Three Gospels, as we have seen, all speak of the Last Supper as being actually on the first day of the feast of unleavened bread, which is the Passover. (*b.*) It has been conjectured that the Galilean usage as to the Passover may have varied from that of Judæa ; but of this there is not the shadow of evidence ; nor is it likely that the priests, who had to take part in the slaying of the Paschal lambs, would have acquiesced in what would seem to them a glaring violation of their ritual. (*c.*) Stress has been laid on the fact that in the later ritual of the Passover week a solemn meal was eaten on the day that followed the sacrifice of the Paschal lamb, which was known as the *Chagigah* (festivity, or festive meal). This also was a feast upon flesh that had been offered in sacrifice ; and it has been thought by some who seek to reconcile the four narratives, that this was the feast for which Judas was supposed to be ordered to make provision, that this was "the Passover," the prospect of which led the high priests to keep clear of entering under the roof of the Prætorium. In many ways this seems, at first, an adequate solution of the difficulty ; but there is no evidence that the term, "the Passover," which had such a strictly definite significance, was ever extended to include this subordinate festivity.

(4.) It remains to examine the narrative somewhat more closely, and with an effort to realize, as well as we can, the progress of the events which they narrate. As a preliminary stage in the inquiry, we may note two or three facts which cannot well be excluded from consideration. (*a.*) The narrative of the first Three Gospels, probably independent of each other, represents on any assumption, the wide-spread tradition of the Churches of Judæa, of Syria, and of Asia ; of St. Matthew, St. Peter, and St. Paul. It is antecedently improbable that that tradition could have been wrong in so material a fact. (*b.*) The Fourth Gospel, whether by St. John or a later writer, must, on any assumption, have been written when that tradition had obtained possession of well-nigh all the Churches. It is antecedently improbable either that such a writer should contradict the tradition without knowing that he did so, or that, if he knew it, he should do so silently. and without stating that his version of the facts was more accurate than that commonly received. It is at least a probable explanation of his omitting to narrate the institution of the Lord's Supper, that the record of that institution was recited whenever the disciples met to break bread at Ephesus as elsewhere (1 Cor. xi. 23—26) ; and that he felt, therefore, that it was better to record what others had left untold than to repeat that with which men were already familiar. If he was not conscious of any contradiction, then his mode of narrating, simply and without emphasis, noting facts as they occurred, was natural enough.

(5.) It remains to be seen whether there is, after all, any real discrepancy. Let us picture to ourselves, assuming for a time that the Last Supper was the Paschal meal, what was passing in Jerusalem on the afternoon of that 14th of Nisan. The Passover lamb was, according to the law (Ex. xii. 6 ; Lev. xxiii. 5 ; Num. ix. 3, 5) to be slain "between the two evenings." The meaning of the formula is not certain. If, some have supposed, it meant between the evening of the 14th and that of the 15th of Nisan, it gives a space of twenty-four hours within which the lamb might be slain and eaten, and then the whole apparent contradiction between the two narratives disappears. It was open to the disciples to eat their Passover on the 14th of Nisan ; to the priests to eat theirs on the 15th. The occurrence, however, of the same expression in the rules as to the daily evening sacrifice (Ex. xxix. 39, 41 ; Num. xxviii.

4), excludes this interpretation; and it seems more probable that it covered the period that preceded and followed the setting of the sun. (Comp. Deut. vi. 2.) Looking to the prominence given to the ninth hour (3 P.M.) by the connection with the evening sacrifice and prayer (Acts iii. 1), it would be probable enough that the slaughter of the Paschal lambs would begin at that hour; and this conclusion is expressly confirmed by Josephus, who states that they were slain from the ninth to the eleventh hour, *i. e.* from 3 to 5 P.M. ("Wars," vi. 9, 3). It is clear, however, that the process would take up the whole of the time, and would tend to stretch beyond it. Josephus (*ut supra*) reckons the number of lambs that had to be sacrificed at 270,000. Some were certain to begin their Paschal meal two hours before the others.

(6.) Everything indicates that the disciples were among the earliest applicants for the priests' assistance. The Galileans abstained from work, as a rule, on the feast-day more rigidly than the dwellers in Judæa, and this would naturally lead to their making their preparations early. Peter and John are accordingly sent to prepare "when the day came." They get the room ready. They hasten, we may believe, to the Court of the Temple with the lamb. They sit down to their meal "at evening," *i. e.* about sunset, or 6 P.M. (Matt. xxvi. 20; Mark xiv. 27; Luke xxii. 14). It was in the nature of the case certain that the priests would be the last to leave the courts of the Temple, where they had to wait till the last lamb was offered, to burn the fat and offer incense, and cleanse the Temple, and purify themselves by immersion from the blood of the sacrifices; and that their Paschal meal would therefore be the latest at Jerusalem. They could scarcely expect in any case to eat their Passover before 9 or 10 P.M.

Now let us turn to the upper room, in which our Lord and His disciples were assembled. At a comparatively early stage of the meal, before the fourth, or possibly before the third, of the four cups of wine which belonged to the ritual of the feast, Judas leaves to do his traitor's work. He has reason to believe that his Master will go out that evening, as was His wont, to Gethsemane. He goes at once to the priests, say about 8 or 9 P.M., with the welcome tidings. The urgency of the case, the sacred duty of checking the false and blasphemous Prophet Who called Himself the Son of God, the urgency of the policy which sought to prevent the tumult which might have been caused by an arrest in the day-time, are all reasons for immediate action. *The Paschal meal is postponed.* They will be able, by-and-by, to comply with the rule that it must be consumed before the morning (Ex. xii. 10). The guards are summoned and sent on their errand, as they had been once before on the "great day" of the Feast of Tabernacles (John vii. 37—45). Messages are despatched to all the members of the Sanhedrim (or at least a sufficient number for that purpose) to the hurried meeting, which was held before dawn. Assume these facts, and all runs smoothly. When Judas leaves, the disciples, looking forward to the usual festive *Chagigah* on the following day, the *feast,* as distinct from the *Passover,* suppose that he is gone to prepare for that; and there is no ground for thinking that at that hour the markets would be shut; or that lambs, and bread and wine might not be purchased, or at least ordered, for the following day. When the priests, on the other hand, refused to enter into the Prætorium, "lest they should be defiled," it was because they, and they alone, perhaps, in all Jerusalem, had still to eat the Passover, which had been eaten by others on the previous evening. Had their meal been due on the evening that followed the Crucifixion their scruples would have been needless. They had but to wash and wait until sunset, and they would have been purified from all defilement. With them the case was more urgent. Probably even the pressure of hunger made them anxious to finish the untasted meal of the previous evening. It was then "early," say about 4 or 5 A.M. When Pilate gave his sentence it was "about the sixth hour," *i. e.* assuming St. John to use the Roman reckoning of the hours, 6 A.M. Then their work was done. As soon as they had left the matter in Pilate's hands they *could eat their Passover*, turning the supper into a breakfast. This they had time for while their Victim was being mocked by the Roman soldiers and led out to Calvary. When it was over, they were able to reappear between 9 A.M. and noon, and to bear their part in the mockings and blasphemies of the multitude (Matt. xxvii. 41 ; Mark xv. 31). The disciples on the other hand, who had eaten their Passover, found nothing to hinder them (this is obviously true at least of the writer of the Fourth Gospel) from going into the Prætorium, hearing what passed between Pilate and his Prisoner (John xviii. 33—40), and witnessing, it may be, the scourgings and the mockings. Joseph of Arimathæa was not deterred by any fear of defilement from going to Pilate, for he too had, we must believe, eaten his Passover at the proper time (Matt. xxvii. 57).

(7.) So far then, on this view, all is natural and consistent. St. John omits the fact of the meal being the Passover, as he omits the institution of the Lord's Supper, because these were things that were familiar to every catechumen ; and confines himself to points of detail or of teaching which the current tradition passed over. He is not conscious that he differs from that tradition at all, and therefore neither emphasises his difference, nor is careful to avoid the appearance of it. On the other hand, the assumption that the Passover followed the Crucifixion involves the almost incredible supposition that the chief priests could remain by the cross until 3 P.M. and then go to Pilate (John xix. 31) regardless of their previous scruples ; that nearly the whole population of Jerusalem, men and women, instead of cleansing their houses from leaven, and preparing for the Passover, were crowding to the scene of the Crucifixion ; that Nicodemus and Joseph of Arimathæa, and the Maries, were burying the body of Jesus, and so incurring, at the very hour of the Passover, or immediately before it, a ceremonial defilement, which would have compelled them to postpone their Passover for another month (Num. ix. 10). They go, the first at least of them, to Pilate, and both the visits are, it will be noted, recorded by the same Evangelist, who recorded the scruples of the priests, without any explanation of what, on the other theory, is the apparent inconsistency.

(8.) There remains only a few minor points above noticed. And (*a.*) as to the *Preparation*. Here the answer lies on the surface ; the name (*Paraskeüe*) was given to the day of the week, our Friday, the day before the Sabbath, and had absolutely nothing to do with any preparation for the Passover. The Gospels show this beyond the shadow of a doubt (Mark xv. 42 ; Matt. xxvii. 62 ; Luke xxiii. 54). If any confirmation were wanted, it may be found in the fact that the name is applied in a Græco-Roman decree, quoted by Josephus, to the week-day which answers to our Friday. Even the phrase which seems most to suggest a different view, the "preparation of the Passover," in John xix. 14, does not mean more, on any strict interpretation, than the "Passover Friday," the Friday in the Passover week, and coming therefore before a Sabbath more solemn than others (John xix. 31). It may be noted further, that the term *Paraskeüe*, was adopted by the Church, Western as well as Eastern, as a synonym for the *Dies Veneris* or Friday. (*b.*) The supposed difficulty as to Simon of Cyrene is of the slightest possible character. There is nothing to indicate that he was coming from field-labour. And if he had eaten his Passover on the previous day either in Jerusalem or its immediate neighbourhood, there was nothing either in law or custom to prevent his entering the city on the following morning. (*c.*) The questions connected with the action of the priests, and the thoughts of the disciples as to the meaning of our Lord's command to Judas, have been already dealt with.

John 19:38-42

A THREEFOLD POWER

" And after this Joseph of Arimathæa, being a disciple of Jesus," &c.

EXEGETICAL REMARKS.—Ver. 38.—
" *And after this* (R. V. THESE THINGS)
*Joseph of Arimathæa, being a disciple
of Jesus, but secretly for fear of the
Jews, besought* (R. V. ASKED OF) *Pilate
that he might take away the body of
Jesus: and Pilate gave him leave. He
came therefore, and took the body* (R. V.
AWAY HIS BODY) *of Jesus.*" An account
of the burial of Christ we have also
in Matt. xxvii. 57—61 ; Mark xv. 45
—47 ; Luke xxiii. 50—56. The death
of Christ seemed to rouse Joseph to
some boldness, so that he went to
Pilate and begged the body of Jesus.
Nicodemus, too, of a similarly cowardly
nature, seemed to be actuated by the
same impulse. " The foes of Jesus
have gone into the background, and
He is now with His friends for
evermore. No apostle appears present
at the embalming or entombment ;
but one whose name is hitherto un-
mentioned but for this act steps
forward. So for the just man Providence ever raises new friends. And
so may the weakest faith grow strong,
and take its proper post at the required hour."

Ver. 39.—" *And there came also
Nicodemus, which* (R. V. HE WHO)' *at
the first came to Jesus* (R. V. HIM) *by
night, and brought* (R. V. BRINGING)
*a mixture of myrrh and aloes, about
an hundred pound weight.*" " This
myrrh is a gum exuding from a tree
found in Arabia, and more plentifully
in Abyssinia. It is a very ancient
article of commerce among Egyptians,
Jews, Greeks, and Romans. It is
first- mentioned in Exodus xxx. 23.
It was celebrated in ancient times as
a perfume, and burned for an agreeable fumigation, it was esteemed as a
medicine. It was an ingredient used
by the ancient Egyptian embalming.
In the middle ages of Europe it
was held that it would render a
man's body immortal if there were
any method of completely imbuing
the system with it. The ' *aloes* ' here

mentioned are not to be identified
with the drug which bears that name
in the *Materia Medica*, which is a
very bitter and somewhat stimulant
stomachic purgative ; on the contrary,
the article here named is an odor-
iferous wood, celebrated for its agreeable qualities in ancient literature.
Thus in Ps. xiv. 8 : ' All thy garments smell of myrrh, and aloes, and
cassia.' The Hebrew word *ahil* became
identified both in the Greek and
modern languages with the word
' *aloes*,' simply from the verbal resemblance. It is curious that the
Malay name of the article is *agila*,
which besides bearing a strong resemblance to the Hebrew word has
also a resemblance to the word *eajle*,
and hence the same article has received
the name of eajle-wood."—*Whedon*.
" At the funeral of Gamaliel," says
Livermore, " eighty pounds of spice
were used, and when Herod was buried
there was a procession of five hundred
servants carrying costly unguents and
aromatics. The large quantity which
Nicodemus brought, and by which he
testified his affection, was not, therefore, incredible."

Ver. 40.—" *Then took they* (R. V. SO
THEY TOOK) *the body of Jesus, and
wound* (R. V. BOUND) *it in linen clothes*
(R. V. CLOTHS) *with the spices, as the
manner* (R. V. CUSTOM) *of the Jews is
to bury.*" " In the last two verses
John has mentioned Joseph and
Nicodemus each in the singular, and
adds the part which each performed ;
the former secured the body, the latter
furnished the material for embalming. Now in the plural they both co-
operate in the same work. Hitherto
they have been strangers ; ever after,
doubtless, they were brethren."

Ver. 41.—" *Now in the place where
He was crucified there was a garden ;
and in the garden a new sepulchre*
(R. V. TOMB), *wherein was never man
yet laid.*" (Compare xviii. 1.) " St.
John's account makes the choice of

the sepulchre depend on its nearness to the place of crucifixion: the account in the earlier Gospels makes it depend on the fact that the sepulchre belonged to Joseph. The one account implies the other, and the burial, under the circumstances, required that both the sepulchre should be at hand, and that its owner should be willing that the body be placed in it."
—*Dr. Ellicott's Commentary.*

Ver. 42.—"*There laid they Jesus therefore* (R. V. THERE THEN) *because of the Jews' preparation day* (R. V. OMITS DAY); *for the sepulchre* (R. V. TOMB) *was nigh at hand*" (R. V. THEY LAID JESUS). "The time was so short," says *Dr. Livermore*, "as the Sabbath was about to commence, that is, at sundown, that the burial was hastily performed, leaving something to do afterwards (Mark xvi. 1); and the body was laid in a tomb near at hand, in order to avoid the delay of carrying it to a distance. Thus, in less than twenty-four hours Jesus had been betrayed, seized, tried, crucified, and buried—a concentration of mighty events. To all human appearance His religion perished with Him, and the last ray of hope was quenched in the tomb of Joseph. But to the Sun of Righteousness, as to the natural sun, might the poet's language apply—

'So sinks the day-star in the ocean's bed,
And yet, anon, repairs his drooping head,
And tricks his beams, and with new spangled ore
Flames in the forehead of the morning hour.'"

HOMILETICS

We shall take the conduct of Joseph and Nicodemus, at the burial of Christ, as illustrating a *Threefold Power*—the power of *Worldliness*, the power of the *Cross*, and the power of *Penitence*.

I—THE POWER OF WORLDLINESS

Both of these men had opportunities of being convinced that Christ was the true Messiah, and it is highly probable that both had a sympathy with Him and His cause. And yet they seem to have stood aloof from Him up to the hour of His death. Nicodemus was a member of the Jewish Sanhedrim, and yet he seems to have held his peace, whilst nearly all his fellow-members were calumniating the Son of God, and plotting His destruction. He had not the courage to stand up and denounce their conduct, expressing at the same time his own belief that He was the true Messiah. All that we hear him say was on one occasion, and that in a very timid way, "Doth our law judge any one before it hear him, and hear what he doeth?" The same might be said of Joseph, who is here said to have been "*a disciple of Jesus.*" He makes no bold protest against the enemies of his Lord, nor does he make any open avowal of his discipleship. Why was this? There were, perhaps, three elements of worldliness that influenced them in the matter.

First: The Love of Wealth. It would seem that the Jews resolved, that whosoever should confess that Jesus was the Christ, should be cast out of the synagogue, and entirely excommunicated.

Excommunication amongst the Jews involved the sacrifice of civil as well as religious rights and privileges. The rich man, in those days, who followed Christ would lose his wealth. The home of comfort and luxury would have to be exchanged for a state of penury and want. Decision for Christ was always a question, at that time between principle and property, conscience and cash. Hence Christ frequently told His hearers, that if they followed Him they would have to sacrifice their worldly all. Neither Joseph nor Nicodemus had sufficient moral strength to sacrifice their worldly possessions for Christ. Another element that influenced them was—

Secondly : The Desire for Popularity. They were in elevated positions, members of the Sanhedrim, looked up to and honoured by the populace. The desire for power and the love of social approbation, which belong to us all, would be strengthened in them by their exalted office. Now, if they had followed Christ, all this popularity would have gone at once ; they would have been execrated instead of praised. This popularity they had not moral strength enough to sacrifice. "They loved the praise of men more than the praise of God." What is popularity ? "Popularity," says *Carlyle*, "is as a blaze of illumination, or, alas, of conflagration, kindled round a man, showing what is in him, not putting the smallest item more into him, often abstracting much from him, conflagrating the poor man himself into ashes and *caput mortuum*."

There are three classes of men—(1.) Those who have no moral convictions. This is the largest class. (2.) Those who have moral convictions, but not enough courage to avow them. There are men in Parliament who have moral convictions, but are too cowardly to avow them ; they are mute in the presence of their "party." There are men in the pulpit, who are convinced that much that is being preached is theological fiction, and yet they are mute. Another class—the grander but, alas, the few—are—(3.) Those who have moral convictions, and courageously carry them out, regardless of the frowns of men. These are the heroes, the reformers, the saviours of the world. Another element that influenced them was—

Thirdly : The Power of Caste. They were members of a certain class—the highest class in Jewish society. The whole class not only stood aloof from Christ, but cherished and displayed the most malignant hostility towards Him. Class feelings are always powerful. Because "none of the rulers believed on Him," these men were too weak to come out on His side. Such are the elements of worldly power which probably acted on these men, and prevented them from avowing publicly their attachment to the Son of God. And such elements are as strong here as there, now as then. The conduct of these men illustrates—

II.—THE POWER OF THE CROSS

What was it that now brought forth these timid men, brought them to Pilate to beg the body of him in order to bury Him in the garden?* When Christ was alive, they were afraid to avow their attachment to Him. It was the Cross that nerved them to the effort. There was something about His death that roused them to manly exertion. There were two wonders connected with His crucifixion which would tend to produce this effect—

First: The Material. The rending of the veil, the riving of the rocks, the quaking of the earth, the darkening of the sun at high noon, the raising of the dead, the mysterious quiverings of nature at every point, as if struck with mortal anguish,—these wonders must have produced a deep impression upon the most sceptical spectator. But a much deeper upon those in whose hearts there lurked a latent love.

Secondly: The Moral. To a reflective mind such wonders would be far more impressive. See the moral majesty of Him Who dies between two malefactors, and amidst the furious rage of a maddened populace. Mark His reply to the prayer of the dying thief, the interest He displayed in His mother, the prayers He presented for His murderers, the surrender of His spirit to God, the deep calm and unconquerable love that He displayed. And in all there goes forth "a still small voice"—soul-penetrating withal. All whose spiritual ear could catch the sound must have said, "Truly this was the Son of God." Undoubtedly these men felt the mystic power of all this. As they now handled the mangled, helpless frame, many a tear of self-reproach fell, we may suppose, as they thought of their past unfaithful and unmanly conduct. Thus the power of the Cross overcame in them the Power of the World. This Cross is evermore the power, and the only power, by which we can overcome the Power of the World.

The conduct of these men illustrates—

III —THE POWER OF PENITENCE

Now Christ is dead their consciences are stirred to their centre; and they are, no doubt, deeply stung with remorse, on account of their cowardice. Shame on us, they would probably exclaim, that we should have been so pusillanimous, as to stand aloof from Him during His public ministry! Ah! it is always so with those who have neglected a true friend, when that friend has been taken from them. See now the force of this with these men! Two remarks are suggested concerning this power of penitence.

First: It forced them to a compensatory effort. No doubt this embalming with "*myrrh*" and "*aloes*" was a most costly service. Nothing too good for Him now; even life itself, if needed, might

* See Germ on the next page.

go. What service had they rendered Him during His struggles and His trials? None. But now that He is dead, what are they not prepared to do? All this is the force of moral regret—the force of conscience. Conscience will, sooner or later, drive a man to his duty.

"What conscience dictates to be done,
Or warns me not to do,
This, teach me more than hell to shun,
That more than heav'n pursue."

Secondly: The compensatory effort came too late. Of what use was all this embalming and burying to Christ, now that He was dead? Had they built His sepulchre of diamonds, garnished it with the choicest pearls of ocean, all would have been nothing to Him. The offering was too late. So it often is. The compensatory effort is *made too late.*

Germs of Thought
No. 73   John 19:41

THE GRAVE IN THE GARDEN
" In the place where He was crucified was a garden."—xix. 41.

The history of sin in the Bible is associated with gardens; the darkest things in the moral universe are associated with the fairest in the material. The first *human* sin that " brought death into the world, and all our woe," was perpetrated amidst the beauties of a garden. The greatest *spiritual* suffering ever, perhaps, endured in our world, was endured in a garden. It was in the garden of Gethsemane that Christ exclaimed, " My soul is exceeding sorrowful," &c; and the grave of Him Who is to " swallow up death in victory" was in a garden. It would seem from 2 Kings xxi. 26 that the ancients were accustomed to have sepulchres in their gardens. Amon was " buried in his sepulchre in the garden of Uzza."

Natural affection would suggest the idea of having the grave in a garden. It is far more in accordance with the dictates of the human heart, to bury our dead in the garden, amongst the flowers and shrubs, than to transport them, as is now the custom, to scenes far beyond the reach of family observation. Religion, too, might have suggested the idea. The grave in the garden, would serve as a monitor to those who owned the garden; it would remind them that whatever may be their pleasures and possessions, they would soon have to resign all for the cold and lonely grave. The subject presents to our notice—

I —SIN INTRODUCING THE SAD INTO THE MOST PLEASANT THINGS OF LIFE

Nothing to man is more sad than death, and no scene to him is more pleasant than a well-cultivated garden. But here is death in a garden; and this sin introduced. Because of it Christ Himself died. Here we have the connection of trial with the fairest scenes of life, and it is ever so. Death in a garden! Let a man be in the most propitious circumstances, he is sure to have something to pain his heart. Naaman was a great captain, but he was a leper; Paul a great apostle, but he had a "thorn" in the flesh. Man looks—

First: To new relationships. He fancies that his husbandhood and fatherhood will be a beautiful garden, and hails the entrance thereinto as a scene on which the sun will shine and the dews descend, the flowers bloom and the trees cluster. But, alas! soon he finds a grave there. He looks—

Secondly: To new departments of business. But there he will find a grave. There is some cloud on every landscape, a mildew on every flower. The words present to our notice—

II —BENEVOLENCE RETAINING THE AMELIORATING AMIDST THE SAD SCENES OF LIFE

Death is a great trial, death is brought into the garden, but the garden is left and still blooms on.

First: There are *constitutional* ameliorations to relieve our sadness. There is a self-healing principle in nature. Sever a branch from the tree, wound the body, cut the flesh, or break a limb, and you see the self-healing power exude and work. It is so in the soul. Thought succeeds thought like the waves of the ocean, and each tends to wear out the impression its predecessor has made.

Secondly: There are *incidental* ameliorations to relieve our sadness. New events, new engagements, new relationships tend to heal the wound.

Thirdly: There are *Christian* ameliorations to relieve our sadness. The assurance of an after life, the hope of a future re-union, &c. Such are the reliefs. These, like the flowers and shrubs of a lovely garden, spring up around our hearts, and cover the grave of our sorrows and trials with the shadow of their foliage. Yes; though we have our trials we have still our gardens, and in our garden there is the Rose of Sharon, the Lily of the valley, and more, the Tree of Life for "the healing of the nations." Young life starts up about our graves.

> Life's dreariest path has some sweet flowers,
> Its cloudiest day some sun.

John 20:1-10

A MIRROR OF HUMAN ACTIVITY

*(The visit of the women to the sepulchre.—Mary Magdalene returns.—*Matt. xxviii. 1; Mark xvi. 2—4; Luke xxiv. 1—3; John xx. 1—2.)

*(Peter and John at the sepulchre.—*Luke xxiv. 12; John xx. 3—10.)

"The first day of the week," &c.

Exegetical Remarks.—Ver. 1.— "The (R. V. now on the) *first day of the* week." The Jewish Sabbath was the last day of the week—Saturday. The disciples of Christ seem to have adopted the first day of the week for their spiritual devotion. On that day Christ rose from the dead, and they called it the Lord's day. "*Cometh Mary Magdalene.*" Matthew has "Mary Magdalene and the other Mary." Mark, Mary Magdalene and "Mary the mother of James and Salome;" and Luke, "the women which had come with Him from Galilee." These he enumerates as Mary Magdalene and Joanna and Mary the mother of James, and the other women that were with Him. John only speaks of the woman, Mary Magdalene. There is no contradiction; but the difference shows that there was no collusion, no fabrication. It might be indeed that the different women were at the sepulchre at different times. "*When* (R. V. WHILE) *it was yet dark.*" The mere glimmering of dawn. "*And seeth the stone taken away from the sepulchre*" (R. V. TOMB). This fact is made emphatic in all the accounts, especially in Luke xxiv. 2.

Ver. 2.—"*Then she runneth* (R. V. THEREFORE), *and cometh to Simon Peter.*" Matthew has, "to His disciples." Luke, "to the eleven, and to all the rest." "*The other disciple, whom Jesus loved.*" Thus John describes himself, and with characteristic modesty speaks of himself in the third person. "*And saith unto them, They have taken away the Lord out of the sepulchre* (R. V. TOMB), *and we know not where they have laid Him.*" It is supposed that the plural here included the other women whom the Synoptists mentioned. The language is the passionate cry of a woman's heart. As if she said, They have not only crucified the Lord, but have stolen away His body.

Ver. 3.—"*Peter therefore went forth, and that* (R. V. THE) *other disciple, and came to* (R. V. THEY WENT TOWARD) *the sepulchre*" (R. V. TOMB). The details here are peculiar to this gospel. Luke mentions Peter, but no one else. The scene here is pictured with all the vividness and exactness of one who himself saw and took part in it.

Ver. 4.—"*So* (R. V. AND) *they ran both together.*" She ran, and they ran. "*The other disciple did outrun* (R. V.

OUTRAN) *Peter, and came first to the sepulchre*" (R. V. TOMB). "The histories of the resurrection by the Evangelists betray at every clause their fidelity to nature and truth. There is that agitation, that fear, that hope, that joy, which we should expect. There is running hither and thither: the breathless haste of excited, astonished, conflicting feelings. The women ran, Mary Magdalene ran, and Peter and John ran, as if in competition with each other. There were tears, and prostrations of reverence (Matt. xxviii. 9), and glad reports carried to the absent; and every mark in nature of the reality of this stupendous fact that the crucified Jesus had walked forth from the rent tomb a living being, bringing life and immortality to light."

Vers. 5, 6.—"*And he stooping down, and looking in, saw* (R. V. HE SEETH) *the linen clothes lying; yet went he* (R. V. ENTERED HE NOT) *not in. Then cometh Simon Peter* (R. V. SIMON PETER THEREFORE ALSO COMETH) *following him, and went* (R. V. ENTERED) *into the sepulchre* (R. V. TOMB), *and seeth* (R. V. HE BEHOLDETH) *the linen clothes lie*" (R. V. LYING). How like impulsive Peter is this! He rushed into the sepulchre which John, perhaps, either from reverence or dread, did not venture to do, although it would seem that he was first at the sepulchre.

Ver. 7.—"*And the napkin, that was about* (R. V. UPON) *His head, not lying with the linen clothes, but wrapped together* (R. V. ROLLED UP) *in a place by itself.*" The napkin, it would seem, lay apart from the other pieces of linen. This minute description indicates a complete personal acquaintance with the incident. *Alford* says, "We seem to hear the very voice of Peter describing to his companion the inner state of the tomb."

Ver. 8.—"*Then went* (R. V. ENTERED) *in also* (R. V. THEREFORE) *that other disciple, which came first to the sepulchre* (R. V. TOMB), *and he saw, and believed.*" "*Believed*" what? Evidently, what Mary Magdalene had said, viz.: that they had taken away their Lord. I remember reading, many years ago, a most masterly discourse entitled,

" Unconscious Influence," founded on this incident, by Dr. Bushnell.

Ver. 9.—*" For as yet they knew not the Scripture, that He must rise again from the dead."* What Scriptures ? I am referred by some to Isaiah li. ; Psalm ii. 7 ; xvi. 9, 10 ; but I find no proof whatever that these passages refer to the resurrection of Christ. There may be some other Scriptures that have not come down to us, but Christ himself plainly predicted His resurrection. (See Luke xxiv. 25— 27.)

Ver. 10.—*" Then* (R. V. so) *the disciples went away again unto their own home."* " More exactly, of course, to their lodgings in Jerusalem. They had accomplished the object of their visit to the sepulchre. One, at least, had realized, and he must have told his thoughts to his friend, that the Lord was not to be looked for in the empty grave, and that Mary's fears were groundless. No enemies had taken the body away. They return, then, with hearts filled with this truth, to ponder over its meaning, or to tell it to others of the eleven, or to wonder and wait until He should come again to them, as He had promised." — *Bishop Ellicott's Commentary.*

HOMILETICS

In this remarkable fragment of Gospel History we have a *Mirror of Human Activity.* Man is necessarily an active being : he lives *in* action and *by* it. Inactivity is virtually death ; wrong activity is misery ; right activity, alone, is true living. Hence the world is full of labour. In this incident we see Human Activity *Inspired by strong love, Existing under a strong delusion,* and *Ending in sad disappointment.* Here we see—

I —HUMAN ACTIVITY INSPIRED BY STRONG LOVE

What earnest activity we have here in Mary Magdalene, Peter, John, and the other disciples ! One hurrying to the other, Peter and John hurrying to the sepulchre, Peter bounding into it and carefully examining the linen. All the faculties of mind and body seem on the stretch. What prompted all this earnest activity ? *Love.* Here we see—

First : The Law of Love. What is the law of love ? It is a yearning for the presence of its object. Mary Magdalene and the disciples loved Christ. They had lost sight of Him for some days, and their longing for another glance at Him became irrepressible. Love evermore hungers for a sight of its object ; it will dare mortal epidemics, cross stormy oceans, visit distant islands and continents in order to see, and if possible, to clasp to its bosom, its object. Hence the great attraction of heaven is that we shall see Him as He is. Here we see—

Secondly : The Courage of Love. It was truly a bold thing for Mary Magdalene, either alone or in company with her small sisterhood, to go forth in the dark, enter Joseph's garden, where the Roman soldiers had been all night, and where He was buried, Whom the Jewish authorities hated even unto death. It seemed almost a defiance to the whole Jewish people. But strong love is the spirit of heroism; it will face armies and dare death in its most hideous forms. Here we see—

Thirdly: The Earnestness of Love. On the wide earth could we discover more vehement earnestness, than now around the tomb of Jesus? What strenuous efforts of body, what wrestlings of soul! Strong and sacred love alone is the power to set all the faculties of humanity into vigorous and harmonious action. *Schiller* says—

> "Love, only love, can guide the creature
> Up to the Father-fount of Nature;
> What were the soul did Love forsake her?—
> Love guides the mortal to the Maker."

Here we see—

II —HUMAN ACTIVITY EXISTING UNDER A STRONG DELUSION

These disciples hurried forth in the morning, before the break of day, under the delusive impression that they would find Christ in the tomb. For this false impression they were *blamable*, for He Himself had assured them that He would rise the third day. Their ignorance, therefore, was inexcusable. How much of the world's activity, aye, of the activity of every man, is put forth under illusory impressions! Men seem to be led on by phantasms of their brain; they walk in a "vain show," they act under the influence of day-dreams.

One man runs forth to wealth in search of happiness, another to fame, another to sensual gratification, but when they reach the points whither they direct their efforts, they find happiness is not there. It is all an illusion, and a *guilty* illusion, for they have the means of knowing that the happiness and dignity of humanity can only be found in moral goodness. To the eye of angels, methinks, the tribes of busy men, hurrying hither and thither, appear as so many somnambulists, directed by the wild visions of a disordered brain. Looking around us on all hands, we see men in every department of activity, like Oriental travellers, burning with thirst, hurrying along to what they consider to be lakes of refreshing water, and when they approach the spot they find it is a mere mirage, the whole vanishes into thin air. Each active life is a fiction, and all are pursuing shadows. Why this? Because, like the disciples running to the sepulchre of Christ, they guiltily ignore facts.

Facts tell all men that there is no happiness for them outside of the human soul, that it must well up from within, not stream into them from without. Facts tell men that there is no true honour or dignity to be obtained outside of them, that true greatness, real majesty, consist in noble thoughts, high purposes, and loyalty to the everlasting laws of the universe. That to be great is to be good, and to be good is to conform to the moral image of the God-Man. Solomon sought, with all the earnestness of his nature, for what he considered would make him great and blessed—in fine buildings, splendid gardens, numerous attendants, great wealth, enchanting music, and distinguished knowledge. In all he was acting under the common delusion, and exclaims, " Behold, all is vanity and vexation of spirit." When will humanity be roused from these dreams? When will men see things as they are, and practically recognize eternal realities, look away from the things that are "seen and temporal," and pursue those realities that are "unseen and eternal?" When? "Truly," says *Archbishop Leighton,* " the whole course of a man's life is but a continual trading in vanity, running a circle of toil and labour, and reaping no profit at all." Here we see—

III—HUMAN ACTIVITY ENDING IN SAD DISAPPOINTMENT

" *Then went in also that other disciple, which came first to the sepulchre, and he saw, and believed. . . . Then the disciples went away again unto their own home.*" Yes; now they saw He was not there, and " *believed:* " knew that all their strenuous efforts to find Him were put forth under a delusion. What sadness and darkness this discovery must have spread over their souls! The outward world was " *dark* " when they came forth; no stars shone on them, and the sun had not skirted the horizon. It was dark too, probably, when they wended their steps homeward, but the outward darkness was only a symbol of the depressing darkness that now enwrapped their hearts—the darkness of a terrible disappointment. They felt that all their exertions had been lost labour. They felt, as *Cowper* expresses it, that they had been—

> "Letting down buckets into empty wells,
> And growing old with drawing nothing up."

There are few if any trials in life more distressing than disappointment. But the pain of the disappointment will always be in proportion to the power and influence of the hope that has been blasted. Such experience must be the lot of all who have lived under delusion. As the man in the Gospel, who built his house on the sand, and fully expected a beautiful residence, that would shelter him from the stormy blast and the scorching ray, and just after he had expended much time and great labour to rear it, at the hour when he most required it "the rain descended, and the floods came, and the winds blew and beat upon that house, and it fell, and great was the fall of it."

Ah, what are we all doing in this illusory life, but building houses on the sand, houses that must fall to pieces when we need them most? When the storms of eternal realities, with all their lurid lights and violent forces, will beat upon us. Ah, then comes the terrible conviction that all life's labour has been lost ! " The setting of a great hope," says *Longfellow*, " is like the setting of the sun. The brightness of our life is gone ; shadows of the evening fall around us, and the world seems but a dim reflection—itself a broader shadow. We look forward into the coming lonely night, the soul withdraws itself, then stars arise, and the night is holy."

John 20:11-18

PHASES OF PIETY

(Our Lord is seen by Mary Magdalene at the Sepulchre.—MARK xvi. 9—11 ; JOHN xx. 11—18.)

" But Mary stood without at the sepulchre weeping," &c.

EXEGETICAL REMARKS.—Ver. 11.— " *But Mary stood* (R. V. WAS STAND-ING) *without at the sepulchre* (R. V. TOMB) *weeping.*" It would seem from this that Mary had ran with the two disciples to the sepulchre, and while they went in she stood " *without weeping.*" "*And* (R. V. SO) *as she wept, she stooped down, and looked into the sepulchre*" (R. V. TOMB). How earnestly and intently she must have looked, how anxious to know the result of the search, and weeping all the while !

Ver. 12.—"*And seeth* (R. V. SHE BEHOLDETH) *two angels in white sitting, the one at the head, and the other* (R. V. ONE) *at the feet, where the body of Jesus had lain.*" This appears to have been a distinct vision to Mary, which she probably related to the author of this Gospel. Though John himself might not have witnessed it, he had such faith in her testimony that he records it. These angels were " *in white,*"—emblem of celestial purity, —" *the one at the head, the other at the feet.*" They were the heavenly watch-guards of that Sacred Body.

Ver. 13.—"*And they say unto her, Woman, why weepest thou ?*" A modern expositor says the question was asked, "not because they knew not why she wept, but to open the way to make her know that there was no reason to weep." "*She saith unto them, Because they have taken away my Lord, and I know not where they have laid Him.*" This is the passionate cry of her heart ; the sup-

posed loss of Christ was the source of her agony.

Ver. 14.—"*And when she had thus said, she turned herself back, and saw* (R. V. BEHOLDETH) *Jesus standing, and knew not that it was Jesus.*" As she appears to have turned away from the angels, another form arrested her attention : it was that of "*Jesus,*" but she failed to recognize Him. Perhaps in figure, feature, gait, and garb, He was not as she had seen Him last.

Ver. 15.—"*Jesus saith unto her, Woman, why weepest thou ? whom seekest thou ?*" How different are these words spoken by Jesus, to the same words even spoken by the angels ! How different the feelings that prompted them : how different the tones in which they were uttered ! "*She, supposing Him to be the gardener.*" Perhaps a servant of Joseph of Arimathæa, employed to take care of the garden. "*Sir, if thou have* (R. V. HAST) *borne Him hence, tell me where thou hast laid Him, and I will take Him away.*" Three times she refers to the Lord simply by the pronoun "*Him.*" She has named Him in the previous verse, and, perhaps, thinks that the gardener had heard those words ; but the impression formed from her eager words is that her own mind is so entirely filled with the one subject that she supposes it to be in the minds of others. The same passionate eagerness is heard in the words which follow. Devotion such as hers does not weigh difficulties, a place of safety for that sacred body is the object of her will, and that will neither dreads danger nor sees that the task would be physically impossible, but asserts in the confidence of its own strength,—"*and I will take Him away.*"

Ver. 16.—"*Jesus saith unto her, Mary.*" "This word was, no doubt, pronounced with a peculiar intonation which she recognized at once as that of Jesus." The sound of that voice thrilled her through and through. "*She turned* (R. V. TURNETH) *herself, and saith unto Him* (R. V. IN HEBREW), *Rabboni; which is to say, Master.*" She had heard her own name pronounced in a well-known voice, and it brought back to her memories that flood her with emotions, and in her ecstasy she exclaims in her native Hebrew dialect, "*Rabboni; which is to say, Master.*"

Ver. 17.—"*Jesus saith unto her, Touch Me not.*" The word "*Touch*"

is a Greek word which signifies to cling to, to fasten on to, to clasp. In the ecstasy of her feeling, she cast herself at His feet (Matt. xxviii. 9), and with accustomed reverential embrace, clung to His knees. The reply of our Saviour seems to mean, Do not continue to cling to Me, "*For I am not yet ascended to My* (R. V. UNTO THE) *Father.*" I am about ascending to our common Father, and we shall meet again. "Where I am, there ye shall be also." "*But go to* (R. V. UNTO) *My brethren, and say unto* (R. V. TO) *them, I ascend unto My Father, and your Father; and to My God, and your God.*" This was a grand commission for her.

Ver. 18.—"*Mary Magdalene came* (R. V. COMETH) *and told* (R. V. TELLETH) *the disciples that she had* (R. V. I HAVE) *seen the Lord, and that He had spoken* (R. V. SAID) *these things unto her.*" She sets herself at once to discharge her mission.

HOMILETICS

This fragment of evangelic history may be taken to illustrate a *Threefold Aspect of Piety.* Here we have—

I —PIETY IN SADNESS

"*Mary stood without the sepulchre weeping.*" * She seemed overwhelmed with sorrow. Notice here—

First: The intensity of her affection. What is that which makes bereavement painful? *Love.* Had we no affection for the departed we should drop no tear into their graves. All the anguish at sepulchres streams from love. Mary's great distress therefore on this occasion, demonstrated the strength of her affection to Christ.

Secondly: The greatness of her courage. "*She stood without at the sepulchre.*" The grave has with most a power to excite fear. Few of the bravest men enjoy walking through a graveyard in the dark. Explain it how you may, we feel timid amongst the graves of the dead. But in Mary's case there was something more than this natural fear. To stand by the sepulchre of Jesus was really a perilous position. The Roman soldiers had strict charge to watch the tomb. To show love to Him Who lay there, was to incur the displeasure of the rulers of the country. Yet Mary stood there alone in the dark. Love is courage. Her affection raised her above the fear of the ghosts of the dead and the drawn swords of

*See Addendum at end of volume on "Words of the Angels to Mary."

the living. The tears of love are not the expressions of weakness, but the symbols of a force unconquered and unconquerable.

Thirdly : The imperfection of her faith. He, Whose loss she was mourning, was at that moment standing by her side. She supposed " *Him to be the gardener.*" Ah, me ! how often, through the lack of faith, we degrade the grandest things in the universe ! We only see common labourers, gardeners, etc., where the divinities are present and in action. This lack of faith on Mary's part was very inexcusable ; for had she not been told He would rise from the dead on the third day ? She wept for the very reason that she ought to have rejoiced. What poor blind creatures we are ! We often see nothing but a " *gardener,*" where in reality stands the Divinest messenger of God ! O for eyes to see the Divine, even under the humblest form of life, and to detect blessings under the disguise of trials ! Thus we weep when and where we ought to rejoice ! Like Jacob we say, " All these things are against us," whereas in reality, as in his case, they are for us. Piety has its dark moods ; days when the sea of life becomes very rough, and when neither stars nor sun appear. Here we have—

II —PIETY IN RAPTURE

" *Jesus saith unto her, Mary ! She turned herself, and saith unto Him, Rabboni, which is to say, Master.*" Christ does not condemn the tears. There is no harm in weeping. He Himself wept.

> " The very law which moulds a tear
> And bids it trickle from the source,
> That law preserves the earth a sphere,
> And guides the planets in their course."—*Rogers.*

He only suggests the impropriety of the cause. Her exclamation " *Rabboni,*" and the command of Christ " *Touch Me not* " indicate that she had risen into an ecstasy of soul. It would seem that for a moment she was wild with rapture. Two facts are here to be observed—

First : The *Rapidity of our mental changes.* This woman passed, as in a moment, from anguish to ecsta.y. To such changes we are ever exposed, at least in this world. We can pass with the swiftness of lightning, from one pole of experience to another. Though clouds of darkest gloom and most portentous shape may overspread the heavens of the soul, *one* thought can sweep them clean away, and make the azure arch blaze with the light of noon. The awful swiftness with which we can pass from mood to mood, urges the necessity of implicitly confiding in that God Who alone can keep us in " perfect peace." Another fact to be observed here is—

Secondly : The *Power of Christ's voice.* What effected this change ? One word of His—the word " *Mary !* " He pronounced

it, no doubt, with an intonation which she recognized. She knew
the voice; it rang with the old notes of love. Neither the
mysterious sorrows of Gethsemane, the agonies of the Cross, the
tortures of death, nor the darkness of the grave, had changed that
loving voice. It sounded "*Mary*" now as ever. Thus by a word
Christ can lift the soul into the highest bliss. It was not the voice
of the angels that uplifted her, but that of Christ. Here we have—

III—PIETY IN ACTION

"*Go to My brethren, and say unto them, I ascend unto My
Father, and your Father; and to My God, and your God.*" This
command she promptly attended to. Notice here—

First: Christ's Merciful identification with His disciples. "*My
Father, and your Father.*" The good of all ages are one with Him,
—children of the same Infinite Father. This command indicates—

Secondly: The Heavenward direction which her sympathies
should take. Look upward—"*I ascend.*" "Seek those things that
are above." Notice—

Thirdly: The Right direction of religious feeling. Do not live in
mere sentiment; turn your feelings into action. Action will at
once *express, and utilize your emotions.* Go and work. Piety in
duteous action, is piety in its highest and safest state. Sighs of
sorrow and shouts of rapture, are verily worse than worthless, unless
they pass into duteous deeds, and consolidate the character. Tears
should invigorate the moral heart as rain strengthens the oak.

John 20:19-23

THE UNEXAMPLED KINDNESS OF CHRIST TO HIS DISCIPLES

(*Jesus appears in the midst of the disciples, Thomas being absent. Jerusalem.*
—MARK xvi. 14—18; LUKE xxiv. 36—49; JOHN xx. 19—23.)

"Then the same day at evening, being the first day of the week," &c.

EXEGETICAL REMARKS.—This account of our Lord's appearance to His disciples should be compared with Mark xvi. 14; Luke xxiv. 26—36. It is supposed by some that between the events recorded, immediately preceding, and what we have in this paragraph, there occurred the bribing of the guard (Matt. xxviii. 11—15); and also the conversation on the way to Emmaus (Luke xxiv. 13—25; Mark xvi. 25).

Ver. 19.—"*Then the same day at evening* (R. V. WHEN THEREFORE IT WAS EVENING ON THAT DAY), *being*

the first day of the week." All the evangelists agree that the resurrection occurred on the first day of the week. The event which John here records took place on the evening of the first day. On this evening the disciples had gathered together no doubt for study, conference, and devotion. "*When the doors were shut where the disciples were assembled* (R. V. OMITS) *for fear of the Jews.*" Their Shepherd was struck down, and they were left now as wandering sheep, exposed to the ravenous wolves that surrounded them. Our Lord had told them the danger and persecution that awaited them (chap. xv. 18). "*Came Jesus and stood in the midst.*" Now whilst they were in this room, with the doors closed, Christ appeared. How did He gain admission? Not by force, breaking in the doors. No! His resurrection body was independent of the laws of gravitation. "*And saith unto them, Peace be unto you.*" The same salutation is recorded in Luke xxiv. 36. What words are these falling on their ears in heavenly music midst the darkness of the grave!

Ver. 20.—"*And when He had so said* (R. V. SAID THIS), *He shewed unto them His hands and His side.*" Luke says, "His hands and His feet." None of the other evangelists refer to the piercing of the side. "*Then were the disciples* (R. V. THE DISCIPLES THERE-FORE WERE) *glad, when they saw the Lord.*" They were satisfied as to His corporeal identity, and enraptured at having once more in their midst the presence of their loving Lord.

Ver. 21.—"*Then said Jesus* (R. V. JESUS THEREFORE SAID) *to them again, Peace be unto you: as My* (R. V. THE) *Father hath sent Me, even so send I you.*" Here He identifies Himself with them, in the same Divine mission. He is an Apostle of redemptive love; so are they. The Father sent Him; He sends them.

Ver. 22.—"*And when He had said this, He breathed on them.*" "The word rendered '*breathed*' occurs nowhere else in the New Testament, but was familiar from its use in the Greek (LXX) of Gen. ii. 7. St. John, to describe this act of the risen Lord, uses the striking word, which had been used to describe the act by which God breathed into man's nostrils the breath of life. He writes as one who remembered how the influence of that moment, on their future lives, was a new spiritual creation by which they were called, as it were, out of death into life. It was the first step in that great moral change which passed over the disciples after the Crucifixion, and of which the day of Pentecost witnessed the accomplishment." "*And saith unto them, Receive ye the Holy Ghost.*" "These words," says Pro-

fessor Watkin, "are not, on the one hand, understood as simply a promise of the future gift of the Holy Ghost, for they are a definite imperative, referring to the moment when they were spoken; nor are they, on the other hand, to be taken as the promised advent of the Paraclete (chap. xiv. 16), for the gift of the Holy Ghost was not yet, because Jesus was not 'yet glorified.' The meaning is, that He then gave to them a sign which was itself to faithful hearts as the first-fruits of that which was to come. His act was sacramental, and with the outer and visible sign there was the inward and spiritual grace. The very word used was that used when He said to them, 'Take, eat; this is My body' (Matt. xxvi. 26; Mark xiv. 22). It would come to them now with a fulness of sacred meaning. The Risen Body is present with them. The constant spiritual Presence, in the person of the Paraclete, is promised to them. They again hear the words, '*Receive ye,*' and the very command implies the power to obey."

Ver. 23.—"*Whose soever sins ye remit* (R. V. FORGIVE), *they are remitted* (R. V. FORGIVEN) *unto them; and whose soever sins ye retain, they are retained.*" (Matt. xvi. 19; xviii. 28.) (See my "Genius of the First Gospel" on these passages.) "The medium by which they were to remit sins is the Gospel committed unto them, for the efficient ministration of which they are now empowered by the Holy Ghost breathed upon them by their Divine Master. Through that Gospel they would remit the sins of all who accept it by faith. Our Lord in these words declares the efficacy of the Gospel for this purpose. By the same Gospel the true minister condemns the rejecting sinner. The apostolic hand holds the instrument by which it is enabled to dispense release from the power and guilt of sin to all those who are penitent, and to retain under its condemnation those who are incorrigible. Thus with it in their hands, apostles would go forth discharging the souls of men from sin, or confirming them under its condemnation."

HOMILETICS

The great subject which this fragment of evangelic history presents to us is *The Unexampled Kindness of Christ to His Disciples*. Observe—

I —HE GRANTS THEM HIS PRESENCE, AND IMPARTS TO THEM HIS BENEDICTION

First : He grants them His Presence. *"Jesus came and stood in the midst."* Though the doors of the room where they were assembled were shut, He entered and stood in the midst of them. No granite walls, no iron bolts or bars, can exclude Him from His genuine disciples. He has pledged His presence to all such. "I will come to you," &c. "I will not leave you comfortless," &c. "Lo, I am with you alway."

Secondly : He imparts to them His Benediction. *"Peace be unto you."* This was just what they wanted. They must have been at this time in a wild tumult of anxious thought, memories, and apprehensions. All men want this *"Peace,"* for they are like the troubled sea whose waters cannot rest. They are at war with their Maker, and consequently with themselves, society, and the universe. Christ came to give Peace. "Peace on earth" was the burden of the anthem, which the herald angels carolled over Bethlehem, on the morning of His birth. Observe—

II —HE DISPELS THEIR FEARS, AND ESTABLISHES THEIR FAITH

First : He dispels their Fears. They were not only afraid of the Jews, but His appearance also at first greatly alarmed them. Luke says, "They were terrified and affrighted, and supposed they had seen a spirit." This utterance implies their belief in the existence of disembodied spirits ; in the possibility of these spirits appearing to them ; and that these spirits were not friendly towards them.* Men have always been afraid of spirits. To allay this dread of spirits Christ not only shows them *"His hands and His feet,"* (but according to Luke) says, "Why are ye troubled ? and why do thoughts arise in your hearts ?"

(1.) Here He implies that Spirit may exist apart from Matter, and in that state may appear to Living Men ; (2.) Here He demonstrates the materiality of His body, and urges on them an inquiry into the cause of their superstitious fear. "Why are ye troubled ?"

Secondly : He establishes their Faith. *"Then were the disciples glad, when they saw the Lord."*† In Luke it is said that at first "they believed not for joy," a state of mind which we can appreciate. At the first moment of good news the mind often

*See Addendum.

says to itself, It is too good to be true. He established their faith not only by exposing His resurrection body to their view, but also (as we find from Luke) by eating with them. Observe—

III —HE GIVES THEM A COMMISSION, AND QUALIFIES THEM FOR ITS DISCHARGE

First: He gives them a Commission. "*As My Father hath sent Me, even so send I you.*" What the commission was we find in Luke xxiv. 46, 47. "Repentance and remission of sins should be preached in His name among all nations, beginning at Jerusalem." They were to preach "repentance and remission of sins," preach that to "all nations," and to preach it in a certain order— "beginning at Jerusalem."

Secondly: He qualifies them for its Discharge. "*He breathed on them, and saith unto them, Receive ye the Holy Ghost: whose soever sins ye remit, they are remitted unto them; and whose soever sins ye retain, they are retained.*"

(1.) He inspires them with the Divine Spirit. Rightly to carry out a *new* enterprise, a man must be put into possession of a new *spirit* equal to it. And to discharge this new enterprise of preaching the Gospel through the world, nothing less than the Spirit of God Himself is required. Christ now gives this new inspiration.

(2.) With this new inspiration they became invested with the highest Authority. "*Whose soever sins ye remit, they are remitted unto them; and whose soever sins ye retain, they are retained.*" It is noteworthy that this Authority was not given to Peter, or to any one of the disciples, but to all alike.

CONCLUSION. How transcendent the privileges of the genuine disciples of Christ! He grants them His presence, and imparts to them Peace; He dispels their fears, and establishes their faith; He gives them a commission, and qualifies them for its discharge.

Germs of Thought
No. 74   John 20:19-23
(Luke 24:36-48)

CHRIST'S APPEARANCE TO THE DISCIPLES *

" And as they thus spake, Jesus stood in the midst of them," &c.—xx. 19—23.

This is Christ's *fourth* appearance to His followers after His resurrection; and there are five things in the incident of great practical significance.

* This is one of a Series of Ten Discourses on "Christ's Appearances after His Resurrection." (See "Homilist," Vols. x. and xi.)

I —HE DECLARED HIS BENIGNANCY, IN ORDER TO TRANQUILIZE THEIR HEARTS

" *As He stood in the midst of them, He said unto them, Peace be unto you.*"

First : His glorious benediction expressed the great Want of Human Nature. The disciples now gathered together specially required this benediction of *Peace ;* for their excitement must have been intense. Agitating thoughts about Jesus of Nazareth, His Crucifixion, and His empty grave, must have surged in violent succession through their hearts ; within them " deep called unto deep," and the commotion was furious. They required a voice which would bid the tumult cease, command the storm to be still. But what they in this special sense wanted, human nature everywhere requires ; and the more wicked, the more deep the necessity. "The wicked are like the troubled sea, whose waters cannot rest." Men are alienated from their Maker ; and because of this, they are at war with *themselves,* at war with *society,* and at war with the *universe.*

Secondly : His glorious benediction expressed the great Design of Christ's Mission. He came to give " *Peace.*" He came to reconcile man to his Maker, to Himself, and to the Creation. He came to reproduce in humanity that Supreme Sympathy with God, which is the essential and unfailing security of spiritual tranquillity in all worlds.

II —HE APPEARED TO THEIR REASON, IN ORDER TO ALLAY THEIR FEAR

His appearance amongst them roused their superstitious fear. "They were terrified and affrighted, and supposed they had seen a spirit." Their fear implied three things—

(1.) Their belief in the existence of Disembodied Spirits. (2.) Their belief in the Possibility of these Disembodied Spirits appearing to them. Men have always believed in this ; hence they have peopled every sphere of the world with ghosts. (3.) Their belief that Disembodied Spirits were not Friendly to them. Else why fear them ? " Why are ye troubled, and why do thoughts arise in your heart ? " Why should they be afraid of a spirit ? Were they not themselves spirits, members of the spiritual universe, and soon to be introduced into a conscious connection with its unearthly tenants ? Is not the Infinite Father a Spirit ? And the prophets, patriarchs, and the saints of departed ages, whom they honoured, were *they* not Spirits ? Why then fear a Spirit ? The Spirit-Fear is the symptom of a *guilty* conscience. A guilty conscience urges men to forebode messengers of insulted justice from the invisible. In Christ's appeal to them in order to allay their fear—

First : He assures them that spirits may exist apart from matter, and in this state appear to living men.

Secondly : He demonstrates the materiality of His own resurrection body. "*Behold My hands.*"

Thirdly : He throws upon them an inquiry into the cause of their superstitious fear. "Why are ye troubled?" Inquiry into our mental phenomena will soon expel superstition.

III —HE GAVE THEM EVIDENCE, IN ORDER TO ESTABLISH THEIR FAITH

"*And while they yet believed not for joy.*" Here is one of those developments of simple nature with which Scripture records abound. The state of mind here expressed is common to humanity; when we say that the news is too good to be true, we express the feeling. Observe two things in relation to the evidence He now presents of His Resurrection—

First : Its Nature. It consisted of two things.

(1.) *A palpable exhibition of the reality of His body.* "He said unto them, Have ye here any meat?" &c. He eats before them, showing them that He was Jesus of Nazareth, with Whom they were accustomed to eat, previous to His death. (2.) *A clear showing that His resurrection answered to the predictions of the Scriptures concerning the Messiah.* "All things must be fulfilled which were written in the law of Moses." We are not told all that He said, but the conclusion He thus states : "Thus it is written, and thus it behoved Christ to suffer, and to rise from the dead the third day."

Secondly : Its Effect. "Then opened He their understanding." He thus assured them of His resurrection.

IV —HE PROPOUNDED HIS SYSTEM, IN ORDER TO INDICATE THEIR DUTY

In Luke we have these words, "And that repentance and remission of sins should be preached in His name among all nations, beginning at Jerusalem."

First : He here propounds the *great doctrine* of His system. "Repentance and Remission." Just the two things indispensable to the well-being of man everywhere.

Secondly : He here propounds the *world-wide aspect* of His system. "All nations," &c. It is not for a sect or class, but for all.

Thirdly : He here propounds the order of *propagating* His system. "Beginning at Jerusalem."

V —HE ENDOWED THEM WITH EXTRAORDINARY POWER, IN ORDER TO FIT THEM FOR THEIR EXTRAORDINARY WORK

The account of the event informs us that, "*He breathed on them, and saith unto them, Receive ye the Holy Ghost. Whose soever sins* ye remit, they are remitted unto them ; and whose soever sins ye retain, they are retained." In endowing with the Holy Spirit, Christ does two things—

First: He performs a symbolical act. "*He breathed on them.*" The old prophets often set forth their message by emblematic acts. (See Jer. xiii., xvii.) And Christ here symbolizes the descent of the Spirit on the day of Pentecost, by breathing on His disciples. The same Greek word means *wind* and "*spirit.*"

Secondly: He endows them with an extraordinary authority. He gave them authority to "*remit*" the sins of men—power of absolution.

John 20:24-29

THE HONEST SCEPTIC

(Jesus appears in the midst of the apostles.—Thomas present.—Jerusalem.— John xx. 24—29.)

" But Thomas, one of the twelve, called Didymus, was not with them when Jesus came," &c.

EXEGETICAL REMARKS.—Ver. 24.— "*But Thomas, one of the twelve, called Didymus.*" Both words mean twin. The Jews often had two names, one in Hebrew, the other in Greek or Latin. Thomas is the Jewish, and Didymus the foreign appellation. "*Was not with them when Jesus came.*" Why he was not at that meeting we are not told. Did the Crucifixion destroy all his faith, or did the panic of the Crucifixion drive him too far off to be present ?

Ver. 25.—" *The other disciples therefore said unto him, We have seen the Lord. But he said unto them, Except I shall see in His hands the print of the nails, and put my finger into the print of the nails, and thrust* (R. V. PUT) *my hand into His side, I will not believe.*" He rejects entirely the testimony of the disciples, and demands the testimony of his own senses. This is at once unjust and unreasonable. Yet this seems to be in accord with his mental habit. We find in chapter xiv., when our Lord referred to His departure, Thomas says, " Lord, we know not whither Thou goest,

how can we know the way ? " " *I will not believe,*" which means I will by no means believe.

Ver. 26.—"*And after eight days again His disciples were within, and Thomas with them.*" We are not to suppose from this that they had not met in the interval, but this meeting was special, it was on the Lord's day. "*Then came Jesus* (R. V. JESUS COMETH), *the doors being shut, and stood in the midst, and said, Peace be unto you.*" He again entered preternaturally, and He salutes them as before.

Ver. 27.—" *Then saith He to Thomas, Reach hither thy finger, and behold* (R. V. SEE) *My hands; and reach hither thy hand, and thrust* (R. V. PUT) *it into My side: and be not faithless, but believing.*" He knew Thomas's state of mind, and specially addresses Himself to him, condescending to present him with the kind of evidence he required.

Ver. 28.—"*And Thomas answered and said unto Him, My Lord and my God.*" A confession of resuscitated and re-invigorated faith.

HOMILETICS

This fragment of evangelical history presents to us—

I—AN INTERESTING RELIGIOUS SCEPTIC

"*But he said unto them, Except I shall see in His hands the print of the nails, and thrust my hand into His side, I will not believe.*" Observe—

First: His scepticism was negative, not positive.

Secondly: His scepticism was intellectual, not moral.

Thirdly: His scepticism was candid, not clandestine.

Fourthly: His scepticism was convincible, not obstinate. Here is—

II—AN EXEMPLARY RELIGIOUS GUIDE

How did Christ treat this sceptic? Did He denounce him, or ignore him? No; He finds him out, speaks to him with exquisite tenderness, and condescends to give him the very evidence he required,—"*Reach hither thy hand, and thrust it into My side: and be not faithless, but believing.*" Observe—(1.) The *promptitude;* (2.) The *speciality;* (3.) The *exquisite considerateness;* and (4.) The *moral success* of His treatment of this sceptic. Christ won him. "*Thomas answered, My Lord and my God.*"

III—A SUPER-EMINENT RELIGIOUS FAITH

It is implied,—

First: That it is possible for those who have never seen Christ to Believe in Him. "*Have not seen, and yet have believed.*" It is implied—

Secondly: That those who believe in Him without seeing Him are Peculiarly Blest. "*Blessed are they that have not seen, and yet have believed.*" (1.) Faith without sight is more *praiseworthy* than faith by sight. (2.) Faith without sight is more *accurate* than faith by sight. (3.) Faith without sight is more *enriching* than faith by sight. (4.) Faith without sight is more *invigorating* than faith by sight.*

John 20:30, 31

THE PARTIALNESS AND THE PURPOSE OF THE EVANGELIC RECORD

(*The Ascension.—Bethany.*—Mark xvi. 19, 20; LUKE xxiv. 50—53; JOHN xx. 30, 31.)

"And many other signs truly did Jesus in the presence of His disciples."

EXEGETICAL REMARKS.—Ver. 30.— "*And many other signs truly* (R. V. THEREFORE) *did Jesus in the presence of His* (R. V. THE) *disciples.*" The Greek

---

*For an amplification of these points, see Addendum.

here for "*signs*" is often rendered miracles, for the miracles of Jesus were all signs indicating the Divinity of their Author. The signs were not merely those referring to the resurrection, but included, no doubt, all the manifestations of His power both before and after His resurrection. They refer to His whole work. "*Which are not written in this book.*" The evangelical record then of Christ's life is only partial. It is said in the last verse of the next chapter : "There are also many other things which Jesus did, the which, if they should be written every one, I suppose that even the world itself could not contain the books that should be written." "This," says *Dr. Brown*, "is to be taken as something more than a merely parabolical expression which would hardly comport with the sublime simplicity of this writer. It is intended to let his reader know that even now when he had done, he felt his materials so far from being exhausted, that he was still running over, and could multiply gospels to almost any extent within the strict limits of what Jesus did. But in the

limitation of these matchless histories, in point of length and number alike —there is as much of that Divine wisdom which has presided over, and pervades, the living oracles, as in their variety and fulness."

Ver. 31.—"*But these are written, that ye might* (R. V. MAY) *believe that Jesus is the Christ, the Son of God ; and that believing ye might* (R. V. MAY) *have life through* (R. V. IN) *His name.*" This "*ye*" addresses every reader, to the end of the world. It speaks from John to the person that now reads the words, inviting him to believe on the Lord Jesus Christ, and have life through His name. Jesus is *the* Christ, the Messiah. Christ lived, His apostles preached, and His evangelists wrote, that the world might shape its conceptions to the true idea of the Messiah, not as the Emancipator of the nation, but as the Saviour of the world." We have in these two verses what the best scholars of modern times consider to be a proper summary and ending of the book. The chapter which follows has been considered a later addition.

HOMILETICS.

The subject of this passage is *the Partialness and the Purpose of the Evangelical Record*.

I —ITS PARTIALNESS

"*Many other signs truly did Jesus in the presence of His disciples, which are not written in this Book.*" * Christ was a Worker ; an earnest, diligent, unflagging, and unremitting Worker. He had a wonderful mission to discharge within a brief space of time. "He went about doing good." "The works," He said, "which My Father gave Me to do." "I must work the works of Him that sent Me, while it is day ; the night cometh when no man can work." Every day of His life was crowded with deeds, and these deeds were "*signs.*"

First : They were "*signs*" of His Preter-natural Might. The works ascribed to Him in the Gospels transcend all human power. No man could do the works that He did.

Secondly : They were "*signs*" of His Matchless Philanthropy. All His works were inspired and directed by a love for man that was disinterested, self-sacrificing, and unconquerable.

* See Germ, p. 187.

Thirdly : They were "*signs*" of His Immeasurable Possibilities. The works He did were only specimens of His Infinite productiveness. His works were but the "Hiding of His Power." But though the works recorded were only a miserably small portion of what He accomplished—

(1.) They are sufficient for our purpose. They reveal Him as the All-loving and Almighty Saviour. (2.) They suggest a wonderful history for future study. Will not all the unrecorded deeds of His which He wrought on earth, as well as all His works since He left the world, be unfolded for our study in the future ? Into these things "the angels desire to look." Concerning this Evangelical Record observe—

II —ITS PURPOSE

" *These are written, that ye might believe that Jesus is the Christ, the Son of God.*" *

First : The facts of His life are written in order to reveal Him. They are revelations of (1.) His power, (2.) His love, (3.) His transcendent excellence. The works of a man are the *Revelations of himself.* "By their fruits ye shall know them."

Secondly : The facts of His life reveal Him in order that men may Believe in Him. How could they believe in Him of Whom they have not heard ? Faith in Him is at once—(1.) The most essential and (2.) The most practicable of all faiths. It is easier to believe in a Person than in a Proposition ; easier to believe in a Transparently Good Person than in any other.

Thirdly : Men are to believe in Him in order that they may have the highest life. " *That believing ye might have life through His name.*" What is the highest life ? *Supreme Sympathy with the Supremely Good.* Men lost this at their fall, and the loss is their guilt and ruin. The mission of Christ is to resuscitate this lost *sympathy,* and to fill souls with the love of God. This is the great Moral Resurrection that is going on in the world, and which comes, and comes only, out of faith in Him Who is the "Resurrection and the Life."

Germs of Thought
No. 75   John 20:30, 31

THE QUICKENING WORKS
" And many other signs truly did Jesus," &c.

Every man in his life may be compared to a book ; and every day adds a fresh page to the book. Notice—

I —THE RECORD

" *These are written.*" The subjects of the publication are the wonderful works and sayings of our Lord. His deeds were such

* See Germ, p. 189.

as no human power could accomplish. The miracles of Christ were performed for three special purposes. (1.) As acts of Humanity. (2.) As proofs of His Divinity. (3.) As illustrations of the works of Salvation. Their *publicity* is particularly noticed in the text. These "*signs*" were done in the *presence* of His disciples. Imposture seeks concealment; works in the dark. But "*these things* were not done in a corner*," but openly,—on the stage of public society. The miracles said to every doubter, "Come and see." The *number* of these miracles is also noted. "*Many other signs*," &c. Not only are the miracles of Christ recorded, but also His *sayings*. With what dignity, authority, and power, does He speak! &c. "*These things are written.*" The way by which the Divine Will has been revealed to mankind, has been by directing and inspiring certain persons to record it in *writing*. Many advantages are derived from this method.

(1.) There is the advantage of *Universality*. A man's writings reach further than his voice.

(2.) There is the advantage of *Appeal*. "To the law and the testimony," we appeal. This is the judge that ends strife.

(3.) There is the advantage of *Security and Permanence*. The word uttered perishes; the letter written remains. Everything of consequence we desire to have in *writing*. What do we know of ancient history, but by streamlets that have flowed down to us in books and writings? Let us be thankful, then, for two great blessings; for the Book; the book written in our own tongue— and for an ability to read it. Let all possess the Bible, read it, love it! Notice—

II—THE REASON

"*These things are written, that ye might believe*,"—

First: In the *Real Existence* of Jesus. Some have been so sceptical as to doubt whether such a Person as Jesus Christ ever appeared in the world. They never doubt the historic existence of such men as Julius Cæsar or Mahomet. But have we not much higher proof of the existence of Jesus Christ? "*These things are written, that ye might believe*,"—

Secondly: In the *True Character* of Jesus. "*That Jesus is the Christ, the Son of God.*" He came to "redeem men from all iniquity," &c. The great object is more especially noticed in the next clause of our text, which is—

III THE RESULT

"*And that believing ye might have life.*" Some write books for pecuniary ends. But the Evangelist wrote without any view of temporal benefit to himself, but to bring men to Christ and Heaven. That "*ye might have life.*" Not of course animal or even intellectual life, but Spiritual and Eternal Life. We may, however, form some idea of this spiritual life, by thinking of signs and evidences of animal life. There are at least five signs of life—*sensibility, activity, appetency, appropriativeness, superiority to gravitation.* Have we these signs spiritually?

Take this Record; thank God for it. Christ is the Substance of it. He is the Gospel, so believe in Him, that you may "*have life*" Spiritual, ever Growing and ever Blessed Life.

No. 76   John 20:31

THE SON OF GOD

" The Son of God."

God has many sons. The children of Israel were called His sons, the judges in the theocracy were called His sons, angelic existences are called His sons; but Christ is called "*The Son of God.*" Why this? He must be a Son in a sense which does not apply to any other being in the universe. Wherein is His *uniqueness* as a "*Son of God?*" He was—

I —UNIQUE IN HIS AGE

He was "set up from everlasting." He was in the "beginning with God." He is the "first-born." The oldest of God's other sons are young compared with Christ. He was—

II —UNIQUE IN HIS CONSTITUTION

He was God in a Human Personality. He was not merely Man, not merely God, but *God-Man.* God is in all intelligences, in all creatures; but He was in Christ in a sense in which He is in no other being, giving Omnipotence to His arm, Omniscience to His intellect, Ubiquity to His presence. He was—

III —UNIQUE IN HIS MISSION

He is the Mediator between God and man. He is the only Saviour. "There is no other name given amongst men," &c. There is good reason, therefore, why He should be singled out from all other sons of God, and be called "*The Son of God.*"

John 21:1-14

THE RELATION OF CHRIST TO THE SECULAR LIFE OF HIS DISCIPLES

(*The Apostles go away into Galilee.—Jesus shows Himself to seven of them at the Sea of Tiberias.—Galilee.*—MATT. xxviii. 16 ; JOHN xxi. 1—24.)

" After these things Jesus shewed Himself again to the disciples at the Sea of Tiberias," &c.

EXEGETICAL REMARKS.—Because the last two verses of the preceding chapter seem to close the whole book, some have supposed that John is not the author of this chapter. But the thought, the spirit, and the style seem to stamp it as the production of his pen.—*Westcott* says that " This chapter is evidently an appendix to the gospel which is completed by chapter xx. It is impossible to suppose that it was the original design of the Evangelist to add the incidents of chapter xxi. after chapter xx. 30, which verses form a close to his record of the great history of the conflict of faith and unbelief, in the life of Christ. On the other hand, it is equally clear that it was written by the author of the gospel. The style, the character, and contents of the chapter are peculiar to John. The occasion of the addition is probably to be found in the circulation of the saying of the Lord as to John xxi. 23."

Ver. 1.—" *After these things.*" The expression may not indicate immediate succession, but rather an interval during which other events had transpired. " *Jesus shewed* (R. V. MANIFESTED) *Himself again to the disciples at the sea of Tiberias.*" On the lake of Galilee. Seven of the apostles had returned to their native lake and to their former employments.

Ver. 2.—" *There were together Simon Peter, and Thomas called Didymus, and Nathanael of Cana in Galilee, and the sons of Zebedee, and two other of His disciples.*" " It is probable," says an able modern expositor, " that we have here the names of all in the group of seven who were apostles, and that the two remaining persons were disciples in the wider sense in which the word is used by John. (Chaps. vi. 60, 66 ; vii. 3 ; viii. 31 ; xviii. 19.) If they were Andrew and Philip,

which has been supposed from chap. i. 40—43, it is not easy to understand their position in the list, or the absence of their names. Thomas is not named by the other evangelists, except in the list of the apostles. (Compare chaps. xi. 16 ; xiv. 5 ; xx. 24.) Nathanael is named only by St. John. He is, probably, to be identified with the Bartholomew of the earlier gospels, the latter name being a patronymic. The descriptive note '*of Cana in Galilee,*' is added here only. The sons of Zebedee are not elsewhere given by St. John as a description of himself and his brethren, but this is the only place in which he names himself and his brother in a list with others. In St. Luke's account of the earlier draught of fishes, the sons of Zebedee are named as partners with Simon (chap. v. 10). Their position here agrees with the Johannine authorship of the chapter. In the lists of the other gospels, and the Acts of the Apostles, James and John are uniformly prominent in the first group."

Ver. 3.—" *Simon Peter saith unto them, I go a fishing.*" Literally, I am going to fish. They had no longer a common purse, no longer any reason to believe that they would be fed as they had been by the miraculous interposition of their Master. They were now thrown upon their resources for a livelihood. " *They say unto him, We also go* (R. V. COME) *with thee.*" How often the determination of one man stirs others to action ! Peter's resolve moves the whole circle of the brotherhood. " *They went forth, and entered into a ship* (R. V. THE BOAT) *immediately* (R. V. OMITS) ; *and that night they caught* (R. V. TOOK) *nothing.*" All their efforts, although, probably, most strenuous, proved fruitless.

Ver. 4.—" *But when the morning was now come* (R. V. DAY WAS NOW

BREAKING), *Jesus stood on the shore* (R. V. BEACH) : *but* (R. V. HOWBEIT) *the disciples knew not that it was Jesus.*" The distance and the dimness of the early morning light might account for their not knowing Him.

Ver. 5.—" *Then Jesus* (R. V. JESUS THEREFORE) *saith unto them, Children, have ye any meat ?* (R. V. AUGHT TO EAT). *They answered Him, No.*" "The word rendered ' *Children* ' (or as the margin has it, Sirs) is used in addressing others only by St. John, among the New Testament writers (1 John ii. 14, 18). It is not the word used in chap. xiii. 33, where we have an expression denoting His affectionate tenderness for the disciples which would not have been appropriate here, for He does not at once reveal His identity to them. It is a word which indeed may express His love for them (compare iv. 49), but which appears also to have been used as an address to workmen or inferiors, not unlike our own words—boys or lads. They seem to take it in this sense, as though some traveller passing by asked the question because he wished to purchase some of their fish. The word rendered ' *meat* ' occurs here only in the New Testament. It means anything eaten with bread, and was used as equivalent to the fish, which was the ordinary relish."— *Watkin.*

Ver. 6.—" *And He said unto them, Cast the net on the right side of the ship* (R. V. BOAT), *and ye shall find.*" They knew not which side the fishes were ; He did, and He directs them to fling the net on that side. " *They cast therefore, and now they were not able to draw it for the multitude of fishes.*" In the eighth verse they are described as dragging the net to the shore.

Ver. 7.—" *Therefore that disciple* (R. V. THAT DISCIPLE THEREFORE) *whom Jesus loved saith unto Peter, It is the Lord.*" Here the beloved disciple recognized the mysterious stranger as his Master. Sympathy with a person is the quickest eye with which to see him. " *Now* (R. V. SO) *when Simon Peter heard that it was the Lord, he girt his fisher's* (R. V. OMITS) *coat unto* (R. V. ABOUT) *him, (for he was naked,) and did cast* (R. V. AND CAST) *himself*

into the sea." Instantly, true to his enthusiastic nature, Peter fastened his fisher's tunic about his loins, plunged into the sea, and swam, some hundred yards or more, into the presence of Jesus, and fell at His feet.

Ver. 8.—" *And* (R. V. BUT) *the other disciples came in a little ship* (R. V. THE LITTLE BOAT) ; *(for they were not far from land* (R. V. THE LAND), *but as it were* (R. V. ABOUT) *two hundred cubits,)* (R. V. OFF) *dragging the net with* (R. V. FULL OF) *fishes.*" The words ship and boat are interchangeable. The distance was about three hundred feet.

Ver. 9.—" *As soon then as they were come to* (R. V. SO WHEN THEY GOT OUT UPON THE) *land, they saw* (R. V. SEE) *a fire of coals there, and fish laid thereon, and bread.*" Who kindled that fire on the bleak shore ? Who laid the fish and the bread thereon, and thus prepared a breakfast for the hungry and exhausted ones ? Jesus, undoubtedly, and no one else.

Ver. 10.—" *Jesus saith unto them, Bring of the fish which ye have now caught* " (R. V. TAKEN). It is implied that they did so, and thus they supplied a part of the meal of which they were to partake.

Ver. 11.—" *Simon Peter went* (R. V. THEREFORE) *up, and drew the net to land full of great fishes, an hundred and fifty and three : and for all there were so many, yet was not the net broken* " (R. V. WAS NOT RENT). The net was full of great fishes. They were not tiny and valueless, but large and precious, an hundred and fifty and three.

Ver. 12.—" *Jesus saith unto them, Come and dine* (R. V. COME AND BREAK YOUR FAST). *And none of the disciples durst ask* (R. V. ENQUIRE OF) *Him, Who art Thou ? knowing that it was the Lord.*" Probably they desired Him to declare Himself, although from what John had said, they had the impression that it was the Lord.

Ver. 13.—" *Jesus then cometh* (R. V. JESUS COMETH), *and taketh* (R. V. THE) *bread, and giveth them, and* (R. V. THE) *fish likewise.*" Thus He proves at once the fact of His resurrection, His condescending love, and His tender regard for His disciples.

Ver. 14.—" *This is now the third time that Jesus shewed Himself* (R. V. WAS MANIFESTED) *to His* (R. V. THE) *disciples, after that He was risen from the dead.*" "That is, was manifested to His disciples, that is, His assembled disciples, for if we reckon His appearances to individual disciples, they were certainly more."—*Dr. Brown.*

HOMILETICS

The narrative illustrates *The Relation of Christ to the Secular Life of His Disciples.* There is nothing but Secularity in the whole of these fourteen verses. They contain no reference to the soul, spiritual objects, immortality, moral redemption, or the Eternal Spirit. All is *Secularity.* The passage is not the less religious or Divine on this account. Man is material as well as spiritual; he lives in a material home, and amidst material influences has to form his character for eternity. There are four thoughts here suggested—

I—CHRIST DOES NOT RELIEVE HIS DISCIPLES FROM THE NECESSITY OF SECULAR LABOUR

Several of His disciples we here find busily engaged all night on the Sea of Tiberias, in fishing. To this work they had undoubtedly resorted as a means of subsistence: they felt themselves the subjects of that law which saith, " He that does not work shall not eat." Christ does not relieve a man from this obligation when he becomes His disciple. The duty of Secular Labour continues to rest upon him in all its original force. In truth, a release from this necessity would be an injury rather than a blessing to men. Secular labour is one of the primary conditions of *Physical health, Intellectual vigour,* and *Moral development.*

Inaction, where there is the power of action, is a crime. Heaven's plan is "that man should go forth to work and to labour until the evening," and if he labours not he sins. He hides his talent in a napkin, and his retribution must come. Non-working is a positive injury. Since the Infinite Lawgiver is infinitely benevolent, what is contrary to His will, and therefore morally wrong, must be injurious. Indolence is an injury to the individual himself. Muscular inactivity enfeebles the body; mental inactivity enfeebles the intellect; moral inactivity enfeebles the soul. Look at the men and women who stand "all the day idle" in the vineyard of life! What are they? They are, it may be, graceful in their movements, elegant in their attire, gentle and pleasing in their manners. But have they, as a rule, any robustness of health, any vigour of intellect, any force of character? They are your feeble mothers and delicate sisters, your nervous fathers, insipid and lackadaisical sons, your simpering women, and your moody men— the greatest patrons of medicine, and the greatest grumblers in life. But idleness injures *others* as well as the individual. The idle person is a social thief. He is constantly living on the produce of others. The case seems to me to stand somewhat thus : The All-bountiful Creator has fitted the earth to produce an ample provision for every human being, on the condition of a certain amount of a right kind of labour. So much labour will produce so much of the necessaries and comforts of life and no more; the measure of the agency put forth will determine the amount which nature yields for the supply of human wants. If the supplies, therefore, are not equal to the demands of a population, the scarcity, as a rule, must be referred not to a deficiency in nature's bountihood (for she liberally responds to every touch of proper agency), but to deficiency in human labour. The idle, therefore, must stand responsible for the destitution. He is sinning against the natural and revealed law of God; he is eating without working, consuming without producing. He is dishonestly appropriating the product of other men's labours. We denounce and punish deeds of larceny when brought under our notice, and we do well. But the idler's life is a life of larceny. His bread is not the bread of honest labour. The men and women who take food and raiment from society, without giving back some kind of honest labour in return, live—unconsciously to themselves, it may be—lives of cruel dishonesty, cruel because the energies of others are overtasked to make up for their idleness. They make "bread so dear, and flesh and blood so cheap." Let us not talk of *Providence* as an excuse for indolence. God is good, and He will provide. He has provided richly, but He only grants the provision on condition of the right employment of our powers. There is an inheritance for the good, but only on the condition of their working. There is a heaven of knowledge, but only for the student; there is a harvest of blessedness, but only for the diligent husbandman; there are scenes of triumph, but only for the victorious warrior.

II —CHRIST ALLOWS THE POSSIBILITY OF FAILURE IN THE SECULAR ENDEAVOURS OF HIS DISCIPLES

These disciples toiled all night and *"caught nothing."* A different result, perhaps, might have been expected. Reason, perhaps, would have suggested the belief that the secular labour of Christ's disciples would never prove futile. It is not so in fact. The crops of a godly farmer fail, the plans of a godly merchant break down, the vessels of godly mariners are wrecked.

The settled laws of nature pay no particular deference to Piety. Exemption guaranteed from *secular failure*, however much we may desire it, would be no blessing. It would tend to nourish worldliness, self-sufficiency, and religious neglectfulness. Liability to secular failure is a spur to industry, and a motive for prayerful dependence on Heaven. Let not, therefore, any unfortunate tradesman who righteously conducts his business, conclude that Christ has deserted him. Let not society conclude that such a man is ungodly because he has failed. The disciples toiled all night and "*caught nothing.*" Observe—

III —CHRIST IS DEEPLY INTERESTED IN THE SECULAR CONCERNS OF HIS DISCIPLES

First: His eyes are ever on them in their work, though *they may be unconscious of Him.* Whilst their little ship was tossed on the sea, and they were toiling with their net, Jesus stood looking at them from the beach, though they did not know it. "*Jesus stood on the shore: but the disciples knew not that it was Jesus.*" * So it ever is. When you, His disciples, who are absorbed in your secular undertakings, battling with difficulties and struggling, it may be, even for the means of subsistence, His all-seeing, yet benignant eye is on you, though you may be unconscious of it. "He knoweth the way you take."

Secondly: He sometimes so signally interposes for their help, as *demonstrates His presence among them.* When they had no meat, Jesus commanded them to "*cast the net on the right side of the ship.*" † They did so, and they were not able to draw it for the multitude of fishes. "*Therefore that disciple whom Jesus loved saith unto Peter, It is the Lord.*" The knowledge, the power, and the mercy displayed in this act of Christ, struck home to their hearts the delightful conviction that Christ was amongst them. Peter, with his wonted enthusiasm, was so excited with rapture, that he girt his fisher's coat about him, and cast himself into the sea in order to approach Christ more quickly than the little vessel would bear him. Thus it has often been and still is. He signally appears to His disciples in troubles, and manifests Himself to their delight.

IV —CHRIST OFTEN MAKES THE SECULAR TRIALS OF HIS DISCIPLES THE MEANS OF A CLOSER FELLOWSHIP WITH HIMSELF

When the disciples had come to shore with their extraordinary quantity of fish, "*Jesus saith unto them, Come and dine.*" ‡ Here we have a display of—

First: His Merciful Condescension. The narrative gives the impression that He kindled the fire for them on the beach, and prepared their fish and their bread for food. It gives the impression, also, that He ate with them, and thus condescended to identify Himself with them in the necessities even of their physical nature. Here, too, we have a display of—

Secondly: His Remedial Wisdom. His eating with them, not

* See Germ, p. 195.　† See Germ, p. 195.　‡ See Germ, p. 196.

only demonstrated His real corporeity and settled the question of His resurrection, but did more,—enlisted at the same time the social sympathies and heart confidences of their nature. The man who attempts to elevate his race in the true sense, and descends not to a level with their hearts, enters not their social affections, and enlists not their confidence, will inevitably fail. We must clothe ourselves with the infirmities of the men we would redeem. Thus Christ acted here, and in this has left us an example. What Christ did now with the disciples He ever does, seeks to make the secular trials of His people the means of a more intimate connection with His heart.

Germs of Thought
No. 77   John 21:4

THE LONELY WATCHER ON THE SHORE OF LIFE

" Jesus stood on the shore."

On the shore of Galilee Christ now watched His disciples as they were plying their oars on the sea. Christ is the Watcher of Christly men wherever they are and however engaged.

I —HE KNOWS ALL ABOUT THEM, ON THE SEA OF LIFE

Every gust of wind, every violent surge; every success and defeat He knows.

II —HE IS DEEPLY INTERESTED IN THEM, ON THE SEA OF LIFE

There He stands on the shore. Whoever is absent, He is there; whoever comes and goes, He remains looking on with intense interest.

III —HE IS READY TO HELP THEM, ON THE SEA OF LIFE

He stood now ready to help the disciples. So He ever is *willing and " able to save to the uttermost."*

No. 78   John 21:6

OLD INSTRUMENTALITIES, BUT NEW METHOD, AN EMBLEM OF CHRIST'S REDEMPTIVE METHOD

" Cast the net on the right side of the ship, and ye shall find."

Christ here commands the disciples to cast in the *old* net in a *new* way, in order to catch the fishes. Thus He ever does in redeeming souls.

I —HE EMPLOYS OLD INSTRUMENTALITIES

Christ employs many instrumentalities by which to redeem men, but they are all *old.*

First: The same old Natural Facts. He employs the phenomena of nature to quicken, educate, and elevate souls. We have nothing *more* of nature than what men of remotest generations had.

Secondly: The same old Gospel Principles. Biblical truths are His great redemptive forces, but these are *old ;* the youngest of them is eighteen hundred years.

Thirdly: The same old Mental Faculties. In regenerating men Christ does not give them new faculties, a new intellect, memory, or imagination. He employs the old. Hence He brings out the new moral creature with the old mental idiosyncrasies.

II —HE EMPLOYS OLD INSTRUMENTALITIES IN A NEW METHOD

" *Cast the net on the right side of the ship."* He directs men—

First: To a new method of studying Natural Facts. *Thoughtfully, inductively, devoutly*—regarding them all as mirrors of the Divine.

Secondly: To a new method of studying Gospel Truths. Not desultorily, speculatively, controversially, but *inductively, systematically,* and *practically.*

Thirdly: To a new method of employing Mental Faculties. Turning the mental powers away from the temporalities of time to the spiritualities of eternity, from the creature to the Creator. Brothers, use the old rightly; cast the old " *net "* in a new direction.

No. 79   John 21:12

THE DINNER ON THE GALILEAN SHORE.—AN EMBLEM OF REDEMPTION

" Come and dine."

The context presents a wonderful scene, sublimely romantic and Divinely significant. This dinner which Christ provided, may be looked upon as an emblem of His great Redemptive System.

I —THE TIME WAS OPPORTUNE

The disciples had tried all their resources for means of a livelihood that night, and had failed. " They had toiled all night, and had caught nothing." They were no doubt tired and dejected, and knew not what to do. The dinner came just at the right time. It is just so with the Redemptive System. After the world had tried everything for its salvation—tried poetry, philosophy, religion, civilization, and grew worse—Christ came—" came in the fulness of time."

II —THE PROVISIONS WERE DESIRABLE

The fish they caught they had been toiling to obtain all night. They were craving for such food. The provisions of the Gospel are both exquisitely fitted for man's needs and urgently required. They are (1.) Soul *renovating,* (2.) Soul *cleansing,* (3.) Soul *developing,* (4.) Soul *harmonizing,* (5.) Soul *perfecting.* In Isaiah xxv. 6 we have a description of the Great Spiritual Banquet. How rich, how varied, how abundant the viands !

III —THE HOST WAS CONDESCENDING

What a sight, the great Son of God sitting down on the Galilean shore preparing a feast for the poor fishermen, and dining with them ! Thus He has done in spiritual redemption. He descended into the " lowest parts of the earth," into the lowest Social Grades. " Made Himself of no reputation," &c. He came down to a level with the creatures. He came to save. He came in the likeness of sinful " flesh." He clothed himself with our infirmities.

John 21:15-17

THE REALM OF LOVE THE SPHERE OF RELIGION

"So when they had dined, Jesus saith to Simon Peter, Simon, son of Jonas, lovest thou Me more than these ? " &c.

EXEGETICAL REMARKS.—Ver. 15.— " *So when they had dined* (R. V. HAD BROKEN THEIR FAST), *Jesus saith to Simon Peter.*" During the meal, perhaps, silence reigned supreme. There was the hush of reverent amazement. "*Simon, son of Jonas*" (R. V. JOHN). It is noteworthy that Jesus does not call him Peter, which means rock, the high title which He had conferred upon him before his fall ; but by his natural name. "*Lovest thou Me ?*" "There are two Greek words alike rendered '*love*' in our translation, but which have a different force. The love of this question ἀγαπᾷς signifies the love of will, of judgment, or of moral feeling ; nearly our English word to prize. The other is φιλέω which is simply affectional love, springing from the natural sensibility. In His question Jesus

uses the former word ; in his answer Peter uses the latter." "*More than these.*" Some say that Christ points to the fishes, or the boats, nets, &c., that is, his worldly calling ; others, which is more probable, to the disciples, who were present. Peter had said, in a somewhat boastful spirit : "Though all men shall be offended because of Thee, yet will I never be offended" (Matt. xxvi. 33). Our Lord might here imply the question, "Art thou of the same opinion now, Peter ? Dost thou love Me more than these other disciples?" "*He saith unto Him, Yea, Lord; Thou knowest that I love Thee.*" That is, with the love of affection and tenderness. "*He saith unto him, Feed My lambs.*" More exactly, "little lambs."

Ver. 16.—"*He saith to him again the* (R. V. A) *second time, Simon, son of*

Jonas (R. V. JOHN), *lovest thou Me?*" The same word for love ἀγαπᾷς that Christ used before He uses here, which is the moral term for love, the love of purpose, judgment. In the reply, Peter uses the other term representing tender emotions. Christ says, "Prizest thou Me, Peter?" Peter says, "*Thou knowest that I love Thee.*" "*He saith unto him, Feed* (R. V. TEND) *My sheep.*" Be a shepherd of My sheep. He is now restored to the commission which he received before his fall, after his noble confession.

Ver. 17.—"*He saith unto him the third time, Simon, son of Jonas* (R. V. JOHN), *lovest thou Me?*" Here Jesus uses the term for love which Peter had used, the more affectionate and tender word. True, it does not represent love of such a high form, but it is love of a tenderer kind. They are intimately associated. "*Peter was* grieved because He said unto him the third time, Lovest thou Me?*" Was he grieved because of the demand now made on him, or because his Master deemed such a question necessary? The latter is the reason, I trow. Thrice he had declared, "I know not the Man:" and now, thrice he is required to say, "I love the Man." "*Lord, Thou knowest all things; Thou knowest that I love Thee.*" The question cut to the very quick, and in the agony of the heart, smarting beneath the wound, he appeals, in more emphatic words than before, to the all-seeing eye that could read the very inmost secrets of his life. "*Jesus saith unto him, Feed My sheep.*" Some read, "little sheep." Here Jesus restores him to the high commission he had forfeited, on the dark night of the trial.

HOMILETICS

The subject of these words is the *Realm of Love the Sphere of Religion.* There are some who put religion in the realm of *Sensuousness.* The mere excitement of the senses by paintings, sculpture, music, gorgeous rites, and tragic anecdotes, is regarded as Piety. Tears of mere animal sympathy are regarded as the expressions of godly sorrow, &c. Some put religion in the sphere of *Logic.* It is in some system of human thought, which men call orthodox, and nowhere else. Unless your intellect, however large it may be, will make its home in some little catechism or creed, you are more fiend than saint. And some put religion in the realm of *External Performances.* If you attend your place of worship, pay all secular debts, subscribe to charities, you are a religious man. From these verses we learn that *the deep moral love of the heart is the seat of true religion.* The question is, therefore, what is this Love? From the passage we infer—

I —THAT IT IS A SUPREME AFFECTION FOR CHRIST

"*Lovest thou Me more than these?*" That is, more than these disciples love Me?—aye, "more even than thou lovest aught besides?" Observe—

First: Religion is a Paramount Affection. It is not a common sentiment flowing in the ordinary current of emotions, sometimes rising into fervour and force, and then passing away. It is either the master passion of the heart—the all in all—or it is nothing.

Love never becomes religion until it grows into Supremacy, and becomes the Monarch of the heart. Observe—

Secondly: Religion is a Paramount Affection for Christ. "*Lovest thou Me?*" Not merely My *ideas*. It is almost impossible for men of intellect not to be ravished with Christ's ideas. Not merely My *works*. Who could fail to admire Christ's stupendous works of beneficence and compassion? Not merely My *heaven*. Christ's heaven, the house of His Father, where there are "many mansions," men may long for. But it is love for *Himself* that He demands. But why should Christ be loved supremely "*more than these?*"—more than father, mother, houses, lands, even these wonderful works of nature?

(1.) Because it is *Right in Itself*. Ought not the greatest Benefactor to have the most gratitude? The most perfect Character to have the highest admiration? The sublimest Royalty to have the most absolute devotion? What Benefactor is so great as He Who gave Himself? What Character so holy as He Who died to "put away the sins" of the world? What authority so high as His? He is the "Prince of the kings of the earth." "He is exalted far above all," &c.

(2.) Because it is *Indispensable to Man*. Man's destiny and his happiness depend upon the object of his love. The object of his love becomes either the wing of a seraph to bear him to the highest heaven, or a millstone to crush him to the deepest infamy and woe. Hence the mighty reason of this Paramount Affection. From the passage we infer concerning this Love—

II —THAT IT MUST BE A MATTER OF CONSCIOUSNESS WHEREVER IT EXISTS

Both our Lord's question and Peter's reply indicate this. A man cannot be ignorant of his supreme affection; it is the spring of his activities, the central fact of his experience. Here are the criteria. The object of supreme affection is ever—

(1.) The chief *thought* in the *intellect*. (2.) The chief *theme* in the *conversation*. (3.) The chief *end* in the *design;* and (4.) The chief *object* of the *desire*. All the laws of mind must be reversed before it can be otherwise. Concerning this Love observe—

III —THAT IT IS THE QUALIFICATION FOR OFFICE IN THE EMPIRE OF CHRIST

After Peter's confession, which was sincere, solemn, and thrice repeated, Christ gave him a commission in His kingdom, and that was to feed His sheep. "*Feed My lambs.*" There are three things implied in this commission—

First: That Peter would meet with the Spiritually Needy in his future course. He would meet with hungry sheep and feeble lambs. The world abounds with those young, inexperienced, undisciplined, hungry souls.

Secondly: That Peter would have at his disposal Suitable Supplies for the needy. He could not feed them without food. The doctrines he had received from Christ would be the food.

Thirdly: That Peter had the capacity so to Present the Supplies as to Feed the Needy. Here was his work, and love to Christ was the qualification for it. Nothing can qualify a man properly to help souls but love for Christ. Learning, genius, eloquence—all will not avail without this. This is the only true inspiration.

Hast thou this Supreme Love, not for the theological or conventional, but for the Personal and Living Christ, friend? Is He Who trod the shores of Galilee and climbed the mountains of Capernaum, Who died upon the Cross and ascended to heaven, the central point of thy soul? Is He the home of thy spirit? Dost thou live in Him? Art thou in Christ?

John 21:18-23

THE TRUE SERVICE OF CHRISTIANITY TO MAN

(Conclusion of John's Gospel narrative.—JOHN xxi. 11—25.)

" Verily, verily, I say unto thee, When thou wast young, thou girdedst thyself, and walkedst whither thou wouldest," &c.—xxi. 18—23.

EXEGETICAL REMARKS.—Ver. 18.— " *Verily, verily, I say unto thee, When thou wast young, thou girdedst thyself, and walkedst whither thou wouldest.*" Peter's whole life is here included, reaching from youthhood to the verge of old age. In young life there is freedom and force. At this time, perhaps, Peter was in middle life. " *But when thou shalt be old, thou shalt stretch forth thy hands, and another shall gird thee, and carry thee whither thou wouldest not.*" " This seems to point to his death, which, tradition says, was by crucifixion. Then is Peter girded by the hand when he is stretched forth on the cross."—*Tertullian.* It is supposed by some that the expression " *Stretch forth thy hands*" points to his personal surrender previous to being girded by another.

Ver. 19.—" *This spake He* (R. V. NOW THIS HE SPAKE), *signifying by*

what death (R. V. MANNER OF DEATH) *he should glorify God.*" This is not a mere prediction of the manner of his death, but of the honour to be conferred upon him by dying for his Master. " *And when He had spoken this, He saith unto him, Follow Me.*" " It may be, and the next verse makes it probable, that our Lord withdrew from the circle of the disciples, and by some movement or gesture signified to Peter that he should follow Him; but these words must have had for the Apostle a much fuller meaning. By the side of that lake he had first heard the command, ' *Follow Me.*' (Matt. iv. 19.) When sent forth on his apostleship he had been taught that to follow Christ meant to take up the Cross. (Matt. x. 38.) It was his words which drew from Christ the utterance, ' If any man will come after Me, let him deny himself, and take up his cross and follow Me.'

(Matt. xvi. 23.) To his question at the last supper came the answer, 'Whither I go, thou canst not follow Me now; but thou shalt follow Me afterwards' (chap. xiii. 36); and now the command has come again with the prophecy of martyrdom; and it must have carried to his mind the thought that he was to follow the Lord in suffering and death itself, and through the dark path which He had trodden, was to follow Him to the Father's Home."—*Ellicott's Commentary.*

Ver. 20.—"*Then Peter, turning about, seeth the disciple whom Jesus loved following.*" This was the beloved disciple John. He was now in the rear pursuing Peter and his Master, hence the expression, "*Peter turning about.*"

Ver. 21.—"*Peter* (R. V. PETER THEREFORE) *seeing him saith to Jesus, Lord, and what shall this man do?*" Or, how shall it fare with him?

Ver. 22.—"*Jesus saith unto him, If I will that he tarry till I come, what is that to thee? follow thou Me.*" "From the fact that John alone of the Twelve survived the destruction of Jerusalem, and so witnessed the commencement of that series of events which belong to the last days, many good interpreters think that this is a virtuous prediction of fact, and not a mere supposition; but this is very doubtful, and it seems more natural to consider our Lord as intending to give no positive indication of John's fate at all, but to signify that this was a matter which belonged to the Master of both, Who would disclose or conceal it as He thought proper, and that Peter's part was to mind his own affairs. Accordingly in '*Follow thou Me*' the word '*thou*' is emphatic. Observe the absolute disposal of human life which Christ claims."—*Dr. Brown.*

Ver. 23.—"*Then went this saying abroad* (R. V. THIS SAYING THEREFORE WENT FORTH) *among the brethren, that that disciple should not die: yet Jesus said not unto him, He shall* (R. V. THAT HE SHOULD) *not die; but, If I will that he tarry till I come, what is that to thee?*" This was the inference drawn from the words of the Saviour. Strange that the disciples of Christ should thus misinterpret the meaning of their Master; but with the best men there is no infallibility of judgment.

HOMILETICS

These words are part of an interesting conversation which Christ had with Peter, after His resurrection from the dead. In verse 14 we are told that this was the "*third*" time of His appearing to His disciples. He had appeared before to the women, to Cephas, and to James, and to the two disciples on the way to Emmaus. The Sea of Tiberias was the scene where He now displayed Himself; a sea this whose restless surface and whose silent shores had often felt His presence and witnessed His miracles.

I shall use the incident before us to illustrate *The True Service of Christianity to Man.* Perhaps there is no question so generally discussed in such a variety of forms, and for such different purposes, and upon which such a diversity of opinion prevails, as this: "Of what real service is Christianity to man?" There are three classes, I conceive, who are grossly wrong on this question—

First: Those who maintain that it is a Positive Injury. There are many who aver, by significant and plausible insinuations, as well as by broad and bold statements, that Christianity has injured rather than benefitted the race. They tell us how it has warped the judgments of men, and nurtured morbid sentimentality: how it has sectionized society, reared the throne of spiritual despotism, and served the ends of superstition, priestcraft, and tyranny. They point us to the inquisitions, prisons, and stakes of past ages, and to the property that in its holy name is now wrung from the blood and sinews of the toiling population.

Secondly: Those who maintain that it is one of the many Elevating Forces at work in Society. They say it has done some good as well as much evil; that it is generally of service to men in a low stage of civilization; and that, like the theories and superstitions of old times, it has its mission, which it will fulfil; and then, like them, become obsolete, to be left behind as the race advances in intelligence and manly virtue.

Thirdly: Those who maintain that it does Everything for Man. These say, there is nothing good in the world but Christianity. No good in nature, no good in science, no good in the feelings of man without Christianity; that if a man has Christianity, he needs nothing more; it does everything for him.

Now these conflicting sentiments suggest the propriety, and urge the necessity, of raising the question: " Of what *real* use is Christianity to man?" The incident before us will supply a twofold answer—NEGATIVE and AFFIRMATIVE. Let us look on—

I —THE NEGATIVE SIDE

First: The incident suggests that Christianity does not Counteract the Natural changes to which man's Physical Life is subject. " *When thou wast young, thou girdedst thyself, and walkedst whither thou wouldest: but when thou shalt be old, thou shalt stretch forth thy hands, and another shall gird thee.*" Peter, notwithstanding his defects, was a genuine disciple of Christ. Christianity had penetrated, fired, and transmuted his nature. Yet, notwithstanding this, Christ foretells that he should experience the natural decay of old age; He tells him that the *Christianity in his soul would not prevent time wearing out his body.* It is difficult to conceive of a more solemn idea of the effect of age than that which our Saviour here represents. Christ teaches that *age incapacitates man from executing his volitions.* This is slavery. To have a strong desire to do a thing, without the executive power, is the veriest vassalage. If a man is bound in chains, and enclosed in a prison, yet has no *desire* to walk abroad, he is no slave. The paralytic that was brought to Jesus is the true picture of a slave. He had the will to ply his members and muscles; but he could not. This, Christ here teaches, is the effect of age upon us. " *When thou wast young, thou girdedst thyself, and walkedst whither thou wouldest.*" Thou couldst ply the oar on the water, roam the fields, and scale the hills; there was an energy in thy limbs, a flexibility in the movements of thy young frame, by which thou couldest readily execute thy desires. "*But when thou shalt be old,*" &c. Age leaves the will in vigour, but steals away the executive power. Now, Christianity will not prevent this natural effect of age. It will not prevent the bloom fading from the cheek, the brightness passing from the eye, the strength dying out of the limb. It allows nature to take its course. Christianity neither offers resistance to the regular course of nature, nor any atonement for her violations. This fact shows three things—

(1.) *It shows that physical sufferings are no criteria for individual moral states.* Some of the best men are the greatest sufferers. Some of the most useful die in the zenith of life, and in the midst of beneficent labour. A rankling "thorn in the flesh " is consonant with the Piety of an Apostle.

(2.) *It shows that Christianity respects the ordinances of nature.* However deeply you may drink into you the Spirit of True Religion, however consecrated you may be to its service, if you rebel against nature you must suffer.

(3.) *It shows that if the disciples of Christ would be physically happy, they must attend, like other men, to physical laws.* If you are in want of physical comforts, it is of no use for you to sing, "The Lord will provide," and sit down in indolence and sloth.

Secondly : The incident suggests that Christianity does not guard a man from the Social Oppressions of Life. " *When thou shalt be old,*" &c. It is here foretold that Peter should die of crucifixion. His hands would be stretched forth, his arms would be extended on a cross, and he would be led to a death of violence, at which his nature would revolt. About forty years after this, Peter died a martyr. His Christianity did not deliver him from the *malice of men,* the storm of persecution, and the agonies of a martyr's death. Christianity promises us no escape from the opposition of wicked men; indeed it teaches us to expect it. It teaches us that they who live righteously, "must suffer persecution." "Marvel not if the world hate you." The world has ever persecuted its best men. This fact shows—

(1.) That Christianity *can do without the favour of the world.* It does not require or authorize its disciples, in the slightest degree, to compromise their principles in order to gain the patronage of mankind; but to carry them out in all their fulness and force, even though it cause the world to be in arms against them.

(2.) That Christianity *can do without the lives of its most devoted disciples, rather than without their fidelity.*

Thirdly : The incident suggests that Christianity does not solve the Speculative Problems of Life. Peter seeing him saith to Jesus, " *Lord, and what shall this man do ?* " As if he had said, " Why am I thus to be dealt with ? What is to become of him (John) ?—is he to be crucified also ?—or will he be allowed to live the natural term of life ?" To this question Jesus replies : " *What is that to thee ?* " There are many questions which the events of life force upon us to which Christianity offers no response. Why are we in such suffering, whilst others, who contemn our principles, and despise our God, are exempt from trials ? Why are our lives cut short while we have so much work to do ? Why are we allowed such scope and faculties for working in this world when we have so little time ? Why are our principles so tardy in their progress ? Why are events allowed to spring up which check their advancement ? Such questions as these arise, and to them Christianity makes no reply. The only words she says to the querist are : " *What is that to thee ?* " There are good reasons why Christianity is silent upon such questions :—

(1.) *The encouragement of these questions would strengthen the speculative tendency, rather than improve the heart.* One answer would lead to another question, and so on interminably.

(2.) *An answer to such questions would create emotions that would paralyze moral action.* Suppose we knew what would happen to us and our children in coming years; where we should spend our eternity ; who would go to perdition, &c. Would not the feelings that such knowledge would create, be likely to check all the fire and healthy action of the soul ?

(3.) *An answer to such questions would multiply the forces that divert us from practical godliness.* They would lead us into the realm of boundless speculation.

Fourthly : The incident suggests that Christianity does not invest us with an Infallible Judgment in this Life. " *Then went this saying abroad among the brethren,*" &c. The disciples fell into a wrong interpretation of our Saviour's meaning. Christianity does clear and strengthen the human judgment, and furnish it with certain great truths to guide it in its investigation; but it does not render it infallible.

The dogma of human infallibility in the Church is a wicked invention, and a withering bane. The clergy who claim it grow heartless tyrants; the laity who bow to it become bondsmen and serfs. The " BRETHREN " made this mistake.

But whilst the incident suggests that Christianity DOES NOT ensure any of these things, it also suggests much that it does do. Let us look now on—

II —THE POSITIVE SIDE

First : The incident suggests that it enlists Christ's Interest in the History of His Disciples. What an interest did Christ display in the history of His disciples, both before and after His resurrection ! He even sought to impress upon their minds, that there was the closest spiritual relationship subsisting between them and Him, that He was vitally identified with them. He calls them His "*brethren*," and teaches that kindness shown to them He regards as shown to Him. And what an interest did He show now in foretelling the events of Peter's life, and preparing him to meet them! No truth in the New Testament is more manifest than this—that Christ feels the greatest interest in His disciples. His conversation with them, the night on which He was betrayed, shows how deeply His heart was with them. *Is not this something?* Is it nothing to enlist the interest of the Governor of the universe in our history?

(1.) Having His interest you have the interest of One *Who knows the whole of the present, past, and future of your inner and outer life.* He knows everything which is *now* connected with your being and circumstances; all that ever *has* been, and all that ever *will* be. He sees you now as you may be in some other world ten thousand years to come.

(2.) Having His interest you have the interest of One *Who has ample power, so to control the events of the outward life, and supply the aspirations of the inward, as to crown your existence with perfect blessedness.* "He is able to do exceeding abundantly." If Christianity gives us the interest of such a Being as this, is it not an infinite boon? What thought can be more soul-inspiring and uplifting than this—that He "Who formed the earth by His power, and garnished the heavens with His understanding," has His Heart on me?

Secondly: The incident suggests that it brings Glory to God in the Death of His Disciples. "*This spake He, signifying by what death he should glorify God.*" Ecclesiastical history testifies that Peter suffered martyrdom by crucifixion at Rome, in the reign of the Emperor Nero—probably in the year 65. It is added that this death, and the torture connected with it, were endured by the venerable apostle with marvellous patience and fortitude; and that deeming himself unworthy to die in precisely the same manner and posture as his Lord, he asked and obtained permission, to be crucified with the head downwards; a posture which could not fail greatly to aggravate the tortures of the cross.

But how does the death of a true disciple of Christianity "*glorify God?*"

(1.) It illustrates *the Mercy of God.* Visit the deathbed of a genuine disciple of Christ; mark the unruffled calmness, the gratitude, the resignation, and sometimes the triumphant rapture, which are displayed in the midst of physical anguish the most poignant. What are the attributes in such circumstances but glorious illustrations of Divine mercy? It is mercy that thus raises and sustains the spirit, amidst the mysterious sufferings of dissolution.

(2.) It illustrates *the Fidelity of God.* He has promised to be with His people in the last hour; and when you see all this heavenly composure and triumph, you feel that He is as good as His word—for He is there. Now, is this nothing? To "*glorify God,*" to illustrate His perfections, is the end of creation; the general duty of all intelligent beings; the supreme aim of the holy in all worlds. Is it nothing for Christianity to enable poor, depraved, guilty men to do this, even in the agonies of death—to do in death that which is the highest aim of the highest seraph—to "*glorify God?*"

Thirdly: The incident suggests that it gives a Definite Unity and Attraction to all the Duties of His Disciples. What theories of human duty ethical sages have propounded! How voluminous is the code of human laws! But Christianity reduces *all* duties to these words: "*Follow thou Me.*" "To cherish My spirit, tread in My footsteps, copy My attributes, constitute the totality of human duty, and the perfection of human character." Christianity gives you duty, not in dry propositions, but in a fascinating Life; not in the life of an angel, but in the life of a Man. In Jesus Christ we see it in the most *perfect,* the most *attractive,* and the most *practicable* forms. Is this nothing? Is it nothing to have all our moral problems thus solved—to be freed from cumbrous codes and endless speculations—to have "the whole duty of man" thus brought to us in the Life of One Man?

John 21:24, 25

THE REVEALED AND THE UNREVEALED IN CHRIST'S BIOGRAPHY

"This is the disciple which testifieth of these things," &c.

EXEGETICAL REMARKS.—Ver. 24.— "*This is the disciple which testifieth* (R. V. BEARETH WITNESS) *of these things, and wrote these things: and we know that his testimony* (R. V. WITNESS) *is true.*" There are many different opinions as to who is the writer of these two last verses. In any case the meaning is, that what has been stated in this Gospel is true.

Ver. 25.—"*And there are also many other things which Jesus did, the which, if they should be written every one, I suppose that even the world itself could not contain the books that should be written. Amen*" (R. V. OMITS). "Writings might be added to writings without end to describe the glory of the only begotten Son; this indefinite series of writings would never exhaust such a subject."—*Godet.*

HOMILETICS

The subject of these verses is the *Revealed and the Unrevealed in Christ's Biography.*

I —VERY MUCH HAS BEEN REVEALED OF HIS BIOGRAPHY

His four biographers have said very much about Christ. Each has presented Him in some fresh aspect.

II —MUCH MORE MIGHT HAVE BEEN REVEALED

" *If they should be written every one, I suppose that even the world itself could not contain the books.*" What volumes it would have taken to contain all the words uttered, all the deeds wrought during three years of One Who never spent an idle hour, Who " went about doing good," &c.

CONCLUSION. (1.) We should fully appreciate the amount revealed. It teems with truths, and pulsates with inspiration. A larger amount, perchance, would have been obstructive rather than helpful.

(2.) We may anticipate wonderful studies. All the Unrevealed in Christ's Biography will yet be brought under our observation, and for our devoutest study.

Addendum

CONSISTING OF DISCOURSES ON THIS GOSPEL, THAT HAVE BEEN DELIVERED
AT DIFFERENT TIMES IN DIFFERENT PARTS OF ENGLAND AND WALES.

The Spiritual Universe
No. 1   John 3:5-8

"Jesus answered, Verily, verily, I say unto thee, Except a man be born of water and of the Spirit, he cannot enter into the kingdom of God. That which is born of the flesh, is flesh; and that which is born of the Spirit, is spirit. Marvel not that I said unto thee, Ye must be born again. The wind bloweth where it listeth, and thou hearest the sound thereof, but canst not tell whence it cometh, and whither it goeth : so is every one that is born of the Spirit."

(For Exegetical Remarks, see Vol. I. page 65.)

Both the Hebrew word "*ruach*" and the Greek "*pneuma*," translated "*spirit*," have no less than four different significations in the Bible: their meaning, therefore, in any given place is to be determined by the connection in which they stand.

Sometimes the word in each language stands for *wind*. Thus in Amos, "He that formeth the mountains, and createth the wind;" and in this passage, "*The wind bloweth where it listeth.*"

Sometimes the word in each language stands for the *vital principle*. Thus in the Psalms, "His breath goeth forth;" thus in Ecclesiastes, "Yea, they have all one breath;" and thus in Luke, "His spirit (life) came again, and he rose straightway."

Sometimes the word stands for the *mental disposition*. Thus in Numbers, "The spirit of jealousy came upon him;" thus in Deuteronomy, "Full of the spirit of wisdom;" and thus in Romans, "Ye have not received the spirit of bondage again to fear; but the spirit of adoption." Hence the meaning of the expressions, "spiritual man," and "spiritually minded."

Sometimes the word in each language stands for the *rational nature*. This is evidently the import in Luke, "For a spirit hath not flesh or bones, as ye see Me have;" in Job, "There is a spirit in man;" in Isaiah, "The Egyptians are men, and not God, and their horses flesh, and not spirit."

* This discourse is one of a Series delivered at Stockwell on "The Spiritual Universe."

The subject of these words is—

THE MAKING OF MAN RIGHT IN RELATION TO THE SPIRITUAL UNIVERSE

Man is, as I have said, SPIRIT:—as truly in the Spirit-World, a member and tenant of it now, as he will ever be. But he has lost his normal moral position. His original relations in it are not only disturbed, but dissolved. Like a star that has broken from its centre, the centripetal force of Divine Love has lost its hold on him. He is rushing through darkness on a career of ruin. How to bring him back, and link him to the great Primordial Centre of "light and life" in the Spiritual Universe, is the greatest problem that has ever risen in the history of human inquiry. A problem, whose solution is not in the researches of science, nor in the philosophies of the world's great thinkers, but in the History and Doctrines of Jesus of Nazareth. The text gives us four facts in relation to this problem—

I —THAT MAN'S WELL-BEING IN THE SPIRITUAL UNIVERSE DEPENDS UPON HIS NOW ENTERING "INTO THE KINGDOM OF GOD"

Jesus speaks of entering *"into the kingdom of God"* as that which He supposed Nicodemus would regard as the Chief Good; and of that which He Himself evidently regarded as such. He represented in His teaching, introduction to the kingdom of God as that which men should supremely strive after, and for which they should be prepared to make any sacrifice. The hand, the foot, the eye;—better even to sacrifice these than not to "enter into the kingdom of God" (Mark ix. 43—47). The question arises, What is meant by entering into the *"Kingdom of God?"*

(1.) It does not mean merely *being under the absolute government of God.* In this sense we are in His kingdom, and out of it we can never go. There is no wing to waft us beyond the boundaries. "His kingdom ruleth over all." The animate and inanimate, matter and mind, instinct and reason, physical movements and spiritual operations, agents and actions, intellect and its thoughts, heart and its emotions, will and its efforts, Paradise and Hades, are all under the dominion of God. Our connection with His kingdom in this sense, is independent alike of our choice or conduct. Whether we are freemen or serfs, loyal citizens or rebels, tread the fair fields of immensity with the joyous step of liberty, or sigh in dungeons with the "spirits in prison," we are in His kingdom, and bound indissolubly to His throne.

(2.) It does not mean merely *being under the Gospel dispensation.* It is true, the expression *"kingdom of God"* is sometimes used to designate the Gospel economy. Thus John the Baptist used it when he said, " Repent, for the kingdom of heaven is at hand;" thus Mark used it when he speaks of Joseph of Arimathæa as " waiting for the kingdom of God;" and thus Jesus uses it when, at the commencement of His ministry, He said, " I must preach the kingdom of God to other cities also." But this cannot be the meaning here. For in this sense the *"kingdom of God"* comes to every man to whom the Gospel is preached.

What, then, does it mean? The general meaning, I think, may be expressed thus:—*The reign of God over the individual soul with its hearty concurrence.* God's kingdom over souls may be divided into two provinces. The one He rules *without* the concurrence of the subject; and the other *with its hearty wish and choice.* Wicked men and fallen angels belong to the former; true Christians and celestial intelligences belong to the latter. The latter is the reign spoken of here. And in other places where the *"kingdom of God"* is represented as being " within;" as coming " not with observation;" as being not " in word but in power;" as consisting " not in meat and drink, but in righteousness, and peace, and joy, in the Holy Ghost;" as being that which Christ states to be the duty of every man to " seek first." It means, having God as the chosen Monarch of the soul; to marshal all its faculties, direct all its operations, and turn the whole current of its thoughts and sympathies into the channel of His own will. Now that this entrance into the *"kingdom of God"*—this cordial, spiritual obedience to the Divine will—is indispensable to man's well-being, will appear from the following considerations—

First: Without it there is no true Liberty of Soul. Liberty and slavery may both be expressed by one word—*subjection.* Subjection to the senses, the opinions, the passions, the caprice, either of ourselves or others, is serfdom. Physical slavery is but a very faint image of spiritual; and civil despots are but the shadows of those enthroned in a corrupt soul. But, whilst *subjection* will represent slavery, it will also represent Liberty. Absolute submission to God, the adoption of His will as our law in everything, the surrendering of self and all to Him, are the eternal conditions of true liberty in a moral creature. His will alone affords scope for the full and everlasting play of all our powers. A supreme sympathy with that will is the only inspiration, that can set and keep the soul in the enchanting music of harmonious action. Philosophically, men may as well strive for physical vigour without obedience to the laws of health, as strive for liberty without submission to the will of God. His will is the universal, inflexible, and absolute law of the creation; opposition to it is necessarily confusion and slavery; a loving submission to it is harmony, freedom, and bliss.

Secondly: Without it there is no true Peace of Conscience.

A *feeling* that the Supreme Will should be obeyed, underlies all our consciousness, and baffles all the attempts of scepticism to obliterate. Men, everywhere, whatever their theological views or measure of intellectual culture and development, *feel* that the will of their Deity is the supreme law which they are *bound* to obey. Conscience will own allegiance to no sovereign but the ABSOLUTE. Other lords may usurp the throne, and obtain mastery over it, but it will never *peacefully* submit to their rule. No time or force can crush its instinct of rebellion against all authorities but the Supreme. It will shake every fibre and faculty of the soul, with the terrible roar of the artillery which it hurls against all potentates but God. Our moral constitution renders peace of soul impossible under any reign but His. But where He reigns all is blessed serenity. Like the noiseless stars, every faculty moves peacefully in a sphere made luminous by the rays it borrows from the central fires. Like the channel of a majestic river into which a thousand streams have flown, the underlying purposes of the soul bear on in calm and mighty flow all the complex tendencies and the sympathies of the heart.

Thirdly: Without it there is no true Growth of Soul. By the growth of soul, I mean, not the growth of any particular faculty, principle, or power; but the growth of the whole—the growth of all its parts: as the tree grows simultaneously and in symmetrical proportions. As *Bacon* says, in relation to moral culture, " We must not proceed as a statuary proceeds in forming a statue, working now on one part and now on another ; but we must proceed, and it is in our power to proceed, as nature does, in forming a flower or any other of her productions; *Rudimenta partium omnium simul parit et producit*; she throws out altogether, and at once, the whole system of every being, and the rudiments of all the parts." I mean growth in *holy, moral* force. Force to subordinate the outward to its will. Force to tread the path of duty with a firm and dauntless step, looking foes the most ruthless and terrible in the eye, and bidding them stand aside. Force to bear the spirit buoyantly over the mountain billows, and under the midnight storm. Force to resist the evil and pursue the good, to subordinate the senses to the intellect, the intellect to conscience, and the conscience to the majesty of Right. Force to meet death with triumph, and, like Stephen, cleave the heavens in the mortal hour, and catch an uplifting glance of the glories of the spiritual world. This is the true Force of the Soul. A force without which, what are we? Machines! Yes; machines worked by external influences; " reeds shaken by the wind ;" slaves under the iron yoke of circumstances—feeling ever the lash of remorse for the past, and of terror for the future. But this Force belongs to no soul where the Moral Monarch is not God. Under every other sovereignty the spirit, in a moral sense, becomes more and more feeble ; the victim not only of outward, but of inward, evils ; scared by the demon ghosts of its own morbid fancies. But under the genial and benign reign of the Eternal Father, the soul strikes its roots deep beside the fountain of life ; and grows pure and beautiful as the lily, and strong and majestic as the cedars of Lebanon.

Sufficient, I presume, has been stated to show the truth of this first proposition, which I deduce from the passage under review, namely, that *man's well-being in the spiritual universe depends upon his now entering into the " kingdom of God."* We must *" enter "* His kingdom ; come at once under His rightful and gracious reign ; have His will done *in* us as it is done in heaven, before we can, from the very necessity of our nature and relations, be happy. And to be thus in His kingdom, is to be in heaven *now* as truly, if not as perfectly, as patriarchs and apostles are there. To have this *" kingdom of God "* within, is to have all the splendours and felicities of the apocalyptic heaven without.

I infer from the text—

II —THAT INTRODUCTION INTO THIS " KINGDOM OF GOD " INVOLVES A GREAT MORAL CHANGE

" Verily, verily, I say unto you, Except a man be born again, he cannot see the kingdom of God." Nicodemus being a Jew, a Pharisee, and a member of the great council of the nation, ought to have known what the expression *" born again "* meant. It was a phrase applied to designate the change which took place in a Gentile proselyte, when he renounced his paganism and identified himself with the Jewish religion. So great was the importance which the Hebrew Rabbis attached to this change, that they regarded the proselyte as no longer akin to his Gentile father or mother ; and he might marry, without committing incest, within the proscribed degrees of physical relationship.

But great as was the change, which the expression was used to designate in relation to the proselytes to Judaism, Jesus employed it to represent a far greater change. It is a *moral* change—moral in contradistinction to all physical, theoretical, or institutional changes. It is a change of heart. But *what is a change of heart ?* It is a CHANGE· IN THE SUPREME OBJECT OF LOVE.

Now, that an introduction into this kingdom involves a great moral change, will appear evident from two considerations,—

First : That the object of Supreme Love is evermore the Monarch of the Soul. The real sovereign is that which rules the soul. Monarchs, whose pageantry dazzles the eyes of the populace, whose names ring through obsequious courts and servile crowds, and whose authority is supported by mighty fleets and triumphant armies, are powerless, compared with those unseen potentates that Rule Within.

And who are these? The objects of your *chief* regard. It is a law of being, *that whatever you love the most, rules you most absolutely.* There are, therefore, as many moral empires on earth, as there are objects which men hold in supreme regard. PLEASURE is the sovereign of the sensual; GAIN is the sovereign of the avaricious; POWER is the sovereign of the ambitious; DISPLAY is the sovereign of the vain; and GOD is the Sovereign of the Good. What "principalities and powers" there are even in earth's department of the spiritual universe! Into how many petty provinces is the empire of human souls divided! Another consideration is—

Secondly: That at the outset of man's history, God is *never* the Object of his Supreme Love. To offer illustrations, or evidences of a fact so patent to all, would be unnecessary and tedious; and to explain the various theories which have been set forth to account for it, is neither essential to the argument nor in keeping with my plan. I simply note the fact because, viewed in connection with our first consideration under this head, it shows that to enter into the "*kingdom of God*" involves a great moral change. We are not "*born*" into this kingdom;—"other lords have had dominion over us." As the monarch of the soul is the object of supreme love, and as the object of our chief affection, at first, is not God; if we would come under His Empire—if we would have Him enthroned within us, we must withdraw our hearts from other objects, and set them entirely upon Him. We "*must be born again.*" If the old potentates of the soul are to be deposed, and God have the kingdom within us, the heart must change its chief object of love; *and this is Regeneration.* For a change in the object of supreme love, leads inevitably to a change in all our principles, purposes, and pursuits. It makes us new moral men.

Here hinges our fate. This is *the* crisis. There are other great crises in the history of man. *Birth* is a great crisis. To be ushered, a helpless infant, into this wonderful creation; to breathe a breath of perhaps deathless inspiration; to receive impressions that the rolling current of ages cannot wear away; and to form a character out of which shall spring a Paradise or flame a Gehenna, is a stupendous event. *Death* is a great crisis. To leave the world, to detach ourselves for ever from the scenes of our first impressions and activities, to surrender the body to the noisome worm and the gloomy grave, to leave for ever the stage of probation and the means of spiritual discipline, and to enter the ghastly scenes of retribution, and to go we know not where; this is indeed a Tremendous Crisis. But great as is the crisis of birth and death, this crisis of *Regeneration* is, for many reasons, more important than either. It gives our birth a value, and our death a glory. It introduces us, *even now*, into the "*kingdom of God*"—a kingdom whose sphere is the holy universe, whose citizens are the great and good of all worlds, whose law is love, and whose duration is eternity.

I infer from the text—

III —THAT THE GREAT CHANGE, THUS INVOLVED IN AN INTRO-
DUCTION TO THE "KINGDOM OF GOD," IS EFFECTED BY THE
DIVINE "SPIRIT"

"*Except a man be born of water and of the Spirit, he cannot enter into the kingdom of God.*" The expression "*of water and of the Spirit*" does not refer to two agents, but to one. It is a *Hebraism*, meaning Spiritual Water. John, the illustrious herald of Jesus, had already spoken of *fire* in connection with the Spirit's renovating operation. "I indeed," says he, "baptize you with water unto repentance : but He shall baptize you with the Holy Ghost, and with fire." As John did not mean material fire there, neither does Christ mean material "*water*" here. Jesus may have spoken of the Spirit in connection with "*Water*" for one or two, or both, of the following reasons—

(1.) *To represent the renovating effects of the Divine Agent.* His great aim in all His benign operations upon the human soul, is to cleanse it thoroughly from all the filthiness of erroneous thoughts, corrupt feelings, and perverse volitions, and give it a new and ever-growing life. His action on the human spirit is like that of "fire" and "*water*"—it renovates and purifies. Fire and water, the mightiest forces in the material world, whose incessant action gives every moment new forms to nature, are assuredly the most striking emblems of the operations of the Divine Spirit upon the human soul. Moreover, Jesus may have spoken of the Spirit in connection with "*Water*"—(2.) *To represent the insufficiency of "water" itself to effect this Regeneration.* Jesus was speaking to one who knew, or ought to have known, what a *new birth* among the Jews meant. He knew washing or ablution was the necessary process through which this change was effected ; that no Gentile came over to the Jewish religion who was not washed with material water. Jesus, therefore, might have used the expression to intimate to Nicodemus that the new birth which he required was not like the new birth of the Jewish religion, which required material water. But it was that which required the Spiritual Water—a something that must act purifyingly, not on the body, but on the soul. In the light of this interpretation the passage, instead of affording the slightest support, either to those who hold the absurd dogma of baptismal regeneration, or those who attach so much importance to baptism as to make it a badge of denominational distinction, or a condition of Church membership, throws the ceremony into a very insignificant aspect. The baptism connected with the new birth of which Christ speaks, is a spiritual, not a material, baptism —a baptism that cleanses the soul, and not the body. " Neither circumcision availeth anything, nor uncircumcision, but a new creature."

The language of Jesus here suggests two thoughts in relation to the Spirit's agency in this work of Regeneration—

First : The Indispensable Necessity of the Spirit's agency to effect this Change. Jesus most clearly intimated this. It is a doctrine so evident, both from Scripture and the difficulties of the work, that it is a settled article in the creed of all orthodox Churches. Were it inquired, wherein does the Necessity of Divine agency in the effectuation of this work appear? I would answer in the very *nature* of the work. What is the work ? Recur to the definition already given. IT IS A CHANGE IN THE OBJECT OF SUPREME LOVE. Before the human mind can make God the Object of Supreme Love three things *must* take place. (1.) *A supremely attractive revelation of Him.* Who can love an unknown object ? And God, to be known must be revealed. (2.) *Clearness of moral vision to see Him.* He may be revealed, but if our eyes are so dim and filmy that we cannot see Him, His revelation will answer no practical purpose. What impression does the finest landscape, or the most glorious sky, make on the heart of the blind ? (3.) *A practical determination to direct the eye fairly to Him.* He may be fully and gloriously unfolded to the vision, and the vision in itself may be good ; but if we will not look, no impression can be produced. The Spirit is necessary for these *three* things. Who but the inspiring Spirit, could have given us such a soul-attractive Revelation of God as we have in Christ ? Who but He can so clear the spiritual vision—so scatter, by His refreshing breeze, those clouds and mists of impure feeling that darken the moral horizon, and enable it to see Infinite beauty distinctly as "the pure in heart" alone can see ? Who but He can overcome that strange reluctance of the soul to approach its Maker, and fix its gaze on Him ? Verily, the nature of the work indicates, that if we are "*born again,*" it must be by the " *Water and the Spirit* "—the renovating energy of God. The necessity of the sun and shower, to the production of vegetable life, is not more *reasonably* obvious, and more generally recognized by true Christians, than are the operations of the Spirit to the generating of spiritual life in the souls of men. All good, moral as well as natural, is from God ; all life, of every species, is from one primal Source. The possessors of this new moral life, what-ever their theological views may be, will evermore involuntarily, and by a necessary law of their religious nature, gratefully and adoringly refer it to the "Father of Spirits." Another thought suggested is—

Secondly : There is much in the manner of the Spirit's Operation in effecting this change that is very Mysterious. "*The wind bloweth where it listeth,*" &c. Several ideas have been attached by divines to these words; which, judging from the context, were evidently not intended to be expressed by Christ. For example, they have been supposed to teach the *Sovereignty* of Divine influence. That God works upon men according to His own "good pleasure" is an undeniable doctrine; for it is absurd to suppose that if the Almighty acts at all, He acts from any force but the spontaneous impulse of His own nature. But the idea, however true, is not taught here. They have also been supposed to teach the *Irresistibility* of Divine influence. It has been said that as the "*wind*" is beyond man's power,—as he cannot arrest its course or control its operation, neither *can* he effectually resist the spiritual influence of God. But this idea is *untrue* in itself. It is contradicted by the doctrine of human responsibility, and the consciousness of every regenerated man. All that Jesus intended to teach was, evidently, that it could not be fully traced in all its *modes* of action. *How* does the "*wind*" act? You see the waters lashed into billows, forests bend, fleets tossed in confusion, and all nature struck with wildness, by an invisible agent. But how? How does that invisible agent produce these effects? Aye, how? This is the question. Perhaps a gust of wind swept o'er the scene, where Jesus and Nicodemus now stood; and the Divine Teacher, as *was His wont*, seized the incident to illustrate His doctrine. We cannot explain all about the manner of Divine influence, but though you cannot tell "*whence it cometh,*" nor "*whither it goeth,*" you hear the sound, and you witness the effects.

I infer from the text :—

IV.—THAT THOSE WHO HAVE BEEN THUS INTRODUCED INTO THE "KINGDOM OF GOD," ARE DISTINGUISHED NOT BY THE SENSUOUS, BUT BY THE SPIRITUAL

"*That which is born of the flesh, is flesh; and that which is born of the Spirit, is spirit.*" What is the great distinction here intended by Christ? It is not, of course, *physiological*. The man before regeneration has "*spirit,*" and the man after has "*flesh.*" The spiritual powers and the material organs remain intact. It is no sin in the good man to have "*flesh;*" it is no virtue in the bad man to have "*spirit.*" Both flesh and spirit are the primary constituents of humanity, and the precious gifts of God. The distinction is *moral,* and refers to a change in the relative influence which these two parts of the man exert over his life and conduct. It is a question of ascendency. The unregenerate man, whom

Jesus says is *"flesh,"* and whom the New Testament generally designates as carnal or fleshly, is the man who is *ruled* by the flesh—whose spiritual powers are in utter subjection to the body—"carnal, sold under sin." He is in all his experiences, purposes, and pursuits, *"flesh."* Matter is the centre of his being, the scene of his constant action, the fountain of his pleasures, the source of his motives. His impulses to action are "fleshly lusts," his mind is a "fleshly mind," his wisdom is "fleshly wisdom." He may possess mind of a high order, and educational attainments, and embellishments of the first class, and still, in the Saviour's sense, be only *"flesh."* He may be merchant, artist, author; but the inspiration of his business, the glow of his genius, the tinge and form of his thoughts will be *"flesh"* rather than *"spirit."* Nay, he may be a Religionist, and that of the most orthodox stamp, but his creed and devotions will "be after the law of a carnal commandment." More than half the religion of Christendom is the religion of *"flesh."* Its inspiration is fleshly feeling, its forms of thought are fleshly; its rules of life are fleshly; its Christ is "known only after the flesh." It "judges after the flesh," "walks after the flesh," "wars after the flesh;" it is altogether sensuous and gross. Wherever the *body reigns,* be it in the halls of science, the councils of cabinets, at the altars of devotion, or in the pulpits of Christianity, the man is *"flesh"* and not *"spirit."* He lives in the realm where nothing but forms are valued or seen; the sensuous realm bounded above, beneath, and around, by matter. His atmosphere is animal feeling—an atmosphere too hazy and thick to transmit the effulgent rays of the spiritual universe. " HE IS FLESH."

But—" *That which is born of the Spirit, is spirit."* The spirit has regained its rightful sovereignty, and the man "minds spiritual things." Principles are dearer to him than property; the claims of the soul are to him more imperative than those of the body; the invisible is greater to him than the visible; the "unseen" has a more potent influence over him than the seen. " HE IS SPIRIT." Spirit, in the sense of *vivacity.* He is not sluggish and dull, but agile and blithe. All his faculties are instinct with a new life; the life of conscience, the true life of man. The eye of intellect is brightened, thought is active, imagination is always on the wing. He is *"spirit,"* in the sense of *social recognition.* He is not known as other men are known, as "men of the world," men who seek fleshly distinctions, fleshly wealth, and fleshly pleasure. But as a spiritual man he is known—as a man distinguished by spiritual convictions, sympathies, and aims. He is *"spirit"* in the sense of *Divinity.* He is *"born"* of the Divine Spirit, and has a resemblance to His Eternal Father. He is a partaker of "the Divine nature." His sympathies centre in the Divine, and his life reflects it. From this subject we learn—

First: The infallible Criterion by which to determine our true position in the spiritual universe. Who are now right in the dominion of the Eternal? In harmony of feeling with all holy created intelligences, and one with God? Not the men who are swayed by their senses, and whose chief study is that of appetite; whose highest question is, "What shall we eat, what shall we drink, and wherewithal shall we be clothed?" Not the men who are more interested in the body than the soul—in matter than mind— in the visible forms of goodness than the hidden principles. No, not these, however high their religious profession, punctual their attendance on religious services, zealous and self-sacrificing their efforts to promote their religious views. They are without the pale of the religious kingdom. They are in a sensuous realm. They may denounce materialism as a system of thought, but in it, as a reality, "they live, and move, and have their being." The men who are in the holy, moral kingdom of God, and whose position in the spiritual universe is right *now*, are "spiritually minded" men—men of spiritual insight, aspirations, and fellowship—men who *practically* make matter, in all her combinations and forms, their absolute subject and efficient servant, the means of spiritual growth, and the organ of Divine communion. They are *now* in that transcendental world, of which philosophic Germany has some delightful dreams—a transcendentalism this, not of mere intellect, but of heart; not of mere thought, but of being; not transcendental idealists, but transcendental *men*. Their "citizenship *is in* heaven." They are "in heavenly places" now.

Our subject shows—

Secondly: The great Agent on whom we are dependent to make us right in the spiritual universe. The celebrated *Fichte*, speaking of his supersensuous philosophy, says: "I now first truly understand the first power that can enable the imprisoned Psyche to break from the chrysalis and unfold her wings; poised on which, she casts a glance on her abandoned cell before springing upward to live and move in a higher sphere." Great sage! I feel with thee the importance of enabling the "imprisoned Psyche" of humanity to "break from the chrysalis" of flesh and "unfold her wings." But I am at issue with thee, mighty thinker, in supposing that thy philosophy, profound, suggestive, and spiritual though it is, is the "first power" to effect this glorious disimprisonment. No; the "first power" is the power of the *Eternal Spirit*. They only that "*are born of the Spirit, are spirit.*" It is the Divine Spirit that must call up the human from its sensual prison-house where it is "carnally sold under sin"—unchain its limbs, lead it out into the open universe of spiritual thought and life, give it eyes to see the spiritual beauties, and wings to follow the flight of angels, under the unclouded sky of intelligence and love.

Blessed Spirit! help us ever to honour Thy work, follow Thy monitions, and adore Thy love!

My brother! Whilst I would have thee gratefully remember that it is the Spirit of God that must introduce thee to this gracious kingdom, if ever thou art introduced; I would have thee remember also, that that Spirit will do it only *in connection with thine own efforts*. He will help thee as the teacher helps the pupils, through the exercise of their faculties; as nature helps the agriculturist, by giving effectiveness to all the adapted processes of cultivation; as the winds help the mariner on his watery way, by filling the skilfully hoisted canvas with their breathing force. Wait not for miracles. The kingdom of heaven cometh not "with observation." It comes not like the noisy cataract dashing from the hills, but like the silent dew, full of life; it comes not as ocean billows come to the shore, under the furious blast of the storm, but like the deep river it rolls unheard at your feet, and gives life to all who drink; it comes not as the lightning flash, but as the morning sun, silently touching the fields into new life and melting clouds into luminous ether. The Spirit speaks not in the roar of thunder, or the crash of earthquake, but "in the still small voice" of thought, conscience, and truth.

Christ "Above All" As a Teacher
No. 2   John 3:31-36

"He that cometh from above is above all : he that is of the earth is earthly, and speaketh of the earth : He that cometh from heaven is above all. And what He hath seen and heard, that He testifieth ; and no man receiveth His testimony. He that hath received His testimony hath set to his seal that God is true. For He whom God hath sent speaketh the words of God : for God giveth not the Spirit by measure unto Him. The Father loveth the Son, and hath given all things into His hand. He that believeth on the Son hath everlasting life : and he that believeth not the Son shall not see life ; but the wrath of God abideth on him."

(For Exegetical Remarks, see Vol. I. page 77.)

These verses set forth in the most striking and sublime manner, *The Pre-eminence of Christ as the Great Teacher of humanity.* So exalted is the view here presented of Him as a Teacher, that some critics have concluded that the words could not have been the utterance of John the Baptist; that they transcend his conception of the Messiah. With such a conclusion I cannot agree, for elsewhere the views of the Baptist concerning the Messiah chime in with those set forth in the text (Luke i. 29, &c.). As the Teacher of humanity Christ is "ABOVE ALL."

The text teaches that—

I —AS A TEACHER HE IS "ABOVE ALL" IN THE SUBLIMITY OF HIS ORIGIN

John speaks of Him, as "*He that cometh from above*"—from heaven. All other teachers, from Enoch down to Malachi, were "*of the earth.*" They came into existence in the natural order of generation; offspring of depraved parents, receiving from earliest childhood a bias to error and to wrong; and though called in their manhood by God to the high office of teaching, they never lost entirely their *earthliness.* On the contrary, Christ came down from the pure heavens of God, from regions free from all ignorance and error. He had a pre-incarnate existence. (Prov. viii.; John i.) He saw God. He lived with God. He communed with God. "He was in the bosom of the Father." During His existence here He received no taint of moral earthliness. Whilst here He was

morally *"above all."* To use the language of one of the greatest
thinkers of this age (and one of my oldest acquaintances), the late
Dr. Bushnell: "We notice the perfect originality and independency
of Christ's teaching. We have a great many men who are original,
in the sense of being originators, within a certain boundary of
educated thought. But the originality of Christ is uneducated.
That He draws nothing from the stores of learning can be seen at
a glance. The impression we have in reading His instructions
justifies to the letter the language of His contemporaries when
they say, 'This man hath never learned.' There is nothing in
any of His allusions or forms of speech that indicates learning.
Indeed there is nothing in Him that belongs to His age or country
—no one opinion, or task, or prejudice. The attempts that have
been made, in the way of establishing His mere natural manhood, to
show that He borrowed His sentiments from the Persians and the
Eastern forms of religion, or that He had been intimate with the
Essenes, and borrowed from them, or that He must have been
acquainted with the schools and religions of Egypt, deriving His
doctrine from them—all attempts of the kind have so palpably
failed, as not even to require a deliberate answer. If He is simply
a Man, as we hear, then He is most certainly a new and singular
kind of man, never before heard of: One Who visibly is quite as
great a miracle in the world as if He were not a man. We can
see for ourselves, in the simple directness and freedom of His
teachings, that whatever He advances is from Himself. Shakspeare,
for instance, whom we name as being probably the most creative
and original spirit the world has produced—one of the class, too,
that are called self-made men—is yet tinged in all his works with
human learning. His glory is, indeed, that so much of what is great
in history and historic character, live and appear in his dramatic
creations. He is the high-priest, we sometimes hear, of human nature.
But Christ, understanding human nature so as to address it more
skilfully than he, never draws from its historic treasures. He is
the High Priest, rather of the Divine nature, speaking as One that
has come from God, and has nothing to borrow from the world.
It is not to be detected by any sign that the human sphere in
which He moved imparted anything to Him. His teachings are
just as full of Divine nature as Shakspeare's of human." The text
teaches that—

II—AS A TEACHER HE IS "ABOVE ALL" IN THE CHARACTER OF HIS DOCTRINES

What does He teach? The passage replies—
First: Realities of which He Himself is Conscious. He teaches
that which *"He hath seen and heard."* That which to Him was
not a matter of speculation, but of experience, consciousness.

What had Christ "*seen and heard?*" Ah, what? What are all the forms and voices of eternal truth? What did He teach?

Secondly: Realities which are Moral in their Influence. I use the word *moral* here to signify that which stands opposed to that which is *irresistible* in its influence. Mathematical truths are irresistible. They force their way into man's conviction irrespective of his choice. Not so with the truths which Christ represented. Some did not accept His doctrines. "No man (comparatively few) received His testimony." He spoke eternal realities. But through the pride, the prejudice, and the carnality of His hearers they were rejected. Some, on the contrary, "*believed.*" "*He that hath received His testimony hath set to his seal that God is true.*" When His truths are received in faith, the receiver of them is assured in his own consciousness that "*God is true.*" Christ's doctrines are so congruous with man's sense of right, consciousness of need, feeling of God, desire for immortality, that the believing soul sees them as Divine reality, and admits no more reasoning against them. What did He teach?

Thirdly: Realities which are Pre-eminently Divine. "*He Whom God hath sent, speaketh the words of God.*" The realities are concerning God Himself, His words, His very thoughts, feelings, purposes. Christ does not teach what men call *sciences*. He teaches God Himself, the Root and Branch, the Centre and Circumference of all science. The text teaches that—

III —AS A TEACHER HE IS "ABOVE ALL" IN THE AFFECTION OF HIS FATHER

"*The Father loveth the Son.*"

First: No Teacher Shared so much of the Divine Love as Christ did. The Father loveth all. He is Love. All the true teachers of the world participate in His affection, but He loveth the Son *pre-eminently*. He is His "well-beloved Son." He loves Him with an infinite complacency, and because He is His well-beloved Son, He says to the world, "Hear ye Him."

Secondly: No Teacher Deserved so much of the Divine Love as Christ did. He never offended the Father in His conduct. He never misrepresented the Father either in His spirit, actions, or teaching. "He did no sin, neither was guile found on His lips."

Thirdly: No Teacher gave such Demonstrations of Divine Love as Christ did. "*He hath given all things into His hands*"—the administration of all spiritual blessings; all authority over souls. The text teaches that—

IV —AS A TEACHER HE IS "ABOVE ALL" IN THE EXTENT OF HIS ENDOWMENTS

"*For God giveth not the Spirit by measure unto Him.*" The other inspired teachers had the Spirit in a limited degree. But

Christ had that Spirit *fully*. That Christ was thus fully endowed with the Divine Spirit is clear from the fact that "He knew what was in men," and also from the stupendous miracles He performed. But that He had *more* of the Divine Spirit than any of the old prophets had, is manifest by comparing—

First: Their Theology with His. How narrow, material, and one-sided their views of God often appear to be, as compared with Christ's! Their God seemed no more to them at times than a Local, Vindictive, Passionate Divinity. Christ's God was an *Infinite* Spirit and an *All-Loving* Father. By comparing—

Secondly: Their Spirit with His. They shun sinners and pray for their destruction. "Let the sinners be consumed out of the earth, and let the wicked be no more." Language breathing this spirit, frequently occurs in their address. Christ loved His Enemies, mingled with Sinners, came to "call them to Repentance." By comparing—

Thirdly: Their Lives with His. The best of them often displayed great moral infirmities. Moses lost his temper; Elijah lost heart in duty; Jeremiah grew sulky, saying, "I will speak no more in Thy name." But through the whole life of Christ not a shadow of defect! He challenged His enemies to "convince" Him of sin.

There is no teaching like *Life* Teaching. All mere verbal and professional teaching is as the tinkling cymbal to this true trump of God. It is the most *intelligible* teaching. The language of the lip is different in different countries. It requires in some cases years of study to understand it. The language of the *life* men interpret by the instinct of their nature. The eye, the tone, the smile, the gait: the spirit of the man leaps out to light in these. It is the most *undebatable* teaching. Verbal teaching is frequently so hazy as to provoke discussion. Words are addressed to the understanding, and the understanding will criticize. But what life teaches is unmistakable. A noble deed strikes right to the hearts of men. A real true life is a Divine poem which sets men to music rather than discussion. Men reason against your Paleys; but they cannot reason against those whose lives commend themselves to "every man's conscience in the sight of God." It is the most *constant* teaching. Letter and logic teaching are only occasional. Sometimes they are expressions of the teacher's life, and sometimes they are not. But life teaching is constant. Its light streams through all the acts and events of every day life. It is not the brooklet that rattles after the shower, and is silent in the drought, but it is the perennial river rolling in all seasons, skirting its pathway with life and beauty, and reflecting on its bosom the heavens of God. The text teaches that—

V —AS A TEACHER, HE IS "ABOVE ALL" IN THE NECESSITY
OF HIS MISSION

Trust in Him is *essential* to man's eternal well-being. "*He that believeth on the Son hath everlasting life: and he that believeth not the Son shall not see life; but the wrath of God abideth on him.*" Here are suggested two points which show Christ's pre-eminence as a Teacher—

First: The Faith which He requires as a Teacher is Faith in Him. It is not merely faith in the facts of His history, or in the truth of His propositions, but *in* Himself as the Son of God and the Saviour of the world. We are not called upon to put unbounded trust in the character even of inspired teachers. Nowhere are they held up as an example. Indeed, were we to trust even in the best of them we should be ruined.

Secondly: Faith in Him determines the destiny of the soul. Those that believe *in* Him "*hath everlasting life,*" *i. e.* life without any evil in connection with all good, and life without end—"*everlasting life.*" *Hath* it; not shall have. They that believe in Him *hath* this life now. "This *is* life eternal," &c. Heaven is not something then and yonder, but now and here. What of those that believe not? "*The wrath of God abideth on him.*"* Wrath in God is not like wrath in man—passion, revenge, malignity. It is opposition to all that is unjust, irreverent, malignant, wicked in His universe. God is against bad men as the morning sun is against the burglar and the assassin—checking, baffling, exposing, and confounding them.

CONCLUSION. Christ is our MORAL monarch. "One is your master, even Christ."

* See next page.

Wrath in God
No. 3   John 3:36

" The wrath of God."

(For Exegetical Remarks, see Vol. I. p. 77.)

THE word ὄρχη, translated "*wrath*," occurs about twenty-five times in the New Testament. It is sometimes rendered "anger," "vengeance," and "indignation." The Bible is a book for men: it speaks after the manner of men, in order that men may reach its meaning. Hence it presents even the Infinite in human forms, ascribes to Him attributes that are purely human. The Eternal is spoken of as seeing and hearing, going and coming, working and resting, loving and hating. Much mischief has been done by such a literal interpretation of all this as to humanize the Deity. The word "*wrath*" as applied to God has been thus treated.

It may be useful as well as suggestive briefly to compare the Difference and Agreement of "*wrath*" in God and "*wrath*" in man.

I —THE DIFFERENCE BETWEEN WRATH AS IT IS IN GOD AND AS IT IS IN MAN

First: In man it is an *Exciting* Passion. How wrath excites a man! It shakes him to the very centre of his being. It is seen in his countenance, sometimes in a ghastly pallor, and sometimes in scarlet fire. The eyes, ever true to the soul, flash out the fury. The joints tremble, and the blood boils and quivers. Wrath in man is a most agitating passion. Not so in God; it makes no ripple on the infinite river of His being. In Him it cannot be a state of mind that ever had a beginning, or that will ever have an end. He is ever of one mind. There is no succession of feeling in the Infinite heart.

Secondly: In man it is a *Malignant* Passion. It is rancorous, spiteful, and resenting. It burns with a desire to make miserable its object. But there is no malevolence in the heart of God. "Fury is not in Me." He Who alone understands His own nature thus declares Himself. "God is love," says John. The whole construction of the universe confirms this. Had the Creator been malevolent, what a different universe we should have had! All

His other attributes are but so many forms of His Love. All His commandments are but Love speaking in the imperative mood. All His threatenings are but Love, raising its warning voice to prevent His creatures from falling into ruin.

Thirdly: In man it is a *Painful* Passion. Wrath in man is a tormenting fiend. So long as it exists there is no inward rest or pleasure. Hence the man who treasures anger gives his enemy an advantage over him, inflicts a greater injury on himself than he can on the object of his hate. But nothing can disturb the peace of the "ever blessed God." He knows no pain. He is the God of Peace; He is eternally tranquil.

Fourthly: In man it is a *Selfish* Passion. Man's wrath is excited because something has occurred which he supposes injuriously affects himself in some way or other: his reputation, his influence, his interests. Wrath raises him up to defend himself. There is nothing of this kind in the wrath of God. No creature can injure Him. "If thou be righteous what givest thou Him, or what receiveth He of thine hand?" "Thy wickedness may hurt a man as thou art, and thy righteousness may profit the son of man." Some speak of human sin as something challenging the Almighty to efforts as to how best to defend His character, reputation, and government. Blasphemy this! Notice—

II — THE AGREEMENT BETWEEN WRATH AS IT IS IN GOD AND AS IT IS IN MAN

There must be some things common to both which warrant the application of the same word. What are they? There are at least two things—

First: Repugnance. Wrath in man raises his whole nature against the offences, or the offender, or both. There is at once a recoil and an antagonism. All friendly connection and amicable intercourse are at end. Is there nothing answering to this in the Wrath of God in relation to sin?

(1.) Wickedness is repugnant to His *Nature*. He is essentially holy, and moral evil in all its forms must be necessarily disagreeable to Him. Solomon specifies seven things that are an abomination unto the Lord (Prov. vi. 6). But *all* things contrary to the ineffable purity of His nature must be abhorrent. This His Word declares over and over again. "O do not the abominable thing which I hate."

(2.) Wickedness is repugnant to His *Procedure*. The construction of the universe, the moral constitution of souls, the essential conditions of happiness, personal, social, and national, show that God's whole conduct as Creator and Governor is opposed to sin. As wrath in man separates him from his offender, Wrath in God detaches Him from wickedness. He has no fellowship with wrong. The other point of agreement is—

Secondly : Retribution. There is in the wrath of man an *avenging* instinct : something that craves for the punishment of the offender. Its cry is,

> " O that the slave had forty thousand slaves.
> One is too poor, too weak for my revenge :
> I would have nine years a killing."—*Shakspere.*

There is this Retributiveness in the Wrath of God. Not as a Passion, but as an Eternal and unalterable Principle. The principle of Retribution runs through the whole universe, so that the wrong never fails to meet with punishment. Retribution as it runs through the judiciary arrangements of our own country, is an imperfect expression and form of it as it runs through the great universe of God. Retribution even in our Law is too well organized to be a tumultuous passion : it is a calm, all-pervading principle, having its administrators everywhere. The constable that lays hold of the culprit, and takes him to his cell, has no passion for revenge. The judge who tries his case maintains the utmost calmness. The jury pronounces the verdict without any personal feeling. The final executioner acts as emotionless as a machine. It is somewhat thus, but in a far more quiet and effective way, that God's retribution runs through all life. The Nemesis steps closely on the heel of the transgressor, dealing out retribution for every single sin. Thus the wicked now and here are "going away into everlasting punishment." Every sin is a step adown. Every sinful heart is a nest where the Furies hatch their swarming brood.

CONCLUSION. This subject—

First : Corrects a Theological Error. This error is, that Christ's death was an appeasement of Divine vengeance. Popular hymns are full of this abhorrent and execrable sentiment.

> " Thus saith the Ruler of the skies,
> Awake, My dreadful sword,
> Awake My wrath, and smite the man
> My fellow, saith the Lord.
>
> Vengeance received the dread command,
> And armed down He flies ;
> Jesus submits t' His Father's hand,
> And bows His head and dies."—*Watts.*

Though I venerate the author of these lines, and class some of his compositions amongst the choicest productions in the hymnology of Christendom, I condemn such utterances as these as repugnant to every rational idea of God, and to the whole tenor of Gospel-Teaching. Christ's Mission was the Effect, not the Cause, of God's Love. This subject—

Secondly : Supplies a Terrible Warning to Sinners. "Be sure your sins will find you out." There is wrath ! Beware ! Wrath in the heart of God. Wrath running through all the Laws of the universe. Wrath that must inevitably fill the wrong-doer with misery. Have I stripped His wrath of terrors ? By no means. Of all wrath it is the most distressing in its effects upon its object.

Suppose a man suffering the penalty of having committed some great offence against his brother man. What the offence is it scarcely matters : it may be defamation, robbery, wounding, manslaughter, or even murder. He is in the cell, at the wheel, or in the convict settlement, enduring the punishment which the law had righteously attached to the crime. Now, will not the bitterness of his misery greatly depend upon the state of his mind in relation to the man against whom he had committed the offence ? If he regards him as a man of *malevolent* nature, ever ready to cause misery to his fellow-creatures, will he not feel almost an inner satisfaction that he has inflicted upon him the wrong for which he is suffering ? But if, on the other hand, he regards him as a meek and kind-hearted man, ready ever to render service to his fellow men, the bitterness of remorse will greatly enhance the painfulness of his punishment. It will be thus with the impenitent sinner when judgment overtakes him. He will feel that he has wronged not a *malevolent* God Whose rancorous wrath is a curse to the universe, but a God of Infinite goodness. That the wrath under which He is suffering is not the wrath of a malicious nature, but the wrath of Love—the " wrath of the Lamb." It is the wrath that sets Him in antagonism, not to the rights, the interests, or to the happiness of His creatures, but which raises Him in resistless hostility to all that is opposed to their holiness, their liberties, and their everlasting progress in intelligence, goodness, and bliss. This is the terrible wrath, this wrath of Love. To endure it is the hottest and deepest hell of souls. The wrath of malicious persons you may resent ; you may struggle against its savage fury, and even die under its severest tortures with a moral satisfaction. But, O Heavens ! who can stand against the wrath of Love ! An ocean of oil in flames ! This subject—

Thirdly : Urges the Necessity of Regeneration. The only way to avoid this Wrath is to avoid sin ; the only way to avoid sin is by Repentance towards God and faith in our Lord Jesus Christ.

"Unless ye repent, ye shall all likewise perish." " Marvel not that I say unto you, Ye must be born again."

True Worship
No. 4   John 4:20-24

"Our fathers worshipped in this mountain ; and ye say, that in Jerusalem is the place where men ought to worship. Jesus said unto her, Woman, believe Me, the hour cometh, when ye shall neither in this mountain, nor yet at Jerusalem, worship the Father. Ye worship ye know not what : we know what we worship : for salvation is of the Jews. But the hour cometh, and now is, when the true worshippers shall worship the Father in spirit and in truth : for the Father seeketh such to worship Him. God is a Spirit : and they that worship Him must worship Him in spirit and in truth."

(For Exegetical Remarks, see Vol. I. p. 87.)

Man is constitutionally a Worshipper. There is an element within him, which prompts him to seek, qualifies him to recognize, and compels him to render homage to, a God. This element I regard not as a something transmitted to him by education, or attained by any effort on his part, but as an essential constituent of his spiritual being. It is the incorruptible germ of his manhood, which no power can uproot, no catastrophe destroy. It lives through all ages, and develops itself in every part of the globe, and in every stage of civilization. Man by the necessity of his nature is a worshipper; his being "crieth out for the living God." This worshipping element is the proof of a God. Where this element is, there is no need of logic; it is a matter of consciousness, and where it is not, the soul of the man is gone, and there is no power to appreciate any argument on the subject. The existence of a Supreme One is a fact inscribed on the ever-unfolding page of man's consciousness. The man who endeavours to prove to you that there is a sun, at the moment when its rays are penetrating your eyeballs and surrounding you with its brightness, acts wisely compared with him, who essays to prove to you the existence of God whilst His existence is implied in the very structure, as well as in all the operations of the soul.

"Where'er I turn my restless eye
Wandering from earth to heaven, from sphere to sphere,
Great God ! I feel Thy present Deity,
Everywhere feel Thee—Thou art everywhere.

Yes ! Thou art here—above the empyrean high
Veiled all in light:
Filling creation with Thy presence bright ;
With the proud splendour of Thy majesty.
The little flower that grows
Beneath me ; the gigantic mountain steep
Whose brow is covered with eternal snows,
Whose roots are planted in the deep ;
The breeze that murmuring blows
Among the green leaves, rustling in the sun,
And yonder glorious star advancing on,
Gladdening earth, heaven, and all things as he goes :
These tell me that 'tis Thou
Who givest that sun that brightness ;
And that the flower which breathes and blooms alone,
Breathes, blooms all in Thy pure sight."—*Melendez.*

The *Perversion* of this instinct of worship is the Ruin of
Humanity. If this is wrong, the mainspring is disordered and
every part of the machinery is out of joint. If this is wrong
the very fountain of our being is poisoned, and all the streams
are pernicious. Its misdirection, alas ! is general ; and hence the
disorder and misery of the world. False worship lies, perhaps, at
the root of all the evils that afflict our race.

The great world of false worshippers may be divided into three
classes :—*Those who worship a wrong God ; those who worship a
right God in a wrong way ; and those who worship the right God in
a right way from a wrong reason.*

There are those who worship a *Wrong God.* History tells us
that no less than thirty thousand Divinities were embraced in
that vast system of idolatry which prevailed in Greece and
Rome. In ancient Egypt a similar system prevailed ; the meanest
and most contemptible creatures in nature, receiving the religious
homage of human souls. The less enlightened races of antiquity,
were of course not less idolatrous. The Phœnicians, the Syrians,
the Canaanites, the Babylonians, the Arabians, the Ethiopians,
the Carthaginians, the ancient Gauls and Britons, were even
more deeply sunk in idolatry than classic Greece or Imperial
Rome. Nor in this age are false gods less numerous ; for the
heathen world is crowded with them. The prevalence of idolatry
throughout all ages is awfully significant. It argues the strength
of man's religious nature. What are idols but the idea of
human souls personified ; outward symbols of man's deep craving
and tremendous capacity for worship ? It argues, too, the
dense moral darkness that shrouds the spirits of men ; and it
teaches the lesson which every philanthropist should learn ; namely,
that to improve the human race effectively, to raise it from its
savagism, its depravities, and its miseries, you must take hold
upon the religious nature, pour light into it, and "turn it from

dead idols to serve the living God." Unless you take hold of man's religious element you can never raise him.

There are *false* worshippers, too, who worship the right God *in a Wrong Way*. There are thousands who profess to worship the One True and Living God, but whose methods of worship are false. There are those who employ a *wrong mediation* in their worship, such are those who approach Him through priests, human merit, and sacrifices. And there are those who employ a *right mediation in a wrong way in their worship ;*—such are mere nominal Christians—those who recognize the atonement only theoretically and formally in their devotions.

There are also false worshippers who worship the right God in a right way, from a *Wrong Reason*. Thoughtless multitudes repeat Christian Creeds in Christian temples, bow before Him in the attitude and with the language of devotion, because it is the fashion of the country in which they live. Others kneel before Him with crouching terror and servile alarm, as slaves before a tyrant, hoping to appease His wrath and escape His fierce displeasure. Wrong motives in religion are, it is to be feared, prevalent where there are the Right God and the true method of worship.

If, then, the misdirection of this worshipping element in man is man's ruin, and this misdirection is so general in false worship, the all-important question is, What is True Worship? Worship we must; it is a *necessity* of our nature. But how shall we do it rightly? Will nature instruct us? Far am I from disparaging nature as a religious revelation. But the idolatry of ages has demonstrated its insufficiency rightly to direct the human soul. Christ is the Infallible Teacher on this question. In these few words with the woman of Samaria He throws out a theory of worship, which the greatest sages of the ancient world had never reached, and which agrees at once with our reason and our heart.

I —HE REVEALS THE TRUE OBJECT OF WORSHIP

In these words He reveals that glorious One, Whom the human soul was made to worship with supreme love and adoration. The view here given of the great Object of worship is exactly fitted to the reason and heart of humanity. He teaches—

First : That the Object is a Person. " *They that worship Him.*" Christ gives no pantheistic idea of God : does not speak of Him as the underlying substance, the eternal *All*. Nor as the Eternal River of which all other existences in the universe are bubbles, made of it, rising from it, and breaking into it, in an unending succession. Such an idea is but a dream ; a splendid dream, it is true ; still, only a dream. It may interest a highly speculative intellect and charm a poetic imagination, but it does not satisfy the reason or meet the cravings of the heart. Christ says, " *They that worship Him* "—not *it ;*—a Being Who has personal attributes ;— (1.) Affection, (2.) Will, (3.) Freedom, (4.) Power to recognize and to reciprocate our love. He teaches—

Secondly : That the Object is One. " *The Father.*" There is but *one* God, " the Father of all, and by Whom are all things." The One Whom the old patriarchs worshipped, and the apostles worshipped, and Jesus worshipped, and Whom the good in all ages worshipped, and all in heaven worship, we are to worship. There is but *One.** Then in our worship let us give Him our *undivided* hearts ; let there be no restraint in our affections ; let the whole soul flow forth in Supreme love towards Him. He teaches—

Thirdly : That the Object is a Spirit. What is a Spirit ? No philosopher has yet been able to answer that question. We attach certain ideas to spirits : such as indivisibility, invisibleness, intelligence, affection, unbounded power of thought or action.† " *God is a Spirit.*" The universe echoes this ; creation develops plan ; plan implies Spirit. Man's nature teaches that God is a Spirit. Instinctively we believe in spirits. What we admire in art are the attributes of spirit ; what we admire in nature are the attributes of spirit. " *God is a Spirit ;* " an all-seeing, all-present, all-powerful, all-loving Spirit. We have to worship a Spirit. He teaches—

Fourthly : That the Object is Paternal. " *The Father.*" " *Our* Father." We have His *Nature ;* for children participate in the nature of their parents. The human soul is the fairest image of God. The magnanimity of Moses, the genius of Isaiah, the zeal of Paul, the flight of Milton, the reasoning of Butler, and the philanthropy of Howard, give to me a nobler idea of God, than I can get from the finest sceneries of earth or the brightest orbs of heaven. They are rays from the Father of lights. But as a Father we have not only His nature, but His *Love.* A paternal relationship is a relationship of love. "As a father pitieth his children," &c.

Christ taught us to worship God, not as an insulted Sovereign, but as a Loving Father. He taught His disciples to address Him as a Father. (1.) When Christ tells us to worship God, as a Father, we have an *intelligible* idea of worship. The relationship of a Creator to the creature, who can understand ? The relation of an Infinite Sovereign to the universe is also too vast for our comprehension ; but the relation of a parent to a child we can all appreciate. Our first look of reverence, our first emotion of love, our first feelings of obligation, were directed to parents—they were the first gods we worshipped. When Christ tells us, therefore, to worship God

*See Addendum on Monotheism.

as a Father, we can understand something of what worship is. (2.) When Christ tells us to worship God as a Father we have an *attractive* idea of worship. Men have been taught to regard God with superstitious fear and trembling. They have been taught to approach Him rather as a tyrant requiring flattery and tears to obtain His favour, than as a Father full of love, delighted with the approach of His erring children;—running to meet the prodigal son "when a great way off." Let men feel that the God to be worshipped is a Father, and then they will hasten to His presence : they will say with an old Hebrew: "I was glad when they said unto me, Let us go into the house of the Lord."

Such, then, is the Glorious Object of Worship as presented by Christ. He has *Personality, Unity, Spirituality,* and *Fatherliness.*

II —HE REVEALS THE TRUE METHOD OF WORSHIP

" *They that worship Him must worship Him in spirit and in truth.*"

First : " *In Spirit,*" in contradistinction to *Ritualistic* Service. Under the law there was a great deal of ritualism in connection with worship.

(1.) There were rites referring to the *Body* in worship. There were ablutions, fastings, and feastings;—there was much bodily service required. Bodily service now in worship profiteth but little ; nothing, in truth, except as it expresses and propagates the devout feelings of the soul.

(2.) There were rites referring to *Place* in worship. The Temple of Jerusalem was the appointed place of worship; thither the tribes were to repair to celebrate their religious devotions ; and worship became identified with that place. An idea this too prevalent still ; an idea, alas ! encouraged by a priestly consecration of places. But Christ teaches that place has little to do with worship ; that all places are equally sacred. The mountain on which the Temple stood for ages; the brow of Calvary stained with the blood of the world's High Priest ; the marble sepulchre where the mighty Redeemer slept, and whence He rose as the " Conqueror of death and the Captain of human salvation "—are no more consecrated to worship than those rude hills which the foot of man has never trod, and from which a breath of worship has never ascended. " *Neither in this mountain nor that,*" but in the spirit now.

(3.) There were rites referring to *Time* in worship. There were certain days specially appointed for worship—holy days;—but now all days are equally sacred for devotion. We bless God that we have a seventh portion of our time devoted to the purpose; but the proper use of this day is to enable us to make all days equally devotional and Sabbatic.

(4.) There were rites referring to *Officers* in worship. There were men set apart to appear in the presence of God on behalf of the people; but that age is over. Worship now is an individual act; each man is to be priest for himself—to go to God on his own behalf. We are to "*worship Him in Spirit.*" It matters not in what form as to the body, in what attitude, or in what language; it matters not in what place—in the conventicle, or in the cathedral, in the pauper's cottage, or in the monarch's palace, on the seashore, or on the mountain brow. It matters not as to *time*—what day of the week, or what hour of the day; it matters not as to those who may *conduct* our devotions. The hour of sacerdotalism is gone. "*God is a Spirit: and they that worship Him must worship Him in Spirit and in Truth.*" The Eternal Father's Spirit is everywhere; everywhere can we worship Him.

Secondly: "*In Truth,*" in contradistinction to *Hypocritical* Service. There has always been an immense amount of hypocrisy in connection with religious worship. Every word uttered in prayer or praise, not true to our convictions and aspirations, is an act of hypocrisy.

> " He asks no taper lights on high surrounding
>   The priestly altar and the saintly grave ;
> No dolorous chant, nor organ music sounding,
>   Nor incense clouding up the twilight nave.
> For he whom Jesus loved hath truly spoken,
>   The holier worship which He deigns to bless ;
> Restores the lost, and binds the spirit broken,
>   And feeds the widow and the fatherless !
> Types of our human weakness and our sorrow,
>   Who lives unhaunted by his loved ones dead ?
> Who, with vain longing, seeketh not to borrow
>   From stranger eyes the home-lights which have fled ?
> Oh, brother man ! fold to thy heart thy brother,
>   Where pity dwells the peace of God is there ;
> To worship rightly is to love each other—
>   Each smile a hymn, each kindly deed a prayer.
> Follow with reverent steps the great example
>   Of Him Whose holy work was 'doing good :'
> So shall the wide earth seem our Father's temple,
>   Each loving life a psalm of gratitude.
> Then shall all shackles fall, the stormy clangour
>   Of wild war music o'er the earth shall cease ;
> Love shall tread out the baleful fire of anger,
>   And in its ashes plant the tree of peace ! "—*Whittier.*

III—HE REVEALS THE TRUE REASON OF WORSHIP

"*The Father seeketh such to worship Him.*" This is the Reason. We are to worship the Father thus,—not because such worship is recognized by the institutions of our country and the religious customs of our age as a proper and a desirable thing; not because it may be a means of averting Heaven's just displeasure on account of our misdoings, escaping the miseries of perdition, and securing the joys of Paradise. Such reasons for worship, however specious to the judgment of the selfish, palatable to the tastes of the vulgar, and prevalent in the devotions of mankind, must be deprecated as foreign to the essence of true worship. The reason for this worship is, the *"Father seeketh"* it. Why does He seek it? Shall ignorant mortals dare moot such questions? Ask! Can they avoid doing so when they think? Do not such queries oftentimes start within us, without, if not against, our consent? Reverently I suggest as an answer—

First: The *"Father seeketh"* such worship because it is *Right*. Where does the rightness appear? On the ground of the *relationship* which He, the ever-blessed One, sustains to us His intelligent creatures? Are we bound to worship Him because He is our Creator and absolute Proprietor? Not entirely so. Mere relationship, apart from *moral excellence* of character, would not make worship right; nay, would not make true worship even *possible*. Were He, the Almighty Creator and absolute Proprietor of the Universe, *untruthful, unjust, malevolent*, could we worship Him? No. Through that moral constitution of nature which He has given us, we should recoil with loathing and horror from Him—did His moral attributes clash with the spiritual intuitions of our being. He might command us to worship Him: He might threaten us with the tortures of eternity if we disobey: yet if His moral character agree not with our native sense of goodness, we could never feel the command to be binding, nor attempt to obey it as practicable.

Worship is *Supreme Gratitude,* and there must be sovereign kindness; worship is *Unbounded Confidence,* and there must be absolute truthfulness; worship is *Self-Surrendering Adoration,* and there must be transcendent excellence. We look, therefore, at His infinite moral excellence, in connection with the *relation* He sustains to us as our Almighty Creator, and *feel* at once He has a right to the undivided and incessant worship of the soul. Another answer I suggest to the question is—

Secondly: The *"Father seeketh"* such worship because it is *Necessary*. Necessary, I mean, to the well-being of the soul. Why does He require us to worship Him? Not because our poor devotions can be of any service to Him. He is neither to be "worshipped with men's hands," nor with men's souls, as though He "needed anything," seeing He giveth to all "life, and breath, and all things." He requires us to worship Him, because it is the *necessary* condition of our happiness. He has so formed us that we cannot be happy without such worship of Him. Worship is the vital air and sunbeam of the soul; worship is the highest end of our being; it is not the means to a higher end, there is no higher end for creature spirits. Worship is not the *way* to Heaven, *it is Heaven;* and nothing else is Heaven. If you choose happiness, you must worship—there is no alternative. Worship is the heaven of the soul. Hence the loving Father in love *"seeketh us"* to *"worship Him in Spirit and in Truth."*

CONCLUSION. "O come let us worship and bow down; let us kneel before the Lord our Maker." Let us worship Him, not as some transcendent impersonality, the essence of all things, a mystic something—

> "Blowing under foot in clover,
> Beating over head in stars;"

but as a Being having *personal* attributes, ever cognizant of our existence and conduct, and ever ready to reciprocate our love. Worship Him, not as one out of many divinities, claiming the adoration of our spirits, but as the *only One* demanding the undivided love and homage of our natures. Worship Him, not as an Absolute Sovereign before Whom we are to crouch with terror, and Whose clemency we are to gain by servile cries and tears, but as a Father, from Whose tender and unbounded love all the affection of His creatures is derived; and to which the greatest love of the most loving earthly parent is but as a dim spark to the central sun of the universe. Let His Fatherly love draw us with a rapturous affection into His "presence with thanksgiving, and into His courts with joy." Worship Him, not as a corporiety, however majestic its proportions and sublime its attitudes, but as a Spirit Whose presence is everywhere, and Whose eyes, like a "flame of fire," penetrate the profoundest secrets of our existence. Worship Him, not with a mediation of mere human invention, but through the mediation of Him Who is "the Way, the Truth, and the Life." Worship Him, not in the mere forms of custom, or the rites of ceremonialism, or in the unfelt utterances of devotion, but in *"Spirit and in Truth."* Let it be soul-work and real. Worship Him, not because others do it, or to appease His wrath, nor for any selfish ends, but because He *"seeketh"* it; and He *"seeketh"* it because it is right in itself, and indispensable to thee. Worship Him, not here or there, now or then, in this action and department of life or that, but everywhere, and at all times, and in all the functions and phases of every day existence. Let every spot of earth be trod by thee as "holy ground," every deed wrought by thee as religious; let every act, and word, and thought of thy life, form one unbroken psalm, instinctive and melodious with the true spirit of worship. Let worship be the constant attitude and vital atmosphere of thy spirit. "O come let us worship and bow down; let us kneel before the Lord our Maker." What is life without worship?

> "What were men better than sheep or goats, that nourish
> A blind life within the brain ; if knowing God
> They lift not hands of prayer, both for themselves
> And those whom they call friend ?
> For so the whole bound earth,
> Is every way bound by gold chains about the feet of God."
>
> *Tennyson.*

The Philosophy of a Sound Theology
No. 5   John 5:30

"My judgment is just ; because I seek not Mine own will, but the will of the
Father which hath sent Me."

(For Exegetical Remarks, see Vol. I. p. 131.)

THE querulous and meddling spirit of the mere verbal and
turgid religionists of our day, true to its history, is arrogantly
projecting on public notice the heterodoxy of independent students
of the Holy Book.   As this miserable spirit is now constantly
ringing in our ears, it will not be untimely, and I trust not
unprofitable, to devote a little quiet thinking to the subject of
the *Essential Condition of True Theology.**

I shall make my way to the subject by a few consecutive
remarks on the points naturally arising out of the text—

First : There is a Moral Difference in the "*judgment*" of men
concerning Divine truth.   There are "*just*" and unjust judgments.
There is no sphere of study into which man enters, where opinions
are so various and even contentious as that of theology.   In
astronomy, geology, and the physical sciences in general, students
are comparatively agreed.   But in theology there is an incessant,
and frequently a violent collision of sentiment.

The fierce battles that have been fought on the arena of the
Bible, make up no small portion of the history of Christendom.
Chapters, too, of terrible depravity are found in this voluminous
history.—Would, for the honour of our nature, they could be blotted
out !   This diversity of theological sentiment is *remarkable*.   Antecedently, it might have been expected that in whatever other
branch of study men differed in judgment, in the science of the
God of Love and the common Father of us all, our souls would
meet in holy affection, and blend in sweet harmony of thought.
Nor is this diversity merely remarkable ; it is *moral*.   It implies
evil somewhere.   Man is a moral being, and all his judgments
must be either "*just*" or unjust.   Thoughts have a moral character.
The Omniscient penetrates the deepest secrets of the mind, marks
its thoughts as they rise from their invisible source, and registers
them either as good or bad.   Thoughts being either virtuous
or otherwise, their influence must be either advantageous or

* This discourse was delivered at the time of the "*Lynch Controversy*."

pernicious. They are not mere visions that flit before the mind for a moment, and then pass away for ever, making no more impression upon the heart than the feathery clouds of a summer's sky upon the granite hills. They are for the most part germs. The most light and unsubstantial of them are like those tiny seeds that float in their downy bed on the softest zephyr; they drop into a soil where they may germinate and grow. Or, to change the figure, the thoughts that rise in the soul are like the exhalations from the earth, they form clouds in the over-arching heavens —clouds that discharge themselves either in fructifying showers or devastating storms.

Another remark arising out of the text is—

Secondly: The diversity of *"judgment"* on Divine truth is dependent upon our Moral Conduct. Jesus here intimates that if He had been a Self-Seeker, His *"judgment"* would not have been *"just."* It is a fact, patent to every reflective observer of human nature, that our religious creed is rather the outcome of our general life, than the result of intellectual investigation; springs rather from the proclivities of the heart than from the deductions of the head. In moral questions, life rules logic; feeling sways judgment, conduct grows the creed. The ancient philosophers recognized this fact. Aristotle considered a man unfit to meddle with the grave precepts of morality, till the heat of youthful passions and the violence of youthful impulses had passed away. Intellectually we look at moral truth through our lives. Self is our medium of moral vision; the glass through which we look at God and His holy laws. If our moral lives, the medium through which we view Divine doctrine, be coloured or dimmed by sin, all within the sweep of our vision will appear unnatural, unbeautiful, and without truth. You may as well expect to see a green landscape and an azure sky through a crimson glass, as to see truth in its native beauty through a depraved life. The fact is, you must have moral truth in you, as a feeling, before you can see it outside. Could any philosopher impart to you the conception of the taste of a fruit the like of which had never touched your palate, or the fragrance of a flower, the like of which you had never smelt, or the form or colour of an object, the like of which you had never seen before? Impossible. Equally impossible for you to understand the doctrines of love if you are not benevolent; the principles of justice if you are not just. Spiritual things are only spiritually discerned. It is not enough to have the competent intellect. In order to form a *"just judgment"* upon the truth, you must have a pure life. Holy habits are indispensable to the formation of right theological opinions. "The truth as it is in Jesus" is to be reached and realized only by the *spirit* that was in Jesus.

In the moral doings of men, then, you have, as the Heavenly

Teacher intimates, the philosophy of the diverse judgments on Divine doctrine which prevail amongst men.

Another remark arising out of the text is—

Thirdly: Man's moral condition is resolvable into one of two grand principles of action,—Self-Seeking or God-Seeking. *"My judgment is just ; because I seek not Mine own will, but the will of the Father."* Regarding Christ as speaking merely as a Man, three thoughts are here suggested :

(1.) *That man has a Will concerning himself.* He is endowed with the power of free action. He is by nature constituted the sovereign of his own activities. In other words he has a *will*. This will he uses;—he rejects this and chooses that, pursues this in preference to that, because he has a will. He has a *will* concerning his own pleasures, interests, pursuits, self;—an individual purpose in relation to his own life. It is here suggested—

(2.) *That God has a Will concerning man.* *"The will of the Father."* The Almighty did not make us and leave us to ourselves to live and act as we list. He has a purpose as to how we should employ our powers, regulate our conduct, and spend our lives. It is, moreover, here suggested—

(3.) *That man's Will and God's Will are not always in agreement.* It is implied that the doing of our own will would not be the doing of our Father's. True, Christ's own individual Will was ever in perfect and unbroken harmony with the Will of His Father. But of mankind, as depraved, their will is antagonistic to the will of God. In one respect indeed, the will of depraved man and that of the Great God agree. Both are directed to man's happiness. Man's will is bent on his own happiness, and the will of the Infinite Father concerning us is our well-being. It is not His will that any, not even the "least of the little ones, should perish." The difference, however, is in the *method* of obtaining the happiness. Man aims at it as the *end* of his existence. He holds all things cheap in comparison to it : would subordinate the universe to his own gratification. The Almighty, on the other hand, wills that man should be happy, not by selfishly seeking happiness as an end, but by obeying universal laws, going out of himself, losing the very idea of his own interests in the grand idea of universal good ; not by striving to appropriate all to himself, but by giving himself to all, and co-operating with the loving Creator, like stars and suns and holy angels, for the good of the great creation. Which is the wiser of the two methods ? The laws of mind and the experience of humanity unite in answering—God's. Hence, to pray as Jesus taught us, for the universal doing of the Divine will, " on earth as it is in heaven," is the same as to pray for the happiness of the human race the world over. To " glorify God " is to do His will, and to do His will is to promote universal happiness. God's glory is in diffusing His own blessedness through all the districts of His immeasurable creation. There is yet another remark which arises out of these words, and it contains the pith of the utterances, and the point on which I am especially anxious to fasten your attention. Another remark arising out of the text is—

Fourthly: The adoption of the Divine Will is the essential condition of a True Theological Faith. Christ avers that His *"judgment"* was *"just," because He did not His own will, but His Father's ;*—which really means that He was not under the sway of selfishness, but of benevolence. Every mind in the universe is under the domination of one of these two moral dispositions. He is either selfish or benevolent, either doing his own will or *"the will of the Father."* Now the grand point on which I am desirous of fastening attention in this homily is—

That THIS BENEVOLENCE, THIS DOING THE DIVINE WILL, IS THE ESSENTIAL CONDITION OF A SOUND THEOLOGICAL FAITH. The truth of this will further appear both from the nature of the case, and the testimony of Scripture.

I —LOOK AT THE NATURE OF THE CASE

The Selfish Principle gives a False Medium of Vision. Selfishness is a sense which reduces to the smallest point the truly great, and magnifies to the greatest proportions the mere puerilities of existence. It throws all in the moral domain, into false shapes and fictitious proportions, and tinges all with hues untrue to fact. Can a man, for example, who looks at himself through his selfishness, form any truthful idea of himself? Will he not exaggerate his own excellencies and overlook his own defects? Whilst to other men he may appear truly contemptible, to his own eye there is no one so worthy of love and admiration. Selfishness precludes the possibility of self-knowledge. Nor will he be more able to form a *"just"* judgment concerning other men. The noble order of souls, who act on the principle of self-sacrifice, he will not understand, but attribute to them the same self-seeking motives that sway his own life. The great world itself, moreover, he will misinterpret. He will regard it rather as a market for the obtaining "filthy lucre," than a temple for the worship of the Infinite ; as a scene for mere animal gratification and sensual indulgence, rather than as a school for spiritual study and moral training. The character of Christ will also be shrouded in impenetrable mystery to him. The selfish eye cannot reach the springs of self-sacrificing love. His judgments, too, of the ABSOLUTE ONE will be to the last degree *"unjust ; "* He will think the Almighty such as himself. He will judge of His procedure, by the miserable principles of policy that rule himself.

(1.) *Benevolence is the true Medium of Moral Vision.* Through it things appear as they really are; and nothing seems great but God. The man who looks at truth through a selfish heart, is like the man in some dreary wilderness, with the mists of the mountains hanging over him, whilst looking out upon nature. His horizon is contracted and clouded; the azure roof above, and the meads and the mountains around, are shut out from him by the shadows of the wilderness and the haze of the atmosphere. And even the few things which fall under his eye are but dimly perceived; they appear not in the just proportions of nature, nor in the blush of beauteous life. On the contrary, the man who looks at truth through the other moral medium, "*the will of the Father,*" is like the man who, on some cloudless day, looks forth on nature from some Alpine height. The horizon is vast, and all things stand out in just proportion, and form one magnificent landscape to entrance the soul. Not only does "*the will of the Father*" furnish the only true medium of vision, but—

(2.) *Benevolence supplies the healthful Organ of Moral Vision.* Selfishness impairs the intellect, dims its eye, enfeebles its muscles, and fetters its operations. It twines around the reflective faculty as ivy about the oakling, drinking up its vital sap, and tying it down to its own dimensions. Not so with benevolence. Under the influence of godly love, the intellect grows in energy and bounds in freedom. It is to it what the sun is to the eagle— warming its impulses into stimulus and action, and revealing the bright and boundless for the sport of its pinions.

II —LOOK AT THE TESTIMONY OF SCRIPTURE

So full is the *Oracle* of utterances confirmatory of this doctrine that I hesitate what to select as the fairest specimen.

Here is one:—" With the merciful, Thou wilt show Thyself merciful; with an upright man, Thou wilt show thyself upright; with the pure, Thou wilt show thyself pure; and with the froward, Thou wilt show Thyself froward." What mean these words but this—That the character of man's heart conditions the character of God's revelation to him? Man's heart is the mirror of his Maker. Here is another:—" The secret of the Lord is with them that fear Him, and He will show them His covenant." Does not this mean, that the fear of God—reverential love—is the condition of Divine teaching; that where the heart is right, those great ideas of God will come which are secrets or hidden mysteries to the world? Here is another:—" If any man do His will, he will know of the doctrine whether it be of God." This version, I think, gives not the idea with its full force. The idea is not, that we must *actually perform* the Divine Word before we shall understand the Divinity of the doctrine; but that we must *will* its performance, be in thorough sympathy with it, and heartily resolve to live it out. It means this:—" If any man *willeth* to do His will, he shall know of the teaching." * This rendering gives even a stronger attestation to the truth of the *position* we are discussing.

Here is another:—" The carnal mind discerneth not the things of the spirit, neither can he know them, for they are spiritually discerned." What is the carnal mind but the selfish mind ? And the selfish mind can never discern Divine things. Here is another:—" Eye hath not seen, nor ear heard, neither have entered into the heart of man, the things that God hath prepared for them that love Him." What are those "things" but Divine truths ?—and what is the idea therefore but this : That those truths cannot be conveyed to man through eye or ear, or mere natural heart, but only through the organ of a loving soul ? Here is another:—" Blessed are the pure in heart, for they shall see God." And to another and another, and yet another, I might proceed for hours ; but I select one more to crown the whole. It is this:—" HE THAT LOVETH NOT, KNOWETH NOT GOD ; FOR GOD IS LOVE."

We have reached, I trust, the meaning of Christ in these words, and feel something of their deep philosophy and spiritual significance. *" My judgment is just ; because I seek not Mine own will, but the will of the Father."* As if He had said, " I am influenced by no mere personal considerations ; I have no partial system to advocate, no selfish interests to promote ; I am wedded to no class interest, nor swayed by any class prejudices or associations ; I am ruled by the principles of absolute right, and the spirit of universal benevolence. The *" will of the Father"* is everything to Me. By this I test every doctrine, measure every institution, and determine the true worth of every man. What accords with this, I love and encourage. What is contrary to this I loathe and repudiate."

The subject serves several important purposes—

First : To account for the perversion of the Bible by its avowed disciples. There are views enforced, and institutions advocated, by professed believers in the Bible, and in the Bible's name, which I cannot but regard as essentially incompatible with its genius—as a libel on its teaching, an insult to its authority. Why do men, in

---

* "You are to observe," says the *Rev. Archer Butler*, in a magnificent discourse on this text, "that an appeal to the original language of this Gospel at once determines, that the declaration is *not*, that if any man will *actually* perform, or continue to perform, the will of God, he shall know the doctrine ; but that if any man *sincerely wish* to perform that will, he shall discover the Divine original and descent of the doctrine. The knowledge in question is not, in the first instance, suspended upon the cordial voluntary performance of God's will, but purely, upon the purpose to perform it when once discovered ; a qualifying condition for this great gift of knowledge, much more merciful because much more *limited*."

the name of the Bible, preach an *Avenging* Deity? Present the Infinite Governor of the universe to men, as burning with a wrath which never can be appeased, without the infliction of tremendous suffering either on the sinner himself or his Substitute? The answer is, they see Him through their own revengeful nature. Why do men in the name of the Bible preach a *Commercial Atonement*, and represent the ALL-LOVING ONE as consenting to save a certain number of souls, on the condition of a certain amount of suffering being endured on their behalf? The answer is, they see Him through their own sordid feelings and prudential calculations. Why do men in the name of the Bible preach the utter *Impotency of the Human Will*, and represent men as having no more *natural* power to do the right thing than the corpse itself? The answer is, they look at Him through their own morally forceless natures. They are men of feeble purpose, men whose wills have been all but paralyzed by natural impulses and indolent habits. Ultra-Calvinism is the product of intensified selfishness, an impious arrogance, and a powerless will. Why did men in the name of the Bible represent *Slavery as a Divine Institution?* The answer is, They were interested in upholding the accursed system. The fact is, men act from the heart, and then employ the intellect to formulate a theory that shall justify their conduct. This explains all the theological and ecclesiastical corruptions of Hebrew Scripture. The subject serves—

Secondly: To indicate the method in which the Gospel should be preached. If the condition of the heart is thus so fundamentally important; if it so controls the intellect that men cannot form a *"just"* judgment, if they are sordid and self-seeking; then manifestly the grand object of preaching should be to open the heart to right perceptions. But what preaching is suited to this; suited not merely to excite the sensuous sensibilities, but to dispose the moral heart towards truth? Why, the philosophy of your nature as well as experience answers, it must be the preaching not of mere ideas, abstractions, and theories, however true and sublime, but of the heroic deeds, the lofty character, and the stirring inspirations of a morally grand *Individual Life. Individual* life, I say, for the heart is always affected more by particulars than generals; more by one member than the whole species. The *Personal* Christ is the Divine power rightly to influence the heart. The true method of Gospel preaching is to preach HIM; manifestly set HIM forth, as crucified in the midst of sinners. Set HIM forth, not as the Purchaser of Divine love, but as its sublimest Exponent, its highest Type, and mightiest Organ. Set HIM forth, not as a model whose features are to be copied, but as an Example Whose inspiring spirit is to be imbibed and cherished. If you would become a great painter, do not slavishly copy the productions of your master, but seek to catch his genius, and you will produce pictures of your own, that may give you imperishable fame, and inaugurate you as the founder of a new school. Thus let us exhibit not merely the productions, but mainly the genius, of our Heavenly Master—bring out that self-sacrificing benevolence which is the very soul of His history, and make it flash as heaven-purifying fire upon the selfish heart, melting it into love. Set HIM forth ; do not babble about your dogmas, parade not your own abilities, keep far in the background your sect. Humanity wants Christ, not you or yours ; the Christ, not of your dry creed and dead Church ; but the Christ of the Evangelic Record, the Christ of Bethlehem, Capernaum, and the Cross. Our subject serves—

Thirdly : To supply a test to determine a man's fitness for the work of the Gospel ministry. Heaven knows, we do not want less Intellect in the modern pulpit, nor less Learning ; but we want more *noble-heartedness.* We want men of broader sympathies, wealthier natures, and more self-denying impulses. For as self-seeking souls cannot even form a *"just judgment"* of the Gospel, how can they preach it ? For my part, I would not encourage a young man to enter the ministry because he has a clever intellect, a ready tongue, an irreproachable reputation, a pietistic spirit and gait. An opulent, genial, self-sacrificing nature, seems to me fundamental to the holy office. Love alone can interpret love. Nor would I have in our Theological Chairs men of mere mental ability, biblical learning, and religious reputation. Power to inspire the heart of the student with the true spirit of the office ; to breathe into him thoughts that will expel all that is mean, selfish, and sectarian, and make him glow with the benign enthusiasm of the heavenly mission, seem to me essential qualifications for training young men for the ministry of a love that " passeth knowledge." Men of the highest type we want ; men of the noblest intellects, swayed by the noblest hearts. The subject serves—

Fourthly : To indicate the necessity of Divine influence. If a certain state of heart is necessary in order to form a *"just judgment"* of the truth, it is absurd to suppose that the truth of itself can do all that is needed. Must there not be some influence to clear the eye of the soul that it may rightly *perceive* the truth ? So it seems to me. Paul evidently thought so, when he averred that the Divine truths which the " eye could not see," nor the ear hear, nor the heart conceive, had been revealed unto the Corinthian Christians by the Spirit of God. The heart of Lydia was "*opened*" before she could understand the Apostle's words. There is no way by which the Spirit can affect the soul but through truth, says one of your Sapient Theologues. Poor mortal ! What dost thou know about the laws and modes of spiritual influence ? Do not all created spirits float in the immeasurable sea of Divine influence, and breathe in it as their vital atmosphere ? Has not the Almighty direct access to souls, and can He not touch at His pleasure every spring of their being ? Still more; is not the universe to me according to my mental mood ?—And is not that mood dependent on a thousand outward things ? Even the atmosphere rules it. If I am depressed, and gloomy, and indisposed to look at truth or God, let Him but increase a little of the oxygen in the air I breathe, and my mind will grow bright and buoyant at once, and I shall look at all with a grateful and gladdened nature. In such, and in countless other ways, can He not influence me apart from truth ? Avaunt! all dogmatism about the methods of Divine Spiritual Influence, and welcome the practical impression of our dependence upon the living God for all good. " Not by might, nor by power," &c.

CONCLUSION. Brother, let us seek, then, this unselfish, God-loving, and God-obeying heart. This love will make all things clear : it will enable us to see the Holy One "face to face." It is "the unction" by which we shall "know all things." Love is the eye-salve of the soul; it restores the organ of spiritual vision, and makes all things appear in a new, true, and entrancing light. Waken within me a strong love for an artist, and then his picture, which perhaps I saw yesterday in the Royal Academy without much interest, will, if viewed to-day, entrance me with its new-discovered beauties. Oh, let me look at the universe through love, and I shall see beauties and sublimities which are veiled for ever from unloving hearts! The same with the blessed Gospel itself. Let me study it through the medium of a loving affection, and all the hidden mysteries will be revealed. Love breaks open the sealed apocalyptic book, and leads all the powers of the soul to join in their hallelujahs.

In the language of *Archer Butler*, I exhort you, in conclusion :— " Feel and know that the only way to feel and know Christ is to be Christ-like. Be assured that every step you rise in inward holiness, you are obtaining a nearer vision of that God, Who is holiness itself; and that no other organ than purity of heart can ever behold Him. Burst, therefore, the shackles of a mere dogmatic religion, a religion of phrases and periods ! Can you be saved by a proposition in Euclid ? Believe me, you can just as well be saved by a proposition in theology ! Creeds are valuable only when our hearts sway them ! Love God and love each other as the children of God ; and the God of Love will teach you Divinity."

The Duty of Frugality
No. 6   John 6:12

"Gather up the fragments that remain, that nothing be lost."

(For Exegetical Remarks, see Vol I. page 143.)

FRUGALITY is the lesson which Christ attached to the marvellous Work He had just wrought. This deed teaches, amongst other things:

First: That His compassion extends to our Physical Wants. He not only loves souls with a boundless, ever-working, all-conquering love, but takes a deep and practical interest in man's physical needs. This is shown in the ample provisions He has made in nature, as well as in the deeds which He wrought for the relief of man's body while on this earth. It teaches—

Secondly: That His compassion for our Physical Wants is suggestive of His Divinity. It is said: "Then those men, when they had seen the miracle Jesus did, said, This is of a truth that prophet that should come into the world." In the light of this marvellous deed, they seemed to catch a glimpse of the great Moral Deliverer, the Hope of the Ages. Divine deeds in nature are spiritual revelations; they are flashes that light up the invisible. Matter is the creation—the organ and revealer of mind.

Admitting that what men called His miracles were not evidences; that they had no power to prove either the Divinity of His Person or the truth of His Doctrine, they nevertheless served high spiritual ends. They attracted men's attention to the truth. *John Foster* somewhere speaks of miracles as bells which Christ rang, in order to call men's attention to the new doctrines which He propounded. They also symbolized truths. The restoration of bodily organs—eye, ears, feet—symbolized the restoration of lost spiritual feeling and faculty. The hushing of storms figurated His power over the tempests and passions of the human heart. Moreover, they generally had a lesson attached to them. Christ usually introduced or finished His miracles by a lesson. Sometimes His lessons seemed to be very naturally connected with the incident; at other times, very remote, and what could not have been expected.

This is the case with the lesson He attaches to this miracle, namely, *Frugality*. Who would have thought that He Who had just shown power enough to increase " five barley loaves and two small fishes " into an amount of provision that not only satisfied the five thousand, but left twelve baskets full unused, would have inculcated economy ? One might rather have expected that He would have said : " Heed not the fragments ; do not be careful about these temporal matters : rather be lavish in their use, for I can create abundance for you in a moment. I can rain on you oceans of material supplies." But this He did not say, but the opposite. *" Gather up the fragments that remain, that nothing be lost."*

This is just like Him in nature. He is bountiful everywhere, but most frugal. He allows nothing to run to waste. We see this in the *inorganic* world. " Denudation is the inseparable accompaniment of the production of all new strata of mechanical origin. The formation of every new deposit by the transport of sediment and pebbles necessarily implies that there has been somewhere else a grinding down of rock into rounded fragments, sand, or mud, equal in quantity to the new strata. All deposition therefore, except in the case of a shower of volcanic ashes, is the sign of superficial waste going on contemporaneously and to an equal amount elsewhere. The gain at one point is no more than sufficient to balance the loss at some other. Here a lake has grown shallower, there a ravine has been deepened. The bed of the sea has in one region been raised by the accumulation of new matter ; in another its depth has been augmented by the abstraction of an equal quantity. Nothing whatever is annihilated. For ' matter,' says *Roucher,* " like an eternal river, still rolls on without diminution. Everything perishes ; yet nothing is lost.' " * We see this in the *vegetable* world : landscapes wither, flowers decay, forests rot, but nature allows not a particle of their dust to run to waste. It turns their smallest fragments into instruments for new life, and makes their very gases contribute to the healthfulness of the atmosphere. In the *animal* world it is the same. Generations of birds, beasts, fishes, men, die and rot, but frugal nature gathers up all their fragments. All that belong to our own bodies will go to make the blood, the bones, the muscles, the limbs, and the brain of the men of coming times. Christ's Doctrine of Frugality here, therefore, is quite in accord with nature.

> " Each moss,
> Each shell, each crawling insect holds a rank
> Important in the plan of Him Who framed
> This scale of beings : holds a rank, which lost,
> Would break the chain, and leave behind a gap
> Which nature's self would rue."—*Thomson.*

---

* From an admirable book, which every public speaker should possess, just published by Dickenson, Farringdon Street, entitled, ' Scientific Illustrations and Symbols, Moral Truths mirrored in Scientific Facts,' intended for the use of the Senate, the Bar, the Pulpit, the Orator, and the Lover of Nature.

The Duty of Frugality here inculcated, we may look at as binding on men in the two great departments of life, viz. the *Material* and the *Spiritual*.

I —FRUGALITY IS THE DUTY OF MAN IN HIS TEMPORAL CONCERNS

First : Every man should be frugal in the use of *his own secular resources*. The good that Providence has put into your possession you should use, as the steward of God, with a prudent economy. Nothing should run to waste ; the smallest fragment should be turned to a proper use. Why should you do so ? In order that you may have wealth, and gratify avarice ? Christ never meant this. There are men who do this, and damn themselves thereby ; they are always gathering up. They cringe to any patient, client, or customer, if they can only sweep from their very feet that which will enrich their coffers. Why, then, should there be frugality ? Two good reasons may be suggested—

(1.) To prevent us from becoming *burdens* on society. Every man is bound so to manage his temporal affairs, and to husband his resources, as to prevent him from becoming a burden on his contemporaries. Self-respect, as well as social benevolence, will always urge a true man to this. Extravagance is one of the most prolific sources of pauperism as well as crime. It is constantly supplying our courts with bankrupts, our workhouses with paupers, and our gaols with prisoners.

> "Thy Spirit, Independence, let me share,
> Lord of the lion heart and eagle eye ;
> Thy steps I follow with my bosom bare,
> Nor heed the storm that howls along the sky."—*Smollett.*

(2.) To enable us to *help* society. There is a wrong hoarding and a right hoarding. The man who is hoarding up his wealth for his own aggrandizement, to gratify his own vanity and miserly propensities, is one of the most contemptible characters on the face of the earth ; he is an offence to all generous natures, and an abomination in the eyes of heaven.

Such men have abounded in every age, and their ravenous greed has brought starvation and nameless woe on millions of our age here in our England, The "*Land-grabbers*," as they are called, have appropriated to themselves the greater portion of the earth which God gave to "the children of men." They are those men whom Shakespeare represents :

"I can compare our rich misers to nothing so fitly as a whale : 'a plays and tumbles, driving the poor fry before him, and at last devours them all at a mouthful."

Albeit, the man who is hoarding his property, laying it by from day to day, in order to give to benevolent and religious objects regularly, as God prospers him, is a noble man, and a true philanthropist. Frugality should be a servant to fill the hands of generosity. St. Paul teaches us that we ought to work in order to give (Acts xx. 30—35).*

Secondly : Every man should be frugal in the use of that which *others have entrusted to his care.* There is, in the sight of God, as great a sin in a servant or assistant wasting the property or time of his employer, as there is in an actual theft. Indeed such wasting is theft. He who idles away the hours that his employer pays him for, is a thief, whether the employer be an individual, a company, a corporation, or a state. This is true even of Rulers, who receive countless thousands a year from their employers, and yet waste their time, not only in absolute indolence, but in extravagant sensualities. "Obey those which are over you in the flesh, not with eye service as men pleasers, but with singleness of heart, fearing God : Whatsoever ye do, do it heartily as to the Lord, and not as to men." *Employés,* whether princes or peasants, should "*gather up the fragments*" of the property with which they have been entrusted, and the time for which they are paid; allow nothing to be lost, turn all to the advantage of their employers.

II —FRUGALITY IS THE DUTY OF MAN IN HIS SPIRITUAL CONCERNS

First: This duty will apply to the Revelation of Truths contained in the Bible. The various tracts which make up this book contain undoubtedly many great truths, but they are only the fragments of those which God in past ages made known to man. There is every reason to believe that many books, having as much claim to inspiration as the old Hebrew Scriptures, have been lost; gone down irrevocably into the sea of oblivion. And even in relation to that which is the very substance of the Bible, the Life of Christ, we are assured that we have but a "*fragment.*" "Had all His mighty works been written in a book, the world itself would not have contained the books." It is for us to "*gather up the fragments,*" and allow nothing to be lost. Gather up every precept, promise, doctrine, fact; study them well, and turn them to a right account. Fragments though they be, they are wondrously precious. "More precious than gold, yea, than fine gold." Fragments though they be, millions have fed on them, and found them to be the bread of eternal life. Fragments though they be, all the libraries of the world are contemptible in their presence.

Secondly : This duty will apply to the Memory of Holy Impressions. On all hearts many sacred impressions have been made in times that are past—made by parents, teachers, ministers of the Gospel, made by providential events, and books. Many of

*See *Acts of the Apostles,* Kregel Publications, Grand Rapids, Mi. 1980 in loco.

those impressions have, alas! been obliterated for the time; we
cannot call them up at present by any effort of will, but they will
come up one day; their graves will be opened, and they will start
into terrible reality.

> "Forgotten? No, we never do forget:
> We let the years go, wash them clean with tears,
> Leave them to bleach out in the open day,
> Or lock them carefully, like dead friend's clothes,
> Till we shall dare unfold them without pain:
> But we forget not, never can forget."—*D. M. Mulock.*

But, thank God, we have memories of a few now. True, these
are but mere fragments, still let us now gather them up, that they
may not be lost. Let us dwell upon the mercies we have received
in the past, that gratitude may fill and fire us. Let us think upon
our sins, that we may fall down before the great Father and
implore forgiveness.

Thirdly: This duty will apply to the Remainder of our Time.
How much of our time is gone! Some of us have only fragments
left; a few years at most; it may be only a few days, or even less.
There is no waste so criminal, so ruinous, as the waste of time.
The man who wastes time does not only waste his income, he
wastes his capital whence his income springs, and his pauperism
is inevitable.

John Foster says: "If a person were so foolish as to throw away
a valuable piece of money into a pit, or in the sea, he would not
literally throw away anything but the metal: but *virtually* he
would throw away whatever best thing it would have purchased;
as bread, clothing, refreshments, medicine for the sick, instructive
books, &c. Even so a person wasting time throws away, not the
time itself only, but the opportunities and the privileges which
that time represents."

CONCLUSION. "*Gather up the fragments*" of your Sacred
Memories and Remaining Opportunities, turn them to a right
account, and do not let them be lost. If they are lost, all will be
lost—the world lost, heaven lost, God lost, your soul lost. "*Gather
up the fragments.*"

The Object of Soul-Redemptive Faith
No. 7   John 6:29

"This is the work of God, that ye believe on Him whom He hath sent."

(For Exegetical Remarks, see Vol. I. p. 156.)

VOLUMES have been written explanatory of Faith, yet no sane man requires one single word in order to understand it. He knows it as he knows love, hope, fear, and every other natural state of mind—by his own consciousness. What inner feeling reveals to the soul, logic clouds rather than illumines. Intuitive sentiments burn brightly as stars in the firmament within. From childhood up, man's every day life is a life of faith, and it is too real and vital a thing with him to require explanation. If there be a soul that has it not, the study of all the explanatory works of the world's ablest theologians would never reveal it. The grand work, therefore, of the Christian Teacher, is not to give a philosophic exposition of its nature, but to direct it to the true *Object* —the object on which the well-being of humanity depends.

What is that Object? Is it a *Proposition* or a *Person?* Not —I venture to assert—a *proposition*, though representing the greatest facts, and the Divinest principles, no, not even such propositions. It is a *Person*, and the Person no one less than the God-Man. My doctrine is, that faith—faith in the sense of trust exercised in Him—is the only genuine Christian faith, the only faith that will effectuate the Moral Redemption of the Soul. A man may believe in all the facts of Christ's life, and in all the doctrines of the Christian system, and yet not have the faith which Christ urges, and the spiritual restoration of man requires. I admit, nay, I proclaim with conviction, that Faith in such propositions concerning Christ, is necessary to bring Him in a life-like form to the eye of the human soul; but such faith is no more Christian faith than industry is wealth, or study scholarship. Many labour industriously for riches who die paupers; many study earnestly for the honours of scholarship who die without such distinctions; and many believe in propositions revealing Christ, who have *no* faith whatever *in Him.* In illustration of this doctrine, I submit the following remarks—

That faith in the *Person* of Christ, rather than in any *Propositions* concerning Him, is—

I —THE MORALLY TRANSFORMATIVE POWER

That a moral transformation of soul is essential to the true freedom, dignity, and blessedness of man, is demonstrated by universal experience, attested by our own consciousness, and declared with remarkable force and frequency in the Word of God. We must be "born again," "renewed in the spirit of our mind," " changed into the image of the Lord." A new heart, life, and character, are involved in the change demanded—nothing less. Now faith, neither in a Proposition nor in a system of propositions, neither in a fact nor in a series of facts, can effect this moral supreme revolution.

For what is essential to this Transformation ? The *Generating in the Heart of a Love for Goodness.* Our loves are our masters. They inspire our activities, they work our faculties as they please. The strongest love is evermore the monarch of the soul, and the moulder of the character. The love of sin, in the form of carnal pleasure, self-aggrandizement, and gratification, is the sovereign passion of depraved hearts. To dethrone this despot, and to expel him from the soul, there must be generated within, and fostered an all-conquering passion, a love of goodness. Can faith in *Propositions* about virtue and holiness ever accomplish this ? Never. The soul must have goodness incarnated and bodied forth in a living Personality ; must see its radiant countenance, feel its warm breath, and listen to the thrilling music of its lips, in order to feel its heart captivation. In Christ it has all this, and nowhere else. In Him you have the "Beauty of the Lord." Love the tenderest, the deepest, the most universal and unconquerable, blended with a purity radiant with the effulgence of the Godhead. He is "The Truth." This is His title. He is "The Truth" respecting man, embodying in His life the Ideal of humanity ; embodying what God intended all men to be. He is "The Truth" respecting God, the "brightness of His glory, and the express image of His person." In Him you have what Divinity *really* is, what humanity *really* should be. The aroma of all virtues in the universe stream from His robes. The accents of heaven tone their music in all His utterances. The spirit of all goodness is His very life. It is as the eye of faith looks at Him that the soul sees what sin is, and loathes it ; what goodness is, and loves it. Here is the process. "Beholding as in a glass the glory of the Lord, we are changed into the same image," &c.

The living Christ, not a dead creed, is the magnet to draw, and the power to transform, the fallen souls of men. The heart wants heart, not dogma. Heart alone can touch heart. No power can change heart but heart. The true creed for man is the Christ of God; the Bible for man is not letter, but life; not parchments and papers, but the Biography of Jesus.

I observe, moreover, that Faith in the *Person* of Christ rather than in *Propositions* concerning Him is—

II —THE SOUL-SATISFYING CONDITION

There are certain elements in unregenerate souls, such as sense of dependence, consciousness of wrong, and cravings for objects of love, that keep them in restless anxiety. What can answer and allay these? What can satisfy the soul's *sense of dependence?* Our sense of dependence is deep, ineradicable, and ever-operative. Constant, and often terribly painful, is man's consciousness that both his being and his well-being depend every moment upon what is outside of himself. Every day he feels that he has been leaning on objects external to himself that have failed him. All on which he is depending, he sees floating away on the resistless tide of destiny. His soul craves some *permanent* resting-place; some rock on which to stand amidst the surging sea of change; some object on which to centre his soul in implicit confidence. Without this, all inner satisfaction is an impossibility. What will give it? Will faith in *propositions* give it? Never. The soul cannot feel itself secure in words. Words, however true, are but cold statuary; the heart cannot repose on marble. Trust in Christ meets the want. Trust in Him means confidence in Infinite Love, Unerring Wisdom, and Almighty Power. What, again, can allay the soul's *sense of guilt?* Man has not only sinned, but he is *conscious* of it, and the consciousness is universal. It is felt by the strong as well as by the nervous, by the cultured as well as by the rustic, by men of genius as well as by men of the humbler type of mind. This consciousness is connected with restlessness and distress of soul. In it is the serpent of remorse, and before it lowers the thunderstorm of punishment. What will remove this? Will faith in any *proposition* do this? No. What is wanted is a new consciousness, which in its rising flow will submerge the old; and this can only come through a new life, with its new affections, purposes, and aspirations. This new life is in Christ, and faith in Him is the instrument of conveying it into the soul. "He that believeth in Me, out of his belly—his being—shall flow rivers of living waters." These rivers of new thoughts and loves and hopes and aims will drown the old. The man who comes to love Christ—and love for Him can only come through faith in Him—gets his sense of guilt removed, the threatening clouds of his soul dispelled, and his heavens brightened into hope; believing in Him, he rejoices with " joy unspeakable, and full of glory." What can satisfy man's craving for objects of love ? The deepest hunger of man is the hunger of the heart for some object on which to centre his affections. But what object can do it ? The laws of our nature show that there is no object under the sun on which the soul can settle its affections with unbroken repose. All history shows that it has never done so. Men are nowhere fully satisfied with their loves. Christ meets the case, and He only; on Him the heart can centre its affections. As the bee searches the flowers of nature for honey, the soul is ever in quest of some object on which to settle its love. Hearts find no true repose in words. Syllables cannot satisfy souls. As the mariner's needle quivers in restless motion until it finds the pole, so the affections of the heart will heave in agitation until they find infinite excellence embodied in a Living Personality. Faith in the Personal Christ, then, is essential to soul-satisfaction. When souls are brought to faith in Him, they exultingly exclaim, " Lo, this is our God; we have waited for Him." What, too, will meet the *sense of distance from God* which is so soul-disturbing ? Men are separated from God, not of course in a physical sense : this is impossible. Nothing but annihilation could detach us essentially from the Infinite. We are in Him, and He in us; and this by the necessity of being. The estrangement of which we speak is moral —an estrangement of sympathy, and heart, and life; and of this we all are conscious. This separation is the very essence of sin and the font of woe. Its consciousness is universal, and terribly distressing. Separate the stream from the fountain, and its existence ceases; cut a branch from the root, and it dies; detach a planet from its centre, and it rushes into chaos. God is the Fountain, Root, and Centre of the soul; and if detached from Him, its ruin is inevitable and complete. What can bring the wandering spirit back into fellowship with the Great Father ? What keeps it away ? In-difference, fear, enmity. What can remove these ? Faith in *propositions?* Never. Christ, not doctrines, is the " Way." Christ, not doctrines, is the " Mediator" to reconcile. God in *Him*, not in propositions, is "reconciling the world to Himself." Faith in the *Person* of Christ brings the soul and God together, and the twain become one again. Men must come to Christ, not to theo-logical systems or ecclesiastical ritualities, if they would come back to God. He is "the Door" into the loving home of the Great Father of souls. I observe again that Faith in the Person of Christ rather than in *Propositions* concerning Him is—

III —THE GRAND DEMAND OF THE GOSPEL

It has been said by a very able modern theological writer, that in more than thirty passages of the Gospel of St. John, we find with reference to Christ, the expression, *trusting to Me, or trusting to Him, or trusting to the Son.* The same language is employed by the other Evangelists, and also by Peter and Paul. Faith in Him is represented as the great demand which God makes on men. "*This is the work of God, that ye believe on Him whom He hath sent.*" Faith in *Him* is represented as the grand condition of Salvation. "He that believeth on Me hath everlasting life." "He that believeth in Him is not condemned ; he that believeth not is condemned already, because he hath not believed in the name of the only begotten Son of God." Faith in *Him* is also represented as the means of usefulness. "He that believeth on Me, the works that I do shall he do also ; and greater works than these shall he do." Faith in *Him* is represented, moreover, as the great source of spiritual comfort. "Let not your heart be troubled : ye believe in God, believe also in *Me.*" And, furthermore, *He*, not doctrine, is represented as the grand subject of religious commemoration. On the night on which He was betrayed, He turned the minds of His disciples away from the old subjects of religious commemoration and centred them on Himself. Taking the elements used in the Passover, He said, "Do this in remembrance of Me," as if He had said, "This is the last night of Judaism ; My people, henceforth, must remember *Me*, a Person, rather than things." He rang the knell of letterism and ritualism that night—the religion of humanity hence on, had to do with a PERSON. And again, *He*, not doctrine, is represented as the grand Subject of the Christian Ministry. "Whom we preach, warning every man, and teaching every man, that we may present every man perfect in Christ Jesus."

Sufficient has, I conceive, been advanced to show, that the true faith of the Gospel means *Trust in Christ*, and not belief in *Propositions*, whatever the character and amount of faith or doctrine such Propositions may represent.

CONCLUSION. This subject explains—
First : The complaints of Religious Professors concerning their faith. "We feel that our faith is very feeble—how difficult it is to believe ! Oh, how weak our faith is ! We cannot take hold upon the promises." Who has not heard expressions like these in every religious circle ? Such complaints are prevalent. What do they indicate ? This :—That the faith is directed to *propositions* rather than to the *Person.* Do you ever hear the child of noble parents—parents whose love is genuine, and whose honesty is incorruptible—say, "I have a great difficulty in believing in my father or my mother, a great difficulty in laying hold upon their promises ?" Do you ever hear a wife say in relation to a husband, who has always appeared to her incapable of doing a wrong act, "I am distressed that I cannot have stronger faith in him ?"

Such things would be the greatest of social anomalies in this anomalous world. Who feels any difficulty in believing in a person of *undoubted* goodness and integrity? If the faith of religious people were directed *to Christ*, the Incarnation of all Excellence, rather than to *creeds*, we should not hear all this sentimental jargon. What is there in Christ to prevent you believing in Him? Is there not everything to enlist your cordial and implicit trust? In truth, if you believe in Him, you will accept His doctrines, even though you cannot understand them, and acquiesce in His procedure although you fail to appreciate or even to discern its wisdom. If I believe in a man, I take his word. If I believe in Christ, I accept His revelations. Belief in Him is in fact necessary in order—(1.) To believe the truth of His Word, and (2.) To appreciate the meaning of His Word.

This subject explains—

Secondly: The Weakness of the Church in its endeavours to Christianize the World. The nominal Church in all its branches, is confessedly active, and has been active for ages. It does a great deal of a certain kind of work, but not much, I trow, of the work Christ demanded, the work the world wants, which *is to cast out its devils.* The fiends of selfishness, carnality, pride, hypocrisy, avarice, unbelief, practical atheism, are they not as rampant in the world as ever, notwithstanding all the trials of the Church to expel them? Civilization has given them more attractive costumes and more delicate instruments than they had in barbaric ages. But their power is as great and their aims as deadly as ever. Why has not the Church succeeded? When Christ descended from the Mount of Transfiguration, He found that His disciples had been trying to cast out the devil in a man, but had failed; and on their asking Him the cause of their failure, He said, "Because of your unbelief; for verily, I say unto you, if you had faith as a grain of mustard seed, ye shall say unto this mountain, Remove hence unto yonder place, and it shall remove, and nothing shall be impossible to you." The weakness of the Church is its Lack of Faith in Christ. The Church, in truth, has talked a great deal about its faith; has fought for its faith; has bled for its faith; aye, and more, has even *persecuted* for its faith; but what has been its faith? Faith in some verbal articles: in some cases "thirty-nine," in others more, and in others less, rather than in the living, loving, Personal Son of Man and Son of God. This subject explains—

Thirdly: The Cause of all Divisions in the Nominal Church. The Sect life in the Church, whatever may be said to the contrary, I hold to be one of the greatest evils of the world. It is one of the chief devils of Christendom. It narrows the sphere of charity, it nurtures a heartless bigotry, it obstructs the progress of universal truth, it misrepresents the Spirit of Christ. This evil is begotten of a certain faith in certain propositions; propositions in some cases relating to metaphysical theology ; and in other cases referring to some ceremonial observance. Even an idea about *water* creates sects; and the smaller the idea that creates a sect, the more *venomous* that sect becomes. If all the members of all the Churches, believed with a Living Faith in the One Personal Christ, such miserable divisions would cease. Christ would become the Centre. Diversity of opinion must ever exist so long as mind is mind ; but diversity of opinion is the charm of *genuine* fellowship. Does diversity of opinion amongst brothers and sisters in the same family lead to separation, when all hearts centre in their parents ? Never. Where a common love rules, diversity of sentiment heightens the harmony. Diversity of opinion may be one of the great charms in celestial conferences.

This subject explains—

Fourthly : The True Method of Religious Teaching. If Christ is the great Object of faith, the grand work of the religious teacher should be so to present the *Personal* Christ as to inspire the loving confidence of men. The Biography of Christ must be our Bible. In truth, what is all that is written in the tracts of that wondrous volume that we call the Bible, apart from Christ ? Nothing of any vital value. The casket without the jewel, the royal robes without the monarch, the body without the soul. Our every text should be from the Biography of Christ, our every subject Christ *Himself*. The " truth as it is in Jesus," as a *Person*, the world wants, not as it is in the books of theologians, or even in Moses and the prophets; but as it is in Jesus—a loving, symmetrical, Divine, soul-attractive, soul-satisfying thing.

Brothers, let us preach, not traditional doctrinism, or the Christianity of the sects, but the Christ of the Bible—the Christ, not as He is caricatured in portraits, taken in the murky studios of theologians and ecclesiastics; but as He appears livingly photo graphed on the pages of the Evangelic Records.

Genius of the Gospel World Embracing
No. 8   John 6:37

"All that the Father giveth Me shall come to Me ; and him that cometh to Me I will in no wise cast out."

(For Exegetical Remarks, see Vol. I. p. 162.)

I TAKE the words as illustrating three things—

I —THE UNBOUNDED CONFIDENCE OF CHRIST IN THE GOVERNMENT OF HIS FATHER

Faith in the Character and Procedure of the Father, is the perfection of piety, and the condition of a happy existence. Everywhere in the Bible, the great Father seeks to awaken in man the most loving and unshaken trust in Himself and in His procedure. The strength of the old saints was in this. Their heroic lives, as celebrated in Heb. xi., are ascribed to their loyal trust in the wisdom and the love of Heaven. Those illustrious worthies felt one with Job, who said, "Though He slay me, yet will I trust in Him." No Being ever possessed or exhibited this trustfulness as did Christ. In Him it had its most perfect development and force. It buoyed Him up amidst the surges of anguish that rolled over His holy soul. It never deserted Him. In Gethsemane it was as strong as ever, when He said, "Not My will, but Thine, be done." It comes out in the text. He had been speaking to the multitudes, who had followed Him for the sake of the "loaves." He had been exhorting them "to labour for the meat that endureth unto everlasting life." He had represented Himself as the "Bread of God which cometh down from heaven, and giveth life unto the world." But notwithstanding this, they believed not. Such heartless infidelity amongst those whom He had laboured so self-denyingly to enlighten and convince, had a tendency to sadden His spirit and oppress His heart as a Man. Still His trust in God bears Him up. He looks to heaven and says, "*All that the Father giveth Me shall come to Me.*" As if He had said, "My Father overrules the world; all men are at His disposal; I acquiesce in His arrangements; I bow to His will."

This is the spirit of the passage. What is called Calvinism has laid special claim to this text; and Calvinism in some of its vulgar and corrupter forms has sadly marred and mangled these wonderful words. But they have nothing to do with any of your *isms*. Their *Divine* genius overflows the logical boundaries of the most expansive creeds. The text is not uttered as a Theological Dogma, but in a Sublime Spirit of trustful devotion and unbounded philanthropy.

"*All that the Father giveth Me.*" There are certain ideas attached to these words by a certain class of men that they do not necessarily contain; and some of which are certainly inconsistent with the dictates of unsophisticated reason and the whole tenor of Biblical truth.

(1.) The words do not *necessarily convey the idea that the Father has given any Men to Christ.* It is remarkable that the word "all," πᾶν, in the text is neuter, whilst the word τὸν ἐρχόμενον, "*him that cometh,*" is masculine. As if the passage meant, that all things were given to Christ by His Father, and therefore there would be the greatest certainty that no man who came to Him would be, or could be, "*cast out.*" When Christ gave His commission to His disciples after His resurrection from the dead, He said, "All power is given Me in heaven and on earth." The words of the text might have been spoken in anticipation of this glorious event. If so, the words may be thus paraphrased :— "All things (universal dominion) that the Father giveth Me shall come to Me after My resurrection, and consequently the men that come to Me, whoever they may be, I will on no account '*cast out.*'"

(2.) Nor even if the words include the idea of men being given to Christ are they so given,—that the *Father has surrendered any of His claims upon their being or services.* Literally, when we give anything to another, we cease to have any claim over it. A father when he gives his child to another, surrenders his parental claims. With a miserable perversity of judgment, there are some who propound the monstrous idea, that in what they call the "counsels of eternity," there was a contract entered into between God the Father and His beloved Son, by which, on certain conditions, a certain number of souls were made over to Christ. They became His. He bought them, paid for them with His blood; and they are no more amenable to the moral claims of the Great God, as the Creator and Governor of the universe. Such an impious notion clashes with the consciousness of every Christian man, who *feels* evermore his allegiance to the Everlasting One; clashes also with the obligations which God in the Bible enjoins upon the disciples of Christ; and clashes with the fact that the redeemed in heaven ascribe their all to the Almighty Author of all things. Indeed Christ Himself everywhere enforced, with the utmost earnestness, the obligations of His disciples to love, serve,

264 / Gospel of John

and worship His Father. "Thou shalt love the Lord thy God, with all thy heart, and with all thy soul, and with all thy might." This He taught was the "FIRST AND GREAT COMMANDMENT." And again: "The hour cometh, and now is, when the true worshippers shall worship the Father in spirit and in truth: for the Father seeketh such to worship Him." The word "*given*" therefore, in the text, must not be taken in its literal and current sense.

(3.) Nor must the words be regarded as conveying the idea that, supposing men are "*given*" to Christ, they are *compelled to go to Him*. Some have laid wonderful stress upon the "*shall*," as if to express the idea that, whether they will or no, they *shall* come;— come irrespective of their own choice. The word ἥξει, however, has no imperative meaning, but merely expresses what will happen in time to come. The Father does not act upon His children as upon machines. He treats all creatures in accordance with the nature He has given them. Moral beings He moves by moral means. He does not, to use the language of *Luther*, "draw sinners to the Saviour as a hangman draws a culprit to the gallows." He does not either drag or drive. He draws—draws with the "cords of a man." Indeed in verse 44 the Saviour speaks of the Father as "drawing" men, and also explains the nature of the "drawing." "Every man, therefore, that hath heard, and hath learned of the Father, cometh unto Me." The fact that the Almighty presents the strongest inducement to men, and charges those who yield not to them, as *grieving, resisting, quenching* His Spirit, is proof sufficient that there is no coercion; and that in all cases He treats men as moral agents in the matter. In His last prayer (chap. xvii.) Christ speaks of His disciples as being *given* to Him by His Father, and yet did they not freely follow Him? Did He not say to them on one occasion, "Will ye also go away?" As if He had said, "You are free agents: the matter must rest with you."

(4.) Nor even suppose that the words imply the idea of men being "*given*" to Christ—they do not mean that they are so given that they *must necessarily be saved*. Christ speaks of Judas as being *given* to Him by the Father—"Those that Thou gavest Me I have kept, and none of them is lost, but the son of perdition." God gave Judas to Christ;—that is, He induced Judas to follow, and to listen to His teaching. But "Judas by transgression fell, that he might go to his own place." God giving men to Christ, then, does not necessarily involve salvation, for (the same word δίδωσί is employed) Judas was *given* to Christ.

(5.) Nor must the words be regarded as conveying the idea *that the Father is not disposed to give all men to Christ*. Christ had been representing Himself to the multitude as the "Bread of life," and inviting them to come unto Him to participate in the blessing. But they avail not themselves of His kind invitation. Whereupon,

He gives utterance to these words—"*All that the Father giveth Me shall come to Me.*" Language which, in this connection, seems to me to convey but this one idea—that "*all that the Father giveth to feel their need of Me, as the bread of Life, shall come to Me.*" The appetite of hunger awakened within them will prompt them to do so. *Tholuck,* quoting Theophylact, observes, that "as the magnet does not attract everything, but only iron, so also to be connected with Christ there must exist a certain frame of mind,—the feeling of what we should be, and what we are not." This state of mind the Father seeks to give, not to one but to *all.* God, by His Providence, by the human conscience, by His blessed Word, seeks to make men so *feel their need of Christ* that they may go to Him. He says to all, "Wherefore do ye spend money for that which is not bread? and your labour for that which satisfieth not? Hearken diligently unto Me, and eat ye that which is good, and let your soul delight itself in fatness." "As I live, saith the Lord God, I have no pleasure in the death of a sinner." "Turn ye, turn ye, why will ye die?"

Whilst these words, then, contain no such theological notions as these;—notions which some men have substituted for the "glorious Gospel of the blessed God," they do express what I have already said—the *Unbounded Confidence of Christ in the Rule of His Father as the Disposer of Mankind.* It was His habit as the Great Exampler of piety to trace everything to the hands of His Father. When He stood in the court of Pilate, He recognized the power of that temporizing worldling as a power *Given* to him of His Father;— "Thou couldst have no power except it were *given* thee from above." As He lay prostrate under the mysterious agonies of Gethsemane, He regarded His very sufferings as His Father's gift. "The cup which My Father hath *given* Me, shall I not drink it?" And as on the eve of His crucifixion He looked upon the few poor men who had been disposed to receive instructions from His lips, He felt that their discipleship was the *gift* of His Father;—"I have manifested Thy name unto the men whom *Thou gavest* Me out of the world: Thine they were, and Thou *gavest* them Me." Indeed, as He looked upon the great universe above and about Him, He felt that all things to Him were the gift of His Father. "The Father," said He, "loveth the Son; and hath *given* all things into His hand."

Be it ours to cherish that spirit of Unbounded Confidence which our great Master expresses in the words,—"*All that the Father giveth Me shall come to Me.*" Heaven forbid that we should content ourselves, in getting from these words some little dogma for the brain, and strive not after that spirit of sublime trust in God for the heart which they breathe, and are intended to enkindle! Let us bear our trials with the feeling that all that the Father

" *giveth* " even of afflictions shall come to us, and no more : that "our times are in His hand." Let us prosecute our labours with the consciousness that all the success that the Father " *giveth* " us shall come unto us. I shall take the words as illustrating—

II —THE SETTLED CONDITION OF A SINNER'S WELL-BEING

What is it? Coming to Christ. " *Him that cometh to Me.*" Such language is of frequent occurrence in the New Testament. " If any man thirst, let him come to Me," &c.

What sermons have been delivered, and what tracts have been written, on " coming to Jesus ! " But how few understand the meaning of the words ! Can we attach any intelligible and practical meaning to the expression—*coming to Christ* ? We can. There are different ways in which we are constantly coming to the distant and the dead.

First : By taking into us their Ruling Ideas. We come to men intellectually when our general ideas approximate theirs. We feel one with them in intellect as we mingle with them in thought. Thus modern men come to the great thinkers of past ages. Socrates and Plato, Shakespeare and Milton, and other illustrious intellects, we meet in the quiet realms of thought. In the ideas of Jesus of Nazareth, we can thus come to Him. Though His great thoughts transcend them all ;—in their spotless purity, in their unerring truthfulness, in their immortal freshness, in their unbounded sweep, in their soul-quickening and soul-uplifting force, they stand alone. The greatest ideas of others are but the reflected beams of the cold moon ; His the bright rays of day, touching the world into life. Let us "learn of Him," and thus "come to Him," through His great thoughts. We come to Him in His biography, which is living and life-giving. We come to men—

Secondly : By heartily sympathizing with their Spirit and Aim. We are one with those who love the same objects, and sympathize with the same pursuits. Congruity of feeling welds hearts together. The patriot *comes* to Cromwell, the philanthropist to Howard, the missionary to Xavier, because their sympathies are one. Thus by loving the objects that Christ loves, and sympathizing with the pursuits of His heart, we come to Him. Talk of patriotism ! Was there ever patriotism like that which overflowed His great soul, and rolled down in tears, as He beheld the doomed metropolis of His own country ? Talk of philanthropy ! Was there ever philanthropy like that which He displayed, Who died " the just for the unjust," to bring sinners to God, and Who employed His expiring breath in praying for His murderers? " Father, forgive them, they know not what they do." You must come to Christ in these Sympathies. " He that hath not the spirit of Christ, is none of His." We come to men—

Thirdly: By appropriating their Moral Temper. In morals like draws like. We are drawn to those who are like ourselves in temper and in aim. Similarity of character is always a magnet. The good attracts the good. Thus we must come to Christ. We must "learn of Him, Who was meek and lowly in heart, and we shall find rest unto our souls." He is our Model; "He has left us an example that we should follow in His steps." We must imitate Him, not by servilely copying particular acts, but by in-breathing the genius of His Glorious Life. In these respects you must come to Christ. This is the condition of your well-being. There is no happiness for the sinner where Christ is not followed as the Guide to goodness. "There is no other name given under heaven among men, whereby we must be saved." If, then, Soul-Fellowship with the great Father is the only True Happiness of an intelligent being, and if coming to Christ in the sense indicated is the only condition,—what follows? This,—that Christ is the Supreme Necessity of human souls. If we are to be happy, it is not a question as to whether we will come to Christ or not; we must come, or we shall be lost. If you are to see you must have light, if you are to breathe you must have air, if you are to live you must have food, and if you are to be *Happy you must have Christ.*

Here, then, is the *Settled Condition of a Sinner's Well-Being.* He must come to Christ, in *order to be brought into loving fellowship with the everlasting Father.* Who that admits the existence of a Supreme Being can hesitate to conclude, that a loving fellowship with Him is essential to the well-being of all created spirits? But who can be brought into this sublime state of being who comes not to Christ? None. He alone removes the three great obstructions that keep the human soul away from, Him the Source of Human Blessedness. (1.) *Indifferentism.* The mighty millions of the world are dead to God. They have no more feeling about a God than the beasts of the field or the birds of heaven; they are "without God." Christ, through His incarnation, brings the Great Father within the sphere of their Senses, their Conceptions, their Sympathies. Those who come to Him are no longer destitute of interest in the Great First Cause. A series of questions start within them that have a tendency to conduct them into His ineffable presence. He removes—(2.) *Terrorism.* By a law of depraved mind, thoughts of God awaken terror. "I heard Thy voice in the garden, and I was afraid." Terror drives men away from God. Dread of God is the parent of all soul-crushing superstitions, all blasphemous theologies, and atheistic theories. Dread of God is a centrifugal force in depraved souls; it drives men away from the true centre of being. Now he who comes to Christ will have the dread expelled. He brings the dreaded One to them in the most winning aspects of tenderness, compassion, and moral loveliness. Through Him, the Infinite says to all, of every age and land, "It is I; be not afraid." He removes—(3.) *Antagonism*. If a man dread another, he will come to hate him. The object of his dread, his imagination will make so hideous in feature and form, as to be loathed and hated. Hence men's dread of God has invested Him with jealousy, wrath, vengeance, and they hate Him. "The carnal mind is at enmity with God." We shun those we hate, hence men shun God.

Now how can this enmity be removed? Suppose the existence of a man you hate, and have hated for years; so hated that you have always shunned his presence, and glowed with indignation at the mention of his name. The question is asked, how to quench that flame of enmity towards the man in your mind? There is only one way in which that can be done. And that is, by working into your soul, a strong and unquestioning conviction, that he whom you have been hating all these years has never done you any harm, has always been your faithful friend, has always endeavoured to serve you, and stood up for you when your character has been defamed, and has defended your interests; nay, has made sacrifices for your benefit. Moreover, that he is one of the grandest of human characters. The very moment that conviction is worked into your soul, not only will every spark of your enmity be extinguished, but you will feel a burning shame for your past feelings, and there will come into your heart such a strong current of love to that man, that hence on his name will be as music in your ears. Thus Christ removes men's enmity to God. He comes and gives you a demonstration, that however much and long you have hated Him, He has never had one unkind thought towards you; but, on the contrary, has loved you with an everlasting love; so loved you that He has given "His only begotten Son" to bless you with everlasting happiness. Hence, coming to Christ is the Settled Condition of your Loving Fellowship with the great Father.

Notice—

III —THE AMAZING MERCY OF CHRIST IN HIS TREATMENT OF SINNERS

"*Him that cometh to Me, I will in no wise cast out.*" The idea is; "he that applieth to Me for Spiritual Life and Blessedness, whoever he may be, I will on *no account reject.*"

There are at least two general *accounts* on which the best of us do sometimes reject the requests of an applicant.

First: On account of something in connection with Ourselves. (1.) There may be a *Deficiency in our Benevolence*. An individual may apply to us for a favour, and we may have the *power* to render it, but lack the disposition. Our benevolence may be at fault. It is a sad fact that through the ingratitude, the dishonesties, the hollow pretensions of the world, the fountain of kindness even in the most benevolent natures, gets well nigh dried up sometimes. Many a generous heart has grown misanthropic through intercourse with a hollow and heartless age. When our benevolence is at a low ebb, we may turn away from the request of even a deserving applicant. But will Christ ever *" cast out "* *one* on this ground ? Does He lack benevolence ? He has given the world the highest conceivable demonstration of His love; He has given Himself to a death the most excruciating and ignominious. "Scarcely for a righteous man will one die," &c.

The height, depth, breadth, length, of His love, "passeth knowledge." It is an ocean that no line can fathom, no shore can bound. It is infinite; and you cannot exhaust the infinite. Could the wickedness of men have exhausted it, there would have been none after His crucifixion. But lo ! soon after His resurrection, just before His ascent to heaven, He commanded His disciples to go and preach *Forgiving Mercy* even to His murderers at Jerusalem. Christ, therefore, can *"in no wise cast"* a man out on account of any lack of benevolence in His own loving heart.

Or sometimes, where our benevolence is not at fault—
(2.) There may be a *Deficiency in our Resources*. We may not be able to entertain the request. Many a generous man is obliged to say No ! whilst in his heart he feels Yes ! This is one of the greatest trials of truly benevolent natures in this world. Still it is better, a thousand times better, to have the disposition to give and not the means, than to have the means and not the disposition. He who has the one is a pauper in the universe; he who has the other, a prince. The one is a grub moving through his earthly possessions; the other a seraph, on joyous pinion winging his way through regions as rich as love, as beautiful as Paradise, as vast as immensity, as blessed as God. But though our resources fail us, however benevolent we may be, Christ will in *" no wise cast "* a man out on this account. His resources are *Inexhaustible*. Paul speaks of them as "unsearchable riches." Whereunto shall I liken the Redemptive Resources of Christ ? To a Feast ? If so, then, not a feast implying limitation—providing for so many, and no more. But rather it is like that banquet which Jesus spread out upon the mountain of Capernaum, "of which all the thousands did eat and were filled," and stores of fragments still left unused. I scarcely know to what to compare the "Unsearchable riches of Christ." I think of a Masterpiece of Music, every note suited to touch some of the deepest chords in human nature. It has awoke rapture in the men of past generations, and seems as potent in its stirring impulses now as ever. Still it may be exhaustible. The time may come when our Handels, Haydns, and Beethovens will be outgrown, and left behind as relics of the past, All that is human

has its limitations. I think of the great Sun, which has been giving out his beams for I know not how many thousand years, in quickening and gladdening the unnumbered tribes of life that teem in air, and earth, and sea; in annually robing our world with forms of beauty, ever fresh and affluent, and causing the earth "to bring forth and bud, that it may give seed to the sower, and bread to the eater." As I think of this royal orb I am impressed with the vastness of its resources. But though vast, I feel it is not inexhaustible: it is finite. Its beams will grow dim, its fires die out, and the period may dawn when not a vestige of its existence shall be found throughout the districts of immensity. There is nothing that I can think of to which I can compare the Resources of Christ. There is nothing in fact in the creation, for the creation itself is limited. But Christ, the "Sun of Righteousness," although He pours His soul-saving beams on millions of generations, and will light up the heavens of God with blessedness through un-numbered ages, must remain as bright and warm as ever. Christ, then, on the ground of the lack of Resources, "*will in no wise cast out.*"

The other general reason on which the best of men do sometimes reject applications is—

Secondly: On account of something in Connection with the Applicant. Either of the three following circumstances connected with an applicant, would wondrously tempt us to expel him and his requests from our presence.

(1.) *If his character were unusually vile.* Should a man, deeply sunk in the mire of intemperance and licentiousness, or character-ized by systematic dishonesty and daring blasphemy, make applica-tion to us for a favour, we should scarcely tolerate his presence, still less entertain for a moment his case. If we spoke to him, it would be in the language of severe reproof, if not indignant denunciation. We should say, "You deserve more than the misery you are in; starvation is too good for you." But Christ will "*in no wise cast out*" on this account. Take two cases out of many. Christ is at a feast in Simon's house. While there, a woman, notorious as a Sinner in the city, entered into the room where He was, "stood at His feet weeping, and began to wash His feet with tears, and did wipe them with the hairs of her head." This woman was probably known as the corruptest character in the city; odious in depravity. She had turned, perhaps, many a youth from virtue, and stained many an innocent nature with her vice. There she kneels before Christ; she has intruded into His presence. What does He say to her? Does He scathe her with a look of indignation? Does He cast her from His presence? No. He first reproves Simon the Pharisee, who seems astounded at His allowing one so depraved to remain near Him even for a moment;

and then, with a heart overflowing with compassion, He turns to her and says, " Thy sins are forgiven : go in peace." Take another case. On one side of Him on the cross hangs a malefactor in the last agonies of death. Society has cast him off as a wretch unfit to live. Even corrupt humanity could no longer tolerate his presence, or allow him a place amongst the living. He himself owns that his doom is just. But in this, his last hour, he turns imploringly to Christ, saying, " Lord, remember me when Thou comest into Thy kingdom." What answer does he receive ? Does Christ say, " My sufferings are too great to attend to thee ; every nerve of My frame is on the rack, and a mountain of anguish is on My soul ; I can think of nothing but My own condition ? " No. Does He say, " Wretch, why appeal to Me in this the last moment of thy life ? Thou hast spent the days which Mercy has given thee, to cultivate thy spirit, and to find acceptance with thy Maker, in depravity and crime. Away with thee to thine own place !—the place for which thou art fitted, and to which justice dooms thee ! " No. With unutterable tenderness and love, He says, " To-day shalt thou be with Me in Paradise." He " *will in no wise cast out.*"

Let not the sins of any man, however aggravated, however enormous, keep him away from Christ. Stand up before me, Sinner of the greatest enormity, and tell me thy sad tale.

" My character," sayest thou, " is too dark for description. My iniquities, like a thick cloud, roll over my soul, obstructing the light of heaven, and threatening to destroy me with their brooding tempests. I was the child of godly parents ; I had a Mother, who, in my early days, taught me to lisp the name of Jesus, and read His holy life ; a Father, who by his example and his speech, sought to guide me into the way of virtue and of peace. I had Religious Teachers in early life, too. I listened to a faithful and an impressive ministry, received deep impressions and made solemn resolutions. But *they are all gone.* My parents, whose hearts my corrupt conduct had broken, are long since in their graves. The ministers I first heard are no more. The companions of my youth, too, are gone. I am left alone, an old man tottering on the verge of the grave. Fifty years at least, I have spent in a career of wickedness and blasphemous impiety. The thought of the injuries I have done to my species by my depraved conduct and influence appals me. ' I have sat in the seat of the scorner.' I have endeavoured to shake men's faith in God ; I have scouted the Bible as a cunningly-devised fable ; I have denounced Christ as an impostor, and His disciples as hypocrites ; I have made many laugh at sacred things ; I have rifled many of their virtue ; I have turned many an innocent youth into the paths of scepticism and profligacy. Many a wife has cursed my influence over her husband, and many a mother has recoiled with horror at the mention of my name. The memory of my enormities appals me. Here I stand worn out with sin. I feel tottering as on a tremendous precipice. Above me there is a tempest about to break in fury on my hoary head; beneath me there is a yawning retribution. Talk not to me of Mercy. Mercy has exhausted herself on me. She has made her last overture; she has taken her wings and gone for ever!"

Oh! Brother, terrible is thy tale. It is a wonder that thou art not in hopeless perdition! Still I would not leave thee, even *thee*, in despair. "The mercy of the Lord reacheth unto the clouds." Avail thyself of this, thy departing hour of life, and go to Christ, and thou wilt find that He will in "*no wise cast out*" (1 Cor. vi. 10, 11). Again, we reject a man's request—

(2.) *If he has sought to injure us.* Were a man to apply to us for a favour, whom we knew had been acting the part of an enemy towards us for years; endeavouring to stain our reputation, thwart our plans, and injure our interests, should we not be likely to expel him with severe reproof? Perhaps we should say to him, "We wonder how you could have the audacity, knowing as you do the villainous way in which you have acted towards us, to ask for a single favour!" But Christ will not repel on this account. Look at Saul of Tarsus. Lived there ever a man who hated the name of Jesus of Nazareth more than he, who laid himself out with greater determination and force to blot His memory from the minds of men, and to annihilate His influence? Like a furious beast breathing out slaughter, he hastened to Damascus, having "received authority and commission from the chief priests," in order to persecute the men who dared to profess their attachment to this Christ. He said, "I verily thought with myself that I ought to do many things contrary to the name of Jesus of Nazareth." And he did so. To use his own language: "I punished them oft in every synagogue, and compelled them to blaspheme; and being exceedingly mad against them, I persecuted them even unto strange cities." He was indeed a hater of Christ, and he proved his hatred. Yet one day, struck with the heavenly light of moral conviction, he prostrates himself before this Jesus of Nazareth, and says, "Lord, what wilt Thou have me to do?" And how was he received? Did He Whom he had thus hated and opposed, Whose disciples he had persecuted and destroyed, drive him from His presence? No. To the poor prostrate soul He says, "Stand upon thy feet; for I have appeared unto thee for this purpose; to make thee a minister and a witness, both of these things which thou hast seen, and of those things in the which I will appear unto thee; delivering thee from the people, and from the Gentiles; unto whom now I send thee, to open their eyes, and to turn them from darkness to light, and from the power of Satan unto God, that they may receive forgiveness of sins, and inheritance among them which are sanctified by faith that is in Me." Paul, having met with this wonderful reception of unexpected mercy, leaves this testimony to after ages, "This is a faithful saying, and worthy of all acceptation, that Christ Jesus came into the world to save sinners, of whom I am chief."

Still again we reject a man's request—

(3.) *If, after having once granted his application, he has persisted in doing us wrong.* Suppose a man, to whom you had rendered a great favour in answer to his application, and who afterwards disowned you, and displayed the most shameful ingratitude, were again to apply to you, would you not be tempted to drive him from your presence, whatever might be his expressions of sorrow, and promises for future improvement? But Christ *"will in no wise cast out"* on this account. There is Peter, to whom He had shown many special favours, whose applications He had often graciously granted. This Peter denies Him;—denies Him in the hour when friendship was most needed,—denies Him with impious oaths,—thrice denies Him. Yet did not Christ cast a gracious look on him, that stirred his heart and melted him to tears? Far enough am I from encouraging backsliding. It is a dreadful sin. A step backwards is of all actions the most daring and hazardous. But having done so, do not be afraid to make another application to Christ. See how He found this Peter out, and treated him on the Galilean shore immediately after His resurrection! "Come and dine," He says. "Simon, son of Jonas, lovest thou Me?" &c. Come! He *"will in no wise cast out."*

CONCLUSION. I feel well nigh overwhelmed with sadness, when I reflect upon the base and pernicious uses to which this text has been degraded. It has been used as a battle-ground for bigots, instead of an exhaustless field fertile with all that is enchanting in beauty, and choice in fruit. "ALL THAT THE FATHER GIVETH ME." "Here is Calvinism," says one narrow Sect. "HIM THAT COMETH TO ME I WILL IN NO WISE CAST OUT." "Here is Arminianism," says another Sectlet. Thus the first clause and the last, are taken up by two contending parties, the one snarling and howling at the other throughout Christendom. But the passage is not a Theological divisibility, it is a grand Moral unity. It does not articulate an idea for the brain, but glows and beats with a spirit of love vital and universal as the sun. Whilst narrow sectarists use it as a fœtid pool, in which they stir up the offensive vanities of their own foul hearts, let us regard it as an immeasurable lake, clear as crystal, reflecting on its bosom the Infinite Mercy of God.

The grand question for each to ask is, What is our relation to Christ? Have we come to Him? Are we now through Him enjoying friendship with the Holy One, and blessed intercourse with Heaven? Is He our Moral Guide, leading us on to a higher acquaintance with His doctrines, a closer identification with His sympathies, and a more perfect assimilation to His character? If so, let us gratefully adore the everlasting Father for thus *Giving* us to Christ. The work of the Spirit, by Providences and Gospel ministries, is to *Give* human souls to the ever-blessed Son. Take heed that you "resist not the Spirit." For He has said, "My Spirit shall not always strive with men." *

* This Discourse was delivered in Churches in different Towns in England and Wales, where the congregations were known to be extremely Calvinian in their theology.

Soul-Adjudication*
No. 9   John 7:24

"Judge righteous judgment."

(For Exegetical Remarks, see Vol. I. page 193.)

ADJUDICATION is one of the many avocations of civilized man. There are *Commercial* adjudicators. In almost all departments of action, where men ply their energies for a livelihood, there are those who are recognized as authorities; men whose judgment upon the value of commodities, properties, and productions are accepted and acted upon. There are *Literary* adjudicators. Men who for the most part constitute themselves as authorities on literary productions. In their various journals they arraign our authors at their tribunal, examine their works, and pronounce upon their excellences or defects. Although it comes not within my purpose to discuss the value of such functionaries, or to criticize the way in which their duties are generally discharged, I cannot but express my profound regret, that so many of them are utterly disqualified for the position they have assumed. There are *Legal* adjudicators. Men who preside in our courts of justice, who sift evidence, balance probabilities, and always in the name, if not always under the sense of justice, pronounce upon the merits of the case before them. There are *Theological* adjudicators. Men who profess to know the whole truth of God, pronounce judgment upon the religious opinions of their fellow-men, and at whose feet sit weak-minded religionists, who accept their dictates and call them Rabbis. The true, the honest, and the independent searchers after the Truth, repudiate their authority, and denounce their arrogant and impious assumptions.

Whilst, however, there is a great deal of Adjudication going on in the Commercial, the Legal, the Literary, and Theological departments of human life, there is an Adjudication which transcends all others in importance, and which devolves not upon any

---

* This is one of a series of articles, on "Emblems of Soul-Work," that appeared in the "Homilist," Vol. xxiii. The remainder of the series will re-appear in a subsequent volume.

particular class of men, but upon each man as the most urgent obligation of life. I mean the Adjudication of those subjects which are vitally connected with our *Spiritual* and *Undying Interests*, subjects concerning which each must form his own estimate, and where the judgment of one can never become the substitute for that of another. Subjects concerning which Heaven commands us to *"judge righteous judgment"*—to "prove all things, and to hold fast that which is good." What are those subjects? I shall mention only a few of the most important, and they may be comprehended under four general heads:—MAN, THE GOSPEL, RELIGION, and PROVIDENCE.

We should *"judge righteous judgment"* concerning—

I —MAN

It is of paramount importance that men should form a *"righteous judgment"* of themselves. "To know thyself," is at once the condition and guarantee of all true knowledge.

> "By all means use sometimes to be alone;
> Salute thyself—see what thy soul doth wear;
> Dare to look in thy chest, for 'tis thine own,
> And tumble up and down what thou find'st there."—*Wordsworth.*

What is a *"righteous judgment"* of man's *Nature?* What is man? Widely different estimates are given and circulated. The thoughtless millions *practically* declare that he is corporiety, and nothing more; that the body, with its limbs, appetites, organs, sensations, constitutes the entirety of his being. Hence for mere animalism they live. Their grand question is, "What shall we eat, what shall we drink, and wherewithal shall we be clothed?" The sciential materialists agree in this. They say, "The body is everything; man is nothing more than organized matter. Dust, and nothing else. All are of the dust, and all return to dust again." Here, then, is a subject of which it becomes every man to form a true estimate. For myself, my judgment is formed. My philosophy, such as it is, and my Bible, as I interpret it, assure me that man is a *Spirit;* that the body is no more him than the house is the tenant, the telescope the astronomer, the harp the lyrist. When I say Spirit, I mean *Responsible* Spirit. There may be spirits existing that have neither the attributes nor the sense of accountability. Such is not man; he is not an engine, moved hither and thither by the force of another; a mere spoke in the wheel of the universe; a mere log of wood tossed about on the black surging sea of destiny. He is a Responsible Agent, Self-Moving, Self-Directing. I have no debate upon the point; my reasoning, my consciousness, and my Bible, have placed for me the question beyond the pale of discussion long, long ago. I *feel* that I am free. The sense of responsibility permeates my nature, throbs in every pang of remorse, and in every thrill of self-approval.

What is a *"righteous judgment"* of man's *Mission?* Wherefore is man here? Wherefore sent into the world? Is there a purpose in his creation? If so, what? The voluptuary says, "I am here to gratify my senses;" the worldling, "I am here to amass wealth;" the intellectualist, "I am here to struggle after the philosophy of things." But are these *"righteous judgments?"* I trow not. They outrage reason, they clash with conscience, they contradict the teachings of the Holy Book. Brothers, it seems to me that we are here in order that, by searching after truth, and struggling after holiness, we may form a character that will qualify us for the Fellowship and the Service of God, through all the Æons that await us.

What is a *"righteous judgment"* concerning man's *Chief Needs?* What are his primary necessities? Men have come to call food and raiment, with emphasis, "the necessaries of life." But are they so? Cannot man live without them? Does he not so exist in the other world? To me the chief needs of man appear to be freedom from sin, purity of heart, moral nobility, harmony with the universe, and unbroken peace with Heaven.

Form, then, a true estimate of *Man.* You can never exaggerate his importance. "What shall it profit a man if he gain the whole world and lose his own soul?" The *World is great.* All men, though for very different reasons, are impressed with its greatness. It is great to the *Poet*, whose imagination glows in the presence of its scenes of enchanting beauty, and aspects of stirring grandeur. It is great to the *Philosopher*, who in every step of his research, is amazed with the subtlety of its elements, the regularity of its operations, the fitness of its means to its ends, and the boundless variety of its combinations and its life. It is great to the *Christian*, who feels its moral significance, regards it as vocal with the thoughts, overflowing with the goodness, filled with the Presence, and radiant with the Majesty, of the Great Father of all. It is great even to the miserable *Worldling.* He navigates its oceans, traverses its shores, cultivates its soil, and works its mines, in order to appropriate to himself its treasures. But great as the world is, the Soul is Greater. The world cannot think of its Creator; the Soul can. The world cannot act contrary to the will of its Creator; the Soul can. The world will not exist for ever; the Soul may. As a leaf, this planet shall fall from the forest of existence; as a passing cloud it shall melt into thin air. But the Soul has peradventure an imperishable existence. Who can tell its value? Think of its *Capabilities!* Recall the wonders it has achieved, and is still achieving. Think of the *Influence* which it exerts! One soul can pour into an age, a flood of sentiment that shall beat through the heart of centuries. The one wrong act of Adam vibrates in all hearts to-day. Think of what has been given for the *Redemption* of a Soul! "Ye are not redeemed with corruptible things," as silver and gold . . . . but with the precious blood of Christ."

Another subject on which we should *"judge righteous judgment"* is—

II —THE GOSPEL

The great God has submitted the Gospel to our judgment. What is it? This is a vital question—vital to every man. Sadly diversified and even contradictory, are the estimates that men have formed of the Gospel. Some pronounce it a *"cunningly-devised fable."* They consider it a story which, with some amount of historic foundation, was wrought out of the imaginations of the *wily and superstitious* of past times. This is simply absurd. Its *Incongruity* with the popular ideas, spirit, and character of the age and country from which it sprung, and its *Congruity* with itself, with our *à priori* ideas of the Divine character, and with the common intuitions and exigencies of human nature, expose the atrocious preposterousness of such a view. Besides, could a fable have done what the Gospel has achieved? Could it create a Christendom, with its civilization, its freedom, morality, and religion? Could it command the homage and the advocacy, of the greatest thinkers, authors, and sages of all times? If it be a fable all things are fabulous, and we live in dreams.

Others say that it is nothing more than a *Wonderful History.* It is indeed a wonderful history! The advent of Christ to this world—His Teachings, Sufferings, Death, Resurrection, and Ascension, are the grandest and most influential facts that ever occurred in the annals of our race. But the Gospel is more than a history. The history is but its form and manifestation. There is something underlying the facts, producing the facts, throbbing in the facts; that something is the heart and essence of the Gospel. What is that something? We shall see as we advance.

Some say it is a *System of Theology.* But a theology is man's production; the thoughts of poor erring men systematized—nothing more. Our *conception* of the Gospel is not the Gospel itself. The Gospel is as independent of our theology, as the stellar universe is independent of astronomic theories. What, then, is the Gospel? It is a *Revelation of God's Love to Sinners.* This is its essence: "God so loved the world," &c.

You can never over-value this Gospel. It is the *Essential Means of Spiritual Life.* It is to the soul what light and air, food and water, are to the body—that without which there can be no life or growth. The loss of the Gospel, as I regard it, would be a greater loss to humanity, than if you were to quench all the lights of the firmament and leave the heavens in sackcloth, or seal up the clouds so that the fertilizing showers shall no more visit the earth. Another subject on which man should *"judge righteous judgment"* is—

III — RELIGION

What is Religion? Some *"judge"* it to be a *Creed*. I have no words to express the high importance I attach to a well-digested system of truth; but a Creed, however Scriptural, is not Religion; devils have an orthodox creed. What is religion? Some *"judge"* it to be a *Ritual*. I share not the spirit of those who, with the exclusiveness of the bigot and the ignorance of the unthoughtful, indiscriminately denounce all ceremonies in connection with religion. I like the æsthetic in form, the harmonious in song, the graceful in gesture, and the sublime in expression. But this is not religion. When the ritual is the expression of a Divine thing it is beautiful, useful, and good. When it is *Form*, and nothing more, it is utterly worthless. What, then, is Religion? It is the *Spirit of Christ—His Moral Temper—in the man*. "If any man hath not the Spirit of Christ, he is none of His." His Spirit is the Spirit of True freedom, incorruptible honesty, self-sacrificing philanthropy, and adoring worship. This is Religion, and nothing else. "Pure religion and undefiled before God and the Father is this: to visit the fatherless and widows in their affliction, and to keep himself unspotted from the world." You are perhaps ready to exclaim—What, is this all? Is the thing about which a million books have been written, and ten thousand sermons are preached every Sunday, nothing more than a Christ-like Temper? It is reported of a man, that on seeing the sea for the first time, he exclaimed, "What, is this all? Is this the mighty ocean?" It was all that he *saw* of the ocean; but if he could only launch out upon the piece of water he saw, trust himself to it, sail over its billows, it would take him round the world. It is so with the Religious Spirit. It may appear small to your vision, but it extends to everything that is sacred in the universe; it reaches the throne of God. Trust yourself to it; sail forth on the tidal wave, and it will bear you to the calm and sunny shores of eternity. Another subject on which you are called upon to *"judge righteous judgment"* is—

IV — PROVIDENCE

By Providence here, I mean that ever-changing world of external circumstances in which we "live and move and have our being." Circumstances are *vital* things to man; they not only affect his senses, but stir his deepest soul. How do you estimate them?

There are different estimates current and advocated. Some regard them as Fatalistic Occurrences; others, as Divinely ordered. The former declare "that all things come alike to all;" the events of life, like the billows of ocean, break on all shores alike. The latter consider that they are all Divinely directed and come with a Divine purpose. Some regard circumstances as their masters, others as their servants. The former bow to them, and ascribe to them their condition and their character; the latter use them as the horseman his steed, the mariner the winds, the telegraphist the lightning—to carry out their purposes and to do their work. Some regard them as beneficial, only as they tend to the gratification of the body and the amassment of wealth; others as beneficial in proportion as they serve to discipline the character, to spiritualize the affections, and to lead the soul to God. All souls make their own appraisement of circumstances. Which estimate is yours? Do you consider Circumstances as coming by Chance, or as ordered by God? My view is the latter. Not a sparrow falleth to the ground unnoticed by the Great Father. Do you regard them as Tyrants or as Slaves? Are you groaning under them, or are you battling with them, and making them subserve your spiritual good? Do you regard them as serviceable only when they promote your temporal interest?—or as blessings, however painful, if they tend to school you into virtue and to religion? The latter is the right idea. The worldly man, in taking stock, estimates the year as profitable, only as it has served to augment his wealth. He will say, "It has been a good year" if he has prospered; and a "bad one" if his worldly resources have not increased. But this is not a "*righteous judgment.*" That is really the good year that has deepened your sense of the spiritual, strengthened your confidence in God, and invigorated your sympathies with the spiritual, the religious, and the Christ-like. The year that has wrecked your fortune, robbed you of your health, bereaved you of your friends; if it has led you into closer fellowship with the Infinite, has been a good year. Thus Paul felt: "What things were gain to me,"—my learning, my social status, my worldly prospects,—"I counted loss for Christ."

CONCLUSION. You see how much the Soul has to do in the great Work of Appraisement. It has to form a true estimate of *Man*, of the *Gospel*, of *Religion*, and of *Circumstances*. False estimates prevail concerning all these, and false estimates are ever dangerous. "*Judge righteous judgment,*" brothers. You have a judiciary function to fulfil in life. No man in ermine requires more scrutinizing thought, more gravity of spirit, than you. The great God is submitting, every day, questions for your decision which are of paramount moment. As one single figure wrong amongst a million in arithmetical sums, will vitiate all the calculations and give a wrong result, so one mistake upon these vital points, may involve you in a terrible calamity.

What is called Education is valuable only as it stimulates and guides man to a "*righteous judgment*" on these questions. Education of the true type is the supreme want of humanity. By Education I mean the bringing out of all the latent faculties of the soul in harmony with themselves, the laws of the universe, and the Will of Heaven.

This is the Education for which I have lived and laboured for many years, and in which I continue to feel a vital interest.*

---

* This discourse was preached at Stockwell, when I was deeply interested in a great Educational Scheme for Wales. Some twenty years ago, when I was recruiting my health in the romantic neighbourhood of Caswell Bay, I became so impressed with the sad lack of Education in my native country, as a Welshman, that I made a solemn resolution to do all I could to supply the deficiency. I wrote at once to the "CAMBRIA DAILY LEADER" (the first Daily Paper ever started in Wales, of which my son, David Morgan Thomas, Barrister-at-Law, was the Proprietor) a letter, urging my countrymen to establish a University. When I returned home to London, the late Dr. Nicholas, then President of Carmarthen College, inspired by my appeal, called on me. And in my own library I drew up the first Resolutions on the question, Resolutions which, in the course of a fortnight, were moved and carried at the first meeting held in London on the subject, presided over by my old friend, William Williams, Esq., M.P. for Lambeth, from whom I obtained the first £1000. I continued to work on the committee (whose meetings were held for some years alternately in my son's chambers in the Inner Temple, and in the chambers of Morgan Lloyd, Esq., Q.C. and M.P.,) until £20,000 were obtained, and the splendid building at Aberystwith purchased ; and with the late Dr. Nicholas and Hugh Owen went down to the inaugural meeting presided over by the then Lord Lieutenant of the county. This fact is stated here, not merely to show my interest in Education, nor to claim credit for the great undertaking from vanity, but for the sake of historic truth. There are those who, now that it has become a success, claim credit for its origination, who not only stood aloof from it at the commencement, but even strenuously opposed it. (For an account of the movement, see "Homilist," Vol. XL. p. 461.)

Biblical Monotheism
No. 10   John 8:50

"There is One that seeketh."

(For Exegetical Remarks, see Vol. I. p. 254.)

CHRIST here proclaims the fact that there is One God, and One only. In the old Hebrew Scriptures the Infinite is represented as saying, "I am the First, and I am the Last, and besides Me there is no God." On this Monotheistic Doctrine I offer three preliminary remarks.

First: It is supported by the Order and Structure of Nature. So far as the universe has come within the sweep of scientific observation and research, it appears as one complete whole. All its parts are beautifully harmonized, all its forces are nicely balanced. Nature has no contradiction in her utterances, no jarring in her orchestra, no deviations from her original habits and ways. Her march is stately and unswerving. The same causes under the same circumstances, produce evermore the same effects. Nature, as a Temple, has endless sections and compartments, yet the whole is manifestly the draft of One Architect, the work of One Artificer. Nature, as a Machine, is wondrously complicated, with wheels within wheels, yet the whole is obviously the invention of One intellect, the arrangement of One mind. On the front of the grand fabric of the universe there appears, in bold, clear, imperishable characters, the declaration, "There is but One God." Concerning this declaration, notice—

Secondly: It is in direct antagonism to Certain Prevalent Opinions. It is opposed to *atheism*, which declares there is no God; that whatever is, has either always been, or else was produced by chance. It is opposed to *feticism*, the worship of any material object that a capricious superstition may select. Also to *polytheism*, which holds the plurality of gods: and to *pantheism*, which regards nature as identical with Deity, and thus destroys a Divine Personality. The lie is given to all such miserable theories. Concerning this declaration, notice—

Thirdly: It is accepted as a Fundamental Truth in all Evangelical

Churches. There is a class of men professing faith in the Bible, who call themselves Unitarians. They have no more right to assume that name than have Evangelical believers. No orthodox Church believes in a plurality of deities. They believe in One God, and only One. Monotheism is the religion of Christendom. But my object in this discourse is briefly to consider the practical uses of Biblical Monotheism.

I —IT REVEALS THE GREATNESS OF THE CREATOR

Survey the wondrous universe. Gaze upon the vast, and examine the minute, in the clearest and broadest light of modern science, and what do you see? *Wisdom?* Yes—manifold wisdom —in every blade and insect, as well as in every intellect, world, and system. All this wisdom is the product of *One* mind. The archetypes of all you see existed once in One Intelligence. He had no "Counsellor to instruct Him." Do you see *Goodness?* Yes, like an everflowing tide, overflowing all, streaming in every ray of light—breathing in all life, beating in all pulsations, giving a happy glow and a beauteous form to all things. All this goodness is an emanation from One heart, the Eternal Fountain of all life. Do you see *Power?* In rearing the stupendous fabrics, building up the mountains, pouring out the oceans, stretching out the heavens, moulding, adjusting, burnishing, propelling the worlds and systems that fill immensity? The hand of One Being did the whole. It was God Himself formed the earth, and made it: He hath established it. Do you see *Wealth* in all this? If you attach value to one acre of earth, what is the value of the globe? But what is the earth to the universe? A leaf to the forest. A sand-grain to the shores over which all oceans roll. There is but One Proprietor of all this wealth. He can say, "All is Mine: the sea is Mine; the earth is Mine; the Heavens are Mine; all souls are Mine; the souls of the Father and Son are Mine." Oh, if there be but One God, how great must He be! All nations are nothing to Him—and less than nothing, and vanity. "Thou, even Thou, art Lord alone: Thou hast made heaven, the heaven of heavens, with all their host; the earth, and all things that are therein; the seas, and all that are therein, and Thou preservest them all; and the host of heaven worshippeth Thee." Another practical use of this glorious fact is—

II —IT REVEALS THE DEFINITENESS OF MORAL OBLIGATION

Deep in the souls of all men is the sense of duty. It may be deadened, but it can never be killed, never be eradicated. Hence, thoughtful men in every age have earnestly inquired into the principles of moral obligation, and very numerous and often conflicting theories have come forth as the result. Some have propounded one standard of virtue and some another. My definition of virtue is this—*Following a Right Rule from a Right Motive.*

From this the question arises what is the *Rule?* Clearly if there be but One God, the will of that One God must be the *Rule.* What is the *Motive?* Clearly if there be but One God, supreme love to that One God must be the motive. Were there a plurality of gods, there would be a difficulty in finding out what virtue is. We should have to determine whose will to obey—the will of each, or some, or all. And we should also have to find out who of all the gods we should love the most. But as there is but *One* God, our duty becomes definite, and clear as day. His Will alone is Supreme law. *He alone demands Supreme Regard.* The Bible urges this argument. "Hear, O Israel: the Lord our God is one Lord : and thou shalt love the Lord thy God with all thine heart, and with all thy soul, and with all thy might. Know, therefore, this day, and consider it in thine heart, that the Lord He is God in Heaven above, and upon the earth beneath : there is none else. Thou shalt keep, therefore, His statutes, and His commandments, which I command thee this day, that it may go well with thee, and with thy children, which the Lord thy God giveth thee for ever."

Another practical use of this glorious fact is—

III —IT REVEALS THE FITNESS OF RELIGION TO THE CONSTITUTION OF THE SOUL

There are three psychological facts that scarcely admit of disputation, and that every preacher of the Gospel should ever practically recognize in his discourses.

First : The human heart has a Centralizing Tendency. Deep in our emotional heart is a craving for some *One* object, on which to place entire confidence, and centre the deepest love. The soul, like the planet, is made for a centre ; it requires something on which to hang as its chief support ; something to circle round as its glory, something to serve by reflecting its attributes, and transmitting its influence. There is not a soul whose love does not point to some *one* object, as the needle to the pole.

Secondly : The moral character of the soul depends upon its Central Object. By a law of our nature we become like that we most love. Love is a transfiguring force. It moulds us to the character of its object. He who loves the character of the devil becomes like him. He who loves God becomes a partaker of the Divine nature.

Thirdly : The soul's happiness is determined by the Character of the Object most loved. All experience shows that most of our happiness and misery come out of our Supreme love. He that loves supremely a faithless, worthless, suffering, dying object, must inevitably suffer sooner or later. Elsewhere I have shown, that the Object of supreme love, to make us happy, must be supremely excellent, always blessed, ever reciprocating our affection, and continuing with us without end. Here are the eternal conditions of human happiness, and this One God is necessary to the fulfilment. Thus it is that all in every age who have loved the One God supremely, have felt with the Psalmist, who said : " Whom have I in heaven but Thee ? and there is none upon earth that I desire beside Thee. My flesh and my heart faileth; and God is the Strength of my heart, and my Portion for ever."

Another practical use of this glorious fact is—

IV — IT REVEALS THE UNIVERSAL BROTHERHOOD OF SOULS

" To us," says Paul, " there is but one God the Father of all things, and we in Him." It seems to me that spirits stand in a different relation to God to what material existences do. God is the Creator of matter, God is the Father of souls. We are His offspring : the highest seraph in eternity, as well as the poorest clod on earth. Between souls and God there is an essential resemblance and involuntary reciprocity. Those of His offspring who have always been obedient, feel and recognize their brotherhood, and are banded together with the tenderest feelings of love. They look on each other through their love for their One Father, and feel the vast universe their Father's House. Men, alas ! have proved wayward and rebellious children. Humanity is the lost sheep that has gone away from the ninety-and-nine in the great fold; the prodigal that has left the Father's House. Because they have proved disobedient to their Father, they have lost the true spirit of Brotherhood amongst themselves. What a moral anomaly in the universe is war ! Children of the same Father burning with mutual malice, and earnest in mutual murder ! What shall end this ? What shall annihilate all the unkind feelings of men toward their race ?—what shall generate the loving spirit of brotherhood ? Nothing but a common love for the One Father can do it. He who loves not God as His Father, will never love his fellow-men. Piety is the parent of philanthropy. Genuine religion is the inspirer of human brotherhood.

Another practical use of this glorious fact is—

V — IT REVEALS THE WONDERFUL IN MEDIATION

" God so loved the world, that He gave His only begotten Son, that whosoever believeth on Him should not perish, but have everlasting life." Here is love passing knowledge.

First : What a disparity between Him Who loves, and they who are loved. What a disparity in *Natures !* God, the Almighty, the All-wise, the Eternal : man, the feeble, the ignorant, and the dying. What a disparity in *Character !* God, the Essence and Fountain of all holiness : man, vile and polluted with sin.

Secondly: What a Manifestation of the greatness of His love ! He so loved that He gave What ? A World, a system, the universe ? No ; all this is nothing compared to what He gave—He gave His " only begotten Son." " Herein is Love." I see Divine Love everywhere. It rises high, and drowns the hills. It floods the universe. But all I see elsewhere is nothing compared with what is here. " Herein is Love." Love, free, and unbounded, and unquenchable.

Brothers, is this One God our God ? Have we no idols ? Is there nothing greater in our hearts than He, nothing that engrosses more of our sympathies, and engages more of our thoughts and powers ? Let us look well to this. Away with all idols of the heart ! Let Him be the All-in-All of our souls. " For of Him, and through Him, and to Him are all things."

Man's Cry for Fellowship With God
No. 11   John 14:8

Shew us the Father, and it sufficeth us."

(For Exegetical Remarks, see Vol. II. p. 12.)

An accurate and full Delineation of the Fitness of the Gospel to the Spiritual Constitution of Man, would supply an evidence in favour of its Divinity, of a force unequalled in any existing theological literature. Several such Delineations have been attempted, with more or less ability, and, so far as they succeed, they furnish the best book-evidences we have. The congruity of the essential truths of the written Word, with the faculties and sentiments of the human soul, goes a great way towards the demonstration of the Divinity of that Word. Albeit, there is, I think, a more conclusive evidence even than this, which may be reached, and which the sceptical tendencies of the age seem to demand. It is that which will be found in the absolute necessity of the Gospel in order to appease all the profoundest *Cravings of the Human Heart*—cravings which exist in man under all dispensations, in all ages, climes, and stages of human development. I have long watched the more philosophic portion of the Religious Press, awaiting with earnestness the advent of such a production. It is an undoubted desideratum. The adaptation of the Gospel to the Spiritual faculties and sentiments of the soul, is unquestionably an evidence of considerable potency. But the *Necessity* of it to meet those deep and universal *longings* of the heart, which work the mental faculties and sway the emotions, yields an argument whose force is unequalled and well-nigh resistless. The adaptation of a system to humanity is one thing, the *necessity* of it is another. There may be adaptation where there is not Divinity; but where there is a *necessity* to men's spiritual life, a question of its Divinity is scarcely admissible.

It is to an attempt at the development of this Necessity that I shall now give myself.* Though painfully conscious of my

* This is one of a series of Homilies that appeared in the "*Homilist*," Vols. xiii. and xiv.

insufficiency for the task, my impression of the *need* emboldens me in the effort. Urgency justifies acts of daring, which in other circumstances might be fairly regarded as culpably presumptuous. If I can approximate, in any measure, even to my own ideal of the work required, I may effect something in placing the Divinity of the Gospel, amongst the irresistible evidences of human consciousness.

That there are certain Cravings in Man's Spiritual Nature, wide as the race, deep as the deepest springs of being, and restless as the sea, will become undebateably obvious as we advance in our path of inquiry. The first of these to which I shall call attention is that expressed here by Philip, the disciple of Christ. It is a craving after Fellowship with God; a quenchless thirst for Communion with the Living One. The questions for solution are not those of the *Speculative Intellect*, but of the deep and ever-anxious heart of the world. Of course, the Being of God is implied in this longing—underlies it, is the spring of it. The Being of a God requires no logical proof; it is written in legible and imperishable characters in the constitution of the human soul. "I deny," says *Cousin*, the great French philosopher, "that there are people who have no idea of God." So do I. It is true that the judgments of men differ widely, and have ever differed, as to who the true God is. They figure Him in different images, they ascribe to Him different attributes, and they call Him by different names. But their belief in Him is accordant, and their craving for fellowship with Him is the same the world over and the ages through. The soul-attitude of the race is that of a suppliant. Man is constitutionally prayerful. The heart of the world is on its knees; its face is upturned to the heavens, and its cry is—"Oh, that I knew where I might find Him!" Men, everywhere and for ever, feel after Him, if "haply" they may find Him. The philosophy of all the divinities, temples, and priesthoods of ancient and modern heathendom, is found in this deep longing of the soul for Fellowship with God.

"Humanity," says Edmund de Pressensée, in his 'Religions before Christ,' "taken as a whole, has never erred in its mode of propounding the religious problem. It has ever held religion to be not a mere communication of ideas concerning the Divinity, but a solemn effort to reunite the broken bond between heaven and earth; to establish an effectual union between man and God. The religions of the Ancient World all had presentiments of this union, and strove to realize it. In the East it manifested itself under the form of frequent incarnations; in the West, in the apotheoses. In the East, it is the Divinity that stoops to man; in the West, humanity rises to the Divinity; but neither in India nor in Greece was the real union between man and God effected. In

India incarnation was but illusory, and was, to borrow the expression of *Pouramus*, 'but a kind of mask with which the friendly Divinity invested himself, like an actor who puts on a costume to perform a part.' If we consider attentively, we shall find that those repeated incarnations were striking proofs of the contempt which this pantheistic and ascetic religion, professed for the human individual, which was, in its eyes, but an evanescent form of an absolute being. Brahma of Vishnu alone possesses real existence. The worshippers seek to become merged in them, and to utterly annihilate the human element. In Greece it is the Divine element which is compromised. Humanity in its natural state is declared to be Divine, if adored in its grandeur; it is so likewise in its passions and in its weaknesses. The Olympian god is but a hero placed beside an altar. Thus we see that the religious problem is far from being solved. Efforts were made to simplify it by reducing all to a factitious unit, alternating, ignoring either the Divine or the human side. In India, we find all is one vast divinity, devouring the universe which it creates and destroys at the same time. In Greece we find nothing but one presumptuous humanity, trying to cheat, by adoration of itself, its own infinite wants; and hiding its shortcomings under the graceful veil of Polytheism. Nevertheless, and in spite of these radical imperfections, the aim and endeavour of those religions of the East and the West, even under their grossest myths, was the union of Divinity with humanity."

Now is there anything suited to satisfy this Craving? Or is the longing something—unlike any other creature-desire of which we have any knowledge—left to gnaw the heart and burn the soul without any provision whatever? We can only determine this question, by ascertaining what *kind* of provisions are equal to the demand. I think that the Provisions must involve a threefold Manifestation of God—a *Personal*, a *Benevolent*, and a *Propitiable*.

I —THE PROVISION TO SATISFY THIS LONGING MUST INVOLVE A PERSONAL MANIFESTATION OF GOD TO THE SOUL

It is not for some *thing*, though grand and beautiful as the magnificent universe itself, that the soul cries after. It is for a *Person*—for an existence endowed with the personal attributes of Knowledge, Love, Will, Reciprocity. Pantheism may gratify the instinct of the speculative or the sentiment of the poetic; but it meets not this profoundest craving of our nature. It may seem very intellectual and poetic to talk of God as the great Ocean, of which all other existences are but billows, rising out of it and breaking into its abysses again; as the One Life of which the universe is the ever-changing branch and leaf; as the One Underlying Substance, of which all else is but everchanging vesture. But all this is no more suited to meet the deep cravings of the soul, than the strains of the musician the wants of a hungry man. The soul wants a Personal God; One to Whom it can speak, in Whom it can confide, and Who will reciprocate the deepest sentiments of its nature.

II —THE PROVISION TO SATISFY THIS LONGING, MUST, MOREOVER, INVOLVE A BENEVOLENT MANIFESTATION OF GOD TO THE SOUL

The soul will never cry for Fellowship with a being of mere Almighty Force, or of mere All-knowing Intellect; a being without emotions—passionless and heartless. Still less will it crave for fellowship with a *Malevolent* being, one who finds his pleasure in the misery of his creatures. From such an one it would recoil with loathing and with horror. For an *Unemotional* God it has no affinity; for a *Malevolent* one it has a dread. It craves for One kind and loving, One on Whom it can put its supreme affection, and place its undoubted trust. Its cry is for "*the Father.*" "*Show us the Father.*" Nothing else will do.

III —THE PROVISION TO SATISFY THIS LONGING MUST INVOLVE, STILL FURTHER, A PROPITIABLE MANIFESTATION OF GOD TO THE SOUL

A sense of sin presses heavily on the race. Even the savage feels that he has offended the Great Spirit, and he is anxious to propitiate Him. "O wretched man that I am!" is the moral groan of all. The sacrifices, pilgrimages, self-inflicted tortures, priesthoods—all express the deep feeling which the world has—that it has offended its Maker. Now a Propitiable Manifestation it must have, in order to satisfy its longing. Mere benevolence will not do. He may be benevolent and yet not propitiable; nay, benevolence in some cases may demand implacability. Would the soul cry for fellowship with an unappeasable deity? It is not possible.

Now, if such a threefold Manifestation of God is *necessary*, to satisfy this deep spiritual craving of humanity, the question is, Does the Gospel furnish such a Manifestation? It would be easy to show that man, by the light of nature, has failed to discover such Manifestations of the Deity. Poor human reason, through the thick mists of depraved passions and moral remorse, has scarcely seen any Personal Deity, save one that is malevolent and unappeasably wrathful. Nay, it has seen not one Divinity, but many, and these Divinities amongst the most vile and contemptible of objects. But my point is, not whether nature supplies the provision, but does the Gospel do so? If so, then it meets the Supreme *Necessity* of human nature.

Does it give a *Personal* God? Take a specimen of its revelations on the point. "I am the first, and I am the last; and beside Me there is no God" (Isa. xliv. 5). Again: "I am the Lord; and there is none else" (Isa. xlv. 18); "I, even I, am He, and there is no God with Me" (Deut. xxxii. 39). Again: "Of Him and through Him, and to Him, are all things: to Whom be glory for ever. Amen" (Romans xi. 36). "I Am that I Am. This is My name for ever, and this is My memorial unto all generations" (Exod. iii. 14, 15). But it is not in mere *language* that His Personality is announced, it is in a *living history*—the history of Christ. "Great is the mystery of godliness; God was manifest in the flesh, justified in the Spirit, seen of angels, preached unto the Gentiles, believed on in the world, received up into glory" (1 Tim. iii. 16). Christ is the "brightness of His Glory, and the express image of His Person" (Heb. i. 3). The God of the Gospel is a Personal God.

Does it give a *Benevolent* God? Take again a specimen of its revelations on this point. "The Lord is good to all: and His tender mercies are over all His works" (Psalm cxlv. 9). "Like as a father pitieth his children, so the Lord pitieth them that fear Him" (Psalm ciii. 13). "The eyes of all wait upon Thee; and Thou givest them their meat in due season. Thou openest Thine hand, and satisfiest the desire of every living thing" (Psalm cxlv. 15—16). "Who in times past suffered all nations to walk in their own ways. Nevertheless He left not Himself without witness, in that He did good, and gave us rain from heaven, and fruitful seasons, filling our hearts with food and gladness" (Acts xiv. 16, 17). Again: GOD IS LOVE.

Does it give a *Propitiable* God? Here is the revelation: "And the Lord descended in the cloud, and proclaimed the name of the Lord. . . . The Lord, the Lord God merciful and gracious, longsuffering, and abundant in goodness and truth, keeping mercy for thousands, forgiving iniquity and transgression and sin" (Exodus xxxiv. 5—7). Again: "Thus saith the high and lofty One that inhabiteth eternity, whose name is Holy; I dwell in the high and holy place, with him also that is of a contrite and humble spirit, to revive the spirit of the humble, and to revive the heart of the contrite ones" (Isaiah lvii. 15). And again: "Let the wicked forsake his way, and the unrighteous man his thoughts: and let him return unto the Lord, and He will have mercy upon him; and to our God, for He will abundantly pardon. For My thoughts are not your thoughts, neither are your ways My ways, saith the Lord. For as the heavens are higher than the earth, so are My ways higher than your ways, and My thoughts than your thoughts" (Isaiah lv. 7—9). Again: "God so loved the world, that He gave His only begotten Son, that whosoever believeth in Him should not perish, but have everlasting life" (chap iii. 16).

Such, then, is the God of the Gospel, the very God after Whom the soul of humanity has been ever craving. " Oh that I knew where I might find Him ! " To the millions who utter this question, I hold up the Gospel and say, " Here He is." The very God you seek is here. *" Shew us the Father, and it sufficeth us."* O ! ye wandering prodigals from your Father's house, here is the very Father Whom ye seek, overflowing with love, and Almighty to help you. In this blessed Book you have a solution of the profoundest questions of your nature—a solution which the Zoroasters, the Confuciuses, and the Platos sought, in vain. The Bible meets the deepest longings, and matches the loftiest aspirations of the soul. All who have ever rightly sought for God here, have exclaimed with rapture, "This is our God ; we have waited for Him."

The Miraculous and the Moral
No. 12   John 14:12

" Verily, verily, I say unto you, He that believeth on Me, the works that I
do shall he do also ; and greater works than these shall he do ; because
I go unto My Father."

(For Exegetical Remarks, see Vol. II. page 16.)

THE question which meets us at the outset is—What is the
comparison herein implied ?—What are the " *greater works* ? "
The comparison, I think, must be either between the *miraculous*
works of Christ and the miraculous works of the apostles ; or
between the *moral* works of Christ and the moral works of the
apostles ; or between miraculous works in themselves, and moral
works in themselves. Which of these is the most probable ? This
is the question which we have now to settle. Is it the First ?
Does the Heavenly Teacher mean to say that if they, His disciples,
believed on Him, they should perform " *greater*" miraculous works
than they had seen Him perform ? The history of the case
precludes this supposition. If you compare the miracles wrought
by Christ with those effected by His apostles, you will find that
their miraculous achievements were neither so great in their
nature nor in number as those ascribed to the Son of God.
We are told, in hyperbolical language it is true, that if all the
deeds He wrought were written, "The world itself could not
contain the books that should be written." Is it the Second ?
Is the comparison between the moral works wrought by Christ
—works to enlighten the human mind, purify the human sympathies, and emancipate the human will—and the moral works
wrought by the apostles ? Does the Divine Teacher mean to say
that the apostles would excel Him in this the highest department of action ;—that their works of this class would be " *greater* "
than His ? I think not.

I am aware that there is a popular impression that the Spiritual
Usefulness of Christ was very limited as compared with that of
His apostles ; that His ministry of Truth was ineffective as

compared with theirs. I cannot admit this. When I think of the truths which Christ propounded in His ministry,—truths so fresh and powerful, so adapted to meet man at every point of his nature, and quicken his faculties into the higher life ; when I think of His method of proclaiming those truths, so natural, so reasonable, so conversational, so earnest, and so devout; when I remember His indefatigable diligence in His work, and call to memory the fact that there was perhaps scarcely an adult in Judæa on whose ear His blessed voice did not fall, pregnant with those soul-quickening truths ; I cannot believe that either of the apostles, or all combined, did anything like the amount of real *Spiritual* work as that which He Himself accomplished. His voice roused the mind of Judæa from the religious slumber of ages. When He came to this earth, there was little or no religious thinking throughout the whole of Judæa. The Hebrew mind was like a stagnant lake; it had no throb of Spiritual energy in it; there was not a ripple of independent thought upon its surface. Christ's doctrines, like the winds of heaven, lashed that lake into a tempest, and its billows of fresh thought surge through the world to this hour. Or, to change the figure, when He came the great engine of independent thought in connection with religion had been all but motionless for centuries. He touched its springs, and set it a-going ; and its revolutions have been proceeding in an accelerating ratio from that hour to this, and will thus proceed, I trust, under God, until the complete regeneration of our fallen world is realized.

If, then, the comparison is neither between the Miraculous works of *Christ* and those of His *apostles*, nor between the Moral works of *Christ* and those of His *apostles*, we are shut up to the alternative, that the comparison is between *Miraculous* works in themselves and *Moral* works in themselves. It must be borne in mind that the personal history of Christ on earth seemed to be marked more by the *Miraculous than the Moral;* more by the wonderful signs He wrought in such abundance, than by the doctrines He taught. On the other hand, the history of His disciples is distinguished more by the strange facts they propounded, and the sublime doctrines they taught, than by the material miracles they achieved. The meaning of Christ in all probability (I say no more), might be this: " You are struck with My miraculous works as great; but if you believe in Me you shall perform *moral* works—and moral works are the greater. Moral works—works connected with the spiritual regeneration of mankind—are greater than miraculous works; and these moral works you shall perform if you believe on Me." Supposing this to be the idea, the subject I take for discussion as suggested by these words is, *The Work of Moral Reformation*. Observe—

I —THAT THE WORK OF MORAL REFORMATION IS A "GREATER" WORK THAN THAT OF A MIRACLE

It is implied that to perform a miracle is a *great* work. I do not say that a miracle is a Supernatural event. As Nature itself transcends all human thoughts, it is absurd for us to talk of the supernatural! But whatever definition you give of a miracle —call it a suspension of the laws of nature, or a deviation from the laws of nature, or an infraction of the laws of nature, or the development of an old unknown Law of nature, it matters not. All men *feel* that no being but the Author of Nature Himself, can effect that which they unanimously *consider* miraculous. I do not say that philosophy or logic would conduct the mind to the conclusion, that the Maker of the universe alone could accomplish that which we consider miraculous. All I say is, that men instinctively *feel* this to be the case. The strange in nature, in all lands and times, starts as by a resistless impulse in all minds, both civilized and savage, the belief that God Himself is at work. Account for it how you will, Miracle and Divinity seem indissolubly associated in the instinctive feelings of humanity. It is this *intuitive feeling* that always reaches the highest truths—that grasps those verities that lie high up in those regions of Divine light to which the wing of philosophy has never mounted. To perform a miracle, therefore, is a great work; but great as it is, to *convert a soul* is "*greater.*" Why is this?

First: The Morally Reforming Power works on a Higher Nature. Matter is the theatre of what we consider to be Miraculous Agency. We see it nowhere but outside of us; out on the scenes of Material nature. We see its force arresting the orbs of heaven and mantling all in gloom; heaving the mountains from their foundations, and turning the flinty rocks into refreshing streams; hushing the raging sea and the stormy atmosphere into peace; healing the diseases of suffering humanity; unlocking the flinty graves, and bringing the dead to life again. Such works as these, we have seen miraculous agency accomplish, and they are all in the *Material* realm. But in *Conversion* the work is in a higher sphere—the Spiritual. What is matter to Spirit? What is a dead instrument to a free and living agent? What are a decaying form and a passing shadow to an enduring essence and a deathless reality? "Heap worlds on worlds, one soul outweighs them all."

Secondly: The Morally Reforming Power achieves a Higher Good. (1.) It is a good *Unmixed*. Miracles, whilst they have been in many instances useful in meeting the wants and alleviating the distresses of humanity, have in other instances been very disastrous. They were what are called miracles that destroyed the old world, engulphed Pharaoh and his host, burnt to ashes the cities of the plain, swept from the field on one night the mighty army of Sennacherib. But in Conversion there is nothing disastrous; it is good, and good only. Nothing is destroyed but error, and wrong, and misery, that which tends to destroy the freedom, the force, the purity, the grandeur, and the blessedness of the undying spirit. (2.) It is a good in *Itself*. Miracles, even when they were free from everything disastrous, and served the physical interests of men, were only really good as they served to promote the cause of truth and virtue. Though a miracle raise a dead man to life, what avails that new life to him if he spend it in depravity? But conversion is a good in itself. The growth, development, and perfection of Divine knowledge, and true holiness in God's spiritual offspring, constitute the highest end of the creation. The Great One Himself works to make human spirits "meet for the inheritance of the saints in light." (3.) It is a good *Ever-Enduring*. The men who were benefited by miracles did not *permanently* enjoy the good conferred. Those who were fed grew hungry again; those who were healed sank again under infirmities; those who were raised to life, died again. Not so with a Spirit that is thoroughly renewed. The old disease will never crush it again; spiritual death will never seize it any more. When Christ raised Lazarus from the dead, that new life was only temporary. Lazarus would have to descend to his grave again. But when in Conversion a corrupt soul is thoroughly quickened into the Divine life, that soul will not die again; the man thus quickened may reverentially adopt the words of Christ and say: "I am He that liveth and was dead, and behold I am alive for evermore." (4.) It is a good *Ever Extending in its Influence*. The good conferred by a miracle is limited to the particular sphere in which it is wrought. Thus the manna that descended from heaven, and the water that gushed from the rock, continued only forty years, and were confined to Arabia. Others who lived beyond those districts, or in later times, might have required the heavenly bread and the refreshing streams, yet they had them not. But there is no limit to the salutary influence that springs from the conversion of even one soul. Such an event originates a series of thoughts, sympathies, and actions, that can never be circumscribed by place, nor bounded by time. In every true conversion to God, there is a new fountain of Divine influence opened up in the soul, whose streams extend from district to district in ever-widening circles, until they encompass the globe, and roll down from age to age, until perchance they touch with life the heart of the last man. It achieves, then, a higher good, inasmuch as the good is *unmixed*; is in *itself* a good; a good *ever-enduring* and *ever-widening* in its influence.

Thirdly: The morally Reforming Power requires a Higher

Energy. All the power necessary to perform a miracle is a Divine volition. It is the mere fiat; God has only to will that a certain effect shall be produced in material Nature, and forthwith it is. Not so in Conversion. As a fact His mere volition does not accomplish it, and we see not how of itself it could do so. Take an illustration. I see Christ sailing in a little skiff with His disciples on the Galilean lake; a terrific storm comes suddenly on, and the waters are lashed into fury. The frail bark seems doomed to sink: the disciples, panic-struck, cry to their Master, Who, exhausted with the toils of the day, is asleep in a corner of the vessel. He hears them, ascends the deck, looks serenely out on tempestuous nature, and says, "Peace, be still." The winds and waves obey Him, and there is "a great calm." This same Jesus I see a short time afterwards standing on the Mount of Olives, and looking upon the doomed metropolis of His country, with a soul overflowing with compassion, and tears rolling down His blessed cheeks, exclaiming, "Oh Jerusalem, Jerusalem, that killest the prophets, and stonest them that are sent unto thee, how often *would* I have gathered thee, as a hen gathers her chickens under her wings; but *ye* would not!" Mark, Christ *willed* that the storm which swept over the Galilean lake should subside; *because He willed* it, the storm passed away. Christ willed that the population of Jerusalem should go to Him as their Saviour; that population remained in depravity and sank into ruin. Now why was this? Why did that Will, which took immediate effect upon tempestuous nature prove powerless upon the depraved people of Jerusalem? It was not, of course, that there was more earnestness thrown into the *will* in the former case than in the latter. The reverse is obviously the fact. His whole being seemed to have been imported into that Will which He expressed over doomed Jerusalem. The fact is, there are two things connected with the human soul, that are not found in material nature, and that require something more than Divine volition to influence.

(1.) *The Existence of a Moral Element.* There is a power in humanity enabling it to resist outward appeals—enabling it to say yes or no to the wishes or behests of another. I care not what you call this power. If you dislike the expression, Free Agency, be it so. Give it what name you please, I challenge you to deny its existence. You see it everywhere at work in society. You feel it in your own experience—you are conscious of it as one of the chief elements of your existence. No argument can destroy the consciousness which I have that I am free. This fact links us to Moral Government; this fact makes us men: this fact invests human nature with an importance, before which we may well stand in reverent awe. I look upon a child of five or six years old; and because I see that he has this power, I feel that he is greater than any object in the material universe. Neither the rolling ocean nor the revolving planets have this power. If God of old really commanded the sun to stand still in Gideon, and the moon on Ajalon, neither the royal orb of the day nor the majestic queen of the night had the power to say " No." They were bound to pause in their career, by a force over which they had no control. But when God says to a little child, " Love Me with all thy heart, soul, and strength," that child can say, " No, God." It does so frequently. In connection with this moral element there is—

(2.) *The Existence of a Depraved Element.* Human nature has not only the power to say " *No* " to its Maker, but somehow or other it has the *disposition* to do so. The possession of the power is a blessing, but neither a virtue nor a vice. The disposition to employ this power in opposition to God, is the sin and ruin of humanity. Angels have the power to say " No." This makes them free, and makes their actions virtuous. But they have not the disposition; their whole nature goes with the Infinitely Good.

In consequence of these two elements, something more than a mere Divine volition is necessary to rectify and regulate the springs of moral action. In connection with the volition there must be Means — there must be Argument, Suasion, Heart, Example. When God performs a miracle in outward nature He has only to show, as it were, His finger. When He had to spiritually reform a world He had to bow the heavens and come down and show Himself; He had to bring His own great thoughts and loving sympathies into close and vital contact with the depraved heart of the world. "The Word was made flesh, and dwelt amongst us." It is this moral power—not the miraculous—that is to convert souls.

This fact requires to be brought boldly out and impressed upon the public mind, in order to dissipate fatal misconceptions as to the Divine Influence. I remember some years ago being invited to spend an evening in the house of a sceptic, who was at that time intellectually interested in my ministry. In our conversation the greatest objections that he brought forward to the Bible he stated somewhat thus: "You say that the Bible reveals the fact that God is willing to save humanity?" My reply was: "Yes: as I interpret the Holy Word it seems to me to have but one voice, 'As I live, saith the Lord God, I have no pleasure in the death of a sinner.'" "Well, then," he said, "how is it that the world is not saved? According to the theology of the sects, generations after generations come and go, and are not saved; the millions in every passing age drop into hell. He, the Great One, has the Will to save all—why does He not do so? All that is required on the part of an agent to accomplish a work is the *disposition* and the *power*. Give me the disposition to do a work, and an adequate amount of executive energy, and forthwith the thing is done. If there be a God, nature shows that that God is all-powerful—has sufficient power to do whatever He wills. He Who piled up the mountains, spread out the heavens, and poured out the sea, has certainly the power to save whomsoever He wills." "My friend," said I, "your reasoning is plausible, but fallacious, and the root of your fallacy is in your misconception of the *power* required to convert souls." There was a little boy in the room, and I illustrated my meaning by saying, "Suppose I *will* that that little boy leave the room. There are two ways in which I could give effect to that will. I could take him in my arms, and by superior muscular power remove him: or I could take him on my knee, speak lovingly and persuasively to him, in order to induce him to leave the room himself. If I adopted the former I should merely have removed his body; his volitions would be all against me, and he would feel I had done him violence. If I succeeded in the latter I should have influenced his mind, and he himself would use his own little limbs, and with a happy smile depart."

There are, then, obviously, two kinds of power—what is called the Miraculous, and the Moral; and the latter is that by which God converts souls. I find in the New Testament God has employed as much of this Moral Power as it is possible for me to imagine. The elements of moral power are *Truth, Rectitude,* and *Love.* The more of these together, the more power. These, stated in the form of propositions, are powerful; these embodied in living examples are more powerful. These, in the example of a child, are powerful; in the example of a man more powerful; in the example of a God are Moral Omnipotence. In this last form the Gospel gives them to me. In Christ these elements of power exist in their highest degree, and come out in their mightiest forms. Christ is not only the Wisdom of God, but the "Power of God." If a man in his deep dark cave of depravity is to be reached, and brought out into the light of holiness, it is not by the great and strong wind that may rend the mountains and break in pieces the rocks about him; nor by the yawning earthquake, nor the raging fires; for there is no way by which coercion can travel into the moral hiding-places of a man's soul. It is the "still small voice" of Truth, Rectitude, and Grace breathed forth by the life of Christ that will reach him, stir his energies, and lead him out to light and duty again. The words teach—

II —THAT FAITH IN CHRIST WILL QUALIFY ANY MAN TO PERFORM THIS "GREATER" WORK

"*He that believeth on Me.*" What is it to believe on Christ? Men of different theological schools will of course return different answers to this question. It is foreign to my purpose to discuss it controversially. It admits of but one true answer, but that answer may be presented in a variety of forms: and I shall therefore give it in the form that will best serve the purpose of my argument. The faith in Christ that qualifies a man to effect this, the greatest of all works, includes at least three things.

First: Faith in Him as the Atonement. What is called the "doctrine of the atonement" has been, of all theological subjects, the most fertile in polemics. It has been a fierce battle-ground for creed-makers and creed-defenders. In no physical campaign have more fiendish passions been displayed. Volumes on the subject have been written; not one satisfactory either to the intellect or heart. The last, perhaps, the least satisfactory of all. The fact is, the Atonement is not a Doctrine at all, it is a Life— *the* Life of Christ. He, not the mere facts of His history, or the truths of His teaching, but He Himself is the Atonement, the Reconciler; He atones not God to man, but man to God.

The Infinite Father is in Him, "reconciling the world unto Himself." By Him we receive the καταλλαγὴν, the thorough moral change of heart in relation to God. He does not appease Divine wrath; He demonstrates and communicates Divine love. He does not expiate human sins; He "puts away sins" by the sacrifice of Himself. The law He satisfies, is not something outside of Himself, but the law of His own Self-Sacrificing Love. He effects no change in the mind of God towards man; such a change, if possible, would be supremely undesirable. The change He effects is a change in the human mind. In this view how absurd the questions of our technical theologues! In what part of Christ's history is the atoning element to be found? Did He die for all, or for some? *He is the Atonement*, and the Atonement for *all*. "He loved us, and gave Himself for us." Another thing included in this faith is—

Secondly: Faith in Him as the Moral Commander. There are those who regard Christ rather as a Victim than a Victor. They wail and weep over His mysterious sufferings in Gethsemane, and His poignant agonies on the cross. The "bleeding Lamb" is the theme of their thoughts and the burden of their songs. This is the murky atmosphere in which their spirits live. *Goethe* somewhere represents what are called Evangelical preachers, as trading in the agonies of Christ, as spreading out those mysterious sufferings of Christ, from which the great sun hid his face. The other view of Christ, methinks, is the most Scriptural, ennobling, and God-honouring,—as the Triumphant Victor, the Captain of Salvation. We are told that as He was bearing His cross on His lacerated shoulders up the brow of Calvary, crowds of women, as they witnessed His agonies, broke into tears, and poured their wailings into His ears. How did He treat those tender-hearted women? Was He pleased with their compassionate wailings? Did He utter a word of commendation to them on account of the sympathy they expressed? No; on the contrary, He said, "Weep not for Me, but weep for yourselves, and for your children." As if He had said: "You misunderstand Me: I am not here by necessity, but by choice. I am not a Victim in the hands of Necessity. I am a Captain in the battle against sin; if you knew My mission, you would commend rather than compassionate: 'I have power to lay down My life, and power to take it up again.'" Another thing included in this faith is—

Thirdly: Faith in Him as the Efficient Restorer. The soul of mankind although made for freedom is a slave. It is enslaved by passions, by prejudices, by habits, by worldliness, and legions of other inner tyrants. There is One Being in the universe—and only One—Who can break its prison-doors, snap its chains, and bring it into the true liberty of the "sons of God." Christ is a Moral Necessity. Had there been only one man to have been saved, there must have been Christ; and what one man required will meet the wants of all. Had the Almighty Maker intended only one man to have lived on this earth, that one man must have had the glowing light of heaven, the rolling atmosphere, the refreshing waters, and all the gases that work on this planet now. What that one man would have required to make his existence even tolerable, has done for millions that are gone, and will do for millions more, when this generation shall be sleeping under ground. So it seems to me with Christ. Had our merciful Maker intended only to have saved one man, that one man must have had the Hero of Calvary. What has done for the innumerable multitudes now in heaven, will do for the countless millions who are yet to come.

Now it is this *Faith* in Christ, as the Atonement, as the Moral Commander of souls, and as the only Efficient Restorer of mankind, that qualifies a man to do these "*greater works.*" Practical trust in Him in these respects will equip me for this, the sublimest of missions. It will give me a kind of moral omnipotence; make me mighty through God, to the accomplishment of these "*greater works.*" I ascribe all the great achievements of the most distinguished labourers in the interest of souls, of whom we read in history, to simple but earnest faith in these verities. I see the apostles meeting together towards the evening of their active life, and in the language of devout congratulation, saying, "Thanks be unto God, which always causeth us to triumph in Christ, and maketh manifest the savour of His knowledge by us in every place." Their brilliant victories I ascribe to this Faith. I see

302 / Gospel of John

Luther, rising up a lonely man before a frowning hierarchy; he speaks, and his words fall like a flaming thunder-bolt upon the heart of the papal system, inflicting a wound that never has been healed, and never will. I refer his renowned achievements to his Faith. I see Whitfield leaving the University at Oxford, going through the length and breadth of the United Kingdom, crossing the Atlantic, standing up in every place he visited, and addressing thousands of men with a power that was well-nigh overwhelming, and with results that will gladden the ages. I ascribe his matchless conquests, not to his genius, his logic, his learning, or his eloquence, but to his Faith in Christ. Yes, this is it: "He that believeth in Me,"—not in what men say about Me, not in Church theories concerning Me, but in Me, the living, loving Son of God, and the Saviour of the world,—shall do these the "*greater works.*"

Truly wondrous is the difference of the influence of faith in Propositions to Faith in a Person. Faith in Propositions divides men; faith in a Personality unites them. Faith in propositions can never make men heroes; faith in a Grand Personality has and does. The millions who believed in Garibaldi became heroes through their faith. It is said that on one occasion, Garibaldi called for forty volunteers for an operation, in which half of them were certain to be killed, and the other half mortally wounded. The whole battalion rushed forward to offer themselves, and he had to draw lots. On one occasion at Rome, Garibaldi called all well-disposed men to follow him, and it is said that officers and soldiers sprang up as if the ground had brought them forth. On another occasion, at the close of the siege of Rome, when the surrender was voted by the Assembly, he had made up his mind to depart, and he put forth this order: "Whoever chooses to follow me, will be received among my own men. All I ask of them is a heart full of love for our country. They will have no pay and no rest. They will get bread and water when chance may supply them. Whoever likes not this may remain behind. Once out of the gates of Rome, every step will be one nearer to death." *Four thousand infantry and five hundred horsemen* accepted immediately his terms. Faith in Garibaldi made heroes of thousands. Christ, in wisdom, justice, benevolence, moral nobility, is infinitely greater than Garibaldi. Why are the millions who call themselves Christians, weak, morbid, craven, almost entirely destitute of the heroic element? Because the Faith which they have is in human propositions *concerning* Christ: not in *Him.* Because their Faith is in a dying Victim rather than in an All-Conquering Hero.

The words teach that—

III —THE ASCENSION OF CHRIST TO HEAVEN IS A GUARANTEE OF
SUCCESS IN THE PROSECUTION OF THIS "GREATER" WORK

"*Because I go to My Father.*" "It is expedient that I go away.
If I go not away the Comforter will not come;" and when He is
come, He will "convince the world of sin, of righteousness, and judgment." In heaven He has the power of sending forth His Spirit
to renew the souls of men. His disciples were not equipped for
their work until He ascended into heaven. He commanded them
to tarry in Jerusalem until He should send them "power from on
high." On the day of Pentecost He dispensed that power, and
"suddenly there came a sound from heaven, as of a rushing mighty
wind." Christ in Heaven, then, is a Guarantee of success in the
earnest prosecution of this work. Without the Spirit all human
labours would be utterly useless.

CONCLUSION. Brother, realize the sublime grandeur of thy
work ! There is no work in dignity equal to that of endeavouring
to convert a soul. Yet worldly men see no glory in it. On a
calm Sabbath morning there stood in the street of one of our
country towns two men engaged in conversation. As they talked
a young female passed by with a New Testament in her hand.
"Who is that ?" said one to the other. "She is only a Teacher
in the Sunday School," was the reply. Only a Teacher in the
Sunday School! Who art thou, proud mortal? Mayor, statesman, hero,—I care not who thou art. I tell thee that the young
woman who, on the holy day of God, gathers around her a few
little children, and seeks to inbreathe into their young natures
the living, loving thoughts of Jesus of Nazareth, does a more
glorious work for the universe, than any magistrate as magistrate,
statesman as statesman, hero as hero ever achieved. Those
thoughts shall live and spread and work beneficently in the realm
of spirits, long after the most enduring thrones have crumbled
into dust, and the most illustrious of earth's magnates have been
blotted from the roll of memory. Tell me of a "*greater*" work,
my brother ! You say Moses performed a great work when with
his mystic rod he smote the rock of Horeb, and caused it to
send forth living streams to refresh the Israelites for forty long
years. But with that old Gospel you can perform a "*greater*"
work than that. With this moral rod you can break the rocky
heart of humanity, and cause it to send forth vivifying sympathies
and life-giving thoughts that shall roll down the ages with a soul-
renewing power. You say that Elijah did a great work, when
on Carmel's lofty brow he confounded the idolators of his day,
by bringing from heaven a Divine fire to consume his sacrifice.
You can do a "*greater*" work than that. With this old Gospel
you can kindle a fire in the hearts of men, that shall burn up

their depravity, consume their lusts, and transmute their nature into the image of their Maker. You say that Christ did a great work when on the Galilean Sea He hushed the furious storm. I would not say a word to depreciate any work wrought by the Son of God; still I say that you can do a "*greater*" work than that. With this old Gospel thou canst hush more fierce and furious storms. Thou canst go to the poor widow whose spirit is tossed with grief, and say to her, "Sorrow not as those without hope; if you believe that Jesus died and rose again, even so them also, which sleep in Jesus, will God bring with Him." And under Heaven's gracious influence she will have peace. Thou canst go to the young man whose spirit is being borne hell-ward by the furious tempests of polluted passions, and thou canst say to him, "Acquaint now thyself with God, and be at peace, and thereby good shall come unto thee :" and by God's grace he will have peace. Or thou canst go to the poor sin-convicted one beaten by the tempest of a guilty conscience and say, "Believe on the Lord Jesus Christ, and thou shalt be saved," and he shall find "joy and peace in believing."

There is no work in the universe greater than that of enlightening, quickening, enfranchising, and raising to the ever-heightening blessedness and ever-advancing honours of Immortality, souls that are sin-benighted, enslaved, degraded, and lost.

Gifts of the Spirit and Son Compared
No. 13   John 3:16, 14:17, 1 John 4:13

" He will give you . . . the Spirit."
" He hath given us of His Spirit."
" He gave His only begotten Son."

(For Exegetical Remarks, see Vol. I. p. 66, also Vol. II. p. 17.)

THESE passages present to our mind *God's Greatest Gifts* to mankind. My object in bringing them together is to show, that *There is as much Divine Love displayed in the gift of the Spirit, as there is in the gift of the Son.*

This is a point we are probably prone to overlook. We often think and speak of God's Love in the gift of His Son, and never can we be too much impressed with it. But His Love in the gift of His Spirit does not so frequently engage our attention, nor, it is to be feared, so deeply impress our hearts. I shall endeavour to illustrate the subject by four remarks—

I —THE "SPIRIT" IS AS INTRINSICALLY GREAT AS THE "SON"

The Son is great—transcendently great. " In Him dwelleth all the fulness of the Godhead bodily." But the Spirit is *equally* great. The same attributes are ascribed to Him, the same prerogatives belong to Him, and the same Divine words are ascribed to Him. They are in truth One in essence, but multiform in aspect. If you test, therefore, the extent of Love by the Greatness of the gift, you have as much in the one case as in the other.

II —THE "SPIRIT" IS AS ACTIVELY ENGAGED FOR THE BENEFIT OF THE WORLD AS THE "SON"

Christ was active when on earth for the world. He seems to have devoted every hour to the great work. " I must work the works of Him that sent Me." But had not the Spirit been active ? Did He not strive with the old world ? Did He not inspire the men who wrote this Book ? Has there ever been a Soul regenerated and saved without His Agency ? Has there ever been a conscience

that He has not touched ? In *every* solemn thought and expression
of every mind, is He not working ?

III —THE "SPIRIT" HAS BEEN AS WICKEDLY TREATED BY THE WORLD AS THE "SON"

The cruel treatment which the Son received is recorded in this
Book, and will be transmitted to all future ages as the most
humiliating and astounding exhibition of Human Depravity. But
the ill-treatment of the Spirit has been as wicked, and far more
extensive and *lasting.* The people of Judæa alone *personally* ill-
treated Christ; the population of the world "do always resist the
Spirit." About thirty-three years measured the period of our
Saviour's personal ill-treatment. The ill-treatment of the Spirit
extends over well-nigh twice that number of centuries.

IV -—THE "SPIRIT" IS AS NECESSARY FOR MANKIND AS THE "SON"

Two things are necessary to man's salvation : Deliverance from
the GUILT of sin, and from the POWER of sin. Christ was necessary
for the first, and the Holy Spirit for the second.

It is sometimes said, in opposition to the doctrine of the
Necessity of the Spirit's Agency, that a man wants nothing but
sufficient evidence, and the free use of his faculties, to believe.
This is readily admitted in relation to every other system of Truth.
But why should we make this an exception ? Do we find any
particular circumstances identified with it antagonistic to faith,
which are not found in connection with other departments of
truth ? If there are none, the exception is not allowable ; but if
there are such circumstances, then right reasoning justifies us in
taking it. Such circumstances exist.

First: There is Moral Habit. The habits which most persons
contract before the Gospel comes fairly under their attention, are
such as the whole tenor of its truths condemn. Their habits
become their ruling principles, and when assailed, they marshal
every power of the soul to their defence.

Secondly: There is Servile Fear. The man in business, who
feels that the current of events is hastening him to insolvency,
frequently develops a great reluctance to go into his accounts.
In all the world there is no book to him so fearful as the Ledger.
It is repulsive to him ; for too well he knows that it will confirm
what his foreboding heart suspects; and what he is afraid to look
in the face—afraid to believe. Nothing but sheer urgency will
ever induce that man to open that book, and to reveal its figured
page. Is there not something similar to this in man's soul, in
relation to the Bible? Often has his conscience whispered that
he is on the losing side—that he has contracted a fearful debt
—and has nothing to pay. He knows that the full assurance

of such a fact would confound him with terror—would fill him with anguish. He quiets his inward Monitor. His delusive peace he retains by persuading himself that the suggestion is not true. Meanwhile, the Bible is presented to him as a book from God. He is told that it will shed light upon the conjectures which have been harassing his brain, and reveal in light to him the whole truth about his state and condition. In such a case, I ask, how is the man likely to regard the document? Would he dread it as an enemy, or would he hail it as a friend? Is it not probable that a fear of being convinced of a truth, whose very suspicion has filled him often with pain, would cause him to shun the book which contained it, would prevent him from giving to it that examination, without which he could not ascertain its truths and therefore could not believe?

Thirdly: There is Social Influence. From the great law of sympathy man is ever influenced by others. The mass of Mankind have no faith in Christianity, and therefore the great bulk of human influence runs directly counter to a belief in the system.

Fourthly: There is Satanic Agency. "The God of this world blindeth the eyes of men." Now, it may be said, We grant that these Moral Habits—this latent Dread of Condemnation—this general current of Social Influence, and this Satanic Agency, are all opposed to faith in Christianity. But are they not found existing in connection with other departments of truth? I think not. Man's moral habits are not generally opposed to physical or mental Truth. Nor is Fear: he is not afraid to look any abstract principle in the face; the fields of general science and literature he can traverse with a buoyant heart and a fearless step. Nor is Social Influence; the more general intelligence he possesses the more respect would he command from society. And with regard to Satanic Agency, we argue that the more knowledge a man obtains, if his heart remains depraved, the more capacity for evil; and therefore the "prince of darkness" has no reason for checking the mere progress of the intellect. One may penetrate the earth's heart, bring up old worlds to life, and add a thousand centuries to our history. Another may walk the starry vaults, weigh the systems in his balance, and gauge them with his Euclidian lines. A third may enter into the Divine arcana of spirit, analyze its operations, and ascertain its laws. What motive could the master spirit of darkness have to check these noble intellects in their striving after knowledge? Does he not know right well, that such knowledge, whilst it has no power to destroy moral depravity, has, nevertheless, a capacity to make that depravity less offensive— to enrobe it in beauty, and to invest it with power? But the case is different in relation to Christianity. Belief in its truths emancipates the Spirit from his empire, and raises it into the "marvellous light" of holiness and God.

If, then, there are circumstances connected with Christianity repugnant to faith, which you find not associated with the general system of mere physical and mental truth, is it not fair to infer, that whilst, in general, all that a man requires to produce faith is clear testimony and a free intellect, yet that, in relation to Christianity, something else may be necessary? Yes; and unless it has some auxiliary, we may well despair of its ever effecting that moral reformation which it proposes, and which is the great demand of our fallen nature.

When I say that the Spirit is *Necessary*, I mean that He is necessary in a sense *apart from the Truth*. There is, indeed, a sense—a sense not sufficiently appreciated—in which the Spirit is in the Word. His all-living and life-giving inspirations are in the Document. Are there not fountains of quickening thought down "in the deep things of God;" never seen—never tasted yet? But it is something more than the *Book Spirit* that I mean—something that uses this as its instrument—the *Spirit Himself*. The human writer infuses his spirit into his book, and whatever influence his book produces upon the mind of the reader, may be called the influence of his spirit. This is sometimes taken to illustrate the doctrine of Divine influence; but very partial is this representation. So far as the mere influence of the Book-spirit is concerned, there is a parallelism,— but no further. Infinitely short is this, however, of the Bible-idea of God's agency. Let us not be deceived by analogies. God's Spirit is not only *in* the book, but *with* the book. The personal, conscious spirit of a human author goes not with his work. It may enter regions of which he is ignorant, fall into the hands of thousands of whom he knows nothing, and receive a million misinterpretations of which he is happily unconscious. Not so with the Author of the Gospel. He is everywhere. He pervades the soul of every man who takes it into his hand. And there is not a thought which it awakens with which He is not conversant. Am I to suppose that the Infinite Author, Who is thus ever-present with every reader of His Book, cognizant of every thought which it suggests, having at all times His finger upon every spring of the mind, does nothing to facilitate a right impression of His Word? Is He a mere spectator? Has He no interest in the processes and results of the thoughts which His own revelation originates? When the reader is striving after a correct idea of a passage, can He help? Or is He impotent? Will He? Or is He heartless? I confess that the very supposition that in such a case He exerts no personal agency, is repugnant to my instinctive notions of a God—to all my reasonings too. He paints the lily—He directs the sparrow in its flight—and, oh! Will He not help the struggling soul? The Great Parent, will He not solve the questions of His anxious child? Would any human author be thus present with the mind of his reader, having a power to help—help needed—help, perhaps, sought—and not help? "If ye, then, being evil, know how to give good gifts unto your children; how much more shall your Heavenly Father give the Holy Spirit to them that ask Him?"

Christ's Estimate of Death and Paul's
No. 14   John 16:7 Phil. 4:24

"It is expedient for you that I go away."

"Nevertheless to abide in the flesh is more needful for you."

(For Exegetical Remarks, see Vol. II. p. 49.)

BETWEEN Jesus and Paul, when each uttered the words before us, there was a remarkable correspondence.

First: Both were in the immediate Prospect of Death. The words of *Christ* were a part of that tender and consolatory address which He delivered to His disciples in the immediate prospect of dissolution. They were, no doubt, full of sadness at the thought of being separated from Him, Who had changed the whole current of their sympathies and thoughts, introduced a new and glorious era into their experience, and with Whom they had mingled on terms of the most endearing friendship for at least three years. He knew their distress, and condescended in this conversation with them, on the night before His death, to administer the necessary relief. Every sentence is charged with consolation. The expression before us is a sample of the whole. He assures them that it was "*expedient*" for them that He should depart, and bestow upon them a Comforter, that should not only be with them, but *in* them; and that, not for a season, but for ever.

The words of *Paul* are part of an address which he delivered to the Philippian Christians, when he was in the immediate prospect of being separated from them by a cruel and an ignominious death. Death, in forms of horrid torture, was before the eye and heart, both of Jesus and Paul, when they uttered the sentences before us. Both are the utterances of those about to grapple with "the King of Terrors," and step into the mysterious scenes of disembodied spirits.

Secondly: Both were under the master influence of the same principle of Self-Sacrificing Philanthropy. The strongest desire of Christ when He spoke, was the good of those to whom He addressed Himself, and this was also the strongest desire of Paul. Both wished well to their race; both were supremely anxious to serve it.

Now the remarkable point to which I wish to draw your attention is this, that Jesus should regard His *departure from the world as necessary to serve the interests of His disciples, and that Paul should regard his continuance in the world as the most necessary to serve the interest of his converts.* Jesus considered His death, so far as the good of the Church was concerned, highly "*expedient.*" Paul, on the other hand, considered his death inexpedient for the Church. The One thought that He could do more good by going to heaven; the other thought that he could do more good by remaining on earth.

Now I think that an inquiry into the *cause* of this difference of judgment between Christ and Paul, concerning Usefulness, will not only be interesting but profitable. I assume, of course, at the outset, that both were correct in their judgment. It would be blasphemy to suppose that the Mediator had not formed a true judgment; nor would it be much else to suppose that the Apostle had not, since he "spake as he was moved by the Holy Ghost." Why, then, should it be *better* for the world for Christ to depart, and for Paul to remain? I suggest two reasons—

I —BECAUSE MANKIND WOULD LOSE LESS BY THE DEPARTURE OF CHRIST, THAN IT WOULD BY THE DEPARTURE OF THE APOSTLE

There are three things which men probably lost by the departure of the Apostle, which they did not lose by the departure of Christ.

First: His *Personal Presence.* When the Apostle departed this life, it is probable that his person left all the scenes of his mortal life, so that he had no more connection with the earthly affairs of mankind. At any rate the Bible does not give any reason to believe that, after death, a man continues in any personal connection with this terrestrial state. He passes away to some other world. He returns no more to his house. "His sons come to honour, and he knoweth it not." The places that once knew him, know him no more for ever. The world loses him. Paul, after his departure, would not be found in Corinth, or Rome, in Ephesus, or Philippi, or with any of the Churches which he had planted.

But it is not so with Christ. Death did not take Him from the world. He was as present after His decease as before. "I will not leave you comfortless. I will come to you." Christ is Personally with every section of His Church—with every disciple. "I am with you always, even unto the end of the world."

Secondly: His *Personal Agency.* After Paul's decease, not only was his person absent from this world, but, of course, his personal agency. He wrote no more letters, his tongue pronounced no more addresses, his pen was still, and his voice was hushed on earth for ever. When we die, we finish our *personal* agency on earth. We leave our work; we return not to complete any undertaking—not to finish even the education of our children. We leave the work for ever when we die. But it is not so with Christ. He continues to carry on His designs. He works in His disciples "to will and to do His own good pleasure." The Acts of the Apostles are the acts of Christ through the Apostles; and all the true achievements of the Church are but the operations of Christ.

Thirdly: His *Personal Intercession.* The Apostle, during his mission on earth, prayed earnestly and constantly for the Church; —he "prayed always with all prayer." But when he died, perhaps this intercession ended; I say *perhaps*—for it does not behove us to speak positively here. Indeed reason would suggest that intercession is the act of all holy souls; and that those for whom we interceded in earnestness here, we shall remember in our aspirations in the heavenly state. The Bible, however, gives us no absolute authority for believing this, and therefore it is, at any rate, a matter of doubt.

But the Intercession of Christ continues. That is a beautiful prayer in chap. xvii.; but it is only a short specimen of His intercession for mankind in the heavenly world. "He ever liveth to make intercession." "If any man sin, we have an advocate with the Father." His intercession is not Persuasion; that is not needed with Infinite Mercy and Immutable Love. It is the Representation of Mankind in the presence of God and His holy universe. Another reason suggested is—

II —BECAUSE MANKIND WOULD GAIN MORE BY THE DEPARTURE OF CHRIST, THAN BY THE DEPARTURE OF PAUL

Humanity would gain more of three things by the Departure of Christ, than by the Departure of the Apostle.

First: More Sanctifying Truth. I know not of any truth that came out in Paul's death, that we have not in his life and teaching. But oh! what a new flood of truth burst upon this world when Christ died, and rose from the dead! Indeed these facts involved the very essence of the Gospel. What is the Gospel? "How that Christ died for our sins, according to the Scriptures. And that He was buried, and that He rose again the third day, according to the Scriptures; and that He was seen of Cephas, then of the twelve; after that He was seen of about five hundred brethren." Here is the Renovating and Sanctifying Power of Truth. Humanity would gain—

Secondly: More Heavenly Attraction, The departure of Paul,

indeed, increased the attraction of the heavenly world. The members of the various Churches who knew Paul and heard him preach, would assuredly feel drawn toward heaven after his departure. Has not the death of the good ever this power? The celestial world comes with meaning and uplifting power to us when we think of heaven as the home of all the great and good men whom we have known and loved. But how little is this attraction, compared with the attraction which flows from Christ! Christ in Heaven is the magnet which draws the heart of humanity Heaven-ward. "Whom having not seen we love, rejoicing with joy unspeakable, and full of glory." Humanity would gain—

Thirdly: More Secure Guardianship. Were we to suppose, what some hold, that those departed spirits of the good, who loved us most, become our guardian angels; yet what is their guardianship compared with a guardianship secured to us by Christ, in consequence of His departure to the other world? "All power," said He, "is given to Me." All things are under His control;—all elements, laws, beings, agencies, actions, worlds, systems, matter, mind. "Things visible," &c. "He is head over all things to the Church," &c. Humanity would gain—

Fourthly: More Divine Influence. It is true that when a good man leaves the world, the remembrance of the noble deeds he has wrought, and the Christly Spirit he has exemplified will bring some measure of Divine influence to his survivors. This, however, will be insignificant in measure compared with the tide of influence that came down from heaven when Christ ascended on high. The windows of heaven were opened then. A new and mighty power came down. "And when the day of Pentecost was fully come, they were all with one accord in one place. And suddenly there came a sound from heaven as of a rushing mighty wind, and it filled all the house where they were sitting. And they were all filled with the Holy Ghost."

CONCLUSION. The subject teaches—

First: That our Privileges are superior to the privileges of those who were the Contemporaries of Christ.

Sentimental saintlets are constantly extolling the privileges of the past. But in these last times "God hath provided some better things for us."

'Twas good to have lived in that old Hebrew land,
  When Thou, our Redeemer, wast there;
Men stood by Thee then, and were touched by Thy hand,
  Still better, far better, be here.
'Twas good to have heard from Thine own loving voice,
  Thy words bidding sinners come near;
Yet reason assures us, and we would rejoice,
  Tis better, far better, be here.

Peter grew wonderfully in moral energy by the departure of Christ. How weak in "the High Priest's house" when Christ was present! (Luke xxii. 54—62.) How strong when confronting the Sanhedrim a few days after Christ's departure! (Acts iv. 5—12, &c.) (See Exposition on John xvi. 7.) The subject teaches—

Secondly: That the earth is probably the one Sphere in which we can serve our Race. Paul felt this. Whatever you desire to do in the way of spiritually improving your children, servants, neighbours, must be done *now*. What can the mighty hosts that have entered Heaven do for us poor mortals? The subject teaches—

Thirdly: That the death of the good is a real Loss to the World. The death of a good man is the drying up of a well-spring in the desert of life, the quenching of a star in our heavens already too clouded by depravity.

Christ and the Human Race
No. 15   John 17:2, 3

" As Thou hast given Him power over all flesh, that He should give eternal life to as many as Thou hast given Him.   And this is life eternal, that they might know Thee the only true God, and Jesus Christ, whom Thou hast sent."

(For Exegetical Remarks, see Vol. II. p. 69.)

As these words now stand before us, the idea is, That the Eternal Father gave to Our Lord a certain number of men, to whom He was to give "*eternal life,*" and to none besides.   "Here," says a popular expositor, pointing to this text, "is the Father making over the elect to the Redeemer, and giving them to Him as His charge and trust; as the crown and recompense of His undertaking.   He has a sovereign power over all the fallen race, but a *peculiar* interest in the chosen remnant.   And here is the Son undertaking to secure the happiness of those that were given Him, that He would give eternal life to them."   Is this the idea contained in the original Greek?   If so, we are bound to accept it.   The idea of the Infinite Father, acting on the principle of favouritism, and handing over a certain number of His children to Christ to be saved, leaving the others to be damned, may be revolting at once to our intellectual conceptions and our moral instincts. What of that?   Am I a judge of the Infinite?   Can I span immensity?   "Who am I, that I should reply against God?"   But is it contained in God's *real* Word?   If so, I accept it, though it confounds my judgment, and strikes hard against my intuitions.

Whether such an idea as this is contained in other parts of the Scriptures is a question on which I have not to enter now.   It may be so, though, to say the least, I have never found it.   But that it is contained in the Original of the text, I venture, with all humility, to deny.   I have submitted, in my Exposition, the translations of *Dean Alford* and *Dr. Davidson* as more faithful than that of our version : "*According as Thou gavest Him power over all flesh, that whatsoever Thou hast given Him, to them He should give eternal life.*"

The idea seems to be this: INASMUCH AS THOU GAVEST HIM AUTHORITY OVER ALL MANKIND, THAT HE SHOULD GIVE TO ALL MANKIND WHAT THOU HAST GIVEN HIM—ETERNAL LIFE.

Taking this as the idea contained in the text, we have, then, several glorious truths brought under our notice.

I —CHRIST IS THE MASTER OF THE HUMAN RACE

He has "*power over all flesh.*" The word ἐξουσία, here translated "*power,*" is rendered authority in about thirty other places in the New Testament, and this is undoubtedly its meaning here. The word flesh, σαρκὸς, which in the Bible sometimes means all animal existences, sometimes a constituent part of the human body, sometimes moral corruption, and sometimes spiritual sensibility, here unquestionably means human nature, as in Luke iii. 6, "All flesh shall see the salvation of God." The text, therefore, asserts that Christ has authority over all humanity; that He is in fact the Master of the Human Race. This is taught elsewhere in the New Testament: taught with great clearness, force, and frequency too. We are told that when He ascended from the grave, He said unto His disciples, "All power is given to Me in heaven and on earth." It is said that He is gone into heaven, and "sitteth on the right hand of God," and angels and authority are made "subject" to Him. And we are also informed that He "hath on His vesture and His thigh a name written—King of kings, and Lord of lords."

Now, as Master of the race, several things are noteworthy—(1.) *His power over all is absolute.* His authority is more than legislative and judicial. It extends to life itself. He kills, and He makes alive. He has "the keys of death and of hell at His girdle." None come into existence but by His bidding; none continue an instant longer than He wills; and not one departs without His permission. As Master of the race—(2.) *He is infinitely independent of all.* He is not on the throne by the suffrage of any. Did men wish Him there? Not they. They struggled hard to confine Him in the dark chambers of mortality. Their cry was, and is, "We will not have this Man to rule over us." They neither placed Him there, nor can they depose Him. He is sublimely independent. The "heathen may rage; the people imagine a vain thing; the kings of the earth set themselves, and the rulers take counsel together, against the Lord and against His Anointed, saying, Let us break their bands asunder, and cast away their cords from us. He that sitteth in the heavens shall laugh; the Lord shall have them in derision." As Master of the race—(3.) *He interferes not with the freedom of any.* Absolute as is His power over them, He exerts no coercion. Each of the millions is left free—free to obey, and free to rebel. He allows conquerors to deluge continents with blood, and proud ecclesiastics to sit in the place of God. Each is *conscious* of his freedom. As Master of the race—(4.) *He does not value service by its amount, but by its motive.* Men look at the *measure* rather than the *motive* in service : not so with Him. The cup of cold water, and the widow's mite, to Him, are more valuable than cathedrals reared for His worship, or lordly inheritance bequeathed to carry on His cause. As Master of the race—(5.) *He has no misgivings about the results.* He is sitting down, "expecting His enemies to be made His footstool." He has established an agency on earth to work out His mediatorial purposes. He has no fear of failure. He can afford to wait. He has plenty of time. He cannot be disappointed. As He sees the golden autumn creeping through the tempests, snows, and desolation of winter, so, amidst the wreck of kingdoms, the desolations of war, the opposition of infidels, and the revolution of ages, He sees the millennium coming on. Notice—

II —CHRIST IS THE MASTER OF THE HUMAN RACE BY DIVINE APPOINTMENT

" *As Thou hast given Him power over all flesh* "—over *all* mankind. "The Father loveth the Son, and hath given all things into His hands." "God hath highly exalted Him." "Thou hast put all things in subjection under His feet." Unto the Son He saith, "Thy throne, O God, is for ever and ever," &c. Thus He reigns by *Divine Right*. The Divine right of human kings is an *impious fiction*, a fiction which for ages has licensed the most ruthless tyrannies, and entailed the most terrible calamities upon the nations of the earth. In the march of general intelligence this fiction is rapidly losing its power; and will, thank God, very soon be buried with the blasphemous absurdities of the dark ages. That Christ reigns by Divine right is, however, no fiction. It is a glorious truth. "God hath highly exalted Him."

First : He being our Rightful Master, *we should obey Him*. "Ye call Me Master and Lord : and ye say well, for so I am." "And why call ye Me Lord, Lord, and do not the things which I say ? " "Whoso honoureth the Son, honoureth the Father." "Kiss the Son, lest He be angry." Our governments should be moulded by His laws. Our creeds should be founded on His teaching. Our business should be regulated by His principles. Our lives actuated in all by His Spirit. "One is your Master, even Christ."

Secondly : He being our Rightful Master, we should *rejoice in the government under which we live*. He is not only All-wise, All-just, and All-powerful, but All-loving. Blessed be the Great Father for making Christ the Master of our race ! He might have put the world under the government of some Satanic being, who would have gratified his malign nature by rendering our existence a torture, and turning the world into a pandemonium. Or He might have placed us under an inexorable Nemesis, who would have pursued us with the red-hot rod of punishment, and compelled us every instant to eat of the bitter fruits of our own doings. But He has placed over us One Who wears our nature ; One Whose love for us is unconquerable, stronger than death itself ; One Who died for us on the cross, and now lives on the throne, and works through the universe, in order to bless us with the felicities of His Father and Himself. Notice—

III —CHRIST IS THE MASTER OF THE HUMAN RACE IN ORDER TO MAKE IT HAPPY

" *That He should give eternal life.*" Eternal life is the great boon which Christ gives to the world. This is stated with great frequency and explicitness in the New Testament. " The gift of God is eternal life, through Jesus Christ our Lord." " Whosoever believeth on Him shall not perish, but have everlasting life." " Thou hast the words of eternal life." " He that receiveth My word shall have everlasting life." Jesus said to Martha when her brother Lazarus was in the tomb, " Thy brother shall rise again." She replied, " I know that he shall rise again in the resurrection at the last day." Jesus answered, " He that believeth in Me, though he were dead, yet shall he live : and he that liveth and believeth in Me shall never die."

But what is ETERNAL LIFE ? Is it merely *endless* existence ? This humanity might have had, had He never interposed ; and this is not necessarily a blessing. It might be a curse : a curse even worse than annihilation itself. The germ of this eternal life is *Eternal Goodness.* Goodness is essentially eternal. Finite existence is not so. Finite existence every moment depends upon His will. God can blot out of being in an instant the strongest of His spiritual creatures. To talk of the *essential* immortality of creatures, is a contradiction in true philosophy. But can He annihilate goodness ? Never. It is the soul of Himself. Goodness is the true immortal life of souls. " The incorruptible seed," the perennial river of life, the unfading crown. The immortality of the soul consists *not* in its constitution, but in its *character*. The Divine elements of rectitude, love, truth, godliness—in these are " *eternal life.*" Alas, the converse of this is true. What is death ? *Sin* is death. Unholiness is soul-mortality. The spirit in which moral evil dwells and works, dies—dies to all that gives worth and bearableness to existence, dies to God and all the blessings of His happy universe. Christ, then, is made the Master of the race, *in order to make the race happy.* "I am come that ye might have life, and that ye might have it more abundantly." Glorious truth!

CONCLUSION

First: This subject furnishes a ground for the Highest Gratitude. Who would have wondered had He been enthroned to wreak vengeance upon the world, and to have rendered human existence an intolerable curse? But not so; He is made Master to hush all the discords, remove all the diseases, and crush all the evils of the world. He is on the throne in order to "wipe away all tears" from all faces, and to make the world happy with the happiness of God Himself. "He that sat upon the throne said, Behold, I make all things new." A "new heaven and a new earth, wherein dwelleth righteousness." Love, amazing love, is this!

Secondly: This subject furnishes a ground for the Sublimest Catholicity. He does not work to bless any mere section of humanity, but to bless the race. "In this was manifested the love of God toward us, because that God sent His only-begotten Son into the world, that we might live through Him." The sphere of His redemptive mercy is co-extensive with His dominion; and His dominion is over all mankind. Christ is the Saviour of *all* men. "The Light that lighteth every man that cometh into the world." Bigot, cease to look upon all outside thy little sect as the reprobate of God, and cease to exult in the vain and impious thought that thou art a special favourite of Heaven! Thy miserable exclusiveness is a decisive proof that thou art a moral anomaly in the empire of Christ. Christ is for the race, and "if any man hath not the Spirit of Christ, he is none of His."

Thirdly: This subject presents a ground for the Strongest Confidence. Let us rejoice in the authority of Christ. The race for whom in love He died, is now under His control. His love for it now on the throne is as strong as when He bled for it on the Cross. He is using His vast authority for its restoration, and it is getting better and brighter. Its moral agriculture is improving. A layer of loam is being spread over the world, in which the old weeds and thistles wither and die, and new plants of heavenlier climates are springing up in every direction. Governments, religious institutions, and customs, that once grew here luxuriantly, are losing their root-hold and are rotting away. Every plant which His heavenly Father hath not planted He is plucking up. Its moral atmosphere is becoming more salubrious; the lungs of conscience breathe freer; old diseases are gradually disappearing; and souls are getting stronger in resolve and deed. Its moral firmament is growing more luminous, new lights break through the clouds, new constellations rise on the horizon, and fresh rays come down from the sky of thought, upon regions where mental midnight has long prevailed. Thus, under the Masterhood of Jesus, humanity is advancing. To us, the impatient children of a day, the progress may appear slow. But time to Him is nothing, and He has a far higher estimate of moral achievements than we have. The conversion of one soul is not much to us; but to Him it is a stupendous event, producing a thrill of rapture through His holy universe. "There is joy in the presence of the angels of God over *one* sinner that repenteth."

Christ's Imprisonment
No. 16   John 18:12, 13

" Then the band and the captain and officers of the Jews took Jesus, and
bound him, and led him away to Annas first ; for he was father in
law to Caiaphas, which was the High Priest that same year."

(For Exegetical Remarks, see Vol. II. p. 109.)

THE word *"prison,"* in Isaiah liii. 8, should not, perhaps, be
taken to designate a particular place of incarceration ; for there is
no evidence to show that Christ was ever confined in any such
penal cell.   He was, however, a Prisoner.   His limbs were bound,
and He was held in the custody of the iron-hearted officers of the
Roman Government.   The verses we have selected contain the first
account we have of such Imprisonment.   Up to this time He seems
to have been free.   Though the demon eye of envy and malice
was ever on Him, He had, till now, power to move about at
pleasure ;—no limb was manacled.   From this time on, however,
He is in bonds.   During this imprisonment His enemies seem
to have been intensely active : all their faculties were on the
stretch from this time up to the hour of the Crucifixion.   The
closing hours of the Thursday night, and the opening hours of
the Friday morning, form a period of *intense* activity.   For
earnest, concentrated, and strenuous action, they will ever be
memorable in the history of the universe.   Heaven and earth
and hell were all wondrously busy.   The devil and his emissaries
were all astir.   It was the " hour " of darkness.   The Scribes, the
Pharisees, the Chief Priests, the Rulers, and the Roman officers
were straining every nerve, and turning every moment to the
infernal end they contemplated—the destruction of the Son of
God.   Christ Himself was none the less active.   He had been
busily employed every minute.   He had attended the Passover,
and there answered the many questions, and corrected the many
errors, of His disciples.   There, too, He foretold His betrayal;
delivered that beautiful discourse to His sorrowing disciples,
commencing with the words, " Let not your hearts be troubled," and
offered up that prayer of inexpressible sublimity contained in

John xvii. Having sung a hymn with the disciples, He retired
to the Mount of Olives—His accustomed retreat; and soon after
we find Him in the mysterious solitude of Gethsemane, in an
unknown agony of soul, praying to the everlasting Father for help.
Truly, His activity during these few hours was marvellous. It
would seem that He compressed the work of unnumbered ages
into a few hours.

Our subject is *Christ's Imprisonment ;* and we shall look upon it
in three aspects—

I —AS THE MOST THRILLING EVENT IN THE HISTORY OF CHRIST

Just look at what takes place during His *Imprisonment !* I
shall endeavour to give the history in the order in which it
occurred, as I gather it from a comparison of the various
Evangelical records.

First : He was first taken a Prisoner from Gethsemane to
Annas. *"Then the band and the captain and officers of the
Jews took Jesus, and bound Him, and led Him away to Annas
first ; for he was father in law to Caiaphas, which was the High
Priest that same year."* Why was He led to Annas *"first ?"*
Annas was not in office now, and had not the legal power to deal
with the matter. Why, then, was this glorious Prisoner brought
first to him ? There was a deep, cunning, crafty policy in this.
The old man, it is true, was not in office, but in all likelihood he
had more real power than any other one man in the Jewish
kingdom. For a long time he had been the High Priest himself,
and no less than five of his sons had filled that most elevated of
Jewish offices. And now it was Caiaphas, his son-in-law, who
was invested with its authorities and honours. By taking the
Blessed Prisoner to him first, the old man would be so compli-
mented, have his pride as well as his curiosity so gratified, that
his great influence in effecting their infernal design on Christ
would be assuredly secured. What was the character of this
interview,—what words exchanged,—what insults offered ? We
know not.

Secondly : He was then taken as a Prisoner from Annas to
Caiaphas. *"Now Annas had sent Him bound to Caiaphas the
High Priest."* And they that laid hold on Jesus, led Him away to
Caiaphas, the High Priest's house, where were assembled all the
Chief Priests, and elders, and the Scribes. "The High Priest then
asked Jesus of His disciples, and of His doctrine." Here is His
reply, "I spake openly to the world ; I ever taught in the synagogue,
and in the temple, whither the Jews always resort ; and in secret
have I said nothing. Why askest thou Me ? ask them which
heard Me, what I have said unto them : behold, they know what

I said. And when He had thus spoken, one of the officers which stood by, struck Jesus with the palm of his hand, saying, Answerest Thou the High Priest so? Jesus answered him, If I have spoken evil, bear witness of the evil: but if well, why smitest thou Me?" (John xviii. 19—24.) "Now the Chief Priests and elders, and all the council, sought false witness against Jesus, to put Him to death; but found none: yea, though many false witnesses came, yet found they none. At the last came two false witnesses, and said, This fellow said, I am able to destroy the temple of God, and to build it in three days. And the High Priest arose, and said unto him, Answerest Thou nothing? what is it which these witness against Thee? But Jesus held His peace. And the High Priest answered and said unto Him, I adjure Thee by the living God, that Thou tell us whether Thou be the Christ, the Son of God. Jesus saith unto him, Thou hast said: nevertheless I say unto you, Hereafter shall ye see the Son of man sitting on the right hand of power, and coming in the clouds of heaven. Then the High Priest rent his clothes, saying, He hath spoken blasphemy. What think ye? They answered and said, He is guilty of death. Then did they spit in His face, and buffeted Him; and others smote Him with the palms of their hands, saying, Prophesy unto us, Thou Christ, Who is he that smote Thee?" (Matt. xxvi. 59—68.)

Here, at the outset, the High Priest pressed on Him questions of a general nature, touching His "disciples" and His "doctrine."

The Reply of our Saviour is sublimely characteristic. With the fearlessness and frankness of the highest magnanimity, and with the adroitness of unerring wisdom, He directs them to the multitude around, for any information concerning His disciples and Himself. "I spake openly to the world; ask them that heard Me." He had spoken to multitudes. No One was better known amongst the millions of Judæa at that moment; and He challenged the verdict of public sentiment. With the insolence of base hirelings, who courted the favour of their master, the officer, we are told, which stood by, struck Him, saying, "Answerest Thou the High Priest so?" To this insult the noble Prisoner said, "If I have spoken evil, bear witness of the evil: but if well, why smitest thou Me?" False witnesses were now sought to convict Him. There seems to have been a great difficulty in finding any; and many of those who were found proved useless on account of the disagreement in their testimony. At last, however, two false witnesses came, who seemed to agree in the testimony, that they heard Him say, "I am able to destroy the temple of God, that is made with hands, and within three days I will build another, made without hands." The High Priest now interposed; he arose and stood up in the midst, and asked Jesus, saying unto Him:

"Answerest Thou nothing? What is it which these witness against Thee?" Christ remained silent. He knew that speech was useless in such a case. Again the High Priest addressed Him: "I adjure Thee by the living God, tell us whether Thou be the Christ, the Son of the Blessed." An answer to this question would decide the case, and determine His fate. To this appeal Christ could not be silent; it was an opportunity for Him to declare Himself, and He said, "Thou hast said I am; nevertheless I say unto you, Hereafter shall ye see the Son of man sitting on the right hand of power, and coming in the clouds of heaven." This declaration was thought to be sufficient; the High Priest rent his clothes, saying, "He hath spoken blasphemy." *Blasphemy* was the charge brought against Him here, and for it He was now pronounced worthy of death. In this court and at this hour Peter denied Him thrice; and His enemies smote Him, spat on His face, blindfolded Him, &c. Having been pronounced in this court to be guilty of death, the men that held Him, like infuriated monsters, began to insult and torture Him. "And the men that held Jesus mocked Him, and smote Him; and some began to spit on Him, and to cover His face, and to buffet Him; and the servants did strike Him with the palms of their hands. And when they had blindfolded Him, they struck Him on the face, and asked Him, saying, Prophesy unto us, Thou Christ, who is he that smote Thee? And many of these things blasphemously spake they against Him."

Thirdly: He was next taken a Prisoner from the palace of Caiaphas to the Hall of the Sanhedrim. Notwithstanding the condemnation which had been pronounced upon Him before the High Priest, and in which the people seemed most heartily to concur, the authorities themselves, the authors of the sentence, do not seem thoroughly satisfied with the result. Conscience makes them uncomfortable, and prompts them to seek further evidence to justify their decision. Accordingly they resolve on holding another court, and having another formal trial. Hence they adjourn from the "High Priest's palace" *to the great hall of Session*, which was one of the buildings of the temple. The morning which succeeds that horrible night is just breaking, when the Grand Council of the nation assemble in that hall. Jesus was conducted by an armed escort up Moriah's hill into their presence. Can you picture to your mind this court? The hall, we may suppose, was spacious and magnificent, fraught with many heart-awing associations. Seventy-two of the most distinguished men in Israel were there clad in authority. They are the rulers; they form the great Council of the nation—the Sanhedrim. Though night has just broken, they are all there to adjudicate on the charges brought against this Nazarene. The High Priest is the president; next to him sat those who had previously held the higher office;

next to them the representatives of the four-and-twenty classes of the priesthood. Then follow the elders or rulers of the synagogues, and some of the most eminent doctors of the law; men well versed in the laws of Moses and the traditions of the Rabbis. It was to the Jewish people the most august assembly. Here the blessed Prisoner now stands. The inspired biographer gives the circumstances of the trial with a simplicity and brevity alike inimitable. "And as soon as it was day, the elders of the people and the Chief Priests and Scribes came together, and led Him into their Council, saying, Art Thou the Christ? tell us." And He said unto them, "If I tell you, ye will not believe: and if I also ask you, ye will not answer Me, nor let Me go. Hereafter shall the Son of Man sit on the right hand of the power of God. Then said they all, Art Thou then the Son of God? And He said unto them, Ye say that I am. And they said, What need have we of any further witness? for we ourselves have heard of His own mouth. And they took counsel against Jesus to put Him to death." Their cause gained nothing by this second trial. They only furnished posterity with another and fuller revelation of the enormous wickedness which they were capable of perpetrating in the name of law and religion. Truth, however, gained not a little even on this occasion; it received another glorious confession of Christ's Messiahship. "Hereafter shall the Son of Man sit on the right hand of the power of God."

Fourthly: He was next taken as a Prisoner from the hall of the Sanhedrim to Pilate. The morning is advancing, and all Jerusalem is astir. The streets are in commotion, and crowds are moving about with unusual haste. All the members of the Sanhedrim and every officer in the State look and move as if under a strange excitement. "Then led they Jesus from the hall of Caiaphas unto the hall of judgment: and it was early; and they themselves went not into the judgment hall, lest they should be defiled; but that they might eat the Passover" (Matt. xxvii. 11—14; Mark xv. 1—5; Luke xxiii. 1—7; John xviii. 28—38). What do we see on this occasion? Outside of that hall there is a strange scene. All the members of the great Council of the nation were there. Christ, the Prisoner, had been thrust into the hall by the force of the Roman officers; but there, His malignant accusers would not cross the threshold. Why? Oh! the base villainy of a sanctimonious religion. "They went not in, lest they should be defiled." That judgment hall was not sacred enough for these demons masked in religion. Take care of the men who are afraid to be polluted by places! "Pilate then went out unto them, and said, What accusation bring ye against this Man? They answered and said unto him, If He were not a malefactor, we would not have delivered Him up unto thee." Here again, their foul-hearted sanctimoniousness comes out. "If He were not a male-factor!" Wickedly assuming that He was, and with an unblushing arrogance declaring their pretended incapability of bringing aught but a malefactor to him for trial. "Then said Pilate unto them, Take ye Him, and judge Him according to your law." What reply did they make to this? Had they the candour to say, "We have tried Him?" No! With their wonted hypocrisy they said, "It is not lawful for us to put any man to death." Rome, it would seem, had deprived the Sanhedrim of the power of ad-ministering capital punishment. What charge must they bring against Him, then, in order to get the Roman authority to put Him to death? A religious one?—the same that was against Him before the High Priest? There the charge was blasphemy. No! Rome tolerates all religions; and they could not gain His death on such a charge. With the wiliness of the great serpent himself, their moral master, they say, "We found this fellow perverting the nation, and forbidding to give tribute to Cæsar, saying that He Himself is Christ, a King." This charge, though as baseless as the former, came within the jurisdiction of Pilate. Now he leaves these arch-hypocrites outside, enters the judgment hall again, and summons Jesus into his presence. No sooner had the judge seated himself, and the Prisoner confronted him, than he felt himself embarrassed by another strange and unexpected difficulty.

His own wife despatches a strange and startling message to him, in which she says, "Have thou nothing to do with that just Man, for I have suffered many things in a dream because of Him." The judge, notwithstanding, felt that his position bound him to proceed with the case. He appeals to the Prisoner at the bar, "Art Thou the King of the Jews?" To which Jesus replied by the question, "Sayest thou this thing of thyself, or did others tell it thee of Me?" Christ perceives the question was asked, not for information, but in the spirit of ridicule; and He shapes His reply accordingly. In this reply He reminds Pilate that the testimony of enemies was suspicious, and that it ought not to influence him in his decision. To this Pilate replies, "Am I a Jew?" That is, "Dost thou suppose me to be a Jew, and to be acquainted with Jewish quarrels? I am a Roman, and disclaim any knowledge of any such miserable squabbles. I am here to do justice—'What hast Thou done?'" Jesus then declares His Kingship. "I am a King. Though poor and miserable in aspect I appear before thee; though thou didst laugh to scorn the idea, yet I am a King; but My kingdom is not of this world," &c. "To this end was I born, and for this cause came I into the world, that I should bear witness of the truth. Every one that is of the truth heareth My voice. Pilate saith unto Him, What is truth?" At this question Christ stood sublimely mute. He knew that explanations would be useless. Pilate's heart was not in a condition to understand truth. You cannot make truth evident to souls clouded with depravity. The judge is silent. He gets an impression of the innocency of the Prisoner. He withdraws from the court, goes again outside to the Chief Priests and the people, who felt themselves too holy to enter, and He emphatically declares, " I find no fault in this Man." This, instead of satisfying them, only excites them the more in urging their accusations. " The Chief Priests accused Him of many things." Amongst other things they said, " He stirreth up the people, teaching throughout all Jewry, beginning from Galilee to this place."

Fifthly: He was then taken as a Prisoner from Pilate to Herod. We have seen that the Chief Priests in the charges which they brought against Christ before Pilate referred to His connection with Galilee. " He stirreth up the people," &c. Pilate, strongly desiring to rid himself of a work which he felt repulsive to his nature, when he heard of Galilee, and found that Christ was a Galilean, determined to send the Prisoner for trial to Herod; Galilee being within Herod's jurisdiction, and Herod being now at Jerusalem. This was Herod Antipas, the tetrarch of Galilee, the wretched libertine whom the Baptist reproved; the murderer who put to death that illustrious reformer for charging him with his guilt; that cruel and crafty one whom the Son of God designated a "fox." Before this Imperial monster Christ now stands. "And when Herod saw Him, he was exceeding glad," &c. (Luke xxiii. 8—12.) This meeting was *complimentary* to Herod. " The same day Pilate and Herod were made friends together," for before they were at enmity between themselves. Though, perhaps, Pilate sent Christ in order to relieve himself of a painful duty, Herod took it as a compliment, and was pleased; and thus a friendship was established between them. This very circumstance reflects honour on Christ. Had these men in power felt that Christ was only a common criminal, a religious enthusiast, or an impostor, would Herod have felt the compliment? This meeting was *gratifying* to Herod. "When Herod saw Jesus he was exceeding glad: for he was desirous to see Him for a long season" (Luke xxiii. 8, 9). It seems strange that Herod had never seen Jesus, Who had been so often in Galilee and laboured there. But Herod resided at Tiberias, and Christ, though near to the spot, had never actually visited it. Herod no doubt considered the smallest effort in his own district to see and listen to Christ beneath his dignity. Herod had heard a great deal of Him, and now his curiosity was gratified; "He was pleased." The meeting was *disappointing* to Herod. He hoped to have seen some miracle done; he expected to be interested in some display of the marvellous: but he is mistaken. The mighty

Prisoner could have wrought the most stupendous miracles before him; but He stands passive. The king puts questions to Him; but the Prisoner answered him nothing. Question after question perhaps was pressed, yet sublimely mute stood Christ; "He answered not a word." This silence was profoundly significant; it shows that even the holiest speech is sometimes useless and inexpedient. This meeting was *mortifying to Herod.* He wanted miracles; and will not Christ perform them? Not a finger will He move to gratify his wish. He wanted answers to certain idle questions. Will not Christ reply? No! "Not a word." Herod is therefore enraged. His dignity is wounded. "And Herod with his men of war set Him at nought, and mocked Him, and arrayed Him in a gorgeous robe, and sent Him again to Pilate."

Sixthly: He was then taken as a Prisoner back from Herod to Pilate. Herod "sent Him again to Pilate" (Matt. xxvii. 15—26; Mark xv. 6—15; Luke xviii. 13—35). On this occasion Pilate calls together at the outset the Chief Priests and the rulers of the people, and declared unto them that he had examined Christ touching all things of which He had been accused, "and that he could find no fault in Him;" that he had also sent Him to Herod, and that Herod found nothing worthy of death in Him. He proposes, therefore, to chastise and release Him. He reminded them of the custom of the governor to release at the Passover a criminal, and he leaves them to decide as to who it should be; Barabbas, who was a robber and a murderer, or Jesus Who was called Christ. "Whether of the twain will ye that I release unto you?" "Then cried they all again, Not this man, but Barabbas." This seemed to be the verdict of the Jewish people, the verdict of public sentiment, which Pilate had not the courage to withstand. Still he recoils from the idea of putting Christ to death, and appeals to them again. "What will ye then that I should do unto Him, Whom ye call the King of the Jews? And they cried out again, saying, Crucify Him, crucify Him." Pilate seems confounded. Within his heart there is a tremendous battle, between his love of popular favour and the demands of his conscience. He makes another appeal to them, "Why, what evil hath He done? I have found no cause of death in Him: I will therefore chastise Him, and let Him go. And they cried out the more exceedingly, Crucify Him, crucify Him; and the voices of them and the Chief Priests prevailed"—prevailed over the clearest dictates of his own judgment and the strongest protests of his own conscience. Still, though the sentence is pronounced, and Christ delivered up to their will, his conscience is yet asserting her rights. Several efforts after this he seems to have made to conciliate his outraged conscience. *He washes his hands before the multitude,* and says,

"I am innocent of the blood of this just person; see ye to it." He declares again and again that "he had found no fault in Him." In order to touch them into a compassion that should reverse their decision, he brings Christ forth to them, wearing the crown of thorns and the purple robe, and the reed of mock royalty in His hand, presenting an appearance enough to break the hardest heart—and he says, "Behold the Man!" Still all this is of no avail: the cry, "Away with Him, away with Him; crucify Him, crucify Him," rose louder and more vehement every minute. "Then delivered he Him unto them to be crucified."

Seventhly: He was finally taken as a Prisoner from Pilate to Calvary. "Then the soldiers of the governor took Jesus into the common hall, and gathered unto Him the whole band of soldiers. And they stripped Him, and put on Him a scarlet robe. And when they had platted a crown of thorns, they put it upon His head, and a reed in His right hand: and they bowed the knee before Him, and mocked Him, saying Hail, king of the Jews! And they spit upon Him and took the reed and smote Him on the head. And after that they had mocked Him, they took the robe off from Him, and put His own raiment on Him, and led Him away to crucify Him" (Matt. xxvii. 27—50). What a view of Him as a Prisoner you have here! Never was there such a journey as that from the hall of Pilate to the brow of Calvary. It was not a long one; but most momentous to the universe. Never was there such a period as that which transpired between Pilate's sentence and the Prisoner's dying cry. Though embracing only three hours, the scenes and circumstances connected therewith, will extend their influence over all minds, and take eternity to study. The Cross is the sublime culmination of the whole.

> "At last the word of death is given ;
> The form is bound, the nails are driven ;
> Now triumph, Scribe and Pharisee !
> Now, Roman, bend the mocking knee !
> The cross is reared. The deed is done !
> There stands Messiah's earthly throne !
> Still from His lips no curse has come ;
> His lofty eye has looked no doom ;
> No earthquake burst, no angel band
> Crushes the black, blaspheming hand ;
> What say those lips by anguish riven ?
> God, be My murderers forgiven !"

Look at *Christ's Imprisonment*—

II —AS THE GREATEST ENORMITY IN THE ANNALS OF CRIME

First: His imprisonment combined all the chief Elements of Crime. Here was the foulest *Injustice*. Imprisonment is for criminals; but had Christ ever been guilty of a crime ? Had He contravened any law human or Divine? Had He rebelled against any righteous authority? Had He violated any of the rights of His race? No! He challenged His enemies in full assembly to convict Him of sin, and they were silent. Judas, whom He had admitted into the inner sanctuary of His social life, and who had the best opportunity of knowing His character, and who, to appease his own conscience, would readily have declared any delinquency of Christ if he had discovered it, leaves the world and passes into the dread presence of his Judge, attesting His unimpeachable excellence; " I have sinned," he says, " in that I have betrayed innocent blood." Even the charges that were brought against Him in the various courts in which He was arraigned, if true, could be vindicated on the principles of everlasting right. Was He charged with blasphemy for making Himself the Son of God? He *was* the Son of God. Was He charged with political rebellion in making Himself a king? He was a King—a King by eternal right. How often did Pilate, who, overborne at last by priestly intolerance and popular clamour, condemned Him, declare that "he found no fault in Him!" Truly He was the holy, the harmless, and the separate from sinners; He rendered in His life the highest homage to every righteous law in the universe. O Justice, never, never wast thou so outraged as in the imprisonment and death of this illustrious Galilean! Here, too, is the basest *Ingratitude*. Was there one man in Judæa, or Galilee, or Samaria, who could refer to one single act of unkindness which He had ever committed towards any? Not one. "He went about doing good." His breast heaved and glowed with love for all. How many thousands of the population had been the personal recipients of His kindness! He had given health to many a diseased frame, fed many a hungry one, and brightened many a home. He had injured none; He had blessed thousands and sought to save all. Here is *Astounding Impiety*. The Prisoner was the "Son of God." He was the "Prince of Life." Had these men not heard, had they not witnessed, those stupendous acts of His which attested His Godhead? How astounding their hardihood in daring to lay hands on Him, Who in a moment could consume them with the breath of His mouth!

Secondly: His imprisonment was effected in the name of Law and Religion. The Law they referred to (Deut. xviii. 20) had no just application to the case of Christ, and they must have been conscious of its irrelevancy. Christ was not a "prophet" Who had presumed to speak a word in the "name of Jehovah" which "He had not commanded," nor had He spoken in the name of "any other god," and therefore by the law of Moses He was not guilty of death. Still, knowing as they did its inapplicability, they plead it. Sin is essentially a vile thing anyhow; but its blackness deepens when perpetrated in the name of law. But what, if a law authorized a morally criminal act, is the act less criminal? In no measure. So depraved is our world that even in States the most civilized, the moral errors and corrupt wishes of men have often been organized into law, guarded by Imperial pomp, and backed by national power. But a crime is not less a crime because law sanctions it. Great professions of loyalty to law, and loyalty to religion, the dark past urges us to look upon with a suspicious eye. Law has sanctioned martyrdom with all its nameless horrors, and war with all its bloody enormities. It is often more virtuous to break a law than to obey it. Have not the greatest benefactors of the world broken laws? Daniel and his three brethren in Babylon, the apostles, and reformers, set the law at defiance—and we bless their memories. But it was in the *name* of *Religion* as well as law. This makes the crime greater still. The men that instigated the Crucifixion of the Son of God were professedly religious men; they were the religious authorities of the country. Under profession of respect for truth and God, they wrought all the enormities which blackened the page of evangelic history. The greatest outrages on justice, humanity, and religion, have often been enacted by those who have vaunted most their loyalty to civil order and sacred truth. The devil is never so mighty in his rule on earth as when he robes himself in a garb of rectitude, and quotes the words of Heaven. This he did now in Jerusalem, and this the Heavenly Teacher Himself emphatically declared was "his hour"—the hour when he seemed to hold the mind of the Jewish nation in his grasp, and when his empire on earth reached its culmination—

"Hell howled, and heaven that moment let fall a tear."

Look at Christ's Imprisonment—

III —AS THE MOST WONDERFUL ENIGMA IN THE GOVERNMENT OF GOD

I know of nothing more wonderful in the universe than the sight of Jesus in bonds. Three questions start in the mind, to which unaided reason can give no soul-satisfying solution.

Why does Eternal Justice allow unsullied Holiness thus to suffer? Under the rule of a righteous government we should reasonably infer that an absolutely holy Being would be absolutely free from sufferings and trials of every kind—would be absolutely happy. How, then, comes it to pass that here we find not merely innocence, but incarnate virtue and truth in its highest form; the bleeding Victim of a tyranny the most intolerant and the most cruel? How comes it to pass that we have here the purest and loveliest Character on earth the most tried and afflicted of any amongst the sons of men? Where is the justice of the universe?

The justice that often vindicated itself in the ages that were gone? If ever in the history of the race interposition of justice seemed called for, it was now, to crush wickedness at its height, and to help agonizing virtue in its sublimest aspects. But there is no indication of it. Where is it? If it exists, it has shrouded itself in such thick clouds of darkness that human reason cannot penetrate it.

Why does Almighty God give men the power to perpetrate such enormities? All the power wicked men have comes from God. "In Him they live and move." They cannot think a thought or move a limb without Him. Why does the Almighty, Who is so holy as to charge the angels with folly, and to declare the Heavens unclean in His sight, allow these wretches to inflict such torture upon His blessed Son? He could frustrate their designs, paralyze their power, and quench their existence in a moment. Why did He not do so? Why does the Almighty, "Who as a Father pitieth his children, pitieth them that fear Him," not come to the help of His well-beloved Son now in agony and blood?

Why does the All-powerful Emmanuel Himself submit to these enormities? He could have delivered Himself. Is not this tortured Man in bonds He Who had wrought such wonders in Galilee during the last three years? Is it not He Who raised the buried dead, and hushed the furious storm? Why does He submit to these indignities now? By a wave of His hand He could drive them in confusion and dismay from His presence; by a glance of His eye He could scath them to ashes. Why does He allow His *Almightiness* to slumber within Him, and submit to this ignominious and excruciating infliction? Why? Reason has no answer. All the oracles of nature stand mute before these questions. We turn to the Bible; and the blessed oracle responds to our interrogations; and though in its communications on the subject there is much that seems still inexplicable we rest our faith in its teaching.

"Even as the Son of man came not to be ministered unto, but to minister, and give His life a ransom for many."

"For when we were yet without strength, in due time Christ died for the ungodly: For scarcely for a righteous man will one die: yet peradventure for a good man some will even dare to die. But God commendeth His love towards us, in that, while we were yet sinners, Christ died for us."

"For I delivered unto you first of all that which I also received, how that Christ died for our sins according to the Scriptures."

"For He hath made Him to be sin for us, who knew no sin; that we might be made the righteousness of God in Him."

"Who His own self bare our sins in His own body on the tree, that we, being dead to sins, should live unto righteousness : by Whose stripes ye were healed."

"For Christ also hath once suffered for sins, the just for the unjust, that He might bring us to God, being put to death in the flesh, but quickened by the Spirit."

Does not the VICARIOUS principle stand out in these verses in sunny prominence ? I profess not to explain this principle, so as to solve all our speculative questions concerning the Sufferings of Christ. In truth when we take it up for discussion in every aspect it starts questions still more perplexing to our poor intellects. I accept the principle, not as it stands in the fog of human theories, but as it stands in the clear light of such Divine utterances as I have quoted. As it stands in such utterances it invests the Sufferings of Christ with a moral significance powerful enough to break the heart into humble penitence and adoring gratitude.

Human Crimes Repeatable from Age to Age
No. 17   John 19:6, Heb. 6:6

"Crucify Him, crucify Him."

"Crucify to themselves the Son of God afresh."

(For Exegetical Remarks, see Vol. II. p. 137.)

THE Crucifixion was, perhaps, one of the greatest crimes ever perpetrated on this earth.

In the history of this world, which teems with crimes, it stands forth with pre-eminent enormity.   Political tyrannies under which empires have groaned, through the round of many centuries; Religious superstition and Priestcraft with their bloody inquisitions, their torturing racks, and fires of martyrdom; War—hell's chief offspring, which has desolated the fairest portions of the globe, dyed oceans with blood, and hurled millions into eternity—all these are an aggregation of crimes whose enormity no finite intellect can estimate.   But great as they are, are they to be compared with the Crucifixion ?   No! sooner compare atoms in the sunbeam to the cloud-capped mountains that block out the great sun itself.   Every sinful passion you can conceive of was brought out and worked to its utmost tension to accomplish this Crucifixion.

The expression in the Hebrews, "Crucifying the Son of God afresh," proclaims the Repeatability of this crime.

Two remarkable things strike us at the outset, concerning the Apostle's charge.

First : It was a Charge made against Professed Religionists.   The persons who are represented as "crucifying the Son of God afresh" had gone a great way in the religious life.

(1.) They had been *enlightened*.   True spiritual ideas had broken in upon the darkness of their minds.

(2.) They had *participated in the Divine*.   They had been made "partakers of the Holy Ghost."   The Divine Spirit had come into them.

(3.) They had *relished the truth*.   "Tasted the good Word of

God." They had experienced a certain amount of delight in their religion.

(4.) They had been *subject to spiritual forces.* "Brought under the powers of the world to come." Considerations drawn from the invisible, the spiritual, and the eternal, had begun to influence them.

These are the persons of whom the writer to the Hebrews speaks. And are not such persons Christians to a great extent? Anyhow they are as much Christians as the best conventional Christians of our day. The startling point is, that these Christians are spoken of as *"crucifying the Son of God."* Had they been heathens, atheists, profligates, one would not have marvelled. Conventional Christians crucify Christ.

The other remarkable thing that strikes us concerning the Apostle's charge is—

Secondly: It was made against Professed Religionists, thirty years after Christ had left the World.

Where now was Judas, who betrayed Him? He had "gone" to his own place. What had become of Pilate, who condemned Him? He was, no doubt, sleeping in his grave. The rabble who cried, "Away with Him! Away with Him!" where were they? Sleeping most of them in the dust. And the soldiers too? During the thirty intervening years most of them probably had gone the "way of the whole earth."

A Generation of men had well-nigh passed away since the tragedy of the Crucifixion, and yet here is an inspired person charging the crime upon living men who had never seen Christ! How is this to be explained? The *Repeatability* of the crime of the Crucifixion is true of all crimes. The moral spirit of men is transmitted from generation to generation. The criminal act of one man strikes a chord that will vibrate through all the centuries. The souls of past ages animate the men of these times. Adam lives in all unregenerate men to this day. How can this be? The following propositions may contribute to the solution of this fact—

I —THAT THE ESSENCE OF AN ACTION CONSISTS, NOT IN ITS EXTERNAL FORM, BUT IN ITS SPIRIT

The moral character of an action, is not in the *muscular exertion,* but in the *mental volition.* "As a man thinketh in his heart so is he." This is Heaven's idea of moral conduct. With what clearness, force, and constancy, did the Heavenly Teacher insist on this! True philosophy agrees with Christ in teaching that a man might be *a thief* who had never taken a fraction of another man's property; *a liar* who had never uttered a word of falsehood; *a blasphemer* who had never given utterance to a profane expression;

a murderer who had never struck a blow. Real moral actions are performed, battles are fought, victories are won and defeats endured, crimes perpetrated and virtues displayed, down deep in regions of the soul into which no eye penetrates but God's. In this way the Apostle regarded men as being guilty of perpetrating the dreadful act of *crucifying* Christ who had never seen Him.

First: This fact agrees with our sense of Moral Propriety. Who does not feel that if his character were to be estimated only by his *overt* acts, without any reference to the inward motives that prompted them, he would be grossly misjudged? Would not the verdict upon the conduct clash with the sense of what is reasonable and right?

(1.) Our outward actions often misrepresent our motives, *either by mistake or intention.* We know, for instance, that outward actions, which often appear good to others, and which have apparently a good tendency, spring from motives that conscience cannot approve, and we know the reverse.

How often, for example, do men from the influence of passion, say or do something that their whole nature disowns the moment after it has been done! From a sudden rush of passion, an expression leaps from the lips which the whole nature of the man disowns, before the echo of the last word has died away; which he disclaims and would recall at once if he could. The man feels, "It is not I that have said this." On the other hand, how often do men perform deeds which society accepts at once as morally meritorious and signally generous, from motives which are unvirtuous, and which the author's own conscience condemns!

For instance, a man may be regarded by public sentiment as a prince amongst the philanthropists of the age, a peer in the realm of benevolence, whose outward charities are inspired and ruled by unworthy motives.

In some cases, *Greed*, love of money, prompts men to what the world consider Munificent acts of charity. A man embarks in a commercial undertaking; his success requires that he should make known as widely as possible his warehouse and his wares. What is the best advertisement? Let him contribute handsomely and persistently to the most popular benevolent institutions; and his name shall be emblazoned in reports, and shouted on platforms. Verily, no advertisement in the "Times" newspaper would be so commercially valuable as this. The beneficiaries of the institutions he patronizes will wend their way to this man's establishment.

In other cases *Vanity*, love of praise, prompts men to what the world considers munificent acts of charity. Vanity, in some natures, grows into a regal passion. There is a hungering for praise. Hence the abounding of fawning sycophants in all circles. Let a man contribute largely to popular benevolent institutions, and what will be the result? Though he may have no sterling moral character, and but little brains, he shall be voted to the Chair, and be made for the time being the king of the Assembly. Hireling Secretaries will pour into his ear the most fulsome adulations, and audiences will thunder out his name with acclamations. All this Greed and Vanity, therefore, the blind world will credit as sublime philanthropy, whilst the holy Heavens will scowl down upon it as putrescent Hypocrisy and Cant.

Therefore it is just and right we should be tried and judged by our *motives* rather than by our Overt acts.

(2.) Our outward actions are insignificant in number *compared with our volitions.* Outward actions, both good and bad, amount to very little when we consider what their authors would do if they had the capacity and the means. Thank God, there is a *Restraining* power in the Divine government. There are potential Napoleons, and Czars all about us bound in chains. They cannot do what they list. Moreover—

(3.) We instinctively associate the *intention or motive with the outward action.* We condemn the actions of some, and frequently laud those of others, simply because of the character of the intention which we suppose prompted the performance. Our consciences approve not of any act we put forth because it seems good to others, but simply because it was *intended* as good by ourselves. If the whole world condemn our conduct, conscience will smile upon us, if the motives which have controlled us are pure. But should our actions, on the contrary, awaken the hosannas of the age, our consciences will damn us if they have not sprung from motives in accordance with our convictions of the True, the Beautiful, and the Good.

Secondly: This fact urges the Necessity of a thorough Discipline of the Heart. The productions depend upon the soil, the streams upon the fountain. Look well, therefore, to the soil; keep the fountain pure; let the roots be healthy. "Keep thy heart with all diligence." The parts which the actor on the open stage performs with such striking effect before the gaze of applauding thousands, he has many times before acted over and over again in solitude. So with *overt* crimes. Those deeds of atrocity that shock for a time the feelings of a whole age, the perpetrator has acted several times before in the hidden regions of his own foul heart.

Thirdly: This fact suggests unexpected Revelations at the Last Day. Men judge each other here by outward appearances. Hence many great sinners pass for great saints. But it will not be so on the great day of final assize. The hidden things of darkness will then be brought to light. Motives will be everything. We are told that then we are to give an account of things done "*in* the body." Whether this little preposition was intended to express the idea I am attaching to it or not, the idea itself is undeniably true. What we have done *by* the body is trifling indeed compared with what we have done *in* it. All that each man has done *in* his body will be revealed in the eternal sunlight of retribution. What is the history of your conduct? The mere catalogue of your outward muscular deeds? I tell you, nay; it includes the unexpressed wishes, the inarticulate longings, the unwrought purposes of the heart. And what is the record of the *outward* life to this? What is one short verse of the Bible to the great thousand chaptered book itself? It is for all in that great unsealed book that you will have to answer when called to give an account of "all the things done *in* the body." Great heavens! What revelations will there be in the last day! Notice—

II —THAT THE SPIRIT THAT ANIMATED THE PERPETRATORS OF THE LITERAL CRUCIFIXION, IS PREVALENT AMONGST MEN AT THE PRESENT DAY

Now, my point is, that this crowning crime corrupt humanity everywhere is capable of perpetrating.

Who were the Instigators of the crucifixion? "The Chief Priests and the Pharisees" moved the nation to the deed. What was the feeling that stimulated them? ENVY. They were envious of His growing popularity, and grew malignant as they saw the people turning away their attention from them to Christ. The Resurrection of Lazarus from the dead, seemed first to call out this feeling into practical determination. Then from that day forth "they took counsel together for to put Him to death."

Is not *envy* prevalent now? Merchant envies merchant, statesman envies statesman, sect envies sect, even preacher envies preacher, and author envies author. This passion burns everywhere. It is that which a poet represents "as a coal that comes hissing hot from hell." The infernal fire which flamed in the breasts of these Chief Priests and Pharisees smoulders with more or less intensity in the breasts of all.

What prompted Judas to betray Christ? Was it any unkind feeling towards Him? Was it malice? The overwhelming distress he experienced when he heard that Christ was delivered to be crucified, unmistakably shows that it was no malign impulse which inspired his treacherous deed. No; it was simply LOVE OF MONEY. "What will ye give me?" was the question. It was a pure matter of cash. If he could have had a larger sum for protecting his Master, would he not have done so more readily? Supposing that when Judas was making his bargain some one had stepped up to him and said, "Judas, I will give you five more pieces of silver than the priests have offered you, to stand by Jesus and follow Him to the end." Do you suppose that Judas would not have rapturously accepted the offer, and frowned the other barterers from his presence? He would have stood by the Cross to the last moment, and fronted with a defiant bearing the wild fury of the mob, had sufficient silver been offered.

Is this passion extinct? Extinct! Never did it reign and rage more than now. "What will ye give me?" is the great question. "My time and influence, my mind and muscles," says the Englishman, "are yours for money." The man who neglects duty for gain, who suppresses a truth, or sacrifices a principle for interest, is a modern Judas.

What inspired Pilate to condemn Him? LOVE OF POPULARITY. Did he believe Him guilty? No! Before the Chief Priests, the rulers, and the people, he repeatedly declared that he "found no fault in Him;" and after he had, contrary to his convictions, pronounced the sentence, he called for a "basin of water" in the open court, and thus symbolically corroborated his verbal declaration: "I am innocent of the blood of this *just Person*." Oh, Pilate, Pilate! all the waters of the Atlantic could not wash out that stain! His conscience declared His innocence. It was the fear of becoming *unpopular*. He attended to the voice of the populace, rather than to the voice of his own conscience. He thought more of *popularity* than of *principle*.

Does not this sentiment prevail now? Are not the great bulk of mankind governed more by conventionalities than by convictions?—disposed ever to relinquish what is true for what is popular? The spirit of Pilate is common. Popularity hunters will be found now in every walk of life, not only in the State, amongst the garrulous members of our Senate House, but in the Church amongst our clap-trap pulpiteers.

What induced the people to cry out for the deliverance of Barabbas rather than Christ? A STRONGER SYMPATHY FOR BRUTE FORCE AND COURAGE, THAN FOR SPIRITUAL GOODNESS AND MORAL HEROISM. Did they feel in their consciences that Barabbas was a better man? No. They preferred *brute* force to moral. Barabbas may be considered the type of the one, Christ of the other. Barabbas was a seditious person, a thief, a "murderer," a man of physical daring, violence, and blustering pretence. They voted for him.

Is not this common? Remove the conventional discredit from the weaker thief, exalt him to the majesty of the military despot, and who now will not vote for Barabbas? Let the man who is imprisoned for a *petty* theft, or condemned to be hanged for *one* murder, rifle whole cities and lay ten thousand dead upon the battlefield, and this Barabbas shall receive the loud plaudits of a whole nation.

Is not this common? Two men who have gone out from England to foreign lands each on a mission shall return home the same day. The mission of the one was to indoctrinate the heathen mind with the soul-renovating and ennobling elements of Christly truth and goodness. He has lived and laboured amidst human scenes the most revolting to his moral intuitions and the social decencies of his nature, amidst perils the most alarming, and deprivations the most crushing. He has won converts to truth and rectitude. The other has gone forth on a military campaign. In prosecuting his mission he has rifled thousands of their virtue, enwrapped homes, cities, villages, in conflagration, shed rivers of human blood, covered hundreds of green acres with tens of thousands of the dead and the dying, broken the hearts of thousands of parents, and widows, and orphans. He, too, shall return from his mission. Mark how each is received back to his home!

The one goes to his Mission House, whence he received at first his commission. There, perhaps, are gathered together a few men unknown to fame, who welcome him with a warm shake of the hand, and say a few kind words to him,—and that is all.

How is the other received? Flags float from lofty towers, bells peal out from churches and cathedrals, hundreds of grandees are present to welcome with their congratulation, crowds gather on all hands to shout their hurrahs. The Premier goes to the Senate House, and delivers his panegyric in the choicest language, and in the sweetest tones he can command. Bishops and Archbishops preach, and seek to inspire congregations with gratitude to the "GOD OF PEACE" for the life and labours of such a murderer. The Parliament votes him a handsome fortune and a splendid annuity, and the Sovereign makes him a Baronet or a Lord. What does all this mean? *"Not this Man, but Barabbas."*

"Honour," says Carlyle, "Barabbas the Robber, thou shalt sell old-clothes through the cities of the world; shalt accumulate sordid moneys, with a curse on every coin of them, and be spit upon for eighteen hundred years. Raise statues to the swollen Gambler as if he were great, sacrifice oblations to the King of Scrip;—unfortunate mortals, you will dearly pay for it yet. Quiet as Nature's counting-house and scrip-ledgers are, no faintest item is ever blotted out from them, for or against; and to the last doit that account will have to be settled. Rigorous as Destiny;—she *is* Destiny. Chancery or Fetter Lane is soft to her, when the day of settlement comes. With her, in the way of abatement, of oblivion, neither gods nor men prevail. 'Abatement? That is not our way of doing business; the time has run out, the debt it appears is due.' Will the laws of gravitation abate for you? Gravitation acts at the rate of sixteen feet per second, in spite of all prayers.

Were it the crash of a Solar System, or the fall of a Yarmouth herring, all one to gravitation."

What inspired the soldiers who nailed Him to the cross, and plunged the spear into His side, who wagged their heads and mocked Him? What was the spirit that stimulated them? A MISERABLE SERVILITY TOWARDS THEIR SUPERIORS. They did it to please their masters. This flunkeyism runs through all classes— one class bowing and cringing to those above them; the class next to the throne the most servile of all. Courtiers with emphasis are they. Now do not these feelings run through all modern society, *envy, greed, love of popularity, admiraton of brute force, servility,* and *flunkeyism?* I say that I can find nothing in the breasts of any of those men who were employed in the Crucifixion, that I cannot find now in the hearts of the men about me. Notice—

III —UNDER SIMILAR CIRCUMSTANCES THIS SPIRIT WILL BE
DEVELOPED IN SIMILAR FORMS

Let a being appear amongst us similar to Christ, and these existing germs of evil would probably develop themselves in as aggravated a form as they did at the Crucifixion. Suppose the son of an humble mechanic, from one of the most obscure parts of the country, to appear amongst us. Let him be the very picture of penury and want,—his countenance "marred more than any man's." Let him go through the length and breadth of the land, denouncing in no measured terms the religious leaders of the age, and sapping the foundation of their influence. Let him go into our Temples, and call them his own, and cast out all the "money changers" that are found within their precincts, and turn the heart of the people against their priests. Let him deal as severely with our Magistrates, Mayors, Senators, and ecclesiastics, as Christ did with the various members of the old Sanhedrim. Let him denounce wealth, pleasure, and military glory, and in fact, all the idols of the people. Let him take a firm stand against the flowing tide of popular sentiment, and strike every hour without mercy at the tenderest prejudices and the dearest objects of the people's devotion. And in the Senate House, the market, the judicial Courts, the Exchange, and in the scenes of fashion thunder out, "Woe unto you; woe unto you!" Let him talk about destroying his enemies and setting up a "kingdom" himself, that shall extend over the world and grind into powder all other dynasties. How long, think ye, would such a man be tolerated in England? *Three years?* I trow not. Many months would not elapse before all London, all England, would echo with the cry, "*Away with him!*" Before three months he would be in Newgate, and perhaps hanged on the gallows for high treason.

Do you say the case is not parallel, inasmuch as Jesus of

Nazareth was the Son of God? True. But the Jewish people did not know it; "for had they known it they would not have crucified the Lord of glory." The parallel, therefore, is complete, so far as the feelings of the people are concerned.

I confess that I do not discover a single passion or impulse, in any of the actions in the tremendous tragedy of our Lord's Crucifixion, that I see not pulsating in the bosoms of men around me. In this respect as well as in others, "that which hath been is now." That which raged in hellish riot on Calvary's brow, eighteen centuries ago, is here in England now, speaking essentially the same thing, though in a different language, and working out the same master aims, though by different instruments and methods. The germs of that harvest of appalling crime, which shocked creation's nerves, and made the sun put on his mourning veil, are lying thickly in the heart of our age, under the gilded roof of a Conventional Christianity.

CONCLUSION. The subject teaches us to—
First: Be careful, in denouncing the great Criminals of History, that you are not as bad as they are. Do you denounce the Chief Priests, Judas, Pilate, the populace, the soldiers? I know you do, nor can I blame you. On the world's black roll of crime their iniquities appear in aspects that thrill my nature with a quivering horror. But in condemning them let us take care that we do not foredoom ourselves. The portrait of that criminal which Nathan the prophet held up to the eye of David, woke in the heart of the king the most indignant denunciations. And looking at the demon-figure, he exclaimed, "As the Lord liveth, the man that hath done this thing shall surely die." But David, "*thou art the man*" that hast perpetrated that moral enormity, and in thy severe sentence thou hast foredoomed thyself! In like manner, the picture of the "Husbandman"—who first killed the servants of the "Householder" and last of all killed his son—which the Heavenly Artist drew, and held up to the Chief Priests and Pharisees, roused their indignation. They declared that such "wicked men" should be "miserably" destroyed. But they *themselves* were those wicked men, and they did not know it. Let us, therefore, be modest in our denunciations of others.

The subject teaches us to—
Secondly: Realize the urgency of Heart-Renovation. Nothing will effectually serve us but a change of heart. "Marvel not; ye must be born again." Embedded in the depraved heart are the seeds of all wickedness, and so thickly cluster those seeds amidst the central fibres of the soul, that the heart itself must be taken away before they can be removed. There is no hope for the world but in a new "heart of flesh," a heart of tender moral

sensibilities, and warm truthful sympathies, in which the "incorruptible seed" of truth and virtue will germinate and grow.

Secular Philanthropist! I give thee credit for purest motives, and I yield to none in my admiration of thy ingenuity in constructing measures for the world's improvement, and of thy zeal in seeking to work them out; but I have no faith in any of thy efforts to make man as man one whit the better. Thou art only patching the rotten garment; thou art only seeking to purify the streams whilst the fountain is filthy in its springs; thou art only lopping off a few branches from the Upas—and thereby strengthening the roots, and striking them deeper in the soil; thou art only anointing with thy salves the few eruptions on the outside of the body, whilst the whole current of blood is poisoned in the veins. Thy work is a quackery, under which I fear our poor humanity is getting worse. "*Marvel not that I say unto thee, Ye must be born again.*" The world wants moral renovation;—nothing less. The subject teaches us to—

Thirdly: Estimate the transcendent value of Christianity. The philosophy of our nature shows, that there is no other instrumentality on earth that is at all suited to effect this *moral renovation,* and all history demonstrates that nothing else seems to have done it. The Cross of Christ is the soul-renewing force.

Herein is a marvellousness of Divine plan. The Cross, which required all the depravity of the world to erect, has in it a power to *destroy* all the depravity of the world. That in which all evil found its climax is that in which all evil shall find its death. That which the "principalities and powers of darkness" in the human heart built up, shall one day "triumph over them all, and make a show of them openly." The blow which the hellish spirit inflicted in the Crucifixion rebounds, and will bruise the very head of the world's serpent. The Cross on which Christ was crucified is to crucify the world unto itself.

> "Hail! Son of the most High, Heir of both worlds,
> Queller of Satan! On Thy glorious work
> Now enter; and begin to save mankind."—*Milton.*

Spirits
No. 18   John 19:30

" He gave up the ghost " (Spirit).

(For Exegetical Remarks, see Vol. II. p. 155.)

NOTICE here—

I —THERE IS A SPIRIT-WORLD

Two questions arise here—

First : What is Spirit ? I confess my utter inability to solve a problem on which the greatest sages of all times have pleaded ignorance. To say that it is a something that is *immaterial*, instead of answering the question, only states it in another form. What is *immateriality* ? Or to say that it is a thinking and reasoning principle is as far from a solution : the question comes up again, What is that principle ? Yet though Spirit transcends all our definitions, there are certain ideas we attach to it, which mark it off, in broad and clear outline, from all which we consider to be material existences—at least from all the material existence of which we have any knowledge. What are those ideas ?

(1.) We attach the idea of *Elementalness* to Spirit. By this I mean that its existence is not made up of parts, but that it is an uncompounded and unmixed entity. All material lives are combinations. All vegetables and animals are compounded of various elements : abstract one of their constituent principles, and they cease to be. Indeed, it is probable, there is nothing that we know of, even in the inorganic world of matter, that is a simple substance. Probably, the next race of chemical analysts will find that oxygen, nitrogen, and such substances, which are now considered elemental, are but compositions. But we think of Spirit as an *Uncompounded Principle*—as something that is not made up of parts—something that you cannot divide, that you can take nothing from, and add nothing to.

(2.) We attach the idea of *Moral Activity* to Spirit. Inertness is a quality of matter. Neither atom nor globe would ever move were it not set in motion by a foreign force. And whilst life in trees and flesh moves, it ever moves by impulses over which it has no control : and thus in these forms it moves in the beaten track of ages. Each plant moves under the same circumstances in the same way—rejects and appropriates, as did the first parent of its kind which grew in the garden of Eden. Each sentient individual of the various tribes of earth and air and sea, does the same thing, in the same manner, as did its primal sire. But Spirit we consider self-moving and self-controlling; each chooses its own line of action and determines its own pace. Each is a distinct fountain of influences, outpouring streams that never flowed before : a self-acting machine performing evolutions and producing results, the like of which has never been before, and never will be again. No two Spirits have the same history. Each has chapters of thought, feeling, and deed, which find no record in the other. To Spirit, therefore, we attach the idea of an existent which acts, but which acts not *necessarily :* neither from an inward impulse, nor an outward force, but from itself.

(3.) We attach the idea of *Reflectiveness* to Spirit. By this I mean, the power to turn back upon itself, study its own nature, translate its own sensations into ideas, and create a world of thought of its own—a power to rise from the particular to the universal, the discordant to the harmonious,—the creature to the Creator—a power to link the most solitary fact in fellowship with an eternal principle, and bring the wildest and harshest sounds into the scale of intellectual music—a power which, from the facts of its own consciousness, builds up a superstructure for itself in which it can live as an independent monarch, secure from all foreign invaders, and independent of all help : where it can worship as a seraph under the ever-lightening rays of God. A power by which the mind reads the philosophy, feels the poetry, and chants the anthems, writ on creation's hieroglyphic page. Brutes have no such power as this. The universe is nothing but sensation to them : it gives them no idea ; they cannot spell a word of meaning from any part of its various and vast revelations.

(4.) We attach the idea of *Religiousness* to Spirit. By this I mean a tendency to, and a capacity for, worship. In the tribes of irrational existences around us we discover no such principle as this. None display any knowledge of a Great First Cause, nor therefore any desire to worship Him. The sunlight of ten thousand days gives to them no idea of their Creator, nor do the blessings which they receive through a long life, filling up every sense with pleasure, and satisfying every appetite and want, awaken in them one sentiment of gratitude toward Him. The mind of the most sagacious of their class is a blank in relation to Him. It has neither the eye to see Him, nor the sensibility to feel His spiritual touch.

But *Spirit* we regard as the offspring of the " Father of Spirits," partaking of His essence, possessing the filial element as its primary impulse : and having therefore both a native tendency and a moral obligation to reverence, praise, and serve Him. Spirit feels itself morally related to Him ; has its eye wistfully fixed upon Him ; and its heart "cries out for the living God." The language of an old Hebrew expresses the experience and attitude of all Spirits in their normal state. "Unto Thee I lift mine eyes, O Thou that dwellest in the heavens. Behold, as the eyes of servants look unto the hand of their mistress, so our eyes wait upon the Lord our God."

(5.) We attach the idea of *Self-Modification* to Spirit. There is nothing in nature which seems to us to possess the self-modifying attribute but Spirit. The mountains cannot make themselves higher, nor the stars make themselves brighter ; the ocean can make itself neither broader nor deeper, nor the earth increase its verdure or fecundity by its own act. Irrational life also seems destitute of this self-modifying power. Brutes change not their condition ; their habits are fixed : they seem as incapable of deviating from the laws of instinct as the stars of swerving from their pathway. The birds that warble in our groves are neither wiser nor better perhaps than their first parents, that poured their music into the ear of Adam. But Spirit has a Self-forming and a Self-altering power. No one Spirit is compelled to act like another, nor even to act as it has itself acted heretofore. It has a power to map out new pathways for itself, to widen its own domain, to increase its own energy, and augment its own wealth ; to rise through all the stages of glory, or sink through all the degrees of degradation.

(6.) We attach the idea of *Absolute Personal Identity* to Spirit. There is no permanent identity in any corporeal organization. Such organization is composed of particles, all of which are in a state of constant flux. Corporeally the man cannot say that he is the same as he was when a youth : every particle of his frame has changed since then. Since then, perhaps, many of the particles which once belonged to other men, have helped to build his frame, and in their turn gone off to form parts of other frames. The body is like a river, every particle is in rapid flow— in constant circulation, and is the same only in form and function : never a moment the same in all its materials. But we think of Spirit as being the same in Essence ; a simple indivisible substance that can never lose a particle of itself, and that can never have any new element wrought into its being. It may change its condition, it may vary its moods, it may alter its realms of action, and new thoughts and feelings may stream through it in endless succession. But in essence it is evermore the same ; the ever-lastingly identical *Ego* of being. Truly does *Dr. Reid* remark, "that all mankind place their personality in something that cannot be divided, or consist of parts."

(7.) We attach the idea of *Power* to Spirit. We see power everywhere round us. We see it in the inanimate world, as the effect which one element produces upon another, and in the motion which one body produces upon another. We see it also in the world of life : in the plant that turns to its use and trans-mutes into its own essence, the elements that play about it; in the beast that drags along the farmer's harvest wain, and in the bird that rises on the wing and chants its victories over the force that binds the earth and links it to the sun. All these powers are manifestly effects, not ultimate causes—are derived, not primal. All true science proves this, and the Bible declares it. Spirit is the fontal force. It was Spirit that gave to the elements the proclivity to act and react on each other, and that so poised the masses of the universe that one should gently press its fellow into lines and ratios of motion, and thus conduce to the harmony and well-being of all. And the forces of life, too, whether in the fibres of plants or the muscles of flesh, are but the breathings of that Spirit which "reneweth the face of the earth." " He stretcheth out the north over the empty place, and hangeth the earth upon nothing."

I turn now to the question of evidence.

Secondly : What proof is there that there are such beings as Spirits ?

(1.) The structure of the visible universe indicates the *Existence of Spirit*. The universe seems to be produced by and designed for Spirit. Matter is essentially inert; but every part of nature is in motion : matter is blind; but every part of nature indicates the most consummate contrivance : matter is heartless; but every part of nature is warm and instinct with goodness. The whole system of creation, so far as it comes within my narrow vision, is a reflection of the ideas I attach to Spirit. In part of its wondrous structure the "invisible things" as from a burnished mirror are "clearly seen." And then, too, it seems designed *for* Spirit. Does not its exquisite contrivance appeal to thought, its warm and ever-gushing streams of goodness to gratitude, its enchanting realms of beauty to admiration, its infinite grandeur and sublimity to reverence and awe ? Indeed the whole system of visible nature seems to me to imply Spirit, and to be incomplete without it. Let landscapes unfold their beauty and oceans roll in grandeur; let the immeasurable dome above display its radiant worlds by night, and its glorious sun by day, all is meaningless without Spirit. Without Spirit there is no eye for beauty, no heart for goodness, no soul for sublimity and grandeur. What is this fair universe without Spirit but a magnificent mansion without a tenant; a theatre disclosing the most enchanting scenes and inspiring plots without a spectator; a temple filled with the glories of the Shekinah, but containing no worshipper? I infer, therefore, that wherever there is a streak of beauty, a ray of glory, or a note of music, in whatever orb, however far away, there are Spirits to study, adore, and love.

(2.) The *concurrent impressions of mankind sustain the belief in Spirits.* Men, from remotest times, in all places, and in every stage of culture, from the lowest point to the highest, have believed in a spiritual world. The philosophy of the sage, as well as the superstition of the savage, and the fancy of the poet, has peopled the atmosphere with ghosts. The Chaldæans, Egyptians, Greeks, Romans, and Jews, as well as the polytheistic world in all times, regarded every section of nature as filled with Spirits (demons). The gods of the heathen were but the forms which man devised to represent his ideas of mysterious Spirits that tenanted the earth, ruled the elements, and presided over the destinies of our race. Man cannot shake off faith in spiritual existence; the child believes in it without evidence; and the old man who has passed through a life of scepticism, as in the case of Robert Owen, becomes a firm believer in tales of ghostly exploits. Men see Spirits, not only in dim twilight, but in the high noon of civilization. A belief so universal must be intuitive, and an intuitive belief must be true, otherwise there is no truth for man.

(3.) The *Bible most unequivocally declares the existence of Spirits.* They are ascending and descending between heaven and earth— they are ever moving the vast and complicated wheels of Providence, and are ever on the wing to execute the behests of their Sovereign. It tells us that there are legions of such existences; that they exist in various orders and states; and that there is One Infinite Spirit—the Parent, Sustainer, and Judge of all: Who is above all, and in all, and through all, God blessed for ever.

I am bound to believe, thn, that the universe is something more than I can see: something more than can be brought within the cognizance of my five senses: something distinct from the terraqueous globe on which I live, and the huge worlds of flame that roll around me, and shed their brightness on my path: something behind all, or rather in all, and above all. Aye, the angels, demons, genii, sylphs, and ghosts, of which all the nations have thought and spoken, are something more than the airy offspring of a superstitious imagination. They are existences answering, in some degree at least, to the notions which humanity has ever attached to such mystic terms.

I am not disposed to pronounce all who have stated that they have seen Spirits—either fanatics or impostors. The *à priori* wonder is, not that they should be seen, but that they are not more generally perceived. We are related to the material world, and we have senses to discern material existences. We are confessedly more intimately and solemnly related to the Spiritual, and is it not natural to expect that we should have a sense to see spiritual beings? Were such a sense to be opened within us, as the eye of Elijah's servant was opened of old, what visions would burst upon us! The microscope gives us a new world of wonders; but were God to open the spiritual eye, what a universe of Spirits would be revealed! Observe—

II —MAN IS A MEMBER OF THIS SPIRIT-WORLD

I say member, for man is but a very inconsiderable section of the great universe. Still he is a part. "There is a Spirit in man." Christ was now parting with this Spirit in the article of death. Man has Spirit in him; or more properly, perhaps he is Spirit. Man has a something in him to which we attach all the ideas we associate with Spirit in general: a something in which he places his identity: a something which originates moral activity, and which turns back upon itself, and reflects upon its own states: a something which points him to God, and fills him ofttimes with a solemn sentiment: a something by which he is constantly modifying his condition: a something which, whether it be *immaterial* in its essence or not—for over the essence of all things there is a veil through which the keenest eye of science has never pierced—is universally felt to be different to all material organizations, and which we denominate Mind or Spirit: a something in which our personality inheres, and which we regard as *Self*.* Let men call it what they please, all have the principle answering in every point to the afore-mentioned ideas which we attach to Spirit. If different phenomena indicate different substances, then Spirit is essentially different from matter: and if Spirit be essentially different from matter, then we have stronger philosophical evidence for its existence than we have for the existence of matter. Three facts duly pondered and estimated will indicate our authority for these remarks—

(1.) All the evidence, either for the existence of matter or Spirit, is *derived exclusively from phenomena.* We have nothing but the operations and appearances of either: the essence of both is alike hidden. It is under the impenetrable shadows of the ever unknown.

(2.) The Essence whose phenomena appeals *most directly to consciousness is the most conclusively proved.* Consciousness is

---

* Pantheistic philosophy denies this, and teaches that there is but One Substance—the Absolute and the Eternal—in the universe, and that all phenomena, even the most apparently diverse—such as thought and extension—inhere in it.

evermore our ultimate standard, our infallible judge. The senses deceive and so does the understanding, but consciousness never.

(3.) The *phenomena of mind alone appeals directly to consciousness.* We are not conscious of the phenomena of matter; we are only conscious of certain impressions made upon our senses. But the phenomena of mind, thought, emotion, volition, hope and fear, are immediate subjects of consciousness. But the men who theoretically deny to man a Spirit, are few indeed compared with those vast multitudes who hold it in their creed and deny it in their practice : who live as if they had no soul, and as if the body was the all in all of man. I would impress on such three considerations—

First : *They are now in the Spiritual world.* There is a popular idea that man enters the Spiritual world at death, and that he is separated from it now. Let this idea be banished. We are as truly in the Spirit-world now as we ever shall be. Where is the sphere of Spirit ? Where is it not ? Spirit fills the universe. The body does not separate me from Spirit : it is the residence of Spirit, and its medium of communication. There is naught that separates me from the Spirit-world but my unbelief—and that is my sin. Death perhaps will not take me farther into it : but it will open my faithless eyes and make me see it. Jesus walked the earth as the scene of Spirits, and the apostles wrought their mission under the impression that a "cloud of witnesses" were looking on from the spiritual world. Add to my body another sense, and you will give me a new material world. Give my Spirit an earnest evangelical faith, and I shall look at "things unseen" through the medium of all the palpable and material around me.

Secondly : *They are now amenable to all the laws of the Spiritual world.* One law governs all mankind : and one law governs the Spiritual, and that is Love. "Thou shalt love the Lord thy God with all thy heart, and with all thy soul, and with all thy strength, and thy neighbour as thyself." This law is as binding upon man now as it ever will be :—as binding upon him here in his degradation and weakness, as it is upon a seraph in the zenith of his dignity and strength. This is the royal law of the Spiritual world.

Thirdly : *They are now forming a character which will determine their lasting condition in the Spiritual world.* What will decide my abiding position and circumstances in the great universe of disembodied Spirit ? Things done *in* the body. Material wealth and splendour, however great, will go for nothing there. Earth's mightiest patricians are there on a level with the poorest plebeians. The hand of death strips princes of all their earthly garniture, and leaves their Spirits bare to the common eye of souls, and to the searching eye of God. Not merely things done *by* the body. It is but a small portion of our life deeds that we perform by the body; that we allow to take a palpable form. Our works are *really* done before a hand is uplifted or a muscle moved. Heart and brain are our workers: limbs are but our instruments, which we may use or not. Things done *by* the body are but contingent and occasional exhibitions, or specimens of the innumerable and complicated things done *in* it. Volitions, with all their train of thought and feeling and impulse, are the deeds done *in* the body. The theatre of moral action is not the spot of ground on which the actor stands, but the state of the heart he is in :—it is never space, but always soul. It is the unseen things done *in* the body that will determine our destiny *out* of it.

Let us, then, rise to a sense of the greatness of that nature with which the great God has endowed us ! We are SPIRITS. Emanations of the Infinite Mind, and members of that Spiritual System, for which matter, in all its functions and forms, was made. Let us assert our Supremacy over the material; use the world as not abusing it. In one sense we can never think too highly of ourselves. "What shall it profit a man, if he gain the whole world, and lose his own soul ?"

Angel's Words to Mary
No. 19   John 20:11-23
(See also Matthew 28:5-7, Mark 16:5-7, Luke 24:5-7)

"But Mary stood without at the sepulchre weeping: and as she wept, she stooped down, and looked into the sepulchre. And seeth two angels in white sitting, the one at the head, and the other at the feet, where the body of Jesus had lain. And they say unto her, Woman, why weepest thou? She saith unto them, Because they have taken away my Lord, and I know not where they have laid Him."

(For Exegetical Remarks, see Vol. II. p. 175.)

AT the outset our attention is called to the *various versions of the same fact*. Matthew and Mark speak of one angel—Mark describing the angel as a young man, clothed in white raiment, sitting at the right side. Luke speaks of two angels; he says, "Behold, two men stood by them in shining garments;" and John also speaks of two angels in white. Then, too, some of the evangelists record words which these angels spoke, which the others have omitted. And as to the women, Matthew mentions two Marys, Mark adds Salome to them, Luke speaks of women generally; he says, "It was Mary Magdalene, and Joanna, and Mary the mother of James, and other women that were with them." In these varied versions there is no *contradiction*. The strange and startling circumstances of the occasion, would strike some spectators in a way that they would not affect others; each would record what came most clearly under his eye, and struck most powerfully on his ear. No two minds are exactly alike; hence it would be impossible for the same objects and events to make exactly the same impression upon different persons. The diversity of their version, being just what might have been expected as *natural*, proves that each was independent in his narrative, and that there was no collusion between them. Had each given the same identical account of this fact, there would have been something like a good reason for doubting their honesty and discrediting the fact which they attested.

* This is one of a Series of articles on the "Words of Angels to Men on Earth," preached at Stockwell. They will re-appear in subsequent volumes of the Homilistic Library.

The Bible informs us that in the Spirit-World there are innumerable intelligences existing in an immeasurable chain of gradation reaching from man up to archangels. From the representations made of them in the Sacred Record, we are given to understand that they possesss attributes which distinguish them from men. They have unusual vitality, hence they are called "living ones;" they excel in strength; they have vast intelligence; "full of eyes;" incalculable celerity; the "speed of angels time counts not." We learn further, that they not only possess attributes that distinguish them from men, but attributes also that distinguish them from one another. They are not all of the same mould, poŝition, rank, or formation. Hence we read of "thrones," "principalities," "dominions," &c.

Sometimes when angels appeared to men, they did their work *mutely*, and dropped no word. Neither the angel that smote the camp of the Assyrians, the angel which walked in the fiery furnace with the three Hebrew youths, the angel that guarded Daniel in the lions' den, nor the angel that smote Herod that he died, seem to have uttered a word. In profound silence each discharged his heavenly mission. On the other hand, the angels that appeared to Hagar, Abraham, Sarah, Lot, Isaac, Jacob, Balaam, Joshua, Gideon, Manoah and his wife, to the kings and elders of Israel, during the three days' pestilence in the time of David, to Orma and his four sons, to the prophets, Elisha, Elijah, Isaiah, Ezekiel, Daniel, and Zechariah, to Zecharias, father of John the Baptist, to the Virgin Mary, Joseph, to the shepherds watching their flocks, to the disciples as they gazed on their Lord ascending, to the company of Apostles, to Philip the deacon, to Peter in prison, to Cornelius, to Paul on the Adriatic, to John in Patmos, and to the women at the sepulchre—all these spoke—spoke the thoughts of heaven in human language to men on earth.

In reference to the language of the angels here recorded, I notice—

I —IT IS SUGGESTIVE OF THEIR TENDER CONSIDERATION FOR THE INFIRMITIES OF GENUINE DISCIPLES

There are two infirmities in human nature, even in its Christian state.

First: A Tendency to *dread* the Preternatural. "The thought of the supernatural," says *Tulloch*, "abides with man, do what he will. It visits the most callous, it interests the most sceptical. For a time—even for a long time—it may lie asleep in the breast, either amidst the sordid despairs, or the proud, rich, and young enjoyments of life: but it wakens up in curious inquiry, or dreadful anxiety. In any case it is a thought of which no man can be reasonably independent. For so far as he retains his reasonable being, and preserves the consciousness of moral susceptibilities and relations, in so far will his thought of a higher world, of a life enclosing and influencing his present life—be a powerful and practical thought with him." We are told, that when the angel descended from heaven, the earth quaked, the stone rolled from the grave, and the Roman guards did shake and become as dead men. These women perhaps participated in the terror, hence the considerateness of the angel in saying to them, "Be not affrighted."

Secondly : A Tendency to *doubt* the Preternatural. It would seem, when the angel told the disciples that He was not there, but was risen, they were somewhat incredulous, hence he says (according to Matthew), "Come, see the place where the Lord lay ; "—"come, look for yourselves. Here is the spot where He lay ; but it is vacant, He is gone." What the angel said to these women, Christianity says to all men—"Come and see for yourselves." May we not conclude from this tender consideration of human infirmities, that angels are acquainted with the workings of the human soul ? And in all the anxieties and sorrows of the genuine disciples of Christ do they not feel a profound and practical interest ? Indeed, how else can they succour us ? How else can they scatter our doubts, dispel our fears, strengthen our hopes, and nerve our courage ? "He shall give His angels charge over thee," &c.

In reference to the language here, notice—

II —IT IS SUGGESTIVE OF THEIR REPUGNANCE TO HUMAN ERROR

Luke says that the angel asked Mary, "Why seek ye the living among the dead ?" There is something like reproof in these words, as if the angel had said, "I know that you are seeking Jesus, and that is well; but you are seeking Him in the wrong place, He is not here, He has risen." The reproof contains—

First : A Glorious Truth. Christ is the "*living*" One. The living, τὸν ζῶντα, Him Who liveth. Christ not only lives, but He is *the* living One. "I am He that liveth, and was dead, and am alive for evermore." The living One that never changes with circumstances, never decays with time, that never dies, "Who only hath immortality, dwelling in the light," &c. The reproof suggests—

Secondly : A Common Error. Men are everywhere seeking the living among the dead. They do it—(1.) *Socially*. What a tendency is there in all bereaved hearts to think of the loved ones who are gone as *in the grave !* In spirit, if not in body, we repair oftentimes to the sepulchre where sleep the remains of those ever dear to our hearts. We seek them there ; but they are not there, they are living elsewhere,—living a holier, happier life, somewhere in God's bright universe. Heaven says to the mourner bending over the grave of his dead one, "He is not here, He is risen." They do it—(2.) *Religiously*. The men who seek Christ in the dogmas of creeds, the ceremonies of Churches, the relics of saints, the ministries of priests, the fellowship of nominal Christians, seek the living among the dead. Christ is not in these. He is not in this Church or that Church, in this theology or that theology, in this society or that society, He is risen. "If ye then be risen with Christ, seek those things which are above."

In reference to the language here, notice—

III —IT IS SUGGESTIVE OF THEIR INTIMATE KNOWLEDGE OF CHRIST AND HIS DISCIPLES

Luke gives the following words of the angels : " *Remember how He spake unto you when He was yet in Galilee, saying, The Son of man must be delivered into the hands of sinful men, and be crucified, and the third day rise again.*" A reference is here, perhaps, to Matt. xvi. 21. When Christ thus spoke to His disciples concerning His crucifixion and resurrection, we have no account of angels being present. Anyhow, the Evangelists did not observe them, otherwise we may rest assured they would have taken some notice of their appearance. Albeit they were there, heard, felt, and pondered the conversation. They were always present with Christ, ever attending on Him as His ministers. "I am not alone," He said. He knew that there were legions of angels about Him. Remember the words He spake to you; I heard them, they were memorable words, words never to be forgotten. Christ was the grand subject of angelic study when on earth. "Into which things the angels desired to look," said Peter; and Christ is the Object of angelic worship now in heaven. Though we are not known by our fellow-men—even our nearest friends, and though we are ignorant of ourselves, there are intelligent creatures in the universe who know us, who from infancy up to the present hour have attended us, who have never by day or night been absent from us, who have marked our every act, and peered into our very hearts. The fact that we do not see them is no proof that they do not exist. The surrounding atmosphere teems with existences too small for the keenest unaided eye to detect. Each is busy working out its little destiny, playing its little part in life's universal drama. They encompass us in untold millions. Albeit we see them not. Put to your eye a microscope sufficiently powerful, and you will feel yourself present with the innumerable legion,—you have a new universe.

> " Millions of spiritual creatures walk the earth
> Unseen, both when we wake and when we sleep.
> All these with ceaseless praise His works behold
> Both day and night. How often from the sleep
> Of echoing hill or thicket have we heard
> Celestial voices to the midnight air,
> Sole, or responsive each to other's note,

> Singing their great Creator !   Oft in bands
> While they keep watch or nightly rounding walk
> With heavenly touch of instrumental sound
> In full harmonic number joined, their songs
> Divide the night, and lift our thoughts to heaven."—*Milton.*

In reference to the language here, notice—

IV —IT IS SUGGESTIVE OF THEIR DESIRE TO HAVE MEN RIGHTLY AND QUICKLY DIRECTED TO CHRIST

Matthew says that the angels said to Mary :—"And go quickly, and tell His disciples that He is risen from the dead ; and, behold, He goeth before you into Galilee; there shall ye see Him : lo, I have told you." He is gone into Galilee, where He had spent most of His public life, and Matthew (xxviii. 16) informs us that upon a mountain of Galilee, Christ, according to appointment, met with eleven of His disciples. And some suppose that on that occasion the five hundred referred to by the Apostle (1 Cor. xv. 6) also met Him. "Go quickly, and tell His disciples He is risen from the dead." Remove their anxieties, dispel their doubts, by meeting Him according to His appointment on a mountain in Galilee. Why should angels be so anxious for men to know Christ ?

First : Because, of all the Beings in the universe, He is the *Most Worth Knowing.* He is the "Image of the invisible God," the Fountain of all intelligence, the Root from which all the branches of science break forth, live, and flourish.

Secondly : Because, of all the Beings in the universe, none is so *Necessary for Man* to know. A knowledge of Christ is essential to restore man to the image, the fellowship, and the enjoyment of God.

In reference to the language here, notice—

V —IT IS SUGGESTIVE OF THEIR COMPASSIONATE INTEREST IN THE SORROWS OF EARNEST SOULS

"*And they* (the angels) *said unto her, Woman, why weepest thou ?*" Mary was in tears. Her tears were perhaps those of disappointed hopes, bereaved love, sad apprehensions. Piety is often found in tears. "*Why weepest thou ?*" "*They have taken away my Lord.*" We mourn our losses. What does this angel know about human tears ? Had he ever wept for the dying or the dead ? Had he ever wept the tears of pain, bereavement, or moral regret ? "*Why weepest thou ?*" Thy tears mean unbelief, for did He not tell thee He would rise again ? Thy tears are the tears of ignorance, for didst thou know the fact thou wouldst rejoice. He is not dead, but living.

CONCLUSION. The subject addresses itself to Four classes of men.

First: To the Enemies of Christianity. It says to them, All your efforts to suppress truth must prove futile, and in all you will be baffled and confounded. The Sanhedrim and the Jewish people so hated Christ, that they put Him to death. They buried Him in a grave, they sealed the stone of His sepulchre, and set Roman guards to watch it. Having done so no doubt they concluded that His voice was hushed for ever, and His influence gone ; but lo, on the third day, the God of Truth despatched a messenger from the skies. The approach of that messenger made the earth quake and the guards fall as dead men to the ground. Christ arose, invested with a power to spread His truth through the world and His influence through the universe. Infidels try to suppress truth ; they may apparently succeed for a short time. They put a stone on its grave, seal the stone, guard it with civic power ; but, like Christ, it shall rise. "The kings of the earth set themselves, and the rulers take counsel together against the Lord and against His anointed. He that sitteth in the heavens shall laugh ; the Lord shall have them in derision." The subject addresses itself—

Secondly: To the Worldly-Minded. To those whose spiritual natures are so thoroughly materialized that they "walk after the flesh," and are influenced only by the things that are seen and temporal,—I would say, There are beings and things about you that you do not see and hear, that are more real and lasting a thousand times, than all the objects that come within the realm of your senses. Wherever you are, there is a ladder by your side reaching to heaven, a ladder which the angels of God are ascending and descending. If the eye of your soul was truly opened, you would exclaim, "Surely God is in this place, and I knew it not." Angels crowd about us, and we know it not. The subject addresses itself—

Thirdly: To Conventional Christians. What thousands there are in this country and throughout Christendom seeking the living among the dead, seeking Christ in hoary systems, Church ceremonies, and institutional religions, and judging of Him as seen there. Judge not Christianity even by its most perfect embodiment in the life of its disciples here. The best are imperfect, and Christianity itself teaches this, and points to perfection as yonder. Do not judge the science of the organ-builder by the half-finished instrument in the workshop. There is but little in that to please the eye, and from it scarce a note can be evolved to charm the ear. Judge not the artistic character of the painter by the first rough outline which you discover on the canvas in his studio. There is scarcely a touch of life in it, or any perceptible resemblance to the original. Judge the organ-builder by the instrument as it stands in the great cathedral, pouring forth by the touch of a master-musician, pealing strains of music electrifying the congregated thousands. Judge the artist by the picture as hung up in the Academy of Art, looking, throbbing, and blushing at you as a thing of life, gathering round it a crowd of admiring spectators. Even so judge Christianity. Its organ—the Christian life—is not half-finished here: in the workshop yonder, in the great Cathedral of Eternity, you will see it in perfection and feel the inspiration of its harmonies. The painting is not finished here in its studio; its figure is half formed and blotched, and scarcely a feature is accurate. See it in the great gallery of the heavens finished, an exact copy of the Son of God Himself. Say not in thine heart, "Who shall ascend to heaven?"—that is, to bring Christ down from above, or "Who shall descend into the deep?" The subject addresses itself—

Fourthly: To Sorrowing Disciples. How many there are of the truly good, who, like Mary Magdalene, are in tears! But "blessed are they that mourn, for they shall be comforted." Comforted perhaps at the very place where they were made sad. It was the sight of the empty grave that broke this woman's heart into tears; but at that very grave the angel of mercy appeared, and spoke to her words about Christ suited to hush her sorrows and to transport her soul with rapture. "*He is not here, He is risen.*"

> "Deem not that they are blest alone
> Whose lives a peaceful tenor keep,
> For God, Who pities man, has shown
> A blessing for the eyes that weep.
>
> The light of smiles shall free again
> The lids that overflow with tears:
> And weary hours of woe and pain
> Are promises of happier years.
>
> There is a day of sunny rest
> For every dark and troubled night;
> Though grief may bide an evening guest,
> Yet joy shall come with early light.
>
> Nor let the good man's trust depart
> Though life its common gifts deny;
> Though with a pierced and broken heart
> And spurned of men he goes to die.
>
> For God has marked each sorrowing day,
> And numbered every secret tear;
> And heaven's eternal bliss shall pay
> For all His children suffer here."—*Bryant.*

The Honest Sceptic, How to Treat Him
No. 20   John 20:24-29

" But Thomas, one of the twelve, called Didymus, was not with them when Jesus came. The other disciples therefore said unto him, We have seen the Lord. But he said unto them, Except I shall see in His hands the print of the nails, and put my finger into the print of the nails, and thrust my hand into His side, I will not believe. And after eight days again His disciples were within, and Thomas with them : then came Jesus, the doors being shut, and stood in the midst, and said, Peace be unto you. Then said He to Thomas, Reach hither thy finger, and behold My hands ; and reach hither thy hand, and thrust it into My side : and be not faithless, but believing. And Thomas answered and said unto Him, My Lord and my God. Jesus said unto him, Thomas, because thou hast seen Me, thou hast believed : blessed are they that have not seen, and yet have believed."

(For Exegetical Remarks, see Vol. II. p. 184.)

WONDERFUL day was that on which the Great Mediator rose from the dead as the Conqueror of death and the " Captain of human salvation." In it all past and future eras in the annals of redeemed man meet as in a central epoch. It is a bright orb, in the sky of earth's moral history, throwing its radiance on all events, however distant and minute.

On the evening of this ever-memorable day, the disciples, drawn by a common interest in the wonderful facts of Christ's history, assembled together, probably for conference and devotion. " The doors being shut "—for they were afraid of the Jews. They knew that the men who had imbrued their hands in their Master's blood, would not hesitate to inflict agony and death on them. Whilst in this room Jesus appears to them. No iron doors, no granite walls, no massive bolts can exclude Him from His people. "*He stood in the midst, and said, Peace be unto you.*" To assure them that He was not a spectre, but the same veritable Jesus that two days before was nailed to the accursed tree, He shows to them the hands through which the rugged nails were driven, and the side into which the heartless soldier plunged the spear. The fear of the disciples departed, their faith was established, and they " were glad when they saw the Lord." Christ repeats His benediction, gives to them a commission, and qualifies them to discharge it by breathing on them the inspiring influences of Heaven.

There were two disciples absent from this remarkable meeting, Judas and Thomas. Poor Judas could not be there; he had gone " to his own place " of retribution, he had done with such meetings for ever—he was somewhere in eternity in the iron grasp of avenging justice. Alas! Judas, no more Christian conferences and godly devotions for thee!

But where was Thomas? Was he unacquainted with the hour or place of meeting? Did he flee too far off at the Crucifixion to be able to attend? Or, had he other engagements which precluded the possibility of his joining his brethren on this occasion? It is idle to speculate about the causes; all we know is, that he was not present. Whether his absence was unavoidable or otherwise is not stated.

Some time in the course of that week, perhaps immediately after the meeting had broken up, the disciples met Thomas and told him that they had " *seen the Lord.*" But he could not believe their statement, and he candidly told them so. " *Except I shall see in His hands the print of the nails, and put my finger into the print of the nails, and thrust my hand into His side, I will not believe.*" Whilst there is an energy in this man's scepticism rather startling, there is a manly outspokenness about it which one is disposed to admire.

Eight days roll by, the second "*Lord's day*" dawns, and the disciples meet again. Thomas is present now. The doors are shut as before; Christ appears. After pronouncing His benediction, He singles out Thomas, and says to him, " *Reach hither thy finger, and behold My hands; and reach hither thy hand and thrust it into My side: and be not faithless, but believing.*" Such is the wonderfully suggestive incident before us.

An *interesting religious sceptic*, an *exemplary religious Guide*, and a *super-eminent religious faith*, are the three prominent objects in this narrative. They stand out in bold relief and commanding attitude on the canvas of this fragment of evangelical history. They are not characters foreign to our times and spheres, at which we have to gaze with a little curiosity and then pass on; in them, we, the men of this age, and of this island, have a vital interest. They demand, and will repay our deepest and devoutest study. Let us, then, bestow some earnest attention on each separately. We have here—

I —AN INTERESTING RELIGIOUS SCEPTIC

An interesting religious sceptic! What an abuse of language— what a profanity of sentiment! A sceptic! his name should be mentioned with abhorrence, he should be shunned as a leper, denounced as a criminal; at his head the faithful of all Christian sects should hurl their severest fulminations! Such, probably, will be the utterance of those pious dogmatists who have reached a blessed certitude in all departments of theological inquiry. Albeit I cannot but regard *doubters* like this Thomas, as characters of peculiar interest.

> "Who never doubted, never half-believed ;
> Where doubt, there truth is,
> 'Tis her shadow."—*Festus.*

And as *Tennyson* says:

> "There lives more faith in honest doubt,
> Believe me, than in half the creeds."

There are certain features in this Scepticism of Thomas that mark it off from the conventional and common scepticism of mankind.

First: The scepticism of Thomas was Negative, not Positive. Thomas did not put himself in antagonism to the fact announced, and meet it with a dogmatic and positive denial. He did not echo the everlasting NO that thunders evermore in the infidel world; all he said was, I cannot believe it without more evidence. He did not manifest any affinity of feeling with that presumptuous herd of mortals who arrogantly proclaim Gospel facts impossibilities, Gospel doctrines absurdities, and Gospel believers brainless fanatics, or cunning knaves. Had he fully expressed his feelings he might have said,—" I do not deny its possibility, this would be to arrogate to myself infinite intelligence; nor do I impeach the veracity of you, my brother disciples; all that I say is, that such is the character of my intellect that I cannot believe such a strange and unheard-of fact on your unsupported testimony."

Secondly: The scepticism of Thomas was Intellectual, not Moral. The wish is often the father to the thought—the creed the offspring of the heart; but it was not so here. There is evidence that his love to Christ was fervid and forceful. About three months before this, when Lazarus lay dead, Christ said to His disciples, "I go, that I may awake him out of his sleep,"—Thomas, being present, said,—" Let us go that we may die with Him." A noble burst of generous feeling this, indicative of his strong attachment to Christ. His heart, then, we may presume, was in favour of the fact. Only too glad, we may suppose, would he be to welcome the beloved dead to life again. The difficulty was purely intellectual. The circumstance of a dead man coming to life, rising from a grave on which a large stone had been placed, and firmly sealed; a grave sedulously guarded, too, by the Roman soldiers, was altogether so stupendous and unique that his intellect could not yield it credence without extraordinary evidence. In this, too, his scepticism differed widely from the general scepticism of mankind. Men's difficulties in believing now are not so much intellectual as moral.

Thirdly : The scepticism of Thomas was Frank, not Underhanded. To whom did Thomas avow his unbelief ? To the sordid worldlings who felt no interest in those things—to the sneering infidel who would readily nurse his doubts into atheism ? Or, to Scribes and Pharisees, who would be only too delighted at the indications of his apostasy from this new and odious faith ? No ; to the ten men who told the fact, he avowed his unbelief; like an honest man he expressed his disbelief in the face of the believers. Let modern sceptics imitate his example in this. Let them be ingenuous and manly in their deportment; let them, instead of appealing to the thoughtless crowd, and seeking to work insidiously their infidel notions by jeers and jokes, innuendoes and tales, into the minds of the unreflecting multitude, go at once to the Church, to the men that believe, and say openly and respectfully, as did Thomas, " We cannot believe in the doctrines you offer unless you give us more evidence." This would be manly and honest, and this might serve the common cause of truth and the common interest of our race.

Fourthly : The scepticism of Thomas was Convincible, not Obstinate. There are some men so inveterate in their prejudices that no amount of evidence will modify their opinions. You may as well argue with granite as with them ; as well endeavour to remove Snowdon from its rocky foundations as to uproot old notions from their brain. Such was not Thomas. After he first avowed his unbelief, did he seek, as is generally the case with sceptics, every possible means to establish himself in his infidel views ? Nay, did he even avoid opportunities for obtaining evidence that would shake him in his foregone conclusions ? The reverse of all this is the fact. He remained open to conviction, he sought new evidence. " *Eight days* " after he declared his scepticism, we find him with the disciples, no doubt in search of sufficient proof, to convince him that Christ had risen from the dead. It is not improbable that he spent the whole of the intervening week in the same earnest endeavour. He was an Honest Doubter. Honest doubt is active—active, because it is a law of mind to seek certitude.

Such, then, was the Scepticism of Thomas—it was negative, not positive; intellectual, not moral; ingenuous, not mean; convincible, not obstinate. Such scepticism stands in striking contrast to that impertinent dogmatism, moral grossness, underhanded obliqueness, and stolid obstinacy, which mark too many of the sceptics of this age. I confess to a kind of sympathy with the scepticism of Thomas's type. It indicates intellect of the higher species, honesty of heart, activity of thought, and often an agony of feeling. I have more faith in the virtue, more hope in the destiny of such scepticism, than I have faith in the virtue, or hope in the destiny of mere traditional faith. Honest Scepticism is better than Technical Sainthood.

Another far more interesting object which we have in this narrative is—

II —AN EXEMPLARY RELIGIOUS GUIDE

We have here detailed the method in which Jesus, the Heavenly Guide of mortals, dealt with this poor sceptic. How does He act towards him? Does He denounce him as a heretic, and expel him from the circle of His disciples? Does He treat him even with cold indifference, which to sensitive natures would even be worse than actual severity? No. How then? Let the ministers, who fulminate from the pulpit denunciations against all who cannot subscribe to their tenets; let the sectarians who with self-complacency consign to perdition all beyond the pale of their little church, mark well the conduct of Christ towards this Thomas. Eight days after Thomas had avowed his scepticism, Christ finds him out, enters the room where he was with his brother disciples, fastens His loving looks upon him, singles him out, and says,—"*Thomas, Reach hither thy finger, and behold My hands; and reach hither thy hand and thrust it into My side: and be not faithless, but believing.*" Three things are observable here—

First: The Direct Specialty of His Merciful Treatment. He dealt with Thomas Personally. He did not address some general remarks bearing on the subject of doubt, to the whole company, leaving Thomas to apply them if he would to his own individual case. He deals directly with him. He knew the highly critical state of his mind; He saw that the man was on the margin of the cold, dark, chaotic world of infidelity, and that he required prompt and special attention or he would be irrevocably gone. Men in this doubting state require special treatment—the case is special. The bulk of mankind are either too weak or too indolent in soul, ever to get into a state of doubting; credulity is their weakness and their bane. The doubter therefore requires what Christ gave Thomas,—special attention.

Secondly: The Exquisite Considerateness of His Merciful Treatment. The request of Thomas was objectionable on many grounds. There was an indelicacy of feeling, and a presumptuous extravagance about it, more or less revolting to our finer sensibilities. Nor can we see that the request went for anything like rational and conclusive evidence. He might touch the wounds, and the fact of Christ's identity would remain open to debate. Still though the request is thus open to objection, Christ with exquisite considerateness condescends to grant it. He might have reproved him with severity for venturing such a demand; but instead of allowing a word of reproach to escape His lips, He at once, and lovingly, accedes :—" *Reach hither thy finger, and behold My hands; and reach hither thy hand, and thrust it into My side : and be not faithless, but believing.*"

Thirdly : The Moral Influence of His Merciful Treatment. What was the effect this produced upon the heart of Thomas ? He answered and said, "*My Lord, and my God.*" As if he had said, " I am more than convinced, more than satisfied; I am subdued by Thy merciful condescension, I am won by the majesty of Thy love." It was not, I trow, the mere touch of the wounds that produced this sublime effect upon his ' soul; it was the moral royalty of His merciful treatment. It is the *spirit*, not the letter of argument that will overcome scepticism. Far enough am I from disparaging the efforts of your Paleys, your Butlers, and your Lardners ; but I believe that he whose life and words are inspired with the benign spirit of Christianity, though he may have no logic and no learning, will do more to subdue scepticism than your most cogent argumentations or your most eloquent appeals.

Mark well, then, my brothers, Christ's method of treating scepticism, and take heed to the fact that in this respect He has left us an example that we should follow in His steps. But how has the Church acted towards sceptics ? Has it treated them with tender consideration, singled them out, as Christ did Thomas, for special acts of kindness suited to touch their hearts, the seat of the disease ? The volumes of history that lie about me unite in one emphatic No. History tells us, that for many ages the Church branded honest doubters as heretics, delivered them to the bloody inquisitors, and consigned them to the fiendish horrors of martyrdom. But how in our own times are they treated ? In theological controversy their opinions are often caricatured, their motives often impugned, and their feelings often wounded, by a language coarse and contemptuous, and a spirit imperious in insolence and menace.

Take some modern Churches. Let one of the members be known to doubt the truth of certain of the statements that fall from the pulpit, or certain of the tenets held by the community, and that man shall be looked upon with cold suspicion, if not with pious horror. He may be signally honest, generous, devout ; yet because he has some doubts, which he is manly enough to state, he shall, if not dismissed from the fellowship, be simply allowed the formalities of toleration. Selfishness and sleepiness, ignorance and vulgarity, shall be tolerated in a Church member rather than honest doubting. When will pastors and deacons of Churches treat earnest doubters in the spirit of Christ ? When will theological tutors have that moral majesty that shall win the confidence of the young student whose intellect is active enough to doubt, and who is honest enough in heart to declare the failings of his faith ?

The other interesting object in this narrative is—

III—A SUPER-EMINENT RELIGIOUS FAITH

" *Jesus saith unto him, Thomas, because thou hast seen Me, thou hast believed: blessed are they that have not seen, and yet have believed.*" These words imply two facts—

First : That it is Possible for those who have never seen Christ to believe in Him. Wherever His Gospel goes, there goes evidence sufficient to produce faith without any personal manifestation of Christ whatever. There is—

(1.) *The Testimony of Competent Witnesses.* A competent witness is one who has sufficient knowledge of the fact whereof he affirms, and a truthfulness of principle that would guard from any temptation to deceive. The declaration of such a witness I cannot but receive. Society could not go on, could not exist, were men to repudiate such testimony. Now, are not the Gospel witnesses pre-eminently of this class ? Had not the apostles every opportunity of thoroughly knowing those facts of Christ's history which they propounded ? Had they any possible motive to deceive ? On the contrary, were not their inducements to deny the facts far stronger than those to declare them ? There is—

(2.) *The Testimony of our Consciousness.* There is such a congruity between the doctrines of the Gospel and the intuitive beliefs of mankind, between the provisions of the Gospel and the deep-felt wants of mankind, that it comes with a self-evidencing power. It commends itself to " every man's conscience " in the sight of God. On this ground rather than any other, I imagine it is generally believed. Consult the great body of believers on the question, and they would say what the Samaritans of old avowed, " Now, we believe not because of thy saying, but because we have *heard him ourselves.*"

Thank God, it is possible to believe without seeing ! In ordinary matters we are doing so every day. " Faith is the evidence of things not seen." The illustrious believers, whom the writer celebrates in the eleventh chapter of the Hebrews, believed without seeing. Abraham believed in a city he never saw. Noah, in a deluge, long years before the windows of heaven were opened and the floodgates of the great deep broken up. Ever since the departure of Christ from this material sphere of being, the language of the Church has been—" Whom having not seen we love, in whom though now we see Him not, yet believing, we rejoice with joy unspeakable and full of glory."

The other fact implied in these words is—

Secondly : That those who believe in Him, without seeing, are Peculiarly Blessed. We are apt to think that the contemporaries of Christ, that the apostles who saw Him, heard Him, touched Him, were privileged above all the rest of the human family. This is a delusion. The unseeing believer is the most signally blessed. "*Blessed are they that have not seen, and yet have believed.*" Why ? For the following reasons—

(1.) *Faith without sight is more Praiseworthy than faith by sight.* There are some I know who deny all moral character to faith ; they say, that man is no more accountable for his belief than he is for the colour of his skin. This I admit to be true of a certain kind of faith. There are two very different kinds of belief ; the one *voluntary*, the other *involuntary.* The one comes by a proper inquiry into evidence, and the other springs up irresistibly whenever a fact is visible to the senses, or a proposition is obviously truthful to the mind. The evidence both of the bodily senses and the mental intuitions renders faith involuntary, and takes away from it therefore all moral merit. For such faith, I say, man is not responsible. But the *voluntary* is a very different thing. This depends upon a man's agency. There is a universe of facts that lies beyond the realm of my senses and that transcends all my *à priori* ideas. Belief in those facts—and it may be shown that the belief is indispensable to our well-being—requires evidence, and the evidence requires careful, honest, and earnest investigation. Man may examine evidence or he may not ; he may examine it in a right or a wrong way. Here, then, is the responsibility. This voluntary faith has a moral character. Why do men not believe in Christ ? It cannot be said for the want of evidence—for as a fact there is evidence that has satisfied millions, and that will satisfy millions more—but because that evidence is either entirely neglected, or if examined,—examined improperly. Now the faith of Thomas sprang from the senses, and had in itself but little if any moral merit. "*Blessed are they that have not seen, and yet have believed.*"

(2.) *Faith without sight is frequently more Accurate than faith by sight.* The senses are deceptive, the eye especially makes great mistakes : "Things are not what they seem." Nature is not what it seems ; men are not what they seem. The eye would have us believe that the heavenly bodies are but lamps of various sizes hung up in the heavens ; that the earth beneath our feet is the largest object brought within our notice, and that it sits like a queen in the midst of the system, serene and motionless, while all the heavenly luminaries like attendant angels pass round it, ministering evermore to the requirements of its life, and to the brightness and beauty of its forms. In all this the eye deceives; and in a thousand other minor matters it is busy with its delusions. Reason collects evidence and corrects those mistakes. It weighs the heavenly bodies and tells their density to a grain, it measures them and tells their dimensions to an inch. It calculates their velocity with the utmost accuracy. Reason has evidences on which to build a faith of unquestionable truthfulness.

(3.) *Faith without sight is more Ennobling than faith by sight.* (*a.*) It involves a higher exercise of mind. Whatever tends to stimulate and work the mental faculties is good. Faith founded on rational evidence implies and demands this mental action. Sensuous faith does not require this; the mind may sleep while it comes and remains. The history of the apostles furnish a striking illustration of this. How morally weak, because mentally inactive, were their minds, during their personal connection with Christ! Their faith in Him was more or less the faith of *sight*. Hence how weak and timid they were! Peter had not power to avow Him, none of the disciples had force enough to stand by Him in His dying hour. "They forsook Him, and fled." But after His ascension, when they are thrown upon themselves, and upon rational evidence, how giantly strong they become in a few days! They make the Sanhedrim tremble, they brave the most terrible powers of opposition, they turn the world upside down. (*b.*) It ensures a higher mode of life. Were our faith in Christ to be merely built upon the senses, I can scarcely see how it could raise the mind from its present earthly and material state. Indeed, faith founded on the senses must confine the soul more or less to the sensuous department of life. Hence as a fact, the disciples, so long as their faith rested on this ground, had the most material notions of the Saviour. On the contrary, the faith that comes without seeing, that depends upon evidence requiring an examination that brings us in contact often with the most stirring facts, the most glorious principles, and the most quickening spirits, transports us beyond the realm of sense, and introduces us into the world of invisible forces:— the things not seen and temporal, but unseen and eternal. (*c.*) It gives a wider sphere of being. The man whose faith is bounded by the evidence of his senses must have but a very narrow world. With the places he has not actually seen, he will have no interest, no connection. The stupendous systems that roll away in the boundless districts of space, and the mighty principalities of spirits that populate those systems, will be nothing to him. Nay, life which is invisible, mind which is invisible, God Who is invisible, will be nothing to him, if he believes only what he sees.

From all this it is clear that especially " *blessed are they that have not seen, and yet have believed.*"

The subject serves several important purposes.   It suggests—
First: An Incidental Argument in favour of Christianity. The fact that there was such a man as Thomas amongst the disciples, who could not believe without extraordinary evidence, and who manfully avowed his belief before the whole, plainly shows that there was no *collusion* between these witnesses of Christ; and that they were not a body of superstitious and credulous men.   It suggests—

Secondly: The Superiority of our Advantages to those of the Contemporaries of Christ.   In certain sentimental moods we are disposed to say, Would that we had lived in the days of Christ, and enjoyed the privileges of His disciples! Would that we had gone with Him on some of His journeys! walked with Him the shores of Galilee, sailed with Him over the Sea of Tiberias, sat down with Him on the mountain brow, entered with Him the villages and cities which He visited! Would that we had heard Him preach, and witnessed the wonderful things He suffered and wrought! Ah! this is not only useless wishing, but unwise.   It is *better* to be where you are.   "We have a more sure word of prophesy, unto which ye do well to take heed."   It suggests—

Thirdly: The Duty of the Church in relation to Doubters.   Who are the men in the Church that are most severe with doubters? Not the men who have the most intelligent, earnest, practical, faith in Christ; but the men whose faith is either traditional, and therefore arrogant and blustering; or superstitious, and therefore moody, whining, and shaken with every breeze of doctrine.   These in every age have been the fierce denouncers and the heartless persecutors of souls struggling with doubt.   But as *Gilder* says—

> "Against the darkness outer,
> God's light His likeness takes,
> And He from the mighty doubter
> The great believer makes."

If we would be true to our profession, as disciples of Christ, we must imitate His example in His conduct with doubters. "If a man be overtaken in a fault, ye which are spiritual, restore such an one in the spirit of meekness; considering thyself, lest thou also be tempted."

> "Let not this weak unknowing hand
> Presume Thy bolts to throw,
> And deal damnation, round the land,
> On all I judge Thy foe.
> If I am right, Thy grace impart
> Still in the right to stay;
> If I am wrong, O teach my heart
> To find the better way."

This subject suggests—

Fourthly: The Relationship to Christ we should seek to attain. It is that which Thomas expressed, when he exclaimed, "*My Lord, and my God.*" This man's faith reached the highest point. It was more than a satisfaction with the fact of Christ's resurrection, more than a trust in His Divine Person, more even than a confidence in His personal relation to him: it was a loving and loyal surrender of his being to Him. "*My Lord, and my God!*" I am entirely Thine;—my intellect, my affections, my powers, my energies, my all, are Thine. Thou art mine;—mine to guide me in difficulties, guard me in dangers, supply me with all I need through all the coming ages of being.

This is the Blessed Transcendentalism :—a loving self-abandonment to Christ; a moral absorption in Him.

CONCLUSION. Do not denounce Honest Scepticism, or treat it either with superciliousness or indifference. Do not regard the first disciples as being more privileged than yourself. You can believe without seeing, and this is the highest kind of faith. Do not regard the witnesses of Christ's resurrection as too weak-minded, prepossessed, and credulous, to have required evidence. Thomas says: "*Except I thrust my hand into His side, I will not believe.*" Do not fear to display special brotherly interest in an honest sceptic. He is a far more interesting character than a traditional believer. He is a living Spirit, the other is a mental fossil. Traditional faith is more obstructive to the spread of the Gospel than earnest doubt.

Introduction to Gospel of John

1
Discussion About Its Authorship

WHEN a man takes into his hand a document, whether ancient or modern, if he is in genuine quest of truth for its own sake, his grand question is, not when, where, by whom, and for what purpose was this document written ?—But what is the quality, measure, and practical bearing of the truth it contains ? The other questions, as to date, authorship, and purpose, would perhaps naturally arise and stimulate inquiry. Such inquiry might become very interesting, and result in the discipline of mental faculties, and in enriching the mind with much information. Albeit, the truth contained in the document is absolutely independent of all such inquiries. It is the nature of truth to carry with it its own intrinsic worth and convincing evidence. The mathematical truth contained in Euclid is independent of the writer, and it is believed, not because of Euclid, but because of itself.

Notwithstanding this, many readers of such a Work as this will naturally look for some solution of problems that have agitated the minds of students for ages in connection with this Gospel of St. John. If I were to take no notice of these points, whilst some would be disappointed, others, perhaps, would say that I know nothing of these subjects, and am therefore disqualified for the work of Homiletic interpreter. I shall, therefore, endeavour to bring into the smallest compass nearly all the information which the most distinguished scholars and Biblical critics have furnished.

DR. GODET, PROFESSOR OF THEOLOGY, NEUCHATEL—by general consent one of the greatest Biblical scholars of this age—supplies the following information concerning the discussions relating to the authenticity of this Gospel. He says—

" In the rapid view of the history of the discussions on the Gospel we might bring together, in a single series, determined by chronological order, all the writings upon the subject before us, whatever be the tendency to which they belong. But it seems preferable to us, with a view to clearness, to distribute the authors whom we intend to quote into three series, chronologically parallel. (1st.) The advocates of the entire spuriousness of our Gospel ;

(2nd.) The defenders of its absolute authenticity; (3rd.) The sup-
porters of the different middle terms proposed.

I —THE ADVOCATES OF THE ENTIRE SPURIOUSNESS OF THIS GOSPEL

" Down to the end of the seventeenth century the question had
not even been raised. It was known that in the primitive Church,
a small sect, mentioned by Irenæus and Epiphanius, attributed
the fourth Gospel to Cerinthus, an adversary of the Apostle John
at Ephesus. But the learning of theologians, as well as the feeling
of the Church, ratified the almost unanimous decision of the first
Christian communities, and of their leaders, who saw in it the
work of St. John.

" Some attacks of little importance, proceeding from the side of
the English Deists, who flourished two centuries ago, commenced
the struggle. But it did not burst forth seriously till a century
later. In 1792, the English theologian Evanson raised for the
first time some noteworthy objections against the general belief.
He took his stand especially on the differences between our Gospel
and the Apocalypse. He attributed the composition of the former
of these books to some Platonic philosopher of the second century.

" The discussion was not long in being transplanted into Germany.
Six years after Evanson, Eckermann controverted the authenticity,
whilst allowing that certain Johannine traditions must have formed
the first foundation of our Gospel. Several German theologians
carried on the attack thus begun. They urged the contradictions
with the first three Gospels, the exaggerated character of the
miracles, the metaphysical tone of its discourses, the manifest
theological relations between the theology of its author and that
of Philo, the scarcity of literary traces establishing the existence of
that writing in the second century. From 1801, the cause of the
authenticity seemed to be already compromised to such a degree
that a German Superintendent, Vogel, allowed himself to cite the
Apostle John and his interpreters to the bar of the last judgment.
This, however, was still only the first phase of the struggle, the
time of skirmishes which generally preludes that of pitched
battles.

" It was again a German Superintendent who opened the second
period of the controversy. Bretschneider, in his " Probabilia," published in 1820, concentrated in one vigorous attack all the
objections which had been previously raised, and to these added
new ones. He developed with much force the objection drawn
from the contradictions with the first three Gospels, whether from
the point of view of the form of the discourses, or from that of the
Christological teaching. The fourth Gospel must be the work of
a Christian of pagan, probably Alexandrian, origin, who lived
during the first half of the second century. The learned and

skilful work of Bretschneider called forth numerous replies, of which we shall speak further on; and at the close of which this theologian declared, in 1824, that he had attained the end he had proposed to himself, viz., that of calling forth a more vigorous demonstration of the authenticity of the fourth Gospel. But the seeds sown by the hand of Bretschneider were not eradicated from the soil by this somewhat equivocal retractation. De Wette, in his 'Introduction,' published for the first time in 1826, without positively taking part against the authenticity, confessed the impossibility of demonstrating it in an unanswerable manner. In the same year, Reuterdahl, following in the footsteps of Vogel, assailed as a forgery the tradition of the sojourn of John in Asia Minor.

"The publication of the 'Life of Jesus' by Strauss, in 1835, exercised a much more decisive influence upon the criticism of the history of Jesus than upon that of the *documents* in which that history has been transmitted to us. Strauss evidently had not devoted himself to a special study of the origin of these latter. He set out, as regards the Synoptics, from two ideas which had been disseminated before him,—the theories of Gieseler and of Griesbach, according to which our Gospels are a redaction of the apostolic tradition, which, after having circulated for a long time in a purely oral form, was at last slowly fixed in our Synoptics (Gieseler); this at first in the redactions of Matthew and of Luke; then in that of Mark, which is only a compilation of the two others (Griesbach). As for John, he admits as proved the conclusions of Bretschneider. And if in his third edition, in 1838, he recognized that the authenticity of that Gospel was no longer so absolutely unmaintainable in his eyes, he was not long in retracting that concession in the following edition in 1840. In reality, the slightest tergiversation upon this point unsettled the whole of his edifice of mythical legends. The axiom which forms its basis, that the ideal is not exhausted in one individual, would be demonstrated to be false if the fourth Gospel were the narrative of an eye-witness. Nevertheless, the great excitement produced in the learned world by the work of Strauss could not fail soon to react upon the criticism of the Gospels.

"Christian Hermann Weisse was the individual who first drew attention, in a remarkable work, to the close connection between the criticism of the history of Jesus and that of the Gospels. From 1838, he studied in a special manner the nature and origin of these writings. He positively rejected the authenticity of the fourth Gospel, but not without recognizing in that book an apostolic foundation. The Apostle John, with the view of fixing the image of his Master, which, in proportion as the reality receded from his view, became more and more indistinct in his mind, and in order to render to himself a clear account of the impression which he had preserved of Jesus, had drawn up certain 'studies,' which, when enlarged, became the discourses of the fourth Gospel. To these portions, more or less authentic, there was adapted at a later time an historical framework altogether fictitious. It is not impossible to comprehend how, from this point of view, Weisse could defend the authenticity of the first Epistle of John. At this moment there appeared in the criticism of our Gospel a revolution similar to that which was taking place at the same time in the manner of regarding the first three Gospels. Wilke was endeavouring at that very time to prove that the differences which distinguish the Synoptic narratives from one another were not, as had always been believed, simple and involuntary accidents; but that it was necessary to recognize in them modifications, introduced in a manner savouring of reflection and of deliberate purpose, by each author into his own narrative or that of his predecessors. Bruno Bauer extended this method of explanation to the fourth Gospel. He maintained that the Johannine narrative was not at all, as the treatment of it by Strauss supposed, altogether the simple deposit of a legendary tradition; but that this narrative was the reflective work of a thinker and of a poet conscious of his procedure—the product of an individual conception. The history of Jesus thus became a philosophical and poetical romance; which, according to the witty expression of Ebrard, who reduced the narrative of it to a single line : ' At that time it came to pass . . . that nothing came to pass.'

" In that same year Lützelberger attacked, in a more decided and thorough manner than Reuterdahl, the tradition of the sojourn of John in Asia Minor. The author of our Gospel, according to him, was a Samaritan, whose parents had emigrated to Mesopotamia, between 130 and 135, at the time of the new Jewish revolt against the Romans, and had composed that Gospel at Edessa. That 'disciple whom Jesus loved,' whom the author is pleased to bring upon the stage, was not John, but Andrew.

" We here reach the third and last period of this prolonged controversy. It dates from 1844, and has for its point of departure the famous work published at that date by Ferdinand Christian Baur. The first phase had lasted upwards of twenty years, from Evanson to Bretschneider (1792-1820); the second, in like manner, twenty and odd years, from Bretschneider to Baur; the third has now lasted more than thirty years. It is that of the struggle to extremity. The dissertation which gave the signal to it is certainly one of the most ingenious and brilliant compositions which theological science has ever produced. The purely negative results of the criticism of Strauss demanded for their complement a positive construction; on the other side, the arbitrary and subjective character of the procedure of Bruno Bauer did not respond to the wants of an age eager for positive facts. The discussion found itself then enclosed, as it were, in an inextricable difficulty. Baur understood that his task was to withdraw it from that position, and that the only efficacious means for that purpose was to discover in the progress of the Church of the second century a clearly defined historical situation, which might present itself as the soil on which there could have been raised an edifice so grand as that of the fourth Gospel. He believed that he had discovered that situation towards the middle of the second half of the second century. *Gnosticism* was then flourishing, alongside of which our Gospel marches throughout its entire course. At that time thoughtful men were above all preoccupied with the idea of the *Logos,* which is precisely the theme of our work. The need was then making itself more and more felt of uniting in one great and single Catholic Church the two parties, hostile to each other, of which the Primitive Church was composed, but which a series of numerous transactions had gradually drawn closer together. The fourth Gospel appeared as the desired treaty of peace. The spiritualistic reaction of Montanism was at that time displaying itself against the Episcopate. Our Gospel supports this tendency, by borrowing from it whatever it contains of truth. Finally, there was then kindling up the discussion between the Churches of Asia Minor and those of the West on the Paschal rite. Now it seemed evident to Baur that our Gospel modifies the history of the Passion in such a manner as to draw away minds toward the Western rite. While thus placing in a determinate historical situation the composition of our Gospel, Baur, following in the footsteps of Bruno Bauer, demonstrates with wonderful skill the reflective and systematic unity of that work ; he explains its logical march and its practical applications, and thus destroys at a single blow both the hypothesis of unreflective myths, on which rested the work of Strauss, and every attempt at selecting between certain authentic and other non-authentic parts in our Gospel. Baur admits, then, the unity and the integrity of the writing, and fixes as the date of composition about the year 170, when all the circumstances indicated above meet together. He has not attempted, however, to designate 'the great unknown,' to whose pen we owe this masterpiece of high mystical philosophy and skilful ecclesiastical policy which has exercised so decisive an influence over the destinies of Christianity. From that moment the discussion had a precise object. All the forces of the school agreed in supporting the work of the master in its different parts. Zeller completed it by the study of the Ecclesiastical testimonies; and that labour had as its result the sweeping away from the history of every trace of the existence of the fourth Gospel before the epoch indicated by Baur. Schwegler, in his treatise on the period which followed that of the apostles, assigned to each one of the writings of the New Testament its place in the development of the struggle between the apostolic Judæo-Christianity and Paulinism, and presented the fourth Gospel as the final and rich product of that long elaboration of the primitive Christian thought. Köstlin, in a famous work on the *pseudonymous literature* in the Primitive Church, endeavoured to prove that the pseudographic procedure, to which Baur attributed the composition of four-fifths of the New Testament, was in conformity with literary precedents and the ideas of the epoch. Volkmar laboured to ward off the blows with which the system of the master had been incessantly threatened by the quotations, less and less indisputable, of the fourth Gospel in the writings of the second century, those of Marcion and of Justin, for instance, and the ' Clementine Homilies.' Hilgenfeld finally treated, in a more profound manner than Baur had done, the dispute about the Passover, and its relation to the authenticity of our Gospel. Thus learnedly supported by that Pleiad of distinguished critics, devoted not without marked variations to the common cause, the opinion of Baur might appear for the moment to have gained a complete and definite triumph. Nevertheless, in the bosom of the school itself there was already manifesting itself a divergence of a secondary nature doubtless, but which, nevertheless, in many respects, struck a blow at the hypothesis so skilfully designed by the master. Hilgenfeld abandoned the date fixed by Baur, and in consequence the advantages of the situation chosen by him; he removed the composition of John's Gospel backward from thirty to forty years. According to him, the origin of that writing was connected with the development of Gnosticism, especially of the *Valentinian* heresy. According to his own expression, he hoped ' to succeed in throwing light, by the torch of Gnosticism, upon the sanctuary of Johannine theology.' The author of the Gospel had proposed to himself to cause the Gnostic teaching to penetrate into the Church under a modified form. Already towards 150, the existence of that writing could scarcely be any longer called in question. It must then date from 130 to 140.

"Volkmar took an intermediate position. He spoke of the year 155; and the Dutch professor, Scholten, in a work published in 1864, likewise removed back the date of the composition as far as 150. The author was, according to him, a Christian of pagan origin, initiated in Gnosticism, and who had taken it as his task to render that tendency profitable to the Church. It contained at the same time, within wise limits, the Antinomian reaction of Marcion, and the exaltation of the Montanist spiritualism, which were at that time displaying themselves. He interposed, finally, in the question of the Passover; not to decide in favour of the Western usage, as Baur thought, but to ensure the triumph of the principle of Pauline spiritualism, according to which there ought no longer to be any festival days in the Church. The author of the fourth Gospel then skilfully appropriated the truth contained in all the tendencies of that epoch (the middle of the second century); and without sliding into any of their exaggerations, he presented to the world, under the figure of a purely ideal disciple of him whom Jesus loved, the perfect spiritual Christianity which alone could become the universal religion.

"In 1866, this same point of view was developed by M. Réville in the 'Revue des Deux Mondes.' M. d'Eichthal in like manner expressed his assent to the idea of a relationship between our Gospel and Gnosticism. The work which M. Stap published the same year, in his collection of critical studies, is only a reproduction without originality of all the ideas of the school of Tübingen. These first retrograde steps in the date of our Gospel were followed by a third, still more considerable.

"In 1865, appeared the 'History of Jesus,' by Keim. He energetically opposes, in the part of the introduction which he devotes to the study of the sources, the authenticity of the fourth Gospel. He takes his stand especially on the philosophical character of that writing, and upon the contradictions which the narrative contains, with the nature of things, with the data furnished by the writings of St. Paul, and with the synoptic narratives. But, on the other hand, he establishes the traces of the existence of that work as far back as the most remote times of the second century. 'The testimonies,' he says, 'go back even to the year 120; so that the composition dates from the beginning of the second century, in the reign of Trajan, between 100 and 117.' The author was a Christian of Jewish origin, belonging to the *Diaspora* of Asia Minor, in perfect sympathy with the heathen, and thoroughly acquainted with all that concerns Palestine. In a more recent writing, a popular reproduction of his great work, Keim has gone back from that early date, assigning as his reason for the change of opinion, arguments which, we may say, contain nothing serious; he now fixes its composition in the year 130.

"Of what importance here is a decade of years? It would follow from the one as well as from the other of these latter dates, that twenty or thirty years after the death of John at Ephesus, the fourth Gospel was attributed to him by the very presbyters of the country where he had spent the end of his life, and where he had died. How can we explain the success of an act of falsehood in such circumstances? Keim felt that difficulty; and in order to remove it, he found no other means than to take up the idea let fall by Reuterdahl and Lützelberger, and to represent the alleged

sojourn of John in Asia Minor as a mere fable. By this decided
step he went beyond the school of Tübingen. Baur and Hilgenfeld did not doubt for an instant the truth of that tradition.
Their criticism even rests essentially on the reality of that fact;
at first, because the Apocalypse, the Johannine composition of
which serves them as a lever for overturning that of the Gospel,
demands the sojourn of John in Asia; and afterwards, because all
their reasoning, drawn from the alleged contradiction between the
Paschal tradition, bequeathed by the apostle to the Churches of
Asia, and the day of Jesus' death in the fourth Gospel, would fall
to the ground with the sojourn of John in these countries. At
the present day, on the contrary, since the criticism which is
hostile to our Gospel feels itself embarrassed by this sojourn, it
throws it overboard without ceremony. According to Keim, all
that tradition is only the result of a misunderstanding of Irenæus,
who applied to John the apostle what Polycarp had related before
him of quite a different person. Scholten then came to the rescue,
in a special work, but with an important difference. That false
tradition is to be explained, according to him, by a confusion of
another kind. In the Church, the author of the Apocalypse, who
was not the Apostle John, but who had borrowed his name, was
taken for the apostle himself, and in this way they had come to
suppose that John must have lived in Asia, where the Apocalypse
seems to have been composed. Whatever be the real state of the
case, and however the error retailed by the tradition is to be
accounted for, the discovery of that error 'takes away,' as Keim
says, 'the last point of support to the idea of the composition of
the Gospel by the son of Zebedee.' In this way two of the
bases of Baur's criticism—the authenticity of the Apocalypse,
and the sojourn of John in Asia—are at this hour undermined
by those very men who continued his work, because such a
negation appears to them the only means of making an end of the
sacred book.

" In 1868, the Englishman Davidson ranked himself amongst the
opponents of the authenticity. Holtzmann, like Keim, sees in our
Gospel an ideal composition, but nevertheless one not entirely
fictitious, dating from the epoch of the Epistle of Barnabas (the
first third of the second century), and which since 150 has been
favourably welcomed by the Church. Krenkel, in 1871, defended
the sojourn of the apostle in Asia; he attributed to him the
composition of the Apocalypse, but not that of the Gospel.

" We close our review by mentioning a work, published recently,
in which is summed up with immense erudition all the critical
labour of past times and of the present epoch. It is Hilgenfeld's
'Introduction to the New Testament.' In that work the author
continues to defend the cause to which he consecrated the firstfruits

of his pen,—viz. the composition of the Gospel of John under the influence of the Gnosticism of Valentinus.

II —THE DEFENDERS OF ITS ABSOLUTE AUTHENTICITY

" This persevering attack by one party of modern critics against the authenticity of the fourth Gospel, resembles the siege of a fortress on which depends the fate of a country. In face of all these onsets, the defenders, let it be understood, did not remain inactive,—they also felt the supreme importance of that scientific struggle ; and the numerous transformations which the tactics of their opponents underwent, sufficiently demonstrate the continuous action exerted upon the assailants by the works of defence. We shall rapidly enumerate the writings published in favour of the authenticity.

" The oldest attack—that of the sectaries of the second century, called *Alogi*—did not remain unanswered ; for it seems certain that the work of *Hippolytus* (beginning of the third century), the title of which thus appears in the catalogue of his works, ' In favour of the Gospel of John and of the Apocalypse,' was directed against them.

" The attacks of the English Deists were repulsed in Germany and Holland by Le Clerc and Lampe ; by the latter, in his celebrated Commentary upon the Gospel of John. Two Englishmen, Priestley and Simpson, replied at once to Evanson. Storr and Süskind resolved the objections raised shortly after in Germany ; and that with such success, that Eckermann and Schmidt declared that they retracted their doubts.

" In the train of this first phase of the struggle, Eichhorn, Hug, Bertholdt, in their well-known Introductions to the New Testament, Wegscheider in a special work, and others also, unanimously declared themselves in the direction of the authenticity ; so that at the beginning of this century the storm seemed calmed down and the question decided in favour of the traditional opinion. The historian Gieseler, in his admirable little work on the origin of the Gospels (1818), decided in the same way, and gave expression to the opinion that John had composed his book for the instruction of those heathens who had already made some advance in the Christian religion.

" The work of Bretschneider, which all at once broke this apparent calm, called forth a multitude of replies, amongst which we shall cite only those of Olshausen, of Crome, and Hauff, and the first edition of the commentary of Lücke. At the close of the first of these publications, Bretschneider declared, as we have already said, that his objections were solved ; so that once again the calm seemed restored, and Schleiermacher, with all his school, could devote himself, without encountering any opposition worthy of note, to the predilection which he felt for our Gospel. From the very beginning of his scientific career, Schleiermacher, in his *Discourses on Religion*, proclaimed the Christ of John as the true historic Christ, and maintained that the synoptic narrative must be subordinated to our Gospel. Critics so learned and independent as Schott and Credner in like manner supported at that time, in their Introductions, the side of the authenticity. De Wette alone at that moment let a somewhat discordant voice be heard.

" The appearance of the ' Life of Jesu' by Strauss, in 1835, was thus like a thunderbolt bursting in a serene sky. That work called forth a whole legion of apologetic replies; above all, that of Tholuck on the credibility of the evangelical history, and the ' Life of Jesus' by Neander. The concessions made to Strauss by the latter have often been erroneously interpreted. They had for their aim only to secure a minimum of indisputable facts, by giving up what might be the subject of attack. It is precisely this work, so moderate and impartial, and in which we feel at every word the unchangeable love of truth, which seemed for the moment to have made the greatest impression upon Strauss, and to have drawn from him, in reference to the Gospel of John, the species of retractation announced in his third edition.

" Gfroerer and Hase, although setting out from quite different points of view from the two preceding writers, defended the authenticity of our Gospel against Strauss. Frommann, on his side, refuted the hypothesis of Weisse. In the following years there appeared the work of Ebrard on the evangelical history, the truth of which he valiantly defended against Strauss and Bruno Bauer and the third edition of the commentary of Lücke (1848). But the latter made such concessions in regard to the credibility of the discourses, and of the Christological teaching of John, that his opponents did not fail soon to turn his own work against the very thesis he had desired to defend.

" We reach the last period—that of the struggle maintained with Baur and his school. Ebrard was the first to appear in the breach. At his side a young savant presented himself, who, in a work filled with rare patristic erudition, and a science derived from the primary sources, sought to recall to the right path historical criticism, which, in the hands of Baur, seemed to him to have strayed from it. We speak of Thiersch, whose work, modestly entitled an ' Essay,' is, even at this day, for beginners, one of the most useful means of discovering one's true position in the domain of the history of the first two centuries. Baur could not bear this call to order which was addressed to him—to him, a veteran in science—by so young a writer. Under a feeling of irritation, he wrote that violent pamphlet in which he accused his opponent of fanaticism, and which assumed almost the character of a denunciation. The reply of Thiersch was as remarkable for its propriety and dignity of tone as for the excellence of the general observations which are there presented on the criticism of the sacred writings. We may call in question the correctness of several of Thiersch's opinions, but it cannot be denied that his two works abound in ingenious and original points of view. A strange work appeared at that epoch. The author is usually quoted in German criticism under the name of ' *The Anonymous Saxon.*' He is a Saxon theologian who then belonged to the Thurgovian clergy. He defended the authenticity of our Gospels; but with the intention of demonstrating by that very authenticity how the apostles of Jesus, authors of these books, or rather of these pamphlets, had only laboured to decry and vilify each other.

" The most skilful and learned reply to the works of Baur and of Zeller was that of Bleek in 1846. Alongside of this writing the articles of Hauff deserve to be especially mentioned. In the following years, Weitzel and Steitz discussed with great care and erudition the argument derived by Baur from the Paschal controversy at the end of the second century. Following in the footsteps of Bindemann (1842), Semisch demonstrated the use of our four Gospels by Justin Martyr.

" The year 1852 saw appear two very interesting writings, that of the Dutchman Niermeyer, designed to prove, by a discriminating and thorough study of the writings attributed to John, that the Apocalypse and the Gospel could and must both have been composed by him, and that the differences of substance and of form which distinguish them are to be explained by the profound spiritual revolution which took place in the apostle after the fall of Jerusalem. A similar idea was at the same time expressed by Hase. The second work is the commentary of Luthardt on the fourth Gospel, the first part of which contains a series of characteristic portraits of the principal actors in the evangelical drama, drawn after St. John, intended to make palpably visible the living reality of all these persons. These portraits are full of fine and correct touches.

" We shall here bring together three authors : Hase, Reuss, and Ewald, whose point of view in respect of our Gospel seems in general to agree. All the three defend the authenticity of the writing ; but, what is almost inconceivable, they accord scarcely any historical credibility to the discourses which the apostle represents Jesus as delivering, and even to the miraculous deeds which He relates. That is an inconsistency on which Baur has severely animadverted in his reply to Hase. Such defences of a gospel are almost equivalent to sentences of condemnation pronounced against it,—or, rather, they mutually destroy each other. We may say of these almost what we say of the opinion of Bunsen, who views the Gospel of John as the only monument of evangelical history which proceeded from an eye-witness, who declares even that otherwise 'there is no longer an historical Christ,' and who yet consigns to the domain of fable a fact so decisive as that of the resurrection. Guericke and Bleek in their Introduction to the New Testament, Meyer, Hengstenberg, Lange in their commentaries, have pronounced in favour of the authenticity, as well as M. Astié (who adopts Niermeyer's point of view), as also the author of these pages. The Johannine question in its relation to that of the synoptic Gospels has been treated in an instructive manner by MM. Sabatier and de Pressensé.

"Let us here mention a strange notice which was published by Nolte, after a chronicle of the ninth century—that of George Hamartolos. It is a narrative attributed to Papias, according to whom the Apostle John was killed by the Jews.

"The study of the patristic testimonies has recently formed the subject of two works, the one of a very popular character, the other more strictly scientific: the small work of Tischendorf on the date of the composition of our Gospels, and the academic programme of Riggenbach in 1866, relating to the historical and literary testimonies in favour of John's Gospel. The solidity and impartiality of this latter work have been recognized by those who were opposed to the views of the author. To these two writings we may add that of Hofstede de Groot, professor at Groningen, in which he treats of the question of the date of Basilides, and of the Johannine quotations, especially in the Gnostic writers. The cause of the authenticity has likewise been maintained by the Abbé Déramey (1868). The tradition of the sojourn of John in Asia Minor has been valiantly defended, against Keim, by MM. Steitz and Wabnitz. Wittichen, regarding it from a point of view which is peculiar to himself, gives up the sojourn of the Apostle John in Asia; but in order the better to support the authenticity of our Gospel, he maintains that it was composed by that apostle in Syria, to refute those Ebionites who had tendencies to Essenism. That writing would then date from the times which immediately followed the fall of Jerusalem. As to the John of Asia Minor, that would be the presbyter, author of the Apocalypse. We have here the antipodes to the theses of Tübingen.

"In two works, the one by Zahn, the other by Riggenbach, the question of the existence of the Presbyter John as distinct from the apostle has been discussed. These two authors, after a very careful study of the famous passage of Papias relative to that question, came to a negative conclusion. This is the case, in like manner, with Leimbach in a very recent study, and with Professor Milligan, of Aberdeen, in an article in the 'Journal of Sacred Literature,' entitled 'John the Presbyter' (Oct. 1867).

" The historical credibility of the discourses of Jesus in the fourth Gospel has been defended against modern objections by Gess, in the first volume of the second edition of his work on the person of the Saviour; and more especially by M. H. Meyer, in a very remarkable thesis for the degree of licentiate. From the year 1872 dates the English work of Sanday; and from 1873 that of the Superintendent Leuschner,—a courageous little work, which specially attacks Keim and Scholten.

" We have pleasure in concluding this review by mentioning two remarkable works : the critical study of Luthardt on the origin of the fourth Gospel, forming in a special volume the introduction to the second edition of his commentary, the first volume of which has just appeared ; and the brilliant article of Beyschlag in the ' Studien und Kritiken,' which perhaps contains the most decisive and intellectual answers to all the objections of present criticism.

III —THE SUPPORTERS OF THE MIDDLE TERMS PROPOSED

" Urged by the force of the reasons for and against, a certain number of theologians have sought a middle position, suited to give satisfaction to both sides. Some have tried to make a selection between portions which are truly Johannine and those which are not authentic, but which have been interpolated at a later date. It is in this way that Weisse, whom we cannot exempt from including amongst the opponents of the authenticity, on account of the important place which he occupies in the development of that manner of view, would nevertheless be disposed to attribute to John himself some verses, such as ch. i. 1—5 and 9— 14; also, certain passages in ch. iii.; finally, the discourses of ch. xiv.—xvii., while cutting off from them the dialogistic and narrative parts.

" Schweizer has tried another mode of selection. According to him, the narrations which have Galilee for the theatre of action must be eliminated from the Johannine writing; they have been added at a later time to facilitate the agreement between the narrative of John and that of the synoptic Gospels. Schenkel proposed to consider the discourses as the primitive work forming a whole, and the historical parts as added at a later date. But since the unity of the composition of our Gospel has been triumphantly demonstrated, the division of it externally into parts of diverse origin has been given up. Weizsäcker maintains that there is certainly a difference to be established in that narrative; but it is not of a quantitative nature,—it is the whole narrative which, from the first to the last line, presents a double character, an historical character on the one side, a speculative one on the other. In this way, then, the author himself comes to be made two different persons : the one, the witness, from whom have proceeded in an oral form the information which constitutes the substance of the book; the other, the editor, who has collected this information from the mouth of the former, and from it has composed our Gospel. Thus Paulus, in his account of the work of Bretschneider, proposed to attribute the redaction to a disciple of the Apostle John,—a disciple who had himself attended the ministry of the Lord in Palestine, and who composed that didactic work with the aim of blending the Judæo-Christian belief in the Messiah manifested in Jesus with the idea of the Logos as it was taught by Philo. It is almost the same idea which reappears in the hypothesis which has been developed by M. Michel Nicolas. One of the members of the Christian society of Ephesus took as a guide the teaching of the Apostle John, and sketched a tableau of the work of Jesus Christ. That writer was the person who in the smaller Epistles is called *the Elder*, and with whom history has made us acquainted under the name of *John the Presbyter.*

"Tobler, in like manner, maintains that alongside of the ideal character of the narrative there are features truly historical, chronological and geographical notices for example, which can rest only upon testimony of a very exact nature. The witness was the Apostle John, according to whose instructions Apollos, the author of the Epistle to the Hebrews, composed our Gospel before the end of the first century.

"In the 13th edition of his 'Life of Jesus,' M. Renan, after having scrupulously weighed the reasons in favour of these different hypotheses, arrives at this conclusion, that a half Gnostic sectary constituted himself the editor of the narratives of the aged apostle; perhaps he even possessed some notes dictated by the latter, and which formed the primary materials of his work. Thus M. Renan explains, on the one side, the obvious features of authenticity; and, on the other, the not less indisputable characters, in his eyes, of a composition of later date and of an artificial nature.

"Finally, Weizsäcker, in a work which we may be allowed to call masterly, thinks that he can discover, even in the text of the Gospel, traces of a distinction between the evangelistic editor and the apostolic witness, on whose credibility the former gives the narrative. The editor has carefully worked up what he had gathered from John's narratives, and believes that he is able to put into the mouth of Jesus Himself what he had heard related by that apostle of the impression produced on him by the person of the Saviour. We may compare with this result certain expressions which have proceeded from the pen of Holtzmann, in the articles of Schenkel's 'Biblical Dictionary.' We conclude this exposition by again mentioning the third edition of the 'Introduction to the New Testament' of Bleek, which we owe to the care of Professor Mangold. Whilst Bleek maintains in that noble work the authenticity of the fourth Gospel, his present editor accompanies ·his argument with very instructive critical notes, which put the reader *au fait* with all the details of recent discussions, and the bearing of which is tolerably sceptical. The external evidences would appear to the author sufficient to confirm the authenticity; but the internal difficulties seem to him, up to the present time at least, insurmountable.

"This long enumeration, in which we have included only the more remarkable works, proves of itself alone the gravity of the question. A century will soon have elapsed since all the forces of science have been drawn up to sweep away or to defend this position. Long ago the Emperor Julian already indicated its supreme importance in that saying which is attributed to him, 'It is this John who, in declaring that the Word was made flesh, has done all the evil.' The Johannine question has become the decisive question, not only in the domain of criticism, but also in that of Christology,—that is to say, of Christianity itself."

2
John the Author of the Gospel

(A Supplement to the article in Vol. I. page 1.)

JOHN the Divine, called the beloved disciple (xiii. 23; xix. 26; xx. 2; xxi. 7, 20, 24), and one of the Sons of Thunder, was son of Zebedee and Salome (Matt. iv. 21; xxvii. 56; Mark xv. 40). His father was a fisherman, probably of Bethsaida, and apparently in good circumstances (see and compare Mark i. 20; Mark xvi. 1; Luke xiii. 3; xxiii. 55; John xix. 27, and xviii. 15). His mother is said to have been daughter of Joseph (Mary's husband) by a former wife; so, she was our Lord's sister, and John His nephew. John followed his father's occupation till his call to the Apostleship (Matt. iv. 21, 22; Mark i. 19, 20; Luke v. 1—10), at about twenty-five years of age. He remained with Christ till His ascension; was present at the Council at Jerusalem, A.D. 49 or 50 (Acts xv.); is said to have gone to Asia Minor as pastor of the Seven Churches; resided chiefly at Ephesus; was banished thence by Domitian, A.D. 95 to Patmos, where he wrote the Apocalypse; was recalled on accession of Nerva, A.D. 96; returned to Ephesus, where he died about A.D. 100, aged about 100 years, in the third year of Trajan. That he was thrown, prior to his exile, into a caldron of boiling oil, by order of Domitian, before the Porta Latina at Rome, rests mainly on the authority of Tertullian.

3
The Logos

THIS Work would be undoubtedly incomplete without some elucidatory remarks on the word "*Logos.*" Having consulted some of the best critics on the question, such as Meyer, Bengel, Luthardt, Westcott, Godet, Hengstenberg, &c., I avail myself of the observations of one of our ablest modern authorities. It is not only the last production on the subject, but the most condensed.

"As early as the second century *Sermo* and *Verbum* were rival translations of the Greek term LOGOS = Word. Tertullian (fl. A.D. 195—210) gives us both, but seems himself to prefer *Ratio. Sermo* first became unusual, and finally was disallowed in the Latin Church. The Latin Versions all adopted *Verbum*, and from it comes our translation, 'the Word.' None of these translations are at all adequate; but neither Latin nor any modern language supplies anything really satisfactory. *Verbum* and the "*Word*" do not give the whole of even one of the two sides of *Logos*: the other side, which Tertullian tried to express by *Ratio*, is not touched at all; for ὁ λόγος means not only the "spoken Word," but the thought expressed by the spoken Word: it is the spoken word as expressive of thought. It is not found in the N. T. in the sense of 'reason.'

"The expression '*Logos*' is a remarkable one: all the more so, because St. John assumes that his readers will at once understand it. This shows that his Gospel was written in the first instance for his own disciples, who would be familiar with his teaching and phraseology. Whence did St. John derive the expression *Logos?* It has its origin in the Targums, or paraphrases of the Hebrew Scriptures, in use in Palestine, rather than in the mixture of Jewish and Greek philosophy prevalent at Alexandria and Ephesus, as is very commonly asserted.

"(1.) In the *Old Testament*, we find the Word or Wisdom of God personified generally as an instrument for executing the Divine Will. We have a faint trace of it in the 'God said' of Gen. i. 3, 6, 9, 11, 14, &c. The personification of the Word of God began to appear in the Psalms xxxiii. 6 ; cvii. 20 ; cxix. 89 ; cxlvii. 15. In Prov. viii. and ix. the Wisdom of God is personified in very striking terms. This Wisdom is manifested in the power and mighty works of God : that God is *love,* is a revelation yet to come.

" (2.) In the *Apocrypha* the personification is more complete than in the Old Testament. In Ecclesiasticus (*c.* B.C. 150—100) I. 1—20 ; xxiv. 1—22 ; and in the Book of Wisdom (*c.* B.C. 100) vi. 22 to ix. 18, we have Wisdom strongly personified. In Wisdom xviii. 15, the Almighty Word of God appears as an agent of vengeance.

" (3.) In the Targums or Aramaic paraphrases of the Old Testament the development is carried still further. These, though not written down, were in common use among the Jews in our Lord's time. And they were strongly influenced by the growing tendency to separate the Godhead from immediate contact with the material world. Where Scripture speaks of a direct communication from God to man, the Targums substituted the *Memra* or 'Word of God.' Thus in Gen. iii. 8, 9, instead of 'they heard the voice of the Lord God,' the Targums have, 'they heard the voice of the *Word* of the Lord God :' and instead of 'God called unto Adam,' they put 'the *Word* of the Lord called unto Adam,' and so on. The '*Word of the Lord*' is said to occur one hundred and fifty times in a single Targum of the Pentateuch. In the theosophy of the *Alexandrine Jews,* which was a compound of theology with philosophy and mysticism, we seem to come nearer to a strictly personal view of the Divine Word or Wisdom, but really move further away from it. Philo, the leading representative of this religious speculation (fl. A.D. 40—50), admitted into his philosophy very various and not always harmonious elements. Consequently, his conception of the *Logos* is not fixed or clear. On the whole his *Logos* means some intermediate agency, by means of which God created material things and communicated with them. But whether this *Logos* is one Being or more, whether it is personal or not, we cannot be sure : and perhaps Philo himself was undecided. Certainly his *Logos* is very different from that of St. John ; for it is scarcely a Person, and it is not the Messiah. And when we note that of the two meanings of Λόγος, Philo dwells most on the side which is less prominent, while the Targums insist on that which is more prominent in the teaching of St. John, we cannot doubt the source of his language. The LOGOS of Philo is preeminently the DIVINE REASON. The *Memra* of the Targums is rather the DIVINE WORD ; *i. e.* the Will of God manifested in personal action ; and this, rather than a philosophical abstraction of the Divine Intelligence, is the starting-point of St. John's expression.

" To sum up : The personification of the Divine Word in the Old

Testament is *poetical*, in Philo *metaphysical*, in St. John *historical*. The Apocrypha and Targums help to fill the chasm between the Old Testament and Philo; history itself fills the greater chasm which separates all from St. John. Between Jewish poetry and Alexandrine speculation on the one hand, and the Fourth Gospel on the other, lies the historical fact of the *Incarnation* of the *Logos*, the life of Jesus Christ.

"The *Logos*, therefore, of St. John is not a mere attribute of God; but the Son of God existing from all eternity, and manifested in space and time in the Person of Jesus Christ. In the *Logos* had been hidden from eternity, all that God had to say to man: for the *Logos* was the Living Expression of the nature, purposes, and Will of God. Human thought had been searching in vain for some means of connecting the finite with the Infinite, of making God intelligible to man and leading man up to God. St. John knew that he possessed the key to this enigma. He therefore took the phrase which human reason had lighted on in its gropings, stripped it of its misleading associations, fixed it by identifying it with the Christ, and filled it with that fulness of meaning which he himself had derived from Christ's own teaching."

A. PLUMMER

4
The Analysis of the Gospel

CHAP. i. 1—18. THE PROLOGUE

(1.) The Word in His own nature (1—5)
(2.) His revelation to men, and rejection by them (6—13)
(3.) His revelation of the Father (14—18)

Chap. i. 19; xii. 50. THE MINISTRY

I. (i. 19; ii. 11.) *The Testimony*

  (1.) The testimony of the Baptist (i. 19—37)
    (*a.*) To the deputation from Jerusalem (19—28)
    (*b.*) To the people (29—34)
    (*c.*) To Andrew and John (35—37)
  (2.) The testimony of the disciples (i. 38—51)
  (3.) The testimony of the First Sign (ii. 1—11)

II. (ii. 13; ix. 41.) *The Work*

  (1.) The work among the Jews (ii. 13; iii. 36)
    (*a.*) First cleansing of the Temple (13—22)
    (*b.*) Belief without devotion (23—25)
    (*c.*) The discourse with Nicodemus (iii. 1—21)
    (*d.*) The baptism and final testimony of John (22—36)
  (2.) The work among Samaritans (iv. 1—42)
  (3.) The work among Galileans (iv. 43—54)
  (4.) The work and conflict among mixed multitudes (v.—ix.)

    (A.) Christ the *Source* of Life (v.)

      (*a.*) The sign at the Pool of Bethsaida (1—9)
      (*β.*) The sequel of the sign (10—16)
      (*γ.*) The discourse on the Son as the Source of Life (17—47)

    (B.) Christ the *Support* of Life (vi.)

      (*a.*) The sign on the land, feeding the five thousand (1—15)
      (*β.*) The sign on the lake, walking on the water (16—21)
      (*γ.*) The sequel of the two signs (22—25)

(δ.) The discourse on the Son as the Support of Life (26—59)

(η.) Opposite results of the discourse (60—71)

(C.) Christ the Source of Truth and Light (vii. viii.)

(α.) The controversy with His brethren (vii. 1—9)

(β.) The discourses at the Feast of Tabernacles (10—39)

(γ.) Opposite results of the discourses (40—52)

(δ.) The woman taken in adultery (vii. 53; viii. 11)

(η.) Christ's True Witness to Himself and against the Jews (12—59)

(D.) Christ the Source of Truth and Light illustrated by a sign (ix.)

(α.) The prelude to the sign (1—5)

(β.) The sign (6—12)

(γ.) Opposite results of the sign (13—41)

(E.) Christ is Love (x.)

(α.) Allegory of the Door of the field (1—9)

(β.) Allegory of the Good Shepherd (11—18)

(γ.) Opposite results of the sign (19—21)

(δ.) The discourse at the Feast of the Dedication (22—38)

(η.) Opposite results of the discourse (39—42)

(F.) Christ is Love illustrated by a sign (xi.)

(α.) The prelude to the sign (1—33)

(β.) The sign (33—44)

(γ.) Opposite results of the sign (45—57)

III. (xii.) *The Judgment*

(1.) The judgment of men (1—36)

(α.) The devotion of Mary (1—8)

(β.) The hostility of the priests (9—11)

(γ.) The enthusiasm of the people (12—18)

(δ.) The discomfiture of the Pharisees (19)

(η.) The desire of the Gentiles (20—33)

(θ.) The perplexity of the multitude (34—36)

(ι.) The judgment of the Evangelist (37—43)

(κ.) The judgment of Christ (44—50)

Chaps. xiii.—xx. THE ISSUES OF THE MINISTRY

I. (xiii.—xvii.) *The inner Glorification of Christ in His last discourses*

(1.) His love in humiliation (xiii. 1—30)

(2.) His love in keeping His own (xiii. 31 ; xv. 27)
    (α.) Their union with Him illustrated by the allegory of the vine (xv. 1—11)
    (β.) Their union with one another (12—17)
    (γ.) The hatred of the world both to Him and them (18—25)
(3.) The promise of the Paraclete and of Christ's return (xvi.)
    (α.) The world and the Paraclete (xvi. 1—11)
    (β.) The disciples and the Paraclete (12—15)
    (γ.) The sorrow turned into joy (16—24)
    (δ.) Summary and conclusions (25—23)
(4.) The prayer of the Great High Priest (xvii.)
    (α.) The prayer for Himself (xvii. 1—5)
    (β.) The prayer for His disciples (6—19)
    (γ.) The prayer for the whole Church (20—26)

II. (chap. xviii.—xix.) *The outer Glorification of Christ in His Passion*

(1.) The Betrayal (xviii. 1—11).
(2.) The Jewish or Ecclesiastical Trial (12—27)
(3.) The Roman or Civil Trial (28 ; xix. 16)
(4.) The Death and Burial (xix. 17—42)
    (α.) The Crucifixion and the title on the Cross (17—22)
    (β.) The four enemies, and the four friends (23—27)
    (γ.) The two words, "I thirst," "It is finished" (28—30)
    (δ.) The hostile and the friendly petitions (31—42)

III. (chap. xx.) *The Resurrection and Threefold Manifestation of Christ*

(1.) The first evidence of the Resurrection (1—10)
(2). The manifestation to Mary Magdalene (11—13)
(3.) The manifestation to the Ten and others (19—23)
(4.) The manifestation to St. Thomas and others (24—29)
(5.) The conclusion and purpose of the Gospel (30—31)

Chap. xxi. THE EPILOGUE, OR APPENDIX

(1.) The manifestation to the Seven, and the miraculous draught of fishes (1—14)
(2.) The commission to St. Peter, and prediction as to his death (15—19)
(3.) The misunderstood saying as to the Evangelist (20—23)
(4.) Concluding notes (24, 25)

5
Latin Hymn

"SACRED Latin poetry," says *Professor Plumptre,* "scarcely possesses anything grander or loftier than the following composition. Many readers will be glad of an opportunity of reading that hymn in the unapproachable majesty of the original. Others will appreciate it even in the weaker medium of a translation. The writer is unknown, but he was clearly one who had been trained in the school of Adam of St. Victor, and was not inferior to his master."

Verbum Dei Deo Natum
Quod nec factum nec creatum
Venit de cœlistibus ;
Hoc vidit, hoc attrectavit
Hoc de cœlo reseravit
Joannes hominibus.

The Word of God the Eternal Son
With God the Uncreated One
Came down to earth from Heaven ;
To see Him, handle Him, and show
His heavenly life to man below,
To holy John was given.

Inter illos primitivos
Veros veri fontis rivos
Joannes exiliit
Toti mundi propinare
Nectar illud salutare
Quod de throno prodiit.

Among those four primeval streams
Whose living fount in Eden gleams
John's record true is known ;
To all the world he poureth forth
The nectar pure of priceless worth
That flows from out the Throne.

Cœlum transit veri rotam
Solis vidit ibi totam
Mentis figens aciem ;
Speculator spiritalis,
Quasi Seraphim sub alis
Dei vidit faciem.

Beyond the heavens he soared, nor
   failed,
With all the spirit's gaze unveiled,
To see our true Sun's grace ;
Not as through mists or visions dim
Beneath the wings of Seraphim,
He looked, and saw God's face.

Audiit in gyro sedis
Quid psallant cum citharœdis
Quater seni proceres ;
De sigillo Trinitatis
Nostrœ nummo civitatis
Impressit characteres.

He heard where songs and harps
   resound
And four-and-twenty elders round
Sing hymns of praise and joy.
The impress of the One in Three
With print so clear that all may see,
He stamped on earth's alloy.

Volat avis sine metâ,
Quo nec vates nec propheta
Evolavit altius ;
Tam implenda quam impleta
Nunquam vidit tot secreta
Purus homo purius.

Sponsus, rubrâ veste tectus
Visus, sed non intellectus
Redit ad palatium ;
Aquilam Ezechielis
Sponsæ misit, quæ de cœlis
Referret mysterium.

Dic dilecte, de Dilecto
Qualis, adsit, et de lecto
Sponsi, sponsæ nuncia
Dic quis cibus angelorum
Quae sint festa superorum
De sponsi præsentia.

Veri panem intellectûs,
Cœnam Christi super pectus,
Christi sumptam resera ;
Ut cantemus de Patrono
Coram Agno, coram Throno
Laudes super æthera.

As eagle winging loftiest flight
Where never seer's or prophet's sight
Had pierced the ethereal vast.
Pure beyond human purity,
He scanned with still undazzled eye,
The future and the past.

The Bridegroom, clad in garments red
Seen yet with might unfathomed,
Home to His palace hies.
Ezekiel's eagle to His bride
He sends, and will no longer hide
Heaven's deepest mysteries.

O loved one, bear, if thou can'st tell
Of Him Whom thou did'st love so
    well,
Glad tidings to the Bride ;
Tell of the angels' food they taste,
Who with the Bridegroom's presence
    graced,
Are resting at His side.

Tell of the soul's true bread unpriced,
Christ's supper, on the breast of Christ
In wond'rous rapture ta'en.
That we may sing before the Throne
His praises whom as Lord we own,
The Lamb we worship slain.

See *Rev A. Watkin, M.A.*, in BISHOP ELLICOT'S COMMENTARY

Topical Index

Noteworthy aspects of Christ and His disciples, ii. 68
Novalis quoted, i. 5

OBEDIENCE, Christian, ii. 154
Obedience to Christ, ii. 19, 34, 38
Object, the, of faith, i. 108 ; ii. 255
Object, the, of worship, ii. 234
Objections to the Bible, ii. 128
Obligation, moral, ii. 283
Obligation, social, i. 15, 406
Obligations do not go beyond capacity, i. 63
Obligations to Christ, i. 127
Obliquity, moral, ii. 147
Obsequiousness, ii. 141
Obstinate scepticism, ii. 362
Occurrence, a common, but significant, i. 338
Office in the empire of Christ, ii. 199
Officers of worship, ii. 237
Officiousness, ii. 115
Old age, ii. 202
Omnipresence of God, ii. 232
Omniscience a proof of Divinity, i. 108
One Christ, the Transcendent, i. 24
One event with many revelations, ii. 149
One, the, God, ii. 282
Operation, God's unremitting, i. 128
Operations, the, of nature, i. 18
Operations, the, of the Spirit, ii. 218
Opinions concerning Christ, i. 208
Opinions, persecution on account of religious, i. 303
Opponents, Christ's malignant, i. 202
Opportuneness, the, of Christ's advent, ii. 196
Opportunities for knowing Christ, i. 272
Opportunities, great, i. 70
Opposition, truth maintained in spite of, i. 275
Oppression, the removal of a painful, i. 401
Oppressions, social, ii. 203
Organ, a special, ii. 15
Origin, the sublimity of Christ's, ii. 223
Originality, the, of Christ's teaching, ii. 224
Orphanhood, soul, ii. 22
Owner, the, of the universe, i. 12

PAINFUL, a, passion, ii. 229
Pantheism, ii. 13

Paradise, the, of God, i. 287
Paramount affection for Christ, ii. 198
Parasites, the, prevalence of, ii. 116
Parent, the, of lies, ii. 113
Parental affection, ii. 107
Parental distress, ii. 152
Parents, a lesson for, ii. 124
Parents, the, of moral character, i. 247
Partialness, the, of the evangelic record, ii. 186
Participation in Christ's joy, ii. 83
Participation in Divine peace, ii. 21
Partridge, the, John and, i. 7
Pascal quoted, i. 192
Passion, ii. 228
Passion, a revengeful, ii. 146
Passion, animal, i. 214
Path, the, to heaven, i. 405
Paul's estimate of death, ii. 310
Peace, Divine, ii. 21, 68
Peace, man's need of, ii. 180, 182
Peace of conscience, ii. 213
Pedigree, the, of true men, ii. 44
Penitence, evangelical, ii. 160
Penitence, the power of, ii. 168
Perdition, the son of, ii. 82
Perilous, a, position, ii. 119
Perniciousness, the, of spurious sanctity, ii. 123
Perniciousness, the, of unbelief, i. 169
Perplexities, intellectual, ii. 57
Perplexity, a distracting, ii. 157
Persecution, hatred, developing, ii. 42
Persecution on account of opinions, i. 303
Person, a, belief in, ii. 255, 302
Personal, a, manifestation, ii. 289
Personal holiness i. 178
Personal, the, identity of Spirit, ii. 346
Personality, a Divine, ii. 15
Personality, an appreciable, ii. 15
Personality, the, of God, ii. 234
Perversions of the Bible, ii. 246
Perversity, moral, i. 208
Perversity, the, of unbelief, i. 230
Peter, an enemy of, ii. 120
Peter and Malchus, ii. 103, 107
Peter brought to Christ, i. 40
Peter, Christ's commission to, ii. 199
Peter denying Christ, ii. 113, 119
Peter refuses to have his feet washed, i. 385
Peter, the crucifixion of, ii. 203
Peter's impulse, i. 408
Peter's inquiry, i. 407

Sons, the, of light, i. 366
Soothing, nature's, influence, i. 122
Sorrow turned into joy, ii. 59
Soul, a Christ-loving, ii. 19
Soul, a, satisfying condition, ii. 257
Soul adjudication, ii. 275
Soul food, i. 154
Soul glory, ii. 72
Soul growth, ii. 214
Soul, liberty of, ii. 213
Soul, meanness of, i. 273
Soul orphanhood, ii. 22
Soul quickening, ii. 9
Soul-redemptive faith, ii. 255
Soul, the, constitution of, ii. 284
Soul, the, destiny of, ii. 227
Soul, the, immortality of, i. 164
Souls, the intuitions of, i. 18
Soul, the monarch of the, ii. 215
Soul, the, value of, ii. 277
Soul, true unity of, ii. 82
Soul truth, i. 22
Souls, the brotherhood of, ii. 285
Souls, the Creator of, i. 17
Souls, the true life of, ii. 65
Sound, a, theology, ii. 241
Sovereignty, the, of Divine influence, ii. 219
Special revelations of Heaven, i. 18
Special, the, Heaven of Christ's disciples, ii. 4
Speculative interest in Christ, i. 267
Speculative problems of life, ii. 203
Sphere, the, of religion, ii. 198
Spirit, a bad, i. 294
Spirit, a, God is, ii. 235
Spirit, different meanings of, ii. 211
Spirit, the, agency of, i. 69
Spirit, the, day of, ii. 62
Spirit, the, descent of, ii. 64
Spirit, the Divine, ii. 22, 52, 217
Spirit, the, exemplified by Christ, i. 68, 155
Spirit, the, gift of, ii. 305
Spirit, the, necessity of, ii. 308
Spirit, the, of Christ, ii. 226
Spirit, the, of God, ii. 235
Spirit, the, of Independence, ii. 252
Spirit, the, of Truth, ii. 55
Spirit, the, of worship, i. 90
Spirit, the, with you and in you, ii. 22
Spirit, the, world, ii. 212, 344
Spirit, the world-restoring, ii. 46
Spirits, ii. 344
Spirits, man's fear of, ii. 180, 182
Spiritual adversity, ii. 81
Spiritual cannibalism, i. 175

Spiritual cleansing, i. 78, 79, 386 ; ii. 213
Spiritual concerns, ii. 253
Spiritual connection with the Father, ii. 10
Spiritual culture, i. 100
Spiritual fruitfulness, ii. 37
Spiritual guidance, ii. 55
Spiritual health, i. 79
Spiritual improvement, i. 342
Spiritual life, i. 174, 289 ; ii. 33, 278
Spiritual moods, i. 387
Spiritual reformation, ii. 17
Spiritual, the, cry of man, ii. 12, 289
Spiritual, the, good of man, ii. 81
Spiritual, the, history of man, ii. 70
Spiritual, the, presence of Christ, ii. 20
Spiritual, the, universe, ii. 211
Spiritual, the, work of Christ, ii. 294
Spiritual truth, i. 71
Spiritual vision, i. 79
Spiritually, the, needy, i. 198
Spoliation of death, ii. 149
Spurious sanctity, ii. 122
State hirelings, ii. 160
Steward, the Father's, i. 165
Strikingly, a, suggestive trial, i. 313
Student, a distinguished, i. 66
Studiousness, the, of Christ, i. 211
Subjection, ii. 213
Sublimity, the, of Christ's origin, ii. 223
Success, a guarantee of, ii. 303
Success, Christ's ultimate, ii. 30
Success, the, of a truth-seeker, i. 47
Success, true ministerial, i. 81
Successful prayer, ii. 37
Suffering, human, i. 121, 126, 263
Suffering, mental, i. 361
Suffering, the right way to accept, ii. 109
Sufferings cannot quench love, ii. 153
Sufferings no criteria of character, ii. 203
Sufferings, the, of the good, ii. 108, 144
Sunday School Teachers, ii. 303
Superciliousness, i. 210
Super-eminent, a, religious faith, ii. 185, 365
Superiority, arrogated, ii. 126
Superiority, the, of Christ, i. 151 ; ii. 30
Supernatural power of Christ, i. 51, 57
Supernatural relief through prayer, i. 117
Supernatural, the, dread of, i. 150

418 / *Topical Index*

Superscription, the, on the cross, ii. 146

Superstition, wretched, i. 344

Superstitious fear, ii. 182

Supplementariness of John's Gospel, i. 5

Suppliant, the Divine, ii. 81

Supplies for the needy, i. 198

Supreme affection for Christ, ii. 198

Supreme, the, object of love, ii. 215

Supreme things in man's history, ii. 70

Surprising simplicity, i. 92

Surrender, the, of the soul, ii. 157

Sustainer, the, of Life, ii. 10

Sycophancy, an act of, ii. 116

Sycophancy, crouching, ii. 126, 141, 160

Sympathies directed Heavenward, ii. 178

Sympathy a great blessing, i. 319

Sympathy, religious, ii. 107

Sympathy with brute force, ii. 339

Sympathy with God, i. 284

Sympathy with Truth, i. 299

Synagogue, the, banishment from, ii. 48

System, Christ propounding His, ii. 183

System, Christ's redemptive, ii. 195

System, a, of theology, ii. 278

Swain quoted, ii. 39

Sword, Peter's, ii. 107

TABERNACLES, the Feast of, i. 191, 194, 201, 204, 208

Taylor, Jeremy, quoted, i. 50

Teacher, a, Christ above all as, ii. 223

Teacher, a religious, i. 32

Teacher, the transcendent, i. 68, 192, 211

Teachers, Sunday School, ii. 303

Teaching, Christly, ii. 61

Teaching, Life, ii. 226

Teaching, true method of religious, ii. 261

Teachings, the, of Christ, i. 156, 208, 236, 375 ; ii. 225

Tears, the, of Peter, ii. 120

Technical saints, ii. 159

Technicality, i. 269

Temple, a special, ii. 15

Temple, the ideal and the actual, i. 56

Temporal calamities, i. 119

Temporal prosperity, ii. 81

Temporal, the, concerns of life, ii. 252

Tempting, a, society, ii. 119

Tendency, the, of unbelief, i. 168

Tenderness, the, with which Christ reproves, ii. 48

Tennyson quoted, ii. 240, 361

Terrorism removed, ii. 267

Test, the, of piety, ii. 39

Testimony, a, to Christ's Messiahship, i. 146

Testimony, the, of Scripture, ii. 245

Theologians, dogmatism of, ii. 96

Theological, a, error, ii. 230

Theological adjudicators, ii. 275

Theology, a sound, ii. 241

Theology, a system of, ii. 278

Theology, the heavenly, i. 68

Theology, the, of Christ, ii. 226

Theology, the, of Churches, i. 156

Thirst, the, sufferings of, ii. 156

Tholuck quoted, ii. 265

Thomas Didymus, i. 317

Thomas, the unbelief of, ii. 184, 359

Thomson quoted, ii. 251

Thought, a stimulant to, ii. 58

Thought, a threefold subject for, ii.135

Thousand, Christ feeding the five, i. 146

Three facts relating to Christ, i. 400

Threefold, a, power, ii. 166

Threefold, a, subject for thought, ii. 135

Threefold, a, type of sinners, ii. 139

Tiberias, the disciples on the Sea of, ii. 192

Time, wasting, ii. 254

Times for worship, ii. 236

Timidity, moral, i. 67

Titles of Christ, i. 68

Tortures, physical, ii. 156

Traditional believers, i. 62

Training, religious, i. 2

Traitor, the unmasked, i. 398

Transaction, a wicked, ii. 147

Transactions, the, at a remarkable meeting, ii. 102

Transcendent, a, gift, i. 161

Transcendent, the, element in moral character, i. 292

Transcendent, the, Teacher, i. 68, 192, 211

Transcendent, the, worth of Christianity, i. 184

Transcendentalism, true, ii. 221

Transformation, moral, ii. 256

Treachery, atrocious, ii. 101

Treatment, Christ's merciful, ii. 363

Trial, a strikingly suggestive, i. 313

Trials do not go beyond capacity, i. 63

420 / *Topical Index*